The Palgrave Handbook of Applied Ethics
and the Criminal Law

Larry Alexander • Kimberly Kessler Ferzan
Editors

The Palgrave Handbook of Applied Ethics and the Criminal Law

palgrave
macmillan

Editors
Larry Alexander
University of San Diego School of Law
San Diego, CA, USA

Kimberly Kessler Ferzan
University of Virginia School of Law
Charlottesville, VA, USA

ISBN 978-3-030-22813-2   ISBN 978-3-030-22811-8   (eBook)
https://doi.org/10.1007/978-3-030-22811-8

This Palgrave Macmillan imprint is published by the registered company Springer Nature Switzerland AG.
The registered company address is: Gewerbestrasse 11, 6330 Cham, Switzerland

PREFACE

This handbook addresses ethical questions within the criminal law. It gives an unparalleled overview of topics within the criminal law, while simultaneously including the author's unique perspective on the issues. These chapters include entries not only on "traditional" topics such as death penalty and civil disobedience but also chapters that take on the contemporary concerns of the criminal law, including revenge porn, targeted killing, and the role of neuroscience.

Just as our topics merge the traditional and the contemporary, so, too, do our contributors. All contributors are extraordinary theorists within the criminal law, and this handbook includes not only established theorists but also more junior scholars who are already making a lasting impression on the field.

This handbook should be of interest to both undergraduate and graduate law and philosophy students, philosophers, and criminal law theorists.

We are grateful for the institutional support of our two law schools, including Dean Stephen Ferruolo at the University of San Diego and Dean Risa Goluboff at the University of Virginia. Noah Gaarder-Feingold (JD, USD) and Pol Minguet (LLM, UVA) provided invaluable support in preparing this manuscript.

San Diego, CA, USA   Larry Alexander
Charlottesville, VA, USA   Kimberly Kessler Ferzan

CONTENTS

Notes on Contributors

Larry Alexander is Warren Distinguished Professor at the University of San Diego School of Law.

Christian Barry is Professor of Philosophy at the Australian National University.

Samuel W. Buell is Bernard M. Fishman Professor of Law at Duke University.

Vincent Chiao is an associate professor at the University of Toronto, Faculty of Law.

Kevin Cole is Professor of Law at the University of San Diego.

Andrew Cornford is Lecturer in Criminal Law at the University of Edinburgh.

Tom Dannenbaum is Assistant Professor of International Law, the Fletcher School of Law and Diplomacy, Tufts University.

Candice Delmas is Assistant Professor of Philosophy and Political Science and Associate Director, Politics, Philosophy, and Economics Program at Northeastern University.

Michelle Madden Dempsey is Professor of Law and Harold Reuschlein Scholar Chair at Villanova University.

Antje du Bois-Pedain is Reader in Criminal Law and Philosophy at the University of Cambridge, UK, and a fellow of Magdalene College, Cambridge.

James Edwards is Associate Professor of Law at the University of Oxford, Tutorial Fellow in Law at Worcester College, and Lecturer in Law at Brasenose College.

Benjamin Ewing is an assistant professor at Queen's University Faculty of Law.

Chad Flanders is Professor of Law at Saint Louis University.

Mary Anne Franks is Professor of Law at the University of Miami School of Law.

Stephen P. Garvey is Professor of Law, Cornell Law School.

Stuart P. Green is Distinguished Professor of Law, Rutgers Law School.

Deborah Hellman is David Lurton Massee, Jr. Professor of Law and the Roy L. and Rosamond Woodruff Morgan Professor of Law at the University of Virginia School of Law.

Heidi M. Hurd is Ross and Helen Workman Chair in Law, Professor of Philosophy, and Co-Director of the Program in Law and Philosophy at the University of Illinois.

Douglas Husak is Distinguished Professor of Philosophy, Rutgers University.

Margo Kaplan is Professor of Law, Rutgers Law School.

Leo Katz is Frank Carano Professor of Law at the University of Pennsylvania.

Kimberly Kessler Ferzan is Harrison Robertson Professor of Law and the Joel B Piassick Research Professor of Law at the University of Virginia School of Law.

Adam J. Kolber is Professor of Law at Brooklyn Law School and Visiting Fellow at NYU School of Law, Center for Research in Crime and Justice.

Youngjae Lee is Professor of Law at Fordham University School of Law.

Michael S. Moore is Charles R. Walgreen, Jr. Professor of Law and Co-Director of the Program in Law and Philosophy, at the University of Illinois.

Stephen J. Morse is Ferdinand Wakeman Hubbell Professor of Law, Professor of Psychology and Law in Psychiatry, and Associate Director of the Center for Neuroscience & Society, University of Pennsylvania.

Alvaro Sandroni is E.D. Howard Professor in Political Economy at the Kellogg School of Management, Northwestern University.

Alex Sarch is Reader (Associate Professor) in Legal Philosophy at the University of Surrey School of Law.

Kenneth W. Simons is Chancellor's Professor of Law and Philosophy, University of California, Irvine School of Law.

Patrick Tomlin is Reader in Philosophy at the University of Warwick.

Alec Walen is Professor of Law and Philosophy at Rutgers University.

Peter Westen is Frank G. Millard Professor of Law Emeritus at Michigan Law School.

Gideon Yaffe is Wesley Newcomb Hohfeld Professor of Jurisprudence and Professor of Philosophy and Psychology at Yale Law School.

Ekow N. Yankah is Professor of Law at Cardozo Law School.

CHAPTER 1

Introduction

Larry Alexander and Kimberly Kessler Ferzan

There are myriad ways that one might approach the relationship between ethics and criminal law. One might begin with what one takes to be the best ethical theory and then apply it in a top-down way to determine what ought to be a crime. Or one might begin with a pre-existing concept in our legal or ordinary discourse and seek to unearth its ethical presuppositions, holding true to most of its current conceptual features. Still others might be interested in the institutional aspects of law, reasoning that criminal law is not solely about moral philosophy but also about political philosophy, thereby implicating questions of the state. And hybrids of the political and moral questions appear when the state may use only some, but not other, reasons to criminalize. All of these approaches are on display in this handbook.

We have chosen to order this handbook alphabetically by topic, and each chapter is a stand-alone entry on a particular subject within criminal law. We believe that this organization will be the most accessible approach for those who are likely to read this handbook to gain knowledge about a subject or two. Nevertheless, we will use this introduction to impose a different structure (or perhaps simply a structure) on the myriad entries that follow. It is our hope that this introduction will provide a useful guide to how one can approach the wide-ranging, disparate questions of applied ethics and the criminal law.

L. Alexander (✉)
University of San Diego School of Law, San Diego, CA, USA
e-mail: larrya@sandiego.edu

K. K. Ferzan
University of Virginia School of Law, Charlottesville, VA, USA
e-mail: kferzan@law.virginia.edu

© The Author(s) 2019
L. Alexander, K. K. Ferzan (eds.), *The Palgrave Handbook of Applied Ethics and the Criminal Law*, https://doi.org/10.1007/978-3-030-22811-8_1

1

Notably, this introduction does not impose the "typical" structure on the criminal law. Many criminal law theorists approach the criminal law by dividing the criminal law between the general and special parts. The special part is the actual criminal offenses, such as rape, murder, and theft. The general part, as its label denotes, applies generally. This part includes the voluntary act requirement, the definition of the mental states that crimes can contain, causation, as well as provisions for attempts and accomplice liability that apply across offenses. But this handbook, which deals with applied ethics, is not the best venue to pursue the philosophy of action inherent in the voluntary act requirement, or the philosophy of mind underpinning various mental states, or the metaphysics of causation. Some of the general part topics do relate to applied ethics, as, for example, the entries on inchoate criminality and complicity reveal. But in our view, a systematic approach to applied ethics and the criminal law cannot be best discerned through the traditional general/special part division of labor.

Instead, particularly for the reader unacquainted with criminal law theorizing, we suggest a different structure. We begin first with the "big picture" questions about the relationship between morality and criminalization, in terms of both whether the law should reflect morality and how we should deal with uncertainty about what morality requires. From here, we turn to the wide-ranging criminalization questions presented by many of the entries in this handbook, and we juxtapose the top-down and bottom-up strategies imposed by the authors. We then note how some crimes that appear to be stand alone are instantiations of more general principles and how different crimes ultimately depend on the same underlying theoretical presuppositions or otherwise draw connections to other debates within criminal law. Next, we turn to the notions of responsible agency upon which just punishment depends. The questions of who counts as a legal person for punishment, when can a person be held responsible, and how particular features of a person's psychology or circumstances affect just punishment are considered. Finally, we direct our gaze to punishment and the role of the state, asking about the mode and amount of punishment, as well as the justness of the state's imposition of punishment.

CRIMINALIZATION

Morality and Criminalization

Many of the entries within this handbook are concerned with particular crimes and what justifies their criminalization. What is the role of moral wrongfulness in justifying the prohibition of a particular act? Criminal law theorists continue to debate the appropriate reasons to criminalize, ranging from forms of legal moralism, that require, as either a necessary or sufficient condition, that the behavior be morally wrongful, to more harm-centered theories, that justify punishment based on harm to others, offense to others, or harm to self. The intricacies of these topics justify book-length treatments. James Edwards' *No*

Offense nicely explores the complexity of these questions at this high level of generality with respect to offensive behavior. The question is how an action's offensiveness justifies criminalization. Interestingly, Edwards concludes that the justification for criminalization is neither that an act is offensive nor that it is wrong, but rather some further fact by virtue of which the act is offensive and wrong. Edwards also counterintuitively defends the proposition that sometimes offensiveness dictates against, not in favor of, criminalization, whereas lack of offense may dictate in criminalization's favor.

But even when moral wrongfulness directly bears on criminalization, how do we even know if something is wrong? Drawing on a new line of inquiry within applied ethics, Christian Barry and Patrick Tomlin's *Moral Uncertainty and the Criminal Law* asks how we should approach criminalization (and punishment) if there is doubt that an act is morally wrong. After demonstrating the complexity of this question for individuals determining what they ought to do, Barry and Tomlin address the modifications that ought to be made as we ask this question through the prism of the state.

Should law and morality diverge? Two chapters address different aspects of this question. In *Role Morality*, Leo Katz and Alvaro Sandroni ask whether a defense attorney is subject to a special role morality that permits her to violate ordinary moral standards in representing a defendant. How can a lawyer assist the client without being complicit in his wrong? How can we condone the lawyer while condemning the criminal without inviting "moral combat?" How should we understand the duties owed to a "personless corporation?" Katz and Sandroni think that there can be special role moralities, that they are, in their terms, "non-option stratified," and that if law and morality were option stratified, we could not condone role morality. However, their non-option-stratified law and morality allows role morality as it produces interesting forms of intransitivity among possible choices. And, in *Ignorance of Law: How to Conceptualize and Maybe Resolve the Issue*, Douglas Husak quarrels with the long-accepted criminal law maxim that ignorance of the law is not an excuse. Instead, he argues that legal ignorance should generally be treated the same way as is factual ignorance. If the defendant's ignorance is culpable, that culpability should be taken into account the same way as is culpability regarding the nature or consequences of the criminal act. And if ignorance of the law is nonculpable, the legally ignorant defendant should be regarded as nonculpable.

These chapters explore the relationship between law and morality on a more abstract level, as opposed to focusing on discrete crimes. They require us to ask whether moral wrongfulness and our beliefs about such wrongfulness bear on what and when the state should punish.

Analyzing Crimes: Why Prohibit?

Ideally, when one seeks to criminalize certain conduct, one would understand the nature of the conduct and have clear ideas about what justifies punishing it and how. That is, criminalization would proceed in a top-down manner, thereby *applying* ethics. Many of the entries in this handbook attend to specific crimes and what justifies their prohibition.

A useful glimpse at ideal pre-criminalization theorizing is provided in Mary Anne Franks' *The Crime of Revenge Porn* chapter. The recent use of "revenge porn," or as Mary Anne Franks would have us call it, "nonconsensual pornography," has challenged legislators and theorists to think about what makes this problematic behavior of concern to the criminal law. Franks' *The Crime of Revenge Porn* demonstrates how we ought to look at the criminalization question, from understanding the conduct, to explaining why it ought to be criminalized, to working through the ultimate features of the defense, to engaging with the struggles with understanding how and why laws pass and fail.

In most instances, however, legislatures rarely have clear ideas about what they are prohibiting and why. Rather, theorists often engage in ex post inquiries, searching for the sorts of ideas that can justify a particular law. This traditional method of inquiry is clearly on display in Heidi Hurd's *Crimes Against Animals*. Hurd's contribution is an example of a systematic inquiry in which a scholar probes every justification for criminalization to determine how and why something ought to be punished. In light of Hurd's searching and scathing critique of existing laws, we are left wondering why we so inconsistently protect animals and whether this protection is truly about animals at all or whether it is simply about protecting humans from themselves and each other.

Like Hurd's attempt to locate animal cruelty statutes within the various justifications for criminalization, Kenneth Simons systematically analyzes various arguments about hate crimes. Simons' *Hate (or Bias) Crime Laws* scrutinizes when and why hate crimes should be punished differently than other offenses. He thus works through reasons to think there is greater harm, a different wrong, or more culpability and then examines how one would frame the crime so as to speak to these potential reasons for differential punishment. Although both of these entries focus on particular laws, they take a somewhat top-down approach in that they apply the different categories of moral thinking, displaying a willingness to give up the existing law in favor of better moral accounts.

An alternative approach to the normative question is to start with the law that we have and try to see what theories both fit and justify the law. This analysis is more bottom-up than top-down. One exemplar of this sort of approach is Deborah Hellman's *Understanding Bribery*. What makes trading money for a vote a bribe but trading a vote for a vote permissible logrolling? To Hellman, bribery is best understood as an exchange across domains that is prohibited by the relevant decision-maker. This allows us to unearth what those things we take to be "bribes" have as their common core. In a similar vein, in *Incest*, Stuart P. Green offers what he calls a "normative reconstruction" of the law of incest. He first looks at incest as a complex cultural taboo, then considers the various ways the criminal law has dealt with it. He then asks whether incest with juveniles substantially duplicates statutory rape laws and whether incest laws should be applied to putatively consensual acts between adults. And in a similar effort, in *Blackmail: A Crime of Paradox and Irony*, Peter Westen takes up, as have countless others before him, the paradoxical crime of blackmail—what its various definitions have been historically and what Westen believes it should be limited to as a normative matter. Westen painstakingly reviews a multitude of statutory definitions of the offense and the defenses thereto, and he then confronts head-on the so-called paradox of blackmail—that its illegality consists of a threat to make a legal disclosure to induce a transaction that is also legal. He concludes that blackmail should be restricted to threats that are criminal or tortious, rejecting approaches of others that focus on the defendant's purpose.

Finally, even when starting with the crime as the point of inquiry, there are those crimes that seem to evade precise definitions themselves. In *Fraud*, Samuel Buell examines the concept of fraud, which he argues escapes being reduced by criminal law into anything resembling bright-line rules. Fraud, says Buell, is really a common law crime, despite the fiction that our law has eliminated such things. He illustrates his thesis by canvassing a number of white-collar crimes and prosecutions.

These entries, then, approach the same question from two distinct methodologies. Some theorists are inclined to get the morality right, thus leading us to condemn our existing legal practices. In contrast, others are seeking to find the morality that undergirds the pre-existing legal practice. Although both are willing to trim the law when necessary, the former privileges the moral and the latter privileges law.

Drawing Connections

There are also interconnections between criminalization questions. Some crimes do not stand alone, but rather operate within a backdrop of other crimes and justifications.

Consider the entries by Andrew Cornford and Margo Kaplan. In *Inchoate Criminality*, Cornford takes up the criminalization of acts that are merely preparatory to committing a crime or an attempted crime. Although Cornford takes seriously various skeptical arguments against the creation of preparatory crimes, he believes that the issue is more complicated than the skeptics aver, and that the creation of some such crimes is justified. Kaplan's *Sex Offenses and the Problem of Prevention* questions whether laws against enticement and solicitation of minors can be justified as inchoate offenses. She then probes the potential justifications for the commitment of sexually violent predators, including detaining the dangerousness, self-defense, and punishment. Hence, in analyzing inchoate offenses, one discovers that other crimes that appear to be aimed at a specific wrong are, in fact, inchoate offenses in disguise.

Similarly, Alec Walen and Tom Dannenbaum take up related questions. As Walen argues in *Targeted Killing and the Criminal Law*, the justifiability of targeted killing depends upon whether it is justified as an act of self-defense. Hence, Walen introduces novel ways to think about why one may kill someone to eliminate the threat he poses, how confident the defender must be, and why the selection of the target must also pass moral muster. Just as Walen writes about targeted killing against the backdrop of individual self-defense, Dannenbaum's *War Crimes and Just War Theory* looks at war crimes more broadly against the backdrop of just war theory. In recent years, revisionists have claimed that the morality of war is reducible to the morality of individual self-defense, and both revisionists and their interlocutors have assumed that this creates a chasm between existing law and morality. Dannenbaum explores the criminalization questions, ultimately arguing that the divide is far narrower than theorists suppose.

Accomplice liability necessarily entails the conjunction of the accomplice's acts and another's crime. In *Complicity*, Antje du Bois-Pedain asks when should an actor who does not herself commit the actus reus of a crime be held responsible for the criminal act of another. Du Bois-Pedain describes the two modes of complicitous involvement—joint enterprises and accessorial participation. She rejects the idea that complicity is based on causation, a view most recently defended by Michael Moore, and defends a view based on the accomplice's influence on the principal actor. She then examines what responsibility the accomplice should bear when the principal actor's crime is more serious than the accomplice contemplated.

Finally, some connections are not between crimes, but between different criminal law approaches. In *Affirmative Consent*, Kevin Cole analyzes the approaches and puzzles with respect to consent in the criminal law. One important strain of his argument is that questions of mens rea and, in particular negligence, are connected to questions about proxy crimes. Hence, through the prism of one question, we can see that seemingly disparate questions within criminal law are interconnected. In addition, as Cole and one of us (Alexander) argue in *Reckless Beliefs*, sometimes the connections are problematic. Through the prism of rape reform, Alexander and Cole demonstrate that legislatures sometimes create conceptual problems by positing mental states that simply are not possible.

Many of the entries in this handbook thus address specific offenses. With respect to these offenses, a reader can see distinct methodologies as the authors seek to best understand criminal statutes and can see significant dependencies and connections between crimes.

RESPONSIBLE AGENCY

Even when it is appropriate to criminalize a particular act, it may, nevertheless, be inappropriate to punish any particular offender. Although as a matter of substantive law many of the questions addressed are often treated as a question of when an agent should be *excused*, these are ultimately questions about the idea of responsible agency that undergirds the criminal law.

Undermining Responsibility

As Stephen Morse explains in *Neuroscience and Criminal Law: Perils and Promises*, new scientific advances raise a host of concerns in the criminal courtroom, perhaps most significantly regarding the law's conception of responsible agency. Morse gives grounds for caution, though he optimistically believes that neuroscience will inform, rather than replace, the folk psychological concepts on which the law relies. Stephen Garvey's *Insanity* focuses on the more localized concern that a lack of rational or volitional capacity or some sort of irrationality can undermine responsibility. Garvey finds philosophical weaknesses in each of the tests the law uses to define when it is that we exempt someone from responsibility. We lack a firm grip on the conditions under which one ought not to be punished because of one's mental illness. In *Addiction and Responsibility*, Michael Moore asks whether addiction should be a defense to crimes committed as a result thereof. He first explains what addiction is and why people become and remain addicted. He then turns to addiction as a possible defense and concludes that the threat of withdrawal symptoms is not an excuse, and that addiction is not sufficiently incapacitating to excuse addicts as a general matter.

Assumptions About Agents

In contrast, Adam J. Kolber's chapter, *The Subjectivist Critique of Proportionality*, demonstrates an altogether different way in which presuppositions about who we are affects how the criminal law can treat us. If two people experience the same punishment differently, then it seems possible that at least one of the punishments is disproportionate, a result that Kolber thinks is particularly problematic for retributivism. And, Alex Sarch's chapter, *Skepticism about Corporate Punishment Revisited*, explores the outer boundary of whom we take to be an appropriate subject of the criminal law, as he explores whether corporations can be punished. Sarch answers this question in the affirmative, finding that corporations can be the subjects of criminal law rules.

In contrast to those chapters that probe the responsible agent, Benjamin Ewing's chapter denies that many sorts of mitigation are warranted by the agent's partial excuse or justification. His chapter thus has us cast our gaze to claims that agents may have that are not grounded in their agency being undermined. Ewing notes that we intuitively take into account an offender's disadvantaged background, lack of criminal history, or acceptance of responsibility, yet current theories struggle to justify these practices. In *Mitigating Factors: A Typology*, Ewing argues that these mitigating factors are not exculpatory—they do not lessen the actor's culpability or wrongdoing—and yet, they are, indeed, moral claims that offenders have to lesser punishment. According to Ewing, our traditional thinking about mitigation, that it is often grounded in the undermining of responsibility, is wrong.

In sum, when the criminal law aims to prohibit someone from acting or seeks to punish someone for violating its prohibitions, it must be fair to condemn that person. Hence, one question is whether certain actors are exempt from the criminal law, the question that both Sarch and Garvey's entries take on. But flawed human beings also raise challenges for whether they should be excused for a particular crime, whether neuroscience will explain our behavior and undermine our responsibility, and how to understand our punishment practices. Finally, some practices that appear to fall within this category cannot be explained in this way, as they ultimately serve altogether different masters.

Punishment and the Role of the State

Punishment

When a criminal law is violated, an offender may be punished. Although myriad issues may be raised about punishment, this handbook focuses on two essential questions. The first is how to determine that the punishment is proportionate, and the second is whether capital punishment can be justified.

Punishment is stigma and harsh treatment that is responsive to crime. In *Proportionality in Punishment*, Youngjae Lee asks what makes a given punishment "proportional" or "fitting." He considers both the currency of punishment—is it years in prison? the suffering experienced? and so on—and whether we should consider that proportionality should be a function of how other offenders have been treated (comparative proportionality) or how others should have been treated (noncomparative proportionality). He concludes by looking at a variety of issues that raise the problem of proportionate punishment.

In *Capital Punishment and the Owl of Minerva*, Vincent Chiao's focus is on one particular punishment—capital punishment. Are there reasons not to use this particular form of punishment? Chiao closely examines various arguments for its abolition but finds them inconclusive. He concludes that capital punishment might be justifiable if it deters serious crime more effectively than alternatives, though he also believes its racial impact might militate against its use notwithstanding its benefits.

The State

In thinking about the criminal law, one can inquire why the state is permitted to harm its citizens, either to achieve retributive justice or to advance consequentialist ends. Chad Flanders' chapter, *Political Philosophy and Punishment*, asks the question, not what justifies punishment, but what justifies the state in imposing punishment. Here, he helpfully surveys various approaches within political philosophy, while demonstrating that many political theories will find this to be a more difficult question than it first appears.

Not only must we consider why the state is justified in punishing, but we must question the impacts of the state having an institution of criminal justice. Ekow Yankah's *Race, Criminal Law, and Ethical Life* examines the criminal law through the prism of race. Yankah shows the pervasive effects of structural racism that extend far beyond questions of hate crimes, to the ways that the criminal justice system criminalizes, investigates, prosecutes, incarcerates, and employs collateral consequences. Yankah ends with thoughts as to the duties one has in such an unfair world.

Yankah's chapter is an interesting juxtaposition to two other chapters. First, in *Prostitution*, Michelle Madden Dempsey grapples with the criminalization of prostitution. She notes that prostitution can be understood transactionally or structurally. Whereas Yankah eschews individual acts of criminalization for the wide-angle lens of structural defects, Dempsey suggests (and Yankah would likely agree) that the criminal law itself is best deployed for transactional, and not structural, problems. Hence, Dempsey's ultimate approach is like many of the earlier criminalization chapters, but she is keenly aware of the larger structural question about the subordination of women that pervades her inquiry.

Second, Candace Delmas' *Civil Disobedience, Punishment, and Injustice*, likewise, explores the relationship of citizen and state. Delmas begins with two traditional questions within the civil disobedience literature: (1) Should the state punish those who engage in civil disobedience and (2) should those actors accept punishment? But Delmas' conclusion dovetails with Yankah's, as she questions whether we have been asking the correct question all along—perhaps, she suggests, individuals are morally required to be disobedient in unjust societies.

Civil disobedience is not the only criminal law defense to directly implicate the relationship between citizens and the state. One of us (Ferzan) has written *Stand Your Ground*, and the conclusions reached therein also lead us back to the state. If, as Ferzan argues, "stand your ground" laws are ultimately a delegation of police law enforcement authority to private citizens, then we must ask whether states ought to delegate and, more importantly, whether even states should have the power they are delegating.

Finally, we must inquire into what the state owes its citizens in terms of due process. In *When Does Evidence Support Guilt "Beyond a Reasonable Doubt"?*, Gideon Yaffe asks when is evidence sufficient to meet the constitutional requirement of proof beyond a reasonable doubt. He discusses probabilistic accounts of the beyond a reasonable doubt standard and contrasts them with psychological accounts. He concludes that a successful account is more likely to be a psychological one.

Ultimately, the state creates and implements criminal law. Thus, a central question within the criminal law is the stance of the state to its citizens. These chapters address why the state may punish, when is a state illegitimate and unable to punish, whether a state is delegating its enforcement role, and how confident must the state be before it punishes.

PART I

Addiction

CHAPTER 2

Addiction and Responsibility

Michael S. Moore

Introduction

Addiction to substances generally, and to opioid drugs specifically, is a major problem in the United States. Indeed, it seems to be getting to be a worse problem with every passing year. We have over two million opioid addicts in our population, of whom approximately 42,000 die of overdosing opioids every year. By the US Surgeon General's estimate, substance addiction generally costs us $442 billion annually in health-care costs, criminal justice costs, and loss of productivity; that figure is $93 billion for drug addiction alone (the rest due to alcohol addiction) (New York Times 2016, p. A-14).

Most of the current attention to the addiction crisis is, rightly enough, focused on methods of prevention and cure. Thus, the National Institute of Health, for example, in April 2018 announced its HEAL Initiative, the acronym standing for Helping to End Addiction Long-Term. My interest in this chapter, however, is not with these much discussed issues of prevention and cure, important as they are. Rather, I focus on the relation of addiction to the criminal justice system. My question is whether addicts who commit crimes deserve to be punished for those crimes or whether instead they should be fully or partly excused whenever their crimes were motivated or otherwise caused by their addiction. In short, my question is whether addiction is a moral and legal excuse for responsibility for acts done because one is an addict.

I thus seek to assay the responsibility of addicts for the acts they do because they are addicts. This, too, like the issues of prevention and cure of addiction, is an important contemporary topic. A recent study found that 65% of the jail and prison population of the United States—some 1.5 million inmates—meet

M. S. Moore (✉)
University of Illinois, Champaign, IL, USA
e-mail: micmoore@illinois.edu

© The Author(s) 2019
L. Alexander, K. K. Ferzan (eds.), *The Palgrave Handbook of Applied Ethics and the Criminal Law*, https://doi.org/10.1007/978-3-030-22811-8_2

the criteria for being diagnosed as suffering from a "substance use disorder" (the American Psychiatric Association's label for substance addiction when severe) (Center on Addiction 2010). While most of such incarcerated addicts are not imprisoned for doing related crimes, surely many are. If addiction should be a legal defense or mitigating factor because it is a moral excuse, then a very large number of those we have imprisoned are being unjustly punished.

Addiction as such is not a defense to crime in any US state or federal jurisdiction.[1] The few jurisdictions that have considered a defense of addiction as a matter of common law have refused to countenance such a defense.[2] At most, under present law, addiction poses the theoretical possibility of being raised via the insanity defense. Yet even this possibility exists only in those jurisdictions: (1) retaining an insanity defense at all; (2) having a "loss of control" (or "volitional") prong to that defense; and (3) considering addiction to be a legally cognizable mental illness for purposes of the insanity defense. There are almost no instances where jurisdictions in the United States meet these three requirements, particularly the last (Morse 2017).

Despite the unavailability of any defense of addiction as a matter of ordinary (statutory and common) law, in 1968 the US Supreme Court came very close to requiring addiction to be a constitutionally required defense for those accused of using the drugs or alcohol to which they were addicted. In *Powell v. United States*, five members of the Court were prepared to hold that those addicted to alcohol could not be constitutionally punished for such addicted use; addiction, it was thought, compels use of that to which one is addicted, and compelled behavior is excused behavior that could not constitutionally be punished. Only Justice White's fine distinction in his concurring opinion—that although use of alcohol is compelled for alcoholics, *appearing in public* drunk was not compelled—saved the Court from holding addiction to be a constitutionally required defense to convictions for use or possession of alcohol or drugs. Despite these five votes for the Constitution requiring such a defense, *Powell* has subsequently been interpreted by the lower courts *not* to constitutionally require a compulsion excuse for addicts who use;[3] rather, the only constitutional prohibition is one prohibiting federal or state laws from conviction of addicts for a *status* rather than an *act*. One cannot thus be punished for being an addict (because that is a status), while one can be punished for acts of possession and use as an addict (because those are acts).

Thus as a matter of statutory, common, and constitutional law, addiction does not presently serve as any kind of defense in Anglo-American criminal law. But that doesn't answer the normative question of whether the law is not mistaken in this regard. Does doing some wrongful and illegal act in order to satisfy a desperate craving for the drug to which one is addicted reduce or eliminate one's moral blameworthiness for doing that act? If so, then by standard theories of punishment (Moore 1996, ch. 2–4), there should be some mitigation or legal defense. It is to that moral question that this chapter is devoted.

Conceptualizing What Addictions Are

It is a common injunction to those who write about anything that they should first "define their terms."[4] So I began with some description of what it is we talk about when we describe, explain, or evaluate "addiction."

To keep the topic manageable, I have restricted my focus to drug, alcohol, and tobacco addiction, the so-called substance addictions. And usually I focus on the central one of these: addiction to the use of opioid drugs. The concept of addiction has of course been much more widely employed than that, having been extended to cover what are called "behavioral addictions" such as the addiction to gambling, to sex, to eating, and the like. What is said about substance addictions can sometimes also be said about behavioral addictions, but there are also enough differences that in this chapter I seek only to deal with what are paradigmatically addictions, leaving to others to assess the degree to which one can analogize the less central cases of addiction to the central case.

Given the prevalence of the notion of disease in modern discussions of substance addiction (hereinafter, just referred to as "addiction"), a place to start in conceptualizing what we talk about is with the medical profession's definitions of "substance use disorders." Consider the latest and fifth edition of the American Psychiatric Association's *Diagnostic and Statistical Manual's* ("DSM-V") definition of the most relevant of substance use disorders, that which is called "Opioid Use Disorder." A "severe" case of Opioid Use Disorder is when someone exhibits "at least six to seven" of the following 11 symptoms:

1. taking the opioid in larger amounts and for longer than intended
2. wanting to cut down or quit but not being able to do it
3. spending a lot of time obtaining the opioids
4. craving or a strong desire to use opioids
5. repeatedly unable to carry out major obligations at work, school, or home due to opioid use
6. continued use despite persistent or recurring social or interpersonal problems caused or made worse by opioid use
7. stopping or reducing important social, occupational, or recreational activities due to opioid use
8. recurrent use of opioids in physically hazardous situations
9. consistent use of opioids despite acknowledgment of persistent or recurrent physical or psychological difficulties from using opioids
10. tolerance as defined by either a need for markedly increased amounts to achieve intoxication or the desired effect or a need for markedly diminished effects with continued use of the same amount. (Does not apply for diminished effects when used appropriately under medical supervision)
11. withdrawal manifesting as either a characteristic syndrome or the substance is used to avoid withdrawal (does not apply when used appropriately under medical supervision)

There are a number of observations to be made about this definition. The main one is that this is a definition of a *medical* disorder for use by the *medical* profession. The general purposes guiding such a definition are in line with the general aims of the medical profession: to diagnose, cure, and prevent those harmful and unwanted conditions of human beings known as diseases (Moore 1978, 2015). Defining particular diseases such as "Opioid Use Disorder" serves these general medical purposes by isolating clinically distinct syndromes, syndromes whose distinctness requires distinct forms of explanation and thus distinct methods of prevention and cure. Whether this definition is a good definition for medical professionals to use depends on how well it serves these medical purposes.

As I explained in the introduction, my interests in this chapter are not the medical interests of prevention and cure. Rather, the three tasks undertaken by this chapter are (1) to describe addiction, (2) to explain the behavior of addicts, and (3) to evaluate whether the condition so described explains the wrongful behaviors in addicts in ways tending to excuse them from moral responsibility and legal liability. Those tasks have very little to do with the diagnosis, prevention, and cure guiding medical definitions of addiction, so one might reasonably wonder why I start with a medical definition.

If the medical definition just given were a purely stipulative definition—making a word mean whatever the speaker wants it to mean to serve his purposes in using that word on some particular occasion—then we could ignore medical definitions of addiction in this context. Yet regarding medical definitions of discrete diseases as stipulative definitions would rob them of their ability to serve medical purposes; this is thus the wrong way to regard them. Medical nosology can serve the diagnostic, preventative, and curative purposes of medicine, only if that taxonomy of diseases describes a natural clumping of disease entities that exist independently of doctors so labeling them. Successful medical definitions capture, but do not create, the clumping together of symptoms into the disease entities that doctors can separately diagnose, explain, prevent, and cure.

This gives moralists and lawyers some interest in medical conceptualizations of those natural conditions that doctors regard as diseases, conditions that existed long before there were doctors or lawyers. For there is a shared search in all professions, medicine and law included, for both an accurate description of what a condition such as addiction is and a true explanation of how addiction explains the drug-related behaviors of addicts. This overlapping interest in accurate description and true explanation persists in the face of the fact that medical professionals use such descriptions and explanations for different purposes than do moralists and lawyers. Successful location of excuse in morals and law depends upon accurate descriptions and true explanations of those conditions thought to be excusing, just as successful prevention and cure in medicine depends on such accurate descriptions and true explanations.

So let us begin our discussion of what the nature of addiction is by attending to the medical definition of a central case of addiction, addiction to the use of opioid drugs. Stephen Morse has extensively reviewed this and similar medical definitions of addiction (Morse 2000) and has raised a number of relevant considerations. First of all, notice that the definition is intentionally imprecise in the mode of combination of its 11 symptoms. These 11 conditions do not even purport to give *criteria* in the old logical positivist sense of *merkmal* (necessary and sufficient conditions of correct applications), as for example the definition of "bachelor" as (1) unmarried, (2) male, and (3) person purports to do. Rather, the conditions constitute criteria for addiction only in Wittgenstein's looser, "criteriological" sense: no single condition is necessary for a clump of conditions to be an addiction—in Wittgenstein's famous simile, addiction would be like a piece of rope that is truly one piece of rope even though it is made up of many strands, no one of which runs its entire length—and it is unclear what conjunctions of conditions are sufficient, short of the entire set.[5]

Second, as Morse notes, several of the conditions considered separately are degree vague in their specification of the quantities required to satisfy them. Third, Morse notes that such definitions lack a center of gravity, an essence, to addiction; each of these 11 conditions is treated as if they are equally important and interchangeable in determining when someone is severely disordered, whereas in truth some conditions seem much more important than others. Morse himself, for example, believes that "craving, a subjectively experienced strong desire, is (or almost always is) a central part of the condition" (Morse 2000, p. 13), whereas some doctors believe that the essence of addiction lies in "compulsive drug seeking and use, even in the face of negative health and social consequences" (Leshner 1997, p. 45).

Morse laments these three characteristics of medical definitions of addiction, and he is right to do so—if we were regarding the medical definition as a finished theory as to the nature of addiction. Yet if we regard this definition from the self-consciously tentative and unfinished viewpoint of our current collective understanding of addiction, these three characteristics are but expressions of the provisional nature of our current theory. When we only partially know the nature of something, we would be pretending to know more than we do, and we would freeze inquiry so as to cut off learning more, by stipulating an artificially precise nature to addiction. We might in years past have analogously stipulated, for example, that any person whose heart and lungs have ceased spontaneously functioning is *dead*—cutting off the insight that actually some of such persons (if they have been immersed in very cold water) are not really dead because death is *not* a state whose nature is fixed by the long-used heart/lung definition of death.[6]

So it is no defect in the medical conceptualization of addiction that it is provisional and thus somewhat vague: about how its criteria are to be combined, about the quantitative variables in those criteria, or about the essential versus the accidental properties of addiction. The scientific nature of the enterprise of describing and explaining addiction cautions patience and thus tolerance of imprecision here.

We have exposed two reasons to begin with a *medical* definition of addiction: one, having to start somewhere with someone's conceptualization of the phenomena and two, law having enough overlapping interests with medicine to start there. There is also a third reason to broach our subject by beginning with medicine's ideas about addiction. This reason is constituted by the fact that, despite the admirable restraint shown by the medical profession in not regarding its definition of addiction as complete and final, nonetheless, in this context, the medical profession has badly overreached. I refer to what is known as "the disease model of addiction." That label has become the slogan for the view that addiction is a brain disease and that because of this fact alone bad acts done by addicts cannot fairly be either blamed or punished.

This would be a much shorter chapter if this last moral conclusion were true, for addiction is a brain disease—or at least there is nothing improper about the medical profession classifying addiction as a disease in light of the fact that it is at least partially amenable to medical treatment.[7] But it is a serious mistake to infer from that premise the conclusion that therefore addiction must be both a moral excuse and a legal defense to crime. As I see it, there are three routes by which this mistaken inference is drawn. The first and least thoughtful is to believe that "sick" and "bad" are exclusive categories in which to describe states of persons. That is, such terms are either contradictories or at least contraries: if one is sick, one is not bad, and if one is bad, one is not sick. Yet stated this baldly, this is silly: a murderer who has a cold—or pneumonia, cancer, or spinal meningitis for that matter—is still a murderer, that is, a culpable killer deserving of blame and punishment. Being sick and being bad are not, on their face, mutually exclusive categories.

The second route attempts to add some precision to the first route. Of course murderers can have colds while they kill and still be judged to be bad people; but the point is that the conditions that make them bad cannot be the same conditions that make them sick, and it is in this sense that the categories of the sick and the bad are said to be exclusive. The argument for this more precise conclusion begins with the observation that all illnesses involve incapacitation of some kind. This is made explicit in overall definitions of disease. Consider, for example, the definition of "medical disorder" proposed by the then chairman of the American Psychiatric Association's Committee on Nomenclature and Statistics for inclusion in the *Diagnostic and Statistical Manual, Third Edition*: being diseased is to suffer dysfunction, distress, disability, and disadvantage (Spitzer and Endicott 1978).[8] The argument then proceeds by observing that all forms of volitional excuse are based on the offender being in some sense *incapacitated* from doing better than he in fact did (Moore 2016a). Therefore, the argument concludes, to be properly classified as being diseased is to be excused.

The problem for this version of the inference (from disease to excuse) lies in the middle terms of that inference, disability, and incapacitation. Put simply, the disability that makes for being diseased need not be the same as the incapacity that makes for excuse. This obvious enough mistake is obscured by the fact that there *is* a large overlap between the disability that makes for disease and the incapacity that makes for excuse. It is this overlap that makes it absurd to blame and punish *all* conditions properly classified as diseases, for most diseases are not our fault. Samuel Butler caricatured this absurdity in his invention of a country, Erewhon ("Nowhere" almost spelled backward), where all diseases are punished as offenses against the state. Butler describes an Erewhonian sentencing hearing for the offense of having pulmonary consumption:

> Prisoner at the bar, you have been accused of the great crime of laboring under pulmonary consumption, and ... you have been found guilty ... yours is no case for compassion: this is not your first offence ... you were convicted of aggravated bronchitis last year: and I find that though you are now only twenty-three years old you have been imprisoned on no less than fourteen occasions for illnesses of a more or less hateful character. ... It is all very well for you to say that you came of unhealthy parents, and had a severe accident in your childhood which permanently undermined your constitution; excuses such as these are the ordinary refuge of the criminal. ... There is no question of how you came to be wicked, but only this—namely, are you wicked or not? ... you may say that it is not your fault. ... I answer that whether your being in a consumption is your fault or no, it is a fault in you ... you may say that it is your misfortune to be criminal; I answer that it is your crime to be unfortunate. (Butler 1872)

Butler is of course correct: it would be absurdly unjust to punish all diseases, because most diseases are things that happen to us and are not conditions constituted by things we do. In the ancient etymology of "patient," most sufferers of diseases are passive not active, in both the bringing about of their condition and the symptoms manifesting that condition.

But overlap is not co-extensiveness. Some diseases we do culpably cause to exist in ourselves (e.g., cigarette-caused lung cancer), and the symptoms of some diseases are actions we do and not conditions we suffer under (e.g., using drugs). We can thus be at fault for having such a disease and for manifesting its symptomatic behaviors. It would be absurdly unjust to punish people *because* their condition and behaviors are rightly classified as being a disease, but such absurdity does not infect the idea that we may punish people for their conditions and behaviors *despite* those conditions and behaviors being rightly considered to be diseases. Being diseased is not a reason to punish people but it is also not a reason not to punish them.

Unfortunately it is easy to confuse these two relations between diseases and justified punishment such that the absurdity of one (punish because diseased) is thought to infect the other (punish despite being diseased). Consider these two statements from the opinions of the US Supreme Court in *Robinson v. California*. Justice Stewart wrote for the majority of the Court, holding that no one can constitutionally be punished for being a drug addict, on the rationale that being a drug addict was to be diseased:

It is unlikely that any State at this moment in history would attempt to make it a criminal offense for a person to be mentally ill, or a leper, or to be afflicted with venereal disease ... a law which made a criminal offense of such a disease would doubtless be universally thought to be an infliction of cruel and unusual punishment. ... Even one day in prison would be a cruel and unusual punishment for the 'offense' of having a common cold. (370 US at 666–667)

Justice Douglas echoed Stewart's disease rationale in his concurrence in the same case:

the prosecution [of addiction] is aimed at penalizing an illness. ... We would forget the teachings of the Eighth Amendment if we allowed sickness to be made a crime and permitted sick people to be punished for being sick. This age of enlightenment cannot tolerate such barbarous action. (370 US at 678)

Stewart and Douglas get it wrong: while it would be unjust to punish someone just because doctors had properly classified his condition as a diseased one—Butler's point—it would not necessarily be wrong (and certainly not "barbarous") to punish someone for morally blameworthy acts even if those acts were causative of or symptomatic of a condition properly classified as a disease. The correct inclusion of a condition as a disease cannot rule out moral blameworthiness and legal punishment even though that inclusion is not itself a basis for such blameworthiness and punishment.

I come then to the third route by which the medical profession and its acolytes have sought to show how addiction being a disease *ipso facto* means that addicts are to be excused from responsibility. This route depends on a feature of the "disease model of addiction" that we have not yet addressed. This feature is the deeper, physical nature to addiction that scientists believe they have discovered in the human brain. Consider this early but well-known summary of the brain pathology that is thought to underlie the behavior and phenomenology of addiction to drugs:

Although each drug that has been studied has some idiosyncratic mechanism of action [within the brain], virtually all drugs of abuse have common effects, either directly or indirectly, on a single pathway deep within the brain. This pathway, the mesolimbic reward system, extends from the ventral tegmentum to the nucleus accumbens, with projections to areas such as the limbic system and the orbitofrontal cortex. Activation of this system appears to be a common element in what keeps drug users taking drugs. This activity is not unique to any one drug; all addictive substances affect this circuit. (Leshner 1997, p. 46)[9]

Such seeking of some deeper, unifying nature to the natural kinds that disease entities have long been supposed to be[10] is an expected and legitimate part of science. In our daily life we brush into surface indicators that things like water, gold, polio, or addiction might be natural kinds, and we expect science to investigate and reveal to us whether such surface indicators are or are not underlain by some deeper, unifying nature that marks a kind as a natural kind. Such natures can themselves be of different kinds, but for behavioral/phenomenological surface indicators like the symptoms of addiction, underlying states of the brain are plausible places to look.

So there is nothing suspect about the disease model of addiction seeking a unifying nature for addiction in some pathological states of the brain. This is good science doing the work it is supposed to do. It is the second step of the inference from disease to excuse that is the trouble-maker here. The third way that that step is taken is when one assumes that any behavior that is physically caused is, by virtue of that causation, to be excused.[11]

There are two stunning problems for this bald assertion of an "incompatibilism" existing between physical causation of behavior and responsibility for that behavior. The first and main one is that the assertion is demonstrably false. For several hundred years—roughly since David Hume—philosophers have worked through a series of "compatibilisms." Recently I surveyed ten of these compatibilisms for neuroscientists, who like other scientists seem woefully ignorant that such a literature even exists, let alone what its content might be (Moore 2014, 2016b).

All forms of compatibilism share a denial of the supposed incompatibility of (1) being caused to do what we do and (2) being responsible for what we do. Of course, such compatibilists owe us an account of what it means to say that some action is excused because "he couldn't have done other than he did." If ability in this principle (usually called the "Principle of Alternative Possibilities" or "PAP") does not mean "uncaused," compatibilists need to tell us what it does mean.[12] On my own version of compatibilism—known as "classical compatibilism" or, in its revised form, "new conditionalist compatibilism"—one *could* not have done other than they did on some occasion, if and only if that person *would* not have done other than they did even if he were presented with very strong reasons to do so.[13] The relevant question of excuse is whether a wrongdoer lacked the capacity to do better, in this counterfactual sense of "capacity"—not whether his wrongdoing was caused by events in his brain.[14] Although Leshner's "activation of the mesolimbic reward system" may figure in an account of why addicts are rightly to be excused, that will not be because such reward system activation is a physical cause of addicts' behavior. Rather, such activation of the reward system will have to be shown to cause an incapacitation in the morally relevant sense.

The second problem for the asserted incompatibilism of cause and responsibility is that even if the asserted incompatibilism were true, it could not provide a theory of why addicts are excused *from a responsibility that non-addicts bear.* For given the plausibility of there being physical causes in the brain for all that we choose and do,[15] physical causation of addictive behavior can hardly be the basis for excusing addicts; rather it could only be the basis for excusing everybody from any responsibility for anything. Such a theory of *universal* excuse is not a theory of excuse at all; it is a theory why no one needs excuses because no one is responsible for anything anyway.

The only way of avoiding this unwelcome extension to universal excuse is by hedging one's bets about the physical causation of non-addicts' behaviors. Thus one might say that addicts' behaviors are "fully caused" by events deep in the brain, but that non-addicts are only "partly caused" to do what they do; or that addicts are "mechanically caused" to take drugs, whereas non-addicts are only "predisposingly" or "incliningly" caused to do wrongful acts; or that brain-event causation forms a larger part of the set of factors sufficient to explain addicts' behaviors but that such brain-event causation plays a more minor role in the set of factors sufficient to explain non-addicts' behaviors; and so on.[16] Such strategies aim to dilute the kind, degree, or strength of the physical causes of non-addicts' behaviors so that they can be held responsible, while the more strongly caused behaviors of addicts can then be excused without leading to universal excuse. One should say of all these maneuvers what Peter Strawson (1962) once said about one of them: the metaphysics such maneuvers require is "grotesque" in its nature and "desperate and panicky" in its motivation. No respectable science of human behavior should find these maneuvers even slightly tempting.

The upshot is that the disease model of addiction's thesis—that the behavior of addicts is physically caused by events deep in the brain—is a valid piece of scientific theorizing that is nonetheless not relevant to responsibility. If addiction excuses, it won't be because addiction is a physical cause of the behavior of addicts.

This allows us to put aside the shortcut offered up by the disease model of addiction to answering the concerns of this chapter. And now we can more generally put aside all three forms of the thought that medical classification of a condition as a disease carries any moral freight with regard to moral excuse. This frees us to look at medical definitions such as that with which we began in their proper light: these are attempts to pick out a natural phenomenon, addiction, by a profession with as much interest as that of the law in getting its descriptions and explanations of that phenomenon right. The stamp of the medical profession upon such a definition adds nothing to the authority that is has for us; it has such authority as it does possess only by virtue of its accuracy, not its provenance. Such a definition can nonetheless aid us in the task of providing some conceptualization of addiction with which to work.

The definition can use considerable simplification and compression, however. Morse is right: there is no seeming center of gravity to the definition.[17] Here I think that we can put both Leshner and Morse together, combining their views into the following idea about the essential features of addiction: addiction is indeed a state characterized by the phenomenology of craving for the thing to which one is addicted, as Morse holds, and such cravings characteristically bring with them behaviors characteristic of being compelled by them, as Leshner holds, inasmuch as behavior that yields to such cravings goes against other things the addict needs, desires, and values.

Very little turns on whether this is a complete (or even accurate as far as it goes) account of the essence of addiction. Given the provisional nature of any definition of addiction—provisional before the insights of an advancing science—all we need are indicators that succeed in referring to the natural kind of phenomenon that is an addiction. We more completely explore the nature of that thing as we explain why it exists and how it works to produce its symptomatic behaviors. It is to those two explanatory tasks to which we now turn.

The Explanation of Becoming an Addict

With this conceptualization of addiction under our belt, we can now turn to the explanations of addiction. Such explanations are the necessary precursors to seeing whether addiction can be an excuse.

We should distinguish two kinds of behaviors by addicts about which we need explanations: (1) at t_1, the using of drugs, alcohol, and so on, while not addicted but its use eventually causes one to become addicted, and (2) behavior at t_2 while addicted when that behavior is motivated or otherwise caused by the addict's need/desire for drugs, alcohol, and so on (the latter category includes both possession and use of such items and behaviors such as theft, assault, and murder when done in order to fund acquisition of such items). While I am in this chapter interested in the addict's responsibility for the second of these two sets of behaviors, it is commonly said that explaining the first of these behaviors will obviate the necessity of worrying very much about the explanation of the second. The thought is that if the explanation of why non-addicts use the drugs that eventually hook them is such that there is full responsibility at t_1 (for becoming an addict), then *a fortiori* there will be responsibility at t_2 (when they are an addict) as well, no matter how excusingly the t_2 behavior might otherwise be explained. Put simply, addicts are responsible for using as addicts no matter what might be the deteriorated state of their minds at t_2, because they were responsible at t_1 for becoming so deteriorated in the first place. On such a view we only need to explain the behavior of non-addicted users in order to know all we need to know to evaluate the behavior of addicted users. Before seeking an explanation for why addicts use and acquire drugs at t_2, I shall first examine this thought that we don't need such an explanation in order to evaluate the use and acquisition of drugs by addicts.

There is a well-known tendency in discussions about responsibility generally (not just the responsibility of addicts) to engage what is known in the trade as the "tracing strategy" (Vargas 2005; Fischer and Tognazzini 2009).[18] The general idea is this: if at the time of causing harm to another (call that time "t_2") the actor suffers under some debilitating and excusing condition—an epileptic seizure, say—the actor is at fault at some earlier time ("t_1") for getting himself into such a debilitating condition, than a condition that normally excuses for bad acts at t_2 doesn't excuse. The excuse the actor would have had at the later time is forfeited by tracing his fault back to some earlier time when he brought about the conditions for his later excuse.

In the case of the behavior of addicts who acquire and use drugs (t_2), they themselves earlier acted when they were not addicts (t_1) in ways that made them addicts. According to the tracing strategy, therefore, they are responsible for their acts at t_2, no matter how excusing addiction might otherwise be.

This is a terrible argument about the responsibility of addicts because the tracing strategy itself is generally a terrible argument for responsibility. The stunning problem for the tracing strategy lies in its equation of an actor's blameworthiness at t_1 with the blameworthiness that actor would have had at t_2 if he were not in the debilitating condition he culpably (at t_1) caused himself to be in. There is no reason whatsoever to think that such an equation is necessarily (or even often) true.

Take duress as an example. Suppose at t_2 the defendant badly beats a victim, but he does so because the defendant was threatened with unlawful force against his children unless he did what the threatener told him to do. Suppose the threat at t_2 is sufficiently credible, proximate, and onerous to excuse the defendant from most or all blame. The tracing strategy would eliminate this defendant's excuse of duress if at t_1 the defendant culpably placed himself in a position where he might be subjected to such a threat. This means that a defendant who is only negligent at t_1 in unreasonably risking that he might be coerced into doing some minor wrong is to be blamed as an intentional beater at t_2 with no account taken of the ordinarily excusing threat. An unexcused, intentional beating (for which this defendant is blamed under the tracing strategy) is much more blameworthy than a merely negligent risking of some minor wrong being done; yet the tracing strategy equates the two, blaming slightly culpable, minor wrongdoers as if they were seriously culpable, major wrongdoers.

While the Model Penal Code (with two partial exceptions related to the excuses of duress and intoxication) rejects the tracing strategy, the common law of crimes persists in the strategy and gives it its own doctrinal name, "actio in libera causa" (an act that is free and responsible in its cause even if not free and responsible in itself). Why does the tracing strategy persist in the face of its obvious potential for disproportionate blame and punishment? Mostly because there is another analysis that is not unjust and with which the tracing strategy is confused.[19] According to this alternative analysis, when someone culpably does some wrong at t_1, the doing of that wrong can cause a further state of affairs to exist at t_2 for which the defendant is properly blamable. Suppose, for example, that the defendant in the above duress hypothetical wanted to beat up the person he did in fact beat up but lacked the courage to do so on his own. So at t_1 he coerces another to coerce him at t_2 to beat up the intended victim. Under the alternative analysis, at t_2 the defendant does not lose his excuse as he would under the tracing strategy—he was coerced into beating up the victim and he retains that excuse of coercion; but at t_1 the defendant's act (of coercing another) causes the threat which causes the defendant to beat the victim up—that is, at t_1 the defendant has intentionally caused contact on the victim's body with his fists and should be blamed accordingly. He is guilty of assault, but it is a t_1 assault for which he has no excuse, not a t_2 assault where he has the excuse of coercion.

Unlike the tracing strategy this alternative analysis blames and punishes people proportionate to their desert. It recognizes that sometimes one can equally well cause a bad state of affairs to exist at t_2 *by some act as some earlier time t_1* as well as by some later act at t_2, and that when one does so one is blameworthy in proportion to the culpability with which one acted at the relevant time. There is no fictional equation of blameworthiness here, as there is with the tracing strategy.

Let us apply all of this to addiction. The relevant t_1 is when the addict is not yet addicted but takes the drugs that make him addicted. (This of course occurs over an interval of time, not all at once, but this nuance can be ignored for these purposes.) Are non-addicted users to blame for using the drugs that make them into addicts? Surely in many cases that answer is "yes," although it is a qualified "yes."

It is yes because the conditions of culpability are often met at t_1. Each user may intend to become addicted (think Timothy Leary types), or more often they may know that they will or that they might become addicted. Or they should know of such a risk even if they do not in fact know. In all such cases, such non-addicted users satisfy the conditions of culpability with respect to the consequence of being an addict.

The qualification to this "yes" lies in the second aspect of blameworthiness in addition to culpability, which is wrongdoing: one might doubt that becoming an addict is a wrong at all (or perhaps it is a wrong that one had a right to do) (Moore 1998). The worry is that perhaps ruining one's own life prospects, abusing one's own talents, and so on are one's own business, and that is not wrong to do because it is not a wrong to someone other than the actor. True, the criminal laws currently on the books criminalize the acts of use that produce addiction, but one might well doubt that laws have the capacity to make morally wrong behaviors that were not, prior to the law's enactment, antecedently wrong.

For purposes of argument here, however, we should concede that at t_1 non-addicted users who use sufficiently to addict themselves are both culpable and wrongdoers, that is, blameworthy. Can one use this (at least arguendo-conceded) moral conclusion as sufficient to find them blameworthy at t_2 for acquiring and using drugs when they are addicted? The tracing strategy would answer affirmatively, but that simply illustrates the general injustice of the tracing strategy. Non-addicted drug users' culpability and wrongdoing at t_1 need bear no relationship to the culpability and wrongdoing that they would have had if they robbed, stole, or used drugs at t_2 in some counterfactually non-addicted state.

So using the tracing strategy is out, here as it is generally. Does the alternative analysis outlined above show that addicts are blameworthy for their acts of theft and use at t_2 by virtue of their culpable acts of using at t_1 having caused these later bad actions at t_2? It does not. First of all, the causal connection—between the much earlier acts of use that made an addict an addict and the later acts of acquisition and use of drugs—is much too attenuated to support responsibility. Even if a later theft at t_2, for example, counterfactually depended on earlier, addiction-producing acts of use at t_1, the t_1 using is neither the wrong of a t_2 stealing nor the proximate cause of such a wrong. Second, the culpability needed for serious wrongs like theft or robbery is lacking at t_1 when the soon-to-be addict uses drugs. Such a user at t_1 at most might be aware of a risk that if his present use leads to addiction, he might later resort to theft or robbery to support his habit. Such recklessness is a lesser culpability than that of an intentional thief or assaulter.

The upshot is that there is no legitimate basis for holding addicts responsible for their acts as addicts because they are (arguably) responsible for becoming addicts in the first place. The tracing strategy is unavailable because generally unjust, and the alternative, analysis does not justify such responsibility in the particular case of addiction. The result is that we must explore the moral responsibility of addicts for their acts of use and acquisition on its own terms, unaffected by whatever responsibility addicts might have for becoming addicts.

The Second Explanatory Question: What Explains Why Addicts (Despite the Known Costs to Their Lives) Continue to Acquire and Use Drugs?

The upshot of the discussion just completed is that we must seek our answer about the responsibility of addicts for addiction-motivated behaviors while they are addicts, in the explanations of those behaviors themselves. There is no cheap and easy substitution of the responsibility addicts may have for becoming addicts, for their responsibility for their acts as addicts.

The striking feature of such behaviors—the feature pricking our curiosity and raising at least intuitions of compulsion and excuse—is that they typically seem so self-destructive and irrational. Addicts often ruin their lives, their relationships, their jobs, their hopes and ambitions for themselves, in ways and to extents that are puzzling and suggestive of being driven by "forces" not under their control.

The beginning of wisdom here is to recognize how diverse the explanations for addicts' behaviors may be. Even the "self-destructive" characterization does not fit all addicts. Decades ago Harry Frankfurt distinguished what he called the "willing addict" from the unwilling addict (Frankfurt 1971). Willing addicts choose to continue to use the drugs to which they are addicted as a matter of rational choice: although perhaps conflicted about it, the willing addict most wants to take drugs over all the other things he also desires at a given time; he values the experience of intoxication (perhaps as Aldous Huxley's "voyage of discovery for those with the courage to take it")[20]; he believes correctly that satisfying such a desire will rule out satisfying the other, conflicting, but less strong, desires that he also has; he also acts on rational beliefs about how to obtain drugs, exhibiting means/end rationality; despite the costs that he acknowledges his drug use causes, the willing addict nonetheless feels as satisfied by his theft, possession, and use as he predicted he would feel when he decided upon this course of action. One might add that such an action, choice, desire, evaluation, and enjoyment ("liking") are all in character for this addict. And we might further add that he has such a personality in part because that is the kind of person he has chosen to be. The willing addict, in short, is rational in his choices to act in ways that continue his addiction.[21]

Unwilling addicts will be of greater interest to our moral question. This is because the willing addict just described evinces no defects of rationality that give even a hint of excuse. Willing addicts take drugs because that is what they most want to do, just as people cheat on their taxes, murder their enemies, rob banks, and so on, because that is what they most want to do. Such drug users are ordinary criminals (again with the caveat that the law may well be wrong in its current criminalizing of mere use or possession of drugs). But it is implausible to think that all addicts are willing addicts, so we should turn to consider unwilling addicts. Detailing how and why such unwilling addicts nonetheless behave as they do is a delicate and nuanced task, in part because there is no one answer that holds for all unwilling addicts. Consider the range of explanations that follows.

The Conative Failure to Form an Intention: The "Automaticity" Model of Addiction

Surprisingly prominent in the literature describing the psychology of addiction is one or other of various models according to which addicts use drugs and steal to get drugs while they are on so-called automatic pilot. Addiction is presented as a case where choice/intention is (largely) absent so that one's desire to use drugs never gets integrated with one's other desires or with one's evaluative beliefs in the way that they do when we deliberately choose to do something. Such failures to form an intention are one way that addicts may use drugs despite that act not being what they most want or most value. As Jeanette Kennett sees it, "drug-related stimuli … cue action *automatically*," which she believes results in a "subsequent loss of self-control" (Kennett 2013, p. 271).[22]

Addictive Cravings as a Kind of Emotion-Driven Bypassing of Intention

Undeniably one of the salient markers of addiction is how addicts experience their desires (to do that to which they are addicted) as cravings. Cravings are rightly seen as a kind of emotion. It is commonly thought that strong emotions can "unhinge the will" in the sense that intention and choice are bypassed or sidelined by the frenzy of such emotional storms. The thought is not unique to cravings. Some such explanation is given for actors who are provoked to do things they would not otherwise do by the outrageous behavior of their victims, behavior that makes such actors so *angry* that their anger is said to unhinge their reason. Likewise to explain why some actors again do acts they otherwise would not do, and know that they should not do, when driven by the *fear* aroused by a threat of another. Nor is the thought, when it is confined to cravings and not other emotions, limited to the cravings of addicts. I take the depiction of the craving for high social position in Theodore Dreiser's *An American Tragedy* (Dreiser 1925) to be an accurate portrayal of how strong emotions of cravings that are not those of an addict can cause an actor to do what he cannot bring himself to do through intention and choice—in Dreiser's example, strike the blow, capsize the boat, and fail to rescue the victim he so wants to be rid of in order to satisfy his craving for high social position.

Cognitive Failures to Keep Degrees of Beliefs Responsive to the Evidence Available to Support It

Part of the phenomenology of addicted behaviors seems to be the erosion of belief in three distinct ways. (1) Dieters, for example, may come to believe momentarily that they can eat the dessert in front of them and that somehow such consumption will not be inconsistent with losing weight. Or (2), a person who has reached a level of tolerance so as not to have found enjoyment in taking drugs in the recent past may yet believe (without further evidence) that this time the taking of drugs will produce the satisfaction, pleasure, and enjoyment that has previously eluded him. Or yet again (3), an addict who has tried to quit before and failed may come to believe that failure is inevitable (despite the social science showing that it is not) and, being thus resigned to such failure, does not try to resist his temptations. Jeanette Kennett dubs addicts suffering from this last kind of erosion of beliefs, "resigned addicts" (Kennett 2013, p. 160).

Such erosions of belief—erosions that result in the actor temporarily believing things contrary to what the evidence available to him would support—seem to be due to wishful thinking, itself a kind of self-deception. One craves the drug so powerfully that this causes one to temporarily "forget" what one knows and instead believes (1) that one can "have his cake and eat it too," (2) that pleasure is just an injection away, and (3) that success in quitting is impossible.

Motivational Failure: Not Integrating One's Desires into What One Most Wants

Just as an actor's decisional processes may skip the forming of a choice or intention (as described before), an actor may skip the forming of an all-things-considered desire, what I have called elsewhere what he *most wants*. The beliefs of some schizophrenics give us a model for how this can work. A delusional belief that one is being persecuted, for example, can be "frozen" in the sense that it is immune to correction or outweighing by other, contrary beliefs. Frozen beliefs don't "play nice" with their fellow beliefs, that is, don't combine with those other beliefs the way that ordinary beliefs do.

The cravings of addicts can operate vis-à-vis competing desires the way frozen beliefs operate against competing beliefs in the minds of schizophrenics. Such cravings are "asocial" vis-à-vis their fellow desires in the way that frozen beliefs are asocial vis-à-vis their fellow beliefs. Being not combinable with their fellows, they are not amenable to correction by desires that are, in some sense at least, stronger. The result is an unresolved conflict of desires whereby the craving may directly cause choice in accordance with it, without there being any overall want operating as a causal intermediary.

This "non-combinability" characteristic of the cravings of addicts is not so much a feature of the cravings themselves, as if they possessed some intrinsic "reverse magnetism" vis-à-vis other desires. Rather, it is that addicts are robbed of one of our main tools for integrating conflicting desires into an overall want, namely, *attention*. In resolving conflicts of desires we need to be able to put aside attention to one desire while we attend to the other items that we also desire. Whereas this is just what addicts have a difficult time doing: the craving monopolizes attention on the cravings' object, precluding attention to the other desires that may be of greater strength (Wallace 1999, pp. 645–647; Sinnott-Armstrong 2013, p. 128). In this too addictive cravings resemble the frozen beliefs of paranoid schizophrenics: in both cases the craving or belief is an obsessional mental state, a state the actor cannot easily cease focusing on and a state that drives out focus on other states (of desire or belief) and thus prevents them from being considered, compared, and integrated into overall desires and overall beliefs.

Normative Failure: Acting and Wanting Against One's Better Judgment

Perhaps most common to the phenomenology of addiction is the failure of the content of what one most wants to match the content of what one values, that is, judges one should want. In such cases one's evaluative beliefs fail to match one's desires and wants. Although choice and action lines up with what one most wants in such cases, they do not line up with one's evaluative judgments of desirability. The addict chooses to take drugs against his own best judgment. Victor Tadros generally speaks of desires that are not "accepted [by the agent] in light of the agent's values" (Tadros 2005, p. 343). This way of putting things finds resonance in the contemporary literature on addiction: addicts are said to want what they don't value (Holton and Berridge 2013; Kennett 2013).

Addiction by Akrasia: Failures to Execute One's Intention Not to Take Drugs

I turn now from the unwilling addict's failings that occur before choice to failings that occur after choice is made. I turn, that is, from failures to choose in light of what one most wants and most values to cases where one fails to do what one chooses. (Notice that in either case, one ultimately *acts* in ways not fulfilling of what one most wants or most values.) Relevant here are not cases of ordinary failure of our intentions to produce what we intended to produce; rather, of concern here is where the addict doesn't even try to do what he intended to do (which in the cases in which we are interested was to abstain from taking drugs). Eaters may choose, for example, not to eat the dessert in front of them, and such choice may be fully in line with what they most want and most value, but they intentionally eat the cake anyway, despite their choice not to do so and despite the wants and values that motivated that choice. Such persons are classically considered to be akratic, that is, to suffer from weakness of will.

Many would deny that anyone actually intends at the time he is acting not to do A, and then despite or perhaps even because of that intention does A anyway. Yet we should separate criticizable irrationality from psychological impossibility. The akratic who acts against his present intention is indeed highly irrational, but that does not mean there are no such cases. Moreover, if we move from synchronic cases to what are called diachronic cases, weakness of will seems quite familiar. A diachronic case of weakness of will is where the addict changes his intention over time so that at the moment he takes drugs his act is in line with his new intention, but such an agent is still irrational because both before and after his taking of drugs his intention is *not* to take drugs. I characterize such vacillating intentions as "non-sticky" intentions.[23] Unlike ordinary (which is to say sticky) intentions, non-sticky intentions do not preclude constant re-evaluation of what the agent most wants to do or thinks, all things considered, that he should do. Such non-stickiness is criticizably irrational because intention is not performing its conflict-resolving function; but it is psychologically possible (and is indeed, quite common and familiar).

Where Liking Doesn't Match Wanting or Valuing: Failures of Satisfaction

Even if all else is in perfect working order, an addict's drug-taking may still represent a failure in practical rationality because the state of affairs desired, valued, intended, and caused by one's acts may give the actor little or no satisfaction when that state of affairs is realized. Berridge and Holton, for example, have argued that addicts have this kind of mismatch between their wants and what they truly like ("like" in the sense of predict that it will give pleasure or be more generally pleasing to one) (Holton and Berridge 2013). They argue that for such addicts getting high gives no pleasure even though such state of intoxication is wanted in advance and motivates acts to achieve it. Worse, such addicts may repeat the action that disappointed them in the past knowing full well that it will disappoint them again. This is a failure of practical rationality for such addicts, a failure constituted by desires that do not do what desires are supposed to do, namely, produce pleasure in their satisfaction.

*   *   *

In each of these seven ways unwilling addicts do things (use, steal, etc.) that are irrational. The right way to see these seven irrationalities is not as omnipresent in the behaviors of each unwilling addict. Rather, behaviors by addicts are no doubt best explained on a case-by-case basis, each addict behaving as he does on each occasion for his own, relatively unique combination of irrational factors. Still, each such unwilling addict does behave irrationally in one or more of these senses. This is enough to place such addicts within the ballpark of moral excuse. Whether such addicts are in fact excused is the topic of the next and last part of this chapter.

ADDICTION AS A MORAL EXCUSE AND LEGAL DEFENSE

Lessened Opportunity as Excuse: The Threat of Withdrawal Faced by Addicts

We turn from the explanation of addiction to the moral question of whether addiction excuses those who act because of their addiction. I earlier put aside several ways of clouding this moral issue. One lay in the confusion that if addictions are diseases, responsibility for them evaporates. Another lay in the notion that if addictions *cause* the criminal behavior of addicts—irrespective of whether such causes mark addicts as diseased or not—then behavior is excused by that fact alone. A third unnecessary clouding of the moral issue lay in the illicit substitution of the responsibility users may well have for becoming addicts, for the responsibility addicts might have for their behavior as addicts. I now put aside a fourth consideration that clouds the relevant moral issue here.

There is a fundamental misunderstanding of the nature of excuses that has unfortunately invaded the discussion of whether addiction is an excuse. The misunderstanding is perhaps best seen by adverting to the standard excuse of duress. Duress is the doing of a wrongful action required by another who threatens us with adverse consequences if we do not do it. Some (including my former self) have thought that duress at least sometimes excuses because our *opportunities* to do the right thing are so constricted by the threat of adverse consequences that we cannot fairly be blamed for yielding to the threat by doing what the threatener wants (Moore 1990). Although there is no threatening second agent in the use or acquisition of drugs by addicts, the analogy drawn is to the "threat" of nature: if the addict doesn't do what he needs to do to acquire and use drugs, then he will suffer the adverse consequences of withdrawal. Given the painfulness and inevitability of withdrawal following on nonuse of some drugs by those addicted to them, the addict is said to have much less opportunity than the non-addicted person to refrain from using and acquiring drugs. Thus Walter Sinnott-Armstrong concludes that the threat of withdrawal can constitute a kind of excusing loss of control because "the addict cannot quit" (Sinnott-Armstrong 2013).

The misunderstanding common to this loss-of-opportunity version of both duress and addiction is this: although lessened opportunity to avoid doing wrongful acts may lessen blameworthiness, it does not do so by lessening culpability (it does not, in other words, *excuse*). What lesser opportunity can do is lessen the degree of wrong done; it does this, when it does this, by showing that something good came out of the wrongful act in question so that *net*, less wrongdoing was done. Such lessened opportunities thus operate as partial justifications, not as excuses. When such opportunity costs of ordinarily rightful action get high enough, they may not *partially* justify the omission of such ordinary rightful action, they may fully justify it. Thus, Jay Wallace assesses addicts to have lesser blameworthiness because of withdrawal, not because the threat of withdrawal excuses but because the threat of withdrawal may make the addict's use *permissible* whereas for non-addicts such use is *impermissible* (Wallace 1999 p. 644).

Even with this misunderstanding removed so that withdrawal's potential to lessen blameworthiness is properly categorized, withdrawal-related loss of opportunity does not do much moral work with respect to the responsibility of addicts. Withdrawal does not exist for non-drug- and non-alcohol-related addictions, and it is almost nonexistent for some addictive drugs such as cocaine (Holton and Berridge 2013, p. 244). Even when withdrawal does exist, with perhaps the exception of alcohol, it is not that adverse a state to suffer through to constitute much of a diminution of the addict's opportunity set. Some have likened withdrawal from non-use of opioids to be no worse than having an average case of the flu, and we do not let flu sufferers off the hook for stealing flu medicine that they cannot afford to buy (Richard and Pearce 2013).

The Alleged Incapacitation of Addicts by Their Addiction

In any case, the proper question of *excuse* for addicts is a question about their diminished capacities, not their diminished opportunities. We thus need to repair to the explanations earlier advanced in Part IV to see whether any of them instantiate some plausible version(s) of an incapacity that excuses the behavior of unwilling addicts.

If one took the automaticity model of addiction literally, addicts would not be responsible for their addiction-motivated behaviors. This would not be because addicts were *excused* for such behaviors; rather, it would be because these behaviors were not actions and so there would be nothing to excuse. But no one (I think) thinks that the supposed automaticity of addictive behavior is to be taken so literally. Addicts *act* when they use drugs and they act when they steal so that they can acquire drugs. As Holton and Berridge recognize in dubbing the automaticity model of addiction the "habit account," addictive automaticity is much more like the preconscious actions described by William James about ordinary life, where habits and skills have developed to the point that *conscious* intention and choice is not needed to successfully execute these routines (James 1890). Yet such preconscious actions are ones for which the actor is fully responsible because they are within the control of the actor. So if addicted behaviors are simply the bypassing of conscious intentions, no diminishment of responsibility is to be found here.

Does this moral conclusion change if our behavior surprises us when we do find ourselves engaged in it—such as finding ourselves nibbling on cake when we had resolved not to have dessert today or speeding through traffic when we had decided there was no reason to hurry today? Wittgenstein once famously quipped that actions are marked "by an absence of surprise" (Wittgenstein 1953)—should we reverse that and think that the *presence* of surprise marks a bit of behavior as being a non-action? Surely not. When I munch or speed preconsciously and am surprised and irritated at myself when I see that that is what I have been doing, I rightly regard this as my fault, something for which I can justly be blamed. We control these behaviors as we control the routines of skills and beliefs that do not surprise us when we eventually turn our attention to them.

To the extent that addicted behavior is automatic in the absent-minded way of preconscious behaviors, no excuse is to be found for it. Does it change this moral conclusion if we add strong emotion (such as the cravings of an addict) to the mix? Do actions that are automatic—that bypass intention—become more excusable to the extent that this automaticity is due to strong emotion? Surely strong emotionality as the genesis of action does not by itself tend to diminish responsibility. Being passionate about one's commitments, whether good or bad, does not diminish one's praiseworthiness/blameworthiness for acting on those commitments. Indeed, save for some unrealistic Kantian fantasies about willing against all inclination, it would seem that some emotionality must be built into all motivated action.

It is more specifically the unhinging of will by emotion that gives rise to some intuition of excuse here. Emotions can incapacitate the will in the sense of making it more difficult to exert self-control. The criminal law is thus not wrong when it eliminates or reduces responsibility for those who do wrongful acts because of their fear of the threat of others (duress when it operates as an excuse), their fear of the "threats" in nature (necessity when it operates as an excuse), their craving to preserve their own life (self-defense when it operates as an excuse), and their anger at the provoking act of the victim (provocation when it operates as an excuse). Might one say the same about the excusability of actions done because of emotions involved in the strong cravings typical of addiction?

Although there is a there there (as Gertrude Stein might say) with regard to the excusing quality of emotional unhinging of decisions, it is a very slim slice of moral landscape even for anger or fear. For addictive cravings, it is almost nonexistent. Most yieldings to emotion are decisions made in the service of those emotions; it is not a preclusion of such decision and choice. This is even more true of addicts yielding to their cravings than it is for defenders defending themselves in self-defenses, those threatened yielding to the threats of others, and so on. The former are deliberate, intentional, decisions made by the addict.

That the cravings cause the choice to take drugs is not enough; anger, fear, and other emotions frequently cause choices by us that are in no sense excused.

We should next examine how we should assess the responsibility of those who, through wishful thinking, conflicts of desire, or conflicts between desire and evaluative beliefs, do not choose to do what they most want to do or most value doing when they choose to use drugs. There are all defects of rationality, as we earlier explored. Are they also excusing?

Let us begin with the addict whose cognitions have been eroded by his craving for some drug. Some addicts' cravings seemingly cause them to believe (1) that there is no conflict between what one most wants and most values, on the one hand, and taking drugs now, even though there is such a conflict; (2) that this time one will find the drug experience pleasurable, even though one's past experiences should tell one that in fact it will not be pleasurable; or (3) that one will fail if he tries to quit, even though there is good evidence available to him supporting the opposite belief.

Although one can say, very generally and paraphrasing Aristotle, that ignorance joins compulsion as the other of two kinds of excuses, in point of fact only ignorance (or mistake) about certain things lessens one's responsibility. To lessen responsibility, such ignorance must be about some wrong-making characteristics of one's actions. To be ignorant that there is poison in the drink one is serving, or to mistake a man for a stump at which one is shooting, is relevant to the diminishment/elimination of responsibility, for these are mistakes about the causal properties of an act that make it wrong. To be mistaken about the color of the hair of one's intended rape victim, or to not know her parentage, is not relevant at all to our responsibility assessments.

This negative verdict—about the irrelevance of immaterial mistakes to responsibility—does not change when the ignorance or mistake was a necessary condition of the actor doing the wrong that he did. Suppose a rapist would not have raped the victim he did had he known that she was pregnant or had he known that she wasn't a natural blond. Ignorance or mistake about such matters was thus necessary for him to have done what he did, because the presence or absence of these factors happened to be motivationally significant for this rapist. Even so, such mistakes/ignorance about facts that are immaterial to the wrongness of what was done—even if material to this particular individual's motivation—are in no way diminishing of responsibility.

We can thus put aside worries about the excusability of addicts whose mistakes were necessary for them to use and acquire drugs. Mistakes about whether drug use will give them pleasure, whether they can or cannot quit, or whether their cravings are or are not consistent with what they most want or most value are all by the by for assessment of their responsibility.

Some would resist this conclusion by thinking that addictive cravings interfere with the processes of rational belief formation, and for mistaken beliefs that are necessary for addicts to act as they do in using and acquiring drugs, such interference with belief formation is therefore a causing of a lessening of the addict's capacity for rational action. The paradigm here might be the interference in belief formation done to Patty Hearst by the coercive indoctrination ("brainwashing") done to her by her kidnappers, the Symbionese Liberation Army (SLA). The SLA indoctrinated Patty to believe that her wealthy parents had disowned her and abandoned her to her fate. Suppose this mistaken belief by Patty, although immaterial to the wrong she did (bank robbery), nonetheless was motivationally significant for her, that is, she would not have robbed the Hibernia Branch of the Bank of America in San Francisco had she known the truth about her parents. The analogy for addicts would be to liken the disturbance in the formation of motivationally significant beliefs done by addictive cravings to the disturbance done by brainwashing. In each case, the argument is, the actor wouldn't have done the wrong she did if she had not been mistaken about some facts, and that mistake was not her fault because such a mistake was caused by interfering factors outside her control.

The error in this argument lies in its assumption that cravings (or brainwashings for that matter) interfere in a morally relevant way with belief formation. The deeper error here is to conceive of belief formation as some hyper-rational process whereby no factor that is itself not probative evidence for the truth of a belief can have any causal role in the production of that belief if that belief is to be rationally held. This is an error because it ignores the commonness of beliefs being influenced by all kinds of factors having little to do with the probative evidence supporting of those beliefs' truth. Who we are taught by, what happens to grab our attention, what mood (of receptivity) we happen to be in when we confront evidence, and so on, all have influence on what we believe. Even though the standard by which we adjudge a belief to be rational lies in a proportionately of degree of belief to the evidence available to support it, many beliefs that are rational by that standard are not formed through a process focusing exclusively on such evidence. Finding excuse for addicts in this cognitive locale would be to romanticize the processes by which rational beliefs are formed.[24]

The moral issue we next face (which is about desires) bears some resemblance to the issue just resolved about beliefs, namely, is there some rational mode of (now desire rather than belief) formation with which addictive cravings unduly interfere, which interference gives rise to excuse? On this model of addiction, cravings are said to monopolize attention, freezing stronger desires out from competition with them and resulting in choices (to use and acquire drugs) that are not in accordance with what one most wants.[25] Does this diminish the addict's responsibility?

As with belief formation, this forces us to confront whether responsibility depends on some normal mode of both (component) desire acquisition and (overall) want formation existing such that deviation from this mode is excusing. There is a rationalistic picture of this mode that is hopelessly romantic about human capacities and that must for this reason be put aside. This is the view that we form evaluative beliefs about what is desirable and then choose desires to conform to such evaluative beliefs. Yet like factual beliefs, our desires—both componential and overall—are not (much) up to our choice and our will in this way. Our desires arise within us more than they spring from our choices about them. So it cannot be that addicts are to be excused because their desires do not obediently proceed from their evaluative beliefs. For all of us, non-addicts and addicts alike, would be excused if this were the case.

Holton and Berridge have no romantic illusions about how our desires generally arise, but they nonetheless conclude that:

> something goes badly wrong with the process by which substance addicts ... form their desires ... substance addiction results from the malfunctioning of a normally rational system for creating intrinsic desires. (Holton and Berridge 2013, p. 265)

The malfunctioning they have in mind consists of drug-induced spiking of desire into the kind of intensively experienced desire we call a craving, the asociability of such cravings with other, more normal desires, and the monopolization of attention that marks such asociability and makes it as potent as it is in the prevention of overall want formation.

Taking these one at a time: surely the intensity of a craving does no excusing work (so long as it does not unhinge the will, as above discussed). Strength of desire, as Aristotle remarked long ago, is surely not by itself excusing of action done to satisfy such a desire.

As to the "asociability" of desires, whether this is excusing depends on whether one had some fair opportunity to integrate such component desires into an overall want.[26] And such fair opportunity, on the Holton/Berridge account, depends on what control one has of the monopolization of attention, so let us turn to that aspect of the problem.

Everyday life confirms the limited control we have of obsessional thoughts. The melody that we cannot get out of our head, the insult we cannot forget, and the image of a loved one that will not disappear are familiar experiences of obsessional thoughts by persons who are neither addicts nor obsessive-compulsive neurotics. Such experience confirms two truths about this phenomenology of addicts here: (1) it can be difficult to be rid of the thought of using drugs once that thought has come into existence by some drug-related cue in the environment and (2) yet it is not impossible to do, mostly via indirect strategies of distraction and supplantation rather than by a direct strategy of willing away. The first of these truths is enough to reduce the responsibility a little in line with the small break we accord to obsessional neurotics; the second is enough not to eliminate such responsibility entirely.

Consider next the striking experience of many addicts that their own wants and choices fly in the face of their better judgment. Acting against one's own best judgment is a phenomenon to be found in a far broader range of cases than just those of addicted behavior. It is the favored form of locution of many spurious claims of excuse, from the pathetic males who cannot take a rejection by their supposed love object and therefore kill her, through the righteous religious zealots who proclaim their sinfulness yet repeatedly choose to do what their evaluative beliefs tell them they should not do, to the childish, "the

Devil made me do it." The interesting question is whether there are any genuine forms of such an excuse, and, if there are, whether any cases of addictive behavior present a plausible instance of such excuse.

The weakness of the case for there being any excuse to be found in these environs can be glimpsed by noting that some quite respectable moral theorizing regards such cases as the very paradigm of responsible and blameworthy action. Gideon Rosen, Michael Zimmerman, and Douglas Husak have all urged recently that those who choose contrary to their own best moral judgment are the *most* blameworthy of wrongdoers, not the least (Rosen 2002; Zimmerman 2008; Husak 2016). Their point: acting in the face of knowing the facts by virtue of which some act is wrong is bad enough because it reveals a will that is nonresponsive to moral reasons, but to act in the face not only of that knowledge but also of knowledge that what one is doing is morally wrong reveals a will that is truly vicious. Acting contrary to one's better judgment on this view becomes a harbinger of culpability, not a defeater of it.

Those who find excuse for addicts in these quarters seek to distinguish the addicts' kind of choosing against their own best moral judgment from the cases envisioned by Husak, Rosen, and Zimmerman. Addicts, they say, experience their choices as not their own. As Freudians say, such addicts see their choices, and the cravings behind them, as "ego-alien," as belonging to a "not-me," an alien thing, an it, an "id" (Eagle 1983). Yet where there is no break in the continuity of the consciousness of the actor (so that the "not-me" or disavowed decision is made in an altered state of consciousness, as where one is asleep, unconscious because in shock, has the amnesia between the personalities of a multiple-personalitied person, is under hypnosis or posthypnotic suggestion, is in some fugue state induced by torture or brainwashing, etc.), those items that are "not-me" are identified solely by the sense of identification of the actor. This is troublesome for reasons I expressed in earlier work (not particularly in relation to addiction):

> [T]he worry [is] that we as moral agents have limited normative power to map out the domain of excuse for ourselves by our self-identifications … that our own self-identifications … can make us excused … is troubling. Seemingly the size and boundaries of our moral agency is not up to us in the way or to the degree that this doctrine of excuse suggests. (Moore 2016a, p. 200)

Even Freud himself once scornfully remarked that he would "leave it to the jurist to construct for social purposes a responsibility that is artificially limited to the metapsychological ego" and that this would be to "disregard the evil in the id" and "not make my ego responsible for it" (Freud 1961, p. 133). True responsibility is based on the choices of the entire self, and that self includes both the choices and desires behind them that go against what one most values.

The akratic addict exhibits no defects of rationality up to and including his choices; his irrationality lies after such choices in that he cannot effectuate those choices in action. Our current question is whether such gross and plain irrationality excuses. As a first cut at answering this moral question, surely the intuitive answer is no. Such weakness is not only not excusing; it is itself a form of moral shortcoming. When St. Paul complains in Romans vii that "the good which I want to do, I fail to do" and that "what I do is the wrong which is against my will," he was not exonerating himself, he was blaming himself. Such weakness to do what one knows is right has perhaps a contemptible cast to it that fully affirmed and willed evil does not (Duff 2013, pp. 165–165), but both on their face are morally condemnable, not excusing (Hill 1986, pp. 135–137). True, we have limited capacities to strengthen our will in general by will power-building exercises and even less strengthening capacity in particular cases by willing our self to be stronger of will. But that is true of our ability to shape our desires too—yet no one thinks that my insufficient concern for others, my hatred of some virtuous person, or my fondness for watching others suffer, excuses me just because these attitudes, desires, or emotions are difficult to eliminate or even substantially change very much. Some aspects of who we are ground our blameworthiness for our actions even when those aspects are not subject to our willing them to be otherwise.

I take it that Anglo-American criminal law recognizes this moral truth in its doctrines of duress and provocation. Model Penal Code section 2.09 allows the excuse of duress only when the threats are such that a "person of reasonable firmness" would have been unable to resist them. Such a restriction seemingly eliminates weakness of will as a legal excuse in that akratics do not have a reasonable firmness of will. Similarly, the common law's partial, provocation defense to murder requires that the provoking act of the victim be such as would make a "reasonable person" lose his powers of self-control over his anger (Duff 2006). One of the attributes that makes a person "reasonable" in this context is that he has the power to control emotions (like anger) possessed by a person of reasonable firmness. The hot-tempered, impulsive, pugnacious, emotionally explosive, unthinking brutes get no excuse under such a standard, no matter how deeply and how demonstrably they lack the power to control their emotions because their will to do so is weak.[27]

Consider, lastly, the addict who continues to want to take drugs even though they bring him no satisfaction and he knows it. Isolated instances of this form of irrationality do not on their face tempt one toward excuse. Andre Gide's Lafcadio is disquieted by his pushing an old man out of a moving train to that man's death, whereas he had anticipated some feelings of satisfaction (at proving his surmounting of conventional morality) (Gide 1927). Lafcadio's lack of satisfaction in no way excuses his gratuitous killing of an innocent. Holton and Berridge distinguish such cases by observing that addicts *recurringly* desire to use drugs despite their prior experience of doing so giving them no pleasure. Holton and Berridge paint this as part of the "bruteness" of addicts' cravings for drugs, such cravings being isolated from *both* anticipations of pleasure and judgment of value (Holton and Berridge 2013).

To think that there is excuse to be found here would require that one thinks that the formation of the component desires that make up overall wants must include judgments of anticipated pleasure on the satisfaction of such desires. Yet as we have seen, desire formation is largely an arational process that is beyond the powers of the will for all of us, non-addict and addict alike. We cannot choose our desires nearly to the extent that we can choose whether or not to act on them. Responsibility thus doesn't depend on some normal route of desire acquisition, a route that addicts can then be said not to follow. This was (I argued earlier) true of implanted desires and implanted evaluative beliefs; it is also thus true of desires arising in ways not responsive to anticipations of pleasure or displeasure.

* * *

I conclude that the case for excusing addicts for their acquisition and usage of drugs while being addicts is largely but not entirely nonexistent. Moreover, to the extent there is mitigation of blame for addicts because they are addicts, notice how occasional that is and how specific to particular attributes of addiction that not all addicts share. There is no excuse for addicts across the board in the offing, only ad hoc mitigation occasionally available on a case-by-case basis.[28]

NOTES

1. To my knowledge, addiction is also not a defense in any Western penal code. This is a bit of a surprise in countries such as Portugal, the Netherlands, and Canada, given that the legal systems of each regard addiction as a disease that in its origins and its symptoms are not the fault of the addict. Portugal and the Netherlands have rendered the issue of defense largely moot by decriminalizing use and possession, thus eliminating the need for any defense of addiction for those behaviors that would be crimes elsewhere. Despite Canada's interpretation of its human rights laws against disability-based discrimination so as to prohibit loss of job or housing because one is an addict (*see* Stewart v. Elk Valley Coal Corp., 2017-1 SCR 591, 2017 SCC 30), nonetheless addiction remains not a defense to crime in Canada as in the rest of the English-speaking world. (For the state of the law in Australia, see Kennett 2014.)

2. The leading case here is United States v. Moore, 486 F2d 1139 (D.C. Cir. 1963), where the District of Columbia Court of Appeals rejected any addiction-based defense to the charge of possession of a controlled substance. The case is notable for its two dissents by two well-known liberal judges (Bazelon and Wright) arguing vigorously for the existence of a defense in these circumstances. The recent decision of the Supreme Judicial Court of Massachusetts in *Commonwealth v. Eldred*, 101 N.E. 3d 911 (Mass. 2018), is in line with *Moore*. The issue in *Eldred* was whether Ms. Eldred's parole could be revoked for use of controlled substances to which she was addicted and thus (she claimed) she was compelled to use; the Court held that use of drugs by those addicted to them is not necessarily so compelled (or otherwise not a matter of responsible choice) as to make revocation of parole for such use unfair or impermissible. The *Eldred* Court was aided in its decision by an amicus brief signed by myself and most of those thanked in this chapter's final footnote.

3. The sole exemption to this is the recent decision of the Fourth Circuit Court of Appeals in *Manning v. Caldwell*, case no. 17-1320, decided July 16, 2019.

4. The injunction is to be taken with a grain of salt. Definitions can aid both speaker and audience to secure the reference of words like "addiction," but such definitions should not themselves be thought to be analytically necessary criteria for the proper use of such terms. *See* generally Moore (1981, 1985a). It is also and for the same reasons an oversimplification to think that one can entirely separate the definition of "addiction" from the explanation and the evaluation of addiction.

5. The differences between these two senses of "criteria" are explored by me in Moore (1981).

6. Death is a much discussed example of the point being made in the text, in Moore (1985a).

7. Amenability to medical treatment is what I called the "jurisdictional" justification for medical definition, that is, the marking out of a jurisdiction for professional treatment by labeling conditions, "a disease." Lawyers do the same thing when they mark out a condition as a "legal problem," that is, a problem with which only law-trained professionals can deal. *See* Moore (1978).

8. As a consultant to Spitzer's APA Committee on Nomenclature and Statistics, I urged a narrowing of this overall definition of medical disorders (Moore 1978). Some of my suggested narrowings found their way into the overall definitions of medical disorders to be found in the third, fourth, and fifth editions of the *Diagnostic and Statistical Manual. See* Stein (2010).

9. For an update of the same view, see Volkow et al. (2016).

10. Hilary Putnam used diseases as examples of natural kinds in his early papers on the famous "Kripke-Putnam" theory of direct reference to such natural kinds. *See* Putnam (1962, 1965). For some doubts about whether the diseases of *DSM-V* really are natural kinds, see Graham (2013).

11. What I dubbed long ago, "the causal theory of excuse" (Moore 1985b), and that Stephen Morse has long called "the Fundamental Psycho-Legal Error" committed by scientists and others (Morse 2006).

12. At least my brand of compatibilism needs to do so. The so-called source compatibilists follow Harry Frankfurt (Frankfurt 1969) in denying that an actor need satisfy the Principle of Alternative Possibilities (PAP) (in any sense) in order to be responsible and thus do not require an analysis of the meaning of PAP. *See* Moore (2014, 2016b), for a brief explication of source compatibilism.

13. In Moore (2014), I present a more nuanced account of the counterfactuals involved here. Classical compatibilism stems from G.E. Moore (1912), and much of what classical compatibilism now consists of are the ten or so amendments one must make to (G.E.) Moore to accommodate the century of criticism that has intervened.

14. Notice that one may have the capacity to do other than he did (in this counterfactual sense of "capacity") even though his action and the choice behind it were sufficiently caused by factors not under the actor's control.

15. The brain is the "bottleneck" through which all genetic and environmental causes have their causal influence on mind and behavior (Greene and Cohen 2004).

16. I explore five such "partial libertarianisms" in Moore (1985b, 2015, pp. 666–669).

17. It is arguable that the idea that addiction essentially involves a craving that compels is *implicit* in the first 9 of the 11 symptoms of substance use disorder earlier quoted.
18. I and Heidi Hurd discuss the tracing strategy generally and then as applied to negligence, in Hurd and Moore (2011).
19. The alternative analysis is laid out in Robinson (1985). Sometimes adherence to a tracing strategy is not due to confusing it with the alternative analysis explored in the text. Rather, the tracing strategist applies a kind of forfeiture morality: if someone is doing something they should not be doing in the first place (like shooting up when not yet an addict), then they are responsible for all the effects of that initial wrongdoing no matter how unintended, unforeseen, or unforeseeable those effects might be. Such wrongdoers' initial wrongdoing is said to "forfeit" our normal concerns to grade their culpability by their actual mental states at the time they act. One sees this crude, forfeiture view on vivid display with the notorious felony-murder rule in Anglo-American criminal law.
20. Huxley's description to me when I was an undergraduate when Huxley had just returned from experiencing the hallucinogenic effects of LSD (lysergic acid diethylamide) in Mexican mushrooms.
21. Notice that there is nothing in such a rational choice explanation of addictive behaviors that evaluates the addict's chosen action, choice, and so on, as actually being desirable, morally permissible, or prudentially wise. What I mean by the rational choice explanation of addiction is thus not what economists such as Gary Becker seem to mean when they refer to the rational choice model of addiction (Becker and Murphy 1988; Schwartz 1989). What I mean by rational choice here takes no position on the normative correctness of an addict's choices and actions—these may well be the best a person in the addict's situation can get, or they may not. Rather, what is rational in my sense of a rational choice explanation is the way the addict's character, beliefs, desires, evaluations, choices, actions, and enjoyments line up together. The addict described above is rational because these items for him line up in the way that constitutes practical rationality. No position is taken whether the fully practically rational addict just depicted is actually choosing and doing the right or even the sensible thing. (Of course if one's ethics is that of a monistic utilitarian—where the only intrinsically good state of affairs is the satisfaction of human preference—that will blur this distinction between objective vs. subjective rationality, because on such an ethics satisfying subjective desire will necessarily also be objectively valuable.)
22. Richard Holton and Kent Berridge call this the "habit account" of addiction (Holton and Berridge 2013, pp. 244–245).
23. "Stickiness" is my nontechnical term for the rational commitments having an intention commits us to (Bratman 1983). Of particular relevance here is the rational commitment to non-reconsideration of the pre-decision desires that incline one in different directions (Yaffe 2010, pp. 148–156). Joseph Raz has long conceptualized such commitments to non-reconsideration, in terms of negative second-order reasons (Raz calls them "exclusionary reasons," so called because they exclude what were formerly good reasons pro or con some past decisions). Such reasons are reasons not to act for certain reasons (Raz 1975, 1986, ch. 2–4). For several interpretations of Raz's exclusionary reasons, see Moore (1989).

24. Another aspect of the genesis of these mistaken beliefs of addicts is the motivated nature of the mistakes: addicts make such mistakes because they so want (because of their cravings) such beliefs to be true. Surely the self-deceptive nature to such wishful thinking does not decrease an addict's responsibility; if a passively experienced mistake does not excuse, why would an actively caused one do so?

25. Or wants *most of the time*, on diachronic versions such as that of Yaffe (2013).

26. The same point was often made about the supposed "implantation" of evaluative beliefs in cases of brainwashing like that of Patty Hearst. Even if such beliefs were suddenly implanted through no act, choice, or fault of Patty, still, after the passage of enough time in which Patty could integrate such beliefs into her evaluative system one way or the other, she was responsible for acting on such beliefs. Whether Patty had such a fair opportunity to accept or reject such implanted beliefs depended not just on the amount of time but also on whether she was in some fugue-like, disassociated state, making it difficult or impossible for her to compare her implanted beliefs with the contrary beliefs she had long held.

27. Anglo-American criminal law does recognize a limited excuse of weakness of will in duress and provocation doctrines that individualize the standard of reasonable firmness of will to those defects of will (such as those typically possessed by the young or the grieving) that are not the actor's fault for possessing. The strength of will judged reasonably firm in such cases is one that can be fairly demanded of persons with such incapacities.

28. My thanks to Douglas Husak, Stephen Morse, and Gideon Yaffe for their comments on this specific chapter and to the same individuals (plus Hedy Kober, Alan Schwartz, and Richard Holton) for their co-teaching or consulting with me on the university-wide seminar on addiction at Yale University Spring Semester, 2017. This chapter is a considerably shortened version of the last chapter of my forthcoming book, *Mechanical Choices: The Responsibility of the Human Machine* (OUP).

References

Commonwealth v. Eldred, decided July 16, 2018.

Stewart v. Elk Valley Coal Corp., 2017-1 SCR 591, 2017 SCC 30.

United States v. Moore, 486 F2d 1139 (D.C. Cir. 1963).

Becker, Gary, and Kevin Murphy. 1988. A theory of rational addiction. *Journal of Political Economics* 96: 675–700.

Bratman, Michael. 1983. *Intentions, plans, and practical reason*. Cambridge, MA: Harvard University Press.

Butler, Samuel. 1872. *Erewhon*. London: Trubner and Ballantyne.

Center on Addiction. 2010. *Behind bars II: Substance abuse and America's prison population*. New York: Columbia University.

Dreiser, Theodore. 1925. *An American tragedy*. New York: Boni and Liveright.

Duff, R.A. 2006. The virtues and vices of virtue jurisprudence. In *Values and virtues: Aristotelianism in contemporary ethics*, ed. T.D.J. Chappell. Oxford: Oxford University Press.

———. 2013. Virtue, vice, and criminal liability: Do we want an Aristotelian criminal law? *Buffalo Criminal Law Review* 6: 147–184.

Eagle, Morris. 1983. Anatomy of the self in psychoanalytic theory. In Vol. 2 of *Nature animated*, ed. Michael Ruse. Dordrecht: D. Reidel.

Few Drug Addicts are Treated, U.S. Finds. 2016. *New York Times*, November 18, p. A14.

Fischer, John Martin, and Neal Tognazzini. 2009. The truth about tracing. *Nous* 43: 531–556.

Frankfurt, Harry. 1969. Alternate possibilities and moral responsibility. *Journal of Philosophy* 66: 829–839.

———. 1971. Free will and the concept of a person. *Journal of Philosophy* 68: 5–20.

Freud, Sigmund. 1961. Moral responsibility for the content of dreams. In *Standard edition of the works of Sigmund Freud*, ed. James Stratchey. London: Hogarth Press.

Gide, Andre. 1927. *The counterfeiters*. Trans. and Ed. Dorothy Bussy. New York: Alfred A. Knopf.

Graham, George. 2013. *The disordered mind: An introduction to philosophy of mind and mental illness*. 2nd ed. London: Routledge.

Greene, Joshua, and Jonathan Cohen. 2004. For the law neuroscience changes nothing and everything. *Philosophical Transactions of the Royal Society of London* 359: 1775–1785.

Hill, Thomas. 1986. Weakness of will and character. *Philosophical Topics* 14: 93–115.

Holton, Richard, and Kent Berridge. 2013. Addiction between compulsion and choice. In *Addiction and self control*, ed. Neil Levy. Oxford: Oxford University Press.

Hurd, Heidi, and Michael Moore. 2011. Blaming the stupid, clumsy, selfish, and weak: The culpability of negligence. *Criminal Law and Philosophy* 5: 96–148.

Husak, Douglas. 2016. *Ignorance of law: A philosophical inquiry*. Oxford: Oxford University Press.

James, William. 1890. *Principles of psychology*. Cambridge: Harvard University Press.

Kennett, Jeanette. 2013. Addiction, choice, and disease. In *Neuroscience and legal responsibility*, ed. Nicole Vincent. Oxford: Oxford University Press.

———. 2014. Why shouldn't addiction be a defense to low-level crime? *The conversation*. Symposium on blame and biology. June 12.

Leshner, Alan. 1997. Addiction is a brain disease, and it matters. *Science* 278: 45–47.

Moore, G.E. 1912. *Ethics*. Cambridge: Cambridge University Press.

Moore, Michael. 1978. Discussion of the Spitzer-Endicott and Klein proposed definition of mental disorder (illness). In *Critical issues in psychiatric diagnosis*, ed. R. Spitzer and D. Klein. New York: Raven Press.

———. 1981. The semantics of judging. *Southern California Law Review* 54: 151–295.

———. 1985a. A natural law theory of interpretation. *Southern California Law Review* 58: 277–398.

———. 1985b. Causation and the excuses. *California Law Review* 73: 1091–1149.

———. 1989. Law, authority, and Razian reasons. *Southern California Law Review* 62: 827–898.

———. 1990. Choice, character, and excuse. *Social Philosophy and Policy* 7: 9–58.

———. 1996. *Placing blame: A general theory of the criminal law*. Oxford: Oxford University Press.

———. 1998. Liberty and drugs. In *Morality, legality, and drugs*, ed. P. deGreiff. Ithaca: Cornell University Press.

———. 2014. Compatibilism(s) for neuroscientists. In *Law and the philosophy of action*, ed. E. Villanueva. Dordrecht: Rodopi.

———. 2015. The search for a responsible responsibility test: Norwegian insanity law after Breivik. *Criminal Law and Philosophy* 9: 645–693.

———. 2016a. The neuroscience of volitional excuse. In *Philosophical foundations of law and neuroscience*, ed. Michael Pardo and Dennis Patterson. Oxford: Oxford University Press.

———. 2016b. Stephen Morse on the fundamental psych-legal error. *Criminal Law and Philosophy* 10: 45–89.

Morse, Stephen. 2000. Hooked on hype: Addiction and responsibility. *Law and Philosophy* 20: 3–49.

———. 2006. Brain overclaim syndrome and criminal responsibility: A diagnostic note. *Ohio State Journal of Criminal Law* 3: 397–412.

———. 2017. Addiction, choice, and criminal law. In *Addiction and choice*, ed. N. Heather and Gabriel Segal. Oxford: Oxford University Press.

Putnam, Hilary. 1962. Dreaming and depth grammar. In *Analytical philosophy*, 1st Series, ed. R.J. Butler. Oxford: Oxford University Press.

———. 1965. Brains and behavior. In *Analytical philosophy*, 2nd Series, ed. R.J. Butler. Oxford: Oxford University Press.

Raz, Joseph. 1975. *Practical reason and norms*. Oxford: Oxford University Press.

———. 1986. *The morality of freedom*. Oxford: Oxford University Press.

Richard, Hanna, and Steve Pearce. 2013. Addiction in context: Lessons from a personality disorder. In *Addiction and self-control*, ed. Neil Levy. Oxford: Oxford University Press.

Robinson, Paul. 1985. Causing the conditions of one's own defense. *Virginia Law Review* 71: 1–63.

Rosen, Gideon. 2002. Culpability and ignorance. *Proceedings of the Aristotelian Society* 103: 61–84.

Schwartz, Alan. 1989. Views of addiction and the duty to warn. *Virginia Law Review* 75: 509–562.

Sinnott-Armstrong, Walter. 2013. Are addicts responsible? In *Addiction and self-control*, ed. Neil Levy. Oxford: Oxford University Press.

Spitzer, Robert, and Jean Endicott. 1978. Medical and mental disorder: Proposed definition and criteria. In *Critical issues in psychiatric diagnosis*, ed. R. Spitzer and D. Klein. New York: Raven Press.

Stein, Dan. 2010. What is a mental/psychiatric disorder: From DSM IV to DSM-V. *Psychological Medicine* 40: 1759–1765.

Strawson, Peter. 1962. Freedom and resentment. *Proceedings of the British Academy* 48: 1–25.

Tadros, Victor. 2005. *Criminal responsibility*. Oxford: Oxford University Press.

Vargas, Manuel. 2005. The trouble with tracing. *Midwest Studies in Philosophy* 29: 269–291.

Volkow, Nora, G.F. Koob, and A.J. McLellan. 2016. Neurobiologic advances from the brain disease model of addiction. *New England Journal of Medicine* 374: 363–371.

Wallace, Jay. 1999. Addiction as defect of the will: Some philosophical reflections. *Law and Philosophy* 18: 644.

Wittgenstein, Ludwig. 1953. *Philosophical investigations*. Trans. G.E.M. Anscombe. Oxford: Basil Blackwell.

Yaffe, Gideon. 2010. *Attempts*. Oxford: Oxford University Press.

———. 2013. Are addicts akratic? Interpreting the neuroscience of reward. In *Addiction and self-control*, ed. Neil Levy. Oxford: Oxford University Press.

Zimmerman, Michael. 2008. *Living with uncertainty: The moral significance of ignorance*. Cambridge: Cambridge University Press.

PART II

Affirmative Consent

CHAPTER 3

Affirmative Consent

Kevin Cole

As a way of educating people about respecting others in sexual matters, "affirmative consent" is a helpful slogan. As a legal standard, it is controversial.[1]

Some of the controversy arises because "affirmative consent" means different things to different people. In popular debate, the phrase is often taken to mean that sexual contact requires verbal authorization—hence the slogan "yes means yes," shorthand for "*only* yes means yes." Few scholars and fewer legislatures embrace that view, as it is out of touch with popular conceptions of how people generally behave in intimate encounters.[2] At a minimum, "affirmative consent" means that mere passivity does not signal consent to sexual activity but words or actions might. Thus stated, the requirement would accomplish very little. If we turn back the clock far enough, we can always find action by a sex partner, even if it is just agreeing to meet for coffee. Some further explication is necessary as to the types and timing of actions that suffice.

Fleshing out affirmative consent reveals that the concept belongs in one of two classifications that retributivists have found problematic. Either affirmative consent constitutes a proxy crime (explained more fully below), is a thinly veiled (and more problematic) form of negligence liability, or is some combination of the two. As a negligence standard, affirmative-consent provisions may temporally limit the acts that may be considered in determining whether the actor reasonably inferred willingness and may alter the degree of risk that a reasonable person would perceive without violating the provision. Moreover, affirmative-consent provisions might be interpreted to require actions indicating more than willingness—but rather enthusiasm—for particular sexual activity.

K. Cole (✉)
University of San Diego, San Diego, CA, USA
e-mail: kcole@sandiego.edu

© The Author(s) 2019
L. Alexander, K. K. Ferzan (eds.), *The Palgrave Handbook of Applied Ethics and the Criminal Law*, https://doi.org/10.1007/978-3-030-22811-8_3

47

I further argue below that explicating affirmative consent reveals an interesting connection between proxy crimes and negligence liability—negligence liability is a proxy crime in which the details are not disclosed in advance but rather are articulated by jurors case by case. In the context of sex, most "rules" compatible with current practice will be vague enough to devolve into negligence liability.

Whether the special difficulties posed by sexual assaults justify employing these measures is debatable. The benefits of an affirmative-consent standard are often exaggerated,[3] and a full assessment requires careful consideration of alternative means of improving the law at lower cost to those who cause harm without subjective awareness that they are risking it. While many of the arguments in favor of affirmative-consent provisions are overstated, however, the question remains whether such standards are justified as a way to avoid harmful sexual contact. Moreover, social changes may ultimately make affirmative-consent provisions easier to justify even for retributivists.

Affirmative-consent standards have proliferated on college campuses, in part because of pressure from the US Department of Education (Gersen and Suk 2016). They have also begun to appear in criminal codes. Sometimes the standard is diluted because it appears in conjunction with requirements of force or resistance. Tuerkheimer stated in 2016 that the standard applied in 1400 institutions of higher education but, in pure form, in only three US criminal codes (Tuerkheimer 2016, pp. 450–451). The recent efforts of the American Law Institute (ALI) to amend the sexual assault provisions of the influential Model Penal Code (MPC) have intensified the debate over affirmative-consent provisions. Notwithstanding that the ALI membership rejected the reporters' effort to incorporate an affirmative-consent provision (Johnson and Taylor 2017, pp. 231–235), the draft proposal was carefully developed and hence is a valuable window into the problems such standards raise.

Alternatives to Affirmative Consent

Talking about affirmative consent is facilitated by having a clear sense of alternatives. This section considers a typical approach to criminalization as supplemented by the so-called no-means-no rule.

A Standard Focus

Consider the approach the Model Penal Code usually takes to criminalization. A social harm—like killing—is identified. Liability is then imposed on those who culpably bring about that social harm. Generally, the Code required subjective culpability—MPC recklessness—as the minimum culpability for punishment. MPC recklessness requires that an actor be consciously aware of a substantial and unjustified risk regarding elements of the offense, the disregard of which would be a gross deviation from the standard of conduct a law-abiding person would observe (American Law Institute 1985, § 2.02(2)(c)). For killings, however, the Code imposed liability based on an objective, negligence standard (ibid., §210.4), though the required degree of negligence was greater than that needed for tort liability (ibid., §2.02(2)(d)).

Applying this formula to sexual assault requires identification of the harm in sexual assault. The better view is that harm occurs when an actor imposes sexual contact on a partner in the absence of the partner's willingness to experience sexual contact (Alexander 2014; Ferzan and Westen 2017, p. 788; Hurd 1996). (For simplicity of expression, I will sometimes refer to an "unwilling" partner as shorthand to include cases in which a partner has not adverted to sexual contact. But consent does not occur in the absence of the partner's advertence.) Such contact violates the partner's autonomy. Willingness does not require enthusiasm. People often make decisions they would prefer not to. They sell their houses at lower prices when markets are down but they need to move; they have sex because their partner desires it even if they'd rather not. Assent to sexual contact establishes legally effective consent so long as the partner has sufficient capacity to make the decision and does so under conditions that we do not identify as vitiating consent (like under certain threats of force or harm).

Some have argued that the harm in sexual assault results when sex occurs in the absence of objective manifestation of the partner's willingness. It may be that a legal requirement of objective manifestation is justified—the debate about affirmative consent is largely about whether that is true and what those manifestations should be. But the stronger argument in favor of that position focuses on the long-term effects of requiring objective manifestations as a means of avoiding the harm of sexual contact with an unwilling partner (Ferzan and Westen 2017). On the question of when the social harm in sexual assault occurs, assume a jurisdiction requires a verbal "yes" as a predicate to sexual penetration. Neither partner is aware of the rule, and they engage in mutually desired sexual intercourse. It is hard to see how either has been harmed, though each might be liable under the posited rule. The strongest case for the rule is that it would avoid harms in cases in which a partner was not willing to engage in the sexual activity, not that harm actually occurs on the above example.

Arguably, an objective standard of consent would avoid offensive conduct. But the effect should not be overstated. A focus on willingness need not exalt sexual desire independently of the circumstances in which people prefer to have sex. In other words, people might be unwilling to engage in sex because of their partners' presumptuousness, regardless of some residual sexual desire. An objective standard differs from a focus on willingness only in those cases in which a person is miffed by her partner's conduct but not so miffed as to be unwilling to engage in sexual activity. Having sex despite the wish that someone treated you better seems indistinguishable from having sex despite the wish that your partner wasn't interested during your favorite TV program.

No-Means-No

Given the nature of sexual encounters, the MPC's typical approach to criminalization might justifiably be supplemented by what is typically called a no-means-no rule. The rule is a proxy rule, and the retributive case against them is discussed below. The case for no-means-no, however, is stronger than the case for many proxy rules. Accordingly, in considering the justifiability of affirmative-consent provisions, a comparison might profitably be made not only to the MPC's typical approach to criminalization but also to that approach as supplemented by a no-means-no rule.

AFFIRMATIVE CONSENT AS PROXY CRIME

Proxy crimes have been described in different ways (Husak 2017, p. 355). Here, I use the phrase to refer to crimes that can be committed without the criminal's adverting to the risk of bringing about a widely recognized harm. For example, the crime of knowingly discarding batteries in a landfill does not require that the criminal be aware of the environmental risks of the practice and thus is a proxy crime (Husak 2016, p. 32); the crime of recklessly risking water pollution is not, even when an actor's risky conduct does not in fact cause pollution (perhaps because the actor's spouse removed the batteries upon seeing that they had been thrown in the trash).

For retributivists, proxy crimes are problematic because they impose "substantive strict liability" (Simons 1997, pp. 1087–1088). Even if most or even almost all people would understand the connection between battery disposal and environmental harm, the statute permits conviction of those who do not. Given that ignorance of the law is usually not an excuse, proxy crimes may be committed by those unaware of either the illegality or the pertinent riskiness of their conduct. And retributivists sometimes doubt that awareness of illegality alone would suffice to establish culpability anyway, in the absence of awareness of the underlying risk—that is, the risk that justifies criminalization.

Given what has been said, it should be clear how affirmative-consent standards may constitute proxy crimes. Consider the rarely advocated, extreme version, the requirement of a verbal "yes." If mutual foreplay is taken to signal willingness to engage in escalating sexual activity, many actors may not perceive any risk—much less a substantial risk—that the absence of a verbal "yes" indicates unwillingness. Punishing an actor who engages in sexual activity in the absence of a verbal "yes" thus risks that the actor is punished in the absence of subjective culpability.

"No means no" might similarly be criticized. So long as some partners say "no" when they don't mean it, actors in some situations may not perceive a substantial risk that the "no" is genuine. Punishing the actor simply based on sex after the "no" thus risks punishment of those who are not subjectively culpable.

The case in favor of insisting that a "no" be taken at face value, however, is substantial. In sexual encounters between persons of different sizes and strengths, the stronger actor's proceeding in the face of a "no" might well signal to the weaker partner that her unwillingness is irrelevant to her intimate. Often the weaker partner might fear that further resistance will be overcome by force. And while studies have sometimes indicated that women say "no" when they don't wish sexual encounters to end, verbal resistance certainly increases the risk that a partner is unwilling. Many of the reported opinions regarding consent include a woman's claim of verbal resistance.

On the other hand, the cost of requiring that "no" be respected is modest among those who know the rule. The rule merely requires a cessation of planned activity to clarify the partner's wishes. As with any rule, some complicated borderline questions will need working out. Is blocking someone's hand a "no"? What words or conduct undo a "no"? How long is a "no" effective? These issues require sensitive attention to ensure that the "no" rule imposes only acceptable costs.

Those who do not know that a jurisdiction follows a "no" rule pose the problem of punishing the nonculpable. When a proxy rule jibes with common experience, the problem is decreased. Even without knowing that a jurisdiction has a "no" rule, most people would probably recognize that proceeding in the face of a "no" runs a substantial risk that the partner is unwilling. And while the edges of the rule might be imprecise, the basic idea is fairly easy to communicate, decreasing the risk that actors will be unaware of the rule. While we can imagine subjectively innocent actors punished under such a scheme, the population is likely a small one.[4]

AFFIRMATIVE CONSENT AS COVERT AND DILUTED CRIMINAL NEGLIGENCE

Most affirmative-consent provisions and proposals stop short of requiring verbal authorization. They share a requirement of some external manifestation of a partner's willingness but they go farther than that—they do not simply say, for example, that an actor is guilty if he either infers willingness without reference to external manifestations or otherwise proceeds recklessly. Instead, most affirmative-consent provisions define "consent" in terms of some other vague concept or series of concepts, some of which themselves suggest a focus on how a reasonable person would interpret the signals. While the articulation of affirmative-consent standards stressed their difference from negligence standards (Schulhofer 1998, pp. 257–259)—a position reiterated in the ALI draft (Cole 2016, p. 552)—they turn out to share significant features. Accordingly, the criticisms retributivists have directed at explicit negligence standards (Moore and Hurd 2011) apply as well to affirmative-consent standards.

Sample Affirmative-Consent Provisions

Tuerkheimer identifies three "pure affirmative-consent" jurisdictions and collects some other examples from colleges. Wisconsin defines "consent" as "words or overt actions by a person ... indicating a freely given agreement to have sexual intercourse or sexual contact." Vermont's definition requires "words or actions by a person indicating a voluntary agreement to engage in a sexual act." The key New Jersey judicial opinion defining the standard speaks in terms of "permission to engage in sexual penetration [that] must be affirmative." Yale insists on "positive, unambiguous, voluntary agreement at every point during a sexual encounter—the presence of an unequivocal 'yes' (verbal or otherwise), not just the absence of a 'no.'" The University of Iowa says that consent "must be freely and affirmatively communicated between both partners in order to participate in sexual activity or behavior. It can be expressed either by words or clear, unambiguous actions. ... Silence, lack of protest, or no resistance does not mean consent" (Tuerkheimer 2016, pp. 442, 451).

The Negligence Connection

The standards that speak in terms of "agreement" strongly suggest that the fact-finder should inquire how the partner's manifestations should reasonably be interpreted. In law, agreements are formed based on reasonable appearances, at least in the absence of evidence that a party did not mean what reasonably appeared. Even without that gloss, the requirement of "agreement" suggests something independent of an actor's mental state regarding a partner's willingness. The same is true of "permission." And the actor's belief that an "agreement" or "permission" exists would not exculpate. The actor's misunderstanding of the facts might exculpate—for example, did the partner say "now" or "no"—but whether those facts should be *interpreted* to constitute "agreement" or "permission" is likely a legal question on which mens rea is not required.

A judge might instruct a jury in a way that would prevent these general terms from devolving into negligence liability. A judge might instruct, for example, that a partner's verbal "yes" or manual assistance in an act of penetration is required to show "agreement" or "permission." If so, the resulting proxy rules would be analyzed as in the preceding section.

If the fact-finder is instead guided only by the general language in the affirmative-consent provision, it is likely to default to the equivalent of a negligence standard.[5] It would likely attempt to surmise why the provision exists. If most people agree that the harm in sexual assault results from sex with an unwilling partner, they are likely to ask whether the objective indicia of willingness were of the type that justified the sexual contact. But if this is the goal of affirmative-consent provisions, it would be better to speak directly in terms of negligence liability regarding the partner's willingness. Doing so would incorporate general provisions requiring criminal negligence to be gross negligence;

without instruction, a fact-finder might well not put that thumb on the scale in favor of the accused. Moreover, words like "agreement" and "permission," by not specifying the social harm to be avoided, leave fact-finders free on an ad hoc basis to impose liability because the partner was not eager to engage in sex. If this is to be the law, as some have suggested, it should be adopted clearly.

Unambiguous Conduct

Both of the college provisions cited above, as well as an early draft of commentary to the MPC revision, refer to the need for "unambiguous" conduct to satisfy the affirmative-consent standard. This requirement might be thought to modify the ordinary criminal negligence standard. The MPC's general "negligence" definition is satisfied only if an actor should have known of a "substantial and unjustifiable risk"; failure to perceive that risk must constitute a "gross deviation from the standard of care that a reasonable person would observe in the actor's situation" (American Law Institute 1985 §2.02(2)(d)). All human behavior poses some interpretive doubt—even a "yes" could involve misspeaking or a misheard question. But the insistence on "unambiguous" conduct might be practically implemented to mean that an interpretive risk can be less than "substantial" but still enough to render the conduct ambiguous. And fact-finders might not view the running of such risks as a "gross" deviation from how reasonable people would behave, if the fact-finder were allowed to apply that part of the negligence definition. Accordingly, the insistence on "unambiguous" conduct could supplement the negligence standard by removing the limitations the criminal law normally places on it.

One might respond here that the requirement of "unambiguous" conduct simply substitutes the legislature's judgment for the jury's about what counts as negligence in a particular context. After all, the defendant's view that risk-taking was on balance justified is not committed to the defendant's judgment even under the MPC's recklessness standard. Perhaps running even a small risk of sex with an unwilling partner is in fact grossly negligent. And some have argued that the "substantiality" requirement is unsound generally, though the examples used to demonstrate this point involve motivations substantially more antisocial than the desire for consensual sex.

Whether sex with an unwilling partner is such a serious problem as to justify deviating from our usual approach even to negligence liability might depend on the range of sexual contact covered by the standard. The ALI proposal originally applied to any sexual contact between individuals not in an intimate, cohabiting relationship (Cole 2016, p. 513). But even an affirmative-consent standard limited to penetration will often apply to acts of digital penetration that might be thought less harmful than other kinds of penetration.

Of course, if "unambiguous conduct signaling agreement" were as easy to decode as "throwing a battery in the garbage," these provisions would belong solely in the discussion of proxy crimes. Because of the room for disagreement about the meaning of the standards, however, the "covert negligent" label seems more apt. People can know that "affirmative consent" is the rule without knowing how it would apply.[6] And as reforms take hold—some admirable and some less so—one would expect more complaints in borderline cases, increasing the risk of misunderstanding.[7]

Connecting Proxy Crimes, Vague Statutes, and Negligence Liability

This discussion in part illustrates an interesting connection between proxy crimes, negligence liability, and vague criminal provisions. In proxy crimes, legislatures specify *ex ante* conduct that will subject the actor to punishment, regardless of whether the actor perceived the connection between the crime's elements and the risk of harm. Vague statutes and negligence liability allow fact-finders to engage in this kind of law making after the fact. While one might object that the legislature is morally incapable of making conduct culpable simply by saying so, at least a proxy crime gives those who disagree greater opportunity to avoid the criminal law's (arguable over)reach.

COMPARISON TO OTHER COMMON APPROACHES: FLESHING OUT AFFIRMATIVE CONSENT

Thus far, affirmative-consent standards have been compared to an idealized approach to consent based on the MPC's general approach to criminality, which reflects the commonly held academic view that criminal liability for negligence is suspect. Many jurisdictions, however, deviate from that approach already. A brief comparison of affirmative-consent standards to those other common approaches is useful to situate what is at stake in the affirmative-consent debate.

Many jurisdictions classify rape as a general-intent crime and follow the common-law rule that mistakes of fact must be reasonable to constitute a defense. Accordingly, such jurisdictions require mistakes about consent to be reasonable to exculpate. In such jurisdictions, affirmative-consent standards do not effect a change from a subjective to an objective focus to liability; the focus is already objective.

How adopting an affirmative-consent standard in such a jurisdiction would change the law depends on how the standard is cashed out. The standard will to some degree constrain the facts that can be considered in determining whether a mistake is exculpatory. Obviously, if only-yes-means-yes, the reasonableness inquiry is displaced. But if other conduct can unambiguously signal agreement (e.g.), the affirmative-consent standard may narrow the temporal scope of conduct that the fact-finder may consider in deciding whether agreement occurred.[8] For example, the Yale policy's insistence on agreement "at every point during a sexual encounter" might imply that conduct cannot be considered in inferring agreement if the conduct occurred very far before a disputed sex act. Commentary to the MPC proposal suggests the same result.[9]

If these temporal limits are designed to preclude the inference that going to someone's dorm room signals consent to sexual penetration, one doubts how often a fact-finder would draw that inference even without having temporal limits placed on the evidence to be considered (even if recklessness were the standard). And in a no-means-no jurisdiction, mistaken inferences can quickly be corrected in ways that do not require the fact-finder to engage in reasonableness inquiries anyway.

In the common setting of mutually escalating foreplay, however, limits on what the fact-finder may consider could be imposed by judicial instruction or inferred by the fact-finder from the general language of the standard. And here the limitations might make a difference. If activity levels commonly fluctuate during sexual encounters, juries might think that some pre-passivity conduct would signal agreement to certain kinds of sex acts if the jury were permitted to consider such conduct. The point here is not that engaging in some sex acts constitutes consent to any sex act—rather, a jury might think that clear agreement to engage in some sex acts implies agreement to engage in moderately more intimate activity, in the absence of indications to the contrary, including the absence of any indication that the partner had lost the ability to communicate a desire to stop the encounter.

Consent to Opaquely Anticipated Acts

By emphasizing that consent to one sex act does not entail consent to others, affirmative-consent provisions might exacerbate a problem that also needs attention in any consent-based approach that rejects the need to show force. People are often happy to have their partners engage in activity that is, at least to some degree, unexpected.[10] Just as you can't tickle yourself, something is lost in a sexual experience that is entirely predictable. Exceeding expressed limitations cannot be justified by a desire to surprise, and the desire to surprise is no license to offend. A recklessness standard focused on willingness can accommodate this idea—one can ask whether the actor was reckless about whether particular surprising sexual contact would offend by considering how substantially it deviated from anticipated contact. Affirmative-consent standards could be construed similarly, but the focus on "agreement at every point during a sexual encounter" might incline interpreters to a different view.

Defenses of Affirmative-Consent Standards

Criticism of affirmative-consent provisions has generated responses along two lines. One is that the concerns expressed by critics are misplaced. Others deal with the alleged advantages gained by adopting an affirmative-consent provision. These arguments are addressed below.

Miscommunication as a Nonissue

The principal reporter for the ALI's reform project, Stephen Schulhofer, recently commented on the opposition his affirmative-consent proposal has confronted. He classified the frequent concern with miscommunication as the domain of "low-information people" (Schulhofer 2017, p. 350):

> [B]uilding a consensus for reform requires changing the narrative. We must work to shake people free of the media's obsession with young, inexperienced, middle-class peers in college settings. ... These low-information people have to be reminded of the wide range of very different contexts in which current rape law fails. They must be made aware of what the rape reform effort is really about.[11]

Similarly, Deborah Tuerkheimer recently recounted published appellate opinions from the jurisdictions that follow a pure affirmative-consent standard. She concluded that most of the cases involve sleep, intoxication, or fear, and "in none of these categories are the cases characterized by 'mixed signals' or, more to the point, a reasonable mistake as to consent" (Tuerkheimer 2016, p. 452).

The Schulhofer critique is misleading. Many of the examples he provides have little to do with the affirmative-consent standard itself: "The situations in which the serious inadequacies in current rape law become most salient and consequential include domestic violence, physically and mentally disabled victims, and gross discrepancies in age, power, or authority" (Schulhofer 2017, p. 349). Situations like this, as some frame the issue, defeat the legal inference from assent to consent (Ferzan and Westen 2017, p. 762). A rape victim who complies at the point of the gun may have chosen sex rather than being shot, but regardless of whether we follow an affirmative-consent regime, we view assent in this setting as without legal effect. Situations that vitiate consent can be legislated about independently of an affirmative-consent standard, as the MPC draft itself did, and such limitations are perfectly compatible with the other general approaches to the consent question.

Does the affirmative-consent standard add anything to express prohibitions on acquiring sex through indirect threats of violence, exploitation of the disabled, or capitalizing on discrepancies in age, power, or authority? Perhaps if the standard is interpreted to require manifestations of enthusiasm rather than of willingness. But if this is what the standard means, it is even more problematic when applied to specific acts of mutually escalating foreplay than a requirement of simple willingness to engage in those acts. Everyone agrees that it is wrong for a police officer to insist that a woman fellate him to avoid getting a speeding ticket. Relying on the affirmative-consent standard to guard against this outcome, however, makes the standard less workable in more common settings.

Moreover, in cases involving truly bad actors, one doubts that the affirmative-consent provisions will do much. The large problem with prosecuting most sexual assaults is that they occur in private, in situations equally (or sufficiently) consistent with consensual encounters to reduce to swearing contests between the complainant and defendant. Nothing prevents a defendant from lying about the presence of conduct unambiguously signaling agreement or even about verbal authorization. The affirmative-consent standard will most likely affect outcomes when those who think they did nothing wrong report truthfully when questioned by authorities.

It is unclear whether Schulhofer thinks the miscommunication concern is based on "low information" solely because the risk is outweighed by the benefits of the standard in addressing pressing social concerns. As to whether miscommunication is itself a risk worth considering, it is of a piece with what has animated retributive objections to proxy crimes and negligence liability across the board—concerns that were largely embraced by the MPC. One study has suggested that "[t]he nature of hooking up makes effective communication about one's sexual limits difficult to achieve" and that many men "seem to believe that women want the same level of intimacy that they do"; it found that 78% of the instances of unwanted sexual intercourse on a college campus occurred during a hookup (Flack et al. 2007, pp. 146, 154).

One might respond that uncertainty about consent is easier to resolve than uncertainty about other elements of criminal offenses—just ask the partner. But negligence standards operate even when actors harbor no conscious doubts. If actors have substantial conscious doubts, even a recklessness standard would punish them. Of course, a negligence standard could make people more careful,[12] and care may seem especially useful in certain settings, like penetrative acts involving unfamiliar partners. A recklessness standard would take this intuition into account too, however, without the other costs of an affirmative-consent standard. And spontaneity in intimate relationships is imperiled as deterrence is pursued.

Tuerkheimer acknowledges the difficulties of relying on published appellate opinions to discern the impact of affirmative-consent standards (Tuerkheimer 2016, p. 464). But she understates the problem. One might well expect prosecutors trained in an earlier era to start by employing affirmative-consent laws to address especially egregious conduct. As prosecutors, judges, and juries educated in colleges having affirmative-consent requirements achieve substantial numbers, one would expect malleable standards to be applied in more situations. Moreover, even today the large percentage of cases resolved by plea will be missed by surveying appellate case law. Less egregious cases are especially prone to substantial sentencing discounts that make guilty pleas the sensible course, even for the innocent.[13]

The cases identified by Tuerkheimer, however, illustrate some of the overbroad claims made regarding the necessity of an affirmative-consent standard to effect needed reform, and they overlap with arguments Schulhofer makes regarding why rape reform is essential. They are addressed below.

Sleep

Obviously, a sleeping person cannot give affirmative consent. But well before the affirmative-consent movement, sex with an unconscious partner was treated as rape. If penetration occurs before a person wakes up, the crime of rape is complete regardless of what happens afterward and regardless of the approach taken to consent. The victim has not plausibly assented to what comes completely by surprise, and assent is a necessary component of consent.[14]

Other cases involve victims who wake up right before the actor engages in sexual activity, or after the actor makes sexual contact but before other contact, like penetration, for which the actor is now prosecuted. Both of the cases raise a similar problem—the possibility that fear might keep the victim from resisting, even verbally (though the case Tuerkheimer cites involved a victim who verbally resisted). Fear is an especially likely response when the actor was not present when the victim went to sleep. While these cases are easy under an affirmative-consent standard, they should also be easy even if recklessness regarding willingness were required. A defendant would face an uphill struggle convincing a fact-finder that he appreciated no substantial risk that fear precluded resistance. Perhaps the showing could be made in cases of ongoing relationships,[15] but here the likelihood of fear will also be diminished, in the absence of past evidence of violence, permitting the no-means-no rule to operate.

Intoxication and Inadequately Considered Sex Generally

Intoxication plays a large role in many sexual assaults. At one extreme, intoxication can render a victim unconscious. As in the sleep cases, this end of the intoxication spectrum is easy under an affirmative-consent standard but also easy under other approaches.

In other cases, Tuerkheimer argues, the affirmative-consent standard is more significant (Tuerkheimer 2016, p. 457)—

> [w]here intoxication does not render a victim unconscious, but nevertheless results in significant impairment. ... [A] victim's ability to "resist" is undermined by alcohol, and her unwillingness to engage in sexual activities may manifest as resignation. However, since unresponsiveness does not qualify as consent under an affirmative definition, the inebriated victim who does nothing—whether or not she is fully unconscious—is deemed not to have consented.

But the affirmative-consent standard resolves these cases only on the assumption that, to be considered, acts must immediately precede the sexual contact in question. In many cases, the woman has engaged in some cooperative sexual activity. In those cases, if acts need not immediately precede the sex act in question, the affirmative-consent standard still leaves questions to be resolved that are similar to those under a general negligence standard—whether a reasonable person would have perceived the entire course of the woman's action as indicating a willingness to engage in the sex act in question. Even under a general negligence standard, the woman's intoxication would be germane in assessing the reasonable inferences to draw from the woman's actions, including her failure to object. The affirmative-consent standard can simplify these cases if the woman's relevant acts are strictly temporally limited. But those same temporal limitations simply increase the chance of convicting those who are not subjectively culpable (or even reasonably mistaken) about the woman's willingness—even in cases involving less severe intoxication or no intoxication at all.[16]

Moreover, the affirmative-consent standard does nothing to address the significant problem of the inauthentic choice.[17] Drinking loosens inhibitions. Drunk people make choices that predictably they would not have made if sober; in fact, they sometimes consciously drink to overcome inhibitions. And even those who are so drunk that they cannot remember what happened are still capable of the kinds of cooperative activity, including verbal permission, that satisfy an affirmative-consent standard (Shaw 2016, pp. 1369–1370).

A tightly temporally limited affirmative-consent standard might reduce the incidence of two related problems. First, it decreases the risk that a person might be subjected to a sex act in the absence of assent. Presumably, in some cases, a reasonable actor might think that a person has made a conscious choice to engage in a sex act but the person (perhaps because of intoxication) has not processed information sufficiently to have understood what was about to happen. Requiring affirmative consent immediately prior to the act decreases this possibility.[18] Second, the standard allows the person to make decisions about sex acts on her own timetable. For example, notwithstanding reasonable appearances that a person is prepared to engage in a sex act, the person might prefer time to mull the matter over. If no-means-no is the rule, the person can buy time with verbal resistance. But in a rapidly escalating sexual encounter, the person—especially a drunk person—might forget about that option or be reluctant to employ it. With a bit more time, even a drunk person might decide against activity that will be regretted later. Whether these benefits offset the costs of a strict affirmative-consent standard is a matter on which people will differ.

Fear

Fear was previously addressed briefly in conjunction with the problem of the sleeping victim. In other settings, proponents have trumpeted affirmative-consent standards as a cure for the problem of "frozen fright." A woman overwhelmed by the aggressiveness of her physically stronger partner retreats into passivity rather than engaging in what she perceives to be fruitless or dangerous resistance. A strict affirmative-consent standard allows conviction in these cases.

Many of the cases involving frozen fright involve an actor's persistence in the face of verbal resistance.[19] Failing to respect a "no" reasonably signals to the partner that further sex acts are inevitable. A no-means-no rule reduces the need to rely on affirmative-consent standards to cure this problem. Education about the significance of a "no," and about the dynamics that lead people not to say "no," could also reduce the incidence of frozen fright unaccompanied by any verbal protest. Encouraging education about how to avoid sexual assault is sometimes perceived as blaming the victim, but that charge is less serious than the fabrication that legal doctrine can altogether prevent undesired sex.

Among the cases Tuerkheimer finds in her review of the fear category are those involving young victims and familial relationships. But cases like this can, often are, and should be addressed by categorical prohibitions on sex in certain kinds of unequal relationships. The affirmative-consent standard isn't needed to address them. More generally, she finds that the cases in this category "tend to reflect predatory behavior, not confusion. Put differently, the fear cases feature behavior designed to capitalize on a victim's vulnerability, as opposed to conduct resulting from 'miscommunication.'" But precisely the features that support this characterization should also result in finding that the defendant was reckless regarding whether fear vitiated consent. While conviction is easier under an affirmative-consent standard, it should also occur under a properly constructed recklessness standard in these troubling cases.[20]

Past Violence

Schulhofer includes "domestic violence" among the "most salient and consequential" situations demonstrating the "serious inadequacies in current rape law," and Tuerkheimer praises affirmative-consent standards for permitting conviction when "violence is conceived as 'past'—that is, as temporally preceding the intercourse, without regard to how little time has lapsed or the fear that lingers," as an alternative focus on "'force' may not be satisfied." Of course, affirmative-consent standards are not the only alternative to force requirements. But it is true that other consent-based approaches may not reach certain cases of sex in violent relationships that an affirmative-consent standard would.

Should the domestic-violence tail wag the dog of consent in sexual relations generally? No one denies that the tail is much longer than it should be, even those who reject more extravagant views of the corrupting influence of inequality on sexual relations. Here too, however, some of the cases can be handled by a no-means-no rule or by focusing on the defendant's mental state regarding whether fear vitiated consent. In the much-discussed case involving a history of domestic violence, State v. Alston,[21] "[t]he evidence tended to show" that the victim had said, "no, that I wasn't going to bed with him," and the victim cried during intercourse.

But assume a case in which past violence leads a woman to be entirely passive when sexually approached by her partner. If the partner is aware of a substantial risk that the woman acquiesces because of fear—notwithstanding the absence of any verbal protest—conviction is appropriate under any consent-based approach.[22] But is conviction appropriate in the absence of that showing?

One question involves the incidence of no-verbal-resistance passivity in domestic violence situations. Another involves the percentage of those cases that involve fear, rather than reflecting a form of modest protest. And a third involves how often passivity occurs throughout a sexual encounter rather than only at times during the encounter. Perhaps in domestic violence cases the difference between a strictly temporally limited affirmative-consent standard and a more capacious view of acts that signal willingness is less significant than in the date-rape context. If domestic violence victims express unwillingness by declining to participate in even preliminary sexual activities, the concern about misunderstanding passivity is reduced—pervasive passivity is more probative of unwillingness than sporadic passivity.

I doubt the ability of any legal rule to influence a violent person's sexual conduct in an ongoing battering relationship. If it could affect behavior, it might simply lead the batterer to insist, explicitly or implicitly, on the victim's more active sexual cooperation. But whether the rule can influence conduct or can only help us identify whom to incapacitate, we could fashion the rule to apply only to those who have engaged in certain acts of past violence with the partner. Doing so could achieve whatever benefits the affirmative-consent standard might have in this area without untoward consequences in situations in which sporadic passivity is less probative. But if incapacitation rather than deterrence is the goal here, we also need to think about whether punishment for the prior acts of violence would suffice in cases in which the defendant credibly claims to have been unaware of the risk that his partner's willingness was induced by fear. Punishing past violence does not compensate the victim for unwilling sexual imposition, but criminal law isn't supposed to compensate victims anyway.

Shifting the Focus from the Victim's Mental State

Affirmative-consent standards are sometimes supported on the grounds that they shift attention from what the victim thought to what the victim did. Questions about what the victim was willing to do invite wide-ranging and potentially embarrassing inquiries into the victim's general predilections and desires. Rape-shield laws limit some of these questions. Even limited questions about the victim's desires at the time in question, however, seem offensive when what the defendant knew makes his culpability evident.

This is a wound that the criminal law inflicts on itself by generally punishing cases in which harm results more severely than those in which it does not. A simple focus on the partner's willingness seems to require a showing that the partner was unwilling, notwithstanding the defendant's obvious risk-taking with respect to willingness. Rather than applying a murky affirmative-consent standard to address this concern, however, the criminal law could simply define sexual assault in terms of the defendant's culpability. Doing so would not make the victim's willingness irrelevant, as her mental state is some indirect proof of the actions she engaged in that might disprove the defendant's culpability. But the same is true of an affirmative-consent standard—what the victim wanted is indirect proof of whether she engaged in acts that met the affirmative-consent standard.

Beyond Willingness

An affirmative-consent standard might nudge the law toward requiring something more enthusiastic that mere willingness to engage in sexual relations. The connection is inexact. Even a verbal "yes" can be expressed without enthusiasm, by a person willing to accommodate a more eager partner. But perhaps "actions unequivocally signaling agreement" will be interpreted in a way to correlate strongly with a high degree of manifested enthusiasm for the sex acts in question. Some affirmative-consent provisions suggesting that cajolery can vitiate consent support this view,[23] as do parts of the commentary to the MPC draft.[24] Moreover, a vague standard of unequivocally signaled agreement might be interpreted in the future to require these kinds of acts.

Feminist scholarship has long criticized the prevalence of undesired but acquiesced-in sex. Two recent feminist takes on rape law arguably seek to nudge the law toward requiring more than willingness.

In a series of articles, Tuerkheimer has advocated focusing on the "agentic quality of sexuality." And she ties the view expressly to affirmative-consent standards (Tuerkheimer 2015, pp. 42–43):

> [S]exual agency explains the cultural ascendance of consent and provides impetus for reforming its legal definition. Statutory language that describes consent as "words or overt actions … indicating freely given agreement" contemplates the interaction of sexual subjects; not objects. On this view, women and men are deemed capable of having and of expressing an intention to engage in sexual conduct. Without somehow expressing this intent, one cannot be said to have acted as a subject.
>
> Affirmative consent definitions—like the campus disciplinary codes that have become commonplace—construct sexuality to underscore its agentic qualities. By doing so, these definitions have the greatest potential to promote agency

Clearly, the agentic focus is designed to distance itself from a focus on autonomy, which Tuerkheimer criticizes for assuming that people "can operate largely free of external influences" (ibid. p. 41). But it is unclear how positive expressions of intentions to engage in sexual conduct are less socially influenced than are passively accepted sex acts—which may reflect a mild rebuke to the aggressive boor. Nor is it clear why an agent cannot decide to engage in sexual activity in ways that do not accord with the preferences of extensively educated people who write about sex. In the end, "agentic" may convey nothing more than "people like sex they enthusiastically desire enough to ignore why they are enthusiastic about certain partners and certain situations."

Catherine MacKinnon has criticized rape law's focus on consent as impractical because of power differentials between parties to sexual encounters. She advocates reorienting rape law to focus on those inequalities, suggesting the following definition: "a physical invasion of a sexual nature under circumstances of threat or use of force, fraud, coercion, abduction, or of the abuse of power, trust, or a position of dependency or vulnerability." In part, the goal is to move to center stage the conditions commonly considered to vitiate consent. But consent (and then some) sneaks back into the analysis as a way of showing when the powerful will not be held to have exploited their power (MacKinnon 2016, p. 476):

> If sex is equal between partners who socially are not, it is mutuality, reciprocity, respect, trust, desire – as well as sometimes fly-to-the-moon hope and a shared determination to slip the bonds of convention and swim upstream together – not one-sided acquiescence or ritualized obeisance or an exchange of sex for other treasure that makes it intimate, interactive, moving, communicative, warm, personal, loving.[25]

MacKinnon does not tie her proposal to affirmative-consent standards—indeed, she claims to be dismissing consent altogether. But one might think of her proposal as affirmative consent with a vengeance.

No one exalts reluctant sex. However, we criticize (or at least disapprove of) many activities that we do not criminalize. Some harms we think are too slight—or are at least regarded as slight by many people—to justify imposition of the formal apparatus of criminal condemnation. Others are close enough to desirable conduct that we worry about the effects of criminalization. When the victim can avoid the harm by saying "no," the case for criminalization is weaker. And when the victim perceives that her world would be worse if she lacked the power to engage in reluctant sex, the case is weaker still. Everyone's decisions are constrained all the time. While treating decisions about sex differently is defensible, it is by no means inevitable.

The Future

At bottom, this chapter identifies the harm in sexual assault from the subjective viewpoint of the partner. It argues in favor of criminalizing conduct only when an actor subjectively runs a substantial risk that his partner has not consciously decided to permit the sexual activity (putting aside the conditions that vitiate consent). It criticizes affirmative-consent standards for diverting the inquiry into proxy rules, devolving into particularly harsh forms of negligence liability, or some mixture of the two.

In two ways, the case against affirmative-consent standards could weaken over time. First, social consensus could grow that unwelcome but acquiesced-in sex is a harm of the degree that justifies the intervention of the criminal law. While affirmative-consent standards protect against this harm only imperfectly, as noted previously, they do protect against it to some degree. The greater the perceived harm, the stronger the case for prophylactic rules to guard against it. Even if some risk to the nonculpable persists, the risk should be reduced as social consensus grows regarding the harm, as more people will come to understand that steps are necessary to avoid the harm.

Second, social consensus could grow that certain sexual behavior offends dignitary interests.[26] It may be, for example, that over time, more people will agree that sexual penetration should never occur in the absence of verbal authorization, at least among first-time sex partners.[27] In such an environment, a narrow affirmative-consent requirement might protect against sexual overtures that offend and, as the social norm becomes widely known, impose reduced costs on the nonculpable. Any criminal prohibition reflects a judgment about harm that any particular actor might not understand. As the norms become widely shared, the costs of punishing the morally innocent are regarded as acceptable (Cole 2018). Vague, unarticulated standards, applicable across the vast range of sexual interactions, will pose larger risks for a longer time.

When general social norms deviate from a particular individual's subjective preferences, we normally employ consent as a safety value—hence our ability to box or play football or poker without being at risk in the grocery store of being punched, tackled, or deceived into surrendering money. Those who take no offense—and even pleasure—in somewhat unpredictable sexual encounters perhaps will be permitted to accommodate their preference by opting out of affirmative-consent regimes in the same way devotees of sadomasochism opt out of current conventions for expressing unwillingness.[28]

NOTES

1. Many of the arguments and some of the expressions of those arguments in this chapter first appeared in Cole (2016).
2. Antioch College's policy in the 1990s, however, stated:

   > Verbal consent should be obtained with each new level of physical and/or sexual contact/conduct in any given interaction, regardless of who initiates it. Asking "Do you want to have sex with me?" is not enough. The request for consent must be specific to each act.

   The standard was parodied on the TV show *Saturday Night Live*. Verbal authorization was not required when a sex act was "mutually and simultaneously initiated" (Johnson and Taylor 2017, pp. 219–920).
3. An example is the canard that affirmative-consent standards are needed to displace a presumption of female sexual availability and protect women from being fondled by strangers on a bus before they have a chance to object, appropriately rejected by Ferzan (2016, p. 429).
4. Proxy crimes are less troubling when they address a closely regulated industry whose participants can easily be educated about the rules. Obviously, no-means-no does not satisfy that criterion.
5. For a white paper aimed at higher education that explicitly advocates cashing out affirmative-consent standards in reasonableness terms, see the NCHERM excerpt quoted in note 6.
6. Consider Shaw (2016, pp. 1412) on campus affirmative-consent policies, discussing a 2015 survey:

   > Eighty-three percent of students, both men and women, indicated they were familiar with the "yes means yes" standard. While they were well aware of the standard, they differed greatly in its application. When asked if undressing, getting a condom, and/or nodding in agreement established consent for further sexual activity, over forty percent said "yes" and over forty percent said "no." ...

A higher education consulting group "widely credited with helping to popularize and institutionalize consent-based policies in higher education" has recently expressed concern about their application by campus "sex police" (The NCHERM Group 2017, pp. 3, 5–6):

> "Affirmative consent" policies ... need to be used correctly or the entire concept will get a bad name. ... Some of you are off track because you are applying a utopian lens to consent. ...
>
> ... [Y]ou should look at consent more as transactional and contextual, meaning that we view the entire sexual interaction and the context of the larger relationship. We contrast that to an approach that is more particularized and occurrence-based, where finders-of-fact tend to hyper-focus on each touch within a sexual interaction and ignore the larger context of the relationship. ... [Y]ou will be best served by evaluating consent based on the perspective of a reasonable person who is viewing the totality of the circumstances. That means we look at the whole relationship or interaction (the transaction), not just one time that someone might have touched someone else problematically (the occurrence).

Adding to the risk of confusion: some campuses may have classified instances in which a person assented to sex but regretted it as not involving consent. For a case reporting on plaintiff's allegations that a Title IX coordinator had publicly taken the position that "regret equals rape," see *Doe v. Washington and Lee University* (p. 3). If legality depends on a prediction of how a partner will feel in the future, the risk of mistake increases. *See also* Flack et al. (2007, pp. 148–149) (women reporting "unwanted" vaginal intercourse listed "thought I wanted it at the time" among the top three reasons 37.5% of the time).

7. On procedures on campus that could not be used in the criminal law, see Johnson and Taylor (2017, ch. 4).
8. A higher education consulting group has identified this tendency toward temporal limitation among some colleges in applying their affirmative-consent standards. *See* note 6.
9. American Law Institute (2015, p. 164) defends exempting some persons from the affirmative-consent standard because "the Code makes clear that the consent must accompany the specific disputed act."
10. *See* Simons (2006, p. 588) for a similar suggestion.
11. The ALI reporters have previously employed the strategy of "chang[ing] the narrative." After criticism of its self-consciously styled affirmative-consent proposals, the reporters recast it as a "contextual-consent" proposal without significantly altering its substance (Cole 2016, p. 512).
12. One commentator praised the vagueness of a proposed California affirmative-consent standard because of its ability to deter, hoping the law would "create a haze of fear and confusion over what counts as consent" (Klein 2014).
13. In the college disciplinary system, problems have been well documented. An instructive survey of troubling cases appears in Johnson and Taylor (2017).
14. Tuerkheimer discusses a case in which the defendant claimed to believe the victim was feigning sleep but did not point to any conduct or communication by the victim that led to this belief. Conviction would be likely even under a recklessness standard in the absence of some compelling account of why the defendant did not perceive a substantial risk that the victim was actually asleep.

15. American Law Institute (2015, section 213.9(2)) exempts "spouses and intimate partners" from liability when specific facts show the actor "honestly and reasonably believed" the sleeping partner "would welcome the act."

16. Even Tuerkheimer acknowledges that the intoxication cases "more often seem to feature expressions of non-consent" (Tuerkheimer 2016, p. 457), which of course could be handled by a simple no-means-no rule.

17. Indeed, the drafters of the MPC proposal thought this problem was beyond solution. For discussion and critique, see Cole (2017).

18. Flack et al. (2007, pp. 148–149) found that women who experienced unwanted vaginal intercourse listed "happened before I could stop it" 50% of the time among the top three reasons that it occurred.

19. Tuerkheimer says that "many of [the fear] cases also feature a communicated lack of consent. On these facts, the conduct alleged would qualify as nonconsensual under any definition, affirmative or otherwise" (Tuerkheimer 2016, p. 458).

20. In one of the cases addressed, the victim was "shaking and crying throughout" the sexual encounter, strong evidence that the defendant was consciously aware of a substantial risk that the victim's cooperation was induced by fear. Other cases involve a "surprise attack," another scenario in which only a sociopath would fail to recognize the risk that fear had induced cooperation. For example, in *State v. Benitez*, a 17-year-old was driven home by the 40-something husband of her church pastor following a church event. After dropping off everyone else, the defendant drove away from the victim's house and stopped on a dead-end street. He "began to rub the inside of [victim's] thighs, kissed and bit her neck, put his hands under her shirt and rubbed her breasts." The victim did nothing to encourage the activity. And in yet another, the victim did not say "no," but the defendant had held his hand over her mouth—pretty good evidence that he was aware of a risk that she was unwilling (State ex rel. K.B.).

21. 310 N.C. 399 (1984).

22. Presumably, if fear induces a woman to say "yes," and her partner is aware that her affirmative consent is induced by fear, the standard will be elaborated such as to permit conviction.

23. One model code, promulgated by a firm that advises academic institutions, includes the following illustration as vitiating consent (The NCHERM Group 2010, p. 9):

> Amanda and Bill meet at a party. They spend the evening dancing and getting to know each other. Bill convinces Amanda to come up to his room. From 11:00pm until 3:00am, Bill uses every line he can think of to convince Amanda to have sex with him, but she adamantly refuses. He keeps at her, and begins to question her religious convictions, and accuses her of being "a prude." Finally, it seems to Bill that her resolve is weakening, and he convinces her to give him a "hand job" (hand to genital contact). Amanda would never had done it but for Bill's incessant advances.

Johnson and Taylor (2017, pp. 99, 101) identify one college discipline case in which responsibility was based on the conclusion that the accused had "directed unreasonable pressure for sexual activity toward [the female student] over a period of weeks" and another in which consent was vitiated because a woman was "pressured ... seemingly by the general college environment," not by the accused.

24. See the discussion in Cole (2016, pp. 535–537). Relatedly, Ferzan (2016, p. 406) suggests that affirmative-consent standards might be interpreted to require "requests" rather than "permissions."

25. Presumably, the generally powerful might be rape victims even under an equality approach. The generally powerful, for example, might occasionally be in a vulnerable position, like unconsciousness. But in other situations, the powerful party's simple willingness to engage in sex apparently will defeat claims of vulnerability, and the less powerful person will not have exploited inequality even if the more powerful person was not enthusiastic.

26. For an argument that conduct should be criminalized on dignity grounds only when violations constitute "severe humiliations," see Hornle (2012).

27. Some criticize the idea that different rules should apply to first-time sex partners, apparently believing that such rules imply that consent to sex is never ending. Early ALI drafts exempted some long-term relationships from the affirmative-consent requirement (Cole 2016, p. 513). A general recklessness or negligence standard would take into account whether partners had a sexual history against which to evaluate a sexual encounter. Certainly, no one would overlook that a woman had on prior occasions emphatically rejected intercourse with a partner in evaluating the meaning of signals in later encounters.

28. American Law Institute (2015, §213.9(1)) would have created a defense for those who prove by a preponderance of the evidence that they reasonably believed their partner had given "explicit verbal consent" to applying physical force and ignoring indicia of unwillingness.

References

Doe v. Washington and Lee University, 2015 WL 4647996 (W.D. Va. 2015).

State ex rel. K.B., 2013 WL 3340654 (N.J. Appel. Divn. 2013).

State v. Benitez, 2010 WL 4811893 (N.J. Appel. Divn. 2010).

Alexander, Larry. 2014. The ontology of consent. *Analytic Philosophy* 55: 102–113.

American Law Institute. 1985. *Model penal code*. Philadelphia: American Law Institute.

———. 2015. *Model penal code: Sexual assault and related offenses*. Discussion draft no. 2. American Law Institute, Philadelphia.

Cole, Kevin. 2016. Better sex through criminal law: Proxy crimes, covert negligence, and other difficulties of "affirmative consent" in the ALI's draft sexual assault provisions. *San Diego Law Review* 53: 507–577.

———. 2017. Sex and the single malt girl: How voluntary intoxication affects consent. *Montana Law Review* 78: 155–185.

———. 2018. Real-world criminal law and the norm against punishing the innocent: Two cheers for threshold deontology. In *Moral puzzles and legal perplexities*, ed. Heidi M. Hurd. Cambridge: Cambridge University Press.

Ferzan, Kimberly Kessler. 2016. Consent, culpability, and the law of rape. *Ohio State Journal of Criminal Law* 13: 397–439.

Ferzan, Kimberly Kessler, and Peter Westen. 2017. How to think like a lawyer about rape. *Criminal Law and Philosophy* 11: 759–800.

Flack, William F., Jr., Kimberly A. Daubman, Marcia L. Caron, Jenica A. Asadorian, Nicole R. D'Aureli, Shannon N. Gigliotti, Anna T. Hall, Sarah Kiser, and Erin R. Stine. 2007. Risk factors and consequences of unwanted sex among university students: Hooking up, alcohol, and stress response. *Journal of Interpersonal Violence* 22: 139–157.

Gersen, Jacob, and Jeannie Suk. 2016. The sex bureaucracy. *California Law Review* 104: 881–948.

Hornle, Tatjana. 2012. Criminalizing behaviour to protect human dignity. *Criminal Law and Philosophy* 6: 307–325.

Hurd, Heidi M. 1996. The moral magic of consent. *Legal Theory* 2: 121–146.

Husak, Douglas. 2016. *Ignorance of law: A philosophical inquiry*. New York: Oxford University Press.

———. 2017. Drug proscriptions as proxy crimes. *Law and Philosophy* 36: 345–366.

Johnson, K.C., and Stuart Taylor Jr. 2017. *The campus rape frenzy: The attack on due process at America's universities*. New York: Encounter Books.

Klein, Ezra. 2014. "Yes means yes" is a terrible law and I completely support it. *Vox*. https://www.vox.com/2014/10/13/6966847/yes-means-yes-is-a-terrible-bill-and-i-completely-support-it. Accessed 25 Feb 2019.

MacKinnon, Catherine A. 2016. Rape redefined. *Harvard Law and Policy Review* 10: 431–477.

Moore, Michael S., and Heidi M. Hurd. 2011. Punishing the awkward, the stupid, the weak, and the selfish: The culpability of negligence. *Criminal Law and Philosophy* 5: 147–198.

Schulhofer, Stephen J. 1998. *Unwanted sex*. Cambridge, MA: Harvard University Press.

———. 2017. Reforming the law of rape. *Law and Inequality* 35: 335–352.

Shaw, Lori E. 2016. Title IX, sexual assault, and the issue of effective consent: Blurred lines—When should "yes" mean "no"? *Indiana Law Journal* 91: 1363–1423.

Simons, Kenneth W. 1997. Criminal law: When is strict liability just. *Journal of Criminal Law and Criminology* 87: 1075–1137.

———. 2006. The conceptual structure of consent in criminal law. *Buffalo Criminal Law Review* 9: 577–653.

The NCHERM Group. 2010. NCHERM model sexual misconduct policy. The NCHERM Group. https://www.ncherm.org/wp-content/uploads/2017/08/MODELSEXUALMISCONDUCTPOLICY1-10.pdf. Accessed 25 Feb 2019.

———. 2017. Due process and the sex police. The NCHERM Group. https://www.ncherm.org/wp-content/uploads/2017/04/TNG-Whitepaper-Final-Electronic-Version.pdf. Accessed 25 Feb 2019.

Tuerkheimer, Deborah. 2015. Rape on and off campus. *Emory Law Journal* 65: 1–45.

———. 2016. Affirmative consent. *Ohio State Journal of Criminal Law* 13: 441–468.

PART III

Animals

CHAPTER 4

Crimes Against Animals

Heidi M. Hurd

Few areas of law are as schizophrenic as the criminal law's prohibitions of animal cruelty. Varying markedly between the 50 states, the District of Columbia, and America's 5 inhabited territories, criminal provisions governing the treatment of animals reflect deep-seated ambivalence about who counts as the victim of animal cruelty, what constitutes the wrong of animal cruelty, and what role punishment ought to play in response to animal cruelty. Indeed, the defining criteria of an "animal" and of "cruelty" are matters of considerable legal disagreement, and qualitatively identical deeds perpetrated on members of the same species within the same jurisdiction can invite markedly dissimilar legal liability. As I shall argue in this chapter, animal cruelty laws are thus an embarrassment to the criminal law, and they will remain an embarrassment until the law embraces a consistent set of answers to fundamental philosophical questions about what sorts of wrongs the criminal law can properly address and what sorts of wrongs are at issue in cases of animal cruelty.

In the first part, I shall sketch some of the most basic doctrinal contradictions that make manifest the criminal law's need for philosophical clarity. As I shall demonstrate, animal cruelty laws flagrantly flout, misuse, and abuse doctrines and principles that have been long settled within the general part of criminal law, and for this reason alone, quite apart from their unprincipled impact upon animals themselves, they ought to be of concern to those who devote their scholarly energies to harmonizing the core conditions of criminal responsibility.

In the first part, I shall reveal how the contradictions that pervade animal cruelty laws in part follow from, and in part capitalize on, the long-standing debate about the very point of criminal law. As scholars of the criminal law well appreciate, there are at least five theories—five principles—concerning the

H. M. Hurd (✉)
University of Illinois, Urbana, IL, USA
e-mail: hhurd@illinois.edu

L. Alexander, K. K. Ferzan (eds.), *The Palgrave Handbook of Applied Ethics and the Criminal Law*, https://doi.org/10.1007/978-3-030-22811-8_4

legitimate scope and limits of the criminal law.[1] These principles are not mutually incompatible, although several of them have been famously propounded by theorists who have advanced them as exclusive justifications for criminalization. As I shall argue, one way to bring a modicum of order to the chaos of animal cruelty provisions is to recognize that their cross-cutting prohibitions and permissions respond to, and perhaps exploit, competing understandings of whether one, some, or all of these five principles of legislation appropriately inform the reach of the criminal law. I shall, accordingly, unpack the significant doctrinal disagreements about when and why punishment ought to be visited upon those who harm animals by working through the ways in which animal cruelty provisions appear to be responsive to inconsistent views about the very point of the criminal law.

DOCTRINAL CONTRADICTIONS

Criminal statutes that construe forms of animal treatment as significant legal wrongs extend back to the nineteenth century when Massachusetts (1804), Oklahoma (1887), and Rhode Island (1896) enacted legislation that felonized certain types of physical abuse and neglect (Campbell 2013, p. 276 n. 38). A century later, Wisconsin (1986) became the fourth state in the nation to categorize at least some acts of animal cruelty as felonies (Otto 2005, p. 312 n. 1). Over the 30 years that followed, the remaining states in the nation followed suit; the final three—Idaho (2012), North Dakota (2013), and South Dakota (2014)—doing so only recently (JAVMA 2014). Today, while most first-time violations, however egregious, continue to constitute mere misdemeanors, state criminal laws that apply to animals reach a wide variety of acts and omissions, including animal cruelty (physical abuse, torture, or neglect); sexual animal assault or bestiality; organizing and attending animal fights; live vivisection; animal slaughter; poaching, baiting, poisoning, and trapping animals; animal theft, concealment, and animal identification tampering; improper confinement and transport of animals in vehicles and at agricultural operations; animal abandonment; animal hoarding; animal breeding methods; artificial coloring of animals; the keeping of dogs deemed dangerous; the possession and distribution of depictions of animal cruelty; and forms of bodily mutilation such as tail docking, ear cropping, and devocalization. At the federal level, the Animal Welfare Act (7 U.S.C. §§ 2131–2159 (2012)) sets minimum standards of care and treatment for certain animals bred for commercial sale, used in research, transported commercially, or exhibited to the public as is "necessary to prevent and eliminate burdens upon such [interstate] commerce"[2] (7 U.S.C. §§ 2131 (2012)), and in recent years Congress has invoked the Commerce Clause to criminalize the sale and distribution of animal "crush videos" (18 U.S.C. § 48 (2012); Serafino 2011, pp. 1128–1129) and the organization of animal fights for sport or entertainment under circumstances that implicate interstate commerce (7 U.S.C. § 2156 (2012)).[3] And not only is there now a multitude of criminal prohibitions against particular actions, at least with regard to particular animals, but there is also a wide variety of investigation, reporting, enforcement mechanisms, financial penalties, and other adverse consequences that attend infractions, from expanded investigative permissions,[4] to veterinary-reporting obligations and immunities,[5] psychological evaluation requirements,[6] costs-of-care bonds,[7] liens,[8] and forfeiture demands,[9] to offender registration laws.[10]

It is tempting to assume that the passage of multiple animal cruelty laws[11] and the expansion of investigative and reporting capacities on the part of authorities evidence the recognition that the misery of animals is of sufficiently grave moral concern to merit the attention of criminal law. But it would be a mistake to think that these laws either originally expressed or manifest today the law's embrace of the view that animals themselves are legally recognizable victims of wrongdoing when they are neglected, abused, forced to fight, physically altered, trapped, confined, experimented upon, or even tortured. Indeed, unlike most criminal laws, the points of which appear abundantly clear, animal cruelty laws reflect a deep ambivalence about their very purpose—a deep uncertainty about who counts as the victim, about whose interests are of paramount concern, and about whose rights are being vindicated by the threat of punishment.

By way of illustration, consider the most basic definitions that are at work in these laws. What, for example, is an "animal?" What constitutes "cruelty?" Legislators are remarkably unwilling to construe the first question as a biological inquiry, preferring instead to define as "nonanimals" creatures whose painful treatment they are content to countenance. An animal, in short, is a nominal kind, not a natural kind. It is a status bestowed on creatures to whom cruelty matters to humans; it is not a status possessed by all creatures to whom cruelty matters to them.[12] Georgia thus excludes from its definition of "animal" "any pest that might be exterminated or removed from a business, residence, or other structure" (Ga. Code Ann. § 16-12-4(d) (West 2018)); Texas excludes from its definition any creature that has not been "domesticated" or at least "previously captured" (Tex. Penal Code Ann. § 42.092(a)(2) (West 2017)); Iowa's animal cruelty statute specifically provides that, "'animal' does not include any of the following: livestock … game, any fur-bearing animal, fish, reptile, or amphibian … unless a person owns, confines, or controls the game, fur-bearing animal, fish, reptile, or amphibian … [and] [a]ny nongame species declared to be a nuisance [under state law]" (Iowa Code Ann. § 717B.1 (West 2018)).[13]

In other words, it simply is not possible to be cruel to house mice in Georgia, Texas, or Iowa because house mice are not "animals" under the laws of those states. They can be poisoned, left to die in sticky traps, dismembered, microwaved, skinned alive, or repeatedly electrocuted, without amounting to even prima facie cruelty in these states. But pet mice are different.[14] In Georgia, Texas, and Iowa, if someone poisons, dismembers, microwaves, skins alive, or repeatedly electrocutes a mouse purchased at PetSmart, this counts as a crime, and potentially a felony, because animals who are owned or conventionally considered "pets" are "animals" to whom it is possible to be cruel.[15]

Yet how can members of the same species be both animals and not animals? How can the harsh treatment of one constitute a felony, while the same treatment of another count as an extermination job well done? It would be preposterous to exempt naughty youngsters from the category of "children" in order to ensure that child abuse prohibitions do not inhibit the harsh treatment of those who misbehave. Why is it not equally preposterous to vary the legal definition of an "animal" by the degree to which the avoidance of a creature's pain while managing its behavior constitutes an inconvenience? Such obvious definitional gerrymandering provides the first take-away concerning animal cruelty laws: they lack a coherent understanding of their very subject matter. (Satz 2009, p. 70) As a result, within any given state, animal cruelty provisions generate morally perverse results. Further, the wide variations between states' definitions of what counts as an animal result in a national patchwork of laws that embody contradictory prohibitions and permissions.

Just as animal cruelty laws lack a coherent conception of what constitutes an "animal," so do they also belie both moral and legal confusion about what constitutes "cruelty." Animal cruelty is very commonly defined as "the unreasonable" (Tenn. Code Ann. § 39-14-202 (West 2018)), the "unnecessary" (S.C. Code Ann. § 47-1-40 (2018)), the "unjustifiable" (Del. Code Ann. Tit. 11, § 1325 (West 2018)), or the "needless[ ]" infliction of suffering (Ohio Rev. Code Ann. § 959.13 (West 2018)). If a state's criminal law defined domestic abuse as an unnecessary battery of a domestic partner, or if it defined rape as unreasonable nonconsensual intercourse, the criminal law would imply that there is such a thing as necessary domestic battery and reasonable sexual assault. It would further imply that when such acts are necessary or reasonable, they are not in any way morally objectionable, and hence, they are not even of prima facie legal concern. How preposterous would that be? But animal cruelty laws make clear that when animals suffer for the sake of ends deemed "reasonable," suffering is not in any way morally problematic and hence is not even of prima facie legal concern.

Of course, the devil is in the details. If animal suffering is deemed reasonable only in circumstances in which the criminal law would otherwise accord perpetrators a traditional justification, then animal cruelty laws effectively allow the infliction of suffering on animals only when it would be justified by standard defenses within the criminal law (e.g., self-defense, defense of others, true necessity). But this is not the case. All sorts of activities that cause great pain and suffering to animals are thought to be "reasonable," and most of these come nowhere close to being the moral equivalent of acts that save lives or constitute the least harmful means of preventing far greater evils to the larger community. For example, a great many practices that cause animal suffering within agricultural operations are exempted from animal cruelty laws.[16] Inasmuch as 98 percent of the world's animals that are used by humans are raised for consumption and 9.5 billion farm animals are raised and slaughtered for commercial purposes each year in the United States alone (Ibrahim 2006, p. 180), the standard exclusion of farm animals from animal cruelty laws guarantees that the vast majority of animals with whom humans have contact are not protected from even the grossest forms of abuse.[17] Thus, to take but one example, Ohio prohibits persons from "keep[ing] animals *other than cattle, poultry or fowl, swine, sheep, or goats* in an enclosure without wholesome exercise and change of air" (Ohio Rev. Code Ann. § 959.13(A)(4) (West 2018); italics added). Ohio further makes it a crime to "impound or confine an animal without affording it …access to shelter from wind, rain, snow, or excessive direct sunlight" but goes on to make clear that "this section does not apply to animals impounded or confined prior to slaughter" (Ohio Rev. Code Ann. § 959.13(A)(2) (West 2018)).

Consider the notorious example of how veal is still produced in numerous facilities across the nation. The goal of veal production is pale, white, anemic meat (Matheny and Leahy 2007, p. 332). Male calves who are birthed in dairies (which of course, have no use for males) are fed a synthetic formula that lacks iron while being deprived of water in enclosures that are kept miserably warm so that in their desperate need to cool themselves, they will drink yet more of the formula (Cohn-Sherbok 2006, p. 87). These calves live their entire lives in wooden crates (Friend and Dellmeier 1988, p. 59). Why? Because if their crates were made of metal their craving for iron would cause them to lick the bars in ways that would pinken their flesh (Cohn-Sherbok 2006, p. 87). They often are so tightly confined that they cannot turn around, lick themselves, or scratch themselves (Matheny and Leahy 2007, p. 332). Why? Not just because this guarantees that their muscles remain soft, but because if they could turn around, their desperate craving for iron would induce them to lick their own waste, and this would again pinken their meat (Cohn-Sherbok 2006, p. 87). Bucket-feeding (as opposed to nursing) the formula has a laxative effect, so the calves suffer from severe digestive problems that lead to searing open sores and scours on their legs (Friend and Dellmeier 1988, p. 55). For these sad creatures, death simply cannot come soon enough, because their short lives are nothing if not the definition of misery. Yet, this brutalizing treatment of crating veal calves is still deemed legally "reasonable" in 42 states in the nation (Rowland 2017).

The same legal conclusion attaches to a great many other practices that would count as torture if done to a cat or dog. Dehorning, tail docking, debeaking, branding, castration, ear notching—without any anesthesia—all count as "reasonable" practices under virtually all animal cruelty laws.[18] And as states across the nation are rapidly prohibiting the confinement of dogs in cars when high temperatures pose a source of danger to them,[19] the suffocating confinement that animals experience in concentrated animal feed operations (CAFOs) remains perfectly legal. And the same is true of numerous painful practices that are routine within rodeos, fairs, zoos, circuses, fishing, hunting, trapping, and industry and university research.[20] For example, both rodeo horses and bulls are encouraged to buck more vigorously by tightening a flank strap above their genitals that induces them to kick wildly (Soehnel 1992) and calves during calf-roping competitions can reach speeds of 27 miles per hour before being lassoed around the neck and jerked to an abrupt stop in ways that commonly cause punctured lungs, internal hemorrhaging, and paralysis ("Special Report on Rodeos" 1973, pp. 1–2). All of these practices fall well short of being "necessary" in the sense that the criminal law standardly employs that term. For the notion of necessity in the criminal law is never otherwise unpacked as that which is "economically profitable," or "economically efficient," or "conducive to human entertainment," or "in the service of human convenience," or "a time-saving means of reducing human irritation." What constitutes "the reasonable infliction of suffering on animals" thus cannot be thought to coincide with what our standard criminal law doctrine of necessity would otherwise exonerate.

So how are we to understand what makes the suffering of animals reasonable or unreasonable, necessary or unnecessary, within the meaning of typical state laws? In answer, some states and local jurisdictions have adopted the practice of assigning panels of citizens and delegates of industry the task of determining what constitutes cruel treatment.[21] But these panels, like the courts in states that simply leave questions of interpretation to judges, are required to honor statutory exemptions for the following: *commonly accepted* agricultural and husbandry practices used in the commercial raising of livestock[22]; *normal* animal training and use of trained animals in hunting[23]; *customary* uses of animals in *normal and usual* events at fairs, circuses, rodeos, and zoos[24]; *accepted and best* animal husbandry practices in private animal custodianship[25]; *traditional* veterinary practices[26]; and bona fide scientific experimentation.[27] Thus, in these states, panels are not entitled to rethink the legitimacy of practices that are "standard," "normal," "usual," "customary," "traditional," or "accepted." What is ordinary is per se reasonable. It follows that so long as animal industries do not innovate, so long as they do not break ranks, so long as they adhere to custom, they insulate themselves from moral scrutiny—and therefore from legal intervention.

What other professions are so perfectly self-immunized from liability? In most professions what is customary is evidential of what is reasonable, but it is not its perfect measure. As Learned Hand famously insisted in *The T.J. Hooper*, entire industries can "unduly lag[ ] in the adoption of new and available" practices, and what is ordinary and customary can become unreasonable in light of new technologies and changed circumstances (ibid. p. 737). "[T]here are precautions so imperative that even their universal disregard will not excuse their omission" (ibid. p. 737). If the universal disregard of precautions cannot insulate factories, railroads, coal mines, automobile manufacturers, fracking operations, airlines, shipping companies, and tunnel-builders from legal liability, what explains the willingness of the law to allow the "universal disregard" of animal suffering to insulate animal operations from legal consequences?

In the next part, I shall suggest that there are at least five distinct moral agendas that explain the cross-cutting provisions within crimes against animals.

These agendas coincide with the five theories of legislation that have been defended by those who have been concerned with the scope and limits of criminal punishment.[28] As I shall suggest, once one appreciates the competing moral concerns that underlie animal cruelty provisions, and once one recognizes how that battle reignites long-standing disputes over the reach of the criminal law, it becomes possible to make sense of (but hardly to justify) the interstate doctrinal contradictions and intrastate doctrinal perversities that cumulatively result in the vigorous protection of a few animals and the simultaneous indifference to the suffering of the vast majority.

FIVE PRINCIPLES OF ANTI-CRUELTY LEGISLATION

The Principle of Democracy

Let us begin with the position defended by those who believe that there are no principled limits to a democratic state's authority to criminalize conduct.[29] On this theory, criminal legislation is justified if and only if it has been enacted democratically—namely, through a legislative process that procedurally realizes the value of ensuring that the majority of citizens live under their own laws.[30] Procedural fairness, on this view, guarantees substantive justice.

There is a significant sense in which this first theory of criminal legislation is a non-theory (or, at best, a theory about why one needs no such theory). Yet it is sadly all too easy in this day and age to imagine electoral enthusiasm for any number of legislative initiatives that would appear morally unjustified despite their democratic pedigree—for example, travel bans predicated on race or religion and prohibitions against demonstrators or journalists at political events. For this reason, most legal theorists believe that just as judges are bound by a defensible theory of adjudication, so too are legislators bound by a defensible theory of legislation that includes area-specific constraints that derive not from the whims of an electoral majority but from the best justification(s) that can be advanced for each area of law in question. For most criminal law scholars, then, the task is to articulate a theory of criminal legislation that harmonizes with persuasive defenses of our criminal justice system, generally, and our practices of punishment, more specifically.

Yet nothing will drive theorists back to claims about the constitutive moral authority of democratic dictates faster than discussions about how our legal treatment of animals can be justified. For little else seems to morally vindicate why animal cruelty laws allow cattle to be branded but not dogs; why they allow rodeos but not dog fights; why they allow owners, without anesthesia, to use hot irons, pliers, hacksaws, and rotary tools to de-spur roosters but attach felony liability to anyone who employs such methods to extract the claws of cats. More generally, the distinctions that many states draw between pets and other animals, both domestic and nondomestic, that license harms to the latter that would be decried if inflicted on the former, appear morally justified only if the raw fact that they were democratically approved is morally validating. Few doubt, of course, that the sheer fact that the majority prefers things one way rather than another gives ample justification for plenty of legally recognized practices. Majoritarianism validates the rules of the road, the seasonal schedule of taxes and holidays, the administration of a social security system, the structure of a nation's health-care system, and so forth. But can the raw fact that a majority prefers to protect only some animals from practices that inflict equal misery on a great many more morally vindicate the law's willingness to do so? We do not consider a majority's desire to discriminate between people on grounds of race, religion, gender, and so on as a legitimate basis for our legal institutions to do so. Why would we think there is any moral relevance to the distinction that a majority draws between members of the same species (birds kept as pets vs. birds kept for experimentation) or between species all of whose members similarly suffer when subjected to similarly brutalizing treatments?

The Harm Principle

The second theory of criminal legislation answers the call for a more principled basis upon which to criminalize actions, including those that impact the fates of animals. It takes its leave from John Stuart Mill's famous claim that "the only purpose for which power may be rightfully exercised over any member of a civilized community, against his will, is to prevent harm to others" (Mill 1963–91, vol. 18, pp. 223–224). Those who defend this so-called Harm Principle permit the state to eliminate choices from citizens' opportunity sets only when those choices will proximately result in harm to others (e.g., by causing physical injury to their persons or property or by exacting unfair advantages through fraudulent means). On this theory, democratically elected legislators are not at liberty to employ their power in any manner that might comport with the will of the majority. Rather, legislators satisfy the obligations of their legislative role if but only if they employ criminal law to prevent conduct that is harmful to others.

If "others" were to include animals, then the Harm Principle would clearly demand a radical overhaul of animal cruelty laws. Indeed, Mill's own utilitarianism, which committed him to a concern for the suffering (disutility) of all things that can suffer, clearly contemplated that animals should be protected from harm no less than human beings: "The reasons for legal intervention in favour of children, apply not less strongly to the case of those unfortunate slaves and victims of the most brutal part of mankind, the lower animals" (Mill 1892, p. 578). Yet while the Harm Principle has standardly found favor amongst utilitarians, it has also standardly been given an anthropocentric interpretation (White 2013, p. 142). None have insisted that its consistent application would commit the criminal law to criminalizing actions that harm animals in ways that would be illegal if directed at humans. Instead, the Harm Principle is taken to license the prohibition of actions that cause physical harm only to human beings and their property.

This is not to say that animals have not been protected under this Principle. Indeed, the concern for human welfare has instrumentally motivated a concern for animal welfare for two reasons. First, animals have standardly been thought of, and protected, as human property. In fact, the original purpose of animal cruelty laws was explicitly to protect animal owners from economic injuries resulting from harms inflicted by others on their valuable domestic animals (Chiesa 2008, p. 9; Serafino 2011, p. 1120). The first animal cruelty law enacted in Vermont in 1846, for example, made it a crime to "willfully and maliciously kill, maim, injure or disfigure … any horse or horse kind, cattle, sheep, or swine *of another person*" (1846 Vt. Acts & Resolves 34).[31] Animal cruelty laws thus first emerged as a species of laws concerned with theft or destruction of property (Chiesa 2008, p. 9; Serafino 2011, p. 1120). This understanding of the gravamen of animal cruelty has endured in many states.[32] Iowa's "Animal Abuse" provision, for example, explicitly limits criminal liability to one who "intentionally injures, maims, disfigures, or destroys an animal *owned by another person*" (Iowa Code Ann. § 717B.2 (West 2018)), making clear that its concern is to protect the property interests of animal owners.

Indeed, I would suggest that it is the concern for animal owners, rather than animals themselves, that motivates the law to equate animal cruelty with unreasonable suffering and then to deem reasonable any animal suffering that follows from human activities that are profitable, recreational, educational, entertaining, or merely convenient.[33] After all, if animal cruelty laws are fundamentally about protecting the material interests of humans, then it is unsurprising that they will permit whatever is deemed reasonable by the owners of ranches, feedlots, dairies, CAFOs, rodeos, circuses, fairs, zoos, and corporate and university research labs. But should what counts as cruelty really turn on the human value associated with the creature that does the suffering? And if humans value an animal more when it is subjected to suffering (e.g., a deer that is hunted, a rodeo bull that is cinched to buck, a veal calf that is closely confined), should infliction of suffering on that animal be deemed less cruel than it would be if it were inflicted on an animal that is valued most when not in a state of misery (e.g., a pet dog, a nimble show horse)?

The second argument for passing animal cruelty legislation as an instrumental means of advancing human welfare stems from the claim that animal cruelty is a gateway crime that makes more likely future acts of violence against humans (Kruse 2002, pp. 1668–1669). There is certainly substantial evidence that this is the case (Kruse 2002, p. 1669).[34] Animal abusers are deemed five times more likely to commit violent crimes than are those without such a history, and most of the infamous serial killers of the last century bragged of engaging in animal torture (Lacroix 1998, p. 8; Sauder 2000, p. 14 n. 114).[35] Further, 71 percent of pet-owning women who enter domestic shelters report that their abusers also targeted their pets, and about one-third of these women report that their children have harmed or killed animals (142 Cong. Rec. S4630-05).[36] Thus, animal cruelty laws are very much like other "proxy crimes" that prohibit acts prophylactically—for example, laws that prohibit the possession of burglary tools, counterfeiting technologies, firearms by ex-felons, and drugs in quantities that indicate an intent to sell. The problem with animal cruelty, on this account, is not animal cruelty; the problem is that it is a harbinger of cruelty to humans.

If animal cruelty laws are fundamentally about preventing future violence to humans, then it is unsurprising that the cruelties inherent in animal husbandry, hunting, fishing, trapping, rodeoing, zoo keeping, and animal research are exempted, because nothing suggests that pig farmers, duck hunters, bronco-busters, and psychology professors are the next serial killers or school shooters. But again, it seems important to ask whether what counts as cruelty to animals today should be limited to what we fear will happen to humans tomorrow. Why should acts that cause suffering to animals matter only when they are likely to be repeated on people?

The Offense Principle

On the third theory of criminal legislation, prohibitions backed by the threat of punishment may be enacted as a means of preventing actions that cause offense or psychic injury to others.[37] It is as a result of legislators implicitly invoking the Offense Principle that laws against public nudity, prohibitions against public displays of intimate sexual conduct, restrictions on noise and light pollution, sex-segregated restrooms, and so forth are commonplace. By conceiving of offense-generating behaviors as legitimate objects of criminal legislation, this theory expands the criteria that will justify limitations on liberty by making both the Harm Principle and the Offense Principle independently sufficient justifications of prohibition.

This third account of the scope and limits of criminal legislation has long licensed the view that animal cruelty is a matter of public concern because it is an offense to public sensibilities (Kruse 2002, p. 1655). Soon after the emergence of animal cruelty laws, in fact, courts began to find violations not only when valuable property interests were infringed, but also when acts of cruelty were thought to infringe upon the sensibilities of innocent onlookers.[38] In the language of one prominent Delaware attorney: "While the brutes have no legal rights, to inflict cruelty on animals *in public* injures the moral character of those who witness it—and may therefore be treated as a crime" (Gerry 1875). This concern that animal cruelty will impact the public by offending their sensibilities, or worse, desensitizing their moral emotions, remains a theme in contemporary legal debates about the regulation of animal cruelty.[39] It is this concern—that humans not lose their humanity by witnessing animal cruelty—that appears to make sense of why the law prohibits organized displays of bear wrestling, kangaroo boxing, and bull, dog, and cockfighting, even when the owners of these animals consent to their involvement. And it is this account that best explains why numerous states have followed Illinois in adopting prohibitions analogous to child pornography laws[40] that punish those who create, sell, market, or simply possess images of animal cruelty.

It is also the claim that animal cruelty is problematic when and because it is a spectacle that makes sense of why the law leaves untouched practices that are conventionally accepted by industry practitioners who are ostensibly living proof that these practices are not character corroding. It is this notion that makes sense of why the law leaves untouched practices that are out of sight, out of mind—practices that inflict as much suffering in private as do animal exhibitions in public but that go on behind the closed doors of puppy mills, pig farms, poultry barns, veal operations, dairies, CAFOs, pelt producers, animal research labs, and animal entertainment training facilities. Yet it now seems incumbent to ask whether what counts as cruelty should really turn on the size of the crowd that witnesses an animal's suffering. Should animal cruelty be present when some group believes it is witnessing the deliberate infliction of suffering on an animal—even if what it, in fact, witnesses is a mere depiction generated by computer simulation? Should animal cruelty be absent when an animal unowned by another is made to suffer in isolation?

A second category of animal cruelty decisions beyond those that have adjudicated public displays of animal brutality appears to be best explained by the Offense Principle. According to these cases, the problem with animal cruelty is that it is a harm to those who share emotional bonds with the animal and who are thus psychologically pained by its suffering. This concern is manifestly at work in the case of *People v. Garcia*,[41] in which a father threw his son's goldfish bowl across the room and then forced his 9-year-old son to watch him stomp on the goldfish that flopped on the carpet. Because the act appeared to be intended to "inflict[ ] emotional pain on … *the boy*," it was deemed a "sadistic and depraved act" (ibid. p. 852) that reflected the state of mind on the part of the perpetrator that both the trial and appellate courts deemed definitional of aggravated cruelty to an animal. In other words, it was on the basis that the boy was psychologically offended, not on the basis that the fish was physically tortured and killed, that the father was found guilty of a felony.

It is this concern for protecting the psychic tranquility of humans by protecting the objects of their sentiments that appears to ground the distinctions that many states make between harms to pets and harms to other animals. In several states, it is a felony to abuse an animal that is conventionally considered a pet, with some states elevating penalties for harms to dogs and cats in particular, while the very same acts of abuse, if perpetrated upon animals that do not commonly share people's homes, constitute misdemeanors at most.[42] In these states, it is a felony to cut off the paw of a pet rabbit, but not the paw of a trapped jack-rabbit; it is a felony to use a hook and line to catch a goldfish in a fish tank, but not to catch a trout in a stream; it is a felony to skin a cat, but not to skin a raccoon. Animal cruelty on this model is a function of whether humans suffer when the animal in question suffers because what matters on this second application of the Offense Principle is protecting those things that people love because they love them. But now we ought to ask again whether what counts as cruelty should turn on whether the suffering creature is deemed eligible to live in a house. Should cruelty to an animal be found only when humans are subjectively offended by its suffering?

The Paternalism Principle

The fourth category of actions that may be usefully distinguished from those categories that are targeted by the Principle of Democracy, the Harm Principle, and the Offense Principle comprises actions that are harmful to actors themselves—actions that are of concern to those who consider the Paternalism Principle a legitimate basis for criminal legislation. Such actions may cause indirect third-party harm or offense, or they may appear independently immoral, but what distinguishes them is the fact that their wrongfulness resides principally in their self-injuring nature and the principal legislative motivation for their prohibition is paternalistic. Those who consider such actions eligible for criminal punishment add to the menu of reasons that may be independently sufficient to criminalize behavior the fact that such behavior will cause setbacks to the health, wealth, or psychological interests of the actor herself, independently of any harm or offense to others that it may also cause.

Several types of crimes against animals appear to be motivated by a concern for the humans who do the harming as much or more than the animals who are harmed. Animal hoarding, for example—generally defined as keeping a higher-than-usual number of animals as domestic pets without the ability to properly house or care for them, while at the same time denying this inability—is often described as traumatic to hoarders themselves and only incidentally harmful to the animals who are the objects of their obsession (Animal Hoarding, n.d.). "Obsessive hoarding consumes all available resources of time, money, and emotion; squeezing family and friends out of the picture. Social isolation sets in as acquaintances eventually become exasperated and give up their failed attempts to help. People who hoard animals may use them to fulfill emotional needs that had been previously met by human interaction, according to recent studies" (ibid.).[43]

But paternalism appears most apparent in the statutes governing bestiality—generally defined as sex acts with animals—which exist in 45 states (Wisch 2017). In those states whose provisions date back a century or more, bestiality is categorized not with acts of animal cruelty but rather with "crimes against nature" that govern acts described as "unnatural or perverted" (Md. Code Ann., Crim. Law § 3-322 (West 2018)), "abominable and detestable" (11 R.I. Gen. Laws Ann. § 11-10-1 (West 2018)), or simply "buggery" (S.C. Code Ann. § 16-15-120 (2018)). When five states and the District of Colombia recently repealed their bestiality provisions, they did so as a consequence of repealing the crime of sodomy (Wisch 2017). Their equation of these two categories of actions clearly revealed their view that if consensual sodomy is within someone's constitutional rights, so too is bestiality. Such a view presupposes that bestiality has nothing to do with the impact it has on animals, who are obviously dis-analogous to consenting adult partners in their inability to provide morally transformative consent to others' actions. Instead, it reveals that these states take bestiality to be a wrong only if it is a wrong to offenders themselves.

While several states have recently proposed or enacted bestiality provisions and have done so under the auspices of "animal cruelty," it is striking how much more severe their penalties can be than are those that attach to other forms of animal abuse, torture, and neglect. About half of the states that have criminalized bestiality have been willing to categorize it as a felony—a proportion far greater than those that categorize grotesque acts of animal torture and prolonged neglect as felonies (Wisch 2017). In Michigan, for example, offenders can be sentenced to life imprisonment (Mich. Comp. Laws Ann. § 750.158 (West 2018)). In Rhode Island and Massachusetts offenders can receive sentences as long as 20 years (11 R.I. Gen. Laws Ann. § 11-10-1 (West 2018); Mass. Gen. Laws Ann. ch. 272, § 34 (2018)). It is hard to imagine that these penalties are motivated by a concern for animals, since anyone seeking to advance animal welfare would, for example, be more outraged by the commonplace rodeo practice of cinching a bull's genitals to make it buck (which is not a crime) than by someone seeking gratification through a bull's sexual stimulation.

As discussed above, one explanation for these enhanced penalties is that bestiality is being used as a proxy crime—a predictor of further, future criminality against other human beings. This explanation draws strength from the fact that bestiality is a significant predictor of sexual assault on other human beings (particularly children) and thus, in several states, those convicted of bestiality are subject to mandatory sex offender registration (DaSilva 2016). But this explanation, which would squarely locate bestiality provisions under the Harm Principle, appears to under-explain the law's treatment of bestiality, for there are numerous behaviors that are significant predictors of violence toward other humans that do not invite sentences of the sort that some states impose upon those convicted of bestiality. It is thus hard not to conclude that bestiality inspires longer sentences because it signifies to many legislators a violation of a duty that offenders owe to themselves. On this interpretation, states are imposing their judgments of what constitutes healthy sexual practices on citizens who have broader appetites, not because they are concerned for the animals who are the objects of those appetites, and not because they are protecting others from harm or offense, but because they consider incarceration to be a means of rescuing offenders from their own unfortunate choices.

The Legal Moralism Principle

The fifth theory of criminal legislation which lends support to aspects of animal cruelty provisions denies that harm ought to be the touchstone of criminal legislation—whether physical or psychological, whether to other human beings or to oneself. After all, it is easy to find harms that are not morally wrongful—say, the economic injuries that befall competitors when one is successful in attracting away their customers within a free market—and it is easy to find acts that Mill would have declared harmless to others that nevertheless appear eligible for legal regulation—say, the desecration of a corpse. Inasmuch as some harms are not wrongful and some wrongs are not harmful, those who defend the Principle of Legal Moralism argue instead that criminal legislation is justified if but only if it prohibits moral wrongdoing. On this fifth theory of criminal legislation, the legitimate jurisdiction of the criminal law is coextensive with actions that constitute (non-*de minimis*) moral wrongs.[44] While some such actions may be harmful or offensive to oneself or others, other such actions may be wrong even though they neither harm nor offend anyone. The eradication of a plant species or the destruction of privately owned artistic masterpieces, for example, may constitute "free standing wrongs," and when sufficiently serious, such actions may justify criminal prohibition in their own right. While there may be both prudential and moral reasons to stay the hand of the state in response to certain sorts of moral wrongdoing—reasons well explored by "liberal perfectionists," for example[45]—these reasons would need to be weighty enough to overcome the prima facie legitimacy of extending the reach of criminal prohibitions to all forms of behavior that breach moral duties or infringe moral rights.[46]

It is this fifth and final account of the proper purpose of the criminal law that best makes room for the view that animals themselves are the true victims of animal cruelty and thus the appropriate legal beneficiaries of animal cruelty prohibitions. On this view, animals themselves can be morally wronged, and it is with these moral wrongs that animal cruelty laws are, or ought to be, concerned. Perhaps animals can be morally wronged because animals themselves have moral rights, and their wrongs correspond with rights violations. Or perhaps animals can be morally wronged because their sentience generates interests that ground free-standing moral duties to them. Or perhaps animals can be wronged because they are third-party beneficiaries of moral obligations that humans have with regard to them (but not *to* them), which, when violated, represent wrongs *tout court*. Whatever the basis for the moral claims that animals make upon humans, animal cruelty laws are defensible when they enforce those claims, and they demand amendment and revision when they do not.

There are certainly code provisions and case decisions that appear to be best explained by this view of the gravamen of animal cruelty. In the textbook case of *State v. Tweedie* for example, James Tweedie placed a cat in a microwave oven in his workplace cafeteria, turned it on, and left the room. After the cat emerged with agonizing burns covering its entire body and had to be euthanized, Tweedie's only stated concern was that he hoped he had not "jeopardized his job" (ibid., p. 858). He then challenged his conviction claiming both unconstitutional statutory vagueness and legally insufficient evidence of guilt. The Rhode Island Supreme Court felt no need to reach to arguments about how Tweedie's gruesome deed could adversely impact either himself or others. Instead, it rejected the defendant's appeal on the basis that "no idiosyncrasy of a trier of fact is required to conclude that the killing of the cat in this case was cruel," and while "animals are not capable of communicating verbally," "reasonable inferences of severe suffering are easily drawn from the evidence in this record" (ibid., pp. 857–858).

Still, while those who love animals are likely to assume that this account is the most obvious, rather than the least obvious, rationale for criminal protections against animal cruelty, this fifth account is surprisingly dissonant with the patchwork of prohibitions and the broad exemptions that define the category of crimes against animals.[47] After all, if animal cruelty laws *are* fundamentally about protecting animals from suffering, it is surely puzzling that they do not prima facie prohibit the infliction of all suffering on all creatures that can suffer—as laws against mayhem prima facie prohibit all forms of human disfigurement; as laws against battery prima facie prohibit all forms of nonconsensual physical contact; and as laws against theft prima facie prohibit all acts of dispossession. It is puzzling that we do not limit justifications for acts that cause animal suffering to those that ordinarily exonerate defendants who commit prima facie infractions, instead of extending them to those who cause misery in the name of profit, entertainment, fashion, recreation, convenience, or custom.[48]

NOTES

1. These principles include (1) the Principle of Democracy, (2) the Harm Principle, (3) the Offense Principle, (4) the Paternalism Principle, and (5) the Legal Moralism Principle.
2. Federal sources of animal protections also reside within the Fish and Wildlife Act (16 U.S.C. §§ 741-754a (2012)), as well as within numerous conservation statutes. These provisions, however, do not embody protections for individual animals, except only incidentally; they rather seek to regulate the harvesting of, or activities that have an impact on, larger collectivities of animals, whole species, habitats essential to species preservation, and so on.
3. For a non-exhaustive list of very helpful overviews and critical appraisals of the body of crimes against animals, see Chiesa 2008, pp. 1–68; Ibrahim 2006, pp. 175–204; Livingston 2001, pp. 1–74; Madeline 2000, pp. 307–340; and Otto 2005, pp. 131–166.
4. See, for example, Me. Rev. Stat. Ann. tit. 17, § 1034 (2018) (allowing issuance of search warrants to humane agents).
5. See, for example, Me. Rev. Stat. Ann. tit. 7, § 4018 (2018) (granting veterinarians immunity for reporting or testifying about suspected animal cruelty); Mich. Comp. Laws Ann. § 333.18827 (West 2018); Or. Rev. Stat. Ann. § 686.445 (West 2018).
6. See, for example, 510 Ill. Comp. Stat. Ann. 70/3.03(c) (West 2018) (allowing courts to order psychiatric evaluations of persons convicted of depictions of animal cruelty).
7. See, for example, La. Stat. Ann. § 14:102.2(c) (2018) (requiring bonds to cover animal care costs for 30 days).
8. See, for example, Ga. Code Ann. § 4-11-9.3(b) (West 2018) (allowing liens for animal impoundments).
9. See, for example, Cal. Penal Code § 597(f) (West 2018) (requiring forfeiture of animal upon conviction).
10. Rhode Island was the first to introduce legislation containing an offender registration provision (H.B. 7789 at 4-1-46(d), 2004 Gen. Assembly (R.I. 2004);

H.B. 5817 at 4-23-23(d), 2003 Gen. Assembly (R.I. 2003); Otto 2005, 157 n. 70). See also, S.B. 1232, 85th Leg. (Tx. 2017); Tex. Code Crim. Proc. Ann. art. 62.001(5) (West 2017) (categorizing bestiality as a "reportable conviction or adjudication" for a sexual offender registration program).

11. While the term "animal cruelty" is often used within state and federal provisions to refer solely to physical abuse, torture, and neglect (perpetrated intentionally or recklessly), I shall employ the term more generously and shall describe "animal cruelty laws" as all substantive and procedural criminal law enactments that have been devised in answer to forms of animal alteration, injury, neglect, and suffering.

12. Thus, for example, the Animal Welfare Act (7 U.S.C. § 2131(g) (2012)) exempts from the definition of an "animal" birds, rats, and mice that are "bred for use in research."

13. Utah has similarly excluded livestock from the definition of "animals," "if the conduct toward the creature, and the care provided to the creature, is in accordance with accepted animal husbandry practices or customary farming practices" (Utah Code Ann. § 76-9-301 (11)(b)(ii) (West 2018)).

14. For another example of a state that varies the meaning of "animal" between pet rodents and rodents considered pests, see Wisconsin, which prohibits cruelty to rodents except when poison is used on them within one's own premises for purposes of pest control (Wis. Stat. Ann. § 951.06 (West 2018)).

15. Versions of this puzzle reappear in numerous animal cruelty statutes. For example, in Illinois, "aggravated cruelty," a felony, is only possible in cases that involve the abuse of a "companion animal" (defined as an animal "commonly considered to be, or is considered by the owner to be, a pet") (510 Ill. Comp. Stat. Ann. 70/2.01a (West 2018); 510 Ill. Comp. Stat. Ann. 70/3.02 (West 2018)). Thus, one who tortures a pet rabbit in Illinois invites felony liability, while one who tortures an ensnared wild rabbit invites only misdemeanor liability.

16. As several authors have made clear, while at least 13 states do not statutorily exempt either agricultural practices or animal experimentation from their anticruelty provisions, courts in those states have interpreted these statutes not to prohibit the infliction of even extreme suffering so long as it is incidental to accepted practices (Francione 1996, p. 58; Ibrahim 2006, pp. 191–194).

17. "Anti-cruelty statues … are intended to protect animals from the kinds of behavior that no responsible hunter or farmer would defend" (Frasch et al. 1999, pp. 75–76).

18. For example, Illinois' Humane Care for Animal Act (510 Ill. Comp. Stat. Ann. 70/3.03 (West 2018)), which has been celebrated as one of the five toughest animal cruelty prevention measures in the nation by the Animal Legal Defense Fund, explicitly states:

> (b) For the purposes of this Section, 'animal torture' does not include any death, harm, or injury caused to any animal by any of the following activities:
>
> …
>
> (3) any alteration or destruction of any animal by any person for any legitimate purpose, including, but not limited to: castration, culling, declawing, defanging, ear cropping, euthanasia, gelding, grooming, neutering, polling, shearing, shoeing, slaughtering, spaying, tail docking, and vivisection.

19. "28 states have laws that either prohibit leaving an animal in confined vehicle[s] under dangerous conditions or provide civil immunity (protection from being sued) for a person who rescues a distressed animal from a vehicle" (Wisch 2018).

20. In *State v. Cleve*, for example, a defendant was convicted of animal cruelty after snaring two deer in ways that caused one to die of strangulation and the other to die of fatigue, starvation, or dehydration. The New Mexico Supreme Court reversed the defendant's conviction on the basis that the state game and fish laws preempted the state's animal cruelty laws. As the court observed, otherwise "the lawful hunting of deer would appear to subject [all] hunter[s] to potential prosecution for cruelty to animals" (ibid., p. 36).

21. See, for example, Maine's Animal Welfare Act (Me. Rev. Stat. Ann. tit. 7, § 3906-C (2017)), which specifies the membership and role of an Animal Welfare Advisory Committee. See also the Baltimore Animal Services Advisory Commission which "advise[s] the County Council and the County Executive on issues pertaining to animal care and welfare" (Baltimore County Code § 3-3-2401), as well as the Kankakee County Animal Welfare Advisory Committee which consists of nine members who advise the Kankakee County Board (Illinois) (Shapiro 2017).

22. See, for example, Colo. Rev. Stat. Ann. §§ 18-9-201.5, 18-9-202 (2)(a.5)(VII) (West 2018); Mont. Code Ann. § 45-8-211(4)(b) (West 2017); Utah Code Ann. § 76-9-301(1)(b)(ii) (West 2018).

23. See, for example, Neb. Rev. Stat. Ann. § 28-1013(8) (West 2018); Wyo. Stat. Ann. § 6-3-203(f) (West 2018).

24. See, for example, Mich. Comp. Laws Ann. § 750.50 (11)(d) (West 2018); Mont. Code Ann § 45-8-211(4)(c) (West 2017); Or. Rev. Stat. Ann. § 167.335(2) (West 2018).

25. See, for example, Me. Rev. Stat. Ann. tit. 7, § 4011 I-A (2018) (also permitting the shooting of one's own cats and dogs).

26. See, for example, Alaska Stat. Ann. § 11.61.140(c)(3) (West 2018); Conn. Gen. Stat. Ann. § 53-247(b) (West 2018).

27. See, for example, Idaho Code Ann. § 25-3514(3) (West 2018); Tex. Penal Code Ann. § 42.09(e) (West 2017).

28. This taxonomy owes a debt to Luis Chiesa's similar effort to explain animal cruelty offenses in terms of five distinct social interests that are implicated by the injurious treatment of animals (Chiesa 2008, pp. 30–50). Others have similarly recognized some combination of these interests as doing work to explain various kinds of animal protections (Ibrahim 2006; Livingston 2001; Madeline 2000).

29. This is the position that Robert Bork ultimately took in defending majoritarianism as the only principled basis for settling contested questions of law (Bork 1971, pp. 1–35). Similarly, John Ely insisted that "as between courts and legislatures, it is clear that the latter are better situated to reflect consensus," and absent objective moral values that could constrain either individual citizens or legislators, governance by consensus is the best that can be hoped for (Ely 1980, p. 67). On both Bork's and Ely's views, then, if the process by which values compete is kept democratic, then whatever the outcome of that competition, it will be fair and just in the only sense in which those terms make sense. For a critique of the "relativist jurisprudence" inherent in these views, see Hurd (1988, pp. 1417–1510).

30. This vague formulation clearly disguises large issues concerning how to preserve the consent of the people when direct democracy is replaced with representative democracy; when the views and values of representatives often have little or no direct impact on the formulation of legislation upon which those representatives are asked to vote; when legislators often vote for legislation without any real appreciation of its justification or impact; when legislators have conflicting reasons for, and intentions with regard to, legislation for which they vote so as to defeat any notion that there is any shared majority intention with regard to the legislation in question; and when not all legislators vote for all legislation so as to leave at least some constituencies altogether unrepresented in the legislative process.

31. Today, special criminal provisions protect service animals for much the same reason that horses were protected in the nineteenth century, namely, because they are essential to the full participation of their owners in the life of the community. See, for example, Col. Colo. Rev. Stat. Ann. §§ 18-9-202 (2)(b)(III)(d)(I) (West 2018). ("If a person is convicted of cruelty to a service animal … the court shall order him or her to make restitution to the agency or individual owning the service animal for any veterinary bills and replacement costs of the service animal if it is disabled or killed as a result of the cruelty to animals incident.")

32. But see Chiesa (2008, p. 62) (warning against over-stating the degree to which modern animal cruelty statutes perpetuate a property-based conception of animals).

33. "Human interests are protected by rights in general and by the right to own property in particular …. As far as the law is concerned, [a conflict between human and animal interests] is identical to that between a person and her shoe" (Francione 1996, p. 127). It follows that "[b]y viewing animals as mere objects, animal welfare laws, like property laws, allow owners to determine the 'proper uses' of their animal property" (Madeline 2000, p. 329 n. 129).

34. See generally Lockwood and Ascione (1998) (a collection of studies demonstrating the correlation between animal abuse and human-directed violence).

35. See also Chiesa (2008, p. 32).

36. Senator Cohen's statement references studies by The National Research Council and the Federal Bureau of Investigation that demonstrate significant connections between child abuse and childhood cruelty to animals and between childhood cruelty to animals and violence to others during the perpetrator's life (142 Cong. Rec. S4630-05). As William Ritter recounts, 25 percent of male offenders and 36 percent of female offenders incarcerated for violent crimes report prior histories of animal cruelty, and 48 percent of convicted rapists and 30 percent of convicted child molesters admit to childhood animal abuse (Ritter 1996). See also Bershadker and Clark 2015.

37. Recall Joel Feinberg's famous "ride on a bus"—an exercise designed to persuade readers of the legitimacy of employing criminal law to punish and prevent conduct that causes non-*de minimis* affronts to the senses, strong sensations of disgust, shocks to moral sensibilities, inducements of annoyance, and significant anxiety (Feinberg 1985, pp. 10–13).

38. "Thus, many early animal welfare laws were housed in chapters of the criminal code entitled, 'Of Offenses Against Chastity, Decency and Morality.' This was the case in New Hampshire, Minnesota, Michigan, and Pennsylvania among others" (Favre 1993, p. 11).

39. California Senate Bill 313, known as the Circus Cruelty Prevention Act, was recently introduced by Senator Ben Hueso to prohibit the use of wild or exotic animals in traveling acts. Among the rationales for this Act is that those who witness animal abuse become desensitized to cruelty and thus impoverished in their empathetic capacities. Numerous studies of childhood exposure to animal abuse support this claim. For useful summaries of these, see Ascione and Arkow (1999) and Linzey (2009).

40. In *United States v. Stevens*, when "analyzing the constitutionality of a statute regulating videos depicting animal cruelty, [Justice Alito] stated that the most relevant prior decisions of the United States Supreme Court concerned child pornography" (Serafino 2011, p. 1124). Both acts involve "record[ing] the actual commission of a criminal act" that "inflicts severe physical injury" (Stevens, p. 494 (Alito, J., dissenting)).

41. This case inspired Luis Chiesa's insightful examination and critique of anti-cruelty offenses (Chiesa 2008, pp. 1–68).

42. See, for example, New York's "Buster's Law" (N.Y. Agric. & Mkts. Law § 353-a (McKinney 2018)), which reserves the crime of aggravated cruelty, which alone merits felony liability, for injurious act to a companion animal.

43. Additionally, "hoarders fail to acknowledge the ... negative effect of their behavior on their own ... health and wellbeing" (Arluke and Killeen 2009, p. 112).

44. Consider the trilogy of articles by Michael S. Moore defending legal moralism and its relation both to retributivism and liberalism (Moore 1997, pp. 637–795). See also his more recent works (Moore 2014, pp. 182–212, 2017, pp. 441–64).

45. See, for example, Hurd (2002, pp. 385–465, 2004, pp. 37–69), Moore (1997, pp. 739–95), Raz (1986, pp. 369–399, 1989, pp. 761–786), and Wall (1998, pp. 145–161).

46. It is worth recognizing that there is logical space for a second version of this theory that effectively collapses the distinction between paternalism and legal moralism. Were one to believe that criminal legislation is an appropriate means of safeguarding the moral well-being of individuals, rather than their health, welfare, economic well-being, or psychological interests, then the demands placed on the criminal law by paternalism would be co-extensive with those of legal moralism. Gerald Dworkin labels such a theory "moral paternalism" and very capably explores its implications and problems (Dworkin 2005, pp. 305–319).

47. Still, in Chiesa's view:

> [I]t is a strategic blunder to ignore that ... people "virtually universally" accept the proposition that "the primary purpose of [anti-cruelty] laws is to protect animals." Thus, instead of decrying statutes that criminalize animal abuse as another example of how animals are treated as "fungible" and 'disposable' goods, we should argue against the existence of the many exemptions that plague such laws by tapping into the basic sentiment that has led people to call for enactment of anti-cruelty statutes in the first place. (Chiesa 2008, p. 62; quoting Tannenbaum 1995, p. 580; Bryant 2006, p. 76)

48. Special thanks to Heather Simmons, Stephanie Davidson, and the rest of the research team at the University of Illinois College of Law Library for their very helpful and expeditious research assistance. Thanks also to Lauren DeCarlo (Illinois Class of 2020) for her excellent editing and bibliographic assistance. And much appreciation to Adam Kolber for his thoughtful comments on the piece.

REFERENCES

11 R.I. Gen. Laws Ann. § 11-10-1 (West 2018).

18 U.S.C. § 48 (2012).

142 Cong. Rec. S4630-05 (statement of Sen. Cohen).

510 Ill. Comp. Stat. Ann. 70/2.01a (West 2018).

510 Ill. Comp. Stat. Ann. 70/3.02 (West 2018).

510 Ill. Comp. Stat. Ann. 70/3.03 (West 2018).

510 Ill. Comp. Stat. Ann. 70/3.03(c) (West 2018).

1846 Vt. Acts & Resolves 34.

Alaska Stat. Ann. § 11.61.140(c)(3) (West 2018).

Animal Welfare Act, 7 U.S.C. §§ 2131–2159 (2012).

Baltimore County Code § 3-3-2401.

Cal. Penal Code § 597(f) (West 2018).

Cal. Senate Bill 313 (2019-20 Regular Session) (California Legislative Information, http://leginfo.legislature.ca.gov).

Colo. Rev. Stat. Ann. §§ 18-9-201.5, 18-9-202 (2)(a.5)(VII), (2)(b)(III)(d)(I) (West 2018) (West 2018).

Conn. Gen. Stat. Ann. § 53-247(b) (West 2018).

Del. Code Ann. Tit. 11, § 1325 (West 2018).

Fish and Wildlife Act, 16 U.S.C. §§ 741-754a (2012).

Ga. Code Ann. § 4-11-9.3(b) (West 2018).

Ga. Code Ann. § 16-12-4(d) (West 2018).

H.B. 5817 at 4-23-23(d), 2003 Gen. Assembly (R.I. 2003).

H.B. 7789 at 4-1-46(d), 2004 Gen. Assembly (R.I. 2004).

Idaho Code Ann. § 25-3514(3) (West 2018).

Iowa Code Ann. § 717B.1 (West 2018).

Iowa Code Ann. § 717B.2 (West 2018).

La. Stat. Ann. § 14:102.2(c) (2018).

Mass. Gen. Laws Ann. ch. 272, § 34 (2018).

Md. Code Ann., Crim. Law § 3-322 (West 2018).

Me. Rev. Stat. Ann. tit. 17, § 1034 (2018).

Me. Rev. Stat. Ann. tit. 7, § 3906-C (2017).

Me. Rev. Stat. Ann. tit. 7, § 4011 I-A (2018).

Me. Rev. Stat. Ann. tit. 7, § 4018 (2018).

Mich. Comp. Laws Ann. § 333.18827 (West 2018).

Mich. Comp. Laws Ann. § 750.50(11)(d) (West 2018).

Mich. Comp. Laws Ann. § 750.158 (West 2018).

Mont. Code Ann. § 45-8-211(4)(b) (West 2017).

Mont. Code Ann § 45-8-211(4)(c) (West 2017).

Neb. Rev. Stat. Ann. § 28-1013(8) (West 2018).

N.Y. Agric. & Mkts. Law § 353-a (McKinney 2018).

Ohio Rev. Code Ann. § 959.13 (West 2018).

Ohio Rev. Code Ann. § 959.13(A)(2) (West 2018).

Ohio Rev. Code Ann. § 959.13(A)(4) (West 2018).

Or. Rev. Stat. Ann. § 167.335(2) (West 2018).

Or. Rev. Stat. Ann. § 686.445 (West 2018).

S.B. 1232, 85th Leg. (Tx. 2017).

S.C. Code Ann. § 16-15-120 (2018).

S.C. Code Ann. § 47-1-40 (2018).

Tex. Code Crim. Proc. Ann. art. 62.001(5) (West 2017).

Tex. Penal Code Ann. § 42.09(e) (West 2017).

Tex. Penal Code Ann. § 42.092(a)(2) (West 2017).

Utah Code Ann. § 76-9-301(1)(b)(ii) (West 2018).

Utah Code Ann. § 76-9-301(11)(b)(ii) (West 2018).

Wis. Stat. Ann. § 951.06 (West 2018).

Wyo. Stat. Ann. § 6-3-203(f) (West 2018).

State v. Cleve, 980 P.2d 23, 36 (N.M. 1999).

People v. Garcia, 777 N.Y.S.2d 846 (N.Y. Sup. Ct. 2004).

People v. Garcia, 812 N.Y.S.2d 66 (N.Y. App. Div. 2006).

The T.J. Hooper, 60 F.2d 737, 737 (2d Cir. 1932).

State v. Tweedie, 444 A.2d 855 (R.I. 1982).

2018. *Animal hoarding: An in-depth look at the phenomenon.* http://animalhoarding.com/. Accessed 23 Aug 2018.

Arluke, Arnold, and Celeste Killeen. 2009. *Inside animal hoarding: The story of Barbara Erickson and her 522 dogs.* West Lafayette: Purdue University Press.

Ascione, Frank, and Phil Arkow. 1999. *Child abuse, domestic violence, and animal abuse: Linking the circles of compassion for prevention and intervention.* West Lafayette: Purdue University Press.

Bershadker, Matt, and Rep. Katherine Clark. 2015. Protecting all the victims of domestic violence. *ASPCA.* https://www.aspca.org/blog/protecting-all-victims-domestic-violence. Accessed 22 Aug 2018.

Bork, Robert. 1971. Neutral principles and some First Amendment problems. *Indiana Law Journal* 47: 1–35.

Bryant, Tammie L. 2006. Trauma, law and advocacy for animals. *Journal of Animal Law and Ethics* 1: 63–183.

Campbell, Danielle K. 2013. Animal abusers beware: Registry law in the works to curb your abuse. *Valparaiso University Law Review* 48: 271–328.

Chiesa, Luis E. 2008. Why is it a crime to stomp on a goldfish?—Harm, victimhood and the structure of anti-cruelty offenses. *Mississippi Law Journal* 78: 1–68.

Cohn-Sherbok, Dan. 2006. Hope for the animal kingdom: A Jewish vision. In *A communion of subjects: Animals in religion, science, and ethics,* ed. Paul Waldau and Kimberley Patton, 81–90. New York: Columbia University Press.

DaSilva, Jessica. 2016. Bestiality laws matter in preventing, prosecuting sex crimes. Bloomberg Law. https://www.bna.com/bestiality-laws-matter-n57982070635/. Accessed 23 Aug 2018.

Dworkin, Gerald. 2005. Moral paternalism. *Law and Philosophy* 24: 305–319.

Ely, John Hart. 1980. *Democracy and distrust.* Cambridge, MA: Harvard University Press.

Favre, David S. 1993. The development of anti-cruelty laws during the 1800s. *Detroit College of Law Review* 1993: 1–35.

Feinberg, Joel. 1985. Offensive nuisances. In *Offense to others.* New York: Oxford University Press.

Francione, Gary L. 1996. *Rain without thunder: The ideology of the animal rights movement.* Philadelphia: Temple University Press.

Frasch, Pamela D., Stephan K. Otto, Kristen M. Olsen, and Paul A. Ernest. 1999. State animal anti-cruelty statutes: An overview. *Animal Law* 5: 69–80.

Friend, Ted H., and Gisela R. Dellmeier. 1988. Common practices and problems related to artificially rearing calves: An ethological analysis. *Applied Animal Behaviour Science* 20: 47–62.

Gerry, Elbridge T. 1875. Address before the bar of Delaware county. August 16.

Hurd, Heidi M. 1988. Relativistic jurisprudence: Skepticism founded on confusion. *Southern California Law Review* 61: 1417–1510.

———. 2002. Liberty in law. *Law and Philosophy* 21: 385–465.

———. 2004. When can we do what we want? *Australian Journal of Legal Philosophy* 29: 37–69.

Ibrahim, Darian M. 2006. The anticruelty statute: A study in animal welfare. *Journal of Animal Law and Ethics* 1: 175–204.

JAVMA. 2014. South Dakota is last state to make animal cruelty a felony. *JAVMA News.* https://www.avma.org/News/JAVMANews/Pages/140615f.aspx. Accessed 6 Sept 2018.

Kruse, Corwin R. 2002. Baby steps: Minnesota raises certain forms of animal cruelty to felony status. *William Mitchell Law Review* 28: 1649–1680.

Lacroix, Charlotte A. 1998. Another weapon for combating family violence: Prevention of animal abuse. *Animal Law* 4: 1–32.

Linzey, Andrew, ed. 2009. *The link between animal abuse and human violence.* Eastbourne: Sussex Academic Press.

Livingston, Margit. 2001. Desecrating the ark: Animal abuse and the law's role in prevention. *Iowa Law Review* 87: 1–74.

Lockwood, Randall, and Frank R. Ascione, eds. 1998. *Cruelty to animals and interpersonal violence: Readings in research and application.* West Lafayette: Purdue University Press.

Madeline, Beth Ann. 2000. Cruelty to animals: Recognizing violence against nonhuman victims. *University of Hawai'i Law Review* 23: 307–340.

Matheny, Gaverick, and Cheryl Leahy. 2007. Farm-animal welfare, legislation, and trade. *Law and Contemporary Problems* 70: 325–358.

Mill, John Stuart. 1892. Book 5, Chap. 11, § 9. In *Principles of political economy.* London: Longmans, Green, and Co.

———. 1963–91. On liberty. In Vol. 18 of *The collected works of John Stuart Mill*, ed. John M. Robson. Toronto: University of Toronto Press.

Moore, Michael S. 1997. *Placing blame: A general theory of the criminal law.* Oxford: Clarendon Press.

———. 2014. Liberty's constraints on what should be made criminal. In *Criminalization: The political morality of the criminal law*, ed. Antony Duff, Farmer Lindsay, S.E. Marshall, Massimo Renzo, and Victor Tadros, 182–212. Oxford: Oxford University Press.

———. 2017. Legal moralism revisited. *San Diego Law Review* 54: 441–464.

Otto, Stephan K. 2005. State animal protection laws—The next generation. *Animal Law* 11: 131–166.

Raz, Joseph. 1986. *The morality of freedom.* Oxford: Clarendon Press.

———. 1989. Liberalism, skepticism, and democracy. *Iowa Law Review* 74: 761–786.

Ritter, William, Jr. 1996. The cycle of violence often begins with violence toward animals. *Prosecutor* 30: 31–33.

Rowland, Michael Pellman. 2017. State laws are creating anxiety for food producers. *Forbes.* https://www.forbes.com/sites/michaelpellmanrowland/2017/05/19/new-laws-are-creating-anxiety-for-food-producers/#69e3efc3364f. Accessed 6 Sept 2018.

Satz, Ani B. 2009. Animals as vulnerable subjects: Beyond interest-convergence, hierarchy, and property. *Animal Law* 16: 1–50.

Sauder, Joseph G. 2000. Enacting and enforcing felony animal cruelty laws to prevent violence against humans. *Animal Law* 6: 1–22.

Serafino, Laurie. 2011. No walk in the park: Drafting animal cruelty statutes to resolve double jeopardy concerns and eliminate unfettered prosecutorial discretion. *Tennessee Law Review* 78: 1119–1172.

Shapiro, Allison. 2017. County adds animal welfare committee. *Daily Journal.* https://www.daily-journal.com/news/local/county-adds-animal-welfare-committee/article_bb23baa0-ad0b-5142-8553-5c3455ce5378.html. Accessed 6 Sept 2018.

Soehnel, Sonja A. 1992. What constitutes offense of cruelty to animals—Modern cases. *American Law Reports* 6: 733.

Tannenbaum, Jerold. 1995. Animals and the law: Property, cruelty, rights. *Social Research* 62: 539–607.

The Human Society of the United States Special Report 6. 1973. Special report on rodeos. The human society of the United States special report 6. https://animal-studiesrepository.org/sp_reps/6. Accessed 6 Sept 2018.

Wall, Steven. 1998. *Liberalism, perfectionism, and restraint.* Cambridge: Cambridge University Press.

White, Rob. 2013. *Environmental harm: An eco-justice perspective.* Bristol: Policy Press.

Wisch, Rebecca F. 2017. Table of state animal sexual assault laws. Animal Legal & Historical Center. https://www.animallaw.info/topic/table-state-animal-sexual-assault-laws. Accessed 6 Sept 2018.

———. 2018. Table of state laws that protect animals left in parked vehicles. Animal Legal & Historical Center. https://www.animallaw.info/topic/table-state-laws-protect-animals-left-parked-vehicles. Accessed 6 Sept 2018.

Beyond a Reasonable Doubt

CHAPTER 5

When Does Evidence Support Guilt "Beyond a Reasonable Doubt"?

Gideon Yaffe

Consumers of courtroom dramas, not to mention elementary school students, can tell you that in our system, a person can be punished for a crime only if shown "beyond a reasonable doubt" to have committed it. Very few people, however, perhaps no one, can tell you exactly what that means. We know that the standard is supposed to be more demanding than others we find in the law, such as the "by the preponderance of the evidence" standard used in civil trials, which is usually interpreted as "more likely than not," or the "clear and convincing" standard, which serves various purposes. But knowing what the standard is not is different from knowing what it is. Under what conditions has a body of evidence, E, established that defendant D has committed crime C *beyond a reasonable doubt* (BARD)?

The answer is of great importance as a matter of both theory and practice. The practical side is obvious: when we vary the standard of proof we apply in criminal trials, we also vary the distribution of true and false positives and negatives among our convictions and acquittals. The lower the bar, the more convictions, and so the more we have of both convictions of the guilty and convictions of the innocent. Raise the bar and we drive down the conviction rate, letting more guilty people go free and saving more innocent people from unjust conviction. So, while we agree that the standard of proof is BARD, but disagree about what that means and ought to mean, we disagree about what mix of true and false positives and negatives we have and ought to have.

In addition, the question of what, exactly, the BARD standard is implicates the fundamental issue of the conditions under which it is appropriate for the

G. Yaffe (✉)
Yale Law School, New Haven, CT, USA
e-mail: gideon.yaffe@yale.edu

© The Author(s) 2019
L. Alexander, K. K. Ferzan (eds.), *The Palgrave Handbook of Applied Ethics and the Criminal Law*, https://doi.org/10.1007/978-3-030-22811-8_5

state to exercise its power against one of its citizens in the form of criminal punishment. To know the exact conditions under which a person has been shown to be guilty BARD is to know something important about the limits we place on our government's power to decide who is to be free, and who is not, who is to live, and who is to die. The BARD standard, that is, is a bar on state power and so to know what the standard is, is to know something about the very nature of government authority.[1]

Broadly speaking, there are two ways one might answer the question of what, exactly, is necessary and sufficient for a showing BARD. First, there are *probabilistic* answers. One might think that the BARD standard has been met just in case the probability of guilt, in light of the evidence, is above a certain threshold. More carefully, advocates of probabilistic accounts of the BARD standard hold that the standard is met just in case $P(H|E) > t$, where P is the probability function, H is the hypothesis that defendant D committed crime C, E is a body evidence, and t is some threshold number between 0 and 1, such as 0.9 or 0.8. Someone advocating a probabilistic account might offer an actual number for t or might, alternatively, give some other description of a number. One theorist might say that t is 0.75. Another might be more circumspect, saying that t is whatever probabilistic threshold results in the best overall mix of convictions and acquittals. This latter kind of theorist then defers to criminologists, or others involved in empirical study, to determine what number t is and leaves open the possibility that the number will change as conditions change. But in addition to identifying t, directly or indirectly, a probabilistic account of the BARD standard must explain why it is that it is permissible to punish someone for a crime only if $P(H|E) > t$. Probabilistic accounts, that is, must build a normative bridge between a descriptive fact about a conditional probability and a normative fact, a fact about how we, and our government, ought to behave in light of that conditional probability.

Second, there are *psychological* answers. One might think that the BARD has been met just in case actual or hypothetical jurors are in a certain psychological state. Maybe the actual jurors in the case need to *feel certain* the defendant did it, or something like that. Or maybe *an ideal, unbiased* juror would *believe* the defendant guilty in light of the evidence. Or perhaps an actual or bias-free juror must be in a mental state that *constitutes knowledge of guilt if the defendant is in fact guilty*. Taking this kind of approach requires describing (a) the psychological state of relevance (e.g. belief, knowledge, subjective certainty, etc.) and (b) the people who must be in such a state (e.g. the actual jurors in a trial, a hypothetical bias-free person, someone biased in the defendant's favor, etc.). But it also requires, most importantly and elusively, an answer to the following question: why is it appropriate to subject a person to criminal punishment only if the people described in (b) are in the psychological state described in (a)? That is, those offering psychological accounts of the BARD standard, like the advocates of probabilistic accounts, must build a bridge linking the psychological and the normative. The heart of any psychological account of the BARD standard will be that bridge.

This chapter canvasses a variety of possible probabilistic and psychological accounts of the BARD standard. Section "Probabilistic Accounts" examines the pros and cons of probabilistic accounts. Section "Psychological Accounts" turns to the psychological. Unfortunately, no definitive conclusions are reached. No particular account is defended. However, some small progress is made: it is argued here that psychological accounts are more likely to be able to adequately build a normative bridge than are probabilistic accounts. So the ambitious theoretician, aiming to specify what the BARD standard is with precision, should expend her efforts in trying to develop a psychological account.

Probabilistic Accounts

Imagine that I hand you a card with a picture of a man's face on it. I explain that this is the face of an innocent man. Would you be willing to convict this man of murder and send him to prison for life? "Of course not!" you say, "You just told me he was innocent of that crime!" Fair enough. Now I hand you two cards, with two new faces. One of the two is a murderer, the other is innocent, but I don't tell you which is which. Your choice is all or nothing: either both go to prison for murder or neither do. Are you willing, now, to send both to prison for life? No? What if there are three cards in the stack, only one of whom is innocent? Or 9? Or 1000? At what point are you willing to send all of them to prison, including the one innocent person? How many guilty murderers are you willing to release in order to avoid condemning an innocent to life in prison? The famous judge and scholar William Blackstone seemed to think that 12 was the magic number of cards. Or, rather, that is one natural interpretation of this famous remark: "[I]t is better that ten guilty persons escape, than that one innocent suffer" (Blackstone 1915, Book 4, ch. 27, p. 523). Naturally interpreted, this implies that it was *not* better that 11 guilty persons escape than that one suffer; the suffering of the one is worth 11 true convictions, although not 10. So, if Blackstone were handed 12 cards—11 guilty and 1 innocent—he would send the lot of them to prison. Putting Blackstone's ratio this way can make you shudder. But it's not because 12 is too few. There's deep discomfort attached to any answer one might give. How could anyone choose a stack, of any size, and thereby knowingly destroy a life, sending an innocent person away forever?

One might try to diagnose the discomfort here like so: let's vary the hypothetical slightly. You are handed the stack of cards and know that exactly one person in the stack is innocent. But instead of having to convict or acquit the lot of them, you need to decide only about one person, chosen randomly from the stack. So, if there are X cards in the stack, the probability that this randomly chosen person is innocent is $1/X$. Is there any value of X such that it would be unreasonable for you to doubt the guilt of the person chosen? One might think not. To doubt that the person is guilty is to believe the following: *he might be innocent*. This is a belief in a modal proposition; it is not the belief that the person *is* innocent, only that he *might* be. That doubt is reasonable if there is a good reason for it. But there is a good reason for the belief that the randomly chosen face *might* be the face of an innocent person: there is one innocent person's face in the stack, and the card was chosen from the stack. That's a good reason for that belief. So the doubt—the belief that the person *might* be innocent—is supported by a good reason. And that in turn implies that it is reasonable to doubt that the person is guilty. If this is right, then any probabilistic account of BARD must necessarily fail for conceptual reasons: if there's a chance that the defendant is innocent, then there's ipso facto a reasonable doubt about his or her guilt.

The argument just stated might be thought to work, if it works at all, *for any value of X*. But someone pressing the argument need not go that far in order to object to probabilistic accounts of the BARD standard. At least as an intuitive matter, there are enormous values of X such that it is unreasonable to believe that the chosen card *might* show the face of an innocent. Perhaps if there are a billion cards in the stack, it is unreasonable to believe even that the card *might* be the one innocent. (Although try telling that to players of the lottery; of course, they think they *might* win, or else they wouldn't play.) However, even if we grant this point, it would be remarkable if the BARD standard required such high probabilities. Surely, if there are 100 cards in the stack, the chosen one *might* be the one innocent person in the stack; it would not be unreasonable to believe that. And the same is true if X is 500, or maybe even 10,000. But if a jury should convict only if $P(H|E) \geq 0.9999$, there should be next to no convictions at all and far fewer than we actually find. We frequently convict, and justifiably, on the evidence of two witnesses, for instance, both of whom independently pick out the defendant in a five-person lineup as the one who threw the punch. Setting aside complicating factors, the probability is $24/25$, or 0.96, that this testimony was not due to chance.[2] And there may be other factors, thanks to which $P(H|$this witness testimony$)$ is higher than that; hopefully, the witnesses are credible enough that the probability that each picked out the perpetrator is higher than $1/5$. But, still, such testimony is very unlikely to support the hypothesis of guilt above such very high probabilities as 0.9999. What this shows is that we cannot exclude the belief that the defendant might be innocent from the category of the reasonable doubts solely on the grounds of probability.

But the defender of a probabilistic account of BARD should not fold in the face of these reflections. What they show is that we set our standards too high if we suggest that a reasonable belief that the defendant might be innocent suffices for a reasonable doubt about her guilt. The sun *might* not rise tomorrow. Belief in this proposition is not just reasonable, it can amount to knowledge; we know the sun might not rise. But the proposition that the sun *will* rise tomorrow is proven BARD, despite this; proof BARD is not defeated by the belief that the sun might not rise tomorrow. By contrast, the coin might not come up heads; it would be reasonable to doubt that the coin will come up heads, given this belief. What we need to know is this: when does the reasonable belief that the defendant might be innocent amount to a reasonable doubt about guilt, a doubt sufficiently strong to warrant withholding a guilty verdict? This is just another way of asking exactly what the BARD standard is. That is, what the worry so far raised does is point us squarely at what we are seeking: an account of the BARD standard.

But we should not reach the conclusion from these reflections that it is a mistake to recoil from the prospect of sending away all X people in the stack of faces when we know for sure that one of them is innocent. Instead, we should seek an alternative account of the source of our uneasiness. The important scholar of Constitutional law, Laurence Tribe, gives voice to a different kind of concern that might be animating the discomfort that many feel at the idea of condemning all those people in the stack of cards when we know that exactly one of them is innocent. More than 40 years ago, he argued that it is normatively unacceptable to equate the BARD standard with any particular probability of guilt. Tribe's central concern is that a juror who convicts while recognizing a possibility that the offender is innocent must think conviction of an innocent worth risking in order to achieve something—security, vindication of the victim's rights, or crime reduction, for instance. But then, thinks Tribe, that juror uses the innocent person as a means to the attainment of that further end. This is morally objectionable. And yet it is not morally objectionable to convict those proven to be guilty BARD. The result: proof BARD cannot be modeled probabilistically, as a conditional probability above a certain numerical threshold. If it could, then it would be acceptable for a juror to convict in moral consistency with the belief that there is a probability of $(1-t)$ that the defendant is innocent. Equivalently, one would be on firm ground in convicting in the face of evidence that supported the hypothesis of innocence some small amount. In a representative passage, Tribe writes:

> [I]n precisely what sense does our society willingly tolerate the conviction of innocent individuals in order to confine the guilty? When we say "better that ten (or a hundred) guilty men go free than that one innocent man be condemned," do we thereby suggest that we would countenance the deliberate conviction of one innocent man to prevent the erroneous acquittal of twenty (or two hundred) guilty ones? Surely these celebrated formulas do not mean that society may knowingly sacrifice innocent men so long as the terms of the trade are sufficiently favorable to the community as a whole…[Such a decision] cannot be made without greatly undermining society's commitment to the dignity of the individual as an end in himself. (Tribe 1970, pp. 385–386)

Here Tribe makes his point through appeal to the Kantian maxim that one should treat others always as ends in themselves and never as means. His claim is that if the BARD standard is modeled probabilistically, then a juror who convicts uses at least innocent defendants, and perhaps guilty ones too, as a means to whatever goods are achieved through the punishment of the guilty.[3]

In an important recent paper, Alec Walen identifies a few problems with Tribe's argument and goes on to defend a probabilistic account of BARD

(Walen 2015, pp. 380–381). The main point animating Walen's criticisms is that Tribe is trading on ambiguity in the notion of "using someone as a means." In some ways of understanding that phrase, it describes necessarily impermissible behavior, and in others it does not. Walen notes that it cannot be that to knowingly adopt an imperfect social policy—one that helps a lot of people at the expense of harm to some—is to impermissibly use people as a means. Say that BARD is not to be interpreted probabilistically. Still, we know that there are innocent people whose guilt it would be unreasonable to doubt, whatever exactly that means. What's the percentage? Is it one in a hundred who cannot be reasonably thought innocent who are so in fact? Or is it one in ten? There must be some answer to this question. Let's say it is 1 in X. In adopting the BARD standard, we are accepting that when you are handed X cards and exactly one person in the stack is innocent, the thing to do is to send them all to prison. But that implies that *whatever* account of BARD we adopt—whether probabilistic or what have you—the legislature is accepting a policy that condemns some innocent people. And they do that because the legislature believes that the evils realized in the punishment of the innocent are outweighed by the goods achieved through the punishment of the guilty. That cannot, all by itself, imply that the legislature is thereby acting impermissibly. If the legislature is "using some people as a means" in adopting such a policy, then there are some forms of use of others that are not impermissible.

One could try to respond to this point by distinguishing between the perspective of the juror and the perspective of the legislator. In fact, sometimes Tribe seems to make such a move (Tribe 1971, p. 1375). Perhaps it is acceptable to *legislate* the use of the BARD standard, while recognizing that there is a percentage of innocent people who meet that standard for guilt, *so long as jurors never adopt the legislator's perspective.* Say that the legislature decides that we get the best mix we can hope for of false and true convictions when we convict only if $P(H|E) \geq 0.99$. Say that if we convict in all and only those cases, we get a 1% false conviction rate and an acceptably low false acquittal rate.[4] And imagine, for instance, that after exhaustive empirical study, we find that when jurors are told that they should not convict unless "they know for sure" that the defendant is guilty, this is exactly what we get: jurors instructed that way convict only when $P(H|E) \geq 0.99$, and only 1% of the resulting convictions are of innocents. So a way for a legislator to engineer things so that what she judges to be the best results are achieved is to pass a law requiring that this is how juries are to be instructed. We now have two different standards of proof: the legislator's probabilistic above −0.99 standard and the jurors' know-for-sure standard. The empirical facts stipulated in the hypothetical are such that when jurors apply their standard, the legislature's standard is met.

Notice that the jurors in this example are not in the mental state of believing that there's a 1% chance of guilt when they convict. They are, instead, if they follow the instruction to convict only if they "know for sure," in a mental state of *certainty* of guilt; they think the chances of guilt are zero and the legislature knows that they are wrong 1% of the time. The jurors, therefore, do not even knowingly impose *a risk* of unjust conviction on anyone, for they believe them-selves to be imposing no risk at all on the defendants they convict. Everybody wins: we all reap the benefits of a system of punishment with a low-enough non-zero false conviction rate that its evils are outweighed by the goods achieved through it, and jurors never objectionably use the defendants they convict as a means since they never convict without belief to a certainty in guilt. We might say that legislators are justified in handing the stack of cards to the juror, knowing that one in the stack is innocent, and jurors are justified in con-victing the lot provided that they are in the dark about the fact that there's an innocent in the stack and take themselves, instead, to be certain that all in the stack are guilty.

In this hypothetical, jurors employ a non-probabilistic standard of proof, the know-for-sure standard. In the example, this standard, when employed by jurors, sorts cases in accordance with the legislature's goal of convicting only if $P(H|E) \geq 0.99$ and of having a false conviction rate no higher than 1%. But it is an empirical question about juror psychology whether the standard they are to employ in order to reach this goal could be, or need be, probabilistic. Perhaps the best way for the legislature to reach its goal is for jurors to convict only if they themselves judge $P(H|E) \geq 0.99$. Maybe they should be asked to make this probabilistic calculation. Or perhaps jurors tend to underestimate probabilities, and so they should instead be told to convict only if they think $P(H|E) \geq 0.95$. Thanks to their tendency to underestimate, perhaps by follow-ing this instruction, they would end up convicting when, in fact, $P(H|E) \geq 0.99$. However, given what we know about ordinary people's capacities to make probability judgments, chances are it will be a bad idea to ask jurors to employ a probabilistic standard. (The well-spring of such work is Tversky and Kahneman (1954).) People make a lot of errors in their probability calculations. They might get closer to the 99% threshold by convicting when "certain of guilt," or when "their gut tells them the defendant's guilty," or even when instructed to convict when convinced "beyond a reasonable doubt," no matter how they interpret that phrase. It is an empirical question, that is, what standard to be applied by jurors will result in what is optimal from the legislator's point of view (DeKay 1996, pp. 95–132). Further, and importantly, there might be additional constraints that we have reason to impose on the standard to be adopted by jurors. Perhaps, for instance, they cannot be asked to employ a standard that would result in their using defendants as a means to securing crime reduction; perhaps they cannot be themselves motivated by the goal of general deterrence. Such a constraint might, for the kinds of reasons Tribe identifies, rule out a probabilistic standard to be employed by jurors, even if employing it would result in the right mix, from the legislature's point of view, of false and true convictions and acquittals.

When we understand things in this way, the term "the beyond the reason-able doubt standard" is ambiguous. It could be referring either to the standard the legislature does or ought to set or to the standard jurors do or ought to use. We make room, then, for the possibility that the *legislative* BARD standard is probabilistic, while the *factfinder* BARD standard is not. The advocate of such a view needs to explain why it is that behavior that is permissible for the government would be impermissible for jurors. Why is it that it is permissible for the government to use convictions of the innocent in order to achieve crime reduction, while it is not permissible for jurors to do exactly the same thing? If the two parties are to be held to the same moral standards, then either they both act wrongly in employing a probabilistic standard, or neither does, in which case the two-level approach is neither better nor worse than one in which jurors are to employ a probabilistic standard.

But it's likely that this burden can be discharged. There are good reasons to think that the government is permitted to use people in ways that ordinary folk are not. If a consent-based theory of political authority is correct, for instance, then the government is permitted to act against a citizen precisely because the citizen consented, directly or more likely tacitly, to such treatment by consenting to be governed. But citizens have given no such blanket consent to each other, and so it is no surprise that the government is permitted to use people in ways that ordinary citizens are not. (The same point follows even if we refuse to give the label "use" to a form of treatment to which someone consented.) The point here is not special to the case of a consent-based theory of political authority. Any adequate political philosophy must explain why it is permissible for the state to manipulate, cajole, and coerce, for valuable ends, in a wide variety of ways impermissible for ordinary people, acting in their private capacities.

Even taking this point on board, however, there is a concern about the two-level approach which one might take to speak decisively against it: it lacks transparency in ways that appear to undermine the possibility of a democratic rationale for criminal punishment. It's plausible, that is, to think that the legislature is permitted to enshrine a particular standard of proof in criminal trials only if jurors are permitted to *knowingly* apply it. To see this, step back and ask why we think it important that a criminal defendant has the opportunity to be judged by "a jury of his peers?" The answer has something to do with joint ownership by The People of the guilty verdict, and subsequent punishment. The attraction of such an approach derives from the thought that the government is authorized to punish only because The People support punishment; the government is authorized to act only as The People's proxy. Under the two-level approach proposed, however, jurors are being conscripted into doing something for the government while kept in the dark about what they are doing. The government is using the innocent, and using jurors to do that on its behalf, while leading jurors to believe it is doing no such thing. The government is trying to cleanse from moral taint its use of the innocent by manipulating jurors into blamelessly convicting. But in so doing, it alienates its conduct from the conduct of jurors, the representatives of The People. Rather than government acting as The People's proxy, in the two-level approach proposed, The People are serving unwittingly as the government's proxy. They are doing the government's dirty work of convicting some innocents for the sake of lots of convictions of the guilty.

The advocate of a probabilistic account of BARD might agree that something has gone wrong if government demands that jurors employ a different standard of proof from the one that the government takes to be optimal, and yet, at the same time, respond to Tribe's using-as-a-means objection. The point has already been made that any adequate account of government authority must explain why it is permissible for the government to do things to people that would constitute impermissible use of others, if done by ordinary citizens. But this point can help us to see that there need be no particular moral problem with jurors using a probabilistic standard. A juror, after all, is not an ordinary citizen. She is a temporary government worker, sworn into service for the length of a trial. If it is permissible for the government to use some innocent people by sending them to prison for the sake of the goods that come from the punishment of the guilty, then it is permissible for a *juror* to do that while doing his duty as a temporary government official.

However, the advocate of a probabilistic account must do more than show that there is no principled objection to a probabilistic account; she must also show that there is some way to normatively ground a choice of probabilistic threshold. She must build a bridge between the descriptive and the normative. How are we to decide whether a threshold of, say, 0.9 is better or worse than a threshold of 0.75? What values or principles are to guide such determinations and why? A probabilistic account of BARD has to have an answer to this question and an argument for the answer, an argument grounded in the point or purpose of criminal punishment. We need to know why a 0.9 threshold gets us closer to serving the purpose of criminal punishment than a 0.75 threshold does (if it does).

If one holds, with deterrence theorists, that systems of criminal punishment are worth having just in case they reduce crime sufficiently to outweigh the system's costs, then the right choice of probabilistic threshold becomes a problem to solve with the help of empirical work in criminology. How many incidents of crime, and of what magnitudes, are prevented by a conviction rate of 99 out of 100? 50 out of 100? How does the choice of standard of proof affect the conviction rate? What is the false conviction rate when the overall conviction rate is 99 out of 100? 50 out of 100? Are the magnitudes of punishment the same for the falsely convicted as for those who are actually guilty? Do we have variations in conviction rate or deterrent value of convictions, across different types of crime? What are the collateral effects of punishment on the families of offenders? Are the collateral effects greater or less when the offender was guilty than when he was innocent? What is the effect on jurors of convicting? Of acquitting? Do those effects vary between false and true convictions? And so on. None of the answers to these questions mean much unless they are coupled with a metric of value—how bad is false imprisonment? How much of a benefit is it to prevent a murder? a theft? and so on—but there is no way to calculate a probabilistic threshold, with which a deterrence theorist will be happy, without answers to at least some of them. The choice of probabilistic threshold has potential effects on all those intertwined with the criminal justice system. If the point of having such a system is to add overall value to the world, then there is no principled way to guide that choice that avoids reliance on empirical studies of the effects of the choice.

Larry Laudan has argued, quite persuasively, that if we take seriously this broadly consequentialist perspective of the point of criminal punishment, and incorporate what is known about the myriad effects of conviction rates, we will find that the right threshold for the BARD standard is surprisingly low (Laudan 2011, pp. 198–226). Among other things, Laudan thinks that there is strong evidence that the rates of guilt among those charged are very high and so the total number of false convictions would be very low, even if the threshold were set as low as 0.5, requiring conviction if guilt is more likely than not, given the evidence. True, in that case, given some assumptions (e.g. that the quality of evidence does not vary with the guilt of charged defendants), we can expect as many as half the innocents who are charged with crimes to be found guilty. But if there are very few innocents who are charged, there would still be very few false convictions. Further, these false convictions would be offset by true convictions, and subsequent crime prevention, of those guilty people of whose guilt we have only relatively weak evidence, too weak to meet higher thresholds. It might allow conviction, for instance, in cases in which the evidence consists of only one eye witness who testifies to the defendant's guilt and another who offers an alibi. A jury who found the former witness slightly more credible than the latter might convict, if they were to do as instructed. If it is true that the vast majority of those charged are guilty, and if that percentage does not alter with the probabilistic threshold, then the 0.5 threshold would secure conviction of many guilty people who are currently acquitted since the evidence falls far short of meeting a threshold of 0.7, much less 0.9 or 0.95.

Walen, engaging with Laudan, has noted a variety of factors that any unflinching consequentialist would also need to weigh in determining the appropriate probabilistic interpretation of BARD (Walen 2015). For instance, he notes that it is natural to hold that one of the costs of false conviction is that the actual perpetrator remains free and potentially commits more, similar, crimes. But, notes Walen, this oversimplifies, for in many criminal trials (although it is an empirical question how many), the defendant makes no claim of mistaken identity. In a well-known recent Supreme Court case, for instance, defendant Elonis admitted that he had posted remarks on Facebook that his ex-wife interpreted as threats to her and their child's safety. He claimed that he was just joking and was unaware that his posts would be interpreted as being in earnest. If his contention was true, the court ruled, then he was to be acquitted (Elonis v. United States, 575 U.S. ____ (2015)). But had it been true, and had he been falsely convicted, there would not have been any Facebook-posting threatener at large, ready to terrorize the community. The question was not whodunit, but whether in doing it Elonis committed the crime charged. So, there is at least one downside of false conviction—namely future crime by the real perpetrator—that would not attend Elonis's false conviction. And Elonis's case is far from unique. All cases that turn on mens rea, like Elonis's, are of this form. But also cases in which self-defense is claimed, for instance, fall into this category, as do all cases in which the defendant attempts to raise doubt about elements of the crime's actus reus that do not involve denying that he himself was the performer of the act. If we take such factors into account, and couple them with the consequentialist position under consideration, we find that the BARD should be even lower than suggested by Laudan.

Combining a variety of points of this sort, and coupling them with empirical evidence, Walen has shown that a threshold of *well below* 0.5 could be on balance beneficial *when the death penalty would be imposed.* This would have the perverse implication that we should have a *lower* standard of proof in a criminal proceeding where the ultimate penalty is at stake than we have in comparatively trivial civil trials where the standard of proof is more likely than not. Walen sees this argument, and with good reason, as providing a *reductio ad absurdum* of the unflinching consequentialist's efforts to explain the normative significance of a probabilistic standard of proof. If the only point of the BARD standard for the system of punishment is to generate more good, primarily in the form of crime prevention, than it generates harm, then a very low probability threshold is appropriate. The right response is to reject the premise: we need a new normative bridge from the probabilistic facts to our practices of punishing; a consequentialist theory will not do.

Most who have followed this kind of train of thought have given up on probabilistic accounts of BARD. But Walen is different from most in this regard. He argues, instead, that an adherent of a retributivist theory of punishment—a theory according to which the point of a system of punishment is to give offenders what they deserve—ought to accept a probabilistic account of BARD involving a high threshold. His idea is that a retributivist ought to hold that some consequences of punishing, no matter how good they are, cannot be taken into account in our calculation of the benefits associated with adoption of a particular standard of proof. They are, as it were, "screened off" from deliberative consideration. In particular, a retributivist is barred from choosing a standard of proof thanks in part to the good consequences of punishing the innocent. To place this value on the scale in the calculation of the ideal probabilistic threshold is to violate the retributivist's belief that the value of punishment is not to be measured by the value of its consequences but, instead, by its conformity or disconformity to the principle that the deserving should be punished. The primary thing that a retributivist can take into account in choosing a probabilistic threshold is the resulting mix of true and false convictions and acquittals, considered independently of the downstream positive consequences of such a mix. The result, when coupled with something like Blackstone's ratio, is a very high probabilistic threshold, probably above 0.9 at least.

One almost irresistible way to defend this position involves endorsing what Robert Nozick once called "a utilitarianism of rights" (Nozick 1974, p. 28). Walen himself eschews such a view, defending an alternative picture of rights from that assumed by the utilitarian of rights; the details, however, are beyond the scope here (Walen 2019). Jeffrey Reiman, however, gets close to endorsing an account of BARD deriving from a utilitarianism of rights (Reiman and van den Haag 1990, pp. 230–234). The utilitarian of rights holds with other consequentialists that an act's permissibility is a function of the value of its consequences. But unlike other consequentialists, the utilitarian of rights thinks that the value of those consequences must be measured in part by examination of the magnitude of the rights vindications and violations they involve, if any. The innocent have the right not to be punished, so if an act has the result of causing an innocent to be punished, then the act's consequences are substantially worse than they would be if they involved, for instance, exactly the same amount of pain, but no violations of right, as in the punishment of the guilty. A utilitarian of rights who is also a retributivist about punishment might adopt from Walen the idea that one is not permitted to consider the positive consequences of punishment, such as the reduction of crime, when choosing a probabilistic threshold for a standard of proof. Instead, the *only* positive value of moral relevance, when it comes to punishment decisions, is found in the vindication of right found in punishing the deserving. On such a view, there is some equivalency of value—one difficult to articulate—between the rights vindications involved in the punishment of some large number of guilty people, on the one hand, and the harms that attend any system of punishment including the disvalue involved in the violation of right resulting from the punishment of the innocent. Such a utilitarian of rights holds that the BARD standard is whatever probabilistic threshold is such as to tip the balance into the black.

The basic logic of such a defense of a probabilistic account of BARD is no different from that which guides a thinker like Laudan. And so it is perhaps no surprise that such a position is subject to the same kinds of criticism that have been levied against Laudan. Consider Walen's point, rehearsed above, that in many actual cases the punishment of the innocent will not also involve the failure to punish someone guilty, for there is sometimes no guilty party at all. The point is that if you embrace the idea that the appropriate standard of proof is sensitive to the consequences of true and false convictions and acquittals, then you have to go where the facts about the consequences lead. That can mean accepting a standard so low as to be morally intolerable. But the utilitarian of rights imagined here, too, cares about consequences, just not all of them; such a theorist excludes consideration of crime reduction, for instance, as good as it is; the achievement of true convictions is the only positive reason to punish. But the limitation does not help. For instance, there will be cases in which thanks to the conviction of someone on very weak evidence we are able to convict many guilty people. For instance, say that the conditional probability that D is guilty, given the evidence is only 0.1, but if he is convicted and sent to prison he will become an informant and aid in the prosecution and conviction of 11 guilty gang members who would have evaded justice but for his presence in prison. By the metric of value proposed, coupled with Blackstone's ratio, this conviction is worth imposing. How common are such cases? It's an empirical question. But if they are sufficiently common, then this will provide a reason, under the proposed schema, to lower the probabilistic threshold.

If every person convicted could be conscripted into service as an informant of this kind, for instance, then we would be wise to convict all defendants, no matter how little evidential support there is for guilt. But that can't be right. We are led to the same kinds of absurdities that attend Laudan's view. It cannot be that we could buy our way into a very low probabilistic threshold for proof of guilt thanks to more and more effectively using the innocent as jailhouse snitches.

The problem here is deep. It is not possible to construct a consequentialism that accords with the full set of moral intuitions about permissibility. It is always possible to construct cases in which very good consequences follow on intuitively impermissible conduct or very bad ones follow on intuitively permissible conduct. The utilitarian of rights has no immunity against this kind of concern. Here, the act in question is the act of convicting when $P(H|E) > t$ and t is quite low. To say that such acts are intuitively impermissible is to report a fact about what we think we're achieving in employing the BARD standard: we think we are thereby convicting *permissibly*, even if we are, in the end, mistaken. But then if the intuitions are to be taken seriously, we must reject any probabilistic account of BARD built on a utilitarianism of rights. Or to put the point in a less conclusory way, a probabilistic account grounded in a utilitarianism of rights is only as defensible as that form of consequentialism, and so it must overcome the same kind of worries that generally plague consequentialist theories, worries of a sort that Walen has raised with respect to consequentialist views like Laudan's.

Psychological Accounts

Broadly speaking, the probabilistic accounts under discussion in the previous section were guided by the idea that the purpose of the BARD standard is to strike the right balance between protecting the innocent from conviction, on the one hand, and enjoying the benefits of an inevitably imperfect system of punishment, on the other. However, there is little reason to think, at least as a matter of historical fact, that the BARD standard was created to serve this purpose. James Whitman, in the most thorough and rigorous study of the history of the BARD standard, shows that it has Christian roots, and surprising ones. Whitman demonstrates that the BARD standard was introduced not to protect the accused from unjust conviction, but, instead, to protect jurors who feared that they would be condemned to hell for condemning the undeserving. Punishing the deserving was, it was assumed, to do God's will, a thought strengthened by the Divine Right of Kings. But since human beings, endowed with original sin, are innately fallible, no matter how sure of guilt they are, they, unlike God, might be mistaken. And when they punish the undeserving, they thereby act contrary to God's will and so face the possibility of condemnation themselves. This could be avoided, the thought went, provided that the juror had no reasonable doubts; perfect certainty was not required for the juror to avoid condemnation for acting contrary to the will of the creator. The BARD standard, then, functioned to encourage convictions, convictions that jurors might have been too frightened to issue without assurance that they could avoid condemnation (Whitman 2008).

So understood, the BARD standard is directly linked to the medieval and early modern notion of "moral certainty": the epistemic state with respect to p that one needs to be in to be blameless for wrongful action that would not have been wrongful were p true. If you are morally certain that the cup contains sugar, when it really contains arsenic, you are blameless for poisoning another. Not so if you fall short of moral certainty. Similarly, if you are morally certain that the offender is guilty, when he is actually innocent, you are blameless for the punishment. To be convinced BARD, on this view, is to be morally certain.

What the history offers is a functional characterization of the BARD standard, not an intrinsic characterization. To say that the psychological state of being convinced BARD serves to shield a mistaken juror from blame is not to say which doubts are reasonable and which are not. "Convinced BARD" and "morally certain" are just names for whatever cognitive state of mind serves to shield from blame and involve no characterization of that mental state's intrinsic qualities. Still, functional characterizations can be useful; they provide us with a description of a defining criterion for the success of a philosophical account. If the account of the BARD standard is not such as to absolve mistaken jurors from blame, then it does not do the work that, historically, was hoped for from the BARD standard. Of course, a philosophical account of the BARD standard need not be constrained in any way by its traditional, historical rationale, or purpose. Practices and doctrines admitting of a certain normative rationale are often developed for entirely different reasons. Still the historical motivation for the BARD standard, assuming Whitman is right, points the way toward a psychological account of the standard, rather than a probabilistic one. One might think that the BARD standard is met just in case a rational person who considered the evidence would come to believe the accused is guilty and, at the same time, be shielded from blame for the resulting punishment and condemnation of the accused, if mistaken. Guided by this idea, we can ask what psychological state one must be in to be shielded from blame for a false conviction. The answer to this question will be a psychological account of the BARD standard.

In approaching this question, start by considering a norm of the form "Don't C unless X!" Norms of this form prohibit a type of conduct—type C—and specify conditions under which tokening that type is not a violation of the norm—conditions X. A consideration that a person offers to shield herself from blame for the violation of a norm with this form can be of one of three well-known sorts: excuse, justification, and what I will call "denial." As often understood, excuses demonstrate diminished responsibility for a norm-violating, wrongful act, while justifications demonstrate that the act in question was not, despite initial appearances, norm-violating. Denials involve asserting that the act was not, despite appearances, of the prohibited type. Excuses involve asserting that one was not responsible for C-ing in the absence of X; justifications involve asserting that although one C'd, X obtained; denials involve asserting that one did not C. Denials are akin to justifications since both demonstrate that the relevant norm was not violated.[5]

It is controversial whether an agent's epistemic state can justify his conduct. The question turns on the defensibility of what is sometimes called "the objective theory of wrongdoing" under which what is permissible or impermissible does not depend on an agent's mental states. But it is uncontroversial that an agent's epistemic state can sometimes supply an excuse, and sometimes a denial. For instance, there's a moral norm, admitting of exceptions, that says, "Don't lie!" However, a person lies only if she believes that what she says is false. So, someone who speaks falsely and says in her defense, "But I thought it was true!" offers a denial. She claims that she did not lie, and so did not engage in the wrongful act of which she was accused but only the potentially permissible act of speaking a falsehood. If her speaking a falsehood is shown to be, itself, wrongful, despite not being a lie, because, for instance, it is very harmful, then the agent's belief that she was telling the truth might not serve as an excuse from blame for that distinct form of wrongdoing.

The norm that every well-meaning juror hopes not to violate is this one: "Don't condemn the innocent!" We are seeking a description of the mental state of the juror who falsely convicts, and so tokens the type of act prohibited by this norm, and yet is absolved from blame. Belief in guilt is necessary for absolution of this kind but it does not suffice; when such a belief is formed capriciously or from prejudice, for instance, the juror is blameworthy for the false conviction. So we are looking for some additional features of a false belief in guilt such that when they are present the juror has either an excuse, a justification, or a denial.

There is some reason to think a juror's belief BARD in an innocent defendant's guilt does not shield the juror from blame by providing either an excuse or a justification. To see why it's not likely to provide an excuse note that excused agents are in an asymmetrical position with respect to those they harm: they are not both victims of circumstance; rather, the injured party is a victim of circumstance and the excused party has engaged in wrongful conduct. This asymmetry makes it appropriate for the excused at least to apologize to the injured party. They do not commiserate together as equal victims of fate. By contrast, when a juror believes BARD that an innocent is guilty and convicts in light of that belief, the two parties are in a position to commiserate. Of course, the innocent has suffered much more than the juror, but the juror has been cast by fate into the role of the dupe and owes no apology—except perhaps of the diluted form "I'm sorry *but*...." This point is not decisive, of course, but it is suggestive: it suggests that it's unlikely that a belief BARD in an innocent's guilt provides an excuse for inflicting punishment on the innocent.

Such a belief is also unlikely to provide a justification. After all, the considerations that an agent cites in justification of his action are such as to alter the moral quality of the act that tokened the prohibited type. Killing intentionally *in self defense* is morally different from other tokens of that type of act. But the act of condemning an innocent to a prison term *because you believed him BARD to be guilty* has no morally significant features that distinguish it from other tokens of the type. What is morally significant about condemning an innocent person is that *an innocent person is condemned* and that is just as true when the juror who causes this result does so from a false belief BARD in guilt. One might push back against this point by noting that condemning an innocent to a prison term *because you believed him BARD to be guilty* is to participate in a valuable social practice: the practice of participation in an institutional criminal justice system, thanks to which we enjoy many benefits, including security and crime reduction. But no one with a retributivist impulse will take such a line of thought to involve *a justification*. We cannot justify punishing the innocent by appeal to the good things that we thereby achieve through doing so. Again, while this line of thought is not decisive, it is suggestive. What we want to know is how a false belief, held by a juror BARD, shields the juror from blame. It could be that our best prospect for answering this question is to consider whether the false belief provides neither an excuse nor a justification, but a denial.

This way of framing the issue provides us with a tool for appreciating the important work on the BARD standard of R. A. Duff (Duff et al. 2007, pp. 87–92; *see also* Kitai 2003, pp. 1163–1187). Duff claims that conviction and punishment, when justified, are expressive acts: they express the community's condemnation of the offense and the offender. This form of expressive act is not just permissible, but essential to a community's flourishing. But a person has engaged in this permissible form of expression only if convinced of the offender's guilt. That level of conviction, the level required to be genuinely expressing community condemnation, is what the BARD standard is. The BARD standard is met, that is, just in case jurors meet the necessary epistemic conditions of the act of expressing community condemnation for crime. Another way to put the point: what every juror should avoid is expressing condemnation of innocent conduct. But one expresses condemnation of *impermissible* and *criminal* conduct when one is convinced BARD of the guilt of the person one convicts *even if the person is in fact innocent*. The sentence "J condemns innocent conduct" admits of a *de re* and a *de dicto* interpretation. *De re*: J condemns conduct that is in fact innocent (whatever J happens to believe). *De dicto*: J condemns whatever conduct in fact meets the description "innocent." Under its *de re* interpretation, the sentence is true of any juror who falsely convicts; the juror's verdict had the effect of sending to prison someone whose act was innocent, although not represented as such in the mind of the juror. But if a juror is convinced BARD in guilt, then the sentence is not true in its *de dicto* interpretation: it is not the case that the juror condemns any innocent conduct; he condemns only conduct that meets the description "criminal"; and so he does not even condemn the defendant's innocent conduct. Add that what jurors must avoid is for such *de dicto* sentences to be true of them, and we reach the conclusion that showing that one was convinced BARD in guilt is a denial, and so shields the juror from blame for that reason. If J does not believe that the defendant is innocent, then she has not acted in such a way as to make true the *de dicto* sentence "J condemns innocent conduct."

This way of thinking of the BARD standard has the virtue of continuity with the standard's history. The juror is shielded from blame for false conviction if his act of convicting, despite being erroneous, was of the distinctive type he was given the job of performing. He was tasked with expressing the community's condemnation, if condemnation was what was called for. And he did his job, provided he met the relevant epistemic conditions. He is thus blameless, despite his error.

However, Duff's approach rests on a view of the act of expressive condemnation that may not, in the end, bear scrutiny. To see this point, consider the following appealing idea: what the community condemns, a condemnation it tasks jurors with expressing, is not just criminal conduct, but rather conduct *that has been shown beyond a reasonable doubt* to be criminal. That is, it's appealing to think that the community leaves to God or the Fates the job of condemning conduct that is not shown to be criminal BARD. If this is right, then there is no way to follow Duff's line of thought without circularity. When has the BARD standard been met? Answer: when the juror is in the epistemic state, it is necessary to express the community's condemnation. What epistemic state is that? Answer: the state of believing BARD in the defendant's guilt since what the community condemns is conduct that has been shown BARD to be criminal. Under what conditions is a juror in that state of belief as opposed to some other state that fails to qualify his conduct to be expressive of the community's condemnation? In other words: when has the BARD standard been met? We are brought in a circle.

In other words, Duff's answer requires that the BARD standard is not, itself, incorporated into the definition of what the community condemns. But there is no reason to think that a community cannot choose to conceptualize the fitting objects of its condemnation in part by reference to the standard of proof. In fact, one might think that any community dedicated to a "presumption of innocence" does just that. To presume innocence, one might think, is to refuse to condemn in the absence of proof BARD—it is to take a person's conduct to be an unfitting object of condemnation unless shown BARD to be criminal. To put the point more circumspectly, it would be surprising, at least, if an adequate account of the BARD standard precluded this way of conceptualizing the presumption of innocence.

But it is important to separate the promise of Duff's particular account with the promise of the general strategy that he pursues in offering it. Say we identified a sufficient condition of the permissibility of an act of conviction and punishment. Duff takes that sufficient condition to be that the act is "expressive of the community's condemnation"; but set that particular account aside and imagine we have some other condition such that an act of conviction and punishment is permissible when it is met. And imagine that that condition includes tacit or explicit epistemic conditions: a person has met the condition only if in a particular epistemic state with respect to the proposition that the defendant is guilty. The strategy is to assert that the BARD standard is met just in case the juror is in this epistemic state. Such an approach provides us, immediately, with the normative bridge that is needed. The psychological state is necessary to meet the condition that is sufficient for the permissibility of the act of conviction and punishment. The question, then, of what the BARD standard is reduces to the identification of the relevant sufficient condition and the articulation of its epistemic requirements. If there is reason to think that there is some sufficient condition of this kind, then there is reason to be optimistic about the prospects for an adequate psychological account of the BARD standard. And there is reason to think this. As has been emphasized throughout, conviction and punishment is *government* behavior—sometimes performed by ordinary citizens, jurors, conscripted into service, but still—and if there is a way for a government to do it legitimately then there is a sufficient condition, bringing with it epistemic conditions, for its permissibility. Filling in the details means offering a genuine political philosophy, an account of the nature and limits of the state's authorization to harm those who violate its criminal prohibitions. I do not have such an account to offer, and so, correlatively, I do not have a positive psychological account to propose. But I'm optimistic about the possibility of such an account—or, rather, as optimistic as I am about the prospects for a political philosophy of the kind that would be needed to support such a psychological account.

Conclusion

Reflection on the nature of the BARD standard is an entry point for thought about fundamental issues of criminal justice. What do we want from our criminal justice system? What prices are we willing to pay for it? What do we require of a state tasked with meting out punishment? What do we demand of those ordinary citizens who find themselves in the role of factfinder, required to pass judgment on their fellow citizens, invariably with serious consequences and sometimes with lethal? What has been suggested here is that taking seriously the way in which the BARD standard is the tip of a philosophical iceberg suggests that a successful account of its nature is more likely to be a psychological account than a probabilistic one. There is a plausible, if schematic, normative bridge from a description of a psychological state, on the one hand, and condemnation and punishment, on the other. What we need to identify is the psychological state necessary to be engaged in the state's authoritative activity of condemning and punishing, the activity that it is licensed to perform, and jurors are licensed to aid it in performing.[6]

Notes

1. Should the BARD standard also apply to the findings of nongovernments, like churches or corporations, which are also sometimes in the business of finding people guilty of wrongdoing? While a picture of the BARD standard as a distinctively political standard will be sketched by the end, this question is not fully

reached here for it is possible that other institutions besides governments ought to operate under similar constraints.

2. The probability here is calculated like so: the probability that D was chosen randomly by Witness #1 is $1/5$; the same for Witness #2; so the probability that they both randomly chose D is $1/5 \times 1/5 = 1/25$. In real cases, "complicating factors" cannot be set aside. For instance, a jury presented with the testimony of two witnesses who picked the same person from separate lineups also know that the witnesses witnessed the crime; that the police picked the defendant to place in the lineup; that the police thought the witnesses credible enough to request that they view the lineup; and so on. These are all pieces of evidence over and above the mere facts that the two witnesses picked out the person in the courtroom who is facing the charge.

3. Others have expressed this same concern about probabilistic accounts (cf. Stein and Allen 2013, pp. 557–605).

4. We can reach this conclusion only, given the assumption that the likelihood that the evidence supports conviction above the threshold is independent of the guilt of the defendant. If the evidence of guilt is typically worse when the defendant is innocent, then the false conviction rate will be lower than 1% even when the threshold is 0.99.

5. We sometimes define a type of action as all and only those acts that violate a particular norm, as when we say that murders are all and only those killings that violate the norm of the form "Don't kill unless X." This then gives us an exceptionless norm: don't engage in such acts, period. With respect to that exceptionless norm, there are only denials, and no justifications. The general point here is that the denial-justification distinction is norm-relative and so relative to the type of action prohibited by the norm.

6. Thanks to Vincent Chiao and Alec Walen for comments on an earlier version of this chapter.

REFERENCES

Elonis v. United States, 575 U.S. ____ (2015).

Blackstone, William. 1915. In *Blackstone's commentaries abridged*, ed. W. Sprague, 9th ed. Chicago: Calahan and Company.

DeKay, Michael L. 1996. The difference between Blackstone-like error ratios and probabilistic standards of proof. *Law and Social Inquiry* 21: 95–132.

Duff, Antony, Lindsay Farmer, Sandra Marshall, and Victor Tadros. 2007. *The trial on trial: Towards a normative theory of the criminal trial*. Oxford: Hart Publishing.

Kitai, Rinat. 2003. Protecting the guilty. *Buffalo Criminal Law Review* 6: 1163–1187.

Laudan, Larry. 2011. The rules of trial, political morality, and the costs of error: Or, is proof beyond a reasonable doubt doing more harm than good? In *Oxford studies in philosophy of law*, ed. L. Green and B. Leiter, 198–226. Oxford: Oxford University Press.

Nozick, Robert. 1974. *Anarchy, state and utopia*. New York: Basic Books.

Reiman, Jeffrey, and Ernest van den Haag. 1990. On the common saying that it is better that ten guilty persons escape than that one innocent suffer: Pro and con. *Social Philosophy and Policy* 7 (2): 226–248.

Stein, Alex, and Ronald Allen. 2013. Evidence, probability and the burden of proof. *Arizona Law Review* 55: 557–605.

Tribe, Laurence. 1970. An ounce of detention: Preventive justice in the world of John Mitchell. *Virginia Law Review* 56: 371–407.

———. 1971. Trial by mathematics: Precision and ritual in the legal process. *Harvard Law Review* 84: 1329–1393.

Tversky, Amos, and Daniel Kahneman. 1954. Judgment under uncertainty: Heuristics and biases. *Science* 185: 1124–1131.

Walen, Alec. 2015. Proof beyond a reasonable doubt: A balanced retributive account. *Louisiana Law Review* 76: 355–446.

———. 2019. *The mechanics of claims and permissible killing in war.* Oxford: Oxford University Press.

Whitman, James. 2008. *The origins of reasonable doubt: Theological roots of the criminal trial.* New Haven: Yale University Press.

PART V

Blackmail

CHAPTER 6

Blackmail: A Crime of Paradox and Irony

Peter Westen

The criminal prohibition of blackmail comes laden with irony. Blackmail derives its archaic name from a 1601 English statute that has hardly anything to do with the modern offense of blackmail. Every US jurisdiction today criminalizes what the lay public regards as blackmail, and yet few do so in the name of "blackmail." Prosecutors rarely enforce the crime in practice (Posner 1993, pp. 1841–1847), and yet lawyers, philosophers and economists continue to obsess over it. The lay public accepts blackmail as a legitimate criminal prohibition, and yet legal experts question its legitimacy. Ultimately, blackmail remains the only major offense that is commonly said to constitute a "paradox."

I shall (1) define what I mean by blackmail; (2) describe how American penal codes frame it in relation to offenses of theft, larceny, extortion, threat, coercion and intimidation; (3) describe the variable scope of state and federal blackmail prohibitions; (4) address variations in the existence and content of defenses to blackmail and (5) define the so-called paradox of blackmail, arguing that, though the paradox is genuine, it is narrower than generally supposed and endeavoring to explain, though not justify, its persistence.

Defining "Blackmail"

No consensus exists in law regarding the meaning of the term "blackmail," a failing that is due in part to the term's heterogeneous history.

The term "blackmail" stems from two archaic terms: "mail" or "mayle" from the French word "maille," referring to coins that freebooting Scottish Highland chiefs historically extorted from English landowners across the Scottish border by promising to keep the landowners safe from marauding

P. Westen (✉)
Michigan Law School, Ann Arbor, MI, USA
e-mail: pkw@umich.edu

© The Author(s) 2019
L. Alexander, K. K. Ferzan (eds.), *The Palgrave Handbook of Applied Ethics and the Criminal Law*, https://doi.org/10.1007/978-3-030-22811-8_6

brigands (whom the Highland chiefs implied were they themselves), and "black" from an English statute of 1601 which prohibited the payment or receipt of such "black mayle" (43 Eliz. ch.13, § 2).[1] For much of its history in England, blackmail referred to what was traditionally called extortion, that is, the crime of demanding protection money from others in return for not criminally harming them. English law was extended in the mid-eighteenth century to criminalize the practice of obtaining, or attempting to obtain, property of others, by threatening otherwise to accuse them of infamous crimes (Ginsburg and Shechtman 1993, p. 1851; Yehudai 2009, pp. 296–812). And the offense was further extended under Queen Victoria to criminalize what today is often called "informational blackmail," that is, the practice of obtaining or attempting to obtain property of another by threatening otherwise to disclose information that incriminates or subjects another to hatred, contempt or ridicule (McLaren 2002, pp. 31–38).

The 50 states and the US government all prohibit informational blackmail to a greater or lesser extent. But they rarely do so in the name of blackmail. Among the 50 states plus the District of Columbia, only 7 jurisdictions possess crimes denominated "blackmail," and of those 7, only 4 confine the crime to acts of informational blackmail,[2] the rest encompassing acts of extortion as well.[3] The District of Columbia and Wyoming statutes are examples of the former and latter, respectively:

D.C. Code § 22-3252

(a) A person commits the offense of blackmail, if, with intent to obtain property of another or to cause another to do or refrain from doing any act, that person threatens:

(1) To accuse any person of a crime;
(2) To expose a secret or publicize an asserted fact, whether true or false, tending to subject any person to hatred, contempt, or ridicule; or
(3) To impair the reputation of any person, including a deceased person.

Wyoming Statutes § 6-2-402

(a) A person commits blackmail if, with the intent to obtain property of another or to compel action or inaction by any person against his will, the person:

(i) Threatens bodily injury or injury to the property of another person; or
(ii) Accuses or threatens to accuse a person of a crime or immoral conduct which would tend to degrade or disgrace the person or subject him to the ridicule or contempt of society.

The remaining jurisdictions, as discussed below, also punish informational blackmail, but they do so under the rubric of other offenses. Some confine blackmail to being a property offense, while others broaden it to include the use of threatened disclosures to abridge a person's freedom of action (*see "Broadening Extortion to Include Infringements of Personal Freedom," infra*).

I shall henceforth use "blackmail" to refer solely to acts of informational blackmail. I do so for two reasons. First, doing so is consistent with the lay public's use of the term. "Blackmail" is a legal term that has become part of popular discourse, where it refers to coercive threatened harms of a certain kind, namely, threats by _A_ to disclose incriminating or other reputation-damaging information about _B_.[4] Second, and more importantly, the paradigmatic example of the "paradox" of blackmail is the criminalization of informational blackmail.[5]

BLACKMAIL WITHIN AMERICAN PENAL CODES

Just as jurisdictions differ over the meaning of blackmail, they differ, too, over the meaning of "theft," "larceny," "stealing," "extortion" and "coercion." To appreciate the differences, it is useful to start with a baseline, in this case ordinary-language usage. The lay public commonly uses the terms as follows:

> _Theft_: "Theft" is a property offense that _A_ commits against _B_ by depriving _B_ of property without _B_'s consent, by means of deception, stealth or other non-forcible means (Merriam Webster's Collegiate Dictionary 1997, pp. 1222, 1150).
> _Larceny_: "Larceny" is a synonym for theft and stealing, and vice versa.
> _Stealing_: "Stealing" is a synonym for theft and larceny, and vice versa.
> _Extortion_: "Extortion" is a property offense that _A_ commits against _B_ by depriving, or attempting to deprive, _B_ of property with the latter's consent[6] by either threatening to otherwise inflict unlawful harm in the future (e.g., "Pay me or your house will be vandalized") or, while being a public official, violating public trust by threatening to otherwise withhold or take official action (e.g., "Pay me or I'll deny you a zoning variance").[7]
> _Coercion_: Coercion is an offense against the person that _A_ commits against _B_ by compelling _B_ to do or refrain from a lawful act by either threatening to otherwise inflict unlawful harm without consent (e.g., "Submit to sexual intercourse or I will strike you") or unlawfully threatening to otherwise inflict harm (e.g., "Submit to sexual intercourse or I will fire you from your at-will position.") (Merriam Webster's Collegiate Dictionary 1997, p. 222).

Some jurisdictions use theft, larceny, stealing, extortion and coercion in the aforementioned way (_see_, e.g., Calif. Pen. Code §§ 484, 518; Calif. Gov. Code § 8313). Most jurisdictions, however, use the terms in different and occasionally overlapping ways, including by (1) broadening extortion to include blackmail; (2) broadening theft, larceny and stealing to include all wrongful deprivations of property (other than by immediate force or threats of immediate force); and (3) broadening extortion to include not only wrongful deprivations of property but also infringements of personal freedom of the kind associated with coercion.

Broadening Extortion to Include Blackmail

The District of Columbia mirrors lay understandings of extortion and blackmail by confining extortion to threats of unlawful harm and of abuses of public trust and confining blackmail to threatened disclosures of information (D.C. Code §§ 22-3252, 22–3251). Most jurisdictions, however, do otherwise. Rather than possessing offenses denominated "blackmail," they broaden the crime of "extortion" to encompass acts of blackmail as well. Thus, Hawaii subsumes traditional offenses of extortion and blackmail within a generic offense of "extortion":

> Hawaii Rev. Stat. § 707-764
> A person commits extortion if the person does any of the following: (1) Obtains ... control over the property ... of another ... by threatening ... to (a) Cause bodily injury in the future to ... any ... person; ... (c) Accuse some person of any offense; [or] (g) Expose a secret or publicize an asserted fact, whether true of false, tending to subject some person to hatred, contempt, or ridicule ....

Broadening Theft, Larceny and Stealing to Include All Unlawful Deprivations of Property (Other Than by Means of Immediate Force or Threats of Immediate Force), Including Blackmail

Some jurisdictions, following the Model Penal Code (MPC), use "theft" as a generic offense to include all deprivations of property (other than deprivations by means of immediate force or threats of immediate force, the latter being the offense of robbery) (*see*, e.g., Ark. Code § 5-36-102). Other jurisdictions define "larceny" (*see*, e.g., Conn. Gen. Stat. Ann. § 53a-119(5)) and "stealing" (*see*, e.g., Mo. Rev. Stat. §§ 570.010, 570.030) in the same generic fashion. The consequence in such jurisdictions is that "theft," "larceny" and "stealing" cease being synonyms for deprivation of property by stealth and deception and, instead, become umbrella concepts in which blackmail is a subset. The state of Pennsylvania is an example. Theft in Pennsylvania is a generic offense of which "theft by unlawful taking," "theft by deception" and "theft by extortion" are subsets (18 Pa. Comp. Stat. §§ 3921-23), the latter of which also encompasses the offense of obtaining property by threats of accusation or exposure (18 Pa. Comp. Stat. § 3923(a)(2-3)).

Broadening Extortion to Include Infringements of Personal Freedom

Some jurisdictions are content to confine blackmail to being a property offense (*see*, e.g., Ariz. Rev. Stat. § 13-1804). Others, however, extend blackmail to include using threats of accusation or exposure to abridge freedom of action as well. They do so in two distinct ways. Some, like Pennsylvania (which has committed itself to making it a crime of "theft" to obtain property by threats of accusation or exposure), follow the MPC and make it a separate crime of "coercion" to use threats of accusation or exposure to restrict a person's freedom of action:

Criminal Coercion
    (Pa. Comp. Stat. § 18-2906)
    A person is guilty of criminal coercion, if, with intent unlawfully to restrict freedom of action of another to the detriment of the other, he threatens to: (a) commit any criminal offense; (2) accuse anyone of a criminal offense; (3) expose any secret tending to subject an person to hatred, contempt or ridicule; or (4) take or withhold action as an official, or cause an official to take or withhold action (emphasis added).
    (A few jurisdictions do the same thing by adopting statutes denominated "intimidation" rather than "coercion"; *see*, *e.g.*, Burns Ind. Code § 35-45-2-1(d).)

Other states eschew Pennsylvania's two-statute approach. Rather than framing extortion and blackmail as subsets of property offenses of theft, stealing and larceny and enacting separate offenses against coercion or intimidation, they define blackmail and extortion as offenses encompassing deprivations of freedom as well as property. Thus, the Wyoming statute, quoted earlier, defines "blackmail" as the offense of using threatened disclosures of incriminating or shaming information *either* "to obtain property of another" *or* "to compel action or inaction by [another] against his will." Other jurisdictions define "extortion" in the same way (*see*, e.g., Iowa Code § 711.4).

Pennsylvania's two-statute approach and Wyoming's one-statute approach have advantages. Wyoming's approach has the advantage of subsuming separate offenses against property and freedom into a single offense, thus obviating the need for a separate offense of "coercion" or "intimidation." In contrast, Pennsylvania's approach has the advantage of enabling Pennsylvania to criminalize certain threats with respect to *property* that it does not criminalize with respect to threats to infringe *freedom of action*. Thus, Pennsylvania is able to make it a crime of extortion to obtain property by threats to "inflict any ... harm which would not benefit the actor," while *not* making it a comparable crime of coercion to abridge a person's freedom of action by such means (*compare* 18 Pa. Comp. Stat. § 3923 *with* 18 Pa. Comp. Stat. § 2906).

The Variable Scope of State and Federal Blackmail Prohibitions

The earliest English statutes that criminalized informational blackmail distinguished between two kinds of threatened disclosures, which they penalized differently: threats to accuse persons of *crimes*, which they penalized by up to life in prison, and threats to disclose information that subjected persons to *hatred, contempt or ridicule*, which they punished by no more than three years in prison (Libel Act of 1843 § 3).

    A few US jurisdictions criminalize only one or the other of the two kinds of threatened disclosures. Thus, a half-dozen jurisdictions solely criminalize threats to accuse persons of crimes,[8] while Ohio does the opposite by criminalizing only threats to expose persons to hatred, contempt or ridicule (Ohio Rev. Code §

2905.11). Still other jurisdictions subsume both kinds of threatened disclosures within a single phrase (*see*, e.g., 17A Me. Rev. Stat. § 355(2)(B)). Nevertheless, the great majority of jurisdictions continue to distinguish between the two kinds of threatened disclosures, though they no longer penalize them differently. Thus, Iowa makes it an offense, punishable by up to ten years in prison to do "any of the following with the purpose of obtaining ... anything of value: (b) Threatens to accuse another of a public offense; (c) Threatens to expose any person to hatred, contempt or ridicule" (Iowa Code §§ 711.4).

Blackmail statutes vary considerably from jurisdiction to jurisdiction. But the principal differences concern the following: (1) whether threats must be in verbal form; (2) whether threatened disclosures must be of information that is outside the public domain; (3) whether the threatened disclosures must be false; (4) whether the threatened disclosures must harm reputations; (5) whether threatened persons must be identical to or personally intimate with persons whom threatened disclosures would harm; (6) whether threats to disclose public wrongdoing are confined to accusations of crime; (7) whether statutory limitations on what constitutes blackmail are subject to broader catchall prohibitions; and (8) penalties for violations.

Threats in Verbal Form

Some jurisdictions, being apparently concerned about issues of proof, confine criminality to verbal threats, whether the latter are oral or written (*see*, e.g., Fla. Stat. § 836.05). Others extend the crime to all threats, regardless of how the threats are communicated, whether through words, innuendo or actions (*see*, e.g., La. Rev. Stat. § 44-66(A)). Most, however, merely state that it is a crime to "threaten" to make certain disclosures without specifying any particular form of communication (*see*, e.g., D.C. Code § 22-3252(a)).

Information Not Yet in the Public Domain

Jurisdictions differ regarding the criminality of threats to disclose information that is already in the public domain. Some jurisdictions require that threatened disclosures concern compromising information that is "confidential" (Alaska Stat. § 11.41.520), "secret" (18 Penn. Comp. Stat. Ann. § 3923) or "not previously in the public domain" (Miss. Code § 97-3-82(2)), while others make it an offense to threaten to disclose "*any* asserted fact" (New Jersey Stat. § 2C:20–5), or "any information sought to be concealed by the person threatened" (N.D. Cent. Code § 12.1-23-10(12)(g)), that subjects a person to hatred, contempt or ridicule. It is unclear why the offense should be confined in the former way. Assume, for example, that a nursing-care attendant threatens that unless paid, he will reveal to an aged and institutionalized patient that her grandson has been publicly accused of pedophilia. If it is wrongful to extort money on such grounds *before* an accusation is made public, is it not also wrongful to do so *after* an accusation is made if the target of disclosure is unaware of the information (*see* People v. Bollaert, pp. 727–728)?

False Information

As discussed earlier, blackmail statutes commonly make it an offense to extort money or conduct by threatening to subject a person to "hatred, contempt or ridicule." Because the phrase "hatred, contempt or ridicule" is a term of art from the law of defamation, and because truth is a defense to allegations of defamation in the US,[9] at least one court in the US has construed the phrase as criminalizing threatened disclosures only if the disclosures are false (*see* Landry v. Daley; *see also* Burns Ind. Code § 35-42-2-1(d)(7) (making it a crime to threaten to harm a person's credit or business reputation only if threatened assertions are "false")). The majority view, however, is overwhelmingly to the contrary. Whether states do so by explicit statutory provision (*see*, e.g., Ark. Code § 5-13-208(a)(5)) or by judicial statutory construction (*see* Annotation), states overwhelmingly take the position that truth is not a defense to blackmail.

The consequence is that criminal prosecutors nearly everywhere do not have to concern themselves with whether threatened disclosures are true or false. Absent some other defense (*see* "Defenses to Blackmail," *infra*), it constitutes blackmail to threaten another that, unless demands are met, the actor will make or release statements that subject the other to hatred, contempt or ridicule, regardless of truth. However, this does not mean that truth is never relevant under extortion statutes. Within jurisdictions in which actors have defenses to blackmail only if they *believe* their threatened disclosures to be true, truth is relevant as circumstantial evidence of such belief. Truth is also relevant within jurisdictions that, in addition to criminalizing blackmail, separately make it an offense for an actor to threaten another with "libel" (*see*, e.g., Nevada Rev. Stat. § 205.320(3)), or "calumny" (*see*, e.g., Ohio Rev. Code § 2905.11(A)(4)), unless the actor's demands are met.

Harm to Reputation

England confined the offense of blackmail to accusations of crime and other disclosures that subject persons to hatred, contempt or ridicule, all of which are injuries to a person's character and reputation. Some jurisdictions, like Rhode Island and West Virginia, follow England by confining the offense to accusations of "crime" or disclosures that injure a person's "reputation" (R.I. Gen. Laws § 11-42-2) or "character" (W. Va. Code § 61-2-13). Others go further and extend the offense to disclosures that impair a person's "credit or business repute" (*see*, e.g., Alaska Stat. § 11.41.520(a)(3)) or reveal a physical "deformity" (*see*, e.g., La. Rev. Stat. § 14:66(A)(3)). Still others like Hawaii extend the offense to "any information" that is "sought to be concealed by the person threatened or any other person" (Hawaii Rev. Stat. § 707-764(1)(g)), regardless of whether information would injure a person's reputation. To illustrate the difference, assume that <u>A</u> threatens, unless paid, to disclose medical information about <u>B</u> that, though not damaging to <u>B</u>'s reputation, is nevertheless private. <u>A</u> commits an offense in Hawaii but not in West Virginia.

Relationship Between Threatened Parties and Victims of Threatened Disclosures

Most jurisdictions make it an offense for an actor to threaten that, unless he is compensated, he will disclose compromising information about "any" person, regardless of whether the person whom the compromising information implicates is related to those being threatened (*see*, e.g., Code of Ala. § 13A-8-1(14) (f)). And some go further and criminalize threatened disclosures about persons, regardless of whether they are living or dead (*see*, e.g., N.D. Cent. Code § 12.1-23-10(12)(f)). Yet other jurisdictions prohibit threatened disclosures only if the disclosures implicate the very persons being threatened, while still others prohibit threatened disclosures only if the disclosures implicate persons who stand in an intimate relationship to those being threatened. Thus, Indiana makes it an offense to threaten to expose "the person threatened" to hatred, contempt or ridicule (Burns Ind. Code § 35-45-2-1); California makes it an offense to threaten to accuse a person of a crime, provided that the latter is the threatened person himself or "a relative" or "member of his family" (Calif. Pen. Code §§ 518–19); and Louisiana makes it an offense to threaten to accuse a person of a crime, provided that the latter is the threatened person himself, a family member or someone "held dear" to the threatened party (La. Rev. Stat. § 14-66). The latter limitations appear to reflect the view that, given the penalties for blackmail, punishment for blackmail should be confined to persons whose threats inflict severe emotional distress upon their targets.

Notice that jurisdictions that make it an offense to threaten to disclose reputation-damaging information about "any" person raise the question of whether it is a crime for a person who possesses reputation-damaging information about a public official or public figure to offer an exclusive right to information to whichever tabloid or scandal sheet pays the most for it. Since the threat to each tabloid is to disclose the information to another tabloid unless the former matches or exceeds the highest bid, the threat violates the terms of such statutes. To be sure, courts within such jurisdictions might interpret their statutes to apply only to threats to disclose that are also accompanied by *offers to suppress*, not threats to disclose in any event. However, even then, the statutes would prevent a person from offering to sell the information to whichever tabloid agreed to pay the most, provided that the latter agreed to pay more than a certain stated amount.

Threats to Disclose Legal Wrongdoing

Nearly all jurisdictions make it a crime to obtain property or abridge a person's freedom of action by threatening to accuse a person of a crime, though North Carolina limits the offense to accusations of crimes that are punishable by "death" or "imprisonment in the state's prison" (N.C. Gen. Stat. § 14-118). Other jurisdictions go further and also make it an offense to threaten to "bring charges" against a person, say, by declaring oneself willing to prosecute an offense that has previously been reported (*see*, e.g., Ariz. Rev. Stat. § 13-1804(A)(5)). Still others also make it an offense to threaten to report a person's actual or suspected immigration status (*see*, e.g., Calif. Pen. Code § 519(5)). And at least one jurisdiction makes it a crime to threaten to report a person's violation of a civil statute (Miss. Code § 97-3-82(2)).

The Relationship Between Statutory Limitations and Catchall Prohibitions

The aforementioned limitations on blackmail liability can be effective. However, in jurisdictions that have adopted the Model Penal Code's catchall prohibition regarding extortion, the limitations can be illusory. The MPC not only makes it a crime to obtain property of another by threatening to accuse another of a criminal offense or disclose secrets that subject another to hatred, contempt or ridicule but also makes it a crime to obtain property by threatening to inflict "*any other harm which would not benefit the actor*" (MPC § 223.4(7)). Now, it might be thought having addressed a specific kind of conduct (e.g., threats to "accuse" others of "crimes" or disclose "secrets" that subject others to "hatred, contempt or ridicule"), the MPC intends such limitations to control in any case involving threatened *disclosures of information*. However, the MPC commentary makes it clear that it intends the catchall prohibition to apply to all cases encompassed by its terms (Model Penal Code and Commentaries 1980, pt. 2, vol. 2, pp. 214–216). This suggests that, within states that have made the MPC catchall part of their blackmail statutes, specified limitations on blackmail liability, for example, the requirement of "secrets" or harms of "hatred, contempt or ridicule," may be overridden.

Penalties

Jurisdictions differ regarding the degree to which they grade the offense of blackmail and the severity with which they penalize violations.

Sentencing Ranges
Sentencing judges have discretion to sentence with prescribed ranges and, hence, discretion to sentence blackmail less severely than other forms of extortion that carry the same potential sentences. Yet prescribed sentencing ranges themselves vary considerably from one jurisdiction to another. Thus, although Michigan and North Carolina both make it an offense to threaten to accuse another of a crime, Michigan penalizes such threats by up to 20 years in prison, while North Carolina penalizes it by no more than 45 days in jail (*compare* Mich. Comp. L. § 750.213 *with* N.C. Gen. Stat. Ann. §§ 14.188, 15A-1340.23(c)). Similarly, Louisiana penalizes blackmail by up to 15 years in prison, while Missouri penalizes it by no more than 1 year in jail (*compare* 14 La. Rev. Stat § 66 *with* Mo. Rev. Stat. §§ 570.030(8) & 578.011(6)).

Grading Blackmail

Jurisdictions also differ regarding whether and, if so, how to grade penalties for blackmail. Some jurisdictions penalize extortion by violence identically with blackmail, while others distinguish between them (*compare* Iowa Code § 711.4 (no difference in penalty range), *with* Ariz. Rev. Stat. § 13-1804 (penalizing extortion by violence more severely than blackmail)). Other jurisdictions grade demands for money more severely than demands for actions, while others do not (*compare* Code of Ala. §§ 13A-8-15 and 13A-6-25 (penalizing demands for money more severely than demands for actions) *with* Fla. Stat. Ann. § 836.05 (penalizing both offenses the same)). Other jurisdictions grade black- mail by the amount of money extracted, while others do not (*compare* Tex. Pen. Code Tex. § 31.03 (grading by amount appropriated) *with* 11 Del. C. § 846 (2) (no grading by amount appropriated)). And still other jurisdictions grade blackmail by whether threats succeed, while others do not.[10]

DEFENSES TO BLACKMAIL

The English Libel Act of 1843 was unqualified: it made it an offense, without exception, to extort money by threatening to disclose information about a person (Libel Act of 1843, § 3). Interpreted literally, the English statute would have criminalized practices that are common in civil litigation, for example, pre-litigation demand and offer letters, and offers under seal by plaintiffs in civil suits to dismiss the suits and preserve confidentiality in return for pay- ments by defendants. It would also have made it a crime for a person to make threats such as "Pay for the damage you caused in spraying racist graffiti on my car or I'll tell the newspapers what you did" or "Stop your affair with my daughter-in-law or I'll tell your wife about it."

Not surprisingly, a majority of US jurisdictions provide statutory defenses to blackmail (Robinson et al. 2010, pp. 309–11 & nn. 74, 79–80) and others create judge-made defenses (*see*, e.g., United States v. Jackson)—some of which con- sist of offense-negating elements (*see*, e.g., Code of Ala. § 13A-8-15) and oth- ers which are true "affirmative defenses" (*see*, e.g., Ohio Rev. Code § 2905.12).[11] Thus, some statutes condition the state's *prima facie* case on threatened disclo- sures being "wrongful" (*see*, e.g., Calif. Pen. Code § 518) or "malicious" (*see*, e.g., Florida Stat. Ann. § 836.05), while others contain detailed defenses based on those of the Model Penal Code (*see*, e.g., Alaska Stat. §§ 11.41.520(c) (adopted verbatim from MPC § 223.4) and 11.41.530(b) (adopted verbatim from MPC § 212.5)).

As previously mentioned, the MPC contains two provisions for criminaliz- ing blackmail: an extortion provision, which criminalizes demands for prop- erty, and a coercion provision, which criminalizes demands for action or inaction (e.g., "Stop your affair with my daughter-in-law or I'll tell your wife about it"). The two MPC provisions contain two respective defenses—a defense to extorting property and a defense to coercing action or inaction. Thus, it is defense to extortion of property under the MPC that the actor "honestly claimed" the "property" as "restitution or indemnification for harm done in the circumstances to which [the disclosure] relates" (MPC § 223.4), and it is a defense to coercion of behavior under the MPC that the actor "believed [the disclosure] to be true" and that his purpose was limited to compelling the other to behave in a way reasonably related to the circumstances that were the subject of the [disclosure]" (MPC § 212.5).

Defenses to blackmail all share at least one thing in common: they apply only when actors threaten disclosure in order to obtain redress for perceived misconduct or to induce others to begin conducting themselves as it is believed they ought to. Given that limitation, however, defenses differ regarding the permissible scope of threatened disclosures and the permissible kinds of property, action and inaction that actors may demand. The principal differences concern: (1) whether the defense extends beyond demands for property to include demands for conduct as well; (2) whether the defense extends to threats to accuse persons of criminal conduct; (3) whether the defense extends to threatened disclosures that are broader than needed for legal redress; (4) whether the defense extends to demands for property in excess of what is needed for redress; (5) whether the defense extends to demands for action or inaction beyond action to redress perceived wrongs; (6) whether actors must believe the threatened disclosures to be true; and (7) whether a nexus must exist between the property demanded and the subject of the threatened disclosure.

Extension of the Defense to Include Demands for Action or Inaction

As we have seen, some states follow the MPC by enacting blackmail statutes against both demands for property and demands for action or inaction. Some of these states also follow the MPC in providing statutory defenses to both offenses (*see*, e.g., Alaska Stat. §§ 11.41.520(c), 11.41.530(b)). Yet, strangely enough, and perhaps unconstitutionally as well, other state statutes do not: they prohibit both sorts of demands, and they provide statutory defenses to demands for property, but they provide no defenses to demands for action or inaction. Thus, Arkansas possesses separate statutes against blackmail demands for property and blackmail demands for action or inaction (*see* Ark. Code §§ 5-36-101(B), 5-36-103(a)(2)). The former statute states that it is a defense to blackmail for property that the property is "restitution or compensation for harm done in the circumstances to which the [threatened] accusation [of crime] or exposure [of secrets] relates" (Ark. Code § 5-36-101 (11)(B)). But the latter statute provides no defense at all to blackmail demands for action or inaction. (Interestingly, several states do the converse by providing a defense to coercion but not to larceny.)[12]

The failure to provide defenses to blackmail—as well as the enactment of stingy defenses—raises constitutional questions because it effectively criminalizes threats that may deserve First Amendment protection. Consider, for example, an employee or an airline company who discovers that a company pilot has recently experienced epileptic seizures. The employee could respond to the danger by directly notifying the company, "Your pilot has been having epileptic seizures." If the employee did so, the First Amendment would protect the employee in prohibiting the state from punishing him for the statement. But now assume that the employee decides to respond to the danger by telling the pilot, "If you don't immediately get help with you seizures, I am going to tell the company about them." Given that the First Amendment would prohibit the state from punishing the employee for directly notifying the company, and given that employee now threatens to notify the company unless the pilot resolves the very danger that the threatened notification concerns, a court could reasonably conclude that the First Amendment also prohibits the state from punishing the threat (*see* State v. Robertson, pp. 577–590).

Courts respond in two ways to constitutional inadequacies in defenses to blackmail, whether the inadequacies arise from an absence of defenses (*see*, e.g., Whimbush v. People) or from excessively stingy defenses (State v. Robertson, p. 590). Some courts avoid declaring blackmail statutes unconstitutional by inserting judicially fashioned defenses into statutes that lack explicit defenses (*see*, e.g., United States v. Jackson). Other courts, believing that only legislatures should fashion defenses, feel obliged to invalidate blackmail statutes on First Amendment grounds (*see*, e.g., State v. Robertson).

Extension of the Defense to Include Accusations of Criminal Conduct

We have seen that most blackmail statutes prohibit both threats to accuse others of *crimes* and threats to injure *reputations*. Among statutes that do so and that also contain defenses to blackmail, most statutory defenses apply to both types of threats (*see*, e.g., Ky. Rev. Stat. §§ 509.080(2), 514.080(2)). However, at least one statute provides no defense to actors who threaten that, unless they obtain redress, they will *contact criminal authorities* or otherwise *pursue criminal charges* against wrongdoers. Thus, California has held that it is extortion for retail company's attorney to tell a store employee who has been caught stealing goods that, unless the employee pays the owner as compensation, the store will criminally prosecute the employee for theft—the court declaring that "the law does not contemplate the use of criminal process as a means of collecting debt" (People v. Umana, pp. 638–41).

The two aforementioned rules—California's rule as well as the majority rule—both serve legitimate state interests. California's rule prevents persons from suppressing criminal prosecutions of criminal wrongdoers when wrongdoers are willing to provide them with civil redress.[13] The majority rule, in turn, embodies the view that criminal law may legitimately assist victims in recovering compensation[14] and that, given the costs and burdens of bringing civil suits for wrongs that are also criminal in nature, victims should be allowed to invoke the criminal process in order to obtain civil redress. In contrast, neither policy supports the Washington statute, which provides a defense to actors who threaten to accuse others of crimes but not to actors who threaten to expose others to hatred, contempt or ridicule (*see* Wash. Rev. Stat. §§ 9A.56.120(28)(d-e); 9A.56.130(2)).

Extension of the Defense to Include Threats of Disclosure Broader Than Needed for Legal Redress

The defendant in *State v. Gile* was the husband of the ex-daughter-in-law of a wealthy couple with several grandchildren. The defendant believed that his children had been sexually molested by two of the couple's other grandchildren. The defendant threatened the wealthy couple that unless the couple provided a home for him and his sexually molested children and provided therapy for his children, he would make the sexual molestation public by bringing a tort action against the couple's son and grandsons and disclose the molestation to every available media outlet, both local and abroad.

If the defendant in *Gile* had made the threat in Ohio, he would have had a defense because it is a defense to blackmail in Ohio that the actor's sole purpose was to redress a wrong. However, in the Kansas court in *Gile* held that the defendant's threatened disclosure exceeded what he had a right to threaten in order to obtain legal redress. He had a right, the court held, to threaten the couple that, unless they compensated his children for the wrong the couple's grandchildren had committed, he would bring a civil lawsuit that would expose the couple and their family to ridicule, contempt or degradation. But he had no right to go further and also threaten to contact "every available media outlet, local and abroad, with overwhelming evidence" of sexual abuse (State v. Gile pp. **18–19).

Extension of the Defense to Include Demands for Property in Excess of What Is Owed

Some jurisdictions provide that in order for a defendant to possess a defense to blackmail, his demand for property cannot exceed or, at least, not unreasonably exceed what he claims is owed to him. Others impose no such requirement. Thus, Tennessee provides a defense only if a person "reasonably believes" that he is entitled to the compensation demanded (Tennessee Code § 39-14-112(b)), while Arkansas provides a defense to a person who merely "claims" that he is entitled to the property demanded, without reference to the reasonableness of his claim (Ark. Code § 5-36-101(11)(ix)).

To illustrate the difference, consider *United States v. Jackson*, where Autumn Jackson, who claimed to be famous comedian Bill Cosby's illegitimate daughter from an extramarital affair, threatened to make her allegations public unless Cosby paid her US$40 million. Jackson would have had a defense in Arkansas, provided that she showed that she actually believed she was entitled to US$40 million of Cosby's wealth. However, she probably would have lacked a defense in Tennessee, just as she lacked one in the federal court that ruled that she did not "*reasonably* believe she ha[d] a claim of right" to the property demanded (p. 71).

Extension of the Defense to Include Demands for Action or Inaction Beyond Action to Redress Perceived Wrongs

We have seen that, in addition to making it an offense to use threats of disclosure to demand property, some jurisdictions also make it an offense (which they typically call "coercion") to use such threats to compel persons to take unwanted actions or inaction. Some of these jurisdictions also provide statutory defenses to making threats of disclosure in order to induce action or inaction.

Among such jurisdictions, some provide a defense to threats of disclosure to induce actions or inaction but only if the induced actions or inactions provide redress for past wrongs. Thus, Delaware confines its defense to coercion to actors whose sole purpose is to compel a targeted person to take "reasonable action to make good the wrong" that is the subject of the threatened disclosure (*see* 11 Del. Code § 792).

Other jurisdictions provide defenses to actors whose purposes go beyond redressing past wrongs. Thus, Connecticut makes it a defense to coercion to "compe[l] the other person to behave in a way reasonably related to the circumstances which were the subject of the [threatened disclosure]," including not only making good a "wrong done" but also "desisting from further misbehavior" (*see* Conn. Gen. Stat. § 53a-192(b)). And other jurisdictions make it a defense not only to act to redress past behavior or prevent future misbehavior but also to protect others from self-regarding harm. Thus, Pennsylvania provides a defense to actors who intend that another "refrain[n] from taking a[n] action or responsibility for which the actor believes the other disqualified" (18 Pa. Comp. L. § 18-2906(b)) and North Dakota provides a defense to an actor whose primary purpose is to "cause the other to conduct himself in his own best interests" (N.D. Cent. Code § 12.1-17-06(2)(a)).

An Actor's Belief in the Truth of Threatened Disclosures

As we have seen, blackmail threats are actionable without regard to the truth of threatened disclosures. Yet with respect to actors who make threats of disclosure for the alleged purpose of obtaining rightful redress, jurisdictions differ regarding whether, in order for the actors to possess a defense, they must believe the disclosures to be true. Thus, Connecticut takes the position that an actor lacks a defense to demands for action or inaction unless he "believe[s]" threatened accusations or revelations to be true (Conn. Gen. Stat. § 53A-192(b)), while North Dakota imposes no such requirement (N.D. Cent. Code § 12.1-17-06(2)). Consider, for example, an actor who, in order to compel another to pay a debt he owes, threatens to accuse the other of adultery of which the actor believes the other to be innocent. The actor would have a defense in North Dakota but not in Connecticut.

The MPC is strangely ambivalent on whether an actor must believe in the truth of threatened disclosures in order to possess a defense to blackmail. The

MPC requires such a belief of actors who claim a defense to demands for action or inaction, but it does not require such a belief of actors who claim a defense to demands for property (*compare* MPC § 212.5 (action or inaction) *with* MPC § 223.4 (property)). As a consequence, under the MPC, an actor may obtain property by threatening to make a disclosure that he does not believe to be true, provided that he honestly believes he is owed the property as compensation.

A Nexus Between the Subject of the Threatened Disclosure and the Property Claimed

Some statutes provide that, in order for a defendant to possess a defense to blackmail, a nexus must exist between the subject of his threatened disclosure and the property or action he demands. Other statutes require no such nexus. Thus, Alabama states that a defendant has a defense to extortion if the property he demands is claimed as restitution or indemnification for harm done in "the circumstances to which such accusation [or] exposure ... relates" (Code of Ala. §13A-8-15(b)). In contrast, Tennessee states that a defendant has a defense to extortion if the property he demands is appropriate restitution or indemnification for "harm done," regardless of whether the threatened disclosure concerns the property claimed (Tenn. Code § 39-14-112(b)(1)).

To illustrate the difference, consider *State v. Pauling*, where an ex-boyfriend tried to collect a debt from an ex-girlfriend against whom he had a default judgment by threatening her that unless she paid what she owed him, he would send nude photos of her to her neighbors. The ex-boyfriend would have a defense to blackmail in Tennessee because he used the threat to obtain what he claimed was owned him. But he would not have a defense in Alabama because the nude photos did not "relate" to whether his ex-girlfriend owed him money.

THE PARADOX OF BLACKMAIL

The paradox of blackmail is best illustrated by a crime that is not paradoxical, for example, the traditional offense of extortion. Extortion is not paradoxical because *both* what an extortionist threatens to do (e.g., murder, maim, assault, vandalize or otherwise criminally wrong another) *and* the verbal act of threatening to inflict such wrongs are themselves crimes. It is hardly surprising, then, that it is also a crime for an actor to use such criminal threats to extort property or conduct from another against his will.

Blackmail is different. Neither what a blackmailer threatens nor what he offers in lieu thereof and neither his threatening to disclose information nor offering to withhold disclosure is itself criminal. Thus, it is not a crime to truthfully accuse a person of a criminal offense; nor, with rare exceptions (*see* subsection "Broadening Extortion to Include Blackmail," *infra*), is it a crime to refrain from accusing person of a crime. Similarly, with rare exceptions (*see* "Conclusion," *infra*), it is neither a crime to disclose reputation-damaging information about a person, nor a crime to refrain from doing so. Nor, apart from those exceptional areas, is it a crime to utter unconditional threats or unconditional offers regarding any of the aforementioned disclosures or non-disclosures (e.g., "I intend to disclose photos of your love child to the *National Inquirer* by noon tomorrow, and there is nothing you can do about it"). Finally, it is not a crime to commercialize criminal or reputation-damaging information by selling disclosure on the open market. Yet it *is* a crime, that is, the crime of blackmail, to condition threats of disclosure and offers of silence on demands for property or conduct. The paradox of blackmail is said to be that the law makes it a crime for a person *to demand property or conduct from another by making conditional threats and offers of disclosure and non-disclosure, respectively, that are neither criminal in themselves nor criminal to announce as unconditional intentions.*

Commentators have grappled with the paradox for decades. To understand them, it is useful to recognize that blackmail demands for property or conduct fall into three distinct categories: (1) demands in return for suppressing accusations of crime; (2) demands in return for suppressing information that, from a legal standpoint, is not only private but also of insufficient interest to the public to merit disclosure; and (3) demands in return for suppressing information, the disclosure or suppression of which is legally discretionary, that is, information such that people's interests in favor of disclosure and people's interests in favor of suppression are in equipoise. As we shall see, blackmail demands in category (1) are not paradoxical because a blackmailer's act of making the demands transforms otherwise permissible silence regarding the existence of a crime into a public wrong. And blackmail in category (2) is not paradoxical because the disclosures which blackmailers threaten are civil wrongs, and criminal law is uniquely suited to deterring threats to make such disclosures. In contrast, criminalizing blackmail demands in category (3) remains both paradoxical and problematic.

The Public Wrong of Offering to Suppress Accusations of Criminal Wrongdoing in Return for Property or Beneficial Conduct

George Fletcher pointed long ago that there is nothing paradoxical about making it a crime to demand compensation for actions or inactions that persons are permitted to perform (Fletcher 1993, p. 1617). Examples are offers to engage in sexual intercourse for money and threats or offers by public officials to grant or withhold public services in return for personal gain. Persons are ordinarily permitted to engage or refrain from engaging in sexual intercourse, as they may wish, and public officials are often permitted to exercise discretion in granting or withholding public services. Nevertheless, it is a crime, that is, the crime of prostitution, to offer sexual intercourse in return for money, and it is the crime of extortion for a public official to threaten or offer to grant or withhold public services in return for personal gain. There is nothing paradoxical about criminalizing prostitution and extortion because communities can legitimately conclude that the quid pro quo of personal gain corrupts legitimate grounds for engaging in sexual intercourse and for granting or withholding public services, respectively.

The same analysis justifies blackmail statutes that make it a crime for a person to demand property or conduct in return for not accusing another of a crime. Many jurisdictions once possessed misprision-of-felony statutes but, with rare exceptions, they no longer do (*see* Westen 2012, p. 605, n. 83). Jurisdictions have allowed misprision-of-felony statutes to lapse because jurisdictions are reluctant to prosecute the very persons who are most likely to offend such statutes: namely, persons who fear retaliation if they make accusations; persons who naturally shrink from betraying family members or other intimates; and persons who dread the exposure and demands of being involved in the criminal process.

As Mitchell Berman has insightfully observed, however, the very act of demanding money or conduct in exchange for not accusing persons of crimes negates existence of these grounds for refraining from prosecuting misprision of felony: actors who threaten to accuse others of crime reveal themselves *not* to fear retaliation, *not* to shrink from any betrayal and *not* to dread the criminal process (*see* Berman 1998, pp. 833–51). On the contrary, they reveal themselves to be ready to assist the police in enforcing the law. Allowing an actor who is willing to inform the police of criminal wrongdoing to suppress the wrongdoing in return for a personal payoff is wrongful for the same reason that it is wrongful to allow an actor who is willing to testify to suppress sworn testimony in return for a personal gain. Both actors can be justly punished because both are willing for no legitimate reason to deprive the public of information of significant social value: both actors are willing to suppress information that the actors' very act of making conditional threats and offers reveals rightly belongs to the public, namely, the identity of criminal wrongdoers and sworn testimony on matters of criminal and civil justice, respectively, that the actors' manifest willingness to suppress or disclose depending upon receipt of personal benefits reveals to be information that the actors have no legitimate grounds to suppress.

The Public Wrong of Conditional Threats to Disclose Private Shameful Secrets of No Legitimate Interest to the Public

The defendant in *People v. Payne* secretly videotaped sexual encounters with numerous men whom she had enticed into sexual liaisons and then threatened to disclose the videotapes unless the men paid her up to US$50,000 to suppress them (*see* "More Victims"). The defendant *Regina v. Rose* threatened to reveal "intimate" and "sordid" stories about his ex-girlfriend's sex life unless she paid him £200,000 (*see* "Ex-boyfriend"). The defendants in *Payne* and *Rose* would not have committed crimes if they had unconditionally disclosed the information they possessed.[15] Yet by making conditional threats of disclosure, that is, threats conditioned upon their not being paid, they ended up committing crimes of blackmail.

Contrary to what is often said, criminalizing conditional threats like those in *Payne* and *Rose* is not paradoxical, for two combined reasons. First, although unconditional disclosure of such information would not have been criminal, it would have been tortious. The defendant in *Payne* threatened her sexual partners' privacy by threatening to reveal embarrassing information about them that she had secretly accessed by an "intentional ... intrusion [that] would be highly offensive to a reasonable person" (Restatement (Second) Torts § 652B). The defendant in *Rose* threatened his sexual partner's privacy by threatening to reveal "private facts," the revelation of which would be both highly offensive to a reasonable person and of no legitimate concern to the public (*see* Restatement (Second) of Torts § 652D; Prosser 1960, pp. 392–98; Lake v. Wal-Mart Stores, Inc.). In addition, the two disclosures might have constituted the tort of intentional infliction of emotional distress (*see* Restatement (Second) of Torts § 312; State v. Pauling; Prezioso v. Thomas).

Second, although tort remedies may suffice for privacy and emotional-distress victims *once* disclosures are made, tort remedies are an inadequate remedy for blackmail. The tort remedy of damages is inadequate because, for most blackmail victims, their reputation is worth more to them in money than the monetary compensation they would receive in return for being deprived of it. And the tort remedy of injunctive relief is inadequate because, in order to bring a suit for injunctive relief, a blackmail victim would have to disclose the very information she seeks to suppress (*see*, e.g., Vafaie v. Owen (a blackmail victim must disclose her identity as a condition for suing to prevent disclosure)). Criminal condemnation and punishment by the state are appropriate protections for such blackmail victims because, given the extent to which blackmail victims fear reputation-damaging disclosures, victims are not likely to avail themselves of civil remedies that are theoretically available to them (Westen 2012, p. 603, n. 74).[16]

The Paradox of Criminalizing Blackmail Cases in Which Legitimate-to-Disclose Reputation-Damaging Information and Legitimate Reasons to Withhold it Are in Equipoise

Robert Halderman, a CBS employee, threatened CBS late-night talk show host David Letterman that, unless Letterman paid him US$2 million, Halderman would make public that Letterman had a history of sexual relations with female members of his talk show staff (*see* "David Letterman"). Given Letterman's status as a public figure and the public's legitimate interest in his late-night show, it would not have been a crime or a tort for Halderman himself to have unconditionally made Letterman's indiscretions public. Nor would it have been a crime or a tort for Halderman to conditionally offer to sell the information to a media organization, conditioned upon receiving sufficient remuneration. Nor, except possibly within a few jurisdictions (*see* "Relationship Between Threatened Parties and Victims of Threatened Disclosures", *supra*), would it have been a crime or a tort for Halderman to conditionally offer to sell exclusive rights to the information to a media organization that wished to suppress it. Nor, finally, would it have been a crime or a tort for Halderman to unconditionally withhold the information from the public out of regard for the privacy of all involved. Yet, paradoxically, it was a crime, and, indeed, one for which Halderman was sentenced to prison, for Halderman to try to sell Letterman exclusive rights to the information for a price that, for all Halderman knew, Letterman was willing to pay.

Commentators in law, economics and philosophy have long struggled with the paradox of punishing blackmail, including cases like Halderman's.[17] Some commentators deny the supposed contrast between blackmail and extortion, arguing that, like extortionists, blackmailers threaten their targets with harms that are wrongful in themselves.[18] Other commentators accept the contrast between blackmail and extortion. That is, they concede that blackmail laws criminalize threats to make disclosures that do not themselves wrongfully harm their targets yet seek to justify the prohibition by claiming that the act of black-mailing—the act of obtaining or attempting to obtain property of another by threatening to disclose reputation-damaging information—either itself operates to wrong persons, whether the wronged persons are the targets of the actor's threats (see, e.g., Shaw 2012), or independent third parties (see, e.g., Lindgren 1984), or has the effect of imposing net costs on society, whether the costs are social or economic (see, e.g., Ginsburg and Shechtman 1993), or does both (see Elhauge 2016). Still other commentators deny that the paradox can be either negated nor justified and, hence, conclude that blackmail should be decriminalized (see, e.g., Block and Gordon 1985).

Blackmail doubtless tends to have deleterious social and economic effects. But economic effects cannot account for popular intuitions that have long supported blackmail's criminalization (see Katz 1993, p. 1582). To justify the law's long-standing criminalization of blackmail like Halderman's against Letterman, one must show that it inflicts unjustified deontic harm. Like others, I doubt that such a showing has yet been made.[19]

The fact that criminalization cannot be normatively justified, however, does not mean it cannot be psychologically explained. The most plausible explanation, I believe, is that criminalization responds to the psychological intuition that underlies the Doctrine of Double Effect ("DDE"). DDE is a contested moral proposition regarding the effect of an actor's motive on the permissibility of his inflicting a harm that would otherwise be justifiable. DDE comes in various versions. However, a common formulation is that with respect to persons who are fully aware of what they are doing and otherwise act identically, the moral permissibility of their inflicting harms may depend upon whether inflicting harm is their reason for acting or merely a known consequence of what they purposely do.[20] To illustrate, DDE advocates would say that, even if it is morally acceptable for a tactical bomber pilot in a just war to purposely bomb an enemy munitions plant knowing that the ensuing blast will kill a certain number of nearby civilians, it may be morally unacceptable for a fellow pilot who is aware of the same facts to take the former pilot's place and purposely bomb the munitions factory in identical fashion and cause identical casualties for the subjective purpose of killing those civilians in order to demoralize the population (Kamm 2004, p. 666).

DDE, having ancient roots in the Catholic doctrine, evidently reflects people's shared intuitions regarding blackmail (*see* Robinson et al. 2010, p. 296). The doctrine also manifests itself from the earliest to the latest scholarly efforts to resolve the paradox of blackmail (Gordon 1993, pp. 1758–59). These efforts come in several variations, but they are identical in claiming that blackmailers like Halderman are wrong to conditionally threaten targets like Letterman with disclosure in the event their targets refuse to pay because their threatened disclosures are improperly motivated. One variation comes directly from DDE, claiming that the reason conditional threats render otherwise permissible disclosures impermissible is that in order to coerce their targets into paying, blackmailers necessarily reveal it to be their purpose to harm their targets in the event the latter refuse to pay rather than advance any good that disclosure serves (*see*, e.g., Gordon 1993, pp. 1758–59; Katz 1993, p. 1598; Rivlin 2015, pp. 405–413 (describing the theory without embracing it)). Another variation is that, even where blackmailers do not reveal their conditional purpose to be to harm their targets, their threats render otherwise permissible conduct impermissible because they conditionally threaten to inflict what they know to be justified harm without being motivated by justifying purposes: they know that their threatened disclosures will inflict reputational harm, and they know that the disclosures may serve public purposes, but they cannot claim to be motivated by those purposes because if they were so motivated, they would be revealing the information unconditionally (Sachs 2006, pp. 260–261; Lamond 1996, pp. 231–232). Still another variation is that, even where conditional threats do not reveal motives that render otherwise permissible disclosures impermissible, they reveal motives that render otherwise blameless actors criminally culpable (Berman 2006, pp. 785–795; Berman 1998, pp. 847–849, 854).[21]

These subjectivist rationales for criminalizing blackmail, and the intuitions that underlie them, depend directly or derivatively on the validity of DDE itself. That is true regarding subjectivist versions that claim that the wrongfulness of threatened blackmail disclosures results from blackmailers' threatening to purposefully harm their targets for refusing to pay. However, it is also true with respect to subjectivist variations that the claim that the wrongfulness or culpability of threatened blackmail disclosures results from blackmailers' threatening to inflict what they know to be justified harm without being motivated by justifying purposes. For if DDE is mistaken to claim that *acting with a malevolent purpose* to inflict what actors know to be justified harm renders the harm unjustified, one is also mistaken to claim that *failing to act with a beneficent purpose* renders such harm unjustified or renders persons culpable for inflicting it (Westen 2012, pp. 627–628).

Blackmail laws, at least as applied to cases like David Letterman's, are suspect because DDE itself is suspect. Most commentators today reject DDE, denying that the intuitions that animate DDE are grounded in reason (*see* authorities cited in Overland 2014, p. 482, n. 3). If these commentators are correct that DDE lacks a grounding in reason, then insofar as blackmail laws are predicted on intuitions that underlie DDE, blackmail laws and the intuitions that underlie them lack grounding in reason as well.

Conclusion

Blackmail is one of several offenses regarding threatened and actual disclosures of reputation-damaging information. Thus, it is a crime of "revenge porn" to intentionally post sexually explicit photos or videos of another online without the latter's consent (*see* "Revenge porn laws by state"). It is a crime of "harassment" to intentionally cause another substantial emotional distress by sending sexually explicit photos of him to friends or acquaintances (*see*, e.g., U.S. v. Osinger). It is a crime of "unauthorized use of private identifying information" to maintain a website for soliciting and posting photos and private information about persons until they pay to have the information removed (People v. Bollaert).

None of the first three crimes is paradoxical. Nor is it paradoxical to criminalize threats to commit the aforementioned crimes, nor paradoxical to make blackmail a crime when it consists of threats of criminal accusation or threats of reputation-damaging disclosures that are tortious in themselves. But it is paradoxical to criminalize blackmail when it consists of offers by actors to sell suppression of information that actors are free to suppress, free to disclose and free to disclose for a fee.

Notes

1. *See* Helmholz (2001, p. 35); McLaren (2002, pp. 12–13); Ginsburg and Shechtman (1993, p. 1851). The "Waltham Black Act" of 1722, which was enacted in response to a gang of extortionists who called themselves "blacks" and painted their faces black, further solidified the use of "black" as a pejorative description of extortion. *See* ibid. p. 1851. For an alternative etymology of the term, see Mackay (1888, pp. 11–12).
2. *See* D.C. Code §22-3252; Kan. Stat. §21-5428; 21 Okla. Stat. §1488; 13 Vt. Stat. §2651.
3. *See* N.C. Gen. Stat. §14-118; S.C. Code §16-17-640; Wyo. Stat. §6-2-402.
4. For the frequency with which "blackmail" is used in common discourse, see *Oxford English Dictionary* (n.d.). For the popular meaning of "blackmail," see how it is defined in Google, *Dictionary* ("the action, treated as a criminal offense, of demanding money from a person in return for not revealing compromising or injurious information about that person").
5. This is not to say that the paradox is confined to information blackmail. To the extent the paradox exists, it extends more broadly to include statutes that, like the Model Penal Code, make it an offense to obtain property of another by threatening to "inflict any … harm which would not benefit the actor." Model Penal Code §223.4(7); Conn. Gen. Stat. Ann. §53a-119(5)(I).
6. The term *with [B's] consent* is designed to distinguish extortion, which functions by inducing victims to cooperate for fear of the consequences, from robbery, which can function by brute force, as in purse grabbing or mugging (*see* In re Stanley E.).
7. Merriam Webster's Collegiate Dictionary (1997, p. 412) ("extortion"). Some jurisdictions extend extortion to include private individuals who, while possessing legal authority to act on behalf of others, threaten to use such authority to

obtain personal benefits for themselves rather than those they represent. *See* Oregon Rev. Stat. §164.075(1)(f) (extortion for a union leader to demand monies in return for not causing a labor strike, provided the leader demands money for the benefit of himself rather than for "the group in whose interest [he] purports to act").

8. *See* 18 U.S.C. § 873; Mass. Code § 265-25; Mich. Code § 750.213; Miss. Code §97-3-82(2); North Carolina Code §14-118; Vermont Code §13-1701.

9. A majority of states treat truth as a defense to libel and slander, though some require in addition that speakers act from good motives. *See* Note (1993) (arguing that requiring a truth-speaker to act with "good motives" violates *New York Times v. Sullivan*). In contrast, in the nineteenth century in England truth was not a defense to criminal libel. *See* Yehudai (2009, pp. 799–800).

10. *Compare* W. Va. §61-2-13 (grading based on success) *with* D.C. Code §22-3252 (no grading based on success). Other jurisdictions implicitly grade based on success by, first, *defining* blackmail in terms of success and, then, separately criminalizing *attempted blackmail* but punishing it less severely. *See*, for example, Code of Ala. §§13A-8-13, 13A-4-2.

11. Under the MPC, affirmative defenses shift burdens of production to defendants but not burdens of persuasion; see MPC § 1.12(2)(a). In some states, however, affirmative defenses shift both burdens to defendants. *See* Ohio Rev. Code §2901.05(A).

12. *See* Conn. Code §§53a-119 (larceny); 53a-192 (coercion); 53a-192(b) (defense to coercion); N.D. Cent. Code § 12.1-23-10 (theft); 12.1-17-06(1) (coercion); 12.1-17-06(2) (defense to coercion).

13. But see *State v. Pauling*, stating in dictum that victims of vandalizing property have a constitutional right to threaten criminal prosecution in order to obtain compensation.

14. Consider the common practice of conditioning reduced sentences on payment of restitution. *See*, for example, 18 U.S.C. §§ 3663-64 (the "Victim Witness Protection Act").

15. New York did not have a criminal statute against revenge porn at the time Payne acted.

16. Exceptions to this may be victims of libelous blackmail. Victims of threatened disclosures of *false* information may have an adequate remedy in civil court because in contrast to victims of threatened disclosures of true information, victims of threats of libel may welcome the opportunity to litigate the truth in public.

17. *See* Lindgren (1993, p. 1975) (describing blackmail as "one of the most elusive intellectual puzzles in all of law") and articles in 2016, 2015, 2012, 2011 and 2007, referenced in note 19, infra.

18. *See*, for example, Levy (2007, pp. 1082–84). Others, including this author, seek to *partially* negate the paradox's existence by arguing that some instances of blackmail are no different from extortion. *See*, for example, Feinberg (1988, pp. 240–258); Westen (2012, pp. 599–611).

19. For critiques of older efforts to resolve the paradox of blackmail, see Westen (2012, pp. 614–632); Christopher (2006, pp. 750–769); Berman (1998, pp. 799–832). For critical commentary on more recent efforts by Einer Elhauge (2016), Ram Rivlin (2015), James Shaw (2012), Mitchell Berman (2011) and Ken Levy (2007), see Westen (2018).

20. Thomas Aquinas appears to have such a case in mind in arguing that, when A̲ knowingly kills a person, B̲, who is wrongfully threatening his life, A̲'s conduct is permissible if A̲'s purpose is to defend himself but impermissible if A̲'s purpose is to kill B̲. *See* McMahan (1994, p. 211). But see Cavanaugh (1997, p. 109).

21. Ram Rivlin argues that even where conditional threats do not reveal motives that render otherwise permissible disclosures impermissible, they reveal motives that render any consequent transfer of hush money nonconsensual. *See* Rivlin (2015, pp. 418–423). For criticism of Rivlin's view, see note 19.

REFERENCES

STATUTES

11 Del. Code § 846 (2017).
13 Vt. Stat. § 1701 (2017).
13 Vt. Stat. § 2651 (2017).
17-A Me. Rev. Stat. § 355(2)(B) (2017).
18 Pa. Comp. Stat. § 2906 (2017).
18 Pa. Comp. Stat. § 3921 (2017).
18 Pa. Comp. Stat. § 3922 (2017).
18 Pa. Comp. Stat. § 3923 (2017).
18 U.S.C. § 3363 (2017).
18 U.S.C. § 3364 (2017).
18 U.S.C. § 873 (2017).
19 Del. Code § 792 (2017).
21 Okla. Stat. § 1488 (2017).
43 Eliz.. ch.13, § 2.
Alaska Stat. § 11.41.520(a) (2017).
Alaska Stat. § 11.41.530(b) (2017).
Ariz. Rev. Stat. § 13-1804 (2017).
Ark. Code § 5-13-208(a)(5) (2017).
Ark. Code § 5-36-101(11)(B) (2017).
Ark. Code § 5-36-102 (2017).
Burns Ind. Code § 35-45-2-1(d) (2017).
Calif. Gov. Code § 8313 (2017).
Calif. Pen. Code § 484 (2017).
Calif. Pen. Code § 518 (2017).
Calif. Pen. Code § 519 (2017).
Code of Ala. § 13A-4-2 (2017).
Code of Ala. § 13A-6-25 (2017).
Code of Ala. § 13A-8-1(14)(f) (2017).
Code of Ala. §§ 13A-8-15 (2017).
Code of Ala. § 13A-8-13 (2017).
Conn. Gen. Stat. § 53a-119(5) (2017).
Conn. Gen. Stat. § 53a-192 (2017).
D.C. Code § 22-3251 (2017).
D.C. Code § 22-3252 (2017).
Fla. Stat. § 836.05 (2017).

Hawaii Rev. Stat. § 707-764 (2017).

Hodges v. Gibson Prods. Co., 811 P.2d 151 (Utah 1991).

In re Stanley E., 81 Cal. App. 3d 415 (1978).

Iowa Code. § 711.4 (2017).

Kan. Stat. § 21-5428 (2017).

Ky. Rev. Stat.. § 514.080(2).

Ky. Rev. Stat. § 509.080(2) (2017).

La. Rev. Stat. § 14-66(A) (2017).

Lake v. Wal-Mart Stores, Inc., 582 N.W.2d 231 (Minn. Sup. Ct., 1998).

Landry v. Daley, 280 F. Supp. 938 (S.D. Ill., 1968), *rev'd on other grounds sub nom Boyle v. Landry*, 401 U.S. 77 (1969).

Larceny Act of 1861, § 44 (Eng.).

Libel Act of 1843, § 3 (Eng.).

Mass. Gen. L. ch. 265, § 25 (2017).

Mich. Comp. L. § 750.213 (2017).

Miss. Code § 97-3-82(2) (2017).

Mo. Rev. Stat. § 570.010 (2017).

Mo. Rev. Stat. § 570.030 (2017).

Mo. Rev. Stat. § 588.011(6) (2017).

N.C. Gen. Stat. § 14-118 (2017).

N.C. Gen. Stat. § 15A-1340.23(c) (2017).

N.D. Cent. Code § 12.1-17-06 (2017).

N.D. Cent. Code § 12.1-23-10(12) (2017).

N.J. Stat. § 2C:20-5 (2017).

Nev. Rev. Stat. § 205.320(3) (2017).

New York Times v. Sullivan, 376 U.S. 254 (1964).

Ohio Rev. Code § 2901.05(A) (2017a).

Ohio Rev. Code § 2905.11 (2017).

Ohio Rev. Code § 2905.12 (2017b).

Ore. Rev. Stat. § 164.075(1)(f) (2017).

People v. Bollaert, 248 Cal. App. 4th 699 (2016).

People v. Umana, 138 Cal. App. 4th 625 (2006).

Prezioso v. Thomas, 2000 U.S. App. LEXIS 7740 (4th Cir.).

R.I. Gen. Laws § 11-42-2 (2017).

Rev. Code of Wash. § 9A.56.120 (2017).

S.C. Code § 16-17-640 (2017).

State v. Gile, 2014 Kan. App. Unpub. LEXIS 209.

State v. Haugen, 392 NW2d 799 (N.D. Sup. Ct., 1986).

State v. Pauling, 108 Wash. App. 445 (2001), *rev'd on other grounds*, 149 Wn. 2d 1001 (2002).

State v. Robertson, 649 P.2d 569 (Ore. Sup. Ct., 1982).

State v. Strong, 167 Wash. App. 206 (Ct. App., 2012).

Tenn. Code § 39-14-112(b) (2017).

Tex. Pen. Code § 31.03 (2017).

U.S. v. Osinger, 753 F.3d 939 (9th Cir. 2014).

United States v. Jackson, 180 F.3d 55 (2d Cir. 1988), *rev'd on other grounds*, 196 F.3d 383 (2d Cir., 1999).

Vafaie v. Owens, 1996 Tenn. App. LEXIS 557.

W. Va. Code § 61-2-13 (2017).

Whimbush v. People, 869 P.2d 1245 (Colo. Sup. Ct. 1994).

Wyo. Stat. § 6-2-402 (2017).

American Law Institute. 1962. *Model penal code*. Philadelphia: American Law Institute.

———. 1965. *Restatement (Second) of torts*. Philadelphia: American Law Institute.

———. 1980. *Model penal code and commentaries*. Pt. 2, Vol. 2. Philadelphia: American Law Institute.

Annotation. 2017. Truth a defense to state charge of criminal intimidation, extortion, blackmail, threats, and the like, based upon threats to disclose information about a victim. *American Law Reports* 4th 39:1011.

Associated Press. 2007. More victims possible in L.I. sex blackmail case. Feb. 2.

Berman, Mitchell. 1998. The evidentiary theory of blackmail. *The University of Chicago Law Review* 65: 795–878.

———. 2006. Meta-blackmail and the evidentiary theory: Still taking motives seriously. *Georgetown Law Journal* 94: 787–812.

———. 2011. Blackmail. In *The Oxford handbook of philosophy of criminal law*, ed. John Deigh and David Dolinko, 37–105. Oxford: Oxford University Press.

Block, Walter, and Gary Anderson. 2001. Blackmail, extortion, and exchange. *New York Law School Law Review* 44: 541–561.

Block, Walter, and David Gordon. 1985. Blackmail, extortion and free speech. *Loyola of Los Angeles Law Review* 19: 37–54.

Cavanaugh, Thomas. 1997. Aquinas's account of double effect. *The Thomist: A Speculative Quarterly Review* 61: 107–121.

Christopher, Russell. 2006. Meta-blackmail. *Georgetown Law Journal* 94: 739–786.

Elhauge, Einer. 2016. Contrived threats and uncontrived warnings: A general solution to the puzzles of contractual duress, unconstitutional conditions, and blackmail. *The University of Chicago Law Review* 83: 503–584.

Feinberg, Joel. 1988. *Harmless wrongdoing*. New York: Oxford University Press.

Fletcher, George. 1993. Blackmail: The paradigmatic crime. *University of Pennsylvania Law Review* 141: 1617–1638.

Ginsburg, Douglas H., and Paul Shechtman. 1993. Blackmail: An economic analysis of the law. *University of Pennsylvania Law Review* 141: 1849–1876.

Google. *Dictionary*. https://www.google.com/search?source=hp&ei=d9J0W-TtGqjO jwTa067ADA&q=blackmail+definition&oq=blackmail+definition&gs_l=psy-ab.3..0 l9.3110.8556.0.8700.20.20.0.0.0.0.100.1585.18j1.19.0..2..0...1.1.64.psy-ab..1.1 9.1583...0i131k1j0i10k1.0.qf6NaEuYfIM

Gordon, Wendy. 1993. Truth and consequences: The force of blackmail's central case. *University of Pennsylvania Law Review* 141: 1741–1785.

Helmholz, R.H. 2001. The Roman law of blackmail. *The Journal of Legal Studies* 30: 33–52.

Kamm, Francis. 2004. Failures of just war theory. *Ethics* 114: 650–692.

Katz, Leo. 1993. Blackmail and other forms of arm-twisting. *University of Pennsylvania Law Review* 141: 1567–1615.

Lamond, Grant. 1996. Coercion, threats, and the puzzle of blackmail. In *Harm and culpability*, ed. A.P. Simester and A.T.J. Smith, 214–238. Oxford: Clarendon Press.

Levy, Ken. 2007. The solution to the real blackmail paradox. *Connecticut Law Review* 39: 1051–1096.

Lindgren, James. 1984. Unraveling the paradox of blackmail. *Columbia Law Review* 84: 670–717.

———. 1993. Blackmail: An afterword. *University of Pennsylvania Law Review* 141: 1975–1989.

Mackay, Charles. 1888. *A dictionary of lowland scotch.* Edinburgh: Ballantyne Press.

McMahan, Jeff. 1994. Revising the doctrine of double effect. *Journal of Applied Philosophy* 11: 201–212.

McLaren, Angus. 2002. *Sexual blackmail: A modern history.* Cambridge, MA: Harvard University Press.

Mish, Frederick, ed. 1997. *Merriam Webster's collegiate dictionary.* 10th ed. Springfield: Merriam Webster.

Note. 1993. The truth will not set you free in Nebraska. *Nebraska Law Review* 72: 1236–1274.

Overland, Gerhard. 2014. Moral obstacles: An alternative to the doctrine of double effect. *Ethics* 124: 481–506.

Oxford English Dictionary. n.d. 3rd ed. Oxford: Clarendon Press.

Posner, Richard. 1993. Blackmail, privacy, and freedom of contract. *University of Pennsylvania Law Review* 141: 1817–1848.

Prosser, William. 1960. Privacy. *California Law Review* 48: 383–423.

Revenge porn laws by state. http://criminal.findlaw.com/criminal-charges/revenge-porn-laws-by-state.html

Rivlin, Ram. 2015. Blackmail, subjectivity and culpability. *Canadian Journal of Law and Jurisprudence* 28: 399–424.

Robinson, Martin. 2013. Ex-boyfriend of Tamara Ecclestone found guilty of £200,000 blackmail plot to reveal her "intimate secrets." *Daily Mail*, February 25. http://www.dailymail.co.uk/news/article-2284229/Derek-Rose-ex-boyfriend-Tamara-Ecclestone-guilty-200-000-blackmail-plot.html

Robinson, Paul, Michael Cahill, and Daniel Bartels. 2010. Competing theories of blackmail. *Texas Law Review* 89: 291–352.

Sachs, Stephen. 2006. Saving Toby: Extortion, blackmail, and the right to destroy. *Yale Law & Policy Review* 24: 251–261.

Shaw, James. 2012. The morality of blackmail. *Philosophy and Public Affairs* 40: 165–196.

The Guardian. 2009. David Letterman foils $2 m sex blackmail plot. October. 2.

Westen, Peter. 2012. Why the paradox of blackmail is so hard to resolve. *Ohio State Journal of Criminal Law* 9: 585–636.

———. 2018. Critical Commentary. University of Michigan. http://www.umich.edu/~pkw/criticalcommentary

Yehudai, Chen. 2009. Information blackmail: Survived by technicality? *Marquette Law Review* 92: 779–828.

PART VI

Bribery

CHAPTER 7

Understanding Bribery

Deborah Hellman

What is bribery? And what makes bribery wrong, when it is wrong? Bribery involves an exchange of some sort, but of what sort? As most exchanges between people do not constitute bribery, we must identify the features that distinguish bribery from other exchanges. If a person offers a painter money for her painting and the painter agrees to sell the painting, the buyer doesn't bribe the painter to sell the painting. If a person offers her representative money for her vote on a proposed bill and the representative agrees to sell her vote, this is bribery. What distinguishes these cases? According to the dominant view, bribery involves an agreement that violates a professional or positional duty.[1] On this view, the second case is a bribe because the agreement violates the duty that the representative owes to her constituents to decide how to vote guided only by their interests (or something along these lines) rather than for the sake of personal financial gain. The painter, by contrast, has no obligation to restrict the reasons for which she decides to sell or not sell her own painting. Because this conception of bribery involves a violation of duty, bribery is *pro tanto* wrong. Violating one's professional or positional duties is wrong and thus so is bribery.

This chapter challenges the view of bribery as a violation of professional duty. Instead, it proposes an account of bribery according to which one of its central features is an exchange of goods of different types. It is for this reason that the exchange of money for a legislator's vote is bribery but an agreement between two legislators to exchange votes on bills that the other favors (logrolling) is not. Yet most exchanges of values of different types do not constitute bribery, as the money for art example described above makes clear. Rather,

D. Hellman (✉)
University of Virginia School of Law, Charlottesville, VA, USA
e-mail: dh9ev@virginia.edu

L. Alexander, K. K. Ferzan (eds.), *The Palgrave Handbook of Applied Ethics and the Criminal Law*, https://doi.org/10.1007/978-3-030-22811-8_7

bribery involves an exchange of goods of different types when the exchange across domains is prohibited by the relevant decision-maker. On this account, what distinguishes the sale of art for money from the sale of a legislative vote for money is the fact that the painter authorizes the first sale but the legislature forbids the second.

WHAT IS BRIBERY?

According to the dominant view, bribery involves an acceptance, or an agreement to accept, something of value in exchange for an act or omission, or an agreement to perform an act or omission, that violates a professional or positional duty. This duty is usually understood as a duty of loyalty. This loyalty-based account of bribery grounds bribery's wrongfulness in the violation of duty. In what follows, I argue that while bribery often involves a violation of professional or positional duties of loyalty, it need not. Some agreements to exchange something of value for acts that violate duties of loyalty do not constitute bribery, and some bribery involves no duty violation. Instead, I argue that bribery involves an exchange, or agreement to exchange, something of value from one domain for something of value from another. The central feature of this account is the crossing of a boundary between domains that a person, society, or institution has determined should be kept distinct. As exchanges between spheres of social life or domains of value are not in themselves wrong, the upshot of this boundary-based account of bribery is that bribery may not be inherently wrong. Whether it is wrong will depend on how we understand the concept of the relevant decision-maker. Does positive law or social practice determine who is the relevant decision-maker? Or do moral considerations determine who occupies this role? Either way, when bribery is wrong, its wrongfulness derives from diverse sources on the account presented here. In addition, the boundary-based account of bribery makes two important normative questions salient. First, what exchanges should be avoided and second, who decides the answer to the first question?

Bribery as a Violation of Professional or Positional Duty

Stuart Green offers the most carefully articulated version of this dominant view. Green defines bribery in the following way:

> X (a bribee) is bribed by Y (a briber) if and only if: (1) X accepts, or agrees to accept, something of value from Y; (2) in exchange for X's acting, or agreeing to act, in furtherance of some interest of Y's; (3) by violating some duty of loyalty owed by X arising out of S's office, position, or involvement in some practice. (Green 2005, p. 145)

This account seems appealing because it appears to explain why quintessential examples of corrupt exchanges constitute bribery and why they are wrong. Consider the following example which we might call *Classic Bribe*.

Classic Bribe: X, the owner of a business located within the district of Y, an elected official, calls Y and says the following: "If you promise to vote "no" on bill A (which would be detrimental to X's business), I will give you a large sum of money that you can use for whatever you like." Y answers: "Great, I accept."

According to Green, elected officials owe a duty to their constituents to act in ways that further the interests of their constituents. If he is right about this,[2] then it is easy to see that *Classic Bribe* is a bribe and that the reason it is wrong is that Y has agreed to vote for the bill in order to get the money rather than because the bill at issue would advance the interests of Y's constituents. In addition, bribery statutes generally target exchanges with people who have such positional duties, thus enhancing the plausibility of Green's account.[3]

Green emphasizes that an agreement violates the duty of loyalty owed by the elected official to constituents even in cases where what the official agrees to do (here, vote on a bill) would *in fact* be in the interests of the constituents. If Y votes for the bill because X has paid him to do so, rather than because the bill would help his constituents, then Y has violated his duty of loyalty to his constituents, according to Green.

This feature of the duty-based account of bribery opens the view up to significant problems. On this view, a well-motivated elected official cannot commit bribery. Consider the following example:

Practical Politician: X, an elected official, is running for reelection against an independently wealthy challenger, Y, who has promised to spend millions of her personal fortune to defeat X. Z, an equally wealthy private individual, offers to spend her own personal fortune on advertisements in support of X if X will agree to support an issue favored by Z. X accepts the offer, reasoning as follows: "My policies will benefit my constituents far more than Y's would. If I support the issue Z wants me to, I do so because, overall, this will benefit my constituents as I will thereby get the spending of Z and more likely win the election."

This example illustrates a fatal problem of the duty-based account. An official who accepts money for official action *because* she believes the receipt of the money will benefit the person or group to whom she owes the duty of loyalty does not commit bribery. For elected officials who honestly believe that their own election will benefit their constituents more than the election of their opponents, the duty-based account seems to allow such politicians to make all sorts of deals that certainly seem like bribes.

Perhaps the duty-based account can be rescued by modifying the manner in which we understand the duty of loyalty. For Green, what mattered was whether the official acted in a manner that she believed was in the best interests of constituents. Instead, we might say that the official complies with her duty of loyalty so long as she actually acts in her constituents' interests. This modification is not likely to be helpful. It may correctly label some practical politicians as guilty of bribery but not necessarily all. When the politician at issue is correct in her assessment that her constituents are better off overall in the world in which she accepts the payment and gets elected, there will be no breach of the duty of loyalty and thus no bribery.

In addition, there may well be instances in which an official, X, agrees to accept something of value from Y, in exchange for X's agreeing to act in furtherance of some interest of Y which violates a duty of loyalty that X owes Y, understood *objectively*, yet which does not seem to be bribery. Consider the following example:

> *Campaign Promise*: X, a legislator up for reelection, makes a speech at a campaign event in which she says: "If you promise to vote for me in the next election, I promise not to raise your taxes." At the end of the speech, Y, a voter attending the event approaches X and says, "great, I accept."

In this example, X accepts something of value from Y (a promise to vote for X) in exchange for X's promise to act in furtherance of some interest of Y's (not raising Y's taxes). Thus, whether or not this case in an instance of bribery depends, according to the duty-based account, on whether or not raising Y's taxes actually is in the interests of X's constituents. If not raising taxes violates the duty of loyalty that X owes her constituents because the tax revenue is needed, then this case would be an instance of bribery, according to that account. This result also seems incorrect.

Consider another example.

> *Logrolling Legislator*: X, a legislator of one party says to Y, a legislator of another party: "I will vote yes on bill A if you will vote yes on bill B." Y, the second legislator, agrees.

Here too, if the deal between X and Y does not serve the interests of the constituents of either party *in fact* (even if X and Y believe it does), then the duty-based account (understood in objective, rather than subjective, terms) would consider this case to be bribery. This result also seems incorrect.

The duty-based account of bribery fails because we must interpret the duty of loyalty that grounds the account either subjectively or objectively. If the duty permits X to do anything that she *honestly believes* will serve the interests of those to whom she owes the duty, it would seem to countenance (or mislabel)[4] clear instances of bribery. If we understand the duty objectively such that it requires X to do what in fact serves the interests of those to whom it is owed, the account fares no better. Where accepting what looks like a bribe does serve constituent interests overall, the objective version of the account also appears to leave out clear cases of bribery. At the same time, the objective account would label many exchanges that the official mistakenly believes serve her constituents' interests, but which objectively do not, as bribery, including campaign promises and legislative logrolling, which seems inapt.

Defenders of the duty-based account might object that what matters is not whether the politician acts for good reasons overall, but instead what matters is his or her proximate reason for action. In *Practical Politician*, X accepts Z's offer in order that Z will spend her money in support of X. While X believes that this expenditure of money will make X's reelection more likely and that her reelection will benefit her constituents, it would be hard to argue that X believes her proximate reason for action on its own will benefit her constituents. And so, Green and the defenders of the duty-based account might argue that once we focus our attention on the proximate reason for action, *Practical Politician* poses no problem for that account.

This reply generates its own problems, however. If we focus on the proximate reason for action, rather than the wider reason for action, then *Logrolling Legislator* becomes an instance of bribery. The *Logrolling Legislator* doesn't believe that the bill she agrees to support benefits her constituents. Instead, she believes the deal as a whole is beneficial. Her agreement to support it thus violates the duty of loyalty she owes to her constituents. If she agrees to vote on a bill in violation of her duty of office in exchange for another legislator's vote on a bill she favors, she thus commits bribery.

In response, one is tempted to reply that the legislator does not violate her duties of office if she believes that the deal (the exchange of votes) will benefit her constituents. However, if we accept that this legislator can bundle the two acts together when assessing whether the combination will benefit her constituents, the same approach will be open to *Practical Politician*, and we are back where we began.

Defenders of the duty-based account might reply that the *Logrolling Legislator* doesn't commit bribery, even if she violates her duty of office, because she receives no personal benefit. This line of argument also has problems. It is difficult to delineate a *personal* benefit from one that is not *personal* in instances where professional success is also personally beneficial, as is often the case. Consider *Practical Politician* again. Z offers to spend money in support of X, an elected official. Is this spending a personal benefit to X? It seems it is, even though none of the money goes into X's own pocket. If one is tempted to say that *Logrolling Legislator* does not commit bribery because she does not personally benefit, it seems that one would have to conclude the same thing about a *Practical Politician*.

Alternatively, perhaps the logrolling example is not a counter-example to the duty-based account but instead a data point in support of it. Maybe *Logrolling Legislator* is an instance of bribery. Several states prohibit logrolling either by statute or via their state Constitutions and some even define it as bribery.[5] In my view, this approach is a mistake. *Campaign Promise* illustrates the fact that there is a gap between the violation of professional duty and bribery. An agreement by a legislator to take a position in exchange for the votes of her constituents may well violate her duties of office. Yet, it seems odd to call this exchange bribery, at least in my view. If this is correct, this suggests that state prohibitions on logrolling are better explained as grounded in the view that these exchanges violate legislative duty rather than that they constitute bribery.

Bribery as an Exchange Across Boundaries

The mischaracterizations of *Campaign Promise* and *Logrolling Legislator* (if the reader shares my intuitions about that case) provide a clue as to what is missing from the duty-based account of bribery. Take the campaign promise first. A campaign promise is an agreement by an elected official (or prospective elected official) to exchange an official act for a voter's vote. While the return promise by the voter to vote for the official does benefit the official and the promise by the official to vote a particular way may violate the official's duty of loyalty to her constituents (depending on how one conceives of this duty),[6] this agreement does not seem like bribery because a voter's vote for the elected official and an official's vote for a piece of legislation are species of the same genus, to speak metaphorically, or are both acts within the domain of politics. The *Logrolling Legislator* is similar. To exchange a vote on one bill for a vote on another is to exchange two things of the same type. This observation leads to a hypothesis. Perhaps the reason these agreements do not constitute bribery is because bribery requires that the exchange, or agreement to exchange, be of something of value from one domain for something of value from another. Call this view the "boundary-crossing theory of bribery" because it requires that the exchange at issue cross a boundary between different types of goods or domains of value.[7]

Bribery requires that the values exchanged be of different types. An exchange of money for a vote *can* be an instance of bribery because money is a different sort of good than a vote. An exchange of a vote for a vote (logrolling) cannot because the things exchanged are valuable in the same domain. It was for precisely this reason that Judge Easterbrook rejected the claim that the former Governor of Illinois, Rod Blagojevich, solicited a bribe when he asked President-elect Barack Obama to appoint Blagojevich to the President's Cabinet in exchange for Blagojevich appointing Valerie Jarrett to fill the Senate seat vacated by Obama.[8] The judge reasoned that "a proposal to trade one public act for another, a form of logrolling, is fundamentally unlike the swap of an official act for a private payment."[9] Judge Kozinski made a similar point in a concurring opinion in *United States v. Dorri*, explaining that "[a] judge, for instance, wouldn't be acting corruptly if he conditioned a shorter prison sentence on payment of restitution for the victim; but he would if conditioned the lower sentence on defendant's cutting the judge's lawn."[10]

While bribery requires a crossing of boundaries or an exchange of goods of different types, not all such exchanges constitute bribery. Consider the following case.

Ordinary Sale: A painter (P) signs an agreement with an art gallery owner X which provides that X will endeavor to sell P's painting and that if she succeeds in doing so, X will retain 30% of the purchase price. Y is a prospective art purchaser who enters X's gallery and admires P's painting. Y offers to pay X the price marked in exchange for the painting, with the understanding that X will keep some part of that amount and give the rest to P.

Ordinary Sale is an agreement to exchange money for a piece of art—values that arguably belong in different domains. Yet, clearly this agreement does not constitute bribery. The boundary-crossing account must be supplement by another element. An agreement across boundaries only constitutes bribery when the relevant decision-maker has prohibited such boundary crossing. In this case, we presume, the artist has authorized it.

Bribery as an Exchange Across Boundaries Prohibited by the Relevant Decision-Maker

As *Ordinary Sale* illustrates, an exchange of different values only constitutes bribery when prohibited by the relevant decision-maker. To see the importance of this criterion, consider the following pair of cases.

> *Greedy Official and Unqualified Applicant*: X is an admissions officer at a public university. Y is an applicant. The university's president, together with a committee of faculty and administrators, has determined the admissions procedures and set the admissions criteria. Y recognizes that if the University applies these criteria, she is unlikely to be accepted. As a result, Y approaches X and offers to pay X a sum of money to gain admission. X accepts.
>
> *Confused Official and Unqualified Applicant*: X is an admissions officer at a public university. Y is an applicant. The admissions procedures are the same as in *Greedy Official*. Y recognizes that if the university applies these criteria, she is unlikely to be accepted. So, Y approaches X and offers to donate a large sum of money to the university in exchange for admission. X is unsure what to do and so consults with the university president. The president decides that accepting this offer is in the best interests of the university and directs the official to accept the "gift" and admit the student.

Greedy Official is a clear instance of bribery. Two different types of goods are exchanged (money for admission) and this exchange is prohibited by the relevant decision-maker, as the setting of admissions criteria implicitly excludes other criteria (or so we suppose). But what about *Confused Official*? What makes this case difficult, at least in part, is the ambiguity about whether the president of the university is the relevant decision-maker. Can she alone determine whether this exchange is permissible? Or is this a decision for the Board of Trustees or for the faculty?

Suppose that the university's regulations make it clear that the president of the university has unilateral authority to determine what admissions criteria the university should employ. If so, her decision in *Confused Official* to supplement the prior criteria with an additional one—admission should be granted in exchange for large donations to the university—makes this case *not* an instance of bribery. Yet still, it would not be odd for faculty at the university who learned of the president's decision to complain that the university accepted a bribe. Why? The faculty might respond this way because they believe that the president made the wrong decision, that she should not have permitted such an exchange. They use the term "bribery" to signal their view that this exchange across domains *ought* to be prohibited.

Greedy Official and *Confused Official* differ in an important way that bears emphasis. In *Greedy Official,* the official is the one who accepts a bribe. In *Confused Official,* it is the university that arguably does so. The boundary-crossing account of bribery permits institutions themselves to be bribed; the duty-based account does not. If one thinks that an institution, like a university, can itself accept a bribe, this is another reason to reject the duty-based account.

These examples also illustrate how discussions about bribery take place in either a descriptive or a normative voice. When we ask whether the relevant decision-maker has drawn a boundary forbidding exchange between two domains, we are asking about whether such exchanges are permitted by relevant decision-makers. This is a descriptive question. However, the relevant decision-maker himself or herself must make a judgment about whether to permit the exchange and so engages in a normative inquiry to determine how to draw such lines. Sometimes we call something "bribery" in order to say that we think the relevant decision-maker has made the wrong choice.

The following example illustrates this fusion of descriptive and normative ways of discussing bribery.

> *Worried Parent:* X is the parent of Y, a procrastinating high school student. X is worried that if Y persists in his habits of putting off his homework, he will earn poor grades in school and have few opportunities. X offers to pay Y $10 for each A grade and $5 for each B he receives on all quizzes and tests. As a result, Y changes his behavior and begins to do well in school. When X is asked by friends how she managed this turn around in Y's behavior, she responds "I bribe my kid to get good grades."

Does X bribe Y to get good grades, or does she merely pay him?[11] According to the boundary-crossing view of bribery, the answer to this question depends on the answer that *the relevant decision-maker* provides to *the normative question* of whether exchanges between the academic domain and the market are permissible. As a preliminary matter, one must first ask whether this is an exchange between goods of different domains. If the answer is yes, as it appears to be, one must go on to ask whether the exchange is permitted by the relevant decision-maker. There are two place holders in this account, each of which must be filled in to determine whether *Worried Parent* bribes her teen. The first question is *who decides* whether the parent may pay money to her child in exchange for good academic performance. The answer to this question depends on normative questions about the scope of parental rights. I will assume, plausibly, that it is the parent who properly makes this decision. The second question is descriptive: Does the relevant decision-maker allow the exchange? When the parent describes her own conduct as a "bribe," she asserts (assuming she means this remark seriously) that payment is the wrong sort of reward for academic accomplishment and thus that in some sense she makes the wrong decision when she offers payment to her child in exchange for study.[12]

If the relevant decision-maker, in this case the parent, determines that exchanges across these domains are appropriate, then this payment is not a bribe. As the parent is the one paying, she seems to have clearly authorized it. And yet, she describes the payment as a bribe. In so doing, she simultaneously asserts that she makes a mistake of some kind in paying her child for grades. The parent thus exploits the ambiguity of her status as both the person authorized to make the decision (and thus to determine if the payment is a bribe) and the critic who regards the exchange as one that ought not to be permitted (and thus as a bribe).

While the descriptive and the normative questions are conceptually distinct inquiries, in practice people will often fuse them. For example, education critic Alfie Kohn argues that grades bribe kids to do well in school (Kohn 2011). When he describes grades as bribes, he isn't claiming that school officials, who have the relevant authority to determine whether grades should be awarded for academic performance or not, have in fact forbidden this "exchange." In other words, he isn't making a descriptive claim. Rather, he is engaging in the normative argument about whether a boundary should be drawn between the domain of learning and any external reward.

Similarly, a critic of the current campaign finance regime might describe campaign contribution as bribes. For example, in August 2015, Senator Bernie Sanders exhorted: "Let us be frank, let us be honest, the current political campaign finance system is corrupt and amounts to legalized bribery" (Carney 2015). Again, Sanders isn't making a descriptive claim about what exchanges the relevant decision-makers have, in fact, forbidden. Rather he is asserting that Congress or a state legislature should forbid contributions of the size or kind at issue because these contributions induce official actions and so should be prohibited.[13]

Is Prostitution Bribery?

The boundary-based account seems too capacious. If any exchange of goods of different types that is prohibited by the relevant decision-maker constitutes bribery, it seems that prostitution is bribery and illegal organ sales are bribery. While this result may seem to doom the boundary-crossing account, these seeming counter-examples are not as devastating as they might initially appear. Indeed, as others have noted, including Michael Sandel and Michael Walzer, there is a core of similarity between these offenses (Walzer 1983, p. 9). We may reserve the term "bribery" for a subset of offense of this type but there is a family resemblance among them.

What Makes Wrongful Bribery Wrong?

The wrongfulness of wrongful bribery derives from different and varied sources. According to the boundary-crossing account, bribery requires an exchange across boundaries that is forbidden by the relevant decision-maker. But who is the relevant decision-maker? There are two ways to understand this idea. The relevant decision-maker could be determined by positive law and by the social practices of the society. Alternatively, the relevant decision-maker could be understood in normative terms—such that the decision-maker has moral authority or such that others have a moral obligation to defer to the decisions of this person or entity about what exchanges are prohibited.

If the relevant decision-maker has the authority to make the decision at issue, this can be for several different reasons. The wrongfulness of wrongful bribery can then be traced to these different sources. If legislatures prohibit the exchange of money for official actions of various types, such exchanges constitute wrongful bribery for democratic reasons. Both the briber and the bribee have reasons to defer to elected officials that rest on commitments to democracy. If a university president prohibits the exchange of admissions for donations to the university, and an admissions official accepts such an offer nonetheless, the official acts wrongly because she has a professional or contractual obligation to defer to the judgment of the university president on this matter. If a parent prohibits paying her children for good grades but a grandparent pays the children over the parent's objection, the wrongfulness of this bribe relates to the interference with parental rights. And so on.

In addition, bribery can be wrong for reasons that have their source in violations of professional duty (as the duty-based account envisions) or in violations of the internal norms of an institution or valued practice. When bribery violates professional duty, it may be wrong for this additional reason. But not all violations of professional duty constitute bribery.

Bribery is sometimes wrong and sometimes not. An agreement to exchange goods of different types that is forbidden by a decision-maker to whom the briber has an obligation to defer is wrong. An agreement to exchange goods of different types that is forbidden by a decision-maker to whom the briber has no obligation to defer could be wrong but need not be. When bribery is wrong, its wrongfulness comes from different sources. It might be wrongful because it violates professional duty. It might be wrongful because democratic decision-makers have prohibited it. It might be wrong because it corrupts the internal norms of a valued institution and so on.

Key Ancillary Normative Questions

A claim that an exchange constitutes bribery gives rise to two questions. First, are the goods exchanged of different kinds or types, as understood in that society? Second, if they are different, has the relevant decision-maker prohibited or forbidden their exchange? However, there are two ancillary normative questions to which this analysis gives rise. First, who is the relevant decision-maker? Second, should that decision-maker permit or prohibit the exchange? Many of the debates about whether particular cases are or should be considered to be instances of bribery focus on these normative questions.

Who Is the Relevant Decision-Maker?

We already saw how this issue can become important and subject to disagreement in *Confused Official*. Can a university president himself or herself determine what the admission criteria are? If so, then *Confused Official* is not an instance of bribery. If not, perhaps it is. The real-world case of the bribery prosecution of the former Governor of Virginia Robert McDonnell also illustrates the importance of this question. In 2016, a unanimous Supreme Court vacated the conviction of McDonnell on charges of bribery.[14] The problem, according to the Supreme Court, lay with the jury instructions. Those instructions permitted the jury to convict McDonnell if they found *either* that McDonnell had agreed to set up meetings between a businessman and relevant government officials in exchange for various goodies (including paying for McDonnell's daughter's wedding and shopping trips for his wife) or that McDonnell had pressured or directed the government officials to make a particular decision. The statute at issue prohibited the exchange of something of value for an "official act," so the jury instructions were acceptable only if the proper understanding of that term included both parts of the instructions (i.e. setting up meetings and pressuring officials to make decisions). Interpreting the statute, the Court determined that while directing or pressuring a government official is an "official act," setting up a meeting with a government official is not.

For the most part, the Supreme Court's decision in this case rests on an exercise of statutory interpretation. As such, the reason that sale of access does not constitute bribery is that Congress has not proscribed this exchange, in the Supreme Court's view. But there is a suggestion in Chief Justice Roberts' opinion that a legislature could not criminalize the sale of access without running afoul of the Constitution.[15] If this is indeed his view, he is asserting that the Constitution sets limits on what exchanges a legislature may prohibit.

This example illustrates that answering the question of who the relevant decision-maker is may well require normative analysis. In *Worried Parent*, it depends on a theory of the family. In *Confused Official*, it depends on a theory of the university. And in *McDonnell*, it depends on US constitutional theory.

How Should the Relevant Decision-Maker Decide?

As we have seen, sometimes, controversy arises because critics object to the exchanges the relevant decision-maker has decided to permit. Should parents or teachers pay kids for good grades? Should universities accept large "donations" in exchange for lowering admissions standards for the children of these donors? Should legislatures permit the sale of access to public officials? While the relevant decision-maker is the one whose decision on each of these questions determines whether each case is an instance of bribery, that decision is open to criticism. Our "bribery talk" sometimes fuses the descriptive question (Has the relevant decision-maker permitted the exchange?) with the normative question (Should she?). The critic who objects to what the relevant decision-maker has permitted or prohibited sometimes calls the transactions "bribes," in order to signal disagreement with the decision-maker's determination.

REMAINING CONCEPTUAL QUESTIONS

In this final section, I address three conceptual questions related to the law of bribery that have arisen in either case law or legal scholarship. First, must the briber derive a personal benefit from the exchange or is the fact that he or she agrees to the exchange of values all that is required? If we use the language of *quid pro quo*, we can restate this question by asking whether the *quid* must personally benefit the briber. Second, how specific must the *quo* be? This issue arises in the context of what are termed "stream-of-benefits" cases in which, at the time of the alleged bribe, the recipient of the bribe (the bribee) has not specified what, precisely, she or he will do for the briber. Third, bribery is often equated with the concept of a *quid pro quo* exchange. In other words, something of value must be given or received *for* something else. What is not emphasized is the presence of an agreement to exchange the *quid* for the *quo*. Is a *quid pro quo* without an agreement sufficient for bribery or do cases and commentators err by insufficiently stressing the importance of a promise or agreement?

Is a Personal Benefit Necessary?

If X and Y make an agreement in which Y agrees to give *a* to X and X agrees to do *b*, should we inquire as to whether X's doing *b* benefits Y? Stuart Green's definition of bribery, while not crystal clear on this point, appears to make personal benefit an element of the offense. In his definition, "(1) X accepts, or agrees to accept, something of value from Y; (2) in exchange for X's acting, or agreeing to act, in furtherance of some interest of Y's" (Green 2005, p. 145). The main federal bribery statute, 18 U.S.C. § 201, also emphasizes the idea of the briber's personal gain but adds that the briber may also be acting for another person or entity. According to this statute, "whoever, being a public official or person selected to be a public official, directly or indirectly, corruptly demands, seeks, receives, accepts, or agrees to receive or accept anything of value personally or for any other person or entity, in return for being influenced in the performance of any official act"[16] commits bribery.

Why is it necessary to include the element of personal benefit? If Y gives X value in exchange for X's act, must we also ascertain whether this act is in Y's interest? Either the fact of the exchange serves to demonstrate that the act serves Y's interest, in which case we don't need this element, or the element has independent force. But if it has independent force, then it would seem to require that we rule out as bribery some exchanges that do not in fact serve the briber's interest. Consider the following example:

> *Ill-conceived Exchange*: Y is the owner of a pharmaceutical company which has several new drugs that it wishes to bring to market. In order to do so, rigorous and expensive testing is required. X is the Governor of a state and as such has authority to determine whether the state universities will pay for and conduct studies on various drugs (let us suppose). Y offers to pay the expenses for the extravagant wedding of X's daughter if X will direct the state's flagship university to conduct studies on drug A, the drug Y believes is most promising. X agrees. The studies demonstrate that A is without benefit. Had the exchange not taken place, and the drug's potential remained unclear, Y would have been able to sell his company for much more than he can now. Alternatively, had the exchange not taken place, independent scientific review would have selected another of Y's drugs to evaluate and the result would have been more promising.

The deal in *Ill-conceived Exchange* does not actually benefit Y. But surely Y's mistake about his own benefit does not render the exchange not bribery.

It thus appears that actual benefit to the briber (or a third party for whom the briber acts) is not necessary. Instead, all that is required is that Y acts in furtherance of a benefit for himself or another as he perceives it. If this is correct, it is hard to see why this is a necessary element. The fact that Y makes an agreement with X is sufficient to demonstrate this.

The Specificity of the Quo?

Courts have not required that the *quo* for which the briber gives value be clearly specified.[17] Rather, a commitment to provide benefits as the occasion arises has been sufficient. Consider the following example:

> *Stream of Benefits*: Y, the Chief Executive of a company that produces air pollution offers to pay X, a Congressman, a sum of money if X will vote against any proposed bills that increase the stringency of the air quality regulations. X agrees.

This result, while correct in my view, has been seen as a difficult case due to the fact that the Supreme Court, in both campaign finance cases and the *McDonnell* bribery case, has emphasized that "ingratiation and access" do not constitute corruption.[18] The issue here is distinguishing a mere gift, which may well engender return favors, and a bribe. A grateful politician who expresses his gratitude for campaign contributions from a coal company executive by voting against bills that would regulate air quality is not guilty of bribery. The reason that he is not, however, is because the two have not entered into an agreement (explicit or implicit) to exchange the campaign contribution for favorable votes as they arise. Admittedly stream-of-benefits bribery cases and gifts that engender return favors resemble each other in the following respect. The benefits received by briber/donor are not specified in both instances. However, this similarity is not sufficient to determine that both are permitted. When the *quid* the alleged briber gives to the public official is a campaign contribution, the courts have insisted that there be an agreement to exchange the contribution for some *quo*. However, they have not insisted that the *quo* be specified.

This issue was specifically addressed in *United States v. Menendez*.[19] Senator Menendez argued that the Supreme Court's decision in *McDonnell* undermined the stream-of-benefits theory of bribery. The District Court did not accept this argument: "A reading of the Supreme Court decision [in *McDonnell*] reveals an absence of definite conflict between the now-limited definition of official acts of a public official, and the stream of benefits theory, a tool long used to prosecute bribery charges against public officials."[20]

When the agreement is implicit rather than explicit, the campaign gift which is followed by favorable action by a public official and the bribe look even more similar. But what distinguishes the two scenarios, at least in theory, is the fact that in the first case, there is an agreement, albeit implicit. Thus, the fact finder must determine that the briber or bribee intended to form an agreement in order to be guilty of bribery.

Quid Pro Quo *Versus Agreement*

The criminal law of bribery and the constitutional law governing campaign finance require that one be able to distinguish a legitimate campaign contribution from a bribe. Both bodies of doctrine rest on the premise that a difference exists. In addition, constitutional law increasingly insists that campaign finance regulation that limits the amounts of money that people can give to candidates is only permissible when it is needed to prevent what the Court terms "*quid pro quo* corruption." This aspect of the doctrine suggests that the Court believes that bribery is distinguished from a legitimate campaign contribution by the presence of a *quid pro quo* exchange. Is this correct? Consider:

> *Ingratiating Campaign Contribution*: Y, the Chief Executive of a coal company, regularly makes large campaign contributions to X, an elected official. Each of these contributions is properly reported and within legal limits. Y makes these contributions because X has been a supporter of policies favored by Y and beneficial to the coal industry. Y intends the contributions to have the effect of inducing X to continue to support these policies. In fact, Y includes a note with his last contribution which reads as follows: "Thanks so much for your support of coal. I hope you will continue to support this great American industry!"

Is *Ingratiating Campaign Contribution* a bribe?[21] Under current law, it clearly is not. Yet equally clearly, there is a *quid pro quo*. Y provides the contribution in order to induce X to continue to support goal. In other words, the contribution is given *for* the official action or actions. What is missing is a promise by X to accept the contribution in exchange for the action.

While the criminal bribery cases recognize that an agreement is required in addition to a *quid pro quo* exchange when the *quid* at issue is an otherwise legal campaign contribution, the campaign finance cases are unclear on this point. Yet it is elementary from the law of contracts that consideration (the *quid pro quo*) and promise are distinct elements. If the term *"quid pro quo* corruption" is meant to include more than bribery, this might explain why. While I think *quid pro quo* corruption ought to include the *Ingratiating Campaign Contribution*, so that campaign finance laws intended to prevent the gratitude such contributions give rise to would be permissible, I do not think the current Supreme Court shares this position. If that is correct, the doctrine should focus on agreements rather than merely on the presence of a *quid pro quo*.

Conclusion

On the dominant view, bribery involves an agreement to exchange things of value in a manner that violates a professional or positional duty. This chapter argues against that view. Instead it proposes that bribery involves an agreement to exchange values of different types. But not all boundary-crossing exchanges constitute bribery. Agreements to exchange values of different types constitute bribery when they are prohibited by the relevant decision-maker. This account has two variants—one descriptive and one normative. If the relevant decision-maker is determined by positive law or social practice, then bribery is a non-moralized concept. If the relevant decision-maker is determined by moral considerations, then bribery is a moralized concept. On either account, the relevant decision-maker herself has an important decision to make. Should such exchanges be prohibited or permitted? The answer to this question depends on many and varied moral concerns. For this reason, bribery can be wrong for many different reasons.

Notes

1. On this account, the definition of bribery also includes other elements, but the duty violation is one of its central features.
2. There are multiple ways of understanding the duty that elected officials owe to constituents. For example, some accounts focus on constituent interests (as does Green's), while others focus on constituent preferences.
3. Those with the positional duties targeted by bribery statutes include sports officials (N.Y. Penal Law § 180.40 (Consol. 2000)), bank officers (18 U.S.C. App. § 2B4.1), lawyers and doctors (Fla. Stat. § 838.15), and witnesses (18 U.S.C. § 201 and Wis. Stat. Ann. § 946.61 (West 2015–16)).
4. It is not exactly clear whether the duty-based account is an account of what bribery *is* or if it is an account of what makes bribery wrong.
5. Examples of such states include Colorado (Colo. Const. art. 5, § 40), Wyoming (Wyo. Const. Art. 3, § 42), and North Dakota (N.D. Const. art. 4, § 9).

6. Whether the legislator's promise not to raise taxes does violate her duty to her constituents depends, in part, on how one understands those duties. Depending on whether one understands the duty as requiring the legislator to do what the constituents want or instead what the legislator believes to be in the interests of the constituents, this promise might violate the legislator's duties. For a discussion of several ways to understand how these factors interrelate, see Hellman (2017, pp. 1965–70).

7. For similar accounts of bribery as involving exchanges across domains of value, see Sandel (2012), see also Alldridge (2000).

8. United States v. Blagojevich, 794 F.3d 729 (7th Cir. 2015).

9. Blagojevich, 794 U.S. at 734.

10. 15 F.3d 888, 894 (9th Cir. 1994). For a discussion of how the boundary-crossing account better explains why plea bargaining is not bribery, see Hellman (2017, pp. 1947–1992).

11. Sandel discusses a similar example (Sandel 2012, p. 78).

12. This view is consistent with the parent holding the view that while paying kids for good grades bribes them, nevertheless, paying for good grades is the right thing to do, all things considered. Of course the parent might not mean the comment seriously. However, even in this case, the fact that this language functions metaphorically in the way that it does is illuminating.

13. Under current law, an agreement to exchange a campaign contribution for an official act does constitute bribery, see Evans v. United States, 504 U.S. 255 (1992) and McCormick v. United States, 500 U.S. 257 (1991), but a contribution that merely induces official action (without an implicit or explicit agreement) likely does not constitute bribery. This question isn't definitively settled because bribery statutes themselves do not require an agreement and in fact explicitly state that a "gift, offer or promise" of something of value for an official act constitutes bribery. Yet, when the thing of value being offered for the official act is a campaign contribution, courts insist on an agreement rather than simply that the contribution is given *for* (i.e. in order to induce) the official action. For an analysis of the distinction between *quid pro quo* and an agreement, see Hellman (2017, pp. 1958–1961).

14. McDonnell v. United States, 136 S. Ct. 2355 (2016). McDonnell was charged under four statutes, among them 18 USC § 201, which prohibited bribery. The Supreme Court remanded the case after setting parameters for the definition of "official act," and the government subsequently dropped the charges.

15. Ibid. at 2372 (suggesting that a definition of "official act" that includes setting up meetings will lead to a situation in which "officials might wonder whether they could respond to even the most commonplace requests for assistance, and citizens with legitimate concerns might shrink from participating in democratic discourse").

16. 18 U.S.C. § 201(b)(2)(A).

17. *See* United States v. Malkus, 696 Fed.Appx. 251 (9th Cir. 2017); United States v. Repak, 852 F.3d 230 (3d Cir. 2017); United States v. Bruno, 661 F.3d 733 (2d Cir. 2011); United States v. Bradley, 173 F.3d 225 (3d Cir. 1999).

18. Citizens United v. Fed. Election Comm'n, 558 U.S. 310, 360 (2010).

19. 291 F.Supp.3d 606 (D.N.J. 2018).

20. Ibid. at 613.

21. This, under 18 U.S.C. § 201(c)(1)(B), would still be considered an illegal gratuity. Illegal gratuities do not require an intent to influence or be influenced, and thus there does not need to be a *quid pro quo* for an official to be charged with violating the statute. The requirement is that an official receives something of value "for or because of any official act." *See*, for example, United States v. Verrusio, 762 F.3d 1 (D.C. Cir. 2014) (where the defendant, former policy director of the House Transportation Committee, violated the gratuities statute by accepting comped travel, hotel stays, and World Series tickets from a lobbying group which were offered because of his work on a federal highway bill).

References

18 U.S.C. § 201.

18 U.S.C. App. § 2B4.1.

Citizens United v. Fed. Election Comm'n, 558 U.S. 310, 360 (2010).

Colorado Const. art. 5, § 40.

Evans v. United States, 504 U.S. 255 (1992).

Fl. Stat. § 838.15.

McCormick v. United States, 500 U.S. 257 (1991).

McDonnell v. United States, 136 S. Ct. 2355 (2016).

N. Y. Penal Law § 180.40 (Consol. 2000).

North Dakota Const. art. 4, § 9.

United States v. Blagojevich, 794 F.3d 729 (7th Cir. 2015).

United States v. Bradley, 173 F.3d 225 (3d Cir. 1999).

United States v. Bruno, 661 F.3d 733 (2d Cir. 2011).

United States v. Dorri, 15 F.3d 888, 894 (9th Cir. 1994).

United States v. Malkus, 696 Fed.Appx. 251 (9th Cir. 2017).

United States v. Menedez, 291 F.Supp.3d 606 (D.N.J. 2018).

United States v. Repak, 852 F.3d 230 (3d Cir. 2017).

United States v. Verrusio, 762 F.3d 1 (D.C. Cir. 2014).

Wisc. Stat. Ann. § 946.61 (West 2015–16).

Wyoming Const. Art. 3, § 42.

Alldridge, Peter. 2000. *Relocating criminal law*. Dartmouth: Dartmouth Publishing Company.

Carney, Jordain. 2015. Bernie Sanders to fight for campaign finance reform. *The Hill*. http://thehill.com/blogs/ballot-box/presidential-races/250187-sanders-campaign-finance-system-amounts-to-legalized. Accessed 26 Feb 2019.

Green, Stuart P. 2005. What's wrong with bribery? In *Defining crimes: Essays on the special part of the criminal law*, ed. Antony Duff and Stuart P. Green, 143–165. Oxford: Oxford University Press.

Hellman, Deborah. 2017. A theory of bribery. *Cardozo Law Review* 38: 1947–1992.

Kohn, Alfie. 2011. The case against grades. http://www.alfiekohn.org/article/case-grades/?print=pdf. Accessed 20 July 2018.

Sandel, Michael J. 2012. *What money can't buy: The moral limits of markets*. New York: Farrar, Strauss and Giroux.

Walzer, Michael. 1983. *Spheres of justice: A defense of pluralism and equality*. New York: Basic Books, Incorporated.

PART VII

Civil Disobedience

CHAPTER 8

Civil Disobedience, Punishment, and Injustice

Candice Delmas

From the Birmingham Bus Boycott to the Freedom Rides in the Jim Crow South, from the anti-Vietnam War student protests to Act Up (AIDS Coalition to Unleash Power), civil disobedience has played a crucial role in bending the proverbial arc of the moral universe and remedying injustice. This valuable role is widely recognized, at least in democratic states. Martin Luther King, Jr., has a national holiday named after him, and children celebrate the Civil Rights movement during Black History Month. This recognition of the value of civil disobedience tends to rest on a twofold contrast between civil and criminal disobedience, on the one hand, and civil and revolutionary disobedience, on the other.

Civil disobedients are thought to be neither ordinary criminal offenders acting for their own profit nor revolutionary actors bent on overthrowing the state. On the standard understanding of civil disobedience, agents break the law publicly, openly, nonviolently, and with the intention of persuading the public to change certain laws or policies. They exhibit seriousness, discipline, and selflessness. In contrast, criminals typically break the law covertly and for self-interested reasons; they evade punishment and use or threaten force. Revolutionary actors, like civil disobedients, are moved by moral and political principles to break the law, and they, too, often seek to address the community. However, revolutionaries share with criminals their willingness to use violence and their evasion of punishment. Crucially, on this standard account, civil disobedients are supposed to accept (while criminals and revolutionaries reject or don't care about) the legal system's legitimacy, and thereby to manifest respect for the rule of law, where criminals and revolutionaries show none.

C. Delmas (✉)
Northeastern University, Boston, MA, USA
e-mail: c.delmas@northeastern.edu

© The Author(s) 2019
L. Alexander, K. K. Ferzan (eds.), *The Palgrave Handbook of Applied Ethics and the Criminal Law*, https://doi.org/10.1007/978-3-030-22811-8_8

Even thus demarcated from criminal and revolutionary disobedience, civil disobedience is deemed presumptively impermissible in decent, democratic societies, given the moral duty to obey the law. It can nonetheless be justified under certain circumstances to protest against systematic, deeply entrenched injustice (such as clear violations of the basic equal liberties principle, on John Rawls's (1999) account). Justified or not, civil disobedience is liable to legal punishment. Civil disobedience, Hugo Bedau noted, "is not just done; it is committed. It is always the sort of thing that can send one to jail" (Bedau 1961, p. 654). And sending one to jail it has: antislavery abolitionists, feminist suffragists, civil rights workers, gay rights activists, anti-abortion campaigners, and Occupy demonstrators, along with countless others, have been arrested, prosecuted, fined, and imprisoned. Over 35,000 anti-nuclear activists were arrested between 1983 and 1992 in the United States, under charges of trespass or disturbing the peace (Lippman 1994, p. 345).

Many people don't see any tension between the democratic appreciation of civil disobedience and its punishment. After all, civil disobedients break the law; and their sacrificial acceptance of punishment is often deemed crucial to their power of moral suasion, as the canon of civil disobedients' prison writings (e.g., King's "Letter from a Birmingham Jail") and trial speeches (e.g., Nelson Mandela's "I Am Prepared to Die") indicates. This view nonetheless begs the question: is it right to punish civil disobedients? For if civil disobedience is (sometimes) morally justified, then engaging in it is (sometimes) not wrongful, and so there is (at least then) nothing to punish (*see* Sandalow 1969).

This tension between the punishment and justification of civil disobedience becomes clear when one considers the criminal law's function, which is to punish and prevent crimes, that is, *wrongful* conduct. Unlike civil wrongs, which are privately brought, criminal wrongs are public wrongs: the polity, not the victim (there may not be any), prosecutes them. Punishment, depending on one's overarching account, serves to dissuade people from committing the types of conduct identified as wrongful (Bentham 1907), appropriately respond to those who culpably commit them (Moore 1997), and/or express the community's moral disapproval of such conduct (Feinberg 1965). So, one way to answer the question whether it is right for states to punish civil disobedients is to determine whether civil disobedience is a public wrong that people ought not to engage in and that the community is right to condemn. If so, then criminal punishment (assuming certain constraints such as proportionality are met) may be found to be an efficient means toward a worthwhile end—deterring civil disobedients; an appropriate response to agents' culpably engaging in it; and/or a way to express the community's warranted disapproval of civil disobedience.

The first part of this chapter surveys the prominent positive, then negative answers to that very question, whether the state should punish civil disobedience, focusing on two concerns—stability and democracy—that are central to US courts' stated rationales for punishing civil disobedients. The second part examines "non-evasion," the requirement that civil disobedients accept punishment, which I take to demand that the agent (1) willingly submit to arrest and prosecution, (2) plead guilty in court, (3) not try to defend her crime, and/or (4) not complain for the punishment received. After presenting the scholarly debates on pleas and defenses, I put forth some instrumental and intrinsic reasons in favor of evasion of legal sanctions. While philosophical and legal discussions focus on these two questions—should the state punish civil disobedience? and should civil disobedients accept punishment?—the third part takes a step back to ask anew: how *should* we think about civil disobedience? In the concluding section, I will uncover the presuppositions behind the common theoretical approach to the "problem" of civil disobedience.

Should the State Punish Civil Disobedience?

"Yes"

There are well-known reasons for treating civil, not just criminal, disobedience as a kind of public wrong against the polity. Socrates formulated several such reasons, in the voice of the Laws of Athens personified, in Plato's *Crito* (2002, 46b–50a). They include the notion that Socrates ought to be grateful for the benefits he received from Athens and that he tacitly consented to submitting to all the polity's laws by being a resident and citizen of Athens. Both these arguments serve to establish a moral duty to obey the law that makes his contemplated escape from jail wrong. For Socrates, this duty is absolute. For contemporary theorists, it is defeasible: countervailing moral reasons sometimes outweigh it.

Socrates advances two other arguments that still resonate loudly today, and which I'll focus on. One is that disobedience, even civil, is wrongful because it destabilizes society; the other is that civil disobedience is impermissible in democracies that afford citizens lawful avenues of dissent. On these bases, Socrates denies that (even civil) disobedience can ever be justified. Many officials and theorists nowadays concede that civil disobedience can be morally justified, while maintaining the need to criminally punish civil disobedients, on the basis of arguments very much like Socrates'.

Stability

The Laws of Athens begin their oration by painting the act of disobedience contemplated—Socrates' escape from jail—as an act intended to "destroy us" (Plato 2002, 50b). On this first argument, disobedience, be it criminal or civil, is wrong and cannot be tolerated because it destabilizes society and invites anarchy. It does so both through example, by signaling to others that anyone can disobey if they feel the urge, and in principle, by expressing disrespect for law's authority. The conscientious and principled character of civil disobedience does not preclude its destabilizing tendency, on this view. On the contrary, if everyone were to violate the law each time one finds it unjust, society would be thrown into a disorder akin to the state of nature.

One familiar version of this argument brings us to Hobbesian shores. It goes something like this: the state cannot achieve its rights-preserving function without political stability; stability requires universal compliance with the law; disobedience (even civil) undermines political stability; disobedience (even civil) thus hinders the state's rights-preserving function; and disobedience (even civil) must therefore be punished. Of course, the state can withstand *some* disobedience without descending into chaos, contra the second premise—but the idea is that civil disobedience invites its own proliferation and escalation (uncivil and criminal disobedience), and, basically, that the state can only withstand so much disobedience. Criminal punishment, here, is primarily a matter of deterring actual and would-be civil disobedients so as to protect stability.

A second version of the objection paints disobedience as an impermissible and dangerous expression of contempt for the legitimacy of the legal order: it risks destabilizing society and "destroying" the legal system (to use the Laws' phrase) by eroding its authority. Justice Abe Fortas (1968), for instance, viewed civil disobedience, which he only referred to as "open lawlessness" in this early essay (thereby suggesting that civil disobedients' openness could be worse than criminals' covert lawbreaking in being more disrespectful and provocative), as a great societal menace and one of the gravest "dangers to the rule of law." Civil disobedience is thus wrongful conduct and appropriately condemned as such. Criminal punishment is then conceived as retribution toward those who culpably flout the rule of law and hinder the state's rights-preserving function.

Concerns about political stability pervade the jurisprudence of civil disobedience in the US. Judges in the nineteenth century sometimes raised the specter of Southern states' secession and invoked the need for political stability to defend their harsh prosecution of Abolitionists who broke the law to aid slaves to escape or reach safety (Lippman 1994, p. 323). Judges claimed that violating slaveholders' property rights was the first step on a slippery slope to anarchy and systematically privileged these property rights over slaves' rights to life and liberty. One judge wrote a propos the deliberate violation of the Fugitive Slave Act by Abolitionists:

> When every man may transgress a law with impunity because he dislikes it, our government will have become a vain mockery, not worth preserving, for it will have ceased to afford protection to the rights either of property or of life. (United States v. Cobb)

Court decisions especially in the South of the United States, but also in the North, are replete with such attempts to rationalize the harsh treatment of Abolitionists and ignore the horrors of chattel slavery by appealing to the state's mission to protect rights.

The judicial approach to civil disobedience did not change much after the Civil War, as Lippman (1994) has shown. Civil rights activists protesting the racial caste system were painted as dangerous, seditious "rabble-rousers," endangering political stability and undermining the rule of law with their disobedient activities. In *Walker v. Birmingham*, the Supreme Court put respect for judicial process above all else, as it upheld the arrests of activists, including Martin Luther King, Jr. and Ralph Abernathy, for their decision to march in violation of Birmingham's injunction, even though the court admitted the injunction in question would not have withstood constitutional scrutiny. The ruling described activists as "impatient" and implied they were "uncivil, disrespectful, and dangerous" (*see* Sarat 2014, p. 304). The Court's reasoning was that by refusing to abide by a court order—albeit an unjust and unlawful one issued out of racist animus—activists disrespected the judiciary and jeopardized the social order.

Legislatures also tend to respond harshly to widespread civil disobedience. Southern legislatures met anti-segregation protests with new bills outlawing civil rights groups and curbing the right to peaceful assembly. In the wake of a string of mass protests covering everything from police brutality to the inauguration of President Trump, at least 31 US states have considered over 60 anti-protest bills, all in the name of public order and safety. North Dakota enacted a new bill (HB 1293) expanding the scope of criminal trespass, which civil disobedients engaged in sit-ins are often charged with. Florida's HB 1419 (ultimately defeated) would have criminalized the obstruction of traffic during an unpermitted demonstration and eliminated civil liability for a driver who unintentionally injures or kills a protestor interfering with traffic during an unpermitted demonstration. Georgia successfully passed a bill mandating sanctions for campus protesters (SB 339), and Missouri now bars certain public employees from picketing (HB 1413). Clearly, concerns for law and order still weigh heavily in the balance against civil disobedience; and they are often used to rationalize its harsh treatment.

Democracy

According to the Laws of Athens (Plato 2002, 51b–c), "whether in battle or in a court of law, or in any other place, he [Socrates] must do what his city and his country order him; or he must change their view of what is just." Socrates had the opportunity to do the latter during his trial before a jury of his peers (the legislature and judiciary are one and the same assembly in Athens). But since he failed to persuade them that he was innocent of the charges brought against him, he must now "endure the punishment in silence": "If not persuaded, [the polity shall be] obeyed."

One plausible interpretation of this second central argument deems civil disobedience a proper object of punishment because of its anti-democratic nature: it flouts democratic decision-making processes. The "persuade or obey" argument, as it is dubbed, assumes that democratic procedures are in place, which give citizens meaningful opportunities to dissent and to seek legal reforms. When and to the extent that there are such opportunities, there can be no liberty right to civil disobedience. In Justice Fortas's view (1969), by protecting voting rights and freedom of speech, the US Constitution affords citizens effective—and sufficient—means of protesting governmental policies with which they disagree. The Laws of the United States might thus say, like those of Athens: persuade the community to change us or obey us. Civil disobedience cannot be tolerated where the constitution affords citizens legal, democratic ways of protesting.

Officials and judges often argue that laws can only be altered through the democratic process, however slow and ponderous the latter may be, and that any unlawful attempt to bypass this process endangers it. An appellate court faced with defendants who had seized and intended to destroy registration cards from a Selective Service office (they were convicted of "willfully and knowingly attempting to hinder and interfere with the administration of the Military Selective Service Act of 1967 by force, violence, and otherwise") brought together the stability and democracy concerns thusly:

> We counsel only that the fabric of our democratic society is fragile, that there are broad opportunities for peaceful and legal dissent, and that the power of the ballot, if used, is great. Peaceful and constant progress under the Constitution remains, in our view, the best hope for a just society. (United States v. Kroncke)

Another version of the democratic argument draws the wrongfulness of civil disobedience from what it represents and expresses, even when it is otherwise socially beneficial. The idea is that civilly disobedient agents are guilty of a form of moral self-indulgence: they accord themselves a larger say in public matters, objectionably taking the law into their own hands and making themselves an exception to prevailing rules (Cohen 1971, pp. 138–145; Weinstock 2016, p. 709). Civil disobedients claim, in effect, to better understand what the public good requires than do their fellow citizens. Justice John Paul Stevens expressed this sentiment in a 1971 case involving the religiously motivated burning of draft registration cards in protest against the war in Indochina:

> One who elects to serve mankind by taking the law into his own hands thereby demonstrates his conviction that his own ability to determine policy is superior to democratic decisionmaking. Appellant's professed unselfish motivation, rather than a justification, actually identifies a form of arrogance which organized society cannot tolerate. (United States v. Cullen)

Civil disobedience betrays a kind of arrogance because it appears like an assertion of moral superiority, a way to say, "I know better than everyone else what is right and wrong." It is wrong, presumably because it neglects the democratic ideal of lawmaking as a collective enterprise and reflects one's misplaced sense of entitlement.

These arguments from stability and democracy thus support the notion that civil disobedience constitutes a special kind of public wrong in democracy, which the state is correct to punish—as deterrent, retribution, and expressive condemnation. Meanwhile, theorists who want to concede the value and justification of civil disobedience, while still defending its punishment make a proceduralist argument based on courts' proper functions. The idea is that even if civil disobedience is justified and socially valuable, it is not courts' job to distinguish between just and unjust law (or between law that is or isn't subject to reasonable disagreement) or between justified and unjustified acts of civil disobedience. Courts are to determine what the law says and apply it impartially, treating like cases alike (at least from the perspective of criminal law). For instance, in a case involving an Abolitionist defendant, one court insisted that it was not judicial province "to consider abstract principles in regard to slavery. We deal with legal rights and established law. From these we cannot depart, without a violation of our duty" (Driskill v. Parrish). Per the federal separation of powers, the legislative assembly is the one tasked with the work of making and changing laws, whereas courts are to focus on the letter of the law, without considering the moral merits or demerits of established law. Hence, courts' neutrality is supposed to provide a weighty, pragmatic reason for punishing and not attempting to evaluate civil disobedience.

"No"

Others, however, insist civil disobedience is a public *good* that should be, if not praised, at least tolerated, but not punished.

Stability

Some theorists deny as fallacious the concerns underlying the stability arguments. Howard Zinn (2002), for instance, stressed that the stability of oppressive legal orders is a bad thing, that the latter don't deserve any respect, and that mass civil disobedience to unjust law (contra the worry with proliferation) is a valuable tool to help close the gap between legality and justice. Citizens ought not to respect the rule of law when it is the rule of unjust law, in Zinn's view, and civil disobedience can both highlight its injustice and undermine it.

But most theorists take both law-and-order and rule-of-law objections seriously. Their strategy has been to show that *civil* disobedience reduces, even disarms, its disruptive potential. Thus, Rawls stresses that civil disobedients violate the law but act "within the limits of fidelity to law." He contends:

> The law is broken, but fidelity to law is expressed by the public and nonviolent nature of the act, by the willingness to accept the legal consequences of one's conduct. This fidelity to law helps to establish to the majority that the act is indeed politically conscientious and sincere, and that it is intended to address the public's sense of justice. (Rawls 1999, p. 322)

Publicity (as openness and communicativeness), nonviolence (which is key, for Rawls, to constituting the disobedient act as a speech-act), and non-evasion (i.e., acceptance of legal sanctions) are what makes disobedience *civil* and thereby defuse its destabilizing potential. The act also accords with decorum: the agent seeks to be respectful in her behavior and tone even as her act is transgressive. Civil disobedience is thus defined and identified in a way that signals a concern with political stability. Rawls further orients his account of the justificatory conditions of civil disobedience toward minimizing the disruptive effects of civil disobedience by requiring that the act (1) target a serious injustice (preferably involving a denial of citizens' equal basic liberties), (2) be undertaken as a last resort, and (3) be coordinated with other groups with similar grievances (Rawls 1999, pp. 326–328). For Rawls, then, agents must carefully weigh their resort to civil disobedience, choosing it reluctantly, as it were, and taking great precaution to avoid its proliferation.

While Rawls sought to neutralize the stability argument against disobedience, other theorists go further by putting the argument on its head. In response to the rule-of-law concern in particular, some theorists have argued that, far from undermining the stable system of rights, civil disobedience can instead strengthen it. For Hannah Arendt (1970), what really disrupts social order is not civil disobedience; it is instead the state's exclusion of certain groups from the political association, since it makes rebellion inevitable. And so, mass civil disobedience always occurs under unstable political circumstances and ultimately steadies society by reenacting the horizontal social contract and strengthening civic bonds.[1] Far from destabilizing society, civil disobedience can thus help correct injustice and reinvigorate democracy. Incorporating Arendt's republican insights into Rawls's liberal model, William Scheuerman (2018) highlights civil disobedience's fidelity to law, which imposes constraints on the lawbreaking conduct (including nonviolence and publicity) and seeks to deepen law's legitimacy and efficacy. In his view, rather than undermining it, civil disobedience buttresses the rule of law.

Ronald Dworkin (1968, 1985) conceived of the civil disobedients of his time as challenging the constitutionality of racial segregation and the Vietnam War (while later finding that anti-nuclear activism failed in this regard). In Dworkin's view, it is crucial that civil disobedients articulate legal arguments and show their actions to be grounded in a plausible interpretation of the law. Civil disobedients, like judges, engage in constitutional disputes. Contra the rule-of-law concern, he thus argued that civil disobedience tests positive law by appealing to the spirit of the law, and contributes in that way to law's integrity and stability.

These responses to the stability concerns debunk the state's general casting of civil disobedience as a public wrong. In doing so, they seriously challenge the appropriateness of punishing its practitioners, as we shall see in a moment.

Democracy

Liberal philosophers like Rawls highlight civil disobedience's potential to enhance justice, against flawed democratic majoritarian decisions (*see also* Bedau 1961; Cohen 1966; Dworkin 1985; Sabl 2001). Although they generally concede its anti-democratic character, their arguments, nonetheless, help weaken the anti-democratic blow. In particular, these champions of civil disobedience allay the charge of moral self-indulgence, by stressing that the agent who follows the strictures of civility communicates that she is neither disobeying lightly nor taking advantage of others' compliance with the law. Theorists and practitioners alike have highlighted the significant burdens and risks incurred by civil disobedients. These include legal sanctions, such as arrest, fines, and imprisonment; social sanctions (e.g., employer retaliation, community ostracizing); and extralegal risks to one's life and physical integrity, especially from mobs and police.

Theorists have struck other parts of the democratic edifice against civil disobedience. They have challenged the supposedly democratic character of decision-making procedures in societies like ours, thus contesting that the latter successfully generate the "persuade or obey" imperative. They have argued that civil disobedients often denounce and seek to correct serious democratic deficits, including curtailed avenues of political participation (e.g., Markovits 2005; Smith 2013; Delmas 2018, ch.3). Robin Celikates (2014) contends that civil disobedience offers a "dynamizing counterweight to the rigidifying tendencies of state institutions" and constitutes a form of democratic empowerment. Arendt (1970) finds that civil disobedient groups are formed with "the same spirit" that informed political and civic voluntary associations earlier in US history and that they strengthen mutual trust by enacting a public space in which people, as free and equal citizens, act and deliberate together. Democratic and republican theorists thus paint civil disobedience as instrumentally valuable, given its potential to correct democratic deficits and intrinsically valuable, given its democratic nature.

To recap, champions of civil disobedience have shown, against its detractors, that civil disobedience can make society more stable, reinforce the rule of law, correct injustice and democratic deficits, heighten legitimacy, and even express democratic sovereignty. Together, these rationales evince the value of civil disobedience and rebut its characterization as a kind of public wrong: it suggests that those who engage in it should be praised or at least tolerated—and certainly not punished. What does this imply exactly for how the state should treat civil disobedients?

Implications

Officials at all levels have the discretion to *not* sanction civil disobedients, and they should use it. The police have no obligation to arrest them when they commit minor violations of the law. As the Burlington police chief noted the day after University of Vermont student protests, "blocking traffic is a violation of the law that police officers have the discretion to enforce based on their experience, judgment and the totality of the circumstances" (Del Pozo 2018). He justified his department's decision not to make any arrests thusly: "When the reason people are blocking traffic is to engage in political protest on matters of great interest to the community, officers are required to be judicious in the use of their powers to remove protesters from the road" (ibid.). In this vein, William Smith (2013, ch.5) defends a "policing philosophy," which orientates law enforcement strategies toward accommodation rather than prevention or management of civil disobedience. On this view, "the police should, where possible, cooperate with civilly disobedient activists in order to assist in their commission of a protest that is effective as an expression of their grievance against law or policy" (Smith 2013, p. 111).

In turn, prosecutors have and should use their discretion not to press charges against civil disobedients in some cases, or to charge them with the least serious offense possible. Dworkin (1985) urged judges to engage in an open dialogue with civil disobedients (at least those who articulate legal arguments in defense of their actions) and dismiss their charges after hearing them, or to use their discretion in sentencing, for instance by accepting guilty pleas or guilty verdicts but imposing trivial punishments.

However, Dworkin's proposal could amount to letting judges evaluate the worthiness of individual civil disobedients' causes, which would not on its own guarantee judicial leniency. To the contrary, judges might well systematically decide against civil disobedients, upholding the special interests of the elite they are part of. The proceduralist insistence on courts' neutrality avoids this pitfall and generally warns against turning courtrooms into political forums. Yet the latter transformation might not be so insidious and may indeed be part of a necessary institutional reform to provide civil disobedients with a platform, perhaps along the lines of Arendt's (1970) proposal to treat civil disobedients as a kind of people's lobbyists (*see* Smith 2010).

Other theorists have taken a different path, arguing that *no* civil disobedient should (presumptively) be punished. They defend a moral right to civil disobedience that is independent of the social benefits of civil disobedience and of the justification of particular exercises of this right. This moral right designates a protected sphere to engage in civil disobedience, justifiably or not, and entails a presumptive claim-right against censure and punishment (Lefkowitz 2007; Brownlee 2008; Smith 2013).[2] These philosophers understand the right to civil disobedience as a liberal right of conduct. Just as the right of free speech protects illiberal and offensive speech, not just "good" speech, so the right to civil disobedience protects civil disobedients who pursue illiberal, undemocratic, or otherwise problematic causes, and not only those engaged in justified civil disobedience, from state interference.

Joseph Raz (1979), David Lefkowitz (2007), and Smith (2013, ch.4) base this right on political participation rights, whereas Kimberley Brownlee grounds it in the "principle of humanism," which says that "society has a duty to honor the fact that we are reasoning and feeling beings capable of forming deep moral commitments" by allowing conscientious persons who find themselves burdened by law's demands to freely disobey these on the basis of their convictions (Brownlee 2012, p. 7). For Brownlee but not for Lefkowitz, the right to civil disobedience entails a presumptive claim-right protection against *all* forms of state interference, including penalization and punishment.

To recap, for champions of civil disobedience, the answer to the question whether the state should punish civil disobedience is a resounding "no." Instead, they advocate tolerating and accommodating its exercises as much as possible. While a fully accommodating stance would require significant legal reforms (viz., not only allowing criminal defenses but also creating special forums to hear civil disobedients), officials can and should use their discretion to treat civil disobedients leniently. Now let us turn to our second, agent-centered question.

SHOULD THE CIVIL DISOBEDIENT ACCEPT PUNISHMENT?

It is almost an article of faith that civil disobedients are to take responsibility for, and accept the legal consequences of, their actions. Their evading punishment would make them criminals or rebels, not civil disobedients; their submission to the legal system is supposed to demonstrate their endorsement of the state's legitimacy. Carl Cohen fleshes out the necessary connection between civil disobedience and full acceptance of punishment thusly:

> Because the civil disobedient acts within a framework of laws whose legitimacy he accepts, this legal punishment is more than a possible consequence of his act—it is the natural and proper culmination of it. Because his act is essentially one of protest, his submission to public punishment—indeed his invitation of it—is vital in exhibiting his intense concern over the issue at hand. (Cohen 1966, p. 6)

On this view, criminal punishment is not begrudgingly endured, but invited. The point is to sacrifice oneself to demonstrate to the wider public the sincerity and depth of one's conviction: trying to present the latter as an excuse for one's lawbreaking or begging for judicial leniency would defeat the very point and purpose of civil disobedience.

It is helpful to tease out the different attitudes that could fall under the label "non-evasion." Non-evasion may require the agent to (1) willingly submit to arrest and prosecution, (2) plead guilty in court, (3) not try to defend her crime, and (4) not complain for the punishment received. Some theorists (e.g., Fortas 1969; Cohen 1971; Woozley 1976) may be read as supporting all four elements. The state's treatment of civil disobedients suggests it expects all four as well. This is manifest in the trials of civil disobedients that involve evidentiary hearings only, and which legally bar defendants from explaining the rationale for their civil disobedience (per (3) above). In such cases, defendants who try to explain why they civilly disobeyed may be held in contempt, removed from the courtroom, and further sentenced.[3] In what follows, I focus on pleas and defenses ((2) and (3)), before examining reasons to evade legal sanctions (contra (1) and (4)).

Pleas

For Cohen (1966, p. 5), civil disobedients must plead guilty to their offense in court to demonstrate that they do not put themselves above the law. Matthew Hall (2007) endorses requirements (1) through (4) above but proposes that civil disobedients on trial be allowed a "Guilty But Civilly Disobedient" (GBCD) plea, and that jurors be allowed to reach a GBCD verdict if they find the defendant acted conscientiously, openly, and respectfully. Hall sees this as a reconciliation of civil disobedience with the criminal law because it allows to "distinguish one kind of guilt from another, not to distinguish guilt from innocence" (Hall 2007, p. 2115). Hall stresses that GBCD is *not* a criminal defense.

His objections to allowing anything more than GBCD in the courtroom fall under two rubrics. First, the possibility of seeking judicial leniency, jury nullification, or acquittal by introducing defenses would present problematic incentives in civil disobedients' calculus: it would potentially turn the selfless nature of civil disobedience into a self-interested effort to win acquittal, in his view; and it would open the floodgates to civil disobedience by decreasing the likelihood of punishment. Second, tolerating criminal defenses means introducing political argumentation into the courtroom and converting trial into a tool of publicity for the civil disobedient's cause, which is supposedly anathema to courts' proper role, as we discussed. For these reasons, according to Hall, civil disobedients should not count on being treated any differently from nonpolitical lawbreakers.

However, other theorists have pushed back against the notion that non-evasion requires pleading guilty and not contesting the charges. Piero Moraro (2012) argues that agents should plead "not guilty" in court, either denying responsibility of having committed the action as alleged by the prosecutor or admitting responsibility but denying liability ("Yes, I did X, but X does not represent a criminal action"). According to Moraro, pleading not guilty is a way of denying the state's characterization of the civil disobedient act as a public wrong and appealing to a higher form of legality ("what the law is meant to implement").

Dworkin's (1985) distinction between policy and principle seriously weakens Hall's floodgate objection: while the legislature is to decide on matters of policy, courts are to apply the law and respect defendants' rights without concerning themselves with the social (dis)utility of their rulings. And contra Hall's second objection, Dworkin's proposal to let defendants articulate their arguments in the courtroom, couched in legal terms, is compatible with either "guilty" or "not guilty" pleas. Indeed, it is not clear why a "not guilty" plea would rob the civil disobedient act of its selflessness, as Hall alleges. While a "guilty" plea dramatizes the self-sacrificial element, a "not guilty" plea might better communicate the defendant's insistence that she lacked the malice typically required for findings of criminal liability and invite jury nullification.

Defenses

Excuses

The Supreme Court affirmed requirement (3), according to which civil disobedients on trial should not seek any excuse for their lawbreaking. In *United States v. Berrigan*, the court ruled that a "good motive" will not "save the accused from conviction," and that civil disobedients could not appeal to their principled motivations as an excuse for their commissions of crimes (U.S. v. Berrigan). Yet good motive, at the very least, indicates lack of malicious intent—usually a sine qua non of criminal liability. Jeremy Horder (2004, ch.5) thus defends individuals' right to raise a "demands-of-conscience" defense, an excusatory defense that allows defendants to point to the deep and sincere reasons they had for believing they were justified in acting the way they did. On Horder's view, this defense is grounded in the requirement to treat people with equal respect as autonomous beings.

Whereas Horder restricts the demands-of-conscience defense to conscientious objectors and denies that it extends to civil disobedience, Brownlee argues that the defense (which she recasts as the "demands-of-conviction" defense[4]) "applies most readily to civil disobedience" (2012, p. 167). Her general argument is that the criminal defenses and legal protections available to conscientious objectors apply a fortiori to civil disobedients, given their willingness and efforts to communicate their convictions—something conscientious objectors do not always exhibit. This is especially true of the demands-of-conviction defense, which, in her view, should (presumptively) fully exculpate civil disobedients.

However, one may object that even if the defense were available to civil disobedients, it is not one they should, or would want to, appeal to. Excusatory defenses typically convey admissions of wrongdoing. When we present an excuse, we seek to explain why we had reason to believe we were doing the right thing even though we didn't, in fact, have sufficient reason to act the way we did. It makes some sense for conscientious objectors who say they couldn't help disobey the law while recognizing they had weighty reasons to obey it. Martin Luther's "Here I stand I can do no other" epitomizes this attitude. But civil disobedients don't seek excuses: they claim justification. Think of Martin Luther King, Jr.'s (2003, p. 293) insistence that "one has a moral responsibility to disobey unjust laws." Civil disobedients claim they had good reasons for acting the way they in fact acted and they wish to share these reasons with the public, since they find that these reasons bind everyone else, too.

Martha Minow makes a similar point in her analysis of the ethics of representing politically motivated lawbreakers, as she urges lawyers not only to take on such clients (Minow 1991, p. 741), but also to choose defense tactics that reflect their client's actual views. She warns against the danger of using particular arguments that "besmirch or degrade the client's commitments" even though they may promise judicial leniency (Minow 1991, p. 748). For instance, a challenge to anti-sodomy statutes on the grounds that gay sexuality deserves constitutional privacy protection despite being distasteful would not properly respect a gay client's commitments. Likewise, a lawyer who compels her client to express regrets and contrition for his civil disobedience would disrespect his commitments. Instead, lawyers ought to learn to "make vivid and understandable the perspective of a client who may seem entirely wrong from the perspective of the prosecutor or the court" (Minow 1991, p. 749).

Thus, even if a demands-of-conscience or -conviction defense could help reach a reduced sentence, it may fail to authentically represent the disobedient's own view about her lawbreaking. An excusatory defense cannot do justice to the public and political orientation of civil disobedience, and thus does a disservice to disobedient actors. Only justificatory defenses can adequately reflect and respect disobedients' commitments.

Justifications

Chief among justificatory defenses is the necessity defense, which can lead to an acquittal if defendants can persuade the jury that they violated the letter of the law in order to further some greater good. In particular, they are supposed to show that: (1) they were faced with two bad options and chose the lesser; (2) they acted to prevent imminent harm; (3) they reasonably believed that their action could prevent that harm; and (4) they had no reasonable legal alternative. Anti-war, anti-nuclear, and anti-abortion activists all regularly invoke the necessity defense; and some have done so successfully in state courts, which tend to apply the necessity requirements less stringently than federal courts (see, e.g., Boxerman 1990; Lippman 1991; Cohan 2007; Germanos 2018).

However, in *United States v. Schoon*, the Ninth Circuit created a per se rule barring the application of the necessity defense to cases of indirect civil disobedience (where the law broken is not the law being protested, as when environmental activists trespass on a nuclear plant), claiming that the imminency standard ((2) above) could never be met in such cases (U.S. v. Schoon). A number of philosophers, legal scholars, and activists have argued that this is an unfair and arbitrary restriction of defendants' rights. Lippman (1991) urges courts to adopt a flexible interpretation of necessity, focused on the magnitude of the harms activists protest (e.g., nuclear annihilation or war) compared with the minor offense they commit. Lippman (1994) illustrates such flexible interpretation of the imminency standard with Judge Spaeth's concurring opinion in *Commonwealth v. Berrigan* (involving anti-nuclear civil disobedience):

> Appellants do not assert that their action would avoid nuclear war (what a grandiose and unlikely idea!). Instead, at least so far as I can tell from the record, their belief was that their action, *in combination with the actions of others*, might accelerate a political process ultimately leading to the abandonment of nuclear missiles. And that belief, I submit, should not be dismissed as "unreasonable as a matter of law." A jury might—or might not—find it unreasonable as a matter of fact. (Commonwealth v. Berrigan)

At the very least, then, letting defendants appeal to necessity and letting a jury determine the reasonableness of such appeal would be showing proper respect to civil disobedients.

Civil disobedients also appeal, sometimes successfully, to the criminal defense known as the Nuremberg Principles defense. The Allies codified the Nuremberg Principles at the end of World War II, to try Nazis charged with crimes against peace, crimes against humanity, and war crimes. Not only government officials but also private citizens can be held responsible for participating in these crimes, according to the notion of personal responsibility central to the Nuremberg Principles (art. 6 of the 1946 London Charter). The Nuremberg defense is a version of necessity insofar as it asserts the need to violate the letter of the law to prevent massive human rights violations (*see* Cohan 2007, pp. 166–172).

Anti-war and anti-nuclear activists have sometimes argued that they were bound by the Nuremberg Principles to nonviolently protest in order to prevent or halt their government's commission of international crimes. In 1987, Brian Willson was kneeling on the railroad tracks at the Concord Naval Weapons Station, in the context of a series of "Nuremberg Actions" to protest US militaristic involvement in El Salvador. Willson lost his two legs and suffered other grave injuries as a train carrying ammunition to El Salvador ran over him. In *United States v. Montgomery* and several other cases, however, courts held that the Nuremberg defense was limited to individuals who could demonstrate that they were ordered to engage in war crimes. Activists have nonetheless continued to appeal to the Nuremberg Principles to defend their civilly disobedient protests of US domestic and foreign policy.

To recap, legal scholars and philosophers have criticized courts' refusal to permit civil disobedients to rely upon the necessity defense (e.g., Brownlee 2012, ch.6) and to raise international law arguments (e.g., Turenne 2004).

In Defense of Evasion

Accepting punishment has a symbolic appeal, which didn't escape Henry David Thoreau (2002, p. 134): "Under a government which imprisons any unjustly, the true place for the just man is in prison." But is it really a moral imperative for civil disobedients? Critics answer "no." Some point out that civil disobedients' acceptance of punishment is often a strategic choice or a matter of prudence under the circumstances—and definitely not a manifestation of their endorsement of the system's legitimacy (*see*, e.g., Lyons 1998; Pineda 2015). Other theorists argue that demonstrating respect for law is crucial to the disobedient act's civility, but they note that it can be done without submitting to legal sanctions. For instance, although Edward Snowden evaded legal sanctions after he leaked classified information, Scheuerman (2018) sees evidence that evasion does not necessarily manifest contempt for the rule of law in Snowden's many public appearances, during which he justified his actions through "appeals to standing law and an implicit notion of the rule of law."

Howard Zinn (2002, pp. 27–31) went further in arguing that since the state's arrest and imposition of punishment is itself problematic and impermissible, civil disobedients' demands of amnesty (which were common among anti-war student activists) and further protests against their arrests, prosecutions, and sentences are justifiable. But for Zinn, as for Brownlee and Celikates, civil disobedients can evade apprehension or refuse punishment without compromising the civility of their civil disobedience. Contra these broad, inclusive accounts of civil disobedience, I conceive of non-evasion as a necessary mark of civility, and thus deem evasive acts of principled disobedience "uncivil." In this last section, I present some reasons principled disobedients may have to evade apprehension and punishment and further explain why disobedients' evasion or refusal of punishment can manifest a meaningful kind of incivility.

There are, first, instrumental reasons for evasion. Some stem from the expectation of draconian punishment. In the United Kingdom last year, 15 activists who locked themselves together around an airplane to prevent it from deporting undocumented migrants were convicted under terror-related legislation (Perkin 2018). Snowden risks a 30-year sentence under the charges brought against him. In addition, covertness and non-evasion may be necessary for the disobedient action's success. For instance, before *Roe v. Wade*, which guaranteed access to abortion services in the United States, a number of doctors illegally, covertly, and evasively provided abortion to women. If physicians were to break the law openly and non-evasively, they would risk prosecution, conviction, or loss of medical license, which could jeopardize their ability to provide abortion services in the future. Women to whom such physicians provided services could be also harmed (viz., through the shame of public exposure and potential liability; *see* Reagan 1996).

However, there are also, second, some non-instrumental reasons to evade punishment. If accepting punishment is taken to manifest respect for law, then expressing disrespect toward the legal system, when it doesn't deserve our respect, may be apt. Elizabeth Cady Stanton exposed her reasons not to submit to the legal system in a letter to Matilda Joslyn Gage (Tenafly June 25, 1873 (1969, p. 143)):

> The insult of being tried by men—judges, jurors, lawyers, all men—for violating the laws and constitutions of men, made for the subjugation of my sex; to be forever publicly impaled by party, press, and pulpit, so far transcends a petty verdict of butchers, cab-drivers, and plough-boys, in a given case, that my continuous wrath against the whole dynasty of tyrants has not left one stagnant drop of blood in my veins to rouse for any single act of insult.

Stanton voices an intense distrust toward the state and its rules. This distrust is warranted: Why ought she (morally) submit to legal sanctions meted out by a state that treats her and her peers as inferior human beings, unfit for self-rule? Why should she take, or act as if she took, this system as morally authoritative and politically legitimate? She had good reason to evade and reject—not submit to—the state's prosecution and punishment of her disobedience. And such evasion and rejection could express better than civil, non-evasive disobedience her denial of the state's democratic legitimacy.

These non-instrumental reasons against submitting to legal sanctions hold (albeit not always decisively) even if evasion were demonstrably counterproductive to activists' cause and were sure to alienate the public. Agents bent on moral suasion may well elect non-evasion, but they still have good (defeasible) reasons to withhold deference to the legal system by uncivilly refusing to submit to it. This also explains why theorists should not try to shoehorn evasive principled disobedience in the category of civil disobedience: activists may deliberately evade punishment, in a gesture that radically breaks with the standard template of civil protest.

Conclusion: How Should We Think About Civil Disobedience?

In 1917, 33 suffragists were arrested for picketing outside the US White House for the right to vote. They were clubbed, beaten, and tortured by the guards at the Occoquan Workhouse in Northern Virginia. In 2017, 234 protesters and bystanders, including journalists, medics, and legal observers, were arrested at an anti-Trump rally near the White House and charged with felony inciting to riot, rioting, conspiracy to riot, destruction of property and assault on a police officer, which together carry sentences of at least 50 years in prison.[5]

According to the scholarly framework I presented in this chapter, brutalizing civil disobedients and punishing them excessively do not raise significant philosophical issues: this is simply not how the state should respond to civil disobedience. The issue, for a number of legal scholars and philosophers, is instead to reconcile the value and justification of civil disobedience with the moderate punishment of its practitioners. Theorists propose to do so by distinguishing civil, criminal, and revolutionary disobedience, and showing that civil disobedience is compatible with respect for legality, which it conveys through non-evasion of legal sanctions. Even champions of the moral right to civil disobedience are engaged in a kind of reconciliatory project, as they argue that liberal democratic societies' duty to respect agents' political participation rights (Lefkowitz 2007) or freedom of conscience (Brownlee 2012) entails their duty to accommodate civil disobedience. These theorists' arguments, too, rest on the contrast between civil, criminal, and revolutionary disobedience and on the notion that civil disobedience does not necessarily destabilize society or flout democracy.

The tripartite distinction between civil, criminal, and revolutionary disobedience, which is central to legal and philosophical thinking on the topic, crumbles under scrutiny. Take the criterion of nonviolence, which is supposed to demarcate civil from the other kinds of disobedience. In fact, much crime is nonviolent and harmless, especially in a legal system that overcriminalizes; some revolutions, such as Estonia's Singing Revolution, are entirely nonviolent; and Henry David Thoreau, American paragon of civil disobedience, defended the use of violence in the fight against slavery in his 1859 *Plea for Captain John Brown*. Neither is the contrast between the selflessness of civil disobedience and selfishness of crime clear: consider that some people resort to criminal activity to feed their family, that oppressed people personally have a lot to gain from their anti-oppression struggles, including better life prospects, improved material conditions, and heightened self-respect, and that some behavior commonly read as criminal may in fact be undertaken, or should be interpreted, as a kind of resistance (*see*, e.g., Smith and Cabrera 2015; Shelby 2016). Pierre Bourdieu's structural analysis of delinquency as not only effect of but also reaction to the structural violence of neoliberal politics and the demolition of the welfare state, per what he calls the "law of the conservation of violence," is also relevant here, as it challenges the partition upon which defenses of civil disobedience tend to rest (Bourdieu 1998, p. 40).

The tripartite distinction is not only conceptually simplistic but it also serves particular political and ideological purposes, by suggesting that civil disobedience is the only kind of disobedience that can ever be permitted under "normal" circumstances, where one is typically bound to obey the law. Pervasive racial, gender, and economic injustice (among other kinds of structural injustice) cast doubt both on the supposition of a general obligation to obey the law and on the narrow scope of justifiable disobedience. Tommie Shelby (2016) thus argues that the US legal system, insofar as it subjects ghetto residents to systematic injustice and deprivation, especially through the criminal justice system, fails to morally bind them (*see also* Yankah, this volume, Chap. 22): the latter may engage in various criminal activities, including prostitution, drug trafficking, welfare fraud, tax evasion, and selling stolen goods. Criminal activities like these might count as forms of resistance to systematic injustice, while clearly falling outside the scope of civil disobedience. And I have argued (Delmas 2018) that some forms of uncivil—that is, covert, violent, evasive, or offensive—disobedience can be justified within societies like ours on the very basis of the normative principles commonly used to support the duty to obey the law.

Beyond their many disagreements, most theorists presuppose the decency and commitment to mutual respect of the society in which civil disobedients are acting. They suppose that the state does its job of protecting people's rights and that the legal system is entitled to our respect and worth preserving. This theoretical framing is not by accident but by design: as Rawls stresses, civil disobedience is only a problem in near-just societies, while there is no need to justify civil disobedience in unjust, tyrannical, or autocratic states, where one has a right not just to disobey but to overthrow the government. This makes sense. However, theorists think about and seek to justify *real-world* civil disobedience, against democratic disenfranchisement, racial segregation, police brutality, and even colonial domination. In doing so, they imply that the disobedience in question requires justification and that the society in which it took or takes place could reasonably be deemed near-just. Yet these targets of civil disobedience suggest the opposite: that a society with these injustices is not "near-just," and that civil disobedience is not presumptively impermissible.

When the state fails to protect everyone's basic rights to life and liberty, when the police persecutes and terrorizes those it is supposed to protect, when thousands of innocent people are told to plead guilty to crimes they didn't commit, when hundreds of thousands of people spend decades behind bars for minor offenses, and when large swaths of the population are prevented from voting,[6] we have reason to be skeptical of the presuppositions built into the common approach to civil disobedience. Rather than trying to soften the blow of what opponents see as the destabilizing potential of civil disobedience, we should pursue it: disrupting the status quo is a good thing, when that status quo perpetuates systemic injustice. Rather than fearing the anti-democratic nature of civil disobedience, we should force a reassessment of society's own professed commitment to democratic ideals. And rather than restricting the scope of legitimate protest to its civil manifestations, we should scrutinize the ways in which the idealized category of "civil disobedience" has been used to delegitimize all kinds of dissent, from the Dakota Access Pipeline protests to the Movement for Black Lives.

By framing disobedience as a problem to solve, legal scholars and philosophers ignore a deeper one: that *compliance* with, rather than disobedience to, an unjust, undemocratic, exploitative, or discriminatory legal systems is presumptively wrong. Once we see obedience under systematically unjust sociopolitical conditions as the problem, we might approach civil disobedience as a moral duty rather than an occasionally permissible conduct.[7]

Notes

1. Agents ought to act nonviolently and openly and present their civil disobedience as an appeal to the foundational principles of consent, freedom of association, and the right to dissent (*see* Smith 2010).
2. To say that the right against punishment is presumptive is to recognize that there may be weighty countervailing reasons to punish or penalize civil disobedience. However, Brownlee contends that even when judges are justified to punish civil disobedients, they ought to apologize to the latter for infringing upon their rights.
3. A Plowshares case illustrates the state's rigid stance and what's at stake when civil disobedients fail to satisfy some of the non-evasion requirements identified above. Four anti-nuclear Plowshares defendants who insisted on explaining why they had trespassed a Johns Hopkins University research facility were found in contempt and removed from the courtroom. Daniel Berrigan shouted from the audience, "Let them speak, judge" and later added, "This court is a disgrace." The judge demanded an apology and Berrigan defiantly replied, "I will change my position when you allow people in this court… to explain their actions." Vaughn responded by holding Berrigan in contempt and sentenced him to five years in prison. *See* Buckley (1992).
4. Brownlee (2012) draws a distinction between conscience and conviction, which explains her change of terminology. "Conscience," in her view, consists of "a set of practical moral skills that stem from an inward knowledge of the working of our own mind and heart," while "conviction" refers to serious and sincere, though possibly mistaken, belief in a moral norm (Brownlee 2012, p. 52).
5. A portion of these protesters was part of a black block that smashed some windows.
6. I could summon many references here, but Anderson (2016) fits particularly well.
7. I am grateful to Chris Bennett, Koshka Duff, Ben Ewing, Kimberly Ferzan, Thomas Fossen, Robert Jubb, David Lyons, Andrei Poama, William Smith, and Aart Van Gils for their valuable feedback on earlier drafts.

REFERENCES

Commonwealth v. Berrigan, 325 Pa. Superior Ct. 242 (1984).

Driskill v. Parrish, 7 F. Cas. 1100 (C.C.D. Ohio 1845) (No. 4,089).

Florida House Bill No. 1419 (2017).

Georgia Senate Bill 339 (2017–2018).

Missouri House Bill No. 1413 (2018).

North Dakota House Bill No. 1293 (2017).

Roe v. Wade, 410 U.S. 113 (1973).

United States v. Berrigan, 283 F. Supp. 336 (D. Md. 1968).

United States v. Cobb, 25 F. Cas. 481, 482 (D.C.N.D. N.Y. 1857) (No. 14,820).

United States v. Cullen, 454 F.2d 386, 392 (7th Cir. 1971).

United States v. Kroncke, 459 F.2d 697 (8th Cir. 1972).

United States v. Montgomery, 772 F.2d 733 (11th Cir. 1985).

United States v. Schoon, 939 F.2d 826 (9th Cir. 1991).

Walker v. Birmingham, 388 U.S. 307 (1967).

Anderson, Carol. 2016. *White rage: The unspoken truth of our racial divide*. New York: Bloomsbury.

Arendt, Hannah. 1970. Reflections on civil disobedience. *New Yorker*, September 12, 70–105.

Bedau, Hugo. 1961. On civil disobedience. *Journal of Philosophy* 58: 653–665.

Bentham, Jeremy. 1907. *An introduction to the principles of morals and legislation*. Oxford: Clarendon Press. (Orig. pub. 1789).

Bourdieu, Pierre. 1998. *Acts of resistance: Against the tyranny of the market*. New York: The New Press.

Boxerman, Arlene D. 1990. The use of the necessity defense by abortion clinic protesters. *Journal of Criminal Law and Criminology* 81: 677–712.

Brownlee, Kimberley. 2008. Penalizing public disobedience. *Ethics* 118: 711–716.

Brownlee, Kimberley. 2012. *Conscience and conviction: The case for civil disobedience*. Oxford: Oxford University Press.

Buckley, Stephen. 1992. Berrigan released while appealing contempt term. *The Washington Post*, March 28.

Cohan, John Alan. 2007. Civil disobedience and the necessity defense. *Pierce Law Review* 6: 111–175.

Cohen, Carl. 1966. Civil disobedience and the law. *Rutgers Law Review* 21: 1–17.

Cohen, Carl. 1971. *Civil disobedience: Conscience, tactics, and the law*. New York: Columbia University Press.

Del Pozo, Brandon. 2018. Recent civil disobedience in Burlington. *Burlington Free Press*. https://www.burlingtonfreepress.com/story/new s/local/vermont/2018/02/23/why-didnt-police-arrest-uvm-protesters-burlington-chief-explains/368156002/. Accessed 26 Feb 2019.

Delmas, Candice. 2018. *A duty to resist: When disobedience should be uncivil*. New York: Oxford University Press.

Dworkin, Ronald. 1968. On not prosecuting civil disobedience. *New York Review of Books*, June 6.

Dworkin, Ronald. 1985. *A matter of principle*. Cambridge, MA: Harvard University Press.

Feinberg, Joel. 1965. The expressive function of punishment. *The Monist* 49: 397–423.

Fortas, Abe. 1968. Dangers to the rule of law. *American Bar Association Journal* 54 (10): 957–959.

Fortas, Abe. 1969. *Concerning dissent and civil disobedience.* New York: The New American Library, Signet Books.

Germanos, Andrea. 2018. Judge drops charges against 13 who argued pipeline civil disobedience action was "necessary" to save planet. *Common Dreams.* https://www.commondreams.org/news/2018/03/28/judge-drops-charges-against-13-who-argued-pipeline-civil-disobedience-action-was. Accessed 26 Feb 2019.

Hall, Matthew R. 2007. Guilty but civilly disobedient: Reconciling civil disobedience and the rule of law. *Cardozo Law Review* 28: 2083–2132.

Horder, Jeremy. 2004. *Excusing crime.* Oxford: Oxford University Press.

King, Martin Luther, Jr. 2003. *A testament of hope: The essential writings and speeches.* Ed. James M. Washington. New York: HarperCollins.

Lefkowitz, David. 2007. On a moral right to civil disobedience. *Ethics* 117: 202–233.

Lippman, Matthew. 1991. Towards a recognition of the necessity defense for political protesters. *Washington & Lee Law Review* 68: 235–251.

Lippman, Matthew. 1994. Liberating the law: The jurisprudence of civil disobedience and resistance. *San Diego Justice Journal* 2: 317–394.

Lyons, David. 1998. Moral judgment, historical reality, and civil disobedience. *Philosophy and Public Affairs* 27: 31–49.

Markovits, Daniel. 2005. Democratic disobedience. *Yale Law Journal* 114: 1897–1952.

Minow, Martha. 1991. Breaking the law: Lawyers and clients in struggles for social changes. *University of Pittsburgh Law Review* 52: 723–752.

Moore, Michael S. 1997. *Placing blame: A theory of criminal law.* Oxford: Oxford University Press.

Moraro, Piero. 2012. A dilemma for the civil disobedient: Pleading "guilty" or "not guilty" in the courtroom? In *The public in law: Representations of the political in legal discourse,* ed. Claudio Michelon, Gregor Clunie, Christopher McCorkindale, and Haris Psarras, 99–111. Edinburgh/Glasgow: Ashgate.

Perkin, Charlotte. 2018. Stansted 15: Activists who stopped deportation charter flight convicted of terror-related charges. *Novara Media.* https://novaramedia.com/2018/12/10/stansted-15-activists-who-stopped-deportation-charter-flight-convicted-of-terrorism-charge/. Accessed 26 Feb 2019.

Pineda, Erin. 2015. Civil disobedience and punishment: (Mis)reading justification and strategy from SNCC to Snowden. *History of the Present* 5: 1–30.

Plato. 2002. *Five dialogues: Euthyphro, apology, Crito, Meno, Phaedo.* Trans. G.M.A. Grube and revised by John M. Cooper. Indianapolis: Hackett Classics.

Rawls, John. 1999. *A theory of justice.* Rev. ed. Cambridge, MA: Harvard University Press. (Orig. pub. 1971).

Raz, Joseph. 1979. *The authority of law.* Oxford: Clarendon Press.

Reagan, Leslie J. 1996. *When abortion was a crime.* Berkeley: University of California Press.

Robin, Celikates. 2014. Civil disobedience as practice of civic freedom. In *On global citizenship James Tully in dialogue,* ed. David Owen, 207–228. London: Bloomsbury Press.

Sabl, Andrew. 2001. Looking forward to justice: Rawlsian civil disobedience and its non-Rawlsian lessons. *The Journal of Political Philosophy* 9: 307–330.

Sandalow, Terrance. 1969. Review of *Concerning dissent and civil disobedience,* by a. Fortas. *Michigan Law Review* 67: 599–612.

Sarat, Austin. 2014. Keeping civility in its place: Dissent, injustice, and the lessons of history. In *Law, society, and community: Socio-legal essays in honour of Roger Cotterrell*, ed. Richard Nobes and David Schiff, 293–308. Abingdon: Routledge.

Scheuerman, William E. 2018. *Civil disobedience.* Cambridge, UK: Polity Press.

Shelby, Tommie. 2016. *Dark ghettos: Injustice, dissent, and reform.* Cambridge, MA: Harvard University Press.

Smith, William. 2010. Reclaiming the revolutionary spirit: Arendt on civil disobedience. *European Journal of Political Theory* 9: 149–166.

Smith, William. 2013. *Civil disobedience and deliberative democracy.* Cambridge, UK: Routledge.

Smith, William, and Luis Cabrera. 2015. The morality of border crossing. *Contemporary Political Theory* 14: 90–99.

Stanton, Elizabeth Cady. 1969. *Elizabeth Cady Stanton: As revealed in her letters & diary.* Vol. 2. Eds. Theodore Stanton and Harriet Stanton Blatch. New York: Arno.

Thoreau, Henry D. 2002. In *The essays of Henry D. Thoreau*, ed. Lewis Hyde. New York: North Point Press.

Turenne, Sophie. 2004. Judicial responses to civil disobedience: A comparative approach. *Res Publica* 10: 379–399.

Weinstock, Daniel. 2016. How democratic is civil disobedience? *Criminal Law and Philosophy* 10: 707–720.

Woozley, A.D. 1976. Civil disobedience and punishment. *Ethics* 86: 323–331.

Zinn, Howard. 2002. *Disobedience and democracy: Nine fallacies of law and order.* Cambridge, MA: South End Press. (Orig. pub. 1968.).

PART VIII

Complicity

CHAPTER 9

Complicity

Antje du Bois-Pedain

Phenomena of complicity raise the question on what ethical basis one person—call her S, the "secondary party"—can be held responsible for some wrong that another person—call him P, the "perpetrator" or "principal"—has committed, just because of something that S said or did in respect of P's wrong that did not as such amount to the commission of this wrong by S. They raise, second, questions concerning the extent and reach of this responsibility, particularly in cases where there is some mismatch between what P and S, respectively, knew or intended, and/or between what (S thought) P set out to do and what P eventually did.

This chapter addresses complicity as a question of individual responsibility—the primary mode in which complicity matters in criminal-law contexts—in contradistinction to treating it as a question of collective responsibility, which is how complicity, especially of members of collectives, is sometimes addressed in political discussions and in some philosophical writings (for a comprehensive review of these arguments, see Smiley 2017). That said, the philosophical literature also contains rich treatments of complicity as a mode of individual responsibility (e.g., Kutz 2000; Mellema 2016). This chapter draws on some of these works, as well as on the traditions of doctrinal legal scholarship in different jurisdictions, to answer two main questions: (1) what is the ethical basis on which one person can, by reason of something she has said or done, be considered responsible for some wrong that another person has committed, and (2) how far does this responsibility extend, particularly in cases where there are

A. du Bois-Pedain (✉)
Faculty of Law, University of Cambridge, Cambridge, UK
e-mail: alp22@cam.ac.uk

© The Author(s) 2019
L. Alexander, K. K. Ferzan (eds.), *The Palgrave Handbook of Applied Ethics and the Criminal Law*, https://doi.org/10.1007/978-3-030-22811-8_9

significant discrepancies between what each of the parties thought, intended, or set out to do (what I refer to as "divergent trajectory cases")?

The discussion is divided into three parts.

Part I ("Mapping the Legal Territory") explains the two main modes of complicitous involvement recognized by most legal systems: joint enterprises (also referred to as common purpose crimes) and accessorial participation mainly through behavior that encourages or assists the principal's crime (what we might think of as secondary participation in a narrow sense). It also explains the often contentious application of either of these doctrines in cases of spontaneous violence and the specific challenges faced in all these scenarios when P's actions, and/or their outcomes, to a significant extent differ from or go beyond the core of what P initially set out to do (or what P was thought/ intended by S to set out to do).

Part II ("The Distinctive Wrong(s) of Complicitous Contributions to Crime") addresses, and rejects, the view expressed in the literature that responsibility for complicity is reducible to responsibility based on causation.[1] My main argument here is that causality is an insufficiently nuanced basis for responsibility-ascription in these cases. It may identify a workable prerequisite of responsibility-ascription for the crimes of others qua "results" of one's own behavior (at least if it is interpreted widely so as to encompass behaviors having the concrete capacity to psychologically influence P or be otherwise causally potent), but it *does not* accurately identify the *distinctive ethical basis* on which S shares moral responsibility for P's acts or acquires moral responsibility for P's crime. To identify this ethical basis in an appropriately nuanced manner, we need to distinguish between cases where S acts (1) together with, (2) through, and (3) alongside P.

Part III ("What to Do in Divergent Trajectory Cases") takes up the main practical challenge of criminal participation: cases where what P did is in some significant way worse than what S expected, thought, or meant for P to do (the "target crime"). In this section, I argue against various forms of quasi-constructive liability for S in these cases—and, in particular, against the view that it could be sufficient for S to bear full moral and legal responsibility for P's actual crime(s) that the crime(s) P did commit were a "natural and probable" consequence of P embarking on the commission of the target crime. What is more debatable is whether it could suffice for S to be held responsible for the outcome of P's acts that P's divergent behavior was subjectively foreseeable for S (or even that it was actually foreseen by S as a real possibility). If we think this suffices, we effectively endorse a risk-based mode of responsibility-ascription. Importantly, there are not only objective but also subjective elements to consider for this risk-based mode of responsibility-ascription. This has important implications for the designation of S's crime. The relationship S's behavior bears to P's crime is, here, one of negligent or reckless causation/support. This should be accurately reflected in the type of offense for which S is held responsible.

Mapping the Legal Territory

When a person (S) has not fulfilled the preconditions of criminal liability set down in the criminal offense definition by her own conduct but nevertheless appears to have influenced the commission of a crime by another person, P (who is referred to as the direct perpetrator or principal), criminal law has to decide whether S (who is not a direct perpetrator) can and should be held responsible for the crime's commission. There are three situations in particular where criminal law answers with a resounding "yes."

The first situation concerns cases where S uses P as an innocent agent. In such cases, the criminal law effectively short-circuits S's responsibility for P's actions by treating P as akin to a mere tool or instrument in the hands of S. Imagine that S, a young mother, gives a bottle containing poison to her baby's wet nurse (P), telling P falsely that the bottle contains medicine for the child and intending for P to give the contents of the bottle to the baby, thereby killing the child. When P, as instructed, feeds the poison to the child with fatal consequences, S is in law treated as the perpetrator of the wrongful act despite the fact that P performed the conduct specified in the offense's definition.[2]

The second situation, which is of far greater practical relevance, concerns instances where people act together to achieve a shared goal—that goal consisting in the commission of one or more criminal offenses. Take a standard case of residential burglary, where A stands watch in front of the building, B disables the building's security cameras and alarms from a security station in a nearby garage, and C climbs the fence and forcibly enters and searches the premises for valuables, while D sits in a parked car behind the premises waiting for C to emerge from the building with the stolen goods and to drive both away. All along E, the criminal mastermind of the whole operation, who provided the others with instructions of which house to burgle and which goods to steal, waits at his warehouse for the arrival of the getaway car. This situation is one where (on slightly different doctrinal tracks) the criminal laws of different jurisdictions reach an outcome where all involved are held liable for the burglary (in most modern systems, as joint principals or co-perpetrators notwithstanding the fact that some of those involved were not present at the scene of the crime).

There has been much discussion in recent years, especially among scholars focusing on English criminal law, whether such cases—referred to in the literature as "joint enterprises" or "common purpose crimes"[3]—can be made sense of by applying an accessorial liability route to anyone but the participant who in his own person performs the actus reus of the offense (in our example, C who breaks into and enters the premises and takes the goods).[4] The better view is that this is a strained perspective that does not accurately reflect how the different parties to this crime are invested in its commission—to wit: equally strongly. Nor does it capture the crime's mode of commission, which is co-operative rather than by everyone else proffering C with various types of ancillary support. It is also a view that runs into insoluble difficulty when there is no single participant who performs all the conduct elements of the actus reus in his own person (think of a robbery where one participant applies force to the victim while the other takes V's property). For these cases, the aim of the criminal law must be to ascribe responsibility for the acts performed by each of the participants in the joint enterprise to all others—and, based on that mutual act-attribution, to hold them each responsible for the commission of the crime.[5]

The third situation is one where there is one central actor who carries out the offense, around whom are grouped various others who influenced or supported this central agent. For these cases, criminal-law systems have developed modes of accessorial liability to hold these other, ancillary actors, responsible for their contribution to the main actor's crime. It is here that we find the classical modes of secondary participation—variously referred to as instigation or facilitation, as aiding/abetting/counseling or procuring, or as "assistance and encouragement."

Two matters are important here: what is attributed to the accessory is *not* the principal's physical act as if it were performed by the accessory (in contrast to co-perpetratorship, described earlier, where such mutual act-attribution is at the heart of the parties' individual responsibility as co-perpetrators). Rather, what is attributed is a degree of responsibility for the principal's *crime*, based on a certain contributory activity performed by the accessory with a certain mental state referring to both this contribution and the envisaged target crime of the principal. Second, legal systems face a choice about whether they treat this type of liability as derivative or as freestanding. If they treat it as freestanding, they effectively create an inchoate crime of "attempted assistance or encouragement."[6] Most systems opt against this inchoate strand and instead make the liability of the would-be accessory depend on whether the principal committed (or at least attempted to commit) the target crime. But even systems where the basic mode of accessorial liability is derivative in this sense allow for some modifications of the accessory's liability that can result in a degree of divergence between the crime for which the principal is held responsible and the crime which constitutes the target crime of the accessory's contributory act. (Later, in the chapter, I further elaborate on the rationale behind this form of responsibility-attribution. I will also say something about the fairly important distinction between instigators, on the one hand, and facilitators, on the other hand.)

In what follows, I use the notion of "complicity" or "secondary participation" in a wide sense to cover all the scenarios described earlier, as involving complicitous contributions to crime. When I speak of "the standard form of secondary participation/accessorial liability," I only mean to refer to scenarios of the third type. I refer to the envisaged main offense to which the secondary party's liability attaches as the "target crime" or "envisaged main offense."

Few things in life go exactly as planned or intended, and this is just as true on those occasions where we act together with or through others as it is when we act on our own. This, in turn, leads to the practically very significant question whether participants other than the direct agent can be held liable for further or divergent action taken by one of their number—particularly when these further or divergent acts constitute a different criminal offense than the target crime. This problem is particularly acute when the direct agent is aware that she is deviating from or going beyond the original criminal objective. The time-honored principle, that "if any of the offenders commits a crime foreign to the common purpose, the others are neither principals in the second degree nor accessories unless they actually instigate or assist its commission," appears unchanged in the final edition of Sir James Fitzjames Stephen's famous *Digest of the Criminal Law* (Stephen 1950, p. 17). Yet it has always coexisted with other rules that made it difficult for other parties to effectively rely on this principle, particularly rules that included a large range of unplanned acts within the common purpose as acts done in furtherance of it.

Two patterns can be observed in actual legal systems:

1. Most systems operate ascription rules for further/divergent acts/crimes (also referred to as collateral offenses).
2. The applicable ascription rule can differ as between standard secondary liability cases and joint enterprise/choate conspiracy-cases.

Wisconsin's criminal code provides a good example of this practice (although the fault line runs between aiders and abettors, on the one hand, and parties to a conspiracy and those who have advised, hired, counseled, or procured the perpetrator's crime, on the other hand). Wis.Stat. §939.05 provides, in the relevant subsection (2):

A person is concerned in the commission of a crime if he:

(a) Directly commits the crime; or
(b) Intentionally aids and abets the commission of it; or
(c) Is a party to a conspiracy with another to commit it or advises, hires, counsels or otherwise procures another to commit it. Such a party is also concerned in the commission of any other crime which is committed in pursuance of the intended crime and which under the circumstances is a natural and probable consequence of the intended crime. [...]

Wisconsin law thus restricts the application of the liability extension for collateral crimes that were a "natural and probable consequence of the intended crime" to co-conspirators and instigators and does not apply this extension to mere helpers. (Similarly, the extended common purpose doctrine in Australian law applies only to parties linked by a common purpose, which does not include all cases where a person assists or encourages another to commit a crime.) Where the liability extension applies, it is strict in the sense that no subjective fault of the other party is required in respect of the collateral crime, even if that crime does require subjective fault on the part of the direct agent. It is also harsh in that liability is ascribed for the direct agent's collateral crime *of intent* despite the absence of such intent in the secondary party. Note, however, that the Wisconsin provision reflects only one fairly typical but by no means an inevitable legislative approach. Israeli criminal law, whose earlier rules on liability of accomplices for collateral crimes (set out in Ohana 2000, pp. 328–329 nn. 23–24) used to be very similar to Wisconsin's scheme,[7] in a 1994 reform introduced the following rule:

> Where in the course of committing an offence a perpetrator also commits a different or an additional offense, the possibility of the commission of which, in the circumstances of the case, a reasonable person could have been aware of:
>
> (1) his co-perpetrators shall also bear liability for it; however, if the other or additional offense was committed with intent, then the other co-perpetrators shall bear liability for it as an offense of indifference only;
> (2) a person who was an instigator or aider shall bear liability for it as an offence of negligence, if there is such an offense with the same factual elements. (Section 34A(a) of the Preliminary and General Part of the Israeli Criminal Code of 1994 (Penal Law 5737-1977), translation adapted from Ohana 2000, p. 328).

This rule differs from the Wisconsin scheme in several important respects: first, the fault line now runs between jointly committed crimes, on the one hand, and standard secondary participation by instigating or abetting, on the other hand. Second, in both scenarios liability for the other party is extended (by contrast, the Wisconsin scheme does not extend liability for those who have merely provided help). But third, and perhaps most importantly, the new Israeli law changes *the offense* for which the secondary party is held liable: it is no longer (in either of these cases) the primary party's crime of intent as such, but (in respect of jointly committed crimes falling under subsection (1)) an offense where indifference suffices as the mental element, and (in standard accessorial liability scenarios covered by subsection (2)) a crime of negligence, provided that negligence in respect of what the primary party has done is a criminal offense.

Which assumptions underpin these different approaches and whether any of them are defensible are addressed in Part III. First, however, we need to clarify the conceptual and ethical bases of an accomplice's liability for the target crime.

THE DISTINCTIVE WRONG(S) OF COMPLICITOUS CONTRIBUTIONS TO CRIME

Some philosophers have queried whether the different kinds of complicitous behavior set out above really require distinct normative bases for responsibility-ascription. Michael Moore, for instance, has argued: "Aiding another to cause some bad result is not an independent desert basis. It is a mere stand-in for one of the four general bases on which we are rightly blamed" (Moore 2007–2008, p. 395). These general bases (causation, counter-factual dependence, chance-raising, and purely subjective culpability) are (as Antony Duff summarizes Moore's argument) "not peculiar to complicity"; rather, they are the bases "for criminal liability generally, of 'principals' as much as of 'accomplices'" (Duff 2008, p. 444). Stewart sums up Moore's approach as "subsum[ing] [accomplice liability] within generic principles of attribution" (Stewart 2014, p. 543).

Moore's argument involves defending a particular theory of causation, which (if one accepts it) allows one to put to one side Sanford Kadish's main argument for a necessary distinction between complicity and causality: as Kadish puts it, "Causation applies where results of a person's action happen in the physical world," but not "where results take the form of another person's voluntary action," such that "Complicity emerges as a separate ground of liability because causation doctrine cannot in general satisfactorily deal with results that take the form of another's voluntary action" (Kadish 1985, p. 327). Indeed, without wanting to enter here into the complexities of Moore's theory of causation, which counts "counter-factual dependence" as a separate general desert base, one can for the purposes of this discussion simplify and summarize Moore's argument as contending that all criminal liability is grounded in causing, risking, or attempting to cause harm, including in cases of complicity.[8] The point I want to make in reply to Moore does not deny the relevance of these notions also for cases of complicity. Rather, the point I wish to make is that even if it is possible (and important) to analyze the influence exerted by secondary parties over principal offenders in these terms, they do not enable us to capture the nature of the *wrongdoing* involved in complicitous conduct.

To appreciate this difficulty, take the causal view of the wrong of complicity to its logical conclusion. If it were indeed the case that anyone who causes another to engage in a wrongful act is herself implicated in the commission of that wrong, any victim whose conduct in some way inspired or provoked the offense by P would for this reason be implicated in P's wrong against her— which is hardly a plausible result. It is not just that we would need to "exclude" V's responsibility for P's offense under some description,[9] but that the very classification of P's conduct as an offense becomes questionable when the ostensible victim is suddenly identified as a co-perpetrator/participant (albeit perhaps one who is not criminally liable under some special rule). Victim conduct cannot be rendered "participatory" or "complicitous" merely by being *causal* for P's reaction (nor, for that matter, by being chance-raising or counterfactually necessary in respect of it). Whatever the wrong of complicity is, it cannot simply consist in somehow "inspiring" another through some feature of one's personal existence to commit a criminal offense. The problem that raises for Moore's view is that despite the presence of these general desert bases in the victim examples, we do not believe that they do constitute any sort of desert base in this context. This raises doubts as to whether the general desert bases constitute appropriate desert bases for complicitous behavior.

Perhaps Moore could respond that although V is complicit in P's offense against her, that complicity is not culpable because it is she who is running the risk from P's conduct, not some unwary person. But this response would simply beg the question whether causality does, after all, constitute an appropriate desert base in cases of complicity. In contrast to situations where V harms herself directly, here it is P who causes harm to V. In *this* harm, which is classed as wrongful, V is causally implicated.

This allows us to turn to the question what the specific *wrong* of participatory conduct consists in. I argue that the answer depends on the kind of participatory conduct in question. We should distinguish between situations where persons join together to share the tasks involved in the commission of a particular crime, situations where a person instigates or facilitates the commission of a crime by someone else, and situations where people act alongside each other toward a similar end. In the first kind of case, the wrong is the commission of the target crime as such, shared among those who work together to make it happen. In the second kind of case, the wrong consists in S affecting P's choices in a particular, morally odious way. In the third kind of case, the wrong lies in the goal-directed behavior engaged in by each party rather than in any influence one party has or may have exerted over the actions and choices of other parties (which may in any event be difficult or impossible to trace). I explore these distinctive wrongs in du Bois-Pedain (2020, 2016) and draw on this discussion here.

The best way of understanding the first type of case is provided by Christopher Kutz's analysis of collective action (Kutz 2000; *see also* Bratman 1999, p. 124ff., for a similar approach). Kutz identifies as a "common structural feature" of a group act (which he calls a "collective action") that "individual members of a group intentionally do their parts in promoting a joint outcome" (Kutz 2000, p. 69). For this structural feature to be present, the participants (at a minimum) (1) have to have a particular outcome in mind, which is broadly the same outcome intended by them; they (2) have to have the notion that they will bring about this outcome by acting together (rather than by each of them trying to bring about the outcome on his or her own); and this notion of acting together also usually requiring (3) some plan or shared idea about how they will collaborate and coordinate their activities in order to bring the outcome about.[10] Kutz maintains that "what makes a set of individual acts a case of jointly intentional action is the content of the intentions with which the individuals act" and, specifically, that "jointly intentional action is primarily a function of the way in which individual agents regard their own actions as contributing to a collective outcome" (p. 74, referred to by Kutz ibid. as "participatory intention"). What is special about collaborating actors, according to Kutz, is that "Jointly acting individuals do not merely act in parallel: Each responds to what the others do and plan to do" (ibid., p. 76). Kutz's final and most important criterion is a sort of horizontal intention that all the participants have "to do his or her part of promoting the group activity or outcome," which, according to Kutz, is a "further intentional component, by which agents conceive of their actions as standing in a certain instrumental relation to the group act" (ibid., p. 78). When Kutz's criteria for collective action are made out, it is legitimate to treat the actions of each group member as if they were performed by all group members, and to ascribe individual responsibility for such acts to each and every group member. (See also Lepora and Goodin's (2013, pp. 36–39) differentiated treatment of agents who should count as co-principals: those who engage in "full joint wrongdoing" based on a shared plan for whose implementation each participant is essential; those who execute a conspiracy, and those who co-operate or collude in performing the wrongful act. Of these forms, their notion of co-operation is closest to Kutz's conception of collective action.)

Kutz's criteria for joint action help us see how cases of spontaneous violence involving more than one participant differ from the classic group action paradigm. The participants in spontaneous violent encounters will typically lack Kutz's last criterion, the horizontal intention that all the participants have "to do his or her part of promoting the group activity or outcome." For this criterion to be made out, participants would at least have to know what their "part" is and how it serves the collective aim. Once we realize the importance of participatory intention for the responsibility of group members for acts performed by other group members, we can also see why the notion of a "common design" as it is applied in certain US judgments is unsupportable. This is so because "common design" blurs the boundaries between simple "multi-party" activities and the kind of "concerted action" that is typical of genuine group-acts. The latter consist in the organized joint execution of a plan. Mutual act-attribution between the participants is only appropriate in genuine cases of co-perpetration where, in addition to the common plan, one also seeks co-operative execution of the plan. The parties' actions link to each other like cogs in a wheel, and the product of their actions—the target crime—is brought about by this well-oiled execution in which each participant does his thing, building toward the common whole. And note that while each of the participants in such a joint endeavor may only perform one small part of the joint act that constitutes the actus reus of the crime, each of them has the commission of the target crime in his sights and thus has full mens rea. He intends to carry out his part of the crime with the intention that the full crime be committed jointly. The mens rea is direct in that he intends for the crime to be committed by him and the others acting in concert. This mode of participation is therefore best understood as co-perpetration. Each participant not only wills his own contributory actions but also expects and authorizes the others to perform theirs—an authorization that is implicit in the formulation of the criminal plan. What matters decisively is not whether each of the parties is "on the scene," and even less whether her behavior as such fulfills a component of the actus reus definition, but whether she is assigned a role in the execution of the plan that contributes in some way to the commission of the target crime. The contrast between such common purpose-based crimes, on the one hand, and the looser modes of multi-party action from which the defining elements of a group act are absent, on the other hand, was put by one German commentator thus: "joint enterprises involve the deliberate and intentional co-operative behaviour of a multitude of individuals (not merely that people act from within a group)" (Lackner and Kühl 2018, §25 marg.n.9). Where people act from within a group toward the same aims but without cooperation between them, they ought to be held responsible only for their own actions and their consequences (note, though, that the latter can include harms directly or immediately caused by the actions of other agents if their own actions created or increased a risk that others would engage in such harm-causing acts). Philosophers concur. As Mellema (2016, p. 6) observes: "[A] group of people combining their efforts does not automatically qualify them as accomplices. They may well share responsibility for a common outcome, but this is not enough to justify labelling them as accomplices."

The second kind of case described above, where a person instigates or facilitates the commission of a crime by someone else, is the sort of case for which the standard doctrines of accessorial liability have been developed. (As mentioned in Part I, some legal systems take the view that the "joint enterprise" cases discussed in the preceding two paragraphs are reducible to this kind of case.) The key to understanding the nature of the accessory's wrong in this kind of case lies (as Richard Buxton explains) in

> ...the relation of the accessory to the will or intention of the perpetrator to do those things which constitute the principal crime, rather than his relation to the principal crime as such, since the accessory differs from the perpetrator in that he interposes between himself and the legally-prohibited harm the volition of another party. (Buxton 1969, p. 270)

The distinction between the accessory's relation "to the will or intention of the perpetrator," on the one hand, and to "the principal crime as such," on the other hand, is what matters here. The accessory's relation to the latter is usually seen to consist in causation (although some argue that it can also reside in risk creation; a point discussed further below). As we have seen earlier in our discussion of Moore's view, and as Buxton's statement also makes clear, *this relation* between the accessory and "the principal crime as such" is not the decisive one. Rather, the specific character of accessorial wrongdoing resides in the accessory's relation to "the will or intention of the perpetrator to do those things which constitute the principal crime." The wrong of accessorial involvement, which is brought about by the influence S exerts over P's commission of the crime, is a composite wrong that in one part lies in the way in which S influences P's choices and corrupts P's commitment to law-abiding behavior, and in another—subordinate—part lies in P's wrong in committing the target crime reflecting badly on S due to S's deliberate contribution. The accessory's wrong is the combined wrong of leading or supporting P on the path to crime, *and* of thereby conducting an indirect attack (via P) on the interest protected by the target crime in question.

Two important implications follow: (a) The mere creation of a tempting opportunity, or provocative behavior, by S is not enough to make S liable under this paradigm when P goes on to commit an offense. These behaviors by S merely create a broadly causal connection between S's action and P's crime, which by itself is not enough. (b) The inherently goal-directed quality of an action properly conceived of as helping or instigating the commission of P's unlawful act gives the accessory's conduct a purposive dimension. This affects the appropriate mens rea of the accessory. It must be such that S intends for P to carry out the act which amounts to the external element of the principal offense, and also such that S directly intends for his own act to provide encouragement or assistance.[11]

This analysis of the secondary party's wrong also explains why the wrong of complicity cannot be committed negligently. Someone who is merely negligent in respect of his behavior somehow enabling or facilitating the commission of a crime by P cannot properly be said to have set out to help or instigate P's actions. Negligent complicity is not complicity—although it may, in appropriate circumstances, amount to independent negligent commission. Whether the secondary party can encourage or assist P recklessly is more debatable, mainly due to the greater proximity of a mental state of conscious risk creation to broader notions of intention (for discussion of reckless complicity, see Kadish 1997). But note that it does not follow from the purposive dimension of the secondary party's own conduct that P's envisaged main offense must be a crime of intent. The "complicity object" (Herlitz 1992) of the secondary party, that which she sets out to assist or encourage P to do, may well be a crime of recklessness or negligence provided only that the secondary party intends for P to perform this unlawful act and intends to exert her influence over P's conduct in the manner that amounts to assistance or encouragement of P.

Armed with Buxton's distinction between the accessory's relation "to the will or intention of the perpetrator" and "the principal crime as such," we can now also return to the question what the relationship between S's conduct and P's wrongful act should be in order for P's wrongful act to indeed reflect badly on S due to S's deliberate contribution (the second part of the accessory's composite wrong I identified above). In particular, we can address the question whether it is enough for that connection to be a mere abstract one—through risk-enhancement of a general sort—or whether it needs to be causal in some traditional sense. Kutz contends that "[the] normative justification for accomplice liability generally is the risk-enhancing character of aiding or encouraging another's criminal efforts. That is, accomplice liability is best conceived as a form of inchoate liability at the level of act-type criminalization" (Kutz 2011, p. 150). Yeager similarly maintains that complicity should be "conceptualised as an inchoate or risk-based, as opposed to consequence- or harm-based, mode of criminality" (Yeager 1996, p. 25). There are effectively two claims here: that the secondary party's wrong is of the inchoate kind, and (connected to this) that the secondary party's relation to the outcome is not necessarily causal in the standard sense in many cases where our moral intuitions would support the conclusion that the secondary party was "complicit" in some way (e.g., think of the person who "stands by" but is never drawn upon to help, of the person whose inept efforts to assist the crime are a hindrance rather than a help to the main agent, and of the person whose contribution is simply superfluous in that the crime would most certainly also have taken place without it). I argue, in response, that it is a mistake to think of the secondary party's wrong as inchoate. The secondary party's wrong is, as I have explained, a composite wrong: it is partly the wrong of exerting some influence over another person's route toward the commission of a crime (and that part of the wrong is indeed in place once the contributory act has been done), but it only matures into the full-fledged wrong of complicity when the envisaged main offense is indeed attempted or committed. As French explains: "An action only becomes complicitous when another person commits an offence," and our task as moral philosophers is to explain how the complicitous agent's earlier action acquires that special moral gravity that comes from its connection to P's wrongful act when P performs that act (French 2016, pp. 578–579). This means that the secondary party must have a traceable connection to P's wrong at that later stage—and risk-enhancement as an effect of S's conduct in the world is not the right sort of connection between the accessory's conduct and the principal's crime as such.

To some extent, these different positions on the nature of the secondary party's wrong relate to the general debate over whether results matter to criminal desert. Authors who deny that outcomes affect desert will treat an "inchoate" connection (such as conscious risk-enhancement without proof that the risk thus enhanced materialized) as sufficient for linking S's actions to P's crime (for such a view see, e.g., Alexander and Ferzan 2018, ch. 2). To my mind, this position misses the importance of "owning outcomes," as Brudner (1998) put it—the extent to which harms are not just happenings in the world but products of our acts, and thus stand in a specific moral relation to us. So while "causation" (as a natural fact) does not "increase" the actor's blameworthiness, he is blameworthy for an imputable outcome, and while it is true that imputation depends on more than just factual causation of the outcome, particularly on the extent to which the outcome is a product or consequence of our agency, it is *the outcome* which is placed at our door, not just the mental attitudes and cognitive realizations bound up with our agency.

Kutz and Yeager, by contrast, are in principle open to what Yeager describes as "consequence-based modes of criminality" (Yeager 1996, p. 25). Yeager's argument turns on the character of S's *wrong* as being "relational" rather than "causal" (ibid., p. 25). Kutz likewise does not deny the relevance of causal harm-doing to the criminal law. Rather, his point is that the very project of conceptualizing P's crime as "caused" by S's contributory acts is mistaken. This is so because for Kutz, "complicity doctrine … elid[es] individual inquiries into causation by treating the harm intended … as the basis for criminal liability"

(Kutz 2011, p. 157). What matters to Kutz about complicity is that it is a different pathway for responsibility-ascription for P's crime than causation. Viewed from this angle, Kutz's argument (like Yeager's) is really about the distinctive nature of the secondary party's wrong. Hence my disagreement with them turns on the proper conceptualization of this wrong. By reducing (as Yeager does) S's wrong to the first, "relational" part of the composite wrong of complicity identified above, and by "shift[ing] accomplice liability from a harm to a risk, or inchoate, basis," as Kutz does (Kutz 2011, p. 157), both authors forego the requirement of a salient connection between S's conduct and P's crime in the concrete case. In doing so, one of the crucial components of the distinctive wrong of secondary participation slips from their grasp.

It is, of course, true that standard "but for" causation is unlikely to obtain between S's contributory actions and P's crime—and this is so even if we accept the metaphysical possibility that one person's act can be a cause of another person's freely chosen act. The main difficulty lies in explaining how certain sorts of conduct that one would typically want to recognize as complicitous do connect S to P's crime despite appearing (in causal terms) superfluous for P's venture (say, the overcautious person who unnecessarily stands watch, or the person who suggests a modification to the criminal plan that is not accepted). This difficulty has led some writers to settle for a connection through causal potency (as, e.g., Kadish (1985, p. 360) does when he asserts that "in complicity, the possibility of a but-for relationship suffices.") Formulated in this way, however, it is difficult to see how the test for causal potency differs from a test for risk-enhancement, which as I have argued earlier does not suffice. I therefore find preferable Lepora and Goodin's analysis of the appropriate connection in terms of "definitively essential or potentially essential" contributory actions by S to P's wrong (Lepora and Goodin 2013, p. 63). What they mean by this is that (from a forward-looking perspective) S's actions serve to make P's venture more likely to occur or to succeed, even though in retrospect they may have been unnecessary, superfluous, or unhelpful. S's actions make the venture more secure in this way because (in worlds very close to the actual world, in which S's contribution was unnecessary) his contribution would have been essential for the success of the venture. Lepora and Goodin's way of unpacking causal potency thus avoids collapsing this notion into risk and allows us to link S's earlier behavior to P's crime such that S's wrong is, at that later stage, no longer merely the wrong of an inchoate crime. Its wrongness now in part resides in its connection to what P has done.

Beyond these common features of accessorial contributions, there are certain important differences between instigators and helpers that need to be recognized. In the main, these differences pertain to the more subordinate role played by a helper compared to the influence exerted by an instigator—and, connected to this, the fact that the instigator tends to have greater personal "investment" in P's commission of the target crime than the typical assister. It is for this reason that some legal systems treat the instigator, but not the facilitator, as "on a par" with the direct perpetrator when it comes to punishment (*see*, e.g., German Criminal Code, §26 (making instigators liable to the same punishment as perpetrators) and §§27 II, 49 I (setting out mandatory sentence reductions for aiders and abettors); Israeli Criminal Code, §32 (setting out reduced penalties for assisters as defined s31)). It also explains why mere helpers, who need not be personally invested in the commission of the crime, are sometimes held responsible based on a less demanding mens rea requirement than instigators. While (following the judgment of Learned Hand in *United States v. Peoni* (100 F. (2d) 401 (1938)) and the Model Penal Code's later adoption of that standard in § 2.04 (3)(a)) US jurisdictions tend to require that S acts with the purpose of instigating or assisting P's crime, many other jurisdictions require purpose only in respect of instigators but let knowing assistance suffice for liability—a position arrived at by judicial interpretation of the concepts of instigation and facilitation rather than by legislative definition (see, e.g., Israel, Germany). From a philosophical perspective, Lepora and Goodin (2013, p. 83) maintain that culpable ignorance should be viewed as equivalent to knowledge, although this is debatable outside the narrower notion of willful blindness.

What to Do in Divergent Trajectory Cases

In some cases, the crime(s) P commits diverge significantly from the crime(s) S set out to co-perpetrate, assist, or encourage, and yet the laws of different jurisdictions have evolved modes by which S is, despite that divergence, held liable for the crime(s) that P did commit. The most important factual scenarios where this becomes an issue are so-called further act cases, where P initially embarks only on crime A but then, in reaction to situational factors, decides to commit a more serious crime, B, as well (either in lieu of or in addition to crime A). In terms of the burglary example we have discussed before, imagine that D (the person waiting in the getaway car behind the house) suddenly becomes aware of a person V who is unexpectedly present in the vicinity and about to stumble upon the crime scene. What if D now takes it upon himself to do something about this, gets out of the car, knocks V unconscious and ties him up, and then leaves the immobilized V behind? And what if V later dies from hypothermia, having been unable to either free himself or call for help? Would the other parties also be liable for these further crimes committed against V? The problem can, however, also arise in cases where there was a discrepancy from the start between the crime S intended for P to commit, or believed himself to be a contributor to, and the crime that P intended to commit or was by the situation led into committing. Think of a fight erupting between supporters of different football clubs in a pub. Initially, everyone just uses their fists, but as things heat up, someone on the "losing" side of the fight suddenly resorts to the use of knuckle-dusters, seriously injuring or even killing one of the opposing side. There are jurisdictions where S is in such cases held liable for the same crime of intent that P committed, provided only that P's further/more serious crimes were foreseeable/foreseen by S.

In US law, this is achieved by the "natural and probable consequence" doctrine, which finds its near legal equivalent in Australia's "extended common purpose doctrine," and which, until recently, used to be accepted in English law as a form of parasitic accessorial liability.[12] (US jurisdictions which accept this extended form of liability tend to employ an objective test of foreseeability, whereas Australian law and formerly English law focus on the question whether P's further crimes were foreseen by S as possible developments.)

KJM Smith gives the central question posed by divergent trajectory cases a tellingly negative formulation: "What, if anything, must the errant principal do to completely absolve the 'accessory' from any responsibility for the principal's [further/divergent] actions [that lead to serious further harms]" (Smith 1991, p. 226)?[13] This negative or exculpatory phrasing ("absolve") presupposes that the accessory is already implicated in any harmful outcome that arises from the (attempted) commission of the target crime, such that he will incur liability for the principal's further crime unless grounds of exculpation can be found. This may well be an accurate reflection of the assumptions underlying the old common law rule—still prevalent (though now usually enshrined in legislation) in a significant number of US States: that the accessory is liable for any further offenses committed by the principal which are a "natural and probable consequence" of the principal's embarking on the commission of the target crime (see Robinson and Williams (2018, p. 110) for a map of US jurisdictions which accept the "natural and probable consequences" rule). The companion rule for implemented (or "choate") conspiracies, the so-called Pinkerton doctrine, is that a co-conspirator "can be held liable for all of the substantive offences of co-conspirators committed in furtherance of the agreement, even if the conspirator did not assist in any of the offenses" (Robinson and Williams 2018, p. 118). Indeed, the extended common purpose rule nowadays recognized in some common law jurisdictions (which makes such extended liability hinge on the accessory's foresight that the principal might commit these further crimes) marks, from this perspective, a narrowing of broader ascription principles that were historically prevalent (*see* du Bois-Pedain 2020; Krebs 2010).

Philosophically speaking, however, this presumption of responsibility is far from evident. As Gregory Mellema has recently reminded us: "Although … a person who is complicit in the wrongdoing of a principal actor bears moral blame for his or her contributing action, such a person does not necessarily bear moral blame for the outcome produced by the contributions of everyone involved" (Mellema 2016, p. 3). Mellema then suggests that outcome responsibility would not arise when the person is "only mildly complicit in the wrongdoing of another" (ibid.), but he does not specify what contributions belong to that category. While Mellema appears to ask this question with the accomplice's moral responsibility for what lawyers would call the target offense in mind, it arises with equal force in relation to the accomplice's liability for any collateral offenses.

Another important question is whether the difference between cases falling under the standard secondary liability paradigm, on the one hand, and cases where participants act in furtherance of a common plan in ways that allow us to invoke the notion of a collective or group act, on the other hand, also matters with respect to responsibility-attribution to participants other than the direct agent for any collateral crimes.

As argued in Part II, the basic modes of responsibility-ascription under these paradigms are significantly different. For behaviors that amount to support for, assistance to, or the instigation of another person's criminally wrongful act, the accessory incurs liability because of the specific manner in which she has attached herself to the principal's wrongdoing. Conceptually speaking, the accessory is not viewed in these cases as if she was herself performing the act the principal offender carries out. Rather, the accessory commits the wrong of exerting an influence over the principal such that the principal's wrongful act is enabled or facilitated. I contrasted this mode of responsibility-ascription with the perspective appropriate in cases of genuinely joint action—scenarios John Gardner (2002) has explored under the heading "teamwork." Where persons act co-operatively in settings such as these, it is appropriate to attribute the actions of each participant to all others. Liability then arises for the "totaled up" group act in conjunction with the mens rea each participant possesses in respect of the target crime.

Andrew Simester has suggested that these different bases and modes of responsibility-ascription would support different ascription principles for collateral crimes. He argues that: "Whereas aiding and abetting doctrines are grounded in S's contribution to another's crime, joint enterprise is grounded in affiliation. S voluntarily subscribes to a co-operative endeavor, one that is identified by its shared criminal purpose. As such, joint enterprise doctrines impose a form of collective responsibility, predicated on membership of the unlawful concert" (Simester 2006, p. 599).

For Simester, it is the latter that makes the ascription of responsibility for collateral crimes legitimate:

> Through entering into a joint enterprise, S changes her normative position. She becomes, by her deliberate choice, a participant in a group action to commit a crime. Moreover, her new status has moral significance: she associates herself with the conduct of the other members of the group in a way that the mere aider or abettor, who remains an independent character throughout the episode, does not. (Simester 2006, p. 598)

Simester's position thus, in effect, rests on the mutual act-ascription that (also on my view) lies at the hard of the "acting together" liability paradigm. But it is not fully defended by mutual act-ascription. That this is so is evident from the careful distinction drawn by post 1994 Israeli law (quoted in Part I) between the direct perpetrator's liability for a crime of intent, and any co-perpetrator's liability for that same act as a crime of indifference (a lesser mens rea state than intent, and one which the secondary party herself is taken to have exhibited in respect of P's further or divergent act). Even on its own terms, the argument therefore falls short of its mark. The fact that S has, indeed, under-written the risk of certain additional acts being committed by others in further-ance of the joint goal—and accompanied with whatever intent the direct agent has at the point of performing this additional act—does not, as such, show that she would deserve to be held liable for a collateral crime of intent.

What, then, about the attribution of responsibility for collateral crimes to those who are standard secondary parties? Here, again, it appears to me that Israeli law gets it right: it is possible to conceive of the secondary's contribution as contributing to the risk that a further, collateral crime will be committed by P. Where an appropriate crime of negligence exists, the fact that P's collateral crime also results from a further intention P has only formed at that later stage should not block attributing responsibility for the outcome of that further act to S "qua" realization of a risk to which S has negligently contributed.

NOTES

1. Note to readers: another major "single principle" view was developed by Kadish, who unpacks secondary participation as exerting an influence over the princi-pal's will. I address Kadish's view when discussing what I consider the second mode of complicitous behavior—acting "through" another.

2. These facts are adapted from *Michael* ((1840) 9 C&P 356). Note that there are certain offenses where the conduct description is such that it cannot be per-formed through a (human) instrument. In such cases legal systems either forego liability on S's part or exceptionally allow for accessorial liability to be imposed on S in the absence of any principal liability. See, for example, *Cogan and Leak* (1976) Q.B. 217 where S, V's husband, convinced P of V's eagerness to have sexual intercourse with P, which (as S well knew) was completely against V's wishes. P was acquitted of rape on appeal (at that time, an honest belief in con-sent precluded mens rea). P's acquittal notwithstanding, S's conviction for aid-ing and abetting the rape of V was upheld.

3. The factual scenarios covered by this notion cover much of the same ground as what in analyses of the criminal laws of many US States is referred to as the complicity liability of co-conspirators (*see*, e.g., Robinson and Williams 2018, ch. 13). The conceptual boundaries of a choate conspiracy are usually drawn somewhat differently from a joint enterprise, though. On the one hand, all par-ties to the prior agreement, even if they have no role whatsoever in carrying out the plan, are potentially liable for complicity as co-conspirators if the conspiracy is carried out. On the other hand, a joint enterprise can arise through spontane-ous co-operation on the scene without the need for any prior agreement. To complicate matters further, many US court judgments and state legislatures employ the notion of liability based on "common design" (*see*, e.g., 720 Illinois Comp. Stat.Ann. 5/5-2(c))—a notion capacious enough to cover parties linked to a principal agent through standard forms of aiding and abetting as well as implemented conspiracies.

4. *See*, for example, Smith (1997, 1998), Simester (2006), Baker (2016), and Simester (2017). For a more detailed discussion of their views, see du Bois-Pedain (2020).

5. In addition to the modes of perpetration addressed in this chapter, some legal systems also recognize indirect perpetration of a crime through a criminally responsible agent. This notion has proven particularly influential in international criminal law, where it has been developed further into a concept of indirect co-perpetration. *See* Ambos (2013, ch. 4–5) and Eldar (2014).

6. Polish criminal law follows such a model, and England and Wales have recently created a second, nonderivative and inchoate track of accessorial liability through new statutory offenses of "assisting" and "encouraging" crime contained in the Serious Crime Act (2007, §§ 44-46). For liability under these new statutory crimes, it does not matter for S's liability whether P embarks on the commission of the target crime. Confusingly, the terminology of "assisting and encouraging" P's crime is also used as a summary term to designate the traditional common law form of (essentially derivative) secondary participation by aiding, abetting, counseling, or procuring P's offense. This form of "choate" accessorial liability continues to exist in English law. Importantly, under it, S is liable to be charged and convicted as a principal; this means that the same punishment (range) applies to S as applies to P.

7. This is perhaps unsurprising, given that the earlier provisions of Israeli criminal law had their origins in the Criminal Code Ordinance of 1936 and thus still in the Mandate period. Wisconsin and Israeli criminal laws thus share some intellectual roots.

8. It also appears to me that risking and attempting harm can be conceived of as ancillary conceptions to causal harm, at least when the notion of attempting harm is unpacked from the subjective perspective of the agent.

9. Which, on the rare occasions where the problem arises under existing secondary liability law, is done in England and Wales based on the so-called Tyrrell principle (established in the case of *Tyrrell* (1894) 1 Q.B. 710 (C.C.R.) where it was held that V, as the protected party of the offense in question, could not be indirectly made liable as a party to an offense against herself).

10. Note that when it comes to group acts, it is perfectly coherent to hypothesize that "accountability appears to accrue first to the jointly acting group, and then derivatively to its individual members" (Kutz 2000, p. 69). Kutz stresses, however, that at the end of the day a collective act will always be "explicable in terms of the intentionality of individuals" who take themselves to be acting on behalf of the collectivity, as well as "the expectations and beliefs of others regarding what [the collective agent] is and what it is capable of" (ibid., p. 71).

11. On what it means to intend to assist another's crime, see Duff (1990). For further distinctions to be drawn between the kind of intention required (requiring "direct intention" for instigation but settling for certain knowledge in respect of assistance), see Williams (1990).

12. The English doctrine was abandoned in the conjoined cases of R. v. Jogee; Ruddock v. The Queen (2016) UKSC 8; [2016] UKPC 7.

13. Smith speaks of "homicidal" actions because his remark is made in the context of discussing the secondary party's liability for a deadly act by the principal that arises in the process of the principal carrying out the crime the secondary party intended to participate in.

References

720 Ill. Comp. Stat. Ann. 5/5-2(c).

Cogan and Leak [1976] Q.B. 217.

German Criminal Code (Strafgesetzbuch), §§26, 27II, 49I.

Michael (1840) 9 C&P 356.

Penal Law 5737-1977 (Israeli Criminal Code of 1994), s. 34A(a).

R. v. Jogee; Ruddock v. The Queen [2016] UKSC 8; [2016] UKPC 7.

Serious Crime Act 2007, ss44-46 (England and Wales).

Tyrrell [1894] 1 Q.B. 710 (C.C.R.).

United States v. Peoni, 100 F.2d 401 (1938).

Wisc. Stat. §939.05.

SECTION

Alexander, Larry, and Kimberly Kessler Ferzan. 2018. *Reflections on crime and culpability: Problems and puzzles.* Cambridge: Cambridge University Press.

Ambos, Kai. 2013. Treatise on international criminal law. In Vol. 1 of *Foundations and General Part.* Oxford: Oxford University Press.

Baker, Dennis J. 2016. Reinterpreting the mental element in criminal complicity: Change of normative position theory cannot rationalize the current law. *Law and Psychology Review* 40: 119–296.

Bratman, Michael. 1999. *Faces of intention: Selected essays on intention and agency.* New York: Cambridge University Press.

Brudner, Alan. 1998. Owning outcomes: On intervening causes, thin skulls, and fault-undifferentiated crimes. *Canadian Journal of Law and Jurisprudence* 11: 89–114.

Buxton, Richard. 1969. Complicity in the criminal code. *Law Quarterly Review* 85: 252–274.

Du Bois-Pedain, Antje. 2016. Violent dynamics: Exploring responsibility-attribution for harms inflicted during spontaneous group violence. *Oñati Socio-legal Series* 6: 1053–1078.

———. 2020, Forthcoming. Participation in crime. In Vol. 1 of *Core Concepts in Criminal Law and Criminal Justice*, ed. Kai Ambos et al., 94–134. Cambridge: Cambridge University Press.

Duff, R.A. 1990. "Can I help you?" Accessorial liability and the intention to assist. *Legal Studies* 10: 165–181.

———. 2008. Is accomplice liability superfluous? *University of Pennsylvania Law Review PENNumbra* 156: 444–451.

Eldar, Shachar. 2014. Indirect co-perpetration. *Criminal Law and Philosophy* 8: 605–617.

French, Peter A. 2016. Complicity: That moral monster, troubling matters. *Criminal Law and Philosophy* 10: 575–589.

Gardner, John. 2002. Reasons for teamwork. *Legal Theory* 8: 495–509.

Herlitz, Carl Erik. 1992. *Parties to a crime and the notion of a complicity object. A comparative study of the alternatives provided by the Model Penal Code, Swedish law and Claus Roxin.* Uppsala: Iustus Förlag.

Kadish, Sanford H. 1985. Complicity, cause and blame: A study in the interpretation of doctrine. *California Law Review* 73: 323–410.

————. 1997. Reckless complicity. *Journal of Criminal Law and Criminology* 87: 369–394.

Krebs, Beatrice. 2010. Joint criminal enterprise. *Modern Law Review* 73: 578–604.

Kutz, Christopher. 2000. *Complicity. Ethics and law for a collective age.* Cambridge: Cambridge University Press.

————. 2011. The philosophical foundations of complicity law. In *The Oxford handbook of philosophy of criminal law*, ed. John Deigh and David Dolinko, 146–167. Oxford: Oxford University Press.

Lackner, Karl, and Kristian Kühl. 2018. *Strafgesetzbuch mit Erläuterungen.* 29th ed. Munich: C.H. Beck.

Lepora, Chiara, and Robert E. Goodin. 2013. *On complicity and compromise.* Oxford: Oxford University Press.

Mellema, Gregory. 2016. *Complicity and moral accountability.* South Bend: University of Notre Dame Press.

Moore, Michael. 2007–2008. Causing, aiding and the superfluity of accomplice liability. *University of Pennsylvania Law Review* 156: 395–452.

Ohana, Daniel. 2000. The natural and probable consequence rule in complicity: Section 34A of the Israeli penal law. *Israel Law Review* 34: 321–351.

Robinson, Paul H., and Tyler Scot Williams. 2018. *Mapping American criminal law: Variations across the 50 States.* Santa Barbara: Praeger.

Simester, A.P. 2006. The mental element in complicity. *Law Quarterly Review* 122: 578–601.

————. 2017. Accessory liability and common unlawful purpose. *Law Quarterly Review* 133: 73–90.

Smiley, Marion. 2017. *Collective responsibility.* The Stanford Encyclopedia of Philosophy. https://plato.stanford.edu/archives/sum2017/entries/collective-responsibility/. Accessed 8 Mar 2019.

Smith, K.J.M. 1991. *A modern treatise on the law of criminal complicity.* Oxford: Clarendon Press.

Smith, J.C. 1997. Criminal liability of accessories: Law and law reform. *Law Quarterly Review* 113: 453–467.

————. 1998. Joint enterprise and accessory liability. *South African Journal of Criminal Justice* 11: 337–349.

Stephen, James Fitzjames. 1950. In *Stephen's digest of criminal law*, ed. Frederick Lewis Sturge, 9th ed. London: Sweet & Maxwell.

Stewart, James G. 2014. Complicity. In *The Oxford handbook of criminal law*, ed. Markus Dirk Dubber and Tatjana Hörnle, 534–559. Oxford: Oxford University Press.

Williams, Glanville. 1990. Complicity, purpose and the draft code – 2. *Criminal Law Review*: 98–108.

Yeager, Daniel. 1996. Helping, doing, and the grammar of complicity. *Criminal Justice Ethics* 15: 25–35.

PART IX

Corporate Punishment

CHAPTER 10

Skepticism About Corporate Punishment Revisited

Alex Sarch

Some ancient societies—and some not-so-ancient ones—imposed liability on inanimate things. Oliver Wendell Holmes noted that in the time of Edward I, "[i]f a man fell from a tree, the tree was deodand"—that is, forfeited as an "accursed thing" and given to God (Holmes 1991, p. 7; *see also* Blackstone 1769, ch. 8). "If he drowned in a well, the well was to be filled up. It did not matter that the forfeited instrument belonged to an innocent person" (Holmes 1991, pp. 24–25). As late as in the reign of Henry VIII, it was held that if a sword kills a person, "the sword shall be forfeit as deodand, and yet no default is in the owner" (Holmes 1991, p. 25). Modern readers are likely to write off this practice as confused, unfair, or even primitive. Are we guilty of similar mistakes when we punish corporations? Some legal scholars think so (Alschuler 1991, p. 312).[1]

Nonetheless, as this chapter argues, the case for punishing corporations is on substantially better footing than the punishment of inanimate objects like swords and wells would be.[2] There are important skeptical challenges to the punishment of corporations. I argue these admit of some plausible answers where corporations are concerned, but at the end of this chapter, we see that analogous answers are of no avail for inanimate objects.

To see the main sources of skepticism about punishing corporations, assume *arguendo* that there are weighty consequentialist reasons to engage in this practice and the benefits outweigh the costs. The dominant case in favor of corporate punishment is grounded in considerations of deterrence and harm prevention (Kennedy 1985, p. 446).[3] Still, even if there is a strong consequentialist case in

A. Sarch (✉)
University of Surrey School of Law, Guildford, UK
e-mail: a.sarch@surrey.ac.uk

© The Author(s) 2019
L. Alexander, K. K. Ferzan (eds.), *The Palgrave Handbook of Applied Ethics and the Criminal Law*, https://doi.org/10.1007/978-3-030-22811-8_10

favor of corporate punishment, important sources of skepticism remain—and these are the focus of this chapter.

First, one might think a corporation[4] simply is not the right *kind of thing* to be subject to punishment. It does not have the right capacities to be culpable, which is widely thought to be a prerequisite for punishment. Call this the *eligibility challenge*. Second, one might object that even if we adequately answer the first challenge, whatever blame or condemnation we might want to direct at the object itself can simply be reduced to blame or condemnation that is more properly directed at the people who are responsible for the accursed object. If my sword slips from its case and causes death, the proper target of blame and condemnation is *me* for failing to store my dangerous belongings safely. So there may be no need for punishing the object itself; we could simply punish the relevant culpable individuals (if any) instead. Call this the *reductionist challenge*. Moreover, besides these philosophical challenges, one might think practical challenges remain in crafting punishments for inanimate objects that are both effective and that don't unfairly spill over onto innocent people (such as shareholders) who rely on or are proximate to the direct target of punishment. However, I mostly set aside this *implementation challenge* and instead focus on the logically prior philosophical questions about whether such a punishment practice even makes sense.

These skeptical arguments, though familiar, are due for a fresh look. I suggest that progress can be made by attending to recent developments in the theory of criminal culpability, as well as by being careful to distinguish questions in moral philosophy from questions of legal design. By focusing on the right questions—questions about law rather than morality—as well as by applying some lessons from the theory of culpability, we see that corporate punishment is substantially less dubious than the punishment of inanimate things would be.

The scope of this chapter is narrow in certain ways. First, as noted, I defer the implementation challenge—which covers different worries about how to design punishments that are effective[5] and fair[6]—until another time. I take it that these concerns about corporate punishment admit of some answers[7] and are in any case more naturally the topic of a separate project. Accordingly, I focus on the skeptical challenges to punishing corporations that arise *even assuming* such punishments can be carried out in fair and effective ways. Thus, my main focus is the eligibility and reductionist challenges.

Second, the chapter is narrow in that it focuses on skeptical worries rather than the affirmative case for corporate punishment. If punishing corporations is justified at all, its protective consequences surely provide the lion's share of the affirmative case in its favor. Still, I won't be concerned with the consequentialist reasons to punish corporations. Instead, I focus on the skeptical objections that might threaten *even granting* that there are consequentialist reasons to punish corporations. Forms of criminal liability that are justified purely on consequentialist grounds sometimes can conflict with core criminal law principles that we are otherwise committed to—for example, our commitment to avoiding punishment of the innocent. Even if we ultimately adopt these forms of liability, we should be clear about what—if anything—we would be giving up in doing so. As Hart noted in discussing the consequentialist reasons for the expedient of vicarious criminal liability, "[i]n extreme cases many might still think it right to resort to these expedients but we should do so with the sense of sacrificing an important principle" (Hart 2008, pp. 12, 47–48). The skeptical arguments sketched above highlight the principles we may be sacrificing by adopting the expedient of corporate punishment. The eligibility challenge implicates some possible tension with the desert constraint—the idea that we should punish actors only if and to the extent that it is deserved.[8] The reductionist challenge raises a putative conflict with the principle that criminal liability (especially new esoteric forms of it) should be used only if really necessary—"as a last resort" (Husak 2004).

Nonetheless, I argue that the sacrifices of criminal law principle involved in punishing corporations are, on closer inspection, not significant enough to render the punishment of corporations wholly unacceptable. Certainly, these sacrifices, such as they are, are less significant than the analogous drawbacks to punishing simple inanimate objects like swords or wells.

Before proceeding, let me address one concern about the project of this chapter. Perhaps you're a pragmatist who thinks it obvious that corporations cannot really deserve punishment or be either culpable or innocent; instead, they are only *deemed* legal persons so we can use the criminal process to impose a variety of desirable legal penalties on corporate members or managers or provide beneficial regulation of corporate activity.[9] If you think this, however, then you've already accepted the sort of philosophical skepticism I'm concerned to test the soundness of here. Is this really the theoretically most defensible view? Plausibly, the criminal law, in convicting corporations of crimes, at least *purports* to treat corporations as culpable actors who acted criminally, and the point of this chapter is to see how far we can get in defending this conceit from the skeptical objections it naturally faces. Can what the criminal law at least *seems* to be communicating about the corporations it convicts (that they acted culpably, etc.) be taken seriously and defended, or is philosophical skepticism and the resulting pragmatist stance the better view? This is the motivation for the questions examined in this chapter. The conceit involved in corporate punishment ends up being more defensible than the analogous conceit involved in punishing swords and wells would be. Seeing why should, I hope, help reveal something interesting about the nature and justification of our practice of corporate punishment.

The Eligibility Challenge

The first skeptical argument I'll investigate arises at the threshold of the criminal law: Corporations, as non-living entities, are arguably not the right kind of thing to be criminally punished, since they seem to lack the practical reasoning capacities to deliberate and be culpable for action. Punishment paradigmatically involves the imposition of harsh treatment in response to actions that are prohibited by law (Hart 2008, pp. 4–5). Such entities seem incapable of acting culpably and therefore ineligible for punishment.

Why, however, is this a problem? Why would it be bad to fine or dissolve a corporation and call it punishment? To sharpen the inquiry, assume *arguendo* there really are sufficiently good preventive benefits to corporate punishment to provide a consequentialist justification for the practice. What, then, is the problem with punishing the corporation itself? What principles would we be sacrificing?

The first half of this section aims to pinpoint why it would be a problem to impose criminal sanctions on things that lack the capacity to deliberate, act, and be culpable. I argue that several natural ways of understanding this cost actually pose no meaningful hurdle. Still, there is a plausible worry here. In the second half of this section, I use recent developments in the theory of culpability to argue that corporations (unlike inanimate objects) possess the right kinds of agential capacities to satisfy the conditions for counting as culpable. This suggests a plausible case for taking corporations to be eligible for criminal punishment. At least it places the burden on corporate punishment skeptics to refute this prima facie case.

Clarifying the Challenge

The eligibility challenge has two premises. First, it asserts that some class of defendants—for example, corporations or inanimate objects—are not the right kind of things to be punished because they lack certain salient agential capacities like the ability to deliberate, respond to reasons, and act, as needed to be culpable. Call this the *ineligibility premise*. Second, the objection asserts that if this premise is true, there would be substantial costs to important values if we nonetheless impose criminal sanctions on this class of defendants. Call this the *costliness premise*. The conclusion is that there are decisive reasons not to punish this class of defendants.

The eligibility challenge is hard to assess because it's not clear what the relevant costs are. I consider four natural ways to spell out the costliness premise. The first two aren't weighty where corporations are concerned, while the third and fourth are more serious. Later, I reject the ineligibility premise as regards corporations.

Conceptual Confusion

The first way to construe the costliness premise is to say that if we impose criminal sanctions on defendants without the agential capacities needed to be eligible for it, then we display a worrisome form of conceptual confusion. Punishment—at least in its paradigmatic, non-defective form—involves the imposition of hard treatment on defendants because of, or in response to, their culpable conduct in violation of a criminal prohibition (Hart 2008, pp. 4–5).

It would be a conceptual mistake to call convicting and fining the corporation (or convicting the sword and smashing it to pieces) *punishment*.

The trouble, however, is that it is not clear why conceptual confusion in its own right is so bad. Suppose we grant that in convicting and fining the corporation, we are not engaging in *real* punishment. At best, it is a bad imitation of punishment—call it punishment∗.[10] Why is this intrinsically bad? Assuming, as we are, that there are weighty consequentialist reasons for punishment∗, is conceptual confusion a substantial hurdle to adopting or continuing with that practice?

Granted, it might be *embarrassing* for us to make such conceptual mistakes. It shows that we're bad philosophers. But I doubt that this is a weighty reason to abstain from a practice that, by hypothesis, is supported by robust consequentialist reasons. If punishing∗ the corporation is a good way to incentivize people to take proper care in running their businesses, then perhaps it's well worth the embarrassment.

What's more, we can reduce the embarrassment by changing the words used to talk about this practice. Instead of calling it punishment, we should just start calling it something else: maybe "quasi-punishment." Then we could keep getting the beneficial consequences of the practice and avoid the shame. Of course, in the end it is an empirical question whether the calculus of costs and benefits ends up supporting the practice. But where corporations are concerned, it's not implausible the empirics will turn out such that this charge of conceptual confusion does not yield a particularly weighty form of the eligibility challenge.[11]

Principle of Legality

Another way to construe the costliness premise involves the principle of legality. Criminal offenses are typically defined so as to require not just conduct (the *actus reus*), but also a culpable mental state (the *mens rea*), like intention, knowledge, recklessness, or negligence. However, if a given category of entities categorically lacks the right agential capacities to be eligible for criminal punishment, then they cannot literally satisfy the elements of core criminal law offenses. If we nonetheless persist in convicting them of such offenses—of homicide, say, or the knowing violation of financial or environmental regulations—then this might seem to conflict with the *principle of legality* (Husak and Callender 1994). It is often grounded in the value of fair notice and holds that for it to be *legally permitted* to convict a defendant of a crime, it must be proved beyond a reasonable doubt that the defendant satisfies each element of the crime (and no defenses are made out, etc.). This principle would be violated if we convict and punish entities known to be incapable of satisfying certain elements of the crime. This would carry weighty costs because routinely violating the principle of legality risks harming public trust in the judiciary and the perception of its legitimacy. Conceivably, this could be on balance justified on consequentialist grounds, but there would be a weighty principle we'd have to sacrifice to attain these good consequences.

Still, there is a problem. Sometimes legal fictions can be justified, and if they become firmly embedded in the law, such that most participants are aware of and can act in light of these fictions, then the concerns behind the principle of legality would be largely satisfied. This would mean that, even if a given category of entity is not formally eligible for criminal punishment because they cannot literally satisfy mens rea elements, say, the costs to the legal system would not be especially weighty.

Indeed, this is arguably what we see with respect to corporate punishment. Even if corporations cannot literally satisfy mens rea elements, there are widely accepted legal principles that permit the imputation of mental states to corporations. Most importantly, under the *respondeat superior* doctrine, the mental states of an agent of the corporation can be imputed to it provided the agent is acting within the scope of her employment and in furtherance of corporate interests.[12] (Sometimes additional restrictions are added.[13]) Given that such imputation principles are well understood and widely accepted, the principle of legality is largely satisfied. Even if one wants to insist that such imputation principles violate the legality principle strictly construed, the costs one would normally fear from violations of the principle—like sapping the public trust in the courts and undermining their perceived legitimacy—are not likely to be very grave. Thus, even if this remains a problem for corporate punishment, it does not seem a very weighty one.

Unfairness

There are better ways to understand the costliness of punishing entities thought to be ineligible for it. I suggest two, though they rely on contestable normative assumptions.

To see the first, return to inanimate objects. Some might think that if we convict and smash the sword, it would violate the desert constraint, a fundamental limit on the criminal law. It holds that it is unfair to punish in excess of one's desert, where desert is understood chiefly as the culpability of one's illegal conduct.[14] This constraint is violated when we punish more harshly than one's culpability merits even if this otherwise is justified by its deterrent benefits. The present construal of the costliness premise is that it's the desert constraint we compromise by punishing entities that lack most agential capacities. If corporations or swords are incapable of deliberating and acting, they cannot be culpable or deserve punishment. Thus, the idea goes, punishing them violates the desert constraint and is unfair.

Let's not misunderstand the argument. Who is supposedly being treated unfairly? Distinguish (a) unfairness to the entity being punished from (b) unfairness to collateral parties, who stand in some proximate relationship to the recipient of punishment. Unfairness to collateral parties is a separate issue which concerns how to design fair and effective mechanisms for imposing the punishments that are warranted. I've set aside implementation problems in this chapter because it is a separate kind of concern that admits of some plausible answers.[15] Assuming tentatively that punishments can be designed to not be unduly burdensome to collateral parties, our main concern here is with possible unfairness to the recipients of punishment themselves. If corporations are not capable of deliberation and action, and thus cannot be culpable, would it be unfair *to them* to get fined, restricted, or destroyed as a punishment? Doesn't this necessarily exceed their desert, which is always zero?

Very likely, there would be no such unfairness. If an entity is ineligible for punishment because it lacks core agential capacities, then very likely there also would be no basis for giving it the benefit of the protections of the desert constraint—that is, regard it as having a right not to be harmed in excess of its desert. This is certainly true for simple inanimate objects like swords. As they are unable to perform any actions, how could it be unfair *to them* to damage or destroy them pursuant to a criminal process? It's not clear why they should get the benefit of the right not to be punished in excess of their desert. Thus, the general trouble is that if the ineligibility premise is true of a particular kind of entity, then very likely the desert constraint would not apply to these entities.

We cannot dismiss the present argument just yet, however. There is logical space for entities that have a *right* not to be punished in excess of their desert but which nonetheless are ineligible for criminal punishment because they do not have the capacities needed to be *culpable* (and thus always have culpability zero). This might be plausible for entities with enough cognitive function— like the ability to act and to experience pain—to give them moral considerability, but who nonetheless are ineligible for criminal punishment because they lack the practical reasoning capacities—like the ability to deliberate and weigh reasons—needed for being culpable for what they do. Perhaps this is true of some animals (or, in the future, highly sophisticated artificially intelligent entities). If a horse lacks the capacities needed to be culpable, it might still be unfair *to the horse* to punish it, given that its culpability is zero.

This suggests a way to rehabilitate the present interpretation of the eligibility challenge where corporations are concerned. Could we show for corporations that even though they are ineligible for criminal punishment they still should get the benefit of the desert constraint? If so, then punishing them could really be unfair *to them*.

While possible, getting this version of the argument to bite for corporations does seem difficult. It requires showing that corporations are like horses in being able to act and have sufficient experiences to acquire the protection of the desert constraint, but they nonetheless do not have sufficient agential capacities to be culpable for what they do, such that punishing them is always unfair. Perhaps this is possible, but it's a tall order. The position is unstable. The more one beefs up the case for thinking that corporations are the kind of things that have moral considerability and get the benefit of the desert constraint, the harder it will be to show that they cannot be culpable for what they do (as the ineligibility premise states).[16] Thus, this seems a difficult position to establish.

Demanding a Retributive Justification

A final interpretation of the eligibility challenge rests on the claim that because "corporate punishment cannot be justified retributively," it does not further one of the essential purposes of the criminal law (Thomas 2017, p. 612). The question is why this is a weighty cost. Even if corporate punishment does not serve one of the major functions of criminal law—that is, provide retribution for culpable conduct[17]—why is this an affirmative *problem*, especially if we assume corporate punishment is robustly supported by its beneficial preventive consequences? Generally, if something scores poorly on one of the dimensions or functions we want it to serve, this can be made up for if the thing scores well enough on the other dimensions or functions. Thus, if corporate punishment fares well enough on deterrence or incapacitation grounds, why couldn't this render the practice on balance justified?[18]

There is a possible answer, but it relies on a surprising picture of how legal practices are justified. In particular, this version of the argument presupposes that if a given legal practice, L, does not serve one of the purposes we want it to serve *sufficiently well*, then L cannot be on balance justified no matter how well it serves the rest of these purposes. Although surprising, there are real-world cases that involve such a justificatory structure. Consider buying a car. If the car has unbelievably bad acceleration, then it's not going to be a justified purchase no matter how good fuel mileage and top speed it has.[19]

Thus, this version of the eligibility challenge amounts to interpreting the costliness premise as the claim that if we punish certain entities in spite of their ineligibility for punishment, then the cost this entails is that we are engaging in a practice that is on balance normatively unjustified. To continue doing so despite recognizing this lack of justification shows our conduct to be irrational and indefensible.

Answering the Eligibility Challenge for Corporations

We have seen two plausible ways to interpret the eligibility challenge, particularly its costliness premise. Where corporations are concerned, however, there is reason to reject the ineligibility premise. By paying attention to what culpability is, we see that corporations plausibly do have the capacities needed to be culpable.

On what has become the dominant view, criminal culpability is to be understood in terms of the actor's insufficient regard for important reasons, interests, or values (Alexander and Ferzan 2009, pp. 67–68; Westen 2006, pp. 373–374; Yaffe 2011, p. 38; Tadros 2005, p. 250).[20] This is an increasingly popular way to understand moral blameworthiness as well (Arpaly and Schroeder 2014, p. 270). On this view, one is criminally culpable for an action to the extent it manifests insufficient regard for legally protected interests or values—that is, what we might call the legally recognized reasons bearing on how to act. The law does not demand that we are motivated by respect for these interests and values, but it does demand that we not put our *disrespect* for them on display by acting in ways that are inconsistent with attaching proper weight to protected interests and values. Insufficient regard thus is a form of ill will or indifference that leads to mistakes in the way one recognizes, weighs, and responds to the applicable reasons for acting. One *manifests* insufficient regard for them by behaving in ways that can only plausibly be explained by one's not attaching sufficient weight to these interests and values (as opposed to, say, not being a competent or rational actor). Thus, if I undervalue John's well-being so much that I act in ways I know will kill him in order to accomplish my personal goal of making money, this manifests insufficient regard for interests that the law demands we not show disrespect for.

Note that criminal culpability may or may not be the same thing as moral blameworthiness. On one view, criminal culpability *just is* moral blameworthiness, such that legitimate punishment requires being morally to blame (cf. Moore 1990, pp. 30–31; Husak 2016, p. 34).[21] Other views emphasize the differences between criminal culpability and moral blameworthiness, which stem from institutional design constraints on culpability that the analogous moral notion is not subject to (D'Souza 2015, p. 453; Sarch 2019, ch. 2). These constraints might be, for example, the pervasive need for the law's prohibitions to be simple enough to serve as a publicly available guide to action, the need to take a clear stand on difficult moral questions, or the need to take account of regular human epistemic limitations.

I won't resolve this question here. Just note that the insufficient regard theory can capture both positions. Each corresponds to one picture of what the reasons are that the law demands we not manifest insufficient regard for. On the one hand, criminal culpability collapses into moral blameworthiness if the reasons the law properly recognizes simply *are* the moral reasons bearing on how to act. By contrast, criminal culpability comes apart from moral blameworthiness if it turns out the law should recognize a different—perhaps narrower—set of reasons that one shouldn't display insufficient regard for (or if the law would give them different weights than morality). Criminal culpability, on this view, could be seen as a stripped-down analog of moral blameworthiness, with the legal notion of tracking a less-fine-grained set of reasons (or perhaps reasons with different weights) than the moral notion.[22] Thus, moral blameworthiness would not be a prerequisite for proper punishment, only criminal culpability would.

Regardless of how one sees the relation between criminal culpability and moral blameworthiness, the crucial point is that if the insufficient regard theory of criminal culpability is true, then corporations plausibly possess the agential capacities needed to count as culpable. This theory entails that an entity cannot be criminally culpable unless it is reason responsive in the right way—that is, unless it can appreciate, weigh, and act on the relevant reasons for action. Insufficient regard cannot be manifested otherwise.

Corporations plausibly have what it takes. Through their members, they can recognize, weigh, and act on the reasons that the criminal law demands we not manifest insufficient regard for. Corporations routinely engage in deliberation and action. They set goals, adopt strategies for attaining their goals, gather information, and deliberate about how to improve their performance in accomplishing what they set out to do. Moreover, they (usually) strive to do so while being sensitive to the demands of the law so as not to incur undesirable penalties. That is, they guide their conduct by attending to the reasons encoded in law, as directed by their lawyers and compliance officers. Corporations often possess complex decision-making structures, with employees feeding information to and receiving orders from management, who in turn are instructed by and accountable to directors and ultimately shareholders. This hierarchical structure allows corporations to engage in exceptionally complex coordinated activities, as illustrated by global logistics operations or sophisticated investment strategies. As a result, corporations are able to function competently in a range of normatively infused activities. For example, they routinely contract with others, which is a practice akin to promising (Thomas 2017, pp. 612–613).[23]

Thus, corporations are capable of recognizing, weighing, acting on, and guiding their activities in the light of the legally recognized reasons. If so, they have the capacities needed to be criminally culpable as understood by the insufficient regard theory. It is not hard to find examples that further support this conclusion. If a corporation learns, through its employees, that its manufacturing processes generate dangerous waste that is seeping into the drinking water in the nearby town, this is a legally recognized reason for altering its conduct. But if the corporation continues its activities unchanged, this demonstrates that it—through its information-sharing and decision-making procedures—did not end up attaching sufficient weight to the legally recognized reasons against continuing its dangerous manufacturing activities. This is paradigmatic culpability.

One might object that a corporation's practical reasoning and decision-making capacities merely derive from, or are composed out of, those of the corporation's members. However, this is a worry about reducibility—a question to be directly confronted in the next section. It does not undermine corporations' threshold eligibility for punishment. The mere fact that corporations have composite practical reasoning capacities does not entail that these capacities are devoid of normative significance or otherwise cannot produce conduct that manifests insufficient regard.[24]

To see this more clearly, consider an analogy to individuals. On a plausible view, persons are temporally extended entities, consisting of the fusion of each time-slice in which the person exists. Moreover, such temporally extended entities can deliberate collectively. How? Through decision-making procedures that allow individual time-slices to each have an input into the collective decision. A familiar example is revisiting a decision multiple times before you act so as to make sure that the chosen action really is what you want to do (i.e. a reflection of a stable preference). We can model this as a series of time-slices deliberating collectively about how to behave at some point in the future, say, t5. Suppose each time-slice of the person votes on how to behave at t5: The t1 time-slice votes at t1, then the t2 time-slice votes at t2, then the t3 slice votes, and so on. Each votes on whether the specific action at t5 will be carried out. The decision is structured such that the action is performed only if there are sufficient votes in favor of it at t5—that is, only if it obtained sufficient support by the relevant time-slices. If this is the case, then the temporally extended person can be said "not to have changed her mind." Finally, suppose the action in question is criminally culpable. Each time-slice seems culpable for voting to continue on the path to doing the criminal action—for not blocking the crime. Each time-slice has the necessary deliberative faculties for this, since it can weigh the reasons for or against voting this or that way. Nonetheless, this method of reaching a decision about how to behave at t5 intuitively does not prevent the temporally extended person—the fusion of the time-slices from t1 to t5—from *also* being culpable.

An analogous structure appears among decision-makers within a corporation. If each member is individually culpable for supporting a particular course of criminal conduct, why should this prevent the corporation, which is comprised of and acts through these members, from being culpable as well? Granted, there are reducibility worries lurking nearby. Perhaps there is no distinct, non-reducible culpability that attaches to the corporation. But reducibility is a separate problem, which admits of separate answers. The crucial point here is that it's not clear why the corporation cannot *also* be culpable, in addition to its members, in the same way that the temporally extended person can *also* be culpable, in addition to the individual time-slices it is composed out of.

Accordingly, there is good reason to think that corporations do possess—by virtue of the contributions made by the individual persons that make them up—the agential capacities needed to be criminally culpable. They can perceive, weigh, and act on (i.e. guide their behavior in light of) the legally recognized reasons. Thus they can manifest insufficient regard in their actions when they act in ways that show they have failed to attach the appropriate weights to the relevant legal reasons.

As a result, the ineligibility premise is difficult to defend. Those who embrace philosophical skepticism about corporate punishment because of the eligibility challenge have a steep uphill battle before them, given this prima facie case in favor of corporate eligibility for punishment.

The Reductionist Challenge

Even if the eligibility challenge can be met, a deeper source of skepticism threatens. Do we really *need* to punish corporations, given that we already have extensive criminal liability for individuals? A skeptic might argue that any time it seems apt to blame a corporation, this can be fully reduced to blame that properly belongs to individual actors within the corporation. However, what I argue is that while this worry is hard to answer for the *moral blameworthiness* of corporations, there is a plausible strategy for answering it as to *legal culpability*.

Clarifying the Challenge

Start by clarifying the challenge. It comes in two versions: one metaphysical and one practical. To see the first, suppose corporate culpability is fully reducible to individual culpability. What would follow from this *reducibility premise*? It would be a mistake to infer from it that there is *no such thing* as corporate culpability. We don't infer from the reducibility, say, of water to H20, of software to the machinery running it, or of biological properties to physical properties, that water, software, and biological properties don't exist (Hurd and Moore 2018, p. 31). Rather, what follows from the reducibility of one set of facts (or properties, etc.), A, to another, B, is that B is somehow more basic than A. This plausibly means we would lose nothing of explanatory importance if we eliminate the A-facts from our picture of the world. Granted, there may be pragmatic reasons to retain them: Perhaps talk of the A-facts is convenient shorthand for the B-facts, which lets us more quickly draw out or manipulate relevant information. Still, one might think that when it comes to capturing the truth about the world, nothing would be lost by eliminating the A-facts. We don't *need* them. This version of the reducibility challenge suggests it would be confusing, inaccurate, or gratuitous to punish corporations insofar as corporate culpability is fully reducible.[25]

A second way to understand the reductionist challenge is more practical. From the reducibility premise, we might conclude that corporate punishment is not really needed to accomplish the goals of criminal law—such as preventing harm to victims through deterrence, expressing condemnation of wrongful conduct, or otherwise giving actors their just deserts. Since the machinery of the criminal law is not only costly to apply, but also coercive and violent, in order to justify its use, an especially strong justification is needed. This thought underlies the principle that criminal law should only be used as a "last resort" (cf. Husak 2004). Thus, the thinking goes, if corporate culpability is fully reducible to individual culpability, then familiar versions of individual liability can adequately secure the goals of the criminal law, and so there is no call to adopt a new, more esoteric, and broader form of criminal liability, namely, the imposition of criminal liability on corporations. This line of thinking derives further support from a conservative (in the non-political sense) approach to legal change. On this view, we should always only make the smallest possible change to the existing forms of criminal liability in order to secure the goals of the criminal law. If we can accomplish everything we want without introducing any new, more expansive, and less well-understood legal technology, then better not to introduce the new technology. So, if corporate culpability fully reduces to more familiar forms of individual culpability, then there is no call to introduce the new legal technology of attributing culpability to corporations and punishing them.

Answering the Challenge

Interesting responses have been proposed to the reducibility-based challenge—regardless of which version one prefers. These answers try to show that there really is a need for corporate punishment by highlighting ways in which corporations can incur culpability that is not fully reducible to individual culpability. Thus, they amount to denying the reducibility premise on which the challenge rests. I consider two of the best arguments to this effect, rejecting the first but defending the second.

Judgment Aggregation

The first response involves judgment aggregation. It uses observations about decisions reached through voting in order to show that a corporation can end up making judgments and adopting courses of action not endorsed by any individual within the corporation. Many cases illustrate the point (e.g. see List 2012), but consider a plausibly criminal version of the familiar Employee Safety case (Hindricks 2009, p. 165; Lackey 2012, p. 248). Suppose a company is deciding whether to increase executive compensation or improve worker safety. If the pay increase is not adopted, the funds will be used to improve worker safety. Suppose under the circumstances, the pay increase is justified if three questions are answered "yes": (1) Is the pay raise deserved based on past performance? (2) Are the existing safety measures in line with industry standards? (3) Would the proposed safety measures provide only an insignificant reduction in the level of risk to which workers are exposed? The members vote thus:

	Pay raise deserved?	Safety up to industry standards?	Only insignificant safety gains?	Pay increase?
A	No	Yes	Yes	No
B	Yes	No	Yes	No
C	Yes	Yes	No	No
Majority	Yes	Yes	Yes	Yes

Since a majority answers each question in the affirmative, the company ends up adopting the pay increase and declining to implement the proposed safety measures instead. Still, no individual supports this decision. For different reasons, they would all reject the pay increase and make the funds available for improving safety.

Some theorists use this result to argue that there can be group responsibility that is not reducible to individual responsibility (Copp 2007, pp. 369–388; Pettit and List 2011). Suppose the decision to raise executive pay was in fact unjustified, as indeed the individual members themselves believe. Moreover, suppose this choice directly leads to worker deaths that could have been prevented by increasing safety instead. In that case, it seems a serious wrong has been done. But who should take the blame? The corporation itself seems the best candidate, since each individual decision-maker can plausibly argue that because she did not support the pay raise, she is not to blame. This suggests that corporate culpability may not always be reducible to individual culpability.

However, there are problems with this argument against the reducibility of corporate to individual culpability. First, the individual members can remain culpable—at least morally—for their decision to vote as they did. Hindricks argues that where the issues voted on involve normative questions—as at least (1) and (3) do here—then an erroneous vote with respect to them can manifest insufficient regard for the underlying reasons one should have recognized and responded appropriately to (Hindricks 2009, pp. 170–173). Thus, suppose that in fact, while questions (1) and (2) are actually to be answered "yes," question (3) should be answered "no." The pay raise may be deserved and industry safety standards are met, but it would be morally callous to describe the safety gains from foregoing the pay raise as "insignificant." Thus, both A and B got this issue wrong. Accordingly, their votes plausibly manifest insufficient regard for the interests of the workers, so A and B seem culpable for their votes (at least morally). As a result, grounds remain for thinking that the apparent culpability of the corporation can be reduced to the individual culpability of A and B for their votes.

Voting behavior is not the only possible source of individual culpability here. In addition, it is conceivable that the person(s) who designed this decision-making procedure could incur some culpability for it if it was at least foreseeable that it would yield unjustifiable outcomes too often. Moreover, the decision of the managers who implement the decision to raise executive pay despite the fact that it's not supported by any of the individual voting members could also be a source of individual culpability. Given that plausible sources of individual culpability remain in play, such cases involving judgment aggregation don't definitively rule out the reducibility of corporate to individual culpability. For all that's been said so far, perhaps corporate culpability can always be reduced to individual culpability.

Culpability Deficits

A second answer to the reducibility challenge, then, proceeds in a more careful way. Rather than trying to show that sometimes corporations can be culpable when the individuals are not culpable *at all*, a different strategy is to allow that there are some culpable individuals involved in the group-caused harm but insist that the total amount of culpability attributed to individuals nonetheless can be *less* than the total amount of culpability that seems warranted for the group-caused harm. Following Pettit and List, I'll call this a *culpability deficit*. Where, then, is this leftover amount of culpability to be directed? The idea offered by Pettit and List is that it is the *group agent* itself—that is, the corporation—that should be saddled with the leftover amount.

On Pettit and List's view, a culpability deficit is especially likely to occur when some individuals in the corporation possess an *excuse* that mitigates their individual culpability. They suggest a number of excuses that could lead to culpability deficits:

> It may be that the individuals are *blamelessly ignorant* of the harm they bring about together [or that] they each take themselves *not to make a pivotal difference* to it, as in the awful case of a firing squad in which members each treat the behavior of the others as fixed. (...) Or it may be that they take themselves to make... not the right sort of difference [as when] each driver in a group of dangerously speeding cars may see that he or she dare not slow down, for *fear of making a bad outcome worse*[.] Finally, it may be that...they each *act under such felt pressure that they cannot be held fully responsible* for their contribution to a bad outcome; they can each argue that the circumstances mitigate their personal control and responsibility. (Pettit and List 2011, p. 165, emphasis added)

A number of individual defenses are mentioned here: blameless factual ignorance (mistake), denying causation, a lesser evils justification and duress. Some of these look more like justifications than excuses. Nonetheless, the thought is that if the individuals acted in conditions that lowered their culpability, then the total amount of culpability that seems warranted for the group-caused harm would be *greater* than the sum of individual culpability attributed to each of the at least partially excused or justified individual actors in question. This would be a culpability deficit. This, in turn, explains why we need corporate culpability: We need it to fill the gap left by culpability deficits.

What is the significance of mentioning excuses and justifications here? It's because of a suppressed assumption in the argument.[26] In particular, the argument posits a difference between two quanta of culpability: (a) the overall amount of culpability for the group-caused harm in question, or *global culpability*, and (b) the sum of the separate amounts of culpability attributable to specific individuals for their personal actions that contributed to the harm or *net individual culpability*. There is a culpability deficit if global culpability > net individual culpability. A key premise of the argument, of course, is that there sometimes *are* culpability deficits. For there to be culpability deficits, it must be possible for (a) to be greater than (b). This requires that global culpability tracks something different than net individual culpability. But what?

Thus, for the argument to succeed, we need a story about what global culpability tracks that allows it to be greater than net individual culpability. One possibility, at least loosely suggested by Pettit and List's passage above, is that while individual culpability tracks the insufficient regard manifested by one's wrongful (i.e. unjustified) conduct *after* excuses are applied, global culpability tracks the total amount of culpability incurred by individuals for their wrongful (i.e. unjustified) conduct *before* excuses are applied. Thus, an *individual's* culpability would be found by starting with her wrongful conduct (i.e. conduct that is on balance wrongful even after any justifications are taken into account), and then considering any excuses (i.e. considerations meriting sympathy or a concession to human frailty), and then determining how much insufficient regard that wrongful but perhaps excused conduct manifests. These amounts are then added up for all relevant individuals to determine net individual culpability. By contrast, global culpability is to be found by considering the overall badness of the individuals' conduct *before* personal excuses are considered. Thus, to find the global culpability of some bit of group wrongdoing, we would (a) consider all the relevant bits of individual wrongdoing (i.e. conduct that is not justified even after possible justifying reasons are accounted for), (b) determining, for each one, how much insufficient regard it manifests (now, not considering personal excuses), and then (c) adding up all these quanta of individual pre-excuse culpability. Because excuses figure into net individual culpability but not global culpability, we have a possible story about how the latter can be greater than the former.

This is not the only possible way to explain how global culpability could be greater than net individual culpability. Another proposal is that while individual culpability remains the same as above, global culpability tracks something different—something victim-focused, rather than agent-focused. In particular, perhaps global culpability is tracking the *total amount of wrongfully imposed harm suffered by victims*—as adjusted by the degree of wrongfulness in its imposition. The reason for the latter qualification is that global culpability can't be tracking *just* the amount of wrongfully imposed harm suffered by victims of the group's misconduct. After all, one company might cause severe harm to a large number of people, n, through just a tiny bit of negligence. This wouldn't generate as much global culpability as knowingly causing an equally severe harm to a slightly smaller number of people, $n-1$. The latter surely can generate more global culpability than the former. Accordingly, on this proposal, global culpability equals (a) the total amount of harm that is wrongfully imposed on victims times (b) the degree of wrongfulness in its imposition (which is at least in part a function of the mens rea of the individuals within the group toward the harm in question).

Assuming the idea of culpability deficits can be understood in one of these two ways, does the argument succeed? *Are* there culpability deficits in either of these two ways? This may be doubtful at least if we are concerned with moral blameworthiness. But there is reason to think there both are and *should be* culpability deficits where legal culpability is concerned (thus preserving a need to appeal to the notion of corporate culpability).

On the moral front, the reason to be skeptical of culpability deficits is that whenever a group wrong has been carried out, it seems one could always expand the scope of the inquiry—perhaps with no small amount of creativity by the theorist—so as to identify some defective conduct by some individuals, which should have been avoided. For example, a skeptic might take any case where global culpability initially seems to outstrip net individual culpability but then expand the time-frame further and further back in order to find prior upstream instances of bad behavior (perhaps by people who are no longer around) that are culpable and in this way fill in what at first seemed to be a culpability deficit. To illustrate, suppose a company had sub-standard risk detection and compliance procedures at t1 that led to wrongfully imposed harm at t2, but at neither t1 nor t2 can we identify any individual who behaved without due care. By focusing just on t1 and t2, we might think a culpability gap is present. Nonetheless, the current proposal is to look back to t0 at those who *designed* and *implemented* these faulty procedures or allowed them to decay into a faulty state. In this way, we might identify individuals who were culpable at t0 and thus close the culpability gap that initially seemed present. If expanding the scope of the inquiry temporally does no good, perhaps we can zoom out spatially to other actors and thus identify individual culpability on the part of, say, regulators or other contributors to prevailing market conditions.

Thus, the worry here is that at least for moral blameworthiness, we can always make similar moves in any putative case of a culpability deficit. This yields a recipe that can, in principle, always be used in trying to close the culpability gap, and it seems difficult to generally rule out the success of this recipe ex ante. We seem to be left with a situation where each putative culpability deficit would have to be considered one at a time and dissected in detail to determine if it really is a genuine example of the phenomenon. As a result, I am not optimistic that we will be able to defend the culpability deficit response to the reductionist challenge—at least where moral culpability is concerned.

Notice, however, that the same considerations do not apply when we shift to *criminal culpability*. After all, any defensible legal system would not allow us to expand the culpability inquiry for individuals outward in time and space indefinitely far. There are inherent limits to the culpability inquiry the law performs. The statute of limitations prevents us from looking further and further back in time in search of responsible actors. Jurisdictional boundaries prevent us from zooming further and further out geographically in search of the same. Most importantly, the principle of legality demands that in criminal prosecutions, we adhere to the limitations encoded in the laws in force at the time of the wrongs in question. These laws will not criminalize infinitely fine-grained or minute forms of misconduct, but rather will focus on broader and more serious categories of directly harmful misconduct that can be straightforwardly defined, identified, and prosecuted. Minute wrongs or hard-to-detect misconduct in low-stakes settings will slip through the cracks, at least within balanced and prudent criminal justice systems. This, too, blocks the search for ever-more minute or mundane bits of individual misconduct to which corporate culpability might be reduced.

As a result, legal systems like ours very likely will not allow us to secure *criminal convictions* for all the minute and mundane individual misconduct that goes together to constitute a criminal act by a corporation. Where legal liability is concerned, it's less plausible than in the moral case that any time it seems apt to hold a corporation criminally liable, this liability can always be reduced to separate bits of liability to be imposed on individuals, which fully account for the total criminal liability to be doled out for the corporate crime in question. Individual criminal liability plausibly does not go far enough to guarantee that there will be no deficit left to be apportioned.

To this, the skeptic might reply that this is merely a problem with our laws. If individual criminal liability doesn't go far enough to capture all the blame to be allocated for some bit of corporate misconduct, then the law should be *revised* so there always are enough individual crimes on the books to ensure that all the global culpability that seems due—all the blame that seems warranted—can be attributed to individual actors.

Although I can't fully answer this worry here, here is the sort of answer I think we'll need to give. Expanding individual liability so it always accounts for all the global culpability that seems due, such that there is never a culpability deficit that makes corporate culpability needed, *would be a very bad policy*. This is because doing so would likely require criminalizing very minute misconduct—like momentary lapses of attention, the failure to perceive emerging problems that it would be difficult but not impossible to notice, a tiny bit of carelessness here or there, natural mistakes in judgment calls about how to prioritize one's time or resources, getting carried away with excitement about a project, or not being sufficiently skeptical of the group's agenda. Criminalizing such minute and mundane failures—investigating them and deploying the heavy machinery of the criminal law to hold people to account for them—would be highly invasive and threaten other values we hold dear, such as autonomy or freedom of expression and association. Moreover, this expansion of individual liability would increase the risk of over-prosecution and other abuses of criminal process. Accordingly, it would seem a dangerous policy to expand individual criminal liability as far as would be necessary to ensure that culpability deficits never arise.

This, I suspect, is the best way to push back against the reductionist challenge where criminal culpability is concerned. The answer amounts to pointing out principled *moral* reasons for the criminal law not to be such as to completely rule out culpability gaps. We should expect culpability deficits in any well-designed criminal law system. And so, in such systems, there will remain a *need* for corporate criminal culpability, and hence corporate punishment, as an independent concept that cannot be fully reduced to individual culpability and punishment.

Note that this is a principled, normative argument. As such, it goes beyond merely local, pragmatic arguments for corporate culpability that also are common. It is all too easy to point to the practical difficulties in detecting and prosecuting crimes in corporate settings as the primary reason to accept corporate culpability and punishment. By contrast, the argument developed here against reducibility of corporate culpability is a more principled point than simply that it makes life easier for prosecutors. Rather, the argument offered here appeals to stable principles applicable to legal systems like ours, rather than highly changeable pragmatic considerations that could vary from case to case.[27] There are, in other words, good reasons to think that well-designed legal systems should not allow the legal culpability of corporations to always be reduced to the legal culpability of individuals.[28]

CONCLUSION: ACCURSED THINGS OR CULPABLE ACTORS?

The eligibility and reductionist challenges for corporate punishment thus admit of some promising answers. First, where eligibility is concerned, we have reasons to regard corporations as the kinds of agents that can act in ways that manifest insufficient regard for legally protected interests and values and thus be culpable for their conduct. Thus, there is a stronger case for taking them to be eligible for criminal punishment than inanimate objects like wells and swords. For corporations, we saw a prima facie case in favor of thinking that, through their members, they possess agential capacities of information gathering, deliberation, and decision. Moreover, they routinely engage in normative practices like contracting, acting as fiduciaries, relying on the trust of others, and accounting for their behavior when they cause harm. This is one respect in which corporate punishment is on stronger footing than the punishment of inanimate objects. No similar prima facie case can be made that swords or wells have sufficient agential capacities to manifest insufficient regard in their conduct. They neither gather information, comprise deliberative procedures to reach decisions, nor exhibit any other behavior than passively being moved around. Accordingly, it is much more difficult to contend that simple inanimate objects are eligible for being subject to the criminal law.

Second, there are good institutional design reasons to regard corporations as having culpability that is not reducible to individual culpability. We saw that while it will be difficult to completely rule out the possibility of reducing the moral blameworthiness of corporations to individual moral blameworthiness, well-designed legal systems should not allow the legal culpability of corporations to always be reduced to that of individuals.

Analogous arguments do not apply for inanimate objects. For corporations, it's plausible that were the criminal law revised so there always is sufficient individual liability available to prevent culpability deficits from arising, the law would become highly invasive and would criminalize much broader and more minute types of conduct than a defensible criminal law system should. But the same does not hold for objects like swords or wells. The ways in which conduct can be culpable with respect to the storage, maintenance, or use of such objects seem much less variable. Individual culpability in this context seems to arise chiefly from the failure to take sufficient precautions with respect to how one stores, maintains, or uses the object. Thus, articulating sufficient individual crimes ex ante in order to prevent culpability deficits from arising for simple inanimate objects does not seem as daunting a prospect. But in the corporate context, given how dramatically different their activities are, and all the complex, multifaceted roles that individuals might play in these activities, this task would be extremely onerous.

Furthermore, invasive investigative techniques seem needed to identify every instance of bad individual behavior involved in a corporate crime. The same does not hold for typical inanimate objects. Identifying bad behavior with respect to simple inanimate objects likely can be accomplished by investigating a few kinds of activities: How the object was stored, maintained, and used. Law enforcement would not be likely to need extensive insight into communications, group deliberations, corporate culture, research activities, or risk-management procedures.

As a result, for most inanimate objects, it seems unlikely to be as normatively problematic to revise the criminal law so individual liability always suffices to prevent culpability deficits from arising. While we have strong reasons not to give in to the reductionist challenge as applied to corporate culpability, there is no similar imperative with respect to criminal liability for simple inanimate objects. Where they are concerned, reduce away. Corporate punishment fares better as regards the reductionist challenge than the punishment of inanimate objects would.

We have seen reasons to question the main sources of philosophical skepticism about corporate punishment. Unlike the punishment of inanimate objects, a practice that rightly would be met with skepticism, we can make sense of corporate punishment in ways that promise to render it normatively defensible. Far from merely being accursed things—something akin to a sword or well merely to be declared *deodand*—corporations look remarkably like the kind of actor that can be deemed culpable for their crimes and punished accordingly. It is the skeptic's task to show otherwise.

NOTES

1. For example, Albert Alschuler writes: "To superstitious people, villains need not breath[e]; they may include Exxon and the phone company. The corporation thus becomes for some of us…deodand. Just as primitive people hated and punished the wheel of a cart that had run someone over, or the horse that had thrown its rider, or the sword that murderer had used, some of us truly manage to hate the corporate entity" (*see also* Alschuler 1991, p. 312, *see also* Alschuler 2009, p. 1359).
2. Admittedly, requiring a lethal object to be forfeit is not exactly the same as *punishing* it. But it comes close: a condemnatory label, *deodand*, is applied to the object itself and Holmes suggests this early legal procedure likely was "grounded in vengeance" (Holmes 1991, p. 2). Thus, it is not hard to imagine this practice morphing over time into one that genuinely does involve the imposition of criminal liability on the accursed thing.
3. For example, as Christopher Kennedy notes, "[t]he mainstream of commentary…has settled on a utilitarian rationale for the corporate fine, with deterrence as its center-piece" (Kennedy 1985, p. 446).
4. Analogous questions come up for other entities like partnerships and closely held corporations. But I focus mainly on large publicly held corporations as they tend to have the most sophisticated deliberative capabilities. Thus, the theoretical case for their eligibility for punishment is likely to be on the firmest footing. If we can't justify punishing publicly held corporations, then there's little hope that we'll be able to justify punishing more informal entities. (But bear in mind that these arguments are more affected by the *complexity* of the entity's information-sharing and decision-making procedures than its precise legal form.)

5. Fines are the most common forms of corporate punishment. *See, for example,* U.S.S.G. § 8C1.1 (criminal fines for criminal purpose organizations), U.S.S.G. § 8C2.1-8 (criminal fines for other organizations). One worry about using fines to punish corporations is the "deterrence trap," wherein fines cease to be effective as deterrents as the corporation subjected to them moves closer and closer to insolvency (Coffee 1982, p. 390). Another problem with using fines to punish corporations, as Larry Summers put it, is that "[m]anagers do not find it personally costly to part with even billions of dollars of their shareholders' money" (Summers 2014).

6. The main fairness worry here is often referred to as the "spillover problem" and rests on the observation that punishing corporations through fines inevitably spills over to harm innocent shareholders. As Glanville Williams argued, "a fine imposed on the corporation is in reality aimed against shareholders who are not…responsible for the crime, i.e., is aimed against innocent persons" (Williams 1961, p. 863).

7. One might help solve the efficacy problem by using other kinds of punishments in addition to fines, such as imposing various conditions of corporate probation (U.S.S.G. § 8D1.4) or community service (U.S.S.G. § 8B1.3). If these fail, one might even consider the "corporate death penalty" for repeat-offender organizations, whereby the corporate charter would be revoked and operations halted (Ramirez 2005).

   This still leaves the spillover problem, but it too admits of answers. *First,* one might reply that collateral consequences imposed on innocent shareholders are not intended, only foreseen. I have doubts about this reply, since also knowingly imposing harm on the innocent (even if not intentional) could also be a troubling outcome to be avoided. *Second,* and more plausibly, one might reply that virtually all punishments—and indeed most civil liability and regulatory actions—are prone to spilling over onto innocent people in close proximity to the primary target. Thus, one might reply, corporate criminal fines are no different than individual punishments or other legal actions when it comes to collateral consequences. It is just a general feature of any cost-imposing legal action, and so it can be justified as long as the good substantially outweighs the harm caused. Of course, this will be unsatisfying if one thinks the collateral consequences of *punishment* typically are particularly serious or burdensome, and so the only proper response is to do all we can to minimize *all spillover* onto the innocent caused by our punishment practices. This would apply both to individual punishments (and might ground, e.g. support programs for dependents of the incarcerated) and to corporate punishments. Thus, the *third* reply to the spillover problem specifically for corporate punishments is to seek to fix the problem with our laws by seeking ways to minimize the burdens that corporate punishments impose on shareholders. Some theorists have recently proposed just such reforms. For instance, Will Thomas defends a system of corporate criminal fines where the fines paid by the corporation are clawed back from managers found to be culpably involved in the crime for which the corporation was convicted (Thomas 2017).

8. *See infra* note 14.

9. Thanks to Samuel Buell for pressing me on this point.

10. *See* Hart (2008, p. 5) discussing defective cases of punishment and the illicit "definitional stop" method of defining away difficult cases.

11. One might reply that convicting a corporation or sword is costly not because of conceptual confusion, but because it amounts to a lie. (Thanks to Ambrose Lee for this suggestion.) However, to employ a legal fiction is not necessarily to lie, and even if it is, it's not necessarily wrongful. Some legal fictions (plausibly just as with some lies) can be on balance justified, after all. Moreover, we could reduce the perception of this particular legal fiction being a wrongful lie if we call the practice punishment* rather than punishment. Thus, the current way of understanding the costliness premise needn't generate a very weighty concern.

12. As one scholar notes, "[i]n the United States, the doctrine of respondeat superior has been the most traditionally accepted method of imputing criminal liability to a corporation" (Kircher 2009, p. 157). Under respondeat superior, "a corporation is liable for the deeds of any of its agents or employees...as long as...[t]he agent was acting within the course and scope of his or her employment, having the authority to act for the corporation with respect to the particular corporate business which was conducted criminally [and] the agent acting, at least in part in furtherance of the corporation's business interests" (internal alterations and quotation marks omitted) (Lederman 2000, pp. 654–655).

13. For example, the Model Penal Code adopts a respondeat superior model but restricts it to the mental states of high corporate officials. Model Penal Code § 2.07(1)(c).

14. As Berman describes it, retributivism is roughly the view that punishment is justified if, but only to the extent that, "it is deserved or otherwise fitting, right or appropriate, and not [necessarily because of] any good consequences that individual [punishment] may cause to be realized" (Berman 2015, p. 144). Or as Walen puts it, the retributive view holds that "it would be bad to punish a wrongdoer *more* than she deserves, where what she deserves must be in some way proportional to the gravity of her crime. Inflicting disproportionate punishment wrongs her just as...punishing an innocent person wrongs her" (Walen 2014, § 4.4; *see also* Gardner 2008, pp. xv–xvi).

    Note that some might also think penal desert could encompass more than culpability—perhaps also facts about which wrong one committed (e.g. a killing vs. an attempted killing), which may not directly affect culpability. Still, I set aside this complication here because any plausible version of the desert constraint must at the very least *also* rule out punishments that are disproportionate to culpability. Moreover, it is the ineligibility for culpability that is the primary focus of skeptical arguments against corporate punishment—not the inability to capture different levels of harm.

15. *See supra* note 7.

16. Relatedly, Kenneth Silver argues that there is similar instability in the common view that corporations can be held accountable (or culpable) but do not have moral considerability. Taking corporations to be accountable (or culpable), he suggests, creates pressure to see them as having moral considerability (Silver Forthcoming). Thus, the ability to be culpable and having moral considerability plausibly go hand in hand.

17. *See* 18 U.S.C. § 3553(2)(A), which provides that one of the purposes of punishment that sentencing courts shall consider is the need "to reflect the seriousness of the offense, to promote respect for the law, and to provide just punishment for the offense."

18. Note my discussion here presupposes the falsity of the kind of strong retributivism that sees giving wrongdoers their just deserts to be the *only* fundamental aim of the criminal law (the only thing that could justify criminalizing conduct and imposing punishment). I take it for granted that the criminal law, like most legal institutions, can have multiple purposes or justifying aims. For example, Berman notes the "converg[ence] on a desert-constrained pluralism" about the justifications of punishment and describes it as "something approaching a consensus" view (Berman 2015, pp. 141–42). *See also* 18 U.S.C. § 3553(2)(A)-(D), which lays out a variety of purposes that punishments should aim to serve.

19. Of course, this would not preclude the car from being a justified purchase in some contexts—for example, if one has a use in mind for it that does not require good acceleration. Analogously, were we to reject retribution as one of the core purposes of punishment, then it would be no problem that there are difficulties in justifying corporate punishment on retributive grounds. While this is a possible response to the present challenge that is open to some consequentialist or rehabilitative theorists of the criminal law, I set it aside in what follows and instead continue to assume that retribution for culpable conduct is at least one of the important functions that punishment should serve.

20. For example, Alexander and Ferzan take it that "insufficient concern [is] the essence of culpability" (Alexander and Ferzan 2009, pp. 67–68). For Westen, "a person is normatively blameworthy for engaging in conduct that a statute prohibits if he was motivated by an attitude of disrespect for the interests that the statute seeks to protect" (Westen 2006, pp. 373–374). Tadros similarly takes it that if a defendant "is convicted of a serious offence, the state communicates… that [his] behavior manifested an inappropriate regard for other citizens and their interests" (Tadros 2005, p. 250).

21. Moore's position comes close to this, though includes additional sophistication. Husak puts it more cautiously in arguing "we should recognize a *presumption* that the criminal law should derive from, be based on, conform to, or mirror critical morality" (Husak 2016, p. 34).

22. Thus, one would seem to manifest insufficient regard for the legally relevant reasons by stealing even if it is done with good motives. But morality may reach a different result, holding such conduct to demonstrate *less* insufficient regard for the larger, more fine-grained set of moral reasons. This difference (if genuine) would stem from the requirements of institutional design that constrain criminal culpability but not moral blameworthiness.

23. Similarly, Pettit and List argue that corporations can have decision-making structures that satisfy the three main preconditions for responsibility: (1) facing normatively significant choices; (2) having the *understanding* and *access* to evidence required for making normative judgments about the options; and (3) having the *control* needed to choose among the options (Pettit and List 2011, pp. 158–163).

24. Compare Thomas' claim that "inasmuch as corporate attitudes derive from the contributions of individuals who themselves are uncontroversially moral agents…it would be surprising that every emergent corporate attitude would be stripped of normative content" (Thomas 2017, p. 613).

25. Individuals are composites too. Nobody is inclined to say "there is no such thing as individual action or responsibility, only the action and responsibility of single neurons."

26. Here is the argument schematically spelled out. The suppressed assumption underlies (1).

> (1) In some cases, a culpability deficit exists.
> (2) If (1), then there is a role for the notion of corporate culpability to play that can't be fully accounted for in terms of individual culpability.
> (3) If there is a genuine role for corporate culpability to play that can't be fully accounted for in terms of individual culpability, then (4).
> (4) Therefore, corporate culpability is not always reducible to individual culpability.

27. Admittedly, the argument may not be wholly different in kind, but it is substantially different in degree.

28. Even if one accepts this kind of argument for the legal irreducibility of corporate culpability, objections may remain. (Thanks to Kim Ferzan for these.) Suppose a corporation convicted of a crime consists of four individuals A, B, C, and D. Suppose we are confident that A, B, and C, but not D, are culpable for their actions related to the crime—but the total culpability for the corporation's crime should not be fully legally reducible to the wrongs of A, B, and C for the reasons given above (i.e. how invasive this would make the criminal law, etc.). In this case, would it not be unfair to D (who ex hypothesi is innocent) if the corporation is punished, since the corporation consists of A, B, C, and D?

There are two points in response. While I accept that a corporation consists of its members, there is more to a corporation that just a list of the people within it. The corporation is also to be identified with its organizational structure and its procedures, customs, ethos, as well as goals and priorities, plus ways of sharing information and reaching decisions. Thus, there are a range of properties that plausibly may reflect insufficient regard within a corporation beyond just the insufficient regard within an individual.

The second response is that punishing the corporation is not identical to punishing each of A, B, C, and D. After all, even after convicting the corporation of a crime, there is a separate question of how the punishment—be it a fine or some restriction on corporate activity—is to be distributed among the people within it. There are ways to design corporate punishments of corporations so as to spare some members or employees the pain while focusing it on others. Thus, it does not follow that punishing the corporation in this case will entail imposing any punishment on D—if corporate punishment is carried out in a way that spares D. Cf. Thomas (2017) (distinguishing conviction from distribution of punishment within the corporation). (For similar reasons, it also is not necessarily unfair to punish a corporation of which D is a member in a scenario where D *is* culpable but happens to be outside the jurisdiction. This is not an end run around jurisdictional boundaries because convicting the corporation is not necessarily the same as punishing each of its members individually.)

REFERENCES

United State Sentencing Guidelines (U.S.S.G.).

Model Penal Code § 2.07(1)(c)

18 U.S.C. § 3553(2)(A)

18 U.S.C. § 3553(2)(A)-(D)

Alexander, Larry, and Kimberly Kessler Ferzan. 2009. *Crime and culpability.* New York: Cambridge University Press.

Alschuler, Albert. 1991. Ancient law and the punishment of corporations: Of frank-pledge and deodand. *Boston University Law Review* 71: 307–314.

———. 2009. Two ways to think about the punishment of corporations. *American Criminal Law Review* 46: 1359–1392.

Arpaly, Nomy, and Tim Schroeder. 2014. *In praise of desire.* New York: Oxford University Press.

Berman, Mitchell. 2015. The justification of punishment. In *Routledge companion to philosophy of law,* ed. Andrei Marmor. New York: Routledge.

Blackstone, William. 1769. *Commentaries on the laws of England.*

Coffee, John, Jr. 1982. "No soul to damn: No body to kick": An unscandalized inquiry into the problem of corporate punishment. *Michigan Law Review* 79: 386–459.

Copp, David. 2007. The collective moral autonomy thesis. *Journal of Social Philosophy* 38: 369–388.

Dsouza, Mark. 2015. Criminal culpability after the act. *King's Law Journal* 26: 440–462.

Gardner, John. 2008. Introduction. In *Punishment and responsibility,* ed. H.L.A. Hart. Oxford: Oxford University Press.

Hart, H.L.A. 2008. *Punishment and responsibility.* 2nd ed. New York: Oxford University Press.

Hindricks, Frank. 2009. Corporate responsibility and judgment aggregation. *Economics and Philosophy* 25: 161–177.

Holmes, Oliver Wendell. 1991. *The common law.* Mineola/New York: Dover Publications.

Hurd, Heidi, and Michael Moore. 2018. The Hohfeldian analysis of rights. *The American Journal of Jurisprudence* 63: 295–354.

Husak, Doug. 2004. The criminal law as last resort. *Oxford Journal of Legal Studies* 24: 207.

———. 2016. *Ignorance of law: A philosophical inquiry.* New York: Oxford University Press.

Husak, Doug, and Craig Callender. 1994. Wilful ignorance, knowledge, and the "equal culpability" thesis: A study of the deeper significance of the principle of legality. *Wisconsin Law Review* 1994: 29–70.

Kennedy, Christopher. 1985. Criminal sentences for corporations: Alternative fining mechanisms. *California Law Review* 73: 443–482.

Kircher, Ashley. 2009. Corporate criminal liability versus corporate securities fraud liability: Analyzing the divergence in standards of culpability. *American Criminal Law Review* 46: 157–178.

Lackey, Jennifer. 2012. Group knowledge attributions. In *Knowledge ascriptions,* ed. J. Brown and M. Gerken. Oxford: Oxford University Press.

Lederman, Eli. 2000. Models for imposing corporate criminal liability: From adaptation and imitation toward aggregation and the search for self-identity. *Buffalo Criminal Law Review* 4: 641–708.

List, Christian. 2012. Judgment aggregation: A short introduction. In *Handbook of the philosophy of economics*, ed. U. Mäki, 799. Oxford: Elsevier.

Moore, Michael. 1990. Choice, character, and excuse. *Social Philosophy and Policy* 7: 29–58.

Pettit, Philip, and Christian List. 2011. *Group agency*. New York: Oxford University Press.

Ramirez, Mary Kreiner. 2005. The science fiction of corporate criminal liability: Containing the machine through the corporate death penalty. *Arizona Law Review* 47: 933–1002.

Sarch, Alex. 2019. *Criminally ignorant: Why the law pretends we know what we don't*. New York: Oxford University Press.

Silver, Kenneth. Forthcoming. Can a corporation be worthy of moral consideration? *Journal of Business Ethics*.

Summers, Lawrence. 2014. Companies on trial: Are they "too big to jail"? *Financial Times*. http://www.ft.com/cms/s/0/e3bf9954-7009-11e4-90af-00144feabdc0.html, https://perma.cc/ZCD7-Q6FT. Accessed 23 Feb 2019.

Tadros, Victor. 2005. *Criminal responsibility*. New York: Oxford University Press.

Thomas, W. Robert. 2017. The ability and responsibility of corporate law to improve criminal punishment. *Ohio State Law Journal* 78: 601–732.

Walen, Alec. 2014. Retributive justice. *Stanford Encyclopedia of Philosophy*. https://plato.stanford.edu/entries/justice-retributive/#Pro. Accessed 23 Feb 2019.

Westen, Peter. 2006. An attitudinal theory of excuse. *Law and Philosophy* 25: 289–375.

Williams, Glanville. 1961. *Criminal law: The general part*. 2nd ed. London: Stevens & Sons Ltd.

Yaffe, Gideon. 2011. *Attempts*. New York: Oxford University Press.

PART X

Death Penalty

CHAPTER 11

Capital Punishment and the Owl of Minerva

Vincent Chiao

> The basic concept underlying the Eighth Amendment is nothing less than the dignity of man. … The Amendment must draw its meaning from the evolving standards of decency that mark the progress of a maturing society. (Atkins v. Virginia, 536 U.S. 304, 311–312 (2002), citing Trop v. Dulles, 356 U.S. 86, 100–101 (1958))

> The problem of justifying punishment … may really be that of justifying our particular symbols of infamy. (Feinberg 1970, p. 116)

Although certain parts of the United States retain capital punishment, the rate of executions in the United States has been declining precipitously in recent years. This has led some commentators to speculate that capital punishment is nearing, as one author has put it, the "end of its rope" (Garrett 2017; *see* also Steiker and Steiker 2016).[1] The end of capital punishment in the United States may come with a bang or a whimper, that is, through a landmark Supreme Court decision ("*Furman* II," as Carol Steiker and Jordan Steiker have put it) or through state-by-state abolition, legislative reform and desuetude. In either case, if complete abolition comes to the United States, it will come half a century after abolition in most other liberal democracies (Steiker and Steiker 2016, ch. 8).

Many will regard the end of the American death penalty as a moral triumph, and they may be right. A great many criticisms of the American death penalty have been advanced over the years. Many of them have focused on features specific to the American experience, having to do capital punishment's connection to a legacy of racial oppression, its arbitrariness, the lack of firm evidence

V. Chiao (✉)
Faculty of Law, University of Toronto, Toronto, ON, Canada
e-mail: vincent.chiao@utoronto.ca

© The Author(s) 2019
L. Alexander, K. K. Ferzan (eds.), *The Palgrave Handbook of Applied Ethics and the Criminal Law*, https://doi.org/10.1007/978-3-030-22811-8_11

241

of much effect on public safety, the length of time spent languishing on death row and so forth. However, I shall, by and large, not be discussing those issues in this chapter. If the Supreme Court forces states to categorically abolish capital punishment, it is likely to do so by extending a line of argument that it has already used to narrow the types of crimes and defendants who may permissibly be executed. It is likely to announce that capital punishment is ruled out on grounds of "evolving standards of decency." The recent decline in capital punishment reflects an emergent moral consensus across American society, the Supreme Court is likely to say. The Constitution will encode that consensus, in much the way that it encodes a consensus against whipping, torture or other obviously impermissible modes of punishment (United States v Weems, 217 U.S. 349 (1910); Steiker and Steiker 2017).

The great language of decency suggests that abolition, if it comes in this way, will not be a moral statement from a court that has thrown up its hands in the face of endlessly intractable, but essentially administrative, problems with capital punishment. After all, many of those same problems—racial disparity, arbitrariness and uncertainty as to impact on public safety—plague American criminal justice in general, and courts do not seem tempted by the view that criminal justice as such is unconstitutional. Rather, the language of evolving standards of decency suggests that capital punishment will have become unavoidably indecent, regardless of how it is administered.

The idea that capital punishment can *become* unavoidably indecent might seem odd. In principle, capital punishment is either indecent or it is not. Whether we correctly recognize it as such is a fact about us, not a fact about capital punishment. Yet the idea that the moral status of capital punishment can change is reflected in the Supreme Court's invocation of *evolving* standards of decency. Rather than embarking on extended meditations in moral philosophy, this line of cases, somewhat notoriously, has instead sought to discern emergent consensus—would most Americans agree that it is impermissible to execute someone for rape? What about mentally impaired accused or young people? How the Supreme Court has gone about discerning such a consensus has varied over time, but the underlying commitment is to justify its rulings by a thin, but broad, consensus on outcome, as opposed to thick, but potentially contentious, philosophical principle (Lee 2007, p. 72).[2]

The aim of this chapter is to defend a preference for thin consensus over deep principle in the context of capital punishment. In part, this is because of the inconclusive status of capital punishment in moral and political philosophy. I first consider some recent moves in the (extensive) literature and explain why, although in some cases plausible, those arguments remain inconclusive. I argue in the next section that the inability of abolitionists, thus far, to show that their view is the only reasonable one on the table, along with the historical ubiquity of capital punishment, and its continued popularity in many parts of the world, support a consensus-oriented, minimalist jurisprudence. I conclude by considering a modest case for abolition in the United States.

Dignity, Evil and the Social Contract

It is frequently observed that the evidence about the deterrent impact of capital punishment is inconclusive. If, as some studies have purported to show, the death penalty has a substantial downward effect on murders, and perhaps other forms of violent crime, that would be a powerful reason in favor of it. However, despite numerous studies of the issue, there is no clear consensus among social scientists about whether capital punishment deters homicide. The history of that literature, as with the history of the philosophical literature, is marked by continual change, from Sellin's early skeptical conclusions in the 1960s to Ehrlich's forceful rebuttal in the 1970s, which was in turn challenged by newer statistical studies but then re-defended by yet newer ones (Paternoster 2011; Donohue and Wolfers 2005). Ultimately, executions are so rare that conclusions about their impact on homicide are difficult to detect. After surveying this literature, Donohue and Wolfers conclude that the impact of capital punishment on homicide—whether deterring it or causing it, through brutalization—is a matter of "profound uncertainty" (Donohue and Wolfers 2005, p. 794). "We can be sure," Donohue and Wolfers write, "that the death penalty does not cause or eliminate large numbers of homicides, but we learn little else from the data" (Donohue and Wolfers 2005, p. 844). Just as importantly, the majority of empirical work on capital punishment has focused on the United States. Yet, because differences in culture, institutions and law may well affect the deterrent impact, if any, of a system of capital punishment, it is hard to generalize from studies in the United States to unqualified statements about what capital punishment does or does not achieve in terms of public safety (Shepherd 2005).

In any case, many philosophers believe that the basic morality of capital punishment does not depend on whether it turns out to be socially beneficial and prefer instead to appeal to more abstract moral concepts, such as dignity. Capital punishment, Markel has claimed, categorically offends dignity as the "exalted moral status that all human life possesses by virtue of human existence itself" or at least in virtue of "the distinctly human capability for acting in accordance with autonomy and reason" (Markel 2005; *see also* Steiker and Steiker 2017, p. 581; Steiker 2011). The trouble with this line of thought is that, rhetoric aside, it is no more conclusive than empirical studies. Dignity is a notoriously protean concept. Those on opposing sides of the issue are likely to have different opinions about dignity, and it is not entirely clear how to resolve those differences of opinion. "[C]apital punishment is surreal," Hsu writes, but "only because extravagantly evil crimes are surreal to the rest of human sins. Such extreme crimes convey messages that contravene what humanity stands for. To counter such messages, the only proper counter message is death" (Hsu 2015; Pojman 2004). This is not an idiosyncratic view: Kant and Hegel, for instance, regarded capital punishment as consistent with human dignity. Who is right? Both views seem equally plausible.

Kramer has recently insisted that respect for morality positively requires a political community to execute some of its members—namely, those responsible for bringing "extravagant evil" into the world. Someone who has acted in an "extravagantly evil" manner, Kramer avers, "has pitted his life against the nature of humanity generally. His life therefore stands as an affront to the dignity of humankind and as a blot on the relationship between humankind and his community, especially if his community is assigning large quantities of resources to the sustainment of his existence." A failure to execute such an individual, Kramer claims, "is a persistent wrong against humankind" (Kramer 2011, pp. 236–237).

Kramer's "purgative" rationale for capital punishment has come in for a fair amount of criticism (Danaher 2015; Steiker 2015; Lernestedt 2015; Lenta 2015; but see Kramer 2015). A common objection is that Kramer fails to adequately explain why people who do not share his view that the continued existence of evil people is itself a moral wrong should come around to his position. This is a serious flaw because Kramer's view is rather extreme—deontological rigorism *ne plus ultra*—in how it construes the alleged wrong of non-execution. On Kramer's view, a society that refuses to execute someone responsible for extravagant evil is "responsible for perpetuating an affront to humankind" (Kramer 2015, p. 386). This suggests that Norway is currently wronging humankind because it has thus far refused to execute notorious mass murderer Anders Behring Breivik. Not only does this seem rather unlikely, but the claim that failure to execute constitutes an affront to humankind depends on the claim that the only appropriate response to those who reject humanity in their actions is to reject them through execution. That is the point at issue between Kramer and his critics.

Kramer presents his view in rigorously deontological terms. He does not suggest that purgation is a means to an end (or, at least, any end more specific than "restore the moral order") (Danaher 2015, pp. 232–234). It is thus odd that Kramer's account ends up appealing, in a fairly crucial way, to the "minimal invasion principle," the principle that state power exercised for a public purpose must "employ the least restrictive means that is sufficient to achieve that purpose" (Kramer 2011, p. 4, n. 3). Kramer insists that capital punishment satisfies the minimal invasion principle, for no punishment short of death will satisfy the demand to purge the affront to humanity of extravagant evil. His critics are unconvinced, insisting that punishments short of death, such as banishment and life imprisonment, do the job just as well (Danaher 2015, pp. 236–244; Lenta 2015, pp. 58–59).

What is odd about this exchange is simply that Kramer purports to accept the minimal invasion principle. Not only does there appear to be no principled way of deciding whether death or life imprisonment adequately achieves the end of purgation (in part because of disagreement about what counts as successful purgation), but the appeal to instrumental rationality is incongruous, given the otherwise thoroughly deontological flavor of Kramer's theory.

A more consistent deontology would reject the minimal invasion principle, as it is but a thinly disguised version of the Benthamite claim that punishment is always and everywhere an evil and hence must be used sparingly. That principle has no place in the moral architecture of a consistently deontological account of capital punishment, for on such a view, purgation of evil through execution is right intrinsically, not because it is the most efficient means of achieving an independently specified end.

Ultimately, I suspect that what really divides Kramer and his critics are their views as to whether execution is morally fitting in response to extravagant evil, not its efficiency at achieving some clearly specified, and valuable, social end. Although this reading is inconsistent with the letter of Kramer's text, it appears to more adequately explain its spirit: it is not that the resources spent on keeping someone incarcerated themselves matter, nor that banishment is only partially as effective as execution.[3] Rather it is simply that the only way in which the affront to humanity of extravagant evil can be purged is through execution. This may or may not seem plausible to you, but what has thus far remained unanswered is how we come to know whether this is so.

However, it is not clear that the abolitionist's opposing claim that dignity prohibits capital punishment is in an epistemically better position. The question is not about truth (which, as we have seen, is contested) but about warrant. Perhaps, a skeptic might suggest, whether one regards the "exalted moral status that all human life possesses by virtue of human existence itself" as requiring or prohibiting purging extravagant evil has as much to do with deeply held and emotionally resonant moral commitments, upbringing and peer pressure as with dispassionate reasoning from shared premises or impartial analysis of the evidence. For his part, Kramer insists that this is not so. He insists that how people feel about capital punishment is irrelevant to the truth of his theory. He thinks that societies, like Norway, that do not execute those responsible for extravagant evil, undermine the justification for anyone, including someone on the other side of the world, to feel self-respect (Kramer 2015, pp. 387–388). (Perhaps worse still are those countries that refuse even to extradite to countries that *are* willing to stand up for self-respect.) Kramer may well be right that the truth about capital punishment's in-principle permissibility is independent of human judgments and attitudes. It just seems hard to say whether his account of its judgment-independent status is more or less likely to be true than the abolitionist's opposing account.[4]

Turning to abolitionism, Claire Finkelstein has recently sought to defend an abolitionist conclusion without appeal to such contentious concepts as dignity. Rather, Finkelstein seeks to show that instrumental rationality alone will suffice to rule out capital punishment. On Finkelstein's view, instrumentally rational agents with a desire for self-preservation will not agree to a legal system that includes capital punishment, even if they might regard it as consistent with dignity and even if they believe it effective in preventing crime. This line of thinking has roots in Hobbes, who argued that although the sovereign retained a right to kill its subjects, its subjects also retained the right to resist any such effort. For, Hobbes argued, the purpose of entering into the social contract was the preservation of life and liberty; faced with the immediate prospect of the complete extinction of those interests, no contract could be rationally binding.[5] Hence, in capital punishment, "we reach the bounds of legality" (Heyd 1991, pp. 122–123).

Although Hobbes himself did not view capital punishment as illegitimate, others, holding a less sanguine view of the sovereign's powers, have made that argument. Finkelstein's view is recognizably Hobbesian because it rests on the idea that any agreement to the contrary is nullified when the other party seeks to kill you. Since Finkelstein regards punishment as legitimated by consent, if successful, her argument would show that rationality alone rules out the legitimacy of capital punishment. This would be a massive achievement, as it would mean abolitionists could press their case without appealing to a conception of dignity that their interlocutors reject. Consequently, it is worth attending carefully to her argument.

Finkelstein starts by observing that consent can change the moral status of many otherwise impermissible actions, including punishment. While it is not generally permissible for me to kick you in the shins, perhaps it *is* permissible if you have agreed to let me do so under certain conditions. Notoriously, however, the degree to which consent really matters to philosophers in the social contract tradition is a matter of some dispute. By emphasizing hypothetical consent over actual consent, the consent of representatives of groups rather than individuals, by restricting what the contractors know about themselves and their society, and by requiring (or assuming) motivation by ethically loaded attitudes, contractarian political philosophers have found myriad means of legitimating (or de-legitimating, as the case may be) a wide range of social arrangements. For her part, Finkelstein claims to draw upon a robust notion of consent. She foreswears hypothetical consent by representatives in favor of actual consent of individual people, and she imposes no additional veil of ignorance upon contractors beyond "ordinary doubt about one's future" (Finkelstein 2002, 2006, p. 1316). Her version of contractarianism accordingly lies on the more voluntarist end of the spectrum. According to Finkelstein, assuming you live in a society that permits emigration, once you have become a mature adult, capable of making independent decisions about your life, your decision whether to emigrate or stay in your society constitutes your decision as to whether to tacitly consent to your society's system of criminal law, a decision you plainly make in light of everything you believe about yourself and your society at that time (Finkelstein 2006, p. 1314).[6]

There are, however, limits to consent, even for Finkelstein. The most important limit for our purposes is Finkelstein's claim that for your consent to legitimate punishment, it must reflect a rational belief, "in an ex ante position of choice," that the system of punishment to which you are consenting will benefit you (Finkelstein 2006, pp. 1314, 1317). The idea is that it would be irrational for you to agree to a burden without some more-than-compensating benefit. This "benefit requirement" shows, Finkelstein argues, that one cannot rationally consent to a system that includes capital punishment. This is because, when it comes to your "most fundamental political and economic protections," a rational agent would not agree to accept any social rules or institutions (such as a scheme of punishment) that impose a risk of loss (Finkelstein 2006, p. 1317). Consequently, when contemplating a system of punishment, rationality compels you to ask whether you, personally, stand to gain even in the eventuality that you are convicted and facing a punishment of that kind (Finkelstein 2006, pp. 1319–1320). Yet, Finkelstein claims, even if capital punishment has a significant deterrent effect, thereby improving your *ex ante* odds of a long and violence-free life, that gain is insufficient to outweigh the loss of welfare from being executed. Ergo, even though consent legitimates a system of punishment, consent to a system including capital punishment would be irrational and hence void.

Or is it? One might question both Finkelstein's insistence that rationality categorically prohibits "gambling" with one's basic interests, as well as the application she makes of the benefit principle, thus interpreted, to this case. As to the first concern, Finkelstein points out that other contractarian philosophers have also endorsed highly risk-averse bargaining positions, such as Rawls' defense of maximin. However, Rawls' defense of maximin has proven to be highly controversial (Harsanyi 1975, p. 595). It is not clear why rationality requires you to treat uncertain losses as if they were certain, nor is it clear why a sufficiently important and sizable gain, no matter how significant, could never outweigh even a very slight risk to one's basic interests. Moreover, Rawls is an inapposite authority for Finkelstein, as Rawls defends maximin as a principle of rational choice *behind* the veil of ignorance, when contractors cannot rule out the possibility of even quite atrocious outcomes. In contrast, Finkelstein insists that the consent that matters is the actual consent of actual people knowing whatever actual people know about themselves and their society. For instance, you are entitled, Finkelstein says, to draw upon your store of knowledge to decide whether to remain in your country or to leave. But if so, then if anything what rationality seems to require is for you to draw upon your knowledge to estimate how likely it is that you will commit a capital offense and be executed if you do. It's one thing to be highly risk averse when you know nothing about yourself or your society, but if you actually know quite a lot, then it is far from clear that reason requires you to pretend that you know nothing. Yet, by drawing upon your knowledge of yourself and your society in deciding whether it is worth it to you to consent to your society's system of criminal law, you are thereby drawing on your estimation about your personality and circumstances, as well as those of your society's system of law, in determining whether a system of capital punishment benefits you. Since Finkelstein is willing to concede that capital punishment may well deter, she must also concede that it is possible that for some people this cost-benefit calculation will net out positive (Finkelstein 2006, p. 1309).

In any case, it is not clear rational contractors would rule out capital punishment even given Finkelstein's strict no-gambling view. To see this, suppose that, as a young adult, you reflect upon your society's criminal law and ask whether you stand to gain from it, and suppose, further, that being highly risk averse, you imagine that you will be subject to the punishments in question. However, believing *that* you will be punished does not resolve the further question of *when* you will be punished. You might rationally believe, for instance, that although you will be executed, it won't be for many decades (Finkelstein 2006, p. 1316). Hence, in evaluating whether a system of capital punishment is on net good for you, you will have to ask which of these two possible worlds is best for your overall welfare (Finkelstein 2006, p. 1317). Is a world in which you will ultimately be executed, but in which you enjoy a safer life, and a potentially longer one, better or worse for you than a world in which you will not be executed but in which your life is nastier, more brutish and shorter than it would be if there were capital punishment to deter criminals? How people go about answering *that* question would not seem to be resolvable by the austere logic of instrumental rationality alone but rather depends on how each person gives meaning and value to her or his life. (Is there a Platonic form for the shape of *that* utility curve?) It hardly seems appropriate to resolve this kind of question for everyone by philosophical ipse dixit. Consequently, it is doubtful that rational contractors, as Finkelstein conceives them, must necessarily reject capital punishment.

These difficulties reflect a deeper problem for Finkelstein's contractarian theory of punishment. This is that her efforts to motivate strongly egalitarian conclusions are in some substantial tension with her focus on the actual agreement of actual people, operating to secure their own private gain. Consider Finkelstein's claim that rational agreement about fair terms of social cooperation must show net benefit to *each* concrete individual in society, effectively imposing a unanimity requirement upon contexts of social choice (Finkelstein 2006, p. 1320). Why must rational contractors agree to such a condition? After all, the basic source of political legitimacy on Finkelstein's view is each person's considered judgment as to whether to consent to her society's laws. Far from suggesting that a society's laws are illegitimate if they disadvantage you, Finkelstein's emphasis on tacit consent suggests that if you do not like your society's laws, you can take your custom elsewhere. True, we might think it noble or ethically worthy for each party to the social contract to care as deeply about the interests of others as of himself or herself. But for a theory focused on rational, self-interested choice, that kind of altruism appears optional at best.

Like Finkelstein, Corey Brettschneider has argued that abolition is rooted in widely shared political values. However, unlike Finkelstein, Brettschneider does not argue on the basis of each individual person's rationally granted consent (Brettschneider 2007b, p. 812). Instead, according to Brettschneider, the central question is what kinds of punishment free and equal citizens, "motivated to engage in a good-faith effort to find a legitimate balance between rights against coercion and the need to fulfill social goods such as security," could reasonably reject (Brettschneider 2007a, p. 178). "Some policies," Brettschneider claims, "violate the fundamental status of citizens to such a great extent that no reasonable citizen could endorse them as consistent with the core values of a democratic society" (Brettschneider 2007a, p. 178, b, p. 813). For Brettschneider, it is reasonableness, not rationality, that rules out capital punishment.

How does capital punishment violate the fundamental status of citizens? Brettschneider offers two arguments. First, reasonable citizens could reject as unreasonable the punishment of the innocent. Yet, because no human institution is likely to be infallible—and, more strongly, because our actual institutions of punishment are known to make mistakes, even in capital cases—there is always the possibility, however slim, that those we punish are innocent. This doesn't mean that no one can ever be punished, but rather that those who are punished must always have the possibility of proving their innocence. Capital punishment extinguishes that possibility. Moreover, and perhaps more importantly, capital punishment extinguishes the possibility of rectifying mistakes (Brettschneider 2007a, pp. 190–191). Call this the argument from fallibility.

The argument from fallibility is a familiar warhorse in debates about the morality of capital punishment (Brooks 2011). Despite its popular appeal, the argument is far from conclusive. Error is ubiquitous, in criminal justice as elsewhere.[7] Death is an unusually harsh punishment, but that suggests merely that our epistemic burden is greater than usual, not that it is infinite.[8] More to Brettschneider's point, while it is impossible to compensate a person who has been wrongly condemned and executed, it is also impossible to really compensate anyone who has spent a significant period of his life wrongly imprisoned. Society clearly owes something to those who are wrongly imprisoned, but the currency of that debt is not payable in any currency that modern societies transact in. Regret for serious moral error is an ineliminable part of any criminal justice system, with or without capital punishment. This is not changed by the possibility of financial compensation; it is not as if we are morally entitled to convict and punish as many innocent people as we like so long as we compensate them afterward. So if death is not so cruel or degrading as to be impermissible, the inability to make amends does not distinguish it from other penal practices, notably lengthy custodial sentences, that currently enjoy widespread support.

In any case, Brettschneider's more fundamental argument starts from the premise that a society committed to the democratic values of equality, autonomy and reciprocity is one that stands in a certain justificatory relationship to its members, *qua* citizens. Not only must a democratic society justify punishment to the guilty, in the sense of asking what kinds of punishment even the guilty could reasonably accept as a fair balance between their interests and the interests of others (Brettschneider 2007a, p. 179). It must also "never terminat[e]" its relation to its citizens, for it is only in virtue of providing ongoing justification of its coercive practices to its citizens—constantly ensuring, that is, that its policies and actions are such that no one, including the guilty, could reasonably reject them—that the state can legitimately claim authority (Brettschneider 2007a, p. 193). Since capital punishment is nothing if not the termination of the relationship between the citizen and state, capital punishment is inconsistent with the ideals of a democratic society. Call this the argument from ongoing justification.

Dagger has challenged the requirement that a democratic state never terminates its relationship to its citizens (Dagger 2011, pp. 366–367). Does contractualism really show, Dagger asks, that no one, no matter what they do, can lose their status within a democratic polity? Maybe *some* democratic communities are like that, but must *every* democratic community adopt that attitude toward membership? Perhaps not. Contractualism requires "ongoing" justification in the sense that a society's laws and policies be at all times justifiable to reasonable citizens. The question then is whether a law that terminates a person's civic membership necessarily fails that test. Recall that contractualism idealizes from actual people to reasonable citizens. While it is of course true that capital punishment renders an actual person inaccessible to reason, it does not follow that a reasonable citizen must therefore reject capital punishment. Why couldn't a reasonable citizen, as distinct from an embodied person, regard termination of civic membership as a justifiable way of dealing with people who show themselves unwilling to comply with a democratic society's most basic values?

It is at this point that Dagger's objection begins to pinch. It does not seem self-evident that reasonable people could not regard society as in large part a cooperative venture and could not regard their status in that venture as dependent upon their own demonstrated willingness to cooperate with their society's most basic standards of conduct. Against Brettschneider, one might argue that this does not involve discounting the interests of the guilty as against the innocent, for, one might argue, the rule requiring compliance with a society's terms of fair cooperation applies equally to everyone. No doubt those who have committed capital offenses and are facing a death sentence as a result will regard execution as incompatible with their basic interests. But for a contractualist, the legitimacy of a system of punishment does not ride on the consent of concrete people, but rather on what idealized reasonable people, motivated to find fair terms of cooperation, could endorse. (This is the gist of Kant's objection to Beccaria (Kant 1996, pp. 475–476, AA 6:335–336).) Dagger's objection is that reasonable people might well view it as fair to terminate one's membership in the polity if that person has proven to be unwilling to comply with society's basic terms of cooperation.[9] The contractualist's insistence upon ongoing justification does not appear to categorically rule this out.

Evolving Standards

Probably every society has regarded some types of punishment as simply off the table. In liberal democracies today, that list typically includes punishments that involve direct physical manipulation of the body, such as whipping; punishment that is designed expressly to cause pain or fear, such as torture; and punishment that is too obviously meant to humiliate or degrade, such as pillorying or branding. For us, today, there is little reason to discuss the permissibility of these types of punishments (Kahan 1996, but see Kahan 2006). This is probably not because we have good reason to believe that they would be ineffective at securing valuable social aims (do we know torture wouldn't be an effective deterrent?) or that deductive inference from obviously true moral principles rules them out. (Is it obvious that incarceration is less painful, less humiliating or more dignified than whipping?) The formation of a culture's moral *habitus* is likely to be rather more contingent and historically determined than this rationalistic picture suggests (Elias 2000).

Abolitionists would like to add the death penalty to the list of socially unthinkable punishments. It has already been added to that list in most liberal democracies, including most of the United States. There are other punishments that may soon be added to the list. Life without parole and solitary confinement are the two most obvious candidates, but perhaps long periods of incarceration generally should be added to the list. But why stop there? Perhaps future generations will think incarceration, full stop, is cruel and unusual, and will regard present-day societies as barbaric in their reliance on imprisonment of any kind, for any length of time. And who knows? They may be right (Boonin 2008; Chiao 2018, ch. 3; Flanders 2013, pp. 615–619; Garrett 2017, ch. 10).

That said, abolition is, relatively speaking, a historical novelty. Capital punishment has been an accepted practice for thousands of years, across a wide range of human civilizations and legal systems: "[e]very form of government … in every historical period and virtually every country has used the death penalty" (Paternoster 2011, pp. 760–761; Garland 2010, pp. 72–73). Serious efforts toward abolition, in comparison, only date back to the nineteenth century, with most of the movement occurring in the last 50 years (Steiker and Steiker 2016, pp. 56–57; Paternoster 2011, p. 761; McGowen 2016). Moreover, in addition to being recent, this consensus is geographically limited. Although a great deal of the conversation about capital punishment has focused on the United States, many other countries retain capital punishment. Japan, Taiwan and India, all populous democratic nations, retain capital punishment, as do many Asian, Middle Eastern and African nations. As Garland notes, "[t]he age of abolition is a decidedly Western phenomenon" (Garland 2010, p. 73). Perhaps emblematic of this cross-cultural disagreement, in the same year that the Pope proclaimed capital punishment to be in all cases inconsistent with Catholic teaching, Japan quietly executed the ringleader and 12 members of the Aum Shinrikyo cult, who were responsible for sarin gas attacks in the mid-1990s, with 29 deaths attributed to their actions ("Pope Francis Declares Death Penalty Unacceptable in All Cases," Associated Press, August 2, 2018; "Japan Executes Cult Leader Behind 1995 Sarin Gas Subway Attack," Associated Press, July 5, 2018; "Japan Executes 6 Members of Cult Behind Sarin Attack," Associated Press, July 26, 2018).

While many of the nations that retain capital punishment are not democratic, some are. Indeed, as of 2018, the world's largest democracy (India) formally retains capital punishment, as do parts of the world's oldest democracy (the United States). Moreover, far from being inherently inimical to democratic values, part of the explanation for capital punishment's continued existence in the United States has to do with the relatively shorter line between popular sentiment and public policy there than in many abolitionist countries, where political elites more easily enact counter-majoritarian policies (Garland 2010). European elites abolished capital punishment despite high levels of support that would, in the American context, "normally spell trouble" (Zimring 2003, p. 11, 22–24). Moreover, it is not clear that the movement toward abolition in Europe was itself consistently democratic. Abolition did not always reflect the considered moral judgment on the part of citizens and officials, but in some cases reflected economic and political pressure from the European Union and the United Nations (Paternoster 2011, pp. 761–762; McGowen 2016, p. 629; Zimring 2003, p. 36). Finally, depending on one's views about the democratic bona fides of judicial review, one might raise similar concerns about the outsize role played by the American Supreme Court in this context; as Steiker and Steiker have noted, the American experience with capital punishment abolition is idiosyncratic in its intense focus on litigation. "Contrary to the abolition of the death penalty achieved by most of our peer countries," they write, "American abolition almost certainly will arrive, if it does, by constitutional ruling rather legislative repeal" (Steiker and Steiker 2016, p. 256).[10]

Of course, novelty and disagreement do not show that there isn't a moral fact of the matter. For one thing, not all disagreement is reasonable. Often disagreement is uncharitable, polemical, immune to fact or otherwise unworthy of respect. But even when disagreement doesn't take those forms, disagreement alone is not enough to show that it is impermissible to override, rather than persuade, those we believe to be in error. For instance, it might be that those who disagree with you on some subject do not have access to the same information as you, or share your level of moral insight. If that were the case, then all else being equal, we would do better to trust your judgment as against theirs, even if their opinions reflect their sincere best efforts to arrive at the truth. To be sure, it might seem boorish to make too much of a fuss about being better informed or more sophisticated than one's peers. But equality does not entail that no one is smarter or has better judgment than anyone else; it entails only that each person is of equal moral worth, however wise or foolish they may be.

What should perhaps give pause to proponents of philosophically ambitious accounts of capital punishment is the failure, thus far, of either side to produce a decisive argument in favor of their preferred view. There are, to be sure, many *plausible* arguments, but plausibility is an insufficient standard to show that those who remain unconvinced are therefore behaving unreasonably. After all, both p and not-p might be plausible. A more stringent standard of proof is required before one can reasonably dismiss those who take opposing views. Yet here it is surely telling that even the greatest thinkers on punishment have disagreed among themselves. Beccaria and Bentham famously opposed capital punishment, whereas Kant and Hegel defended it. If the paragons of Enlightenment reason were of two minds about it, if contemporary philosophers have thus far failed to produce decisive arguments one way or the other, if the empirical evidence is generally inconclusive (and in any case largely drawn out of one country), and if there are substantial numbers of apparently reasonable people arrayed on both sides, then perhaps there is reason to be modest in one's philosophical attitudes about capital punishment.

As I have noted, in recent years, the United States Supreme Court has regulated capital punishment by appeal to an evolving standard of decency, as revealed in a trend among the states toward limiting the types of crimes, and types of individuals, eligible for death. Admittedly, the Supreme Court's implementation of this idea has been anything but consistent, lending support to the suspicion that it merely camouflages the personal views of the justices (Matusiak et al. 2014). Some of the Supreme Court's judgments strongly suggest that what the justices will count as evidence of an emergent consensus is highly dependent upon personal conviction about the punishments in question (Stinneford 2010, p. 89). Nevertheless, the persistence of reasonable disagreement as to the moral permissibility of capital punishment lends support to a jurisprudence that is oriented toward thin consensus around an emergent norm, rather than one that seeks agreement on controversial moral propositions.[11] Seen from this vantage, the Supreme Court has wisely resisted the blandishments of abolitionists who would prefer it to take a more principled, and categorical, stand against capital punishment. It seems unlikely that the Supreme Court, even with Herculean effort, could do what generations of philosophers have failed to do, namely provide an account of the moral permissibility of capital punishment that will be convincing to all reasonable people. It is not yet the case that all reasonable and decent people must be abolitionists. That may well change, but until it does, the value of democratic self-governance weighs in favor of a light judicial touch. As Waldron puts it, "when decisions about justice or the common good need to be made in a given society, all the members of that society are empowered to form a view and contribute to the public decision" (Waldron 2012, p. 194). On this view, the role of the court is appropriately limited to sweeping up stragglers; like Minerva's owl, the Constitution announces a philosophy of punishment only in hindsight.[12]

One might object that given how divided opinions about capital punishment currently are, modesty is certain to result in grave moral error. If abolitionism is ultimately vindicated, one might come to regret that powerful Western abolitionist countries did not act more forcefully to coerce or inveigle other countries to be like them. One might regret that the United States Supreme Court caved in *Gregg* and did not act sooner to encode moral truth into the Eighth Amendment.

I do not think we should accept this objection. By seeking to minimize the risk of moral error, it makes permissibility contingent upon the most abstemious of views, even when those views are highly unlikely to be correct (Barry and Tomlin 2016, this volume, Chap. 19). Some people think it is morally wrong to put cream into your coffee. So long as that view has *any* chance of being correct, no matter how miniscule, a commitment to minimizing moral error means that you should not put cream into your coffee. Should you never leave the house because you might step on a bug, which might turn out to be a moral wrong? The precautionary principle is no more convincing in moral philosophy than it is in administrative law (Sunstein 2005).

More plausibly, one might argue that the costs of moral errors if abolitionism turns out to be correct are grave—people are executed when they ought not to have been—whereas the costs of errors if abolitionism is false are not serious. Hence, even if abolitionists and retentionists are equally likely to be correct, we should nevertheless accept abolition on grounds of a higher expected moral cost (Kolber 2018; Barry and Tomlin this volume, Chap. 19).

It is not clear how one is to calculate the costs of moral error in this context. On the one hand, death penalty proponents are likely to point out that there are serious moral costs associated with failing to respond appropriately to grave rights violations. Retributivists may additionally claim that the world is made a morally worse place if those who truly deserve death escape a fitting punishment. Moreover, if it turns out that capital punishment does have meaningful deterrent value, then erroneously endorsing abolition means tolerating serious, but preventable, crimes. On the other hand, the costs of erroneously permitting capital punishment are also difficult to estimate. The true cost of error of that kind is net of life imprisonment, capital punishment's most likely substitute. One might well wonder about the permissibility of life imprisonment, but even if one does not, it remains unclear how to assess the marginal harm of execution as compared to that of life imprisonment, much less how to compare those potential harms to the potential harms of failing to protect people from serious victimization and appropriately vindicating their rights when they are victimized. That said, the underlying intuition—that, in cases on uncertainty, it is wise to hedge one's bets by considering the possibility of error—is sound. Arguably, one way of operationalizing that intuition is to replace a single large bet for a series of smaller bets, at least until the correct answer becomes clear enough to warrant final disposition; in a federal system, that is what the incrementalist, "evolving standards of decency," approach represents.

To be clear, none of this is to imply that letting the people decide is the epistemically most reliable way of discerning the truth whenever there is moral uncertainty. It has long been appreciated that democratic governance does not always result in wise policy. The predictable epistemic failures of democratic governance have been a knock against democracy at least since Aristotle; accepting some degree of unwise, sub-optimal or otherwise unjustified social policy seems to be an unavoidable cost of democratic government. Probably the only way to ensure that there will be no regrets about missed opportunities or unwise policies is to forego democracy in favor of epistocracy—that is, rule by the wise (Estlund 2007). Yet even one of democracy's sharpest contemporary critics does not actually suggest replacing democracy with full-blown epistocratic government, but rather merely limiting the franchise to educated and informed people (Brennan 2016). That might well decrease a democracy's margin of error, but seems unlikely to eliminate it entirely. Nor is the claim that democratic values take precedence over any possible moral error. Perhaps in some cases, getting it right is more important than making everyone feel included. But while the costs of moral error in capital punishment are obviously grave, they are also very difficult to assess, and, in any case, to establish their primacy over democratic rights would require further argument, perhaps along the lines sketched by Finkelstein and Brettschneider.

The arguments I have been considering are focused on the permissibility of capital punishment in principle and prescind from any concerns one might raise about how concrete systems of capital punishment are implemented. The consensus-oriented approach I have been recommending is limited to the question of whether a Supreme Court should permit or prohibit capital punishment *in general*. That is consistent with the existence of other, less consensus-oriented, reasons for restricting capital punishment in particular contexts. Suppose, for instance, that the evidence shows that capital punishment is frequently administered in a racially biased manner. That would constitute an independent basis for scrutinizing the permissibility of capital punishment schemes, in the sense that it would not require taking sides on the question of capital punishment's permissibility in principle. Whether the Supreme Court should have been more aggressive in invalidating capital punishment schemes on the basis of racial equality depends in part upon one's view of the ethics of judicial review and in part on one's view of the facts relating capital punishment in the United States to racial oppression (McClekey v. Kemp, 481 U.S. 279 (1987); Steiker and Steiker 2016, ch. 3). My point here is only that the proposition that American death penalty states in the second half of the twentieth century had failed to produce a system of capital punishment that treated people of different races fairly does not have any direct implications for the moral status of capital punishment in (for instance) contemporary Japan or eighteenth-century France or imperial China.

CONVENTION AND CRITICISM

In a justly renowned paper, Joel Feinberg pointed out that punishment serves a variety of important expressive roles: not only does it vindicate law and clarify responsibility, but it also represents a society's authoritative disavowal and symbolic repudiation of wrongdoing (Feinberg 1970, pp. 101–115). Yet, as Feinberg recognized, this does not resolve the question of the specific form punishment should take. Feinberg did not seem to regard this question as calling for much philosophical analysis; the symbols a society uses to vindicate, disavow and repudiate are, in his view, largely conventional in nature. As Feinberg put it, "certain forms of hard treatment have become the conventional symbols of public reprobation," analogously to how champagne is conventionally used at celebrations or how black is the conventional color of mourning (Feinberg 1970, p. 100).

Perhaps convention—historically and culturally contingent as it is—may explain why different groups of people have, at different times and places, come to regard some punishments as acceptable but others as completely off the table. Yet to observe that such is our convention does not show that we ultimately have reason to endorse it. Some conventions can be better than others or, in any case, less cruel. "There was a time," Feinberg imagines a skeptic musing, "when the gallows and the rack were the leading clear symbols of shame and ignominy. Now we condemn felons to penal servitude as the way of rendering their crimes more infamous. Could not the job be done more economically? Isn't there a way to stigmatize without inflicting any further (pointless) pain to the body, to family, to creative capacity?" (Feinberg 1970, p. 115).

Feinberg raised this skeptical doubt at the end of his essay and did not seek to answer it. Yet it is, in my view, a crucially important question for philosophers of punishment. In one form or another, this skeptical challenge has plagued every so-called expressive or communicative theory of punishment since. No expressive or communicative theorist of punishment has ever been able to explain why, as Scanlon rhetorically put it, we should go in for harsh punishment rather than expressing ourselves "with weeds" (Scanlon 1988, p. 214; *see also* Hanna 2008; Ewing 2015).

In this context, it is worth recalling Feinberg's essay, and the skeptical doubt he raises, because once we set aside the empirical issues of deterrence and prevention, what we are left with is the expressive symbolism of death as a response to evil. Retributivists may balk at this characterization, and insist that retribution is about deserved suffering, not symbols. Yet it is unclear how we are to decide this issue; that is, it remains unclear how we can be so confident that suffering must take the precise form it does in any given context. Feinberg leaves us with the vaguely uncomfortable thought that the only answer to the question of why death is uniquely appropriate in response to evil is convention. This is unlikely to satisfy either side. Abolitionists insist that dignity and/or rationality prohibits execution; proponents insist that dignity, morality and/or rights vindication demands it. What both sides can agree on is that convention is a poor response to Feinberg's skeptic.

For those who think the morality of capital punishment is properly fought out in the terrain of a symbolic economy of purgation, or vindication of rights, or dignity or desert, there is, I think, little hope of progress beyond the assertion that death either is, or is not, intuitively fitting in response to a certain class of crimes. By turning up the rhetoric, human rights activists and retributively minded moral philosophers have made capital punishment into a Manichean argument between good and evil, rather than a technocratic problem of criminal justice policy (Zimring 2003, ch. 3).[13] The rather extraordinary amount of attention given to capital punishment in the United States far outstrips its practical significance for criminal justice. This suggests that the struggle over capital punishment may predominantly be a struggle over symbols.[14] So far, there appears to be no answer to the question of why the symbolic functions of punishment must be concretized in one or another form. It just seems fitting, in something like the way that black seems like the color to wear at a funeral, until one day it doesn't.

Abolitionist critics who want to press their claims further by insisting on minimal invasiveness as a precept of reason should reflect on what endorsing that principle suggests. If it turns out that capital punishment is a uniquely effective deterrent, then it might well turn out, as Vermeule and Sunstein have noted, that what is "minimally invasive" is a system of capital punishment (Sunstein and Vermeule 2005a, b). After all, what gives minimal invasiveness its appeal is its solicitude to each person's vital interests. Abolitionists focus on the interests of perpetrators of terrible wrongs, but even so, the interests of the victims of those terrible wrongs *also* count. So, abolitionists who want, like Feinberg's skeptic, to insist that our existing conventions are pointlessly cruel must by the same token acknowledge that their conviction rests, at bottom, on a highly plausible, but unproven, empirical hypothesis that capital punishment is not a uniquely effective deterrent, and they should be prepared to revise their position if the evidence were to undermine that hypothesis (Donohue and Wolfers 2005, p. 844). Abolition in the name of pointless cruelty is, ultimately, an instance of welfarist policy analysis. That mode of analysis has its benefits, most notably its egalitarian concern for the welfare of all, including the most vicious of criminals, but it also has what some regard as drawbacks, including its sensitivity to empirical fact.

For my part, I am inclined to think the gamble worth taking and regard the in-principle permissibility of capital punishment as largely, if not exclusively, dependent upon its actual impact in preventing serious crime. If it is of marginal significance in that respect, then I do not think deontological impulses, of the kind Kramer gives voice to, suffice to answer the skeptic who observes that these impulses may rest on little more than social convention and unbearably cruel ones at that. In my opinion, in liberal democracies the burden of proof for justifying a system of criminal sanctions lies on the state; in default of that burden, less punishment is to be preferred to more, even if there are plausible, but not decisive, moralities that would encourage more rather than less. Admittedly, this is unlikely to be compelling to those who, like Kramer, are convinced that death is the uniquely appropriate response to extreme evil.

On the other hand, the question is rather more complex if new and better evidence emerges that capital punishment does, at least in parts of the United States, significantly reduce victimization of serious crime. Here, questions of how capital punishment compares to other policies, including how its benefits and burdens are allocated, become crucial. To be relevant in this context, the comparison class must be drawn in reasonably realistic terms: clearly, Norway can prevent crime very effectively without capital punishment, but that is of limited practical significance for the United States, where both the will to enact

Scandinavian social welfare policies and the demographic, economic and social prerequisites for a Scandinavian social welfare state are lacking.

But though the political morality of the death penalty is, in my view, sensitive to the empirics, it is not uniquely determined by them. The symbolic economy of punishment is important as well, even if only because of its ultimate impact, through perceptions of legitimacy, on people's willingness (and perhaps moral obligations) to cooperate with a legal system (Shelby 2017, ch. 7). Even if what capital punishment says is that society is committed to ridding itself of extravagant evil, in the context of a United States still struggling with a legacy of racial oppression, that symbolic message is likely to be garbled, if not outright undermined, by countervailing symbolic messages of racial hierarchy, as reflected in the history of trial and execution as a sanitized alternative to lynching (Steiker and Steiker 2016, ch. 3; Garland 2010, pp. 12–13, 27–36). Perhaps even that message could be countered in some way—the perennial promise of better procedures, for instance—but in a society with democratic aspirations, that is ultimately a matter for contestable political judgment.[15]

NOTES

1. Garrett suggests much of this decline can be attributed to improved defense lawyering (Garrett 2017, ch. 4–5).
2. As Franklin Zimring has pointed out, the process of abolition in Europe was not the result of reasoned consideration of philosophical principles; it was, rather, "an era of change without discourse" (Zimring 2003, p. 26).
3. Although Kramer repeatedly invokes the resources used to sustain the life of an extravagantly evil person sentenced to life imprisonment, he ultimately concedes that this is not a concern about inefficiency but rather about discharging a society's responsibility for negating an extravagantly evil person's repudiation of humankind. Hence, Kramer's invocation of resources—like his invocation of the minimal invasion principle—is a red herring (*see* Kramer 2015, p. 386).
4. Kramer is clear that he does not expect his defense of capital punishment to "convert staunch opponents … into supporters" (Kramer 2015, p. 379).
5. As Alice Ristroph has emphasized, on Hobbes' view, the right to resist, while perhaps most clearly exemplified in the case of capital punishment, extends more broadly, encompassing imprisonment and assault as well (Ristroph 2009, p. 617). After all, as Hobbes puts it, "[a] covenant not to defend myself from force by force, is always void" (Hobbes 1994, pt.1, ch. 14). By "force," Hobbes seems to have in mind "death, wounds, and imprisonment."
6. On Finkelstein's view, what one's continued presence in a country establishes is consent "to a general institution of punishment," rather than a particular imposition of punishment upon an individual (Finkelstein 2006, p. 1313).
7. The commandment that the innocent are not to be punished cannot be interpreted to be an absolute bar on practices that have the effect of punishing the innocent since that would rule out *all* punitive practices, given that error is always possible. It is more reasonably understood as the principle that evidence of actual innocence is always material.

8. Contra Brooks, who appears to suggest that a person on death row is morally entitled to an infinite number of appeals (Brooks 2011, p. 239).

9. Termination of civic membership does not necessarily entail execution. But if we take the idea of "civil death" seriously, then this may just boil down to the difference between killings committed by the state and killings committed by private citizens (Chin 2012).

10. Abolition in earlier generations was less court centric. Over the course of the nineteenth century, legislatures in five American states (New York, Pennsylvania, Rhode Island, Michigan and Wisconsin) abolished the death penalty (McGowen 2016, p. 622).

11. This is what Lee refers to as a "norm-centric," as opposed to a "reason-centric," approach (Lee 2007).

12. "Philosophy, as the thought of the world, does not appear until reality has completed its formative process, and made itself ready. … When philosophy paints its grey in grey, one form of life has become old, and by means of grey it cannot be rejuvenated, but only known. The owl of Minerva takes its flight only when the shades of night are gathering" (Hegel 2005, p. xxi).

13. Concerns that the categorical moral question does not admit of a rational answer may have contributed to the turn toward procedural arguments about fairness in its imposition. But, as David Dolinko showed long ago, the procedural turn did not yield the hoped-for rational certainty (Dolinko 1986).

14. Of the nearly 56,000 felony defendants processed through the 75 largest counties in the United States in 2009, only 374—approximately 0.7%—were charged with murder (Bureau of Justice Statistics 2009, table 1, "Felony Defendants in Large Urban Counties, 2009").

15. This chapter grew out of an extended discussion with Chad Flanders about capital punishment. I am grateful as well to Steve Garvey, Adam Kolber and Youngjae Lee for detailed comments and suggestions on an earlier draft.

References

Atkins v. Virginia, 536 U.S. 304, 311–312 (2002).

McClekey v Kemp, 481 U.S. 279 (1987).

Trop v. Dulles, 356 U.S. 86, 100–101 (1958).

Barry, Christian, and Patrick Tomlin. 2016. Moral uncertainty and permissibility: Evaluating option sets. *Canadian Journal of Philosophy* 46: 898–923.

———. this volume. Moral uncertainty and the criminal law (Chapter 19). In *The Palgrave handbook of applied ethics and the criminal law*, ed. Larry Alexander and Kimberly Kessler Ferzan. Cham: Springer.

Boonin, David. 2008. *The problem of punishment*. Cambridge: Cambridge University Press.

Brennan, Jason. 2016. *Against democracy*. Princeton: Princeton University Press.

Brettschneider, Corey. 2007a. The rights of the guilty. *Political Theory* 35: 175–199.

———. 2007b. Unreasonable disagreement: Reply to Lovett. *Political Theory* 35: 811–815.

Brooks, Thom. 2011. Retribution and capital punishment. In *Retributivism: Essays on theory and policy*, ed. Mark White, 232–246. Oxford: Oxford University Press.

Bureau of Justice Statistics. 2009. *Felony defendants in large urban counties, 2009.* Bureau of Justice Statistics. https://www.bjs.gov/content/pub/pdf/fdluc09.pdf. Accessed 25 Feb 2019.

Chiao, Vincent. 2018. *Criminal law in the age of the administrative state.* Oxford: Oxford University Press.

Chin, Gabriel. 2012. The new civil death: Rethinking punishment in the era of mass incarceration. *University of Pennsylvania Law Review* 160: 1789–1833.

Dagger, Richard. 2011. Social contracts, fair play, and the justification of punishment. *Ohio State Journal of Criminal Law* 8: 341–368.

Danaher, John. 2015. Kramer's purgative rationale for capital punishment: A critique. *Criminal Law and Philosophy* 9: 225–244.

Dolinko, David. 1986. How to criticize the death penalty. *Journal of Criminal Law & Criminology* 77: 546–601.

Donohue, John J., and Justin Wolfers. 2005. Uses and abuses of empirical evidence in the death penalty debate. *Stanford Law Review* 58: 791–846.

Elias, Norbert. 2000. *The civilizing process.* Malden: Blackwell.

Estlund, David. 2007. *Democratic authority.* Princeton: Princeton University Press.

Ewing, Benjamin. 2015. The political legitimacy of retribution: Two reasons for skepticism. *Law and Philosophy* 34: 369–396.

Feinberg, Joel. 1970. The expressive function of punishment. In *Doing and deserving*, 95–118. Princeton: Princeton University Press.

Finkelstein, Claire. 2002. Death and retribution. *Criminal Justice Ethics* 21 (2): 12–21.

———. 2006. A contractarian argument against the death penalty. *New York University Law Review* 81: 1283–1330.

Flanders, Chad. 2013. The case against the case against capital punishment. *New Criminal Law Review* 16: 595–620.

Garland, David. 2010. *Peculiar institution: America's death penalty in an age of abolition.* Oxford: Oxford University Press.

Garrett, Brandon. 2017. *The end of its rope: How killing the death penalty can revive criminal justice.* Cambridge: Harvard University Press.

Hanna, Nathan. 2008. Say what? A critique of expressive retributivism. *Law and Philosophy* 27: 123–150.

Harsanyi, John. 1975. Can the maximin principle serve as a basis for morality? A critique of John Rawls' theory. *American Political Science Review* 69: 594–606.

Hegel, G.W.F. 2005. *Philosophy of right.* Trans. S.W. Dyde. New York: Dover.

Heyd, David. 1991. Hobbes on capital punishment. *History of Philosophy Quarterly* 8: 119–134.

Hobbes, Thomas. 1651. *Leviathan.* Ed. E. Curley. Indianapolis: Hackett, 1994.

Hsu, Jimmy Chia-Shin. 2015. Does communicative retributivism necessarily negate capital punishment? *Criminal Law & Philosophy* 9: 603–617.

Kahan, Dan. 1996. What do alternative sanctions mean? *University of Chicago Law Review* 63: 591–653.

———. 2006. What's really wrong with shaming sanctions. *Texas Law Review* 84: 2075–2095.

Kant, Immanuel. 1996. The metaphysics of morals. In *Practical philosophy*, ed. M. Gregor. Cambridge: Cambridge University Press.

Kolber, Adam. 2018. Punishment and moral risk. *University of Illinois Law Review* 2: 487–532.

Kramer, Matthew. 2011. *The ethics of capital punishment.* Oxford: Oxford University Press.

———. 2015. The purgative rationale and the death penalty: Replies to Steiker and Danaher. *Criminal Law and Philosophy* 9: 379–394.

Lee, Youngjae. 2007. International consensus as persuasive authority in the Eighth Amendment. *University of Pennsylvania Law Review* 256: 63–120.

Lenta, Patrick. 2015. The *lex talionis*, the purgative rationale, and the death penalty. *Criminal Justice Ethics* 34: 42–63.

Lernestedt, Claes. 2015. Review of *The ethics of capital punishment: A philosophical investigation of evil and its consequences. Mind* 124 (493): 361–366.

Markel, Dan. 2005. State, be not proud: A retributivist defense of the commutation of death row and the abolition of the death penalty. *Harvard Civil Rights-Civil Law Review* 40: 407–480.

Matusiak, Matthew C., Michael S. Vaughn, and Roland V. del Carmen. 2014. The progression of "evolving standards of decency" in U.S. Supreme Court decisions. *Criminal Justice Review* 39: 253–271.

McGowen, Randall. 2016. The death penalty. In *The Oxford handbook of the history of crime and criminal justice*, ed. P. Knepper and A. Johansen, 615–634. Oxford: Oxford University Press.

Paternoster, Ray. 2011. Capital punishment. In *The Oxford handbook of crime and criminal justice*, ed. Michael Tonry, 757–792. Oxford: Oxford University Press.

Pojman, Louis. 2004. Why the death penalty is morally permissible. In *Debating the death penalty: Should America have capital punishment?* ed. Hugo Bedau and Paul Cassell, 51–75. Oxford: Oxford University Press.

Ristroph, Alice. 2009. Respect and resistance in punishment theory. *California Law Review* 97: 601–632.

Scanlon, Tim. 1988. The significance of choice. In *The Tanner lectures on human values*, ed. Sterling McMurrin, vol. 8, 149–216. Salt Lake City: University of Utah Press.

Shelby, Tommie. 2017. *Dark ghettos*. Cambridge, MA: Harvard University Press.

Shepherd, Joanna M. 2005. Deterrence versus brutalization: Capital punishment's differing impacts among states. *Michigan Law Review* 104: 203–256.

Steiker, Carol. 2011. The death penalty and deontology. In *The Oxford handbook of philosophy of criminal law*, ed. John Deigh and David Dolinko, 441–466. Oxford: Oxford University Press.

———. 2015. Can/should we purge evil through capital punishment? *Criminal Law and Philosophy* 9: 367–378.

Steiker, Carol, and Jordan Steiker. 2016. *Courting death: The Supreme Court and capital punishment*. Cambridge, MA: Harvard University Press.

———. 2017. Abolishing the American death penalty: The court of public opinion versus the US Supreme Court. *Valparaiso Law Review* 51: 579–603.

Stinneford, John F. 2010. Evolving away from evolving standards of decency. *Federal Sentencing Reporter* 23: 87–91.

Sunstein, Cass. 2005. *Laws of fear*. Cambridge: Cambridge University Press.

Sunstein, Cass, and Adrian Vermeule. 2005a. Is capital punishment morally required? Acts, omissions, and life-life tradeoffs. *Stanford Law Review* 58: 703–750.

———. 2005b. Deterring murder: A reply. *Stanford Law Review* 58: 847–858.

Waldron, Jeremy. 2012. Democracy. In *The Oxford handbook of political philosophy*, ed. David Estlund, 187–203. Oxford: Oxford University Press.

Zimring, Frank. 2003. *The contradictions of American capital punishment*. Oxford: Oxford University Press.

PART XI

Fraud

CHAPTER 12

Fraud

Samuel W. Buell

INTRODUCTION

It has been said that the central problem—indeed characteristic—of white-collar crime is the difficulty of distinguishing permissible, even if novel or "aggressive," commercial practices from those that ought to be met with criminal punishment (admittedly, especially by this author (Buell 2015, 2014)). This is both a normative and a forensic problem. Decisions must be made about what to tolerate and what to condemn, while tools must be designed that help legal actors to locate correctly the lines between the two categories.

This is of course a general characteristic of public law. But the task can be acutely difficult with sophisticated commercial behaviors because such conduct evolves rapidly and grows ever more complex and specialized. Detailed black-letter rules do not fare well on the ground in these circumstances, even if lawmakers can achieve consensus on which sorts of commercial conduct ought to be punished.

The criminal law of fraud has developed as a means of managing this problem. Fraud is more of a conceptual category than a particular behavior. And criminal fraud laws are far from black-letter rules. Typically they articulate a broad, question-begging standard: Do not intentionally commit fraud while dealing in securities, or using the interstate wires, or doing business with a federally insured bank or the US government, and so on. (While criminal fraud law shares important concepts with the law of fraud in tort, contract, and other aspects of private and regulatory law, I do not address those bodies of law here. The question whether to punish fraud is of course unique, and thus has produced its own doctrines and practices.)

S. W. Buell (✉)
Duke University, Durham, NC, USA
e-mail: buell@law.duke.edu

L. Alexander, K. K. Ferzan (eds.), *The Palgrave Handbook of Applied Ethics and the Criminal Law*, https://doi.org/10.1007/978-3-030-22811-8_12

This makes fraud, in spite of modern edicts against such things, a common law crime. Fraud law is a flexible tool in the hands of prosecutors, judges, and juries for working out the line between allowable and punishable commercial conduct on a contextual basis—which is the only way that line can be managed. Fraud is thus both the most interesting and most important of white-collar criminal prohibitions. It is, at once, the most common such crime, the broadest prohibition against economic wrongdoing, the most frequently enforced white-collar offense, and the residual crime designed to deal with hard cases.

The objectives of this chapter are threefold. First, it shows why the black-letter law of fraud, to the extent it exists—and in spite of what courts may say about that body of law—cannot govern, in any nearly complete way, the realm of behaviors at issue with the subject of fraud. Second, it shows why a narrower, rule-based antifraud regime would be an impractical alternative and thus, not surprisingly, cannot be found in the Anglo-American law of fraud.

Third, examining the actual practices of prosecutors and judges in fraud cases reveals how the law of criminal fraud, particularly its mens rea analysis, actually works. Finally, this chapter demonstrates to the reader how this method of analysis can be used to properly frame arguments about whether the next scandalous outrage in the corporate sector ought to be punished as a criminal fraud or is only an outrage or, perhaps, something that "oughta be a crime."

THE BLACK-LETTER LAW OF FRAUD

Statutes

In the United States, where fraud is prosecuted much more frequently and with harsher punishment than elsewhere in the world, there is a plethora of fraud statutes in federal and state criminal codes. These laws do not say much. Take, for example, the two bulwark statutes for white-collar prosecutions—the securities fraud prohibitions and the all-purpose wire fraud law. To commit securities fraud, punishable by up to 20 years in prison, is to "employ any device, scheme, or artifice to defraud," to "engage in any act, practice, or course of business which operates or would operate as a fraud or deceit upon any person," or "to defraud any person" in connection with any security or commodities future (15 U.S.C. §§ 78a-78oo, 17 C.F.R. § 240.10b-5). To commit wire fraud, punishable by 20 years in prison, is to send a signal over interstate wires (e.g., the Internet) after "devising or intending to devise any scheme or artifice to defraud" and in furtherance of such scheme (18 U.S.C. § 1343).

This approach is not unique to the United States. When overhauling its theft and white-collar crime statutes with the Fraud Act 2006, the United Kingdom made it a crime, for personal gain, to "dishonestly make a false representation," whether express or implied, and to "dishonestly fail[] to disclose to another person information which [an actor] is under a legal duty to disclose"

(UK Fraud Act 2006). The legislation also criminalized "dishonestly" abusing a position of trust for personal gain.

On the question of fraud's object, criminal statutes typically define their coverage in three ways: (1) by using the word "property," a term that can cover not only money, land, and the like but also informational and intellectual assets and interests; (2) by using terms like "fiduciary duty" and "right to honest services," terms that cover schemes targeting non-property interests like professional duties of loyalty; or (3) by requiring that the fraud, whatever it may be after, affects a particular sector of commercial activity, like securities dealing, business with federally insured banks, health-care payments implicating federally funded programs, or indeed any business with the federal government. It would be fair to say that Congress has created a framework under which a federal prosecutor would have some difficulty failing to locate an applicable fraud statute for deceptive commercial conduct of substantial size in any significant industry.

The federal courts in the United States have long understood that Congress means to invoke the common law of fraud when it uses the word "fraud" in a statute (Durland v. U.S.). This helps some. It is widely agreed that the law of tort and contract has long required at least proof of deception (by false representation or omission), materiality, reliance, and loss to sustain a cause of action (Buell 2011). But this is not criminal law and, as far as I have been able to tell, there never really was any *criminal* common law of fraud. (There was, instead, the familiar and somewhat tortured development in English and early American common law of the theft offenses (Green 2006).) A criminal fraud case, of course, requires no proof of reliance or damages: the crime of fraud would be inchoate even if there were not also readily available attempt and conspiracy doctrines in federal and state criminal law. Finally, a civil fraud case requires no proof of mental culpability.

What Courts Say

If one looks to see how federal courts, where the vast majority of substantial fraud cases are prosecuted, have recited the elements of the crime of fraud, one often finds something like the following: "To convict a person under [the wire fraud statute], the government must prove that he '(1) was involved in a scheme to defraud; (2) had an intent to defraud; and (3) used the wires in furtherance of that scheme'" (U.S. v. Weimert). A court will typically go on to explain that a scheme to defraud requires a material false representation or omission when there is a duty to disclose and reiterate that there must be a specific intent to defraud.

Courts have sometimes editorialized that the mail and wire fraud statutes, in particular, function as flexible stop-gap laws that can be used to catch novel and alarming behaviors that have not yet been specifically prohibited by statute or regulation (McNally v. U.S., pp. 372–373). Even as some judges lament the dangers of punishing "innocent" conduct with such generally phrased and broad criminal statutes, the courts resist narrowing fraud law for fear that doing so will prevent federal prosecutors from reaching seriously harmful and condemnable behaviors.

The exception proves the rule. The only significant narrowing of federal criminal fraud law occurred, after a two-decades-long campaign by academics and a few judges, around an area of fraud law that had greatly expanded. American judges had found that a "scheme to defraud" in the mail and wire fraud statutes could include something like the new UK offense of abusing a position of trust. This was known as "honest services fraud." In 1986, the Supreme Court vitiated this line of cases, ruling, as a matter of statutory interpretation, that the statutes covered only schemes targeting property interests (McNally v. U.S.). Congress promptly countermanded the Court, amending the mail and wire fraud statutes to explicitly cover "honest services" deprivations (18 U.S.C. § 1346).

Eventually the ground shifted to constitutional law. Concerned about the potential vagueness in a criminal prohibition covering limitless forms of self-dealing and conflicts of interests, the Supreme Court ruled (with flimsy statutory support) that the honest services theory of mail and wire fraud, to satisfy constitutional standards, requires proof that the offender received either a bribe or a kickback in exchange for breaching the relevant duty (Buell 2010; Skilling v. U.S.). Thus, honest services fraud is now mostly a fallback option for proving a bribery case, with different jurisdictional elements.

Why the Black Letter Is No Answer

It is easy to see why the fraud statutes, and judges' recitations of their elements, accomplish little in terms of drawing lines between permissible and punishable commercial behaviors. Deficits lie in both the actus reus and mens rea elements of the offense.

With regard to actus reus, the crime of fraud requires at least an attempt to deceive in some way. Deception is a relational concept, best defined along the following lines: leading "the hearer to believe something to be true that the speaker believes to be false" (Solan 2018, p. 74); "the communication of a message with which the communicator, in communicating, intends to mislead" (Green 2006, p. 76); "to intentionally cause [another] to have a false belief that is known or believed to be false" (Mahon 2015).

Defined in this manner, deception is commonplace in social and economic life and can be accomplished in a limitless diversity of ways. In order to prevent easy evasion of antifraud rules, fraud law cannot require an affirmative false statement and must allow for deception through partial misleading statements and omissions. This leaves two principal problems. Are all deceptive statements potential frauds? And which sorts of deceptive partial truths and nondisclosures are potential frauds?

Fraud by False Statement

The first question might appear easy to answer. One might think that all lies could be treated as attempts to commit fraud, as long as the liars were proved to have been out to get something through the lie. But that approach would be overbroad. A lot of lies designed to gain advantage do not belong anywhere near the law of fraud, at least not in its criminal form.

If I pretend to be someone important to gain entry to a fancy party because I would like to make some good contacts, I have lied for personal gain and cheated the hosts out of their right to control the guest list. But no one would suggest that I be prosecuted for fraud. My deception in social relations just is not the sort of thing that fraud law ought to be concerned with.

Even more so if I told a friend I would meet her for lunch, knowing I would probably get lazy and decide not to show up, leaving her to waste a half hour waiting outside a restaurant. Soon I might earn a reputation for being "a fraud." But I would not deserve a fraud conviction.

One could argue that such examples simply point to a kind of *de minimus* principle, or a norm by which all can rest assured that prosecutors will not trifle with pointless cases. But, if one kept spinning out similar examples, I think one would have to conclude that there is something more substantial going on—analogous to the idea that not all lying is immoral and to the fact that criminal law does not punish most common lying (Alexander and Sherwin 2003). It would be a moral, and thus also legal, overstatement to say that I deserve any sort of substantial punishment, as opposed to social and reputational censure, for deceiving hosts and friends. Thus, the interests at stake and the context in which deception occurs are critical to knowing whether an instance of deception might count as a fraud (for further similar examples, see Klass 2018, pp. 733–735).

The problem of determining which lies make out frauds is still more difficult. Even in consummately commercial activities involving parties unknown to each other, deception is normatively allowed. The used car lot, of course, is the paradigm example. The dealer may not tamper with the odometer, that is, lie about the age of the engine. But, at least in the absence of specific regulations, he typically can use shoddy paint to conceal rust and make efforts to avoid disclosing known mechanical defects. If the buyer fails to hire her own inspector to ferret out problems before a sale, then it is too bad.

A more common and practical example is commercial negotiations, in which parties routinely falsify the facts of what will be an acceptable settlement. These are false statements about state of mind rather than facts like market value, of course. But lying about mental state can constitute fraud, such as in cases of fraud based on a false opinion from a position of expertise (Virginia Bankshares, Inc. v. Sandberg).

Or consider huge sectors of sales activity in which sellers commonly make highly misleading claims about the virtues of their products. Some of this may be carved out of fraud law by the concept of puffery (Hoffman 2006, pp. 1400–1420; Klass 2012, p. 459). But that concept does not itself tell one how to determine when a lying salesperson is merely a puffer.

The hard issue for fraud law with sales talk is not whether the salesperson is not really a liar but rather what some have called a "bullshitter," that is, a person who does not know or care whether he is telling the truth (Solan 2018, p. 75). Criminal fraud law's requirement of culpable mental state makes those, including "bullshitters," who might accomplish deception without intent—which requires awareness or willful blindness as to the deception (Buell 2011)—ineligible for punishment (for comprehensive treatment of deceit's place in all realms of law, see Klass 2012). The real problem is that even self-conscious liars, depending on context, may not be committing fraud.

One might say the doctrinal issue here is reliance, since these are examples in which buyers typically do not rely on the relevant talk. But it is not civil fraud we are discussing. It is criminal fraud, which punishes attempts ("devising a scheme"). The question is rather whether a negotiator, for example, would or should believe a statement about someone's walk-away position, given the sort of negotiation in question and the practices and expectations that inhere in that market or sector of commercial activity.

One might say that such claims are not material. But that can be a stretch, since often the relevant factual assertions go to the heart of the deal, even though those assertions—"our cellular signal is the best in the country," "the market for mortgage bonds will keep rising," "there has never been a better time to put your money in condominiums"—are false or misleading, and known to be so by the seller.

Fraud by Omission or Misleading Conduct

The second question—how to deal with partial truths and omissions—is even more difficult. It of course cannot be the case that any omission to provide a material fact when discussing a commercial transaction is a crime. That would be a bizarre mode of economic ordering bearing no resemblance to the modern world. People would have to go around disclosing everything they know before doing deals. Inefficient to say the least, exhausting as well.

Though criminal fraud statutes rarely say anything about when omissions matter, the courts have developed an extensive jurisprudence built around the general concept of fiduciary relations. This jurisprudence usually starts with a statement such as that there can be no criminal liability for fraud based on a failure to disclose a fact unless the accused party had a duty to disclose it (U.S. v. Finnerty). This is of course circular. If we move to the question of when duties to disclose exist, we often see statements like "in a fiduciary relationship," "when there is a relationship of trust and confidence," and the like.

This focuses the inquiry a bit, but not much. How is one to know, when examining a particular transaction, whether the parties had such a relationship? It would be relatively easy if fraud law limited this category to actual fiduciary relationships as defined by other bodies of doctrine, such as trustee to beneficiary, lawyer to client, or corporate director to shareholder. But there will be many situations in which the law of fraud will want rules about nondisclosure to reach relationships of trust that have no special legal imprimatur, lest immunity from fraud be easily achieved by structuring the legal niceties of how one does business.

For example, suppose I walk into a local bank to obtain a mortgage having done no prior business with the bank. Banking regulations, of course, will have much to say about what the bank must tell me. But assume for sake of argument that the government has not gotten around to regulating the mortgage business. When will it be fraud for the mortgage banker to fail to bring to my attention an unpleasant fact about the loan, such as a ballooning interest rate or a prohibition against early payoff? May the banker exploit my relative ignorance by actively hiding the ugly stuff? Fraud law must have a means of determining whether the relationship between me (mortgage purchaser) and the bank (mortgage seller) is the sort that carries duties of disclosure—and of determining how far those duties extend. We know the lawyer has those duties and we know that the used car dealer or flea market merchant does not. But what about all the cases in between?

Mens Rea

Now consider the black-letter law of mens rea in fraud. The courts will say that the mens rea for fraud is the "specific intent to defraud." This formulation is, of course, a tautology. If we are conducting an inquiry into mental state to determine whether a deceptive commercial practice counts as a criminal fraud, it does no good to be told to look and see whether the actor intended to commit fraud.

Taken literally, this formulation could mean only one of two things, neither of which could be the law: (1) that fraud is only a crime if the actor knows at the time of the conduct that he is doing something a court will declare to be a fraud (mistake of law is a defense to fraud, in other words) or (2) that fraud is a crime whenever the actor means to be doing whatever he is physically doing and a court later determines it to be a fraud (in which case the mens rea requirement adds virtually nothing to the actus reus inquiry).

In a later section, I explain how criminal fraud law deals with the large deficits in its black letter. But first we should consider another road, one that the law of fraud has not taken.

THE IMPRACTICALITY OF RULE-BASED REGIMES

Fairness

Those who encounter American criminal fraud statutes and the decisions interpreting them for the first time (e.g., my students) sometimes wonder why courts would bother struggling over the question whether certain conduct constitutes fraud. This is criminal law, after all. If there is uncertainty at the level that sophisticated lawyers and judges argue and disagree with each over the matter, shouldn't that uncertainty resolve the matter? In other words, shouldn't fraud be sanctioned with criminal punishment only if the perpetrator has done something that is plainly, historically, recognizably, even paradigmatically fraud?

This line of argument sounds in the venerable (though not reliably honored) principle of lenity in interpreting criminal statutes. But it is more than an argument from constitutional due process doctrine. It is a normative position that rests on fundamental principles of criminal punishment rooted in legality principles. Punishment is not deserved in the absence of fair notice. In a liberal order, *pace* Hart, offenders should be given the opportunity to see clearly the line of criminal wrongdoing and exercise choice about whether to cross it.

Fraud law, therefore, ought to speak clearly and prospectively about where the line rests between acceptable, even if distasteful, business practices and criminal fraud. It could do so, it would seem, along two possible lines. One would be to list and specify prohibited practices, either by attempting to describe them in more detailed fraud statutes or by having fraud statutes incorporate other bodies of law, such as rules governing conduct in the securities industry or the self-regulatory codes of the professions. The other would be to follow a sort of principle of "first one gets a pass," under which courts could say something like, "This looks like a fraud but it's a novel case and we haven't had this before, so we declare it to come within the fraud statute henceforth, but this defendant may not be punished." (That would be a strange sort of ruling, given justiciability commitments in American adjudication, of course.)

Effectiveness

Anglo-American law has not followed anything like this course in articulating the law of fraud. Legislatures have declined to fill out criminal fraud statutes with specific elements and descriptions of conduct. Congress has only added more general "do not commit fraud" statutes to the federal code. And, in the United Kingdom, Parliament enacted a major overhaul of English theft and fraud law in 2006 that moved decisively in the direction of broader American-style criminal fraud provisions.

Judges have gone along, rarely raising constitutional notice and vagueness concerns with respect to criminal fraud law, routinely finding novel and deceptive commercial practices to fit within the statutes, and occasionally explaining the virtues of broad, flexible laws against fraud: "The law does not define fraud; it needs no definition; it is as old as falsehood and as versable as human ingenuity" (Weiss v. U.S.); "To try to delimit 'fraud' by definition would tend to reward subtle and ingenious circumvention and is not done" (Foshay v. U.S.); fraud exhibits "acute imagination," "inventive spirit," "peculiar charm," "craft and guiles of the dramatic arts," "ingenuities," and "nimbleness" (U.S. v. Falkowitz). And so on.

Theories of behavior and political economy surely explain much about this history. But this chapter is not that enterprise. As a functional matter, legal actors, individually and collectively, have responded to innovation in the matter of commercial deception by crafting and maintaining broad, flexible antifraud rules. These rules operate in a catch-all manner. This way, bright people bent on duping others for their own gain cannot expect to escape punishment by designing their way around the criminal law.

Fraud law thus has chosen to tip the scales in favor of effectiveness over notice. Whether this is all for the good is, of course, a normative question. The purpose of this chapter is to explain the law of fraud, not to justify it. But it must be said that, in modern developed economies, it is hard to conceive of a criminal law that would not have some means of responding to sophisticated and novel forms of commercial deception. Without such law, matters ranging from the Enron fraud to the scandal involving the manipulation of global benchmark interest rates (the London Interbank Offering Rate [LIBOR] and related affairs), and countless others between them, would not have been prosecutable. More than with perhaps any other core crime, the law of fraud is addressed to actors who plan in the criminal law's shadow. A law of fraud that were conservative (if that term works here) would allow for prosecution of the Bernard Madoffs of the world—the bald liars barely different from outright thieves—and not many others, at least not in the contemporary worlds of high finance, health care, high technology, and other major industries.

Fraud on the Ground

How, then, does the law of fraud remotely hope to survive the scrutiny of punishment theorists, much less lawyers or even large segments of the general public? It turns out that the law of criminal fraud has means of satisfying, or at least mollifying, the demands of legality and notice. Those means not only explain how fraud law survives in such broad, malleable form. They also constitute the *law* of fraud. In other words, to determine what is or is not a criminal fraud requires examining not the statutes and the dry judicial recitations of the "elements" of fraud but how fraud cases are decided on the ground. On the dimensions of both actus reus and mens rea, fraud law has evolved deeply interesting methods for selecting actors for punishment.

Markets and Context

To further explore the question of actus reus, return to the problem of deception. To repeat, fraud requires deception. Deception is not sufficient for a fraud, but it is the conceptual core of the offense. Again, however, not all deceptions—not even all deceptions in commercial transactions—are frauds. Even some outright affirmative misrepresentations are not frauds. Meanwhile, most nondisclosures (or silences, if one prefers) are not frauds. But some are, and they can amount to quite serious frauds.

When one looks at how legal actors—prosecutors, juries, and judges—decide whether deception constitutes fraud, context is highly explanatory. To be more specific, two concepts do a great deal of work, especially in close cases of uncertainty: markets and expectations. As a rule of thumb if not of law, Party P's deceptive statement or omission potentially counts as a fraud if it is the sort of thing Party V (or perhaps a reasonable person so situated) would not have expected to be on guard for given the norms of the market in question (Gregory Klass articulates a similar principle in his description of the common law of deceit (Klass 2012, p. 456)).

Two stylized examples, one near each pole, will illustrate the principle. (These are hypotheticals, so please treat them as if no relevant background legal regulations existed.) Suppose that a cardiovascular surgeon, while discussing a risky, expensive, and potentially life-prolonging operation with a patient, were to say that the patient had an 80 percent chance of surviving the procedure. Further suppose, however, that 80 percent is the national survival rate and that this surgeon has performed the procedure many times at only a 50 percent survival rate. The surgeon does not disclose his personal performance data. The patient goes forward with the surgery, the outcome of which is not relevant to criminal fraud analysis.

This is clearly a fraud. The surgeon has made a perhaps literally true but deeply misleading statement and he has omitted to disclose highly material information. Critically, the misleading statement and omission deceive the patient because the market for risky surgery is, as a normative matter, one in which patients rightfully expect full and candid disclosure, given enormous informational asymmetry and very high stakes (not to mention cost!). Although the careful patient might do so, the modal patient is not expected to say, "Wait, I need to see your own performance data."

A judge analyzing such a case would likely put it in terms of the surgeon having a "duty" to disclose, given the "fiduciary" nature of the doctor-patient relationship. But "duty" alone is a fairly meaningless word, and "fiduciary" is used in many different contexts in American law. These terms operate as placeholders. The truth is that the law of fraud, by judging this a fraud, would be creating and imposing that "duty" on the surgeon, and declaring him a "fiduciary" for these purposes.

The existence of the duty would be found because of a conclusion about the norms governing the market for surgery and the expectations those norms create about what forms and degree of honesty and disclosure the buyer is owed—norms that can vary not only across markets but also over time (Klass 2012, p. 472). If those expectations are not met in some significant way, then the buyer has been deceived by being led to rely on his background expectations rather than what might be the actual facts of the case, facts he could only discover if he knew that he better ferret them out.

The question is whether, to borrow Stuart Green's phrase, a principle of "caveat auditor" (in addition to, I suppose, "caveat observer") applies (Green 2006, p. 87). In this way, some types of concealed relational transgressions are deceptions—they prey upon the victim's belief that the perpetrator will act one way when he is secretly acting in another (I thus disagree with Green when he asserts that the crime of fraud has broadened beyond the concept of deceit to include a variety of transgressions not grounded in deceit, so that fraud can be "a wrongful act of almost any sort" (Green 2006, p. 149)).

Now consider a classic example that is not a fraud. An elderly woman befriends a man at church who is an antique dealer. She invites him over for tea after church. He remarks on a chest of drawers in her living room: "That's a lovely piece." She replies, "I wish I could get it out of here, I keep banging into it and I never use it." He says, "I'd be happy to take it off your hands and get it out of here for $100." She agrees. He removes it in his pickup truck and sells it the next week at auction for $10,000. As soon as he saw the chest, he recognized it as a rare beauty in excellent condition that would fetch a handsome price.

This is sleazy but not fraud. These two persons have conducted a cash transaction in an arm's length market for household goods. He at least concealed the true value, and arguably affirmatively misled her about the value by verbally offering a price of $100. The facts do not show her to be mentally vulnerable or unable to ask the sorts of questions, or do the kind of diligence in the market, that any seller would be expected to do in the circumstances. *This* buyer lamentably might not have thought to question *this* seller. But *such* buyers should and do pause, probe, and check. In the bazaar, duties are light if not nonexistent, and one must enter on guard. She knew he had superior information and they had no special relationship. (Elderly, competent tea invitee from church will not suffice to generate a special duty.) This is not fraud.

Intent to Defraud

Because this is criminal law, and fraud is a serious felony, the performance of the actus reus will not suffice to justify punishment. The deceiver must also have acted with a blameworthy state of mind.

Like the idea that misleading statements and omissions are fraud when they violate a "duty," the mens rea formulation of "specific intent to defraud" turns out to be a placeholder for a particular inquiry into mental state that is not unique to the law of fraud (one sometimes sees it also, e.g., in the law of obstruction of justice) but that occurs most clearly in fraud law.

As a rule of thumb if not of law, Party P's deceptive statement or omission potentially counts as a fraud if P knew at the time of the conduct that the conduct was wrongful in the context. This inquiry in part turns back on the actus reus question. P will be aware of the wrongfulness of his deceptive conduct if P knows that the norms of the relevant market treat his conduct as out of bounds, such that Party V will have no expectation that P will engage in such conduct and no good reason to be on guard against such conduct by taking protective measures, making further inquiry, and so on.

As I have explored in previous work, this question of "consciousness of wrongdoing," which looms large at least in hard or arguable cases, quickly becomes an evidentiary matter (Buell and Griffin 2012). Prosecutors, judges, and juries confronted with difficult questions about whether the case before them is a fraud will look for evidence that actors destroyed records, made sure not to leave a paper trail, told people not to disclose things to others, constructed false evidentiary records, and the like.

This sort of evidentiary inquiry has long roots in the criminal law. It connects to legal phenomena such as the very old idea of looking for "badges of fraud" as a way of identifying a fraudulent conveyance. Or the more modern idea of the required mens rea of "dishonesty" in English theft and fraud law, which calls for an inquiry into whether the actor's conduct "was honest or dishonest … to be determined by the fact-finder by applying the (objective) standards of ordinary decent people" (Ivy v. Genting Casinos).

This mental state inquiry appears to perform two functions. First, it provides a (less than perfect) method of determining whether an actor's deception does in fact cross the boundaries of a particular market's norms, which is especially useful when legal actors confront novel schemes within unfamiliar markets.

Second, and more critically, the inquiry deals with the notice problem we were left with earlier. The actor who proceeds in the face of knowledge that his conduct is wrongful according to the norms of the market in which he deals has far less ground for complaint than an unwitting actor when the state later comes along to apply broad, flexible antifraud statutes to his conduct (Klass 2012, p. 473). Notice here *both* satisfies worries about adherence to legality values *and* fortifies the case that the actor should be punished in part for having acted with a blameworthy state of mind (Buell 2015).

The solution is imperfect, of course. Wrongdoers may be perfectly aware that their conduct is perfidious but leave no evidence with which a prosecutor could prove that mental state (proof of mens rea being a general problem in criminal law, of course). Fearful, paranoid, or unusually guilt-prone individuals may try to hide and cover up when their conduct is not something that warrants criminal sanction, raising the danger that fraud prosecutions could encroach upon the legality-based edict against punishing legally impossible offenses (for more on this, see Buell and Griffin 2012). And relying on participants in a market to signal what the rules of the road in that market ought to be is not necessarily how one would want to go about regulatory design—although it might be sufficient for criminal fraud, given that criminal law, for error deflection purposes, generally tries to stay back from achieving the optimal level of deterrence.[1]

It may help to recall that we are discussing how to deal with the hard cases of fraud. There will be many cases in which careful and deeper inquiry into market norms and mental states will not be necessary. For example, a massive Ponzi scheme, based on fictitious claims about nonexistent assets and wild investment possibilities that are only fantasies, presents no difficulty. The deception is elaborate and completely unjustifiable with reference to how any legitimate modern market functions. The wrongfulness of such behavior is universally understood within developed economies. Legal actors do not need to dig deeper because they may simply assume that actus reus and mens rea requirements are easily satisfied.

The problem in hard cases of criminal fraud is how the legal system applies a rule as broad as "do not commit fraud" to an unfamiliar market and new or complicated commercial transaction when deception alone is not necessarily criminally wrongful and legal actors are supposed to limit criminal punishment to blameworthy actors who received fair notice. The methodologies with regard to act and mental state described here are means of dealing with that problem.

How to Identify a Criminal Fraud

To see more clearly how the law of criminal fraud works in hard cases, consider a less stylized and more complex example. Some factual detail will be required to understand how the analysis sketched above might work in a modern-day white-collar prosecution in the corporate sector.

In the LIBOR scandal, which has produced a bevy of prosecutions, specialized traders at large global banks dealt with each other in markets for interest rate derivative products (McBride 2016; Vaughn and Finch 2017; Indictment, U.S. v, Robson 2014; Indictment, U.S. v. Connolly 2016; Indictment, U.S. v. Bogucki 2018; Serious Fraud Office n.d.). Stripped down, this was a market in betting on how interest rates would move, usually over periods of months, in various financial markets and in relation to various currencies: what a Euro on deposit in Tokyo would earn in six months, and so on, in many combinations of currencies, markets, and time periods.

It is good to have places people can go to make deals to hedge themselves against volatility in interest rates if their economic plans could make that volatility a barrier to success. It is thus good for there also to be people who would like to get paid to take on more risk with regard to interest rate volatility and would like to sell such hedges. In theory at least, it is also good to have people with no other economic plans who simply want to bet with each other about interest rates, so that markets will be more liquid and pricing information will be more abundant and perhaps more accurate.

The traders in the LIBOR scandal were the latter. They were transacting a lot of volume for numerous very large banks. Deals were priced using the London Interbank Offering Rate (LIBOR) as a benchmark. Terms might say, in substance, that the deal would settle in six months at LIBOR as published on the settlement date, plus an agreed number of "basis points," that is, hundredths of a percentage point. Who wins and who loses on such a deal obviously depends to a great extent on what LIBOR turns out to be on the date on which the deal settles up.

These traders figured out that they could help themselves not only by being good at predicting interest rate movement but also by influencing what LIBOR would *be* on the settlement dates. LIBOR was calculated by the British Banking Authority (BBA) each day. The BBA would ask the largest banks in London to report the rates they were charged to borrow cash on a short-term basis from each other. The BBA would take these submissions, discard the top and bottom quartiles, calculate the mean of the remaining submissions, and report that number as the day's LIBOR.

Derivatives traders at many banks discovered that they could influence the individuals at their banks known as "submitters" to report to the BBA slightly lower or higher numbers on given days if doing so would benefit the traders' positions. "I have a big six month position coming due, any way you could go a little lower with our submission today." To simplify, if the submitter obliges such a trader, and that bank's submission is a tick lower for the day, there is at least the potential that the BBA's math will produce a lower LIBOR number that day and, thus, that the trader (who, in this example, is holding the short position) will make out a bit better on his deal that settles up on that date. (These derivatives deals, of course, were individually and collectively very large, so that tiny differences in the benchmark rate could greatly affect a trader's profit or loss.)

Is there a criminal fraud here? Start with actus reus. We need a story of deception intended to produce some sort of gain, and we need to be able to identify the players in that story: who is deceiving whom and why. Legal doctrine would put this question in terms like "what is the scheme to defraud?" The most likely theory of deception would be that the trader who uses the submitter at his bank to tweak LIBOR on his deal's settlement date is deceiving his counter-party trader, who believed their deal would be priced using actual LIBOR as the benchmark, not the different number that was "seller-tweaked" LIBOR.

But we need to dig a little deeper into this market to see how this theory works out. First, we need to decide whether this is a case of deception by affirmative misrepresentation (lying) or a case of deception by nondisclosure (silence). One might argue that when the seller said at formation of the deal, "Let's do it at LIBOR plus x basis points," the word "LIBOR" was a lie, because the counter-party would understand it to mean real or independent "LIBOR" not "seller-manipulated LIBOR." But that characterization is perhaps a bit too lawyerly. It might make more sense to say that the seller failed to disclose to the buyer the critical fact that he could and would use personnel within his own bank to manipulate LIBOR to his advantage when it came time to settle up.

This brings us to the question of what the courts call "duty" and what we discussed as an inquiry into the norms of a particular market and whether persons doing business in that market regularly and reasonably expect certain forms of disclosure. The relationship between traders at different banks in an over-the-counter derivatives market is highly arm's length and cannot remotely be described as a trust or fiduciary-like relationship. Therefore, any argument about a duty to disclose what the seller's bank is doing behind the scenes faces a steep uphill battle. Perhaps the strained argument that using the word "LIBOR" in this context was an affirmative deception ends up working better after all, at least for a prosecutor.

Second, we need to consider the more difficult question whether the counterparties to these transactions were or could have been deceived in this way. Fraud can be inchoate and need not accomplish deception. But the perpetrator's scheme must contemplate something that would count as a fraud if it succeeded.

In doctrinal terms, one could look at this either in terms of whether there is a deception at all or in terms of whether fraud's materiality requirement is satisfied. Both avenues lead to the same question. The crux of the problem in the LIBOR scandal is this: If the traders in the interest rate derivatives markets at most or all of the big banks were pressuring their submitters to tweak LIBOR in their favor, then any given trader likely expected any counter-party trader to assume the trader would do it and also do it himself.

Arguably there is no deception at all, or even any belief that deception would succeed. Maybe the traders manipulated LIBOR just to maintain a level playing field. In other words, perhaps this was all a big collective action problem resulting from regulatory failure, not a crime.

Now let us consider mens rea. I have not seen a white-collar prosecution with as damning apparent evidence of mental state as exists in the LIBOR cases. The traders created extensive instant messaging records of their communications with the submitters within their banks, with each other, and with brokers in the market who did not work for the banks but were heavily involved in deal creation. These messages include such gems as "There's bigger crooks in the market than us guys" and "I can't make our LIBOR submission too false" (U.S. Dep't of Justice 2013, 2012). Throughout these messages, the traders provide specific terms of deals they have coming up for settlement and exactly how much they need LIBOR to move, and in what direction, to produce precisely what result in terms of profit.

These folks did not make much effort to cover up what they were doing. But they clearly knew they were engaged in wrongful conduct. Perhaps they were not worried about what their own employers would say (weak compliance systems at the banks I would suppose) but they at least understood that the BBA needed to believe that the numbers provided by the submitters were not corrupted by trader tampering.

One might think a promising alternative theory would be that the traders and their accomplices defrauded not their counter-party traders but the BBA, which had some sort of right to honest reporting from the banks and would be at least reputationally hurt if it came out (as it did) that LIBOR was far from a gold standard. The problem here is that the BBA did little to police the banks and, more importantly, was not clear about how much leeway the banks had to exercise judgment in reporting their numbers (Godoy 2018).

Recall that the number submitted to the BBA was supposed to be a simple fact: the cost for Bank A to borrow cash from Bank B in London for 24 hours or so. Apparently that fact did not really exist. In an instant message exchange, one can see a submitter explaining to a trader that the banks had not been doing any such deals for a very long time (U.S. Dep't of Justice 2012, p. 39). The relevant data simply was not there. The submitters were left to guesstimate the matter, without guidance from their superiors or the BBA about how to do so.

Thus, the evidence of awareness of wrongfulness is not quite as one sided as it might have seemed. "There's bigger crooks" and the like must be balanced against the possibility that many traders and submitters thought everyone was doing it and that the regulatory body did not care.

I chose this example because it is current, typical in the complexity and nuance of big-ticket questions about fraud that the law faces in the corporate sector, and in my view somewhat close to the line. When I first saw the LIBOR instant messages, I thought, "These guys are cooked." But the more I dig into the LIBOR cases and follow their development, the less it surprises me that the results have been mixed, on both sides of the Atlantic: some convictions, some acquittals, and some dismissals by judges.

As a matter of prosecutorial discretion, my own view is that the LIBOR scandal eminently deserved close thought and serious creativity in finding a way to fit the traders' conduct into the rubric of criminal fraud. But this chapter is not concerned with enforcement policy. The point is that one has no hope of working out whether a situation like this might be a criminal fraud without an analysis of both actus reus and mens rea like that conducted above. To say that the law of fraud is something like "do not intentionally deceive another for purpose of gain" will not get anywhere near the bottom of a case like the LIBOR manipulation.

Conclusion

Fraud has a claim, at least in our day, to being the most interesting offense in the criminal law's special part. It deals with some of the most important and challenging matters of our time. (This chapter did not even touch on the globally important question of whether persons trading mortgage-backed securities late in the housing bubble of the mid-aughts committed fraud.) It forces prosecutors, judges, and juries to work hard to figure out how to balance the imperatives of law being effective in the face of innovative wrongdoing with the vital demands of notice and fairness in punishment. And it perpetually changes shape and adapts as modern industries and economies produce new and unforeseen ways of attempting to create wealth.

The subject of fraud will never be settled or boring, and it likely will not die. As Edward Coke wrote in 1601, "If you ask why are there so many laws, the answer is that fraud ever increases on this earth" (Twyne's Case 1601).[2]

NOTES

1. Douglas Husak's observations about a defense of "But everyone does that" are informative (Husak 1996). Husak highlights the potential relevance of a claim of "But everyone does that" for crimes "the wrongfulness of which depends on a convention." The question with criminal fraud is not, as Husak asks, whether criminal conduct may be fully justified or excused solely because of a convention within a community to permit, or not to punish, that criminal conduct. The question is whether a necessary element of the crime—purpose to commit fraud—can exist in the absence of the actor's awareness that her plan or conduct exceeds the contours of allowable deception within the relevant community. Still, I take one of Husak's points to be that people who do something that is illegal on the books but, as far as anyone can tell, clearly accepted and not condemned throughout the relevant community should be permitted to argue that they are not blameworthy and therefore may not be punished. This perhaps rests on a similar principle about blameworthiness as does my account of "consciousness of wrongdoing."

2. Many thanks to Stuart Green, Jeremy Horder, and Leo Katz for very helpful comments on a draft.

REFERENCES

15 U.S.C. §§ 78a-78oo.

18 U.S.C. § 1343.

17 C.F.R. § 240.10b-5.

United Kingdom Fraud Act 2006.

Ivy v. Genting Casinos (UK) Ltd., [2017] UKSC 67 (UK Supreme Ct. 2017).

Twyne's Case, 3 Co. Rep. 80b, 82a, 76 Eng. Rep. 809, 815–16 (K.B. 1601).

Durland v. United States, 161 U.S. 306 (1895).

Foshay v. United States, 68 F.2d 205 (8th Cir. 1933).

McNally v. United States, 483 U.S. 350 (1987).

Skilling v. United States, 561 U.S. 358 (2010).

United States v. Falkowitz, 214 F.Supp.2d 365 (S.D.N.Y. 2002).

United States v. Finnerty, 533 F.3d 143 (2d Cir. 2008).

United States v. Weimert, 819 F.3d 351 (7th Cir. 2016).

Virginia Bankshares, Inc. v. Sandberg, 501 U.S. 1083 (1991).

Weiss v. United States, 122 F.2d 675 (5th Cir. 1941).

Indictment, United States v. Paul Robson et al., No. 14 Crim. 272 (S.D.N.Y. 2014).

Indictment, United States v. Matthew Connolly et al., No. 16 Crim. 370 (S.D.N.Y. 2016).

Indictment, United States v. Robert Bogucki, No. Cr. 18 021 EJD (N.D. Cal. 2018).

Alexander, Larry, and Emily Sherwin. 2003. Deception in morality and law. *Law and Philosophy* 22: 393–450.

Buell, Samuel W. 2010. The Court's fraud dud. *Duke Journal of Constitutional Law and Public Policy* 6: 31–48.

———. 2011. What is securities fraud? *Duke Law Journal* 61: 526–581.

———. 2014. "White collar" crimes. In *The Oxford handbook of criminal law*, ed. Marcus D. Dubber and Tatjana Hörnle, 837–861. Oxford: Oxford Univ. Press.

———. 2015. Culpability and modern crime. *Georgetown Law Journal* 103: 547–603.

Buell, Samuel W., and Lisa Kern Griffin. 2012. On the mental state of consciousness of wrongdoing. *Law and Contemporary Problems* 75 (2): 133–166.

Godoy, Jody. 2018. DOJ "sandbagging" with new theory in Libor trial, judge says. Law 360. https://www.law360.com/articles/1044060/doj-sandbagging-with-new-theory-in-libor-trial-judge-says. Accessed on 26 Feb 2019.

Green, Stuart. 2006. *Lying, cheating, and stealing: A moral theory of white collar crime.* Oxford: Oxford Univ. Press.

Hoffman, David A. 2006. The best puffery article ever. *Iowa Law Review* 91: 1395–1448.

Husak, Douglas. 1996. "But-everyone-does-that!" defense. *Public Affairs Quarterly* 10: 307–334.

Klass, Gregory. 2012. Meaning, purpose, and cause in the law of deception. *Georgetown Law Journal* 100: 449–496.

———. 2018. The law of deception: A research agenda. *University of Colorado Law Review* 89: 707–740.

Mahon, James E. 2015. The definition of lying and deception. Stanford Encyclopedia of Philosophy. https://plato.stanford.edu/entries/lying-definition/. Accessed on 26 Feb 2019.

McBride, James. 2016. Understanding the LIBOR scandal. Council on Foreign Relations Backgrounder. https://www.cfr.org/backgrounder/understanding-libor-scandal. Accessed on 26 Feb 2019.

Solan, Lawrence M. 2018. Lies, deceit, and bullshit in law. *Duquesne Law Review* 56: 73–104.

U.S. Dep't of Justice. 2012. Letter to Gary R. Spratling, Esq. Re: UBS AG, Appendix A, statement of facts.

———. 2013. Rabobank admits wrongdoing in Libor investigation, agrees to pay $325 million criminal penalty. *Press Release*, October 29.

UK Serious Fraud Office. n.d. Libor cases. https://www.sfo.gov.uk/cases/libor-landing. Accessed on 26 Feb 2019.

Vaughn, Liam and Gavin Finch. 2017. Libor scandal: The bankers who fixed the world's most important number. *Guardian*, January 18.

PART XII

Hate Crimes

CHAPTER 13

Hate (or Bias) Crime Laws

Kenneth W. Simons

INTRODUCTION

Enhanced criminal punishment for hate or bias crimes, a relatively recent legal phenomenon, continues to grow both in popularity and in scope, in the United States and around the globe. Almost all American states and a significant number of nations impose higher punishment if a crime (such as a murder, robbery, assault, or defacement of a building) is committed because of the actor's hatred toward, or prejudice against, a member of a protected group or because the actor used the group characteristic as the basis for selecting the victim. The groups most commonly protected by hate crime laws are groups defined by race, ethnicity, nationality, religion, sexual orientation, gender, or disability (Jenness 2012).

But enhanced punishment for hate crimes also continues to raise controversial questions about the proper scope and severity of the criminal law, including the following: whether such punishment amounts to punishing for thoughts or character; whether enhancement can be justified, on a retributivist, consequentialist, expressivist, or distributive justice account of the principles underlying the criminal law; deciding which groups should be "protected" by such laws (in the sense that bias against the group is the trigger for greater punishment); whether hatred or bias is the relevant criterion and whether this criterion is best framed as requiring animus toward the disfavored group or a discriminatory method of selecting the victim; whether, if motive is indeed required, the motive must be a necessary cause of the actor's conduct, a sufficient cause, a primary cause, a sole cause, a substantial cause, or some disjunctive or conjunctive combination of these or other possibilities; and whether authorized pun-

K. W. Simons (✉)
University of California, Irvine School of Law, Irvine, CA, USA
e-mail: ksimons@law.uci.edu

© The Author(s) 2019
L. Alexander, K. K. Ferzan (eds.), *The Palgrave Handbook of Applied Ethics and the Criminal Law*, https://doi.org/10.1007/978-3-030-22811-8_13

ishments (which sometimes greatly exceed the permissible punishment for the parallel crime) are disproportionate to the harm or wrong or to the actor's culpability. An additional question, rarely raised, is whether the law should require (as it typically does) that the actor's conduct, apart from the bias motive or selection criterion, constitutes a crime.

In surveying these issues, this chapter demonstrates their interrelationship and offers some tentative answers.

Do Hate Crime Laws Punish for Hate, for Bias, or for Both?

A preliminary question about the topic is worth addressing at the outset. Do "hate" crime laws punish for hate, for hate plus something else, or simply for something else? On closer inspection, actual statutory schemes focus on whether an actor selected his victim or displayed animus toward the victims on the basis of group bias. For this reason, many have plausibly suggested that such laws are better characterized as addressing bias and thus should be labeled as "bias crime" laws (Jacobs and Potter 1998; Lawrence 1994, 1999; Brax 2016; Brudholm 2018). After all, these statutes do not criminalize hate in the absence of bias. If the statutes were this broad, they would encompass a huge number of domestic disputes, gang killings, and anger-fueled assaults. Indeed, on this view, many or most killings that are mitigated from murder to voluntary manslaughter on the basis of "heat of passion" would at the same time qualify for sentence enhancement as "hate crimes."[1] That is certainly not what supporters of hate crime laws envision. At the same time, hatred is arguably a justifiable emotional reaction in some circumstances—for example, when a victim resents an offender for seriously wronging him.[2] Even hatred of a group might sometimes be justifiable—for example, if a particular gang has been terrorizing a community. Acting on the basis of bias or prejudice, by contrast, is seemingly always unjustifiable.

But the question remains: do these laws require proof of *both* hate and bias? May an actor receive an enhanced punishment for a crime prompted by bias but not by hate? This is not merely a theoretical possibility. Consider three examples.[3]

First, suppose D1 selects a victim on the basis of race and punches him in order to impress D1's fellow gang members, but D1 harbors no personal hostility toward the victim. Many jurisdictions would permit punishment of D1 even though he lacks the intense, passionate emotional attitude distinctive of "hate" or "hateful" conduct. Second, suppose D2 is opportunistic: he attacks women, or the elderly, or undocumented immigrants because he believes such victims are less likely to repel his attack or less likely to report him to the police. D2 does not hate the groups that he is victimizing. Indeed, he is grateful for their existence, since they facilitate his criminal success.

Nevertheless, these two examples alone might not be especially telling against a "hate" requirement. In the first, D1's conduct seems condemnable in part because he knowingly gives effect to the hatred of others. In the second, some might object that the conduct is not highly condemnable, or at least not sufficiently condemnable to warrant a greater punitive sanction.

But now consider a third example. D3 selects blacks, or Catholics, or gays, to victimize, not because he has antipathy toward members of that group, but because he is indifferent to whether members of the group suffer. They simply do not register as human on his moral compass. In his view, their physical, economic, and emotional well-being are of no more importance than the well-being of a gnat or a blade of grass.[4] In principle, if an actor who genuinely hates the group that he preys upon deserves an enhanced punishment, this also seems to be true of D3 (*see* Simons 2002).[5] Practical difficulties in defining the precise contours of "selective indifference" and in proving such an attitude might explain and even justify criminal law's reluctance to expand the category of bias crimes in this manner. Nevertheless, this analysis suggests some important and perhaps surprising conclusions: in principle, hatred is not a necessary condition of what is conventionally called a "hate crime," and it is often not a sufficient condition, either.

In the remainder of this chapter, I usually refer to "bias crime" laws, but the reader should understand that some statutory schemes may indeed require proof of a "hateful" animus.

Justifications for Bias Crime Laws

A variety of justifications have been offered for bias crime laws (Dillof 1997; Hurd and Moore 2004). I focus on four.

Greater Harm

One common rationale for enhanced punishment focuses on the greater harm caused by a bias crime than by the parallel crime. A violent act targeting a member of a minority or religious group might cause: (a) more physical harm to the direct victim than an act not so targeted, (b) more psychic harm to such a victim, or (c) fear and outrage in the entire minority or religious community. A standard objection to this rationale is that such a consequence is empirically contingent; moreover, the rationale is arguably insufficient to justify a categorical bias crime enhancement (Hurd and Moore 2004, pp. 1085–1093; Brax 2016, p. 237; Al-Hakim and Dimock 2012, p. 593). Not all bias crimes have all or indeed any of these effects, and even if the effects do ensue, evidence of the effects can and should be admitted in the individual case. Conclusively presuming that such an effect will occur would frequently result in excessive punishment, according to this argument.

This rationale is indeed imperfect but the objection is overstated. The criminal law frequently employs rough proxies for harm. Almost any legislative definition of criminal conduct is inevitably an imperfect surrogate for the harm or wrong that the conduct might bring about or constitute. Sex with a person under age 16 does not invariably result in or amount to exploitation of a person too immature to understand the significance of the act. Assault with a deadly weapon does not invariably cause more physical harm or more fear than simple assault causes. Yet these proxies for the underlying harm are not usually viewed as problematic, in light of the need to develop criteria for punishment that give fair warning to potential defendants and that legal actors can consistently apply.

I do agree that version (a) of this rationale, greater physical harm to the victim, is weak, for it is easy enough to measure such harm case by case. But the subtler effects of (b) causing psychic harm to the immediate victim or of (c) causing fear and outrage in the victim's community are not at all easy to measure. There is thus much to be said for a categorical legislative solution here, under which the legislature considers these effects when identifying and defining those bias crimes that are proper objects of punishment enhancement, rather than an individualized solution, under which we ask a judge or jury to consider these effects only as questions of fact to be investigated and proven case by case.[6]

Perhaps the real objection to this rationale is that punishment enhancements for bias crimes demand stricter scrutiny (as both a moral and constitutional matter) than run-of-the-mill criminal law prohibitions require because of concerns that such enhancements infringe on freedom of speech or thought. I address this deeper objection in the section "Do Bias Crime Laws Improperly Punish for Thoughts or Character?" below.

Finally, whether bias crimes cause greater harm depends crucially on how one characterizes harm. If harm includes social division and personal insecurity *on the basis of race or religion or sexual orientation*, for example, then bias crimes undoubtedly may cause such harm. Members of disfavored groups, as well as other members of society, subjectively do suffer such harm. On the other hand, some might question the propriety of relying upon this type of harm to justify bias crime laws. Thus, some believe that these laws will only inflame racial, ethnic, and social divisions, not reduce them (*see* Lawrence 2007; Jacobs and Potter 1998). If this is so, and if the justification for criminal law is exclusively or partially consequentialist, this inegalitarian effect surely counts against bias crime laws. Moreover, even a nonconsequentialist might find the fact (if it is a fact) that these laws send an inegalitarian message to be relevant to their justifiability. Some nonconsequentialists might also conclude that the state's use of explicit racial, ethnic, or religious categories is simply intrinsically wrong (at least prima facie), in the same way that many believe that affirmative action programs are intrinsically wrong. Nevertheless, it is not plausible to deny that bias crimes can cause group-specific (including racially specific) harms. Thus, the "greater harm" argument is weightier than many critics of bias crime laws believe.

Greater Culpability

Another justification for enhanced punishment is that an actor who is motivated by bias, or who intentionally selects a victim on the basis of the victim's membership in a protected group, is more culpable than an actor not so motivated. Just as a purposeful killing is more culpable than a reckless or negligent killing, and a purposeful defacement of another's property is more culpable than a reckless or negligent defacement, a purposeful killing or defacement that is motivated by bias is more culpable. And both consequentialist and retributive principles support greater punishment for more culpable conduct.

This justification has some plausibility. Although some opponents of hate crime laws suggest that aggravated punishment for aggravated motives has little precedent in the criminal law, in fact this practice is more widespread than they acknowledge. Many states permit increased punishment if the intentional killing of the actor was motivated by a further purpose or aggravated motive such as pecuniary gain. Specific intent crimes such as burglary elevate criminal punishment if the actor possessed a designated further purpose: the actor must not only intentionally enter another's dwelling but must do so for the purpose of committing a crime therein (Hessick 2006; Simons 2000; Steiker 1999).

Thus, the objection that bias crimes improperly punish motives, not actus reus or mens rea, is undermined by existing criminal law doctrine. To be sure, motives are more often treated as relevant when they mitigate rather than aggravate punishment, but it hardly follows that it is illegitimate or unjustifiable for the criminal law to identify especially culpable motives as a proper basis for punishment enhancement.

Nevertheless, this objection does prompt three related concerns. The first is that enhanced punishment for bias motives is indefensibly selective. Such motives arguably are not more culpable than other especially culpable motives that do not automatically or systematically trigger greater punishment. A motive of greed or sadism is highly culpable, yet legislatures have not created or enacted general provisions that aggravate punishment for "greed crimes" or for "sadism crimes."

This concern has merit. It would indeed be desirable if legislatures more thoroughly and comprehensively addressed the question of the relevance of aggravated motives for crimes (Hessick 2006). On the other hand, the practical political constraints faced by those who would reform criminal legislation in a principled way are a serious impediment to systematic treatment of this sort. Legislators and other legal actors involved in criminal law reform have strong incentives to attend only to the issues that are most salient to voters. Thus, it is unrealistic to expect adoption of bias crime legislation to be accompanied by much broader consideration of the relevance of especially culpable motives throughout the criminal law. Under these circumstances, a conscientious legislator might defensibly focus on obtaining half a loaf or less, in the form of bias crimes legislation, rather than give up altogether on the effort to enhance punishment for aggravated motives.

The second concern is that we as agents lack sufficient control over our motives; thus, extra punishment for a bias motive is inconsistent with just deserts. The strongest rejoinder to this argument is that we have at least as much control of our motives as we do over our mens rea, yet it is widely accepted that differences in mens rea properly affect the level of punishment that we deserve. I might strike another in anger, with the purpose to harm him; or with knowledge that the object I throw in his direction will harm him; or with recklessness or negligence. In each case, it might be difficult to control my angry response. Yet I am responsible for purposely, knowingly, recklessly, or negligently harming him. Similarly, I can decide whether or not to act on a bias motive (or a motive of greed or sadism).[7]

Another version of the second concern is that bias "motives" often are not further purposes of the actor; rather, they are dispositions. Perhaps it is justifiable to impose extra punishment on a hired killer whose motive (in the sense of further purpose) is to obtain money for succeeding in murdering a victim. And perhaps it is justifiable to punish more severely the person who not only breaks into a building but also does so with the intent to steal or batter. But bias "motives" often are not higher-level purposes. When A punches B because of B's race or religion, it often is not the case that A had the purpose, not just to injure B, but to achieve some other goal, such as sending a message that B's group is less worthy of respect.[8]

I agree that bias motives often are not properly characterized as higher-level purposes. There often is no further end that the biased offender is trying to bring about; he acts because of bias, not necessarily "in order to" bring about a state of affairs in which members of the target group are denigrated or excluded.[9] Yet it does not follow that bias is therefore not sufficiently within the actor's control that the actor deserves punishment. Suppose B utters a slightly insulting remark to A and A responds with a punch, and suppose that if A had been of the same race or religion as B, A would not have become so insulted, angry, and violent. A nevertheless has sufficient control for moral and legal responsibility: absent extraordinary circumstances such as a brain tumor causing A's responses, A is responsible for his prejudiced attitude, and A is also responsible for permitting his prejudiced attitude to result in violence against B.[10]

A third concern is that enhanced punishment for a bias motive surreptitiously punishes for character, not for the defendant's actual acts. This concern is addressed below in the section "Do Bias Crime Laws Improperly Punish for Thoughts or Character?", in the discussion of the "improper punishment for thoughts" objection.

Expressive Wrong

Perhaps the strongest justification for bias crime laws is an expressive rationale: crimes motivated by bias express profound disrespect or disdain for the group of which the victim is a member, and the criminal law should counteract the offender's message by sending its own message expressing condemnation of such conduct.[11] Like other expressive accounts of legal rules, this rationale has intuitive power but also raises difficult questions.[12] Is the justification based on (a) what the actor expresses in committing the bias-motivated crime or (b) what the government expresses through heightened punishment? Or is it based on both (a) and (b)?

With respect to (a), is it necessary that the actor actually intended to express disrespect for the victim or the victim's group? Is it sufficient that the actor knew that others will so interpret his or her conduct? That the actor *should* have known this? On the other hand, perhaps such knowledge is not necessary. If that is so, if the actor's intention, knowledge, or other state of mind is not critical, then what facts are necessary or sufficient? Should we focus on the meaning that an average observer, or a reasonable observer, or many observers, would attribute to the conduct? Are the reactions of members of the target group significant or even decisive? In some cases, to be sure, these factors converge and there is no need to choose among them. If A paints a swastika on a synagogue or if B chains an African-American person to his truck and drags him through the streets of a city while screaming racist slurs, it is not difficult to conclude that A intends to communicate hatred of Jews and that B intends to communicate hatred of African-Americans; and almost all observers will perceive their conduct as so intended. But in many other cases, the precise criteria of "social meaning" will make a difference to how the facts are interpreted. (Note that even case A would raise interpretive difficulties if A had no idea what a swastika means but painted the symbol at the insistence of his friends.)

With respect to (b), expressive theories of punishment are controversial. A significant worry is the absence of a close fit between what punishment does to an offender and what punishment expresses by way of condemnation or denunciation. Does a 20-year term of imprisonment really express twice as much condemnation as a 10-year term? Twenty times as much as a one-year term? It seems that the more severe punishment in such examples is more persuasively justified by conventional purposes of punishment such as deterrence, incapacitation, and retribution, under which longer prison terms are justified by the greater suffering that they cause the offender or by the greater extent to which the offender is deprived of various liberties. This worry is especially significant in the context of bias crime laws, which often authorize enormous increases in punishment relative to the punishment for the parallel crime. If consequentialist or retributive principles do not otherwise justify this increase, the expressive value of punishment must be enormously weighty in order to warrant this degree of enhancement.[13]

In a recent essay, Duff and Marshall endorse a "communicative" version of the expressive rationale (Duff and Marshall 2018). In their view, the wrong addressed by hate crime prohibitions is "civic hatred," a radical denial of civic fellowship, a wrong against both the target group and the entire polity. One intriguing aspect of their analysis is the argument that punishment enhancements for bias crimes are justifiable, not because such crimes might cause especially serious harms, nor because the agents of such crimes are especially culpable, but because these crimes constitute distinct wrongs. Robbery, they plausibly argue, is not merely theft aggravated by the use or threat to use force; rather, robbery is "a distinctive kind of wrong—distinct both from ordinary theft and from ordinary assault" (ibid., p. 134).[14] Similarly, a bias crime is not just an aggravated version (either because of "greater harm" or because of "greater culpability") of the parallel crime. Rather, the civic character of the wrong makes bias crimes distinctive, for "they concern the offender's unwillingness to recognize their victim's standing as a citizen" (ibid., p. 134). The criminal law thus has a distinctive reason to mark such conduct as criminal.

Duff and Marshall's claim that a bias crime is a distinct type of wrong that is not necessarily "worse" or deserving of "greater" punishment than other types of wrong is provocative and plausible. But I wonder how far it takes us. In the abstract, it helps defuse the objection (discussed later) that bias crimes punish for thoughts or character alone. But concretely, it is not clear that the argument undermines the conclusion that a bias crime should ordinarily be punished more seriously than an otherwise identical parallel crime. On the other hand, the argument does suggest that it is justifiable for government officials to publicly condemn the offender's conduct or engage in other expressive acts that do not themselves constitute punishment. And perhaps the argument warrants a distinct *type* of punishment, different in kind from the punishments that the state otherwise authorizes. For example, it might support the imposition of a shaming punishment on the bias criminal. Still, even if such a sanction is otherwise an appropriate and proportional punishment, it does seem that the punishment for the parallel crime should be treated as a floor, and that the presence of bias necessarily enhances the otherwise permitted punishment.

Greater Vulnerability of Victims

Another justification for bias crime punishment enhancement sounds in distributive justice. According to Harel and Parchomovsky, the state has the duty to distribute fairly the good of protection from crime; thus, it must make special efforts to reduce crime against those who are especially vulnerable because of immutable personal characteristics such as race or ethnicity (Harel and Parchomovsky 1999). Greater enforcement of the criminal law is one way to discharge this duty, but another is harsher sanctions. And bias crime penalty enhancement, they argue, can be justified by this egalitarian duty.

This argument has some merit. The criminal law does occasionally enhance punishment based directly on a group's vulnerability to crime—for example, when the victim is elderly or a child.[15] Moreover, the authors are correct that their approach helps explain why some bias crime laws do not require animus or hostility but extend to actors who select victims on the basis of a prohibited group characteristic. When the basis of selection is opportunistic, in the special sense of preying on vulnerable victims, then their approach helps explains why the criminal law might wish to impose a higher sanction.

But the authors' approach also poses several problems (*see* Simons 2000; Woods 2008). First, it does not plausibly explain actual bias crime legislation. There exist many categories of highly vulnerable victims for which punishment enhancement is not routinely imposed—for example, crimes against persons with an intellectual disability or against prison inmates. Conversely, legislation imposing heightened punishment for bias crimes is not best explained by the extra vulnerability of the victims of such crimes. When an African-American is assaulted because of his race, a Catholic is targeted because of her religion, or a gay person is attacked because of his sexual orientation, voters and legislators believe that additional moral condemnation and punishment is warranted; but they do not believe that the quantum of additional condemnation or punishment that is deserved is a direct function of the protected group's unusual vulnerability to crime. Race, religion, and sexual orientation are personal traits with enormous social significance. Criminal actors who select victims on these bases do not act in a historical and social vacuum: the moral and social significance of their acts is reinforced by centuries of official and private acts of discrimination that have disadvantaged groups along these lines. When bias crimes occur, they reinforce the memories and effects of that discrimination and threaten social division. Heightened vulnerability to crime is only part of the story.

Second, when special vulnerability (e.g., of a child or elderly person) is indeed a legitimate consideration in the criminal law, the actor need not act out of a motive of animus toward the vulnerable, nor need he or she select the person because of their vulnerability. It is sufficient that the actor knowingly victimizes a child or an elderly person. Yet bias crime liability for a person who merely knows that the victim is of a different race or religion, but who neither is motivated by this status nor selects the victim because of this status, seems clearly unjustifiable. Why the difference? Because the justification for punishing crimes against the vulnerable is quite distinct from the justification for punishing bias crimes: in the latter case, only acts that are based on a bias motive or discriminatory selection are likely either to bring about the relevant harm (such as exacerbating racial division) or to express disrespect for the targeted group.

Do Bias Crime Laws Improperly Punish for Thoughts or Character?

One prominent objection to bias crime laws is that they impermissibly (and perhaps unconstitutionally) punish for thoughts or beliefs, contrary to liberal values including the right of free speech.[16] I only address this objection briefly, since it has been amply discussed in the literature. The most persuasive responses to the objection are as follows:

1. It is incorrect to characterize these laws as punishing for thoughts alone, since the laws always require conduct. Indeed, they invariably require that the defendant's chosen conduct, absent a bias motive or selection criterion, must itself constitute a crime (including the usual actus reus and mens rea requirements of that crime) (*see* section "Must a Parallel Crime Already Exist?" below).

2. Punishment enhancement does increase punishment based on a bias motive or discriminatory selection criterion, but it does not follow that the portion of punishment that is thereby enhanced is itself based on thoughts (or character) *alone*. Rather, the "thoughts" or "character flaw" must motivate or be expressed in the actor's conduct. If D steals from V while harboring negative feelings or antipathy toward the group of which the victim is a member, D is not necessarily eligible for an enhanced sentence. In doctrinal terms, D's attitude must at least satisfy criminal law's concurrence requirement. Consider a straightforward example that does not satisfy that requirement: D steals from V in the dark and has no idea of V's race, ethnicity, or religion. The next day, when D discovers that V was African-American or Catholic, D publicly boasts that he is delighted that he succeeded in victimizing a person from this racial or religious group.

   However, the concurrence requirement by itself is insufficient to ensure that bias crimes are consistent with principles of just deserts and of respect for mental autonomy.[17] That requirement would be satisfied, for example, if a white, heterosexual D knew, while committing a crime against V, that V is African-American or gay. Just as knowingly receiving stolen property or acquiring illegal drugs satisfies the concurrence requirement, so does assaulting a person when the actor knows that the person is within a category protected by bias crime laws. But such knowledge (as opposed to motive or discriminatory selection) is properly considered insufficient for bias crime enhancement. Contrast crimes that punish actors who prey upon specified categories of especially vulnerable victims, such as children or the elderly. For these crimes, knowledge that the victim is in the relevant class suffices to satisfy criminal law principles; the actor need not act with the *motive* of taking advantage of a child or elderly person.

3. A related objection emphasizes the supposed selectivity or lack of neutrality of bias crime laws in picking out as objects of enhanced punishment only certain heinous or hateful motives—viz. those based on an ideology that the government classifies as offensive. Assaulting or injuring someone in order to send a message of disapproval of the victim's race or sexual orientation is punished more, but engaging in the same act from a motive of sadism or greed is not.[18] As a criticism of criminal law's ad hoc consideration of culpable motives that aggravate punishment, this objection has merit, for reasons discussed earlier. But insofar as the argument purports to demonstrate that bias crime laws are problematic because of improper *ideological* selectivity, the argument is not fully convincing. The claim that the criminal law should (or even can) be ideologically "neutral" is implausible, for the familiar reason that any justification of criminal law rules must rely on underlying consequentialist or nonconsequentialist rationales that will inevitably be controversial.

Scope Problems

A number of difficult questions of scope arise if a jurisdiction decides to enhance punishment for hate or bias crimes. The answers to these questions clearly depend on which justifications for bias crime laws one finds most compelling.

Bias Against Which Groups?

Bias crime laws today typically apply to bias or animus on the basis of race, ethnicity, religion, disability, gender, or sexual orientation.[19] Some laws also extend to the group characteristics of gender identity or age. Only a small number of jurisdictions extend protection to groups defined by other categories such as homelessness, personal appearance, or political beliefs.

This variation in coverage is justifiable insofar as it reflects the contemporary reality that different groups are targeted by bias in different communities. And as a matter of principle, in determining which groups to protect, it is highly relevant whether some groups have suffered especially serious disadvantage over time, including government-imposed disadvantage. However, the actual variation between jurisdictions that we see in current bias crime laws is undoubtedly also due to jurisdictional differences in values held by legislators and voters (such as different views among constituents about the expressive value of denouncing homophobic crime) and in the political influence exercised by different religious and civil rights interest groups (Jenness and Grattet 2001).

Two additional questions are important here. First, should protection extend not only to disadvantaged minority groups but also to majority groups? Legislation invariably prohibits bias or selection according to group status (such as race or religion), not according to *minority* group status. In *Wisconsin v. Mitchell,* for example, defendant was an African-American youth who specifically encouraged others to beat up a white victim, which they did. Defendant was convicted not only of aggravated battery but also of intentionally selecting the victim because of the victim's race, resulting in a substantial sentencing enhancement. The Supreme Court upheld the conviction even though the victim was white. In principle, the argument for heightened punishment in this type of case seems weaker, if the most persuasive justifications of bias crime laws are that they cause a greater harm or constitute an expressive wrong and if the most defensible characterization of such a harm or wrong is the causation or existence of social division *because the group has suffered social disadvantage.*[20] On the other hand, egalitarian principles, and perhaps expressive wrong principles, might justify ignoring whether a group is relatively disadvantaged. Perhaps it is important that legislative rules not send the message that blacks should receive greater "protection" from such rules than whites, or that Muslims, Jews, or Catholics should receive greater protection than Protestants.

The second question is whether *intragroup* bias should be the basis of punishment enhancement. In a recent case, members of an Amish sect were prosecuted under the federal hate crime law for violently attacking members of another sect, including shearing their hair and cutting off their beards. The court concluded that intragroup bias is indeed covered by the law.[21] Once again, this broad extension of scope seems much less justifiable than the paradigm case in which a dominant religious group preys upon a widely despised, smaller religious group. On this broader view, for example, the internecine strife between factions of the Nation of Islam that led to the murder of Malcolm X would render that murder a bias crime. Struggles within religious groups over power and disagreements within such groups about dogma seem rather remote from the central concerns of bias crime laws.

Animus or Discriminatory Selection?

Bias crime statutes are often ambiguous about whether animus is required or whether selection on the basis of a group status is sufficient. The statutes often simply state that the actor must have committed a specified crime "because of" race, religion, or another listed group characteristic. But it remains useful to discuss these two distinct models as ideal types and to consider which model is more justifiable.[22]

The animus model insists on proof that the actor was motivated by hatred of members of the victim's group or by a similar disrespectful attitude toward the group. The discriminatory selection model requires only that the victim was selected because of membership in the relevant group.

The discriminatory selection model is normally significantly broader in scope.[23] Accordingly, that model prompts significant concerns about proportionality and fair notice. For example, this model would seem to justify punishment for *opportunistic* bias, a kind of bias that is arguably less culpable than paradigm instances of animus-motivated crime.[24] If an offender deliberately selects transgender or Muslim victims to attack, not because of animus, but because the offender believes that such victims are less likely to report the crime, perhaps his conduct does not express fundamental disrespect in the way that paradigm animus-motivated crimes do. Similarly, if an offender preys upon the elderly or the disabled only because she believes that they are less likely to resist the attack successfully, the conduct again seems less culpable or wrongful. On the other hand, if the group that is opportunistically selected is a group that is quite frequently the subject of animus-motivated attacks, such as transgender or Muslim victims, the fact that a particular offender merely had an opportunistic motive might not be a decisive argument against enhanced punishment.[25]

Even under the narrower animus model, significant questions of scope can arise. Must the actor be *personally* motivated by bias, or is it sufficient that her motivation is to curry favor with a gang or other group that she knows is motivated by bias? The latter seems sufficient: the harm or wrong caused or expressed when *reflected* prejudice or bias motivates a crime is not appreciably less than in a paradigm bias crime.

Should animus be understood to include culpable indifference—a disposition to care less when one's conduct will harm a member of a protected group? If culpable indifference is interpreted broadly, then such an extension would be very problematic. Compare animus in the sense of hatred or antipathy: in such cases, there will often be supporting evidence that an offender uttered racial epithets just before, during, or immediately after the crime, or that the offender planned to target a member of the protected group. But in the case of culpable indifference, supporting evidence will be much more difficult to gather. Only in the rarest case will the offender admit that he victimized X because he simply didn't care whether X suffered harm or because he cared less than if X were a member of the offender's racial or religious group. Moreover, the concurrence requirement properly insists that it is not sufficient that an actor merely possessed an indifferent attitude or disposition while engaging in the relevant conduct. To be sure, it is also true that merely possessing a standing attitude of dislike or hostility toward another group— that is, animus in the narrow sense—is also not sufficient for enhanced punishment if that attitude merely accompanies criminal conduct and does not motivate it. But it is even more difficult in the case of culpable indifference to define and prove the requisite connection between the agent's attitude and his resulting conduct (Simons 2002).

For similar reasons, it would not be defensible to include, within the definition of animus, cases in which the agent's animus or hostility was *unconscious*. Here, the concern about criminal punishment turning on factors that are not sufficiently within the actor's control is indeed powerful and should be decisive against enhanced punishment.

Bias Must Be a Cause, but What Kind of Cause?

Even if bias motive (or targeting a victim because she is a member of a protected group) can be a proper basis for punishment enhancement, the question remains: what causal connection is required between the bias motive or selection criterion and the defendant's action? The most difficult question here is how to resolve mixed motive cases (Verstein 2018). Consider the following perspectives and possible approaches.

1. *Bias as sole or primary motive.* Suppose A has no plan to commit a crime, but happens upon V1, and because of animosity toward V1's group, A assaults V1. Here, we might conclude that bias is the sole or primary motive for the crime. Bias would be a primary motive but not the sole motive if A had another, less compelling reason for engaging in the assault—for example, to prove to himself that he could successfully assault someone without suffering injury himself.

2. *Distinguishing motive for crime from motive for selection.* Suppose B plans to steal a wallet from someone. After patrolling the neighborhood for a few minutes, he decides to victimize V2, in part because V2 is Muslim, and B hates Muslims. B could just as easily have victimized many others. Here, we might conclude that bias is the but for cause of B committing the crime of stealing from V2. But it would not be correct to characterize bias as the sole motive: obtaining financial profit from the crime was plainly another potent motive. Indeed, that was B's initial reason for committing a theft. Perhaps we should say that B's sole motive for committing a theft was financial profit, while B's sole or primary motive for selecting V2 as the victim of the contemplated theft was V2's religion. These characterizations seem more precise and helpful than trying to answer the undifferentiated question, "What reasons motivated B to commit the crime that he committed?" And for similar reasons, it is unhelpful to frame the question as whether it is true that "B intentionally stole from a Muslim."[26]

   Conversely, suppose C decides to victimize V3 because V3 is Muslim, but C initially gives no thought to what crime to commit against V3. When C is in V3's presence, C decides to steal V3's bicycle because he would benefit from owning it. Here, too, it seems most precise to differentiate two questions: What reason did C have to target V3? And what reason did C have to commit the crime of theft?

   Another variation is this: C2 settles upon the crime of stealing V3's bicycle because he knows how much V3 relies upon the bicycle and how difficult it will be for V3 to replace it, and C2 wishes thereby to make life more difficult for V3 as a Muslim. In this variation, unlike the previous two examples, C2 acts out of animus both in selecting a person as a victim and in deciding what crime to commit against the person. This appears to be the somewhat rare case in which an actor's sole motive or reason, along both dimensions, is animus against members of a protected group. (Defacing the home of a member of a group out of animus toward the group is another such case.[27])

3. *Bias as a necessary or but for cause.* Many courts adopt the necessary or "but for" cause (or "straw that breaks the camel's back") approach to mixed motives in bias crime cases.[28] This approach has the advantages of simplicity and also of realism: it is exceedingly rare that an offender engages in a particular form of criminal conduct, victimizing V for the *sole* reason that V is a member of a protected group.[29] However, the approach is highly problematic in overdetermination cases, that is, cases in which the actor has another sufficient motive for the conduct, as in the example in the next paragraph.

4. *Bias as a sufficient but not necessary reason or cause.* Suppose D, who is white, is angry with V4 because D's girlfriend just broke up with him in order to be with V4. And suppose D also dislikes V4 because V4 is African-American, a group toward which D has general antipathy. The next time D sees V4, D gives V4 a shove while uttering a racial slur. Here, the fact finder might conclude that bias was a sufficient but not a necessary (or but for) reason for D's committing the crime of assaulting V4 and might draw the same conclusion about jealousy. If bias and jealousy are each independently sufficient causes of D's conduct, a bias crime enhancement might be warranted. Why should D be treated more favorably by the criminal law just because he happens to be moved both by jealousy (which does not trigger greater punishment) and by bias (which does)?

   Notice, too, that a strict "necessary cause" requirement would have the absurd result of precluding a sentence enhancement if the actor is motivated by two sufficient (but not necessary) reasons, *each* of which is an impermissible bias motivation. Suppose E, who is white and able-bodied, attacks V5 both because V5 is African-American and because V5 is disabled, and suppose that race and disability are each a sufficient reason for E's crime. It would surely be unacceptable to strictly apply a necessary cause test here: because neither reason taken alone was a necessary cause, the result would be no penalty enhancement. (However, a supporter of a necessary cause requirement might respond that the requirement should apply in all cases except for this specific subcategory of overdetermination cases in which two different prohibited reasons are each sufficient but not necessary.)

5. *Bias as a "substantial" or "significant" motivating factor.* Some jurisdictions employ this test.[30] Unfortunately, it borders on incoherence.[31] How much motivating weight is necessary or sufficient under the test? Employing this test amounts to an admission that justifiable causal criteria cannot be identified in advance and that the fact finder should simply

muddle through. Moreover, if the threshold of substantiality or significance is too low, this approach creates problems of proportionality and, perhaps, of punishment for mere thought or bad character.[32] This would be the case, for example, if a reason were considered "significant" simply because it was a reason that the actor consciously considered before acting, even if it played absolutely no role in his decision—that is, even if it did not increase by one iota the probability that the actor would victimize a member of a protected group.

6. *Bias as a primary motive.* If we were to require that bias was the "primary" or "predominant" motive of the actor's conduct, what would this mean? On Andrew Verstein's recent illuminating account,[33] it would mean that bias was a stronger reason for the conduct than any other reason motivating the actor. A primary motive requirement is distinct from either a but for or sufficient cause requirement: The primary motive might have greater motivational force than the secondary motive even if both motives are but for causes and even if each motive is independently sufficient to bring about the actor's conduct.

7. *Characterizing the object of the actor's motive or reason.* Another complication in analyzing mixed motive cases is how to characterize the object of the motive. In an earlier example, I supposed that D would have shoved V4 (a) even if V4 had not been black but also (b) even if D's girlfriend had not left D for V4. In that sense, each motive is a sufficient cause, and neither is a necessary cause. But suppose that D inflicted a *harder* shove on V4 because of the combination of motives than D would have inflicted if only one of these motives had been operative. Should we still say that "the shove" or "the crime of assault" was overdetermined? It seems more precise to say that each motive is a necessary cause of *the extra force of the shove.* In many cases, this extra precision will not make a legal difference. But in other cases, it will. Suppose that the extra force caused V4 to die, while the force that V4 would have used if only one motive had been operative would have caused V4 to suffer injury but not death. On this supposition, both motives are but for causes of the more serious crime of homicide (rather than assault), a fact that might well make a difference to whether we conclude that a bias motive caused that crime.

8. *Bias as a cause but not a motive.* Finally, bias could have a causal effect on the actor's conduct without being a reason or motive for that conduct at all. Suppose a racist individual F, arguing with V5 of a different race, impulsively strikes V5; and suppose it is clear that F would not have struck V5 if V5 had been of the same race as F. So long as it is still within the control of such an actor not to act in response to such a cause, criminal responsibility is at least an open question. Perhaps F harbors unconscious bias toward V5's race. Or perhaps F is simply indifferent to whether members of V5's race suffer harm.

However, authorizing a greater penalty in this category of cases is extremely problematic. I am doubtful that it is feasible for the criminal law to clearly define and consistently apply this criterion. Also, it will often be the case that the practical capacity of an agent to avoid acting out of unconscious bias or indifference is highly diminished, at least as compared to his or her capacity to avoid acting because of a bias motive or reason. These concerns militate strongly against enhanced punishment in this category of cases.

9. *Suggested resolution.* The most defensible causal approach, I believe, is the primary motive test because it is a practical test widely employed in the law and because the strongest justifications for bias crime laws (that bias crimes cause group-specific harm and are expressive wrongs) provide greater support to this test than to the alternatives. If, for example, bias has much greater motivational force than jealousy in inducing an offender to commit a crime, these justifications plausibly support punishment enhancement. And framing the question in terms of "greater or lesser" motivational power is, although somewhat arbitrary, a familiar and accepted doctrinal technique. At the same time, the necessary cause test (if accompanied by an exception for certain overdetermination cases) is also a workable and defensible test. And insofar as the latter test makes conviction more difficult than the primary motive test, it should be appealing to those who are apprehensive about the potential breadth and harshness of bias crime laws.[34]

Must a Parallel Crime Already Exist?

It is widely assumed that bias crimes should merely enhance punishment for conduct that is already criminalized. But is this assumption justifiable? Why, exactly, must a parallel crime already exist?[35] In principle, shouldn't the state be permitted to criminalize conduct that is otherwise not quite serious enough to deserve criminalization, if the conduct is accompanied by a bias motive? In other contexts, the criminal law sometimes recognizes that inculpatory motives may convert noncriminal into criminal conduct. For example, simple possession of burglary tools might not be a crime, but if the actor possesses these items with the intention to break into a dwelling or vehicle, the conduct might become a crime (*see* Hessick 2006, p. 96). Moreover, given the realities of criminal law enforcement, police and prosecutors might not find it worthwhile to fully investigate or pursue a parallel crime (especially if it is a minor crime such as a misdemeanor), yet they would pursue the crime if it was accompanied by a bias motive that could result in a more significant punishment.

In practice, to be sure, there are reasons to require the existence of a parallel crime. It is much simpler, in revising criminal codes, to add a sentencing or crime-level enhancement than to create an entirely new crime. Moreover, punishing for bias-motivated conduct that is not otherwise criminal fosters the appearance that the state is punishing only for bad character or biased thoughts.

Yet the question remains: is this merely appearance? After all, eliminating a parallel crime requirement is entirely consistent with retaining the requirement that the actor's bias motive must bear an appropriate causal connection to the actor's conduct. Suppose, for example, that defacement of the personal property of another is considered too trivial an interference with the person's proprietary and dignitary interests to warrant criminalization. Writing "you suck" in magic marker on a classmate's backpack is annoying behavior but arguably insufficient to justify a criminal record. But now suppose that the defendant writes a racial or religious slur on the backpack, for the purpose of upsetting the backpack's owner and insulting the group to which the owner belongs. I see no principled reason not to permit criminalization of this conduct. At the same time, a bias motive should not permit criminalization unless the underlying conduct was otherwise *eligible* for criminalization—for example, because that conduct could legitimately be criminalized absent countervailing values or pragmatic concerns, or because the conduct does not quite satisfy justifiable principles of criminalization but comes very close to doing so.

Proportionality Problems

Bias crime laws often permit a dramatic increase in punishment relative to the punishment for the parallel crime. Thus, it is common to elevate a misdemeanor to a felony (resulting not only in a lengthier term of incarceration but also in the lifelong collateral consequences of a felony conviction) or to increase the authorized sentence for a parallel felony quite substantially. For example, the Wisconsin hate crime statute upheld in Wisconsin v. Mitchell increased the maximum punishment for aggravated battery from two years to seven years.[36]

Even if some enhancement in punishment for a bias motivation is justifiable, the question remains whether current statutory schemes are too harsh and violate principles of proportionality. Unfortunately, there is nothing close to a scholarly or judicial consensus about what those principles require, on either a consequentialist or retributivist account of the justifications for punishment. Consider, for example, that in some criminal law areas such as theft and sexual assault, the differentiation and grading of different subcategories is largely accomplished by variations in actus reus, whereas in other areas, most notably homicide, variations in mens rea make all or almost all of the difference. No obvious explanation exists for why mens rea has greater significance for some crimes than for others. It is similarly difficult to explain why motive is irrelevant to punishment for some crimes, modestly relevant for others, and highly relevant for yet others. Absent such explanations, the task of developing defensible proportionality rules for aggravating motives is extremely difficult.

One suggestion, offered by Al-Hakim and Dimock, is that proportionality principles permit no more than a doubling of the penalty when group hatred is an aggravating factor. Their rationale is as follows:

> The primary target of our penalty must be the underlying crime, which must be a public wrong worthy of criminal condemnation independently of the motivation(s) that might lead to its commission. That is permissible on liberal grounds. But if we enhance the punishment that the underlying crime deserves by more than 100 percent, ... the primary target of our condemnation is the hatred, rather than the public wrong. (Al-Hakim and Dimock 2012, p. 610)

Such an enhancement, they conclude, would be illiberal and unjustifiable.

This proposal and rationale will not satisfy skeptics who believe that any substantial enhancement, or indeed any enhancement, of punishment because of bias or hatred is inconsistent with liberal principles. Nor will the rationale satisfy others who worry that the offender's actus reus and mens rea should matter much more than his motive. If a violent attack on a stranger deserves 10 years in prison, or arson of a large building deserves 20 years, does an additional bias motivation really warrant a punishment that is almost double that amount (almost 20 years for the attack, almost 40 years for the arson)?

One obvious general approach to proportionality is as follows: calibrate the severity of punishment to the principles that justify the punishment in question. Thus, suppose that, as a matter of just deserts, an actor who purposely harms a victim is much more culpable, or characteristically causes additional harm, or commits a graver intrinsic wrong, relative to an actor who harms a victim knowingly or recklessly. Then those mens rea distinctions should result in proportional differences in punishment severity. Alas, this approach only identifies the requisite ordinal differences; it does not take us very far toward identifying the permissible or required cardinal differences.[37]

Another possible response to the proportionality objection is the "distinctive wrong" argument noted earlier: the wrong that bias crimes target is incommensurate with other criminal wrongs. Just as it might be incorrect or misleading to characterize a minor sexual assault as either more or less grave than a nonsexual physical assault threatening bodily harm, it might be incorrect to characterize the bias "portion" of a bias-motivated crime as more or less grave than the parallel crime. In principle, we might punish the parallel crime (such as the theft or assault) with one type of punishment (such as incarceration for a specified term) but punish the additional bias "portion" of the crime with a different type (such as temporary loss of specified voting or other civil rights). A distinctive wrong arguably deserves a distinctive form of punishment. Whether such a solution is practically realizable in our current criminal justice system is an open question, however.

My own tentative views about proportionality in the present context are as follows. Punishment for the most serious crimes—such as murder or rape—should only be enhanced modestly, perhaps 10%, if motivated by bias against a historically disfavored group. Greater enhancement would implicitly express the false message that bias matters almost as much to the actor's just deserts as the highly condemnable serious crime itself. But at the lowest end, punishment may appropriately be enhanced significantly and in some cases more than 100%—for example, for defacing a building. Nevertheless, in the absence of a comprehensive approach to aggravated motives, I would err on the side of parsimony. Perhaps the existence of a terroristic motive or purpose warrants a large enhancement in the punishment for any crime, while a bias motivation should be treated more like a motive of pecuniary gain, only modestly enhancing punishment, especially for parallel crimes that are already punished severely.

CONCLUSION

This chapter has tried to identify the strongest justifications for bias crime laws and the most potent and troubling challenges. However, such laws are by no means the only or best solution to the serious social problem of bias-motivated violence. Nationalist leaders throughout the world increasingly inflame passions against immigrants, refugees, and racial and ethnic minorities. There is also evidence that the incidence of bias crimes in the United States has increased significantly in recent years.[38]

Bias crime laws may or may not be an effective means of reducing the incidence of bias crimes. They may or may not diminish racial, ethnic, religious, and other social divisions. They may or may not express appropriate condemnation of bias and prejudice. They may or may not impose the punishment that offenders justly deserve. But at the very least, they target a genuine problem, a problem that demands serious attention. I hope we can agree that the principles of equality, tolerance, and mutual understanding that these laws aim to further and uphold are fundamental values, values that demand a fervent defense.[39]

NOTES

1. To be sure, a small number of mitigated murders also do qualify as "hate crimes" in the sense of crimes motivated by bias. See State v. Castagna.
2. See Murphy (1988) (discussing "retributive hatred"); Hampton (1988) (discussing "moral hatred"); and further discussion in Moore (2010).
3. A similar range of examples can be found in Tribe (1993).
4. A similar notion of selective sympathy or indifference has been endorsed as justifying strict scrutiny for equal protection purposes (Brest 1976, pp. 7–8). But compare Baron (2016, p. 506) (concluding that it would not be a hate crime for a thief to intentionally choose Jews as victims of burglaries, not because he hates Jews, but because he likes them less than the others whom he could victimize).
5. At the same time, many racists and homophobes might sincerely claim to "care" a great deal about African-Americans and gays, based on outrageous stereotypes

that assume the intellectual incompetence or moral failings of these groups. Some supporters of slavery asserted benevolent motivations for the practice. To be sure, the credibility of such a claim is dubious if the actor has engaged in an act of violence against a member of the group. How does punching someone in the face demonstrate genuine concern for his welfare? But suppose the actor engaged in a different type of criminal wrong, such as locking the victim in a workplace until the end of the workday out of a misguided, paternalistic belief that the victim is a member of a group that cannot be trusted to return to work after a lunch break. In such a case, the actor's claim that he acted out of a paternalistic and benevolent motive might occasionally be credible. Needless to say, the sincerity of such a motive or belief does not make it justifiable.

6. To be sure, victim impact statements about the effect of a bias crime on the victim's group are one way to provide more individualized case-specific evidence (cf. Hurd and Moore 2004, p. 1091). But such statements create serious problems of their own, such as inconsistency, undue weight accorded to especially articulate victims, and undue favoritism toward more wealthy defendants. These problems are less likely to plague group-based criteria for sentencing enhancement.

7. See Brax (2016, p. 240): "We can choose whether or not to treat a reason *as a reason.*"

    The lack of control argument might, however, provide some support for the argument that bias "motive" should be required and that culpable indifference should be insufficient. See discussion infra. The argument also might be relevant to which causal test of motive should be adopted.

8. See Hurd and Moore (2004, pp. 1122–1123), arguing that hatred "motivates" action only in the limited sense that the action is a product of that emotion, and bias "motivates" action only in the limited sense that bias is a standing disposition to draw false beliefs about members of a group.

9. Similarly, most of those who act out of anger do not act for the purpose of expressing their anger. Contrast the (unusual!) actor who makes a deliberate decision to react in anger, heeding his therapist's advice that expressing anger will benefit his mental health (*see* Simons 2002, pp. 244–245).

    An analogous issue arises with mitigating motives. As a doctrinal matter, self-defense requires that the actor's forcible response to a threat was (at least partially) for the purpose of defending herself. But in many self-defense cases that should result in acquittal, such a purpose is lacking. If D lashes out in fear in response to an unjustified attack, but not with a conscious purpose to prevent further harm to herself, and if D's conduct satisfies the objective necessity and proportionality requirements of self-defense, the absence of a defensive purpose should not be, and probably is not, fatal to her self-defense claim (*see* Simons 2008).

10. But see Garvey (2008), Hurd and Moore (2004).

11. See Kahan (1996), Lawrence (1999), Duff and Marshall (2018) (endorsing a "communicative" rationale). For a general account of expressive theories of law, see Anderson and Pildes 2000. Expressive theories of punishment are discussed in Duff and Hoskins (2017).

12. For a general critique of expressive theories of law (including punishment), see Adler (2000). For a critique of expressive theories as justifications for hate crime laws, see Hurd and Moore (2004).

13. See Hurd and Moore (2004, pp. 1114–1115), arguing that the mere enactment of bias crime laws may send a strong message, while the imposition of actual punishment on actors who do not get the message "is rank injustice" if the punishment exceeds their just deserts.

14. For a similar analysis of felony murder, see Simons (2012).

15. See U.S. Sentencing Guidelines Manual § 3A1.1 (b)(1) & cmt. n. 2 (2016) (authorizing increased punishment by two levels if defendant knew or should have known that a victim of the offense was a vulnerable victim, defined as "a person ... who is unusually vulnerable due to age, physical or mental condition, or who is otherwise particularly susceptible to the criminal conduct").

16. Addressing the constitutional question, the U.S. Supreme Court invalidated a cross-burning statute in *R.A.V. v. City of St. Paul* as a violation of the First Amendment because the law selectively silenced speech based on its content, but in *Wisconsin v. Mitchell*, the Court upheld a very broad bias crime statute that enhanced defendant's punishment based on his discriminatory selection of a victim on the basis of race. In *Virginia v. Black*, the Court upheld a cross-burning statute that, unlike the law in *R.A.V.*, applied to all cross burnings that are intended to intimidate, without regard to the race or ethnicity of the victim.

17. Gabriel Mendlow identifies an additional, implicit criminal law requirement, beyond concurrence of actus reus and mens rea, that he believes bias crime laws might not satisfy—the requirement that the state may not treat a person's thoughts as objects of punishment, even if those thoughts are realized in his conduct (*see* Mendlow 2019).

18. More precisely, bias crime laws permit enhancement of punishment by a specified amount, while factors such as sadism or greed are more likely to be discretionary, aggravating factors that a judge may or may not consider when sentencing the defendant within the range otherwise specified for the crime.

19. These are the most common "protected" categories that trigger potential punishment for a hate crime. See https://www.adl.org/adl-hate-crime-map. The District of Columbia includes a broad list of categories: "race, color, religion, national origin, sex, age, marital status, personal appearance, sexual orientation, gender identity or expression, family responsibility, homelessness, physical disability, matriculation, or political affiliation." D.C. Code § 22-3701(1) (2018). Belgium's list of protected categories is also extensive:

> race, color of skin, descent, national or ethnic origin, nationality, sex, sexual orientation, marital status, birth, age, wealth, belief or philosophy of life, current and future state of health, disability, language, political conviction, or physical or genetic characteristic or social origin.

> (Articles 33–42 of Belgium's Law of 10 May 2007, from OSCE Report, p. 35)

20. See Baron (2016, p. 521), expressing concern about extending bias crime laws to groups that are not especially vulnerable to oppression.

21. *U.S. v. Miller, U.S. v. Mullet.* An analogous issue arises when one Latino prison gang targets a different Latino gang.

22. See Lawrence (1994, 1999); Grattet and Jenness (2001) (describing different phraseology in hate crime laws, including (a) requirement of animus or hatred; (b) requirement that actor had intent to harass and intimidate victim on the

basis of a specified group status; and (c) requirement merely that actor committed offense because of a specified group status).

23. "Normally," but perhaps not always, depending on what other criteria are part of each model. Suppose the discriminatory selection model requires that the selection criterion was a necessary cause of the actor's criminal conduct, while the animus model only requires that animus was a sufficient cause. Then it would sometimes be easier to establish animus than to establish discriminatory selection.

24. See Ginsberg (2011), Lawrence (1999). For arguments in favor of enhancement for opportunistic bias, see Wang (2000), Woods (2008).

25. For a similar view, see Duff and Marshall (2018, p. 145), arguing that the key question is not whether the offender was motivated by bias, but whether the perpetrator demonstrated and "enacted" group hatred "in the very commission of the offense." In their view:

> I can enact hatred of another group in an attack on one of its members, even if what motivates me is just a desire to earn the money I have been promised, or to curry favor with a group to which I want to belong, and I feel uncomfortable about what I "have to" do. To criminalize enactments of hatred is to criminalize actions that carry a certain meaning, not to criminalize thoughts, feelings, or motives that lie behind the action. (Duff and Marshall 2018, p. 139)

26. On one (referentially *transparent*) description, the quoted proposition is true even if B did not know that the victim was Muslim, so long as he intended to steal from a person he identified on some other basis and it turns out that the person was a Muslim. On another (referentially *opaque*) description, the proposition is true only if V2's status as a Muslim was part of the reason that B victimized him. See Schwitzgebel 2015); Ferzan (2008) (rejecting the view that the characterization of an intention is just a matter of what is motivationally significant to the actor).

27. Defacing a house of worship is a similar case except that the persons harmed are not individualized.

28. See *U.S. v. Miller* (concluding that a faith-inspired manner of assault does not necessarily prove a faith-inspired motive for assault). One of the court's examples is highly instructive:

> [I]magine that a child tells his parents he is gay. As a result of their faith, the parents ask the child to undergo reparative therapy. The child resists, the parents dig in, all three fight verbally about everything from faith to family obligations. At some point, the child snaps. He assaults the parents and does so in a faith-offensive way—by physically forcing them to eat non-kosher food, by tattooing 666 on their arms or by taking some other action that deeply offends their faith. No doubt faith entered the mix from both sides of the assault, but there *is* doubt about whether the parents' faith broke the camel's back in terms of why the child committed the assault. That the means of assault involved religious symbolism confirms only that he knew how best to hurt his parents. It does not seal the deal that his parents' faith, as opposed to their lack of support for him, was a but-for motive of the assault. (ibid., p. 596)

29. See *State v. Hennings* (upholding bias crime charge against a defendant whose motive for running over an African-American boy with his truck might have included not only the victim's race but also anger that the victim was standing in the road rather than on the sidewalk).

30. Some state statutes require only that the victim be chosen "in whole or in substantial part" because of the group characteristic. See N.Y. Penal L. § 485.05(1) (a), (b) (2016).

31. The analogous "substantial factor" test in tort law employed by many courts was firmly rejected in the Restatement of Torts, Third. See Restatement Third of Torts: Liability for Physical and Emotional Harm § 26, comment j (2010). Interestingly enough, a recent empirical survey found that the "substantial factor" test did a better job than the "but for" test and other legal tests in capturing survey participants' views about the meaning of legal causation (especially in overdetermination cases involving independent sufficient causes) (*see* Macleod 2019). However, the survey did not examine whether a test that explicitly imposed liability on sufficient but not necessary causes would perform even better.

32. See *U.S. v. Miller* (p. 592).

33. See Kaiserman (2018), Verstein (2018, pp. 1134–1136) (pointing out that a primary motive requirement is employed in a wide range of legal contexts).

34. One recent article explores ordinary understandings of legal causation standards (including causation in the context of bias crimes). The author's conclusions are broadly consistent with my suggested resolution:

    > [T]he "substantial factor" standard for causation comes much closer to tracking common sense and statutory causality attribution than does the "but-for" test, the "contributing factor" test, or the "sole factor" test, and the *sufficiency* of the relevant "cause" is far more predictive of causality attribution (and blameworthiness assessments) than the Court's "but-for" standard. (Macleod 2019, p. 962)

35. Federal hate crime laws do create federal crimes out of conduct that would not be a federal crime but for a prohibited bias motive (*see* https://www.justice.gov/crt/hate-crime-laws).

36. For other examples of the degree of punishment enhancement that bias crime laws permit or require, see Simons (2000, p. 266 n. 67). For example, Alabama increases the punishment for a Class B felony from a minimum of two years to a minimum of ten years if the crime is motivated by bias. AL Code § 13A-5-6, § 13A-5-13 (c)(1)(b) (2016).

37. See Walen (2016, § 4.4) (discussing ordinal and cardinal proportionality).

38. The Federal Bureau of Investigation announced a 17% increase in reported hate crimes in 2017 as compared to 2016 (Hohmann 2018). Moreover, "[a]ccording to the Center for the Study of Hate and Extremism, there were a total of 1,038 hate crimes recorded in the 10 largest American cities last year, an increase of 12 percent from 2016 and the highest figure in more than a decade" (Fausset 2018).

39. I thank Kim Ferzan, Jeff Helmreich, Val Jenness, Jamie Macleod, Gabe Mendlow, and participants in the Law, Reason, and Value Colloquium of the Center for Legal Philosophy, UC Irvine, for helpful comments.

References

AL Code § 13A-5-6, § 13A-5-13 (c)(1)(b) (2016).

Articles 33–42 of Belgium's Law of 10 May 2007, cited in Organization for Security and Co-operation in Europe. 2009. *OSCE report, hate crimes laws: A practical guide*, 35. Vienna: Organization for Security and Co-operation in Europe.

D.C. Code § 22-3701(1) (2018).

N.Y. Penal L. § 485.05(1)(a), (b) (2016).

U.S. Sentencing Guidelines Manual § 3A1.1 (b)(1) & cmt. n. 2 (2016).

Virginia v. Black, 538 U.S. 343 (2003).

State v. Castagna, 870 A.2d 653 (Super. Ct. NJ 2005).

State v. Hennings, 791 N.W.2d 828 (Iowa 2010).

U.S. v. Miller, 767 F.3d 585 (6th Cir. 2014).

Wisconsin v. Mitchell, 508 U.S. 476 (1993).

U.S. v. Mullet, 868 F. Supp. 2d 618 (N.D. Ohio 2012).

R.A.V. v. City of St. Paul, 505 U.S. 377 (1992).

Adler, Matthew. 2000. Expressive theories of law: A skeptical overview. *University of Pennsylvania Law Review* 148: 1363–1502.

Al-Hakim, Mohamad, and Susan Dimock. 2012. Hate as an aggravating factor in sentencing. *New Criminal Law Review* 15: 572–611.

Anderson, Elizabeth, and Richard Pildes. 2000. Expressive theories of law. *University of Pennsylvania Law Review* 148: 1503–1576.

Baron, Marcia. 2016. Hate crime legislation reconsidered. *Metaphilosophy* 47: 505–523.

Brax, David. 2016. Motives, reasons, and responsibility in hate/bias crime legislation. *Criminal Justice Ethics* 35: 230–248.

Brest, Paul. 1976. The Supreme Court, 1975 term—Foreword: In defense of the anti-discrimination principle. *Harvard Law Review* 90: 1–54.

Brudholm, Thomas. 2018. Hatred beyond bigotry. In *Hate, politics, law: Critical perspectives on combating hate*, ed. Thomas Brudholm and Birgitte Johansen. Oxford: Oxford University Press.

Dillof, Anthony. 1997. Punishing bias: An examination of the theoretical foundations of bias crime statutes. *Northwestern University Law Review* 91: 1015–1081.

Duff, Antony, and Zachary Hoskins. 2017. Legal punishment. The Stanford encyclopedia of philosophy, https://plato.stanford.edu/archives/fall2018/entries/legal-punishment/. Accessed 23 Feb 2019.

Duff, R.A., and S.E. Marshall. 2018. Criminalizing hate? In *Hate, politics, law: Critical perspectives on combating hate*, ed. Thomas Brudholm and Birgitte Johansen. Oxford: Oxford University Press.

Fausset, Richard. 2018. Rally by white nationalists was over almost before it began. *New York Times*, August 12.

Ferzan, Kimberly Kessler. 2008. Beyond intention. *Cardozo Law Review* 29: 1147–1192.

Garvey, Stephen P. 2008. Self-defense and the mistaken racist. *New Criminal Law Review* 11: 119–171.

Ginsberg, Alex. 2011. How New York's bias crimes statute has exceeded its intended scope. *Brooklyn Law Review* 76: 1599–1634.

Grattet, Ryken, and Valerie Jenness. 2001. The birth and maturation of hate crime policies in the United States. *American Behavioral Scientist* 45: 668.

Hampton, Jean. 1988. Forgiveness, resentment, and hatred. In *Forgiveness and mercy*, ed. J.G. Murphy and J. Hampton, 35–87. Cambridge: Cambridge University Press.

Harel, Alon, and Gideon Parchomovsky. 1999. On hate and equality. *Yale Law Journal* 109: 507–540.

Hessick, Carissa. 2006. Motive's role in criminal punishment. *Southern California Law Review* 80: 89–150.

Hohmann, James. 2018. The Daily 202: Hate crimes are a much bigger problem than even the new FBI statistics show. *Washington Post*, November 14. https://www.washingtonpost.com/news/powerpost/paloma/daily-202/2018/11/14/daily-202-hate-crimes-are-a-much-bigger-problem-than-even-the-new-fbi-statistics-show/5beba5bd1b326b39290547e2/?utm_term=.888e344270a6

Hurd, Heidi, and Michael Moore. 2004. Punishing hatred and prejudice. *Stanford Law Review* 56: 1081–1046.

Jacobs, James, and Kimberly Potter. 1998. *Hate crimes: Criminal law and identity politics.* Oxford: Oxford University Press.

Jenness, Valerie. 2012. Hate crimes. In *The Oxford handbook of crime and public policy,* ed. Michael Tonry, 524–546. Oxford: Oxford University Press.

Jenness, Valerie, and Ryken Grattet. 2001. *Making hate a crime: From social movement to law enforcement.* Washington, DC: American Sociological Association.

Kahan, Dan. 1996. What do alternative sanctions mean? *University of Chicago Law Review* 63: 591–654.

Kaiserman, Alex. 2018. "More of a cause": Recent work on degrees of causation and responsibility. *Philosophy Compass* 13. https://doi.org/10.1111/phc3.12498

Lawrence, Frederick. 1994. The punishment of hate: Toward a normative theory of bias-motivated crimes. *Michigan Law Review* 93: 320–382.

———. 1999. *Punishing hate: Bias crimes under American law.* Cambridge, MA: Harvard University Press.

———. 2007. The hate crime project and its limitations: Evaluating the societal gains and risks in bias crime law enforcement. In *Social consciousness in legal decision making,* ed. R.L. Weiner, B.H. Bornstein, R. Schoop, and S.L. Wilborn. New York: Springer.

Macleod, James. 2019. Ordinary causation. *Indiana Law Journal* 94: 957–1029.

Mendlow, Gabriel. 2019. The elusive object of punishment. *Legal Theory* 25: 105–31.

Moore, Michael. 2010. The moral worth of retribution. In *Placing blame: A theory of the criminal law,* 104–152. Oxford: Oxford University Press.

Murphy, Jeffrie. 1988. Hatred: A qualified defense. In *Forgiveness and Mercy,* ed. J.G. Murphy and J. Hampton. Cambridge: Cambridge University Press.

Organization for Security and Co-operation in Europe. 2009. *OSCE report, hate crimes laws: A practical guide.* Vienna: Organization for Security and Co-operation in Europe.

Schwitzgebel, Eric. 2015. Belief. The Stanford encyclopedia of philosophy. https://plato.stanford.edu/archives/sum2015/entries/belief/. Accessed 23 Feb 2019.

Simons, Kenneth. 2000. On equality, bias crimes, and just deserts. *Journal of Criminal Law and Criminology* 91: 237–268.

———. 2002. Does punishment for "culpable indifference" simply punish for "bad character"? *Buffalo Criminal Law Review* 6: 219–316.

———. 2008. Self-defense: Reasonable beliefs or reasonable self-control? *New Criminal Law Review* 11: 51–90.

———. 2012. Is strict criminal liability in the grading of offences consistent with retributive desert? *Oxford Journal of Legal Studies* 32: 445–461.

Steiker, Carol. 1999. Punishing hateful motives: Old wine in a new bottle revives calls for prohibition. *Michigan Law Review* 97: 1857.

Tribe, Laurence. 1993. The mystery of motive, private and public: Some notes inspired by the problems of hate crime and animal sacrifice. *Supreme Court Review* 1993: 1–36.

Verstein, Andrew. 2018. The jurisprudence of mixed motives. *Yale Law Journal* 127: 1106–1175.

Walen, Alex. 2016. Retributive justice. The Stanford encyclopedia of philosophy. https://plato.stanford.edu/archives/win2016/entries/justice-retributive/. Accessed 23 Feb 2019.

Wang, Lu-in. 2000. Recognizing opportunistic bias crimes. *Boston University Law Review* 80: 1399–1437.

Woods, Jordan. 2008. Comment. Taking the "hate" out of hate crimes: Applying unfair advantage theory to justify the enhanced punishment of opportunistic bias crimes. *UCLA Law Review* 56: 489–541.

Ignorance of Law

CHAPTER 14

Ignorance of Law: How to Conceptualize and Maybe Resolve the Issue

Douglas Husak

Should ignorance of a moral or criminal rule preclude moral responsibility and/or penal liability? Never, always, sometimes? If the correct answer is "sometimes," as everyone should concede, under *what* circumstances should ignorance bar responsibility and/or liability? Why are responsibility and/or liability precluded in these circumstances but not elsewhere? Moral and legal philosophers differ radically in their answers. Quite a bit (but of course not all) of their disagreement stems from uncertainty about how to conceptualize this issue. My chapter has two sections. In section "A Framework to Conceptualize the Issue," I construct a framework in which I believe this topic is best approached. In section "A Theory of Moral Blameworthiness and its Application," I employ this framework to suggest how I think the controversy might be resolved. Admittedly, my thoughts on the latter topic are fairly unusual and perhaps even radical. Thus it is important to stress at the outset that the positions I take in these sections are largely (but not wholly) independent of one another. That is, the conceptualization I offer in section "A Framework to Conceptualize the Issue" might be adopted even if my answers in section "A Theory of Moral Blameworthiness and its Application" are rejected. But I believe the framework I build helps to show why some positions about ignorance of law are preferable to others.

First, however, I hazard a brief word about one of the motivations for my project. I have long been worried about the related phenomena of overcriminalization and over-punishment. Today, almost everyone shares this concern.[1]

D. Husak (✉)
Rutgers University, New Brunswick, NJ, USA
e-mail: husak@philosophy.rutgers.edu

L. Alexander, K. K. Ferzan (eds.), *The Palgrave Handbook of Applied Ethics and the Criminal Law*, https://doi.org/10.1007/978-3-030-22811-8_14

I have tended to focus on the justifiability of *offenses*, and drug offenses in particular, to combat these problems. In what follows, however, I move away from the content of the substantive penal law to focus on a *defense*. After all, a reduction in the scale of punishment can be accomplished just as effectively by enlarging the parameters of defenses as by contracting the scope of offenses. In my judgment, the unwillingness to enlarge the defense of ignorance of law produces overcriminalization because it imposes penal liability on those who do not deserve it. Except perhaps for a radical reform of our punitive drug policies, an expansion in the availability of the defense of ignorance of law has the potential to make a non-trivial dent in over-punishment—the phenomenon that, above all others, fueled the concern about overcriminalization in the first place.

Existing law, as nearly every schoolchild is aware, is very restrictive about the conditions under which ignorance of law will exculpate. *Ignorantia juris non excusat* is the general rule to which a few exceptions are recognized. But these exceptions do not conform to a clear rationale. To be sure, some statutes include elements that explicitly require defendants to be aware their acts are illegal before they can be liable for committing them. As far as I can tell, however, no principle explains why some statutes but not others contain such elements. In any event, unless a defendant is prosecuted for violating such a statute, her prospects of evading liability because of her ignorance are slim. In most jurisdictions, she will succeed in avoiding liability only if *notice* is somehow defective—that is, only if the state has failed in some way to disseminate adequate information about the existence or content of the law she has breached. The requirement of notice is largely formal; it is not interpreted to entail that a defendant has actually noticed (i.e., is actually aware) that her conduct is unlawful. As a result, an ignorance of law defense is seldom recognized. In my judgment, the availability of this defense should be greatly expanded. This expansion will promote justice inasmuch as it will treat defendants who are ignorant of law as they deserve while simultaneously reducing the number of people subject to punishment.

A Framework to Conceptualize the Issue

In this section, I introduce seven features of a framework for thinking about whether and under what circumstances ignorance of a rule should preclude moral and/or penal responsibility. Although each of these features is important, some are more philosophically debatable and merit more discussion than others.

First, we must construct the general schema to keep in mind when deciding whether and under want circumstances ignorance of a rule should be exculpatory. I contend that we should focus on a case in which A and B engage in the same wrongful conduct Ø that violates the same rule R. A knows his conduct Ø violates R, but B does not know his conduct Ø violates R. Assume B does not know Ø violates R not because she is mistaken about some *factual* property of her act or circumstance, but rather because she is mistaken about the existence, content or application of R itself. Further clarifications of some of the parts of this schema are provided below.

Three features of this schema are worthy of explicit mention. First, A and B must commit the *same* act Ø that violates the *same* rule R. If they commit different acts or breach different rules, too many variables are at play in our judgments about the case, and we are bound to be less certain about which of these variables explains any difference in the severity of the blame and/or punishment we believe should be imposed on A and B. For the same reason, I take both A and B to be *sane adults*. Neither has some other defense—such as insanity or infancy—for violating R. Finally, I stipulate that Ø is *wrongful*. Perhaps persons should be blamed and/or punished when they engage in conduct they mistakenly *believe* to be wrongful—for an *attempt*, for example. And perhaps other circumstances exist in which individuals should be blamed and/or punished even though their conduct is permissible. But blame and/or punishment for permissible conduct or for attempted wrongs raise complex issues better addressed separately. I propose that moral and legal philosophers assess the relative blameworthiness of A and B when their conduct is wrongful before extending their analysis to more unusual situations.

With the foregoing schema in mind, we need to answer what I call the *basic question: Ceteris paribus,* how should the severity of the blame and/or punishment A deserves for Ø compare to that of B? Should B be blamed and/or punished less severely than A, or should A and B be blamed and/or punished to the same extent? Three aspects of this basic question are noteworthy.

First, the basic question is *comparative*. We need not make judgments about *how* severely A or B should be blamed and/or punished for Ø. These judgments are notoriously difficult to defend; disagreements about how to identify the *cardinal* amount of blame and/or punishment of the given offenders are intractable and painfully familiar to theorists of the criminal law. Instead, we must only make the more manageable judgment of how severely A and B should be blamed and/or punished relative to each other. Because the basic question is comparative, several of the cases included in criminal law textbooks may not be useful in posing it. Most such cases involve a single defendant who breaches a rule of which she was allegedly unaware. Readers are then invited to decide: Is she responsible or not? The basic question, by contrast, necessarily involves *two* defendants whose quanta of blameworthiness and/or punishment must be determined *relative* to each other.

Moreover, the contested issue involves the relative blame and/or punishment deserved by A and B *for Ø*. Quite a few of the efforts to assess the fate of B focus on some *other* act Ω alleged to bear a close relationship to the blameworthiness or responsibility of B for committing Ø. For example, perhaps B has breached a duty of inquiry (call it Ω) to learn whether Ø is wrong. If so, the outstanding question is how his blame and/or liability for violating this duty Ω can make him blameworthy and liable *for Ø*. Perhaps this question can be answered or perhaps it cannot. In either event, however, the fundamental question is whether and to what extent B deserves blame and/or punishment *for Ø*, not for some *other* act that bears some relation to Ø.

Finally, the basic question contains a *ceteris paribus* clause. Even if A and B are identical in their degree of blameworthiness, it does not follow that, all things considered, they must be punished with equal severity. Admittedly, theorists may disagree about which specific considerations this clause should be construed to preclude. But no one should assume that desert is the only or even the most important factor to take into account in sentencing.

What *kind* of judgment is needed to answer the basic question? I assume the basic question asks for a *moral* judgment. In other words, in asking whether A deserves more blame and/or punishment than B for Ø that violates rule R, the sense of desert and blame is *moral*. But why, if the relevant inquiry is about ignorance of *law* and state *punishment*, should we be interested in moral rather than legal judgments? I offer two answers. We are interested in whether, to what extent and under what circumstances the criminal law *should* punish or exculpate persons who are ignorant of the rules they violate. If there is a separate sense of *legal* (as opposed to *moral*) desert and blame, I submit we should be uninterested in it if we aspire to decide whether and under what circumstances ignorance of law should exculpate—unless, of course, this separate sense is somehow relevant to a moral inquiry.

Second, I hold the controversial view (which I believe most philosophers share but for which I cannot argue here) that the law per se provides no moral reason for action. If the law proscribing Ø provides no moral reason for action, no such reason is provided by knowledge of the law, and ignorance of the law cannot defeat a reason that did not exist in the first place. Thus no inculpatory or exculpatory work is literally done by knowledge or ignorance of *law*, but rather by knowledge or ignorance of the morality that underlies it. This novel way to conceptualize the problem has at least two implications that should be noticed. First, if *no* morality underlies the law, so that Ø is not wrongful, it is hard to see why those who commit it deserve blame and/or punishment *at all*—whether or not they are aware of Ø. Second, the topic of ignorance of law becomes more intimately related to the well-traveled philosophical issue of responsibility for moral wrongdoing if we accept that morality, rather than the law itself, is what creates reasons for compliance. In any event, this controversial view requires a clarification of the general schema and basic question with which I began. When A but not B realizes her act Ø violates R, what is relevant to A's blameworthiness and to B's case for exculpation is that A but not B recognizes her act is morally wrongful. Conversely, if B realizes his act is morally wrongful but not that it is illegal, B recognizes that which bears on his desert.

Once we try our best to answer the basic question from a moral perspective, I assume we have a powerful basis to shape our legal practices accordingly so that they conform to our moral judgments. In other words, I recognize a *presumption* that our theory of penal liability should mirror our moral theory about when punishment is deserved. Conformity between law and morality represents the ideal to which we should aspire. Of course, this presumption might be overridden if the argument for doing so is compelling. If the implications of my reasoning turn out to be too hard to accept in the real world, we have little choice but to *compromise* on the principles I believe typically favor exculpation or substantial mitigation for offenders who are ignorant of law. But a retreat from a principle for pragmatic reasons should not be confused with the principled position itself. We should always insist on a strong reason if our theory of criminal blame and/or punishment is to deviate from our theory of the conditions under which blame and/or punishment is deserved from a moral point of view. Quite a bit of uncertainty about ignorance of law derives from disagreement about when such a deviation might be warranted. Some theorists will regard the ideal position I defend as so unenforceable and subject to abuse that the rules and doctrines we eventually enact into law will turn out to have little resemblance to it. In any event, I provisionally hold it to be irrelevant to our inquiry whether the rule R violated by A and B is moral or legal. Ideally, the conditions under which B deserves less blame and/or punishment for her violation are identical in both domains, that is, in the domain of morality and in the domain of law.

To answer the basic question, I further assume we need to decide whether B is less *deserving* of punishment than A, is less *morally culpable,* less *blameworthy* and/or is less *responsible* than A for his wrongful conduct Ø that violates R. I am aware that culpability, blameworthiness and responsibility have a multiplicity of distinct meanings which for several purposes must be carefully distinguished. For present purposes, however, I use them interchangeably. The important point is that if ignorance of law bears on the severity of the punishment that should be imposed, it does so because it alters the moral desert, culpability, blameworthiness and/or responsibility of the ignorant offender.

In framing the basic question in terms of desert, I mean to preclude reference to the sorts of consequentialist considerations that have loomed so large in scholarly discussions of whether ignorance of law should be exculpatory. Our inquiry does not depend on conjectures about the *effects* of withholding or granting an excuse to the ignorant defendant. Perhaps imposing blame and/or punishment on ignorant wrongdoers is an efficient use of judicial resources and has beneficial effects in deterring subsequent offenders—although I am skeptical. Nonetheless, I assume that determinations of desert require judgments based upon what persons have done in the past, rather than on predictions about how to shape the behavior of persons in the future. One need not frame the basic question in terms of desert to resist consequentialism. Obviously, however, moral philosophers who (mistakenly) accept a consequentialist perspective on penal liability will regard this part of my framework as unacceptable.

With the foregoing schema and basic question in place, we might describe and evaluate any number of specific examples that exemplify the problem. Unfortunately, intuitions about different kinds of situations involving ignorance of a rule turn out to vary, so it would be dangerous to generalize too readily from any particular case. Still, the following three examples might be kept in mind.

(1) A few years ago I first observed a stranger on a mobile phone in an area where I counted four signs that explicitly indicated that such use is prohibited by Homeland Security. It is easy to anticipate how the offender reacted when an authority confronted him. He did not reply, "I have nothing to say on my own behalf; ignorance of law is no defense." Instead, he responded, "I am sorry; I did not know I was not allowed to use my phone here." I make two observations if I am correct to assume that this latter reply is nearly universal and the former is unusual or non-existent. First, the offender must have believed he was entitled to leniency—some degree of exculpation—if his plea were accepted as true. Second, and just as importantly, the plea of ignorance is often *accepted* as wholly or partially exculpatory by the authority who confronts the offender. One would be surprised to learn that this person did not actually *receive* some degree of leniency, and probably no sanction whatever, relative to that of an offender who knew mobile phones were prohibited. If the intuition that ignorance of law is no excuse was as entrenched as many commentators allege, we would be puzzled by the fact that ordinary persons plead it so frequently and authorities accept it so readily. But these facts are *not* puzzling. A comprehensive perspective on the culpability or blameworthiness of legally ignorant defendants must explain rather than neglect these truisms.

(2) Arguably, the foregoing example is special in one or more respects. To test our intuitions further, we should consider a second example. Hittites who lived 30 centuries ago apparently had no moral qualms about enslaving captives caught in battle. Let me stipulate what I regard as obvious: slavery is an unjust institution and owning slaves is wrongful. Suppose a modern slave-owner in some part of the world (call her "A") understands perfectly well that slavery is an unjust institution, but cannot be bothered to do what she knows to be right because she does not want to do the hard work her slaves perform on her plantation. How should we assess her blameworthiness relative to that of the ancient Hittite (call him "B") who I again stipulate to lack the moral knowledge common today? Reasonable minds can and do disagree,[2] but I am inclined to hold the blameworthiness of slave-owners who know better to be significantly greater than that of slave-owners who are morally ignorant. The latter may not be blameworthy to any degree.

(3) Many reformers are unhappy with the current test used by many legal jurisdictions to establish consent for sexual offenses such as rape. They propose to alter statutes so that only something like "express affirmative consent" will make the sexual encounter consensual. Whatever the exact details of the standard they propose to substitute for the existing law, one can be confident that a great many defendants will be unaware the content of the law has been

changed. These defendants can be expected to proceed with sex whenever they receive what they have regarded as consent before the law was altered. If arrested, they will insist the encounter was consensual, and be shocked to learn that a new statute holds them to be mistaken. Suppose B, who believes the old test still applies, engages in a sexual act Ø believing he has obtained consent. A, on the other hand, understands fully well that his partner has not consented. On this supposition, the basic question asks how the blameworthiness or responsibility of A and B should be compared. On the level of intuition, I find it fantastic to suppose they deserve a comparably severe punishment. Even if we agree that the new test is preferable to the old, its codification does not settle the issue of whether and to what extent persons are blameworthy and responsible when they act wrongfully while mistakenly believing the latter standard continues to apply.

No handful of examples should be used to generalize about all cases in which the foregoing schema is instantiated. If I am correct, we should ask what *additional* information might be needed about A, B, Ø and/or R to answer our basic question. In what follows, I mention a few bits of additional information that might be required in order to provide a general answer.

First, I mentioned that the first of the above examples may be special. Perhaps its special character derives from the supposition that a proscription of mobile cell use is a regulatory, *malum prohibitum* offense, prohibiting conduct that is not wrongful prior to or independent of law. Thus I chose a different kind of case for my second example, involving what I hope everyone would agree to be *mala in se*: slave-owning. My third example, a sexual offense, is a *malum in se* too, although there is considerable controversy about what morality demands about consent. Our intuitive responses to these examples may or may not differ. In any event, quite a few commentators have suggested that the contrast between conduct that is wrongful prior to and independent of law and conduct that is not wrongful prior to and independent of law plays a central role in answering the basic question. In my judgment, these commentators should be pressed to explain why they believe this distinction is crucial. It is true, of course, that sane adults are far more likely to be ignorant of the existence of a *malum prohibitum* than of the existence of a *malum in se*. But this truism does not settle what we should say about the blameworthiness and/or criminal liability of persons in those relatively unusual circumstances in which they *are* ignorant of the existence or application of a *malum in se*.

Next, do we need to know whether a reasonable person in B's situation *would have known* Ø is wrongful? In other words, do we need to know whether B's mistaken belief that Ø is permissible is *reasonable*? Again, legal theorists have been far more willing to reduce the extent of B's blame and/or punishment relative to that of A when the her mistake is non-negligent, that is, when a reasonable person in her circumstances would have made the same mistake

(Husak and Hirsch 1993, p. 157). The judgment that their mistake is non-negligent probably underlies our reluctance to blame the Hittites. In my judgment, however, inquiries about what reasonable persons would have believed and done are probably irrelevant. If the ignorant offender is merely negligent, we have answered the basic question in favor of some degree of exculpation, since no one thinks negligent offenders are as culpable as those with actual knowledge. Moreover, negligence is and ought to give rise to penal liability infrequently and perhaps never; we should not invoke it any more in the domain of mistake of law than in the domain of mistake of fact.

Perhaps we need even more facts to answer the basic question. I stipulated that B violated Ø *in* ignorance, but must we also inquire whether B violated Ø *from* ignorance? In other words, must we know whether B would *still* have done Ø even if he *had* known it to be wrongful? Reasonable minds again disagree. Admittedly, the case for exculpation seems stronger when B's ignorance *makes a difference* to his conduct. If B would have persisted in his wrongful behavior even if he had he known the truth about Ø, perhaps his mistake is immaterial and exculpation should not be granted. Nonetheless, I am tentatively inclined to believe the answer to the foregoing counterfactual is probably irrelevant. Notice that the answer to the comparable counterfactual is rarely if ever deemed important when persons are mistaken about the wrongfulness of Ø because of their ignorance of *fact*. Suppose a hunter is accused of murder but believed his victim was a deer rather than a human being. Would we acquit him even if we know he would have fired the same lethal shot even if he had been aware his victim was human? Reasonable minds disagree. But if this counterfactual is immaterial when defendants are mistaken about the facts, it is hard to see why it is material when defendants are mistaken about whether their conduct is wrongful.

Finally, must we also know *why* B is ignorant of the wrongfulness of Ø? This question has played an enormous role in scholarly attempts to explain why ignorance of law rarely exculpates. B typically deserves blame and/or punishment for Ø, many commentators allege, because B breached some *other* duty: a duty to know the law. We might call this duty Ω to contrast it from the duty not to Ø. If B had not breached his duty Ω, the argument continues, his ignorance of Ø would have been rectified. The popularity of this explanation helps to account for the limited circumstances in which positive law *does* recognize exculpation for B. As I have said, nearly all jurisdictions recognize a defense when *notice* of Ø is somehow defective so that B could not have known it to have been wrongful despite conforming to his duties of inquiry. Even so, I think this rationale for typically denying exculpation to B is unsuccessful. In a great many cases, B could not reasonably have known Ø to be wrongful despite making diligent inquiries. But my main reason to reject this explanation is less obvious. Any blame and/or punishment B deserves for breaching Ω—his alleged duty to find out that Ø is wrongful—is seldom if ever equivalent to the blame and/or punishment A deserves for breaching Ø when aware of its wrongfulness. Thus it is hard to see how any blame and/or punishment B deserves for breaching his duty of inquiry Ω can substitute for or be equivalent to the amount of blame and/or punishment A deserves for doing $\emptyset$.

To my mind, commentators are often misled by searching for a reason why B, the ignorant wrongdoer, deserves *less* punishment than A, who knows his conduct is wrongful. Instead, I suggest it may be more perspicuous to ask why the knowledgeable wrongdoer A frequently deserves *more* punishment than B. After all, these questions are logically equivalent; if A deserves more punishment than B, it follows that B deserves less punishment than A. Posing an old question in a new way can help us gain novel insights. What is it about *knowledge* that $\emptyset$ is wrongful could make A more responsible and blameworthy than B? Instead of trying to understand why *ignorance* of wrongdoing might *mitigate* blameworthiness relative to a baseline of *knowledge*, we might try to ascertain why *knowledge* of wrongdoing might *aggravate* blameworthiness relative to a baseline of *ignorance*.

My seventh and last point is the simplest but most important: No one can hope to answer the basic question, to decide why A's knowledge that $\emptyset$ is wrong may make him more deserving of blame and/or punishment than B, without at least implicitly invoking some general principles—perhaps an entire *theory*—of responsibility. Legal philosophers should struggle to make this commitment explicit. Producing and applying such a theory is the missing piece in nearly all normative investigations into the significance of ignorance of wrongdoing. Without such a theory, we have only our intuitions on which to rely—and these intuitions are notoriously divided and unreliable. We cannot decide whether B deserves less blame and/or punishment for $\emptyset$ than A without deciding why A is blameworthy in the first place. Defending such a theory, however, is extraordinarily difficult. Perhaps no project in contemporary moral philosophy is as problematic and divisive as producing a general theory of responsibility. It is to this inquiry we must turn if we hope to make much progress in answering the basic question.

A THEORY OF MORAL BLAMEWORTHINESS AND ITS APPLICATION

If the framework I have constructed thus far is roughly acceptable, we are in a better position to propose a solution to whether and under what circumstances ignorance of a rule reduces or precludes blameworthiness and/or the severity of the punishment B deserves relative to A. To answer this question, we need a theory (or at least a set of principles) to help identify when criminal responsibility is deserved. Philosophers have defended any number of candidates. In what follows, I discuss what I regard as the two most plausible competitors, ignoring the vast array of novel alternatives some philosophers have proposed. On either theory, the scope of a defense of ignorance of law should be far broader than what the current law allows. That is, according to either position, we should conclude that A, who knows he is violating the rule, is almost always more blameworthy and responsible than B, who does not. If (*ceteris paribus*) the severity of punishment should track the extent of moral blameworthiness, B should almost always receive a lesser sentence than A. I am aware that my conclusion deviates dramatically from positive law. Ultimately, however, I believe my position will turn out to be less radical than initial appearances might suggest. Still, no philosopher of criminal law, to my knowledge, explicitly accepts as far-reaching a position about when ignorance of law is partly or wholly exculpatory.

It is natural to suppose that questions about whether persons are responsible for conduct Φ should be resolved by invoking the same framework that shows why persons possess the capacity for responsibility in the first place. We persons are unlike animals; attributions of blame are appropriate for us. Why? According to the position I accept, agents become eligible for attributions of responsibility generally, and for a given act in particular, by having and being able to exercise our capacity to be *reason-responsive* with respect to it. Roughly, we become morally blameworthy for wrongful conduct when our capacity to respond to moral reasons is intact but we utilize it incorrectly. I propose to briefly elaborate on this position before turning to a discussion of what I take to be its main rival. Although my explication is woefully short of the nuance and detail that philosophical specialists would prefer, I hope to say enough to motivate my conclusion that a reason-responsive account of responsibility—when construed most plausibly—shows why offenders typically deserve exculpation when they are ignorant that their conduct is wrongful. I will also argue that this conclusion does not depend entirely on accepting a reason-responsive account. Even the most well-known competitor to this view—a quality of will theory—should be interpreted to support quite a bit of exculpation for persons who are ignorant their conduct is wrongful. For present purposes, then, the most important difference between these rival theories is not *whether*, but *to what extent* they support the conclusion that B deserves less punishment than A.

I hope an account of responsibility in terms of reason-responsiveness is compatible with virtually *any* framework for conceptualizing the nature of wrongfulness in first-order morality. In what follows, I invoke what often is called an *objective* account of the latter. Although different conceptions of wrongfulness have been proposed for different purposes,[3] I tentatively presuppose that in any given situation, what a person ought to do is a function of the *moral reasons* for or against the alternative courses of action she is able to perform. Conduct Φ is wrongful when the moral reasons against it are stronger than the moral reasons in favor of it. What these reasons are and how they are balanced does not depend on the beliefs of the defendant; the determination of whether Φ is wrongful (unlike the position I favor regarding responsibility) is thoroughly objective. I recognize that this particular conception of wrongfulness, like any other with which I am familiar, is problematic. I acknowledge that reasons are notoriously difficult to identify and to balance, that some appear to be incommensurable, that moral reasons are hard to distinguish from non-moral reasons and that some might be outweighed while others are excluded. Moreover, an objective conception is of little assistance in guiding action and struggles to capture what is distinctive about moral wrongfulness as opposed to other kinds of irrationality. I hope that the essentials of my position about ignorance of law are not undermined if this objective conception of wrongfulness turns out to be misguided or in need of fundamental qualification.

We routinely exercise our capacity to respond to moral reasons, but sometimes deserve blame when we do so incorrectly. When is this so? Consider the following example, which I hope to be straightforward. Suppose Sabine notices that her neighbor leaves his expensive bicycle unlocked on his porch when he returns from school. When he is away on vacation, she sneaks onto his porch, steals his bike and sells it to her friend, who she knows will be happy to buy a nice bicycle below its market value. Sabine is virtually certain her theft will be undetected. On a purely prudential calculus, she increases her expected utility by taking the bike. Nonetheless, she steals the bike while recognizing that the balance of moral reasons proscribes her act of theft. No excuse (e.g., duress) or justification (e.g., necessity) applies to her behavior. In the event my example is under-described and more detail is needed, I stipulate that Sabine's motive for stealing the bicycle is solely to obtain money to finance her vacation in Miami where she plans to indulge her passion for sunbathing. If *anyone* is blameworthy for *any* act Φ, Sabine is blameworthy for her act of theft. I see little point in proceeding further and trying to make headway on the topic at hand if we cannot agree about attributions of responsibility in this case.

As described, however, Sabine's case is *so* easy that it does little to support a particular conception of responsibility; *any* such theory, including those I reject, had better succeed in finding this case to be unproblematic. Still, it is instructive to investigate *what* is so easy about it. Different answers would be given. In my view, Sabine's case is straightforward because she herself is fully cognizant that her conduct is wrongful. Expressed more colloquially, Sabine *knows better* than to steal the bicycle. In the simplest, clearest and least controversial examples of moral blameworthiness, persons agree that the balance of moral reasons requires them not to Φ, but decide to Φ anyway, that is, to act contrary to the balance of the moral reasons they recognize. As far as I can see, the only meaningful point of contention among moral philosophers (who do not advocate the abolition of responsibility altogether) is whether persons are ever blameworthy for wrongful actions *other* than those that conform to this description.

To be sure, *some* such defendants have a plausible claim for a partial excuse from blame on other grounds. Some degree of exculpation may be deserved in those situations in which the defendant battles mightily but unsuccessfully against the temptation to offend. Consider, for example, the stereotypical kleptomaniac. He realizes theft is wrongful, would prefer not to accede to his impulse to steal, but eventually surrenders after an internal struggle. Perhaps he merits some amount of exculpation because his desire, although probably not literally irresistible, makes compliance with the law too onerous. Of course, a central obstacle to any proposal to allow some degree of exculpation for these "hard choices" is to draw the line between those desires that are too difficult and those that are not too difficult to resist. But equally problematic lines must be drawn for defendants who plead *any* excuse. In any event, in what follows I confine my attention to knowledgeable offenders whose temptation to act wrongfully is not sufficiently strong to warrant a partial excuse. I do not believe the defendants I have in mind are exceptional; I think quite a few persons are aware their acts are wrongful, could desist with minimal effort, but decide to offend anyway. I take Sabine to be an example.

Sabine behaves irrationally, that is, she exhibits a deficiency in her rational agency in failing to conform to what she knows morality requires.[4] According to the conception I am inclined to favor, deliberation is deficient in the way that supports blameworthiness only when agents such as Sabine respond incorrectly to the balance of moral reasons *according to their own lights*. Of course, philosophers have distinguished countless conceptions of rationality. Many of these conceptions are wholly objective or externalist; rationality consists in responding to whatever reasons actually exist. Why, then, should the standard of assessment be subjective or internal for judgments of responsibility? Clearly, this part of my theory is the most controversial. Neil Levy defends this component of my view as follows: "It is only reasonable to demand that someone perform an action if performing that action is something they can do rationally; that is, by means of a reasoning procedure that operates over their beliefs and desires. But what agents can do rationally in this sense is a function of their internalist reasons" (Levy 2011, p. 128). Consider the contrary view that would hold persons to be blameworthy because they fail to act as they have most reason to do from an externalist perspective, that is, from the vantage point of the reasons they objectively have, despite being unaware of them. Levy continues: "Suppose that there is a divergence between internalist and externalist reasons: what I have most reason to do, externalistically, is not something that I take myself to have any reason at all to do. In that case, if I do what I have most (externalist) reason to do, I do so not as a result of weighing reasons or any other reasoning procedure. I do so by chance, or through a glitch in my agency, or what have you" (ibid., p. 128). Thus I believe judgments of moral responsibility should require an *internal* assessment of the reason-responsiveness of agents, that is, an assessment from the subjective perspective of the agents themselves. Internalism or subjectivism about reason-responsiveness is the preferable standard of responsibility even though assessments of the reasons that make conduct wrongful proceed externally, according to the true facts that govern the situation.

As I have indicated, no contemporary penal theorist openly embraces a subjectivist theory of rationality to undermine conventional wisdom about *ignorantia juris*. But is this account of blameworthiness really so alien to philosophers of criminal law? It is hard to be sure. I tend to scold legal philosophers for failing to develop a theory of the foundations of criminal responsibility. Of course, penal theorists have not been altogether silent about this matter. They overwhelmingly favor a *choice* theory of culpability and blameworthiness. It has never been entirely clear what this theory is supposed to involve; it is invoked mostly in opposition to a *character* theory. In any event, no philosopher of criminal law, as far as I am aware, has worked out the details of a choice theory, even though they almost uniformly pledge their allegiance to it. Choice theorists owe us an account of the *content* of choice, of *what* must be chosen by the agent before her choice renders him blameworthy. Here is where a reason-responsive theory is explicit. Sabine chose to commit a wrong (*de re*) under that description (*de dicto*). My reason-responsive account certainly qualifies as the most consistent version of a choice theory, as defendants would not be blameworthy unless they *chose to do wrong* (both *de re* and *dicto*).

I am not the first philosopher to argue that the class of wrongful actions for which persons are fully morally responsible consists of those that are contrary to the agent's own subjective judgment of what is best. Most notably, variations of this position have been elegantly defended by Rosen (2002) and Zimmerman (2008), and I readily acknowledge my debt to each of them. In a very important respect, however, my position is *less* radical than that of either Rosen or Zimmerman. *Far* less radical, in fact. The conclusions I have defended admit of a crucial qualification: I hold a class of persons to be *somewhat* blameworthy even when they are *not* sure they are acting contrary to the balance of moral reasons. A defendant B who is aware his conduct Φ creates a substantial and unjustifiable *risk* of violating a moral rule R is responsible and subject to punishment for his act, albeit to a lesser extent than A, who knows his conduct is wrongful. These defendants are *reckless* about whether their conduct is wrongful, even though they do not know it to be. How *much* less punishment should be inflicted on defendants who are reckless about whether their conduct is wrongful relative to defendants who know their conduct is wrongful? Judgments of relative proportionality are notoriously problematic in any context. Still, codes have some experience dealing with similar problems; perhaps the severity of the sentence of the reckless defendant should be a specified fraction of the punishment to which the fully culpable, knowledgeable defendant is subject: one-half, for example.

Let me express my position thus far by relating it to the parallel treatment of ignorance of fact, as I propose to treat mistakes of law and fact *symmetrically* by replicating the same normative structure in each domain. That is, an initial but somewhat oversimplified statement of my theory of ignorance of law is that it applies to mistakes of law the same culpability hierarchy that is familiar in the context of mistakes of fact. Applications of the culpability hierarchy in the *Model Penal Code* would hold a defendant to be fully responsible for Φ if she intends or knows she is acting wrongfully, responsible to a lesser extent if she is reckless about whether Φ is wrongful and not responsible at all if she does not even suspect that Φ is wrongful. Although it is controversial, I regard my proposal to apply the same normative framework about the exculpatory significance of ignorance of fact to judgments about the exculpatory significance of ignorance of law to be relatively simple and intuitively appealing. Actually, if we believe that the primary function of the legal requirement of mens rea is to confine penal liability to the blameworthy, I think we should conceptualize persons who are wholly unaware they are acting wrongfully as lacking mens rea.

The usefulness of the above distinctions is not merely the product of a fertile philosophical imagination. Recklessness with respect to the wrongfulness of conduct is not merely a *possible* culpable state; it is common in cases we are likely to encounter every day.[5] As I hope is clear, the complete absence of suspicion that a *malum in se* is wrongful is exceptionally rare among sane adults. But a suspicion that falls short of knowledge is not the least bit unusual when a *malum prohibitum* is involved. A person who throws away batteries he knows might have to be recycled because they may be damaging to the environment is an example of someone who is reckless about the wrongfulness of his act. Whether we pigeon-hole his mistake into the category of law or fact is irrelevant in my view. If mistakes of fact and mistakes of law are treated symmetrically, the quantum of blame he deserves is somewhere between that of the wrongdoer who *knows* his batteries should be recycled and the amount deserved by the wrongdoer who is not even cognizant of the risk that his batteries should be recycled. The current doctrine about *ignorantia juris* is woefully deficient because it is all or nothing, and does not contain the resources to allow us to adequately represent his degree of blame. A major advantage of a theory that treats mistakes of fact and law symmetrically is that it allows us to do so.

I now return to the underlying philosophical theory of responsibility that affords exculpatory significance to ignorance of law. We can understand the strengths and weaknesses of a subjectivist reason-responsive theory more easily by contrasting it with its main rival. Many moral philosophers who agree that persons are responsible for much of what they do offer competitive criteria of when this is so, and some of the plausible options have different implications for the blameworthiness of persons who are unaware their acts are wrong. In what follows, I provide a brief description of the single most popular alternative, ignoring the vast array of novel theories that have recently been defended. The most serious rival to the conception of responsibility I have presupposed involves a family of views that might be called *quality of will* theories. These theories do not locate moral responsibility in an agent's defective practical reasoning—at least as I understand these terms. Instead, they purport to ground responsibility for a wrongful action Φ in the *will*: agents are blameworthy when their acts proceed from a will that is morally objectionable. Expressed somewhat differently, an individual is morally responsible when her action expresses negative attitudes that reveal something bad about her as a person. Countless variations and permutations of quality of will theories have been proposed, but a sustained evaluation of this family of views is well beyond my scope. Suffice it to say that their central differences consist of the accounts they offer of the exact factors that make the quality of a given will objectionable. The candidates mentioned most often include contempt, hostility, indifference, lack of consideration for the welfare and interest of others and even disrespect for law.

Philosophers who hold a quality of will theory would agree that Sabine's case is easy but tell a different story about why this is so. What makes her clearly blameworthy for her theft of the bicycle, they will insist, is that her behavior manifests whatever quality of will grounds her responsibility. Since Sabine elevates her own interests over those of others, her act exhibits the very attitudes that any quality of will theorist would cite as the foundation of blameworthiness. Some of these theories explicitly deny that her beliefs about morality are relevant to her responsibility. According to these accounts, Sabine exhibits an objectionable quality of will *regardless* of what she happens to think about the morality of her theft. Philosophers who hold such theories sometimes express bafflement (or even outrage) about criteria that take seriously the possibility that ignorance of wrongfulness might exculpate as widely as my own account allows. And they would not hesitate to blame the ancient slave-owning Hittite—even when no reasonable person in his circumstances would have recognized the wrongfulness of slavery.

Before saying more about quality of will theories directly, it is crucial to mention that philosophers who hold such views are bound to have a difficult time preserving the doctrine of *ignorantia juris* in anything resembling its current form. After all, the particular negative properties most often mentioned that make a will objectionable—such as contempt, hostility, indifference and disrespect for the welfare and interest of others—are not clearly displayed when wrongdoers commit a great many penal offenses, especially those that are *mala prohibita*. These traits are *probably* exemplified when defendants print counterfeit money or evade their taxes. But it is a stretch to say that these traits are manifested when defendants commit money laundering or drive an unregistered vehicle. Why, then, are these persons blameworthy at all? If such persons are *not* blameworthy, quality of will theories also have radical implications for the orthodox rules and doctrines that govern ignorance of law—even though they are *less* radical than my own position.

Moreover, criminal theorists need to be cautious before uncritically adopting a quality of will theory. If the ultimate basis of responsibility inheres in the will, and the will enjoys this status because it represents the core of who we are as persons, quality of will theories become dangerously close to those that ground responsibility in our *character*—in *who* we are. My skepticism notwithstanding, I do not insist that quality of will theorists cannot possibly succeed in explaining why they do *not* locate responsibility in our character. Unless they are able to do so, however, one would expect them to encounter stiff resistance from criminal theorists, many of whom go to great lengths to explain that responsibility attaches to particular choices made by a defendant rather than to the character of the defendant who makes them. As I have indicated, my reason-responsive theory preserves the moral significance of choice—the choice to engage in wrongdoing under that description. Theorists who hold quality of will theories attach less significance to choice. After all, no one chooses the quality of her will or whether it manifests objectionable features when wrongs are perpetrated. In addition, do we really gain deep insights into the will of a person by directing our focus on a single action she performs—as the penal law is prone to do? If our ultimate concern is with the will, why attach such importance to particular crimes? These questions should give pause to penal theorists who are tempted to embrace a quality of will theory. Most philosophers of criminal law explicitly repudiate character theories, and it would be troublesome indeed if the kind of theory they reject could not be distinguished from the kind of theory they accept.

Still, if a quality of will theory really provides a better foundation of moral responsibility, the case for affording general exculpatory significance to ignorance of law *seems* to collapse. But I believe this appearance is deceptive. Although I initially presented quality of will theories as rivals to reason-responsive accounts, they need not be construed as competitors. They might be combined (conjunctively or disjunctively) in various ways, suggesting different bases for holding wrongdoers to be blameworthy. Admittedly, several philosophers who hold quality of will theories expressly advertise their ability to resist proposals to exculpate wrongdoers who act in moral ignorance. I suspect that the difficulty of demonstrating why ignorance of morality does *not* exculpate has boosted the popularity of these theories; philosophers frequently appeal to quality of will accounts in the course of their efforts to refute views they regard as highly counterintuitive, such as those of Zimmerman and Rosen. But I am unmoved. A number of these theorists agree that the agent's beliefs about the wrongfulness of her conduct *should* be included among those factors from which the quality of her will is inferred. To decide whether they are correct, we need to recall that our basic question (Q) is essentially comparative. Consider two bicycle thieves; the first but not the second is aware her theft is wrongful. Clearly, the wills of these individuals *can* be distinguished: their actions express something significantly different about them as persons. Sabine, the first thief, manifests a willingness to act contrary to what she knows to be the demands of morality. But the thief who is unaware of the wrongfulness of her act manifests nothing remotely comparable. On what ground should this difference be regarded as wholly immaterial to an assessment of the quality of their respective wills? On the level of intuition—in which I admit to having limited confidence—the will of Sabine is far more reprehensible. If I am correct, quality of will theorists who reject my judgments about the responsibility of morally ignorant offenders need to establish not only that the will is the locus of blameworthiness, but also that ignorance of wrongdoing is immaterial to judgments about the quality of the will. I doubt they will succeed in meeting this burden.

Thus the two kinds of theories I introduced as competitors need not be conceptualized as rivals at all. They can be used in tandem to undermine the doctrine of *ignorantia juris*. Perhaps a deficiency in reason-responsiveness *just is* (or at least *involves*) a defect in the will that manifests as a failure to assign the proper weight to considerations recognized as moral. If so, even philosophers who hold a quality of will theory should afford some exculpatory significance to persons who act in ignorance of the morality that underlies law. This point requires emphasis, since it is among the most important issue on which my theory of ignorance of law depends. Especially when so-called *thick* moral concepts are involved, it would seem preposterous not to allow awareness of wrongdoing to count toward an assessment of the quality of will and the degree of blame the agent merits. To illustrate, imagine a person who treats others unkindly or cruelly. Surely we distinguish between cases in which the wrongdoer is *unknowingly* unkind or cruel from cases in which she *knows* her behavior is unkind or cruel. We respond to persons who make unkind or cruel remarks without knowing they have done so very differently from how we respond to persons who make the same remarks while fully aware of what they are doing. Admittedly, unlike the view I am inclined to favor, theories that take awareness of wrongdoing into account in assessing the quality of a will might still direct *some* amount of blame toward the individual who is completely clueless that her conduct is wrongful. In the absence of further detail, it is impossible to determine *how much* of a distinction quality of will theorists should recognize between the relative blameworthiness of each wrongdoer. But even if the person is blameworthy in both instances, the amount of blame she deserves is greater in the latter than in the former case.

The statement of my theory would be incomplete without mentioning what I regard as the most important *exception* to my general view that persons are fully responsible for their wrongdoing only when they know it to be wrong. When persons are *willfully ignorant* that their conduct is wrongful, they can deserve as much punishment as persons who are fully aware their conduct is wrongful. In the domain of ignorance of fact, the exact parameters of willful ignorance continue to be debated. Whatever the details, I am reluctant to allow offenders to manipulate or game the normative system. They should not be permitted to deliberately cultivate ignorance *in order* to preserve a defense (or some degree of exculpation) that would be withheld in the event their suspicions are confirmed and they find out their conduct is indeed wrongful. Perhaps additional exceptions to my general view should be recognized, but willful ignorance (as I construe it) is the best candidate for an exception I acknowledge.

Before concluding, I should also describe a favorable result that would probably follow from the adoption of my general theory. I mention this prediction because much of the speculation among consequentialists is pessimistic about what would happen if the defense of ignorance of law was broadened. If my theory were implemented, how would we expect legal institutions to respond over time? I would anticipate that legislatures would be more reluctant to enact laws of which persons are prone to be unaware. It was never a good idea to draft statutes that create legal duties of which persons are ignorant, and the recognition of a wider defense of mistake would retard the tendency to do so. Either existing legal obligations would be more readily cognizable by citizens or genuine notice—promulgation that is actually noticed—would become more commonplace. I return to one of my earlier examples to describe how this result has already occurred. Upon returning from my most recent visit abroad, I counted 11 rather than 4 prominently posted signs prohibiting mobile phone use in areas monitored by Homeland Security. If my prediction about the response of legal institutions is accurate, I expect a wider defense of ignorance of law to eventually make a dent in the problems of overcriminalization and over-punishment with which my chapter began.

I have argued that the case for affording exculpation to persons who are ignorant of law may not depend on which of the two kinds of theories of blameworthiness we accept. The only theories of responsibility that grant *no* exculpation to defendants who act in moral ignorance *either* construe a quality of will theory to hold beliefs about wrongdoing to be irrelevant to assessments of the will *or* invoke an altogether different ground of responsibility than I have heretofore discussed. I do not pretend to have mounted a fatal objection to the former alternative. However implausible their position may appear to me, I am aware that several prominent moral philosophers steadfastly deny that awareness of wrongdoing is material to judgments about the quality of an agent's will. I also concede that the latter alternative should be taken seriously, even though I have neglected to discuss it. The topic of moral blameworthiness is presently in a state of flux; new theories of responsibility appear almost weekly, and substantial refinements of old theories are ubiquitous as well. The proliferation of novel views indicates profound philosophical dissatisfaction with existing efforts. It would be absurd to suppose the last word on this topic has been written. Even so, I conclude we have a powerful theoretical basis to afford quite a bit of exculpation to B relative to A when both commit Φ in violation of rule R—even though we may be uncertain about exactly *how much* exculpation is deserved. Unless there are good pragmatic reasons not to do so, I think we should radically reform the rules and doctrines that apply to persons who make mistakes of law.

NOTES

1. The academic consensus is described in Garland (2018, p. 1); the public consensus is described in Ciaramella (2017).
2. For recent commentary that challenges my position, see Guerrero (2015).
3. The various candidates are nicely described in Zimmerman (2014).
4. For a challenge about whether I am correct to say that Sabine exhibits a deficiency in reason-responsiveness, see Yaffe (2018).
5. For a challenge about whether persons *can* be reckless (as I construe it) about whether an act is wrongful, see Zimmerman (2018).

REFERENCES

Ciaramella, C.J. 2017. ACLU poll: Majority of Americans, including Trump voters, say prison population should be reduced. CrimProfBlog. http://lawprofessors.typepad.com/crimprof_blog/2017/11/aclu-poll-majority-of-americans-including-trump-voters-say-prison-population-should-be-reduced.html. Accessed 6 Mar 2019.

Garland, David. 2018. Theoretical advances and problems in the sociology of punishment. *Punishment & Society* 2: 8–33.

Guerrero, Alex. 2015. Deliberation, responsibility, and excusing mistakes of law. *Jurisprudence* 6: 81–94.

Husak, Douglas, and Andrew von Hirsch. 1993. Culpability and mistake of law. In *Action and value in criminal law*, ed. John Gardner, Jeremy Horder, and Stephen Shute, 157. Oxford: Oxford University Press.

Levy, Neil. 2011. *Hard luck: How luck undermines free will and moral responsibility*. Oxford: Oxford University Press.

Rosen, Gideon. 2002. Culpability and moral ignorance. *Proceedings of the Aristotelian Society* 103 (1): 61–84.

Yaffe, Gideon. 2018. Is akrasia necessary for culpability? On Douglas Husak's "ignorance of law". *Criminal Law and Philosophy* 12: 341–349.

Zimmerman, Michael J. 2008. *Living with uncertainty*. Cambridge: Cambridge University Press.

———. 2014. *Ignorance and moral obligation*. Oxford: Oxford University Press.

———. 2018. Recklessness, willful ignorance, and exculpation. *Criminal Law and Philosophy* 12: 327–329.

PART XIV

Incest

CHAPTER 15

Incest

Stuart P. Green

Since the beginning of this century, there has been a growing interest in the moral and constitutional status of laws prohibiting incest. Inspired by new recognition in the U.S., Europe, and elsewhere of the right to engage in private, consensual, adult *same-sex sexual* conduct (Lawrence 2003; Dudgeon 1981), commentators and litigants have argued that there ought to be an analogous right to engage in private, consensual, adult *incestuous* conduct (e.g., Bergelson 2013; Hörnle 2014). To date, most courts in the U.S. and in Europe have been resistant to such a claim (e.g., Lowe 2009; Stübing 2012), but at least among liberal-minded scholars there is a growing consensus that current prohibitions on consensual adult incest are, if nothing else, ripe for reconsideration.

Most of this recent literature has viewed incest prohibitions through the lens of constitutional and human rights law. It typically asks, if the right to engage in private homosexual conduct is protected by the Substantive Due Process clause of the Fourteenth Amendment or by Article 8 of the European Convention on Human Rights (ECHR), why should the right to engage in private incestuous conduct not be protected as well? Moreover, it asks, if the Constitution protects the right to same-sex marriage, should it not also protect the right to incestuous marriage?[1]

The work of criminal law theorists regarding incest has mostly paralleled that of their constitutional law colleagues, though with an important distinction. Rather than ask if incest laws violate the Constitution or the ECHR, criminal law scholars have asked if such laws can be justified as a matter of moral, political, or legal theory (whether in accordance with the liberal harm

S. P. Green (✉)
Rutgers Law School, Newark, NJ, USA
e-mail: spgreen@law.rutgers.edu

© The Author(s) 2019
L. Alexander, K. K. Ferzan (eds.), *The Palgrave Handbook of Applied Ethics and the Criminal Law*, https://doi.org/10.1007/978-3-030-22811-8_15

337

principle or some alternative principle of criminalization). Like human rights scholars, criminal law theorists have focused primarily on the permissibility of legislation prohibiting putatively consensual incest between adults, paying relatively little attention to incest involving juveniles or to how the two kinds of incest are related. And they have tended to look at adult incest as presenting a binary choice, between criminalization and decriminalization, while mostly ignoring the possibility that such laws might be "tailored" to maximize the right of persons to engage in truly consensual sex, while simultaneously minimizing the dangers of coercion that some incestuous conduct presents.

In taking up these broader issues, I offer what can be thought of as a "normative reconstruction"[2] of the law of incest, consisting of four parts: Section "Incest as Taboo, Incest as Aversion" looks at the concept of incest as a complex cultural taboo, one which has attracted the attention of a wide range of social scientists and theorists. Section "How Incest Is Treated in Criminal Law" considers the striking multiplicity of ways in which incest has been dealt with across systems of criminal law, including the fact that a broad swath of civil law jurisdictions does not treat it as a crime at all. Section "A Rationale for the Law of Juvenile Incest" asks whether and how incest involving juveniles should be criminalized, particularly in light of the fact that we already criminalize statutory rape between unrelated parties. Section "A Rationale for the Law of Putatively Consensual Adult Incest" asks whether and how incest involving only adults should be criminalized, paying special attention to the possibility that some putatively consensual incestuous acts will, on further examination, prove to be coerced or exploitative.

INCEST AS TABOO, INCEST AS AVERSION

Before considering how incest is, or ought to be, dealt with in the law, it will be helpful to view it in a broader cultural context. Incest is a subject that has been of intense interest to anthropologists, sociologists, psychologists, theologians, moralists, dramatists, and others, and it is one that hardly lends itself to easy summary. But we can at least identify some of the key questions that have been raised. As we shall see below, many of the issues that surround the subject of incest as taboo resurface in the discussion of incest-as-criminal-offense.

Let us begin with the idea of "taboo" generally. The term was first used in English in 1777 by the British explorer James Cook, borrowing the Polynesian word for "prohibited," "forbidden," "unclean," or "cursed" (Oxford English Dictionary 2018). It is generally used today to refer to practices that generate strong social disgust or abhorrence. Widely observed taboos apply to conduct relating to sex (e.g., incest, bestiality, necrophilia, pedophilia), death and dying (suicide, necrophilia, cannibalism, and grave desecration), food and diet (cannibalism, eating foods that fail to comply with religious dietary laws), and excretion and other bodily functions (public defecation, urination, and flatulence).

Anthropologists and other social scientists have devoted much effort to determining exactly why and how certain behaviors have come to be regarded as taboo. Many taboos can find support in religious texts and traditions: this is especially true of those relating to sex and diet. Other taboos, such as those involving various bodily functions, reproduction, and corpse desecration, seem to have (or have once had) a rationale based, at least in part, on promoting health and hygiene.

Hardest to assess is the relationship between taboos and morality. Some taboo behaviors can be explained on moral grounds that are independent of religious belief. For example, there are compelling moral rationales for the taboos on pedophilia and racism, which can stand alone without reference to any religious text. Other taboos would be hard to explain without reference to their religious origins. This is true with respect to certain dietary restrictions, as well as restrictions on previously condemned forms of sex, such as homosexuality.

Simply because behavior is widely viewed as immoral, however, does not mean that it will be subject to a taboo: for example, we would not normally speak of a "taboo" on stealing, taking bribes, or lying. To be taboo, there seems to be a requirement that such behavior be regarded as unclean or disgusting. Thus, to label a behavior as taboo often involves not merely a moral judgment, but an aesthetic one too. Moreover, while some taboo behavior is illegal and criminal (e.g., grave desecration, pedophilia, public defecation), much is not (e.g., expressing racist views, talking about bodily functions, using profanity).

The recognition of taboos varies, of course, over time and across cultures. Conduct that was once viewed as taboo in Western culture, such as interracial sex and marriage, is no longer generally regarded as such. And conduct that is now often regarded as taboo, including slavery and hebephilia, has obviously not always been so.

The taboo on incest is a particularly complex one. It has been observed, in some form, in virtually every society through history (Turner and Maryanski 2005, pp. 3–25). Freud regarded it as one of two universal taboos (along with patricide) on which all civilizations are based (Freud 1990). In the mid-twentieth century, anthropologist George Murdock studied 250 societies and found evidence of an incest taboo of one sort or another in all of them (though throughout history there have been exceptions; e.g., marriage between siblings was common within the royal families of ancient Egypt) (Murdock 1947, p. 13).

Despite, or perhaps because of, its universality, the incest taboo has meant different things in different cultures at different historical periods. Sometimes, it has referred exclusively to marriage between close relatives; at other times, it has included sexual relations (whether marital or not), ranging from intercourse, to other forms of penetration, to "lesser" forms of sexual contact. And there has been considerable variation with respect to the nature of the prohibited relation—for example, about whether sex counts as incestuous if it involves cousins or parties that are related by marriage or adoption instead of blood.

The concept of incest also reflects an even more fundamental ambiguity. As we shall see below, many American jurisdictions have a single such offense that criminalizes, without distinction, both cases in which adults have sex with juveniles and those in which they have sex with other adults—this, despite the significant moral, psychological, and sociological differences between the two kinds of act. The first kind of conduct violates two taboos: one on having sex with family members and a separate one on pedophilia, hebephilia, or ephebophilia. The second kind of conduct violates only the incest taboo itself. As for the general public, my best guess is that, when most people hear the term "incest," they do not make a clear distinction between the adult and juvenile varieties. Instead, I suspect that there is something of a spillover effect at work here: part of the animus felt toward adult incest may reflect a displaced animus toward incest involving juveniles.

There are at least two reasons why the line between adult and juvenile incest is less clear than one might expect. First, it appears that some putatively consensual incestuous relationships between adults begin while one or both of the parties are still a juvenile. In such cases, the coerciveness of the earlier stage of the relationship colors the latter; the subordinate party remains vulnerable and dependent even after reaching adulthood. Second, the norms concerning juvenile sexuality have evolved: Until modern times, children were often betrothed even before reaching puberty. Sexual relations between adults and children were criminalized under English law as early as 1576, but the age of consent was, from a modern perspective, extraordinarily low—typically, ten years of age. It was not until the late nineteenth century that the law of statutory rape went through a major transformation, with the age of consent continuing to rise significantly until well into the twentieth century. Thus, it appears that what we would clearly regard as juvenile incest today would not have been recognized as such in earlier times.

An additional problem presented by the incest taboo concerns the relationship it bears to the apparently "natural" aversion that most people feel toward the act. This is a topic that has generated significant interest from generations of social scientists, including such luminaries as Durkheim, Levi-Strauss, and Malinowski (Durkheim 1963; Levi-Strauss 1969; Malinowski 1927).

As first described by the anthropologist Edvard Westermarck in 1891, the vast majority of humans feel an intense aversion to the idea of having sex with close family members with whom they have grown up in a family setting (even if they are not related by blood) (Westermarck 1921). Later researchers have found compelling empirical evidence of what has come to be known as the Westermarck Effect (Sheper 1983).

So, we know that incest evokes a strong aversion in most people and that it is prohibited by a cultural taboo. What is less clear is the direction of the causal relationship: is the aversion felt because of the taboo, or does the taboo exist because of the aversion? Some varieties of aversion, it seems, are learned: parents teach their children to resist the inclination to lie, cheat, steal, settle disputes with their fists, excrete in public, walk around naked, burp, and fart. If parents are successful in acculturating their children, the children begin to develop a kind of "learned aversion" to such conduct. There are other kinds of behaviors, however, in which most people seem to have no inclination to engage in the first place, regardless of any moral instruction or social stigma. For example, the aversions that most people feel to necrophilia, bestiality, pedophilia, suicide, and cannibalism seem to exist "naturally," prior to, and independent of, any taboo.

In the case of incest, little, if any, parental instruction is required to make children averse. Indeed, as Pinker has pointed out, parents often "try to socialize their children to be more affectionate with each other ('Go ahead—kiss your sister!'), not less" (Pinker 1997, p. 455). If this claim of innateness is right, it suggests that the taboo on incest is more like the ban on necrophilia, bestiality, and cannibalism than like that on cheating, stealing, and exhibitionism.

Regardless of whether the aversion to incest is innate or learned, the fact remains that some small number of people are immune to it and instead feel a desire to engage in sexual conduct with one or more close family members, at least in some circumstances. But this raises an even more perplexing question— namely, why should we as society *care* if some adults do not experience aversion and instead wish to engage in putatively consensual incestuous conduct with other adults? Why subject people who engage in such conduct to social stigma and shame? What harm is the incest taboo meant to prevent? And why should antipathy to adult incest remain so strong even while taboos on other forms of once-prohibited forms of sexuality have waned?

These questions have generated an immense outpouring of academic theorizing (*see* Wolf and Durham 2004). While it is not possible to do that literature justice here, we can identify several basic contentions that appear again and again. One is that incest, at least in certain circumstances, creates a significant risk of birth defects. While the ancient societies that developed the original incest taboo obviously had no knowledge of the biological processes that make inbreeding so likely to produce genetic defects, they must have had some awareness of a basic correlation. A second commonly offered rationale for prohibiting consensual adult incest is that the practice is destructive of family integrity—that it causes, or exacerbates, rivalries and jealousies and undermines the traditional allocation of roles, within the family structure. This is a tendency that would have been recognizable even in ancient societies where endogamous marriage, in one form or another, was encouraged. A third rationale is that adult incest, in some cases, will involve coercive or exploitative relationships in which more powerful members of a family (typically, parents and older siblings) use less powerful family members for their own sexual gratification. Whether and when any of these rationales is enough to support the criminalization of incest is a subject that is addressed below. (There is also a fourth rationale for the incest taboo which, though quite significant from an anthropological perspective, does not seem particularly relevant to the modern criminalization debate—namely, that the taboo encourages the development of alliances with other social groups and thereby serves to prevent conflict.)

How Incest Is Treated in Criminal Law

Western legal systems are deeply divided over whether and how to criminalize incest. Indeed, there are few forms of sexual behavior that reflect as much variation in how they are regulated. Such variety is surprising given the apparent universality of the basic taboo. In this section, we begin by considering five basic approaches Western jurisdictions take to criminalizing, or not criminalizing, incest. We then take a more detailed look at how incest is defined across U.S. jurisdictions.

Criminalizing Incest Across Legal Systems

Surveying a wide range of legal systems, we can identify five approaches to incest that the criminal law currently takes. They are:

(1) Criminalize, in the same provision and without distinguishing between them, incest between adults and juveniles and incest between consenting adults. Under this approach, all parties to the incestuous union are potentially liable, including the juveniles having sex with adults. This is the prevailing approach in most U.S. states, under the original Model Penal Code (MPC), in Germany, Canada, and most of Scandinavia (*see* Silverman 2015, p. 23; Model Penal Code §230.2; Canada Criminal Code s. 155(1); German Criminal Code (StGB) §173; Sweden Brottsbalken, kap.6, §7).

(2) Criminalize both incest involving only adults and incest involving adults and juveniles, but distinguish the way in which such offenses are defined, treating the latter as the more serious offense and holding only the adult liable. This is the approach under the English Sexual Offences Act 2003 as well as under Kansas and Louisiana law.[3]

(3) Do not criminalize incest between consenting adults, but do criminalize incest between adults and juveniles. This is the approach followed in Michigan, Ohio, and New Jersey, and in France since 2010 (French Penal Code Article 222-31-2; Ohio Rev. Code Ann. §2907.03(A)(5); New Jersey Stat. Ann. §§2C:14-2(a)).

(4) Do not criminalize incest as such, but treat an incestuous relationship as an aggravating circumstance for statutory rape (the approach apparently followed in Brazil) (Laws Regarding Incest).

(5) Criminalize statutory rape, but accord no criminal law significance to the fact that the offender and victim are related. This is the law in Rhode Island and in a wide range of civil law jurisdictions that follow the approach first used in the French Criminal Code of 1791—including Argentina, Belgium, China, Côte d'Ivoire, Japan, the Netherlands, Portugal, Russia, South Korea, Spain, and Turkey (though, as indicated above, France itself reinstated a law making incest involving juveniles a crime in 2010).

We talk more below about which of these regimes makes the most sense, but for now it is worth noting simply that this is an exceptionally wide range of variation in the way that a given form of sexual conduct is treated in the criminal law. If nothing else, it suggests that the norms regarding incest-as-crime are far from settled.

How Incest Is Defined Under U.S. Law

Even among those jurisdictions that follow the majority U.S. approach to incest, there is considerable variation in how the offense is defined. Here, we can identify five basic variables: (1) the kind of sexual conduct covered, (2) the nature of the familial relation, (3) whether the offender must know of the existence of a familial relation, (4) how the offense is classified, and (5) how the age of the parties affects liability.

The majority of incest statutes in the U.S., as well as the Canadian Penal Code, prohibit "sexual intercourse" or an "act of sexual penetration" with a relative, but do not prohibit "lesser" sexual acts, such as oral sex (e.g., Canada Criminal Code s.155(1); Georgia Code Ann. §16-6-22; Hawaii Rev. Stat. §§707-741, 572-1; Mass. Gen Law ch.272, §17). A few state statutes also explicitly prohibit anal intercourse, sodomy, or "deviate sexual conduct" (e.g., Kansas Stat. Ann. §21-3602; Arkansas Code Ann. §5-26-202), though some limit the offense to heterosexual relations (e.g., N.M. Stat. Ann. §30-10-3; Wisconsin Stat. Ann. §§944.06, 765.03). A small handful of states take a potentially broader approach to defining the sexual act, making it a crime to have "sexual contact with" or "perform a sex act" with a relation (e.g., Michigan Comp. Laws Ann. §§750.520b, 750.520c; Iowa Code Ann. §709.4).[4]

There is also a good deal of variation regarding the nature of the family relationship between the parties. Virtually all incest statutes apply to sex between parents and their children and between siblings. But beyond that, they vary. A majority of U.S. statutes include sex involving uncles, aunts, nephews, and nieces.[5] Slightly more than half criminalize sex between step-parents and their step-children. A handful of statutes also apply to sexual relationships between first cousins, though several states, interestingly, create an express exemption for cousins to have sex or marry if they are beyond child-bearing age or at least one is sterile.[6]

Another way in which the statutes differ is with respect to the origins of the relationship. The majority approach is to prohibit sex only between blood, biological, or consanguineous relatives (e.g., Kan. Stat. § 21-3601). A few statutes specify that the relationship can be "whole" or "half-blood" (e.g., Oregon Rev. Stat. §163.525). Many specify that the relationship can be "without regard to legitimacy" (e.g., Kentucky Rev. Stat. Ann. §530.020). A significant minority extend the law to non-blood relatives, including relatives by marriage or adoption (e.g., Alabama Stat. §13A-13-3).

Incest statutes also differ with respect to the requirement of mens rea. Under the common law approach, it was enough that the defendant committed the actus reus of having sex with someone to whom he was related; there was no need that he be aware of the relation. Following the original Model Penal Code recommendation, a majority of states now require that the offender know of the prohibited relationship (Silverman 2015, p. 21; e.g., Conn. 53a-191; Alabama 13A-13-3).

Yet another way in which U.S. incest statutes differ is with respect to classi-fication. The traditional approach was to classify incest as an offense "against morality or decency" (Silverman 2015, p. 16). Other states, and the original MPC, treated it as an offense "against the family" or "affecting marital rela-tionships" (MPC § 230.2). The more modern method is simply to classify incest as a "sexual offense."

Finally—and, from a moral perspective, most significantly—statutes differ in how they deal with the age of the parties. As noted above, the majority of U.S. incest statutes do not distinguish between cases involving juveniles and those involving only adults. Nor do they distinguish, for purposes of liability, between the adult "predator" and juvenile "prey." Thus, under the typical U.S. statute, a parent having sex with a juvenile child, the juvenile child herself, two adult siblings having sex with each other, and two juvenile siblings having sex with each other would all be potentially liable to the same degree. In England and Wales, by contrast, the statutes treat juvenile incest and adult incest as entirely separate offenses, contained in separate provisions of the Sexual Offences Act, defined differently and subject to different penalties (Sexual Offenses Act 2003, ss.25, 27).

A Rationale for the Law of Juvenile Incest

Under what circumstances is it justifiable to subject incest to criminal sanc-tions? To answer that question, we first need to have an idea of when it is justifi-able to subject *any* conduct to criminal sanctions. That is, we need a theory of criminalization. But that is a highly complex and controversial matter and no place more so than in the realm of the sexual offenses. Rather than try to devise or defend a foundational theory of criminalization, I shall simply *assume* a ver-sion of the liberal, civil libertarian stance, one that is influenced by the work of J. S. Mill, H. L. A. Hart, and especially Joel Feinberg—a stance that reflects a strong presumption in favor of personal liberty, liberal neutrality, and against government interference in citizens' private affairs. In adopting this approach, I shall be doing so to the exclusion of leading alternative approaches, such as legal moralism and paternalism (though, near the end of the chapter, I shall consider what might be characterized as a "quasi-feminist" approach to crimi-nalizing adult incest).

Under the approach I shall be following, criminal sanctions can be justified only when they will efficiently prevent harm (or possibly "offense") to others (or possibly self). According to Feinberg, "harm" should be understood as comprising a significant "setback to interests" (Feinberg 1984, pp. 37–38).

Typically, this occurs through the infringement of some tangible aspect of V's "welfare interests," in life, bodily integrity and function, freedom of movement, shelter, or sustenance. Acts that set back interests of this sort—including killing, raping, battering, and stealing—are considered "harmful." A corollary of the harm principle is sometimes referred to as the "wrong principle" (Green 2012, pp. 69–73). Not only must conduct cause or threaten harm, it must also be wrongful, typically in the sense that it violates another's rights. Under the traditional liberal approach, harmfulness and wrongfulness constitute necessary, but not sufficient, conditions for criminalization; other factors would also have to be satisfied before criminal sanctions could be fully justified.

So, does incest satisfy the harm and wrong principles? To answer that question, we need to distinguish, at least initially, between incest involving adults and juveniles (discussed in this part) and incest involving only adults (discussed in the next part) (I leave to the side cases of incest between juveniles).

Before we can consider whether and how the fact that an adult and juvenile *are related* should affect the analysis, however, we first need to consider why it should be a crime for an adult to have sex with a minor who is *not* related to him—that is, we need to consider the rationale for criminalizing the standard case of statutory rape. Virtually all legal systems agree that adults who have sex with juveniles should be subject to criminal sanctions, but explaining exactly why this is so is more difficult than it might at first appear. The traditional understanding of statutory rape is that, like people who are unconscious, severely intoxicated, or intellectually disabled, juveniles are "incapable" of consenting. Non-consent, and the violation of sexual autonomy that follows from it, is therefore presumed. I have argued elsewhere, however, that this understanding is problematic and that a better understanding of the strict liability rule in statutory rape would rest on something other than cognitive incapacity (Green 2015, pp. 246–251). I have suggested that a more plausible justification would rest on the notion that when adults have sex with juveniles, there is, in virtue of their age difference, such a significant potential for exploitation that such conduct should be categorically banned.

Fortunately, this issue need not be resolved definitively here. Regardless of the precise nature of wrongs and harms involved in statutory rape, we can still ask if there is any significant moral difference between cases in which an adult and child are related and those in which they are not. In particular, we can ask if the fact that they are related makes the act any *more* wrongful or harmful.

A reasonable argument could be made that, other things being equal, it is typically even worse for an adult to have sex with a related juvenile than with one who is unrelated. Often, the adult will have a special duty of care to the related juvenile. Parents, in particular, have a duty to look out for their minor children's best interests and protect them from harm. When parents (and presumably stepparents) have sex with juvenile children, they invariably engage in a gross violation of such duties. Moreover, the harms done to related juveniles are even worse than those done to unrelated ones. As criminologists

Stephen and Ronald Holmes have explained, "[a] child sexually abused by a relative is different from one abused by a stranger. The incest victim cannot run away and go home for help and comfort" (Holmes and Holmes 2009, pp. 102–103). Researchers have found that juvenile incest victims suffer both short-term and long-term effects, including eating disorders, vomiting, alcohol abuse, suicidal thoughts, and self-mutilation. As the child advances into adulthood, other effects include amnesia, frigidity, promiscuity, and participation in sex work.

Assuming that the wrongs and harms of statutory rape of a closely related juvenile really are greater than those of statutory rape of an unrelated juvenile, it would seem to follow that the former act should be punished more severely. That leaves the question, though, whether such conduct should constitute an entirely separate offense, called "incest," or whether it should simply be treated as an aggravated form of statutory rape.

The question raised is one of fair labeling—the idea that, as Andrew Ashworth has put, "widely felt distinctions between kinds of offences and degrees of wrongdoing are respected and signaled by the law, and that offences should be divided and labeled so as to represent fairly the nature and magnitude of the law-breaking" (Ashworth 2009, pp. 78–80; see also Green 2012, pp. 52–54). How we choose to label and classify offenses sends important signals about why we are criminalizing the conduct, and the priority of wrongs and harms it entails.

If we were to label the offense as "statutory rape of a family member," we would be signaling that the principal wrong was violating a young person's sexual autonomy, which in turn is aggravated by the secondary wrong of doing so with a family member. In contrast, by labeling the offense "incest with a juvenile," we would be signaling that the principal wrong is having sex with a family member, which is aggravated by the fact that the family member is a juvenile.

In my view, the first label, "statutory rape of a family member," reflects the proper prioritization. It sends an accurate signal that the primary wrong or harm in such cases is the sexual exploitation of a juvenile. The alternative, of criminalizing sex with a related juvenile as "incest," leaves the "tail" of breaching a familial duty wagging the "dog" of exploiting a child. To emphasize what is properly the principal wrong, I would therefore make sex with a related juvenile an aggravated form of statutory rape, rather than a form of incest.

Treating sex with a related juvenile as an aggravated form of statutory rape, rather than as a freestanding offense, would also allow us to avoid the possibility of unfair double punishment. The adult who has sex with a juvenile is subject to prosecution for statutory rape whether or not the juvenile is related. If he is also prosecuted on a separate charge of "incest," he faces the possibility of being punished twice for the same conduct. By prosecuting him solely for aggravated statutory rape instead, an unjust result would be avoided.[7]

A Rationale for the Law of Putatively Consensual Adult Incest

Having briefly considered the law concerning incest with a juvenile, we now turn to the law of incest between adults. As noted, it is this form of incest legislation that has attracted the most attention from scholars and courts. Here, there is no chance of redundancy. Assuming that the act is (at least putatively) consensual, that it is not done for pay, does not involve sadomasochism, and is not performed in a public place, there would be no other offense label under which to criminalize it. Thus, we need to ask, straight on, whether consensual adult incest should be a crime. And, if we decide that it should be, then we need to ask exactly how it should be defined, classified, and graded.

In this section, we consider three possible rationales for criminalizing adult incest: (1) it creates a significant risk of birth defects; (2) it confounds well-established family roles and contributes to family conflict; and (3) the putatively consensual nature of such conduct is often illusory and tends to mask deep structural inequalities in family life, especially in those cases in which the incestuous relationship began while one or both of the parties was still a juvenile.[8]

Infringing the Prima Facie Right to Choose One's (Willing) Sexual Partners

Before we consider the possible rationales for criminalizing adult incest, it is important to acknowledge what is at stake here. To prohibit adults from engaging in putatively consensual sex with other (willing) adults to whom they are related is to impose a significant restriction on the prima facie right to choose one's (willing) sexual partners—an important element of sexual autonomy. If such laws are permitted to stand, they will require justification.

How significant an infringement on sexual autonomy would a categorical ban on adult incestuous relationships be? Sherry Colb has sought to compare the burdens imposed by a ban on adult incestuous marriage with those imposed by a ban on same-sex marriage (Colb 2014). Although she is speaking specifically about marriage, her point seems relevant to homosexual and incestuous sexual conduct more generally.

Colb regards bans on incestuous marriage as more defensible than bans on same-sex marriage. As she puts it, "a [same-sex marriage] prohibition effectively prohibits gay men and lesbians from marrying any member of the entire population of potentially desirable partners. The same likely cannot be said of a man who would, absent the incest laws, be inclined to fall in love with his first cousin" (Colb 2014, p. 3). "To my knowledge," she says, "people do not generally have an exclusively incestuous 'sexual orientation.'" Prohibited from having a relationship with a close relative, she seems to be saying, such people can still find desirable partners elsewhere.

I agree with Colb that, given the choice between prohibiting all homosexual sex and prohibiting all incestuous sex, we should certainly choose the latter. But why should we have to make such a choice in the first place? If X and Y desire to have sex with each other and they are siblings, and the state prohibits siblings from having sex, then it follows that both X and Y will be prohibited from having sex with precisely the person with whom they wish to have it. Colb says that a person who is prohibited from having a relationship with a close relative can still find desirable partners elsewhere. But sexual attraction is not normally a fungible good. Think, for example, of the sexual relationship between adult siblings depicted in Paul Auster's novel *Invisible*, as moving as any in contemporary fiction (Auster 2009). Given the passionate attraction Adam and Gwyn feel for each other, it would be little consolation to tell them that they should renounce the relationship on the grounds that there are "other [non-consanguineous] fish in the sea." This is not to suggest that the prima facie right to have consensual sex with a willing, related partner of one's choosing is necessarily indefeasible. It is simply to say that, before prohibiting such conduct, we need a compelling rationale for doing so.

Preventing Birth Defects

Perhaps the most commonly offered harm-based rationale for criminalizing adult incest is that it offers a means of preventing birth defects. It is well settled that procreative sex between closely related, consanguineous partners is substantially more likely to result in birth defects than procreative sex between those who are not related (Wolf and Durham 2004). All of us inherit damaged genes, containing harmful mutations, from our parents. Some genes are dominant, inflict their carriers, and get selected out. Most, however, are recessive and do no harm until the carrier mates with another carrier and they have children together. When we conceive a child with someone to whom we are not closely related, these genes are generally paired with a functional counterpart inherited from the other parent. When close relatives, such as a brother and sister or parent and offspring, have a child together, however, there is a much greater likelihood that the child will inherit two copies of the damaged gene. Inbreeding thus increases the probability that recessive genes will become dominant and activated, with all of the resulting problems that causes. (The risk resulting from unions between first cousins is significantly lower.)

Numerous studies support the view that inbreeding significantly raises the risk of birth defects (most famously, Seemanova 1971). But do such increased risks justify criminalization? One obvious problem is that only a particular subset of all cases of incest poses any such risk—namely, those involving consanguineous fertile partners of the opposite sex having vaginal intercourse without adequate contraception. Under this rationale, incest laws that apply to cases involving people who are not having sex of this sort are clearly overbroad.

How often does adult incest take this form? It is hard to say: the data are sparse; almost all of the studies focus on juvenile, rather than adult, incest (e.g.,

Max Planck Institute 2017). We can, however, carry out a thought experiment: We can ask, what if incest laws were rewritten to apply exclusively to cases involving consanguineous incestuous partners engaged in procreative sex, and what if it were possible to apply such a law only in such cases and not otherwise? Would such a regime be defensible under the harm principle?

Consider, for example, the German case of Patrick Stübing and Susan Karolewski, biological siblings, raised separately, who had four children together, three of whom were born with severe birth defects (Stübing v. Germany). Given such facts, it seems hard to avoid the conclusion that the couple knowingly or recklessly created a risk of serious harm to others that could have been avoided. Isn't that exactly the sort of conduct that should be subject to criminal sanctions in a liberal society?

Perhaps. But note that the criminal law typically views acts as wrongful or harmful based on the effect they have on already-existing victims. Here, however, the act that potentially causes harm to the child is the very one that brings the child into existence in the first place. This fact raises the so-called paradox of future individuals, or nonidentity problem.[9] Had Stübing and Karolewski desisted from conceiving children out of fear they would be born with birth defects, the children would never have come into existence at all. And, assuming that the children's lives are worth living, it could be argued that their conception constituted a net gain in utility. From such a utilitarian perspective, Stübing and Karolewski would arguably have done the right thing.

If this argument were correct, it would have significant implications with respect to criminalization. The liberal harm principle requires that an offender's act cause a victim's interests to be "set back." Here, an argument could be made that the interests of the conceived child were in fact "advanced." If this were true, it would imply that a couple who conceived a child knowing that it was likely to be born with birth defects would in fact have done something good, rather than causing harm or wrong, and for this reason alone, criminalization would be impermissible.

The non-identity problem is no easy one to solve (for an attempt, see Boonin 2014), but there are at least two possible preliminary responses I can think of. One is to reject the utilitarian approach entirely. Conceiving a child whom one knows is likely to have birth defects would be viewed as wrong, deontologically, without regard to any weighing of costs and benefits. To conceive a child in such circumstances would be to risk violating the future child's presumed "right" to live a life unburdened by suffering. The second response is to take on the utilitarian argument on its own terms. I would argue that "existence" is not a basic good against which "bads" like birth defects are to be weighed. Existence itself is neither good nor bad. It becomes good or bad only in reference to the stuff of which it is comprised. To put the matter simply, in some cases, it really is better not to exist at all than to exist in circumstances that involve serious ongoing suffering.

But even if there were agreement that conceiving a child knowing that it was likely to suffer from birth defects was wrong and harmful, and even if adult incest laws could somehow be applied exclusively to fertile consanguineous heterosexual couples having unprotected sex, it is still questionable that such laws would pass muster in a liberal system of criminal law, such as that in the U.S. The problem is countervailing concerns with privacy and sexual autonomy.

The U.S. law involving prohibitions on reproductive rights has gone through a dramatic transformation. During the Progressive Era of the late nineteenth and early twentieth centuries, laws that placed limits on the ability of people with disabilities to reproduce were considered a legitimate method of promoting social progress. In the wake of Nazi-era eugenics practices, however, such policies came to be seen as racist and discriminatory and are now disfavored. Legislation that prohibits individuals with particular characteristics from reproducing seems almost unthinkable today. As a result, *non*-incestuous couples are completely free to conceive children even when they are aware of significant risks of birth defects—such as from Huntington's disease, hemophilia, sickle cell anemia, Down syndrome, Tay-Sachs, or any number of other devastating congenital diseases, many of which can now be prevented through genetic testing and the use of contraception. Yet any attempt to impose criminal sanctions on parents who failed to prevent or terminate such pregnancies, or even obtain genetic testing, would surely be regarded as a gross invasion of privacy and an unacceptable limit on sexual autonomy and reproductive freedom. In short, the idea that incest laws—even when narrowly tailored to apply exclusively to fertile consanguineous heterosexual couples having unprotected sex—can be justified as a means to prevent birth defects seems at odds with contemporary liberal values.

Protecting Family Integrity

Another commonly offered harm-based rationale for prohibiting consensual adult incest is that the practice is believed to be destructive of family integrity: it is said to cause, or exacerbate, rivalries and jealousies and undermine the traditional allocation of roles, within the family structure. Children born of incestuous unions will presumably grow up in highly unconventional family circumstances: for example, a child's father will also be the child's uncle or grandfather; a child's mother will also be the child's half-sibling or cousin. Such blurring of roles, it is argued, is likely to lead to instability and unwarranted stigmatization. Moreover, even when no child is conceived, family relations will be complicated by entangling sexual intimacies: for example, parents will find themselves competing with their own children for the sexual attention of their spouses, and vice versa.

One significant difference between the previously discussed birth defects rationale and the family integrity rationale is that the latter would seem to apply to a much broader range of cases. Family integrity will arguably be threatened regardless of the kind of sexual relations the parties are engaged in (whether procreative or not) and regardless of whether family members are related by blood. If consensual adult incest really did threaten family integrity, that fact should justify a broader definition of sexual activity than under the birth defects rationale.

The problem is, we really do not know the extent to which consensual incestuous relationships between adults affect family stability. As we saw above, there are virtually no data on the incidence of such relationships, their dynamics, or their psychological impact on participants and their families. Almost all of the empirical studies we have concerning the effects of incest on individuals and families involve *juvenile* victims.

Moreover, even if we did have conclusive evidence that consensual adult incest was likely to cause serious family disruptions, that hardly means that criminalization would be justified. Just as the government lacks the authority to prevent people from having procreative sex when the risk of birth defects is high, it would seem to have even less authority to prevent people from engaging in sexual practices that allegedly lead to family dysfunction. The family integrity rationale, relied on by the framers of the original Model Penal Code in justifying the prohibition on adult incest, seems hopelessly dated.[10] In a liberal society such as ours, people are free to engage in all kinds of intimate behaviors. They can be heterosexual, homosexual, bisexual, or asexual; monogamous, promiscuous, celibate, or polyamorous; cisgender or transgender. They can have sexual and romantic relationships with, and marry, people their parents or siblings do not approve of; have affairs; get divorced or separated. They can raise their children in a traditional, heterosexual "nuclear" family, as single parents; in a straight, gay, or lesbian two-parent household; or on a commune or kibbutz. They can be rigid disciplinarians or overly permissive. They can be cosseting "helicopter" parents or parents who leave the job to paid nannies. Any of this conduct may cause great dismay, and even long-term estrangements, within their families. Yet there is little the criminal law can, or presumably should, do about any of it (Bergelson 2013, pp. 48–49; Sebo 2006, p. 49).

If people choose to compete with family members for the sexual attention of other family members, it is arguably their business to do so, even if the impact on their children and other family members itself is highly adverse. In our system of law, children have a right not to be beaten or have their most basic physical needs neglected by their parents. But, for better or worse, they have little legally recognized "right" to be raised in a psychologically healthy household (though such a factor may play a role in child custody decisions). The idea that the law is somehow justified in making it a crime to enter into a particular kind of sexual or romantic relationship because of the impact it might have on family dynamics is illiberal in the same way it would be illiberal to prevent people from conceiving children who are likely to suffer from birth defects.

Preventing Coercive Sexual Relationships

So far, we have been considering the rationale for criminalizing sexual relationships between adult relatives that have been assumed, initially, to be consensual. We now need to consider the possibility that some significant number of adult incestuous relationships, though putatively consensual, will be found, upon further inspection, to be coercive or exploitative.

The suggestion parallels an argument that is frequently made in the context of prostitution laws. Liberals typically argue that prostitution should be legalized to the extent it involves a sexual act between consenting adults (de Marneffe 2010). Many feminists disagree, on the grounds that consent is often illusory; few women, they argue, go into prostitution out of free choice. Understood within what feminists regard as the broader patriarchal social context in which it typically occurs, prostitution seems much less "consensual" than it does through the narrow conceptual lens adopted by liberal theorists (Dempsey 2010). Perhaps adult incest should be understood in an analogous manner: If we dig deeper into the background of adult incestuous relationships, we may find that they are generally less consensual, and more coercive, than liberal theorists might assume.

For purposes of discussion, let us stipulate that at least some subset of cases of adult incest involve sex that *is* genuinely consensual and that the parties who engage in such conduct are exercising important sexual autonomy rights when they do so.[11] Let us further stipulate that a separate subset of cases of adult incest is *not* genuinely consensual and that some of the parties to these encounters will be subject to a significant infringement of their rights in sexual autonomy. Given such as mix, what is the right way to regulate? If we prohibited all cases of adult incest, then some persons would obviously have their rights infringed (by the government): they would be prohibited from engaging in conduct that is truly consensual; the regime would be *overinclusive*. On the other hand, if we prohibited and punished only those cases in which actual non-consent could be demonstrated, we would be bound, as a result of imperfect procedures and incomplete evidence, to miss some cases in which sex was in fact nonconsensual; some infringements of sexual autonomy (by offenders) would thus go uncensured; and the regime would be *underinclusive*.

So how should we achieve an optimal level of enforcement, one which maximizes the rights of people to engage in truly consensual adult incest and minimizes the occurrence of harmful nonconsensual adult incest? One possibility would be to try to narrow the universe of adult incest cases we wish to prohibit. If we could identify those factors that tend to increase the likelihood that a given case of adult incest was nonconsensual, we might be able to reduce both false positives and false negatives.

Though not speaking in the language of under- and overinclusiveness as such, Tatjana Hörnle has identified two types of cases involving adult incest in which she says it is "plausible to assume invalid consent despite the fact that the young woman or young man was legally an adult" (Hörnle 2014, p. 89). The first sort of case occurs when the sexual relationship started while the younger partner was still a juvenile and continued into adulthood. She gives the example of Pola Kinski, whose father, the famed German actor Klaus Kinski, allegedly began to sexually abuse her when she was a child and with whom she continued to have a sexual relationship well into adulthood. Pola describes "how a lonely child's intense need for love creates vulnerability and dependence, and how difficult it can be to free oneself finally from a web of well-established dependencies and psychological pressures" (Hörnle 2014 [quoting Kinski memoir, published in German]). "Under such circumstances," Hörnle says, "it is defensible to deem even those acts that happen at the time when the younger 'partner' became legally an adult as lacking valid consent." A similar kind of abuse, Hörnle says, can occur with siblings and perhaps other relatives.

The second (partially overlapping) type of case occurs when "the social roles are such that there is a clear and evident social split into 'weaker partner' and 'powerful partner.'" What Hörnle has in mind, primarily, are sexual relationships between parents and adult children, so long as the child was raised by the parent for some significant period of time during childhood. This ban would apply even if the relationship began when both parties were already adults and even if the two parties were unrelated by blood.

Hörnle argues that

> Most modern criminal statutes contain norms that extend the definition of "sexual offense" to adults in situations without explicit coercion: for instance, corrections officers and police officers commit a sexual offense if they have sex with an inmate or a suspect in a criminal investigation.... The prisoner's or suspect's approval or disapproval is irrelevant; under such extreme circumstances of dependence, even explicit factual consent does not count as voluntarily given. (Hörnle 2014, p. 91)

In essence, Hörnle's approach to criminalizing (some cases of) adult incest parallels the liberal approach to criminalizing *juvenile* incest: in both contexts, we assume coercion in all cases in order to prevent coercion in some.

I have several concerns with this approach. First, the analogy between adult incest and sex involving corrections and police officers is problematic. In the latter kinds of cases, we are concerned not just with the possibility of sexual coercion but also that justice might be perverted: sex that officers have with inmates and suspects, regardless of whether it is consensual, tends to compromise their duties as officers of the state. In the case of adult incest, such institutional concerns seem less relevant. In a liberal state, as we saw above, criminal law has virtually no legitimate role to play in regulating family life. Moreover, a person who takes on the role of prison guard or police officer does so voluntarily, presumably aware of the limitations such a role places on him, including in the sexual sphere. The same cannot be said of certain familial roles, such as being a sibling. In addition, the relationship between prison guards and inmates, and between police officers and witnesses, is a temporary one; the ban on sex normally ends when the guard or officer leaves the job or when the inmate or witness is released. By contrast, the relationship between family members is enduring; the proposed ban on sex is "for life."

An even more serious problem concerns the lack of empirical data we have concerning incestuous relationships involving adults. If one reads the literature on adult incest, one is struck by the extensive reliance on a small body of anecdotal evidence that may or may not be representative of such cases more generally—essentially, descriptions of cases involving figures such as Patrick Stübing and Susan Karolewski, Klaus and Pola Kinski, and Allen and Patricia Muth.[12] And, though it might be reasonable to speculate that sexual relationships between parents and their children are likely to be coercive, it seems dangerous to base such significant liberty-limiting legislation on non-empirically verified speculations.

For the purpose of discussion, however, let us assume that we did have reliable data indicating a high rate of incidence of coercive sex in one or both of the situations Hörnle identifies. Could a provision that prohibited only adult incest of these sorts survive scrutiny under a liberal theory of criminalization? Note that, even in such narrowed form, such statutes would still be overinclusive: there would still be some set of cases in which truly consensual adult incestuous would be prohibited, thereby infringing the rights of some people to choose the willing sexual partner of their choice.

The problem of overinclusive statutes has attracted the attention of various criminal law theorists. Most of this analysis, however, has focused on the problem of regulatory and *malum prohibitum*-type laws—involving, for example, speed limits and drunk driving. In that context, the problem is this: some skillful drivers will obviously be able to drive carefully even at high speeds or when intoxicated. With respect to them, such laws will be overinclusive; their right to drive safely at high speed or while intoxicated, such as it is, would be infringed. Antony Duff, notably, has argued that such laws *are* tolerable so long as: (1) the burden of obedience is reasonable; (2) we can trust police and prosecutors to recognize, and not to pursue, so-called *de minimis* cases, which do not involve the mischief at which the law is aimed; and (3) their exercise of that discretion can be made appropriately accountable (e.g., Duff 2018, pp. 313–322).

I agree with Duff that there are circumstances in which certain kinds of overinclusive statutes would be tolerable even in a liberal system of criminal justice. In particular, I agree that *mala prohibita* or regulatory statutes of the sort he considers are good candidates for such treatment. The risk and magnitude of harm are high, while the burden of compliance, applicable penalties, and associated stigma are relatively light.

Statutes prohibiting sex between parents and their adult children, however, present a significantly more difficult question. On the one hand, the burden of compliance, penalties, and stigma are all likely to be higher than in the case of speeding and Driving While Intoxicated laws. On the other hand, requiring the state to prove actual coercion in such cases might lead to significant under-enforcement. The kinds of coercion present in such intra-familial cases can be particularly subtle, involving, for example, the withholding of affection as much as the imposition of more direct pressure.

One possible compromise solution would be to treat parent/child-type cases as raising a rebuttable, rather than conclusive, presumption of coercion under a regime of strict liability. Under such a regime, defendants would be permitted to present affirmative evidence that, despite its violating the letter of the law, their relationship was in fact characterized by genuine consent. This would not be a perfect solution: it would intrude into the privacy of some innocent defendants' lives and subject them to stigma that attends even unproved charges of this sort. But it would at least reduce the potentially overinclusive effects of a strict liability regime.

Notes

1. Although the ECHR recognized the right to engage in homosexual conduct much earlier than the US Supreme Court, it has not yet squarely recognized the right to same-sex marriage.
2. For an explanation of how I use that term, see Green (2012, pp. 52–54).
3. Under Section 25 of the Sexual Offences Act 2003, the offender must "intentionally touch" in a "sexual" way a victim who is under age 18 and related to the offender. Section 64, by contrast, applies to those who are over 18 or over 16 (depending on the circumstances), engage in sexual penetration, and are related in the manner described (*see also* Louisiana Rev. Stat. §14:89(A)(2); §14:89.1(A) (2)(a); Kansas Stat. Ann. §21-3602).
4. England and Wales take a significantly different approach. If neither of the parties is a juvenile, then penetrative sex is required (s.64), but if one of the parties is a juvenile, then any "intentional touching" of a "sexual" nature is covered (s.25)—a much broader class of conduct.
5. Among those that do not are Illinois, Kentucky, Montana, Washington, and Wyoming.
6. *See* Arizona Rev. Stat. section 25-101 (cousins may marry if one is 65 or older); Wis. Stat. Ann. Section 765.03 (cousins may marry if woman is 55 or older).
7. Given space constraints, there are three other issues concerning codification that I am unable to address here: (1) how should the sexual act in such an offense be defined?; (2) *which* familial relations should be regarded as relevant aggravators?; and (3) must *D* know that *V* is related to him to be guilty of aggravated statutory rape? Each is dealt in the longer version of this chapter that appears in my forthcoming book titled *Criminalizing Sex: A Unified Liberal Theory.*
8. In the interest of space, I omit consideration of the possibility that adult incest might be justified as an "offense against others."
9. The *locus classicus* is Parfit (1984, p. 361). Interestingly, Feinberg himself, whom I previously cited as a defender of the liberal harm principle, thinks of cases like these as an exception to the harm and offense principles. As he puts it, "for actions and omissions that lead to the existence of new human beings, and perhaps for these actions only, penal legislation based solely on a form of legal moralism would be legitimate" (Feinberg 1988, p. 327).
10. *See* Model Penal Code Commentary §230.2, comment 2(c), p. 406. ("The essentials of a nuclear family are a man and a woman in a relation of sexual intimacy and bearing a responsibility for the upbringing of the woman's children. This institution is the principal context for the socialization of the individual. A critical component of that process is the channeling of the individual's erotic impulses into socially acceptable patterns.")
11. Imagine a case in which children who are biologically related but not raised in the same home meet for the first time as adults and find themselves attracted to each other—a phenomenon that has been called "genetic sexual attraction." It is in some sense the flip side of the Westermarck Effect (*see* Kirsta 2003).
12. The Muths, cohabitating siblings, were defendants in Muth (2005).

REFERENCES

STATUTES

Canada Criminal Code s. 155(1).
English Sexual Offenses Act 2003, ss. 25, 27.
French Penal Code Article 222-31-2.
German Criminal Code (StGB) §173.
Model Penal Code §230.2 and commentary.
Swedish Penal Code (Brottsbalken), kap. 6, §7.
Alabama Stat. §13A-13-3.
Arizona Rev. Stat. section 25-101.
Arkansas Code Ann. §5-26-202.
Connecticut Stat. 53a-191.
Georgia, Code Ann. §16-6-22.
Hawaii Rev. Stat. §§707-741, 572-1.
Iowa Code Ann. §709.4.
Kansas Stat. Ann. §21-3601, 3602.
Kentucky Rev. Stat. Ann. §530.020.
Louisiana Rev. Stat. §14:89(A)(2); §14:89.1(A)(2)(a).
Massachusetts Gen. Law ch. 272, §17.
Michigan Comp. Laws Ann. §§750.520b, 750.520c.
New Jersey Stat. Ann. §§2C:14-2(a).
New Mexico Stat. Ann. §30-10-3.
Ohio Rev. Code Ann. §2907.03(A)(5).
Oregon Rev. Stat. §163.525.
Wisconsin Stat. Ann. §§944.06, 765.03.
Dudgeon v. United Kingdom, 45 Eur. Ct. H. R. (1981) ¶ 52.
Lawrence v. Texas, 539 U.S. 558 (2003).
Lowe v. Swanson, 639 F. Supp. 857 (N.D. Ohio 2009).
Muth v. Frank, 412 F.3d 808 (7th Cir. 2005).
Stübing v. Germany, European Court of Human Rights, Merits and Just Satisfaction (Application no. 43547/08), 2012.
Ashworth, Andrew. 2009. *Principles of criminal law*. 6th ed. Oxford: Oxford University Press.
Auster, Paul. 2009. *Invisible*. New York: Holt.
Bergelson, Vera. 2013. Vice is nice but incest is best: The problem of a moral taboo. *Criminal Law and Philosophy* 7: 43.
Boonin, David. 2014. *The non-identity problem and the ethics of future people*. Oxford: Oxford University Press.
Colb, Sherry. 2014. Is it arbitrary to distinguish incest from homosexuality? Verdict. https://verdict.justia.com/2014/09/17/arbitrary-distinguish-incest-homosexuality. Accessed 23 Feb 2019.
de Marneffe, Peter. 2010. *Liberalism and prostitution*. New York: Oxford University Press.
Dempsey, Michelle. 2010. Sex trafficking and criminalization: In defense of feminist abolitionism. *University of Pennsylvania Law Review* 158: 1729.
Duff, Antony. 2018. *The realm of criminal law*. Oxford: Oxford University Press.

Durkheim, Emil. 1963. *Incest: The nature and origin of the taboo.* Trans. Edward Sagarin. New York: Lyle Stuart. (Orig. Pub. 1897).

Feinberg, Joel. 1984. *Harm to others.* New York: Oxford University Press.

———. 1988. *Harmless wrongdoing.* New York: Oxford University Press.

Freud, Sigmund. 1990. *Totem and taboo* Trans. James Strachey. New York: Norton. (Orig. Pub. 1912–13).

Green, Stuart. 2012. *Thirteen ways to steal a bicycle: Theft law in the information age.* Cambridge, MA: Harvard University Press.

———. 2015. Lies, rape, and statutory rape. In *Law and lies: Deception and truth-telling in the American legal system,* ed. Austin Sarat. New York: Cambridge University Press.

Holmes, Stephen, and Ronald M. Holmes. 2009. *Sex crimes: Patterns and behavior.* 3rd ed. Thousand Oaks: Sage Publications.

Hörnle, Tatjana. 2014. Consensual adult incest: A sex offense? *New Criminal Law Review* 17: 76.

Kirsta, Alix. 2003. Genetic sexual attraction. *Guardian.* https://www.theguardian.com/theguardian/2003/may/17/weekend7.weekend2. Accessed 23 Feb 2019.

Laws regarding incest. Wikipedia. https://en.wikipedia.org/wiki/Laws_regarding_incest#Brazil. Accessed 23 Feb 2019.

Levi-Strauss, Claude. 1969. *The elementary structures of kinship.* Rev. ed. Boston: Beacon Press.

Malinowski, Bronislaw. 1927. *Sex and repression in savage society.* New York: Routledge. (reprint ed. 2002).

Max Planck Institute for Foreign and International Criminal Law. 2017. Incest in criminology and genetics. https://www.mpicc.de/en/forschung/forschungsarbeit/gemeinsame_projekte/inzest/inzest_krim.html. Accessed 23 Feb 2019.

Murdock, George Peter. 1947. *Social structure.* New York: Macmillan.

Oxford English dictionary. 2018. Oxford: Oxford University Press. Online edition.

Parfit, Derek. 1984. *Reasons and persons.* Oxford: Oxford University Press.

Pinker, Steven. 1997. *How the mind works.* New York: Norton.

Sebo, Jeffrey. 2006. The ethics of incest. *Philosophy in the Contemporary World* 13: 49.

Seemanova, E. 1971. A study of children of incestuous matings. *Human Heredity* 21: 108.

Sheper, Joseph. 1983. *Incest: A biosocial review.* New York: Academic Press.

Silverman, Emily. 2015. *The criminalization of incest in the United States of America.* Freiburg: Max Planck Institute for Foreign and International Criminal Law.

Turner, Jonathan H., and Alexandra Maryanski. 2005. *Incest: Origins of the taboo.* Abingdon: Paradigm.

Westermarck, Edvard. 1921. *The history of human marriage.* 5th ed. New York: Macmillan. (Orig. pub. 1891).

Wolf, Arthur, and William H. Durham, eds. 2004. *Inbreeding, incest, and the incest taboo: The state of knowledge at the turn of the century.* Stanford: Stanford University Press.

PART XV

Inchoate Criminality

CHAPTER 16

Inchoate Criminality

Andrew Cornford

Inchoate Crimes: The Case for Skepticism

When we hear the word "crime," we tend to imagine a narrow range of offenses. Murder, assault, rape, robbery, vandalism, theft—for most of us, such offenses of culpably causing harm to person and property constitute the core of the criminal law. However, the criminal law has always extended beyond this core, to encompass offenses—often seriously punishable offenses—that do not involve harm to others or their interests. Notable examples include *inchoate crimes*: offenses that aim to prevent a given ultimate harm by criminalizing conduct prior to the actual causing of that harm.

In recent times, and across jurisdictions, law-makers have radically expanded the scope of inchoate criminality. Inchoate crimes themselves are not a recent invention: the common law tradition, for example, has long criminalized attempting, inciting, and conspiring to commit other crimes. However, these traditional, general offenses are limited in their scope. They typically require an intention that the relevant ultimate harm occur, and they catch only a limited range of conduct: for example, an attempt often requires an act proximate to the actual commission of the intended offense. By contrast, newer inchoate offenses target a wide range of conduct, and sometimes do not require intention—or indeed, any form of culpability—as to the ultimate harm. Metaphorically, these offenses are said to target conduct that is increasingly *remote* from the harm that they aim to prevent.

These newer inchoate crimes serve various purposes and have taken correspondingly various forms (Ashworth and Zedner 2014, pp. 96–102). Some are designed to deal with headline-grabbing threats, such as terrorists, sexual preda-

A. Cornford (✉)
The University of Edinburgh, Edinburgh, UK
e-mail: A.Cornford@ed.ac.uk

361

L. Alexander, K. K. Ferzan (eds.), *The Palgrave Handbook of Applied Ethics and the Criminal Law*, https://doi.org/10.1007/978-3-030-22811-8_16

tors, and organized crime groups. Hence, law-makers have created offenses of *preparing* to commit certain crimes, of *supporting* certain types of criminal activity, and of *membership* or *participation* in certain types of criminal group. Others are designed to deal with more mundane threats. For example, law-makers have created increasingly expansive offenses of *endangerment* and of *possession* of dangerous objects such as weapons or instruments of crime. More subtly, they have also re-defined some traditional offenses in an "inchoate mode": that is, in a way that does not require the occurrence of the relevant ultimate harm. For example, fraud may be re-defined to require only misrepresentation, and not the deception or resulting loss that the offense aims to prevent.

Many are worried by law-makers' increasing readiness to create offenses like these. The reasons behind this readiness are understandable: a key justifying aim of the criminal law is to prevent harm, and all else being equal, it is better to prevent harm by stopping crime before it occurs than by punishing it after it occurs. However, when law-makers focus exclusively on preventive efficacy, they ignore other factors that they ought to consider in making decisions to criminalize. They ignore the fact that criminalization is not like other regulatory tools: it renders citizens liable to punishment, to the stigma of a criminal record, and to the coercive and intrusive enforcement actions of criminal justice officials. This fact, many argue, should lead law-makers to apply special constraints to the creation of inchoate crimes (Ashworth and Zedner 2014, ch. 5; Asp 2013; Husak 2007, ch. 3.III; Simester and von Hirsch 2011, ch. 4–5). Four worries in particular provide reasons for these proposed constraints.

The first and the most serious worry that many people have about inchoate crimes is that they lead to unjust convictions and punishments. States are justified in convicting and punishing their citizens, this worry goes, only if those convictions and punishments are deserved; convictions and punishments are deserved only if they are imposed for conduct that is both culpable and wrongful. To criminalize conduct that is not culpable or wrongful is therefore to facilitate unjust convictions and punishments. The worry is that many inchoate crimes do precisely this because they criminalize conduct that is so remote from the harm that they aim to prevent (Simester and von Hirsch 2011, pp. 59–65, 71–73).

This first worry is easiest to understand if we adopt a *fact-relative* conception of wrongdoing. On such a conception, whether conduct is wrongful depends on the actual facts of the situation. This means that conduct is wrongful only if it actually causes harm to others (or violates their rights, dignity, autonomy, etc.). To help see the point, we can rephrase it in the language of reasons. Wrongful conduct is conduct in which we have decisive reason not to engage. And our reasons against engaging in given types of conduct derive from the actual welfare of others (or their rights, dignity, autonomy, etc.). If conduct has no impact on these things, then there is in fact no reason to avoid it, and it is therefore not wrongful (Raz 1975, pp. 16–20; Gardner and Macklem 2002, pp. 442–450). Herein lies the problem with inchoate crimes: by definition, they criminalize conduct that has no such factual impact.

A second worry about inchoate crimes is their potential disproportionality. Even if an offense criminalizes only conduct that deserves punishment, it might yet be illegitimate because its effects are disproportionate: simply put, its costs might outweigh its benefits. The worry is that inchoate crimes are especially likely to be disproportionate when compared to the traditional core crimes, for two reasons. First, the reasons for their creation are relatively weak: the need to censure and punish the conduct that they target is not as strong as it is for crimes of culpably and directly harming others. Second, the reasons against their creation are relatively strong: they restrict citizens' liberties to a greater extent and afford expansive enforcement powers that are easily abused. Again, law-makers must be sure to weigh these costs and benefits carefully, since an exclusive focus on preventive efficacy will tend to obscure them (Ashworth and Zedner 2014, pp. 103–105; Feinberg 1984, pp. 190–193; compare generally Horder 2012).

A third, related worry is that the creation of these offenses might prove unnecessary. Even if the benefits of criminalization would outweigh its costs, it might still be unjustified, if an alternative to criminalization is available that would be preferable, all things considered. Again, law-makers must consider the unique features of criminalization as a type of regulation. Do they really need to subject inchoate conduct to conviction and punishment or would a nonpunitive response suffice? Since the reasons for creating these offenses are mainly reasons of preventive efficacy, other interventions might prove more appropriate: for example, noncriminal regulation or preventive restrictions of liberty (Ashworth and Zedner 2012, pp. 562–570). Alternatively, even if criminalization is appropriate, law-makers should avoid creating offenses that are more extensive than necessary in their scope (Husak 2007, pp. 153–159, 168–176; compare again Horder 2012, pp. 85–92).

A fourth and final worry is that inchoate crimes are prone to fail even in their own preventive aims. By definition, these offenses criminalize conduct that does not cause the ultimate harm that they aim to prevent; thus, the state need not prove in court any causal connection between the relevant conduct and the relevant harm. Instead, law-makers must satisfy themselves in advance that the former contributes causally to the latter—or at least, that we can prevent the latter by criminalizing the former. However, law-makers are not social scientists: they are likely to get such judgments wrong, and in today's political climate, they are likely to err on the side of risk-aversion. In other words, they will tend to create inchoate crimes where doing so will not actually prevent the relevant ultimate harm. Since prevention is the purported justification for these offenses, law-makers must again take special precautions to avoid such mistakes (Asp 2013, pp. 33–34; Baker 2007, pp. 376–381; Husak 2007, pp. 145–153).

On the face of it, then, we have a strong case for skepticism about inchoate crimes and their expanding scope. But is this case persuasive? I suggest that it is not. While each of the above worries stems from a legitimate concern, they do not justify an attitude of blanket skepticism toward inchoate crimes. The first and the most serious worry—that inchoate crimes lead to unjust convictions and punishments—illustrates this point most clearly. The fact-relative type of wrongdoing described earlier cannot plausibly be required for legitimate criminalization. And once we identify other types of wrongdoing that might suffice for this purpose, inchoate crimes no longer seem problematic, in and of themselves.

The three remaining worries are more persuasive, but, again, fail to justify blanket skepticism about inchoate crimes. Law-makers should certainly consider the necessity and proportionality of all new offenses and the likelihood that they will achieve their preventive aims. But while some inchoate crimes undoubtedly fail on these criteria, others succeed. The reasons against creating such offenses vary in their strength. And the reasons in favor include the strongest reasons for criminalization available to law-makers: the prevention of serious, wrongful harm. In summarizing the legitimacy of inchoate criminalization, the best we can say is therefore: it is complicated. In what follows, I explore some of this complexity, by examining a range of examples of inchoate crimes.

Unleashing Risk: Complete Attempts and Endangerments

Consider first a type of inchoate conduct that has long been criminalized in many jurisdictions: complete attempts. Complete attempters intend to cause harm and have done everything that they need to do in order to do so; but for whatever reason, their plans fail. To take a textbook example: an assassin loads their gun, takes perfect aim, and shoots at their intended victim, only for a passing bird to get in the way and take the bullet. One *could* try to argue that it is illegitimate to criminalize complete attempters like this assassin. They have not done anything wrong, in the fact-relative sense: reasons against action derive from people's actual welfare (or rights or whatever), and no one's welfare is damaged by the assassin's failed attempt. Yet the view that such conduct may not be criminalized seems dangerously false. And, indeed, if legal systems criminalize any inchoate conduct at all, it is conduct like the assassin's.

The obvious explanation for this is that complete attempts are wrongful in a different sense: they unleash an *unjustifiable risk* of harm. When assassins shoot at their targets, they impose risks on them: their conduct is likely to cause them serious harm, and they relinquish full control over whether that harm occurs. Moreover, their conduct is unjustifiable: they lack good reason for imposing such risks. Their conduct is thus wrongful, even though—ultimately and with any luck—the relevant harm might not occur.

The wrongness of unjustified risking is easy enough to understand. Perhaps true wrongness derives from actual harmfulness; but in the real world, the actual harmfulness of our actions is rarely certain in advance. We must therefore rely on judgments about risk: about the harms that our actions might cause, about the probability of their occurrence, and about whether these possible harms outweigh the possible benefits of our actions. Judgments about risk are not, strictly speaking, fact-relative. Rather, they are *belief-* and *evidence-relative*: they are judgments of how frequently we might expect a harm to occur, given what we believe about the situation or the evidence available to us.

However, precisely because we often have only limited evidence about the results of our actions, such judgments can and should play a genuine role in guiding our conduct. Even if risks are not factual wrongs, they can thus be wrongs for which we may fairly be blamed—including, potentially, through criminal conviction and punishment.

By recognizing the wrongness of unleashing risk, we can also explain the potential legitimacy of another group of inchoate crimes: endangerment offenses. Whereas attempts involve risks of intended harm, endangerment involves risks of unintended harm. Most endangerment offenses criminalize only specific types of risky conduct: stock examples are offenses of careless or dangerous driving. But some jurisdictions also criminalize the unleashing of risks more generally, through offenses of reckless endangerment. These offenses are not "general" in the same sense as the traditional inchoate crimes: they do not create an auxiliary form of liability that applies to all offenses. Rather, they criminalize the risking of certain harms (such as death or injury) without requiring conduct of specific types (such as driving). Since such conduct can be wrongful, the state might be justified in convicting and punishing citizens for it, even when the harm risked does not occur.

It does not follow, of course, that law-makers *should* create general offenses of reckless endangerment. Even if these offenses target wrongful conduct, their creation might be disproportionate because of their unwelcome side effects. By definition, these offenses catch a wide range of conduct: often, the only significant limitations on their scope are evaluative criteria, such as the unjustifiability or unreasonableness of the relevant risk. But the inevitable vagueness of such criteria grants significant interpretive power to prosecutors and courts. They are left to make what are effectively policy decisions about the reasonableness of risky conduct of different types—decisions that, arguably, they are not best-placed to make. A powerful example is the widespread use of reckless endangerment provisions to prosecute people for transmitting human immunodeficiency virus (HIV) and other sexually communicable diseases. Whether such conduct should be criminalized is a difficult and delicate issue; arguably, therefore, it should be settled by legislators rather than officials (Tadros 2001; Clarkson 2005, pp. 137–143).

By contrast, law-makers have relatively strong reasons to criminalize some specific types of risky conduct. Doing so ensures that we can prevent and punish the unleashing of serious risks, while avoiding unwelcome effects like those just described. This is true especially in regulated contexts—such as driving, environmental protection, and health and safety at work—where the applicable standards of care can easily be clarified and publicized. Of course, there are also problems with relying solely on specific endangerment offenses. The resulting law is complex and piecemeal: it fails to catch some risky conduct that we might want to prevent and punish. But the desirability of prevention and punishment do not, by themselves, legitimize criminalization. Given the drawbacks of general endangerment offenses, they are less readily justifiable than their specific counterparts (Clarkson 2005; Duff 2005, pp. 57–59).

Preparatory Offenses

To recognize the wrongness of unleashing risk, however, is not a big concession for the inchoate crime skeptic. The most worrisome inchoate crimes target risks of harm that have not yet been unleashed: that is, where the ultimate harm will occur only if further action is taken in the future, whether by the actor him- or herself or by a third party. These offenses are referred to variously as *preventive, pre-emptive, prophylactic,* or *pre-inchoate* offenses. Their most discussed subcategory is *preparatory* offenses: offenses that criminalize conduct performed with the intention of causing harm, but at a relatively early stage in the actor's plan, before the risk of that harm is finally unleashed.

The view that preparatory conduct is not wrongful, and therefore may not be criminalized, has radical implications. It delegitimizes not only many of the newer inchoate crimes but also the traditional, general inchoate offenses. Consider liability for attempting crime. Although jurisdictions vary in the extent to which they do this, many criminalize some preparatory conduct through the general offense of attempt. Put differently, many jurisdictions recognize that there can be *incomplete attempts*: attempts where actors have not yet done all that they need to do in order to cause their intended harm. For example, imagine again an assassin who has loaded their gun, aimed at their victim, and placed their finger on the trigger. This time, however, the police intervene before any shots are fired—before any risk of harm is unleashed. To punish this assassin—indeed, to punish them *as an attempted murderer*—will strike many as unproblematic. Could the criminalization of their conduct really be illegitimate?

Some bite the bullet and answer "yes." To decriminalize such conduct might seem radical, but that is the price we must pay for avoiding unjust punishments. Preparatory actors, even incomplete attempters like our assassin, have not yet done anything wrong: they have not yet caused or unleashed any risk of harm. Such actors, the argument will go, have merely formed an intention to do harm. But forming a harmful intention is not, by itself, a culpable and wrongful act. Intentions are always revocable: as autonomous agents, we can always abandon them, and we retain full control over whether they will lead to harmful action. Of course, we may think badly of those who form harmful intentions. We may even take coercive preventive action against them, if this proves necessary. But when it comes to criminal conviction and punishment, preparatory conduct simply is not wrongful—and so states must give us "room to repent" (Alexander and Ferzan 2009, ch. 6, 2012a, b; for different arguments for similar results, see, e.g., Asp 2013, pp. 35–45; Ramsay 2010, pp. 214–220; Wallerstein 2007a, b).

But while preparatory conduct admittedly neither causes nor risks the relevant ultimate harm, it can arguably be wrongful in other ways. First, although preparatory conduct does not *unleash* a risk of harm, it can increase the probability that such a risk will be unleashed in the future. As criminal plotters progress with their plans, they take more of the steps that are necessary to ensure their success. They also progressively reaffirm and concretize their harmful intentions; they repeatedly confront the opportunity for abandonment and fail to take it (Ohana 2007, pp. 117–126). This line of thought provides a stronger justification for criminalizing the later stages of preparation than the earlier stages: it more readily justifies criminalizing assassins with their finger on the trigger than would-be assassins researching the heights of local rooftops. Nevertheless, it is an attractive explanation of why preparatory conduct might be wrongful, since it remains grounded in the relationship between that conduct and the occurrence of the ultimate harm.

Still, this explanation cannot *fully* rationalize the criminalization and punishment of preparatory conduct. Much preparatory conduct, even late-stage preparatory conduct, does not increase the risk that the actor will succeed: this may remain unlikely, due to external circumstances, the actor's own incompetence, or just plain bad luck. Moreover, the thought fails to capture *why* many are comfortable with the criminalization of some preparatory acts. Compare again the law of attempts. Attempts are not criminalized (only) because they risk completion: some criminal attempts, such as impossible attempts, carry no such risk. Rather, we criminalize attempts because they involve *trying* to commit a crime (Yaffe 2010, pp. 27–31). Analogous things seem true of preparatory conduct: acting on an intention to cause harm can itself deserve punishment, regardless of the probability of eventual success.

This leads us to a second explanation of the wrongness of preparatory conduct: acting on an intention to do wrong is itself wrongful (Tadros 2016, ch. 16). At the outset, we must acknowledge that this explanation is controversial. It requires us to accept that our mental states—the intentions with which we act—can render our otherwise-permissible conduct impermissible. This phenomenon has proved difficult to explain without simply appealing to our shared intuitions. Equally, however, we must acknowledge that these intuitions are strong. Those who have made substantial progress with a criminal plan, but then abandoned it, seem materially different from those who have never made such a plan: we may blame the former for what they have done, at least to an extent. Indeed, the intended victims of such plans could plausibly even feel wronged, were they to learn of them. Such reactions suggest that preparatory conduct might be wrong in itself and therefore potentially a legitimate target for criminalization and punishment (Duff 2012, pp. 134–142; Levenbrook 1980, pp. 58–59).

However, the view that preparatory conduct is wrong in itself might also be thought to have radical implications. It suggests that very early-stage preparatory conduct—conduct that seems outwardly to be entirely innocent—can potentially be legitimately criminalized. To see the problem, consider an example of a very broad preparatory offense: the offense of preparing acts of terrorism, under Section 5 of the UK's Terrorism Act 2006. This offense criminalizes anyone who intends to either commit or assist an act of terrorism and who "engages in any conduct in preparation for giving effect to [this] intention." Suppose a would-be terrorist forms an intention to bomb a city's metro system.

Acting on this intention, they download a metro map, to see which stations might be suitable targets. Downloading a metro map, one might argue, is entirely innocent conduct. Yet in this case, under the UK law, it is a crime punishable by imprisonment for life. Many will find this objectionable, suggesting that action on wrongful intentions does not, in fact, warrant punishment in and of itself.

To infer from this intuition that early-stage preparatory conduct cannot be wrongful is, however, too quick. The wrongness of a given type of conduct might be necessary for its legitimate criminalization, but it is not sufficient: even if it is wrong for prospective terrorists to buy metro maps, it does not follow that this should be criminal. And indeed, law-makers have good reasons to be cautious about criminalizing early-stage preparation. These reasons derive especially from how such conduct must be proved. Early preparatory acts are often distinguished from truly innocent conduct only by the intention with which they are performed. But by definition, this intention cannot be inferred from the acts themselves: it must instead be inferred from circumstantial evidence. Likely sources of such evidence include actors' opinions, demeanor, and associations with other known criminals. It is easy to see how, in relying exclusively on such sources, courts and prosecutors might err in their findings of harmful intent.

Besides this obvious risk of unjust convictions, the criminalization of early-stage preparation also risks intrusive enforcement. Officials will easily form *suspicions* of terrorist intent. But to confirm those suspicions, they will need to investigate suspects' opinions and associations—most probably through covert surveillance, or seizure of their phones or computers. Broad preparatory offenses are thus likely to damage citizens' liberty and privacy. Meanwhile, the wrongness of "buying metro maps with intent" may be relatively modest; a censuring and punitive response to such conduct may not be urgently needed. In short, the costs of criminalizing such early-stage preparation may greatly outweigh the benefits—even if, in theory, conviction and punishment for such conduct would be just.

This need not be true, by contrast, for offenses that criminalize only late-stage preparation. Consider another type of preparatory conduct that is now criminalized in many jurisdictions: the "grooming" of children for sexual purposes. Compared to the terrorist preparation offense described earlier, grooming offenses often criminalize only a limited range of conduct. For example, they might criminalize only adults who have contacted a child over the Internet on multiple occasions and who have actually traveled to meet that child. Those who have reached this stage in their plans are highly likely both to intend to abuse the child and to succeed in doing so. Although some ostensible groomers are indeed fantasists, they quit their plans at earlier stages. By limiting grooming offenses in these ways, law-makers thus minimize their impact on those who are not prospective abusers and focus on the conduct that there is strongest reason to punish (Sorell 2017; Ohana 2006, pp. 30–31). Grooming offenses are thus more likely to be proportionate than offenses encompassing early-stage preparation.

Some might insist, however, that this is not a satisfactory reply to concerns about the criminalization of outwardly innocent conduct. Such criminalization, they might argue, is objectionable *in principle*. While the above reply gives valid reasons against such criminalization, these reasons could be outweighed, if the ultimate harm were serious and extensive enough—as it might be, arguably, in the context of terrorism. But, the argument might continue, this cannot be right. We can and should distinguish between wrongful and innocent types of preparatory conduct. The former might include (say) building a bomb and putting it on a train. The latter might include buying matches or downloading maps. The mere fact that the latter conduct is intended to facilitate the former is not enough to render it wrongful—or at least, wrongful in a sense that should interest the criminal law (Simester 2012; compare Brudner 2009, pp. 108–130).

This purported distinction between wrongful and innocent preparatory conduct cannot, however, be drawn satisfactorily. The idea that some conduct is inherently innocent is perhaps plausible. But it is plausible because of our preexisting ideas about why we would engage in conduct of different types. There are many imaginable innocent reasons for downloading maps; there are no such reasons for building and setting a bomb. The puzzle is how such generalizations about types of conduct could influence the permissibility of token preparatory acts. If I download a map for terrorist purposes, my reasons are not innocent. How could the fact that *other people* regularly download maps for innocent purposes grant *me* the permission to do so for terrorist purposes? True, this fact might make my terrorist purpose more difficult to prove—which, as noted earlier, generates reasons against criminalizing such conduct. But how it could have normative force—how it could render my conduct non-wrongful—is difficult to see (compare Tadros 2016, pp. 314–315).

Conviction and punishment for preparatory conduct, then, do not seem inherently unjust. But even so, there remains a further objection to the criminalization of such conduct: that there are alternative ways of dealing with it that law-makers should prefer. In particular, they could authorize *preventive restrictions of liberty* for those who are preparing criminal attacks. Law-makers should prefer this option, it might be argued, because it is a more parsimonious means of achieving their aims. The main reasons for creating preparatory offenses arise from their potential to prevent harm—and not from the need to censure or punish the conduct that they target. We should thus prefer a legal regime that prevents harm without censuring or punishing. Moreover, such a regime allows the state to tailor its response to the threat posed by specific preparatory actors. It could therefore mitigate the costs of criminalizing preparatory conduct in general terms, such as the expansion of enforcement powers and the restriction of innocent citizens' liberties. Law-makers should thus prefer such a regime, even if conviction and punishment for preparatory conduct can in theory be just (Ferzan 2011; Alexander and Ferzan 2012a; compare Ohana 2006).

This objection highlights an important point, but once again, it is not decisive against all preparatory offenses. If law-makers are considering such offenses solely for reasons of preventive efficacy, then they should certainly also consider other, less costly means of achieving this aim. But as we have seen, the reasons behind preparatory offenses need not be solely preventive. Some late-stage preparatory conduct—which evidences a firm intention to cause harm and makes the occurrence of that harm significantly more likely—may indeed warrant a censuring and punitive response. (Although exactly how serious a response may be difficult to determine: compare Alexander and Ferzan 2012b, pp. 111–117; Duff 2012, pp. 133–134.) Nor are preventive restrictions of liberty necessarily a less costly option than criminalization. Existing regimes of such restrictions are in some ways more costly: they ground liability in predicted dangerousness rather than proven past conduct, and they avoid the procedural protections afforded to defendants in the criminal justice system (see generally Ashworth and Zedner 2014; compare Ferzan 2011, pp. 177–186, arguing that these costs can be avoided). Whether such restrictions are preferable to criminalization must therefore be judged on a case-by-case basis.

In short, while law-makers should indeed be cautious about creating preparatory offenses, there is probably no decisive objection to their doing so. Unless we take the radical view that all wrongs involve harming or risking—in which case, even the criminalization of attempts is illegitimate—we should accept that preparatory conduct can potentially be legitimately criminalized. Admittedly, the view that preparatory conduct is wrong in itself is also problematic. But at least for late-stage preparatory conduct, for which there is no innocent explanation, this view will surely attract support. All things considered, criminalization seems a potentially appropriate response to conduct of this kind.

Indirect Endangerment

A second type of preventive or pre-emptive offense is offenses of *indirect endangerment*. These offenses are similar to preparatory offenses, in that the occurrence of the relevant ultimate harm depends on someone's future conduct. But whereas preparatory offenses concern the actor's own future conduct, offenses of indirect endangerment concern the conduct of third parties. They are, put simply, offenses of *assisting* or *encouraging* the potential harmful conduct of others. Herein lies the fundamental worry about these offenses: by definition, the relevant ultimate harm seems to be the responsibility of the third party rather than the person criminalized. Can it be just to convict and punish citizens for taking a risk that *other people* will cause harm?

Andrew Simester and Andreas von Hirsch (2011) answer that this is not always just. The problem, they say, is *fair imputation*: what makes it fair to impute to one person the autonomous choices of another person? In truth, however, the language of imputation does not accurately capture their concern with offenses of indirect endangerment. For their worry is not that these offenses criminalize those who lack causal responsibility: surely we can contribute causally to ultimate harms *by* contributing to others' harmful actions (Simester and von Hirsch 2011, pp. 59–63). Rather, their worry is that these offenses criminalize those who have not acted wrongly. Ordinarily, they think, our actions do not become wrongful merely because they might lead to other people acting wrongly. In justifying offenses of indirect endangerment, the key question for law-makers is thus the *normative* relevance of the prospect that third parties might cause the relevant ultimate harm. Why does this prospect render the criminalized conduct wrongful (Simester and von Hirsch 2011, pp. 71–73)?

The answer to this question, Simester and von Hirsch argue, depends on the actor's *normative involvement* in the third party's conduct. It is not enough to show a causal link between the actor's conduct and the ultimate harm, even an entirely foreseeable one; the actor must also be responsible for that harm, in the sense that it is his or her "lookout" (Simester and von Hirsch 2011, pp. 63–65). Sometimes, such responsibility will be easy to find: actors may occupy a role that makes them responsible for the third party's conduct. But absent such special responsibility, actors must make *themselves* responsible, by "affirming or underwriting" the conduct. Those who intentionally assist or encourage another's harmful conduct are easily seen as affirming or underwriting it. But the same is not true for those who assist or encourage harm unintentionally—who do things that risk helping or inspiring others to cause harm, but without meaning to do so. To justify the criminalization of such conduct, say Simester and von Hirsch, something more is required (2011, pp. 79–85; for an alternative view, compare Duff 2005, pp. 62–64).

To illustrate the implications of this view, consider conduct that risks encouraging others to cause harm. Law-makers may be justified in criminalizing such conduct, Simester and von Hirsch would argue, if the encouragement is intentional: here, there is sufficient normative involvement in the ultimate harm to render the encouragement wrongful. General inchoate offenses of inciting or soliciting crime, which typically require such an intention, are thus potentially legitimate. By contrast, if the encouragement is unintentional, then the required normative involvement is probably missing. Consider, for example, the offenses of encouraging and glorifying terrorism that have been created in some jurisdictions. These offenses extend beyond direct incitement to criminalize abstract statements of support for certain ideologies, or portrayals of terrorist acts in a way that risks inspiration or imitation (Hunt 2007; Petzsche 2017). Again, the point is not that we lack a proven, foreseeable causal link between such conduct and the ultimate harm of terrorist attacks. The point is that it is illegitimate to criminalize such conduct *even if* there is such a link: without further normative involvement in the ultimate harm, such conduct is not wrongful and thus may not be punished (Simester and von Hirsch 2011, pp. 82–83).

Many have been influenced by Simester and von Hirsch's approach to offenses of contributing to another's crimes (see, e.g., Ashworth and Zedner 2014, pp. 111–113; Baker 2007; Dempsey 2005; Levanon 2012; Wallerstein 2007a). Yet despite its influence, it fails to provide compelling reasons for skepticism about such offenses. The argument is meant to show that conviction and punishment for these offenses is often unjust: that the conduct that they target is often non-wrongful. It therefore rests on a key implicit premise: that the intervening actions of third parties normally cancel our reasons to avoid causing harm to others. Only if we are normatively involved in those actions, the argument must go, are these reasons reinstated. But it is unclear why these reasons would be eliminated, simply because the causal route to (potential) harm goes through a third party. As we saw earlier, it is wrong to unleash an unjustifiable risk of harm to others; so why would this become non-wrongful, simply because the risk takes the form of another person's actions? Simester and von Hirsch do not provide an answer, and as long as we accept that we can contribute causally to one another's actions, it is hard to see where one might be found (Cornford 2013, pp. 492–494; Alexander and Ferzan 2018, pp. 19–24).

It does not automatically follow, of course, that offenses of indirect endangerment are legitimate. While we generally have reasons to avoid assisting or encouraging others' harmful conduct, we also have reasons to be cautious about criminalizing such assistance or encouragement. One reason is that conduct can be socially valuable, all things considered, despite assisting or encouraging harm as a side effect. If the risks of such harm are sufficiently small, and the social value sufficiently large, then such conduct might not be wrongful: although it involves a risk of harm from third parties, that risk might be justifiable. For example, discussions or portrayals of terrorist violence might contribute slightly to radicalization but also contribute greatly to artistic work, academic research, or important debates of social and political morality. The latter benefits might justify the former risk—in which case, it would be unjust to convict and punish citizens in respect of such discussions or portrayals.

A further justification for conduct that might assist or encourage others to cause harm derives from our liberty interests. If we are forced to refrain from such conduct because it might contribute to others' wrongful actions, then in effect, our liberties are restricted by others' propensities to act wrongfully. Again, such interference with our options is no license to ignore the fact that our conduct might assist or encourage harm. But it might contribute modestly to the justification of those risks: plausibly, we have an interest not only in our liberties themselves but also in their immunity from wrongful restriction by others. This interest might help to justify conduct that assists or encourages harm, and thus tell against its punishment, when the risks are sufficiently small (Alexander and Ferzan 2018, pp. 24–26).

Another reason for caution about offenses of indirect endangerment is their tendency to produce chilling effects. These effects result from the enforcement powers that these offenses afford and how these powers can be used in practice. For example, suppose that law-makers try to address the concern just mentioned: they insist that unintended risks of encouragement are criminal only if they are unjustified. Even so, we should remain skeptical about an offense defined in this way. As we saw earlier, an unjustifiability criterion provides little concrete guidance to officials. They are thus likely to interpret it in an unduly risk-averse way: they are likely to prosecute and convict some people whose conduct was actually or at least arguably justified. This is worrying not only because of the unjust punishments to which it will lead but also because of the conduct that it will deter. If citizens wish to avoid involvement with the criminal justice system, then they will have to avoid certain valuable forms of expression—sometimes even justified forms. Worse, this effect will be especially strong among particular cultural and ideological groups—often already marginalized—on whom officials are known to focus. These effects might render these offenses disproportionate, even when they target conduct whose punishment would be just (Cornford 2013, pp. 499–502).

A final reason for caution is that these offenses are prone to fail in their preventive aims—especially where they do not require proof that the conduct criminalized makes the ultimate harm more likely. This is true of some of the terrorist encouragement offenses mentioned above: although these offenses require "encouraging" conduct, they may not require that anyone actually *be encouraged* to commit terrorist acts. Theorists have long doubted whether the causal links between media communications and behavior are strong enough to ground criminalization (see, e.g., Feinberg 1984, pp. 238–240). And more recently, these doubts have been strengthened through empirical research. One recent review of meta-studies suggests that this relationship is highly conditional: it depends on several variables, most of which are unrelated to the form or content of the communication (Valkenburg et al. 2016). Whether conduct is truly "encouraging" is thus a difficult question, and officials and courts may tend to be unduly risk-averse in their answers. Before law-makers criminalize such conduct, they should be satisfied that, in its context, it is truly likely to encourage the ultimate harm.

Once again, then, there is no decisive objection to offenses of indirect endangerment, although there are certainly reasons for caution. The creation of these offenses can have socially damaging implications. And we can easily conclude too quickly that a given type of conduct will actually assist or encourage others to cause harm. However, conduct can be wrongful, and can justly be punished, simply because it might have this result. If law-makers can address the above concerns, offenses of indirect endangerment are potentially legitimate.

POSSESSION OFFENSES

Despite all the above, however, there remain some inchoate crimes that target conduct that seems neither culpable nor wrongful. Consider, for example, offenses of "mere" or "simple" possession: offenses that criminalize the possession of dangerous articles such as weapons, without requiring an intention to use the article to cause harm. Based on what we have seen so far, possession of dangerous articles might sometimes be wrongful. For example, it might be part of one's own plot to cause an ultimate harm, or it might unleash an unjustifiable risk that others will use the article harmfully. But possession offenses also criminalize conduct that involves no such plot or risk. Some argue, therefore, that they can be criticized as *over-inclusive*: they target a narrow range of wrongful conduct, but do so by criminalizing a wider range of more easily proven conduct, much of which is entirely innocent (Ashworth 2011; Dubber 2005; Husak 2004; compare Baker 2009). They therefore risk the unjust conviction and punishment of those who have done nothing wrong.

To illustrate this criticism, consider an article whose criminalization is especially controversial: guns. Imagine that you enjoy shooting as a sport, and that you own a handgun for this purpose. You have no criminal intentions in which your handgun might play a part. Moreover, since you are entirely stable and responsible, you are unlikely to develop any such intention in the future. Of course, it is theoretically possible that a third party might steal your gun and use it to cause harm. But you are alert to this possibility: you keep your gun in a locked case, which you store in a safe; and when the gun is out of its case, you never let it out of your hands. Are you doing anything wrong simply by possessing a gun? Not obviously. Yet in some jurisdictions, you are committing a serious criminal offense, punishable by several years' imprisonment. This, the critics argue, is unjust: in the absence of any culpability for the relevant ultimate harm, you simply do not deserve punishment for your actions (Husak 2004, 2007, pp. 170–173).

How might proponents of handgun criminalization respond to this criticism? First, they might argue that possessing handguns is indeed wrongful, but in a way that we have not considered so far. Some conduct, they might point out, is not wrong in itself but becomes wrongful as a result of its legal regulation. In the familiar jargon: there exist not only *mala in se* offenses but also *mala prohibita*. Sometimes, law-makers have good reason to use the criminal law as a regulatory tool: to create rules that prohibit certain conduct, on pain of punishment, even though that conduct is not otherwise wrongful. And sometimes, breach of such rules becomes wrongful, in part because they are created and enforced by a competent authority. For example, before the state enacts and enforces a tax code, we have no duty to pay specific taxes; but once it does, we do. Tax evasion, in other words, becomes a genuine *malum prohibitum*. Once we acknowledge this possibility, the earlier criticism of possession offenses is no longer necessarily decisive.

To see why some possession offenses might plausibly be seen as genuine *mala prohibita*, return to the example of gun possession. Why might law-makers want to criminalize gun possession, when as we have seen, only some instances of such conduct are *mala in se*? The obvious answer is that they might want to disincentivize gun ownership. Since guns can cause such serious harm, yet are so easy to use, law-makers have strong reason to restrict their availability—not only to prevent wrongful types of possession but also to reduce the risks of, for example, accident, suicide, and future wrongful use. Of course, whether legislation can actually achieve these aims is a contested question. But there is some evidence that it can: in the most comprehensive metastudy to date, relatively strong evidence was found for the effectiveness of restrictions on owning and carrying guns (albeit subject to serious caveats about methodological challenges: see Santaella-Tenorio et al. 2016). If this evidence is sound, then law-makers might have good reason to regulate the mere possession of guns, since this will prevent more harm than regulating wrongful possession alone.

To justify criminalizing gun possession, however, not only do law-makers need good reasons for regulating this conduct; it must also be wrong for citizens to breach the resulting regulation. In this context, breach might be wrongful because of our duties to promote one another's security: if we can take collective action to make each other safer, at a sufficiently low cost to our collective liberty, then we ought to do so. By criminalizing gun possession, law-makers determine one form that such collective action will take. Moreover, this determination becomes binding, since our security will be enhanced only if enough of us obey the regulation. This argument is, of course, controversial: it depends on a particular view of the state's power to obligate its citizens, and any such view will be contested. But for our purposes, it is enough that this view is not obviously unreasonable, and seems acceptable from a range of political viewpoints. Inchoate crime skeptics should thus take seriously the possibility that possession offenses—and indeed, offenses of other kinds—might be justified as *mala prohibita* (Cornford 2015; for related arguments, see Horder 2012, pp. 96–100; Ripstein 1999, pp. 255–260; Tadros 2008, pp. 943–947, 2012, pp. 165–172).

Admittedly, however, even viewing gun possession as a *malum prohibitum* offense might not completely answer the concern about over-inclusion. Any purported such offense will be vulnerable to counterexamples of *harmless disobedience*: cases where a person commits the offense, but without apparently eroding other citizens' security. Imagine again that you are a conscientious gun-owner who enjoys shooting for leisure. If the safety measures that you take are sufficiently stringent, then not only will you avoid committing any *malum in se*; you might avoid imposing any risks to others' security *at all*. In that case, would you have done anything that deserves conviction and punishment— even wrongfully breaching a regulation? Again, the answer will depend on one's view of political obligation, but it seems unlikely (Tadros 2016, pp. 329–332). Even if the earlier argument is sound, the criminalization of gun possession might thus remain unjustifiably over-inclusive.

This leads us to a second potential argument for the legitimacy of possession offenses, notwithstanding their over-inclusiveness: sometimes, conduct may legitimately be criminalized even though it is not wrongful. So far, we have assumed that non-wrongful conduct may *never* be criminalized because when states punish their citizens for such conduct, they act unjustly. But arguably, the premise here does not entail the conclusion. Even if criminalization would lead to some unjust convictions and punishments, it might still be justified, if there are sufficiently strong reasons for criminalization that outweigh this potential injustice. Although many will see this rejection of a "wrongness constraint" on criminalization as the nuclear option, a reasonable case can again be made for it (Cornford 2017; Edwards 2017; Tadros 2016, pp. 96–100). If the potential for undeserved punishment is sufficiently limited, and the reasons for criminalization sufficiently strong, then over-inclusive criminalization might be justifiable.

These conditions can arguably be satisfied for the criminalization of gun possession. First, law-makers can minimize the impact of such criminalization on the truly innocent: they can offer them controlled and/or conditional access to some types of guns, for example, while reserving absolute prohibition for the most dangerous types. Second, law-makers have good reasons to define gun possession offenses in an over-inclusive way: that is, to criminalize possession itself, and not just the various types of wrongful possession. These reasons include clarity and ease of application but also preventive efficacy. As we saw earlier, the criminalization of mere possession will arguably prevent significantly more harm than the criminalization of wrongful possession alone. Increasing the security of the many in this way might justify decreasing the security of a few from conviction and punishment—especially when these latter harms are easy for citizens to avoid (Tadros 2016, pp. 332–333).

By contrast, some other offenses of mere possession will not be justifiable in this way: in particular, those criminalizing articles that are less dangerous than guns. Notable examples are the offenses created in some jurisdictions that criminalize the possession of instructional materials for terrorists, such as training manuals. Law-makers will struggle to minimize the impact of such offenses on the truly innocent, since material that assists terrorists will probably also assist ordinary people in some ways. Likewise, they have only weak reasons to define these offenses in an over-inclusive way. In this context, criminalizing mere possession is unlikely to prevent significantly more harm than criminalizing possession with terrorist intent—partly because criminalization is unlikely actually to reduce the availability of the relevant materials. Additionally, the costs of these offenses include lengthy prison sentences that treat the truly innocent like actual terrorist offenders. These costs are unlikely to be outweighed by the modest security benefits of these offenses (Cornford 2015, pp. 23–27; McSherry 2008; Tadros 2008, pp. 965–969).

Overall, then, there is no decisive argument against even these most inchoate of inchoate crimes. We surely owe some duties to promote one another's security, which may justify the punishment of some criminal possession. And even potential undeserved punishments may be justified by the security benefits of having possession *offenses* (although this raises the difficult further question of how severe such punishments can legitimately be). The charge that these offenses are over-inclusive certainly demands a serious answer—but the prevention of harm can arguably provide that answer. The remaining question for law-makers is how far this justification can be stretched.

Over-Inclusion in Inchoate Crimes

Preventive efficacy is a tempting rationalization for over-inclusive crimes. By defining offenses in an over-inclusive way—for example, by criminalizing all gun possession, rather than just wrongful gun possession—law-makers can prevent more of the ultimate harm with which they are concerned. This is partly because such offenses might deter a wider range of potentially harmful conduct. But also, they afford wider enforcement powers, which can be used to disrupt or incapacitate dangerous actors. It is easier, for example, to arrest a potential killer on suspicion of possessing a gun than of possessing a gun with intent to kill. Yet, as we have seen, there are also strong reasons against creating over-inclusive offenses. To what extent can preventive efficacy justify offenses that authorize the conviction and punishment of the undeserving? We can answer this question here only superficially, but it is worth doing so, since so many recently enacted offenses are most charitably seen as over-inclusive inchoate crimes.

The best-known examples of this phenomenon are offenses of *abstract* or *implicit* endangerment. These offenses target unjustifiable risk-taking, but they do so without making such risk-taking a required element of the offense; instead, they criminalize a more specific type of conduct as a proxy for that risk. Textbook examples include offenses that criminalize exceeding a speed or blood-alcohol limit, in order to target dangerous driving; and offenses that criminalize sexual contact with persons below an age of consent, in order to target the risk of sexual exploitation. However, the phenomenon also extends to offenses targeting other forms of inchoate wrongdoing. Consider crimes of membership in prohibited organizations. These offenses criminalize the status of membership, in order to target both preparatory conduct in which members are involved and their assistance or encouragement of other members' criminal conduct (Levanon 2012). As with offenses of implicit endangerment, the criminalization of proxy conduct renders these offenses over-inclusive, relative to the wrongs that they target.

The most familiar justifications for defining offenses in such a way are *determinacy* and *guidance*. If law-makers wish to avoid over-inclusion, then as we have seen, they will often have to use indeterminate criteria in defining offenses: for example, requiring that the targeted risk be unreasonable or unjustifiable. Such indeterminacy is bad in itself: it makes official decision-making inefficient and inconsistent, and thus makes the law less predictable for citizens. But paradoxically, it can also lead to ineffective guidance on when conduct is actually wrongful. We all have biases and other cognitive blindspots that lead us to misjudge what is reasonable or justified; to help avoid such misjudgments, law-makers thus have reason to avoid relying on such indeterminate concepts. For example, as guidance on risky driving, "Don't drive drunk" or "Don't exceed 30 miles per hour in residential areas" may be more effective than simply "Don't drive dangerously."

Whether over-inclusion of this kind is justified is a question of cost and balance of errors. Which is better: to risk inefficiency, unpredictability, and ineffective guidance, or to prohibit some conduct that, ideally, the law should not prohibit? This question is familiar in the life of the law generally (Alexander and Sherwin 2001; Schauer 1991). But once again, many argue that it requires a special answer in the criminal law context, where "prohibiting" conduct means authorizing its conviction and punishment. To convict and punish the undeserving is an infringement of their rights, and it is debatable whether such infringements can be justified by determinacy alone. At best, the argument goes, such consequences should be grudgingly tolerated, to the extent that they are strictly necessary in achieving sufficient determinacy (Alexander and Ferzan 2009, pp. 288–316; Ashworth and Zedner 2014, pp. 115–116; Husak 1998, 2007, pp. 153–159; compare Duff 2007, pp. 166–172; Simester and von Hirsch 2011, pp. 75–79).

However, in the context of over-inclusion for reasons of prevention, this minimalist approach is too simple. Even if there is a single "sufficient" level of determinacy for criminal offenses, there is no such level of prevention: all else being equal, it is always better to prevent *more* harm. Moreover, as a reason for over-inclusion, the prevention of harm is much stronger than determinacy. To the extent that over-inclusion will actually prevent more harm, there are thus strong reasons in its favor. At the same time, of course, greater over-inclusion also generates stronger reasons *against* criminalization. The more over-inclusive an offense, the more undeserved convictions and punishments it authorizes— and the more people's rights will be infringed. Again, law-makers are left with a difficult judgment call: balancing some citizens' security from wrongful conviction and punishment against others' security from wrongful harm.

For example, consider speed limits in residential areas. A speed limit of 20 miles per hour would greatly reduce pedestrian deaths and injuries, but would also lead to many safe drivers being unjustly convicted and punished. A limit of 50 miles per hour, meanwhile, would avoid many such unjust convictions, but it would also fail to prevent most injury accidents. Or consider the age of consent. An age of 18 would catch many exploitative sexual encounters, but would also criminalize the normal sexual experiences of most of the population. An age of 12, meanwhile, would avoid this result, but it would also fail to catch much exploitative conduct. In seeking the right compromise in either case, it is unhelpful—perhaps even meaningless—to ask what standard is necessary to achieve the offense's preventive aims.

To add further to this complexity, there are different types of over-inclusive offense—some of which are harder to justify than others. So far, we have mainly been considering offenses that, despite their over-inclusiveness, are meant to lead to the deterrence and punishment *of the conduct that they criminalize*. For example, law-makers criminalize gun possession in order to prevent gun-related deaths and injuries, but in doing so, they hope that citizens will actually avoid acquiring and owning guns, and that those who violate this prohibition will be prosecuted. Like all over-inclusive crimes, such offenses are difficult to justify, but they at least treat citizens with a certain kind of respect. In particular, the guidance that they give is at least honest: they are clear as to both the conduct that citizens are expected to avoid and the conduct that officials are expected to pursue, prosecute, and punish.

Some other over-inclusive offenses, by contrast, treat citizens less respectfully and honestly. These offenses are intended not to prevent and punish *all* the conduct that they criminalize, but rather only a sub-set of this conduct. They aim to expand the powers of enforcement officials in relation to this subset, by making it easier for them to arrest, investigate, prosecute, and eventually punish those whom law-makers *really* mean to target. For example, when English legislators criminalized consensual sexual contact between teenagers, they did not intend to deter teenagers from engaging in this conduct—or to facilitate their conviction and punishment if they did so. Rather, they intended to make it easier to prosecute *exploitative* forms of sexual contact, by removing requirements like proof of non-consent. The resulting offense therefore issues guidance that neither citizens nor officials are honestly expected to follow.

Over-inclusive crimes of this second type are especially difficult to justify. They carry the usual costs of over-inclusion, often to a greater degree: they remove further obstacles to unjust conviction and thus further restrict citizens' liberties. But they also infringe other rights that citizens are often thought to have. Most obviously, they undermine an aspect of the rule of law: they deprive citizens of the ability to use the law as a guide to what they may and may not do, without becoming liable to conviction and punishment. They also undermine procedural justice: they deprive defendants of the ability to answer for the conduct that purportedly justifies their conviction, and they free prosecutors from having to prove that conduct in court (Edwards 2010; Tadros 2008, pp. 951–964). In relation to these offenses, citizens' rights against unjust punishment are thus not the only rights at stake—and so we must be especially careful before concluding that they are justified by preventive efficacy alone.

Where does all of this leave, for example, offenses of membership in prohibited organizations? On the one hand, these offenses probably prevent significantly more harm than offenses of preparation, assistance, and encouragement. They deter citizens from conduct that—partly because of the organizational context—can easily lead to such inchoate wrongdoing, and they empower officials to intervene at an earlier stage. Moreover, their costs to citizens' liberties—of removing the option to become a member of a criminal organization—are relatively low. On the other hand, these offenses facilitate unjust convictions and punishments: for example, of merely passive or nominal members, or of members who are involved only in an organization's civic or political activities. They can also be used against those whom the state really suspects of preparing or assisting crimes, in order to circumvent their procedural rights. Arguably, indeed, it is this—and not the deterrence and punishment of mere membership—that is the true aim of these offenses. Whether the efficient prevention of organized criminal activity can justify such infringements of citizens' rights—and if so, just how efficient that prevention needs to be—seems a difficult question indeed.

CONCLUSIONS

We began by noting that many people are skeptical about the expanding scope of inchoate criminality. We can now see that, while this skepticism is in some ways well-founded, we should view this expansion with mixed feelings. The skepticism is well-founded because criminalization is indeed unique among the tools available to law-makers. Justifying criminalization means justifying liability to punishment, conviction, and enforcement action by state officials—and that is no easy task. Our feelings should be mixed because this is not a decisive case, or even a persuasive *prima facie* case, against all inchoate crimes. The prevention of serious harm is a powerful justifying aim—and for at least some of the offenses considered here, criminalization seems an appropriate means of achieving that aim. Like any proposals for new criminal offenses, proposals for new inchoate crimes must be carefully scrutinized. Scrutiny based on blanket skepticism, however, is not careful enough.

REFERENCES

Alexander, Larry, and Kimberly Kessler Ferzan. 2009. *Crime and culpability: A theory of criminal law*. Cambridge: Cambridge University Press.
———. 2012a. Danger: The ethics of preemptive action. *Ohio State Journal of Criminal Law* 9: 637–667.
———. 2012b. Risk and inchoate crimes: Retribution or prevention? In *Seeking security: Pre-empting the commission of criminal harms*, ed. G.R. Sullivan and Ian Dennis, 101–120. Oxford: Hart.
———. 2018. *Reflections on crime and culpability: Problems and puzzles*. Cambridge: Cambridge University Press.
Alexander, Larry, and Emily Sherwin. 2001. *The rule of rules: Morality, rules, and the dilemmas of law*. Durham: Duke University Press.
Ashworth, Andrew. 2011. The unfairness of risk-based possession offences. *Criminal Law and Philosophy* 5: 237–257.
Ashworth, Andrew, and Lucia Zedner. 2012. Prevention and criminalization: Justifications and limits. *New Criminal Law Review* 15: 542–571.
———. 2014. *Preventive justice*. Oxford: Oxford University Press.
Asp, Petter. 2013. Preventionism and criminalization of nonconsummate offences. In *Prevention and the limits of the criminal law*, ed. Andrew Ashworth, Lucia Zedner, and Patrick Tomlin, 23–46. Oxford: Oxford University Press.
Baker, Dennis J. 2007. The moral limits of criminalizing remote harms. *New Criminal Law Review* 10: 370–391.
———. 2009. Collective criminalization and the constitutional right to endanger others. *Criminal Justice Ethics* 28: 168–200.
Brudner, Alan. 2009. *Punishment and freedom*. Oxford: Oxford University Press.
Clarkson, C.M.V. 2005. General endangerment offences: The way forward? *University of Western Australia Law Review* 32: 131–144.
Cornford, Andrew. 2013. Indirect crimes. *Law and Philosophy* 32: 485–514.
———. 2015. Preventive criminalization. *New Criminal Law Review* 18: 1–34.

———. 2017. Rethinking the wrongness constraint on criminalisation. *Law and Philosophy* 36: 615–649.

Dempsey, Michelle Madden. 2005. Rethinking Wolfenden: Prostitute use, criminal law and remote harm. *Criminal Law Review* 2005: 444–455.

Dubber, Markus. 2005. The possession paradigm: The special part and the police power model of the criminal process. In *Defining crimes: Essays on the special part of the criminal law*, ed. R.A. Duff and Stuart P. Green, 91–118. Oxford: Oxford University Press.

Duff, R.A. 2005. Criminalizing endangerment. In *Defining crimes: Essays on the special part of the criminal law*, ed. R.A. Duff and Stuart P. Green, 43–64. Oxford: Oxford University Press.

———. 2007. *Answering for crime: Responsibility and liability in the criminal law*. Oxford: Hart.

———. 2012. Risks, culpability and criminal liability. In *Seeking security: Pre-empting the commission of criminal harms*, ed. G.R. Sullivan and Ian Dennis, 121–142. Oxford: Hart.

Edwards, James. 2010. Justice denied: The criminal law and the ouster of the courts. *Oxford Journal of Legal Studies* 30: 725–748.

———. 2017. Criminalization without punishment. *Legal Theory* 23: 69–95.

Feinberg, Joel. 1984. *Harm to others*. Oxford: Oxford University Press.

Ferzan, Kimberly Kessler. 2011. Beyond crime and commitment: Justifying liberty deprivations of the dangerous and responsible. *Minnesota Law Review* 96: 141–193.

Gardner, John, and Timothy Macklem. 2002. Reasons. In *The Oxford handbook of jurisprudence and philosophy of law*, ed. Jules Coleman and Scott Shapiro, 440–475. Oxford: Oxford University Press.

Horder, Jeremy. 2012. Harmless wrongdoing and the anticipatory perspective on criminalisation. In *Seeking security: Pre-empting the commission of criminal harms*, ed. G.R. Sullivan and Ian Dennis, 78–102. Oxford: Hart.

Hunt, Adrian. 2007. Criminal prohibitions on direct and indirect encouragement of terrorism. *Criminal Law Review* 2007: 441–458.

Husak, Douglas. 1998. Reasonable risk creation and overinclusive legislation. *Buffalo Criminal Law Review* 1: 599–626.

———. 2004. Guns and drugs: Case studies on the principled limits of the criminal sanction. *Law and Philosophy* 23: 437–493.

———. 2007. *Overcriminalization: The limits of the criminal law*. Oxford: Oxford University Press.

Levanon, Liat. 2012. Criminal prohibitions on membership in terrorist organizations. *New Criminal Law Review* 15: 224–276.

Levenbrook, Barbara Baum. 1980. Prohibiting attempts and preparations. *UMKC Law Review* 49: 41–63.

McSherry, Bernadette. 2008. Expanding the boundaries of inchoate crimes: The growing reliance on preparatory offences. In *Regulating deviance: The redirection of criminalisation and the futures of criminal law*, ed. Bernadette McSherry, Alan Norrie, and Simon Bronitt, 141–164. Oxford: Hart.

Ohana, Daniel. 2006. Responding to acts preparatory to the commission of a crime: Criminalization or prevention? *Criminal Justice Ethics* 25: 23–39.

———. 2007. Desert and punishment for acts preparatory to the commission of a crime. *Canadian Journal of Law and Jurisprudence* 20: 113–142.

Petzsche, Anneke. 2017. The penalization of public provocation to commit a terrorist offence. *European Criminal Law Review* 7: 241–257.

Ramsay, Peter. 2010. Preparation offences, security interests, political freedom. In *The boundaries of the criminal law*, ed. R.A. Duff, Lindsay Farmer, S.E. Marshall, Massimo Renzo, and Victor Tadros, 203–228. Oxford: Oxford University Press.

Raz, Joseph. 1975. *Practical reason and norms*. Oxford: Oxford University Press.

Ripstein, Arthur. 1999. Prohibition and preemption. *Legal Theory* 5: 235–263.

Santaella-Tenorio, Julian, Magdalena Cerdá, Andrés Villaveces, and Sandro Galea. 2016. What do we know about the association between firearm legislation and firearm-related injuries? *Epidemiologic Reviews* 38: 140–157.

Schauer, Frederick. 1991. *Playing by the rules: A philosophical examination of rule-based decision-making in law and in life*. Oxford: Oxford University Press.

Simester, A.P. 2012. Prophylactic crimes. In *Seeking security: Pre-empting the commission of criminal harms*, ed. G.R. Sullivan and Ian Dennis, 59–78. Oxford: Hart.

Simester, A.P., and Andreas von Hirsch. 2011. *Crimes, harms, and wrongs: On the principles of criminalisation*. Oxford: Hart.

Sorell, Tom. 2017. Online grooming and preventive justice. *Criminal Law and Philosophy* 11: 705–724.

Tadros, Victor. 2001. Recklessness, consent and the transmission of HIV. *Edinburgh Law Review* 5: 371–380.

———. 2008. Crimes and security. *Modern Law Review* 71: 940–970.

———. 2012. Wrongness and criminalization. In *The Routledge companion to philosophy of law*, ed. Andrei Marmor, 157–173. Abingdon: Routledge.

———. 2016. *Wrongs and crimes*. Oxford: Oxford University Press.

Valkenburg, Patti M., Jochen Peter, and Joseph B. Walther. 2016. Media effects: Theory and research. *Annual Review of Psychology* 67: 315–338.

Wallerstein, Shlomit. 2007a. Criminalising remote harm and the case of anti-democratic activity. *Cardozo Law Review* 28: 2697–2738.

———. 2007b. The state's duty of self-defence: Justifying the expansion of criminal law. In *Security and human rights*, ed. Benjamin J. Goold and Liora Lazarus, 277–303. Oxford: Hart.

Yaffe, Gideon. 2010. *Attempts: In the philosophy of action and the criminal law*. Oxford: Oxford University Press.

PART XVI

Insanity

CHAPTER 17

Insanity

Stephen P. Garvey

Around 4 o'clock, January 20, 1843, a man was walking down Parliament Street, headed to Downing Street. Another man approached him from behind, drew a pistol, put it to his back, and pulled the trigger. A nearby Bobbie seized the assailant, who'd reached for another pistol. The assailant was Daniel M'Naghten, a woodturner from Glasgow. The victim was Edmund Drummond, private secretary to Prime Minister Robert Peel. M'Naghten had planned on killing Peel, not Drummond, but mistook the latter for the former. Drummond died five days later.

M'Naghten was delusional. Members of Peel's Tory party were, he believed, persecuting him, relentlessly. In reality, the Tories weren't after him. M'Naghten, however, wasn't in reality. He was in a world of his own, at least so far as the Tories were concerned. Earlier, M'Naghten had told the Glasgow police commissioner how "he was the object of some persecution, and … thought it proceeded from the priests at the Catholic chapel in Clyde Street, who were assisted by a parcel of Jesuits." Two days later, M'Naghten told the commissioner that the "Tories had joined the Catholics," and thereafter it was the Tories who, as some witnesses later put it, "haunted" him. M'Naghten would today be likely diagnosed as a paranoid psychotic (Moran 1981, p. 208).

M'Naghten was tried for murder. When the defense finished presenting its witnesses, the presiding Judge, Chief Justice Tindal, asked Solicitor General William Follett: "[A]re you prepared, on the part of the Crown, with any evidence to combat [the defense] testimony …, because we think if you have not, we must be under the necessity of stopping the case. Is there any medical evidence on the other side?" "No, my Lord," Follett replied. Tindal then all but

S. P. Garvey (✉)
Cornell Law School, Ithaca, NY, USA
e-mail: spg3@cornell.edu

© The Author(s) 2019
L. Alexander, K. K. Ferzan (eds.), *The Palgrave Handbook of Applied Ethics and the Criminal Law*, https://doi.org/10.1007/978-3-030-22811-8_17

385

directed an acquittal by reason of insanity. M'Naghten was sent to Bethlem Hospital, also known as Bedlam. He was eventually transferred to Broadmoor Asylum, where he died in 1865.

The monarch at the time, 23-year old Queen Victoria, had herself been an assassin's target three years earlier. Her assailant, Edward Oxford, had, like M'Naghten, been acquitted on grounds of insanity.[1] The queen, livid, couldn't fathom M'Naghten's acquittal. The attack looked premeditated, not insane. Some members of the House of Lords, likewise befuddled, decided to ask the common law Judges for an advisory opinion to clarify, once and for all, the law of insanity in England.

The Lords asked five questions. The Judges' answers, filling only seven pages of the English Reports, set the terms for an enduring debate. The Judges' answers weren't the first juridical attempt to say what made someone legally insane,[2] but they've nonetheless become the standard point of departure for most accounts of the Anglo-American law of insanity. This chapter looks at three tests for insanity, two of which (*M'Naghten* and irresistible impulse) are reflected in positive law today. The third (irrationality), though not yet clearly reflected anywhere in positive law, has been proposed as a replacement for the first two.[3]

M'NAGHTEN

When lawyers, courts, and legal commentators refer to the *M'Naghten* Rule, what exactly is the rule to which they refer? The most obvious possibility, of course, is some rule or test for insanity announced in *M'Naghten's Case* itself. Another is some rule or test, recognizable as an offspring of some test announced in *M'Naghten's Case*, but not identical to it. We begin with the test extracted from the original language of *M'Naghten's Case* itself (*M'Naghten's* canonical test), after which we turn to one derived from the original (the new *M'Naghten* test).

M'Naghten's *Canonical Test*

Of the five questions the Lords asked, commentators usually discuss only the second and third, which the Judges answered together. Combined, according to the Judges, the questions asked for something like a pattern jury instruction "when insanity is set up as a defense." The Judges offered this:

> [T]o establish a defence on the ground of insanity, it must be clearly proved that, at the time of the committing of the act, the party accused was labouring under such a defect of reason, from disease of the mind, as not to know the nature and quality of the act he was doing; or, if he did know it, that he did not know he was doing what was wrong. (M'Naghten's Case, p. 722)

Call this M'Naghten's *canonical test*. Seldom in the course of legal history have so few words been subject to so much scrutiny by so many, with so little agreement, beyond broad generalities, on what they mean.[4]

The Judges' answers to the other three questions tend, nowadays at least, to get far less attention. The neglect is puzzling, especially when it comes to the fourth question, which asked: "If a person under an insane delusion as to existing facts, commits an offense in consequence thereof, is he thereby excused?" The Judges replied:

> [T]he answer must of course depend on the nature of the delusions: but, making the same assumption as we did before [in response to question one], namely, that he labours under such partial delusion only, and is not in other respects insane, we think he must be considered in the same situation as to responsibility as if the facts with respect to which the delusion exists were real. (M'Naghten's Case, p. 722) (emphasis added)

In other words, if someone was delusional, and "not in other respects insane," he'd be "excused" if he wouldn't have been criminally responsible had his delusions been true. Call this the *question-four test*.

The question-four test, like the canonical test, raises several questions, two of which bear emphasis. First, what distinguishes someone who labors under "partial delusions," but isn't "in other respects insane"? One response looks to the distinction, usually attributed to Sir Matthew Hale, between "partial insanity" and "total insanity." According to Hale, the "partially insane" suffer from delusions, but their delusions, being limited in scope or subject matter, influence some choices they make, but leave others undisturbed. If someone with "partial delusions" is "partially insane," then someone "in other respects insane" might be someone who's "totally insane," that is, someone suffering from a "total alienation of the mind" or "perfect madness" (Hale 1736, p. 30).

Second, is the question-four test independent of the canonical test, or is it somehow implicit in the canonical test, such that the former adds nothing of substance to the latter? Commentators disagree.[5] If, as some believe, the question-four test adds nothing to the canonical test, then *M'Naghten's Case* bequeaths a single test for insanity. If not, then it bequeaths *two* tests, not just one, in which case we should speak, as some do, of the *M'Naghten* Rules (plural), and not the *M'Naghten* Rule (singular).

Courts and commentators today rarely address these and other questions about question four.[6] Perhaps that's fair. Perhaps the Judges' answers to all the questions, properly understood, do indeed state a single, coherent, and workable test for insanity, condensed in the Judges' answer to questions two and three. Or perhaps not. For example, Chief Judge John Biggs, of the US Court of Appeals for the Third Circuit, writing in 1955, had this to say about *M'Naghten*:

> I think the Queen and the lords put a hot fire to the feet of the judges of England. They were under pressure from the Crown, the lords, and the press and were in a very difficult situation. The judges were in effect called upon to account for

what seemed to be miscarriages of justice in which murderers went unpunished. They answered obliquely and in too many words, embracing several contradictions all too apparent. Their answers are a hotchpotch of the law as laid down from the time of Bracton. (Biggs 1955, p. 107)

M'Naghten's Case was the most important moment in the history of the law of insanity in Anglo-American world, but the Judges' answers leave a number of questions unanswered. For now, however, let's leave *M'Naghten's Case* behind and turn to *M'Naghten*'s most prominent progeny.

The New M'Naghten *Test*

M'Naghten's canonical test asked if the accused was "labouring under such a defect of reason … that he *did not* know what he was doing was wrong." It made no explicit mention of any capacity.[7] Nonetheless, according to the influential Model Penal Code (MPC) Commentaries, *M'Naghten* "call[ed] for complete impairment of *ability* to know" (American Law Institute 1985, p. 171).[8] The Commentaries therefore appear to read *M'Naghten's Case* to state something like the following rule: "A person is not responsible for criminal conduct if at the time of such conduct as a result of mental disease or defect he *lacks the capacity* to know the wrongfulness of his conduct."[9]

Let's call this the *new* M'Naghten *test*. The new *M'Naghten*, unlike its canonical predecessor, grounds insanity in an *incapacity*. A person is insane, under the new *M'Naghten*, if as a result of mental disease or defect, he *lacked the capacity* to know he was doing what was wrong, or in other words, if he *could not have* known he was doing what was wrong. Insanity, says the new *M'Naghten*, is *compelled ignorance*, arising from a mental disease or defect. Not only do the insane believe they're doing nothing wrong, they're *powerless* to believe otherwise.

The new *M'Naghten*, like the canonical one, uses the word "wrong." Which raises the question: Wrong in reference to what? The ambiguity has long been noted. The usual (but not only) answers are "wrong" in reference to the (criminal) law's rules, or "wrong" in reference to the (conventional) moral rules of some community.[10] Whatever the *M'Naghten* Judges meant when they used the word "wrong,"[11] jurisdictions today are divided. Some expressly say "wrong" means "legal" wrong; others that it means "moral" wrong.[12] Still others don't say one way or the other, leaving the ambiguity unresolved.[13] Setting positive law aside, to what *should* "wrong" refer? One answer to this question begins with another famous case.

Some 43 years before Daniel M'Naghten killed Edward Drummond, 29-year old James Hadfield, a former soldier who'd suffered a terrible head wound in combat, fired at King George III while the king was attending a performance at the Drury Lane Theatre. Hadfield, whose shot just missed, was on a mission. His mission was to bring about the Second Coming of Christ, which would come, Hadfield delusionally believed, on the day of his own death, but only if his death came at the state's hands, not his own. What better way to ensure his death at the state's hands than to be convicted (and hung) for high treason? Alas, Hadfield's mission failed. The jury found him insane (Howell 1820, p. 1286).[14]

The jury, let's agree, reached the right result: Hadfield should have been found insane. Now, Hadfield knew killing the king was legally wrong. It was high treason, and high treason meant execution. Indeed, getting to execution was apparently the whole point. On the other hand, Hadfield presumably didn't believe killing the king was morally wrong. He was doing God's work, bringing forth the Second Coming, and sacrificing himself for the greater good. He should have gotten a medal, not a trial for treason. A moral-wrong reading thus yields the right result in Hadfield's case (insane), while a legal-wrong reading yields the wrong result (sane). Hadfield's case (and others like it) therefore makes a good case for the moral-wrong reading.

Or does it? Think about it. Hadfield realized high treason was a crime, and he realized killing the king was high treason. Not only *could* he have known he was committing a crime, he *did* know. Yes, he suffered from delusions. Yes, he was convinced he was acting for the greater good, and maybe nothing could have convinced him otherwise. But why should Hadfield's moral convictions matter, whether or not grounded in delusion? He still realized he was committing a crime, and the law doesn't usually care what we think about its moral merits. Indeed, it usually doesn't care if we think what we're doing is legal or not. We can get to what we've assumed is the right result in Hadfield's case if we adopt the moral-wrong reading, but *why* that's the right reading isn't obvious.

But, you might say, Hadfield probably couldn't have chosen otherwise. His delusions probably compelled him to do as he did, and he should have been excused on that ground. That might be true. But even if it is, what follows? If, as we're assuming, the new *M'Naghten* is the only test we have, nothing follows. Hadfield's capacity to choose otherwise, under the new *M'Naghten*, is neither here nor there, no matter what meaning we give the word "wrong." The new *M'Naghten* turns on the accused's capacity to *believe* otherwise, not *choose* otherwise. The fact that the legal-wrong reading of the new *M'Naghten* gives the wrong result, in cases like Hadfield's, might be a reason to switch to a different test, but it doesn't give much reason to embrace the moral-wrong reading of the new *M'Naghten* over the legal-wrong reading.[15]

For now, stipulate that "wrong" means "legal" wrong. The new *M'Naghten* test would then state: A person is not responsible for criminal conduct if at the time of such conduct as a result of mental disease or defect he lacks the capacity to know the criminality of his conduct. Like any rule, this one doesn't apply itself. A jury bringing it to bear on a set of facts will still need to confront a range of unresolved questions. In order to illustrate some of them, imagine a jury is asked to apply the new *M'Naghten* to the facts of *M'Naghten*: Was Daniel M'Naghten insane under the new *M'Naghten*?

Our imagined jury includes Tom, Dick, and Jane. Tom, chosen to be foreman, happens to be a philosopher. Dick and Jane happen to be lawyers. Tom opens the deliberations:

Foreman Tom: Did M'Naghten suffer from a "mental disease or defect"? That's the first question, because if he didn't, our work here is done.

Juror Jane: I think he did, but I'm not sure. The judge never told us what makes something a "mental disease or defect."[16] The experts talked a lot about different mental illnesses, and which one M'Naghten might or might not have had. I guess we just use our common sense, and my common sense tells me M'Naghten did suffer from a mental disease. I don't think we need to worry about the exact diagnosis.

Foreman Tom: Agreed.

Juror Dick: Me, too.

Foreman Tom: Alright, then here's the next question. Even if M'Naghten suffered from a mental disease or defect, did he nonetheless know he was committing a crime when he shot Drummond? If he did, then again, we can call it a day.

Juror Dick: Of course he knew. He planned it all out. He got the pistols and lurked around waiting for Peel to show up. He must have known the bobbies would try to stop him, and if he could've run, he would have. But he got tackled before he had a chance. So, yes, he knew he was doing something criminal, which obviously means he could've known, which means he wasn't insane.

Juror Jane: I'm not so sure. True, he believed the police would try to stop him, but so far as I can tell, he believed that only because he believed they, like everyone else, didn't know what he knew: that the Tories were out to get him. He might well have thought the powers-that-be would've understood his predicament if only he could have persuaded them to see things his way. If they did, they would've realized he had no other choice. So I'm not sure he really did think what he was doing was a crime.[17]

On top of that, don't forget this. Before M'Naghten headed to London looking for Peel, he told the authorities in Scotland all about the Tories, but everyone thought he was crazy (Schneider 2009, pp. 205–207). From where he stood, though, he probably thought they were the crazy ones. Maybe he thought, "No one believes me. I've got nowhere to turn. Surely it can't be a crime to take matters into my own hands if no one will help me." So, again, I'm not sure he did realize he was doing anything criminal.

Foreman Tom: Fair enough. The judge never told us how we're supposed to tell if M'Naghten knew he was committing a crime. Still, I have to agree with Dick. I think he did know he was committing a crime, but let's agree, just for the sake of argument, that he *didn't*. We still need to decide if he *could* have known. That's the critical question, even if we stipulate that he didn't know.

Unfortunately, the judge didn't tell us how to answer that question either. He didn't tell us how to distinguish someone who didn't know he was committing a crime, but could have, from someone who didn't know he was committing a crime, and couldn't have.

Since the law doesn't help, I think we should go metaphysical. No, don't laugh. I'm serious. If I remember Metaphysics 101, statements about capacities are really counterfactual statements.[18] In other words, in order to tell if M'Naghten *could* have known he was committing a crime, assuming he didn't know, we need to ask if he *would* have known he was committing a crime in a "possible world," which is like the actual world in which M'Naghten didn't know, but also different. The hard part is spelling out the difference. How does the possible world in which we test M'Naghten's capacity to know differ from the actual world in which he didn't know? What's different about it?

How about this. Let's say M'Naghten could have known killing Drummond was a crime in the actual world if he would have known it was a crime in a world just like the actual world, *except* that a judicial magistrate suddenly appeared before him, just as he was about to kill Drummond, and shouted, "Don't do that! It's a crime!"[19] If M'Naghten would've realized he'd be committing a crime if that happened, then we'd say he had the capacity to realize he was committing a crime under the actual circumstances in which he killed Drummond. So, *would* M'Naghten have realized that killing Drummond was a crime if a magistrate had told him it was?

I think it's obvious. Of course he would have known. Nothing we've heard about M'Naghten suggests he wouldn't have understood what our imaginary magistrate was telling him, which means he could've known he was committing a crime, which means he was sane.

Juror Jane: That doesn't seem right to me. If your magistrate test is the right test, then yes, M'Naghten had the capacity to know he was committing a crime. He wasn't *that* far gone, assuming we also stipulate that he wouldn't have thought the magistrate was just another part of the Tory conspiracy. But I still don't think he deserved the gallows. So if your test for capacity makes M'Naghten out to be sane, I think we need a better test.

Ignore the imaginary magistrate. Why not ask if M'Naghten would have known he was committing a crime, not if the magical magistrate had told him so, but if the magistrate had presented him with what any rational person would take to be compelling evidence proving the Tories were *not* persecuting him? Why not ask if he would've known he was committing a crime if he'd been presented with compelling evidence showing him his delusions were patently false?

Of course, if the magistrate presented M'Naghten with evidence of that sort, nothing would change. When someone delusionally believes something he believes it in the face of rationally compelling counter-evidence. That's what makes a delusion a delusion. That means M'Naghten, in my proposed possible world, would end up being in the same position as M'Naghten in the actual world. So, assuming M'Naghten in the actual world didn't know he was committing a crime—and we're assuming he didn't—neither would M'Naghten in my possible world, and that means M'Naghten lacked the capacity to know he was committing a crime, which makes him insane.

Foreman Tom: But if we use your test for capacity, then anyone who suffers from delusions is insane if, as a result of those delusions, he doesn't realize he's committing a crime. Right?

Juror Jane: Right. And what's wrong with that?

Our jurors' deliberations highlight the new *M'Naghten*'s indeterminacy. Its use of the words "know" and "capacity" leaves room, absent further refinement, for reasonable disagreement. Construed in one way, the test can lead to a finding of sanity. Construed in another, it can lead on the same facts to a finding of insanity. The test gives juries discretion, which is a virtue or a vice, depending on what you think about juries. Can they be trusted to use their discretion wisely or not?

Of course, the new *M'Naghten* could be amended to make it even more indeterminate. That's what the Model Penal Code does. According to the Code, a person is "not responsible" for conduct if, as a result of mental disease or defect, he "lack[ed] *substantial* capacity to ... *appreciate* the criminality of his conduct." In other words, the Code begins with the new *M'Naghten*, then alters it in two ways. First, it introduces the word "substantial" to modify "capacity,"[20] and, second, it substitutes "appreciate" for "know."[21] If nothing else, this makes the new *M'Naghten* even more open ended.

Thoughtful commentators have endorsed *M'Naghten*, in one form or another, with some qualifications or another, as a workable test for insanity.[22] Others disagree, believing *M'Naghten*, however refined, is irredeemable. Cases like James Hadfield's are, for them, Exhibit A in the case against *M'Naghten*. One would be hard-pressed to say Hadfield, delusional as he was, didn't realize regicide was high treason. Not only did he realize it was, he wanted it to be, or else his plan for the Second Coming wouldn't work. If so, if Hadfield realized he was committing a crime, then he's sane under *M'Naghten*, no matter how you cut it, unless *M'Naghten* doesn't really mean what it says. But finding Hadfield sane, and sending him to the gallows, is hard to condone.[23]

Let's now turn to a different test, usually proffered as a supplement to *M'Naghten*, but sometimes as a wholesale replacement.[24] The test has different names, but is probably best known as the *irresistible impulse test*.

Irresistible Impulses

An 18-year-old boy, known to us only as McCullough, attended high school in Osage, Iowa. One day, in 1901, he stole a schoolbook worth 75¢ from another student's desk. McCullough "exchanged [the book] at a store ... for a fishing reel or clothes brush." It wasn't McCullough's first theft. He'd been diagnosed as a kleptomaniac, with "an inordinate desire for possessing himself of articles of personal property, with no regard to any special value they might have, and for many of which he could have no use" (State v. McCullough, p. 503).[25]

Charged with larceny, McCullough pled insanity. Had his plea been tested under *M'Naghten*, he'd probably have been found sane. When he stole the book, he apparently knew he was doing what was wrong. Nonetheless, if we assume McCullough's choice to steal was the result of an impulse he couldn't resist, he shouldn't be punished for it. Ought implies can, and McCullough couldn't. An "irresistible impulse" test for insanity excuses those who, as a result of mental disease or defect, lacked the capacity to choose otherwise and thereby conform their conduct to the requirements of law.[26]

The irresistible impulse test is sometimes portrayed as a response to *M'Naghten*'s shortcomings,[27] but language linking insanity with irresistible and uncontrollable impulses can be found in judicial pronouncements predating *M'Naghten's Case*. For example, three years before Daniel M'Naghten killed Edward Drummond, 18-year-old Edward Oxford tried to kill the young Queen Victoria, then just two years into her long reign. Charged with high treason, Oxford pled not guilty by reason of insanity. Lord Chief Justice Denman instructed the jury, in part, as follows:

> The very important question comes, whether the prisoner was of unsound mind at the time when the act was done? ... If some controlling disease was, in truth, the acting power within him which he could not resist, then he will not be responsible. (R v. Oxford 1840, p. 950)[28]

Oxford was acquitted.

The irresistible impulse test, like the new *M'Naghten*, grounds insanity in compulsion. The new *M'Naghten* grounds insanity in compelled *cognition*: A person is insane if, as a result of mental disease or defect, he lacked the capacity to know he was committing a crime, that is, if he believed he wasn't committing a crime and couldn't have believed otherwise. The irresistible impulse test grounds insanity in compelled *choice*: A person is insane if, as a result of mental disease or defect, he lacked the capacity to control some desire the satisfaction of which would require him to choose to commit a crime, that is, if he chose to commit a crime and couldn't have chosen otherwise.[29]

According to the Model Penal Code, the law shouldn't punish someone whose "disorder prevents his awareness of the wrongfulness of his conduct from restraining his action," or in other words, someone whose "mental disease or defect destroys or overrides [his] power of self-control" (Model Penal Code and Commentaries 1985, pp. 166–167). Believing *M'Naghten*-type tests wrongly permitted the law to punish those who were compelled to act as they did, the MPC included compelled choice, alongside compelled cognition, as a condition excluding responsibility, provided the compulsion resulted from a mental disease or defect.[30] As stated in § 4.01(1): "A person is not responsible for criminal conduct if at the time of such conduct as a result of mental disease or defect he lacks substantial capacity to ... conform his conduct to the requirements of law."

The Code's rendering of the irresistible impulse test, like its rendering of *M'Naghten*'s canonical test, leaves the jury with more discretion than meets the eye. In order to get a better sense of how much, let's imagine McCullough is tried before a jury instructed to apply the Code's control-test language. Once again, Foreman Tom leads the discussion, with Jurors Dick and Jane joining in.

> Foreman Tom: When the judge asked us to decide if M'Naghten was insane under the new *M'Naghten*, we first needed to ask if he knew M'Naghten was doing what was wrong. Only if we thought he *didn't* know did we need to ask if he had the *capacity* to know. For McCullough, we can cut to the chase. We don't need to ask if he conformed to the law. We know he didn't, because he stole the book.

Was he substantially capable of conforming to the law? That's the question. Let's set aside the word "substantial" for the time being. Let's just ask if he could've chosen not to steal the book at the moment he did in fact choose to steal it.

What we need is some way to test his capacity to conform. When we tested M'Naghten's capacity to know he was doing what was wrong, assuming he didn't know, we asked a counterfactual question, though we disagreed about what the right counterfactual should be. We need a comparable test for McCullough's capacity to conform. Any suggestions?

Juror Dick: Before we get to that, can I just say what I think was going on in McCullough's mind when he took the book? I think he saw the book sitting there on the other student's desk. I think he experienced a strong desire to take it, stronger than anything you or I can probably imagine. I think he tried to resist that desire with whatever techniques for self-control he had at his disposal. Maybe he tried counting to ten. Maybe he tried to bring to mind how upset his parents would be if they discovered he'd stolen again. Or maybe he just kept trying to tell himself not to take it. Maybe he did all those things. Who knows ....

Using these strategies, he was trying either to decrease the strength of his desire to steal, or increase the strength of his desire not to steal. Either way, or both, he was trying to make sure his desire to steal didn't become his strongest desire. But that wasn't easy. Trying to control a powerful desire is hard. It wears you out. It causes stress. I think mental health professionals call it "dysphoria." Whatever you call it, it's not pleasant. It's painful. As McCullough tried to resist his desire to steal, I think the dysphoria just became too much for him. He decided to stop resisting, and when he stopped, he stole. His desire to steal the book became his strongest desire, which caused him to form an intent to steal the book, which caused him to form a volition to move his arm to reach out and grab the book, which is exactly what he did.

So isn't the real question this: Would a "reasonable person" in McCullough's situation have done the same thing? Would a reasonable person, experiencing all the psychic pain McCullough was experiencing, have given up too? Shouldn't we try to compare the pain McCullough was enduring in order to avoid stealing the book with the harm he caused when he stole it, which he did in order to put a stop to the pain?

Now, if McCullough had suffered from pyromania, and needed to burn down the schoolhouse in order to escape his dysphoria, the case would be different. Likewise if he suffered from pedophilia and needed to molest a child. A reasonable person doesn't burn down buildings or molest children in order to relieve psychological distress, no matter how great. But McCullough didn't burn down a building, or molest a child. He took a book. Comparing the seriousness of the crime with what I imagine was the pain he was suffering, maybe we should acquit him. It seems to me he acted under a kind of internal duress.[31]

Foreman Tom: I might agree with you if McCullough were being tried in a court of morality, but he's not. He's being tried in a court of law, and the judge told us we should only acquit McCullough if we believed he lacked substantial capacity to conform to the law. But you haven't said anything about his *capacity* to conform. Even if everything you say is true, all it tells us is that McCullough faced a hard choice. Break the law and relieve the dysphoria, or continue to resist and continue to suffer. The way you're looking at it, McCullough chose not to conform to the law because conforming was too hard for him, and yes, maybe it would have been too hard for a reasonable person in his situation, too.

Unfortunately for McCullough, that's not the question. Even if we agree a reasonable person in McCullough's situation would have done as McCullough did, our question is different. We need to ask if, as a result of his kleptomania, which I'm assuming qualifies as a mental disease or defect, he lacked substantial capacity to conform to the law. The question is what McCullough could have done, not what a reasonable person in his situation would have done. As I see it, those are two separate questions. Our job is to answer the former, not the latter. True, they both depend for answers on asking a counterfactual question, but the counterfactual questions on which they depend differ. The latter asks what a reasonable person in McCullough's situation would have done. The former asks what McCullough would have done had he been faced with *compelling* reasons not to take the book.

The problem is figuring out what makes a reason to conform to the law compelling, which brings me back to my original question. What's the right test for capacity? At the risk of beating a dead horse, claims about a person's capacities presuppose some counterfactual or possible world. When someone says McCullough couldn't conform to the law, they must have in mind some possible world in which he fails to conform, as he in fact failed to conform in the actual world, even though he's faced in that possible world with a strong reason in favor of conforming. Indeed, he's faced with a reason so strong we can fairly call it "compelling."

What might that reason be? One place to start is with Kant, who apparently thought a person lacked the capacity to choose otherwise only if he would have chosen as he did in fact choose if he believed he'd be immediately hung for it.[32] If we follow Kant, we'd have to ask ourselves what we think McCullough would have done if a gallows had appeared out of the blue as he was about to pinch the book. Would he have taken it? My guess would be no. If so, and if Kant's gallows is the right way to test someone's capacity to conform, then McCullough *wasn't* compelled to steal, no matter how hard it was for him to continue to resist, and if he wasn't compelled, he wasn't insane.[33]

Juror Jane: Don't you think the gallows is a little over the top? I know you told us to ignore the word "substantial," but I want to bring it back in. That would mean McCullough was insane if, as a result of mental disease or defect, he lacked *substantial* capacity to conform. Doesn't that suggest something more forgiving than immediate death as the relevant counterfactual?[34] Apart from compulsives with death wishes, I doubt many people, including some we'd otherwise be inclined to regard as compelled, would fail to choose otherwise in order to avoid the abyss.

Foreman Tom: I see the point, and the word "substantial" probably does imply *something* less extreme than Kant's gallows. Exactly what, I'm not sure. But I wonder if we really need to settle on any specific counterfactual. What if we just asked: Would McCullough have stolen the book if he'd been presented with a reason not to steal it, where the reason presented is such that, had he recognized or acknowledged it, he would've wanted *not* to steal the book *more* than he wanted to steal it? If yes, then we'd say he lacked the capacity to choose otherwise.

Jurors Jane: That doesn't make any sense. If he'd wanted not to steal the book more than he wanted to steal it, he wouldn't have stolen it.

Foreman Tom. Not necessarily. Here's what I have in mind. Not all desires are created equal. Some desires can disable what philosophers call a person's "practical reason," which, as a matter of folk psychology, is the faculty we use to decide what to do all things considered. When it works as it should, practical reason takes into account all the reasons a person has available to him at the moment of choice, balances them off against one another, and thereby yields an all-things-considered judgement as to what he should do.

But sometimes a desire causes a person's practical reason to become impervious to reasons, or at least some range of reasons. We can present a person in the grip of such a desire with all manner of reasons, up to and maybe including Kant's gallows, not to do whatever he needs to do to satisfy the desire. It won't matter. The desire somehow manages to prevent his practical reason from recognizing those countervailing reasons, and if practical reason can't recognize those reasons, it can't respond to them.[35] That might sound odd, but there it is. That, you might say, is the "mechanism" by which a desire becomes irresistible.

Think about it this way. Imagine a kleptomaniac's desire to steal is like a horse trainer, and his practical reason is like a horse. When a trainer puts blinders on his horse, the trainer prevents the horse from seeing anything except what's in front of him. Likewise, when a kleptomaniac's desire to steal puts blinders on his practical reason, it prevents practical reason from seeing or recognizing anything except the object of the desire. When people say "passion has blinded reason," maybe that, or something like it, is what they have in mind.

Juror Dick: Where does that leave us?

Foreman Tom: With a hard decision. Obviously, we can't pluck McCullough out of this world, throw him back in time to the moment before he stole the book, and then arrange for a gallows or whatnot magically to appear so we can see what he would have done. The best we can do is ask what McCullough has done in the past, in like circumstances. Does he steal only when the teacher isn't looking, for example? If he does, that's some evidence he could have conformed, but didn't. Or does he steal even when the teacher *is* looking? Does he steal even though he knows, if he's caught, that his turn-of-the-century old-school father will beat him within an inch of his life? If so, that's some evidence desire blinded his reason.

Whatever the verdict in McCullough's case, if someone really did, as a result of mental disease or defect, lack the capacity, or substantial capacity, to conform his conduct to the requirements of law, not many people would push for him to be punished. As a matter of moral principle, most people agree, incapacity excuses.[36]

Be that as it may, thoughtful critics have argued against an irresistible impulse test becoming law. With or without the test, say the critics, jurors will make mistakes. *Without* the test, jurors will return some number of unwarranted *convictions*, because, with no legal way to acquit, they'll convict defendants who *ex hypothesi* lacked the capacity to conform. *With* the test, jurors will return some number of unwarranted *acquittals* because they'll sometimes erroneously acquit defendants who *ex hypothesi* had the capacity to conform. According to the critics, the number of unwarranted acquittals will, for two reasons, be large enough to tip the moral balance against the defense.[37]

First, even if someone couldn't have chosen otherwise in the moment, chances are he could have (and should have) taken steps beforehand to avoid being put to the choice.[38] Someone afflicted with a desire he can't control at $t = 1$ is obliged, so the thought goes, to take steps at $t = 1 - n$ if he realizes (or perhaps should realize) that not taking those steps will or might unjustifiably risk leaving him powerless at $t = 1$. In other words, if he can't exercise self-control *synchronically*, he'd better exercise it *diachronically*. If he doesn't, the law shouldn't allow him to plead insanity. Finally, if the vast bulk of those who couldn't have chosen otherwise at $t = 1$ could and should have taken steps to avoid having become incapacitated at that time, withholding the defense will seldom produce unwarranted convictions.

Second, even among defendants without prior fault, jurors have no way reliably to distinguish the truly incapacitated from the counterfeits. No one has an "objective" way to sort those who couldn't conform from those who could but didn't. No less an authority than the American Psychiatric Association, writing in the wake of John Hinckley's 1982 insanity acquittal for attempting to assassinate then-President Ronald Reagan, famously observed: "The line between an irresistible impulse and an impulse not resisted is probably no sharper than that between twilight and dusk."[39] With no surefire way to separate the compelled from the weak, jurors will sometimes make mistakes. Moreover, those mistakes will systematically benefit those who should have been convicted. Jurors will too often see compulsion when all they should have seen was weakness. Better, think the critics, to run a small risk of unjust convictions without the defense than a large risk of unjust acquittals with it.

That's fair, but not dispositive. First, the law often makes affirmative defenses contingent on clean hands, or lack of prior fault. The Model Penal Code, for example, withdraws duress as a defense when the defendant "recklessly placed himself in a situation in which it was probable that he would be subjected to duress" (Model Penal Code and Commentaries 1985, p. 367). Strings of this sort are routinely attached to affirmative defenses. The conspicuous exception is insanity.[40] So one option would be to remove the exception. Rather than reject an irresistible impulse test altogether, because the synchronically compelled typically and culpably fail to exercise diachronic control, why not just attach the usual strings? If an accused was compelled at the time of the crime, he would be excused, unless, for example, he "recklessly placed himself in a situation in which it was probable he would be subjected to compulsion."

Second, as for there being no "objective" way to sort the compelled from the weak, the critics are right. No algorithm exists to distinguish compulsion from weakness. Any line between the two presupposes a moral judgment: What *should* the possible world look like in which we test an accused's capacity to conform to the law? Is it a world with Kant's magically materializing gallows or something less draconian? If something less, how much less? Reasonable minds can disagree. Moreover, even if they agreed on a possible world, they might still disagree on what the accused would have done if plopped down inside it.

Irresistible impulse tests don't apply themselves. Their application requires judgment. That, of course, is true of other defenses besides insanity. Killing in self-defense is permissible only if the defendant *reasonably* believed deadly force was necessary to protect himself from deadly force. Jurors have to decide: *Was* the defendant's belief reasonable? The question can't be answered without judgment, but the law typically offers jurors precious little, if any, guidance when it asks them to make it. Maybe that's as it should be. Maybe the considerations involved in judging reasonableness are too many and too complex for the law to say anything more helpful.

Yet when it comes to saying what makes a choice compelled or not, perhaps the law can and should say more than it does now. Insofar as decisions about capacities rest on counterfactuals, perhaps the law should identify the counterfactual on which it wants jurors to rely. Should they be told to imagine Kant's gallows or something else? If something else, what? Or maybe the law should tell jurors the accused was compelled only if desire "drowned out all competing considerations?" (Morse 2011, p. 929). If the law can help jurors discern the moral line between twilight and dusk, why should it stay silent? And if the line becomes more visible, the risk of erroneous acquittals should drop.

IRRATIONALITY

Compelled ignorance and compelled choice. Those are the law's traditional tests for insanity, provided the compulsion resulted from a "mental disease or defect."[41] Dissatisfaction with the traditional tests has led some commentators to propose an alternative theory, according to which insanity is grounded, not in compulsion, but in *irrationality*. Although this theory has yet to find its way into any penal code, irrationality theories represent a sophisticated and thoughtful challenge to the prevailing tradition. Still, for that challenge to succeed, the irrationality theorist needs to elaborate. Saying the insane are irrational doesn't say enough. The insane are irrational or lack the capacity for rationality, but what does that mean?

According to the new *M'Naghten*, a person is insane if he didn't realize he was committing a crime and would have believed as he did even if presented with compelling reasons to believe otherwise. Likewise, according to the irresistible impulse test, a person is insane if he chose to commit a crime and would have committed it even if presented with compelling reasons to choose otherwise. But isn't a belief held in the face of compelling reasons to believe otherwise irrational? And isn't a choice made in the face of compelling reasons to choose otherwise likewise irrational? If so, how does the irrationality of the irrationality theory differ from the irrationality of the traditional tests?[42]

The new *M'Naghten* and the irresistible impulse test associate insanity with dramatic forms of irrationality. Believing in the face of compelling reasons to believe otherwise is a dramatic form of epistemic irrationality. Choosing in the face of compelling reasons to choose otherwise is a dramatic form of practical irrationality. Of course, epistemic and practical irrationality come in less extreme forms.

Self-deception, for example, consists in believing against the balance of one's available epistemic reasons. The self-deceived could have believed otherwise, but didn't, because they didn't want to. That's irrational. Likewise, the weak-willed choose against the balance of their available practical reasons. The weak-willed could have chosen otherwise, but didn't, even though they believed they should have. That's irrational, too. Yet no one says self-deception or weakness of will amounts to insanity. If so, then how does the irrationality associated with the irrationality theory differ from these less dramatic forms of irrationality?[43]

A persuasive irrationality theory should describe with some particularity the irrationality in which insanity consists. It should describe how the irrationality it associates with insanity differs from the irrationality the traditional tests associate with insanity, and it should provide jurors with some criteria enabling them to reliably sort the irrational-and-insane from the irrational-but-sane. An instruction telling jurors to acquit if they think the accused is so irrational as to be non-responsible doesn't tell them very much. Indeed, doesn't it come close to telling them to acquit the accused on grounds of insanity if the accused was insane?

If an irrationality theory wants to avoid risking vacuity, it needs to come forward with a distinct and serviceable test for insanity. What might such a test look like? One place to start is in 1800, and Thomas Erskine's speech in defense of James Hadfield.

Erskine's Test

Hadfield was tried for high treason after attempting to kill King George III. At the time, English law didn't have any authoritative legal statement defining insanity. Hadfield's defense counsel, Thomas Erskine, acknowledged that Sir Matthew Hale (following Sir Edward Coke) had said insanity excused only when it amounted to *total insanity*, and total insanity meant a "total deprivation of memory and understanding" (Howell 1820, p. 1312). As Erskine said:

> in some, perhaps in many cases, the human mind is stormed in its citadel, and laid prostrate under the stroke of frenzy; .... There, indeed, all the ideas are overwhelmed—for reason is not merely disturbed, *but driven wholly from her seat.* Such unhappy patients are unconscious, therefore, except at short intervals, even of external objects; or, at least, are wholly incapable of considering their relations. Such persons, and such persons alone ... are totally deprived of their understandings. (Howell 1820, p. 1313)

The "totally insane," Erskine agreed, were not responsible, but neither, he argued, contra Hale, were the "partially insane." Someone was "partially insane," thought Erskine, if he was delusional and nothing more. Indeed, according to Erskine, "[d]elusion, ... where there is no frenzy or raving madness [as in total insanity]," was "the *true* character of insanity," provided the accused wouldn't have committed the crime had he not been delusional (Howell 1820, p. 1314). Erskine didn't offer a "test" for insanity, but if he had, it might have looked like this: An accused is insane if, at the time of the crime, he suffered from delusions, provided he would not have committed the crime but for those delusions.[44]

The traditional tests ask if the accused was powerless to know or conform to the law. Erskine's test doesn't. It asks only if the accused suffered from delusions and wouldn't have committed the crime but for those delusions. So Erskine's test doesn't reduce to the traditional tests. It also provides decent enough guidance to jurors, who need to resolve two questions: (1) Was the accused delusional at the time of the crime? (2) If so, would he have committed the crime if he hadn't been delusional? Finally, Erskine's test qualifies as an irrationality test inasmuch as it requires the accused to have been delusional, and delusions are irrational beliefs.

A traditionalist, for whom compelled ignorance or choice is the root of insanity, is apt to find Erskine's irrationality test unpersuasive. Stipulate that M'Naghten was delusional when he killed Drummond, and he wouldn't have killed him had he not been delusional. Now stipulate (as many believe) that M'Naghten, despite being delusional, nonetheless realized he was committing a crime, and had the capacity to choose not to commit it. If so, then why, the traditionalist might ask, should the law allow him to escape criminal liability? He realized he was committing a crime, and he could've chosen not to commit it. Case closed. That's the traditionalist objection.

If the irrationality theorist finds this objection persuasive (and she might not), one response would be to amend Erskine's test, in hopes of fixing it to meet the objection. We can imagine at least two possible amendments, resulting in two new irrationality tests. The first adds a condition to Erskine's test. The second supercharges one condition and eliminates another. Each resulting theory has roots in history. The first brings us back to the Judges' answer to question four in *M'Naghten's Case*. The second brings us back to Lord Hale's account of total insanity.

The Question-Four Test

The first response to the traditionalist objection adds a condition to Erskine's test.[45] It recovers the *M'Naghten* Judges' answer to the neglected question four, which asked: "If a person under an insane delusion as to existing facts, commits an offense in consequence thereof, is he thereby excused?" Erskine would say "yes." But the *M'Naghten* Judges would say "sometimes." Just because a crime resulted from delusion wasn't, for them, enough to excuse. Instead, the delusional accused "must be considered in the same situation as to responsibility as if the facts with respect to which the delusion exists were real." Someone experiencing delusions was insane only if he wouldn't have been criminally liable had his delusions been true. Call this the *question-four test*.

Under the question-four test, M'Naghten would have been insane if, had his delusions about the Tory persecution been true, he wouldn't have been, under prevailing legal rules and doctrines, criminally liable for shooting Peel, even if he happened to believe he was committing a crime, and even if he could have chosen otherwise. He's excused because, believing himself the victim of Tory persecution, and being powerless to believe otherwise, the law should in fairness judge him based on what he believed, that is, as if his delusions had been true. That's how the question-four test responds to the traditionalist objection. So far, so good, but the question-four test isn't out of the woods yet.[46]

First, the question-four test requires entering a delusional world. Because a delusional defendant lacks the capacity to respond to evidence at odds with his delusions, it seems only fair to judge his actions based on the facts as he delusionally believed them to be, not as they were, nor even as a reasonable person (who's capable of responding to countervailing evidence) would have believed them to be. Under the question-four test, the law judges the delusional defendant just like any other defendant, save for the fact that it judges the delusional defendant from inside his delusional world. That, of course, is easier said than done. As Glanville Williams remarked over 50 years ago: "The task of analyzing a complicated delusion in order to discover whether it affords a ground for exemption may present insoluble problems" (Williams 1961, p. 502).

Consider again James Hadfield. Hadfield delusionally believed his death was necessary in order to bring forth the Second Coming of Christ. He also delusionally believed his death could not be at his own hands. It had to be at the state's hands; otherwise, the Second Coming would not come. So Hadfield decided he had to kill King George III, which would lead to his execution for high treason, and thus to the Second Coming. Was Hadfield, under the question-four test, sane or insane?

Well, it depends. Is someone who tries to kill the king criminally liable if the king's death is necessary to bring Christ into the world? Compared to not having Christ come again, maybe killing the king was the lesser evil, so maybe Hadfield would have had, if his delusions were true, a defense of necessity. Alas, necessity probably wasn't, circa 1800, a defense to murder, completed or attempted, let alone when the king was in the crosshairs. Then again, it is Christ we're talking about. Would it be permissible to sacrifice the king (in order to sacrifice oneself in order) to bring about the Second Coming? It probably depends on whether you believe in Christ in the first place but set that complication aside. Isn't the real problem the question itself? Isn't the question itself a little crazy? We should probably think twice before embracing a test for insanity that will often enough force jurors to answer other-worldly hypotheticals.

Second, according to some commentators, the question-four test misunderstands and oversimplifies how the delusional mind works. It assumes someone with delusions can't be faulted for being delusional, but it assumes he *can* be faulted if the choices he makes based on his delusions are choices the criminal law would condemn. In other words, it assumes the delusional mind works just like the non-delusional mind, except the delusional mind reasons from delusional beliefs, while the non-delusional mind reasons from non-delusional ones. That assumption has struck many as implausible. As Glanville Williams put it: the test "compels the lunatic to be reasonable in his unreason, sane in his insanity" (Williams 1961, p. 504).[47]

Let's set aside the question-for test, which is the first response to the traditionalist challenge to Erskine's test, and turn to the second, which brings us back to Lord Hale and the idea of total insanity.

The Total Insanity Test

Recall that Erskine's test had two requirements: delusion and causation. An accused was insane if he suffered from delusions and if his delusions motivated him to commit the crime. The question-four test, which reflects one response to the traditionalist challenge, adds a condition: An accused is insane if he suffered from delusions and if his delusions motivated him to commit the crime, *provided* he would not have been criminally liable if his delusions had been true.

The second response deletes the causation requirement and supercharges the delusion requirement. The resulting test *identifies* insanity with *being* delusional and psychotic, but the psychosis must be severe. Insanity just is *severe psychosis*. The test therefore meets the traditionalist challenge. On the one hand, it constitutes an irrationality test insofar as someone who's severely psychotic just is severely irrational. On the other, whereas the traditional tests ground insanity in compelled ignorance or compelled choice resulting from a mental disease or defect, the total insanity test tells us, in contrast, that insanity just is a mental disease or defect: severe psychosis.

What is it about severe psychosis that underwrites a defense? Simple. Someone who's severely psychotic lacks the basic capacities required for moral agency. Lacking those capacities, he's no longer intelligible to us as a moral agent. Moral agents can be *excused* from blame for the wrongs they do, as when they act under duress, but the insane qua non-moral agents are *exempt* from blame altogether, for anything they do. With insanity identified as severe psychosis, the insanity defense becomes a status defense, like the common law defense of infancy. Children under age seven were exempt from criminal liability at common law based on their status: Being children, they weren't regarded as moral agents.[48] When insanity is equated with severe psychosis, the insane are likewise so regarded.

The link between insanity and severe psychosis goes back to 1736, and Sir Matthew Hale's *Pleas of the Crown*, and before that to 1628, and Sir Edward Coke's *Institutes of the Laws of England*. For Hale and Coke, the only form of insanity sufficient to defeat criminal liability was total insanity, that is, a "total alienation of the mind," or "total deprivation of memory" (Hale 1736, p. 30). So far as one can tell, those Hale and Coke described as "totally insane" would today be described as "severely psychotic." If so, then modern-day irrationality theorists who identify insanity with severe psychosis are direct descendants of Hale and Coke,[49] and so their test for insanity might be called the *total insanity test*.

The severely psychotic (and thus totally insane) suffer from delusions and hallucinations. Their speech becomes a "word salad," replete with neologisms. They experience thought blocking: Their speech ends mid-sentence. At one extreme, they engage in agitated and repetitive movements; at the other, they become catatonic. The more florid inmates of the Bridgewater Asylum for the Criminally Insane, depicted in Frederick Wiseman's 1967 documentary *Titicut Follies*, fit the profile. Other words to describe them might include raving, rambling, bizarre, delirious, and incoherent. Or perhaps: "totally deteriorated, drooling, hopeless[ly] psychotic[ ]" (Zilboorg 1943, p. 273). The totally insane are, as one proponent has put it, "stranger to us than birds in our gardens" (Moore 2015, p. 678).[50]

How would M'Naghten have fared under the total insanity test? M'Naghten suffered from delusions, but was he *so* disordered or psychotic we can't make any sense of him? We can't understand why he thought the Tories were out to get him, but if they were, and if killing the prime minster was the only way to stop them, then wasn't that an intelligible thing to do? Nor was M'Naghten so disordered he couldn't figure out how to make the attempt. He was able to come up with a plan and put it into action. It doesn't look like he was "totally deprived" of reason. Disordered as he was, he doesn't look *totally* insane.[51] If so, and if, as many commentators believe, M'Naghten *was* insane, then the total insanity test delivers the wrong verdict. It declares M'Naghten sane when he wasn't.

M'Naghten was delusionally paranoid, but describing him as totally insane or unintelligible seems to go too far. Yet perhaps we've misunderstood the total insanity test. Maybe, properly understood, M'Naghten *would* qualify as totally insane. So let's stipulate, for argument's sake, that he was. Now, rather than killing another human being, let's imagine M'Naghten decided to steal a bowler, not because he was irresistibly driven to it, but just because he wanted to look dapper and didn't want to pay. He knows full well he's stealing; he knows stealing is a crime; and he could have chosen not to steal. Moreover, his theft has nothing to do with his delusions. He doesn't, for example, believe stealing a bowler will strike a blow against the Tories, making it harder for them to carry on their campaign against him.

Is M'Naghten guilty of larceny? Not if we stipulate, as we have, that he's insane under the total insanity test. The total insanity test grounds insanity in status. Insanity is a property of persons, not their choices. If a person is insane, then all her choices are insane. She's not responsible for anything she chooses to do. Under the total insanity test, the insane can literally do no wrong. So if M'Naghten was *ex hypothesi* totally insane, then he wouldn't have been responsible for stealing the bowler, even if he knew it was a crime, even if he could have chosen otherwise, and even if his theft had nothing to do with his delusions. If that conclusion leaves you dubious, you're not alone.[52]

Theories that ground insanity in irrationality need to say what makes the irrationality of insanity special. Under what conditions does a person's choice to commit a crime, or the person herself, qualify as irrational, such that the choice is excused, or the person exempt, from criminal liability? The question-four test and the total insanity test provide two possible answers to that question, but neither test is immune to fair-minded concerns.

CONCLUSION

For centuries that law has tried to identify what makes a mind insane. The quarry has been elusive. Today, the *M'Naghten* test, in one form or another, holds the upper hand in most jurisdictions,[53] but the history of tests for insanity is of change and evolution. No one should be surprised if the winds shift yet again. Perhaps the irresistible impulse test will, for example, regain favor. Or perhaps some other test. Time will tell.

Another possibility, of course, is to give up the hunt altogether. David Bazelon was a Judge on the United States Court of Appeals for the District of Columbia Circuit for over 20 years, between 1950 and 1973. He had a sharp mind and an abiding concern for the plight and welfare of the mentally ill. Bazelon searched for a test, eventually developing his own. Yet in time, he abandoned it. He came to believe jurors should simply be asked: At the time of his conduct, were the defendant's "mental or emotional processes or behavior controls impaired to such an extent that he cannot justly be held responsible."[54] That, of course, approaches the ultimate question itself: Can this defendant be justly held responsible?

Perhaps the ultimate question is the only one we should be asking. Perhaps the best test for legal insanity is no test at all. Perhaps insanity is like pornography: Jurors should be trusted to know it when they see it. No help from the law needed. The no-test test is one solution to the problem of insanity. It might even be the best solution, but it's not a perfect solution. Like any proposal to leave hard questions to a jury's good judgment, it's only as good as the jurors on whose judgment it depends. Then again, those who study jurors tell us the law makes little, if any, difference.[55] On the whole, we're told, jurors follow their intuition and common sense, acquitting and convicting as they see fit, whatever test they've been told to apply. Of course, on the whole is on the whole. In some cases the law might make all the difference, which makes it worthwhile to keep searching for the right test.[56]

NOTES

1. Oxford was the first, but not the last, to make an attempt on the Queen's life. Six more would follow (Murphy 2012).
2. For historical surveys describing earlier efforts, see Biggs (1955); Robinson (1996); Walker (1968); Platt and Diamond (1966); Walker (1985); Platt (1965).

3. This chapter focuses on the law of insanity. The insanity defense has of course been subject to empirical study. For a recent meta-analysis discussing the variables associated with a finding of insanity, for example, see Kois and Chauhan (2018).

4. Among the many questions *M'Naghten*'s canonical test raises: (1) What, if anything, does the language pursuant to which an accused is insane if he "did not know the nature and quality of what he was doing" add to the language pursuant to which he's insane if he "did not know what he was doing was wrong"? Is the former phrase really necessary, insofar as all (or most) cases in which an accused didn't know the nature and quality of what he was doing will also be cases in which he didn't know what he was doing was wrong? *See*, for example, Clark v. Arizona (pp. 753–754); Goldstein (1967, pp. 50–51) (noting that the "phrase 'nature and quality of the act' … is [m]ore often stated to the jury without explanation or treated as adding nothing to the requirement that the accused know his act was wrong," but also noting "[t]here have been [a] few efforts to treat the phrase as if it added something to the rule"). (2) Does the reference to "wrong" mean legally or morally wrong, and if the latter, in reference to what system of "moral" rules is moral wrongness to be determined? (3) Because the Judges' second question, to which the canonical test was a response, asked about "a person alleged to be afflicted with insane delusion," is *M'Naghten*'s canonical test limited to cases in which the accused claims to have been delusional?

5. For example, *compare* Simester et al. (2013, p. 723) ("This express provision for partial delusions [i.e., the question-four test] does not appear to add anything to the substance of the Rules.") and LaFave (2010, p. 408) ("Although some American cases might be read as if they were following somewhat different standards in [cases involving 'partial delusions only,' and 'not in other respects insane'] it is undoubtedly fair to conclude that this particular part of *M'Naghten* does not set up a unique formula differing from the right-wrong test [i.e., the answer to the second and third questions].", *with*, for example, United States v. Currens (p. 764 n.15) (opinion by Biggs, C. J.) ("The answers of the Judges of England can by some simplification be fairly reduced to *two* rules to determine the criminal responsibility of one pleading insanity as a defense to crime," one corresponding to the Judges' answer to questions two and three and the other to their answer to question four) (emphasis added).

6. In contrast, discussions of the law of insanity in the early twentieth century included, with some regularity, an entry under the heading of "delusion," and appear to analyze "delusion" as a separate test for insanity (*see*, e.g., Wharton and Stillé 1905, pp. 547–549; Weihofen 1933, pp. 69–79; Glueck 1925, pp. 245–254). Writing in 1961, however, Glanville Williams noted: "A study [in England] of the directions actually made show that the [test stated in response to question four] is in desuetude. … So also in most American jurisdictions" (*see* Williams 1961, p. 500).

7. The Judges' use of the phrase "defect of reason," in their answer to questions two and three, might be interpreted as a synonym for incapacity. For a suggestion to this effect, see Fingarette (1972, p. 198). If so, then the canonical test would, like the new *M'Naghten*, ground insanity in cognitive incapacity.

Earlier tests for insanity, predating *M'Naghten's Case*, and associated with Hale's notion of "total insanity" or "perfect insanity," *did* ask if the accused had the *general* capacity to know (and distinguish) right from wrong in the abstract, rather than, as *M'Naghten* asked, if he the capacity to know the particular acts charged constituted a crime. For a recent contribution urging a return to these older formulations, see Moore (2015, p. 768).

8. *Accord* Dressler (2015, p. 348) (stating that the *M'Naghten* Rule "has been persistently criticized … because, by its terms, it does not recognize degrees of incapacity"); LaFave (2010, p. 421) (stating that according to the "usual interpretation of *M'Naghten* … a complete impairment of cognitive capacity … [was] necessary").

9. The Supreme Court has read *M'Naghten's* canonical test in the same way. *See* Clark v. Arizona (p. 747) (stating the Judges' answer to questions two and three and then stating that the "second part" of that answer "presents an ostensibly alternative basis for recognizing a defense of insanity understood as a lack of moral *capacity*: whether a mental disease or defect leaves a defendant *unable* to understand that his action is wrong") (emphasis added).

10. For a helpful discussion on the different ways the word "wrong" can be construed, see Sinnott-Armstrong and Levy (2011, pp. 302–306).

11. *Compare* Walker (1968, p. 112) (reading *M'Naghten's Case* to state that "it was [an accused's] *knowledge* of [his act's] objective moral wrongness, together with the *fact* of its illegality, which made him punishable."), *with* LaFave (2010, p. 406) ("The *M'Naghten* judges did not make clear what construction they were giving to the word 'wrong.'"), *and* Manwaring (2018, p. 988) ("[T]he M'Naghten Rules … did not specify the relevant sense of 'wrong'.").

12. *Compare,* for example, U.S. v. Polizz, (pp. 276–281) (Weinstein, J.) (defining "wrongfulness" in 18 U.S.C. § 17(a), in context of child pornography prosecution, to mean "unlawful"); R v. Windle (legal wrong), *with,* for example, U.S. v. Ewing (pp. 617–621) (defining "wrongfulness" in 18 U.S.C. § 17 to mean moral wrong); People v. Schmidt (p. 947) (moral wrong) (Cardozo, J.); People v. Serravo (p. 135) (en banc) (moral wrong). The Model Penal Code is agnostic. *See* Model Penal Code and Commentaries 1985, p. 169 ("The proposal as originally approved in 1955 was in terms of a person's lack of capacity to appreciate the 'criminality' of his conduct, but the Institute accepted 'wrongfulness' as an appropriate substitute for 'criminality' in the Proposed Final Draft.").

13. In these jurisdictions, jurors are simply kept in the dark as to what "wrong" means (*see,* e.g., State v. Morgan (p. 524 n.5)).

14. For more detail on Hadfield's case, see, for example, Walker (1968, pp. 74–78) and Moran (1985).

15. James Fitzjames Stephen, the eminent Victorian jurist, suggests as much when he writes: "Either, therefore, Hadfield ought to have been convicted, or the presence of delusions must have some legal effect other than those which the answers of the judges to the House of Lords expressly recognize" (Stephen 1883, p. 160).

16. The mental-disease-or-defect requirement plays a pivotal role in both the new *M'Naghten* and irresistible impulse tests, but the law rarely defines the phrase "mental disease or defect," although some conditions, like psychopathy and addiction, are often excluded. *See,* for example, Melton et al. (2018, p. 206) ("In short, legal definitions of the mental disease or defect threshold, if they exist at all, are extremely vague and vary from jurisdiction to jurisdiction.").

17. Stephen made a similar observation about Hadfield. *See,* for example, Stephen (1883, p. 167) ("Hadfield no doubt knew [his act] to be wrong in the sense that

he knew other people would disapprove of it, but he would also have thought, had he thought about it at all, that if they knew all the facts (as he understood them) they would approve of him, and see that he was sacrificing his own interest to the common good."). Likewise, the Connecticut Supreme Court has held: "[A] defendant may establish that he lacked substantial capacity to appreciate the 'wrongfulness' of his conduct if he can prove that … he … harbored a delusional belief that society, *under the circumstances as he honestly but mistakenly understood them*, would not have morally condemned his actions." State v. Wilson (p. 640) (emphasis in original). Asking if an accused would *believe* the law or society would regard his actions as wrongful if his delusions were true is similar to, but not exactly the same as, the question-four test from *M'Naghten's Case*, which asks if the accused would *in fact* have been criminally liable if his delusions were true.

18. *See*, for example, Moore (2016a, p. 208) ("While not universally accepted, it is plausible to analyze 'X could have A-ed' in terms of the counterfactual 'X would have A-ed if C', where C represents a change from the actual word (in which X did not A). Such changed worlds philosophers … have called 'possible worlds'."). *See generally* Maier (2014).

19. Judge Weinstein relied on a similar test when he instructed the jury in *U.S. v. Polizzi*: "[W]hen the [federal insanity] statute says 'unable to appreciate' the 'wrongfulness' of his acts, you are, in effect, being asked to determine, '*If he were told that the act was illegal*, would he be able to understand, i.e., 'appreciate,' that he would be breaking the law" by committing the crime charged? U.S. v. Polizzi (p. 277) (emphasis added).

20. *See* Model Penal Code and Commentaries (1985, p. 172) ("The adoption of the standard of substantial capacity may well be the Code's most significant alteration of prevailing tests. It was recognized, of course, that 'substantial' is an open-ended concept, but its quantitative connotation was believed to be sufficiently precise for purposes of practical administration.").

21. *See* Model Penal Code and Commentaries (1985, p. 166) (use of the word "appreciate" is intended to cover cases in which the accused's awareness of the criminality or wrongfulness of his conduct "does not penetrate to the affective level").

What does it mean for knowledge to "penetrate to the effective level"? One possibility is this: Someone "appreciates" the wrongfulness or criminality of his conduct only if, when he engages in conduct he "knows" to be wrong, he experiences, or at least has the capacity to experience, some adverse reactive emotions, like guilt or shame. That's a plausible way to interpret "appreciate," but it would make psychopaths insane, at least if someone is a psychopath just in case he lacks the capacity to experience such reactive emotions. One might agree or disagree with that conclusion, but if psychopaths *aren't* responsible under § 4.01(1) because they can't "appreciate" the wrongfulness or criminality of their conduct, they're nonetheless outside the scope of § 4.01(1), at least insofar as § 4.01(2) is read to exclude "psychopathy" as a qualifying "mental disease or defect" under § 4.01(1).

22. *See*, for example, Fingarette (1972, p. 239) ("Thus, in effect, it seems to me that *M'Naghten* can stand as an adequate test if properly interpreted, retained in full, and rendered somewhat more flexible in certain respects."); Stephen 1883, p. 171 ("I should be fully satisfied with the insertion in a [Penal] Code of

'knowledge that an act is wrong' as the best test of responsibility, the words being largely construed on the principles stated here."); Bonnie (1983, p. 195) ("[R]eviv[ing] the *M'Naghten* test as the sole basis for exculpation on ground of insanity ... is the approach I favor, although I would modify the language used by the House of Lords in 1843 in favor of modern terminology that is simpler and has more clinical meaning.").

23. Again, the right result in Hadfield's case can be reached if "wrong" is given a moral-wrong reading rather than a legal-wrong reading, but that move would raise the problem discussed *supra* notes 15–16 and accompanying text.

24. *See,* for example, United States v. Currens, p. 774 (opinion of Biggs, J.) (holding that substantial lack of capacity to conform to the law, as a result of mental disease or defect, is the exclusive test for insanity); Corrado 2009. English courts have declined invitations to adopt the "irresistible impulse" test. *See,* for example, *R. v. True* (p. 170) ("There is no foundation for the suggestion that the rule derived from *M'Naghten's* case has been in any sense relaxed.").

25. Among the items he apparently stole: "14 silverine watches, 2 old brass watches, 2 old clocks, 24 razors, 21 pair of cuff buttons, 15 watch chains, 6 pistols, 7 combs, 34 jack-knives, 9 bicycle wrenches, 4 padlocks, 7 pairs of clippers, 3 bicycle saddles, 1 box of old keys, 4 pair of scissors, 5 pocket mirrors, 6 mouth organs, rulers, guns, bolts, calipers, oil cans, washers, punches, pulleys, spoons, penholders, ramrods, violin strings, etc." State v. McCullough (pp. 503–504).

McCullough's jury was, on the issue of insanity, instructed in part as follows:

> If you believe from the evidence that the acts charged in the indictment were done by the defendant ... but were caused by mental disease or unsoundness which dethroned his reason and judgment with respect to those acts, which destroyed his power rationally to comprehend the nature and consequences of said acts, and which, overpowering the will, inevitably forced him to their commission, then he is not in law guilty of the crime charged.

Ibid., p. 504. McCullough's conviction was reversed on appeal for instructional errors unrelated to the quoted language. The *McCullough* case figures prominently in Joel Feinberg's important paper on insanity (*see* Feinberg 1970, p. 281).

26. A standard citation for the irresistible impulse test is *Parsons v. State.* According to the *Parsons* court, an accused "afflicted with a disease of the mind" who knew "right from wrong," may "nevertheless not be legally responsible if the two following conditions concur:"

> (1) If, by reason of duress of such mental disease, he had so far lost the *power to choose* between right and wrong, and to avoid doing the act in question, as that his free agency was at the time destroyed; (2) and if, at the same time, the alleged crime was so connected with such mental disease, in relation of cause and effect, as to have been the product of it *solely.* (Parsons v. State, pp. 866–867)

The irresistible impulse test is often associated with impulse control disorders, such as kleptomania or pyromania, but the defendant in *Parsons,* a woman accused as an accomplice in the murder of her husband, suffered from delusions, not from what would today be describe as a control disorder. As such, *Parsons* appears to presuppose that *delusions*, as distinct from desires, can compel choice. Indeed, M'Naghten's defense counsel, Alexander Cockburn, likewise argued that M'Naghten's delusions took "away from him all power of self control." Walker (1968, p. 94). Several witnessed called on M'Naghten's behalf testified likewise. *See*, for example, Eigen (1991, p. 45) ("Nine physicians and surgeons testified [in M'Naghten's trial], many addressing their remarks to the force inherent in the delusion itself which *led* McNaughtan to the offense."). Perhaps the thought is that some delusions become obsessive, such that someone experiencing such a delusion can rationally think of nothing else. So, for example, perhaps M'Naghten, at the moment he attacked the man he believed to be Peel, could have thought of nothing else, much like McCullough, who at the moment he stole the schoolbook, could perhaps have thought of nothing else.

27. Moore (2015, pp. 659–660) ("The irresistible impulse test was formulated as a response to [the] criticism of M'Naghten.").

28. Another example is *Commonwealth v. Rogers*, decided a year after *M'Naghten* but before the judges in *Rogers* had become aware of it.

29. If a choice is voluntary insofar as it results from a distinctive mental state known as a volition, then a compelled choice is nonetheless a voluntary choice. An accused who voluntarily chooses to commit a crime might lack the capacity to have chosen otherwise, but his choice to commit the crime is still voluntary. Referring to the irresistible impulse test as a "volitional" test is therefore misleading insofar as it implies a lack of voluntary action.

30. The Commentaries acknowledge a common line of thought found in the work, among others, of James Fitzjames Stephen and Jerome Hall, according to which *M'Naghten*'s canonical test, and especially its reference to the word "know," if construed and applied in the "right" way, would classify as insane those who couldn't have chosen otherwise than to commit the crime charged. *See* Model Penal Code and Commentaries 1985, p. 167. But see Goldstein (1967, p. 75) (acknowledging Hall's claims but concluding that "[i]t is difficult to avoid the conclusion that Hall is making exaggerated demands on the word 'know'").

31. *See*, for example, Morse 1994, p. 1660 ("The moral test [for internal duress] only asks for phenomenological description and then weighs it in the moral balance. By comparing the intensity of the threatened dysphoria to the conduct chosen to avoid it, we can make the moral and legal decision whether an internal duress excuse is warranted.").

32. Kant (1788, p. 30).

33. Justice Riddell, of the Ontario Supreme Court, echoed Kant when he wrote: "The law says to men who say they are afflicted with irresistible impulses: 'If you cannot resist an impulse in any other way, we will hang a rope in front of your eyes, and perhaps that will help.'" R v. Creighton (p. 349).

Among other proposed tests, besides Kant's, perhaps the most well known is the "policeman at the elbow" test. *United States v. Kunak* (pp. 357–358) is the usual citation for the test. Courts have allowed prosecutors in jurisdictions following the Model Penal Code to ask witnesses if they believe the accused would have conformed had a policeman been at his elbow. *See*, for example, State v. Gaffney (pp. 415–416); People v. Jackson (p. 13). A much earlier observation along similar lines comes from Baron Bramwell, who testified in 1874 before the House of Commons Select Committee, Homicide Amendment Bill:

I tried a man named Dove many years ago for murdering his wife: he called a number of witnesses for the purpose of proving he could not control his actions; there was one of them who, to prove the state of this man's mind, proved that he had shot a cat in the presence of his wife, or something of that sort; and this man gravely said he believed it was an irresistible impulse. I put this question to him. ... "Now, suppose a policeman had been present when he shot the cat, do you think he would have been restrained," and he said, "Yes." "Well, then" I said, "according to your view, an uncontrollable impulse is an impulse acting upon a man when a policeman is not present."

House of Commons, Select Committee on Homicide Law Amendment Bill 1874, p. 27 (testimony of Hon. Baron Bramwell). Dove's case is described in some detail in Stephen (1863, pp. 391–402). Stephen proposed yet another test: "In the Bill of 1878, the test which I suggested was whether the impulse to commit a crime was so violent that the offender would not have been prevented from doing the act by knowing that the greatest punishment permitted by law for the offense would be instantly inflicted" Stephen (1883, p. 171).

34. *See*, for example, Moore (2016a, p. 215) ("Surely no one really subscribes to [tests like the "policeman at the elbow" test]. ... A line less clear in its delineation, but more sensible in its allowance of excuse, is more plausible. If the strength of the [desire not to commit the crime] ... had been 'a lot greater' and yet the accused still would have done what he did, then the level of excuse is reached."); Morse (2016, p. 245) ("The ability of an agent to exercise control [if faced with the threat of instant death] does not entail that he must be responsible. It is sufficient to excuse if the agent lacks 'substantial' capacity, with that lack given varying normative content depending on the general stance of the legal system to the expansiveness of excuses.").

35. *See*, for example, Kennett (2001, p. 157) (An "irresistible desire is usually so phenomenologically salient that the agent cannot stop thinking about it. It may be such as to defy any strategy aimed at distraction and redirection of attention."); Moore (2016a, p. 210) ("[T]he alien nature of the tempting desire [i.e., the desire to commit the crime] *refuses integration* enough to be balanced off against the controlling desire [i.e., the desire not to commit the crime, so that] ... the tempting desire might cause behavior irrespective of the heightened strength of the controlling desire.") (emphasis added); Morse (2017, p. 293) ("[L]ack of control arises from the intensity of desire that seems to *drown out* all the competing considerations that most of us use to control untoward desires.") (emphasis added); Morse (2016, pp. 244–245) ("Generically, the 'ego-alienated' agent's desires [to commit the crime] are *sealed off* from the *reasons-responsive self.*") (initial emphasis added); Ibid., p. 245 (noting that "craving, intense emotion, and ... other variables" can undermine a person's capacity to "think straight," that is, "to access the good reasons not to offend") (emphasis added); Morse (2005, p. 236) ("The claim is that when desires become sufficiently intense, the agent *can think of nothing else* and cannot bring his or her normative competence to bear.") (emphasis added); Watson (2004, p. 333 n.44) ("I should say that what I have in mind by volitional impairments are not merely defects of something called the will, as distinct from reason or intellect. As I see them, impairments of the kind typified by addictions characteristically involve cognitive distortions of various kinds. The *ability to see things straight*, and in

focus, is not entirely separable from the ability to respond to the reasons one knows one has.") (emphasis added).

Inasmuch as an actor lacks the capacity to control a desire to commit a crime only when the desire renders his practical reason non-responsive to some range of countervailing reasons (actual or counterfactual) not to commit the crime, Stephen Morse has long urged the law to define insanity using the language of rationality and irrationality rather than the language of control. *See,* for example, Morse (2011, p. 928) ("If a defendant was sufficiently irrational, no separate control test will be necessary to excuse him."); Morse (2009, pp. 455–459); Morse (2005, p. 236) ("Note that if the desire sufficiently interferes with the agent's ability to grasp and be guided by reason, then a classic irrationality problem arises and there is no need to resort to compulsion as an independent ground for excuse."). The difference in language—rationality compared to control—may well be a difference in form, not substance. *See* Moore (2016b, p. 392) ("Morse calls the excusing condition that I call, 'volitional impairment,' with his own label, 'irrationality'; while I find this usage of Morse's peculiarly broad, it is a harmless enough stipulation if it in fact covers the same conditions as my own label.").

36. Morse (1994, pp. 1587–1588) ("If it is true that an agent really could not help or control herself and was not responsible for the loss of control, blame and punishment are not justified on any theory of morality and criminal punishment."); Bonnie (1983, p. 196) ("Few people would dispute the moral predicate for the control test—that a person who 'cannot help' doing what he did is not blameworthy.").

37. United States v. Lyons (p. 999) (Rubin, J., dissenting) (noting (and rejecting) criticism that a volitional test "invites 'moral mistakes.'"); Bonnie (1983, p. 196) ("I agree with critics who believe the risks of fabrication and 'moral mistakes' in administering the defense are greatest when the experts and the jury are asked to speculate whether the defendant had the capacity to 'control' himself or whether he could have 'resisted' the criminal impulse.").

38. *See* Morse (2011, p. 929) ("Even if one accepts a control theory of mitigation or excuse, in most cases the agent can still be held responsible. During those times when arousal is dormant or low, they do have intact rational capacity and recognize that they will yield in the future. It is therefore their duty to take whatever steps are necessary … to ensure that they do not offend.").

39. American Psychiatric Association (1983, p. 685); Morse (2011, p. 928) ("Although it may seem unfair to blame and punish an otherwise rational agent who cannot control himself, there was good reason to jettison control tests. The primary ground was the inability of either experts or jurors to differentiate the defendant who could not control himself from one who simply did not."); Morse (1985, p. 819) ("I believe that retaining a volitional branch would be a mistake: distinguishing between resistible and irresistible internal states is simply too difficult.").

40. One, and perhaps the only, exception to this generalization is Washington law, which provides that "[n]o condition of mind proximately induced by the voluntary act of a person charged with a crime shall constitute insanity." Wash. Rev. Code § 10.77.030(3) (2017). *See generally* Mitchell (2003, 2004); Maliha (2018).

41. For the most part, neither statutory law nor case law defines the phrase "mental disease or defect," which is striking, considering the phrase looks like it's meant to play an important role in the traditional tests. *See,* for example, Slobogin (2006, p. 251) ("[D]espite centuries of law, the usual tests for insanity still speak simply in terms of 'mental disease or defect,' without further elaboration.").

42. *See,* for example, Sinnott-Armstrong and Levy (2011, p. 317) ("People lack [the] capacity [to be rational] if they cannot form rational beliefs or rationally consider the criminality or wrongfulness of their acts (a defect in theoretical rationality) or if they cannot act according to the reason that they have (a defect in practical rationality). These are exactly the lack that remove responsibility according to the MPC."); Sinnott-Armstrong (1987, p. 1) (arguing that "insanity cannot be analyzed in terms of irrationality unless irrationality is defined so this it implies the very incapacities that excuse and imply insanity on the traditional approach [as reflected in Model Penal Code § 4.01(1)]").

43. Here's another observation about the relationship between insanity and irrationality. Consider Daniel M'Naghten. M'Naghten delusionally believed the Tories were relentlessly persecuting him. Delusions are irrational beliefs. Yet however irrational M'Naghten's beliefs were, once he made Peel's death his end, he rationally put two and two together. He figured out how to execute his delusion-inspired plan. He bought a couple of pistols. He loaded them. He identified the person he thought was Peel, approached him, and fired. He rationally connected means to ends. If instrumental rationality suffices for sanity, then M'Naghten was sane. Yet if we agree that M'Naghten was insane, then someone who's insane can nonetheless be instrumentally rational.

44. Erskine's test is similar to the *Durham* Rule but importantly different. According to the *Durham* Rule, a person was insane if his crime was the product of a "mental disease or defect." Under Erskine's test, a person was insane if his crime was the product of delusions, which are typically associated with psychotic disorders. Erskine's test thus limits the *Durham* Rule's reference to mental disease or defect to delusions, and thus in the main to psychotic disorders. Erskine's theory received greater attention from treatise writers during the early twentieth century than it tends to receive from writers today.

    Erskine isn't usually included in the standard roster of irrationality theorists. Irrationality theories are usually associated with the work, first appearing in the 1960s, of Herbert Fingarette, Joel Feinberg, Herbert Morris, and, more recently, with the work of Michael Moore, Stephen Morse, and Robert Schopp. *See* Garvey 2018 (collecting literature).

45. Another response to the traditionalist objection would be to supplement Erskine's test with a traditional excusing condition, that is, compelled ignorance or choice. An accused would then be insane if as a result of *psychosis* (and not just mental disease or defect), he lacked the capacity to know he was committing a crime, or if he did know, lacked the capacity to choose otherwise. The test for insanity under federal law, which defines a person as insane if, as a result of "*severe* mental disease or defect," he was "unable to appreciate the nature and quality or wrongfulness of his acts," is a version of this approach. *See* 18 U.S.C. § 17 (2018) (emphasis added). Adding a traditional excusing condition would meet the traditionalist's objection, but the result-

ing test would be a traditional test, albeit one limited to psychotic disorders. That's fine, but irrationality theories are supposed to represent a break with tradition.

46. Writing in 1961, Glanville Williams described the question-four test as "obsolete" (Williams 1961, p. 442). True, the test nowadays gets almost no attention, at least not in the academic literature, but in law nothing may ever be truly obsolete. Old ideas sometimes just wait to be rediscovered, and that goes for the question-four test, which Christopher Slobogin has recently tried to revive. *See,* for example, Slobogin (2000); Slobogin (2003, p. 318) (noting that the "partial delusion test [i.e., the question-four test] ... is very closely related" to the alternative he proposes).

47. Earlier critics of *M'Naghten* made the same point. *See,* for example, Parsons v. State (p. 866) ("If [a delusional accused] dare fail to reason, on the supposed facts embodied in the delusion, as perfectly as a sane man could do on a like state of realities, he receives no mercy at the hands of the law."); State v. Jones, p. 388 (The test "is, in effect, saying to the jury, the prisoner was mad when he committed the crime, but he did not use sufficient reason in his madness."); Maudsley (1874, p. 97) ("Here is an unhesitating assumption that a man, having an insane delusion, has the power to think and act in regard to it *reasonably;* that, at the time of the offense, he ought to have and to exercise the knowledge and self-control which a sane man would have and exercise, were the facts with respect to which the delusion exists real; that he is, in fact, bound to be reasonable in his unreason, sane in his sanity."); Ray (1860, p. 47) ("This is virtually saying to a man, 'You are allowed to be insane; the disease is a visitation of Providence, and you cannot help it; but have a care how you manifest your insanity; there must be method in your madness."); Stephen (1883, p. 157) ("[D]elusion ... never, or hardly ever, stands alone, but is in all cases the result of a disease of the brain, which interferes more or less with every function of the mind."); Wharton and Stillé (1905, pp. 548–549); ("This rule is based on the theory that an insane man must act with reason and moderation; he must measure his acts strictly by a rational standard; but insane men do not do this; and for the reason that they are insane.").

48. Besides young children, early writers also analogized the insane to animals. Animals, along with children and the insane, were thought to lack the attributes and capacities necessary to qualify as moral agents. The analogy to animals, in the early sources, later became, thanks to Judge Tracy's charge in the trial of Edward Arnold, an analogy to "wild beasts." Howell (1816, pp. 764–765) ("[A] madman as is to be exempted from punishment ... must be a man that is totally deprived of his understanding and memory, and doth not know what he is doing, no more than an infant, than a brute, or a wild beast, such a one is never the object of punishment."). *See generally* Platt and Diamond (1965).

49. Watson (2012, p. 219) ("Moore's formulation harks back to the 'total deprivation' standard.")

50. Suppose M'Naghten, contrary to fact, had been insane under the total insanity test. If so, he shouldn't have been liable for killing Drummond. Of course, if he'd been that deranged, as disordered as the total insanity test requires for insanity, then he probably wouldn't have committed the crime in the first place. The non-agents of the total insanity test, one imagines, are so disorganized that

it would be miraculous if they could manage to pull off any but the most simple of offenses. If the totally insane do manage to commit a crime, one hopes no prosecutor would insist on bringing them to trial, or if she did, one hopes no jury would convict. *See,* for example, Fingarette (1972, p. 206) ("[T]here are those whose mental powers have generally so deteriorated for one reason or another that the individual has become permanently incapable of the most elementary self-care or interpersonal intercourse."); Morse (2016, p. 241) ("[T]hose people who are omni-disabled are usually too disorganized to engage in criminal conduct other than simple assaultive or disorderly conduct, for which no sensible defendant raises an insanity defense."). As Erskine likewise noted, the totally insane "are not only extremely rare, but never can become the subjects of judicial difficulty" (Howell 1820, p. 1313).

51. Moore maintains M'Naghten *would* qualify as insane under the unintelligibility theory (*see* Moore 2015, p. 662). That's hard to fathom, given what we know about M'Naghten. This disagreement reflects another point Moore makes; namely, that the "line separating persons from non-persons," the intelligible from the unintelligible, is more gray zone than bright line. Still, portraying M'Naghten as having passed some threshold into *unintelligibility*, as having entered a zone wherein he's "stranger to us than birds in our garden," doesn't seem quite right. History's descriptions of M'Naghten, and the unintelligibility theory's description of the insane, don't mesh very well. Here's one account of how M'Naghten behaved while in prison awaiting trial:

> What would become increasingly interesting about M'Naughten was the fact that his demeanor throughout his time in prison was always precisely the same. He always appeared calm and composed. He had a hearty appetite and ate well. He appeared very attentive to conversations between other people in the jail: other prisoners, attorneys, police guards, and is said to have frequently laughed at any jocular observations that were made. (Schneider 2009, pp. 29–30)

On its face, that doesn't sound like someone who's "stranger to us than birds in our garden," and according to one well-informed observer, in "most areas of life" those with "psychotic disorders" are not strange birds. *See* Morse (2016, p. 240) ("People with psychotic disorders may be perfectly capable of substantive and instrumental rationality in some, indeed most areas of their lives. ... [T]hey are not 'stranger to us than the birds in our gardens,' nor are they 'beyond good and evil.' ... Each is recognizably one of us.") (quoting Moore 2015, p. 678.)

52. Fingarette (1972, p. 208) ("[T]here seems no good moral reason why, in general, a person who is persistently irrational about food should not nevertheless be held responsible in connection with his business dealings."); Morse (2016, p. 241) ("[P]eople with severe mental disorders ... may be competent or morally responsible for some conduct."); Kenny (1991, pp. 24–25) ("Treating madness as a status rather than a factor ... gives a certified mental patient a license which is not given to others: he knows there are certain things he may do without being held criminally responsible, while all others not of the same status will be held responsible."). Morse and Kenny add that treating insanity as a status defense or exemption is also, in one way or another, stigmatizing. *See* Kenny

(1991, pp. 24–25) ("Treating madness as a status ... attaches stigma to insanity by assuming, without any need of proof, that insanity predisposes to criminal action."); Morse (2016, p. 243) (expressing concern that treating insanity as a status excuse "would contribute, albeit marginally, to common misunderstandings and fear of mental disorder that continue to stigmatize and exclude people with such disorders").

53. For a recent survey, see Robinson and Williams (2018, pp. 159–170). Five states (Idaho, Kansas, Montana, North Dakota, and Utah) have abolished insanity as an affirmative defense. The Supreme Court has recently agreed to answer the question: "Do the Eighth and Fourteenth Amendments permit the state to abolish the insanity defense?" State v. Kahler, 410 P.3d 105 (Kan. 2018), *cert. granted*, 139 S. Ct. 1318 (2019). For an argument that they don't, see Morse and Bonnie (2013).

54. United States v. Brawner (p. 1032) (Bazelon, C. J., concurring in part and dissenting in part). The Royal Commission on Capital Punishment, almost 20 years earlier, reached a similar conclusion. A majority of the Commission's members recommended replacing the *M'Naghten* Rules. Rather than *M'Naghten*, the Commission believed the jury should be asked to determine if "at the time of the act the accused was suffering from disease of the mind (or mental deficiency) to such a degree that he ought not be held responsible." Royal Commission on Capital Punishment (1953, p. 116).

Two prominent irrationality theorists have also suggested proposals along similar lines. *See* Moore (1997, p. 609) ("[T]he question put to juries should be the moral question framed in terms of the actual criterion by which such moral judgments are made, that is, in terms of the irrationality of the accused: was the accused so irrational that he cannot justly be held responsible?"); Morse (1985, p. 820) ("A defendant is not guilty by reason of insanity if, at the time of the offense, the defendant was so extremely crazy and the craziness so substantially affected the criminal behavior that the defendant does not deserve to be punished.").

55. *See* Robinson and Williams (2018, p. 166) ("There is evidence that, no matter what instruction a jury is given, its members tend to look to their own shared intuitions of justice in deciding whether a particular defendant's mental illness in a given case renders him or her sufficiently blameless to deserve a defense.").

56. Many thanks to Stephen Morse for helpful comments, not to mention his many scholarly works on insanity and mental health in the criminal law.

REFERENCES

Washington Revised Code. 2017.
United States Code. 2018.
Clark v. Arizona, 548 U.S. 735 (2006).
Durham v. United States, 214 F.2d 862 (D.C. Cir. 1954).
M'Naghten's Case, 8 Eng. Rep. 718 (1843).
Parsons v. State, 2 So. 854 (Ala. 1887).
People v. Jackson, 627 N.W.2d 11 (Mich. Ct. App. 2001).
People v. Schmidt, 110 N.E. 945 (N.Y. 1915).
People v. Serravo, 823 P.2d 128 (Colo. 1992).
R v. Creighton, (1908) 14 CCC 349 (Can. Ont. Sup. Ct.)
R v. Oxford, 9 C. & P. 525 (1840).

R v. True, 16 Crim. App. 164 (1922).

R v. Windle, 36 Cr. App. R. 85 (1952).

State v. Gaffney, 551 A.2d 414 (Conn. 1988).

State v. Jones, 50 N.H. 369 (1871).

State v. McCullough, 87 N.W. 503 (Iowa 1901).

State v. Morgan, 863 So. 2d 520 (La. 2004).

State v. Wilson, 700 A.2d 633 (Conn. 1997).

United States v. Brawner, 471 F.2d 696 (D.C. Cir. 1972).

United States v. Currens, 290 F.2d 751 (3d Cir. 1961).

United States v. Ewing, 494 F.3d 607 (7th Cir. 2007).

United States v. Kunak, 5 C.M.A. 346 (1954).

United States v. Lyons, 739 F.2d 994 (5th Cir. 1984).

United States v. Polizzi, 545 F. Supp. 2d 270 (E.D.N.Y. 2008).

American Law Institute 1985. *Model Penal Code and Commentaries*. Philadelphia: The American Law Institute

American Psychiatric Association, Insanity Defense Working Group. 1983. American psychiatric association statement on the insanity defense. *American Journal of Psychiatry* 140: 618.

Biggs, John, Jr. 1955. *The guilty mind: Psychiatry and the law of homicide*. Baltimore: John Hopkins Press.

Bonnie, Richard J. 1983. The moral basis for the insanity defense. *American Bar Association Journal* 69: 194.

Corrado, Michael. 2009. The case for a purely volitional insanity defense. *Texas Tech Law Review* 42: 481.

Dressler, Joshua. 2015. *Understanding criminal law*. 7th ed. New York: Matthew Bender and Company.

Eigen, Joel Peter. 1991. Delusion in the courtroom: The role of partial insanity in early forensic testimony. *Medical History* 35: 25.

Feinberg, Joel. 1970. What is so special about mental illness? In *Doing and deserving: Essays in the theory of responsibility*, 272. Princeton: Princeton University Press.

Fingarette, Herbert. 1972. *The meaning of criminal insanity*. Berkeley: University of California Press.

Garvey, Stephen P. 2018. Agency and insanity. *Buffalo Law Review* 66: 123.

Glueck, Sheldon. 1925. *Mental disorder and the criminal law: A study in medico-sociological jurisprudence*. Boston: Little, Brown, and Company.

Goldstein, Abraham S. 1967. *The insanity defense*. New Haven: Yale University Press.

Hale, Sir Matthew. 1847. *The history of the pleas of the crown*. Vol. 1. Philadelphia: Robert H. Small. (Orig. Pub. 1736.).

House of Commons. 1874. Select Committee on Homicide Law Amendment Bill. *Special Report*.

Howell, T.B. 1816. The trial of Edward Arnold, 1724. In Vol. 16 of *A complete collection of state trials*, ed. T.B. Howell. London: T.C. Hansard.

Howell, Thomas Jones. 1820. The trial of James Hadfield, 1800. In Vol. 27 of *A complete collection of state trials*, ed. Thomas Jones Howell. London: T.C. Hansard.

Kant, Immanuel. [1788] 1956. *Critique of practical reason*. Trans. Lewis White Beck. New York: Macmillan Publishing Company.

Kennett, Jeanette. 2001. *Agency and responsibility: A common-sense moral psychology*. Oxford: Oxford University Press.

Kenny, Anthony. 1991. Can responsibility be diminished? In *Liability and responsibility: Essays in law and morals*, ed. R.G. Frey and Christopher Morris, 13. Cambridge: Cambridge University Press.

Kois, Lauren E., and Preeti Chauhan. 2018. Criminal responsibility: Meta-analysis and study space. *Behavioral Sciences & the Law* 36: 276.

LaFave, Wayne. 2010. *Criminal law*. 5th ed. St. Paul: West Publishing Company.

Maier, John. 2014. Abilities. Stanford encyclopedia of philosophy. https://plato.stanford.edu/entries/abilities/. Accessed on 23 Feb 2019.

Maliha, George. 2018. Noncompliant insanity: Does it fit within insanity? *Harvard Journal of Law and Public Policy* 41: 647.

Manwaring, James. 2018. *Windle* revisited. *The Criminal Law Review* 12: 987.

Maudsley, Henry. 1874. *Responsibility in mental disease*. London: Henry S. King and Company.

Melton, Gary B., John Petrila, Norman G. Poythress, Christopher Slobogin, Randy K. Otto, Douglas Mossman, and Lois O. Condie. 2018. *Psychological evaluations for the courts: A handbook for mental health professionals and lawyers*. 4th ed. New York: The Guilford Press.

Mitchell, Edward W. 2003. *Self-made madness: Rethinking illness and criminal responsibility*. London: Routledge.

———. 2004. Culpability for inducing mental states: The insanity defense of Dr. Jekyll. *American Academy of Psychiatry* 32: 63.

Moore, Michael S. 1997. *Placing blame*. Oxford: Oxford University Press.

———. 2015. The quest for a responsible responsibility test: Norwegian insanity law after Breivik. *Criminal Law and Philosophy* 9: 645.

———. 2016a. The neuroscience of volitional excuses. In *Philosophical foundations of law and neuroscience*, ed. Dennis Patterson and Michael S. Pardo, 179. Oxford: Oxford University Press.

———. 2016b. Responses and appreciations. In *Legal, moral, and metaphysical truths: The philosophy of Michael S. Moore*, ed. Kimberly Kessler Ferzan and Stephen J. Morse, 343. Oxford: Oxford University Press.

Moran, Richard. 1981. *Knowing right from wrong: The insanity defense of Daniel McNaghten*. New York: Free Press.

———. 1985. The origin of insanity as a special verdict: The trial for treason of James Hadfield (1800). *Law and Society Review* 18: 487.

Morse, Stephen J. 1985. Excusing the crazy: The insanity defense reconsidered. *Southern California Law Review* 58: 777.

———. 1994. Culpability and control. *University of Pennsylvania Law Review* 142: 1587.

———. 2005. The jurisprudence of craziness. In *The law and economics of irrational behavior*, ed. Francesco Parisi and Vernon L. Smith, 225. Stanford: Stanford University Press.

———. 2008. Thoroughly modern: James Fitzjames Stephen on criminal responsibility. *Ohio State Journal of Criminal Law* 5: 505.

———. 2009. Against control tests for criminal responsibility. In *Criminal law conversations*, ed. Paul H. Robinson, Stephen P. Garvey, and Kimberly Kessler Ferzan, 449. Oxford: Oxford University Press.

———. 2011. Mental disorder and criminal law. *The Journal of Criminal Law and Criminology* 101: 885.

———. 2016. Moore on the mind. In *Legal, moral, and metaphysical truths: The philosophy of Michael S. Moore*, ed. Kimberly Kessler Ferzan and Stephen J. Morse, 233. Oxford: Oxford University Press.

———. 2017. Mental disorder and criminal justice. In *Reforming criminal justice. Introduction and criminalization*, ed. Erik Luna, vol. 1, 251. Phoenix: Arizona State University.

Morse, Stephen J., and Richard J. Bonnie. 2013. Abolition of the insanity defense violates due process. *Journal of the American Academy of Psychiatry and Law* 41: 488.

Murphy, Paul Thomas. 2012. *Shooting Victoria: Madness, mayhem, and the British monarchy*. New York: Pegasus Books.

Platt, Anthony. 1965. The criminal responsibility of the mentally ill in England, 1100–1843. Master's thesis, University of California, Berkeley, School of Criminology.

Platt, Anthony, and Bernard L. Diamond. 1965. The origins and development of the "wild beast" concept of mental illness and its relation to theories of criminal responsibility. *Journal of the History of the Behavioral Sciences* 1: 355.

———. 1966. The origins of the "right and wrong" test of criminal responsibility and its subsequent development in the United States. *California Law Review* 54: 1227.

Ray, Isaac. 1860. *Treatise on the medical jurisprudence of insanity*. 4th ed. Boston: Little, Brown and Company.

Robinson, Daniel N. 1996. *Wild beasts and idle humours: The insanity defense from antiquity to the present*. Cambridge, MA: Harvard University Press.

Robinson, Paul, and Tyler Scott Williams. 2018. *Mapping American criminal law: Variations across the 50 states*. Santa Barbara: Praeger.

Royal Commission on Capital Punishment. 1953. *Report*. London: Her Majesty's Stationery Office.

Schneider, Richard D. 2009. *The lunatic and the lords*. Toronto: Irwin Law.

Simester, A.P., J.R. Spencer, G.R. Sullivan, and G.J. Virgo. 2013. *Simester and Sullivan's criminal law: Theory and doctrine*. 5th ed. Oxford: Hart Publishing.

Sinnott-Armstrong, Walter. 1987. Insanity v. irrationality. *Public Affairs Quarterly* 1: 1.

Sinnott-Armstrong, Walter, and Ken Levy. 2011. Insanity defenses. In *The Oxford handbook of philosophy of criminal law*, ed. John Deigh and David Dolinko, 299. Oxford: Oxford University Press.

Slobogin, Christopher. 2000. An end to insanity: Recasting the role of mental illness in criminal cases. *Virginia Law Review* 86: 1199.

———. 2003. The integrationist alternative to the insanity defense: Reflections on the exculpatory scope of mental illness in the wake of the Andrea Yates trial. *American Journal of Criminal Law* 30: 315.

———. 2006. *Minding justice*. Cambridge, MA: Harvard University Press.

Stephen, Sir James Fitzjames. 1863. *A general view of the criminal law of England*. London: Macmillan and Co.

———. 1883. Vol. 2 of *A history of the criminal law of England*. London: Macmillan and Co.

Walker, Nigel. 1968. *The historical perspective*. Vol. 1 of *Crime and insanity in England*. Edinburgh: Edinburgh University Press.

———. 1985. The insanity defense before 1800. *Annals of the American Academy of Political and Social Science* 477: 25.

Watson, Gary. 2004. Excusing addiction. In *Agency and answerability: Selected essays*, 318. Oxford: Clarendon Press.

————. 2012. The insanity defense. In *The Routledge companion to philosophy of law*, ed. Andrei Marmor. London: Routledge.

Weihofen, Henry. 1933. *Insanity as a defense in criminal law*. New York: The Commonwealth Fund.

Wharton, Francis, and Moreton Stillé. 1905. *Mental unsoundness*. Vol. 1 of *Medical jurisprudence*. 5th ed. Rochester: The Lawyers' Co-operative Publishing Company.

Williams, Glanville. 1961. *Criminal law: The general part*. 2nd ed. London: Stevens and Sons Limited.

Zilboorg, Gregory. 1943. *Mind, medicine, and man*. New York: Harcourt, Brace and Company.

PART XVII

Mitigation

CHAPTER 18

Mitigating Factors: A Typology

Benjamin Ewing

Every year, students of criminal law pass countless hours parsing the difference between justification and excuse. Both are exculpatory in that, at the least, they negate a defendant's culpability. And both are defenses in that, if accepted, they lead to an acquittal. A justification, however, is traditionally thought to render an otherwise wrongful act permissible. An excuse, by contrast, is typically taken merely to undercut an agent's culpability for what remains a wrongful act. The distinction between justification and excuse is subtle and at times elusive (Greenawalt 1984). Yet it is a familiar, perennially debated part of moral as well as legal reasoning. Legal justifications and excuses have, and draw upon, analogues in ordinary practices of interpersonal accountability outside the law (Berman 2003).

In the shadow of justification and excuse, mitigation remains notably undertheorized. There has long been debate over the extent to which sentencing should be fixed or discretionary, determinate or indeterminate, individualized or standardized. In the United States, a conjoined academic and political attack on judicial sentencing discretion in the late 1970s and 1980s ushered in the federal sentencing guidelines and many similar systems in the states (Stith and Koh 1993; Frase 2005). There have been few attempts, however, to articulate general theories of the nature and normative force of mitigating factors (e.g., Ashworth 2011; Bagaric 2014; Hessick and Berman 2016). It remains true that, as a leading theorist of punishment put it 20 years ago, "[s]cholarly treatments of mitigation are usually superficial and unsystematic" (Husak 1998, p. 174).

To some extent, this is unsurprising. Even where sentencing guidelines shape the contours of mitigation, it remains less formal and consequential than

B. Ewing (✉)
Queen's University Faculty of Law, Kingston, ON, Canada
e-mail: benjamin.ewing@queensu.ca

© The Author(s) 2019
L. Alexander, K. K. Ferzan (eds.), *The Palgrave Handbook of Applied Ethics and the Criminal Law*, https://doi.org/10.1007/978-3-030-22811-8_18

justification or excuse. Yet it is not obvious that we can even understand the moral structure of justification and excuse fully if we distinguish justification from excuse but not excuse from mitigation. Moreover, how we draw the line between guilt-stage factors (i.e., justifications and excuses) and sentencing-stage factors (i.e., mitigating and aggravating factors) may be even more practically important than how we draw the line between factors that eliminate or alter guilt through justification as opposed to excuse.

The aim of this chapter is to begin to clarify the normativity of mitigation—and how it differs from the normativity of justification and excuse—by offering a preliminary sketch of mitigation's normative core that situates it between two poles in a tripartite typology of mitigating factors. The result is a tentative framework for interpreting and organizing mitigating factors, not an attempt to analyze each of its elements equally or exhaustively, or to classify specific factors definitively or comprehensively. I focus on the type of mitigating factor I take to reflect mitigation's distinctive normativity for two reasons. Not only is it undertheorized, but it has the potential to secure a normative autonomy for mitigation that could bring it out of the shadow of excuse and make it a more clearly worthy object of philosophical analysis.

The chapter unfolds as follows. In the section "The Dilemma for a Theory of Mitigation," I present what I take to be the central dilemma for a theory of mitigation: it appears forced to choose between sacrificing either the distinctiveness or the intuitiveness and coherence of mitigation's normative structure. Either mitigation is centrally a matter of partial exculpation at sentencing (in which case its normativity is primarily just that of excuse) or its distinctiveness is secured precisely by its incorporation of non-exculpatory considerations, which are disparate and are often public policy concerns only peripherally connected to the rights and interests of the defendants for whom they might support mitigation.

In the remainder of the chapter, I argue that this is a false dilemma. Mitigation has a normativity of its own that is simultaneously distinctive and coherent. The key is to locate the core of mitigation neither with exculpatory factors considered at sentencing nor with a mix of public policy reasons to punish a defendant less harshly, but with reasons other than a defendant's diminished culpability why a defendant himself has a stronger moral complaint about punishment. These furnish what I call non-exculpatory "claims" to mitigation. They do not show a defendant's conduct to have been less morally reprehensible from what is or ought to be the criminal law's point of view. But neither are they just general public policy considerations that the defendant himself is in no special position to invoke.

In the section "Claims to Mitigation," I offer a preliminary analysis of what it means for a defendant to have a claim to mitigation as opposed to there simply being reasons for mitigation. I draw out the idea by contrasting exculpatory mitigating factors, which seem necessarily to give defendants claims to mitigation, with non-exculpatory mitigating factors, which do not obviously do so.

In the section "Non-Exculpatory Claims to Mitigation: Three Possible Illustrations," I discuss several possible bases of non-exculpatory claims to mitigation, including two I have theorized as such at length elsewhere (a defendant's unfairly disadvantaged background and his lack of criminal history) and one on which I offer some preliminary reflections (a defendant's acceptance of responsibility). My aims are twofold: to provide a clearer sense of the structure and potential importance of the category of non-exculpatory claims to mitigation and to show how we might use the category to refine our understanding of a range of possible mitigating factors.

THE DILEMMA FOR A THEORY OF MITIGATION

Like excuses, mitigating factors are reasons to respond to wrongdoing less harshly. What, then, distinguishes the two?

In criminal law, there is one obvious difference. An excuse prompts a softened response to wrongdoing by rendering a defendant either guilty of no crime at all, or of a less serious crime than he would have committed absent the excuse. By contrast, a mitigating factor does not diminish or negate a defendant's crime but simply elicits a more lenient sentence for it. To guide the conduct of its subjects and administrators, the criminal law must not individuate crimes so finely that the presence or absence of just any factor relevant to sentencing will alter the crime of which a defendant is guilty.[1] If for no other reason than that, the criminal law can hardly do without a distinction between excuse and mitigation.

From a theoretical standpoint, however, it is worth asking: is the apparently clear line between excuse and mitigation just a more-or-less arbitrarily drawn artifact of the criminal law's need to limit the number of distinct crimes? Or is there a moral difference in kind—and not only a practical difference in degree—between excuses and mitigating factors?

It is tempting to assume that there is no such deeper difference. After all, arguably, the most salient and powerful mitigating factors are precisely ones that appear to differ only in degree, and not in kind, from excuses (Husak 1998). Familiar examples referenced in the US federal sentencing guidelines (United States Sentencing Commission, *Guidelines Manual* (Nov. 2018)) include exigent circumstances not rising to the level of legal necessity (USSG §5K2.11 p.s.), coercive pressures inadequate to constitute legal duress (§5K2.12 p.s.), and provocative acts by an offender's victim that would fail to reduce murder to manslaughter or that provoked a crime other than a culpable homicide (USSG §5K2.10 p.s.). Though such mitigating factors do not rise to the level of legal excuses, the former seem, like the latter, to be legally significant precisely because they show a defendant to be less morally culpable for his crime than he otherwise would be.

Indeed, the most obvious and intuitive reason for the criminal law to leave space for aggravation and mitigation at sentencing is to enable punishments to track more fine-grained judgments of defendants' moral culpability than would otherwise be possible. Aggravation and mitigation enable us to maintain simple definitions of crimes and high thresholds for affirmative defenses to them while still tailoring a defendant's punishment to subtler considerations such as, for instance, coercive pressure a defendant faced that fell below the law's threshold for the excuse of duress.

To be sure, many factors that are sometimes mitigating, and plausibly should be, are non-exculpatory—that is, they neither negate nor reduce a defendant's offense of conviction nor otherwise lessen the criminal law's judgment of his moral fault for his crime (*see*, e.g., Husak 1998, pp. 168–169). Such sentencing factors include, among others, assistance provided by a defendant to law enforcement (*see*, e.g., USSG §5K1.1 p.s.), burdens that a defendant's punishment would impose on third parties (particularly dependent children) (cf. USSG §5H1.6 p.s.), and a low likelihood that a defendant would pose a continuing danger to society.

However, it would seem deflating were it only non-exculpatory factors of the kind just referenced that secure for mitigation a normative structure distinct from that of excuse. For although such mitigating factors are conceptually distinct from excuses, they appear to be peripheral and heterogeneous instances of mitigating factors. The reason is that they seem to reflect the rights and interests of third parties and society as a whole, rather than what we owe, in particular, to the defendants in whose cases those mitigating factors apply.

If anything, non-exculpatory factors of the aforementioned sort seem less central to mitigation than exculpatory mitigating factors, which "mitigate" rather than "excuse" only because they fall short, by degree, of legal thresholds for excuses proper. True, partially exculpatory mitigating factors differ from excuses only by degree. Hence, they are poor candidates for core cases of mitigation *as distinct from excuse*. Yet, intuitively, core instances of mitigating factors are not merely reasons to punish a defendant less harshly, but reasons a lighter punishment is appropriate *for him*. Because partially exculpatory mitigating factors reduce a defendant's culpability, and thereby reduce the degree of punishment that would be proportional to it, it is at least clear that their mitigating force is a function of what is a right or good way to treat him—and not just what is a right or good way to proceed so far as it concerns others, or society in general. The same is not true of non-exculpatory mitigating factors as such.

In sum, the theory of mitigation seems to find itself between a rock and a hard place. If a theory of mitigation treats the difference between mitigation and excuse as predominantly a matter of degree, or as defined by the formal difference between sentencing-stage and guilt-stage considerations, then it seems to render the core of mitigation derivative of excuse, justifying moral and legal theorists' relative lack of interest in it. On the other hand, if a theory of mitigation focuses on mitigating factors that differ in kind from excuses, it seems counterintuitively to identify mitigation's core with disparate public policy considerations lacking unified normative force—rather than with considerations relevant to what we owe to defendants themselves.

In the remainder of the chapter, I try to chart a way beyond this dilemma. In my view, there is a normative core to mitigation that is both conceptually coherent and qualitatively distinct from excuse. That core is constituted by mitigating factors that give defendants themselves *claims* to mitigation (and do not merely create reasons for it), yet do so without reducing defendants' culpability and thereby collapsing into partial excuses considered at sentencing.

Readers should bear in mind, however, that this account of the normativity of mitigation—which places at its core *non-exculpatory claims* to mitigation—is not intended to imply that claims with this normative structure ought *exclusively* to be considered at sentencing as opposed to the guilt stage of a criminal trial. The normative structure of a consideration militating against punishment does not, in and of itself, resolve whether that consideration ought to bear on criminal liability or only punishment. For example, despite their *exculpatory* character, partial excuses often bear on sentencing rather than guilt. Conversely, *non-exculpatory claims* against punishment could, and arguably sometimes already do, bear on liability and not merely punishment. It has long been apparent that there are "non-exculpatory" *defenses*, such as diplomatic immunity and the statute of limitations, which negate criminal liability altogether rather than mitigate punishment (Robinson 1997, pp. 71–81). If some of those defenses are grounded not merely in considerations of public policy but defendant *claims* against punishment (a plausible hypothesis, but one I do not defend here), then the criminal law already considers certain non-exculpatory claims against punishment in assessing liability—and not just in determining punishment.

CLAIMS TO MITIGATION

Some mitigating factors are exculpatory. Others are not. That much is familiar and straightforward. The same cannot be said of the idea that certain mitigating factors do not simply constitute or create reasons to punish defendants less harshly but give defendants themselves *claims* to be punished less harshly. Before considering squarely the idea that some *non-exculpatory* mitigating factors may give defendants claims to mitigation, let us first clarify the idea of a defendant having a claim that we mitigate his punishment, as distinct from there merely being a reason for us to do so.

A mitigating factor gives a defendant a claim to mitigation, in my sense of the term, if at least some of the considerations that justify the mitigating status of that factor include, or rest on, rights and/or interests of his, in particular, as a defendant to whom the factor applies. Another way of thinking about what it means for a defendant to have a claim to mitigation is in terms of the contractualist idea (*see generally* Scanlon 1998) of him having a greater "complaint" against punishment than an ordinary defendant, or punishment being harder to justify *to him* than to an ordinary defendant.

We all always have an interest in avoiding punishment. Punishing us less always serves that interest. However, precisely because the general interest of defendants in avoiding punishment is one everyone shares on a presumptively equal basis, it is never a particular defendant's general interest in avoiding punishment that sets him apart from others and gives him a claim to mitigation that other defendants lack.

The way I employ the term here, to say that a defendant has a "claim" to mitigation is not yet to say he has a legal or moral "claim-*right*" (*see* Hohfeld 1913) to it such that the state is under a correlative legal or moral *duty* to mitigate his punishment. It is rather only to say that the state has a special *reason* to mitigate a defendant's punishment *for the defendant's own sake*. Whether a defendant has a claim to mitigation, in addition to there being reasons for mitigation, is a question not of the weight of the reasons for mitigation but of *whose* rights and interests constitute or create the reasons that tend to justify mitigation. It is a question of "what we owe *to each other*" in the sort of sense of concern to Scanlon (1998), though in a sense broader than what we are duty bound to do for one another or must do for one another in order to avoid morally wronging one another.

The easiest way to see the difference between mitigating factors that give defendants claims against punishment and those that do not is to contrast exculpatory mitigating factors with paradigmatically non-exculpatory mitigating factors—that is, those that appear grounded in general considerations of public policy rather than the rights or interests of the specific defendants in whose cases those considerations of public policy arise.

Consider first exculpatory mitigating factors. Most of us do not believe merely that a defendant's punishment should be proportional to his crime and moral culpability for it. We believe that this is not simply a good thing, or even merely the right thing, but something we owe to him specifically. We would not just behave wrongfully, but wrong him, were we to subject him to a punishment beyond what would be proportional to his crime. The Eighth Amendment prohibition on cruel and unusual punishment in the US Constitution is narrower than a right against disproportionate punishment. But it plausibly exemplifies the conviction that individuals do have a moral right against disproportionate punishment—even if its scope should change if and when it is translated into a constitutional legal right.[2] If a mitigating factor is exculpatory, then it appears necessarily to give a defendant a greater complaint about punishment and a corresponding claim to mitigation—even if not yet a legal right to it. What justifies according the exculpatory factor mitigating status is the moral right of defendants who are less culpable to be punished less harshly.[3]

Not all commonly recognized mitigating factors are exculpatory, however. And some of the most familiar non-exculpatory reasons of public policy for punishing a defendant less harshly are such that, were the state to ignore or discount them, it would not seem to do wrong by the defendant in particular but only by society more generally. Consider, for instance, collateral harms that a defendant's punishment will cause third parties and the low likelihood that a defendant will reoffend.

If punishing a defendant will harm innocent third parties, this may be a reason for mitigation whether or not it gives the defendant himself a stronger complaint about punishment than ordinary defendants and a corresponding claim to mitigation. In some cases, the reasons to care about third-party harm have nothing in particular to do with what we owe to defendants themselves but only what we owe to third parties who may be harmed by a defendant's punishment. As Husak (1992, pp. 448–449) has noted: "Arguments of social policy may militate against the punishment of public figures. Richard Nixon may have deserved punishment for his conspiracies, but Gerald Ford believed that the country was not prepared for the spectacle of a former president on trial." Ford may or may not have been right that the likely social and political consequences of allowing Nixon to be prosecuted and punished trumped the reasons for allowing him to be held criminally accountable for his actions. What is important is that in choosing to pardon Nixon, Ford was responding to interests of society as a whole that did not give Nixon in particular a claim against punishment. Had Ford declined to protect the public from the possibly adverse social and political consequences of Nixon's prosecution and punishment, he might have done wrong by the American people, but not by Nixon specifically.

In other more layered cases, punishment may affect a defendant's relationship to a third party in a way that both harms the third party and undermines the defendant's ability to discharge special duties he has to the third party, thereby arguably also giving the defendant himself a claim to mitigation. For instance, if incarcerating a father convicted of a crime will harm his children, this is at least a *pro tanto* reason not to do so—even if that reason may be outweighed by countervailing considerations. The first and foremost reasons to spare a child the harm of her father's incarceration are the rights and interests the child has with respect to her childhood caregiving and relationship to her father.[4] It is the child who has the first and foremost claim that her father not be incarcerated because of the impact it would have on her—not her father himself. Still, a case can be made that a defendant who is a parent also has a claim not to be separated from his or her child. Mothers and fathers have distinctive rights, duties, and interests when it comes to their children, and these may help justify sparing them certain punishments in some cases. A nursing mother, for instance, would seem to have a particularly strong claim against being separated from her child, even as punishment for a crime.[5]

The issues here can quickly become complex and difficult to disaggregate. But for present purposes, my point is simply that mitigation based on punishment's collateral harm to third parties *need not* rest on any claims of defendants themselves to mitigation. If we fail to mitigate a defendant's sentence in recognition of third-party harms it would impose, the defendant himself will not necessarily have any special grounds for complaint.

Were we to mitigate a defendant's punishment on the grounds that it is less necessary or useful to punish him than ordinary offenders—say, because he poses a relatively low risk of recidivism and need not be incapacitated—there might similarly be reasons to mitigate without the defendant in question having a claim to mitigation. The reason that the gratuitousness or inefficiency of punishing a defendant (from the standpoint of crime control) is a basis for punishing him less harshly is not that doing so will satisfy his interest in avoiding punishment. For he shares that interest with all defendants, including those whose punishment is *not* gratuitous or inefficient. What appears to set him apart and gives us a reason to mitigate his punishment is that *his* interest in avoiding punishment can be satisfied at lower cost to the rights and interests of other people.

Insofar as the justification for mitigating his punishment is purely one of efficiency, he just happens to be someone who would benefit from the pursuit of this value. Efficiency itself would give us no reason to insist that the benefit of mitigation remain with him if it could be redistributed without loss.

There are, of course, any number of reasons why some defendants might be at higher and lower risk of recidivism—and certain potential mitigating factors might gain their mitigating force partly through their connection to a defendant's likelihood of recidivism. If, for instance, we mitigate the punishment of first-time, aberrant, or repentant offenders partly on the basis of their assumed lower likelihood of reoffending, then there remains a question of whether there are further reasons why their status as first-time, aberrant, or repentant offenders might give them claims to mitigation. But the mere fact that a defendant is an unusually inefficient target of punishment does not obviously give him a claim to mitigation, even if it creates a reason for the state to mitigate his punishment.

There are often multiple possible explanations of the mitigating force of any given mitigating factor. Even in circumstances in which the primary reasons to mitigate are interests of society, or specific third parties, there may be subtler ways in which defendants' rights or interests in particular are part of what justifies punishing them less harshly. Far from posing a challenge to my argument, this possibility helps lead the way to it. For my central claim is precisely that in addition to exculpatory claims to mitigation and mere non-exculpatory reasons for mitigation, there is a third category of mitigating factors that are non-exculpatory yet nevertheless give defendants claims to mitigation. If, for instance, third-party harms caused by a defendant's punishment sometimes indirectly give the defendant himself a claim against it as well (a claim derivative of the more straightforward claim of the third party), this is simply grist for my mill.

On the other hand, perhaps one reason the category of non-exculpatory claims to mitigation has not yet been clearly identified and theorized is that few non-exculpatory mitigating factors so clearly *fail* to give defendants themselves claims to mitigation as third-party harms. It is often not obvious whether the mitigating force of a non-exculpatory mitigating factor lies merely in general public policy considerations or—at least partly—in what we owe in particular to the defendants in whose cases that mitigating factor is present. Moreover, if a would-be mitigating factor seems necessarily to give a defendant a claim to mitigation (if it mitigates at all), the question is likely to arise whether it is really non-exculpatory.

In the next part of the chapter, I discuss three possible non-exculpatory claims to mitigation: ones based on an offender's (a) unfairly disadvantaged background, (b) lack of prior convictions, and (c) acceptance of responsibility. In so doing, I hope to show that the category of non-exculpatory claims to mitigation and broader typology of which it is a part are useful tools for grouping and distinguishing mitigating factors with fundamentally similar and different moral foundations.

NON-EXCULPATORY CLAIMS TO MITIGATION: THREE POSSIBLE ILLUSTRATIONS

The nature, breadth, and significance of the category of non-exculpatory claims to mitigation will ultimately depend on how we understand criminal culpability. The latter issue is a difficult and contested one that I cannot hope to resolve here precisely or definitively. Fortunately, it is possible to examine several plausibly non-exculpatory claims to mitigation while remaining agnostic about many of the important controversies regarding the nature of criminal culpability. Nevertheless, some preliminary reflections on the nature of criminal culpability may serve as a helpful foundation for the discussion to come.

My working assumption is that an offender's culpability for a crime—as the criminal law does and should conceive of it—is a function, first and foremost at least, of the deficit of adequate regard for other people that an offender's crime manifests. Like such proponents of versions of this view as Westen (2006), Alexander, Ferzan, and Morse (2009), and Sarch (2017), I see this deficit as some function of the extent to which the good reasons for an offender not to commit his crime outweighed any relevant reasons he may have had to commit it.[6]

It is common to suppose that in assessing an offender's moral or criminal culpability, we need to consider more than just the magnitude of the inadequacy of regard for others his wrongdoing manifested. It is frequently suggested that, alternatively or in addition, we must bear in mind an agent's capacity and opportunity. In particular, it is often thought that moral and criminal blameworthiness depend on whether an agent's capacity or opportunity to recognize and respond to the relevant reasons against his wrongdoing was non-culpably diminished due to (a) some agential condition such as the impairment of his practical rationality by mental illness, youth, or involuntary intoxication (e.g., Wallace 1994, pp. 154–194; Morse 2003) or (b) certain extenuating external circumstances in which he acted (e.g., Kelly 2013; Brink and Nelkin 2013).

However, much, if not all, of the exculpatory effect of diminished capacity and opportunity to avoid wrongdoing reduces to their potential to alter an agent's circumstances and perceptions in such a way that his wrongdoing does not manifest as much of a deficit of adequate regard for other people as it otherwise would (*see generally* Ewing 2016, pp. 54–95). For instance, as Alexander, Ferzan, and Morse (2009, p. 156) note: "Mental illness can affect the actor's estimate of the riskiness of his behavior, making him believe the risk to be lower than he would otherwise have estimated it." Likewise, offenses committed under duress are not merely ones their perpetrators lacked a "fair opportunity" to avoid. They are offenses committed in the presence of different reasons for action such that their agents show less disregard for other people than typical perpetrators of their offenses.

Westen (2006, pp. 364–367) seems to go so far as to suggest that diminished capacity and opportunity are not exculpatory as such, but only to the extent that criminal offenders suffering from diminished capacity or opportunity will have had or perceived different reasons for and against their crimes and thereby shown less disregard for other people by their crimes than typical perpetrators of their offenses. For example, with respect to children, Westen (2006, p. 364) writes: "Because children are incapable of appreciating those interests [of other people, which society wishes to protect] in the way adults do, their conduct is incapable of manifesting ... the kind of malice, contempt, indifference, disregard and neglect that the state expresses when it punishes criminal offenses."

Hence, although certain forms of diminished capacity and opportunity may seem intuitively to be exculpatory, it is far from clear that they are so, apart from contingent ways in which they may alter the degree of inadequate regard for others displayed by offenders affected by them. With that preliminary discussion behind us, let us now consider three possible non-exculpatory claims to mitigation.

An Unfairly Disadvantaged Background

In previous work (Ewing 2016), I have argued that if a defendant comes from an unfairly disadvantaged background, this may fail to justify or excuse his crime yet nevertheless give him a claim of fairness to mitigation at sentencing. My aim here is not to recapitulate my theory of what kind of unfairly disadvantaged background should be mitigating and why. Instead, I hope simply to develop the argument in sufficient detail to give a sense of how it might ground a *non-exculpatory claim* to mitigation.

Consider, for example, a defendant who was abused and neglected as a child, and who grew up in an unjustly deprived community in which he had few good lawful opportunities and many diffuse pressures to resort to crime. When he committed his offense, there were no special reasons or pressures to commit it beyond what any ordinary perpetrator of the crime might have faced. The problem was not that his adverse formative experiences made his conduct less worthy of criminal condemnation, but that they deprived him of what I have called fair "moral" opportunity to develop a reliable disposition to give other people their due (Ewing 2016, pp. 96–130). He lacked a fair opportunity to avoid crime not because his circumstances made it harder for him, as a well-intentioned agent, to avoid crime (and thereby made his crimes less disrespectful of other people and their rights and interests) but because his circumstances made it more burdensome for him to avoid becoming the sort of person disposed to wrongdoing that manifests inadequate regard for others.[7]

Assume, for the moment, that I am right about this—that certain kinds of unfairly disadvantaged backgrounds deprive people of a fair chance to avoid crime without, thereby, making them less culpable if and when they succumb to it.[8] If it is not a reason to condemn a defendant any less, why is it a reason to punish him any less?

One answer—which is not mine—is forward-looking and instrumental. It is a bad thing when the options an agent has to avoid crime are wrongfully or unfairly curtailed or worsened. We all have an interest in good opportunities that give us cheap, easy, and reliable paths away from crime. When we are treated wrongfully or unjustly in a way that predictably diminishes those opportunities, we are wrongfully harmed. The state's interest in deterring crime and incapacitating dangerous criminals is not negated by a defendant's lack of fair moral opportunity. Hence, to mitigate the punishment of such a defendant, the state must forgo a measure of crime control, rendering everyone's rights somewhat less secure against violation. However, precisely because the state would prefer not to have to make this sacrifice, the prospect of having to do so creates a new reason for it to redouble its commitment to ensuring that subjects of the law have a fair opportunity to obey it in the first place. For failing to secure such a fair opportunity will now not only be wrong in itself but doubly destructive to the security of everyone's rights. Mitigating the punishment of the unfairly disadvantaged is, in this way, structurally analogous to a weight-loss program in which participants try to coerce themselves into keeping to a diet by pledging in advance to bear some cost if they fail to do so.

If a state is unwilling to do what it takes to secure for all its subjects a fair opportunity to avoid crime, it is doubtful that it will mitigate the punishment of criminals who have lacked such fair opportunity in order to incentivize the state to do better. But I present this possibility not to defend it but to contrast it against—and thereby clarify—the structure of the argument that I do endorse as a basis for treating a defendant's lack of fair moral opportunity as a mitigating factor.

In my view, the reason to mitigate the punishment of those who have lacked fair moral opportunity is not to incentivize the state to better realize for legal subjects a fair opportunity to avoid crime. Rather, the idea is to ensure that lack of fair opportunity to avoid crime does not become lack of fair opportunity to avoid punishment. It is a second-best solution—a form of compensation for a wrongful harm some defendants have suffered: namely, the wrongful diminution of the quality of their opportunities to avoid crime, moral culpability for it, and corresponding burdens of morally culpable crime such as punishment. I do not take a position here on whether the claim to mitigation of a defendant who lacked fair moral opportunity is a *right* and the state has a *duty* to mitigate.

What I claim is only that the reasons the state has to mitigate such a defendant's punishment arise from rights or interests of his in particular, as a victim of unfair criminogenic disadvantage faced with punishment for a crime he was deprived of a fair opportunity to avoid.

Assuming that there is such a thing as lack of fair moral opportunity, and that it ought to be a mitigating factor, it almost certainly gives defendants who have suffered from it a *claim* to mitigation. The harder question, in my view, is whether it gives them a *non-exculpatory* claim to mitigation. If a defendant lacked fair moral opportunity and consequently lacked a fair opportunity to avoid his crime, it is tempting to suppose that he must be less morally culpable for it—and that this must be the reason why he has a claim to be punished less harshly.

This is not the space in which to defend at length my view that a lack of fair moral opportunity does not necessarily diminish a defendant's blameworthiness, so far as the criminal law does and ought to conceive of it—a view I have explained and defended in detail elsewhere (Ewing 2016). In brief, however, my view is that when a defendant has come from social circumstances unfairly hostile to his healthy moral development, the reason this should be mitigating is not that it makes his crimes less worthy of condemnation by the state but that his moral disadvantage has made the usual system of threats and punishments for crimes unfairly onerous for him. To be sure, there is a sense in which he is less blameworthy because there is a kind of blame that cannot be laid at his feet—namely, blame for mistreating others despite having had a fair opportunity for healthy moral development. But criminal justice is not, and should not be, a God's-eye moral assessment of how a person has performed relative to her moral opportunities in life. The fact that a defendant performed better according to that standard is not a good reason to punish her less harshly. The reason to punish less harshly those defendants who have lacked fair moral opportunity is not to temper our condemnation of their conduct with the injection of a more individualized, holistic point of view but simply to mitigate the extent to which they suffer penal hard treatment they lacked a fair opportunity to avoid.

Lack of Criminal History

In a more recent project (Ewing 2019), I have argued that for reasons similar to those that give a claim to mitigation to defendants who lacked fair moral opportunity, defendants with little or no criminal history may have claims to be punished less harshly than defendants with more extensive criminal histories. Without reviewing comprehensively my theory of the moral significance of prior convictions at sentencing, let us consider enough of it to explain this: how does it give first-timers and novice offenders a *claim* to mitigation without supposing that their crimes are necessarily less *culpable* so far as the criminal law is or ought to be concerned?

There are more obvious and powerful instrumental reasons to treat a defendant's lack of criminal history as mitigating than to treat his lack of fair moral opportunity as such. In fact, it is tempting to suppose that the predominant reason that many criminal justice systems display lenience toward first-timers and harshness toward recidivists is to prevent crime more efficiently. If ex-offenders have shown initial sanctions to be inadequate deterrents, then perhaps they require harsher threats to desist going forward. If recidivists have shown a greater likelihood of reoffending, then perhaps incapacitating them can be expected to do more to reduce crime. These hypotheses should not be accepted uncritically. The calculus with respect to deterrence is particularly complex and difficult to assess (Dana 2001). But it is plausible that scaling defendants' punishments to their criminal histories will spare some people needless punishment and increase our return on the punishment we impose.

For reasons considered earlier, however, the mere fact that a defendant is less likely to reoffend or is a less useful object of deterrence or incapacitation would not appear necessarily to give the defendant a claim to be punished less harshly—even if it would give the state a reason to punish him less harshly. If scaling punishment to criminal history is justified because it makes punishment a more efficient means of reducing crime, then it is justified because it is responsive to the interest, which we all share, in avoiding being the target either of crime or of punishment. Scaling punishment to criminal history, on that view, is a way to achieve greater crime reduction for the same amount of punishment or the same amount of crime reduction with less punishment. The identity of those spared the punishment is morally immaterial. They just happen to be the ones who can be spared punishment at lower cost. If sparing them punishment is an imperative of efficiency, that does not make it something to which they have a right, or something that they deserve or that we owe them as a matter of fairness.

It is my contention, however, that the mitigating force of a defendant's lack of criminal history does not owe entirely or even predominantly to calculations about penal efficiency. To see this, it is helpful to make two observations.

First, prior convictions and lack thereof are more layered grounds for aggravation and mitigation than the relative usefulness and uselessness of punishment as applied to particular defendants. It is a broadly and deeply held intuition that our responses to wrongful acts should vary according to their perpetrators' histories of transgression (Roberts 2008). By contrast, it is controversial and to many people counterintuitive that wrongdoers should be punished in proportion to the usefulness of punishing them. That criminal history is a more entrenched and intuitive sentencing factor than other proxies for the usefulness of punishing a defendant suggests that it has moral significance over and above its epistemic and instrumental value to penal efficiency (Ewing 2019).

Second, intuitively, we do not simply have good reasons of public policy to punish offenders more harshly as they accrue more significant criminal histories. The greater a defendant's criminal history, the weaker his complaint about punishment seems to be. The closer a defendant is to having no record of prior criminality, the more plausible it is that he has a claim to lenience.

My account of the moral significance of criminal history locates it in the significance of a prior conviction (and, to a lesser extent, even just a prior crime) for the nature and quality of a person's opportunity to avoid crime. When we do wrong—and especially but not exclusively when we are held accountable for it by others—an important "moral" opportunity arises to learn not only about the rights and interests of other people that we have inadequately regarded but also about ourselves and the particular blind spots and vulnerabilities to which we are subject as individual moral agents. A recidivist will have had an opportunity of this kind that a first-timer will not yet have had. All else equal, the recidivist will therefore have been better positioned to avoid his offense than the first-timer, owing to the moral and prudential wake-up call he already received.

This account of the noninstrumental significance of prior convictions for sentencing could be turned into a theory of recidivists' greater culpability for their crimes—and therefore an *exculpatory* theory of lack of criminal history as a mitigating factor. However, for reasons I discuss at greater length elsewhere (Ewing 2019), and summarize here, I do not believe that recidivists' special opportunities to learn the lessons of their prior crimes necessarily increase their criminal culpability—that is, their moral culpability so far as the law is or should be concerned.

A prior conviction may contingently lead a person to understand certain risks of a crime that he previously failed to register and thus to manifest marginally greater disregard for others if he commits the crime a second time. There is also a sense in which *the failure* even to learn, let alone act on, the lessons of one's prior wrongdoing is a morally condemnable shortcoming. But because prior convictions do not necessarily make subsequent offenses themselves ones that an offender had stronger reasons not to commit, recidivist crimes do not necessarily manifest a greater degree of disregard for other people than the same crimes committed by first-timers.

On the other hand, simply having had a good opportunity to avoid a complained-of outcome can diminish one's complaint against it (Scanlon 1998, pp. 256–267). To the extent that a recidivist had a better opportunity to avoid his second crime owing to the moral opportunity presented by his first offense, all else equal, he has a weaker complaint against punishment the second time around. It is his prior opportunity that does the work of diminishing his complaint about punishment—not his failure to take advantage of it (for which he should be judged more morally blameworthy, but not more criminally blameworthy).

Suppose we were to consider a defendant's criminal history at sentencing on the supposition that it makes him fit for greater state condemnation and greater punishment on that basis. I believe we would thereby make the same mistake as we would were we to suppose that a defendant's unfairly disadvantaged background makes him fit for lesser state condemnation and lesser punishment on that basis. In both cases, we would be erroneously supposing that the criminal law should treat rights violations and acts of inadequate regard for other people as more condemnable and in need of greater deterrence when perpetrated by people whose perpetration of such acts reflects the further fault of failure to make good use of one's moral opportunities. Again, the reason to adjust defendants' punishments in recognition of their differing moral opportunities is not to turn criminal law into a more fine-grained, holistic, fair-opportunity-adjusted practice of moral assessment, but simply to better realize the ideal of making penal hard treatment a harm that its targets will at least have had a fair opportunity to avoid.

Acceptance of Responsibility

Hessick and Berman (2016) have classed acceptance of responsibility among the "consensus" mitigating factors in the United States. The United States Sentencing Guidelines take a defendant's "acceptance of responsibility" to reduce his offense level by 2 or 3 levels (which run up to 43) (USSG §3E1.1). To get the benefit of this form of mitigation, the defendant generally must decline to contest at least "factual guilt" for his crime (§3E1.1, comment. (n.2)). Other factors relevant to whether a defendant accepted responsibility include whether he has done such things as make restitution or attempt rehabilitation (§3E1.1, comment. (n.1)).

Even if it is relatively uncontroversial that there is at least some reason to punish less harshly a defendant who has accepted responsibility for his crime, it is not obvious precisely why this is so. Perhaps we should punish such a defendant less harshly in order to encourage him—and other defendants—to plead guilty, make restitution, undertake rehabilitative efforts, and so forth. Guilty pleas ease the burden of administering the criminal justice system. Hence, they should increase the speed and certainty with which the state imposes deterrent punishments in general, thereby allowing it to achieve more deterrence given the severity of its sentences or as much deterrence with less severe sentences. Restitution aids actual victims, and rehabilitation helps protect potential victims in the future, so each is also something the state should like to incentivize. Finally, perhaps those who have accepted responsibility in certain ways are less likely to reoffend; hence, we would do less to reduce crime by incarcerating them than by locking up offenders who have not accepted responsibility for their crimes.

If we stop at such thoughts, however, acceptance of responsibility may not seem to give the defendant a claim to mitigation. If we deny mitigation to the defendant who has accepted responsibility for his crime, perhaps we simply miss an opportunity to increase the extent to which defendants accept responsibility, thereby missing an opportunity to save criminal justice resources, ease victims' burdens, and encourage defendants to reform themselves. If so, we fail to promote various social goods. But we do not wrong the defendant or fail to recognize a claim that he in particular has on us. Even if we behave wrongfully, we do not wrong him. We do not owe it, in particular, to defendants who have accepted responsibility for their crimes, to maximize the net social good produced by our system of criminal punishment. Nor do we owe them in particular optimal incentives to take responsibility for their actions.

However, on a different view, the reason to mitigate the punishment of those who have accepted responsibility is not (or not merely) to encourage people to accept responsibility, or to apply punishment where it is most necessary or useful, but to give those who have accepted responsibility their due—that is, to respond to their conduct fairly or proportionally. On this view, the defendant who accepts responsibility has a claim to be treated less harshly.

To specify the source of such a claim, one would need a theory of why defendants who accept responsibility for their crimes merit special solicitude in sentencing. Without attempting to develop such a theory in detail, I want simply to flag a possible way in which one might be developed.

Suppose that what makes it permissible to punish a defendant is the enforcement of an obligation that he owes to society in virtue of his crime. If, for instance, as Tadros (2011, pp. 265–292) has suggested, the perpetrators of crime are morally obligated to contribute to general deterrence, and the state is justified in punishing them in order to enforce this obligation, then defendants who contribute to general deterrence by accepting responsibility and thereby easing the administrative burden of the criminal justice system would seem partially to discharge their duty and thereby partially to erode the basis on which they may be permissibly punished.[9] This would not simply be a reason to punish them less harshly, but the basis of a claim (and perhaps even a moral right) they would have to be punished less harshly.

Such a view would be subject to obvious objections,[10] and it is not my goal to defend it beyond the point of an exposition that makes it plausible. What is important to notice here is only that, *should it prove compelling*, the sort of claim to mitigation based on "acceptance of responsibility" I have sketched here would be another example of a claim to mitigation that does not rest on exculpation. Were we to mitigate the punishment of those who plead guilty because they thereby partially discharge the debt that grounds their punishment, the harsher punishment we would impose on those who do not plead guilty would not be grounded in whatever blame they bear for failing to do so. Their relatively greater sentences would be grounded instead in their greater remaining obligation to contribute to general deterrence.

Indeed, it might seem to be a performative contradiction—or something close—for a defendant to invoke his "acceptance of responsibility" to diminish the seriousness of his crime or his moral culpability for it. Because acceptance of responsibility focuses on acceptance of one's legal guilt in particular and encompasses further activities, it would certainly be *compatible* with pleading for mitigation on the basis of a claim of diminished culpability. But it is hard to see how one's acceptance of responsibility could itself ground a claim of diminished culpability for one's crime. To treat acts of accepting responsibility as exculpatory would seem to require us to enlarge the target of criminal condemnation beyond crimes themselves to encompass the moral quality of a range of defendants' behaviors following their crimes. There seem to be good reasons, both conceptual and moral, to refrain from doing either.

CONCLUSION

If I am right that there are mitigating factors that are non-exculpatory yet strengthen a defendant's complaint about punishment (and not merely the "all things considered" case for relative lenience), then we should recognize three different types of mitigating factors: exculpatory claims to mitigation, claims to mitigation without exculpation, and public policy considerations (such as undue harm to third parties) that support mitigation without giving the defendant himself any special claim to it.

I have suggested that non-exculpatory claims to mitigation constitute mitigation's normative core. And I have discussed three possible bases of such claims: a defendant's unfairly disadvantaged background, lack of criminal history, and acceptance of responsibility. It is difficult to place these and other mitigating factors in the category of non-exculpatory claims definitively, however, both because some mitigating factors appear to have multiple moral grounds and because the lines are not always clear between exculpatory and non-exculpatory mitigation, and between mitigation to which a defendant has a claim and mitigation for which there is merely a reason.

Does my formal classification of distinct types of mitigating factors or my provisional thesis about the distinctive normativity of mitigation shed light on the *weight* we ought to accord to different mitigating factors? It seems perilous to generalize about the relative moral importance of different types of mitigating factors. Reasons for mitigation may be weighty even if they issue from the rights and interests of third parties or society as a whole rather than the defendant in particular. Yet in general, and in the typical case, the first, foremost, and most difficult part of justifying punishment is justifying it to those we punish. In that sense at least, all else equal, defendants' *claims* to mitigation—including their non-exculpatory ones—have an analytic and moral priority over other mitigating factors.[11]

NOTES

1. Kelly (2013, pp. 249–252) makes a point about our standards of moral wrongfulness that is analogous to my claim here about standards of criminal wrongfulness.
2. The practical demands of criminal administration may simply be such that an individual's constitutional legal right against disproportionate punishment should be defined more narrowly than his moral right, lest constitutional interpretation become a constant basis for second-guessing initial legislative and judicial sentencing decisions.
3. Jacob Weinrib has helpfully pressed me to consider whether, conceptually at least, we might distinguish *four* types of mitigating factors: exculpatory and

non-exculpatory mitigating factors that do and do not give a defendant a claim to mitigation. It does not seem *conceptually* incoherent that a mitigating factor could apply to a defendant, and be exculpatory, yet fail to give her a claim to mitigation. However, it does appear *morally* implausible, for it would mean that our reasons not to punish a defendant disproportionately have nothing to do with what we owe to her in particular. The assumption that exculpatory mitigating factors give defendants claims to mitigation at least as a matter of *moral* necessity allows us to narrow our typology of mitigating factors to just three categories (rather than four): exculpatory reasons for mitigation (to which a defendant necessarily has a claim) and non-exculpatory reasons for mitigation to which a defendant does and does not have a claim.

4. Though I have contrasted mitigation based on the public policy goal of avoiding "harm" to third parties with mitigation grounded in what we owe to defendants themselves, a defendant's punishment might come into conflict not only with third parties' interests but also with their rights. Third parties' rights and interests may be mere "public policy considerations" so far as the defendant is concerned, but that does not mean they are mere public policy considerations so far as the third parties are concerned, or that they are of marginal importance or only matters of good and bad rather than right and wrong. Thanks to Jean Thomas for pressing me on this point.

5. Moreover, this would not be a claim based on diminished culpability for her crime, so it would be a putative non-exculpatory claim to mitigation. Where culpability is concerned, if a mother commits a crime that she knows or should know is frequently punished with incarceration, then if anything there is at least a moral sense in which she is *more* culpable than she otherwise would have been. Unless the risk to which she exposed her child was itself an independent crime of abuse or neglect, it may be wrong to treat that risk as a ground for punishing her more harshly for her actual crime. Still, arguably the moral culpability she bears for putting her child at risk partially negates or counteracts her claim against separation from her child (though not necessarily her child's claim against it) or it partially erodes her moral standing to be the one to articulate her claim. To claim mitigation to avoid separation from her child, she must demand that the state show adequate regard for a special relationship that she herself has inadequately regarded by recklessly triggering state interests in conflict with respecting that special relationship.

6. Yaffe (2018, pp. 66–97) also sees criminal culpability as a function of the extent of a defendant's failure to act in accordance with a particular set of reasons against his criminal conduct but leaves open the conceptual possibility that some of the reasons may "have nothing to do with the bearing of the conduct on others" (ibid., p. 77).

7. I have focused here and elsewhere on unfairly disadvantaged *backgrounds*, which affect people over long periods of time. However, the argument I have developed might also help explain the normative structure of claims against punishment grounded in more immediate constraints of certain kinds on a person's capacities or opportunities—such as, for example, involuntary intoxication or entrapment. Thanks to Kim Ferzan for a comment that prompted me to reflect on this possibility. The fact that an offender was involuntarily intoxicated, or intentionally induced to commit his crime by the state or another party seeking to entrap him, would not seem in and of itself to show that there were stronger

reasons for, or weaker reasons against, his crime. Hence, it is not obvious that either factor is exculpatory. But either one might be thought to have deprived an offender of a fair opportunity to avoid his degree of culpability for his crime and thereby to have generated a non-exculpatory claim against punishment—whether such claim would appropriately negate criminal liability or merely mitigate punishment. However, to develop such an argument fully, one would need to consider a question to which I have not even sketched an answer in my cursory overview here of fair moral opportunity: under what circumstances can an agent be said to have lacked a *fair* opportunity to avoid being as culpable for a crime as he was, and not just to have had the *bad luck* to have had less capacity or opportunity to avoid his culpability than he might have had, or than "normal" perpetrators of his crime would have had? For my answer to that question, see Ewing (2016, pp. 96–130).

8. That is not to say that an unfairly disadvantaged background never contingently puts a defendant in circumstances that partially justify or excuse his crime by making it a manifestation of a lesser degree of disregard for other people than it ordinarily would be (*see* Ewing 2018, pp. 36–45). It is only to say that a background unfairly hostile to healthy moral development (a) does not, as such, make a defendant's crime a less defective exercise of moral agency, but (b) does, as such, make the ordinary moral expectations enforced by criminal punishment unfairly burdensome for the relevantly disadvantaged agent to meet.

9. This might suggest that when defendants provide what the federal sentencing guidelines call "substantial assistance to authorities" regarding other persons' criminal conduct (USSG §5K1.1 p.s.), they also have claims to be punished less harshly.

10. Perhaps the most salient concern is that "acceptance of responsibility" for a crime is not the only way to contribute to general deterrence. And, intuitively, it seems wrong that offenders who, before their crimes, already made contributions to general deterrence beyond anything they had a preexisting duty to make should therefore receive a credit against future punishment for crimes they commit. My underdeveloped thinking here has been influenced by Tadros's own reflections on potential objections to his duty-enforcement view of the justification of punishment (Tadros 2011, pp. 283–291).

11. I thank Chuck Ewing, Kim Ferzan, Tim Stoll, Jean Thomas, Sabine Tsuruda, Ashwini Vasanthakumar, Grégoire Webber, and Jacob Weinrib for helpful suggestions regarding this chapter.

References

United States Sentencing Guidelines (USSG).

Alexander, Larry, Kimberly Kessler Ferzan, and Stephen J. Morse. 2009. *Crime and culpability: A theory of criminal law.* Cambridge: Cambridge University Press.

Ashworth, Andrew. 2011. Re-evaluating the justifications for aggravation and mitigation at sentencing. In *Mitigation and aggravation at sentencing,* ed. Julian V. Roberts, 21–39. Cambridge: Cambridge University Press.

Bagaric, Mirko. 2014. A rational theory of mitigation and aggravation in sentencing: Why less is more when it comes to punishing criminals. *Buffalo Law Review* 62: 1159–1237.

Berman, Mitchell N. 2003. Justification and excuse, law and morality. *Duke Law Journal* 53: 1–77.

Brink, David O., and Dana K. Nelkin. 2013. Fairness and the architecture of responsibility. In Vol. 1 of *Oxford studies in agency and responsibility*, ed. David Shoemaker, 284–313. Oxford: Oxford University Press.

Dana, David A. 2001. Rethinking the puzzle of escalating penalties for repeat offenders. *Yale Law Journal* 110: 733–783.

Ewing, Benjamin Harris. 2016. Punishing disadvantage: Culpability, opportunity, and responsibility. Ph.D. dissertation, Princeton University.

Ewing, Benjamin. 2018. Recent work on punishment and criminogenic disadvantage. *Law and Philosophy* 37: 29–68.

———. 2019. Prior convictions as moral opportunities. *American Journal of Criminal Law* 45: 253–304.

Frase, Richard S. 2005. State sentencing guidelines: Diversity, consensus, and unresolved policy issues. *Columbia Law Review* 105: 1190–1232.

Greenawalt, Kent. 1984. The perplexing borders of justification and excuse. *Columbia Law Review* 84: 1897–1927.

Hessick, Carissa Byrne, and Douglas A. Berman. 2016. Towards a theory of mitigation. *Boston University Law Review* 96: 161–218.

Hohfeld, Wesley Newcomb. 1913. Some fundamental legal conceptions as applied in judicial reasoning. *Yale Law Journal* 23: 16–59.

Husak, Douglas N. 1992. Why punish the deserving? *Noûs* 26: 447–464.

———. 1998. Partial defenses. *Canadian Journal of Law and Jurisprudence* 11: 167–192.

Kelly, Erin I. 2013. What is an excuse? In *Blame: Its nature and norms*, ed. D. Justin Coates and Neal A. Tognazzini, 244–262. Oxford: Oxford University Press.

Morse, Stephen J. 2003. Diminished rationality, diminished responsibility. *Ohio State Journal of Criminal Law* 1: 289–308.

Roberts, Julian V. 2008. *Punishing persistent offenders: Exploring community and offender perspectives*. Oxford: Oxford University Press.

Robinson, Paul H. 1997. *Structure and function in criminal law*. Oxford: Oxford University Press.

Sarch, Alexander. 2017. Who cares what you think: Criminal culpability and the irrelevance of unmanifested mental states. *Law and Philosophy* 36: 707–750.

Scanlon, T.M. 1998. *What we owe to each other*. Cambridge, MA: Harvard University Press.

Stith, Kate, and Steve Y. Koh. 1993. The politics of sentencing reform: The legislative history of the federal sentencing guidelines. *Wake Forest Law Review* 28: 223–290.

Tadros, Victor. 2011. *The ends of harm: The moral foundations of criminal law*. Oxford: Oxford University Press.

Wallace, R. Jay. 1994. *Responsibility and the moral sentiments*. Cambridge, MA: Harvard University Press.

Westen, Peter. 2006. An attitudinal theory of excuse. *Law and Philosophy* 25: 289–375.

Yaffe, Gideon. 2018. *The age of culpability: Children and the nature of criminal responsibility*. Oxford: Oxford University Press.

PART XVIII

Moral Uncertainty

CHAPTER 19

Moral Uncertainty and the Criminal Law

Christian Barry and Patrick Tomlin

INTRODUCTION

Our aim in this chapter is not to connect an *issue* in applied ethics to the criminal law, but rather to take a nascent, evolving *approach* to applied ethics, and to see what it might have to say about the kinds of questions and positions we find within criminal law theory.

The approach we want to apply to the criminal law is that of what we call "Moral Uncertainty Theory." Applied ethics, broadly speaking, concerns what, morally speaking, real-life agents ought to do in particular real-life circumstances. Ordinarily applied, ethicists argue for the position that they believe to be the moral truth of the matter.[1] So, for example, Philosopher A writes an article arguing that the correct moral position is that abortion is morally permissible, while Philosopher B writes an article arguing that the correct moral position is that abortion is morally impermissible.[2]

This is all well and good, and of course a lot of fine philosophical work gets done in this way. But it's also important to remember the *applied* nature of applied ethics—it is supposed to offer guidance to real-life agents. Imagine that Jane is unsure about whether or not to have an abortion. She thinks it's probably permissible but is deeply unsure. She reads the work of Philosopher A and Philosopher B. This only heightens her sense of uncertainty. She gets the chance to speak to Philosopher A. Philosopher A tries to convince Jane that the moral truth is that she is permitted to have an abortion. But then Philosopher

C. Barry (✉)
The Australian National University, Canberra, ACT, Australia
e-mail: christian.barry@anu.edu.au

P. Tomlin
University of Warwick, Coventry, UK
e-mail: Patrick.Tomlin@warwick.ac.uk

© The Author(s) 2019
L. Alexander, K. K. Ferzan (eds.), *The Palgrave Handbook of Applied Ethics and the Criminal Law*, https://doi.org/10.1007/978-3-030-22811-8_19

445

B tries to convince her of the opposite. Jane remains deeply uncertain about what the right course of action is. What is Jane to do?

This is where Moral Uncertainty Theory comes in. Moral Uncertainty Theory tries to advise Jane on what she ought to do *given her uncertainty*. It starts from the idea that Jane is uncertain and asks what she ought to do given the moral beliefs that she has. Moral Uncertainty Theory asks the question that Jane is surely asking herself: *what should I do, given that I don't know what I should do?*

It might be thought that the answer to this question is obvious: Jane should respond by doing the objectively morally right thing (Weatherson 2014; Harman 2015). Well, of course, she should! But Jane needs to know how she ought to act, given what she believes at the time when she must decide how to act. And she is uncertain about whether or not some of the courses of action open to her are permissible. Perhaps there is another obvious answer to our question: Jane should suspend belief about the matter. That is, when we cannot tell with much confidence whether or not some course of conduct is permissible, we can simply suspend belief about it.

However, whatever Jane may decide to *believe* about competing claims regarding the permissibility of abortion, she is in a situation where she will conduct herself in ways that *reflect a practical stance* toward this practice. Suppose that Jane is committed to the view that, if a fetus possesses the same moral status as a toddler, she has a stringent responsibility not to terminate her pregnancy. Even if she suspends belief about the claims presented by A and B, she must adopt a practical stance toward the issue of abortion. For example, if she terminates her pregnancy, then given her beliefs, she is taking the practical stance that a fetus does not possess the same moral status as a toddler. Adopting the evidently sensible epistemic principle to "suspend belief until you get more information" therefore cannot provide a full answer to the question of what you should do when you don't know what to do.

To capture this, we might distinguish between moral propositions that agents *believe* they have and those that they *assume*. To assume a moral proposition, as we understand this notion, is for it to play a role in your practical deliberations and to provide you with a motivating reason to act in certain ways.

Imagine that, after careful reflection, Jane thinks it is 60% likely that abortion is permissible. Should she then, for the purposes of practical action, assume the proposition that she is permitted to have an abortion? Perhaps. Most applied ethics appears to regard this as the end of the matter. But some theorists disagree. For example, as Dan Moller argues, if Jane is only 60% convinced that abortion is morally permissible, then she has a 40% credence in the proposition that abortion is *not* morally permissible. Imagine that Jane thinks that *if* abortion is impermissible, it is akin to killing a toddler. That means she thinks that if she has an abortion, then by her own lights there is a 40% chance she is doing something very seriously morally wrong. Moral Uncertainty Theory can take this into account (Moller 2011).

We can make a useful, though perhaps imperfect, analogy with empirical uncertainty here. Imagine that Jane is uncertain about whether or not there is a child in her currently empty swimming pool. If she fills it up, then if there is a child in there, it will drown. Jane thinks there is a 40% chance there is a child in her swimming pool. Jane should, of course, take this into account in deciding what to do: there is a 40% chance that she will do something seriously objectively morally wrong. But the same is true, according to Jane's own beliefs, in the abortion case.

When we assess theories of what we ought to do under moral uncertainty, it's important that we don't criticize them *simply* because they allow conduct that we think is morally forbidden (or forbid conduct that we think is allowed). *That* type of claim is the type to be considered in first-order moral deliberation, when we try to decide what is objectively right and wrong, permissible and impermissible. In judging whether a theory of moral decision-making under uncertainty is plausible, we must instead ask whether it is plausible that "*given this agent's beliefs*, it is reasonable for her to *assume x* is permissible (or impermissible) *when choosing what to do*."

In this chapter, we seek to provide an overview of how different approaches to Moral Uncertainty Theory might inform various debates and issues within criminal law theory. Our discussion is tentative for three reasons. First, the *point* of Moral Uncertainty Theory is that it cannot *on its own* provide moral guidance—it seeks to help agents decide what to do given their own moral beliefs. So, what Moral Uncertainty Theory "has to say" about issues in the criminal law will depend upon what the "inputs" are: what moral views people have and what credence they have in them. Second, there remains debate and controversy about what is the right approach within Moral Uncertainty Theory. That is, there is disagreement about how we should take into account the various first-order moral beliefs that an agent has in deciding what they ought to assume for the purposes of action. The literature is in its infancy (the first systematic treatment is Lockhart (2000)) and questions, issues, and problems are still emerging. Third, Moral Uncertainty Theory applies in the first instance to individual moral agents, providing guidance on what they should regard as morally best or morally permissible given their moral beliefs. But when we are considering issues of criminal law, we face social decisions about how to collectively design shared social institutions. That is, it is not immediately clear what the analogue of the individual agent is or how to represent different credences in propositions concerning the moral status of different kinds of conduct when it comes to collective decisions. In many ways, our chapter is an exploration of the difficulties and complexities of trying to apply this approach to applied ethics to issues within the criminal law.

We shall proceed as follows. In the following section, we introduce Moral Uncertainty Theory in more detail, explaining some different approaches to the questions of what we ought to do when we don't know what to do. In the section "Uncertainty in the Criminal Law," we look at the criminal justice process and identify some key actors who might be morally uncertain and the decisions about which they may face moral uncertainty. In the section "Uncertainty and Criminalization," we focus on questions about criminalization—how can morally uncertain individuals or collectives use Moral Uncertainty Theory when deciding how to vote on criminalization matters? In the section "Comparing Wrongs," we discuss the issue of how to compare the wrongs of impermissible criminalization and impermissible failures to criminalize. In the section "Setting Punishments Under Uncertainty," we discuss sentencing. Finally, we offer some "Concluding Remarks."

Moral Uncertainty Theory: Approaches and Problems

It is only recently that philosophers have begun to systematically turn their attention to what we ought to do under moral uncertainty.[3] Their discussions have, broadly speaking, addressed three questions. The first concerns the validity and the nature of the ought in question. As we have phrased it, the question which Moral Uncertainty Theory addresses is *what should I do, given that I don't know what I should do?* Some have denied that this question makes sense. That is, they have denied that there can be an "ought" which is sensitive to our moral beliefs—morally speaking, we simply ought to do what we ought to do (Harman 2015; Weatherson 2002, 2014)! Others believe that there *is* an ought here, but there is some disagreement about what *kind* of ought it is—a rational ought; a moral ought; or a sui generis kind of ought? We largely set these controversies aside in this chapter.

The second question is substantive: what should I do when I don't know what I should do? Here, philosophers have sought to provide theories or frameworks into which agents can plug their first-order moral beliefs and emerge with an answer about what they ought to do, relative to their moral beliefs. Elsewhere (Barry and Tomlin 2016), we have pleaded for a little more precision about exactly what is being asked here. At the first-order moral level, we often make important distinctions between what an agent is permitted to do, what she is required to do, what would be morally best for her to do, and what she should do all things considered. All of these first-order moral questions have their moral-belief-relative (MBR) analogues, and so the question "what should I do given that I don't know what I should do?" is underspecified. Our own interest, both elsewhere and here, concerns moral permissions and so our question is: "what am I (or we) permitted to do, given that I (or we) don't know what I (or we) are permitted to do?" We can call this the question of moral-belief-relative permissibility (MBR permissibility). Why focus on permissibility? Well, judgments of impermissibility carry a special kind of moral gravity, and impermissible actions attract a special kind of moral blame and censure. This focus seems especially important when considering the criminal law. One possible response to actions that are impermissible is to attach legal sanctions to them, including criminal punishment. Imposing criminal sanctions is not a response that is ordinarily thought to be appropriate when it comes to conduct that is merely morally sub-optimal. And when it comes to punishing conduct, we want, first and foremost, to ensure that our punishments will be permissible: the philosophical debates about punishment turn on if, when, and why it is permissible, not whether it is admirable, or supererogatory. The issue of permissibility under uncertainty is, moreover, of special concern when thinking about what kinds of conduct to criminalize, how criminal procedure should be designed, which punishments are proportionate, and so on. We canvass three general approaches that have been taken to MBR permissibility in the literature.

The final question that philosophers have considered concerns intertheoretic comparisons of value. The issue here is that most approaches to the question of what we are MBR permitted to do require us to take into account the recommendations or requirements of several moral theories. We can understand a theory as a set of principles from which we can derive different moral scores for conduct options. But it isn't clear that these theories are trading in a single "currency" and thus whether they can be compared in the right way. We are going to set this issue aside in this chapter.[4] However, we think it's important to remember that while the comparisons that must be made are intertheory, they are *intra-agent*. That is, the individual who is morally uncertain may be able to do the appropriate comparisons (presumably she knows how valuable or disvaluable the options are according to the moral reasons that generate her uncertainty), even if the moral theories *themselves* don't give her the resources for doing so.[5]

It must be acknowledged at the outset that any talk of the theories that an agent has credences in idealizes quite significantly ordinary moral deliberation in a few ways (Unruh n.d.). First, agents do not typically think of themselves as torn between two conflicting *theories* when making choices (they may not even have a clear idea of what a moral theory might look like). Second, agents are unlikely to articulate their commitments in terms of precise credences in rival moral theories.[6] Third, agents don't typically deliberate on the assumption that specific theories they have some credence in value different options in some very precise manner (assigning a "moral score" to, say, to how the theory treats infringing someone's property rights to help someone else in need of shelter). Still, such idealization can be illuminating. It *is* common for people to be in conflict about the moral status of different conduct options, and their reasons for this can be plausibly represented in terms of competing values to which they are drawn (or arguments they find convincing), which in turn can be seen as embodying competing theories. And, surely, we do have at least some intuitive idea, when we are feeling conflicted about the moral status of some conduct option (whether it is permissible to eat meat, terminate a pregnancy, harshly criticize a colleague on social media), about our level of confidence in its permissibility. Finally, we also seem to have some intuitive idea of just how bad some conduct would be, according to some values we are committed to or some argument we are drawn to.

Three Approaches to MBR Permissibility

My Favorite Theory

How, then, can we tell whether some course of conduct will be MBR permitted? We here consider three answers to this question. The simplest view, and the view which much applied ethics tacitly appears to endorse, is that you should follow a course of conduct which the theory in which you have the most confidence deems permissible. That is, once Jane has decided that she is 60% confident in a theory which says that she is permitted to have an abortion, then she should regard herself as permitted to have an abortion. Ted Lockhart (2000, pp. 42–43) calls this the "My Favorite Theory" approach to moral uncertainty. This approach provides consistent advice for agents: regard as permissible whatever, according to the theory you have most credence in, is taken to be permissible. In addition, it does not require the agent to make inter-theoretic comparisons of value, since she need only pay attention to how one theory—the one she has the most credence in—values the conduct options she is considering.[7]

The My Favorite Theory view has been subject to serious criticism (Lockhart 2000; Barry and Tomlin 2016; Bykvist 2017). One problem with My Favorite Theory is that it seems unduly sensitive to the individuation of moral theories. Say that in our abortion example, Jane is 60% confident in the theory that says she is permitted to have an abortion (Theory 1) and 40% confident in the theory that says she is not (Theory 2). According to My Favorite Theory, she is MBR permitted to have an abortion. Now imagine Jane discovers an important distinction within the way that the permissibility of abortion could be established. She is unsure whether, if it is permitted, it is permitted because the fetus lacks the requisite moral status or because there are circumstances in which we are permitted to kill beings with moral status. She is equally confident in each of these views. So, Theory 1 is split into Theory 1a and Theory 1b. Jane now has 30% credence in each of these views. Jane's Favorite theory now turns out to be Theory 2, in which she has 40% credence. By splitting Theory 1 into two distinct theories, even though her credence in the permissibility of abortion remains constant, it becomes MBR impermissible for Jane to have an abortion. However, the basic intuition behind the My Favorite Theory approach might be preserved by shifting from talk of theories to talk of options. That is, it might plausibly direct the agent to regard as MBR permissible any conduct that is such that she has more credence that it is permissible than that it is impermissible.[8] This would have the implication in the earlier case that Jane regards abortion as MBR permissible, even though she is unsure just which theory gives the best account of its permissibility.[9]

A much deeper worry about the My Favorite Theory approach is that it seems to dismiss the idea that moral risk ought to affect what we do, even when the stakes are very high (as they are in Jane's case in the earlier example.) Imagine an agent faces a moral choice between A and B. She has credence in two theories, Theory 1 and Theory 2, and has slightly greater credence in

Theory 1. Theory 1 says A and B are both permitted. According to My Favorite Theory, the agent should then simply choose between A and B, and she can do so on non-moral grounds—both are MBR permitted. Imagine the agent is personally indifferent between A and B, and so she flips a coin. According to My Favorite Theory, this is fine *even if* Theory 2, in which the agent has almost as much confidence as Theory 1, says that B is a very serious moral wrong akin to murder. Surely, when the agent is indifferent between the options, and one carries a high chance of being a serious objective moral wrong, then even if this option would confer a significant personal benefit to her, she has strong reason to choose the other option.

The above argument relies on the My Favorite Theory Approach appearing to deliver the wrong verdict about MBR permissibility. It is important to remember that when we consult intuitions about these cases, we should not be asking ourselves what *we think* is objectively permissible when it comes to the question of abortion, or even what *we* think is MBR permissible, but rather what *the agent who is uncertain* should regard as MBR permissible *given her beliefs*.

Expected Moral Value

The Expected Moral Value approach to Moral Uncertainty Theory addresses what we suggested was the principal defect of the My Favorite Theory approach. That is, the Expected Moral Value approach takes seriously not only the agent's credence in various theories but also the moral value (and disvalue) that such theories attach to different conduct options that the agent is considering. The Expected Moral Value approach tells us, through judging the "moral score" of a conduct option according to a theory, multiplying it by our credence in that theory and then summing the weighted scores of each option, to pursue the option or options with the highest expected moral score (Lockhart 2000; Ross 2006). So to return to our running example, suppose that Jane has a 40% credence in Theory 2 according to which abortion is akin to killing a toddler and a 60% credence in Theory 1 according to which abortion is permissible. While on the My Favorite Theory approach, Jane should assume the view that she can permissibly terminate her pregnancy, the Expected Moral Value approach will imply that she should regard abortion to be impermissible: the expected moral disvalue of terminating her pregnancy is very high, since by her lights she would be taking a 40% chance of doing the moral equivalent of killing a toddler. We wouldn't ordinarily perform some action that carried a 40% chance (or, for that matter, a 20% chance) of being a serious moral wrong (unless moral reasons concerning the alternatives rendered that the best of a very bad set of options), even if that action would produce a significant personal benefit to us.[10]

One of the appealing features of this approach to moral uncertainty is that it treats the requirements of rational choice under moral uncertainty as broadly continuous with those that apply under empirical uncertainty. Still, the very features that make this seem a plausible approach in some cases lead to counterintuitive implications in others. The central problem with the Expected

Moral Value approach is that it will always prioritize certainly permissible options over possibly permissible options. Imagine that, instead of a 40% credence in Theory 2 (according to which abortion is a very serious moral wrong), Jane has only a 0.1% credence in it. What should she regard as her permissible options in this case? Well, she knows that according to one of her theories (Theory 1—the one she has a 99.9% credence in), it is permissible either to terminate or to carry to term, while, according to the other, more restrictive theory, only one of these options is permissible. So, given that each theory will regard carrying to term as permissible, while one regards terminating the pregnancy as a serious moral wrong, this approach will deliver the verdict that it is MBR impermissible for Jane to have an abortion. That is, this approach will often entail that for the purposes of deciding what to do, we must act in accordance with the most restrictive theory that we have *any* credence in, even if we have *very* little credence in it, and even if (unlike in our case) the potential moral wrong is not a very serious one. We call this a "nesting" case, since one theory (the more restrictive theory) "nests" inside the more permissive theory, in that each and every conduct option permitted by the more restrictive theory is also permitted by the more permissive theory, while the permissive theory allows additional options.

Another challenge for the Expected Moral Value approach is posed by what we call "Venn cases." These are cases in which two (or more) theories agree on the permissibility of a limited set of conduct options (making them certainly permissible), but there are other conduct options which some of the rival theories regard as permissible but others do not (making them possibly permissible, from the agent's point of view). The Expected Moral Value approach says only the certainly permissible options should be considered MBR permissible. The Expected Moral Value approach, however, pays no attention to *why* a given theory finds some conduct permissible and ignores the possibility that moral theories may care about the *combination* of permissible options.

Consider the following example. Richard has thought long and hard about the permissibility of suicide. He is certain it is permissible because he believes that people ought to, insofar as is possible, have control over when and how their life ends. Richard knows that next week he will face a moral dilemma. He is uncertain as to whether to visit a friend or a stranger in hospital, given that visiting the stranger will produce more overall well-being. Given that he is unsure, Richard will risk a minor moral wrong whoever he visits. However, since he is certain that suicide is permissible, the Expected Moral Value approach states that Richard is MBR *required* to kill himself—it is the only certainly permissible option. Much of the appeal of the Expected Moral Value approach strategy of always ranking certainly permissible options over possibly permissible options appears to rely on the idea that no theory "loses out" when an agent's MBR-permissible options are restricted to the options that all the theories endorse as permissible. We think, however, that this fails to take into account a potentially important additional moral consideration—how the competing moral theories view the *range or combination of options* that are morally permitted and *why* they recommend that range of options as permissible. Richard, for instance, has no credence in theories that say that suicide is morally required. He has credence in theories that value the combination of the options of committing suicide or not, and these theories *do* lose out if his MBR-permissible options are restricted to the (objectively permissible) option of committing suicide.

Evaluating Option Sets

In sum, the central problem with the Expected Moral Value approach is that it looks at conduct options one by one, and it pays no attention to the fact that more permissive moral theories don't only care about the permissibility of individual options, but the *range* of options open to the agent. For example, theories that support pro-choice care about the agent having the *choice* of whether or not to terminate their pregnancy, and Richard cares about having the *choice* of when to die. An MBR *requirement* not to abort, or to kill oneself in order to avoid risking minor moral wrongs, fails to take adequate account of these concerns.

An approach to Moral Uncertainty Theory that we have defended seeks to avoid these problems by switching the unit of concern from individual *conduct options* to *option sets* (Barry and Tomlin 2016). Option sets are combinations of options which, if accepted, are all permissible. To take an example from first-order deliberation, imagine that Nina is deciding whether to go to the cinema or stay at home tonight. Both of these options are objectively permissible, and so her moral option set includes both going to the cinema *and* staying at home.

To explain how our approach is distinctive when applied to moral uncertainty, imagine that there are basically three conduct options available to an agent—A, B, and C. The Expected Moral Value approach asks us to look at A, at B, and at C independently, and then choose the option with the best score. Our approach looks at, and evaluates, the different potential *option sets* available to the agent. These include A, B, and C but also AB, BC, AC, and ABC. What, we ask, should the agent regard as her MBR-permitted *range* of options, and our answer to that question takes into account both the moral risks of individual conduct options (as the Expected Moral Value approach does) and also how the *range* of options looks. Essentially, we add an additional layer of scrutiny to the Expected Moral Value approach by morally evaluating combinations of options, and we think it will be sometimes worth accepting a small risk of objective impermissibility for a better option set.

To return to the example of Richard, Richard has three options: visit his friend, visit the stranger, or kill himself. These could be combined into different option sets: an option set that *only* includes killing himself, which, if accepted, would mean he is MBR required to do so; an option set that gives him a choice between all three options, which, if accepted, would mean he is MBR permitted to do any of them; and various combinations of two options. The option set that *only* includes suicide does very well in terms of individual options (no risk of objective wrongdoing) but *very* badly as an option set—it doesn't give him any other options, and he only values the option of suicide when and because it is available *alongside* the option *not* to commit suicide. We think Richard should be guided toward a different option set, even though the other option sets risk objectively impermissible conduct. He is MBR permitted to risk some objective wrongdoing.[11]

UNCERTAINTY IN THE CRIMINAL LAW

Moral uncertainty can occur at many points during the criminal justice process. Consider this, somewhat simplified, model of how some particular person ends up being convicted of, and punished for, some particular crime.

I. Voters elect representatives based, in part, on what they (or their parties) have conveyed about their beliefs concerning issues around the criminal law.

II. Elected representatives choose to make Conduct C a crime—Crime C.

III. Police officers enforce Crime C, arresting individuals they suspect of Conduct C. They arrest Bob.

IV. Prosecutors decide to prosecute Bob for Crime C.

V. A jury decides to convict Bob of Crime C.

VI. A judge sentences Bob, handing down Punishment X for Crime C.

VII. Prison wardens and officers must carry out Punishment X.

VIII. A Parole Board decides to release Bob early, before all of Punishment X has been completed.

The actors involved in all of these decisions may experience moral uncertainty (as well as empirical uncertainty, which, for simplicity, we will set aside here). Citizens can be unsure about what general approach to the criminal law is the correct one. Legislators can be unsure about whether to criminalize Conduct C. Police—as individuals and as institutions—are given discretion about what laws they prioritize the enforcement of, and, relatedly, how to allocate spending, and they may be unsure about which offenses to enforce, or which to prioritize. Prosecutors are given discretion over whether to press charges, in particular, concerning whether or not prosecuting the alleged offense would be in the "public interest." They may be morally uncertain about what is in the public interest. Judges may be morally uncertain as to which of the various punishments they could hand down is morally appropriate. Prison wardens may be morally uncertain about whether they are being too harsh, or too lax, on their prisoners. The Parole Board may be morally uncertain about whether or not an offender's behavior warrants early release.

In addition, at each of these points, we can distinguish two main ways in which moral uncertainty theory might be relevant to the criminal law. First, we can consider moral questions that arise *within* any standing practice of criminal law. That is, judges, lawyers, jurors, and others involved in the criminal process face practical decisions about what to do, where they can be morally uncertain about what to do. For example, a prosecutor must decide whether to bring a case; a judge must decide what sentence to pass. Second, we can consider moral questions concerning the design of the criminal justice system itself. For example, we must individually and collectively make decisions about what kinds of conduct should be criminalized, which punishments can attach to which criminal acts, how criminal process should be structured, what evidential standards to employ, and so on.[12] These two sets of questions are of course related. For example, a juror in a criminal trial may be uncertain about the moral character of the criminal legal process or about how to act when you believe certain aspects of such processes are unjust.

UNCERTAINTY AND CRIMINALIZATION

Let's turn to how Moral Uncertainty Theory might be brought to bear on questions concerning the design of criminal justice institutions. To sharpen the focus of our discussion, we consider the question of what kinds of conduct to criminalize. Note first that there are some important differences between the question that faces us here, and the question that is tackled, in general, in the Moral Uncertainty Theory literature. The question that Moral Uncertainty Theory is typically concerned with is *"given that I am uncertain, what am I permitted to do?"* When we're thinking about criminalizing some conduct, however, the question is *"given that we are uncertain, what are we permitted to criminalize?"* This involves two important additional complexities that the first question does not involve.

The first complexity arises from the move from *I* to *we*. Sometimes we might be asking a question about criminalization under moral uncertainty as an individual—either as an individual citizen or as a legislator—but sometimes we might be asking it as a group—as a legislature or as a society. What would it mean to say that we as a group regard some question regarding criminalization as uncertain? It could refer to the fact that each and every individual comprising the group is individually morally uncertain about the conduct. Or it could mean that, while some individuals may indeed be morally certain about the issue, there is no strong consensus on it. That is, the moral status of the conduct is not treated as morally *settled* by the group but is instead regarded as something about which there is reasonable disagreement.[13] This poses important, and complex, questions about what theories we should be taking into account and what credence we should assign to them. When, as a society, we debate criminalizing some conduct, should I, as a member of society, be trying to figure out what *we* are permitted to do, given that *we* are uncertain, thereby taking into account the diversity of beliefs concerning the moral status of that conduct? Or should I be trying to figure out what legislation to fight for, given that *I* am uncertain about the moral status of some conduct, and so taking into account *my* beliefs?

A second issue prompted by the move from *I* to *we* relates specifically to our own preferred approach to Moral Uncertainty Theory (Evaluating Option

Sets). Recall that our approach is concerned that agents should have a *range* of conduct options. But people who have these kinds of concerns about *individuals* often do not have them, or at least have them in the same way, about political institutions. We might be concerned if morality leaves individuals with no space to shape their own lives and make their own choices, and it is this kind of concern that can only be incorporated if we focus on option sets instead of individual conduct options. But when we ask about whether or not to criminalize some conduct, we ask about what *we* should do *as a political community*. And as Thomas Nagel memorably put it, "institutions, unlike individuals, don't have their own lives to lead" (Nagel 1991, p. 59). So it is unclear whether our particular approach to moral uncertainty theory will have much purchase at the institutional level. However, it is possible that we ought to allow political communities leeway to shape themselves through their criminal law. MBR permissibility, of course, already does this—the society's moral values will shape their criminal law. The question is whether, beyond this, they should have scope to choose their criminal laws, beyond the demands of moral-belief-relative morality. Of course, decisions about whether to criminalize conduct need to be sensitive to beliefs about the importance of individuals having a range of options. After all, criminalization limits the freedom of individuals by attaching legal and social consequences to some options. But should we also be concerned that the *group* retains freedom to devise its own criminal laws, and that morality must not demand too much of *it*?

The second complexity introduced by considering criminalization is that decisions of criminalization involve, essentially, evaluating two kinds of conduct. That is, we need to ask ourselves both whether the conduct to be criminalized is morally impermissible *and* whether our criminalizing it is morally permissible. We can be morally uncertain about both. We can be uncertain both about whether some conduct is impermissible and about whether moral impermissibility is a necessary condition of criminalization. We can also be uncertain about what kind of wrongfulness that matters when deciding whether to criminalize conduct—if the conduct is MBR impermissible, is that enough to potentially warrant criminalization, or is it objective moral impermissibility that matters here? If some conduct is criminalized on the basis of its MBR impermissibility, is that ok, or should we factor in the chance that it *might* be objectively permissible?

To illustrate these difficulties, consider again the issue of abortion. Suppose an agent has a 40% credence in a Theory 1 according to which abortion is impermissible and a 60% credence in a Theory 2 according to which it is permissible. Nevertheless, the agent is certain that we should never criminalize conduct that is morally permissible but holds that it is sometimes permissible to criminalize conduct that is morally impermissible. How then should an agent with such credences think that *law* should regard this conduct? Note that this is a somewhat different question than how the agent should regard the question of the moral permissibility of abortion, given her moral uncertainty. Still, if we hold the My Favorite Theory approach, the answer is probably straightforward: she shouldn't regard it as permissible to criminalize abortion since, by the lights of the theory in which she has the highest credence, it is a morally permissible practice (so it is an MBR-permissible practice, and therefore she should regard it as MBR morally impermissible to criminalize the conduct given her belief that it is always impermissible to criminalize permissible conduct.)

While My Favorite Theory is a controversial view about moral uncertainty, it does seem to capture roughly how representative democracies *do* treat the question of criminalization in practice: the majority's favorite theory (which might not be the theory with the highest average credence) wins the day. Unless some measure to criminalize conduct runs up against a constitutional provision, a bare majority is often enough to pass legislation that criminalizes some conduct. Moreover, there are no formal or informal norms about what kinds, or strengths, of beliefs individual legislators ought to have before voting to criminalize some conduct. So as long as more than half of them are convinced enough to decide to vote to criminalize the conduct, it will be criminalized, regardless of how uncertain various legislators or voters are, or what the moral risks are if they are incorrect about this. For example, if individual legislators vote to criminalize some conduct on a balance-of-probabilities basis, and bills pass on a bare majority basis, then the conduct will be criminalized if 51% of legislators have a 51% credence in the proposition that the conduct can permissibly be criminalized *even if* the other 49% of legislators have no credence in this proposition at all. Therefore, conduct can be criminalized even when the average credence in the permissibility of doing so is 26%. In our view, this seems a very good reason to depart from common practice and reject the My Favorite Theory approach to criminalization (see further Tomlin 2013).

If we apply the Expected Moral Value approach to the question of criminalization, things are more complex. There are broadly two different approaches we could take to the criminalization of conduct under the Expected Moral Value approach. On the first, which we can call the *two-step approach*, we *first* ask "is the conduct MBR permissible?" and then, second, we address the question of criminalization. In the case of abortion, then, this two-step approach would first have us ask "according to Expected Moral Value theory is abortion MBR permissible or MBR impermissible?" Let's imagine that, according to Expected Moral Value theory (with a given set of inputs), abortion is MBR impermissible. The two-step approach would then have us ask "given that abortion is MBR impermissible, is criminalizing abortion MBR permissible or impermissible?" If the only relevant question was the MBR moral status of abortion (which it surely isn't), then it would be MBR permissible to criminalize abortion.

An alternative approach is the *one-step approach*. According to this approach, we should ask *directly* "is criminalizing abortion MBR permissible?" and then work out the relevant moral scores of criminalizing the conduct and not criminalizing the conduct, including the probabilities of abortion turning out to be objectively permissible and impermissible.

Essentially, this would involve constructing a two-by-two matrix. On one axis we would have the decision to be made—criminalize or don't criminalize. On the other, we would have our moral uncertainty—is abortion permissible or impermissible?

One risk is that Theory 1 is correct. If we make abortion legally impermissible, then this would involve criminalizing a practice that is in fact morally permissible. This would be in contravention of our stated principle (which, in this example, the agent is fully confident of), that we may only criminalize conduct that is morally impermissible. We would then need to assess how *serious* a wrong the act of criminalizing morally permissible conduct would be. To some extent, this will depend on the magnitude of the criminal sanction. Generally, however, criminalizing morally permissible conduct would be very seriously wrong indeed, given some of the distinctive features of the criminal law. In criminal trials, defendants are faced with the prospect of hard treatment: losing their rights, liberties, and, in some jurisdictions, even their lives. Moreover, by identifying them as "criminal offenders," society expresses an attitude toward them—that their conduct is paradigmatically blameworthy—that can be seriously damaging to them. Criminal sanctions thus stigmatize the offender and substantially affect the way they are treated within their communities. If the criminal law possesses this strong expressive function, convicting an agent of a criminal offense when they engage in morally permissible conduct may carry a morally relevant cost well above and beyond the cost to the person convicted. This is because the agencies that purport to be acting in the name of justice are imposing unjust harm. Unjust harm imposed on people through the agency of the state is often taken to be of particular moral consequence. Many people care that the state agencies that represent them not only bring about desirable end-states, but that they take special precautions not to impose unjust harm on individuals through what they do, even when this may lead them to allow still greater harms brought about by others (Barry 2005). That is, many people are not morally indifferent to the distinctions between what a state brings about directly through its agencies and what it fails to prevent. The idea that someone would be criminally sanctioned in the name of justice and under the color of law for acts that are morally permissible is deeply disconcerting (Husak 2008; Tomlin 2013). And of course there are other significant costs to the population when conduct is wrongly criminalized. Most importantly, it is not only those who nevertheless commit the act and are punished who are wronged. At the very least, those who *would have* committed the act but refrain from doing so because of the threat of criminal sanction can also be wronged. Plausibly, all those who *could have* committed the act are wronged—even if they have no desire to perform the act in question, since they are threatened with sanction if they do so, even though they ought to be able to perform the act in question. How serious this wrong would be would vary from case to case, but in a case featuring our own bodies, and our core rights, it would be a very serious wrong indeed.

These considerations point toward an important disanalogy between how an individual agent reasons about the MBR permissibility of *her* terminating a pregnancy and how *we* as members of a society reason about whether to criminalize abortion. The individual agent must consider how to weigh the moral risk of terminating her pregnancy (insofar as she has some credence in a theory according to which abortion is a serious moral wrong) against the costs that *she* and others will face if she carries the fetus to term. However, when we deliberate about whether to criminalize abortion, we are considering how to weigh the moral risk of making a morally impermissible practice lawful against the costs that *we* will impermissibly impose on others (namely women who might consider terminating their pregnancies but will be prevented from doing so). Therefore, criminalizing abortion carries huge moral risks, and agents should be very wary of proposing it, *even if, when they individually deliberate, they come to regard abortion as MBR impermissible.*

If Theory 2 is correct, and abortion is objectively impermissible, then one moral risk would appear to be in *not criminalizing* the conduct. It is, however, questionable whether *not criminalizing* objectively impermissible conduct is impermissible and therefore whether it poses a moral risk at all. Criminalization theory is largely concerned with providing an account of the conditions under which the criminalization of some conduct is *permissible*. It often proceeds by way of setting up hurdles to criminalization, and criminalization is regarded as permissible if and only if it manages to clear all of the hurdles (*see*, e.g. Husak 2008). For example, there is extensive debate about how best to characterize the harm principle—roughly, that the purpose of the criminal law is to prevent harm—but most versions of the harm principle see it as a *necessary condition* on criminalization (Tomlin 2014a; Tadros 2011; Edwards 2014). This is of course understandable—given our ever-proliferating criminal law, politicians and states hardly need to be given reasons to criminalize (Husak 2008, ch. 1), and so the focus has been on when criminalization *shouldn't* occur. But when we come to Moral Uncertainty Theory, the difference between it being permissible to criminalize some conduct and it being not only permissible but also required becomes very important. That is, if criminalization is merely *permissible*, then our running example is a "nesting case"—if Theory 1 is correct (i.e. abortion is objectively permissible), criminalization will be a serious moral wrong; if Theory 2 is correct (i.e. abortion is objectively impermissible), then criminalization and not criminalizing may both be permissible. Recall that the Expected Moral Value approach is excessively conservative when it comes to risking moral wrongdoing—certainly permissible conduct is *always* favored over possibly impermissible conduct. This is why the Expected Moral Value approach seems destined to say that, where there is any doubt about its permissibility, abortion is nearly always MBR impermissible (since carrying to term is almost always permissible). But for the same reason, if criminalizing some conduct is, at best, merely permissible according to both theories we have credence in but also carries a risk (however small) of being impermissible, while not criminalizing is certainly permissible, then the Expected Moral Value approach would say we are MBR required to not criminalize the conduct.

Because of this kind of case, Moral Uncertainty Theory might play a substantial role in shaping the direction of first-order moral theorizing about the criminal law. As observed earlier, moral theorizing about the criminal law often takes the form of proposing, defending, and examining justificatory hurdles to the *permissibility* of criminalization (for an extremely prominent example, consider the collective title of Joel Feinberg's four-part classic—*The Moral Limits of the Criminal Law* (Feinberg 1984, 1985, 1986, 1988)). But if criminalization is only ever, at best, permissible, then the Expected Moral Value approach to criminalization under moral uncertainty will only allow criminalization when it is *certainly* permissible. Things would be different, however, if criminalization were, at least sometimes, morally *required*. In that case, we would act impermissibly in *failing to criminalize* some conduct. This seems plausible with respect to certain kinds of conduct. For example, a state that failed to criminalize the killing of innocent, non-threatening people would seem to wrong its citizens quite seriously—but we need criminal law theory to tell us more about when and why we are required to criminalize.

If, under Theory 2 (according to which abortion is impermissible), we would act wrongly by *failing* to criminalize abortion, and under Theory 1 (according to which abortion is permissible) we would act wrongly by criminalizing abortion, then we do not have a nesting case. Instead we have a "cross-condemning case," in the sense that we risk acting wrongly whatever we do. Given this, we must assess the moral disvalue of both options, weight them by their subjective probabilities, and see which has the best expected moral score.

We have already looked at the wrongs of criminalizing abortion should it turn out to be objectively morally permissible. What might be the wrongs of *not* criminalizing abortion if it were objectively morally impermissible? Now, one might think that, according to Theory 2, the costs of legally permitting conduct that it regards as impermissible would be negligible. After all, we don't think that all behavior that is morally impermissible (or even seriously wrong) should be subject to criminal sanction—the betrayal of spouses or the failure to deliver on crucial promises, even some that we are contractually obliged to deliver on, are cases in point. And sometimes this seems plausible for all of the reasons mentioned earlier—the moral risks of overcriminalization are typically quite high, whereas the risks of not criminalizing conduct that is morally impermissible may not be so great. However, this will not always be the case. More specifically, if Theory 2 holds that abortion is akin to murder, then it would also regard practices that permit abortion to be at least morally comparable to practices which permit murder. Indeed, advocates of Theory 2 may plausibly claim that the criminal law is not only expressive in what it forbids but in what it *permits*. And if this is so, then it would attach a great deal of disvalue to the option of failing to treat abortion as a criminal offense, unless doing so carries very high countervailing costs.

Still, there might still be important disanalogies between murder and the termination of pregnancy that could change the calculus even if Theory 2 is correct concerning the moral status of abortion. For one thing, there is a great deal of disagreement about abortion, and this might prove relevant to the criminalization question, even at the level of objective morality. For example, that killing innocent, non-threating adults is forbidden is clearly regarded as settled by the society in a way that the practice of abortion is not. This could make a difference to how adherents of Theory 2 might judge the wrongfulness of the conduct of those who terminate their pregnancies, since those who do terminate their pregnancies do not in all likelihood consider this practice wrongful, much less akin to murder. This is where the issue of collective uncertainty may become relevant. A theory could take the cost of imposing criminal sanctions on conduct that, while impermissible, is the subject of a great deal of moral disagreement to be quite substantial. (This might explain why some ethical vegetarians, e.g., would regard it as impermissible to impose criminal sanctions on meat eaters even though they regard eating meat as a serious moral wrong.)

Our own approach to moral uncertainty, Evaluating Option Sets, would differ from the above analysis only in that it would be less likely to regard abortion as MBR impermissible in the first place, since, as we observed earlier, our approach does not always forbid possibly permissible options when certainly permissible options are on the table. This is because, at the individual level, it is concerned to give full voice to theories that care about choice. However, at the state level, the reasoning would likely be very similar to that under the Expected Moral Value approach, since these kinds of concerns about moral restrictiveness do not necessarily have purchase for institutions.

Comparing Wrongs

If an agent is uncertain about the moral status of abortion, and, if she thinks that if abortion were *definitely* impermissible, the state would be *required* to criminalize it, then in deciding whether she should regard the criminalization of abortion as MBR permissible, she must balance the potential wrongs of criminalizing abortion when it should not be, and not criminalizing abortion when it should be, in light of the theories in which she has credence. We have tried, earlier, to identify some of the considerations that these theories might regard as relevant. But how can we gauge their respective weights?

One possible clue is to be found within the prevailing norms of the criminal justice system itself (Tomlin 2013). Consider the "beyond reasonable doubt" principle, which is the so-called Golden Thread of English law. In Viscount Sankey's famous words: "Throughout the web of the English Criminal Law one golden thread is always to be seen, that it is the duty of the prosecution to prove the prisoner's guilt … no attempt to whittle it down can be entertained" (quoted in Ashworth 2006, p. 83). Insofar as both of the theories in which the agent has some credence are committed to this principle, it may provide some guidance as to how agents with credence in these theories should weight the respective wrongs of incorrect criminalization and incorrect failures to criminalize. Of course, the beyond reasonable doubt principle concerns how *juries* should regard the *empirical questions* that relate to whether or not a defendant acted in a way that was legally prohibited. However, the grounding of this principle may be informative in terms of how to weigh the moral risks of criminalizing under moral uncertainty (see Yaffe, Chap. 5, this volume, for further discussion of the beyond reasonable doubt principle).

The basic thought here is that the beyond reasonable doubt principle suggests that when it comes to convicting accused people, we should be very careful not to convict the innocent, even if this means letting the guilty go free. Consider William Blackstone's famous claim that it is better that ten guilty people go free than that one innocent suffer conviction and punishment (Blackstone 1765). Why is this so? It is surely because these people have done nothing to warrant punishment, and, for all the reasons enumerated earlier, we must be very careful not to inflict punishment on them.

If the reasoning underlying the beyond reasonable doubt principle is correct, then any theory that is committed to it will treat punishment as a tool that should be wielded very carefully indeed. And this further seems to suggest that it will wield *criminalization* very carefully. After all, being punished for something that is not punishable is not so very different from being punished for something you didn't do.

While the reasoning underlying the beyond reasonable doubt principle can *inform* the way in which we balance the potential wrongs involved in criminalization, there are important differences between decisions not to criminalize conduct and decisions not to punish some individual for an existing crime. One difference relates to the expressive or declarative functions of the criminal law. Even if nobody is ever convicted and punished for Crime X, there might be an expressive or declarative value to having it on the statute books. Another difference concerns fair warning and reasonable avoidability. That is, those who are convicted of crimes they didn't commit had no reasonable opportunity to avoid conviction. Those who are convicted of crimes which should not be crimes potentially did have such an opportunity (though how "reasonable" the opportunity is will depend upon the legislation in question and the background circumstances of the agent).

SETTING PUNISHMENTS UNDER UNCERTAINTY

Before concluding, let's briefly consider some issues concerning the determination of punishments under moral uncertainty. Imagine that we are certain that Conduct C should be a crime, it is a crime, and Bob has been convicted of it. Bob now stands before the judge, who must decide on Bob's sentence. The sentence will be a combination of two sets of decisions—those made by politicians and other political actors who have established the range of sentences that the judge can lawfully impose for this crime and the decision made by the judge in the individual case. These actors can be reasonably uncertain both about the general principles that ought to govern sentencing and about how those principles apply to a particular kind of conduct or the individual case.[14] Here, we must balance the risks of *overpunishing* against the risks of *underpunishing*. One possible analysis of this balance again draws on the beyond reasonable doubt principle: that principle appears to emerge from balancing failure to deliver warranted punishment against delivering unwarranted punishment. While overpunishment is a form of unwarranted punishment, underpunishment is a failure to deliver warranted punishment. If the reasoning underlying the beyond reasonable doubt principle can inform sentencing decisions, it suggests that punishments at the lower end of the spectrum being considered should be preferred (Tomlin 2014b).

However, things are potentially trickier when the criminal prohibition in question is one that passed despite deep reservations of those supporting it. For example, imagine a society has a long debate about whether to introduce a "good Samaritan" law, one which criminalizes the conduct of failing to assist others in cases of easy, non-costly rescue. In the end, the legislature decides that it will establish the good Samaritan law. They then must decide what sentences can be handed out to those that breach this law. This raises two interesting issues—one of first-order morality, and the other of Moral Uncertainty Theory. First, should the society's uncertainty and disagreement about the status of some law be taken into account in establishing the morally appropriate sentence for breaches of that law? The answer seems to depend on big questions concerning the point of criminal law and punishment, and we don't have space to do more than raise them here. For example, if we are straight-up retributivists, then the correct punishment will reflect the moral gravity of the act—that society is unsure about whether or not to criminalize the conduct is neither here nor there. Either it warrants criminalization and punishment or it doesn't. On the other hand, more expressive or communitarian-oriented theories might see things differently: if sentencing is a form of *communal* sanction, it seems plausible that the sentence attached to the crime should reflect the unease with which the society introduced the legislation.

At the level of Moral Uncertainty Theory, we can also ask whether the uncertainty with which the society introduced the legislation should affect sentencing calculations. Essentially, when an agent is uncertain about attaching a sentence, we need to take account of all the different sentences that different moral theories would endorse. Let's say that when the good Samaritan law is introduced, a member of the Sentencing Commission is torn as to whether failures to assist in cases of easy, non-costly rescue are significantly less seriously wrong than murder (say, on the general ground that doing harm is much worse than allowing harm to occur, all else being held equal), or are morally equivalent to unlawfully killing innocent, non-threatening people. Therefore, she is unsure as to whether a sentence of one or eight years is appropriate. In deciding what sentence to recommend, she must balance the moral risks of over- and underpunishment. But let's say that she, like the wider society, was also deeply conflicted about whether to introduce the legislation at all. That means that she also thinks that it is possible that such failures to rescue should not be criminally sanctioned at all. Should this be taken into account? If so, a one-year sentence *also* risks overpunishment. If not, a one-year sentence carries no risk of wrongdoing at all. Should sentencing under moral uncertainty proceed as if criminalization is warranted—it only remains to be seen what sentence to attach—or should it reflect the uncertainty with which legislation was introduced?

Concluding Remarks

This chapter has explored how we should approach moral questions concerning the criminal law—in particular what conduct we can or should criminalize and what sentences we can or should attach to criminal conduct—under moral uncertainty. Criminal law theory is hard, and so we are often, and often *should be*, reasonably uncertain about what the morally right answers are concerning how the criminal law should be structured. And of course the stakes attaching to how we resolve these questions are very high—the criminal law, and the conduct it often responds to, can wreak havoc in people's lives, innocent and guilty alike. Using the criminal law inappropriately can have disastrous consequences. Failing to use it when we could do so fairly and effectively can also be a grave moral wrong.

Moral Uncertainty Theory is a growing area of applied ethics that seeks to help us to decide what to do when we are morally uncertain. However, what we have seen here is that it is not easy to apply it to the criminal law. Moral Uncertainty Theory ordinarily deals with questions concerning individual morality. We've seen that when we try to apply it to questions of how collectively we should respond to breaches of interpersonal morality, things rapidly become complex. That is why this chapter perhaps raises more questions than it answers.

Nevertheless, we think Moral Uncertainty Theory holds promise for informing our thinking about some of the most pressing questions in criminal law theory. For example, is it good enough that we always act on the theory in which we have the most confidence? Shouldn't we take account of the potential wrongs we will do if we criminalize conduct that ought to be legal? If we should, we have other questions to answer: What would those wrongs be and how serious would they be? Is the state only ever permitted to criminalize conduct or is it, at least sometimes, required? If it is required, when is it so required? What are the wrongs of the state failing to criminalize conduct it should have criminalized? How significant are they compared with those of incorrect criminalization? And, once conduct is criminalized, how should we approach sentence-setting under uncertainty?[15]

NOTES

1. For the purposes of this chapter, we do not make any assumptions about the status of ethical claims. We do sometimes speak of moral claims or principles being "objective," "right," "correct," or "true" but could rephrase these claims in terms more friendly to anti-realists (e.g. as the moral claims or principles to which the agent should commit herself). On moral uncertainty and non-cognitivism, see Sepielli (2012).

2. Abortion is an issue that many writers on moral uncertainty have focused on (*see*, e.g., Lockhart 1991, 2000; Guerrero 2007; Moller 2011; Weatherson 2014; Barry and Tomlin 2016), and of course its moral and legal status remain the subject of heated disagreement, so we use it as our running example throughout this chapter.

3. For a very useful overview of the debates, see Bykvist (2017). Some distinctive contributions to the literature include Ross (2006), Moller (2011), Jackson and Smith (2006), Guerrero (2007), Lockhart (2000), Sepielli (2006, 2009), Weatherson (2002), MacAskill (2016), Barry and Tomlin (2016), Gustafsson and Torpman (2014), MacAskill and Ord (2018).

4. For discussion see Bykvist (2017), Lockhart (2000, ch. 2), Gustafsson and Torpman (2014), Ross (2006), Sepielli (2009).

5. We are grateful for useful correspondence with Peter Vallentyne on this issue. This is not to say, of course, that the typical moral agent will actually engage in such deliberations.

6. Indeed, any attempt to do so might be implausible. It seems plausible that our credences in theories, as in many other propositions, are rather imprecise or indeterminate.

7. Gustafsson and Torpman regard this as a principal advantage of the MFT approach (Gustafsson and Torpman 2014, p. 60).

8. MacAskill and Ord refer to this as the "My Favorite Option" approach (MacAskill and Ord 2018, pp. 9–10).

9. For a more extended response to these worries about individuation, see Gustafsson and Torpman (2014, pp. 171–172).

10. This approach assumes, which the My Favorite Theory approach does not, that we can indeed make meaningful comparisons across theories in terms of how much they value various options.

11. For criticism of our approach, see MacAskill and Ord (2018). The main issue they identify is "double counting" of demandingness or restrictiveness concerns. Our reply to this is outlined at Barry and Tomlin (2016, pp. 916–917).

12. Some of the decisions we must make concern epistemic issues. We must, for example, consider whether ignorance of the law or uncertainty about what it requires can serve as an excuse for criminal acts. See Husak, Chap. 14, this volume, for discussion of this issue. This type of uncertainty, about the law's requirements, is distinct from the uncertainty that we are focusing on here, which concerns what laws we *ought* to make.

13. That the morality of some conduct is considered to be settled by a group is consistent with the fact that some people choose nonetheless to engage in that conduct—the killing of innocent, non-threatening people is an example.

14. Our question here concerns how the moral uncertainty of those deciding the sentence should influence their decision. A further, potentially relevant, source of uncertainty is from the convicted party themselves—should the offender's legal or moral ignorance or uncertainty affect sentencing? On this issue, see Husak (Chap. 14, this volume). Of course, those deciding the sentence may be uncertain over how to handle the offender's uncertainty, and this may influence their decision.

15. We are grateful to Vincent Chiao and Kim Ferzan for written comments on earlier versions of this chapter.

References

Ashworth, Andrew. 2006. *Principles of criminal law*. 5th ed. Oxford: Oxford University Press.

Barry, Christian. 2005. Applying the contribution principle. *Metaphilosophy* 36: 210–227.

Barry, Christian, and Patrick Tomlin. 2016. Moral uncertainty and permissibility: Evaluating option sets. *Canadian Journal of Philosophy* 46: 898–923.

Blackstone, William. 1765. *Commentaries on the laws of England*. Oxford: Clarendon Press.

Bykvist, Krister. 2017. Moral uncertainty. *Philosophy Compass* 12 (March). https://doi.org/10.1111/phc3.12408.

Edwards, James. 2014. Harm principles. *Legal Theory* 20: 253–285.

Feinberg, Joel. 1984. *Harm to others*. Vol. 1 of *The moral limits of the criminal law*. New York: Oxford University Press.

———. 1985. *Offense to others*. Vol. 2 of *The moral limits of the criminal law*. New York: Oxford University Press.

———. 1986. *Harm to self*. Vol. 3 of *The moral limits of the criminal law*. New York: Oxford University Press.

———. 1988. *Harmless wrongdoing*. Vol. 4 of *The moral limits of the criminal law*. New York: Oxford University Press.

Guerrero, Alex. 2007. Don't know, don't kill: Moral ignorance, culpability and caution. *Philosophical Studies* 136: 59–97.

Gustafsson, Johan E., and Olle Torpman. 2014. In defence of my favorite theory. *Pacific Philosophical Quarterly* 95: 159–174.

Harman, Elizabeth. 2015. The irrelevance of moral uncertainty. In Vol. 10 of *Oxford studies in metaethics*, ed. R. Shafer-Landau. Oxford: Oxford University Press.

Husak, Douglas. 2008. *Overcriminalization*. Oxford: Oxford University Press.

Jackson, Frank, and Michael Smith. 2006. Absolutist moral theories and uncertainty. *Journal of Philosophy* 103: 267–283.

Lockhart, Ted. 1991. A decision-theoretic reconstruction of Roe v Wade. *Public Affairs Quarterly* 5: 243–258.

———. 2000. *Moral uncertainty and its consequences*. Oxford: Oxford University Press.

MacAskill, William. 2016. Moral uncertainty as a voting problem. *Mind* 125: 967–1004.

MacAskill, William, and Toby Ord. 2018. Why maximize expected choice-worthiness. *Noûs*. https://doi.org/10.1111/nous.12264.

Moller, Dan. 2011. Abortion and moral risk. *Philosophy* 86: 425–443.

Nagel, Thomas. 1991. *Equality and partiality*. New York: Oxford University Press.

Ross, Jacob. 2006. Rejecting ethical deflationism. *Ethics* 116: 742–768.

Sepielli, Andrew. 2006. Review: Ted Lockhart, moral uncertainty and its consequences. *Ethics* 116: 601–604.

———. 2009. What to do when you don't know what to do. In Vol. 4 of *Oxford Studies in Metaethics*, ed. R. Schafer-Landau. Oxford: Oxford University Press.

———. 2012. Normative uncertainty for non-cognitivists. *Philosophical Studies* 160: 191–207.

Tadros, Victor. 2011. Harm, sovereignty, and prohibition. *Legal Theory* 17: 35–65.

Tomlin, Patrick. 2013. Extending the golden thread? Criminalisation and the presumption of innocence. *Journal of Political Philosophy* 21: 44–66.

———. 2014a. Retributivists! The harm principle is not for you! *Ethics* 124: 272–298.

———. 2014b. Could the presumption of innocence protect the guilty? *Criminal Law and Philosophy* 8: 431–447.

Unruh, Charlotte. n.d. Moral uncertainty as a real-world problem. Unpublished m.s.

Weatherson, Brian. 2002. Review: Ted Lockhart, moral uncertainty and its consequences. *Mind* 111: 693–696.

———. 2014. Running risks morally. *Philosophical Studies* 167: 141–163.

PART XIX

Neuroscience

CHAPTER 20

Neuroscience and Criminal Law: Perils and Promises

Stephen J. Morse

This chapter addresses the potential contributions of neuroscience to criminal justice decision-making and policy, with special emphasis on criminal responsibility. The neurosciences in question are the behavioral neurosciences, such as cognitive, affective, and social neuroscience, because these are the types of neuroscience most relevant to law. There have been major advances in these fields since the beginning of the present century when non-invasive functional magnetic resonance imaging (fMRI) to investigate brain function became widely available for research. The central question for this chapter is whether the neuroscience is relevant to criminal justice. The general conclusion is that it is scarcely useful at present but may become more relevant as the science progresses.

Many readers of this chapter may not be lawyers, so the chapter begins with a brief explanation of the meaning of criminal responsibility that is used throughout. It then speculates about the source of claims for the positive influence of neuroscience. The next section discusses the scientific status of behavioral neuroscience. Then it addresses two radical challenges to current conceptions of criminal responsibility that neuroscience allegedly poses: determinism and the death of agency. The question of the specific relevance of neuroscience to criminal law doctrine, practice, and institutions is considered next. This is followed by a discussion of how neuroscience evidence is being used in criminal cases in five different countries, including the United States. The penultimate section points to some areas warranting modest optimism. A brief conclusion follows.

S. J. Morse (✉)
University of Pennsylvania, Philadelphia, PA, USA
e-mail: smorse@law.upenn.edu

© The Author(s) 2019
L. Alexander, K. K. Ferzan (eds.), *The Palgrave Handbook of Applied Ethics and the Criminal Law*, https://doi.org/10.1007/978-3-030-22811-8_20

THE MEANING OF CRIMINAL RESPONSIBILITY

This chapter employs an expansive definition of criminal responsibility that is equivalent to criminal liability, criminal blameworthiness, or criminal culpability. Crimes are defined by their criteria, what lawyers term the "elements" of the crime. The most important of these for our purposes are the act requirement (often misleadingly termed the "voluntary act") and a culpable mental state, the mens rea. For example, one basic definition of murder is the intentional killing of another human being. In this example, the prohibited act is killing conduct such as shooting or stabbing, and the mental state element is the purpose to kill. The most basic definition of an act is an intentional bodily movement or omission performed in a reasonably integrated state of consciousness. For example, a reflex movement or movements performed in a state of divided or partial consciousness, such as sleepwalking, would not qualify as acts for criminal law purposes, even if they resulted in harm to another. The act element has constitutional status because it is unconstitutional to punish a person for a status, that is, for some attribute of the person, such as having red hair or for being an addict (as opposed to possession of or using a controlled substance, which would be an act) (Robinson v. California).

A mens rea is not required constitutionally for less serious, regulatory crimes, but it is almost certainly required for all serious crimes involving moral turpitude (Morissette v. United States). Mens rea elements, such as purpose, intent, knowledge, conscious awareness of a substantial risk of harm (recklessness), and unreasonable *un*awareness of a substantial risk of harm (negligence), are crucial because they indicate the agent's moral indifference to the rights and interests of others. Harming another "on purpose" is almost always more morally blameworthy than harms caused carelessly. For the most part, these elements have ordinary language meanings.

Together, the elements are known as the prima facie case and must be proven beyond a reasonable doubt by the prosecution. If they are so proven, the defendant is prima facie criminally liable. The defendant nevertheless can avoid liability by establishing an "affirmative defense" of justification or excuse, which defenses are also defined by their criteria. The Constitution permits the state to place the burden of proof for affirmative defenses on either the prosecution or the defense.

In cases of justification, otherwise prohibited conduct is considered right or at least permissible under the specific circumstances of the case. Self-defense is a classic example because the innocent victim of wrongful aggression is justified in intentionally using proportionate force to defend against the wrongful aggression. Excuses obtain if the agent is prima facie liable because the agent has done something wrong, but the agent is not responsible. Classic examples are the insanity defense and duress. In the former, the agent was irrational at the time of the crime because, for example, he did not know right from wrong as a result of severe mental disorder. In the latter, the agent is compelled by being placed in a do-it-or-else situation through no fault of his own and a person of reasonable firmness would have yielded to the threat. Note that in cases of excuse, the defendant may have intentionally engaged in the prohibited conduct, but he lacked the capacity for rationality or was coerced into doing it. For example, a defendant deluded about the need to use deadly self-defense intentionally kills his imagined attacker; a defendant compelled by a threat of death unless he kills an innocent surely intends to kill the innocent party to save his own life.

In sum, criminal responsibility in this chapter means that the prima facie case has been proven and no affirmative defense has been established. Free will as philosophers understand the term is not a legal criterion for criminal responsibility in any sense.

The Sources of Neuroexuberance

This section speculates based on wide reading and research in the intersection between neuroscience and law that bears on normative questions. At various times, the law has considered the findings from many sciences, including economics, sociology, different types of psychology, such as behaviorism and psychodynamic psychology, psychiatry, genetics, and now neuroscience. Although there are ethical and legal subdisciplines that have arisen as a result, such as bioethics, psychiatric ethics, and mental health law, for the most part, none of these has been based on a revolutionary approach to law or ethics. They primarily use familiar legal and ethical concepts to address traditional issues that the new sciences produce. For example, genomic information about individuals might raise acute privacy or human enhancement issues, but these are traditional questions. The most revolutionary claim arising from these sciences is typically the hoary claim that determinism is incompatible with free will and responsibility. Most of the various sciences have presented themselves as the newest proof of determinism that allegedly should upend doctrines and practices based on personal responsibility. Advocates of this approach typically favor one form or another of consequentially based social control that is often mischaracterized as "medical" (Menninger 1968). Nonetheless, none of these has engendered the type of academic and public enthusiasm (and fear) that neuroscience has produced. The supposed challenges were best summed up by an editorial warning in *The Economist*:

> Genetics may yet threaten privacy, kill autonomy, make society homogeneous and gut the concept of human nature. But neuroscience could do all of these things first. (The Economist 2002)

The question is why neuroscience has had such a large impact.

The relation of the brain to the mind and action has been at the center of philosophical and scientific attention for centuries. The "neuroscientific" approach to understanding behavior roughly dates to the case of Phineas Gage, a railroad construction foreman who suffered a severe injury to his frontal cortex in 1848, but who miraculously survived. The traditional narrative, about which there is some doubt, is that, prior to the accident, Gage was a model of probity and rectitude, but after the injury he became disinhibited, and his prior ability to plan and regulate his behavior, known as executive control, deteriorated. Today, we have a better understanding of the relation of frontal cortical function to executive control, but, even then, the case was a powerful demonstration of the relation of brain structure and function to behavior. Not until the advent of non-invasive functional magnetic resonance imaging (fMRI) in the early 1990s, however, and not really until the early 2000s, when scanners (often colloquially referred to as "magnets") became more widely available, was a non-invasive technology available that could investigate large numbers of nonclinical subjects. As a result of the increasing availability of fMRI, there is now an immense and growing literature on the relation of brain to behavior that has fueled the scientific and popular imagination. This work seems to many people, erroneously I believe, more rigorously scientific than previous sciences of behavior, and the images produced (which are *not* "pictures" of the brain) can be ravishingly arresting. In a metaphor that is question-begging because it assumes a form of mind-brain reductionism that is philosophically controversial, many enthusiasts claim we can now "look under the hood" of the acting agent to discern what the driving mechanisms are. The brain is of course the necessary biological foundation for mind and action, and we are discovering neural correlates and sometimes causes of mental states and actions, but acting human beings are usually not thought to be mere mechanisms like automobiles. The thought that we are merely mechanisms is at present scientifically unjustified and some would argue it is conceptually confused (Pardo and Patterson 2013; Gabriel 2017), but the possibility that this is true has created great expectations.

I speculate that there are four sources of what I have termed "neuroexuberance" among philosophers, lawyers, and others. The history of law as action-guiding is overwhelmingly one of conflict and irresolution with no method to establish an obviously right answer. There is no experiment, even in principle, to indicate that humans *should* behave in one way or another. It is all contestable. Hume's caution that we cannot derive an ought from an is still reigns (Hunter and Nedelsky 2018). As Professor Robin Feldman usefully details, law makers often believe they lack the resources to decide the difficult normative questions, so they wrongly turn to science without understanding that science can almost never resolve such disputes (Feldman 2009). Many commentators now seem to believe that the findings of the "hard" science of neuroscience may hold the key. Even the Supreme Court of the United States fell prey to this belief when it incorrectly distinguished neuroscience from social sciences (Miller v. Alabama, n. 5). Neuroscience and other sciences are all sciences. The important distinctions are between good and bad science and between legally relevant and legally irrelevant science.

Second, many philosophers and scientists dismiss the law's implicit folk psychology as prescientific and explanatorily empty. Folk psychology is a causal theory that explains human behavior *in part* by mental state variables such as desires, beliefs, intentions, plans, and willings. There is dispute about how to characterize the basic mental states, but all folk psychologists agree that mental states partially explain human behavior and are the fundamental tools that we all use to explain our own behavior and the behavior of others. The law provides one set of reasons for people to act as the law requires and the crucial criminal law responsibility criteria are virtually all acts and mental states. Thus, if folk psychology has no causal efficacy and explains nothing, then the law's behavioral premises are entirely incorrect. The neuroexuberants, such as Patricia Churchland, believe that neuroscientific understanding of behavior will finally replace folk psychology and give the law's understanding of behavior a genuine basis at last. I return to this topic later.

Third, many philosophers and lawyers are profoundly skeptical of deontology and especially of retributive justifications for state blame and punishment. Some incorrectly think that neuroscience proves that determinism is true, which, when coupled with hard determinist metaphysics, provides the desired conclusions that no one is really responsible for any behavior and that we should replace allegedly outmoded and unjust retributively based responsibility practices with consequences-based social control. As noted, this argument has been made previously based on other behavioral sciences, but again, neuroscience appears to be a more "real" science that at last will provide a genuine scientific basis for the claim.

Last, behavioral neuroscience is inherently interesting and fun, albeit often difficult to perform. It provides a tangible result, not just an "argument" to which some other clever philosopher or lawyer will find a damaging and perhaps even decisive riposte. It thus offers an engaging and welcome respite from the common frustrations and annoyances of normative work.

Again, the preceding is speculation, but the amount of unjustified overclaiming and exuberance that contemporary neuroscience has produced is striking and cries out for an explanation. I have no stake in my speculations and would invite readers to speculate for themselves. I doubt that anyone will rigorously investigate the question.

The Limits of Behavioral Neuroscience

Most generally, the relation of brain, mind, and action is one of the hardest problems in all science. We have no idea how the brain enables the mind, how consciousness is produced, and how action is possible (Adolphs 2015, p. 175; McHugh and Slavney 1998, pp. 11–12). The brain-mind-action relation is not a mystery because it is inherently unamenable to scientific explanation but because the problem is so difficult. For example, we would like to know the difference between a neuromuscular spasm and intentionally moving one's arm in exactly the same way. The former is a purely mechanical motion, whereas the latter is an action, but we cannot explain the difference between the two. Wittgenstein famously asked: "Let us not forget this: when 'I raise my arm,' my arm goes up. And the problem arises: what is left over if I subtract the fact that my arm goes up from the fact that I raise my arm?" (Wittgenstein 1953, §621). We know that a functioning brain is a necessary condition for having mental states and for acting. After all, if your brain is dead, you have no mental states and are not acting. Still, we do not know how mental states and action are caused. Wittgenstein's question cannot be answered yet.

Despite the astonishing advances in neuroimaging and other neuroscientific methods—especially in understanding sensory systems and memory—we do not have sophisticated causal knowledge of how the brain works generally. The scientific problems are fearsomely difficult. Only in the present century have researchers begun to accumulate much data from fMRI imaging. New methodological problems are constantly being discovered (Bennett et al. 2009a, b; Button et al. 2013; Eklund et al. 2016; Vul et al. 2009).[1] This is not surprising given how new the science is and how difficult the problems are. Moreover, virtually no studies have been performed to address specifically normative legal questions. (There are many studies of the neural correlates of legal decision-making, but they have no normative relevance.) Law should not expect too much of a young science that uses new technologies to investigate some of the most intrinsically difficult problems in science and that does not directly address questions of normative interest. Caution is warranted, although many would think the argument of this chapter is too cautious.

Furthermore, neuroscience is insufficiently developed to detect specific, legally relevant mental content. For example, it does not provide a sufficiently accurate diagnostic marker for even a severe mental disorder that might be relevant to many legal doctrines (Francis 2009; Morse and Newsome 2013, pp. 150, 159–160, 167; Rego 2016). Many studies do find differences between patients with mental disorders and controls, but the differences are too small to be used diagnostically, and publication bias may have inflated the number of such positive studies (Ioannides 2011). There are limited exceptions for some genetic disorders that are diagnosed using genomic information or some well-characterized neurological disorders, such as epilepsy, that are definitively diagnosed using electroencephalography (EEG), but these are not the types of techniques that are central to the new neuroscience based primarily on imaging.

Nonetheless, certain aspects of neural structure and function that bear on legally relevant capacities, such as the capacity for rationality and control, may be temporally stable in general or in individual cases. If they are, neuroevidence may permit a reasonably valid retrospective inference, for example, about a criminal defendant's rational and control capacities and their impact on criminal behavior. Some legal questions, such as whether a defendant is competent and what the agent will do in the future, depend on current-state evaluation of the agent. Such an evaluation will be easier than a retrospective responsibility evaluation. Nonetheless, both types of evaluation will depend on the existence of adequate neuroscience to aid such evaluations. With few exceptions, we currently lack such science (Morse and Newsome 2013, p. 150), but future research may provide the necessary data.

Let us consider the specific grounds for modesty about the current achievements of behavioral neuroscience. fMRI is still a rather blunt instrument to measure brain functioning. It measures the amount of oxygenated blood that is flowing to a specific region of the brain (the blood oxygen-dependent level [BOLD] signal), which is a proxy for the amount of neural activation that is occurring in that region above or below baseline activation (the brain is always and everywhere physiologically active). There is good reason to believe that the BOLD signal is a good proxy, but it is only a proxy. There is a sub-optimal time lag between when actual activation occurs and when fMRI measures it, and for a variety of reasons, pinpointing the exact region where activation occurred is also far from perfect (Roskies 2013, p. 37; Hong et al. 2019). The spatial resolution problem can lead to substantial numbers of false-positive findings.

These and similar technical difficulties will surely be ameliorated by technological advances, but studies to date, especially if they used lower power scanners, do suffer from these limitations. (For sophisticated, systematic, and comprehensive reviews of the proper uses and limitations of fMRI, see Logothetis (2008) and Poldrack (2018).)

There are research design difficulties. It is difficult to control for all conceivable artifacts, that is, other variables may also produce a similar result. Consequently, there are often problems of over-inference and of invalid reverse inferences (Poldrack 2006). The same region of interest (ROI) may be associated with opposite behaviors, which also confound inferences.

At present, most neuroscience studies on human beings involve small numbers of subjects, which makes it difficult to achieve statistically significant results and which undermines the validity of significant findings (Button et al. 2013; Szucs and Ioannidis 2017). This problem is termed "low power." This is especially important as research increasingly uses machine learning techniques to understand neural correlates and to make predictions. To ensure that the algorithms derived from a subject sample are generalizable, they must be cross-validated on populations different from the sample population. If sample sizes are small, the risk of error is magnified (Varoquaux 2017). The problem of small samples will improve as the cost of scanning decreases and future studies will have more statistical power, but this is still a major problem.

The types of subjects used also present a problem. Most of the studies in cognitive, affective, and social neuroscience have been done on college and university students, who are hardly a random sample of the population generally. Many of the studies use other animals, such as rats or primates, as subjects. Although the complexity and operation of the neural structure and function of other animals may be on a continuum with those of human beings and there may be complete similarity at some level, there is reason to question the applicability of the neuroscience of behavior of other animals to humans. The human brain is capable of language and rationality, which mark an immense difference between humans and other animals. To the best of our knowledge, other animals do not act for and are not responsive to reasons in the full-blown sense that intact human beings are. Is so-called altruistic behavior in orangutans, for example, the same as altruistic behavior in humans? Although the point should not be overstated, we should be cautious about extrapolating to human action from the neuroscience of the behavior of other animals.

Most studies average the neurodata over the subjects, and the average finding may not accurately describe the brain structure or function of any individual subject in the study. This leads to a more general problem about the applicability of scientific findings from group data to an individual subject, a problem called *G2i* for "group to individual" (Faigman et al. 2014). Scientists are interested in how the world works and produce general information. Law is often concerned with individual cases, and it is difficult to know how properly to apply relevant group data. For example, a neuroscience study that reports increased activation in some brain region of interest (ROI) bases its conclusion on averaging the activation across all the subjects, but no subject's brain may have activated precisely in the area identified. If such group data are permitted, as they now are for functions such as predictions, the question is how to use probabilistic data to answer what is often a binary question, such as whether to parole a prisoner because he is deemed no longer a danger to society. This is a topic under intensive investigation at present, and I assume progress will be made.

A serious question is whether findings based on subjects' behavior and brain activity in a scanner would apply to real-world situations. This is known as the problem of "ecological validity." Does a subject's performance in a laboratory while being scanned on an executive function task that inter alia allegedly measures the ability to control impulses really predict that person's ability to resist criminal offending, for example?

Behavioral neuroscientists have great flexibility in data collection, analysis, and reporting—a phenomenon termed "researcher degrees of freedom" (Simmons et al. 2011). (This situation is improving, however, as research methodologies are becoming more standardized and investigators publish the hypotheses of a study and the methods to be used prior to collecting and reporting the data ("pre-registration").) When this "freedom" is coupled with low power (the limited potential of the study to have statistically significant findings) and the multidimensionality of fMRI data, the probability of false-positive results is increased markedly (Poldrack et al. 2017).

Replications are few, which is especially important for any discipline, such as law, that has public policy implications (Chin 2014). Policy and adjudication should not be influenced by findings that are insufficiently established, and replications of findings are crucial to our confidence in a result, especially given the problem of publication bias (Ioannides 2011) and reproducibility skepticism (Chin 2014; Gilbert et al. 2016; Open Science Collaboration 2015). Indeed, replications are so few in this young science and the power of too many studies is so low that one should be wary of the ultimate validity of many results. A recent analysis suggests that more than 50 percent of cognitive neuroscience studies may be invalid and not reproducible (Szucs and Ioannidis 2017).

Drawing extended inferences from findings is especially unwarranted at present. If there are numerous studies of various types that seem valid, all converge on a similar finding, and there is theoretical reason to believe they should be consistent, then lack of replication of any one of them may not present such a large problem. For example, there are relatively few neuroscientific studies of adolescent behavior (although it is one of the areas well-studied), but they tend to be consistent with both the developmental psychology of adolescence and the neuroanatomical evidence indicating average differences between adult and adolescent brains. But such examples are at present few, especially in legally and morally relevant neuroscience.

What is known about behavioral neuroscience is quite coarse-grained and correlational rather than fine-grained and causal (Miller 2010). What is being investigated is an association between a condition or a task in the scanner and brain structure or function. These studies do not demonstrate that the brain ROI or activity is a sensitive diagnostic marker for the condition or either a necessary, sufficient, or predisposing causal condition for the behavioral task that is being performed in the scanner. Any language that suggests otherwise— such as claiming that some brain region is the "neural substrate" for the behavior—is simply not justifiable based on the methodology of most studies. Such inferences are only justified if everything else in the brain remained constant, which is seldom the case (Adolphs 2015).

Recall the description of criminal responsibility. The law is concerned with human mental states and actions, not brain states. What is the relevance of neuroscientific evidence to decision-making concerning human behavior? If the behavioral data are not clear, then the potential contribution of neuroscience is large. Unfortunately, it is in just such cases that neuroscience at present is not likely to be of much help. I term the reason for this the "clear-cut" problem (Morse 2011). Virtually all neuroscience studies of potential interest to the law involve some behavior that has already been identified as of interest, and the point of the study is to identify that behavior's neural correlates. Neuroscientists do not go on general "fishing" expeditions.[2] There is usually some bit of behavior—such as addiction, schizophrenia, or impulsivity—that investigators would like to understand better by investigating its neural correlates. To do this properly presupposes that the researchers have already well characterized and validated the behavior under neuroscientific investigation. Cognitive, social, and affective neuroscience is thus inevitably embedded in a matrix involving allied sciences such as cognitive science and psychology. Consequently, neurodata can seldom be more valid than the behavior with which it is correlated. In such cases, the neural markers might be sensitive to the already clearly identified behaviors precisely because the behavior is so clear. Less clear behavior is simply not studied, or the overlap in data about less clear behavior is greater between the subjects of interest and comparison subjects. Consequently, the neural markers of clear cases will provide little guidance to resolve behaviorally ambiguous cases of relevant behavior, and they are unnecessary if the behavior is sufficiently clear.

On occasion, the neuroscience might suggest that the behavior is not well characterized or is neurally indistinguishable from other, seemingly different behavior. In general, however, the existence of relevant behavior will already be apparent before the neuroscientific investigation is begun. For example, some people are grossly out of touch with reality. If, as a result, they do not understand right from wrong, we excuse them because they lack such knowledge. We might learn a great deal about the neural correlates of such psychological abnormalities. But we already knew without neuroscientific data that these abnormalities existed, and we had a firm view of their normative significance.

In the future, we may learn more about the causal link between the brain and behavior, and studies may be devised that are more directly legally relevant. My best hope is that neuroscience and ethics and law will each richly inform the other and perhaps help reach what I term a conceptual-empirical equilibrium in some areas. I suspect that we are unlikely to make substantial progress with neural assessment of mental content, but we are likely to learn more about capacities that will bear on excuse or mitigation.

The Radical Challenges of Neuroscience to Law

Neuroscience allegedly poses two radical challenges to current law: determinism and epiphenomenalism about mind, the no agency thesis. These are purely hypothetical, theoretical challenges at present and have virtually no practical purchase, so this chapter deals with them briefly.

The challenge from determinism is the familiar claim that if determinism or something quite like it is true (e.g., physicalism plus causal closure), then no one can be responsible, a position termed "hard incompatibilism" (e.g., Pereboom and Caruso 2018). Many incorrectly believe that neuroscience will prove that determinism is true, but no science can do this. It is a metaphysical speculation about the ontology of the known universe and, roughly, a working background hypothesis for many practicing scientists. Moreover, there is a competing position within the philosophy of responsibility, "compatibilism," which holds that we have enough freedom to ground robust responsibility even if determinism is true. This is the dominant position among philosophers and there is no possible resolution of this metaphysical dispute. Both camps can recognize that humans are agents who act for causal reasons, but they disagree about whether action is sufficiently free to warrant ascriptions of responsibility.

Compatibilism is the theory most consistent with the approach of the ordinary person and the law to agency and responsibility and with a scientific worldview. It is entirely consistent with the moral distinctions the law makes. For example, even if determinism or something quite like it is true, some bodily movements are actions and others are not. Some defendants are deluded and most are not. Some defendants react to a do-it-or-else threat and most do not. These are simply undeniable facts about human behavior that make a moral difference on deontological and consequentialist grounds that we have good reason to accept.

There is simply no compelling reason to upend centuries of legal doctrine, theory, and institutions based on an armchair metaphysical theory, hard incompatibilism, that is not itself demonstrably true and whose implications are unclear even if it were true. Given the history of the law, the burden of persuasion should rest with the radical critics of current doctrines, practices, and institutions. Critics of the possibility of responsibility have a duty to provide the practical implications of their philosophical position, especially if they hope to institute radical change. They have an obligation to propose the details of psychology, politics, and law that would follow. Most have not done so in any real detail. Pereboom and Caruso (2018) have admirably tried, but the "medical model" they propose does not depend on the new neuroscience and it has been intensely criticized (Morse 2018; Sehon 2016).

The epiphenomenal challenge is more radical. It claims that we are just a pack of neurons or victims of neuronal circumstances and that our mental states have no causal power whatsoever. On this view, minds are just the epiphenomenal foam on the neural wave. The existence of agency is thus denied, but agency is foundational for law and legal institutions. If the epiphenomenal claim is true, law and legal institutions rest on a complete illusion that is itself doing no work because illusory beliefs are mental states. Compatibilism cannot deflect this challenge because it begs the question against epiphenomenalism by assuming that we are agents, which is precisely what the radical challenge denies.

The question is whether mental epiphenomenalism is justified conceptually and empirically. Space precludes me from providing the full argument (which can be found in other work (Mele 2009, 2014; Moore 2012; Morse 2015; Nachev and Hacker 2015; Schurger et al. 2012; Schurger and Uithol 2015)), but the present conclusion, and probably the conclusion forever, is that we have no good conceptual or empirical grounds for thinking the epiphenomenal challenge is correct.

A final objection to the radical challenge is the unjustifiable normative implications that allegedly follow from the truth of the challenge. The most common is the claim, discussed previously, that the truth of the challenge implies consequentialism and the rejection of deontology. But if our mental states, including our reasons, are epiphenomenal and doing no work, then reasons do not have force and no normative implications follow at all. Would anyone want to live in a world without normativity (albeit the question itself makes no sense if the radical challenge is true because desires have no motivating effect but are just epiphenomena themselves)?

We are not helpless Pinocchios being dangled and manipulated by our Geppetto brains. Agency is secure, at least for now. Neuroscience will not radically transform the law's view of the person, legal doctrine, and legal institutions for the foreseeable future and probably never.

Legal Relevance

A previous section discussed the reasons to be cautious about the findings of behavioral neuroscience, but this section assumes that the scientific data being adduced to guide the law are valid. For example, it assumes that imaging data were properly acquired and interpreted. In that case, the issue will be whether the science is genuinely legally relevant. If it is not, it can be misleading and will be used primarily rhetorically.

Those who wish to understand the relevance of behavioral neuroscience to law must first understand that law is a thoroughly folk-psychological institution. The primary goal of law is to guide behavior by giving people reasons to behave one way or another. Law is thus like other forms of social interaction and control, such as ethics, etiquette, and social norms and mores. It is addressed to creatures, us, who can understand and be guided by reasons, creatures for whom mental states in part explain their behavior. Adherents of folk psychology may differ about how mental states are individuated and guide behavior, but all are united in the belief that mental states are crucial to a full understanding of human behavior.

The criminal law is also folk psychological because virtually all its criteria for culpability, responsibility, and competence are acts and mental states (Sifferd 2006). Consequently, the crucial question for law and neuroscience is whether neuroscientific data are relevant to a legal question involving acts and mental states. Do the neuroscientific data help answer a specific legal question?

I term this the problem of "translation" (Morse 2011). Neuroscience is a purely mechanistic science. Neuroscience eschews folk-psychological concepts and discourse (although neuroscientific articles are rife with dualistic discourse that suggests that regions of the brain are little homunculi that do things and that there seems to be a struggle between the self and the brain as an independent agent (Mudrik and Maoz 2014)). Neurons, neural networks, and the connectome do not have reasons. They have no aspirations, no sense of past, present, and future. They do not "do" things to each other. These are all properties of persons as agents. Legal rules are addressed to agents.

Is the apparent chasm between those two types of discourse bridgeable? There will always be a problem of translation between the pure mechanisms of neuroscience and the folk psychology of law. This is a familiar question in the field of mental health law (Stone 1984), but there is even greater dissonance in neurolaw. Psychiatry and psychology sometimes treat people as mechanisms but also treat them as agents. These disciplines are in part folk psychological, and the translation will be easier than it is for neuroscience. It is the task of those doing normative neurolaw always to explain precisely how neuroscientific findings, assuming that they are valid, are relevant to a legal issue. No hand waving is allowed.

The brain does enable the mind and action (even if we do not know how this occurs). Facts we learn about brains in general or about a specific brain could in principle provide useful information about mental states and about human capacities in general and in specific cases. Some believe that this conclusion is a category error (Bennett and Hacker 2003). This is a plausible view, and perhaps it is correct. If it is, then the whole subject of neurolaw is empty, and there was no point writing this chapter in the first place. Let us therefore bracket this pessimistic view and determine what follows from the more optimistic position that what we learn about the brain and nervous system can be potentially helpful to resolving questions of criminal responsibility and other criminal justice issues if the findings are properly translated into the law's folk-psychological framework.

The question is whether some concededly valid neuroscience is legally relevant because it makes a proposition about responsibility or competence more likely to be true. Biological variables, including abnormal biological variables, do not per se answer any legal question because the law's criteria are not biological. Any legal criterion must be established independently, and biological evidence must be translated into the criminal law's folk-psychological criteria. That is, the advocate for using the data must be able to explain precisely how the neurodata bear on whether the agent acted, formed the required mens rea, or met the criteria for an excusing or mitigating condition. In the context of competence evaluations, the advocate must explain precisely how the neuroevidence bears on whether the subject was capable of meeting the law's functional criteria. If the evidence is not directly relevant, the advocate should be able to explain the chain of inference from the indirect evidence to the law's criteria. At present, few such data exist that could be the basis of such an inferential chain of reasoning (Morse and Newsome 2013, p. 150), but neuroscience is advancing so rapidly that such data may exist in the near or medium term.

Even if neuroscience does seem relevant to a legal issue, the concerns with prejudice, cumulation (additional evidence that adds nothing new to evidence already adduced), and other worries about the potentially negative impact of concededly relevant evidence must be considered. The common wisdom about imaging data was that they were prejudicial compared to other, equally valid sources of evidence, such as purely verbal expert testimony or psychological testing. That is, juries were likely to give brain images undue weight. More recent, better designed studies have disclosed that this worry appears unjustified. With limited exceptions, decision-makers do not give undue weight to imaging data (Roskies et al. 2013; Schweitzer et al. 2011). The issue is not yet resolved empirically, but the present default should be that the evidence is not prejudicial.

A more pressing concern is the value-added of imaging. A scan is relatively expensive and somewhat time consuming. It thus has the potential for waste and delay unless there is genuine value-added. More important, legally relevant neuroimages must be based on valid, prior behavioral science that identifies clearly the behavior to which the brain structure or function will be correlated. This raises the problem of cumulation. For example, studies of the anatomical abnormalities associated with schizophrenia must have clearly identified whether the subjects in fact met the diagnostic criteria for the disorder using behavioral criteria to make the diagnosis. Thus, we already knew behaviorally that the person suffered from schizophrenia. What does the scan add? For another example, the law has treated adolescents differently from adults for centuries based on undoubted average behavioral differences between adolescents and adults and recall that the criteria for responsibility are behavioral. Now we know from brain imaging data that adolescent and young adult brains are on average less anatomically mature than adult brains. What does this anatomical information add to what we already knew beyond some potentially causal information? It is unsurprising in light of the behavioral differences that there are brain differences, but would we believe adolescents are *not* behaviorally different if the current brain imaging data did not show a difference? Instead, we would justifiably believe that the neuroscience was not yet sophisticated enough to detect the undoubted brain differences.

In individual cases where the behavior is clear, the imaging data will be cumulative and unnecessary. But, might not neuroscience be especially helpful in cases in which the behavioral evidence is unclear? The answer in principle is that of course it would be helpful, but as a practical matter it will not be because the neurodata are based on correlations with clear behavioral data, a problem I described earlier as the "clear-cut" issue (Morse 2011). Where the behavior is unclear, the neurodata will not be sufficiently sensitive to help resolve the behavioral issue even if the neurodata can distinguish the already behaviorally clear cases.

Here is an example of the current limitations of neuroscience for normative conclusions. A neuroscientist and I reviewed all the behavioral neuroscience that might possibly be relevant to criminal law adjudication and policy. With the exception of a few already well-characterized medical conditions that did not employ the new neuroscience, such as epilepsy, our review found virtually no solid neuroscience findings that were yet relevant (Morse and Newsome 2013, p. 150). Similar conclusions were reached after reviews of "brain reading" studies (e.g., "neural lie detection") (Greely 2013, p. 120) and addictions (Husak and Murphy 2013, p. 216).

The generally pessimistic conclusions I have reached concerning the present relevance of imaging to behavioral legal criteria are unsurprising. Behavioral neuroscience is in its infancy and works on one of the hardest problems in science—the relationship of the brain to mental states and action. As discussed previously, most of what we know generally is correlational and coarse rather than causal and fine-grained (Miller 2010). Replications are few, so the database necessary to reach firm conclusions simply does not exist. Virtually no study is done to address a legal question and there are problems with generalizing from the laboratory to the real world.[3] Even among populations of undoubted legal interest that have been studied intensively by neuroscientists, such as addicts, the people who have been studied are not a random sample of the population as a whole. Future conceptual and technological advances will certainly improve our knowledge base, but, for now, modesty is in order about how neuroscience can assist with legal decision-making and policy.

Let us conclude this section with an observation that will always be germane even if neuroscience makes huge leaps forward. For the law, actions speak louder than images with very few exceptions. The law's criteria are behavioral—actions and mental states. If the finding of any test or measurement of behavior is contradicted by actual behavioral evidence, then we must believe the actual behavioral evidence because it is more direct and probative of the law's behavioral criteria except perhaps in cases of malingering (although neuroscience cannot at present reliably and validly identify malingerers).

For example, if an agent behaves rationally in a wide variety of circumstances, the agent is rational even if his or her brain appears structurally or functionally abnormal. We confidently knew that some people were behaviorally abnormal—such as being psychotic—long before there were any psychological or neurological tests for such abnormalities. In contrast, if the agent is clearly psychotic, then a potentially legally relevant rationality problem exists even if the agent's brain looks entirely normal.

An analogy from physical medicine may be instructive. Suppose someone complains about disabling back pain, a subjective symptom, and the question is whether the subject actually does have such severe pain. We know that many people with abnormal spines do not experience back pain, and many people who complain of back pain have normal spines. If the person is claiming a disability and the spine looks dreadful, evidence that the person regularly exercises on a trampoline without difficulty indicates that there is no disability caused by back pain. If there is reason to suspect malingering, however, and there is not clear behavioral evidence of lack of pain, then a completely normal spine might be of limited use in deciding whether the claimant is malingering.

Unless the correlation between the image and the legally relevant behavior is very strong, however, such evidence will be of limited help. If a biomarker were virtually perfectly correlated with a legal criterion and it was less expensive to collect the biological data than behavioral data, then the biological variable might be a good proxy for a legal criterion. But this would be possible only with clear, bright line legal rules and not with standards, such as whether a reasonable person would be aware of a particular circumstance, because the latter have an inevitably normative component for the decision-maker to assess. Further, rules and standards can evolve, and trying to use an external marker to adjudicate them would conservatively inhibit normatively driven evolution. Moreover, such markers are beyond present neuroscientific expertise.

I believe that many of the claims for the relevance of neuroscience are best characterized as more "rhetorically relevant" than genuinely relevant. For example, defense advocates in capital punishment proceedings, in which the threshold for admissibility of mitigating evidence is considerably lower than at trial, hope that the fetching images produced by "real" neuroscience will be more persuasive to decision-makers than evidence provided by apparently more suspect social and behavioral science, even if the advocate cannot say precisely how the neuroscience bears on a genuinely mitigating condition. Having a brain lesion or injury is not a mitigating condition per se. The actual relevance of such brain abnormality evidence therefore requires an account of why the brain evidence makes it more likely than not that a genuine mitigating condition, such as lack of rational capacity, obtains.

An instructive anecdote illustrates the point. At a conference, I was presenting to a group of federal judges the case study of Spyder Cystkopf/Herbert

Weinstein, a 62-year-old retired business executive who had strangled his wife to death during an argument and then threw her out of the 12th-story window of their apartment building (People v. Weinstein 1992; Morse 1995, p. 527; Davis 2017). It was later discovered that on the underside of the middle lining surrounding his brain, the arachnoid layer, he had a large, benign cyst that pressed on and displaced a large amount of his frontal cortex. The brain image showing the displacement is spectacularly arresting. Based on this finding, the defendant was going to raise the insanity defense, claiming that he could not conform his conduct to the requirements of the law. The behavioral history and evidence were entirely *in*consistent with the validity of this claim, however, and after presentation of both the prosecution and defense arguments, 100 percent of the judges voted to convict. I then asked the judges if they would consider the cyst a mitigating factor at sentencing. About a third of them indicated that they would consider it, so I asked them why. The modal response was that the defendant had a proverbial "hole in his head." I asked why, if it did not affect his behavior, it should be considered a mitigating factor. None of the judges who indicated a willingness to consider it had any adequate explanation except to repeat the (true) observation that he had a gross anatomical abnormality. With respect, having such an abnormality is not per se an excusing or mitigating condition unless it produces a genuine mitigating condition such as diminished rationality or diminished control capacity. But there was not a shred of evidence that the defendant had such problems. The judges simply believed that such an abnormality "must" have mitigating implications, but the relevance was rhetorical rather than real.

NEUROEVIDENCE IN THE CRIMINAL LAW COURTROOM

Quite recently, we finally have preliminary data about how neuroscientific information is being used in criminal cases. Six interesting empirical studies from the United States (Farahany 2015; Gaudet and Marchant 2016); Australia (Alimardani and Chin 2019) England and Wales (Catley and Claydon 2015), Canada (Chandler 2015), and the Netherlands (de Kogel and Westgeest 2015) have attempted to discover the extent to which and in what way neuroscientific evidence is used in criminal cases. Recent excitement about the potential legal implications of non-invasive brain imaging by fMRI motivates this work. These studies begin to examine the reality of neuroscientific influence in criminal cases. All focus on appellate cases reported in various databases for somewhat different periods in the range of years from 2000 to 2012, and all are admirably cautious about the extensive methodological limitations of the study sample. None purports to be an accurate representation of the use of neuroscientific evidence throughout the criminal justice system and other methodological quibbles may be raised, such as the failure to use independent inter-rater reliability (the use of independent raters to check for the accuracy of the measurement of a variable) for characterizing the cases. All use a very expansive definition of neuroscience that includes techniques and data that long antedate the new neuroscience. At most, the data are suggestive. Nonetheless, the studies are interesting and innovative.

The late, great baseball scientist, Yogi Berra, was apocryphally quoted as saying "It's déjà vu all over again." The data indicate that the courts make the classic mistakes about the relevance of neuroscience and behavioral genetics to criminal cases that have bedeviled the reception of behavioral science in general and of psychiatry and psychology in particular. The overarching classic mistake is misunderstanding or uncritically accepting the validity of apparently relevant science and misunderstanding the relevance of the science to the specific criminal law criteria at issue, which are primarily acts and mental states. There are no brain or nervous system criteria in criminal law for any doctrine. In particular, courts too often do not understand the following issues. Metaphysical free will is not a criterion for any criminal law doctrine, and it is not even foundational for criminal responsibility in general. Causation in general and brain causation in particular, even causation by abnormal variables, are not per se mitigating or excusing conditions, and causation per se is not the equivalent of compulsion, which is an excusing condition. And, finally, people with the same diagnosis or condition are behaviorally heterogeneous, and, ultimately, it is the behavior that is legally relevant, not the diagnosis. In one form or another, most of these cases exhibit these mistakes and confusions. It is no surprise that one of the authors, Professor Nita Farahany, characterizes the cases as follows: "That use [of neurobiological research in criminal law] continues to be haphazard, ad hoc, and often ill conceived" (Farahany 2015, pp. 488–489).

Not surprisingly, sentencing decisions were the most common context for the introduction of neuroscience evidence, but it was also used to resolve questions about many criminal responsibility doctrines and, surprisingly, competence, which as we have seen, is a functional behavioral determination. Perhaps the most striking finding is how infrequently the new neuroscience of functional imaging and related techniques is used. This varies across jurisdictions, but the large majority of cases involve the "old" neurology or the old neuropsychology that uses classical structural imaging or behavioral methods to assess brain functioning associated with well-characterized neurological conditions, such as epilepsy and frontal lobe injuries or lesions. Such diagnostic methods are far more common than fMRI, and, in the Dutch and Canadian samples, there is virtually no functional imaging evidence.

In sum, these studies suggest that the influence of the new neuroinvestigative techniques applied to individual cases for forensic assessment is quite modest. Even when inferences are drawn in individual cases using group data about the consequences of various neurological conditions, the studies used are often classic behavioral studies rather than neuroimaging investigations. Indeed, careful examination of the expanded case studies that the papers present indicates that, in most instances, the neuroscientific evidence was far less important than the behavioral evidence, and the former was used largely to buttress the latter. The neuroevidence was rarely dispositive, and, in the other cases, it is impossible to know from these papers' summaries of the case reports how influential the additive neuroevidence was.

The first question when considering the admissibility of scientific evidence, as always, is the degree to which the basis of the testimony has been established. We have already seen that legally relevant neuroscience is not well established at present. It is no critique of contemporary neuroscience to note that it is working on one of the hardest problems in science, the relation of the brain to mind and action. For a specific example, the apparently wide but not universal Dutch acceptance of a brain disease model of addiction that guides legal decision-making fails to confront the hard questions about the status of the science. Judges are not yet in a good position to evaluate neuroscience and may be either too critical or too uncritical (*see* Rakoff 2016 for an analysis by a neuroscientifically informed federal judge).

For another example, fetal alcohol syndrome (FAS) plays a large role in the Canadian cases (although not in the other samples), but the potentially legally relevant aspects of the disorder are the cognitive and rationality defects, which are behavioral signs, that sufferers demonstrate from an early age. Are the brains of FAS sufferers different from the brains of those without the disorder? Of course. This is just a necessary truth of biological physicalism. If the behavior is markedly different, so will be the brain. Brain difference is not per se a mitigating or excusing condition, however. If a particular FAS sufferer is somehow sufficiently able rationally to regulate his behavior, then FAS is irrelevant to mitigation or excuse. Moreover, if an FAS sufferer exhibited lifelong cognitive defects, as many do, that sufferer is potentially excusable even if sophisticated neurotechniques cannot identify the brain pathology or brain difference.

Many of the cases in these studies fail to understand the relevance of the neuroevidence. Even if there is clear evidence of brain damage or a neurological disorder, it does not mean that the defendant did not act, lacked mens rea, was less culpable, is incompetent, or will be dangerous in the future. All the criteria depend on direct assessment of the offender's behavior. The alleged relevance of neuroevidence to competence determinations, which occurs in many of the samples, is instructive but especially bewildering. Criminal competencies are behaviorally functional, and, again, defined entirely in terms of mental states. Does the defendant understand the nature of the charges, can he rationally assist counsel, does he understand the consequence of a guilty plea, and does he understand the nature of the penalty about to be imposed on him and why it is being imposed? These normative, mental criteria must all be evaluated behaviorally. Either the defendant can perform these tasks to the requisite degree or he cannot.

These are continuum capacities, however, and it may be asked whether neuroscience can help with the gray area, indeterminate cases. The answer is, no, as a result of the clear-cut problem and the heterogeneity of behavior associated with similar brain function and structure that have already been addressed. In behaviorally unclear cases in which the law needs help the most, neuroscience is least able to furnish it.

A critical reader of the empirical studies will be repeatedly struck by how many of the expanded cases used either irrelevant or weak (or nonexistent) neuroscience—for example, to assess competence or whether a defendant suffered from a mental illness—or could have been fully resolved with more careful behavioral evaluation. Of course there can be conflict about the behavioral evidence, but because act and mental state questions must be resolved, it is the behavioral evidence that is doing the real work.

Much is at stake in criminal cases, and, of course, judges would like scientific help to resolve the vexing normative issues. At present, however, turning to neuroscience will do nothing more in most cases than to provide a rationalization for a result the judge wishes to reach on other grounds or to avoid responsibility for having to make the hard decision directly by relying on the expert. Convergent behavioral and neurodata might help solve some of these problems that cannot be resolved with either type of evidence alone, but such convergent lines of legally relevant evidence are rare.

THE CASE FOR CAUTIOUS OPTIMISM

How can neuroscience plausibly assist the law in the near to intermediate future as the science progresses? To begin, I do not think that contemporary neuroscience raises new issues (Morse 2004, p. 81).[4] Consider the examples of using scanning to detect mental content relevant to culpability or the possibility of using neuroscientifically based techniques to alter the behavior of an unwilling subject. I contend that the moral, political, and legal resources to address these already exist because they are simply instances of well-established theory and doctrine. The application is new, but the problems are old. There are longstanding doctrines available to address whether an investigative tool violates the Fifth Amendment protection against self-incrimination or whether the state may use techniques, such as the involuntary administration of psychotropic medication, to change an unwilling subject's behavior.

Despite having claimed that we should be exceptionally cautious about the current contributions that neuroscience can make to criminal law policy, doctrine, and adjudication, I am modestly optimistic about the near and intermediate-term contributions neuroscience can potentially make to our ordinary, traditional, and folk-psychological legal system. In other words, neuroscience may make a positive contribution even though there has been no paradigm shift in thinking about the nature of the person and the criteria for criminal responsibility. The legal regime to which neuroscience will contribute will continue to take people seriously as people—as autonomous agents who may fairly be blamed and punished based on their mental states and actions.

If a proper framework for the relevance of neuroscience to law is established and if a cautious approach to the science is adopted, I think neuroscience can potentially help refine legal mental state categories, such as mens rea and mental disorder, through a conceptual-empirical equilibrium in which legal categories guide neuroscientific investigation that in turn then help clarify the legal categories. Neuroscience might also help the fairness and efficiency of criminal law decision-making by increasing predictive accuracy. Finally, in tandem with behavioral science, neuroscience might help us more accurately understand legally relevant human capacities, such as the capacity for rationality and for self-control, which would again improve legal policy, doctrine, and adjudication. But all such optimistic outcomes will depend on precise understanding of legal relevance and valid science.

More specifically, there are four types of situations in which neuroscience may be of assistance: (1) data indicating that the folk-psychological assumption underlying a legal rule is incorrect, (2) data suggesting the need for new or reformed legal doctrine, (3) evidence that helps adjudicate an individual case, and (4) data that help efficient adjudication or administration of criminal justice. Categories (3) and (4) overlap to some degree, but individual and systemic concerns can be distinguished. (In an illuminating, similar vein, Professor Owen Jones lists seven ways that neuroscience may be of assistance (2013).)

Many criminal law doctrines are based on folk-psychological assumptions about behavior that may prove to be incorrect. If so, the doctrine should change. For example, it is commonly assumed that agents intend the natural and probable consequences of their actions. In many or most cases, it seems that they do, but neuroscience may help in the future to demonstrate that this assumption is true less frequently than we think. If the question could be neuroscientifically studied, which would be extremely difficult, a neural correlate of the formation of an intention were discovered, and the study further found an unexpectedly weak connection, the rebuttable presumption used to help the prosecution prove intent should be softened or used with more caution. As Jones points out, even if the assumption holds up, the challenge can be helpful to the law.

Second, neuroscientific data may suggest the need for new or reformed legal doctrine. For example, control tests for legal insanity have been disfavored for some decades because they are ill understood and hard to assess. It is at present impossible to distinguish "cannot" from "will not." Perhaps neuroscientific information will help to demonstrate the existence of control difficulties that are independent of cognitive incapacities. If so, then perhaps independent control tests are justified and can be rationally assessed. More generally, perhaps a larger percentage of offenders than we currently believe have such grave control difficulties that they deserve a generic mitigation claim that is not available in criminal law today. Neuroscience might help us discover that fact if proper studies to address that question could be devised. If that were true, justice would be served by adopting a generic mitigating doctrine. On the other hand, if it turns out that such difficulties are not so common, we could be more confident of the justice of current doctrine. Again, the challenge could be helpful.

Third, neuroscience might provide data to help adjudicate individual cases. Consider the insanity defense. As in *United States v Hinckley*, there is often dispute about whether a defendant claiming legal insanity suffered from a mental disorder, which disorder the defendant suffered from, and how severe the disorder was (p. 1346). For example, it was unclear whether Hinckley was deluded when he tried to assassinate President Reagan and others. At present, these questions must be resolved entirely behaviorally, and there is often room for considerable disagreement about inferences drawn from the defendant's actions, including utterances. In the future, neuroscience might help resolve such questions if the clear-cut problem difficulty can be solved. Nevertheless, in the foreseeable future, I doubt that neuroscience will be able to help identify the presence or absence of specific mens rea or of specific mental content, despite some proof-of-concept studies (those that demonstrate that a question can be addressed or that a creation of a technique is possible, even if a study's result is not ready for practical use).

Finally, neuroscience might help us to implement current policy more efficiently. For example, the criminal justice system makes predictions about future dangerous behavior for purposes of bail, sentencing, including capital sentencing, and parole. If we have already decided that it is justified to use dangerousness predictions to make such decisions, it is hard to imagine a rational argument for doing it less accurately if we are in fact able to do it more accurately, a point raised by the President's Commission for the Study of Bioethical Issues (Presidential Commission 2015). Behavioral prediction techniques already exist. The question is whether neuroscientific variables can add value by increasing the accuracy of such predictions considering the cost of gathering such data (Poldrack 2013). Two recent studies have been published showing the potential usefulness of neural markers for enhancing the accuracy of predictions of antisocial conduct (Aharoni et al. 2013, p. 6223; Pardini et al. 2014, p. 73). At most, these must be considered preliminary, "proof of concept" studies because a re-analysis of the Aharoni et al. data demonstrated that the effect size was tiny[5] and that study did not use the best behavioral methodology for comparison. These studies are not ready to be translated into practice, but it is perfectly plausible that in the future, valid, cost-benefit–justified neural markers will be identified, and thus, prediction decisions will be more accurate and just.

A final example of a promising line of neuroscience research that would apply across the legal system to permit more accurate, just decision-making involves the assessment of the accuracy of a subject's memory. Machine learning techniques have shown great promise in successfully retrodicting whether a subject's report of an event is accurate (Rissman et al. 2010, p. 9849, 2016, p. 604). This methodology can be undermined by countermeasures subjects can employ that erase all successful retrodiction. If this problem can be surmounted, however, assessing the accuracy of witness testimony, which so often plays a crucial role in criminal and civil cases, would also be transformative for the law.

CONCLUSION

At present, neuroscience has little to contribute to more just and accurate criminal law decision-making concerning policy, doctrine, and individual case adjudication. This was the conclusion reached when I tentatively identified "Brain Overclaim Syndrome" 13 years ago, and it remains true today. In the future, however, as the philosophies of mind and action, and neuroscience mutually mature and inform one another, neuroscience may help us understand criminal behavior. Although no radical transformation of criminal justice is likely to occur, neuroscience can inform the law as long as it is genuinely relevant and translated into the law's folk-psychological framework and criteria.

NOTES

1. But see Lieberman et al. (2009 p. 299).
2. But see Bennett et al. (2009a, b) for an amusing exception.
3. But see Vilares et al. (2017) for a "proof of concept" exception.
4. But see Jones (2013) for a contrary view.
5. For example, a re-analysis of the Aharoni et al. study (2013, n. 35) by Russell Poldrack, a noted "neuromethodologist," demonstrated that the effect size was tiny (Poldrack, accessed January 11, 2018). The study used good but not the best behavioral predictive methods for comparison.

REFERENCES

Miller v. Alabama, 132 S.Ct. 2455 (2012).
Morissette v. United States, 342 U.S. 246 (1952).
People v. Weinstein, 591 N.Y.S.2d 715 (1992).
Robinson v. California, 370 U.S. 660 (1962).
United States v. Hinckley, 525 F. Supp. 1342 (D.Ct. D.C. 1981).
Adolphs, Ralph. 2015. The unsolved problems of neuroscience. *Trends in Cognitive Sciences* 19: 173–175.
Aharoni, Eyal, Gina M. Vincent, Carla L. Harenski, Vince D. Calhoun, Walter Sinnott-Armstrong, Michael S. Gazzaniga, and Kent A. Kiehl. 2013. Neuroprediction of future arrest. *Proceedings of the National Academy of Sciences of the United States of America* 110: 6223–6228.
Alimardani, Armin, and Jason Chin. 2019. Neurolaw in Australia: The use of neuroscience in Australian criminal proceedings. *Neuroethics* 12: 255–270.
Bennett, Maxwell R., and Peter M.S. Hacker. 2003. *Philosophical foundations of neuroscience*. Hoboken: Wiley-Blackwell.
Bennett, Craig M., George L. Wolford, and Michael B. Miller. 2009a. The principled control of false positives in neuroimaging. *Social Cognitive and Affective Neuroscience* 4: 417–422.
Bennett, Craig M., Abigail A. Baird, Michael B. Miller, and George L. Wolford. 2009b. Neural correlates of interspecies perspective taking in the post-mortem Atlantic Salmon: An argument for proper multiple comparisons correction. *Journal of Serendipitous and Unexpected Results* 1 (1): 1.

Button, Katherine S., John P.A. Ioannidis, Claire Mokrysz, Brian A. Nosek, Jonathan Flint, Emma S.J. Robinson, and Marcus R. Munafo. 2013. Power failure: Why small sample size undermines the reliability of neuroscience. *Nature Reviews Neuroscience* 14 (May): 365–376.

Catley, P., and L. Claydon. 2015. The use of neuroscientific evidence in the courtroom by those accused of criminal offenses in England and Wales. *Journal of Law and the Biosciences* 2: 510–549.

Chandler, J. 2015. The use of neuroscientific evidence in Canadian criminal proceedings. *Journal of Law and the Biosciences* 2: 550–579.

Chin, Jason M. 2014. Psychological science's replicability crisis and what it means for science in the courtroom. *Psychology, Public Policy, and Law* 2: 225–238.

Davis, Kevin. 2017. *The brain defense: Murder in Manhattan and the dawn of neuroscience in America's courtrooms.* New York: Penguin. ("Spyder Cystkopf" was the pseudonym first used in the literature).

de Kogel, C.H., and E.J.M.C. Westgeest. 2015. Neuroscientific and behavioral genetic information in criminal cases in the Netherlands. *Journal of Law and the Biosciences* 2: 580–605.

Economist. 2002. Open your mind. May 25.

Eklund, Anders, Thomas E. Nichols, and Hans Knutsson. 2016. Cluster failure: Why fMRI inferences for spatial extent have inflated false-positive rates. *Proceedings of the National Academy of Science* 113: 7900–7905.

Faigman, David L., John Monahan, and Christopher Slobogin. 2014. Group to individual (G2i) inference in scientific expert testimony. *The University of Chicago Law Review* 81: 417–480.

Farahany, N.A. 2015. Neuroscience and behavioral genetics in US criminal law: An empirical analysis. *Journal of Law and the Biosciences* 2: 485–509.

Feldman, Robin. 2009. *The role of science in law.* New York: Oxford University Press.

Francis, Allen. 2009. Whither DSM-V? *British Journal of Psychiatry* 195: 391–392.

Gabriel, Markus. 2017. *I am not a brain: Philosophy of mind for the 21st century.* Hoboken: Wiley.

Gaudet, L.M., and G.E. Marchant. 2016. Under the radar: Neuroimaging evidence in the criminal courtroom. *Drake Law Review* 64: 577–661.

Gilbert, Daniel T., Gary King, Stephen Pettigrew, and Timothy D. Wilson. 2016. Comment on "estimating the reproducibility of psychological science". *Science* 351: 1037a.

Greely, Henry T. 2013. Mind reading, neuroscience, and the law. In *A primer on criminal law and neuroscience*, ed. Stephen J. Morse and Adina L. Roskies. New York: Oxford University Press.

Hong, Yong Wook, Yejong Yoo, and Choong-Wa Woo. 2019. False-positive neuroimaging: Undisclosed flexibility in testing spatial hypotheses allows presenting anything as a replicated finding. *NeuroImage* 19: 384–395.

Hunter, James Davison, and Paul Nedelsky. 2018. *Science and the good: The tragic quest for the foundations of morality.* New Haven/London: Yale University Press.

Husak, Douglas, and Emily Murphy. 2013. The relevance of the neuroscience of addiction to the criminal law. In *A primer on criminal law and neuroscience*, ed. Stephen J. Morse and Adina L. Roskies. New York: Oxford University Press.

Ioannides, John P. 2011. Excess significance bias in the literature on brain volume abnormalities. *Archives of General Psychiatry* 68: 773–780.

Jones, Owen D. 2013. Seven ways neuroscience aids law. In *Neurosciences and the human person: New perspectives on human activities*, ed. Antonio Battro, Stanislas Dehaene, and Wolf Singer. Scripta Varia: Pontifical Academy of Sciences.

Lieberman, Matthew D., Elliot T. Berkman, and Tor D. Wager. 2009. Correlations in social neuroscience aren't voodoo: A commentary on Vul et al. *Perspectives on Psychological Science* 4: 299–307.

Logothetis, Nikos K. 2008. What we can and cannot do with fMRI. *Nature* 453 (12 June): 869–878.

McHugh, Paul R., and Phillip Slavney. 1998. *The perspectives of psychiatry*. 2nd ed. Baltimore: Johns Hopkins University Press.

Mele, Alfred R. 2009. *Effective intentions: The power of conscious will*. New York: Oxford University Press.

———. 2014. *Free: Why science hasn't disproved free will*. New York: Oxford University Press.

Menninger, Karl. 1968. *The crime of punishment*. New York: The Viking Press.

Miller, Gregory A. 2010. Mistreating psychology in the decades of the brain. *Perspectives on Psychological Science* 5: 716–743.

Moore, Michael S. 2012. Responsible choices, desert-based legal institutions, and the challenges of contemporary neuroscience. *Social Philosophy and Policy* 29 (1): 233–279.

Morse, Stephen J. 1995. Brain and blame. *Georgetown Law Journal* 84: 527–549.

———. 2004. New neuroscience, old problems. In *Neuroscience and the law: Brain, mind and the scales of justice*, ed. Brent Garland. New York: Dana Press.

———. 2011. Lost in translation? An essay on law and neuroscience. In Vol. 13 of *Law and neuroscience*, ed. Michael Freeman. Oxford: Oxford University Press.

———. 2015. Neuroprediction: New technology, old problems. *Bioethica Forum* 8: 128–129.

———. 2018. The neuroscientific non-challenge to meaning, morals, and purpose. In Neuroexistentialism: *Meaning, morals, and purpose in the age of neuroscience*, ed. G.D. Caruso and O. Flanagan. New York: Oxford University Press.

Morse, Stephen J., and William T. Newsome. 2013. Criminal responsibility, criminal competence, and prediction of criminal behavior. In *A primer on criminal law and neuroscience*, ed. Stephen J. Morse and Adina L. Roskies. New York: Oxford University Press.

Mudrik, Liad, and Uri Maoz. 2014. "Me & my brain": Exposing neuroscience's closet dualism. *Journal of Cognitive Neuroscience* 27: 211–221.

Nachev, Parashkev, and Peter Hacker. 2015. The neural antecedents to voluntary action: Response to commentaries. *Cognitive Neuroscience* 6: 180–186.

Open Science Collaboration. 2015. Psychology: Estimating the reproducibility of psychological science. *Science* 349 (6251). https://doi.org/10.1126/science.aac4716.

Pardini, Dustin A., Adrian Raine, Kirk Erickson, and Rolf Loeber. 2014. Lower amygdala volume in men is associated with childhood aggression, early psychopathic traits, and future violence. *Biological Psychiatry* 75 (1): 73–80.

Pardo, Michael, and Dennis Patterson. 2013. *Minds, brains, and law: The conceptual foundations of law and neuroscience*. New York: Oxford University Press.

Pereboom, D., and G.D. Caruso. 2018. Hard-incompatibilist existentialism: Neuroscience, punishment, and meaning in life. In *Neuroexistentialism: Meaning, morals, and purpose in the age of neuroscience*, ed. G.D. Caruso and O. Flanagan. New York: Oxford University Press.

Poldrack, Russell. 2006. Can cognitive processes be inferred from neuroimaging data? *Trends in Cognitive Sciences* 10: 59–63.

———. 2013. How well can we predict future criminal acts from fMRI data? Russpokdrack.com. http://www.russpoldrack.org/search?q=aharoni. Accessed 11 Jan 2018.

Poldrack, Russel A. 2018. *The new mind readers: What neuroimaging can and cannot reveal about our thoughts*. Princeton: Princeton University Press.

Poldrack, Russell A., Chris I. Baker, Joke Durnez, Krzysztof J. Gorgolwski, Paul M. Matthews, Marcus R. Munafo, Thomas E. Nichols, Jean-baptiste Poline, Edward Vul, and Tal Yarkoni. 2017. Scanning the horizon: Towards transparent and reproducible neuroimaging research. *Nature Reviews. Neuroscience* 18: 115–126.

Presidential Commission for the Study of Bioethical Issues. 2015. *Gray matters: Topics at the intersection of neuroscience, ethics and society*. Vol. 2. Washington, DC: Presidential Commission for the Study of Bioethical Issues.

Rakoff, J.S. 2016. Neuroscience and the law: Don't rush in. *New York Review of Books*, May.

Rego, Mark D. 2016. Counterpoint: Clinical neuroscience is not ready for clinical use. *British Journal of Psychiatry* 208: 312–313.

Rissman, Jesse, Henry T. Greely, and Anthony D. Wagner. 2010. Detecting individual memories through the neural decoding of memory states and past experience. *Proceedings of the National Academy of Sciences of the United States of America* 107: 9849–9854.

Rissman, Jesse, Tiffany E. Chow, Nicco Reggente, and Anthony D. Wagner. 2016. Decoding fMRI signatures of real-world autobiographical memory retrieval. *Journal of Cognitive Neuroscience* 28: 604–620.

Roskies, Adina L. 2013. Brain imaging techniques. In *A primer on criminal law and neuroscience*, ed. Stephen J. Morse and Adina L. Roskies. New York: Oxford University Press.

Roskies, Adina L., N.J. Schweitzer, and Michael J. Saks. 2013. Neuroimages in court: Less biasing than feared. *Trends in Cognitive Sciences* 17: 99–101.

Schurger, Aaron, and Sebo Uithol. 2015. Nowhere and everywhere: The causal origin of voluntary action. *Review of Philosophy and Psychology* 6: 761–778.

Schurger, Aaron, Jacobo D. Sitt, and Stanislas Dehaene. 2012. An accumulator model for spontaneous neural activity prior to self-initiated movement. *Proceedings of the National Academy of Sciences of the United States of America* 109. https://doi.org/10.1073/pnas.12104.67109.

Schweitzer, N.J., Michael J. Saks, Emily R. Murphy, Adina L. Roskies, Walter Sinnott-Armstrong, and Lyn M. Gaudet. 2011. Neuroimages as evidence in a mens rea defense: No impact. *Psychology, Public Policy, and Law* 17: 357–393.

Sehon, Scott Robert. 2016. *Free will and action explanation: A non-causal, compatibilist account*. Oxford: Oxford University Press.

Sifferd, Katrina L. 2006. In defense of the use of commonsense psychology in the criminal law. *Law and Philosophy* 25: 571–612.

Simmons, Joseph P., Leif D. Nelson, and Uri Simonsohn. 2011. False-positive psychology: Undisclosed flexibility in data collection and analysis allows presenting anything as significant. *Psychological Science* 22: 1359–1366.

Stone, Alan. 1984. *Law, psychiatry, and morality*. Washington, DC: American Psychological Association.

Szucs, Denes, and John Ioannidis. 2017. Empirical assessment of published effect sizes and power in the recent cognitive neuroscience and psychology literature. *Plos: Biology* 15 (3). https://doi.org/10.1371/journal.pbio.2000797.

Varoquaux, Gael. 2017. Cross-validation failure: Small sample sizes lead to large error bars. *NeuroImage.* https://doi.org/10.1016/j.neuroimage.2017.06.061.

Vilares, Iris, Michael J. Wesley, Woo-Young Ahn, Richard J. Bonnie, Morris Hoffman, Owen D. Jones, Stephen J. Morse, Gideon Yaffe, Terry Lohrenz, and P. Read Montague. 2017. Predicting the knowledge–recklessness distinction in the human brain. *Proceedings of the National Academy of Sciences of the United States of America PNAS* 114. https://doi.org/10.1073/pn.as.1619385114.

Vul, Ed, Piotr Winkleman, Christine Harris, and Harold Pashler. 2009. Puzzlingly high correlations in fMRI studies of emotion, personality, and social cognition. *Perspectives on Psychological Science* 4: 274–290.

Wittgenstein, Ludwig. 1953. *Philosophical investigations.* New York: The Macmillan Company.

PART XX

Offensive Conduct

CHAPTER 21

No Offense

James Edwards

INTRODUCTION

Criminal law is used to tackle wrongdoing: to prevent wrongs that have not yet
occurred and to hold people responsible for wrongs that have. Abolitionists
claim that, however serious a wrong may be, criminal law should not be used
to tackle it. Fundamentalists claim that, however trivial the wrong, criminal law
always should be. In between these extremes, we find moderates of different
stripes. All moderates distinguish between wrongs that criminal law should and
should not be used to tackle. The difficult question is how this distinction is
to be drawn.

On one view, the default position is that criminal law should tackle wrongs.
We should be moderates, rather than fundamentalists, because there are special
reasons for criminal law not to tackle some of them.[1] On another view, the
default position is that criminal law should leave wrongs well alone. We should
be moderates, rather than abolitionists, because there are special reasons for
criminal law to tackle some wrongs. Joel Feinberg calls this second option *the
liberal view* (Feinberg 1984, pp. 14–15, 1988, pp. 151–155). At least among
philosophers, it has proved more popular than the first. Most agree that, if all
we know about X is that X is wrong, the burden is not on opponents of criminalization to explain why X should not be criminalized. Rather, it remains for
proponents of criminalization to explain why X should become a crime.

J. Edwards (✉)
University of Oxford, Oxford, UK

Worcester College, Oxford, UK

Brasenose College, Oxford, UK
e-mail: james.edwards@law.ox.ac.uk

© The Author(s) 2019
L. Alexander, K. K. Ferzan (eds.), *The Palgrave Handbook of Applied Ethics
and the Criminal Law*, https://doi.org/10.1007/978-3-030-22811-8_21

If the liberal view is correct, an obvious question remains. What gives us special reason to use criminal law to tackle wrongdoing? The most familiar answer is that some wrongs cause *harm*. The fact that a wrong is harmful is special reason for criminal law to prevent it and to hold people responsible for its commission (Mill 1859; Feinberg 1984). This does not mean that all harmful wrongs should be crimes. But it does mean that such wrongs are *eligible* for criminalization: they are the kind of thing that criminal law should be used to tackle, such that the default position is no longer that they are to be left alone by criminal law.

Some liberals claim that harm is one of a kind.[2] Others think it has at least one bedfellow. *Offensiveness,* some claim, is also special reason to tackle wrongs using criminal law. The fact that a wrong is offensive converts it from something criminal law should leave well alone into something eligible for criminalization. This is so whether or not the wrong is harmful. Following Feinberg, we can say that these liberals endorse *the offense principle* (Feinberg 1984, p. 26). This chapter asks what can be said for this principle.

The offense principle can be broken down into the following propositions:

(1) The fact that wrongs are offensive is a fact that bears on whether we should criminalize.
(2) Offensiveness bears on whether we should criminalize by giving us reason to use criminal law to tackle offensive wrongs.[3]
(3) The reason given by the fact that a wrong is offensive makes offensive wrongs eligible for criminalization.[4]

Whether we should accept (1)–(3) depends on what offensiveness *is*. Section "Offense and Offensiveness" clarifies the concept. It distinguishes between that which is subjectively offensive and that which is offensive objectively. Section "Offensiveness and Criminalization" pursues two aims. First, it considers the relationship between offensiveness, wrongdoing and eligibility for criminalization. Second, it argues that we should reject (3). The fact that wrongs are offensive—either subjectively or objectively—does not make them eligible for criminalization. The fact that a wrong is objectively offensive does not bear on whether it should be criminalized. The fact that a wrong is subjectively offensive is no reason to tackle it using criminal law. The offense principle, the section concludes, should therefore be rejected.

Section "The Value of Offense" sketches an argument for a stronger conclusion. As Mill claimed, offense has value. There is instrumental value in our encountering some things that offend us. We have reason not to criminalize in ways that prevent these encounters. So while subjective offensiveness does bear on whether wrongs should be criminalized, it does so by giving us reason to think twice about criminalization. There is also intrinsic value in our being offended by some things we encounter. Some wrongs are such that they *ought* to offend. There are cases in which we have reason to tackle these wrongs using the criminal law because people fail to take offense at their commission. So while subjective offensiveness can give us reason to criminalize, its absence, not its presence, is what gives us this reason. If these claims are true, Feinberg's version of the offense principle is not only unsound; it is something close to the opposite of the truth.

OFFENSE AND OFFENSIVENESS

Imagine we are riding the bus. Other passengers join us one by one. The first masturbates. The second defecates. A third eats what the second left. A fourth gives us the finger. The fifth salutes us. It is the Nazi salute. We conclude that it would have been better to have cycled.[5]

Was anything done on the bus offensive? Did any of it cause offense? What is the relationship between these questions? Let us start with the second. Obviously enough, what happens on the bus cannot offend us if we are unaware of it. Nor does it cause us offense if we are indifferent. We are offended by X only if our reaction to X is *aversive*—only if X is something we want to avoid or extinguish and for which we feel displeasure or distaste.

That aversion is necessary for offense is widely accepted (Feinberg 1984, pp. 45–51; Shoemaker 2000, p. 547; Simester and von Hirsch 2002, pp. 270–275; Tasioulas 2006, p. 150). Few, however, claim that it is sufficient. Feinberg is one exception: he uses the language of offense to refer to aversive reactions of all kinds (Feinberg 1985, p. 1). But while many people dislike the rain, and prefer to avoid it, we would not say that rain is something by which many people are offended. Compare this with someone defecating on a public bus. This, too, tends to generate aversion. Many, I assume, would also say that it offends. What explains these divergent conclusions? The answer is given by Feinberg himself. We are offended in what Feinberg calls "the strict and narrow sense" when we not only "suffer a disliked state" but also "attribute that state to the wrongful conduct of another" (Feinberg 1985, p. 2). To be offended, in this sense, is to experience aversion that is *judgment mediated*: it is to want to avoid X, and to feel distaste for it, partly because one judges X to be wrong. My concern here is with offense in the strict and narrow sense.[6]

We can further clarify what it is to be offended by contrasting offense with harm. We are harmed by X when X makes us worse off by diminishing our future prospects (Raz 1987, p. 327; Gardner 2007, p. 244; Simester and von Hirsch 2011, p. 36). X reduces those prospects when X's occurrence makes it more difficult, or more costly, for us to successfully achieve valuable goals.[7] It follows that we can be harmed by X even if we are unaware of its existence. I am harmed when you remove all the money from my account, even if I have no idea that you have done so. It also follows that we can be harmed by X even if we lack any aversion to X and even if we do not judge X to be wrong. Many people are harmed by smoking cigarettes, even though they want to smoke more not less and even though they do not judge cigarette smoking to be wrong.

If this is right, we can be harmed without being offended. We can also be offended without being harmed. We may experience displeasure when given the finger. We may prefer that it not be given, at least to us. We may react this way partly because we judge giving the finger to be wrong. It does not follow that our future prospects are thereby diminished. Having been given the finger, we may quickly forget what happened and carry on with our lives as they were before: there need be no valuable goal that will be more difficult, or more costly, for us to achieve in future.[8] Where there is not, that which offends us does not do us any harm.

None of this, of course, is to say that offense is never harmful. Perhaps we ride the bus in order to get to work. Perhaps cycling would take much longer and expose us to additional risks. Imagine we are offended by the actions of our fellow passengers and no longer feel able to ride the bus because we fear a repeat performance. If this is so, our future prospects are diminished by what the other passengers do: it is now more costly for us to achieve at least one valuable goal. What happens on the bus then not only offends us. It also causes us some harm.[9]

To be offended by X, I have claimed, is to react to X with judgment-mediated aversion. The judgment in question is the judgment that X is wrong. It is an empirical question whether X in fact offends us. Whenever it does, we can sensibly ask a normative question too: we can ask whether that which offends us should (Shoemaker 2000, pp. 550–551).[10] It is worth noting that the same is not always true when X causes harm. While it makes sense to ask whether we should be offended when someone masturbates on a bus, it makes no sense to ask whether we should be harmed when someone empties our bank account of money. To empty our account *just is* to harm us, by making it more difficult for us to achieve valuable goals.

This difference exists for the following reason. We are often passive participants in events that harm us. Everything that is done, to make it the case that we are harmed, is done by someone else. When events cause us offense, we participate actively. Offense, as it is often put, is something we *take*. We are offended, I have claimed, when we form judgments, desires and emotions. These are not things that are done to us. They are things that we do. And there are reasons that count for and against our doing them. This is why it always makes sense to ask, not only whether X offends, but also whether X should offend us. It is why the normative question, though it does not always make sense when X causes us harm, always makes sense when X offends us.

If we are to answer the normative question, we need to know what reasons there are to take offense. Those reasons come in different flavors. Some are given by extrinsic properties of taking offense at X. Others are given by intrinsic properties of X itself. By extrinsic properties I mean properties that are not part of what it is to take offense, such as the valuable effects that taking offense can have in some cases. For an example, imagine we react to public defecation with judgment-mediated aversion. Our reaction helps reduce the incidence of defecation, which helps reduce the spread of disease. This valuable effect of taking offense is an extrinsic property of our taking it, which gives us reason to take offense.

By intrinsic properties, I mean properties that are partly constitutive of X. Where X is something that has a particular meaning for us, that meaning is an intrinsic property of X. For an example, imagine being given the finger while riding the bus. Part of what it is to give others the finger, absent special circumstances, is to express contempt for those others. This expression of contempt is an intrinsic property of giving others the finger, which gives us reason to take offense when it is given.[11] Let us say that, where there are reasons of this kind, it is *fitting* that we take offense. Where there are reasons of the kind discussed in the previous paragraph, let us say that taking offense is *useful*.

We are now in a position to ask what it is for X to be *offensive*. In one sense of the term, what is offensive is up to us. It is our reactions to things that make them offensive and that make other things inoffensive. If many people are offended by use of Comic Sans, then using Comic Sans is offensive in this sense. If few are offended by Avenir, this choice of font is inoffensive. Let us say that,

X is *subjectively* offensive if and only if X causes widespread offense.

When Feinberg claims that offensiveness makes wrongs eligible for criminalization, it is this sense of offensive that he has in mind (Feinberg 1985, pp. 35–37). The subjective sense is not, however, the only one available. We sometimes say that X is inoffensive even though we know that X causes widespread offense: I might deny that it is offensive for homosexual couples to hold hands, even though I know that widespread homophobia means that this offends many. Conversely, we sometimes say that X is offensive even though we know that X offends next to no-one: I might claim that racist slurs are offensive, even though I know that widespread racism means that few will take offense.

These examples suggest that, as well as being subjectively offensive, X can also be offensive objectively (Tasioulas 2006, p. 153). Some suggest that X is offensive in this second sense if there is reason to take offense at X (Simester and von Hirsch 2002, pp. 273–274; Duff and Marshall 2006, p. 62). We have already seen why this proposal is over-inclusive. One reason to take offense at X is that our taking offense at X is useful. Mere utility, however, is insufficient here. Given the right set of circumstances, taking offense at almost anything might have valuable effects. If I drink too much coffee, and you eat too many pies, it might be useful if I came to be offended by drinking coffee and you came to be offended by eating pies. This would not suffice to show either of these things to be offensive. Compare this with giving others the finger or with racist slurs. These *are* plausibly thought of as offensive because of an intrinsic property that they share: because of the contempt that is thereby expressed for others. These examples suggest that we should prefer a narrower definition. Let us say that,

X is *objectively* offensive if and only if taking offense is a fitting response to X.

On a rival view to Feinberg's, it is the fact that wrongs are offensive in this second sense that makes those wrongs eligible for criminalization (Tasioulas 2006, pp. 153–155). The following sections ask whether we should accept either of these views.

OFFENSIVENESS AND CRIMINALIZATION

What is the relationship between offensiveness and wrongdoing? What is the relationship between these two things and eligibility for criminalization? On one view, acts are wrong because they are offensive. That this is so makes them eligible for criminalization. This view is represented by Fig. 21.1.

John Tasioulas writes that "what *makes* certain acts wrong is, to some significant degree, the fact that they are apt to offend others." Where these acts are not apt to offend—because, say, they take place in private—"the wrongfulness essential to the original case for criminalization evaporates" (Tasioulas 2006, p. 150). For an act to be apt to offend is for it to be objectively offensive.[12] For Tasioulas, then, objective offensiveness helps make some acts wrong, which in turn makes them eligible for criminalization.

Feinberg sometimes writes as if his view is structurally similar. For him, the offense principle is only satisfied by that which is morally wrong: X is eligible for criminalization when and because X is (i) a breach of moral duty, that (ii) generates an aversive response (Feinberg 1985, pp. 1–2). Now whether X satisfies (i), and whether it satisfies (ii), may seem to be questions that must be answered on separate grounds. But Feinberg claims that "there will always be a wrong whenever an offended state (in the generic sense) is produced in another without justification or excuse" (Feinberg 1985, p. 2). This remark implies that, where X is subjectively offensive, this makes it the case that X needs to be justified or excused.[13] And this implies that, where neither justification nor excuse is available, subjective offensiveness helps make it the case that X is wrong. As we just saw, under Feinberg's offense principle, this in turn makes X eligible for criminalization.

Both versions of the view represented in Fig. 21.1 should be rejected. As to the first, acts are not wrong *because* they are objectively offensive. That acts are objectively offensive *presupposes* that they are wrong. To see why, recall that for X to be objectively offensive is for it to be fitting that we take offense at X. To take offense at X is, in part, to judge that X is wrong. It is fitting that we judge X to be wrong only if we judge correctly: only if there are facts which make X wrong independently of our judgment. It is fitting that we judge racist slurs to be wrong only if wrong is indeed what they are. If there turns out to be nothing wrong with using Comic Sans, then judgment to the contrary is not fitting. It follows that in order to establish that X is objectively offensive, we must first establish that X is wrong. And if the objective offensiveness of X presupposes X's wrongness, it is not true that X is wrong because it is objectively offensive.

What about the claim that some acts are wrong because they are subjectively offensive? Feinberg says that this is so when no justification or excuse can be provided. To see why we should reject this view, compare two types of act. Acts of the first type are not wrong because there is no moral objection to their performance. Think of saying hello to your neighbor in the morning. Acts of

Fig. 21.1   O ────▶ W ────▶ E

the second type are not wrong despite the fact that there are such objections. Think of punching your neighbor in the morning in order to prevent her from killing you.[14] Feinberg's claims imply that, when people begin to react aversively to X, this converts X from an act of the first kind into an act of the second. We do not need to justify or excuse acts—like saying hello—to which there is no moral objection. And Feinberg claims that subjective offensiveness needs to be justified or excused. On this view, if our saying hello begins to be met with the aversion of bigots, we cannot respond by pointing out that there is nothing morally objectionable about our saying hello. The aversion of bigots *makes* our saying hello morally objectionable.[15] If the aversion extends to our living nearby, or to our very existence, these things become morally objectionable too. Any view with such entailments, it seems to me, is reduced to absurdity by them. Judgment-mediated aversion to X cannot itself make X morally objectionable. That Feinberg's view implies otherwise is reason to reject it.[16]

Before moving on, it is worth returning briefly to the relationship between harm and offense. It is tempting to juxtapose harmful with offensive wrongs. Breaking someone's legs is both wrong and harmful. Uttering a racist slur is both wrong and offensive. If the above discussion is correct, however, the nature of the conjunction is not the same in each case. It is wrong to break someone's legs partly *because* this is harmful. That my breaking your legs reduces your prospects, by making it more difficult for you to achieve valuable goals, helps make it the case that my breaking your legs is wrong. If the last two paragraphs are right, it is not wrong to utter racist slurs even partly because this is offensive. That something is subjectively offensive does not make it wrong. That something is objectively offensive presupposes that it is wrong. What makes racist slurs wrong, then, is not that they are offensive; what makes them wrong is the contempt that they express for others. Such slurs we can call *expressive wrongs*.[17] Leg-breaking, in contrast, is a *harmful wrong*. These labels should not be taken to suggest that racist slurs are never harmful. Nor should they be taken to suggest that leg-breaking never expresses contempt. They should only be taken to suggest that these additional properties are parasitic. Expressive wrongs can cause a great deal of harm. But they cause this, at least in standard cases, partly because of the contempt that they express. Harmful wrongs can express a great deal of contempt. But they express this, at least in standard cases, partly because they are harmful. Wrongs of both kinds may be offensive. But in neither case does their offensiveness make them wrong.

Let us set Fig. 21.1 aside, then, and consider a different view. If acts are not wrong because they are offensive, perhaps acts are offensive because they are wrong. Perhaps their offensiveness makes them eligible for criminalization. This view is captured by Fig. 21.2.

Antony Duff and Sandra Marshall write that "conduct is offensive because it is wrong by some relevant standard that it violates" (Duff and Marshall 2006,

Fig. 21.2   W ⟶ O ⟶ E

p. 59). By offensive, Duff and Marshall mean objectively offensive. They do not—and could not—mean subjectively offensive. What makes X subjectively offensive is not the fact that it is wrong, but the fact that people *judge* X to be wrong, and experience judgment-mediated aversion. Such judgments, I already suggested, may be hopelessly misguided. This cannot be the case if X is offensive objectively. We know that X is objectively offensive only if X is wrong. It does not follow that X's wrongness is what makes X objectively offensive. To see why, we need to draw another distinction. We need to distinguish between (i) the fact that X is wrong and (ii) the facts that make X wrong. Figure 21.2 implies that (i) makes X objectively offensive. If this were so, there would be something offensive about all wrongs, and all wrongs would be eligible for criminalization. To endorse the offense principle would not be to endorse (a version of) the liberal view. It would be to abandon that view for its rival.

Be that as it may, there are independent reasons to reject that which Fig. 21.2 depicts. We act wrongly when we breach a moral duty. But the fact that X breaches such a duty does not itself make X objectively offensive. Consider the duty we have to keep our promises. If I promise to meet you for lunch, I act wrongly if I arrive late because of bad traffic. Nonetheless, there need be nothing offensive about what I have done. Compare a passenger who gives us the finger or who performs a Nazi salute. Here, it is plausible to think that judgment-mediated aversion is fitting. But what makes it fitting is not the fact that a duty has been breached. What makes such aversion fitting is the contempt that the passenger's conduct expresses for others.[18] That it expresses contempt, I suggested above, is also what makes such conduct wrong: giving people the finger, and performing a Nazi salute, are expressive wrongs. If this is right, it is (ii), not (i), that makes conduct objectively offensive: what the passenger does on the bus is objectively offensive not because it is wrong; what the passenger does is objectively offensive because of the facts that make it wrong. Such facts— here, the contempt expressed by the aforementioned gestures—therefore do double duty: they both make X wrong *and* make X objectively offensive. If X is objectively offensive for the very same reason it is wrong, then X is not objectively offensive because it is wrong. It follows that the view captured by Fig. 21.2 should also be rejected.

If Figs. 21.1 and 21.2 both mislead, we may be tempted by a third view. On this view, that X is wrong or offensive does not help make it the case that X is offensive or wrong. But X is eligible for criminalization only when X is both these things. This view is expressed by Fig. 21.3.

Feinberg sometimes writes as if this represents his view. The offense principle, he claims, requires both "offending and wronging": a "disliked state of

Fig. 21.3

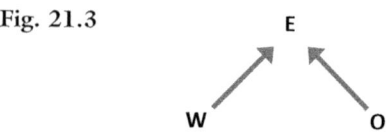

mind" that is "produced wrongfully by another party" (Feinberg 1985, p. 2). These remarks do not commit Feinberg to the claim that, if X is to be eligible for criminalization under the offense principle, X must be wrong (even partly) because X is subjectively offensive. They are compatible with the claim that, where X is wrong, this is always for reasons that have nothing to do with subjective offensiveness. All Feinberg's remarks here require is that, for a wrong to satisfy the offense principle, its commission must be met with widespread offense.

Simester and von Hirsch agree with Feinberg on this point. For them,

> It is not affronting the sensibilities of other persons (even many of them) that should justify possible state intervention, but affront *plus* valid normative reasons for objecting to the conduct. (Simester and von Hirsch 2011, p. 96)

Where X is subjectively offensive, "proponents of criminalisation" must still "put forward reasons *why* the conduct is a wrong" (Simester and von Hirsch 2011, p. 107). Eligibility for criminalization, on this view, requires both subjective offensiveness and wrongdoing. And these must be established separately.

Though this view avoids earlier objections, it has unpalatable implications of its own. We can see this by considering the way in which societal attitudes can change in the face of wrongdoing. Imagine that, at some point in time, X is *both* objectively *and* subjectively offensive: it is a wrong to which judgment-mediated aversion is a fitting response and to which many people respond as is fitting. Figure 21.3 has it that X is eligible for criminalization. Imagine next that, over time, wrongdoers use their power and influence to persuade many that X is not wrong or that wrongdoers commit X so frequently that few people anymore react to X with aversion. On the view taken by Feinberg, as well as by Simester and von Hirsch, these wrongdoers thereby render X ineligible for criminalization.[19] They do so by spreading moral mistakes about their wrongs.[20] It is hard to believe that, simply by spreading such mistakes, wrongdoers can turn a wrong that was eligible for criminalization into one that is ineligible. Tasioulas writes that,

> in a racist society, especially one in which the racially vilified group has absorbed a subordinate self-image, publicly expressed racist abuse might cause serious offence to very few. Such abuse remains, however, objectively offensive. Indeed, the fact that very few are even mildly offended by the public utterance of racist abuse [*pace* Feinberg, and Simester and von Hirsch] gives us additional reason for criminalising it. (Tasioulas 2006, p. 156)

We return below to the claim that the absence of widespread offense might give us reason to criminalize the objectively offensive. The point here is that one cannot render the objectively offensive ineligible for criminalization—where it is otherwise eligible—merely by creating conditions under which offense is no longer widespread.

This last point also holds in reverse. One cannot render conduct eligible for criminalization merely by creating conditions under which that conduct meets with widespread offense. The point is clearest in the case of conduct that is not wrong: that the spread of bigotry leaves many offended by the sight of homo-sexual couples holding hands is no reason to use criminal law to tackle such hand holding (Tasioulas 2006, p. 155; Simester and von Hirsch 2011, p. 97; Tadros 2016, pp. 287–288).[21] The same is true of conduct that is not just wrong but objectively offensive. That receding bigotry leaves many offended by racist abuse does not bring into existence reasons to tackle such abuse using the criminal law. It does not bring these reasons into existence because they existed already: because our reasons to prevent racist abuse, and to hold abus-ers responsible, do not depend on people in fact taking offense at these wrongs. To say otherwise is to say that those who traffic in wrongs like racist abuse weaken the case for criminalization, simply by making it true that enough peo-ple cease to have fitting responses when they or others are wronged.

This does not yet show that we should reject Fig. 21.3. Instead of claiming that wrongs are eligible for criminalization when, and because, they are *subjec-tively* offensive, one might claim that they are so eligible when, and because, they are offensive *objectively*. Though this suggestion is more promising, there are reasons to think that it too proves unsatisfactory.[22]

Recall that for X to be objectively offensive is for taking offense at X to be a fitting response. That Z is a fitting response to X entails that there is reason to do Z when X occurs. What it does *not* entail is that there is reason to prevent X or to hold people responsible for X's commission. We can see this more clearly by considering other examples. If it is fitting that I congratulate you on your achievements, this entails that there is reason for me to congratulate you. It hardly entails that there is reason to prevent you from achieving things worthy of congratulations. If giving a candidate an A+ is the fitting response to her performance in an exam, this entails that there is reason to give the candidate an A+. It hardly entails that candidates should be prevented from performing to such a standard. The lesson of these examples is a simple one: while the fact that Z is a fitting response entails that there is reason to do Z, what *else* that fact entails depends on what *makes* Z fitting. If Z is fitting because X exhibits quali-ties we have reason to foster and support, we have no reason at all—ceteris paribus—to prevent X's occurrence. We have no reason at all—ceteris pari-bus—to tackle X using the criminal law.

Let us return now to the example of racist abuse. Such abuse is a wrong that is objectively offensive. It is also, I assume, a wrong that is eligible for criminal-ization. Does the former fact explain the latter? If the previous paragraph is correct, it does not. Because taking offense is a fitting response to racist abuse, there is reason to take offense. But a reason to do what is fitting is one thing. A reason to prevent or punish is quite another. As we saw with congratulations and grades, that we have a reason of the former kind does not entail that we have a reason of the latter. All the more so when we are talking not about pre-vention and punishment per se, but about preventing and punishing by means of criminalization. There is no small gap between something counting in favor of judgment-mediated aversion and something counting in favor of mobilizing the resources of the criminal law. To bridge that gap, we need to appeal to something other than the fact that offense is fitting. One thing to which we might appeal is that which *makes* it fitting that we take offense: in the case of racist abuse, we might appeal to the kind of contempt that such abuse expresses for others—contempt that may not only have damaging effects on individual self-esteem but may also contribute to unjust inequalities of power and status. Such contempt, it is plausible to think, *is* a reason to prevent racist abuse using the criminal law and to hold abusers responsible in criminal courts. It is a fact that plausibly bridges the gap to a case for criminalization.[23]

If these remarks are correct, the payoff is twofold. First, the fact that wrongs like racist abuse are objectively offensive does not bear on whether we should tackle them using the criminal law. Wrongs are objectively offensive because of further facts about those wrongs. It is these (and other) further facts that give us reason to criminalize. As Tadros puts the point:

> Certain moral properties of conduct make certain negative reactions to that conduct appropriate. ... These moral properties are independent of any judgement about the appropriate response. Because the relevant reactions are appropriate, the conduct is [objectively] offensive—it is conduct about which it is apt to respond in the various ways that constitute taking offence at it. But the morally salient characteristics of the conduct that give us reasons to criminalize it are the grounds that make the conduct [objectively] offensive. The fact that it is [objectively] offensive is not a reason to criminalize it; the facts that make it [objectively] offensive are. (Tadros 2016, p. 287)

The fact that a wrong is subjectively offensive, I claimed above, is also no reason to tackle it using the criminal law. Figure 21.3 should be rejected accordingly.

Second, wrongs like racist abuse are expressive wrongs. It is what they express that makes them wrong, that makes them objectively offensive and that helps make them eligible for criminalization (Tadros 2016, p. 287). We should therefore replace Fig. 21.3 with Fig. 21.4.

Figure 21.4 does not imply that all objectively offensive conduct is eligible for criminalization. It only implies that some facts that make conduct eligible for criminalization also make that conduct objectively offensive. So Fig. 21.4 is consistent with thinking that, where a wrong is objectively offensive, it may be criminalized only when it possesses some additional property, be it publicity (Tasioulas 2006, p. 151; Duff and Marshall 2006, pp. 76–79), or harmfulness (Simester and von Hirsch 2011, p. 118) or something else. What Fig. 21.4

Fig. 21.4   E   W   O
                      F

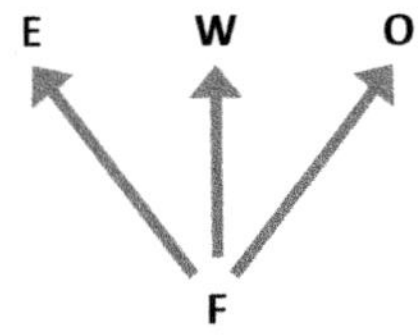

makes vivid, and what matters most here, is that however long the list of eligibility-conferring properties turns out to be, offensiveness—of either kind—is not on it.

Recall next that, according to the offense principle:

(1) The fact that wrongs are offensive is a fact that bears on whether we should criminalize.

(2) Offensiveness bears on whether we should criminalize by giving us reason to use criminal law to tackle offensive wrongs.

(3) The reason given by the fact that a wrong is offensive makes offensive wrongs eligible for criminalization.

If the argument of this section is sound, we should reject (1)–(3). If offensive means objectively offensive, (1) is false. If offensive means subjectively offensive, (2) is false. And (3) is false either way. As Fig. 21.4 shows, the problem with the offense principle is that it casts offensiveness in the wrong role. Where conduct is eligible for criminalization, it may well be offensive. But it is not so eligible because it is offensive. This is why the offense principle is not a sound principle.

It is worth clarifying one final point. To deny that the offense principle is sound is not to say that offensiveness is morally insignificant or that offensiveness is irrelevant to the criminal law. As observed in section II, conduct that is subjectively offensive may be harmful; it may be eligible to be criminalized on the basis that criminalization will prevent this harm. As observed in this section, some conduct is objectively offensive because it expresses contempt; it may be eligible for criminalization on the basis that criminalization will prevent such expression. Simply put, subjective offensiveness sometimes gives rise to facts that make X eligible to be criminalized; objective offensiveness is sometimes the product of facts that make X eligible for criminalization. In neither case, however, does offensiveness itself make X so eligible. It follows that the offense principle should be rejected.

The Value of Offense

An ideal society, it is sometimes suggested, would be one in which we lived together in harmony: in which we did not upset, insult, irritate, offend or otherwise come into conflict with one another. To use a suitably general term, we would not clash as we do now. Many obstacles lie in the path of this supposed utopia. One is the extent to which we disagree about what is good and right. As Rawls and others have argued, such disagreement is all but inevitable in liberal conditions (Rawls 1993). Yet it often leads us to clash, sometimes painfully, with those whose convictions are very different to our own. For those who believe in the harmonious ideal this creates a problem. One response is to try to shuffle moral dissensus—at least of the painful kind—out of our public lives. Where expressive acts are likely to upset, insult, irritate or offend others if performed publicly, steps are to be taken to encourage actors to perform them privately. Much conflict that would otherwise afflict our daily existence can thereby be eliminated.

In *On Liberty*, Mill argues that this line of thought is mistaken from the start. Far from being a place in which we live together in harmony, Mill's ideal society involves a healthy dose of *disharmony*: it is a place in which even the most entrenched convictions are the subject of dissent, such that we all clash, sometimes painfully, with one another. If expressive acts that would upset, insult, irritate or offend others are hidden in private, steps should be taken to encourage their performance in public.[24]

Mill gives several reasons to favor his disharmonious ideal. One is that clashes of conviction help us get at the truth:

> Truth in the great practical concerns of life is so much a question of the reconciling and combining of opposites that very few have minds sufficiently capacious to make the adjustment with an approach to correctness, and it has to be made by the rough process of a struggle between combatants fighting under hostile banners. (Mill 1859)

A second is that clashes of conviction help us develop our deliberative faculties. As Brink puts the point,

> Sharing thought and discussion with others, especially about important matters, improves one's deliberations. It enlarges the menu of options, by identifying new options worth consideration, and helps one better assess the merits of these options, by forcing on one's attention new considerations and arguments about the comparative merits of the options. In these ways, open and vigorous discussion with diverse interlocutors improves the quality of one's deliberations. (Brink 2013, p. 155)

Mill claims that we lead better lives when we develop our deliberative faculties and when we learn the truth about "the great concerns of practical life." For him, both contribute constitutively to how well our lives go for us, whether or not they make us happier or have other valuable effects. Even if this is wrong, it is plausible to think that such effects will often be forthcoming. All else being equal, we are more likely to succeed in achieving worthwhile goals, and in governing ourselves well as a polity, if the quality of our deliberations is high and if those deliberations are not afflicted by falsehoods.

If Mill is right, a society which rid itself of subjectively offensive conduct would move further away from—rather than closer to—the ideal.[25] It does not follow that there is reason not to criminalize each particular offensive act. For one thing, not all conduct that offends does so as part of a clash of conviction. For another, though Mill's ideal demands a dose of disharmony, that dose is not unlimited. What is required is an environment that contains enough moral dissensus to generate the aforementioned gains. Be that as it may, what Mill's argument does imply—assuming it goes through—is that there is reason not to criminalize subjectively offensive acts generally. This *would* threaten to deprive us of the dose of disharmony that Mill's ideal demands. So when people complain that conduct should be criminalized because they find it offensive, it is not only true that this complaint is—in and of itself—without weight. It is also true that, precisely because the conduct attracts such complaints, law-makers should exercise added caution when it comes to criminalization.[26]

We have seen that for some defenders of the offense principle, most notably Feinberg, the fact that a wrong is subjectively offensive is a reason to criminalize that wrong. Section III argued that there is no such reason. What does not follow is that subjective offensiveness never bears on whether to criminalize. In fact, the last few paragraphs suggest that it can. But they suggest that it bears in the opposite direction to that which Feinberg and others assume. That a wrong is subjectively offensive, far from being a reason to criminalize, is a reason to think twice about criminalization.

Various arguments for free expression might be used to buttress this last conclusion. To sketch just one, people are often offended by conduct that forms part of valuable ways of life, particularly where those ways of life are very different from their own. Criminalizing such conduct may be understood to condemn not just the conduct that is criminalized but the valuable ways of life of which that conduct forms part. And public portrayals which help validate different ways of living may become harder to access as a result of criminalization. As Raz writes,

> validation of a way of life through its public expression is of crucial importance for the well-being of individuals whose life it is. It helps their identification with their way of life, their sense of its worth, and their sense that their way of life facilitates rather than hinders their integration into their society. (Raz 1991, p. 312)

Defenders of the offense principle do not, of course, deny the force of such arguments. Feinberg, for instance, accepts that many factors mediate against the criminalization of conduct that offends (Feinberg 1985, pp. 25–49). Boiled down to its essentials, his argument is that we must balance evils. On the one hand, offense is an evil (Feinberg 1985, p. 25). So its prevention is a good. And this makes subjectively offensive conduct eligible for criminalization. On the other hand, there are the evils involved in criminalizing conduct that offends. Criminalization may have bad effects, including those discussed by Raz. It is where effects like these do not obtain, at least in large measure, that we face an evil against which we justifiably use the force of the criminal law.

The importance of Mill's argument is the challenge it poses to this picture. Feinberg would have us see offense as an evil, criminalization of which may rob us of other valuable things. Mill would have us see offense as a valuable thing, of which we may be robbed by criminalization. As Waldron summarizes the view, where "widespread moral distress *is* detectable in the community, then far from being a legitimate ground for interference, it is a positive and healthy sign that the processes of ethical confrontation … are actually taking place." Were law-makers to endorse Feinberg's version of the offense principle,

What ought to be taken as evidence that freedom of thought and lifestyle was promoting progress would be invoked instead as a *prima facie* reason for interfering with that freedom. A sign of vitality would be cited as a necessary condition for legitimately suppressing that vitality. A symptom of progress would be deployed as a justification for acting in a way that would bring progress to a halt. (Waldron 1987, p. 417)

When Waldron makes these claims, he does not make them in his own voice. He is merely telling us what follows from Mill's argument. Whether that argument is sound depends on empirical claims that cannot be verified here. It depends, among other things, on whether offense tends to generate the gains Mill describes. But assume Mill is onto something: that he is right about the ideal and about what is conducive to its achievement. If section III is correct, and Mill's argument goes through, subjective offensiveness bears not in favor of but against criminalization. Feinberg's offense principle is then something close to the opposite of the truth.

Mill's claim is that there is instrumental value in our encountering some conduct that offends us. If some wrongs are objectively offensive, there is intrinsic value in our being offended by some conduct we encounter.[27] That there is value in our taking offense, of course, does not imply that this is what we ought to do. Some writers, however, do claim that we should take offense at some wrongs. Duff and Marshall, for instance, write that offense is sometimes "necessary": this is so where conduct "flouts standards that people ought to care about, in ways that people ought to find offensive (even if they are not in fact offended by it)" (Duff and Marshall 2006, p. 63). Those who meet such conduct with indifference, or positively welcome it, are appropriately criticized for reacting as they do.

Duff and Marshall do not say much about when taking offense is necessary. Let us grant, however, that it is necessary in the case of racist abuse. We can then compare two societies in which such abuse occurs. In the first, people generally do what they ought to do, by taking offense in the face of racist abuse. In the second society, people largely fail to do what they should and meet racist abuse with indifference or enthusiasm.

In both societies, the previous section suggested, there is reason to criminalize racist abuse. This reason is given by the kind of contempt such abuse expresses, combined with the fact that criminalization can both help prevent this expressive wrong and hold wrongdoers responsible for its commission. Feinberg argues that in the first society there is additional reason to criminalize. This is so because in that society racist abuse is subjectively offensive. Like others, I have claimed that there is no such reason. Tasioulas argues that Feinberg has things backward. In his view, there is additional reason to criminalize racist abuse in the *second* society.[28] It is where abuse fails to cause widespread offense, not where it does so, that we have this reason.

Is Tasioulas correct? Here is one reason to think so. We are assuming that, when racist abuse occurs, it is necessary that we take offense. In the first society, this is what happens. People generally react as they should. In the second society, by contrast, offense is rarely forthcoming. Though this is not itself a reason to criminalize, it threatens to send the message—both to (would-be) abusers and to the abused—that racist abuse is a matter of indifference. Just as messages of validation can help foster a sense of self-worth and belonging—recall the Razian argument for free expression sketched earlier—so too messages of indifference can undermine both these things. In this way, widespread failure to take offense can detrimentally affect both individual and group well-being. Criminalizing racist abuse is a means of counteracting the aforementioned message of indifference—and of alleviating its damaging effects—by giving "unequivocal and public expression to our condemnation of such behaviour as wrongful" (Tasioulas 2006, p. 156). That this is so is a reason to criminalize in our second society that does not obtain—at least in equal measure—in the first.

These remarks support the conclusion that whether a wrong is subjectively offensive is of relevance to whether that wrong is eligible for criminalization. This, however, is no help to Feinberg and his followers. For them, there are reasons to tackle wrongs using the criminal law that exist when, and because, those wrongs meet with judgment-mediated aversion. It is where offense is present, not absent, that we have these reasons. The argument here is that something close to the opposite is true. There are reasons to tackle some wrongs using the criminal law that exist when, and because, those wrongs do *not* meet with judgment-mediated aversion. It is where offense is absent, not where it is present, that we have these reasons.

Conclusion

It may help to summarize what I have claimed.

Those who endorse the offense principle claim that:

(A) The fact that wrongs are offensive is a reason to use criminal law to tackle those wrongs.

There are a number of ways in which this claim might be negated. First consider:

(B) The fact that wrongs are offensive is *not* a reason to use criminal law to tackle those wrongs.

I argued for (B) in section "Offensiveness and Criminalization." Neither the fact that a wrong is subjectively offensive, nor the fact that it is objectively offensive, is a reason to tackle that wrong using criminal law.

Next consider:

(C) The fact that wrongs are offensive is a reason *not* to use criminal law to tackle those wrongs.

(C) is too strong, particularly when offensive is used in its objective sense. But I argued in section IV that, when it comes to subjective offensiveness, something close to (C) is supported by Mill's vision of an ideal society. In that society, we all benefit from disharmony: from clashes of conviction that upset, insult, irritate and offend. If we endorse this ideal, the fact that a wrong is subjectively offensive gives us reason to think twice about criminalizing that wrong.

Last consider:

(D) The fact that wrongs are *not* offensive is a reason to use criminal law to tackle those wrongs.

(D) is false if offensive means objectively offensive. But section IV argued that, if it instead means subjectively offensive, we have reason to accept something akin to (D). We have additional reason to tackle some wrongs using the criminal law when, and because, people fail to take offense at their commission.

If (B) is correct, the offense principle is unsound. If (C) and (D) are correct, Feinberg's offense principle—which holds that subjective, not objective, offensiveness makes conduct eligible for criminalization—is something close to the opposite of the truth. None of this is to say—to repeat a point made in section III—that offensive conduct should never be criminalized.[29] But it is to say that offensiveness is not itself a reason to criminalize. And it is to say that where offense does bear on criminalization, its absence may bear in favor, while its presence bears against.[30]

Notes

1. For a view of this kind, see Moore (1997, pp. 661–665). By "special reasons" I mean reasons that do not apply in all cases of criminalization and that—where they do apply—sometimes defeat all countervailing reasons.
2. This is Mill's official position in *On Liberty*: criminal law—like other instances of societal coercion—should be used to tackle harmful wrongs and harmful wrongs alone. *See* Mill (1859).
3. I follow Feinberg in taking reasons to criminalize to be considerations by which law-makers are properly guided and which they properly take to count in favor of criminalization. *See* Feinberg (1984, pp. 4–6).
4. Doesn't (2) entail (3)? It does not. It is one thing to have reason to criminalize. It is another for that reason to be "good enough"—for it to be capable of justifying criminalization (Feinberg 1988, pp. 321–324).
5. This paragraph draws on Feinberg's famous (and even more eventful) ride (*see* Feinberg 1985, pp. 10–13).
6. So understood, offense differs from nuisance. X is a nuisance if we experience an aversion to X that results directly from our senses—from X's smell, taste, sound and so on. Where we judge the creation of a nuisance to be wrong, the judgment is mediated by our aversion. Where we experience offense, the aversion is mediated by our judgment.

7. How difficult X is for us depends on our capacity to achieve X. How costly X is for us depends on what we would have to give up in order to achieve it (Cohen 2000, pp. 171–172).

8. As Feinberg puts it, such experiences often "come to us, are suffered for a time, and then go, leaving us as whole and undamaged as we were before" (Feinberg 1984, p. 45).

9. This does not imply that you have caused me harm whenever my reaction to your doing X worsens my prospects in life. It is consistent with claiming that reactions which are suitably unconstrained and/or unforeseeable break the chain of causation between X and any subsequent harm. What *counts* as suitably unconstrained or unforeseeable is a question that cannot be addressed here.

10. As we will see later, we can also ask whether we should be offended by conduct that fails to offend.

11. Why think that expressions of contempt give us this reason? One answer is that our taking offense amounts to a rejection of the message sent by the expression. Rejecting that message is valuable, it might plausibly be claimed, because rejecting it is part of what it is to respect ourselves (where we are treated contemptuously) or part of showing solidarity with others (where it is they who are so treated).

12. Something is apt to offend, in Tasioulas' sense, when offense is a fitting response. For him, the mere fact that people tend to take offense at X does nothing to make X wrong (Tasioulas 2006, p. 155). More on this point below.

13. Needs in the sense that X will otherwise be a breach of moral duty.

14. To say that X is morally objectionable is to say that there are moral reasons not to do X, which give us a moral duty to refrain from X absent justification or excuse. These reasons explain why, if it were possible to avoid death without punching anyone, we would be morally required to do so.

15. Because (enough) aversion makes our holding hands subjectively offensive, because subjectively offensive acts (Feinberg claims) need to be justified or excused and because acts need to be justified or excused only if they are morally objectionable. Feinberg would no doubt say that holding hands is not wrong because justified. The point here is that this is the wrong kind of reason for concluding that holding hands is not wrong.

16. Here is another way to put the point. Feinberg's comments imply that widespread refusal to tolerate X makes X morally objectionable. Anyone who thinks that conduct which is not widely tolerated can be morally unobjectionable must deny that this is so. They must deny that conduct needs to be justified or excused because it is subjectively offensive.

17. Though a complete account of expressive wrongs is beyond the scope of this chapter, nothing I say here is meant to suggest that all expressive wrongs are expressive of contempt. For other possibilities, see Simester and von Hirsch (2011, pp. 97–104).

18. As Duff and Marshall themselves say, "we should not count all moral wrongs as offensive, *qua* wrong. What offends … is not the mere fact of contravening some standard, but the contemptuous disregard for the standard or for the values it expresses that wrongdoing can display; but not all moral wrongdoing displays such contempt" (Duff and Marshall 2006, p. 65).

19. At least without more. X might remain eligible for criminalization on the basis that X is harmful. But this is a separate matter.

20. The mistake of judging X—which is *ex hypothesi* wrong—to be morally innocuous and the mistake of failing to conform to reasons—which *ex hypothesi* exist—to take offense at X. Note that X becomes ineligible to be criminalized, on the view under discussion, even if the reasons to take offense are *decisive*.

21. Tasioulas calls the contrary view "undeniably grotesque." One reason to think it grotesque is the power it would give the intolerant over those they refuse to tolerate. If subjective offensiveness were itself a reason to criminalize, the desire to extinguish ways of life falsely judged to be wrong would count in favor of criminalization that helps extinguish them. Patrick Devlin is often thought to endorse precisely this view. But it is far from clear that he does. Devlin argues that conduct is eligible for criminalization when its criminalization is necessary to avoid societal breakdown (Devlin 1959). On this view, what gives us reason to tackle conduct using the criminal law is the fact that tackling it is necessary to prevent harm. It is *not* the fact that criminalization is necessary to prevent people being offended.

22. Feinberg reaches the same conclusion for different reasons to those given here. In his view, an offense principle that appealed to objective offensiveness would be illiberal. For criminalization decisions to turn on whether offense is fitting "would require agencies of the state to make official judgments of the reasonableness and unreasonableness of emotional states and sensibilities, in effect closing these questions to dissent and putting the stamp of state approval on answers to questions which … should be left open to unimpeded discussion and practice" (Feinberg 1985, pp. 36–37). If only wrongs that are objectively offensive are eligible for criminalization, unreasonable (or unfitting) aversion cannot make wrongs eligible for criminalization. On Feinberg's view, *any* aversion (however unfitting) can make wrongs so eligible. It is hard to see why the latter view should be thought more conducive to "unimpeded discussion and practice." For detailed criticism of Feinberg's argument on this point, see Shoemaker (2000), Tasioulas (2006, pp. 155–156).

23. To be clear, these remarks do not entail that there is reason to criminalize any action that expresses contempt for others. They are compatible with the claim that the contempt expressed by racist abuse possesses particular properties that are absent when there is no reason to criminalize contemptuous expression. We may, for instance, only have reason to criminalize public wrongs (in some sense of public). There will then be no reason to criminalize contemptuous conduct that is private (in some sense of private).

24. "If there are any persons who contest a received opinion, or who will do so if law or opinion will let them, let us thank them for it … and rejoice that there is someone to do for us what we otherwise ought." There may, of course, be no such persons. But if this is so, we should seek other means of contestation: "some contrivance for making the difficulties of the question as present to the learner's consciousness, as if they were pressed upon him by a dissentient champion, eager for his conversion" (Mill 1859).

25. We can add that the value of some ways of life *resides* in confrontation—in our clashing with others in ways that are liable to offend. A harmonious society would necessarily lack this value and these ways of life.

26. We can add a further reason to think caution appropriate. Mill suggests that exposing people to conduct which offends can help combat prejudice and encourage toleration of valuable ways of life. It can help make it societally

acceptable to act in ways that are not wrong. Ronald Dworkin suggests that the reverse can also be true (Dworkin 2006). Conduct which offends others—by exposing them to ridicule—can help make it societally *unacceptable* to commit serious wrongs. Ridiculing those who peddle bigotry can help expose their bigotry for what it is and encourage us not to tolerate such wrongdoing. Criminalizing subjectively offensive conduct generally would risk robbing us of the exposition. I am grateful to Neil Walker for calling my attention to Dworkin's essay.

27. Because our taking offense is a fitting response.
28. Recall the passage quoted above: "the fact that very few are even mildly offended by the public utterance of racist abuse ... gives us additional reason for criminalising it" (Tasioulas 2006, p. 156).
29. Where criminalization is necessary to prevent great harm it may even be required.
30. I presented a draft at Edinburgh Law School in December 2018. Thanks to my audience on that occasion, and to Vincent Chiao, Kim Ferzan, Doug Husak, Ambrose Lee and Andrew Simester for written comments.

References

Brink, David. 2013. *Mill's progressive principles*. Oxford: Oxford University Press.

Cohen, Gerald. 2000. *If you're an egalitarian how come you're so rich?* Cambridge: Harvard University Press.

Devlin, Patrick. 1959. *The enforcement of morals*. Oxford: Oxford University Press.

Duff, R.A., and S.E. Marshall. 2006. How offensive can you get? In *Incivilities: Regulating offensive behaviour*, ed. Andrew Simester and Andrew von Hirsch, 57–90. Oxford: Hart Publishing.

Dworkin, Ronald. 2006. The right to ridicule. *New York Review of Books*, March 23.

Feinberg, Joel. 1984. *Harm to others*. New York: Oxford University Press.

———. 1985. *Offense to others*. New York: Oxford University Press.

———. 1988. *Harmless wrongdoing*. New York: Oxford University Press.

Gardner, John. 2007. *Offences and defences*. Oxford: Oxford University Press.

Mill, John Stuart. 1859. *On liberty*. London: Parker.

Moore, Michael. 1997. *Placing blame: A theory of criminal law*. Oxford: Oxford University Press.

Rawls, John. 1993. *Political liberalism*. New York: Columbia University Press.

Raz, Joseph. 1987. Autonomy, toleration and the harm principle. In *Issues in contemporary legal philosophy*, ed. Ruth Gavison, 313–333. Oxford: Clarendon Press.

———. 1991. Free expression and personal identification. *Oxford Journal of Legal Studies* 11: 303–324.

Shoemaker, David. 2000. Dirty words and the offense principle. *Law and Philosophy* 19: 545–584.

Simester, A.P., and Andrew von Hirsch. 2002. Rethinking the offence principle. *Legal Theory* 8: 269–295.

———. 2011. *Crimes, harms and wrongs*. Oxford: Hart Publishing.

Tadros, Victor. 2016. *Wrongs and crimes*. Oxford: Oxford University Press.

Tasioulas, John. 2006. Crimes of offence. In *Incivilities: Regulating offensive behaviour*, ed. A.P. Simester and Andrew von Hirsch, 147–171. Oxford: Hart Publishing.

Waldron, Jeremy. 1987. Mill and the value of moral distress. *Political Studies* 35: 410–423.

PART XXI

Political Philosophy and Punishment

CHAPTER 22

Political Philosophy and Punishment

Chad Flanders

Look at any introductory book on contemporary political philosophy from the past 20 years (or similar anthology) and there will be precious little—if any—discussion of punishment (*see, inter alia*, Miller 2003; Kymlicka 2002; Wolff 2016: Goodin and Pettit 2006). This is not a matter of the distinction between "applied ethics" and "political theory," as many of these same books will have lengthy sections on pressing political issues: affirmative action, immigration, or just war. Or look at any of the major works of twentieth-century analytic political philosophy. John Rawls's *A Theory of Justice* has only passing references to punishment; Robert Nozick's *Anarchy, State, and Utopia* does a little better, but there is nothing approaching a theory of punishment in it (Rawls 1972; Nozick 1975; *see also* Flanders 2016a). Scattered references appear in Michael Walzer's *Spheres of Justice*, none in Alasdair MacIntyre's *After Virtue* (Walzer 1983; MacIntyre 2007). Michael Sandel's *Liberalism and the Limits of Justice* does the best among these books—but his treatment of punishment is only in the form of an extended critique of Rawls on distributive justice (Sandel 1998). And again, this is not the result of these books being about political theory rather than "applied ethics" because all of them deal with issues that could fairly be termed "applied," some of them at great length. Surely welfare policy—of which Rawls and Nozick spend hundreds of pages dissecting and debating—is an applied issue, just as much as punishment or criminal justice is.

This is a puzzling state of affairs, one that needs an explanation. Why does punishment get such short shrift from these political philosophers? This certainly was not the case, historically speaking.[1] We can speculate about our present condition, but no explanation fully satisfies. Perhaps punishment was not

C. Flanders (✉)
Saint Louis University, St. Louis, MO, USA
e-mail: cflande2@slu.edu

© The Author(s) 2019
L. Alexander, K. K. Ferzan (eds.), *The Palgrave Handbook of Applied Ethics and the Criminal Law*, https://doi.org/10.1007/978-3-030-22811-8_22

thought to be an especially troubling feature of modern democracies in the second half of the twentieth century, as it is today. But even if this is true—and we have reason to be skeptical—punishment still remains as a theoretical matter an especially important (and troubling) function of state government, seeming to need—as many have articulated—a very strong justification. Or it could be that Rawls's focus on "ideal theory" put questions of what to do in situations of non-perfect compliance off the table, and Rawls's towering (even suffocating) influence dictated the agenda for everyone else (Flanders 2016a, b). But even Rawls talked a *little* about punishment and a lot about some cases of noncompliance (e.g., civil disobedience). And even now, in discussions of the problems with ideal theory, this has not occasioned a rise in looking at political philosophy and punishment in a nonideal mode (Sen 2009). Nor is it at all plausible to put punishment under the heading of "philosophy of law" and so not properly a subject of political philosophy. Even if punishment is sometimes a question of law (which is certainly true), punishment is something that governments do, and one would think that our attitudes and theories about state power generally should inform and condition what it means when the state punishes someone.[2]

So consider: what does a liberal theory of punishment look like? Or a libertarian theory? A communitarian one? Even a Marxist one? Do these theories each entail *one* justification of punishment, or could there be family disagreements about what punishment is for, and when and how the state can punish? It should be obvious that when we talk of state punishment, we are talking about something broader than just the functions that punishment serves, although we are doubtless talking about that. Punishment exists in many contexts—parents punish children, coaches punish players, teachers punish students, employers punish employees, and on and on—and each needs a story of why and how certain agents are empowered to punish.[3] So too do we need theories that connect theories of punishment with the *government's* authority and need to punish in particular. For again, punishment is not only an exercise of government power but one of the more terrifying ones (being punished by a *state* is arguably the worst thing to be punished by, not least because of the power the state has). And so state punishment needs justification, not just in terms of the purposes of punishment (retribution, deterrence, rehabilitation, etc.), but in terms of *what allows a state to engage in the practice of punishing*. It should be obvious that there is a gap between the one thing (what punishment is properly for) and the other (who can rightfully punish).[4] We do have—and this is the exception that proves the rule—a good sense of what a republican theory of punishment looks like, thanks to the work of Philip Pettit and his co-author John Braithwaite (Braithwaite and Pettit 1990). Pettit shows both the necessity of doing the work connecting punishment and state power and also provides an example of how it can be done. Pettit, in fact, is in line with the history of political philosophy, where we have countless examples of philosophers taking the need for a justification of state punishment as fundamental (Flanders and Hoskins 2016; Shuster 2016). Our present situation is, in this regard, an anomaly.[5]

One chapter cannot undo decades of neglect of a subject, but it can make a start. I have two goals here, one descriptive and one normative. The first, descriptive goal involves imagining what debates in recent political philosophy might have looked like had political philosophy taken seriously its burden to give a theory of punishment. This means giving a quick, and admittedly somewhat selective, overview of some major theories of political theory and what I suspect their commitments regarding punishment might be: libertarianism, liberalism, communitarianism, Marxism, and republicanism. Interestingly—and perhaps not surprisingly—I find that these schools of political philosophy all underdetermine the justification for punishment. Different articulations of communitarianism or libertarianism or liberalism may lead to different ideas about the purpose and role of state punishment. But this leads into my second goal. I argue, in part, by showing the sheer number of conflicting ideas about state punishment, that there is a good case to be made for political liberalism *as a political philosophy* and, accordingly, for defending what political liberalism says about the proper function of and limitations upon punishment (*see* Flanders 2016a, b, 2017). Political liberalism takes its cue from the proliferation of a plurality of reasonable "comprehensive" ideas about the good (Rawls 2005). But this "fact of reasonable pluralism" is as real with ideas about the purpose of punishment as it is about the good life for human beings. Political liberalism draws conclusions about what government can—and cannot—do given this reasonable disagreement. And, I argue, this puts constraints on what state punishment is about, just as it puts constraints on other things government might want to do, but can't, without violating political liberalism's principles.

LIBERTARIANISM AND PUNISHMENT

In what follows, I separate out what I take to be libertarian theories of the state from liberal ones when discussing what implications these theories might have for punishment. But it might seem odd to separate out libertarianism and liberalism because they seem to bear at least a family resemblance. Do they not both believe in individual rights? Do they not both trace their lineage to the "classical liberalism" of Locke? Where they differ—and this is no small difference—is in their respective takes on redistribution. The libertarian, presumably, would recoil at the vision of desert and punishment presented by the liberal egalitarian, whom I discuss later.

I leave it to others to trace how distinct liberalism and libertarianism are and whether modern liberalism is an outgrowth of classical liberalism or a perversion of it. For my purposes, however, it serves us well to separate libertarianism and liberalism and to take libertarianism first because libertarianism at best supports a rather spare ideal of punishing, even tending toward the position that there is no legitimate role for the state in punishing. Indeed, libertarians—possibly in contrast to liberals—may in fact come closest to urging the abolition of state punishment, reasoning that the institution itself may be incompatible with the individual rights that the libertarians see as part of their theory. But, and this is a theme throughout this chapter, libertarianism as a political philosophy may underwrite not just one but several justifications of punishment. For libertarians could also see punishment only in terms of public safety and deterrence, and anything beyond this as again fundamentally inconsistent with the protection of individual rights. Finally, and most prominently, several libertarians have defended a theory of restitution as the only theory of punishment consistent with libertarianism.

Abolition

An analysis of libertarian theories of punishment allows us to consider what, in fact, is a perfectly possible option for a political theory in relation to punishment: to abolish it (Boonin 2008). Libertarianism, stated as a theory of fundamental rights which no one can violate—and maybe a rather extreme version of that sort of theory—seems the best candidate to urge this approach to punishment. We have these fundamental rights, the theory goes, and the state simply cannot infringe them (absent of course, a person's consent, in which case we don't really have an infringement) (Nozick 1975; Nagel 1975). Punishment represents a rather serious deprivation of someone's rights; it could involve a serious deprivation of liberty, even if this is only for a short time, and at the limit it could involve putting someone to death. The libertarian could try to reconcile these two seemingly contradictory premises, maybe by invoking a theory of implied consent or a theory of rights forfeiture (Wellman 2017). But suppose the libertarian just sticks to the initial premise, namely, that we have these rights and they cannot be violated, even should the heavens fall. In this case, the institution of punishment, defined as entailing the coercive deprivation of those rights, would be a nonstarter. It is then of course an open question of what would replace it or whether anything would need to. Maybe there would be some small, consensual, and protective associations, where people would somehow have to be shown clearly to consent to their punishment—in a way that might be impossible in a modern state.[6] Or then again, maybe there would simply be people defending themselves, as presumably getting rid of the state institution of punishment would not mean getting rid of the right of people to defend themselves against others who would do them harm.

Is abolitionism worth taking seriously or is it just an option to have out there as a kind of hypothesis, not to be considered as a realistic proposal, but good to have present as something to compare existing institutions against? Abolitionism has always struck me as an underrepresented position in the literature, provided we understand it aright (Boonin 2008; Golash 2005). It is primarily a *negative* argument, to be sure. It is against the very idea that the state could have such power over citizens. As such, it directly addresses the concern that motivates this chapter: what gives the *state* the authority to punish its citizens, to dominate them so completely, so as to put them in cages or even kill them? The answer the abolitionist/libertarian gives is that in fact nothing gives the state the authority to do this, and a state that treats its members this way would be (all else equal) an illegitimate state. I find this in fact a very plausible claim, and if it strikes us as counterintuitive, then we have to do the work to explain the contrary intuition, why it may seem to us natural to say that of course the state has the right to punish its citizens, and that it may even be the case that a state that doesn't have this institution would be illegitimate, and not the other way around.

In other words, the abolitionist, perhaps alone among contemporary political philosophers, really is asking the right question. How could such an institution like state punishment get authority over citizens? The answer to this question would have to get beyond simply saying why punishment might be good—first, because it is not obvious it is really good (especially for the people who suffer punishment) and second, simply because something is good does not mean that it is legitimate for the state to bring it about. What is also helpful about some positive proposals of libertarians/abolitionists (and we look at one in greater detail in the third section in this part) is that they press even more the question of why the state should be engaging in the practice of punishment. Can't there be other, non-state actors that do the job just as well? Couldn't there be practices other than punishment that can fully and adequately substitute for what punishment does? For every political philosophy theory that I present in this chapter, we should then keep in mind the abolitionists sort of null set response to our central question, namely, that there is no good political-philosophical rationale for a state punishing. To the contractarian, they will say that punishment is not something that contractors would agree to—explicitly or implicitly. To the person who emphasizes public safety, they will say that no amount of public safety—even if phrased in terms of a defense of people's rights—can justify the direct violation of another person's right to liberty or to life. These are not easy objections to rejoin, and nothing less than a competing and better political theory can really do the job in answering them. Again, it is not enough to say that retribution makes sense or deterrence brings about value to people. We have to go further; we have to say that not only that these things are true, but that the state is justified in acting in these sorts of ways to bring about these results or to realize these values.

Societal Defense

I associated the abolitionist with the libertarian because there is a certain sort of rights-based libertarianism that can tend in an abolitionist direction. If you are a libertarian who is skeptical about the government's ability to put up stop signs, you will be even more opposed to a government that can imprison you and put you to death. But there is another species of libertarianism that is (broadly speaking) pragmatic but still committed to maximizing a certain understanding of liberty and fundamental rights (Barnett 2014). One part of this more pragmatic libertarianism is, firstly, a recognition of the necessity of some form of "common defense," first in the case of national security and second in the case of societal defense. Indeed, one could see these two things as one sort of a continuum. A libertarian state may have enemies that want to attack it from without. The citizens of that state—if they do not simply want to succumb to a foreign enemy—will have to make some allowances for an army to defend itself. Of course, libertarians may say this should be a volunteer army, but at some point it may simply be necessary for the sake of the survival of the state that provision be made for a draft, to require people to fight and defend the state.[7] So too might there be a further recognition that there are not only enemies from without but also enemies from within. Accordingly, provisions will have to be made for a police force to protect the society against those who may also be members of the state but who may attack those who are also members of the same society. At some point, the realization will be made that there must be a police force, if the society is to survive against attacks made from within the society.

The police are there to defend society, to protect its citizens, and to prevent attacks. But then what happens if someone breaks the law and then evades the police? The libertarian will then have to deal with the problem of the possibility of punishment. For the libertarian would be more than happy to have a police force if it meant that the police deterred crime only by threatening punishment if the laws were broken. The problem comes when the state is asked to make good on that threat (Quinn 1985). If we look at punishment solely through the lens of societal defense—that punishment is simply the extension of a scheme designed to prevent crime—then the question becomes what do we do when prevention fails and the state's bluff is called? It seems that deterrence is the best rationale that fits with this and a very carefully circumscribed version of deterrence. You punish only as much as necessary perhaps to make good on the threat, as a means to deter further violations. Punishment may be a rights violation, *but so are the violations inherent in serious crimes*[8] (libertarians will probably have a lot to say about how small the scope of things the state can criminalize is). Punishment is required to defend society against those who attack it. Best of all is if people take the threat of punishment seriously and never attack society. The second best—and perhaps a very distant second best—is when we have to punish to *prove* that we are serious about defending society, both to the person who committed the crime and to the rest of society. Incapacitation of those who are very dangerous can in theory be an option in some cases, but these cases must be rare because the limitation on liberty inherent in possibly indefinite sentences is very serious indeed.

Again, the abolitionist libertarian will want to know if the state doing this job of societal defense is really necessary. Do we have to set up an entirely separate state institution to do this job of protecting society? Again, the analogy to national defense helps a lot here. Can a private defense force do the job just as well as a state-based institution of national defense? If not, we can then consider the question on the domestic side—maybe we do need a police to both protect people and prevent crime and maybe we do need a separate state institution that punishes when people break the law, that is, when the first line of societal defense fails. The abolitionist libertarian will also want to know whether, even if these kinds of societal institutions are necessary, they are still justified. Can the state under any circumstances violate a person's rights to liberty by punishing them? The societal defense libertarian will have to develop the argument along two dimensions. First, there may just be a first-order disagreement about what rights a person does have—again, we might want to work a sort of rights forfeiture argument, where a person actually loses his right to be free from punishment by violating the law. Second, the libertarian might want to reply that if we want to maximize liberty, we do have to consider both the liberty violated by non-state actors and not only the liberty violated by the state when it punishes. In short, the societal defense libertarian will want to reject the idea of the abolitionist that the rights violations only fall on one side of the equation. Regardless of how this debate gets resolved, it does strike me as the right kind of debate to be having about whether and how the state gets justified in having anything like the institution of state punishment in the first place.

Restitution

The third theoretical possibility for libertarianism is one that has been probably the most discussed and debated in the context of the philosophy of punishment—although not necessarily in the context of political philosophy. In an influential article from the 1970s, Randy Barnett suggested that *restitution* be considered as a possible theory of punishment (Barnett 1977). Although Barnett did not necessarily advertise his libertarian leanings in his initial foray into punishment theory, they seem discernable from the article and are obvious from his later writings (Barnett 2014). One might see Barnett as typifying the libertarian belief in fundamental rights and distrust of government that we saw in describing abolitionism, mentioned earlier, but he also—unlike the straight, null set abolitionist presented—saw a positive possibility for punishment coming out of libertarian premises. On Barnett's theory of punishment, the appropriate remedy for a criminal violation is not punishment but repayment. Briefly, Barnett proposes substituting what is typically considered as a remedy in tort as usable as a remedy in crime. If someone steals my car, I want my car back. It does me no good if the person is punished by a five-year sentence in jail, and I am still without my car. Of course, I may also suffer many other things when someone steals my car—a feeling of violation, a feeling of insecurity—but these may also be things that we can compensate, if only imperfectly, with money. Surely, Barnett reasons, I am better off it I am *paid* for my emotional distress as opposed to the case where my only compensation (if we can call it that) is seeing another person suffer for what he has done. Note how Barnett's proposal both accommodates the abolitionists' worry about punishment and also moves beyond it. Restitution may not violate at all, or not violate as deeply, a person's right to liberty—so it may go down easier as at least an *alternative* to directly liberty-depriving punishment. But restitution does require some state support and coordination. There must be mechanism for me to receive my payment if I am wronged and perhaps to exact payment if the person who wronged me is not forthcoming.

Barnett's proposal immediately got a lot of pushback (Miller 1978; Pilon 1978), but we should look at why. From the perspective of libertarianism, the idea that compensation is superior to punishment seems to follow. If we object to Barnett's proposed replacement for punishment, we have to see where the basis for our objection lies. Is it at the level of an inadequate theory of punishment? Maybe we think that in fact compensation is *not* a sufficient sort of remedy for someone who has been wronged; maybe we think that in fact suffering is somehow required in response to a very serious wrong that has been done. Or maybe we are concerned that restitution would not deter, especially those who are able to pay easily—maybe this doesn't send the signal we want it to send. But we should be sensitive to the political, theoretical constraints Barnett may see himself as working under: it may be that given his (implicit) libertarianism, some options are off the table. Punishment of an especially harsh sort may be off the table because it is so intrinsically liberty denying. If this is the case, then our objections have to also consider this. That is, if we find ourselves objecting to what restitution lacks as a punishment, it may not be enough merely to object to restitution as a punishment without also engaging the higher-order concerns that led Barnett to his solution, the reasons why he felt that principles of political justice might limit and constrain what the state can plausibly do when it comes to punishment.

Our intuitions about state punishment, in other words, may reflect in incipient form deeper intuitions about the function of the state. And of course things can work in both directions. We can see our political philosophy as yielding certain things about what aims the state can pursue in punishing. This is the approach I have been following for most of this chapter. I am asking: what do our beliefs about state power and state authority mean when we look at the possibility and justification of an institution about state punishment? But things can also go in the other direction. We may have strong intuitions about what punishment should really be, and in particular what state punishment must be. Punishment as restitution seems to inspire especially strong responses—mainly responses of how inadequate restitution can come to seem. And again, we can do one of two things with those intuitions. First, we can take them seriously, which means in this context tracing them to see what sort of theory of the state and the state's authority might validate those intuitions—to show how on this or that political philosophy those intuitions against, say, restitution, might be shown to be correct and legitimate. Or we can do what I urged in the earlier paragraph. We can try to figure out what higher-order theory of the state led to the proposal of, say, restitution as a theory of punishment. If we find that theory plausible or persuasive, that may lead us to correct our initial intuitions about punishment, especially if they are inconsistent with that higher-order political philosophy. In either case, the answer is not to rest on those intuitions, but to connect them with political philosophy, where we can then either find them confirmed or find a basis for revising them.

LIBERALISM AND PUNISHMENT

It would be a folly to try to define "liberalism" at the outset, so I won't try to. I instead look at three broad themes in liberal thought and connect them to what I think is a plausible story about the purpose and function of punishment, given those (liberal) themes. The first theme is the idea that society is a contract, an idea that animates both classical and modern liberalism alike. The second theme is the promotion of autonomy. Liberalism has often been thought to take autonomy as one of its main goals—that the goal of a liberal society should be to guarantee the ability of each citizen to act "autonomously" (whatever that means).[9] The third theme is that of equality: liberalism and some form of egalitarianism have long thought to be bedfellows, if not necessary ingredients of one another. In each of these cases, a certain style of liberalism yields what I take to be more or less determinate answers about why we punish and why the state should punish. In pressing each of these theories, I want to focus especially on the question of whether the reasons the broader political theory supplies about the reasons for punishment are in fact reasons that show the state should have the authority to punish. After all, it may be a good thing that the state punish people for doing wrong, but it is a separate question as to whether the state has the legitimate power to do this good thing.

Contractarian Liberalism

On a simple version of the social contract theory, the story of how we get to the state goes something like this.[10] We begin in a state of nature, with perfect liberty, although this comes coupled with nearly total fear—we have liberty, but not security. Liberty is the ability to do what we want, if we have the power to do it, but it comes with no guarantee that others will not stop us from doing what we want, if they are more powerful. So we enter into a bargain with others. We give up some of our liberty in exchange for a guarantee of security, a security that is enforced by the state. The bargain, in fact, is a good one. In the place of a fragile liberty, one that is always at risk of being taken away from us, we get something like a secure liberty. It may be a more restricted liberty—we can no longer do what we want when we want—but it is a surer liberty. If someone wants to take away our liberty, the state steps in and stops them. Although in theory our social contract can be an agreement to do anything, we could agree to set up a religious state, or we could agree to set up a hierarchical society, the liberal version of the contract theory has its roots in the idea that we agree to the social contract not in order to pursue some vision of the good but to preserve the liberty of all, in a way that is fair to all. The contract is, ideally, liberty-maximizing.

But what happens if someone wants to break the law, that is, break the terms of the deal, and succeeds? The deal was that we would accept some burden (restricting our liberty) in exchange for everyone else taking up the same burden. The state is there to secure our liberty, but what if it fails to prevent someone from breaking the law? Such is the question that motivated some early analytic attempts at developing a social contract theory of punishment—one that had its basis in political theory, a theory of the state that saw it as a contract between the members of society (Morris 1968, pp. 477–478; Simmons 1991). When we saw society as a kind of deal between the participants, it seemed to some—Herbert Morris is the classic example (Morris 1968)—that the state's role and purpose in punishing became clear: it was to reassert the original terms of the deal. The deal was that I restrain my liberty for the sake of a greater liberty overall. When I take a greater liberty, then it seems to follow from the deal that I should have to face a new burden, to balance things out again. We need the state not just to threaten that people shouldn't violate the terms of the deal, but actually to (in a way) enforce those terms. Either you obey the law and take the trade-off of less liberty for a more secure liberty or you break the law and you take the trade-off of greater liberty for greater punishment. Both are ways in theory that you can act according to the social contract. Punishment has to be there as sort of an upshot of the idea that you can only have liberty if you accept some restraints on that liberty. Punishing someone who takes a greater liberty by breaking the law gets a greater restraint by being put, for example, in jail.

We can raise all sorts of questions about social contract theory, on the one hand, and (what has been come to be called) the "benefits and burdens" theory of punishment on the other hand. But my purpose here is not to look at the political philosophy aspect of the theory in isolation from the punishment justifying aspect of the theory, nor vice versa. The question is rather, what does the theory say about the authority of the state to pursue punishment? Why should it be the business of the state to set about to enforce the terms of the deal and to reset the balance of benefits of burdens in society? When we look at Morris, again one of the best exemplars of this theory, we get mixed answers. Part of his theory suggests that it is simply an intrinsic good that society be "reset" when someone breaks the terms of the deal; it is only "fair" that if you take an additional benefit, you can an additional burden.[11] Another part of his theory hints that we punish in this way to provide people with an incentive to comply with the law (so that the theory seems justified in terms of public safety).[12] And yet another part of this theory—and here this seems to be the strongest most sustained note—argues that to punish people for breaking the rules is necessary to treat them as "persons" rather than as things that had no choice in the matter (Morris 1968, p. 490; see also Deigh 1984). But these various purposes of punishing may matter less than the device that motivates his theory from the start, that this is an agreement between citizens. Maybe the state has the authority to punish just because citizens have agreed that it has, and the reasons beyond this (fairness, deterrence, and respect for persons) are really secondary to this. If this is the case, then most of the justification of punishment rests not on the goals of punishment but on the legitimacy of the contract—both the act of making it and its terms. We shall return to this point, later, when considering political liberalism, which similarly focuses on the form of justification rather than on the substantive goals of punishment.[13]

Liberal Perfectionism

If we move away from the somewhat formal ideal of a contract at the basis of liberalism, we can look to a much more substantive ideal that motivates some versions of liberalism: that of autonomy. At its heart, many have thought, liberalism does not just have a thin version of liberty—where liberty is noninterference—but a thicker, more robust form of autonomy. Brian Barry memorably embraced this sentiment when he said that liberalism at its best posits a life of reflective freedom, self-authorship, and autonomy—and if you can't handle this, there's beer and television.[14] This is a cartoon of course. In the Rawlsian vocabulary, this focus on autonomy gets cashed out as the "Kantian" interpretation of liberalism, although it is mixed in with some Aristotle (Rawls 1972, Part III). A life well lived, in a liberal society, is not one where we blindly succumb and follow a particular faith or find our meaning in our given attachments to country or to family. It is to our own selves that we must be true. We must be authors of our own story, which no one else can tell for us (or tell us what it is). The state exists to make this type of autonomous life possible, and it must provide the conditions for each of us to realize it—either in the fullness of realizing our goals or in falling flat on our faces. If we are to fail, still it is *our* failure, not something we can blame on anyone else. The society can guarantee us certain primary goods, the necessary preconditions to live an autonomous life, and it can make it possible for us to experience different forms of life to see how they fit. But it cannot guarantee us success: only the (more or less authentic) pursuit of happiness is guaranteed, not the happiness itself.

But what happens when someone breaks the law, and violates the autonomy of others, without justification? What does this sort of autonomy-based liberalism say about punishment? One possible way that punishment can work in such a society is that punishment can make possible the internalization of the right attitudes toward autonomy.[15] The through line from a comprehensive liberalism to a focus on an educative theory of punishment is the idea that society does exist to promote and express certain values. It expresses those values positively, in its embrace of a specific conception of the good and supports for those who follow that good. But it can also express those values in a more punitive vein. Those who do not respect the autonomy of others should be punished, as a means both of expressing the idea that society values autonomy and of communicating to the offender the value of autonomy. Perhaps the person who is being punished can *himself or herself* embrace the message society is trying to send through punishment. He or she can apologize and view his or her punishment as a sort of atonement. Of course, this is up to the offender. A society that values autonomy cannot go *too far* in compelling a person to embrace any values, even the values of autonomy. But surely society can punish the other in the hopes that the offender does come to see the value of the autonomy of others *as truly a value* and also himself or herself come to *autonomously* embrace those values. R. A. Duff's mature theory of a sort of communitarian liberalism represents a possible articulation of this view, although he may not necessarily agree with the outsized version of Enlightenment-autonomy liberalism that I began this section with (Duff 2001). Jean Hampton's early defense of a moral education theory of punishment matches up with her later defense of a sort of comprehensive, metaphysical-type liberalism (Hampton 1984, 1989).

We see later how this emphasis on supporting and promoting a comprehensive doctrine is something that connects this type of liberal communitarianism with communitarianism *proper* (which I cover in Section "Communitarianism and Punishment" of this chapter). But again, we have to return to our question and ask how this type of autonomy liberalism answers it: what gives the state the authority, via punishment, to endorse a comprehensive conception of the good, and to try to facilitate the adoption of that comprehensive doctrine through punishment? This is different than the abstract question of what justifies comprehensive "perfectionist" liberalism and different, as well, than the particular question of whether moral education/atonement is a good theory of punishment. The answer to the question of what gives the perfectionist liberal state the authority to punish must be something like the fact that the promotion of an autonomous life is an intrinsic good[16]—whether we do that via the laws of the state that guarantee people the freedom to pursue that life or via the punishment of those people who do not respect that autonomy and who could benefit from an education in the value of that autonomy themselves. We would, by punishment, be bringing the closer to the good of the autonomous life. So here we have a theory of the state that seems to connect to a particular story about the function of punishment. The answer to why punish and what justifies the state in doing it is a little less ambiguous than the contractarian theory but for that reason perhaps much more objectionable. The focus on possible coercion for the sake of autonomy sounds both paradoxical and even offensive. It may heighten the worries we may have even outside the context of punishment that the goal of the state should not be the promotion of a particular conception of the good.

Egalitarian Liberalism[17]

The past two liberalisms owe some debt to Rawls, as all modern liberalism seems to. The first liberalism goes back to Rawls's (and Hart's) development of a duty of fair play (Dagger 1993). Rawls didn't discuss the theory's application to punishment, but Herbert Morris and Jeffrie Murphy did. The second liberalism owes something to Rawls's development, in Part III of a *Theory of Justice*, an ideal of the "good life" for a liberal. The structure of that ideal was relatively formal, but it did emphasize, if only implicitly, some of the features I listed earlier: autonomy, reflection, and authenticity. But neither of these strands were part of what was, for many, Rawls's greatest innovation, which was the difference principle. According to the difference principle, inequalities in resources would be permitted, but only if those inequalities redound to the benefit of the least well of. For Rawls, this represented a sort of fraternity—we were all in it together (*see* Flanders 2016a, b, p. 83). If some were to get more money, this was only allowed if it was necessary for everybody to be better off on the whole. Even more radically, on one interpretation, the difference principle followed from the idea that we didn't really deserve our initial place in society, or even our God-given talents. These were to be seen as sort of a public resource. The extra wealth that flowed from "your" talents were not, in the end, really yours. They were, in a way, a public good. We each of course had our own lives, but it didn't follow from this that we had an entitlement to all the *profits* we might get from living those lives.

Rawls in *Theory of Justice* made very clear that this idea of wealth redistribution didn't apply in the context of retributive justice (Flanders 2016a, b, pp. 85–86). But suppose we ignore Rawls's warning on this score. In the same way that we might look at inequalities in the distribution of primary goods as only justified if they make everybody better off, so too we might look at punishment in this light. Punishment is justified in those cases where it will end up benefiting everybody. *Contra* Rawls, we should look at punishment as just a scheme of incentives in order to get the greatest benefit overall. Thomas Pogge has developed just such a theory, calling it contractarian-consequentialism—and, indeed, it does look consequentialist (Pogge 1995). But it has an egalitarian core. We only punish insofar as such a redistribution of burdens (rather than benefits) makes everyone better off. Moreover, at the bottom, we are to look at bad character traits—just as much as good character traits—as not really "ours," to the extent that they are accidents of our social situation and of our birth. We do not necessarily deserve our punishment, but punishment may nonetheless be justified insofar as it redounds to the good of society. We don't look at society as existing to reward virtue or punish vice. We look at a structure to promote justice, which means protecting rights and guaranteeing everyone a decent supply of primary goods. Distributive justice isn't just in the realm of primary goods but also the relevant principle in the realm of punishment too. Retributive justice has no place in this type of regime.

Obviously such a theory would need much more spelling out—but we can return to our question: what would give a state the authority to punish *like this?* What would give it the authority to allocate punitive treatment based on some ideal of fair distribution rather than some principle of desert? One answer to this is something we have already canvassed earlier. Maybe it is justified just because it is something that we would agree to in the original position. It is fair on those terms. So we imagine that we do not know our place in society, and so we not only choose principles for fair distribution of primary goods, but we also design a scheme of punishment that is based on something other than desert—something more like what Rawls's proposes for the difference principle. So the punishment scheme, like the difference principle, has its deep justification in a kind of hypothetical social contract and our reflection on the reasonableness of the terms of that contract. Rawls, of course, through his scattered remarks on punishment, did not see things this way. His intuitions, at least, were that we would want to separate out principles of punishment from principles of redistribution. The challenge then in seeing a hypothetical contract leading to *this* justification of punishment would be to show that it is something that we would actually find ourselves agreeing to behind the veil of ignorance, namely, that punishment was not related to desert or to moral education or to fairness. Such a scheme may have its attractions in the abstract, but it would certainly involve radically altering our expectations about what punishment is supposed to be about. Of course, something similar could have been said about the difference principle when it was first introduced.

COMMUNITARIANISM AND PUNISHMENT

The last grouping of political theories (I examine another version of liberal theory in my conclusion) is one which I want to loosely consider as "communitarian." I use this word with some hesitation. Even the so-called communitarians were reluctant to call themselves communitarian.[18] Marxists do not fit easily into conventional communitarianism, still less does republicanism, which some have thought is rather a species of liberalism (although this seems to me incorrect). So take communitarianism here to mean, in the main, anti-liberalism.[19] The theories considered in this part depart from the sometimes radical individualism and even atomism (Taylor 1985, p. 187) championed by the liberal and libertarian theories considered earlier. Communitarianism *proper* does not flinch and instead embraces the idea that society should be governed by a shared conception of the good. Marxism too represents a communal vision of society, and it finds much of its normative attractiveness in opposing the anomie and loneliness of a hyper-individualistic capitalist society. Republicanism takes the picture of negative liberty championed by some versions of liberalism as insufficient and as even missing the point of why we care about that liberty in the first place. So with this admittedly artificial categorization, we should ask: what do these various—and varied—theories have to say, if anything, about the state's authority to punish members of society?

Communitarianism

How does one define modern-day communitarianism? As I just stated, even those frequently labeled as communitarianism deny and even recoil from the label. It would do us well, then, to not be too precise about how we specify the essential features of the communitarian movement. For starters, we can say that it is opposed to liberalism and some of its premises. But what does this mean? It means at least that liberalism has overemphasized the rights of individuals, at the expense of the good of the community as a whole. It has also ignored how we might have affirmative duties to support the community, which at times may frustrate our individual ends—community does not merely exist as a means to serve and satisfy our ends. This, however, puts things in a rather negative and contrastive light. Communitarians see, more positively, our good in a form of community with one another—in Sandel's poignant phrase (especially as he sees community as in decline) in community we find a good that we cannot find alone (Sandel 1998, p. 183). In MacIntyre's scheme, communities are where we exercise the virtues and find our stories (MacIntyre 2007, ch. 15). We almost cannot proceed as individuals unless we first place ourselves in the context of community, a community whose narrative both includes and is larger than our own, as it both precedes us and will succeed us. So too in Taylor's work do our communities provide the horizons on which we see anything as of value, of worth (Taylor 1989). The community stands outside of us, informs us and our judgments, and gives us a horizon of meaning we cannot create just on our own.

Communitarians are sometimes faulted generally for not spelling out the practical consequences of the valorization of community and denigration of the powers and possibilities of the individual. This may not be fair—it is surely not true of the "low" communitarians who write up policy papers, and it is not as if liberal theorists have been all that aggressive in specifying what laws and policy their liberalisms might recommend. But it does seem that we can say something about what communitarians might say about punishment—as indeed some have. If it is in the community that we find our good and even our very selves, then when we break the laws of that community we lose touch with ourselves and our good. We become disintegrated from the community (Kleinfeld 2017). Punishment may be necessary to bring us back into communion with others. This may take the form of a sort of atonement, but not of the liberal form that Duff has recommended. The communitarian vision of punishment means really getting you back in touch with the good and with the community, which in a very real sense are connected. More deeply, a communitarian punishment regime might be a sort of reintegration ceremony; it might even involve a sort of communal shaming (Braithwaite and Mugford 1994). We want to make you *feel* how you have hurt the community, and it becomes necessary as a means to this to make you suffer—suffering is meant to send the message that you have separated yourself from the community, but also to act as the first step of your eventual reconciliation with the community. Joshua Kleinfeld has recently given a full-throated version of this sort of communitarian vision of punishment, based alternatively in Hegel and in Durkheim (Kleinfeld 2016). He represents a recent philosopher who takes seriously the connection between political philosophy and theories of punishment.

But it may also be the case that pointing out the implications that a particular political philosophy has for punishment may make us realize the shortcomings of that political philosophy. Communitarianism has been criticized, abstractly, for not recognizing the existence of plural and conflicting accounts of the good. If communitarianism means finding our shared good in community, what exactly is the content of that good—and what if there are some who dissent from it? A communitarian theory of punishment may in turn exacerbate these worries. Here it is not only that we may believe that there are many conceptions of the good: here the worry is that we *punish* those who disagree with our shared conception of the good, in order to force them back into communion with it. Punishment may be for certain obvious wrongs, but on the communitarian theory, punishment is not about merely preventing future instances of those wrongs, or even to rebalance the benefits and burdens distributed in society. Rather, punishment is to help you realize that you have strayed from the right path, which is in community with others, and to help you go through the paces so that you may (a) apologize to that community and (b) bring yourself back into conformity with it. Of course, what is interesting is that some communitarians will accept this interpretation of the vision but say that it does not follow that harsh treatment is the proper or even preferred mode of bringing about the offender's reconciliation with community. What may be preferable, instead, is a sort of apology ritual or even a restorative justice-type meeting and conversation with the victims one has wronged (Bennett 2016). Whether these alternatives to punishment are appealing, or raise the same sort of liberal anxieties is an important question. It does show, however, that the implication of more than just libertarian theories of punishment may be to move away from punishment, inasmuch as punishment is associated with prison or other forms of harsh treatment.

Marxism

Marxism as such may not be considered a major player in contemporary debates about political philosophy. But it deserves mention here because one of the more significant contributions to the debate about political philosophy and punishment did connect Marxism as an abstract theory to a certain theory of punishment. That essay was Jeffrie Murphy's "Marxism and Retribution" (Murphy 1973). The title to a greater or lesser extent explains the trajectory of the essay. Murphy starts with a Marxist analysis of society and crime and then finds resources within Marx to hold that a Marxist analysis of the material conditions of society might help buttress a Kantian-retributivist justification of punishment. The argument is complicated, clever, and Murphy's essay is one of the real classics of twentieth-century philosophy of punishment. Nonetheless, it seems to me flawed, and a main part of that is precisely in the gap between the political-philosophical and cultural-historical aspects of Marxism that Murphy mines, and the particular theory of punishment he recovers from it. I am critical of it, but I do need to acknowledge the real contribution Murphy's essay makes. He not only considers what Marx would say about punishment, but he ties this closely to what Marx would say about the criminal law, and moreover, what Marx would say about the relationship between cultural conditions and the conditions of criminal responsibility. This is the kind of comprehensive approach that a focus on political philosophy should yield. Murphy sees in Marxism not just a theory of the state and wealth distribution but a theory of the state and punishment. In short, he draws a clear line between the abstract principles of Marxism and a particular social scheme related to crime and dealing with crime.

What, then, does Murphy argue? The *Marxist* part of his argument runs in two steps. First, he looks at a relatively contemporary Marxist account of what causes criminal behavior. The causes are poverty, discrimination, and in general and in general, inequality of opportunities and inequality of resources. Such more or less persuasive causal explanations of criminal behavior sow real doubt as to whether people are ever properly held responsible for their actions, or at least, responsible *enough* so that they can be the subject of criminal punishment. Moreover, and in this way, the critical framework of Murphy's essay becomes apparent. If we look at economic inequality in society, it does not seem plausible to argue that punishment should be a matter of balancing out benefits and burdens. If there is already existing inequality, and at least some of the criminal behavior that is out there is explained by the inequality, then punishment if it is presented as abstractly punishing people for taking on an extra "burden," then punishment may well serve to *reinforce* already existing inequalities rather than rectify them. Surely those who suffer from present-day inequality are not benefitting from such a scheme. And it is with this final argument that we get to the second step of Murphy's argument. If we want to have a scheme of punishment like the one that we looked at earlier in the context of Murphy's mentor Herbert Morris, we must have something like a Marxist revolution, that is, we must have a total change in society where we do have economic equality so that (a) people are free to make choices unconstrained by economic necessity, (b) punishment really will balance out benefits and burdens, and (c) the idea that punishment is a balancing of benefits and burdens can be seen as something that people would genuinely, authentically, consent to.

In other words, Murphy sees his Marxian argument as leading to a sort of back door defense or confirmation of a benefits-and-burdens theory of punishment, now styled not as something that we can do now but something that needs some material preconditions in order to be defensible. The state can only really get the right to punish people if some material preconditions are met (preconditions, it should be noted, that we are nowhere near to meeting in today's society). But such an argument, again clever as it is, seems to be a nonsequitur. Ironically, where Murphy's essay seems to me lacking is precisely when it comes to the question, by what right does the state have to punish? Murphy seems to give a Kantian answer to this question (in that people may have a right to be punished when they break the law), to which he weds a Marxian theory. This makes for an uneasy fit. Why assume that the upshot to a Marxist analysis of the causes of society leads to a Kantian justification of punishment? In fact, Murphy curtly rejects the idea offered by the Marxist social theorist he had been relying on throughout the essay that punishment in a Marxist utopia would be replaced by a sort of therapy (so, on this reading, Marxism too becomes a species of the abolitionist position). "[T]his surely will not do," Murphy says (Murphy 1973, p. 242). Why not? It could be that the Marxist theory of the state—such as the state will exist in a Marxist society— that punishment will be *solely* a matter of therapy and not of harsh treatment. Murphy resists this because in the end he remains a Kantian about the nature and the purpose of the state. So we cannot look to him to provide us a full-out Marxist theory, only a Kantian, liberal one—and indeed, one which may be at odds with the Marxist social theory he throughout the essay relies on.

Republicanism

Republicanism represents a mix of the communitarianism covered earlier in this part and the liberalism of the first section of this chapter. What it rejects is a vision of freedom that sees freedom only as a negative freedom from constraint. Rather, republicanism sees freedoms as being freedom from domination, where one is dominated either when one is actually physically controlled by other and restrained or when one is subject to the arbitrary power of another (Pettit 1997). Spelled out more positively, as a kind of freedom to, republicans speak of having dominion or the power of acting unconstrained in either of these ways or, more positively, having control free from the meddling of the state or other people. This is the basis of republicanism, and beyond this the details can get a little murky. As developed by Pettit, what republicans favor is the *maximization* of freedom from domination, so inherent in republicanism as Pettit sees it is a kind of consequentialism. Writing with John Braithwaite, Pettit has also applied republicanism considered in this maximizing way to criminal justice as a whole. In their book, *Not Just Deserts*, Pettit and Braithwaite develop what they call a systematic theory of the criminal justice system, which includes a republican theory of what things should be criminal, a republican theory of sentencing, and also more broadly a republican theory of the implementation of the criminal law (Braithwaite and Pettit 1990). Braithwaite and Pettit's book stands as one of the rare examples of political theorists taking seriously the idea that state punishment must be given a unique justification, and that one's justification of punishment shouldn't be articulated in isolation from one's larger theory of the state and its purposes (and indeed of criminal justice and its aims). But republicanism may suffer, too, from its too close association—at least in Braithwaite and Pettit's telling—with consequentialism.

In speaking of a republican theory of punishment, Braithwaite and Pettit do strike some communitarian notes. They note especially that a goal of punishment should be some form of social education or socialization about the need to respect the rights of others and to avoid dominating them (domination can come both from state power and private power). Their theory, however, because it is on the lookout especially for state domination, expresses a preference for what they call "reprobation" instead of punishment (Braithwaite and Pettit 1990, p. 10, 88ff). Reprobation is denunciation of a crime, but without any actual punishment of the harsh treatment variety. Even when it comes to punishment itself, they favor depriving a person of his or her property rather than confining that person in prison or taking that person's life. Here it seems important to note that abstract theories of the state and the state's purpose can have implications even for such things as *how* to punish. Borrowing from Braithwaite's criminological work, Braithwaite and Pettit do not shy from the moralizing work reprobation may involve. They see crime (in part) as a sort of alienation from society, and so a necessary part of bringing the criminal back into society can involve social disapproval of them, even a sort of shaming. They see this shaming as comparatively preferable to coercion, which may be "dumb"—the person being coerced may not see why he or she is being coerced. The person who is brought to see that he or she has reason to be ashamed and *does* feel shame, is being punished in many ways more effectively than if that person had been put in jail. This is the more effective punishment and the more effective deterrent, because it will instill in those who violate the law the habits and dispositions to obey the law in the future. It helps, in the words of Braithwaite and Pettit, to make crime "unthinkable" for citizens (Braithwaite and Pettit 1990, p. 89).

The project that Braithwaite and Pettit undertake is an important one but also one that is wide ranging. It deserves serious consideration of those political theorists who see (what should be) the centrality of the question of the right of states to punish. For now, I raise only two points. The first point has to do with how the consequentialism of Pettit's theory fits in with the emphasis on shaming and reprobation in punishment. If the goal of punishment is (ultimately) to reduce the presence of domination, it may in fact be an open—empirical— question as to whether shaming and reprobation do this better than straight out coercion. It may be that coercion in the form of punishment, while it may involve some short-term domination, really does decrease domination (and increase dominion) overall. The second point is somewhat related. Braithwaite and Pettit seem to recognize that an emphasis on shaming and reprobation may raise familiar liberal hackles—is it the job of the government to reprimand and shame others, even those who do wrong? Doesn't this involve the government in a sort of licensed humiliation of offenders, something which James Whitman especially has critically analyzed in the context of shaming punishments (Whitman 1998), and Martha Nussbaum has flagged specifically in the context of crimes involving sex (Nussbaum 2004)? Braithwaite and Pettit may have an answer to this: it may involve being careful about what laws we pass, and to be careful that the laws we enforce via shaming and reprobation are broadly speaking laws which go *only* to the avoidance of domination. But in the end their response seems to be consequentialist. The good of reprobation and social disapproval of crime is that it, in the end, leads to greater freedom from domination than the opposite. This may not satisfy the liberal, even if he or she goes along with the empirical assumption, for the liberal may feel that even if some freedom may be maximized overall, there still could be some impermissible ways of getting to that goal.

Conclusion: Political Liberalism?

There is one political-philosophical option that I have not covered, perhaps conspicuously so, because it represents one of the more interesting and exciting developments in political philosophy in the last quarter century: John Rawls's development of what he calls a "political liberalism" (Rawls 2005). But it is perhaps best to look at political liberalism only after seeing the sheer variety of political-philosophical options when it comes to punishment, not only at a general level (liberalism, libertarianism, communitarianism, etc.) but also within each theory—because we have seen how political philosophies may even underdetermine within themselves as to what their implications are as to punishment. In one respect, this demonstrates the richness of the debate we have missed out on by the almost single-minded focus on issues of distributive justice. Could we have had a number of fully worked out versions of these various theories, now not pivoting on wealth distribution but on issues of criminal justice? Perhaps. But in addition to being a missed opportunity, the proliferation of possible views on punishment derived from these various political philosophies itself is also a data point. It points to if not the actual existence of reasonable disagreement on what punishment is for or what it could be for, at least to the possibility of differing, yet sensible views about what we should be doing when we punish people. Political liberalism takes this disagreement seriously; indeed, it may even be its starting point. As Charles Larmore has written, political liberalism is a "latecomer"—it makes sense after we have seen the diversity of reasonable points of view available, and the difficulty of choosing between them (Larmore 1996, p. 144). This may apply equally to different visions of the good as it might apply to perspectives on punishment. That is, it does not seem wrong to say that we can have reasonable pluralism about opinions about what appropriate to do to people who do bad (keeping in mind that sometimes we may think that punishing people *is* a way of doing what is good for people).

Political liberalism has a family resemblance to contractarian theories in this respect: it takes the measure of the legitimacy of a state program whether it is something which other fellow citizens could reasonably accept. The contract in this sense is not a hypothetical or actual agreement between citizens but more like a constraint on justifiable state action. If a policy cannot be justified in terms of so-called public reasons, then imposing that policy on citizens is not a matter of legitimate state action, but something more like brute coercion.[20] Citizens can object to that policy being done in their name. And the idea of public reason is critically shaped by the existence of reasonable pluralism. If you believe that the good life is one thing and I think it is another, then me proposing a policy that advances *my* idea of the good life cannot get the crucial buy-in from you: it is something that I could reasonably object to. So public reason will constrain, sometimes considerably, the policy options open to a given community, a constraint that applies to punishment no less than any other social policy. A philosophy of punishment that is meant to advance a so-called comprehensive conception of the good will probably be ruled out in a society characterized by pluralism, because someone could reasonably object to *this* personal social good being a matter of state policy. So political liberalism sees a clear dividing line—and here it probably shares a feature of most liberalisms—between what is permissible for persons to pursue in their own individual social lives and what it is permissible for the *state* to pursue in the name of all of its citizens generally. But political liberalism sees this both as a matter of particular policies *and* for the justifications of those policies. States can do the wrong things, but they can also do the right thing for the wrong reasons, which includes the times when they lack the *authority* to do the right thing. Both would be objectionable under political liberalism.

If the justificatory aspect of political liberalism owes a debt to contractarian thinking, the substantive upshot, I think, comes very close to the idea of societal defense or deterrence that I saw as one of the possible libertarian views of the purpose of punishment. Of course, there is a very real possibility that *no* theory of punishment is something that one could reasonably accept in a political liberal society. So abolitionism is—as always—a very real possible outcome, one that we should always keep in mind. Is it the case that the institute of punishment as such is something a person could reasonably reject? Maybe. But I think the better view is that there may be many means of punishment and indeed many crimes that we (currently) punish people for committing that would fail the test of reasonable rejectability. There would still remain, however, a core of things we could punish and ways we could punish people that a politically liberal society could and should accept. At some level, if it is to survive, society must punish—not, however, with the goal of reforming or remolding offenders, as the republican or the atonement liberal would want. These are goals of punishment that would go too far for the political liberal, and do what in the positive context the political liberal would easily reject: they promote a comprehensive conception of the good in the guise of a theory of punishment. Even the idea of punishment as liberal reform or rehabilitation goes too far because again, it is not merely the idea of punishment as reform that is in question, but the state having this as one of its goals. It is reasonably rejectable, I think, to say that the state should have as its purpose not merely to protect others by means of deterrence but to also coerce or shame people into accepting the truth of the good of autonomy or even of non-domination. People should respect each other's rights, and the state can take measures to make this happen, both preventative (especially) and punitive. It is when we go beyond this modest goal of punishment that we risk violating the liberal condition of legitimacy, by advancing state goals that other citizens could reasonably reject.

It is this modest goal that reflects the political liberal's concern with the question, "What right does the state have to punish?" The political liberal's idea of public reason is just a broader version of taking seriously the question, what right does the state have to do anything? The state gets this right only if the underlying justification of its action is something that no citizen can reasonably object to, something which applies just as much if the state is passing some tax measure or if it is proposing some additional new criminal law or criminal sanction. The connection between political liberalism and societal defense seems to me plausible, and rather tight. Because of the legitimacy constraint, I do not see what other goal of punishment—not retribution, not rehabilitation—that could actually meet it. This may seem disappointing; after all, there have been many deep and compelling versions of retribution on offer, many of which propose that theory as a sound (or even the only) possible justification for state punishment. Rehabilitation, although not now in vogue, had many defenders in the mid-twentieth century, who often thought of rehabilitation as the theory most consistent with left-liberal thinking. If the political liberal is right, however, neither of these theories—unless substantially revised and limited—could really be permissible, that is to say, legitimate ends of state policy. Of course, this is not the end of the story. As I noted earlier, if we find this result objectionable, we can challenge it, but this time not merely at the level of punishment theory, but at the level of political philosophy.[21]

NOTES

1. Bentham, Hobbes, Kant, and so on, all had substantial discussions of punishment in the context of their political philosophies. To this list we could also add Beccaria, whose theory of punishment and theory of the state were closely connected.

2. This may also work the other way around: our ideas about the necessity of punishment may inform and shape what we think about the role of the state more generally.

3. On the various kinds of punishment, see Husak (2016).

4. For a good framing of this issue, see the early pages of John Simmons's "Locke and the Right to Punish," (Simmons 1991).

5. Recent works by Chiao (2019), Tadros (2011), Thorburn (2011), and Duff (2001) may seem to be an exception to this sweeping statement. But Chiao, Tadros, and Duff are *philosophers of the criminal law* first and foremost, and political philosophers second. The generalization in the text refers to the lack of attention by political philosophers on questions of the criminal law, and not the other way around. Still, to the extent that Chiao et al. meet political philosophers "in the middle," their emphasis on the "public" and "political" character of the criminal law is a very welcome development. (Again, Braithwaite and Pettit are a good contrast here—they are working out republicanism's implications for the criminal law; that is, they *start* with a political theory and then work down from that.) I discuss Duff's communitarian liberalism in the text *infra*. More recently, Erin Kelly's book, *The Limits of Blame* (2018), approaches the topic in a way that takes political philosophy seriously.

6. An idea canvassed in (Nozick 1975).

7. A related problem—which I cannot consider here—is jurisdictional: what gives the state a right to punish those who might not be citizens of that state?

8. Indeed, this may be the great weakness in the abolitionist argument: the abolitionist considers only rights violations *by the state* rather than by private parties.

9. The libertarian position is one gloss on this idea of "autonomy"—viewing autonomy as mainly (or only) promoted by protecting so-called negative liberty.

10. My analysis here draws heavily from Morris (1968). *See also* (Murphy 1971) and Dagger (1993).

11. Here the benefits-and-burdens theory intersects with a familiar strand of retributivism (Morris 1968, p. 478) ("it is just to punish those who have violated the rules and caused the unfair distribution of benefits and burdens").

12. (Morris 1968, pp. 477–478) (defending punishment as necessary to "induce compliance" and "avoid increasing the number of incidences of people taking what they do not deserve").

13. As I also note in section "Conclusion: Political Liberalism?", the importance of contractarian thought may not be about what purposes of punishment it endorses or allows, but what purposes it *excludes*.
14. *See* (Barry 1973, p. 174) ("Liberalism rests on a vision of life: a Faustian vision. It exalts self-expression, self-mastery and control over the environment, natural and social; the active pursuit of knowledge and the clash of ideas; the acceptance of personal responsibility for the decisions that shape one's life. For those who cannot take the freedom, it provides alcohol, tranquillizers, wrestling on the television, astrology, psychoanalysis, and so on, endlessly, but it cannot by its nature provide certain kinds of psychological security.").
15. I read Antony Duff in some of his books to be advancing just such a theory. *See* Duff (2001) and Flanders (2002).
16. The same applies, modulo some adjustments, to those who believe that punishing criminals is intrinsically good. *See* Moore (1987).
17. Another Rawlsian-inspired theory that deserves consideration in this context is the one developed by Tommie Shelby. *See* Shelby (2007).
18. Sandel, Taylor, and MacIntyre, all have, at one point or another, disclaimed the label.
19. Here I mean to be referencing, but not endorsing, the somewhat tendentious grouping of communitarians with some very illiberal figures in history. *See* Holmes (1993).
20. Importantly, this constraint applies to state action rather than state inaction, although that line is admittedly hard to draw. Still, this may introduce a sort of libertarian bias into political liberalism: one can reasonably reject a welfare policy, but not to the existence of poverty (although one could reasonably reject a state support of an economic system that results in massive poverty).
21. Thanks to Gabe Mendlow, Vincent Chiao, Dan Epps, Alice Ristroph, Raff Donelson, Charlie Lesche, Zac Cogley, and participants at workshops at Northwestern University and at Washington University for comments on an earlier draft.

References

Barnett, Randy E. 1977. Restitution: A new paradigm for punishment. *Ethics* 87: 279–301.

———. 2014. *The structure of liberty: Justice and the rule of law*. 2nd ed. Oxford: Oxford University Press.

Barry, Brian. 1973. The liberal theory of justice; a critical examination of the principal doctrines. In *A theory of justice*, ed. John Rawls. Oxford: Clarendon Press.

Bennett, Christopher. 2016. Punishment as an apology ritual. In *The new philosophy of criminal law*, ed. Chad Flanders and Zachary Hoskins, 211–228. Lanham: Rowman & Littlefield International.

Boonin, David. 2008. *The problem of punishment*. Cambridge: Cambridge University Press.

Braithwaite, John, and Stephen Mugford. 1994. Conditions of successful reintegration ceremonies. *British Journal of Criminology* 34: 139–171.

Braithwaite, John, and Philip Pettit. 1990. *Not just deserts: A republican theory of criminal justice*. Oxford: Clarendon Press.

Chiao, Vincent. 2019. *Criminal law in the age of the administrative state*. Oxford: Oxford University Press.

Dagger, Richard. 1993. Playing fair with punishment. *Ethics* 103: 473–488.

Deigh, John. 1984. On the right to be punished, some doubts. *Ethics* 94: 191–211.

Duff, Antony. 2001. *Punishment, communication, and community*. Oxford: Oxford University Press.

Flanders, Chad. 2002. Review of *Punishment, communication, and community*, by R.A. Duff. *Ethics* 113: 149–151.

———. 2016a. Criminals behind the veil: Political philosophy and punishment. *The BYU Journal of Public Law* 31: 83–110.

———. 2016b. Public wrongs and public reason. *Dialogue* 55: 45–58.

———. 2017. Punishment, liberalism, and public reason. *Criminal Justice Ethics* 36: 61–77.

Flanders, Chad, and Zachary Hoskins. 2016. *The new philosophy of criminal law*. Lanham: Rowman & Littlefield International.

Golash, Deirdre. 2005. *The case against punishment: Retribution, crime prevention, and the law*. New York: New York University Press.

Goodin, Robert E., and Philip Pettit. 2006. *Contemporary political philosophy: An anthology*. 2nd ed. Malden: Blackwell Publishing.

Hampton, Jean. 1984. A moral education theory of punishment. *Philosophy and Public Affairs* 13: 208–228.

———. 1989. Should political philosophy by done without metaphysics? *Ethics* 99: 791–814.

Holmes, Stephen. 1993. *The anatomy of antiliberalism*. Cambridge, MA: Harvard University Press.

Husak, Douglas. 2016. Does the state have a monopoly to punish crime? In *The new philosophy of criminal law*, ed. Chad Flanders and Zachary Hoskins, 95–110. Lanham: Rowman & Littlefield International.

Kelly, Erin. 2018. *The limits of blame*. Cambridge, MA: Harvard University Press.

Kleinfeld, Joshua. 2016. Embodied ethical life & criminal law. In *The new philosophy of criminal law*, ed. Chad Flanders and Zachary Hoskins, 37–54. Lanham: Rowman & Littlefield International.

———. 2017. Three principles of democratic justice. *Northwestern University Law Review* 111: 1455–1490.

Kymlicka, Will. 2002. *Contemporary political philosophy: An introduction*. 2nd ed. Oxford: Oxford University Press.

Larmore, Charles E. 1996. *The morals of modernity*. New York: Cambridge University Press.

MacIntyre, Alasdair C. 2007. *After virtue: A study in moral theory*. 3rd ed. Notre Dame: University of Notre Dame Press.

Miller, Frank. 1978. Restitution and punishment: A reply to Barnett. *Ethics* 88: 358–360.

Miller, David. 2003. *Political philosophy: A very short introduction*. Oxford: Oxford University Press.

Moore, Michael. 1987. The moral worth of retribution. In *Responsibility, character, and the emotions: New essays in moral psychology*, ed. Ferdinand David Schoeman, 179–219. New York: Cambridge University Press.

Morris, Herbert. 1968. Persons and punishment. *The Monist* 52: 475–501.

Murphy, Jeffrie. 1971. Three mistakes about retributivism. *Analysis* 31: 166–169.

———. 1973. Marxism and retribution. *Philosophy and Public Affairs* 2: 217–243.

Nagel, Thomas. 1975. Libertarianism without foundations. *Yale Law Journal* 85: 136–149.

Nozick, Robert. 1975. *Anarchy, state, and utopia*. Oxford: Blackwell.

Nussbaum, Martha Craven. 2004. *Hiding from humanity: Disgust, shame, and the law*. Princeton: Princeton University Press.

Pettit, Philip. 1997. *Republicanism: A theory of freedom and government*. New York: Clarendon Press.

Pilon, Roger. 1978. Criminal remedies: Restitution, punishment, or both? *Ethics* 88: 348–357.

Pogge, Thomas. 1995. Three problems with contractarian-consequentialist ways of assessing social institutions. *Social Philosophy and Policy* 12 (2): 241–266.

Quinn, Warren. 1985. The right to threaten and the right to punish. *Philosophy and Public Affairs* 14: 327–373.

Rawls, John. 1972. *A theory of justice*. Oxford: Clarendon Press.

———. 2005. *Political liberalism*. Expanded, ed. New York: Columbia University Press.

Sandel, Michael J. 1998. *Liberalism and the limits of justice*. 2nd ed. New York: Cambridge University Press.

Sen, Amartya. 2009. *The idea of justice*. Cambridge, MA: Belknap Press of Harvard University Press.

Shelby, Tommie. 2007. Justice, deviance, and the dark ghetto. *Philosophy and Public Affairs* 35: 126–160.

Shuster, Arthur. 2016. *Punishment and the history of political philosophy: From classical republicanism to the crisis of modern criminal justice*. Toronto: University of Toronto Press.

Simmons, John. 1991. Locke and the right to punish. *Philosophy and Public Affairs* 20: 311–349.

Tadros, Victor. 2011. *The ends of harm: The moral foundations of criminal law*. Oxford: Oxford University Press.

Taylor, Charles. 1985. *Human agency and language: Philosophical papers*. Vol. 1. Cambridge: Cambridge University Press.

———. 1989. *Sources of the self: The making of the modern identity*. Cambridge, MA: Harvard University Press.

Thorburn, Malcolm. 2011. Criminal law as public law. In *Philosophical foundations of criminal law*, ed. R.A. Duff and Stuart Green, 21–43. Oxford: Oxford University Press.

Walzer, Michael. 1983. *Spheres of justice: A defense of pluralism and equality*. New York: Basic Books.

Wellman, Christopher Heath. 2017. *Rights forfeiture and punishment*. New York: Oxford University Press.

Whitman, James. 1998. What is wrong with inflicting shame sanctions? *Yale Law Journal* 107: 1055–1092.

Wolff, Jonathan. 2016. *An introduction to political philosophy*. 3rd ed. Oxford: Oxford University Press.

PART XXII

Proportionality and Punishment

CHAPTER 23

Proportionality in Punishment

Youngjae Lee

INTRODUCTION

When the US Supreme Court decided in *Graham v. Florida* that the Cruel and Unusual Punishments Clause of the Eighth Amendment of the Constitution prohibits a sentence of life in prison without parole for a nonhomicide crime committed by a minor, it stated that "[t]he concept of proportionality is central to the Eighth Amendment" and that it is the "precept of justice that punishment for crime should be graduated and proportioned to [the] offense" (Graham v. Florida). These statements make two claims—one legal and one philosophical. The philosophical claim is that justice requires proportionality in punishment, and the legal claim is that this principle of justice is central to the Eighth Amendment ban on cruel and unusual punishments. Both statements are grandiose but abstract and spare enough to be noncommittal, nearly costless for the Court to endorse. At the same time, the idea that justice requires proportionality in punishment is familiar and compelling enough to attract a broad consensus, even if the consensus tends to unravel once we depart from the general formulations either by attempting to articulate philosophical grounds for the punishment or by specifying the notion to implement it into practice. The aim of this chapter is to examine the concept of proportionality in punishment from multiple vantage points—practical, legal, and philosophical—and consider its enduring importance and persistent difficulties.

Y. Lee (✉)
Fordham University School of Law, New York, NY, USA
e-mail: ylee@fordham.edu

© The Author(s) 2019
L. Alexander, K. K. Ferzan (eds.), *The Palgrave Handbook of Applied Ethics and the Criminal Law*, https://doi.org/10.1007/978-3-030-22811-8_23

PROPORTIONALITY: SOME EXAMPLES

Let's start with two sets of examples. The first set is a collection of headlines from recent child pornography possession cases: "Justices Decline Case on a 200-Year Sentence for Man Who Possessed Child Pornography" (Greenhouse 2007), "Life Sentence for Possession of Child Pornography Spurs Debate Over Severity" (Goode 2011), "Ex-School Headmaster Sentenced to 50 Years for Child Porn" (Barrish and Reyes 2015). In all these cases, the offenders violated laws banning possession of child pornography, not production or even distribution. To be sure, people are not exactly lining up to defend the practice of viewing recordings of child sex abuse for pleasure. Nevertheless, it is a commonly held belief that sentences of several decades in prison constitute disproportionate punishments for possessing child pornography, especially compared to similar sentences handed down for crimes like murder (Sulzberger 2010).

Now consider these headlines: "Light Sentence for Turner in Stanford Rape Case Draws Outrage" (Stack 2016a) and "Judge Aaron Persky Under Fire for Sentencing in Stanford Rape Case" (Stack 2016b). In the Brock Turner case, a judge handed down a sentence of six months in jail after Turner was convicted of sexually assaulting an unconscious woman. Two years later, California voters voted to remove him from office through California's recall process (Astor 2018). Or, consider the following answer from a rape victim, who was raped repeatedly by one person when she was a teenager, to the question what she would want as punishment if her rapist were convicted: "I desire a death or natural life sentence for my rapist because that is what seems appropriate given the damage he wrought in my life" (Carlson 2017). Again, these views may be controversial, and the recall movement, in particular, drew much criticism (Del Real 2018), but the sentiment that the sentence for Brock Turner was too lenient, given the gravity of his crime and that, generally speaking, rape is a serious crime calling for a serious response in the form of punishment, is widespread.

These two sets of examples illustrate the ways in which the idea of proportionality in punishment has an intuitive appeal. Even if possession of child pornography is considered to be criminal, it seems disproportionately harsh for a person to lose decades of his life in prison for mere possession, and even if one may generally worry about excessive harshness of state punishments, it is difficult to argue against the proposition that there is such a thing as a disproportionately soft response to a crime as serious as rape. What explains these intuitions? What is this thing called proportionality anyway?

WHAT IS PROPORTIONALITY?

The idea of proportionality is associated with retributivism (Harmelin v. Michigan, p. 989), and retributivism, in turn, may be defined in many different ways, but one common definition is that it is the idea that "wrongdoers deserve to suffer in proportion to the wrong they have committed" (Tadros 2011, p. 26).[1]

To understand what it means for punishment to be deserved or undeserved by an individual, it is helpful to start with an analysis of the general concept of desert. As Joel Feinberg explained in his seminal discussion, every desert statement has at least three elements. In the statement, "S deserves X in virtue of F," S is the deserving person, X is what he deserves, and F is the desert basis—that is, the basis for X (Feinberg 1970a, p. 61). To understand how it is that a person deserves something, we must understand two relationships: the relationship between the person who is deserving and the desert basis (S and F), and that between what is deserved and the desert basis (X and F).

The person who is deserving and the desert basis (S and F) are related, in that the desert basis has to be an attribute of the deserving person. In the relationship between what is deserved and the basis for desert (X and F), the key concept is "fittingness" or appropriateness (Feinberg 1970a). So, a response to criminal wrongdoing is "fitting" or "appropriate" only if it takes a form that symbolizes or expresses the society's condemnatory attitude toward the criminal conduct. This is why it would be inappropriate to reward criminals, whereas infliction of suffering is often seen as an appropriate response. Second, a corollary to this is that not every form of loss is an acceptable form of punishment in every society, depending on the symbolic significance the particular form of loss has in the society. For instance, the sanction of "community service" may appear inappropriate for certain crimes given the mixed signals—either as a sanction or as evidence of the participant's generosity and public spiritedness—such service gives (Feinberg 1970b, p. 114).

The concept of proportionality in punishment follows from the idea of fittingness. In short, the harshness of the punishment should reflect our level of condemnation or disapproval of the criminal act. A punishment would be excessive, then, if the degree of condemnation symbolized by the amount of punishment were too high relative to the criminal's blameworthiness. A punishment also would be excessive in situations where it is imposed on a person who has not committed any acts for which the kind of condemnatory expression that accompanies criminal sanction would be appropriate. A corollary to all of this is that the harshness of the punishment should increase as the appropriate level of condemnation or disapproval increases, which in turn should increase as the gravity of the crime increases (Feinberg 1970b, p. 118).

Fittingness in desert has both comparative and noncomparative aspects (Feinberg 1974). To illustrate, in the punishment context, the noncomparative aspect stands for the view that a person convicted of a given crime should receive a certain amount of punishment, no matter how other people are treated, while the comparative aspect focuses on what the punishment for a given crime is compared to punishments for different crimes of varying degrees of blameworthiness. For example, if a criminal has been sentenced to five years in prison for stealing a car, noncomparative desert asks whether his deed is serious enough to warrant such a response by the state, regardless of how the state is treating other car thieves and criminals of more and less serious crimes. Comparative desert, by contrast, is about whether the car thief is being treated the same way as other car thieves and other comparably serious criminals and how his punishment compares to punishments imposed on those who have committed more or less serious crimes.

Why do both aspects—comparative and noncomparative—matter? Noncomparative desert matters in the following way: when we say that it would be clearly disproportionate to punish parking violation with one year in prison, that statement would be true even if every parking violation were treated the same way and more serious crimes were treated more harshly. In other words, even if a sentencing scheme generates a series of sentences that are in perfect comparative-desert relationship to one another, it is possible for some or all of those sentences to be too harsh.

The comparative aspect matters, too, as what one deserves is sometimes determined in reference to what others deserve. So, when the state punishes, it condemns the behavior it punishes as wrong, and the degree to which the behavior is condemned is expressed by varying the amount of punishment. Therefore, how one's punishment stands in relation to punishments for other crimes supplies a crucial piece of information as to how wrong the behavior punished is viewed by the society. This means that a punishment imposed on a criminal would be "undeserved" if it is more severe than the punishment imposed on those who have committed more serious crimes or crimes of the same seriousness because the judgment it expresses about the seriousness of the criminal's behavior would be inappropriate. For instance, as the death penalty carries a social meaning as the ultimate punishment for the most serious crimes, each time the state imposes a death sentence it shows that it considers the crime at issue to be not only one of the most serious offenses but also an offense that is as serious as other crimes that the society considers to be the most serious. Those who commit offenses less serious than the most serious offenses and are still sentenced to death would be receiving harsher sentences than they deserve because part of what it means for them to receive the punishment they deserve is that they are punished less harshly than the worst criminal.

In this way, comparative desert functions the way an audience at a play responds to various performers at the end of the performance.[2] Assuming that a given production is good enough to merit applause, the audience members vary the length and intensity of their applause to show their relative levels of appreciation for different members of the cast. There may be noncomparative desert at work here, because if the production as a whole is not worthy of applause, no member of the cast may deserve any showing of appreciation. But barring such a situation, what determines how the audience greets each member of the cast is the principle of comparative desert. That is, other things being equal, generally the cast members with bigger and more difficult parts tend to receive the longer, louder, and more intense applause. The reason this has to be so is that there is a limit as to how long, loud, and intense cheering can get, and the audience has to save their longest applause for the cast member they appreciate the most. If they are too quick to unleash their most enthusiastic showing of appreciation and use it on minor characters, they may not be able to express to the ones with the leading parts how much more they appreciate them than those with lesser roles. And if such a situation unfortunately arises, those who deserve more recognition from the audience would not be receiving what they *deserve*, not just what they *comparatively deserve*. It is in this sense that what one deserves cannot be determined without considering both comparative and noncomparative aspects.

Incidentally, it is important to note here that nothing in this account *requires* suffering as a response to criminal wrongdoing, and that is a reason to revisit the definition of retributivism we started with as the idea that "wrongdoers deserve to suffer in proportion to the wrong they have committed" (Tadros 2011, p. 26). According to the account presented, the important feature of desert is that of a "fitting" or "appropriate" response. It is true that what is typically considered to be a "fitting" response to criminal wrongdoing is infliction of suffering, but that is not a requirement of this theory of desert. The right level of condemnation need not be expressed in terms of inflictions of suffering, as a mere symbolic response can suffice (von Hirsch 1993, p. 14).

What Is Proportionality For?

The preceding discussion about desert, though, leaves a crucial question unaddressed. How does it apply to state punishment? Even if we conclude that the principle of proportionality, interpreted as the idea that people should receive the punishment that they deserve and no more, is intelligible, that by itself tells us little about state punishment. That is, simply saying that some people deserve to be punished and by how much does not explain why the *state* must be the one to mete out the punishment people deserve. As a general matter, the state is not in the business of ensuring just deserts. Bad things may happen to good people, just as some people may achieve far more success than they deserve. But it is not the state's job, as a general matter, to intervene and take from those who have more than they deserve and give to those who have less than they deserve. We need to move beyond the simple assertion that some people deserve certain things when attempting to justify the state's role in doling out punishment.

To make some headway into the question of why proportionality in punishment matters, we must first explore the rationales for criminal law. I highlight two, in particular, here. First, criminal law plays an important role in preserving physical security through its system of prohibitions and punishments. That is, harm prevention is an important goal of criminal law. Second, criminal law functions to *displace* feelings of resentment and desires for personal vengeance by punishing wrongdoing. As John Gardner put it, "The blood feud, the vendetta, the duel, the revenge, the lynching: for the elimination of these modes of retaliation, more than anything else, the criminal law as we know it today came into existence" (Gardner 2007, p. 213).

These two aspects of criminal law explain several key features of our criminal justice system, namely that it is *coercive, judgmental,* and *preemptive.* First, its *coercive* aspect reveals itself most obviously through the process of apprehending and punishing offenders. The coercive aspect is essential for ensuring order and physical security—a key function of criminal law.

Second, the criminal justice system is *judgmental* in the sense that when we punish, we also blame, condemn, and stigmatize the offenders (Feinberg 1970b). By stigmatizing offenders, punishment gets "personal" and sends the message that their acts reflect badly on them. This judgmental aspect derives at least partially from the displacement function of criminal law. A core purpose of criminal law and punishment is to manage the punitive and retaliatory emotions of those who have been victims of wrongdoers (as well as others in the community who feel indirectly victimized) and to sublimate, displace, and provide an outlet for feelings of resentment toward the wrongdoers. The success or failure of a society's criminal law system thus depends on how well it responds to the punitive emotions of its citizens.

Finally, the criminal justice system is *preemptive* in that the state is the exclusive agent licensed to punish criminal wrongdoing. Although the basic idea of retribution—that people should receive what they deserve—appears facially neutral on the question of *who* should be the one giving wrongdoers what they deserve, the government is the only legitimate punisher, and the law prohibits private individuals from taking the law into their own hands. This preemptive aspect is essential to both the harm prevention and the displacement functions of criminal law.

How does all this relate to the principle of proportionality? As the exclusive agent of punishment, the state has dual commitments. On the one hand, because citizens are generally prohibited from defending themselves with violence or retaliating against wrongdoers, the state has an obligation to provide physical security to its citizens and respond adequately to any wrongdoing. The outrage surrounding the Brock Turner case can be explained as a manifestation of this idea. On the other hand, as the state enjoys an enormous amount of power, not only to interfere forcefully with people's lives and to brand individuals with the stigma of blameworthiness, but also to prohibit others from doing the same, the state cannot preserve its legitimacy as the sole rightful holder of the power to punish unless it respects the restrictions on its use of force, including proportionality. Respecting proportionality helps preserve the legitimacy of the state's power to punish as the principle ensures that the state punishes in a manner that is fair, by treating the equals equally and the unequals unequally.

According to this picture, the idea that people be punished no more than they deserve is a requirement that flows neither from morality nor from some general principle that people ought to receive only what they deserve. Rather, proportionality is one of several conditions that attach to the state's exclusive control of the power to criminalize and punish, and only by respecting such constraints can the state maintain the legitimacy of its exclusive control.

Is Proportionality in Punishment a Pressing Issue in Criminal Justice Today?

Even if an argument can be made that proportionality in punishment is an important principle of political morality, some contend that it is a mistake to spend much time focusing on this issue (Chiao 2017). Take one of the most pressing problems having to do with state punishment today in the United States: mass incarceration (Alexander 2010; Pfaff 2017). It is tempting to link the size of the prison population to lengths of punishments and interpret the problem of mass incarceration as a problem of proportionality. It stands to reason, it appears, that as people spend more time in prison with longer sentences, the number of people incarcerated at a given moment would increase over time as well. However, some argue that, while long sentences grab our attention, extremely disproportionate sentences are rare and lengths of sentences do not explain the size of the prison population. It is true that prison sentences listed in the books have increased over time as legislatures passed tough sentencing laws, but the actual amount of time prisoners serve in prison appears not to have increased much. What *has* changed, according to these studies, is the number of people who have gone to prison. The reason the prison population has increased over time, then, is not that people are serving longer sentences—they are not—but is simply that more people are going to prison than before (Pfaff 2017).

One might resist this conclusion by arguing that the problem of more people going to prison is still a problem of proportionality because they should not be going to prison in the first place, as many in the prison population are there for nonviolent drug offenses (Alexander 2010). The argument that the problem of mass incarceration has to do with the problem of disproportionate punishments would be that the war on drugs and other government policies that overuse criminal sanctions have led to a broader net of criminal liability than ever before and are catching people for conduct that is innocent, harmless, or not harmful or dangerous enough to warrant criminal sanctions. The problem with this argument, however, is that people who are in prison for nonviolent drug offenses constitute only a small portion of the overall prison population (Pfaff 2017).

It is beyond the scope of this chapter to review the causes of mass incarceration. The point here is to highlight the objection that it is a mistake to be distracted by the problem of disproportionately high sentences, as, the objection goes, outrageously long sentences are an anomaly and sentence lengths have not driven the growth in prison population over time.

So, what if the objection is true? More specifically, what if it is indeed the case that the following propositions are true? (1) Prison sentences that are actually served—as opposed to in the books—have not increased over time as the prison population increased. (2) Most people in prison today are serving sentences for violent crimes, not for low-level, nonviolent offenses (such as drug possession). Is there still a problem of proportionality?

There may or may not be. To start answering the question, we could go back to the diagnosis that much of the prison population growth in the past several decades is attributable to a drastic increase in prison admissions. Why are more people being convicted? Perhaps more people are committing crimes? Or more people are getting arrested? In John Pfaff's work, he argues that neither is the case, as both reported crime and arrests fell over time. While arrests fell, the number of felony cases filed in courts went up, meaning that prosecutors were converting arrests to felony filings at a greater rate than previously (Pfaff 2017). Why would prosecutors behave this way? It is not clear, but one thing we might say is that prosecutors would as a general matter not waste time prosecuting cases unless they believe that there is a reasonable probability of conviction. Prosecutors file charges because they think they can win, and prosecutors think they can win when they see paths that lead to conviction.

What do those paths look like? Did trials get easier over time? It does not appear that way. The proof beyond a reasonable doubt requirement, at least nominally, has not budged, and neither has the right to jury trial (Apprendi v. New Jersey; Alleyne v. United States). Most states continue to require unanimity for verdicts,[3] secrecy of jury deliberation is still protected (Peña-Rodriguez v. Colorado),[4] and acquittals continue to be unreviewable (Martinez v. Illinois), which protects the jury's option to nullify and acquit. The highly burdensome jury selection process, with its system of questionnaires and for cause and peremptory strikes, remains intact as well (Miller-El v. Dretke). So trials do not appear to have become easier for prosecutors over time as a general matter.

How trials go would not make a large difference to the prison population in any event. As commonly noted, 95 percent of cases prosecuted end with guilty pleas (Pfaff 2017). This means that understanding how convictions happen generally requires understanding how the plea process works. Take the case of *Bordenkircher v. Hayes*. Hayes was charged with the crime of forging a check to the tune of US$88.30, a crime which carried the sentence of two to ten years in prison at the time. The prosecutor offered to recommend a sentence of five years in prison if Hayes pleaded guilty. Otherwise, the prosecutor told Hayes, he would seek an indictment and charge Hayes as a habitual offender, which would subject Hayes, with his previous convictions, to a mandatory life sentence. When Hayes refused, the prosecutor carried out his threat, Hayes was subsequently convicted and sentenced to life, and the Supreme Court upheld the conviction and punishment (Bordenkircher v. Hayes). That Hayes was a repeat offender does complicate the proportionality calculation a bit, but a life sentence for the crime of forging a check, even by a repeat offender, seems disproportionate.

For our purposes, the important feature of this example is the five-year sentence offer by the prosecutor. A criminal defendant facing a choice between pleading guilty and going to prison for five years and trying his luck at trial and potentially being sentenced to life would feel an enormous pressure to plead guilty, which would in turn guarantee an easy conviction for the prosecutor. The ease of conviction is accordingly a function of, among other things, what sorts of negative consequences a prosecutor can array against the defendant and the number of options a prosecutor has at his or her disposal to add or drop charges.

Potential negative consequences for a defendant thus strengthen the prosecutor's hand. More specifically, what sorts of things can legislators do to enhance the prosecutor's bargaining position? Here is a partial list, including some that have already been mentioned:

- Increases in sentences: Obviously, by increasing sentences for crimes, legislators strengthen the prosecutor's bargaining position.
- Criminal history enhancements: As we saw in the *Hayes* case, one's sentence for a crime can increase significantly with laws that increase punishments for those with a criminal history.
- Mandatory minimum sentences: If certain charges come with mandatory minimum sentences, they do not just give judges the option of handing down high sentences but require them to sentence at a certain level as a minimum. Mandatory minimums enable the prosecutor to make credible threats with predictable consequences, while leaving no room for the defendant to engage in guesswork or wishful thinking about how a judge might sentence, once all things are considered.
- Criminalization of risk-creation and proxy indicators: Sometimes, the state criminalizes certain conduct not because it directly causes harm but because it is thought to lead to or contribute to harm. Various possession offenses—drugs, weapons, or child pornography—may be categorized in this group of risk-creation offenses. The state also criminalizes conduct that in itself may be morally neutral but is easier to detect and is associated with certain types of criminal behavior. Money laundering is an example of a crime like this, as is the requirement that one declare the amount of currency one is carrying abroad over a certain minimum (United States v. Bajakajian). Drug possession with intent to distribute can fall under this heading, too.
- Overlapping crimes: Sometimes, a single transaction can give rise to violations of multiple prohibitions. Say a person works with another person to sell drugs near a school while carrying a firearm. Such a person may be facing convictions for, among other things, (1) possession of drugs with intent to distribute near a school, (2) conspiring to use a firearm in furtherance of a drug crime, and (3) possessing a firearm near a school (United States v. Cruz-Rodriguez). A prosecutor can threaten to charge and attempt to convict him for all three counts unless the defendant pleads guilty.
- Units of crimes: Sometimes, a person can be convicted of, say, child pornography, under multiple counts if the law permits the prosecutor to charge the defendant one count for every image, even if the defendant acquired all the images in a single transaction. Say that a person has twenty images of child pornography, and the law specifies ten years in

prison per image. In such cases, the prosecutor can decide to charge the person with anywhere between one and twenty counts and tell the defendant to either plead guilty and make most of these counts go away or fight for an acquittal and risk being sentenced to 200 years in prison (State v. Berger).

- Consecutive Sentences: The two factors just outlined—overlapping crimes and units of crimes—would not necessarily increase the overall punishment one faces, as sentences for multiple counts can run concurrently. However, if the option of running them consecutively is available, the stakes rise dramatically for the defendant (Oregon v. Ice).

Of course, prosecutors, once they add these sorts of charges, face the prospect of having to prove them to factfinders, sometimes beyond a reasonable doubt, at trial and sentencing (United States v. Booker), but what some of these methods of strengthening the prosecutor's position do is to lighten the burden of proof prosecutors carry. In other words, "the burden of proof" can be decreased by adjusting crime definitions and sentencing rules without disturbing even one bit the proof beyond a reasonable doubt requirement or the right to jury trial.

We began this discussion with the observation that the problem of mass incarceration appears not to have been caused by excessive punishments (given that lengths of sentences served have not increased over time) or overcriminalization (given that the portion of the prison population attributable to low-level nonviolent risk-creation offenses like drug possession is small). However, this closer examination of the ways in which convictions are generated through the plea-bargaining process shows that increases in punishments and in criminalization on the books can have an impact on the size of the prison population, as such increases strengthen the prosecutor's bargaining position and enhance the government's ability to induce guilty pleas through a use of offers to drop charges or threats to add charges, or both.

It is not easy to conclude one way or the other whether the sort of situation presented in the *Hayes* case is problematic. Here are some reasons to find the *Hayes* situation and other situations like it troubling. First, it is possible that someone who finds himself in a situation like Hayes' is factually innocent of the crime but is still unsure whether the jury would acquit him. If he pleads guilty in order to avoid going to prison for life, he would be pleading guilty to a crime that he did not commit, and the state would be inducing guilty pleas from innocent people and then punishing them. Second, we might also be concerned, whether the defendant is guilty or innocent, that the threats that the prosecutor makes to encourage guilty pleas are themselves improper.

Of course, incentives to plead guilty are not always so troublesome, so the question becomes how to regulate the plea-bargaining process to prevent problematic guilty pleas from the innocent and the guilty alike. It is beyond the scope of this chapter to undertake this task, but here are some options. One may simply ask whether the guilty pleas are voluntary, looking at all the factors

(Brady v. United States). One may also ask whether there has been effective assistance of counsel throughout the process (Missouri v. Frye). These two methods are indirect, process-focused ways of getting at troublesome threats. Yet another way—most relevant for this chapter—is to directly ask whether the threats that prosecutors wield are permissible, and the question of what is permissible can be defined in terms of whether the punishment that would be imposed if the prosecutor carries out his or her threat would be proportionate to the defendant's crime or crimes. That is, according to this view, prosecutors should be permitted to threaten the defendant with negative consequences only if the state would be permitted to impose such consequences, and the state should not be permitted to impose punishments that are disproportionate.[5]

Let us now revisit the initial argument that the problem of mass incarceration is not a problem of excessive punishments and overcriminalization but is rather a problem of too many people entering prisons. The analysis provided here shows that the argument that prison sentences that are served have not increased over time and that most people in prison are not serving sentences for low-level, nonviolent offenses does not necessarily show that the problem of mass incarceration is not a problem of proportionality. We still have a problem of proportionality if prosecutors are wielding threats of disproportionate punishments in order to induce guilty pleas, and the ease of obtaining guilty pleas, of course, translates to more prison admissions, which, in turn, can be linked to the problem of mass incarceration. In order, then, to prevent prosecutors from using threats of disproportionate punishments as tools to generate convictions, we would have to think in terms of proportionality of sentences.

PROPORTIONALITY AND CULPABILITY

To determine whether a punishment is proportionate, we need a way of determining different levels of culpability. Questions of culpability are frequently controversial, and since every offense has a level of culpability, any offense can be discussed under the heading of "proportionality." Here I discuss two issues, mentioned earlier, that are both controversial and important as a matter of practice: the cases of repeat offenders and multiple offenders.

In the United States and in many jurisdictions elsewhere, the most important determinant of punishment for a crime, other than the seriousness of the crime itself, is criminal history (Roberts 2008, p. 12). There may be many reasons for this practice. Some argue that repeat offenders have demonstrated a propensity not to be deterred by ordinary sanctions and must be threatened with especially harsh consequences to prevent them from reoffending. Others argue that the point of harsh punishments on repeat offenders is to keep those most likely to reoffend away from the public so that they can no longer pose a danger to others. Criminal history may also be considered relevant in the way an offender's general personal background and character are considered relevant during the sentencing stage. If rehabilitation is considered to be an important purpose of punishment, then it seems to follow that sentencing should take into account whatever information may aid the legal system in deciding what type and what amount of punishment are appropriate to reform individual offenders. These three rationales—deterrence, incapacitation, and rehabilitation—are prima facie plausible as justifications for the practice of considering criminal history in sentencing (Lee 2009).

However, once we ask whether repeat offenders *deserve* more condemnation than first-time offenders for the same offense, the picture turns fuzzy.[6] It is commonly, and casually, assumed that repeat offenders deserve more punishment than first-time offenders. The Federal Sentencing Guidelines, for instance, justify their heavy reliance on criminal history partly on the argument that "[a] defendant with a record of prior criminal behavior is more culpable than a first offender and thus deserving of greater punishment" (U.S. Sentencing Commission 2018). The political rhetoric surrounding California's Three Strikes law frequently included the language of desert and retribution, with some people saying that repeat offenders deserve draconian prison sentences for being recidivists (Simon 1996). Public perceptions of a crime's seriousness appear to vary according to the criminal record of the offender as well (Roberts 2008, pp. 172–174).

By contrast, desert theorists have been generally critical of sentencing enhancements based on the offender's criminal history (Fletcher 1978, pp. 462–466), and they have criticized recidivist statutes such as California's Three Strikes law on retributivist grounds (Lee 2005). The seriousness of a crime does not change, the argument goes, depending on the criminal history of the person committing it. A robbery is a robbery, whether it is committed by a first-time offender or a repeat offender; therefore, there should be no difference in the way the state responds to repeat offenders and first-time offenders who commit the same crime. Another common objection starts from the view that one should not be punished twice for the same offense. If offenders have already been punished for their crimes, they have paid their debts to society, and this means that increasing the amount of punishment for second crimes on the basis of their criminal histories results in a form of double jeopardy (Lee 2009).

Another controversial issue is the culpability of multiple offenders. As we saw at the beginning of the chapter, a person facing conviction for child pornography possession can face outrageously high sentences for mere possession. In such cases, the offenders have violated laws banning possession multiple times by having multiple images, and the fact that they are facing multiple counts at least partially explains the kinds of punishment they end up facing. For instance, Morton Berger received a 200-year sentence by receiving 10 years per image (State v. Berger). Daniel Enrique Guevara Vilca was charged with 454 counts of possession of child pornography, one count per image found on his computer, and received a life sentence without parole (Goode 2011). Christopher Wheeler had more than 2000 images, was charged with twenty-five counts of possession of child pornography, and received a fifty-year sentence, two years per count (Barrish and Reyes 2015).

The child pornography examples show that one can end up a multiple offender by breaking the same law multiple times over time. But that is not the only way. One can break the same law multiple times in a single transaction, hurt multiple victims in one transaction, break multiple laws in one transaction, break multiple laws over time, and so on. And these crimes can be at varying levels of seriousness and patterns of victimization (Lee 2018).

In cases like these, there is a question as to how to "count" multiple units for the purposes of determining culpability. Should it make a difference not only what crimes people commit, but how many times they commit them? If so, what is the appropriate way of thinking about what each instance of lawbreaking is "worth"? Should every instance of lawbreaking be worth the same amount of time in prison? Should we simply add up the punishment for each charge to arrive at the final sentence, or should there be, as some theorists have dubbed it, a "bulk discount" for multiple offenders through, say, concurrently imposed sentences (Jareborg 1998)? If the punishment for each offense is set at an appropriate level, would simply adding them up ever lead to an excessive punishment? If so, why, and is there a different way of thinking about multiple offenses?

There are multiple approaches to dealing with these situations, and sentences imposed can radically differ depending on which approach is taken. Sentences can be imposed consecutively, concurrently, or with a "bulk discount," which may take the form of concurrent sentences or at least a smaller increase in prison term for each additional crime. The question is how to think about these different approaches theoretically (Lee 2018).

The puzzle is that sometimes the law is draconian and applies consecutive sentencing but at other times applies a "bulk discount," and there is no consensus on how to think about the issue. The idea of a "discount" for those who commit multiple offenses is mysterious. "Bulk discount" is a tactic that commercial enterprises offer to encourage large purchases, and, in the criminal context, of course, multiple offending is not something to be made attractive. In addition, some argue that bulk discounting for repeat offenses is in considerable tension with the recidivist premium discussed earlier (Reitz 2010). To complicate things even further, on its face, theories of sentencing that use principles of desert and proportionality to determine sentences appear to have trouble arriving at a view other than the approach of adding the punishment for each offense and arriving at the final number.

The problem of sentencing repeat and multiple offenders is of enormous practical interest. Not having a clear understanding of how to fairly treat repeat offenders and those who commit multiple offenses could lead to excessively harsh punishments through habitual offender statutes and consecutive sentencing of multiple offenses. In addition, as discussed earlier, as long as a genuine threat of a sky-high sentence, enabled by the possibility of the recidivist premium or consecutive sentencing of multiple offenses, looms, prosecutors' hands are strengthened at the plea-bargaining stage. Even if these defendants thus end up with sentences that look "reasonable," they may still be victims of artificially engineered sanctions prosecutors use to bludgeon them into submission. If certain consecutive sentences and sentencing enhancements can be taken simply off the table on proportionality grounds, such abuses of power can be prevented.

CAN THE PRINCIPLE OF PROPORTIONALITY BE PUT INTO PRACTICE?

Even if theorists can work out the meaning and importance of proportionality, there remains the question of implementation. The short answer to the question whether the principle of proportionality can be put into practice is yes. Or, at least it is the case that legislators, sentencing commissions, prosecutors, and judges, as they operate the criminal justice system, can strive to respect the principle of proportionality. It is, of course, beyond the scope of this chapter to spell out all aspects of the implementation question, so this chapter will discuss just a few issues.

We can start with the question whether the principle of proportionality should be translated and implemented as an individual right, at least as far as the principle is used as placing an upper limit on amounts of punishment. To answer this question, we can look again at the state's "dual commitments"—to provide security and respond to wrongdoing one hand and to refrain from punishing excessively—mentioned earlier. The nature of these commitments suggests that the proportionality-based limitation on the state's power to punish should take the form of an individual *right* that is resistant to tradeoffs.

The harm prevention and displacement functions of criminal law demonstrate how the power to punish can be abused. The pressures the state faces to reduce crime could lead it to use excessive and unwarranted violence, as the state can sometimes provide physical security more efficiently and effectively by ignoring various substantive and procedural safeguards placed on its power. And there will be times when respecting these safeguards may seem downright irresponsible—a dereliction of duty—in that they may get in the way of convicting and punishing wrongdoers. What all of this means is that unless we treat the constraints against punishing people more than they deserve as close to inviolable, proportionality-based restrictions on punishment will give too often and will not be able to provide meaningful limitations on the state's power to punish.

Adopting such a goal-constraint framework to understand proportionality-based limitations on punishments does not necessarily commit one to the position that such constraints cannot be overridden. Rights have limits, need to be specified in particular circumstances with conflicting considerations, and can be traded off, or at least sacrificed at times. What we seek to prevent with the concept of rights or constraints are situations where important interests are given up without special justification (Lee 2005, p. 129).

What would it then mean to implement the principle of proportionality as a right? As we saw at the beginning of this chapter, in the United States, the right could be based in the Cruel and Unusual Punishments Clause of the Eighth Amendment of the Constitution. As rights go, however, the right against excessive punishment is a peculiar kind. This can be seen most clearly by contrasting it to other aspects of the Cruel and Unusual Punishments jurisprudence. Oftentimes, the Eighth Amendment is used as a way of guaranteeing a minimum level of humanity, dignity, and decency for everyone, without any regard to individual culpability of offenders. Prison conditions cases have this logic, and so does the belief that certain forms of punishment, such as drawing and quartering, crucifixion, and torture, are simply not allowed under the Eighth Amendment no matter how heinous the crime or the criminal. The right against excessive punishment is different from these other rights because the scope of the right is tied to the culpability level of the rights holder. When the Eighth Amendment guarantees a minimum standard of decency and humanity, those enforcing the guarantee need not examine the question of what each person deserves, but when the right against excessive punishment is being enforced, the crucial question is what the relevant offender deserves.

This raises the following difficulty. Let's say we have a typical constitutional rights adjudication case, where the legislature authorizes a punishment for a crime and a defendant asks a court to declare such a punishment for the crime unconstitutional under the Cruel and Unusual Punishments Clause. The doctrinal test in such a constitutional challenge would be that the punishment is excessive for the defendant's crime because it is undeserved. The problem with such a test is this. If "the people" believe that, say, child rapists should receive the death penalty, on what basis can a court conclude, under the Eighth Amendment, that "the people" got the desert question wrong?

To elaborate, take, again, for instance, habitual offender statutes. As noted earlier, while the belief that repeat offenders are "deserving of greater punishment" seems widespread, there is far more ambivalence among desert theorists on this issue, which has led one commentator to note that on this issue "[t]he difference between elite and popular conceptions of desert is stark" (Ristroph 1997).

There are two standard approaches to resolving such disagreements between "elite" and "popular" understandings of what people deserve. First, one may believe that the question of what people do or do not deserve are matters of objective moral reality, and "the people," or its frequent proxy, the democratic process, may come out with a wrong answer at times. According to this view, the purpose of the Eighth Amendment is to enforce the retributivist constraint, the content of which does not change with the whims of the democratic majority. This understanding of retribution coheres well with a common image of constitutional rights in general and of the Cruel and Unusual Punishments Clause in particular, as the clause is typically understood as playing the role of holding excessive, and frequently irrational, punitive instincts of the people in check by imposing a moral constraint.

A contrasting approach might go as follows. One may think that there is no gap between what a criminal deserves and what "the people" believe that a criminal deserves. According to this view, what an offender deserves is equivalent to what "the people" believe he deserves, and it is a misunderstanding of desert to believe that courts can second-guess desert determinations made by "the people." If "the people," or their democratically elected representatives, think that child molesters deserve to be punished with death, on what possible grounds can a judge decide that their desert judgment is "incorrect"? If a judge disagrees with what "the people" believe on a question of desert, then it is so much the worse for the judge, is it not?

The position that "the people" are the final arbiters desert judgments that judges may not second-guess has much going for it. If we revisit the idea of "fittingness" in desert judgments, the idea is that when considering whether a punishment is a "fitting" response, the harshness of the punishment should reflect our level of condemnation or disapproval. Such assessment of appropriateness or fittingness, in turn, can be made only within the context of a community of shared values (Duff 2001; Lacey 1988). Given such an expressive dimension of punishment, and what it expresses, it would not make any sense to attempt to answer questions of who deserves what without referring to the ways in which the relevant communities would react to different kinds of stimuli that inspire praise and blame.

Also, it seems ill-advised to ignore community sentiments in formulating a theoretical account of who deserves what punishment. What punishment expresses is not just disapproval, which may be formed from a distance and in a cold, rationalistic, judgmental manner but also an emotive state. Emotions associated with the act of punishing are, for example, anger, resentment, indignation, and hatred. To be sure, while such emotions may be thought to be subjective or irrational in that they can get "out of hand," because of their cognitive content they can be evaluated as appropriate or inappropriate, and rational or irrational (Williams 1973; Nussbaum 2001). When such emotions are felt, their appropriateness can be judged through reflection, and sometimes inappropriately felt emotions disappear once there is a recognition of such inappropriateness, the way, say, anger at a friend based on a misunderstanding can evaporate once the misunderstanding is corrected. But it would be a mistake to ignore the fact that such emotions *are* emotions, part of what Peter Strawson called a "complicated web of attitudes and feelings which form an essential part of the moral life as we know it" (Strawson 2003, p. 91). In addition, take the displacement function of criminal law and punishment discussed earlier. It is not just that the institution of punishment has a close relationship to feelings of resentment but also that a core purpose of criminal law and punishment is to provide an outlet for them. Who will be better judges of whether such punitive emotions are properly attended to than the people themselves?

In short, if ordinary sentiments are so important and central to understanding questions about deservingness of offenders, it may simply be the case that what criminals deserve is whatever the people say they deserve, as expressed through the democratic processes or as reflected in public opinion surveys.

This brings us back to the worry that there may be no role for courts to play as we seek to place proportionality limitations on punishment.

However, there are many problems with this line of thought. First, there is the question of how to interpret legislation and public opinion surveys. As mentioned earlier, the institution of punishment serves a variety of functions, such as deterrence, incapacitation, rehabilitation, and retribution. The question that we are interested in is the question of what people deserve, but if a legislature passes, say, a "three-strikes" law, it is not clear from looking at the end product which purposes—deterrence, incapacitation, retribution, or rehabilitation—have driven the legislation. For habitual offender statutes, the argument that those who have demonstrated an inability to live by the rules of society should be isolated can be a powerful rhetorical tool. Therefore, it is too quick to jump from a passage of a penal legislation to the conclusion that whatever punishments are permitted or required by it are those thought by the people to be deserved. Public opinion surveys, too, are frequently obscure about whether people's approval of harsh sentences for repeat offenders reflect their judgments of what repeat offenders deserve, as opposed to their desire to incapacitate and isolate repeat offenders from the general population. In addition, voters tend to focus on the most recent and salient examples of violent crimes. Due to that and also due to influence by the media and politicians, voters frequently support punitive measures that may go much further than what they otherwise would be willing to support given additional information (Roberts and Doob 1990). Therefore, while we may take into account such imperfect measures of public sentiments in formulating appropriate responses to crimes, public sentiments should be the beginning, not the end, of inquiries about the deservingness of those who come under the reach of those laws.

Second, that a function of criminal law is to displace vindictive impulses of the public does not mean that the punishment that is justly deserved is whatever punishment is perceived to be necessary to satisfy the retaliatory impulses of the people. Even though there is a close relationship between desert and retribution on one hand and vengeance and retaliation on the other, we must be careful not to accept wholesale retaliatory impulses as unfailingly reflecting correct moral sentiments. Punitive passions may be correctly generated by one's sense that a moral wrong has been done, but they can also be excessive and driven by other less desirable, yet no less common, sentiments such as cruelty, sadism, inhumanity, and—particularly relevant in discussing criminal justice in the United States—racial hatred and prejudice. In order to place appropriate proportionality-based limitations on punishment and to filter out effects of impulses that should have no place in our administration of criminal justice system, punitive emotions supposedly felt by the people should be scrutinized carefully and tested against broad principles of desert, both comparative and noncomparative. And this is a task that can be performed by courts as proportionality restrictions are enforced.

It may be argued by some that the democratic process can protect all relevant interests and that we can trust legislative outcomes as reflecting the view of the people that, all things considered, punishments that have been authorized by legislation are appropriate. However, such optimism about the ability of our current political system to reflect all relevant concerns is unwarranted when it comes to criminal justice. As has been much noted, our system has built-in incentives that encourage more and more expansive criminal liability (Stuntz 2001). Politicians cannot appear weak on crime; therefore, there is enormous political pressure to advocate and vote for tougher and tougher laws governing criminal liability and sentencing. Prosecutors have incentives to reach convictions at the lowest cost—either at trial or through pleas—and such an outlook calls for broad definitions of criminal liability and high sentences. Moreover, for several reasons, including felon disenfranchisement and the stigma attached to criminals, effective lobbying on behalf of criminal defendants is difficult. Therefore, we have reasons to doubt that fundamental values of political morality that shield criminals and those accused of crimes from abuse are sufficiently protected through the legislative process (Stuntz 1996).

In sum, despite the special relationship the principle of proportionality has to "the people's perspective," the democratic process can often be insufficiently protective of the principle, and there remains an important role for courts to play in enforcing the principle as a limitation on amounts of punishment.

CONCLUSION

Proportionality in punishment is an important ideal. This chapter has given an account of what proportionality is, what it is for, and why it is important both as a matter of theory and practice. This chapter has also given illustrations of some specific thorny questions about proportionality and has discussed how the principle of proportionality may be implemented in a constitutional democracy. The final picture is not tidy. Punishment—intentional infliction of pain and deprivation of liberty by the government on its citizens, and on behalf of its citizens—is a troublesome practice. And the demands that are put on it—to "displace" retaliatory instincts of citizens without reproducing their excess, injustice, and inhumanity—are difficult to satisfy. But that is no reason to give up on the ideal. The most likely candidate of a criminal justice system that does not rely on the concept of proportionality is perhaps the kind that prioritizes prevention through sophisticated methods of prediction (Mayson 2018). Unless we are ready to wholeheartedly embrace the project of surveillance, prediction, and incapacitation as a replacement of a system that is centered around the principle of proportionality, there is no way to avoid the mess created in the process of making sense of and working with proportionality.[7]

Acknowledgements The author thanks Larry Alexander, Vincent Chiao, Antje du Bois-Pedain, and Adam Kolber for very helpful comments.

Notes

1. Other ways of thinking about proportionality are possible. For instance, retributivism's traditional rival theory, utilitarianism, has its own version of proportionality, derived from the core idea, as stated by Jeremy Bentham, that "all punishment is mischief: all punishment in itself is evil," and that punishment should be allowed "as far as it promises to exclude some greater evil" (Bentham 1789). Built into the utilitarian perspective are various sources of upward and downward pressure on punishment, and such pressures could conceivably generate a schedule of punishments that resembles the one designed on the basis of retributivism. At the same time, the primary concern of the utilitarian theory is to minimize the social loss associated with criminal activities, and attaining the correct relationship between the gravity of crime and the harshness of punishment does not have the kind of special, overriding normative force that the principle of proportionality has in retributivism (Lee 2005). Therefore, I set aside the utilitarian notion of proportionality and focus on the retributivist understanding.
2. I borrow this example from David Miller (Miller 1999, p. 30).
3. Oregon is currently the only state that allows nonunanimous jury convictions (Vogt 2018).
4. *Peña-Rodriguez v. Colorado* did require a narrow exception, however, when it held that "where a juror makes a clear statement that indicates that he or she relied on racial stereotypes or animus to convict a criminal defendant," the Constitution requires breaching the rule of secrecy in jury deliberation for the purposes of potentially reconsidering the jury verdict (Peña-Rodriguez v. Colorado).
5. For a discussion of "coercion" and "threats" that is most conducive to this line of thinking, see Berman (2002).
6. For an interesting argument that challenges the sharp distinction presented here between desert-based sentencing and rehabilitation-based sentencing, see du Bois-Pedain (2017).
7. For a detailed, sustained focus on the principle of proportionality that has produced a set of influential and pragmatically sensible interventions in sentencing theory and policy, see von Hirsch (1985, 1993), and von Hirsch and Ashworth (2005).

References

Alleyne v. United States, 570 U.S. 99 (2013).
Apprendi v. New Jersey, 530 U.S. 466 (2000).
Bordenkircher v. Hayes, 434 U.S. 357 (1978).
Brady v. United States, 397 U.S. 742 (1970).
Graham v. Florida, 560 U.S. 48 (2010).
Harmelin v. Michigan, 501 U.S. 957 (1991).
Martinez v. Illinois, 572 U.S. 833 (2014).
Miller-El v. Dretke, 545 U.S. 231 (2015).
Missouri v. Frye, 566 U.S. 134 (2012).
Oregon v. Ice, 555 U.S. 160 (2009).
Peña-Rodriguez v. Colorado, 137 S. Ct. 855 (2017).

State v. Berger, 134 P.3d 378 (Ariz. 2006).

United States v. Bajakajian, 524 U.S. 321 (1998).

United States v. Booker, 543 U.S. 220 (2005).

United States v. Cruz-Rodríguez, 541 F.3d 19 (1st Cir. 2008).

Alexander, Michelle. 2010. *The new Jim Crow: Mass incarceration in the age of color-blindness.* New York: New Press.

Astor, Maggie. 2018. California voters remove Judge Aaron Persky, who gave a 6-month sentence for sexual assault. *New York Times.* June 6.

Barrish, Cris, and Jessica M. Reyes. 2015. Ex-Headmaster sentenced to 50 years for child porn. *USA Today*, April 24.

Bentham, Jeremy. 2007. *An introduction to the principles of morals and legislation.* Mineola: Dover. (Orig. pub. 1789.)

Berman, Mitchell N. 2002. The normative functions of coercion claims. *Legal Theory* 8: 45–89.

Carlson, Amber Rose. 2017. Is there a "rational" punishment for my rapist? *New York Times*, October 23.

Chiao, Vincent. 2017. Mass incarceration and the theory of punishment. *Criminal Law and Philosophy* 11: 431–452.

Del Real, Jose A. 2018. Activists try to recall judge in Stanford sex attack case. Some say they've gone too far. *New York Times.* February 2.

du Bois-Pedain, Antje. 2017. Punishment as an inclusionary practice: Sentencing in a liberal constitutional state. In *Criminal law and the authority of the state*, ed. Antje du Bois-Pedain, Mangnus Ulväng, and Petter Asp, 199–227. Oxford: Hart Publishing.

Duff, R.A. 2001. *Punishment, communication, and community.* New York: Oxford University Press.

Feinberg, Joel. 1970a. Justice and personal desert. In *Doing and deserving: Essays in the theory of responsibility*, 55–94. Princeton: Princeton University Press.

———. 1970b. The expressive function of punishment. In *Doing and deserving: Essays in the theory of responsibility*, 95–118. Princeton: Princeton University Press.

———. 1974. Noncomparative justice. *Philosophical Review* 83: 297–338.

Fletcher, George. 1978. *Rethinking criminal law.* Boston: Little Brown.

Gardner, John. 2007. Crime: In proportion and in perspective. In *Offences and defences: Selected essays in the philosophy of criminal law*, 213–238. Oxford: Oxford University Press.

Goode, Erica. 2011. Life sentence for child pornography spurs debate over severity. *New York Times*, November 4.

Greenhouse, Linda. 2007. Justices decline case on 200-year sentence for man who possessed child pornography. *New York Times*, February 27.

Jareborg, Nils. 1998. Why bulk discounts in multiple offence sentencing? In *Fundamentals of sentencing theory: Essays in honour of Andrew von Hirsch*, ed. Andrew Ashworth and Martin Wasik, 129–140. Oxford: Clarendon Press.

Lacey, Nicola. 1988. *State punishment: Political principles and community values.* London: Routledge.

Lee, Youngjae. 2005. The constitutional right against excessive punishment. *Virginia Law Review* 91: 677–745.

———. 2009. Recidivism as omission: A relational account. *Texas Law Review* 87: 571–622.

———. 2018. Multiple offenders and the question of desert. In *Sentencing multiple crimes*, ed. Jesper Ryberg, Julian V. Roberts, and Jan W. de Keijser, 113–136. Oxford: Oxford University Press.

Mayson, Sandra. 2018. Dangerous defendants. *Yale Law Journal* 127: 490–568.

Miller, David. 1999. *Principles of social justice*. Cambridge: Harvard University Press.

Nussbaum, Martha C. 2001. *Upheavals of thought: The intelligence of emotions*. Cambridge: Cambridge University Press.

Pfaff, John F. 2017. *Locked in: The true causes of mass incarceration and how to achieve real reform*. New York: Basic Books.

Reitz, Kevin. 2010. The illusion of proportionality: Desert and repeat offenders. In *Previous convictions at sentencing: Theoretical and applied perspectives*, ed. Julian V. Roberts and Andreas von Hirsch, 137–159. Oxford: Hart Publishing.

Ristroph, Alice. 1997. Desert, democracy, and sentencing reform. *Journal of Criminal Law and Criminology* 96: 1293–1352.

Roberts, Julian V. 2008. *Punishing persistent offenders: Exploring community and offender perspectives*. Oxford: Oxford University Press.

Roberts, Julian V., and Anthony N. Doob. 1990. News media influences on public views of sentencing. *Law and Human Behavior* 14: 451–468.

Simon, Stephanie. 1996. Three strikes advocates passionately defend law. *Los Angeles Times*, July 3.

Stack, Liam. 2016a. Light sentence for brock turner in Stanford rape case draws outrage. *New York Times*, June 6.

———. 2016b. Judge Aaron Persky under fire for sentencing in Stanford rape case. *New York Times*, June 7.

Strawson, Peter. 2003. Freedom and resentment. In *Free will*, ed. Gary Watson, 72–93. New York: Oxford University Press.

Stuntz, William J. 1996. Substance, process, and the civil-criminal line. *Journal of Contemporary Legal Issues* 7: 1–41.

———. 2001. The pathological politics of criminal law. *Michigan Law Review* 100: 505–600.

Sulzberger, A.G. 2010. Defiant judge takes on child pornography law. *New York Times*, May 22.

Tadros, Victor. 2011. *The ends of harm: The moral foundations of criminal law*. Oxford: Oxford University Press.

U.S. Sentencing Commission. 2018. U.S. sentencing guidelines manual. Section 4A, introductory cmt.

Vogt, R.J. 2018. Pressure grows on Oregon to end non-unanimous verdicts. *Law360*, November 18.

von Hirsch, Andrew. 1985. *Past or future crimes: Deservedness and dangerousness in the sentencing of criminals*. New Brunswick: Rutgers University Press.

———. 1993. *Censure and sanctions*. Oxford: Oxford University Press.

von Hirsch, Andrew, and Andrew Ashworth. 2005. *Proportionate sentencing: Exploring the principles*. Oxford: Oxford University Press.

Williams, Bernard. 1973. Morality and the emotions. In *Problems of the self: Philosophical papers 1956–1972*, 207–229. Cambridge: Cambridge University Press.

CHAPTER 24

The Subjectivist Critique of Proportionality

Adam J. Kolber

INTRODUCTION

In early America, lobster was so undesirable that it was regularly served to prison inmates. Eating lobster was such an indignity that rules were established preventing prisons from serving it more than once per week (Wallace 2004, p. 55). This bit of history reminds us that the harms of prison depend not only on objective facts about prison conditions but also on the varied ways inmates experience those conditions.

Today, many US prisons are overcrowded, dangerous, and lacking in proper mental and physical healthcare. To some inmates, these conditions are simply difficult and unpleasant; to others, they are agonizing and unbearable. As Jeremy Bentham recognized over 200 years ago: "[O]wing to the different manners and degrees in which persons under different circumstances are affected by the same exciting cause, a punishment which is the same in name will not always either really produce, or even so much as appear to others to produce, in two different persons the same degree of pain" (Bentham 1988, p. 182).[1]

In recent years, the observation that offenders vary in their experience of punishment and in their baseline unpunished conditions has served as the basis for a challenge to retributivism. Retributivism varies in its details but typically holds that we are justified in making wrongdoers suffer (or be punished) in proportion to their wrongdoing.[2] The subjectivist critique argues that, to the extent retributivists ignore variation in the experience of punishment and in offenders' baseline conditions, they will fail to justify punishment practices,

A. J. Kolber (✉)
Brooklyn Law School, Brooklyn, NY, USA

Center for Research in Crime and Justice, NYU School of Law, New York, NY, USA
e-mail: adam.kolber@brooklaw.edu

© The Author(s) 2019
L. Alexander, K. K. Ferzan (eds.), *The Palgrave Handbook of Applied Ethics and the Criminal Law*, https://doi.org/10.1007/978-3-030-22811-8_24

such as incarceration, that invariably inflict experiential harms and worsen offenders relative to their baselines. If, on the other hand, retributivists do attend to such variation at sentencing, they are led to rather counterintuitive results—for example, that the wealthy should generally spend less time in prison or have better conditions than the poor when they commit equally serious crimes.

Some retributivist critics directly challenge the view that offender suffering and deprivation are intrinsically valuable. The subjectivist critique, by contrast, assumes several key retributivist premises to show that they cannot justify punishment practices, such as incarceration, that are even loosely like those we actually use without also leading to conclusions that most will find unappealing. While there are many varieties of retributivism, the critique applies broadly to those forms that aim to justify common punishment practices, such as incarceration, and believe—as is typical—that it is forbidden to purposely, knowingly, or recklessly punish in excess of what offenders deserve.

THE SUBJECTIVE EXPERIENCE OF PUNISHMENT

Suppose that Sensitive and Insensitive are equally blameworthy offenders sentenced to equal time in prison under objectively identical prison conditions. Assume the two are alike in all pertinent respects except that they experience their conditions quite differently. Sensitive is wracked with sadness, anxiety, and insomnia, while Insensitive builds friendships, reads good books, and makes the best of his unpleasant but tolerable situation. The question is whether Sensitive and Insensitive are punished equally when they are incarcerated for the same period of time (Kolber 2009b, p. 183; Husak 1990).

Suffering Retributivism

Some say the dominant retributivist view is that wrongdoers deserve to *suffer* (Berman 2011, p. 438; Tadros 2011, p. 75). Call the view that wrongdoers deserve to suffer in proportion to their wrongdoing "suffering retributivism." Since we are assuming that Sensitive and Insensitive are alike in their wrongdoing, suffering retributivism seems to require that they be made to suffer the same amount. Because Sensitive and Insensitive do not suffer the same amount, they are not both suffering in proportion to their wrongdoing when they serve the same term under objectively identical conditions.

While most retributivists tolerate some underpunishment, few tolerate overpunishment.[3] Indeed, the vast majority accept a firm deontological prohibition on purposeful, knowing, or reckless overpunishment (Alexander and Ferzan 2009, pp. 6, 102 n.33). Call this "the overpunishment prohibition."

If we deliberately ignore the experiences of Sensitive and Insensitive, the state will often inflict suffering in violation of the overpunishment prohibition. If we punish Sensitive and Insensitive with prison terms that would be proportional for those of average sensitivities, we will punish Sensitive in excess of what is proportional. If Sensitive seeks to offer clear scientific evidence of his heightened sensitivity to a sentencing judge who refuses to consider it, the judge has knowingly overpunished (or overpunished with willful ignorance—a rough equivalent) in violation of a firm deontological prohibition. To avoid overpunishment in a system that ignores subjective experience, punishment levels would have to be extremely, perhaps implausibly, light in order to maintain a safe margin of error.[4]

Before considering some objections to these claims, note that retributivists could respond to the subjectivist critique by simply accepting it. In order to punish proportionally, they would have to make serious efforts—aided perhaps by emerging and future technologies[5]—to anticipate the experiences of those being punished and consider them at sentencing. They may also have ongoing duties to monitor the experience of prisoners in case their actual experiences deviate from what was anticipated. Just as we must correct a 16-month prison sentence that bureaucratic error turns into a 60-month sentence, retributivists must correct sentences where sensitivities lead to a sentence that significantly exceeds what proportionality requires. General findings of behavioral psychology may inform experientially sensitive sentencing as well. For example, the initial experience of going to prison is especially difficult, but distress tends to decline as inmates hedonically adapt (Kolber 2009b, p. 225; Bronsteen et al. 2009). If so, sentencing should reflect that severity of confinement is not a linear function of duration.

The Forewarned Is Forearmed Response

Those unpersuaded might argue that Sensitive should have foreseen his sensitivity before he committed his offense (Markel and Flanders 2010, pp. 961–62). While it's questionable whether we are good at predicting our own affective responses to punishment, were it true, one might argue, we needn't feel particularly sorry for Sensitive who should have avoided criminal behavior in light of his heightened sensitivity.

This response, however, fails to rescue proportionality; it merely sidesteps it. If being forewarned of one's punishment were sufficient to make it just, we could ignore all sorts of disproportionality. A statute could punish left-handed thieves with 20 years in prison and right-handed thieves with only 2 years (Kolber 2009b, p. 211). Since people know which side of their bodies is dominant prior to committing crimes and know the statutory punishments, we would be unable to criticize this sentencing arrangement on grounds of disproportionality. In fact, however, advance notice of one's future punishment may reduce the unfairness of disproportionality to some degree, but it does not substantially alter the disproportionality itself.

So the "forewarned is forearmed" response cannot alone fix the disproportionality of Sensitive's situation. If one thinks it unfair to give left-handed and right-handed thieves different punishments due to arbitrary facts about handedness, then one should think it unfair to give Sensitive and Insensitive different punishments based on their morally arbitrary sensitivities. So long as their sensitivities do not reflect different amounts of wrongdoing (as stipulated), then their sensitivities seem just as arbitrary as handedness from the perspective of suffering retributivism.

The Paris Hilton Problem

While retributivists could accept the force of the subjectivist critique and try to adjust punishment accordingly, doing so leads to some rather counterintuitive conclusions. Consider sensitivities resulting from great wealth: a person might be sensitive to punishment because he has so far lived a life of luxury filled with fine food, clothes, homes, and so on. Such people will likely suffer more intensely in prison than those who grew up in deprived circumstances.

When, for example, socialite-turned-celebrity Paris Hilton spends a day in jail, she likely suffers to a greater degree than an equally blameworthy counterpart with average sensitivities (Kolber 2009b, p. 191). To maintain proportionality, suffering retributivists must seemingly jail Hilton for a *shorter* time (or under *better* conditions) than the average person in order to punish her *equally*. Yet punishing Hilton for a shorter time strikes most people as quite the opposite of what justice requires. Most think we punish Hilton equally when she spends the same amount of time in jail as her counterpart, sensitivities be damned. Our intuitions about fair punishment are surprisingly inconsistent with the requirements of retributive proportionality.[6]

One might argue that Hilton, having substantial resources and better life alternatives, is more culpable than the average person who commits the same offense. Hilton herself was convicted of a probation violation stemming from an alcohol-related reckless driving incident (Waxman 2007, p. A1). Presumably, she could have paid for a car service far more easily than the average person and thereby avoided trouble in the first place.

Any heightened culpability she might have is supposed to be screened off in my example, however, as I stipulated that she and her counterpart are equally blameworthy. But suppose she and her counterpart commit crimes that are otherwise identical except for the fact that she was somewhat more culpable because she had resources to more easily avoid criminal behavior in the first place. Would her added culpability allow us to ignore variation in sensitivity?

It would not. Merely being rich is not itself culpable. As a general matter, we permit people to accumulate and spend their wealth so long as they do so legally. Even if there are general relationships between wealth, culpability, sensitivity, and quality of legal representation that subtly infect our intuitions in the Paris Hilton case, these variables do not have simple relationships with each other. Wealth may generally increase both offenders' culpability for bad acts and their sensitivity, but they won't increase at the same rate. It would be a tremendous coincidence if Paris Hilton's heightened culpability for her probation violation just happened to match her increased sensitivity such that she should always be punished for the same duration as others in order to suffer the same amount. Hilton might have an equally rich twin who is as culpable as she is when they commit the same offense, but they may still differ in their sensitivity and, hence, the amount they should be punished.

Sensitivity also varies by punishment modality. Rich people's sensitivities to fines, incarceration, and banishment vary. Hence, Hilton, her twin, and the average inmate are all likely to have different sensitivities across a range of punishment practices in ways that do not follow simple formulae. The claim that wealth increases culpability for some acts, even if it's a fair generalization, is not enough to eliminate the obligation to consider experiential differences.

It, therefore, seems we have to punish the Paris Hiltons of the world for a shorter time (or in better conditions) than average people of equal blameworthiness if we seek to follow a principle that makes suffering proportional to wrongdoing. Because this is such a hard pill for many to swallow, they might instead come to see the proportionality principle itself as in jeopardy.

Retributivists have traditionally challenged pure consequentialist theories on the ground that consequentialism violates deep-seated principles of proportionality. In scenarios, for example, where the town sheriff must choose to hang a person he knows to be innocent or else allow an angry mob to kill three innocents, consequentialists are sometimes thought to be embarrassed by the purported result that they would recommend execution. Retributivism is thought to avoid this result with a firm deontological prohibition on purposeful, knowing, or reckless punishment in excess of proportionality. If the merits of proportionality are in doubt, however, the battle between retributivists and consequentialists might shift somewhat in favor of consequentialism.[7]

The Problem of Inexpensive Tastes

When seeking to distribute limited resources such as food or life-saving organs, some have argued against consideration of purely subjective criteria (Scanlon 1975, p. 659). If, for example, you need a bottle of fine wine to experience the same pleasure I get from a glass of water, some say the state isn't obliged to splurge on wine in order to treat the two of us equally. We can focus instead on equality of resources (such as adequate hydration) rather than equality of welfare (Dworkin 1981, p. 186; but see Alexander and Schwarzschild 1986). We needn't, it is argued, consider "expensive tastes" when allocating scarce resources.

Even if the expensive tastes argument should inform the distribution of positive goods, it is not clear how, if at all, it bears on the distribution of negative goods such as punishment (Kolber 2009b, pp. 233–34 n.144). Importantly, it is much *less* expensive to make wealthy socialites suffer in prison than people like Insensitive. Wealthy socialites suffer more quickly and, hence, *inexpensively* than most. So the expensive tastes argument doesn't explain the common intuition that the Paris Hiltons of the world should be punished as long and in the same objective conditions as ordinary offenders.

Proportionality's Ceteris Paribus Clause

Doug Husak emphasizes that retributivist proportionality has a ceteris paribus ("all else being equal") clause. On his preferred formulation of the proportionality principle, "the severity of the punishment should be a function of the seriousness of the crime" but only ceteris paribus (Husak 2019). In real-world contexts, there will almost always be differences among offenders aside from the seriousness of their crimes. So a proportionality principle with a ceteris paribus clause will almost never provide real-world guidance.

Still, Husak makes use of the clause to argue that retributivists needn't apply the same objectively identical punishments to offenders with different sensitivities because if they have different sensitivities, all else is not equal (Husak 2019). Husak seems to be arguing that retributivism is internally consistent if it adopts what we might call the "capitulation strategy": accept that suffering retributivism requires us to take subjective experience into account at sentencing. Indeed, Husak seems to differ from many retributivists in his potential willingness to capitulate and make Sensitive and Insensitive suffer equally in subjective terms, even if that would mean treating them differently in objective terms.

Capitulation does indeed avoid inconsistency, but we needn't rely on a ceteris paribus clause to reach the conclusion that Sensitive and Insensitive can be punished differently in objective terms. As long as Sensitive and Insensitive suffer in amounts proportional to their wrongdoing, there is no disproportionality from the perspective of the subjectivist critique.

The bullet Husak has to bite, however, concerns the Paris Hilton–style examples. If he accepts the force of the subjectivist critique and holds that Hilton really should spend less time in jail (or have objectively better conditions) than her equally blameworthy counterparts, then he keeps suffering retributivism internally consistent. At the same time, he makes proportionality itself less appealing, as most people seem to firmly believe that Hilton should *not* be given a shorter sentence or better conditions. Arguments for proportional punishment rely heavily on our intuitions—no one has given a satisfactory account of how to translate amounts of wrongdoing into amounts of deserved punishment. To the extent we are already suspicious of the grounding of our proportionality intuitions, the Paris Hilton problem further weakens their foundation.[8]

THE JUSTIFICATION SYMMETRY PRINCIPLE

Some have treated the subjectivist critique as a battle of intuitions about punishment severity (Husak 2019; Simons 2009). For example, were we to punish a 100-pound ballet dancer and a 300-pound football player with a fixed 1500-calorie diet, most would agree that the football player suffers more and receives a more severe punishment (Kolber 2009b, p. 190). On the other hand, if two offenders receive ten-year prison sentences, there is arguably no substantial difference in the severity of their sentences if one sleeps eight hours per day while the other sleeps nine, even though one additional hour of suffering in prison per day adds up to quite a bit over the course of ten years (Gray 2010, pp. 1674–75).

The subjectivist critique, however, extends beyond a mere battle of intuitions. It is a fundamental challenge to the view that retributivism can morally *justify* punishment practices such as incarceration. When we incarcerate, we do all sorts of things to people that are ordinarily prohibited. Were you or I to lock someone up and forcibly separate him from friends and family for years at a time, we would have committed felony abduction—a serious moral transgression. For the state to take the same action in the name of punishment, it must have a moral justification.

A successful justification explains why some behavior is morally permissible without relying on the mere fact of state authority. Under the "justification symmetry principle," state actors must justify any harms to offenders in the name of punishment if you or I would need a justification for causing the same sort of harm to nonoffenders (Kolber 2012, pp. 3–4, 14–16). Because you and I must justify (or otherwise be held to account for) all or most of the non-trivial harms that we purposely, knowingly, recklessly, or negligently cause others, the justification symmetry principle requires the same of state actors. The principle is meant to guard against the possibility that we are surreptitiously allowing the state to act unjustly by holding it to a lower standard than we hold ordinary people.[9]

The serious experiential harms of incarceration are the sort that you or I would have to morally justify were we to inflict them on others. This basic point is reflected in tort law. Those who falsely imprison can be held liable for the emotional distress they thereby cause, and we don't merely count the number of days of wrongful imprisonment. Rather, we bring in actual psychologists or other experts to testify about the amount plaintiffs suffered. If tortious confinement by ordinary people causes emotional distress that requires justification, so too does confinement by the state.

Similarly, were I to somehow separate you from your friends and family and eliminate your sex life, I could again be called upon to justify the emotional harms I caused. If retributivists hope to justify punishment practices such as incarceration, they must justify the harms these practices regularly cause. *If retributivists ignore experiential harms, then they never justify causing such harms and therefore cannot justify the harms of incarceration.*

The Punishment-as-a-Deprivation-of-Liberty Response

Some have argued that, on a better view of retributivism, what wrongdoers deserve is not to suffer but to be deprived of liberty. According to Ken Simons, for example, "When the state imposes criminal sanctions, it deprives the offender of property or liberty" (Simons 2001, p. 243). If we can understand punishment solely as a deprivation of liberty, Sensitive and Insensitive are punished the same amount, one might argue, because they are both equally deprived of liberty when held in identical conditions for equal duration.

There are, however, several reasons why we cannot understand punishment solely as a deprivation of liberty. First, it seems contrary to the pluralistic way most would describe the harm of fines and incarceration (Kolber 2009b, p. 203). Sure, incarceration deprives people of liberty, but that's not all it does. It also causes distress, anxiety, feelings of claustrophobia, and so on.

Second, if punishment were merely a deprivation of liberty, it would seem that we could punish an offender without the offender knowing about it (Kolber 2009b, pp. 203–04). A person unknowingly convicted and subjected to home confinement but who happens not to even try to leave home during the pertinent period does not seem to be retributively punished, even though he was deprived of his liberty (Kolber 2009b, p. 204). The same is true of an inmate who falls into a coma right as his incarcerative sentence begins (Kolber 2009b, p. 204). Thus, there seems to at least be an awareness requirement for some treatment to be deemed punishment, and it's not clear why awareness matters if punishment is merely a deprivation of liberty.

Third, without attending to subjective experience, we cannot easily assess the severity of a liberty deprivation or even choose which liberties ought to be restricted (Kolber 2009b, pp. 204–05). A hypothetical inmate has a variety of liberties you do not have. He has rights to walk around inside his assigned cell, along with rights to prison food and healthcare. You, however, lack these liberties. In what sense, then, is the inmate punished but not you? Even if we concede that the inmate has less liberty than you, what seems most relevant here is not the amount of liberty but its value, and the value of particular liberties will vary by person. Depriving offenders of the right to attend the opera would be a serious punishment for some but an insignificant one for others. The amount of liberty at stake might be the same for both, but the severity of the punishment depends largely on its aversiveness.

More than all these reasons, however, the justification symmetry principle makes clear why the punishment-as-a-deprivation-of-liberty response is inadequate. Even if our punishment practices harm offenders by depriving them of their liberty, they inflict additional harms as well. We don't get to authoritatively characterize the harms we cause. Back to the tort of false imprisonment, we don't allow tortfeasors to authoritatively stipulate that all harms they cause are merely deprivations of liberty. Why? Because they aren't. Any sort of forced confinement will cause experiential harms that vary from person to person. And just as tortfeasors cannot authoritatively determine the harms they cause, the justification symmetry principle tells us that the state cannot do so either. No one can deny that incarceration causes emotional harms. Hence, no one can claim that a proposed justification of inmate liberty deprivation constitutes a full justification of the practice of incarceration.

The Punishment-Must-Be-Intentional Response

According to H.L.A. Hart, a "standard or central" feature of punishment is that it is "intentionally administered" (Hart 1968, pp. 4–5). If punishment must be inflicted intentionally, we can see the basis of another putative response to the subjectivist critique. As Dan Markel and Chad Flanders put it, "if the ancillary burden [an] inmate experiences during his imprisonment lacks authorization, then we cannot *equate* that burden with justified, authorized punishment" (Markel and Flanders 2010, p. 961). Similarly, Ken Simons writes, "[t]he state's responsibility is simply to ensure that the punishment that it directly inflicts is proportionate to desert," and Simons doesn't consider the foreseen distress of prison to be directly inflicted by the state (Simons 2009, p. 4). Assuming we intend to inflict the same deprivation of liberty on Sensitive and Insensitive, say four years of incarceration, then we arguably punish them the same amount because we *intend* the same thing for each.

We must begin, however, by distinguishing two very different ways in which people use the term "punishment." Sometimes they mean it in the way Hart does to describe an *action*. In such cases, punishment is frequently described as a kind of intentional act: "The parent punished the child." Other times, however, punishment is described as a kind of imposed condition in which harms needn't be intentional to count: "The offender was punished with four years' incarceration." While theorists focus on the former use, the latter is more relevant to the justification of our actual punishment practices for our intuitions about *amounts* of punishment pay little heed to the difference between intentional and merely foreseen inflictions:

> Consider two equally blameworthy offenders, Purp and Fore. They are alike in all pertinent respects and receive identical sentences in identical prisons. The only difference between them is that different aspects of their sentences are imposed intentionally. Purp is purposely limited in his liberty to move about, see family, have sex, express himself, possess personal property, vote, and so on. By contrast, Fore is purposely limited in moving about, but all of his other hardships are merely foreseen accoutrements of prison. Because these other hardships are not imposed purposely, they are technically not part of Fore's "punishment" as scholars frequently understand the term.
>
> Despite the different intentions that surround their treatment, we tend to think that Purp and Fore are punished by the same amount. The mental states of their punishers (be they judges, prison personnel, legislators, voters, or some combination of all of these) do not affect the severity of their sentences. So long as the duration of their sentences and the conditions of their confinement are the same, we think that they receive the same amount of punishment. Thus, when assessing amounts of punishment, we consider not only intentional hardships but also certain unintentional hardships as well. (Kolber 2012, p. 3)

Given that our assessments of punishment *severity* depend little on the difference between intentional and merely foreseen inflictions, justifying only intentional aspects of punishment covers only a fraction of what a full justification of incarceration must cover.

Consider, too, that when a pretrial detainee is held in detention awaiting trial, he will receive credit for time spent in detention on a day-for-day basis against any prison time he is sentenced to receive if convicted. This presents a puzzle for retributivists (Kolber 2013, pp. 1143–58; Walen 2014, § 4.4.3). Given that pretrial detainees haven't been convicted of a crime, they are not being made to deliberately suffer anything. Why then do we reduce *punishment* they deserve by time spent unpunished? One answer is that while pretrial detention may not satisfy the definition of punishment as an *action*, it is close enough to actual punishment as a kind of *imposed condition or state of harm*, even though it's not intentionally inflicted, that it can be treated as largely commensurate with punishment.[10]

The key point is that the subjectivist critique is not addressed to the question of whether retributivism can justify punishment narrowly defined as an intentional infliction but whether it can justify our *punishment practices* such as incarceration. Since those punishment practices undeniably implicate more than just intentional inflictions, efforts to justify only intentional inflictions will fail to justify common punishment practices such as incarceration.

As the justification symmetry principle makes clear, you and I must justify far more than the harms we intentionally inflict. Suppose we were to wrongfully imprison someone to prevent the person from voting. Claiming that our purpose was to restrict the liberty to vote but not to inflict suffering—despite knowing that such suffering would ensue—would not relieve us of moral or legal liability for causing that suffering. We would, for example, still have tort liability that takes actually experienced distress into consideration. Similarly, if the state ignores the distress it knowingly inflicts on Sensitive, then it cannot justify that distress.

The Retributivism-Is-a-Limited Justification Response

Some commentators have claimed that retributivism need only justify the intentional aspects of punishment while recognizing that there is more to be justified. For example, Mitch Berman claims that "retributivism is a localized theory of justice, not a comprehensive theory" and "does not claim or aspire to be a theory about what we should do taking all justice-relevant considerations into account" (Berman 2013, p. 104). David Gray has taken a similar position in response to the subjectivist critique, claiming that "no theory of criminal punishment is obliged to justify … the unintended suffering that may incidentally result from punishment," while simultaneously recognizing that "incidental suffering secondary to objectively justified punishment may raise independent moral, constitutional, legal, or institutional questions" (Gray 2010, pp. 1630 n.46, 1653).

Such concessions leave retributivism surprisingly anemic. If all that retributivism purports to do is justify intentional inflictions, then the justification of any punishment practice that involves more than intentional infliction—virtually all plausible punishment practices—is in jeopardy, and retributivism itself is powerless to fill in the justification. This would mean that retributivism cannot, even in principle, justify the *sentence* of a single inmate. While there is surely philosophical merit simply in examining the narrow retributivist claim that we are sometimes permitted to intentionally inflict harm on wrongdoers, this narrow claim, even if successful, is surprisingly far from justifying anything like real-world punishments.

Moreover, many retributivists seem to think retributivism is comprehensive enough to speak to real-world sentencing matters. For example, describing H.L.A. Hart's approach, Doug Husak writes that "the dominant tendency has been to consign the relevance of consequences to the general justifying aim of the institution of punishment" and such "considerations are thought to play no further role once questions of distribution are raised, to answer the questions of who should be punished and to what extent" (Husak 1992, pp. 452–53). If theorists investigate the *extent* to which offenders should be punished, it seems that they are trying to address matters of sentencing that could actually arise in the real world. Gray himself states that the "core challenge to any theory of criminal law" is "to justify punishment generally and to rationalize the punishments inflicted in particular cases more specifically" (Gray 2010, p. 1640). Though Husak and Gray refer to justifying "punishment," it's not clear how we can discuss "the extent" of punishment or the "punishments inflicted in particular cases" without addressing real-world sentencing.

The Doctrine-of-Double-Effect Response

Retributivists could supplement their justification of punishment with the doctrine of double effect ("DDE"). According to the DDE, some foreseen bad consequences can be justified by closely connected intentional good actions. The details of the doctrine vary but, in the standard formulation, the necessary conditions of justifying foreseen harms are that "(a) the intended final end must be good, (b) the intended means to it must be morally acceptable, (c) the foreseen bad upshot must *not* itself be willed …, and (d) the good end must be proportionate to the bad upshot (that is, must be important enough to justify the bad upshot)" (Quinn 1989, p. 334 n.3). Retributivists relying on the doctrine would hope to show that knowingly causing certain bad consequences, such as the side-effect harms of imprisonment, can be justified by the closely connected intentional good actions of giving offenders the punishment they deserve. These side-effect harms could be understood in terms of bad experiences, liberty deprivations, something else entirely, or a combination of these.

As a preliminary matter, not all accept the DDE. In the criminal justice system, we often treat intended acts as on a par with merely foreseen acts. For this reason, appeal to the DDE might even rub up against the justification symmetry principle. At a minimum, for retributivists who rely on the DDE, their total confidence that our punishment practices can be retributively justified is capped by their confidence in the DDE or their ability to find a suitable replacement (Kolber 2018).

But even if the DDE really does relax the burden of justifying the causation of certain foreseeable harms, there are further questions as to whether the doctrine is satisfied in the punishment context. Take the fourth requirement above that "the good end must be proportionate to the bad upshot." Here, we would ask, "Is the good of intentionally giving offenders what they deserve important enough to justify the side effect harms of our punishment practices?" Simply asking the question seems to vindicate at least part of the subjectivist critique: we cannot be confident that the importance of giving offenders what they deserve justifies the magnitude of side-effect harms (such as anxiety and distress) unless we at least roughly measure the magnitude of those side-effect harms.[11]

Moreover, there are reasons to doubt that the purported good of deserved incarceration is valuable enough to warrant its foreseen bad side effects. To see why, imagine, unrealistically of course, that we could disaggregate intentional and side-effect inflictions and that the only way to intentionally punish offenders is to foreseeably harm entirely unrelated innocent people. For example, in order to punish Smith, we must strip away *your* rights to access the Internet, choose the food you eat, and have sex. (These are just some plausible contenders for side-effect harms; the list can be added to or subtracted from in a variety of ways.) Most would say that giving Smith the punishment he deserves is not a good enough reason to justify imposing what should be *his* side-effect harms on *you*. Similarly, were a conjoined twin to commit a crime, say computer fraud, without the other's awareness, we could not justify imposing side-effect harms on the innocent twin without taking further steps to compensate him or otherwise make his treatment justifiable. If punishment of the offending twin were enough to justify the side-effect harms on the innocent twin, it would run contrary to the values underlying the Blackstone ratio which states that it is better that ten guilty people go free than that one innocent person be punished (Blackstone 1765, p. 358). These are values retributivists frequently seem to support.[12]

One reason to oppose inflicting side-effect harms on innocent people is that, unlike offenders themselves, the innocent do not *deserve* those side-effect harms. So it is tempting to say that we can inflict side-effect harms on offenders *themselves* because they deserve it. The problem with this response is that it neglects to consider offenders' "desert debt." If an offender deserves a three-year prison sentence, the suffering or punishment he endures during the course of the sentence presumably diminishes the bad things he still deserves. If his desert makes the intentional inflictions permissible, then he no longer has that bit of desert once the infliction occurs.

Similarly, it would seem, if retributivists justify side-effect harms based on desert, an offender would no longer have that bit of desert once the side effect is inflicted. In other words, just as intentional inflictions reduce offenders' remaining desert debt, suffering side-effect harms reduces desert debt as well. And that would mean we would have to release Sensitive from prison before Insensitive or confine him in objectively better conditions. This would be so even if we thought that offenders have somehow partially forfeited their rights to be free of side-effect harms (Markel and Flanders 2010, p. 964). We would still need to reduce desert debt to the extent the forfeiture was only partial.

There aren't many real-world contexts to test the intuition that side-effect harms reduce desert debt but the following is suggestive: suppose Biff and Marty both believe that, because Marty slept with Biff's lover, Biff deserves to punch Marty in the face. (Despite the machismo, assume this desert claim is true.) Just when Biff is about to punch Marty, Biff notices that his expensive, historically important vase is about to fall. Rushing to save it, Biff knowingly shoves Marty's head out of the way with force equivalent to what his punch would have been. Now suppose Biff *still* wants to punch Marty in the head because even though he made the quick calculation to shove Marty's head and realized that it would hurt Marty a lot, he didn't shove Marty with the *goal* of hurting him. Would we really think that Biff is still entitled to *intentionally* hit Marty? Isn't it enough that Biff got to apply force knowing it would hurt Marty, and he did in fact hurt him? Indeed, it seems a bit sadistic for Biff to insist that Marty still deserves a punch. If so, one would expect that foreseen inflictions and not just intentional inflictions reduce desert debt and that Sensitive would therefore be entitled to relief unavailable to Insensitive.

Notice that, even though I focus on relatively pure forms of retributivism, the vase example still speaks to retributivists who would justify the side-effect harms of punishment on consequentialist grounds. To see why, assume the shove was motivated and completely justified on consequentialist grounds without reference to desert. Nevertheless, even though desert played no role in the shove, an intentional punch after the shove still seems unwarranted. Similarly, even if the side-effect harms of our punishment practices are justified on consequentialist grounds, it seems we must still reduce offenders' desert debt based on those side effects. And that requires officials to measure the side-effect harms to prisoners so as to reduce the severity of intentional inflictions accordingly.

Our intuitions about divine justice may further support the obligation to reduce desert debt based on side-effect harms. Assume that due to Jebediah's misbehavior, his deity proclaims that he will strike Jebediah with lightning in the next two weeks. One week later, Jebediah is struck by lightning and yells to the heavens, "Okay, deity, you have exacted the justice you sought." "I'm afraid not," says Jebediah's deity in a commanding voice. "That was just an ordinary thunderstorm meant to water the fields. Sure, I knew that lightning bolt would hit you, but that wasn't my intent. I won't have my just deserts until the bolt strikes you intentionally." The deity's response might surprise us, even if we believe divine justice is merely hypothetical, for our ideals of justice treat foreseen inflictions as sufficiently close to intentional inflictions that they too can satisfy a desert debt. Both Biff and Jebediah's deity seem unnecessarily vindictive.

Finally, imagine a futuristic method of punishment. Rather than incarcerating offenders, we spray them with "gravitons" that limit their liberty of motion in various ways. Future retributivists have solved problems of proportionality and simply look up an offense's seriousness. If it has 100 units of seriousness, they set their guns to 100 gravitons so that the intentional infliction of punishment precisely matches offense seriousness. But there is a catch. Graviton guns fire 15 extra units 98% of the time. So setting the gun for 100 units will typically spray 115 units.

If the value of retribution is significantly high in some case, retributivists adopting the DDE seem committed to the view that you can set the gun to 100 and fire away, almost certainly leading an offender to receive 115 gravitons total. I think most of us would say that you have to set the gun to 85 units to achieve the ultimate 100 units. We must, in effect, reduce intentional inflictions based on foreseen inflictions, even though doing so falls short of the goal of intentionally inflicting 100 units of punishment.

If that's right, it seems retributivists have to shorten prison sentences in the real world to accommodate harms they knowingly inflict. The intentional portion of sentences must be titrated up or down to adjust for foreseen side effects. The graviton example simply makes this possibility easier to visualize. (One might quibble about what your intentions really are if you set the gun to 100 knowing that it fires in excess so frequently. Yet we sentence people to deprivations of liberty in prison knowing that they will suffer side-effect harms with probability greater than 98%. If graviton side effects are deemed intentional, then so are other similarly foreseen harms in prison.)

The ultimate question, then, for retributivists who refuse to capitulate to the subjectivist critique is the following: why don't you reduce desert debt for foreseen side-effect harms? Retributivists believe that intentional inflictions of harm can be justified by desert. Under DDE principles, foreseen inflictions are usually considered easier to justify than intentional inflictions. So *a fortiori*, one would expect, retributivists *could* justify foreseen inflictions with desert as well.

It would, of course, be awfully inconvenient to monitor side-effect harms in order to adjust desert debt accordingly. But if foreseen inflictions do reduce desert debt, deliberately ignoring them constitutes punishment in excess of desert in violation of the overpunishment prohibition. And it seems that retributivists must reduce desert debt to the extent they support the very common practice of giving credit for time served in pretrial detention. It would be odd to have a right to credit for time spent *unpunished* in pretrial detention yet have no right to credit for foreseen inflictions that occur while punished in prison.

Walen's DDE-Style Response

Alec Walen is one of few to directly address the obligations of retributivists under the justification symmetry principle. Using a variation of DDE-style reasoning, Walen concedes that unintended differences in suffering among prisoners require justification but believes "they can justifiably be caused if (a) the punishment that leads to them is itself deserved, (b) the importance of giving wrongdoers what they deserve is sufficiently high, and (c) the problems with eliminating the unintended differences in experienced suffering are too great to be overcome" (Walen 2014, § 4.3.3).[13]

Walen's first requirement, that the punishment itself be deserved, seems reasonable enough. If the intentional infliction of harm weren't deserved, the punishment practice would already be off-limits from a retributivist perspective. As to Walen's second requirement, he does not himself defend the claim that it is satisfied. I have already suggested that even if the importance of giving wrongdoers what they deserve is sufficiently high that we can impose side-effect harms, we would still need to reduce offenders' desert debt and that would be enough to require treating Sensitive and Insensitive quite differently than we do now. In any event, it is fair to expect retributivists to say more to demonstrate that the condition is satisfied, given that retributivists have said so little about it.

Walen's third condition for justifying side-effect harms is that "the problems with eliminating the unintended differences in experienced suffering are too great to be overcome." This condition is vague as we could surely overcome the problem of unintended differences by not punishing anyone at all. So there is an unstated value judgment here about just how hard it needs to be to take experiential differences into account before we are obligated to do so. Walen goes further, though, to claim that his third condition is arguably satisfied as to most variation in punishment experience:

> The reason is that individual tailoring has a number of problems that would be hard to overcome: (1) it invites gaming the system; (2) it would be perceived by some as unfair because those who claim to be extra sensitive would seem to be given undo leniency, and that would lead to resentment and extra conflict; (3) it would undermine predictability, and it would likely lead to abuse of power; and (4) with regard to those who are relatively insensitive to punishment, it would seem to call for brutality or torture that the state should not want to condone. (Walen 2014, § 4.3.3)

These proposed reasons raise several questions: why refuse to eliminate genuine unfairness simply because some would falsely *perceive* unfairness? While resentment and conflict are certainly bad, *unjustified* resentment and conflict do not seem to be concerns that retributivists would typically use to justify knowingly causing someone harm, especially not in criminal justice contexts. Furthermore, why should we care about undermining the predictability of sentences (presumably in terms of their duration) if duration is an inaccurate metric? Why would less predictable sentences lead to greater abuses of power than do sentences of arbitrary severity (due to a refusal to measure emotional harms)? Wouldn't the call to brutalize and torture insensitive inmates, if there really were one, be offset by the reduced brutalization of sensitive inmates?

Notice that the four reasons Walen offers to support the view that tailoring sentences is too difficult to overcome are heavily reliant on empirical considerations. For example, even if it's true that taking variation in subjective experience into account would incentivize inmates to appear to suffer more than they actually do, it's not clear how harmful this would be or how hard it would be to detect. So if Walen is right, the subjectivist critique could turn to a substantial degree on empirical matters, some of which may change as new technologies develop. Walen's response also has the notable feature among retributivist commentary that, if we had a reliable, cost-effective hedonimeter, Walen would seem to be committed to its use in incarcerative contexts.

I have raised doubts about the condition in both the DDE and Walen's version of it that the good of intentionally giving offenders what they deserve is high enough to permit concomitant side effects. Retributivists certainly need to say more to show that the condition is satisfied. Even if they succeed, they have the still harder job of explaining why they aren't required to reduce intentional inflictions because of known side effects as described in the falling vase example. If side effects reduce desert debt, then retributivists must accommodate sensitive offenders who experience more side-effect harms than average.

PUNISHMENTS ARE WORSENINGS

The subjectivist critique raises a further problem for retributive proportionality that applies even to those liberty-deprivation retributivists who reject the need to consider experiential harms. Namely, we tend to measure the severity of incarcerative punishments in a way that ignores the full harms of those punishments. As a result, liberty-deprivation retributivists must either measure harms correctly and generate results that don't strike people as proportional or continue to measure harm incorrectly and then fail to justify our punishment practices by ignoring the full measure of harms that need to be justified.

Justification Symmetry and the Measurement of Harm

The standard model of harm among both lawyers and philosophers treats harm as a kind of worsening (Feinberg 1992; *but* cf. Shiffrin 2012). To measure the harm of some event, we consider the harmed person's baseline condition and compare that to his condition after the event. The difference between these conditions reveals the magnitude of the harm.[14]

This approach is familiar to tort law. The owner of a wrecked car is harmed based on the value of owning the car before the collision relative to after. Whether we use market prices or subjective valuation, we still measure the harm as a worsening from a baseline to a harmed condition. If, for example, the car was already quite dented before a collision, the driver who negligently caused the incident will have caused less harm than otherwise because the car owner's baseline condition was worse than it would have been had the car still been pristine.

Implications of Measuring Punishment as a Worsening

As the justification symmetry principle reminds us, since you and I must justify the harms we cause as worsenings, so too must the state. Thus, the harms of imprisonment must be measured as worsenings from offenders' baseline conditions to their punished conditions. So even if liberty-deprivation retributivists can somehow avoid the obligation to consider subjective experience, they must still measure deprivations of liberty as worsenings: they must consider not only an offender's liberty while punished but must compare it to the offender's baseline liberty.

One might think the task easy. If all free people have the same liberty, then we can measure the magnitude of liberty deprivations by only measuring liberty deprivation in punished conditions. In fact, however, we vary in the amount of liberty we have. Detained immigrants and those quarantined with communicable diseases do not have the same liberties as everybody else. When they are incarcerated, they are *deprived* of liberty to a much lesser degree than average because they had less liberty to begin with. Similarly, many jurisdictions have juvenile curfew laws requiring teens to be out of public places during certain evening hours. Of course, teens under curfew are not deprived of as much liberty as, say, people under round-the-clock house arrest, but such teens still have less liberty in their baseline conditions than most of us. More generally, we all have different rights to real and personal property. A wealthy rancher in Marin County has more freedom of movement than a homeless person in San Francisco.

Retributivists might respond that prison deprives offenders relative to a generic baseline. We are all said to be equal under the law and the deprivation retributivists seek is relative to this generic baseline. Unfortunately, such a move is precluded by the justification symmetry principle (Kolber 2009a, pp. 1592–93, 2012, pp. 14–16). When you or I purposely, knowingly, recklessly, or negligently harm people by depriving them of their liberty, we measure the deprivation relative to actual liberties, not idealized liberties. I cannot, for example, trespass on a rancher's land and argue that I have not interfered with his property rights because we all have equal property rights under some abstract idealization. Because we quite appropriately punish offenders for interfering with victims' actual (rather than their hypothetical) rights, it would violate the justification symmetry principle to measure deprivations of liberty using some other system that only applies to criminal offenders.

Proportionality Is Measured Inconsistently

We readily treat fines as proportional worsenings. If a rich and poor person are each fined US$1000, they each worsen their total assets by the same objective increment, namely US$1000. It is not obvious why we treat these as equally severe when US$1000 may be an insignificant sum to the rich person and financially devastating to the poor person. But for those who insist on objective measures, note that we do measure fine severity as a kind of worsening.

Our intuitions of proportionality are inconsistent, however, because unlike fines, we do not treat incarceration as a proportional worsening. Consider a person in immigration detention or quarantine slated to remain in such circumstances for at least another year. Suppose the confined person commits a crime for which he is sentenced to one year in prison. If retributivists care about proportional deprivations of liberty, they would need to confine the detainee or the quarantined person under far more liberty-restricted conditions than they would an ordinary person in order to *equally deprive* him of liberty. This result does not correspond with most people's intuitions which likely say that we punish the detainee, the person in quarantine, and the typical inmate the *same* when they are given sentences of equal duration in identical prison conditions.[15] Hence, few truly have the intuition that punishment severity should be measured as a *deprivation* of liberty and that is likely why we do not in fact treat incarceration as a proportional deprivation of liberty.

We can now see how the Paris Hilton problem recurs even when experiences are ignored. The rich generally have more baseline liberty than the poor because they own more land and personal property. When a rich and a poor person are incarcerated in objectively identical situations for equal periods of time, the wealthy prisoner is generally deprived of more liberty than the poor prisoner. So wealthy inmates not only suffer more in subjective terms, even in objective terms they are deprived to a greater extent. Yet few have the intuition that wealthy prisoners should be released sooner than poor prisoners or held in better conditions. Though some theorists describe punishment as a deprivation of liberty, most would find treating incarceration as a proportional deprivation of liberty to be highly counterintuitive.

The even deeper problem for proportionality is that we use two different *methods* of measuring punishment severity based on the punishment modality. We treat fines as worsenings but incarceration as periods of time spent in bad conditions. There is no uniform approach to proportional punishment that applies to both. If one approach is correct, the other is not.

We can more clearly see the contrast between our approach to punishment severity in the fine and incarcerative contexts by imagining what it would look like if we imposed financial punishments the way we impose incarceration. Consider a hypothetical monetary punishment that is *not* measured as a worsening:

> We could punish offenders by setting their wealth to a particular level. People punished by "wealth-setting" would have the total value of their assets reset to a certain dollar amount, say $10,000, and then they could do with their money as they wish. The punishment would make no reference to an offender's assets before punishment. A billionaire who is wealth-set would end up with $10,000, as would a person of very modest means. Even stranger, a wealth-set person with no assets or with debt would have his wealth rise to $10,000. Clearly, [this] approach to punishment strikes us as bizarre. Many people would find it unfair to punish a billionaire, a person of modest means, and a debtor who are equally culpable by setting their assets to the same level.

If wealth-setting seems like an absurd, unjustified form of punishment, know that we do, in fact, punish people with something very much like wealth-setting. The reason is that wealth-setting is part of the punishment of incarceration. For the period of incarceration, we restrict prisoners' rights to use personal property to just the bare essentials. Prison officials wealth-set all inmates to more or less the poverty level for the duration of their sentences. Inmates sentenced to life imprisonment are permanently deprived of most of their baseline property rights. (Kolber 2009a, p. 1576)

The imagined punishment of wealth-setting helps illustrate the very different ways in which we measure the severity of fines (as worsenings) versus incarceration (as periods of time spent in particular conditions). So in addition to retributivists' failure to justify harms when they are not measured as worsenings, the subjectivist critique points out an inconsistency at the heart of proportionality: it can't be the case that our treatment of both fines and incarceration is proportional because we use fundamentally different methods of assessing their severity.

CONCLUSION

Some retributivists deny that they must justify the side effects of punishment because those side effects are not themselves punishment. Rather than get wrapped up in debates about the meaning of punishment, I find it more helpful to speak of the justification of punishment *practices*. Retributivists who purport to only address the intentional inflictions of punishment will have little to say about real-world punishment practices as they invariably include side-effect harms.

The subjectivist critique has two main components. The first charges that, by failing to consider the experiences of those being punished, retributivists either fail to punish proportionally or fail to justify the experiential harms they inflict. The second charges that, whether punishment severity is viewed in experiential terms or not, retributivists who neglect to consider offenders' baseline conditions either fail to punish proportionally or fail to justify the full measure of the harms they inflict. While retributivists might seek to offer some separate justification of side-effect harms, doing so would still require them to adjust sentences to reflect reductions in remaining desert debt as those side effects are imposed. At a minimum, retributivists should offer an explanation of why imposed side effects ought not reduce remaining desert debt.

Retributivists could accept the force of the subjectivist critique and adjust sentences accordingly. Doing so would lead to counterintuitive results however: Paris Hilton would need a shorter sentence or better conditions than an equally blameworthy average offender. Ordinary people would need shorter prison sentences or less restricted conditions than those who had been held in quarantine or immigration detention in order to be equally deprived of liberty. These examples suggest that, when we take experiences and baselines into account, proportionality may not be such an attractive notion after all.

The subjectivist critique gains further strength when seen in the light of related problems with retributivism. For example, how do experiential-suffering retributivists understand the punishment of offenders who benefit from prison? Recently-incarcerated actor Bill Cosby claimed to find prison to be an "amazing experience" (Levenson 2019), a reaction quite unlike the one attributed here to Paris Hilton. Assuming Cosby's reaction is genuine, is he being punished? Can one suffer in prison while finding it net beneficial, perhaps in some spiritual sense? If prison really makes a person better off overall, does it matter that he also undergoes superficial suffering? And if prison can be net beneficial, ought we to encourage that result or does it make prison entirely ineffective?

Other questions are raised for retributivist proportionality by the time frame challenge (Kolber 2019; Tadros 2011, pp. 68–73): should we consider what an offender deserves based only on the usually recent crimes for which he is currently being sentenced or consider what an offender deserves in light of his whole life so far? Focusing only on current crimes arbitrarily examines just a small part of what an offender morally deserves and could lead to punishments that leave offenders with *less* of what they deserve all things considered. By contrast, focusing on an offender's whole life is extremely impractical and could lead to "moral madness" (Ezorsky 1972, pp. xxii–xxvii). Suppose a person is falsely convicted of a crime but, upon release, commits the very crime of which he was falsely accused. Assuming his moral desert was properly aligned prior to the false conviction, under the whole life view, retributivists are prohibited from punishing him for the crime he actually committed.[16] Hence, retributivists cannot inflict proportional punishment without identifying the relevant time frame in which to assess desert; the two most obvious choices come with grave problems.

Our intuitions about proportionality are also quite manipulable. If you ask whether prisoners of different heights should have different-sized cells, many will likely say no. They have a duration fetish that focuses almost exclusively on how long an incarcerative sentence is. But if we define a punishment in an implicitly individualized way, we may get different results. Consider the hypothetical punishment of "boxing" (Kolber 2009b, p. 235) in which offenders are placed in prison cells that are n x n x n, where n is the offender's height. So framed, people are now more willing to deem the boxing of a seven-foot person and a five-foot person as equally severe because the very name of their punishments is the same, even though the taller person will have a cell that is objectively almost three times larger in volume. While boxing is a farfetched punishment, our reactions to it may explain why we tolerate punishments such as home confinement. Two instances of home confinement may share the same name while one restricts an offender to a studio apartment and the other to a sprawling, luxurious estate.

The problems with proportionality are amplified by the fact that no one has a good theory of how to convert serious wrongdoing into amounts of deserved punishment. Inmates might understandably question the fairness and transparency of long sentences grounded in no more than highly debatable intuitions. The familiar problems with proportionality are all the more trenchant when we pile on the proportionality puzzles raised by the subjectivist critique.[17]

NOTES

1. Immanuel Kant made related observations, noting for example that proportional punishment can be achieved "if regard is had to the special sensibilities of the higher classes" (Kant 1999, p. 139). Cesare Beccaria recognized but rejected concerns about variation in subjective experiences, writing that "the measure of punishment is not the sensitivity of the criminal, but the harm done to the public" (Beccaria 1995, pp. 51–52).

2. Not all retributivists make proportionality fundamental to retributivism. According to Mitch Berman, for example, the "core retributivist claim" is "that it is intrinsically valuable or right to furnish wrongdoers with the negative consequences that they deserve" (Berman 2016, p. 35). Proportionality, however, has undoubtedly played a central role in retributivism over the last several decades (Husak 2011, p. 414). Retributivism has little practical use without some measure of what wrongdoers deserve, and proposed answers invariably rely on some form of proportionality.

3. Consequentialists are not committed to proportionality in the way that retributivists typically are, and so the subjectivist critique does not apply to them. Indeed, many consequentialists would be quite receptive to the view that emotional harms are a cost of punishment and that *anticipated* subjective experience may affect optimal deterrence (Kolber 2009b, pp. 216–19; cf. Baer 2009).

4. Suppose, for example, that seven years' incarceration is a proportional sentence for rapists of average sensitivities, and suppose there are some rapists who could present evidence that they are ten times more sensitive than average. In order to punish all rapists without regard to their sensitivities, we couldn't punish *any of them* with more than about eight months' incarceration.

5. While we are a long way from having accurate hedonimeters, Stanford researchers are currently testing a wearable patch that measures levels of cortisol, a hormone that is a rough proxy for certain kinds of stress (Perry 2018). Future developments may give us more accurate and comprehensive information about subjective experience (Kolber 2011).

6. Two empirical studies have examined lay intuitions about the subjective experience of punishment. They both support experientially sensitive intuitions about monetary punishments but reach mixed conclusions as to non-monetary punishments (Montag and Sobek 2014; Montag and Tremewan Forthcoming).

7. Of course, as the number of innocent lives at risk increases enough, say 1000 innocents, threshold deontologists may permit the execution of the innocent despite the prohibition against it. The example in the text is meant to be insufficiently severe to trigger such thresholds as such thresholds are presumably only available in extreme rather than run-of-the-mill circumstances (Moore 1997, p. 719; Alexander 2000; Kolber 2018, pp. 530–31).

8. Alternatively, Husak could invoke the ceteris paribus clause to claim that it's okay for Hilton to suffer more than her equally blameworthy counterpart precisely because all is not equal. I don't think this is the path Husak would choose

as it would lead to violations of the overpunishment prohibition when judges seek to punish her proportionally without considering her sensitivity. It's also not clear how sensitivity can serve as grounds for implicating the ceteris paribus clause. It's one thing to deviate from proportionality when proportional punishment would be too expensive or impractical (Husak 1992), but here we are trying to understand what it means to treat Hilton proportionally even when we're not worried about real-world resource limitations.

9. The state may have obligations to justify conduct that ordinary people do not have. Therefore, satisfying the justification symmetry principle is necessary but may not be sufficient to justify a state punishment practice.

10. Another option is to cease giving credit for time served (Ferzan 2018, pp. 286–87), but many would find that counterintuitive.

11. Use of the DDE also raises questions about the relative rate at which desert and side-effect harms change as sentences are served. If an offender deserved ten years' incarceration as punishment but has already served five, have we already extracted more than, less than, or exactly half of the value of the desert we seek? If we could either give two offenders half of the equal amounts of punishment they deserve or one offender all of it, I suspect most would prefer to give two offenders half. That suggests that the value of desert is not a simple function of the duration of a sentence. Similar questions can be raised about how the magnitude of side-effect harms changes over time (Bronsteen et al. 2009). If desert and side-effect harms change at different rates, side-effect harms on particular inmates might be justified by the DDE during some parts of a sentence but not others.

12. Of course, we do regularly restrict the rights of inmates' friends and relatives to associate with inmates, even though these friends and relatives *deserve* no such harms. The DDE is insufficient to justify such practices as illustrated by the thought experiment in the text. We would not ordinarily think it permissible to dramatically limit *your* freedom to see *your* parents or children if doing so were necessary to give some third party his just deserts. There must be some other principle at play besides the DDE to adequately support the practice.

13. Walen doesn't make entirely clear, however, whether his test aims to justify: (1) unintended harms of punishment as required by the justification symmetry principle, (2) unintended differences in harm among offenders as a matter of equality, or (3) both.

14. Baseline conditions are generally taken to be either a person's condition before some pertinent event or his condition had the event not occurred. We needn't choose between these options for present purposes.

15. Indeed, it's not even clear whether laypeople require sentences of equal duration to be in *objectively similar conditions* in order to deem them equal. Consider how often news articles mention offenders' prison sentences and how rarely they address the severity of their likely conditions of confinement. Many seem to have a kind of "duration fetish" when it comes to incarceration where little but elapsed time seems to matter (Kolber 2013, p. 1159).

16. Larry Alexander and Kim Ferzan adopt a version of the whole life view (Alexander and Ferzan 2018, pp. 200–04). They respond to the get-out-of-jail-free card concern by noting that the person who stands to benefit would not be *morally permitted* to take advantage of the card and that trying to take advantage would itself be culpable. Still, they appear ready to tolerate the "moral madness" of allowing those with get-out-of-jail-free cards to commit crimes

without punishment where, for example, someone is erroneously convicted of a serious crime with a long sentence and then, upon release, commits a far less serious crime. Even if the second crime has additional culpability for trying to take advantage of the system, the offender's total culpability is likely dwarfed by the suffering he has already experienced during the time he was erroneously incarcerated.

17. For helpful comments on earlier drafts, I thank Larry Alexander, Doug Husak, John Oberdiek, Tom Parr, Patrick Tomlin, and Alec Walen. This project was generously supported by a summer research stipend from Brooklyn Law School and a visiting fellowship at NYU School of Law's Center for Research in Crime and Justice.

REFERENCES

Alexander, Larry. 2000. Deontology at the threshold. *San Diego Law Review* 37: 893–912.

Alexander, Larry, and Kimberly Kessler Ferzan. 2009. *Crime and culpability: A theory of criminal law.* Cambridge: Cambridge University Press.

———. 2018. *Reflections on crime and culpability: Problems and puzzles.* Cambridge: Cambridge University Press.

Alexander, Larry, and Maimon Schwarzschild. 1986. Liberalism, neutrality, and equality of welfare vs. equality of resources. *Philosophy & Public Affairs* 16: 85–110.

Baer, Miriam. 2009. Evaluating the consequences of calibrated sentencing: A response to Professor Kolber. *Columbia Law Review Sidebar* 109: 11–20.

Beccaria, Cesare. 1995. *On crimes and punishments and other writings,* ed. Richard Bellamy and trans. Richard Davies. New York: Cambridge University Press. (Orig. Pub. 1764).

Bentham, Jeremy. 1988. *The principles of morals and legislation.* Amherst: Prometheus Books. (Orig. Pub. 1789).

Berman, Mitchell N. 2011. Two kinds of retributivism. In *The philosophical foundations of criminal law,* ed. R.A. Duff and Stuart Green, 35–47. Oxford: Oxford University Press.

———. 2013. Rehabilitating retributivism. *Law and Philosophy* 32: 83–108.

———. 2016. Modest retributivism. In *Legal, moral, and metaphysical truths: The philosophy of Michael S. Moore,* ed. Kimberly Kessler Ferzan and Stephen J. Morse, 35–47. New York: Oxford University Press.

Blackstone, William. 1765. *Commentaries on the Laws of England.* Vol. 4, 1860. Philadelphia: Childs and Peterson.

Bronsteen, John, Christopher Buccafusco, and Jonathan Masur. 2009. Happiness and punishment. *University of Chicago Law Review* 76: 1037–1081.

Dworkin, Ronald. 1981. What is equality? Part 1: Equality of welfare. *Philosophy & Public Affairs* 10: 185–246.

Ezorsky, Gertrude. 1972. The ethics of punishment. In *Philosophical perspectives on punishment,* ed. Gertrude Ezorsky, xi–xxvii. Albany: State University of New York Press.

Feinberg, Joel. 1992. Wrongful life and the counterfactual element in harming. In *Freedom and fulfillment: Philosophical essays,* 3–36. Princeton: Princeton University Press.

Ferzan, Kimberly Kessler. 2018. Defense and desert: When reasons don't share. *San Diego Law Review* 55: 265–289.

Gray, David. 2010. Punishment as suffering. *Vanderbilt Law Review* 63: 1619–1693.

Hart, H.L.A. 1968. *Punishment and responsibility.* New York: Oxford University Press.

Husak, Douglas N. 1990. Already punished enough? *Philosophical Topics* 18: 79–99.

———. 1992. Why punish the deserving? *Noûs* 26: 447–464.

———. 2011. Retributivism, proportionality, and the challenge of the drug court movement. In *Retributivism has a past, has it a future?* ed. Michael Tonry, 214–233. New York: Oxford University Press.

———. 2019 Forthcoming. The metric of punishment severity. In *Of one-eyed and toothless miscreants: Making the punishment fit the crime?* ed. Michael Tonry. New York: Oxford University Press.

Kant, Immanuel. 1999. *Metaphysical elements of justice.* 2nd ed. Trans. John Ladd. Indianapolis: Hackett. (Orig. Pub. 1797).

Kolber, Adam J. 2009a. The comparative nature of punishment. *Boston University Law Review* 89: 1565–1609.

———. 2009b. The subjective experience of punishment. *Columbia Law Review* 109: 182–236.

———. 2011. The experiential future of the law. *Emory Law Journal* 60: 585–652.

———. 2012. Unintentional punishment. *Legal Theory* 18: 1–29.

———. 2013. Against proportional punishment. *Vanderbilt Law Review* 66: 1147–1158.

———. 2018. Punishment and moral risk. *Illinois Law Review* 2018: 487–532.

———. 2019 Forthcoming. The time frame challenge to retributivism. In *Of one-eyed and toothless miscreants: Making the punishment fit the crime?* ed. Michael Tonry. New York: Oxford University. Press.

Levenson, Eric. 2019. Bill Cosby's spokesman says the comedian thinks prison is an "amazing experience". CNN.com. https://www.cnn.com/2019/02/12/us/bill-cosby-prison/index.html. Accessed 23 Feb 2019.

Markel, Dan, and Chad Flanders. 2010. Bentham on stilts: The bare relevance of subjectivity to retributive justice. *California Law Review* 98: 907–988.

Montag, Josef, and Tomáš Sobek. 2014. Should Paris Hilton receive a lighter prison sentence because she's rich? An experimental study. *Kentucky Law Journal* 103 (2014): 95–125.

Montag, Josef, and James Tremewan. Forthcoming. Let the punishment fit the criminal: An experimental study. *Journal of Economic Behavior and Organization.*

Moore, Michael. 1997. *Placing blame: A general theory of criminal law.* New York: Oxford University Press.

Perry, Tekla S. 2018. New wearable sensor detects stress hormone in sweat. IEEE Spectrum.https://spectrum.ieee.org/view-from-the-valley/biomedical/diagnostics/new-wearable-sensor-detects-stress-hormone-in-sweat. Accessed 23 Feb 2018.

Quinn, Warren S. 1989. Actions, intentions, and consequences: The doctrine of double effect. *Philosophy and Public Affairs* 18: 334–351.

Scanlon, T.M. 1975. Preference and urgency. *Journal of Philosophy* 72: 655–669.

Shiffrin, Seana Valentine. 2012. Harm and its moral significance. *Legal Theory* 18: 357–398.

Simons, Kenneth W. 2001. On equality, bias crimes, and just deserts. *Journal of Criminal Law & Criminology* 91: 237–267.

————. 2009. Retributivists need not and should not endorse the subjectivist account of punishment. *Columbia Law Review Sidebar* 109: 1–10.

Tadros, Victor. 2011. *The ends of harm: The moral foundations of criminal law*. Oxford: Oxford University Press.

Walen, Alec. 2014. Retributive justice. Stanford Encyclopedia of Philosophy. https://plato.stanford.edu/entries/justice-retributive/. Accessed 23 Feb 2019.

Wallace, David Foster. 2004. Consider the lobster. *Gourmet*, August, pp. 50–64.

Waxman, Sharon. 2007. Celebrity justice cuts both ways for Paris Hilton. *New York Times*, June 9.

PART XXIII

Prostitution

CHAPTER 25

Prostitution

Michelle Madden Dempsey

Prostitution is controversial in terms of both what it is and what, if anything, the criminal law should do about it. Perhaps the criminal law should take no interest in prostitution. Perhaps it should play a role in enforcing fair labor laws for the regulation of "sex work." Perhaps it should prohibit prostitution or at least some conduct associated with prostitution, such as sex-buying and pimping. Much depends on what we mean by prostitution. All of which is to say normative disagreements regarding what to *do* about prostitution are closely intertwined with definitional controversies regarding what prostitution *is*. Thus, not only does the definition of prostitution determine, in part, what we should do about it, but so too do "our answer[s] to…normative questions… ultimately determine our answer to the definitional one" (Green 2016, p. 66).

This chapter examines ethical debates regarding prostitution and criminalization in three parts. Part one examines different ways of defining prostitution. Part two reviews five objections to prostitution that have framed standard debates regarding criminalization. Part three examines three relatively new issues that have arisen in ethical debates regarding prostitution and criminalization in recent decades.

WHAT IS PROSTITUTION?

One issue in defining prostitution concerns whether it is best understood as transactional or structural. Transactional definitions focus on particular events occurring at a precise place and time, disconnected from the broader social structures that inform the social and political meanings of those events.

M. M. Dempsey (✉)
Villanova University, Villanova, PA, USA
e-mail: dempsey@law.villanova.edu

L. Alexander, K. K. Ferzan (eds.), *The Palgrave Handbook of Applied Ethics and the Criminal Law*, https://doi.org/10.1007/978-3-030-22811-8_25

Structural definitions, conversely, focus on the social institutions in which people participate, emphasizing the structural features that shape participants' relative social statuses and inform the meaning and quality of their interactions. So, while a transactional definition would focus on prostitution as a commercial sex act (trading sex for money), a structural definition would focus on prostitution as a social institution (the commercial sex industry).

Viewed as a transaction, we might take a first pass at defining prostitution as follows: *prostitution is the performance of sexual act(s) in exchange for valuable consideration, typically money or drugs.* This transactional definition focuses on the person who performs the sexual act(s) and receives valuable consideration—that is, the "prostitute," "sex worker," "sex-seller," or "prostituted-person."[1]

One problem with a seller-focused transactional definition of prostitution is that it tends to obscure the role of the person who provides the "valuable consideration" in exchange for sex—the "trick," "John," "punter," or "sex-buyer." Further, it ignores the possibility that a third party is involved in the transaction by selling the prostituted-person—that is, a "pimp," "trafficker," "madam," "manager," and so on. Indeed, where a pimp *is* involved in the transaction, it may be more illuminating to think of the *pimp* as the one who is *selling* and the prostituted-person as the one who is *sold* (MacKinnon 1993, pp. 275–291).

Perhaps, then, it is better to adopt a broader transactional definition: *prostitution is the exchange of sexual act(s) for valuable consideration (typically money or drugs).* One advantage to this definition is that it allows us to conceive of both the sex-seller and sex-buyer as jointly involved in the act of prostitution.[2] Yet even this broader transactional definition of prostitution limits our focus to specific instances of commercial sex exchanges and thus risks obscuring the broader contexts in which these exchanges occur. To avoid this limitation, we might do better to define prostitution structurally.

Structural definitions have the advantage of illuminating and critiquing the inequalities that inform the meaning and practice of prostitution as an institution. Such definitions emphasize the sense in which prostitution "is an inherently unequal practice defined by the intersection of capitalism and patriarchy" (Overall 1992, p. 724). According to structural definitions, prostitution is a form of violence against women (Raymond 1998), which is grounded in men's historical dominance over women and remains both a symptom and a cause of women's continued subordination and economic disadvantage. As such, rather than treating sellers and buyers as ungendered and abstracted from social context, structural definitions take on board and provide an explanation for the fact that, while not all people selling sex are women and not all people buying sex are men, the vast majority of prostitution does follow this gendered pattern (Coy 2016). Evoking a similar theme, Vednita Carter and Evelina Giobbe define prostitution in terms of its "function [as an] institution…[that] allow(s) males unconditional sexual access to females, limited solely by their ability to pay for this privilege…[which is maintained through] economic marginalization, child sexual abuse, rape and battery, as well as racism, classism and heterosexism" (Carter and Giobbe 1999, p. 43).

As these quotes illustrate, structural definitions of prostitution are not designed to clarify the precise actions and mental states that count as a "prostitution act," and thus, they are not well suited to distinguishing marginal cases of prostitution from cases that do not count as prostitution. Rather, structural definitions are designed to critique and illuminate a central case of prostitution, as practiced in a given social context, within the particular social structures that create and sustain prostitution as an institution in that society.[3] While structural definitions of prostitution focus, paradigmatically, on social structures that create and sustain the subordination and economic marginalization of women, especially women of color, relative to more privileged men, the structural definition does not preclude recognition that men sometimes sell sex (albeit most often to male sex-buyers) and women sometimes buy sex.[4]

Criminal statutes are often vague when it comes to defining prostitution, preferring euphemism to clarity. Consider, for example, Pennsylvania's prostitution offense, which defines the prohibited conduct with the unhelpfully redundant phrase, "A person is guilty of prostitution if he or she…is an inmate of a house of prostitution" (18 Pa.C.S.A. § 5902(a)).[5] More clarifying statutes emphasize either the conduct of the sex-seller/prostituted-person—"The performance of…vaginal intercourse…or any sexual contact…for the purpose of sexual arousal or gratification for any money or other consideration" (N.C. Gen. Stat. Ann. § 14-203)—or focus on the conduct of both the seller and buyer: "Prostitution means hiring, offering to hire, or agreeing to hire another individual to engage in sexual penetration or sexual contact, or being hired, offering to be hired, or agreeing to be hired by another individual to engage in sexual penetration or sexual contact" (Minn. Stat. Ann. § 609.321(9)).

It is noteworthy, but not surprising, that criminal statutes adopt a transactional approach to defining prostitution. As Deborah Tuerkheimer has observed, criminal law is "characterized by a narrow temporal lens" (Tuerkheimer 2004, p. 971).[6] "Paradigmatic crimes [such as murder, rape, robbery, and battery] are 'transaction-bound…conceived as occurring at a discrete moment…taking place in an instant of time so precise that it can be associated with a particular mental state or intention'" (ibid., p. 972, citing Lynch 1987). Broader structural considerations that inform the meaning and quality of the phenomena are thereby obscured, in favor of a focus on "demonstrating what happened, in the physical world and in the defendant's consciousness, during the particular transaction under examination" (Lynch 1987, p. 945). As such, adopting "a transactional model of crime…isolates and decontextualizes [prostitution], and conceals the reality" of structural inequalities that create and sustain prostitution as an institution (Tuerkheimer 2004, p. 972).

While a transactional definition may obscure the meaning and quality of prostitution as it relates to structural inequalities in society more generally, it is nonetheless understandable that a liberal criminal legal system would define prostitution-related offenses in terms of precise transactions rather than broader social structures. After all, one important limitation on a liberal criminal legal system is respect for the rule of law's requirement that criminal offenses be clearly defined, such that the law's subjects can guide their conduct to avoid running afoul of the law's dictates (Fuller 1964). Transactional definitions of crimes clearly serve such rule of law values better than structural definitions do. When it comes to prostitution, for example, one can more clearly understand a prohibition on "exchanging sexual acts for valuable consideration" and thus avoid doing so,[7] whereas a prohibition on prostitution defined structurally would provide rather less guidance to law's subjects, leaving the precise scope of prohibited conduct unclear and thus running afoul of the rule of law.

One implication that might follow from these rule of law considerations can be framed as follows: a liberal criminal legal system is designed to target particular instances of wrongdoing, not wrongful societal structures in general— so, even if there *is* a lot wrong with prostitution (understood structurally), it may simply be the case that a liberal criminal legal system is not in a position to address those kinds of wrongs. Below, I push back on this idea and suggest instead that a liberal criminal legal system *can* both target particular instances of wrongdoing and address wrongful societal structures, without sacrificing rule of law values. But first, let us outline the basic definition of prostitution that informs our discussion.

In what follows, we take the criminal law's lead and adopt a transactional definition of prostitution (albeit, a broad rather than a narrow one). Thus, we ask what, if anything, the criminal law should do about prostitution, understood as *the exchange of sexual act(s) for valuable consideration (typically money or drugs)*. In adopting this definition, we limit our inquiry to transactions between buyers and sellers with no pre-existing relationship (e.g., not romantic partners).[8] We also exclude a host of marginal cases regarding what counts as "valuable consideration," such as exchanges in which sex is traded for a promotion at work, a role in a film, a piece of jewelry, and so on. Finally, we focus on sexual acts involving vaginal, anal, or oral penetration, thereby excluding marginal cases involving stripping, lap dancing, spanking, foot-licking, "water play," and so on. (For an illuminating analysis of marginal cases, see Green 2016.)

Importantly, this transactional definition of prostitution does not speak to whether the commercial sex act is consensual, freely chosen, and so on. Thus, it leaves open the possibility that some prostitution transactions are consensual, freely chosen, and even desired by the sex-seller and thus not every prostitution transaction is necessarily harmful/wrongful to the sex-seller/prostituted-person. The point here is not that sex-sellers may sometimes merely *perceive* themselves to be freely choosing, due to a "false consciousness" from which they may eventually awaken.[9] Rather, this transactional definition of prostitution allows for the possibility that some acts of prostitution are consistent with the sex-seller's genuine (non-adaptive) preferences, which reflect a sense of self-worth/entitlement and motivate choices that are properly considered autonomous.[10] As such, in those cases, if prostitution is to be prohibited under a liberal criminal legal system, the justification for doing so cannot be found in any claim that the sex-sellers in those cases are harmed/wronged by the commercial sexual transactions.[11]

With this definition of prostitution in mind, the next section surveys arguments that have framed the ethical debates regarding the criminalization of prostitution until recent decades.

Ethical Debates Regarding the Criminalization of Prostitution: A Brief Retrospective

The criminalization of prostitution became a hot topic in applied ethics following the publication of the UK's Report of the Committee on Homosexual Offences and Prostitution (Wolfenden Report 1957). The brief of the Wolfenden Committee was, in part, to address whether prostitution should be criminalized and, if so, how.[12] As public attitudes toward sex increasingly liberalized during the 1960s, academic and political debate about prostitution flourished in the decades that followed.

Until the late 1980s and early 1990s, debates regarding the criminalization of prostitution typically failed to disaggregate the position of the sex-seller from the sex-buyer. Arguments in favor of criminalizing prostitution were largely assumed to include the criminalization of anyone engaged in prostitution-related activities, although, in practice, criminal law enforcement remained vastly disproportionate, targeting women selling sex, rather than men buying it (Snyder 2012).

This section briefly surveys the main arguments offered during the several decades following the Wolfenden Report, focusing on arguments offered in favor of criminalizing prostitution and responses thereto. While many of these arguments still hold sway in debates regarding prostitution and criminalization, there is now decidedly more agreement regarding the decriminalization of people who sell sex/prostituted-people (Dempsey 2015).

Prostitution Is "Immoral"

One influential and long-standing objection to prostitution is the claim that it is "immoral" (Chesser 1958; Devlin 1959). I place "immoral" in scare quotes here, because in the course of these debates, the term was used simply to refer to social norms that were endorsed by conservative religious teachings or accepted by some significant (and socially powerful) members of society.[13] The argument, as stated most prominently by Lord Devlin (1959), was grounded in concern that a lack of shared social morality would result in societal disintegration.[14] Prominent scholars such as H.L.A. Hart (1963) argued forcefully against the "moral populism" of this view and defended a liberal view of criminal law, according to which it is impermissible to criminalize conduct simply because community standards deem it "immoral."[15] As sexual norms continued to liberalize in the decades that followed, the argument from "immorality" came to hold considerably less sway in debates regarding the criminalization of prostitution. While some modern scholars continue to base objections to prostitution on similar grounds (George 1993), as a matter of legal doctrine (at least in the US), the argument from "immorality" has rather less force than in previous decades (Goldberg 2003).

Prostitution Creates a Nuisance

Another objection to prostitution is that it creates a public nuisance. Indeed, as the Wolfenden Committee remarked, "there is no doubt that the aspect of prostitution which causes the greatest public concern...is the visible and obvious presence of prostitutes in considerable numbers in the public streets..." (Wolfenden 1957, p. 81).[16] While there was and is widespread agreement that street prostitution is perceived as a nuisance (Hubbard 1998), and that street prostitution presents heightened dangers for prostituted-people (Hester and Westmarland 2004), there is little agreement about how to address street prostitution. Should prostitution be legalized and regulated with brothels to reduce street prostitution? Or, as Catherine Benson and Roger Matthews (1995, p. 396) argue, is it the case that "the only parties who actually benefit from these commercialized and exploitative arrangements are the clients and the owners"? Will criminalization "keep the lid" on the problems associated with street prostitution, or as Teela Sanders (2004, pp. 1703–1713) argues, is "street prostitution...made increasingly dangerous for women through punitive policing policies"? The outcome of these debates depends heavily on empirical evidence regarding how prostitution laws and policies will impact street-level prostitution. Thus, debates regarding street prostitution-as-nuisance are indivisible from broader debates regarding the criminalization of prostitution generally.

Prostitution Objectifies and Commodifies the Prostituted-Person

Two closely related arguments in favor of criminalizing prostitution concern ethical issues regarding objectification and commodification of human beings. The objectification argument claims that prostitution does not merely involve the provision of sexual services by the prostituted-person but involves the prostituted-person being used as a sexual object (Anderson 1995). Relatedly, the commodification argument claims that the human being (now reduced to an object) is bought and sold in the prostitution exchange (Pateman 1988; Radin 1996).

This argument bears its greatest force in cases of pimp-controlled prostitution, where prostituted-people do not have a free choice regarding whether, when, with whom, and under what conditions they will be used in any given commercial sex transaction. At its core, however, the argument can apply to any prostitution transaction, even without a pimp. As Carole Pateman puts it:

> When a man enters into the prostitution contract he is not interested in sexually indifferent, disembodied services; he contracts to buy sexual use of a *woman* for

a given period…[thus] when a prostitute contracts out use of her body she is thus selling *herself* in a very real sense. Women's selves are involved in prostitution in a different manner from the involvement of the self in other occupations. (Pateman 1988, pp. 206–208)

Can these considerations justify criminal prohibitions on prostitution that do not involve pimp-involved or pimp-controlled prostitution?[17] At first glance, it seems that the argument bears little to no force when it comes to criminalizing the prostituted-person—since, after all, she is the one being objectified and commodified, rather than a culpable party.[18] Moreover, as Martha Nussbaum (1998) forcefully argued, there is an important sense in which many jobs and professions involve treating one's body as an object and commodifying the use of one's body in commercial exchanges. While arguments from objectification and commodification were once a primary focus in debates regarding the criminalization of prostitution, more recent scholarship tends either to avoid drawing on these arguments (Dempsey 2010, p. 1735, n. 13) or takes a decidedly more positive view of commodification (Lucas 2005).

Prostitution Contributes to the Subordination of Women Generally

Another objection to prostitution is grounded in the claim that it contributes to the subordination of women generally. As Laurie Shrage framed the argument, "[t]olerance for commercially available sex, legal or not, implies general acceptance of principles which perpetuate women's social subordination" (Shrage 1989, p. 356).[19] In response, Igor Primoratz argued that Shrage exaggerated the grip of patriarchal norms in shaping the political and social meaning of prostitution at the time (late 1980s–early 1990s) (Primoratz 1993). Rather than supposing prostitution has a singular political and social meaning which perpetuates women's social subordination, Primoratz claimed that "the beliefs and values of the individuals" engaging in any particular commercial sexual transaction should determine its political and social meaning. "Accordingly," he observed, "there are in our society two rather different conceptions of prostitution…(a) prostitution as commercial *screwing*, and (b) prostitution as commercial sex *simpliciter*" (Primoratz 1993, p. 181). An objection to the former, he argued, does not ground any objection to the latter.[20]

The debate between Shrage and Primoratz illustrates the significance of empirical evidence to debates regarding prostitution and criminalization. What is prostitution like in a given society at a particular point in time? Is it a practice that perpetuates women's social subordination, or is it simply a matter of "commercial sex simpliciter," unrelated to the maintenance and reinforcement of patriarchal norms? For Primoratz, "the practice of prostitution in our society is a question for empirical research" (Primoratz 1993, p. 181). Yet, as discussed later, empirical research is itself influenced by the frameworks researchers employ in conceptualizing the object of inquiry, how they operationalize the relevant concepts, and how they interpret their data. One might easily imagine empirical studies that would provide contradictory evidence regarding what prostitution is like in a given society at a particular point in time. An empirical researcher who shared Primoratz's basic view of the waning influence of patriarchal norms in shaping the political and social meaning of prostitution might easily conclude that the vast majority of prostitution is "commercial sex *simpliciter*"—while another researcher might come to quite the opposite conclusion.[21]

Primoratz's argument seems naïvely optimistic insofar as it rests on the assumption that women's subordination is a thing of the past or, at least, well on its way out the door. As the #MeToo movement continues to shine a light on the impact of male entitlement to sexually harass and assault women, many people report being "shocked" by the extent to which patriarchal norms continue to shape our society and perpetuate women's subordination at work, at home, in politics, in education, in sport, in the arts...everywhere. As Jessica Bennett observed, "the #MeToo moment has become something larger: a lens through which we view the world, a sense of blinders being taken off" (Bennett 2017).

So, too, when it comes to empirical research regarding prostitution, the lens through which we view the world will shape and limit our ability to understand what prostitution is like at any particular time in a given society. If Shrage is correct to suppose that, "ultimately...nothing closely resembling prostitution, as we currently know it, will exist, once we have undermined [patriarchal] cultural convictions" (Shrage 1989, p. 348), then we must ask the further question, how will we know when we've gotten there? Have we *already* undermined patriarchy so much so that any objection to prostitution on feminist grounds demonstrates that the objector misunderstands what prostitution is like in that society? Or are we still in the grip of patriarchal norms, such that anyone who claims to think a substantial amount of prostitution is merely "commercial sex *simpliciter*" is not only blind to women's subordination but fails to understand the way in which it informs the political and social meaning of prostitution?[22]

Prostitution Harms Prostituted-Women

A final objection to prostitution concerns the extent to which prostituted-women are harmed by their participation in the commercial sex industry. There is widespread agreement that prostitution is, indeed, harmful to many people who sell sex, with many experiencing assault and battery, rape, post-traumatic stress, sexually transmitted disease, and facing an estimated 15–20 times greater likelihood of being killed than non-prostituted-women (Matthews and O'Neill 2002; Matthews 2008, 2015, p. 86; Farley 1998; Farley 2003; Farley and Barkan 1998; Farley et al. 2004, 2005; Herman 2003; Vanwesenbeeck 2001; but see Moen 2012; Westin 2014). Yet, there is widespread disagreement as to the significance of these harms. While many of the harms suffered by prostituted-people are not consensual (e.g., battery, rape), many of the harms are simply considered "part of the job."[23] If engaging in "sex work" is consensual, then these "employment-related" harms are not regarded as wrongful. For, if one consents to engage in an activity, so the argument goes, then the harms they experience do not constitute wrongs against them (Feinberg 1984, pp. 115–117; Hurd 1996, 2018). Just as a football player might suffer a concussion, or a factory worker might be exposed to dangerous chemicals, these harms have not (until recently) been regarded so much as wrongs committed against the athlete or factory worker but rather as workplace injuries that are best avoided through harm-reduction strategies.

The best way to reduce harms associated with prostitution, according to this argument, is to conceive of prostitution as "sex work"—to ensure employee benefits, establish and protect collective labor unionized bargaining rights, adopt and enforce occupational health and safety standards, recognize breach of contract claims, and provide anti-discrimination protections—such that prostitution would be treated just like "any other labor" (Law 2000; Bindman and Doezema 1997).[24] If prostitution were recognized and regulated as work, so the argument goes, it would not only remedy the harms that are just "part of the job" but would also reduce criminal victimization of prostituted-people, since the recognition of prostitution as "sex work" would reduce stigma and increase the social status of those who sell sex.[25]

In response to these optimistic arguments, scholars have argued that prostitution cannot be so easily analogized to other labor contexts, since "professional sex is not like 'most' work" (Davis 2015, p. 1250). Factors such as "the culture of alcohol, drinking, and drugs" in which the prostituted-person is not only "working" with "clients" who are often intoxicated, but is expected and often required to consume alcohol herself, distinguish "professional sex" in a manner otherwise inconceivable in most other work contexts (ibid., p. 1245).[26] Further, unlike most work contexts, there is frequently a "blurred line between legitimate re-negotiations and criminal assaults" (ibid.), thus complicating any enforcement of sexual harassment employment anti-discrimination law. When it comes to risks posed by sex-buyers, the proximity required for the performance of sex acts and the isolation of the sex-seller and sex-buyer during the commercial sexual transaction present barriers to effective surveillance and security, since the worker is effectively "isolated from other stakeholders who might provide formal or informal security" (Davis 2015, p. 1255). Finally, when it comes to protection from sexually transmitted disease, the inability to quickly and effectively screen potential sex-buyers frustrates the ability to manage the health risks faced by sex-sellers.

CONTEMPORARY ETHICAL DEBATES REGARDING
THE CRIMINALIZATION OF PROSTITUTION

While none of the arguments surveyed above have entirely faded from view in current debates regarding the criminalization of prostitution, there has been a notable change in strategy and discourse since the mid-to-late 1990s. This section examines the three primary issues which have resulted in a rather seismic shift in debates regarding prostitution and criminalization: (1) the emergence of the Nordic model; (2) the resurgence of "sex trafficking" as a primary focus of prostitution policy; and (3) the entrenchment of conflicting empirical research.

These shifts did not arise suddenly. While the account set out below starts in the late 1990s, the fault lines were in place by the mid-1980s. At the time, the US activist group, Call Off Your Old Tired Ethics (COYOTE), founded in 1973, had been campaigning against the sort of prudish, conservative moralism that informed some of the arguments in favor of criminalizing prostitution.[27] For more than a decade, COYOTE's call for general decriminalization of prostitution (buying, selling, and pimping) was the dominant voice challenging pro-criminalization arguments. It is noteworthy, and indicative of COYOTE's savvy advocacy, that the group named itself in direct opposition to the weakest thread of pro-criminalization arguments: the one which claimed that prostitution should be criminalized because it is considered "immoral" according to conservative social norms. By positioning itself as the chief opponent to the argument from "immorality," COYOTE gained influence in liberal circles, such that the very notion of a liberal approach to sex was seen by many to imply support for prostitution (Bindel 2017, pp. 38–39; Giobbe 1990; Leidholdt and Raymond 1989).

In the late 1980s, however, two radical feminist organizations that viewed prostitution as symptomatic and constitutive of women's social subordination were founded. The first, Women Hurt in Systems of Prostitution Engage in Revolt (WHISPER), was a US organization founded by Evelina Giobbe, a prostitution survivor, in 1985 (Bindel 2017, p. 7). The second, Coalition Against Trafficking in Women (CATW), founded in 1988, was the first international organization to oppose prostitution through the lens of sex trafficking (CATW 2018). These organizations provided the foundation for a genre of anti-prostitution advocacy that has come to be known as "feminist abolitionism"—an approach that seeks to abolish the commercial sex industry generally, as part of a larger set of feminist commitments and goals. As discussed further below, the emergence of feminist abolitionist advocacy around the world has resulted in significant shifts in the strategies and discourse informing these debates.

The Emergence of the Nordic Model

The Nordic model, in its ideal form, is an approach to prostitution that rests on three pillars: (1) implementing social welfare policies that provide people with an adequate range of valuable options for living lives that are conducive to human flourishing, such that no one's choice to sell sex is due to a lack of adequate alternatives; (2) educating people in society regarding the harms of the commercial sex industry; and (3) implementing criminal law reforms that decriminalize the sale of sex, while penalizing pimping and buying sex (Ekberg 2004; Waltman 2011). While the second and third pillars have been adopted in several countries, including Sweden, Norway, Iceland, South Korea, France, Canada, Northern Ireland, and the Republic of Ireland—arguably, no jurisdiction has fully implemented the Nordic model ideal with respect to the first pillar.[28]

The decriminalization of sex-sellers is now largely uncontroversial in most jurisdictions and certainly meets with general agreement in the academic debates regarding prostitution in Western nations, despite the continued criminalization of sex-selling in most US jurisdictions (Dempsey 2015).[29] The major point of controversy in recent debates concerns whether to criminalize sex-buyers. Laws that target sex-buyers, known as "end-demand" laws, are widely supported by feminist abolitionists but strongly opposed by pro-sex-work advocates.

The rationales behind "end-demand" laws vary. Some advocates, adopting a structural understanding of prostitution, argue that prostitution as such is violence against women and thus, men who buy sex should be criminalized. On this view, the distinction between forced and freely chosen prostitution is seen as a false dichotomy (Kelly 2003; Raymond 2013, pp. 20–22). Rather than asking whether it is possible for women to consent to sell sex and how many women actually do genuinely consent, this perspective asks a different question: "If women really choose prostitution, why is it mostly disadvantaged and marginalized women who do it?" (Raymond 2013, p. 21). In creating a blanket prohibition on buying sex, the Nordic model maintains a transactional definition of prostitution, yet still addresses the broader structural inequalities that inform the social and political meaning of prostitution. In this way, the Nordic model uses the criminal legal system both to target particular instances of clearly defined conduct (sex-buying and pimping) and to address wrongful societal structures (prostitution, understood structurally).

While the Nordic model's blanket prohibition on buying sex respects rule of law values regarding the need for clarity in defining criminal offenses, it arguably violates other important liberal criminal law values insofar as it calls for a blanket prohibition on the purchase of sex. For, if some commercial sexual transactions are freely chosen, then liberal criminal law values would weigh against prohibiting those exchanges.

Two arguments in support of the Nordic model have been offered in an attempt to address the concern that a blanket prohibition on buying sex is inconsistent with liberal criminal law values.[30] These arguments, which we will call the liberal defense of the Nordic model, start by conceding both the possibility and actuality that *some* prostitution is freely chosen by sex-sellers. Yet, if the vast majority of prostitution is *not* freely chosen by the person selling (or being sold for) sex, then the liberal defense of the Nordic model offers two lines of argument that might justify a blanket prohibition on buying sex (Dempsey 2010, 2005).

The first is the *complicity argument*, which focuses on the relevance of the *buying* part of "buying sex." Roughly stated, it goes like this: (1) sex-buyers create market demand for prostitution; (2) market demand creates a profit motive for pimps; (3) this profit motive makes a causal contribution to pimps procuring and maintaining a supply of people to sell for sex; (4) in procuring and maintaining this supply, pimps often engage in harmful conduct against these people (e.g., force, threats, and coercion); and (5) thus, by purchasing sex, one makes a causal contribution to the harmful conduct of pimps against the people they sell for sex (Dempsey 2010, pp. 1752–1762).[31]

The second is the *endangerment argument*, which focuses on the *having sex* part of "buying sex." Roughly stated, the argument goes like this: (1) even when prostitution is not pimp-controlled, the conditions that induce people to sell sex are frequently inconsistent with genuine consent to the commercial sex act; (2) having sex with someone who is not genuinely consenting harms/ wrongs that person (in a sense tantamount to rape); (3) thus, in having commercial sex, a buyer runs the risk of having sex with someone who is not genuinely consenting (and thus harming/wronging that person); (4) this risk of harm substantially outweighs the value of the buyer having sex; and (5) thus, in purchasing sex, one engages in conduct that presents an unjustifiable risk of harm to the sex-seller (Dempsey 2010, pp. 1762–1769).

The success of the liberal defense of the Nordic model depends on what most prostitution is like in a given society at a particular time. If people are, for the most part, freely choosing to sell sex (i.e., choosing this option as one they genuinely prefer from among an adequate range of valuable options available to them), then the liberal defense of the Nordic model is weakened. It would be better, in that case, to target a smaller category of sex-buyers: those who purchase sex from the relatively few people who are not freely choosing to sell sex.[32] Yet, if a substantial amount of prostitution is *not* freely chosen, then the liberal defense of the Nordic model is strengthened.

Moreover, the broader impact of criminalizing sex-buying must be considered. Will criminalizing "clients" reduce harms to prostituted-people, or will it make commercial sex more dangerous (Sanders et al. 2017)? If buying sex is simply decriminalized or legalized/regulated, will the market demand for commercial sex increase? And, if so, will that demand be met with a supply of people freely choosing to sell sex or will the increased demand simply expand and exacerbate the harms suffered by people who are *not* freely choosing to sell sex (Cho et al. 2012)?[33] As with the previous debates regarding prostitution and criminalization, these issues must be resolved by drawing on empirical evidence. Yet, as discussed below, the researchers offering empirical evidence regarding what prostitution is like seem to be trapped in a "competing camps" mentality that makes such resolution unlikely.

The Resurgence of "Sex Trafficking"

Shortly after Sweden first adopted the Nordic model, the United Nations (UN) defined human trafficking in the Protocol to Prevent, Suppress, and Punish Trafficking in Persons, Especially Women and Children (Palermo Protocol 2000, Art. 3). While the concept of trafficking already existed in international law in documents such as the International Convention for the Suppression of the White Slave Traffic of 1910[34] and the Convention for the Suppression of the Traffic in Persons and of the Exploitation of the Prostitution of Others of 1949, trafficking had not yet been defined in international law.

Feminist abolitionists and pro-prostitution advocates lobbied UN delegates drafting the Palermo Protocol to adopt a definition of trafficking that reflected their respective understanding of prostitution.[35] Feminist abolitionists lobbied for a broad definition, one that arguably includes nearly all commercial sex acts, while pro-prostitution advocates lobbied for a narrow definition that included only commercial sex acts induced by the use of serious physical force or deception. In the end, the broader definition prevailed (Raymond 2001). According to the Palermo Protocol, Article 3, sex trafficking is defined as:

(a) [T]he recruitment, transportation, transfer, harbouring or receipt of [a child,[36] or an adult if brought about] by means of the threat or use of force or other forms of coercion, of abduction, of fraud, of deception, of the abuse of power or of a position of vulnerability or of the giving or receiving of payments or benefits to achieve the consent of a person having control over another person, for the purpose of exploitation. Exploitation shall include, at a minimum, the exploitation of the prostitution of others or other forms of sexual exploitation...;

(b) The consent of a victim...to the intended exploitation...shall be irrelevant where any of the means set forth in subparagraph (a) have been used...

While perhaps not eloquently articulated, the Palermo Protocol definition of sex trafficking is broad enough to include commercial sex acts brought about by means of an "abuse of power...or vulnerability." Moreover, per the terms of Article 3(b), the consent of the victim to the commercial sex act is irrelevant (Huda 2006, p. 9). The focus of the Palermo Protocol definition is not on *whether* the victim consented to the commercial sex act but *why* she consented. If she consented because someone else held power over her, or because she was in a vulnerable position—and if that power or vulnerability was abused to bring about a commercial sex act—then the elements of trafficking have been established (Dempsey et al. 2012).

As noted above, by securing a broad definition of sex trafficking, feminist abolitionists succeeded in defining sex trafficking in a way that arguably includes nearly all commercial sex acts. As the former UN Special Rapporteur on Trafficking in Persons (Huda 2006, p. 9) observes, "prostitution as actually practised in the world usually does satisfy the elements of trafficking...[since] [i]t is rare that one finds a case in which the path to prostitution and/or a person's experiences within prostitution do not involve, at the very least, an abuse of power and/or an abuse of vulnerability." Thus, while the UN definition of trafficking does not include every possible commercial sex act, the definition may very well include the majority of commercial sex acts. The broad scope of what counts as sex trafficking under the Palermo Protocol means that "State parties with legalized prostitution industries have a heavy responsibility to ensure that the conditions which actually pertain to the practice of prostitution within their borders...are not simply perpetuating widespread and systematic trafficking" (ibid.).

Around the same time that the UN adopted this broad definition of trafficking, the US enacted the Trafficking Victims Protection Act of 2000, providing a similar, albeit somewhat narrower, definition of trafficking (Dempsey et al. 2012).[37] Perhaps most importantly, the US State Department began in 2001 to publish its annual Trafficking in Persons (TIP) Reports, which evaluates nations' responses to human trafficking and ranks them according to three tiers. Since tier rankings are tied to the provision of US economic aid, the TIP Reports have been instrumental in making human trafficking an important issue in international and domestic law.[38]

The resurgence of "sex trafficking" as a primary focus of prostitution policy has created a political climate that is more amenable to feminist abolitionism, which views prostitution as both a symptom and cause of patriarchal structural inequality—but it has not resolved the basic question of what to do about prostitution. Instead, as Liz Kelly observes, "[u]nresolved debates about prostitution...continue to be played out through the lens of trafficking" (Kelly 2005, p. 256).

The Entrenchment of Conflicting Empirical Research

As noted at several points above, ethical debates about prostitution and criminalization frequently turn on empirical evidence. However, the questions that need to be resolved in these debates do not turn solely on empirical evidence, since empirical evidence concerns simply that which can be observed through the senses. In contrast, distinctions between "commercial sex *simpliciter*" and more problematic, exploitative, abusive, coercive, and non-consensual forms of commercial sex depend on *evaluative* concepts such as choice, consent, voluntariness, freedom, and adequate options. As such, it's naïve to suppose that empirical evidence alone will answer fundamental questions regarding what prostitution is like in a given society at a particular time (Dempsey 2012).

From a liberal perspective, consent remains an important consideration in debates regarding the moral quality of conduct and whether it should be criminalized—but the criteria for what constitutes *morally transformative* consent necessarily involves both empirical evidence and moral arguments (Wertheimer 2010, p. 196). Empirical evidence is surely relevant to our conclusions regarding these matters, yet it cannot be determinative. Rather, we must rely on our best philosophical accounts of the evaluative concepts in play (here, consent, freedom, harm, etc.) to design empirical studies that operationalize these concepts adequately.

Unfortunately for anyone looking for a tidy resolution to debates regarding prostitution and criminalization, the quality of empirical evidence regarding the commercial sex industry is not likely to be of much help. Take but two examples. In one empirical study of prostitution (Harding and Hamilton 2009), researchers asked subjects whether they "made a free choice to [engage in] sex work" or were "forced into it by someone else" (ibid., p. 1126). When several subjects responded "yes" to both options, the researchers rightly characterized the responses as a "problematic...(since) it does not seem possible for someone to make a free choice and to be forced at the same time" (ibid.). Nonetheless, the researchers concluded that "these women had been forced into [...] sex work, even though they ultimately believed that they made that decision for themselves" (ibid.). Now, if the researchers had placed these conflicting answers into a broader context that illuminated the conditions under which the women made these choices, their empirical data might form part of a more comprehensive analysis that justifies the conclusion that the women were forced into prostitution. But without more empirical evidence— and, importantly, without philosophical arguments about the relevant concepts under investigation (free choice, force, etc.)—there is little justification for the conclusions reached by these empirical researchers.

While the Harding and Hamilton (2009) study illustrates the risk of overcounting non-consensual prostitution, much of the empirical literature risks undercounting. Consider the example of a subject called Xing-Xing, a Chinese native who (according to the researchers' own evaluation) had been sex trafficked in China and had been brought to South Africa to sell sex (Gould and Fick 2008). When the researchers interviewed her in South Africa, she was unable to speak English, reported "working" 13 hours a day, six days a week, and the "agency" (brothel) kept 65% of the money she earned (Gould and Fick 2008, pp. 138–139).[39] Nonetheless, the researchers concluded that Xing-Xing was not being victimized.

Empirical research regarding prostitution is nowhere close to presenting a coherent understanding of what prostitution is like. Evidence that most prostitution is harmful is dismissed as a "moral panic" (Weitzer 2005b), while evidence that most prostitution is not harmful is viewed as junk science. Matthews (2015, p. 86) puts the point well in his lament regarding the persistence of "'flat earth' theorists who still believe in the myth of the 'happy hooker', despite all evidence to the contrary, or claim that all trafficked women are in fact 'economic migrants' exercising free choice" (citing Agustín 2006; Mai 2009; Weitzer 2007).

If debates in applied ethics regarding the criminalization of prostitution depend in large part on what prostitution is like (as distinct, say, from sex trafficking), and if distinguishing "commercial sex *simpliciter*" from more abusive, exploitative, and/or coercive forms of prostitution depends not only on empirical evidence but on ethical disagreements regarding concepts such as choice, freedom, and consent, then it would be naïve to think that empirical evidence will resolve the question of what to do about prostitution. For, the very concepts that inform our understanding of the empirical evidence are fundamentally ethical concepts. That is to say, we cannot dispense with philosophy in deciding what to do about prostitution—even when it comes to the basic question of what prostitution is.

Conclusion

This chapter has examined the central arguments in applied ethics regarding the criminalization of prostitution over the last six decades. Importantly, it has sought to illustrate the extent to which these debates depend on what prostitution is actually like, as it exists in any given society at any given time. For, the question of what to do about prostitution depends in large part on whether and to what extent prostitution is best understood coextensive with, or distinct from, related phenomena such as sex trafficking. This chapter has highlighted the fact that the answers to such questions depend not only on empirical evidence but on our best understanding of concepts such as choice, freedom, and consent which inform the empirical research regarding commercial sex. As such, this chapter has suggested that empirical evidence alone is unlikely to resolve applied ethical debates regarding what to do about prostitution, since the very concepts that inform our understanding of empirical evidence are fundamentally philosophical concepts.

Notes

1. I use the terms "sex-seller" and "prostituted-person" interchangeably, while intending that the former should be taken to refer to cases without pimp involvement, where the sex-seller enjoys a relatively high degree of free choice in determining the conditions of her prostitution, while the latter should be taken to refer to cases that either involve third-party profiteers (pimps) or in which the prostituted-person's choices regarding participation in, or the conditions of participation in any given commercial sexual transaction, are relatively more constrained.

2. Sex-buyers are typically understood as people to "use the services of a prostitute" but often are not thought of as, themselves, engaged in prostitution. Rather, it is the sex-seller/prostituted-person who is thought to be involved in prostitution, while the sex-buyer is conceived of as engaged in a distinct, but related, act of "soliciting" or "kerb-crawling." Similarly, pimps are often not

understood to be involved in prostitution themselves but simply "promoting the prostitution of others." A broader transactional definition of prostitution can avoid these limitations and illuminate the sense in which all two (or three) parties are equally involved in prostitution.

3. Structural definitions of prostitution do not claim that there are universal structures that perform the work of creating and sustaining prostitution as an institution across cultures. As Andrea Dworkin observed:

> Societies are organized so that men have the power they need, to use women the way that they want to. Societies can be organized in different ways and still create a population of women who are prostituted. For instance, in the United States the women are poor, the women are mostly incest victims, the women are homeless. In parts of Asia, they were sold into slavery at the age of six months because they were females. That is how they do it there. It does not have to be done the same way in every place to be the same thing. (Dworkin 1993, p. 9)

4. While "very little is known about the clients of MSW [male sex workers]...we know that clients are mostly older males" (Galárraga and Sosa-Rubí 2016, p. 293).

5. As Doug Husak observes, such definitions eliminate the act requirement that many (but not Husak) argue is necessary for justified criminalization (Husak 1998, p. 87). To be clear, my argument regarding the deficiencies of structural definitions when evaluated in terms of rule of law values is not simply that structural definitions would eliminate the act requirement but that they are too vague to provide fair warning.

6. Tuerkheimer's argument is made in the context of domestic abuse. She argues that structural conditions which inform the broader phenomena of "battering" are obscured by the criminal law's transactional definition of domestic abuse.

7. This is not to say that transactional definitions are entirely clear. What counts as an exchange? What counts as a sex act? What counts as valuable consideration? For an illuminating discussion, see Green (2016).

8. We leave aside questions about whether "sugar daddy/sugar baby" or "girlfriend experience" cases count as prostitution. But see Green (2016, p. 101), arguing that those who are primarily concerned with prostitution due to structural features ("preventing...exploitation and oppression") will be inclined to include these "arrangements" within the definition of prostitution.

9. Of course, a transactional definition of prostitution can also take on board the fact that many times a sex-seller's self-perceptions of free choice is later recognized as a survival mechanism. Consider the experience of prostitution survivor, Rachel Moran:

> There is a fantasy some women in prostitution indulge in: that they are exceptionally strong, in control of all of this, far above being abused. I know this because I once indulged in it myself...That myth is important to the working prostitute. It enables her to continue to function within the sphere of life she is in Moran. (2015, pp. 110–111)

A similar reflection is illustrated in the words of Evelina Giobbe, founder of WHISPER: "When I was in prostitution I would always say, 'I'm fine, I love what I do.' I had to or I would have gone mad...It is only when we get out, if we are lucky enough to get out alive, we can admit the hell, the horror of what was happening to us" (Bindel 2017, p. 7, quoting interview with Giobbe).

10. On adaptive preferences and autonomy, see Khader (2011, pp. 74–106).

11. The assumption built into this sentence is that a liberal criminal legal system is committed to something like the *volenti maxim*: to one who consents, no harm/wrong is done (Feinberg 1984, 1985, 1986, 1988; Dempsey 2018).

12. At the time, and still to some extent today, the sale and purchase of sex is not criminalized in the UK. However, prostitution-related activities such as solicitation and kerb-crawling have long been criminalized, and as of 2009, buying sex from a victim of sex trafficking is a criminal offense (Policing and Crime Act 2009, amending Sexual Offences Act 2003, §53A).

13. So, the scare quotes signal that I take morality to consist of something other than, but related to, social norms. Social norms can support immoral positions. For an argument that prostitution is genuinely immoral but should not be criminalized, see Yankah (2013).

14. For Devlin, "immorality" in the sense meant here was tantamount to treason (Devlin 1959, pp. 140–141).

15. In the decades that followed, Joel Feinberg published his influential four-volume series exploring the limits and implications of a criminal law committed to a liberal harm principle (Feinberg 1988, 1986, 1985, 1984).

16. While Parliament refrained from criminalizing prostitution itself, the Wolfenden Report was influential in the creation of laws that cracked down on street prostitution (Street Offences Act 1959).

17. Interestingly, though, while these arguments have been used to call for criminalization, neither of the most thoughtful defenders of the objectification and commodification critiques (Anderson and Radin, respectively) called for criminalization, due to concerns that criminalization would simply make things worse for women with few/no better opportunities for survival (Anderson 1995, pp. 150–158; Radin 1996, pp. 132–136). For more affirmative evaluation of commodification arguments, see Ertman and Williams (2005), especially, Lucas (2005).

18. In cases where sex-sellers exercise a sufficient degree of choice, a paternalistic argument can be made to criminalize them on grounds that they are objectifying/commodifying themselves. "Human beings have no right, therefore, to hand themselves over for profit, as things for another's use in satisfying the sexual impulse; for in that case their humanity is in danger of being used by anyone as a thing, an instrument for the satisfaction of inclination.... Nothing is more vile than to take money for yielding to another so that his inclination may be satisfied and to let one's own person out for hire" (Kant 1997, p. 157).

19. Interestingly, while Shrage opposed prostitution, she did not endorse its criminalization. Rather, she simply concluded that "a consumer boycott of the industry is especially important" (Shrage 1989, p. 361).

20. In the next section, we revisit and question Primoratz's conclusion, while granting his premise. That is, even if we grant that there are two (or even more) distinct forms of prostitution in society, the existence of the more problematic/abusive forms can ground an argument against even "commercial sex *simpliciter*."

21. Indeed, the current state of empirical research regarding prostitution illustrates the impact of these contradictory framings, with feminist researchers such as

Melissa Farley producing empirical evidence that strongly supports Shrage's view (Farley 1998; Farley and Barkan 1998; Farley et al. 2009, 2004, 2011), while other researchers, such as Ronald Weitzer, critique the former for adopting an "oppression paradigm" in framing their research (Weitzer 2005a, b, 2010).

22. For a recent, carefully argued explanation of the extent to which patriarchy is still very much with us, see Manne (2017).

23. However, what harms fall within the scope of being "just part of the job" often remain troublingly unclear: "What rape is to others is normal to us" (Farley et al. 2005, p. 254).

24. For an argument that prostitution is not properly conceived as "sex work," see Raymond (2013).

25. For an argument that viewing prostitution as work would have little impact on stigma, see Shrage (1989).

26. "[S]ex workplaces are some of the only ones in which the *workers* are not only permitted but actually expected to consume alcohol. In dance clubs in particular, operators may require dancers to 'hustle' drinks from customers, which the dancers are then expected to drink" (Davis 2015, p. 1245).

27. On the distinction between morality and moralism, and the need for feminist abolitionists to reclaim the language of values and morality from the religious conservative right, see Raymond (2013, pp. 17–18).

28. That said, the robust social welfare afforded in Nordic countries, where the model was first implemented, comes far closer than would be the case in most other jurisdictions.

29. While jurisdictions in the US have been slow to move toward decriminalization of sex-selling by adults, most states have adopted "safe harbor" laws that prevent juveniles from being placed into the criminal or juvenile delinquency system for prostitution-related offenses (Butler 2014). Several local jurisdictions have adopted discretionary policies to stop arresting and prosecuting sex-sellers, while focusing more on targeting sex-buyers. Most notably, in King County, Washington (Tan 2016), where arrests related to sex-selling went from approximately 450 in 2010 to fewer than 10 in 2017, sex-buying/patronizing arrests went from approximately 140 up to approximately 310 (Richey 2018, p. 48).

30. Two of these arguments—complicity and endangerment—have been presented in (Dempsey 2010). The argument from epistemic guidance is presented for the first time here, although now I see that it was previously conflated with the argument from endangerment.

31. On whether it would be possible to disaggregate the commercial sex market, so that buying sex would be permissible so long as the sellers are not pimp-controlled, see Dempsey (2010, pp. 1755–1777).

32. Indeed, this is the approach adopted in England and Wales, and previously in Northern Ireland, until it adopted the Nordic model in 2015 (Policing and Crime Act of 2009, amending Sexual Offenses Act of 2003, §53A; Human Trafficking and Exploitation (Criminal Justice and Support for Victims) Act (Northern Ireland) 2015, repealing Policing and Crime Act of 2009, amending Sexual Offences Act of 2003, §53B).

33. According to a 2010 report from the Swedish government, the law reforms from 1999 resulted in a reduction of street prostitution and a drop in the number of men paying for sex, from 12.7% in 1996 to 7.6% in 2008 (Sweden, Gov't

Offices of., 2010). In response, Jay Levy argues that the Swedish government relied on selective evidence and that the prohibition on buying sex not only "failed to achieve its objective of demonstrably reducing levels of sex work...[it] caused significant harm to sex workers" (Levy 2015).

34. For an argument that the resurgence of trafficking discourse in anti-prostitution advocacy is reminiscent of racist tropes around "white slavery," see Doezema (2000).
35. In the interest of full disclosure, I should note that I was involved in lobbying efforts during the negotiations for the Palermo Protocol in Vienna in 1999, on behalf of the nongovernmental organization Equality Now.
36. Article 3(c) provides that none of the means listed in (a) must be used if the victim is under 18 years.
37. The US Trafficking Victims Protection Act of 2000 defines "sex trafficking" to include all commercial sex acts but limits its focus for funding, criminalization, and so on to "severe forms of trafficking," which includes cases involving minors selling sex and adults selling sex "induced by force, fraud, or coercion."
38. For a critique of US TIP Reports and its use in foreign diplomacy/aid, see Chuang (2006).
39. The researchers interviewed her by phone and provided no information regarding how they translated from Xing-Xing's native language to English. Indeed, they did not even specify Xing-Xing's native language. Space precludes examination of the many other methodological flaws that typically render prostitution and sex trafficking research deficient, but see Kelly (2005), Raphael (2017).

References

Agustín, Laura. 2006. The conundrum of women's agency: Migrations and the sex industry. In *Sex work now*, ed. Rebecca Campbell and Maggie O'Neill. Cullompton: Willan.

Anderson, Elizabeth. 1995. *Value in ethics and economics.* Cambridge, MA: Harvard University Press.

Bennett, Jessica. 2017. The #MeToo moment: When the blinders come off. *New York Times*, November 30.

Benson, Catherine, and Roger Matthews. 1995. Street prostitution: Ten facts in search of a policy. *International Journal of the Sociology of Law* 23: 395–415.

Bindel, Julie. 2017. *The pimping of prostitution: Abolishing the sex work myth.* Basingstoke: Palgrave Macmillan.

Bindman, Jo, and Jo Doezema. 1997. *Redefining prostitution as sex work on the international agenda.* London: Anti-Slavery International and the Network of Sex Work Projects.

Butler, Cheryl Nelson. 2014. Bridge over troubled water: Safe harbor laws for sexually exploited minors. *North Carolina Law Review* 93: 1281–1338.

Carter, Vednita, and Evelina Giobbe. 1999. Duet: Prostitution, racism and feminist discourse. *Hastings Women's Law Journal* 10: 37–57.

CATW. 2018. Coalition Against Trafficking in Women website http://www.catwinternational.org/WhoWeAre. Accessed 3 Aug 2018.

Chesser, Eustace. 1958. *Live and let live: The moral of the Wolfenden report.* London: Heinemann.

Cho, Seo-Young, Axel Dreher, and Eric Neumayer. 2012. Does legalized prostitution increase human trafficking? *World Development* 41: 67–82.

Chuang, Janie. 2006. The United States as global sheriff: Using unilateral sanctions to combat human trafficking. *Michigan Journal of International Law* 27: 437–494.

Coy, Maddy. 2016. *Prostitution, harm and gender inequality: Theory, research and policy.* Abingdon: Routledge.

Davis, Adrienne D. 2015. Regulating sex work: Erotic assimilationism, erotic exceptionalism, and the challenge of intimate labor. *California Law Review* 103: 1195–1276.

Dempsey, Michelle Madden. 2005. Rethinking Wolfenden: Prostitute-use, criminal law, and remote harm. *Criminal Law Review* 2005: 444–455.

———. 2010. Sex trafficking and criminalization: In defense of feminist abolitionism. *University of Pennsylvania Law Review* 158: 1729–1778.

———. 2012. How to argue about prostitution. *Criminal Law and Philosophy* 6: 65–80.

———. 2015. Decriminalizing victims of sex trafficking. *American Criminal Law Review* 52: 207–229.

———. 2018. Volenti non fit injuria. In *The Routledge handbook on the ethics of consent,* ed. Peter Schaber and Andreas Mueller. Abingdon: Routledge.

Dempsey, Michelle Madden, Carolyn Hoyle, and Mary Bosworth. 2012. Defining sex trafficking in international and domestic law: Mind the gaps. *Emory International Law Review* 26: 137–162.

Devlin, Patrick. 1959. The enforcement of morals. In Vol. 45 of *Proceedings of the British Academy,* 129–151. Oxford: Oxford University Press.

Doezema, Jo. 2000. Loose women or lost women? – The re-emergence of the myth of "white slavery" in contemporary discourses of "trafficking in women". *Gender Issues* 18: 23–50.

Dworkin, Andrea. 1993. Prostitution and male supremacy. *Michigan Journal of Gender and Law* 1: 1–12.

Ekberg, Gunilla. 2004. The Swedish law that prohibits the purchase of sexual services: Best practices for prevention of prostitution and trafficking in human beings. *Violence Against Women* 10: 1187–1218.

Ertman, Martha, and Joan C. Williams. 2005. *Rethinking commodification: Cases and readings in law and culture.* New York: New York University Press.

Farley, Melissa. 1998. Prostitution in five countries: Violence and post-traumatic stress disorder. *Feminism & Psychology* 8: 405–426.

———. 2003. *Prostitution, trafficking and traumatic stress.* Binghamton: Haworth Maltreatment & Trauma Press.

Farley, Melissa, and Howard Barkan. 1998. Prostitution, violence, and post-traumatic stress disorder. *Women & Health* 27: 37–49.

Farley, Melissa, Ann Cotton, Jacqueline Lynne, Sybille Zumbeck, Frida Spiwak, Maria E. Reyes, Dinorah Alvarez, and Ufuk Sezgin. 2004. Prostitution and trafficking in nine countries: An update on violence and posttraumatic stress disorder. *Journal of Trauma Practice* 2 (3–4): 33–74.

Farley, Melissa, Jacqueline Lynne, and Ann J. Cotton. 2005. Prostitution in Vancouver: Violence and the colonization of First Nations women. *Transcultural Psychiatry* 42: 242–271.

Farley, Melissa, Julie Bindel, and Jacqueline M. Golding. 2009. *Men who buy sex: Who they buy and what they know.* London: Eaves.

Farley, Melissa, Nicole Matthews, Sarah Deer, Guadalupe Lopez, Christine Stark, and Eileen Hudon. 2011. *Garden of truth: The prostitution and trafficking of native women in Minnesota*. St. Paul: William Mitchell College of Law.

Feinberg, Joel. 1984. *Harm to others: The moral limits of the criminal law*. Oxford: Oxford University Press.

———. 1985. *Offense to others: The moral limits of the criminal law*. Oxford: Oxford University Press.

———. 1986. *Harm to self: The moral limits of the criminal law*. Oxford: Oxford University Press.

———. 1988. *Harmless wrongdoing: The moral limits of the criminal law*. Oxford: Oxford University Press.

Fuller, Lon. 1964. *The morality of law*. New Haven: Yale University Press.

Galárraga, Omar, and Sandra G. Sosa-Rubí. 2016. Male sex workers: HIV risk and behavioral economics. In *Oxford handbook of the economics of prostitution*, ed. Scott Cunningham and Manisha Shah. Oxford: Oxford University Press.

George, Robert P. 1993. *Making men moral: Civil liberties and public morality*. Oxford: Oxford University Press.

Giobbe, Evelina. 1990. Confronting liberal lies about prostitution. In *The sexual liberals and the attack on feminism*, ed. Dorchen Leidholt and Janice G. Raymond. New York: Pergamon Press.

Goldberg, Suzanne B. 2003. Morals-based justifications for lawmaking: Before and after *Lawrence v. Texas*. *Minnesota Law Review* 88: 1233–1312.

Gould, Chandré, and Nicolé Fick. 2008. *Selling sex in Cape Town: Sex work and human trafficking in a South African city*. Pretoria/Tshwane: Institute for Security Studies.

Green, Stuart P. 2016. What counts as prostitution? *Bergen Journal of Criminal Law and Criminal Justice* 4: 65–101.

Harding, Rachel, and Paul Hamilton. 2009. Working girls: Abuse or choice in street-level sex work? A study of homeless women in Nottingham. *British Journal of Social Work* 39: 1118–1137.

Hart, H.L.A. 1963. *Law, liberty, and morality*. Stanford: Stanford University Press.

Herman, Judith Lewis. 2003. Hidden in plain sight: Clinical observations on prostitution. In *Prostitution, trafficking and traumatic stress*, ed. M. Farley, 1–16. Binghamton: Haworth Press.

Hester, Marianne, and Nicole Westmarland. 2004. *Tackling street prostitution: Towards an holistic approach*. London: Home Office Research, Development and Statistics Directorate.

Hubbard, Phil. 1998. Community action and the displacement of street prostitution: Evidence from British cities. *Geoforum* 29: 269–286.

Huda, Sigma. 2006. Integration of the human rights of women and a gender perspective: Violence against women. U.N. Commission on Human Rights. https://www.refworld.org/topic,50ffbce582,50ffbce5121,48abd53dd,0,UNCHR,THEMREPORT,.html. Accessed 27 Feb 2019.

Hurd, Heidi. 1996. The moral magic of consent. *Legal Theory* 2: 121–146.

———. 2018. The normative force of consent. In *The Routledge handbook of the ethics of consent*, ed. Peter Schaber and Andreas Müller. Abingdon: Routledge.

Husak, Douglas. 1998. Does criminal liability require an act? In *The philosophy of criminal law: Selected essays*. Cambridge: Cambridge University Press.

Kant, Immanuel. 1997. *Lectures on ethics*. Trans. Peter Heath. Cambridge: Cambridge University Press.

Kelly, Liz. 2003. The wrong debate: Reflections on why force is not the key issue with respect to trafficking in women for sexual exploitation. *Feminist Review* 73: 139–144.

———. 2005. "You can find anything you want": A critical reflection on research on trafficking in persons within and into Europe. *International Migration* 43 (1–2): 235–265.

Khader, Serene J. 2011. *Adaptive preferences and women's empowerment*. Oxford: Oxford University Press.

Law, Sylvia. 2000. Commercial sex: Beyond decriminalization. *Southern California Law Review* 73: 523–611.

Leidholdt, Dorchen, and Janice G. Raymond. 1989. *The sexual liberals and the attack on feminism*. New York: Pergamon.

Levy, Jay. 2015. *Criminalising the purchase of sex: Lessons from Sweden*. Abingdon: Routledge.

Lucas, Ann. 2005. The currency of sex: Prostitution, law, and commodification. In *Rethinking commodification: Cases and readings in law and culture*, ed. Martha Ertman. New York: New York University Press.

Lynch, Gerald E. 1987. Rico: The crime of being a criminal, parts III and IV. *Columbia Law Review* 87: 927–984.

MacKinnon, Catharine. 1993. Prostitution and civil rights. *Michigan Journal of Gender and Law* 1: 13–32.

Mai, Nicola. 2009. *Migrant sex workers in the UK sex industry*. London: London Metropolitan University.

Manne, Kate. 2017. *Down girl: The logic of misogyny*. Oxford: Oxford University Press.

Matthews, Roger. 2008. *Prostitution, politics & policy*. New York: Routledge.

———. 2015. Female prostitution and victimization: A realist analysis. *International Review of Victimology* 21: 85–100.

Matthews, Roger, and Maggie O'Neill. 2002. *Prostitution, the international library of criminology, criminal justice, and penology*. Burlington: Ashgate.

Moen, Ole Martin. 2012. Is prostitution harmful? *Journal of Medical Ethics* 40 (2). https://doi.org/10.1136/medethics-2011-100367.

Moran, Rachel. 2015. *Paid for: My journal through prostitution*. New York: W.W. Norton & Company.

Nussbaum, Martha. 1998. Whether from reason or prejudice: Taking money for bodily services. *The Journal of Legal Studies* 27: 693–725.

Overall, Christine. 1992. What's wrong with prostitution? Evaluating sex work. *Signs* 17: 705–724.

Pateman, Carol. 1988. *The sexual contract*. Cambridge: Polity Press.

Primoratz, Igor. 1993. What's wrong with prostitution? *Philosophy* 68 (264): 159–182.

Radin, Margaret. 1996. *Contested commodities*. Boston: Harvard University Press.

Raphael, Jody. 2017. Returning trafficking prevalence to the public policy debate: Introduction to the special issue. *Journal of Human Trafficking* 3: 1–20.

Raymond, Janice. 1998. Prostitution as violence against women: NGO stonewalling in Beijing and elsewhere. *Women's Studies International Forum* 21: 1–9.

———. 2001. *The guide to the new U.N. trafficking protocol*. New York: Coalition Against Trafficking in Women.

———. 2013. *Not a choice, not a job: Exposing the myths about prostitution and the global sex trade*. Washington, DC: Potomac Books.

Richey, Valiant. 2018. PowerPoint slides. Presented at 2nd Annual Survivor Symposium. Villanova University Institute to Address Commercial Sexual Exploitation. Philadelphia (on file with author).

Sanders, Teela. 2004. The risks of street prostitution: Punters, police and protesters. *Urban Studies* 4: 1703–1717.

Sanders, Teela, Scott Cunningham, Lucy Platt, Pippa Grenfell, and P.G. Macioti. 2017. Is sex work still the most dangerous profession? The data suggests so. The Conversation. https://theconversation.com/is-sex-work-still-the-most-dangerous-profession-the-data-suggests-so-81854. Accessed 27 Feb 2019.

Shrage, Laurie. 1989. Should feminists oppose prostitution. *Ethics* 99: 347–361.

Snyder, Howard. 2012. Arrest in the United States, 1990–2010. In *Bureau of Justice Statistics, Office of Justice Programs, US Department of Justice*. Washington, DC: Department of Justice.

Sweden, Government Offices of. 2010. Prohibition of the purchase of sexual services. An evaluation 1999–2008 (SOU 2010:49), Stockholm.

Tan, Thanh. 2016. A closer look at King County's groundbreaking efforts to fight sex trafficking. *Seattle Times*, March 10.

Tuerkheimer, Deborah. 2004. Recognizing and remedying the harm of battering: A call to criminalize domestic violence. *Journal of Criminal Law and Criminology* 94: 959–1032.

Vanwesenbeeck, Ine. 2001. Another decade of social scientific work on sex work: A review of research 1990–2000. *Annual Review of Sex Research* 12: 242–289.

Waltman, Max. 2011. Prohibiting sex purchasing and ending trafficking: The Swedish prostitution law. *Michigan Journal of International Law* 33: 133–157.

Weitzer, Ronald. 2005a. Flawed theory and method in studies of prostitution. *Violence Against Women* 11: 934–949.

———. 2005b. The growing moral panic over prostitution and sex trafficking. *The Criminologist* 30 (5): 1–5.

———. 2007. The social construction of sex trafficking: Ideology and institutionalization of a moral crusade. *Politics and Society* 35: 447–475.

———. 2010. The mythology of prostitution: Advocacy research and public policy. *Sexuality Research and Social Policy* 7: 15–29.

Wertheimer, Alan. 2010. Consent to sexual relations. In *The ethics of consent*, 195–219. Oxford: Oxford University Press.

Westin, Anna. 2014. The harms of prostitution: Critiquing Moen's argument of no-harm. *Journal of Medical Ethics* 40 (2): 86–87.

Wolfenden, Great Britain-Home Office. 1957. *Report of the committee on homosexual offences and prostitution*. London: Highline Medical Services Organization.

Yankah, Ekow. 2013. Liberal virtue. In *Law, virtue and justice*, ed. Amalia Amaya and Hock Lai Ho. Oxford: Hart Publishing.

PART XXIV

Race

CHAPTER 26

Race, Criminal Law and Ethical Life

Ekow N. Yankah

Given how integral race is to the construction and application of American criminal law and in turn how central criminal law is to the American racial experience, one might feel that to write about criminal law is unavoidably to write about race. It seems frankly irresponsible to teach the subject without thoughtful consideration of racism and criminal law. Yet despite its pervasive and insidious effects, to describe the role of race and racism in the American criminal law system is no easy task. The sheer scope of the subject makes difficult even knowing where to begin.

This is in part because in the broad criminal theory debate, as elsewhere in society, there remains controversy about the very nature of the question of race in criminal law. While few could deny the importantly disparate outcomes citizens of different races have when encountering the criminal law system, for some the central question of race in criminal law primarily focuses on how criminal law treats those motivated by racial hatred, namely hate crimes, or is affected by explicitly racist motivations of legal actors.[1] Such a view attributes the importance of race in criminal law to undesirable mental states, the defendant, the police officer or prosecutor harboring racist sentiments.

In contrast are those who view the question of race and racism in criminal law as a broader question of structural racism (Massey 2007, pp. 5–6; Lopez 2007, pp. 996–1000, 1005–1006). As is well known, structural racism is concerned not simply, or even primarily, with malicious mental states. Rather, structural racism is focused on the way background institutions conserve racial privilege for White Americans and use criminal law as part of a broader system

E. N. Yankah (✉)
Cardozo Law School, New York, NY, USA
e-mail: yankah@yu.edu

© The Author(s) 2019
L. Alexander, K. K. Ferzan (eds.), *The Palgrave Handbook of Applied Ethics and the Criminal Law*, https://doi.org/10.1007/978-3-030-22811-8_26

625

of racial oppression and control. Structural racism makes sense of how much of the racial damage of criminal law can be done without supposing that some large number of actors within the criminal law system wake up in the morning motivated by explicit racial animus.

It is my sense that most scholars have largely internalized that the most difficult questions of race in criminal law are related to questions of structural racism. Yet even those focused on structural racism face the challenge of delineating the boundaries of inquiry in race and criminal law. First, it is obvious that even drawing a moat around criminal law, broadly defined, will suffer from artificiality (Paul-Emile 2018). Racial injustice in education policy (Glennon 1995), employment law (Bagenstos 2006; Green 2007), welfare distribution (Piven 2003; Harris 2006), property and housing law (Atuahene 2018; Atuahene and Hodges 2018) and countless other fields all have well-known criminogenic effects, making them important in understanding why otherwise "neutral" criminal sanctions may be racially problematic. Even drawing the line more finely to criminal law institutions requires argumentation about how pervasively one views the effects of racial bias. One scholar may limit her view to whether the police enforce minor laws ("broken windows" or "order maintenance" laws) with unjustifiable force against persons of color. Another may point out that quite aside from enforcement, the passing of the legislation itself is racist or at least problematic. That is to say, the legislation itself may be the result of a desire to police certain racial communities or a willingness to aim the power of criminal law at social problems in ways that would never be tolerated in White communities (and certainly not White communities with social power) (McLeod 2016).

This last point brings together the two views, racism as malicious intent and structural racism. To the extent racial hostility and contempt have been central to American history, much of structural racism cannot continue to exist without widespread hostility, implicit racism or deep apathy. This is not to deny the insight of structural racism, that is, racism is not confined to conscious racial hatred. It is to notice that many will react to social problems in ways determined by race. We are far too often willing to impose criminal sanctions on behavior that would be addressed otherwise when it is by "the wrong sort of people." And we are both invested in and collectively skilled at ignoring racial effects.

Taken together, this means examining the role of race in criminal law is to highlight its pernicious role in nearly every facet of our criminal law practices. It is also to question the extent to which racism is not merely a flaw in our criminal law system but part of its purpose, a feature not a bug (Butler 2016). This brief survey can only scan some of the landscape's important features, indicating important conversations and occasionally hinting at work to be continued. Lastly, examining race in criminal law turns our attention to the important question of how we can live ethically under a recognizably unjust criminal law system.

Another important note before beginning. Given America's particularly painful history with chattel slavery of Africans and the enduring stain of racism against African-Americans, it is too easy to treat the question of race and criminal law in America as the question of African-Americans and criminal law; it is a mistake of which I confess my own guilt. It is well remembered that the racial injustices of American criminal law are by no means confined to African-Americans. Hispanic-Americans also experience important inequities in treatment by criminal law institutions (Mann 1993).[2] Much less noted, Asian-Americans and other racial minorities suffer parallel injuries (Gee 2010). Further, race can be a complex component of identity that amplifies or distorts other sites of social vulnerability, most especially class but including sex, gender and sexual orientation. Intersectionality, as it is commonly described, is an important way in which many, perhaps most, experience race (Crenshaw 1989; Delgado 2011); it is sadly a feature which I am not able to even begin to address here.

Lastly, it should be noted that though I focus on racial minorities, racial injustice in the criminal law system imposes serious costs on all, White, Black and Brown alike. Apathetic toward laws we imagine only punish "those people," we allow a ravenous criminal law system that consumes huge numbers of people across all races.[3] Our national inability to address systemic racism in criminal law finally results in a system that is unnecessarily harsh toward all and undermines our ability to build effective coalitions across racial lines (Forman 2012, pp. 64–65).

Racism, Hate Crimes and Intentions

Though the question of how criminal law punishes racial animus is distinct from how racism plays a role in criminal law, they are obviously related. Clearly, they are related by a somewhat unspecified inquiry of the role race plays in criminal law. Their connection (and perhaps contrast) is deeper however. "Hate crime" legislation, as is well known, are criminal sanctions amplifying punishment for criminal violence motivated by some prohibited motivation. Though racial animus is viewed as the archetypal hate crime, hate crime legislation spans much broader, covering a number of protected interests such as religion, gender, sexuality, national origin and age. Here I obviously focus on hate crime legislation as applied to racial animus. Though there is a legal consensus, if not a scholarly one, regarding the culpability of hate crimes, whether malicious racial motivation is justifiably punished is much more academically contested.

There is a particular theoretical tension in hate crime legislation. The legal and popular consensus that racist motivations for committing a crime are reprehensible and worthy of increased punishment is clear. In nearly every American jurisdiction (and many more besides) there is some form of increased punishment for attacking someone because of their race. Yet for some, the justification of such increased punishment is harder to identify (Kim 2006). A prominent line of thought is that state power is justified by and limited to the protection of individual rights. Relatedly, the coercive power of criminal law is often argued to be limited by the Millian "harm principle," that is, the state may only properly punish actions that wrongfully harm other persons (Feinberg 1984). Thus, state power ought not to be marshaled in the pursuit of particular conceptions of "the good." A liberal state is foreclosed from making judgments about better and worse kinds of ethical lives and by extension better and worse kinds of people (Hurd 2001). Unless being attacked because you are Black or Hispanic violates a different set of rights or inflicts a different kind of harm, the state is unjustified in imposing greater punishment. Thus, philosophical liberals fret that hate crime legislation are instances of the state punishing an offender for their odious character (Hurd and Moore 2004).

Of course, there are many responses to this line of thought. The first is that even by the lights of hate crime critics, it is unclear the state may not criminalize hate crimes as a proxy for other harms. Though skeptical hate crime legislation can be justified by the wrongfulness of racist animus, Hurd and Moore note hate crimes may be seen as more wrongful for other reasons, such as instilling widespread fear in racial communities. Such arguments understand the perfectly plain claim that hate crimes are more harmful because they are widely destabilizing. Hurd and Moore argue that the variety of different harms inflicted by hate crimes could be addressed with individual sentencing enhancement. But one might think it simple enough that if the state understands particular harms are nearly universally embedded in a type of action, it may enhance punishment for those harms. That a particular hate crime conceivably did not carry all those harms would at worst make such legislation overinclusive, hardly a new feature in criminal law.

Though such accommodating moves are possible, most responses are more direct in meeting the accusation of illiberality. One might argue liberalism's commitment to neutrality between conceptions of the good is fundamentally premised on equal respect for citizens and their competing conceptions. This same commitment to equality requires the state to ensure that citizens who are disproportionately vulnerable receive greater state protection (Harel and Parchomovsky 1999).

Third, one might view the commission of a crime motivated by racial animus as simply more culpable than the similar crime without racial hatred (Kim 2006; Simons 2000). If hate crimes simply evidence a different and greater level of culpability, then liberals need not necessarily surrender the position that state punishment is entirely justified by individual culpability.

Perhaps the most intuitive position is the expressivist position which understands criminal law as in part expressing society's commitments to certain norms and condemnation of others. This "evaluativist" position argues criminal law unavoidably makes judgments on the content of an individual's actions, including the motives those choices instantiate. On the expressivist position, it is straightforward why a criminal law system would reflect our collective and particularly harsh condemnation of crimes motivated by racial animus (Kahan 2001; Kahan and Nussbaum 1996). Whether described as criminal law's "normativity" (Nourse 2002, 1998), practical reason, underlying character or virtue theory (Huigens 1995, 2004), the ultimate claim is that the law cannot avoid measuring the ethical quality of an offender's choices.

Lastly, though related, one might view hate crimes as violating a particular political right, the right to not be attacked on the basis of intrinsic features such as one's race. Admittedly, putting such a claim in the language of a "right against racist attacks" is infelicitous; it seems to assume the very claim under inspection. The better description argues that state power generally and criminal law in particular is justified by its role in securing our civic equality (Yankah 2015). The reason certain "liberal" views have trouble understanding hate crime laws is because they view criminal punishment as justified by the violation of individually carried rights. But such a view fails to make sense of a broad range of criminal law doctrines. Viewing civic equality as central to criminal law not only harmonizes a number of our practices but makes clear that attacks along vulnerable civic fault lines are a particular threat. While such a view is not wholly violent to liberal commitments, to the extent such explicitly republican justifications reject individual desert as the basis of punishment, they claim so much worse for liberalism (Duff 2007, 2001; Braithwaite and Pettit 1990).

For all of this, the focus on hate crimes as the central interaction of criminal law and race can feel puzzling. First, one might reasonably believe that hate crime legislation is not a radical break from much of criminal law doctrine, which regularly enhances punishments for particularly culpable motives or mens rea (Steiker 1999). Disagreement around hate crime legislation is often a stand-in for disagreements around policy or politics, sometimes disagreements about how to define racism at all.

I, for one, am entirely convinced both by the symbolic importance of our sanctioning hate crime and by the understanding that civic equality is the bedrock justification of our criminal justice system. Yet the emotional debate on hate crime legislation can at times feel distracting, a part of the American habit of trying to cabin the "problem of racism" to the worst kind of explicitly racist acts, ignoring the deeper structural problems of racism in the criminal law system. Indeed, it is no small irony that the first hate crime statutes explicitly protecting people of color in America were passed by slave-owning states, in large part to signal to abolitionists that slavery's gross injustice was tempered by laws protecting otherwise "right-less" slaves (Aaronson 2014). Similarly, early hate crime legislation spread to Northern states who found them an expedient method of addressing complaints of racial inequality without addressing deeper structural racism in criminal law, housing, employment and so on. It is to the deeper questions of structural racism in criminal law we now turn.

STRUCTURAL RACISM AND CRIMINAL LAW

To view criminal law as both a cite and a generator of structural racism is to hold a deeper and more indicting view of the connection between race and criminal law. On the strongest view, the criminal law system is not accidentally infected or corrupted with racism. Rather, the core insight of Critical Race

Studies is that law is a reflection of and important tool in reinforcing and reproducing American racism. This understanding of racism in the criminal law system illuminates that there is no singular racist moment in criminal law; rather, there are countless racial obstacles or "wires," each of which may seem individually minor but represent, into their totality, a powerful source of racial oppression.

Legislation

The most obvious place to start is of course with the law itself. In fields outside of criminal law, it is quite common to inspect the law for evidence of racism, whether a piece of legislation is motivated by racial animus or an otherwise "neutral" law creates or entrenches racial advantages through selective enforcement or disparate impact. Historical versions of the first were both obvious and searing, laws that criminalized a person of color entering certain spaces or marrying outside their race and so on. Their obviousness and constitutional prohibition make it too easy to assume that "racist" criminal laws are a thing of the past. Yet there remains the regular use of criminal law to punish minorities even if explicit racial categories are absent. Indeed, it has been the project of Critical Race Studies to examine the way in which law responds to and entrenches racial dominance without explicit racial categories. (Roithmayr 2000).

One infamous historical example, the disproportionate sentencing difference between powder cocaine, considered a "White drug," and crack cocaine, a "Black drug," is an example of how legislation can be tailored and aimed at different communities without explicit mention of race (Sklansky 1995).[4] A contemporary contrast further illustrates how the very aims of criminal legislation too often depend on race. Notice the current American explosion in drug use, crimes and deaths, particularly the epidemic of opiate addiction.[5] The most striking difference between the current wave of heroin-related deaths and the devastation that accompanied that of the crack-cocaine epidemic in the mid-1980s is the prevalence of harm now found in White and rural communities, as opposed to Black and urban ones. Yet rather than resort to the militarized policing and "civilization versus super-predators" rhetoric that characterized the crack epidemic, this epidemic has been characterized by police officers learning how to administer naloxone in cases of overdose, steering addicts into rehab and addressing crimes as a symptom of addiction rather than as reasons to imprison large portions of a community's young (White) men.[6] The starkly different responses and absence of punishing new legislation illustrates the long-held complaint of minority communities that they are both over- and under-policed (Miller 2006). The point remains that distress in White communities is often seen as a social problem where distress in Black communities is seen as a criminal law problem (Forman 2004).

We need not rely on any one historical example to highlight the point that the structure of legislation itself can be shot through with racism. Loitering laws, long a source of constitutional controversy, directly descend from laws aimed at controlling the newly freed slaves (Lopez 2010). A new generation of scholars have turned their attention to the way misdemeanor legislation not only quietly unravels lives but does so as a method of controlling minority communities (Natapoff 2012; Kohler-Hausmann 2014).

Take another example that has seared itself into our cultural memory, the police killing of Eric Garner on Staten Island in 2014. It has been largely forgotten that the crime for which Garner was confronted by the police was that of selling "loosies," single cigarettes, out of their package, at a slight markup. Ostensibly, the legal justification for the criminal prohibition is that it is a violation of the tax laws.

It is hard to imagine that the revenue lost from selling single cigarettes is a sufficiently serious matter as to require the attention of our criminal law. Put plainly, it is nearly impossible to imagine such a law being passed if there were any realistic possibility that its targets would not be the poor and in particular poor people of color. (By contrast, debates about how to tax the billions of dollars of internet sales lasted for years, costing untold millions without the causal deployment of the police force.) That such statutes overwhelm the American criminal landscape shows how reflexively we rely on criminal law as a primary method of social control, particularly when those to be controlled are racial minorities. Laws from marijuana regulation to those governing Eric Garner are passed because they allow legal control of discrete minority populations (Geller and Fagan 2010). Thus, even the soothing bromide that were we simply to enforce "the laws" neutrally the racism of criminal law would disappear is mistaken.

Policing

By far the topic that has commanded the most attention at the intersection of race and criminal law has been that of policing. The literature over a number of decades is voluminous and rich; indeed, there is no more a consistent thread in the American criminal law experience than the cry of racial injustice in policing (Cottoral 1996; Turner et al. 2006). The basic claim has already been stated. Minority communities often complain of being over-policed and under-protected. Put differently, police surveillance is viewed as not for the benefit of minority citizens but rather as an exercise of power over minority citizens (Capers 2013, 2009).

The historical tension between racial minorities and the police is well known, resulting in a lower perception of legitimacy of criminal law generally and policing in particular in minority communities (Bell 2017; Smith 2010; Brooks 2000; Meares 1997). Confirming the collective memory with empirical evidence is no simple task, in particular given the large number of disparate police forces across the nation and their reluctance to collect and share evidence that would reveal racial bias (to say nothing of the difficulty of disentangling causal relationships even if some perfect data set could be obtained).

Still, the evidence, if not able to answer every question, makes clear that racial minorities, and in particular African-Americans, experience discriminatory policing at every turn. On the streets, a generation of "stop and frisk" policing strategies have institutionalized the disproportionate stopping, searching, harassment and humiliation of millions of overwhelmingly African-American and Hispanic men (Thompson 1999).[7] African-Americans are also more likely to be subject to police attention and arrest for vaguely defined minor crimes and misdemeanors which grant police officers wide discretion. On the roads, African-Americans experience police power as unchecked and biased (Yankah 2019a, b; Carbado 2017; Woods 2015; Epp et al. 2014; Harris 1998, 1997; Sklansky 1997). Thus, despite an absence of any evidence of dissimilar driving, African-Americans and Hispanics are stopped at rates widely disproportionate to their numbers on the road. In some studies, despite being anywhere from 17% to 20% of drivers on the road, minority drivers constituted over 70% of all those pulled over by the police. Still, none of the statistics can fully capture the combination of humiliation and rage that accompanies knowing that a police officer has pulled you over because you are Black and there is no legal recourse—a flat truth revealed in the sardonic understanding that one can be guilty of the crime of "driving while Black."

Finally, one cannot ignore the volatile tinder these interactions create, resulting in spectacular and tragic explosions. In a world soaked in the cultural image of men of color as criminals, such moments lead to murderous violence against Black and Brown men by the police. The last few years have revealed to the nation in heartbreaking images the use of excessive force long complained of by minority communities. The videos of police officers unjustifiably killing unarmed Black men have not only shocked the national conscience but have laid bare the unstable tension between suspicious minority communities and the police—how quickly seemingly innocuous traffic stops can turn deadly (Carbado 2016, 2017; Simmons 2014; Maclin 1998, 1991).

PROSECUTION

Racially disproportionate contact with the police naturally ensnares too many racial minorities in criminal prosecution. Here too the available evidence shows racial minorities are unjustly treated by prosecutors. Because prosecutors maintain vast discretion over who and how to charge and have career incentives that often reward high conviction rates, their conscious or unconscious biases can have devastating ripple effects on African-American, Hispanic and other minority defendants (Pfaff 2014, 2013, 2012). Again, the evidence is difficult to marshal but ultimately suggestive. On the one hand, some studies have suggested that African-American and Hispanic defendants are more likely to have charges dismissed by prosecutors.[8] One might wonder if this is an indicator of prosecutorial leniency or a sign that there was insufficient evidence to warrant a justified arrest in the first place (Butler 2017). Weighing against the hypothesis that prosecutors are lenient on Black men is the evidence that African-Americans are almost twice as likely to be charged with a federal crime that carries a mandatory minimum sentence (Starr and Rehavi 2014). Further, the same study found that Blacks and Latinos are more likely to be held for misdemeanors and receive less favorable plea offers,[9] making the idea that prosecutors are lenient on minority defendants implausible.

SENTENCING

Not surprisingly, racial biases continue into conviction and sentencing as well. Evidence over the last three decades has illustrated that African-Americans are significantly more likely than Whites to be wrongfully convicted of sexual assault and murder (Gross et al. 2017).[10] Whether this is due to persistent racial disparities in jury selection is unknown (Anwar et al. 2012; Alexander 2010). Further, African-American defendants have been found to receive disproportionate sentences; African-Americans are 20% more likely to be sentenced to prison, 21% more likely to receive mandatory minimum sentences[11] and receive sentences that are 10% longer than similarly situated White defendants.[12] Some studies have shown straightforward and raw racial hostility that simply costs years and lives. In one study, defendants perceived to be "Blacker," that is, having darker skin, broader noses or other perceived "African" traits, were more likely to be found guilty and treated harsher (Eberhardt et al. 2006). Most famously, the "Baldus study," the centerpiece of *McCleskey v. Kemp*,[13] illustrated that race played an important role in how we allocate death in capital trials.

RACE AND MASS INCARCERATION

Even when aware of the racial disparities in our criminal justice system, the results never fail to stun. If we as a nation are overenthusiastic in using incarceration generally, the cruel distribution across racial lines invites the view of criminal law as a mode of racial (and interwoven class) control.[14] African-Americans, who constitute roughly 13% of the overall population, are 38% of all inmates in American prisons.[15] Hispanics, roughly the same percentage of population, make up another 20% of all prisoners. These figures, shocking in themselves, insufficiently communicate how our system of criminal punishment consumes so many bodies and souls. American prisons are, in the literal sense, dispiriting places with conditions that should shock any right-thinking person. Our over-reliance on prisons has resulted in such over-crowding that California, the largest state in the country, found its prison conditions violated the constitutional prohibition on cruel and unusual punishment.[16] Further, we have allowed prison cruelty to become a business. Even the perils of profit-driven mass incarceration are haunted by our history of racism; the 13th Amendment which explicitly carves out an exception for prisoners to be pressed into involuntary servitude is widely understood as a tool of racial domination that permitted the domination of the newly freed slaves after the civil war (Lopez 2010).

As noted, the harms of incarceration are not equally spread: poor and minority communities are vastly overrepresented in our country's prisons. It is obvious that spending time in prison is damaging in many ways for a particular person. Yet it would be a mistake to understand the racially disproportionate costs of mass incarceration as simply the piling up of individual suffering without understanding the way harms are shared (and amplified) within a community. With disproportionate numbers of African-Americans and Hispanics in prison, African-American and Hispanic communities, not just individuals, are gutted. In many communities, young men—some of whom could be continuing education or job training, beginning careers or simply being brothers, sons and fathers—are absent for long stretches of time (Yankah 2019a, b; Tonry 1994). All too often, they return with bruised psyches, stunted social and emotional growth and decimated job prospects (Forman 2012, pp. 30–31). Concentrated neighborhoods of marred young men cannot offer each other the type of everyday social support that contributes to a successful life such as a job tip, introduction to a supervisor or admissions counselor or sometimes, simply constructive, as opposed to pathos-tinged, advice (Galster 1993).

Just as within prisons, neighborhoods concentrated with the exiled and the disaffected can replicate a toxic stew of destructive social norms, particularly caustic drug use and volatile urban machismo. Distilled to hazardous levels around tattered barbershops or street corners, these traits are distressing to fellow members of the community. If unable to command, through either personal or political resources, constructive methods of repairing the social fabric, distressed neighbors may resort to accepting or even promoting harsher policing methods to stave off blight or, in the case of the wealthier residents, leave altogether (Forman 2017; Clear 2007; Kelling and Coles 1996, pp. 21–25, 30–37, 242–43, 247–57). The well-known irony is that with the most stabilizing members of a community fleeing, the already-fraying neighborhood may find itself further in tatters, with the already vulnerable ex-convicts ever more likely to become recidivists. Thus, the harm is not simply to one after another Black or Hispanic ex-felon. Given the concentration of mass incarceration in minority communities, the harms visited on the individual person radiate out, corroding entire communities. Further, with a disproportionate number of young men of color, particularly young Black men, imprisoned or under state supervision, it becomes impossible to cabin the social stigma that transforms dark skin itself into a sign of criminality, erecting a social image of Black men as dangerous and criminal (Yankah 2019a, b; Forman 2012, 2004; Alexander 2010; Muhammad 2010).

COLLATERAL SANCTIONS

Once released, ex-felons face a raft of punitive measures, antiseptically labeled "collateral sanctions" (Yankah 2004; Demleitner 1999). Perhaps most visible, many ex-felons find they are prohibited from voting (Fletcher 1999; Varnum 2008; Forman 2012). Voting disenfranchisement rightfully attracts attention because it sends a powerful message—even after serving the required sentence, your voice no longer matters; you are no longer a political equal (Yankah 2004; Hampton 1998). The disproportionate effects of disenfranchisement on minority voting power have long been a practical and symbolic wound.

However symbolically powerful, voting disenfranchisement pales in comparison to the myriad of quieter ways in which ex-felons are exiled from social and economic life. An ex-felon with ambitions to remake their life through transformative education will find opportunities and financial aid foreclosed from most institutions (Manza and Uggen 2006; Thompson 2008). Rebuilding a life through steady work is no little feat; in many jurisdictions, ex-felons are excluded from trades from which a life could be rebuilt—barred from jobs from hairdressers to bartenders (Mitchell 2007; May 1995). If these blockades leave the ex-felon on hard times, there is little remedy. Many jurisdictions prohibit ex-felons from living in public housing, receiving welfare benefits or healthcare. It is hard to imagine a clearer message that society is indifferent to an ex-felon's needs than being denied food stamps. If such collateral sanctions make the reintegration of all former felons difficult, the combination of such laws with already-existing racial discrimination is devastating. One eye-opening study found that Black job applicants without a criminal record received callbacks at a lower rate than White applicants with a criminal record (Pager 2007). The expectation that young Black men are latent criminals makes an already vulnerable population even more so, erecting barriers to work and social mobility even for Black and Hispanic men who have no criminal record and exiling those who do.

Race, Criminal Law and an Ethical Life

All of this has been an over-quick survey of a massive subject at too high an altitude. Important subjects have been merely broached, hinted at and in unfortunate cases, left entirely aside. Hopefully, the method of inspection has at least highlighted an important cleft in how different people approach the question itself. No less in criminal law than in politics more broadly, the question of race and criminal law often suffers when commentators begin with very different views of the phenomenon under inspection. Though by no means innovative, clarifying the distinction between racism as a basic motivation for the law to punish or racism as a problem of the deep structure of our criminal law system, from how we address social problems, to what crimes we punish and to the persistent negative disparities experienced by people of color, may help avoid speaking past one another. As the survey has revealed, I stand firmly in the camp that understands the overwhelming problem of race in American criminal law is one of structural racism rather than cinematic racists motivated solely by hate.

The harder question, taken up in conclusion, concerns the link-up with the subject of this collection, that is, ethical life and criminal law. Though there are obviously many possible links, I wish to suggest that the problem of race in criminal law poses a particular and acute ethical problem for American citizens and suggest some very speculative replies.

To be clear, I take ethical questions to be connected to but different than purely "moral" questions. If the moral is concerned primarily with duties, prohibitions and permissions—what you must do and what you must not do—the ethical is concerned with a broader range of questions concerning how one ought to live more generally. In this rough and ready divide, the ethical is concerned with the kind of character one should cultivate and how one should relate to various worthwhile projects in one's life. An ethical life requires contemplation of the attention one ought to give others even when not duty bound to do so (Yankah 2011).

It has been understood since Aristotle that an ethical life is sensitive to the conditions in which one finds themselves; an ethical life can rarely be created alone from whole cloth and is to some extent hostage to the environment into which one is born. To be born, for example, into fabulous wealth and privilege because one's parents have massive slaveholdings is to have many of one's accomplishments stained even if through no fault of your own. On this view, American citizens also face an important ethical dilemma, if not as dramatic (or perhaps not as immediately temporal), as the heir to a living slave fortune.

The Ethical Challenges of the Racially Disadvantaged

That the criminal justice system is deeply marked with racism will obviously not affect all equally; given the salience of class, it will not even affect all racial minorities equally. But the most vulnerable—racial minorities living in persistent or ghetto poverty—will rightfully view the criminal law as failing to live up to what it rightfully owes them as a fellow citizen. To the extent the many of the most disenfranchised citizens of color are systematically disadvantaged by an unjust criminal law system, I join Tommie Shelby in harboring serious doubts that such citizens have anything like a robust obligation to obey the criminal law (Shelby 2016). This claim ought not to be wildly interpreted to mean that racially disadvantaged citizens are free to commit serious wrongdoing; no one is morally permitted to attack, rape or kill others regardless of legal prohibitions. Outside of their natural duties, however, given they are meaningfully excluded from the legal system of reciprocal benefits, the persistently racially disadvantaged do not have the robust civic obligations that ground a global legal obligation.

That said, disadvantaged citizens, meaningfully excluded from the civic bargain and rightfully rejecting criminal law, will find themselves in an ethically precarious circumstance. Though the failed legitimacy of criminal law does not remove moral prohibitions on violence or serious rights violations, it would be a mistake to imagine that those are the only purposes of criminal law. The criminal law often sets or enforces the boundaries of collectively acceptable behavior, from safety requirements in daycares to how much one must reveal to a buyer in a transaction to how disputes over debts ought to be handled.

Poor racial minorities, finding criminal law systematically indifferent to or even hostile to their well-being, are thrown on their own ethical resources to determine countless difficult questions, from what counts as fair dealing to what norms best regulate public space and interactions. This, of course, is what we see in countless poor minority communities as informal norms replace laws viewed as cynical or oppressive. But we need little imagination to see how such informal norms are susceptible to pathologies.

The Ethical Challenges of the Racially Advantaged

Disadvantaged minorities are not the only citizens for whom the racial illegitimacy of criminal law poses an ethical threat. Outside our admiration for resilience of the most disadvantaged, it seems even more pressing to inspect how ordinarily advantaged Americans, those in whose name the state oppresses, should relate to a substantially illegitimate criminal justice system (Yankah 2019a).[17]

The illegitimacy of the criminal justice system means that when the law does not treat racial minorities as full and equal citizens, particularly across their most important basic liberty rights, severely disadvantaged minorities may reject it as fully binding. But those reasons do not apply to the advantaged citizen, at least not in the same way. She is included in the set of reciprocal benefits secured by the legal system; indeed, to the extent the criminal law exempts her from an unjust allocation of burdens, she appears to be in the opposite position.

Yet advantaged citizens also face a pressing ethical challenge living under a racially corrupt criminal law system. First, they have reason to understand that criminal law's injustice destabilizes their claim to successes in their own lives, devaluing them by rendering them, to some extent, unjust enrichment. Second, this is not simply because the system is suboptimal or unattractive but because she understands that the system is seriously unjust *in her name* (Cooper 2005).

These two points are critical. A seriously unjust legal system anywhere gives reasons to abhor or protest it. But without further explanation, it is not the case that all injustices undermine your relationship with the shape of your own life, with its successes and benefits. Because these injustices are not systematically constructed to favor you, they do not properly indict your goals and projects as the spoils of unjust enrichment (Beitz 2010).[18] Further, serious institutional injustices perpetrated for your benefit, by your own polity and in your name create a different relationship to those wrongs and impose different demands. Of course, this is in part because one stands in a factually different relationship with their own state; one is typically a small but continuous player in a long-running project. But this material difference does not entirely explain the moral distinction. After all, it is perfectly sensible to understand one's duty to work toward goals in one's society that are unlikely to be realized in anything but the distant future (Scheffler 2016, pp. 15–81; MacIntyre 1984). In the case of a consistent injustice in one's polity taken in one's name, there is a felt value of repudiation even if not cashed out in effective reform.

Returning to our thesis, that the criminal law amplifies racial injustices gives many advantaged citizens particular reasons to reject criminal law's claims to obedience. Obviously, not all advantaged citizens, reasonably secure from the worst systemic injustices of criminal law, are White; upper- and middle-class racial minorities are vastly less likely than poor minorities to be subject to criminal law (Forman 2012, pp. 52–58). Nonetheless, our criminal law system systematically treats racial minorities, particularly African-Americans and Hispanics, unjustly. Embedded in a history (and present) where criminal law was used to secure racial hierarchy, there is no way to understand the injustices of our criminal justice system except as expressing that the Black and Brown people are worth less than Whites. Further, knowing such damage can only continue with the implicit support or acquiescence of many White citizens means one has a duty not to be seen as willing to "play along." Thus, White citizens have reasons to reject the racial injustice of the criminal law system and repudiate its claims of their own racial superiority.

The systemic injustices of criminal law secure unjust advantages for too many "ordinary" citizens, rendering their successes and life projects in part unjust spoils. Second, the very law that chews through lives and communities in the ghetto does not only advantage those outside of it but does so in their name. Lastly, White citizens have a unique duty to reject the racist elements of the criminal justice system to repudiate its claims that the lives of racial minorities are worth less than their own. Taken together the racial injustice of the criminal law system presents advantaged citizens with a parallel ethical dilemma as to how to relate to their criminal law system.

That advantaged citizens may rightfully reject a global obligation to comply with criminal law does not mean ignoring criminal law willy-nilly. Just as ghetto residents must think carefully about whether instances of lawbreaking effect positive changes, establishing a fairer criminal law system, even more so do advantaged citizens (Shelby 2016, pp. 222–227). However one engages in lawbreaking as resistance, the justified rejection of criminal law in the service of civic equality fails if the lawbreaking intensifies civic injuries particularly within ghetto communities or deepens corrosive ghetto identities such as "hustlers" and "gangsters."

Though rejecting criminal law highlights the serious duties advantaged citizens have in light of their greater resources, it seems that outside of extraordinary moments, citizens do not have a duty to undertake heroic self-sacrifice. Further, in thinking carefully about particular illegal acts, advantaged citizens in particular must measure not just how their actions will repudiate the injustices of the criminal law system but likely effects on justified (or perhaps excusable) portions of the political order, including harms to vulnerable poor and racial minorities. Taken together, these two tenets generate not only a presumption against general violence toward police officers, already noted in the natural duty against harming others, but caution in how one resists the demands of criminal law. Encouraging indiscriminate violence against police officers not only violates their rights but would utterly rend the already-frayed fabric of the most impoverished communities (and the broader community besides). As scholars have pointed out for a generation, ghetto communities suffer simultaneously from over-policing and under-protection (Gamal 2016). Escalating the serious problems with urban policing into a shooting war promises only to exacerbate the situation.

Precisely because the unjust burdens of criminal law are systematically produced, the first and most obvious duty of advantaged citizens is to engage in systematic reform. Such reform can often feel both glacial and quotidian; reform is often the stuff of ordinary political activity. For most, such reform means at a minimum voting for more just criminal law policies and engaging in a range of political activity meant to produce systemic change, from protesting to running for office, from writing their representatives to writing op-eds. Still, although dedicated systemic reform measures are critical, they do not fully answer the motivating question; given that even plausibly successful systemic reform is a long-term project, what ethical stance should advantaged citizens take toward criminal law while it is still recognizably unjust? I do not pretend to have a detailed menu of permissible lawbreaking by advantaged citizens and in any case circumstances on the ground are likely to be too subtle and changing to create a stable list. I can only nominate a few telling examples, ranging from the quixotic to systematic, that give shape to the kind of repudiation I believe required of advantaged citizens.

In July 2017, following racial justice protests, a mixed-race group of protestors in Durham, North Carolina, pulled down a Confederate war monument in broad daylight with numbers of people filming. Police warned the offending protestors they had been identified and should turn themselves in. In solidarity, dozens of activists appeared to "turn themselves in" along with the identified protesters.[19] Not surprisingly, all charges were eventually dropped.[20]

Along related lines, Paul Butler has argued African-American jurors should refuse to vote to convict African-American defendants of non-violent drug crimes regardless of the evidence (Butler 1995). By using their power of jury nullification, even in contradiction to the law, jurors would be standing with African-American defendants in the face of a criminal justice system which punishes them disproportionately at every stage. My arguments make clear why Butler's proposal if anything is too modest. Given the continued bias in sentencing and institutional barriers suppressing African-American participation in jurors (Anwar et al. 2012), all advantaged citizens and White citizens in particular should deploy this power of jury nullification.

Among the most obvious sites of unjust criminal law enforcement, and its systematic advantages for the well off, is the intricate interaction between race, criminal and immigration law, sometimes dubbed "crimmigration" law (Markowitz and Nash 2018; Vazquez 2017; Hernández and Cuauhtémoc 2015). Again, the advantaged citizens can take it upon themselves to stand against unconscionable laws in ways that clearly repudiate the law rather than seek advantage. I have in mind the advantaged citizen who pays fair market wages to their undocumented employees or who may even file a worker's tax documents on their behalf without identifying the worker.[21]

Of course, as such resistance gets closer to the state's police functions, the tensions to be negotiated are greater still. Over the last few years, it has become increasingly common for citizens witnessing acts ranging from police brutality to unacceptable harassment and intimidation of racial minorities to film and/or admonish the police. Obviously, the tradition of confronting police officers to protest racism or injustice is deeper than the one-off encounters. Various progressive or radical social justice organizations conduct trainings to teach ordinary citizens how to be "street lawyers" or deploy large groups of legally trained observers to events where citizens and police can be expected to clash.[22] In our recent history, socio-political organizations such as the Black Panther Party for Self-Defense were organized around training armed citizen patrols to monitor police behavior and deter misconduct (Seale and Shames 2016).

Though there are countless other examples one could give, one important example causes me disquiet. One obvious way an advantaged citizen can ameliorate uneven burdens in criminal law is by refusing to assist the police in punishing crime (or going even further, actively assisting disadvantaged citizens in committing crimes). The reason for the disquiet is obvious; a culture in which many turn their back on assisting the police globally (as opposed to judiciously combating unjust policing practices) may spin even further into dysfunction and leave crime victims, themselves usually disadvantaged citizens, frustrated and at risk. Many moments where a citizen has the power to restrain the criminal law, to not press charges or withhold information will require careful judgment based on information in which one may lack confidence. Indeed, it is one of the great frustrations of an illegitimate and overly punitive criminal law system that the victim of a crime who otherwise wishes to report a crime and move on with their lives is thrown on their own resources to measure these subtle variables. Is the perpetrator *really* a member of ghetto poor such that inviting criminal punishment adds to the political injustice of their circumstance?

As noted this is precisely the ethical challenge raised by a racially illegitimate criminal law system to which all must respond. Tolerable vandalism, evasion of taxes through under-the-table work, drug use, petty thieving and worse may strike one as at least plausibly reported to authorities in wealthy advantaged communities but should be ignored in already over-punished or distressed communities, not just because they may be expressions of frustration or survival mechanisms but because criminal law is unlikely to help and often exacerbates the background conditions of injustice. But a wise citizen will be thoughtful about the point at which, even under an illegitimate criminal law system, refusing to assist the police in very serious instances of criminality intensifies the damage to distressed communities.

CONCLUSION

In closing it is important to note the duties of all citizens, particularly citizens with the advantages of race and class, to press against the claims of criminal law is not academic fancy or to be taken lightly. As noted earlier, it is overly simplistic to think of political legitimacy as a binary. Criminal law and many of the individual actors within it do tremendous good, protecting citizens and in particular many in the poorest communities. The institutions of criminal law are practically justified to the extent that living our common lives in pursuit of civic goods would be impossible without it (Yankah 2015). Symbolically, a justified criminal law signifies that each citizen must treat each other with a minimum equal civic respect. Yet the very power criminal punishment wields to hold us together threatens immense damage and to the extent that it reproduces our collective history of racial trauma, unraveling lives, banishing individuals to second-class citizenship and imposing a stigma of Black criminality, citizens are obligated to reject its unjust portions and demand it remake itself into something legitimate. But navigating the manner in which we relate to the institutions of criminal law, as well as to each other, under a racially unjust system leaves all citizens negotiating an ethically treacherous civic landscape.

NOTES

1. That is not to say that the distinction between "individual racism" and "structural racism" is at all new (Carmichael and Hamilton 1967, p. 4).
2. U.S. Department of Justice, Office of Justice Programs, Bureau of Justice Statistics, Criminal Offender Statistics. Available at: https://www.bjs.gov/content/pub/pdf/p13.pdf (3/5/19).
3. Sabol et al. (2010): U.S. Department of Justice, Office of Justice Programs, Bureau of Justice Statistics, December 2009, NCJ 228417, https://www.bjs.gov/content/pub/pdf/p08.pdf, p. 2.
4. Anti-Drug Abuse Act of 1986, Pub. L. No. 99–570, 100 Stat. 3207 (codified as amended at 21 U.S.C.§§ 841–904 (2012)). As one might imagine, whether Congress was motivated by or blind to the racial impact of this disparity is now generally denied by those in Congress at the time. 156 Cong. Rec. H6202 (daily ed. July 28, 2010) (statement of Rep. Daniel E. Lungren) (noting that Congress enacted the 100-to-1 ratio "thinking we were doing the right thing at the time"); 155 Cong. Rec. S10491 (daily ed. Oct. 15, 2009) (statement of Sen. Richard Durbin) ("Those of us who supported the law establishing this disparity had good intentions"); ibid., S10493 (statement of Sen. Specter) ("I do not believe that the 1986 Act was intended to have a disparate impact on minorities but the reality is that it does").
5. Kolata and Cohen (2016).
6. Yankah (2016).
7. Report of Jeffrey Fagan, Ph.D. at 22 tbl.3, Floyd v. City of New York, No. 08-01034 (S.D.N.Y. Jan. 31, 2008). In New York City, home of the nation's largest police force, near 4.5 million stop and frisks were recorded between 2004 and 2012. New York's population is roughly 23% Black, 29% Hispanic and

33% White. Nonetheless, in 52% of all searches, the persons searched were Black. In another 31% of the searches, the persons were Hispanic. Blacks and Hispanics were not only vastly disproportionately the target of searches but they also disproportionately experienced police violence. Though over half of these searches were justified as weapons searches, a weapon was found in only 1.5% of these searches. In bitter irony, weapons and contraband were slightly more likely to be found on White persons searched than on either Black or Hispanic persons searched. Just as in *Terry*, the overwhelming stated justifications for initiating the stops are vague descriptors that are easily influenced by racial stereotypes or prejudice such as "furtive movements" and "high crime areas." Examining the record in *Floyd v. City of New York* highlights the obvious: a regime that allows and shields such wildly disparate practices from legal check and all but declares that persons of color live under a different policing regime without recourse.

8. Kutateladze et al. (2014, p. 3).
9. Ibid.
10. Gross et al. (2017).
11. Kerby (2012).
12. United States Sentencing Commission (2010); Spohn (2017, pp. 211–226).
13. McCleskey v. Kemp, 481 U.S. 279 (1987). Specifically, the famous Baldus study, featured in that case, found that a defendant who killed a White victim was vastly more likely to receive the death penalty than one who killed a Black victim. Additionally, the study found that Black defendants were slightly more likely to receive the death penalty than similarly situated White defendants. The study concluded that a Black defendant who killed a White victim was most likely to receive the death penalty.
14. Michelle Alexander comprehensively and eloquently illuminated this problem while giving it a powerful name in her book-length treatment (Alexander 2010).
15. Sabol et al. (2010, p. 2).
16. Brown v. Plata.
17. How confident one has to be in their assessment of the legitimacy of a system is an important issue I leave largely unaddressed. For now, it is enough to note that a thoughtful citizen will not causally decide that his idiosyncratic assessment will be sufficient and begin treating the system as illegitimate. A thoughtful citizen will consult a range of experts across the ideological spectrum and engage in meaningful deliberation with fellow citizens before reaching a conclusion. This does not guarantee that he will not reach deeply mistaken conclusions. The dangers of self-selected sources or simply flawed reasoning are unavoidable.
18. Indeed, to the extent some philosophical cosmopolitans assert that one has equal duties to victims of injustice in other polities, they often ground these duties in the argument that international economic relationships are unjustly created for the enrichment of citizens of rich nations. Beitz (2010).
19. Judge (2017).
20. Bridges and Johnson (2017).
21. As I very roughly understand it, while it is unlawful to file a return without identifying the person, one will be liable for a much more minor offense associated with a failure to file a complete claim rather than a failure to pay. 26 U.S.C. § 6651(a)(1) (2012) (failure to file return); ibid., at § 6651(a)(2) (failure to pay). I am very grateful to tax law colleagues who walked me patiently through this thinking, Mitch Attas, Mitchell Engler and, most especially,

Edward Zelinsky. Highly public claims of avoiding taxes on undocumented workers are too numerous to catalogue but a particularly salient pair of examples can be seen in the President Bill Clinton's twin nominations of Zoë Baird for United States Attorney General and, the following month, Kimba Wood as a federal judge. It became known that both of them had employed undocumented immigrants as childcare workers. Importantly, Baird had avoided paying any associated taxes for her employees. Wood, who had hired her employee when it was legal, had paid the associated social security tax. Following so shortly after Baird's bruising nomination, Wood's nomination was also withdrawn. For our purposes, it is important to note that Wood was in a better position to show that her employment was not exploitative or for her unfair benefit.

22. Among the most prominent of these is the National Lawyers Guild and its various workshops on street lawyering.

References

21 U.S.C.§§ 841–904 (2012).

26 U.S.C. § 6651(a)(1) (2012).

156 Cong. Rec. H6202 (daily ed. July 28, 2010).

155 Cong. Rec. S10491 (daily ed. Oct. 15, 2009).

Brown v. Plata, 563 U.S. 493 (2011).

Floyd v. City of New York, No. 08–01034 (S.D.N.Y. Jan. 31, 2008).

McCleskey v. Kemp, 481 U.S. 279 (1987).

Aaronson, Ely. 2014. *From slave abuse to hate crime: The criminalization of racial violence in American history*. New York: Cambridge University Press.

Alexander, Michelle. 2010. *The new Jim Crow: Mass incarceration in the age of colorblindness*. New York: The New Press.

Anwar, Shamena, Patrick Bayer, and Randi Hjalmarsson. 2012. The impact of jury race in criminal trials. *Quarterly Journal of Economics* 127: 1017–1055.

Atuahene, Bernadette. 2018. "Our taxes are too damn high": Institutional racism, property tax assessments, and the fair housing act. *Northwestern University Law Review* 112: 1501–1564.

Atuahene, Bernadette, and Timothy Hodge. 2018. Stategraft. *Southern California Law Review* 91: 263–302.

Bagenstos, Samuel R. 2006. The structural turn and the limits of antidiscrimination law. *California Law Review* 94: 1–48.

Beitz, Charles R. 2010. Justice and international relations. In *The cosmopolitanism reader*, ed. Garret Wallace Brown and David Held, 85–99. Cambridge: Polity Press.

Bell, Monica. 2017. Police reform and the dismantling of legal estrangement. *Yale Law Journal* 126: 2054–2150.

Braithwaite, John, and Philip Pettit. 1990. *Not just deserts: A republican theory of criminal justice*. Oxford: Clarendon Press.

Bridges, Virginia, and Joe Johnson. 2017. Durham DA drops charges against 3 people accused of toppling Confederate monument. *Herald Sun*. https://www.heraldsun.com/news/local/counties/durham-county/article183661686.html. Accessed 5 Mar 2019.

Brooks, Richard R.W. 2000. Fear and fairness in the city: Criminal enforcement and perceptions of fairness in minority communities. *Southern California Law Review* 73: 1219–1275.

Butler, Paul. 1995. Racially based jury nullification: Black power in the criminal justice system. *Yale Law Journal* 105: 677–725.

———. 2016. The system is working the way it is supposed to: The limits of criminal justice reform. *Georgetown Law Review* 104: 1419–1478.

———. 2017. Race and adjudication. In Vol. 3 of *Reforming criminal justice*, ed. Erik Luna, 211–226. Phoenix: Arizona State University.

Capers, Bennett. 2009. Policing, place, and race. *Harvard Civil Rights-Civil Liberties Law Review* 44: 43–78.

———. 2013. Crime, surveillance, communities. *Fordham Urban Law Journal* 40: 959–992.

Carbado, Devon W. 2016. Blue-on-black violence: A provisional model of some of the causes. *Georgetown Law Journal* 104: 1479–1529.

———. 2017. From stop and frisk to shoot and kill: *Terry v. Ohio's* pathway to police violence. *UCLA Law Review* 64: 1508–1552.

Carmichael, Stokely, and Charles V. Hamilton. 1967. *Black power: The politics of liberation in America*. New York: Random House.

Clear, Todd R. 2007. *Imprisoning communities: How mass incarceration makes disadvantaged neighborhoods worse*. Oxford: Oxford University Press.

Cooper, John. 2005. Political animals and civic friendship. In *Aristotle's politics: Critical essays*, ed. Richard Kraut and Steven Skultety, 65–90. Lanham: Rowman & Littlefield Publishers.

Cottoral, Robert J. 1996. Outlawing outcasts: Comparative perspectives on the differing functions of the criminal law of slavery in the Americas. *Cardozo Law Review* 18 (2): 717–752.

Crenshaw, Kimberle. 1989. Demarginalizing the intersection of race and sex: A black feminist critique of antidiscrimination doctrine, feminist theory and antiracist politics. *University of Chicago Legal Forum* 1989: 139–168.

Delgado, Richard. 2011. Rodrigo's reconsideration: Intersectionality and the future of critical race theory. *Iowa Law Review* 96: 1247–1288.

Demleitner, Nora. 1999. Preventing internal exile: The need for restrictions on collateral sentencing consequences. *Stanford Law & Policy Review* 11: 153–172.

Duff, R.A. 2001. *Punishment, communication, and community*. Oxford: Oxford University Press.

———. 2007. *Answering for crime: Responsibility and liability in the criminal law*. Portland: Hart Publishing.

Eberhardt, Jennifer L., P.G. Davies, Valerie J. Purdie-Vaughns, and Sheri Lynn Johnson. 2006. Looking deathworthy: Perceived stereotypicality of black defendants predicts capital-sentencing outcomes. *Psychological Science* 17: 383–386.

Epp, Charles R., Steven Maynard-Moody, and Donald Haider-Markel. 2014. *Pulled over: How police stops define race and citizenship*. Chicago: University of Chicago Press.

Feinberg, Joel. 1984. *Harm to others*. Oxford: Oxford University Press.

Fletcher, George P. 1999. Disenfranchisement as punishment: Reflections of the racial uses of infamia. *UCLA Law Review* 46: 1895–1908.

Forman, James, Jr. 2004. Community policing and youth as assets. *Journal of Criminal Law and Criminology* 95: 1–48.

———. 2012. Racial critiques of mass incarceration: Beyond the new Jim Crow. *New York University Law Review* 87: 21–69.

———. 2017. *Locking up our own: Crime and punishment in black America.* New York: Farrar, Straus and Giroux.

Galster, George C. 1993. Polarization, place, and race. *North Carolina Law Review* 71: 1421–1462.

Gamal, Fanna. 2016. The racial politics of protection: A critical race examination of police militarization. *California Law Review* 104: 979–1008.

Gee, Harvey. 2010. Asian Americans and criminal law and criminal procedure: A missing chapter from race jurisprudence anthology. *Georgetown Journal of Law & Modern Critical Race Perspectives* 2: 185–208.

Geller, Amanda, and Jeffrey Fagan. 2010. Pot as pretext: Marijuana, race, and the new disorder in New York City street policing. *Journal of Empirical Legal Studies* 7: 591–633.

Glennon, Theresa. 1995. Race, education, and the construction of a disabled class. *Wisconsin Law Review* 1995: 1237–1238.

Green, Tristin K. 2007. A structural approach as antidiscrimination mandate: Locating employer wrong. *Vanderbilt Law Review* 60: 847–904.

Gross, Samuel R., Maurice Possley, and Klara Stephens. 2017. *Race and wrongful convictions in the United States.* University of California Irvine. http://www.law.umich.edu/special/exoneration/Documents/Race_and_Wrongful_Convictions.pdf. Accessed 5 Mar 2019.

Hampton, Jean. 1998. Punishment, feminism, and political identity: A case study in the expressive meaning of law. *Canadian Journal of Law and Jurisprudence* 11: 23–46.

Harel, Alon, and Gideon Parchomovsky. 1999. On hate and equality. *Yale Law Journal* 109: 507–540.

Harris, David A. 1997. "Driving while black" and all other traffic offenses: The Supreme Court and pretextual traffic stops. *Journal of Criminal Law and Criminology* 87: 544–582.

———. 1998. Car wars: The Fourth Amendment's death on the highway. *George Washington Law Review* 66: 556–591.

Harris, Lee A. 2006. From Vermont to Mississippi: Race and cash welfare. *Columbia Human Rights Law Review* 38: 1–50.

Hernández, García, and César Cuauhtémoc. 2015. *Crimmigration law.* Chicago: American Bar Association.

Huigens, Kyron. 1995. Virtue and inculpation. *Harvard Law Review* 108: 1423–1480.

———. 2004. On Aristotelian criminal law: A reply to Duff. *Notre Dame Journal of Law, Ethics and Public Policy* 18: 465–500.

Hurd, Heidi M. 2001. Why liberals should hate "hate crime" legislation. *Law and Philosophy* 20: 215–232.

Hurd, Heidi M., and Michael S. Moore. 2004. Punishing hatred and prejudice. *Stanford Law Review* 56: 1081–1146.

Judge, Monique. 2017. Durham, NC, activists stand in solidarity, crowds gather to turn themselves in for toppling Confederate statue. *Root.* https://www.theroot.com/durham-activists-stand-in-solidarity-crowds-gather-to-1797941708.   Accessed 5 Mar 2019.

Kahan, Dan M. 2001. Two liberal fallacies in the hate crimes debate. *Law and Philosophy* 20: 175–193.

Kahan, Dan M., and Martha C. Nussbaum. 1996. Two conceptions of emotion in criminal law. *Columbia Law Review* 96: 269–374.

Kelling, George L., and Catherine M. Coles. 1996. *Fixing broken windows: Restoring order and reducing crime in our communities*. New York: Touchstone.

Kerby, Sophia. 2012. The top 10 most startling facts about people of color and criminal justice in the United States. *Center for American Progress*. https://www.american-progress.org/issues/race/news/2012/03/13/11351/the-top-10-most-startling-facts-about-people-of-colorand-criminal-justice-in-the-united-states/. Accessed 5 Mar 2019.

Kim, Janine Young. 2006. Hate crime law and the limits of inculpation. *Nebraska Law Review* 84: 846–894.

Kohler-Hausmann, Issa. 2014. Managerial justice and mass misdemeanors. *Stanford Law Review* 66: 611–694.

Kolata, Gina, and Sarah Cohen. 2016. Drug overdoses propel rise in mortality rates of young whites. *New York Times*, January 16.

Kutateladze, Besiki, Whitney Tymas, and Mary Crowley. 2014. Race and prosecution in Manhattan: [specific report]. New York: Vera Institute of Justice. https://storage.googleapis.com/vera-web-assets/downloads/Publications/race-and-prosecution-in-manhattan/legacy_downloads/race-and-prosecution-manhattan-summary.pdf. Accessed 5 Mar 2019.

Lopez, Ian F. Haney. 2007. "A nation of minorities": Race, ethnicity, and reactionary colorblindness. *Stanford Law Review* 59: 985–1064.

———. 2010. Post-racial racism: Racial stratification and mass incarceration in the age of Obama. *California Law Review* 98: 1023–1074.

MacIntyre, Alasdair. 1984. *Is patriotism a virtue?* Lawrence: University of Kansas Press.

Maclin, Tracey. 1991. "Black and blue encounters" some preliminary thoughts about Fourth Amendment seizures: Should race matter? *Valparaiso University Law Review* 26: 243–279.

———. 1998. Race and the Fourth Amendment. *Vanderbilt Law Review* 51: 331–394.

Mann, Coramae Richey. 1993. *Unequal justice: A question of color*. Bloomington: Indiana University Press.

Manza, Jeff, and Christopher Uggen. 2006. *Locked out: Felon disenfranchisement and American democracy*. Oxford: Oxford University Press.

Markowitz, Peter L., and Lindsay Nash. 2018. Pardoning immigrants. *New York University Law Review* 93: 58–106.

Massey, Douglas S. 2007. *Categorically unequal: The American stratification system*. New York: Russell Sage Foundation.

May, Bruce E. 1995. The character component of occupational licensing laws: A continuing barrier to the ex-felon's employment opportunities. *North Dakota Law Review* 71: 187–210.

McLeod, Allegra. 2016. Confronting the carceral state. *Georgetown Law Review* 104: 1405–1418.

Meares, Tracey L. 1997. Charting race and class differences in attitudes toward drug legalization and law enforcement: Lessons for federal criminal law. *Buffalo Criminal Law Review* 1: 137–174.

Miller, Eric J. 2006. Role-based policing: Restraining police conduct "Outside the legitimate investigative sphere". *California Law Review* 94: 617–686.

Mitchell, S. David. 2007. Undermining individual and collective citizenship: The impact of exclusion laws on the African American community. *Fordham Urban Law Journal* 34: 833–888.

Muhammad, Khalil Gibran. 2010. *The condemnation of blackness: Race, crime, and the making of modern America*. Cambridge, MA: Harvard University Press.

Natapoff, Alexandra. 2012. Misdemeanors. *Southern California Law Review* 85: 1313–1376.

Nourse, Victoria. 1998. The new normativity: The abuse excuse and the resurgence of judgment in the criminal law. Review of *Moral judgment: Does the abuse excuse threaten our legal system?*, by James Q. Wilson. *Stanford Law Review* 50: 1435–1470.

———. 2002. Hearts and minds: Understanding the new culpability. *Buffalo Criminal Law Review* 6: 361–388.

Pager, Devah. 2007. *Marked: Race, crime, and finding work in an era of mass incarceration*. Chicago: University of Chicago Press.

Paul-Emile, Kimani. 2018. Blackness as disability. *Georgetown Law Review* 106: 293–364.

Pfaff, John F. 2012. The micro and macro causes of prison growth. *Georgia State University Law Review* 28: 1239–1274.

———. 2013. Waylaid by a metaphor: A deeply problematic account of prison growth. Review of *A plague of prisons*, by Ernest Drucker. *University of Michigan Law Review* 111: 1087–10110.

———. 2014. Escaping from the standard story: Why the conventional wisdom on prison growth is wrong, and where we can go from here. *Federal Sentencing Reporter* 26: 265–270.

Piven, Frances Fox. 2003. Why welfare is racist. In *Race and the politics of welfare reform*, ed. Sanford F. Schram, Joe Soss, and Richard C. Fording, 323–335. Ann Arbor: University of Michigan Press.

Roithmayr, Daria. 2000. Barriers to entry: A market lock-in model of discrimination. *Virginia Law Review* 86: 727–800.

Sabol, William J., Heather C. West, and Matthew Cooper. 2010. *Bureau of Justice statistics bulletin: Prisoners in 2008*. Washington, DC. https://www.bjs.gov/content/pub/pdf/p08.pdf. Accessed 31 Mar 2019.

Scheffler, Sam. 2016. *Death and the afterlife*. Oxford: Oxford University Press.

Seale, Bobby, and Stephen Shames. 2016. *Power to the people: The world of the Black Panthers*. New York: Abrams.

Shelby, Tommie. 2016. *Dark ghettos: Injustice, dissent, and reform*. Cambridge, MA: Belknap Press.

Simmons, Kami Chavis. 2014. The legacy of stop and frisk: Addressing the vestiges of a violent police culture. *Wake Forest Law Review* 49: 849–872.

Simons, Kenneth W. 2000. On equality, bias crimes and just deserts. *Journal of Criminal Law and Criminology* 91: 237–268.

Sklansky, David A. 1995. Cocaine, race, and equal protection. *Stanford Law Review* 47: 1283–1322.

———. 1997. Traffic stops, minority motorists, and the future of the Fourth Amendment. *Supreme Court Review* 1997: 271–330.

Smith, Sandra Susan. 2010. Race and trust. *Annual Review of Sociology* 36: 453–475.

Spohn, Cassia. 2017. Race and sentencing disparity. In Vol. 4 of *Reforming criminal justice*, ed. Erik Luna, 211–226. Phoenix: Academy for Justice.

Starr, Sonja B., and M. Marit Rehavi. 2014. Racial disparity in federal criminal sentences. *Journal of Political Economy* 122: 1320–1354.

Steiker, Carol S. 1999. Punishing hateful motives: Old wine in a new bottle revives calls for prohibition. Review of *Hate crimes: Criminal law & identity politics*, by James B. Jacobs and Kimberly Potter. *Michigan Law Review* 97: 1857–1873.

Thompson, Anthony C. 1999. Stopping the usual suspects: Race and the Fourth Amendment. *New York University Law Review* 74: 956–1013.

———. 2008. *Releasing prisoners, redeeming communities: Reentry, race, and politics.* New York: New York University Press.

Tonry, Michael. 1994. Race and the war on drugs. *University of Chicago Legal Forum* 1994: 25–82.

Turner, K.B., David Giacopassi, and Margaret Vandiver. 2006. Ignoring the past: Coverage of slavery and slave patrols in criminal justice texts. *Journal of Criminal Justice Education* 17: 181–195.

United States Sentencing Commission. 2010. *Demographic differences in federal sentencing practices: An update of the Booker report's multivariate regression analysis.* USSC Government. https://www.ussc.gov/sites/default/files/pdf/research-and-publications/research-publications/2010/20100311_Multivariate_Regression_Analysis_Report.pdf. Accessed 5 Mar 2019.

Varnum, Thomas G. 2008. Let's not jump to conclusions: Approaching felon disenfranchisement challenges under the voting rights act. *Michigan Journal of Race and Law* 14: 109–142.

Vazquez, Yolanda. 2017. Crimmigration: The missing piece of criminal justice reform. *University of Richmond Law Review* 51: 1093–1148.

Woods, Jordon Blair. 2015. Decriminalization, police authority, and routine traffic stops. *UCLA Law Review* 62: 672–759.

Yankah, Ekow N. 2004. Good guys and bad guys: Punishing character, equality and the irrelevance of moral character to criminal punishment. *Cardozo Law Review* 25 (3): 1019–1068.

———. 2011. A paradox in overcriminalization. *New Criminal Law Review* 14: 1–34.

———. 2015. Republican responsibility in criminal law. *Criminal Law and Philosophy* 9: 457–475.

———. 2016. When addiction had a white face. *New York Times*, February 9.

———. 2019a. Pretext and justification: Republicanism, policing, and race. *Cardozo Law Review* 40: 1543.

———. 2019b. Forthcoming. Whose burden to bear? *Criminal Law & Philosophy*.

PART XXV

Reckless Beliefs

CHAPTER 27

Reckless Beliefs

Larry Alexander and Kevin Cole

A recent draft of the revisions to the Model Penal Code's definitions of sexual offenses defines Sexual Penetration Without Consent as an act of sexual penetration without the other's consent when "the actor knows that, *or is reckless with respect to whether*, the act was without consent" (Model Penal Code 2016, §213.2).[1] Our focus here is on the italicized mental state. The more general question we ask is what does it mean to be reckless with respect to whether an element of a crime exists, in this case, whether another has consented? The Model Penal Code revisers obviously think it means something. But what?

The question has implications beyond the Model Penal Code revisions. For example, the infamous English case of *Regina v. Morgan*[2] has been interpreted to require for rape a mens rea of recklessness with respect to consent.[3] So those who so interpret it must have something in mind that counts as that recklessness.

What It Cannot Be: Reckless Belief

Can one's belief that another has consented be reckless? That is, can the belief itself, apart from the acts taken based on it, and apart from acts that could be taken to refine it, be deemed reckless?

It should also be pointed out that the Model Penal Code already contains sections that allude to the existence of reckless beliefs. For example, the choice of evils justification section dictates that when the actor is "reckless … in

L. Alexander (✉)
University of San Diego, San Diego, CA, USA
e-mail: larrya@sandiego.edu

K. Cole
University of San Diego, San Diego, CA, USA
e-mail: kcole@sandiego.edu

© The Author(s) 2019
L. Alexander, K. K. Ferzan (eds.), *The Palgrave Handbook of Applied Ethics and the Criminal Law*, https://doi.org/10.1007/978-3-030-22811-8_27

appraising the necessity for his conduct," he can be prosecuted at the level of recklessness for his actus reus (Model Penal Code, 1962, §3.02(2)). Likewise, when addressing the use of defensive force, "When the actor believes that the use of force ... is necessary for any of the purposes for which such belief would establish a justification ... but the actor is reckless ... in having such belief ... the justification ... is unavailable in a prosecution for an offense for which recklessness ... suffices to establish his culpability" (Model Penal Code 1962, §3.09(2)).

These same sections state that if the actor's belief in the otherwise justifying facts were negligent, he could be prosecuted only for a negligent version of the offense. The drafters of these sections thought that if the actor had an unreasonable belief in the facts that, were the belief true, would justify his conduct, his culpability level was that of negligence. So even if he committed the act purposely or knowingly, he should be treated by the law as if he had committed it negligently—for that was his true level of culpability.

Assuming, as the Code drafters were reluctant to do, that merely negligent actors should face criminal punishment,[4] their treatment of actors who act on negligent beliefs in otherwise justifying facts makes sense. And they obviously thought that if it makes sense to treat negligent beliefs that way, it must make sense to treat reckless beliefs similarly. But they never defined reckless beliefs.

So, what can a reckless belief be? One would assume that the definition of reckless conduct would be the key to understanding reckless beliefs. Reckless conduct is conduct that the actor believes is imposing a risk of harm on others that it is unjustifiable for him to impose. Unlike the negligent actor, who is inadvertently imposing risks of which he should be but isn't aware, the reckless actor is adverting to the riskiness of his conduct (Model Penal Code 1962, §2.02(2)(c)). And there is no specific magnitude that the risk has to exceed in order to deem the actor reckless for consciously imposing it.[5] Sometimes, substantial risks might be imposed justifiably.[6] Conversely, even very tiny risks may be unjustifiable for the actor to impose.[7]

Turn now to beliefs. The actor's belief in some justifying fact—here, whether his partner is consenting to sex—can range from certainty (that she is consenting) to certainty (that she is *not* consenting. Obviously, if the actor's belief is that it is more likely that his partner is not consenting than that she is consenting, then he does not believe he has received consent. So, he does not "recklessly" believe he has received consent because he does not believe he has received consent.

So far, so good. Recklessness cannot be found in cases of nonbelief, including cases of assigning a probability of consent less than 50 percent. Nor can recklessness be found when the actor believes it is 100 percent certain that he has received consent. For in such a case, he is not adverting to a risk of nonconsent of any magnitude.

So, recklessness of belief must be found in the range between more probably than not and less than 100 percent. Only in that range is it possible for the actor to believe in some fact but, at the same time, advert to the risk that he is in error. For error is the risk that is relevant to recklessness of belief, just as *harm* is the risk that is relevant to recklessness of conduct.

So, suppose the actor is more than 50 percent sure that he has received consent but less than 100 percent sure. (Again, if he is less than 50 percent sure, he does not believe he has received consent, and if he is 100 percent sure that he has, he cannot be adverting to a risk of error, for he perceives no such risk.) What would make him "reckless" in believing he has received consent?

Well, he surely should not believe that he has *not* received consent. For that would be irrational, as it would be treating a belief in which he has less than 50 percent credence as true.

Nor can it be that his adverting to the risk that his belief in consent is in error makes his belief reckless. For that would imply that no matter how probable he believes he has received consent to be, unless that probability is 100 percent, he is reckless in believing it. For if he believes it is 95 percent probable, he will necessarily believe it is 5 percent improbable. If adverting to that 5 percent risk of error makes him reckless, then the implication is that adverting to any probability of consent greater than 50 percent but less than 100 percent is a reckless belief in consent. Or, in other words, any belief less than certainty is a reckless belief. In effect, this would require 100 percent certainty for a belief to be nonculpably held. But that would be absurd.

The only remaining alternative is that the actor is reckless if his credence in consent is greater than 50 percent but less than 100 percent by a certain amount. But what is that probability below which one's belief is reckless? And notice that the implication is that the actor should treat as true, not what he believes to be the case, but what he believes *not* to be the case. For whatever degree of credence greater than 50 percent he gives to his belief in consent, he necessarily gives less than 50 percent credence to his belief in nonconsent.

Notice, too, that the same analysis of recklessness regarding belief in consent applies to the Code's notion of recklessness regarding the belief in the facts that would justify the choice of evils or the use of defensive force. Reckless beliefs are as mysterious there as they are in dealing with belief in consent.

Perhaps in the context of sex, the Code revisers believe that one should only act as if one has consent if one believes this with a very high degree of credence, and that one is reckless if one acts as if one has consent on the mere honest belief that one has it.[8] This is a possibility to which we shall return. Notice, however, that the focus here is on the recklessness of the *act* taken with less than the requisite degree of credence regarding consent, not on the *belief* itself.

But with respect to reckless beliefs in the Code's justification article, this solution to the reckless belief mystery seems inapposite. It suggests, apropos of the choice of evils defense, one should not divert the river and flood a farmer's field if one believes that otherwise, a town will be flooded and lives lost, unless one believes that to be the case with a degree of credence greater than a mere 50+ percent level of credence. And it suggests, apropos of self-defense, that one should not use force to defend oneself unless one believes one is being attacked with a degree of credence greater than a mere 50+ percent level of credence. It seems unlikely, however, that this is what the Code means by reckless beliefs, and even more unlikely that it *should* mean this.

The problem is this. One would think that the recklessness of beliefs should be modeled on the recklessness of acts. But they cannot be. One can rationally desist from acting when one believes the act will create but a tiny risk of harm if one has no good reason to take the act in question. But one cannot rationally desist from believing something that one thinks is more than 50 percent likely to be true. *For to desist from believing it would be to believe something that one thinks is more likely than not to be untrue.*

Again, in the context of sex, perhaps it should be deemed reckless to act without a degree of credence in consent much greater than merely a 50+ percent likelihood. Perhaps if the actor perceives a risk of nonconsent that is less than 50 percent but still greater than de minimis, he should refrain from sex, despite the likelihood that the other is consenting. But to say that is to say that an *act* is reckless, not that the *belief* in consent is reckless. Moreover, we doubt the Model Penal Code requires a belief that one is choosing the lesser evil, or that one is defending against an attack, to be a belief greater than one that one believes is 50+ percent likely to be true.

Our bottom line: There is no such thing as a reckless belief.

Live Possibilities

Recklessness in Not Gathering More Information

But perhaps neither the revisers of the sexual penetration provision, the drafters of Model Penal Code sections 3.02(2) and 3.09(2), nor the interpreters of *Regina v. Morgan* are referring to reckless beliefs. Perhaps, instead, they are referring to reckless conduct, a notion that, unlike that of a reckless belief, is surely coherent. Perhaps when referring to whether the defendant is reckless with respect to whether there has been consent, they are asking whether, given the circumstances, the defendant should have taken further steps to determine whether what he believes is most likely consent really is so. For further steps, if not too costly in time, effort, and other costs, may reduce his level of credence regarding consent from above 50 percent to below it. In such a case, he will be aware that his failure to take those steps will be risky, and his awareness of that risk will make his ignoring it unjustifiable and hence reckless.

In *Morgan*, for example, the defendants were surely aware that there was some chance the story they had been told by the victim's husband was untrue, and that the victim's protestations were just what they seemed to be. And there were likely several steps they could have taken to improve their epistemic position. So, they were then undoubtedly aware of a risk that they would be committing rape, a risk sizeable enough to warrant making further inquiries before acting as if they had received the victim's consent.

The same analysis can be applied to section 3.02(2) and its reference to whether the defendant was "reckless ... in appraising the necessity of his conduct." If the defendant believes it is 50+ percent likely that a town will be flooded and lives lost if he does not divert the river onto a farmer's field, but he is aware of steps he can take to refine his level of credence before he can no longer delay his decision, then he might very well be reckless if he acts before taking those steps.

In the context of self or other defense, translating the language of reckless belief into that of reckless conduct is more difficult. For one cannot justifiably use defensive force under the Model Penal Code unless such use is immediately necessary. And that, in turn, implies that no further acts for improving one's level of credence are possible. Still, we can imagine a defendant who believes an approaching person intends him harm, is aware that he might be wrong and that there is something he can do safely to improve his level of credence regarding that person's intent, and fails to take those steps. When it is too late to do anything other than defend himself, he must act on the probability of attack he perceives at that time. And a 50+ percent probability would seem sufficient. But the actor may be deemed reckless for having gotten himself into that epistemic state.

Recklessness in Engaging in Sex with Only a 50 Percent Level of Credence in Having Received Consent

There is another possibility that the reference in the proposed revisions of the Model Penal Code regarding consent to sexual penetration is to reckless conduct, but not the conduct of acting without gathering more information. For, as intimated earlier, acting on the mere belief that one has received consent might be deemed unjustifiably risking nonconsent and thus reckless conduct. If the authors of the revisions believe that the mens rea regarding consent should be higher than negligence—and we agree that it should be—but not as high as belief to a practical certainty, then the question becomes what degree of credence one must have that one's partner is consenting to avoid committing a sexual offense. If mere belief in consent suffices, then one only needs to have a level of credence above 50 percent to avoid culpability. But perhaps a level of credence above 50 percent but less than absolute certainty should be required. In that case, acting on a mere belief that one has received consent to sex, even if one can do nothing to refine that belief, may be deemed reckless with respect to whether one has received consent. Put differently, to avoid being reckless in engaging in sex, one must believe one has received consent with a degree of credence greater than 50 percent but less than certainty. That degree might vary with the nature of the parties' relationship. A first-time "hookup" might require a degree of credence much greater than that of a marriage or long-term sexual relation. That is perhaps because the harm of nonconsensual sex will be greater in the former situation than in the latter ones or because the "justification" for risking that harm is greater in the latter situations than in the former ones. Because reckless conduct is a function of the actor's consciousness of the risk of harm and his justification for taking that risk, this interpretation of recklessness with respect to consent seems quite plausible.[9]

*   *   *

All of this is, of course, speculative regarding the intentions of these provisions and the *Morgan* interpretation. But if the intentions were to refer to reckless beliefs rather than reckless conduct, then they must be rethought. For there is no such thing as a reckless belief.

NOTES

1. A later draft employs different language, imposing liability when the actor "knowingly or recklessly engages in an act of sexual penetration … without the consent of the other person" (Model Penal Code: Sexual Assault and Related Offenses, 2017, §213.4(1)).
2. In *Morgan*, the defendants were told by the victim's husband to ignore her protestations because she was actually consenting to have sex with them.
3. And see § 1 (1) of the Sexual Offenses (Amendment) Act of 1976.
4. Their reluctance was surely justified. See, for example, Alexander and Ferzan (2009); Hurd and Michael S. Moore (2011); Hurd (2014).
5. Consider someone who, merely for the thrill of it, plays involuntary Russian roulette on passersby having placed one live round in a revolver and spun the chambers, then having placed that revolver in a bin containing nine other identical but completely unloaded revolvers, and, finally, having drawn the revolver she is using from that bin. The risk of death or serious injury she is imposing on passersby when she pulls the trigger—1/60—may be far less than the risks imposed by the car chase in note 6. But hers is a case of recklessness, whereas theirs is not.
6. Consider a high-speed car chase by law enforcement officials trying to capture a terrorist in possession of a nuclear device.
7. *See* the example of a reckless act based on a tiny risk in note 5 *supra*.
8. For a similar argument, see Johnson (2006).
9. It is remarkable that although the drafters of the Model Penal Code defined "knowledge" in section 2.02, they did not in that section or elsewhere define "belief." Because knowledge is defined as belief to a practical certainty (plus correctness), beliefs themselves can exhibit less than that degree of credence. Notice that in section 5.01(1)(b), which defines completed (last act) attempts at result crimes, the drafters require only that defendant believe the result will occur without further conduct on his part; they do not require that he be practically certain the result will occur. That might be an oversight on the drafters' part, for it means that a defendant who would be guilty of recklessness but not knowing homicide if his conduct killed would be guilty of attempted homicide—not reckless endangerment—if his conduct did not kill. That is because although he neither intended to kill nor believed to a practical certainty that he would kill, he did, nonetheless, believe he would kill.

   There are, of course, other oddities in the Code's treatment of mental states. Section 2.02(7), for example, states that a defendant who believes there is a high probability that a material fact exists can be said to have knowledge of that fact "unless he actually believes that it does not exist." How one can at the same time believe both that there is a high probability of something's existing and that it does not exist escapes us.

References

Sexual offenses (amendment) act of 1976. 1976. London.

Regina v. Morgan, AC 182 (1976).

Alexander, Larry, and Kimberly Kessler Ferzan. 2009. *Crime and culpability: A theory of criminal law*, 69–86. Cambridge: Cambridge University Press.

American Law Institute. 1962. *Model penal code*. Philadelphia: The American Law Institute.

———. 2016. *Model penal code: Sexual assault and related offenses*. Tentative draft. Philadelphia: The American Law Institute.

———. 2017. *Model penal code: Sexual assault and related offenses*. Tentative draft. Philadelphia: The American Law Institute.

Hurd, Heidi M. 2014. Finding no fault in negligence. In *Philosophical foundations of the law of torts*, ed. J. Oberdiek, 387–405. Oxford: Oxford University Press.

Hurd, Heidi M., and Michael S. Moore. 2011. Punishing the awkward, the stupid, the weak, and the selfish: The culpability of negligence. *Criminal Law and Philosophy* 5: 147–198.

Johnson, Eric A. 2006. Beyond belief: Rethinking the role of belief in the assessment of culpability. *Ohio State Journal of Criminal Law* 3: 503–522.

PART XXVI

Revenge Porn

CHAPTER 28

The Crime of "Revenge Porn"

Mary Anne Franks

INTRODUCTION: "NO CRIME HAS BEEN COMMITTED"

"I will destroy you." These were the words Annmarie Chiarini, a single mother and an English professor, heard her ex-boyfriend say the day after she ended their relationship (Chiarini 2013). When they were together, he had pressured Annmarie into allowing him to take nude photographs of her. Now her ex was threatening to sell a compact disc of those images in an online auction and send the auction link to Annmarie's friends, family, and colleagues. Despite Annmarie's pleas, he began to carry out his threat the next day. He started the auction and posted links to it on the Facebook pages of the college where she taught. Soon Annmarie was receiving emails from various people who had received the link to her nude photos: her ex-husband, friends, and even her babysitter. Annmarie's ex also used the intimate photos to impersonate her on a pornography website, creating a profile that included detailed information about where she lived and worked as well as solicitations for sex. The profile generated more than 3000 views and more than a dozen pages of sexually explicit, often violent, comments within two weeks. When Annmarie repeatedly sought help from law enforcement officials, they leered over the photos, suggested she was to blame for what happened, and told her, "No crime has been committed" (Chiarini 2013).

The officers were not wrong on the last point. In 2010, when these events occurred, "revenge porn" wasn't a crime in Maryland, where Annmarie lived, or in 46 other US states. Beginning in 2013, however, a wave of social, technological, and legislative efforts to combat the problem swept the United

M. A. Franks (✉)
University of Miami School of Law, Coral Gables, FL, USA
e-mail: mafranks@law.miami.edu

© The Author(s) 2019
L. Alexander, K. K. Ferzan (eds.), *The Palgrave Handbook of Applied Ethics and the Criminal Law*, https://doi.org/10.1007/978-3-030-22811-8_28

States (Franks 2017). Mainstream media began featuring victims' stories; major tech companies announced that the content would be removed from their platforms and services (Roy 2015), and the term "revenge porn" was added to the Merriam-Webster Dictionary (Steinmetz 2016). A handful of victims initiated lawsuits against the publishers of their private, intimate material, sometimes resulting in multimillion-dollar judgments. Perhaps the most dramatic and controversial change, however, was the shift in the criminal law landscape.[1] Within six years, high-profile revenge porn website owners like Hunter Moore had received prison terms; 46 states and Washington, D.C., had criminalized the unauthorized distribution of private, sexually explicit imagery; and a federal criminal bill prohibiting the conduct had been introduced in Congress (Franks 2017).

Annmarie herself was part of this push for legislative reform, joining forces with the nonprofit organization Cyber Civil Rights Initiative (CCRI), which began its efforts to fight online abuse and discrimination in 2013.[2] CCRI was founded by Dr. Holly Jacobs, who, like Annmarie, was a victim of "revenge porn," and is now one of the leading nonprofit organizations assisting victims of nonconsensual pornography. One of the chief goals of CCRI's "End Revenge Porn" campaign is the passage of state and federal laws against what the organization refers to as "nonconsensual pornography." The organization was an influential force behind much of the legislative reform on the issue in the United States. Several representatives of CCRI spoke at the introduction of the first bipartisan federal bill addressing the abuse, the 2016 Intimate Privacy Protection Act. In a press release announcing the bill, sponsor Congresswoman Jackie Speier (D-CA) stated: "many predators have gleefully acknowledged that the vast majority of their victims have no way to fight back …. My bill will fix that appalling legal failure" (Speier 2016).

But the push to criminalize "revenge porn" has met many challenges. The federal bill did not receive a vote when it was introduced in 2016, or when it was re-introduced, with slight modifications, in 2017. It was again introduced in May 2019 as the Stopping Harmful Image Exploitation and Limiting Distribution (SHIELD) Act but has not been voted on at the time of this writing. While the number of state laws that have been passed criminalizing nonconsensual pornography is impressive, the majority of them fundamentally mischaracterize the harm as a form of harassment rather than a privacy violation, rendering them under-inclusive and largely ineffective. In many cases, the robust initial drafts of these laws were diluted by aggressive attacks by civil libertarian groups and lobbyists from the tech and entertainment industry.

The passage of weak state laws and the continuing lack of a federal law may be attributed in part to political and social ambivalence regarding criminalization of the conduct. The relatively rapid shift toward criminalization of nonconsensual pornography has, perhaps predictably, been met with praise in some quarters and criticism in others. The grounds for criticism are diverse. Some of these criticisms are advanced in good faith; some are grounded in misogyny, greed, and self-interest. Some ask whether nonconsensual pornography should be a crime at all, questioning whether it is more appropriately addressed by self-help, civil remedies, or existing criminal law. Others worry that the criminalization of nonconsensual pornography might jeopardize freedom of expression generally or endanger journalistic freedom in particular. Others raise concerns about overcriminalization, mass incarceration, and disproportionate impact on minorities and teenagers. Still others agree that nonconsensual pornography should be considered a crime but disagree about how it should be defined or how severe the penalties for it should be. Some fear that criminalization reinforces outdated social norms about sexual behavior or patriarchal views of women.

While some of these objections and concerns are valid, the United States should adopt robust criminal laws against "revenge porn" at the state and federal levels. The unauthorized disclosure of private, sexually explicit images harms not only individual victims but society as a whole. The abuse violates multiple values essential to a democratic society: privacy, freedom of expression, bodily autonomy, and gender equality. While non-criminal remedies are important and necessary, the immediate and often irreparable nature of the harm of "revenge porn" requires the maximum deterrence potential and moral condemnation of criminal law.

To be just and effective, these laws must recognize that the fundamental harm inflicted by nonconsensual pornography is the violation of privacy. In contrast to the majority of recently enacted state criminal laws, which treat nonconsensual pornography as a form of harassment, nonconsensual pornography criminal laws should apply regardless of perpetrators' motives for violating the intimate privacy of their victims.

The second section of this chapter provides a background on the definition, scope, and social harm of the abuse. This is followed by an examination of objections to criminalization. The fourth section details why and how "revenge porn" should be criminalized and includes model statutory language. The fifth section evaluates the current legislative landscape. In the concluding section I offer recommendations for the future of the movement to criminalize "revenge porn."

DEFINING THE ISSUE

What's in a Name?

Much of the confusion and controversy over criminalizing "revenge porn" has to do with nomenclature. "Revenge porn" is a colloquialism that is used in multiple imprecise ways. Most agree that the term refers to the disclosure of sexually explicit images of a person without consent, but the consensus seems to end there.

The most significant difference of opinion has to do with how literally, or narrowly, to take the word "revenge." The most literal and narrow view is that the unauthorized disclosure of a person's private, sexual imagery is not "revenge porn" unless it is committed by that person's former intimate partner for a vengeful purpose. The definition of "revenge porn" offered by the Cambridge Dictionary illustrates this view: "private sexual images or films showing a particular person that are put on the internet by a former partner of that person, as an attempt to punish or harm them." Implicit in this view is that disclosing a person's naked photos without consent is not in itself a harmful act and only becomes harmful if it is motivated by personal malice. This view, which focuses on the motives of a person disclosing the image, can be called the "revenge porn-as-harassment" view.

At the other end of the spectrum is the view that the unauthorized disclosure of private, sexually explicit imagery is a harm in itself, regardless of who does it and for what reason. Whether the discloser is an ex-boyfriend enraged by a breakup, as in Annmarie's case described earlier, or a hacker hoping to make money from stolen celebrity photos, or a sexual predator bragging about his exploits, exposing a person's naked body against her will is an inherently harmful act. This view, which focuses on the impact of the person depicted in the image, can be called the "revenge porn-as-invasion-of-privacy" view.

For these and other reasons, victims of intimate privacy invasions and their advocates caution that the word "revenge" in "revenge porn" is misleading and harmful. In addition to erasing victims who have been targeted by strangers with a range of motives, the word "revenge" also arguably normalizes retaliatory behavior by intimate partners, reinforcing the idea that aggression stemming from the inability to control a partner is a normal and in some cases acceptable impulse. This concern is heightened by the fact that "revenge porn," like domestic violence, sexual assault, and sexual harassment, is a form of abuse that disproportionately involves male perpetrators and female victims.

There are concerns, too, about the word "porn." The word is ambiguous, morally charged, and potentially stigmatizing. One specific concern is that "porn" conveys a negative moral judgment about sexual imagery generally, or of self-created and shared sexual imagery in particular, leading in turn to the denigration of the people who appear in it.

Because of these concerns, many victims and advocates, myself included, avoid the use of the term "revenge porn" in favor of the term "nonconsensual pornography." This term is meant to emphasize the nonconsensual nature of the conduct rather than the particular motivation behind it. It is not a perfect term; in retaining the word "pornography," it risks the stigmatizing effect described earlier. The rationale for keeping the term is that "pornography" is one of the few English words that succinctly describes sexually explicit content aimed at prurient interests and that it is used in this context to describe not the creation of the content but of its distribution without consent.

The term "nonconsensual pornography" is also limited in the sense that it describes the *product* rather than the *action* of the harm. Alternative terms such as "image-based sexual abuse," popular in Australia and the United Kingdom, are superior in this regard. However, the wordiness of these terms, and the fact that they are not in common use in the United States, mitigate somewhat against their effectiveness.

Accordingly, in this chapter, I primarily use the term "nonconsensual pornography," defined as the unauthorized distribution of private, sexually explicit imagery (Citron and Franks 2014). This term includes not only images consensually exchanged within a confidential relationship, but also images originally obtained without consent, such as surreptitious recording, hacked images, and images depicting involuntary sexual acts or nudity, such as sexual assaults.

Scope

According to a nationally representative study conducted by CCRI in 2017, more than 1 in 8 adult social media users have been victimized or threatened with the unauthorized distribution of private, sexually explicit images or videos, and over 1 in 20 adult social media users have engaged in such distribution (Eaton et al. 2017).[3] Experts conducting empirical research on nonconsensual pornography emphasize that victimization figures are likely a low estimate, as they only capture victims who are aware that they have been victimized. Many victims, especially those whose images are shared in restricted online communities, may never discover that they have been victimized.

Nonconsensual pornography is distributed via social media, blogs, emails, texts, DVDs, hard copies, and websites. One victim's images were posted to nearly 10,000 websites.[4] In May 2017, it was revealed that Facebook disabled more than 14,000 accounts related to nonconsensual pornography sexual extortion and handled nearly 54,000 cases of suspected nonconsensual pornography in a single month (Hopkins and Solon 2017).

Nonconsensual pornography is not an equal-opportunity form of abuse. The likelihood of being victimized by nonconsensual pornography is higher for women and sexual minorities. The 2017 CCRI study revealed that women were about 1.7 times more likely to be victimized than men, and men were by far the primary perpetrators of the abuse (Eaton et al. 2017, p. 12). Revenge porn sites are far more likely to feature women than men (Uhl et al. 2013; Whitmarsh 2015).[5] The majority of court cases and news stories to date involve female victims and male perpetrators. A 2016 Data & Society Research Institute study found that young women were the most likely group to be threatened with the conduct: one in ten women under the age of 30 were threatened with disclosure of intimate images (Data and Society 2016, p. 5).[6] The same study also found that individuals who identify as gay or bisexual are more than seven times likely as those who identify as straight to have been threatened with or victimized by nonconsensual pornography (Data and Society 2016, p. 5).

Social Harm

The harm caused by nonconsensual pornography is often immediate and irreversible. Once an explicit image of a victim is made available on a website or social media platform, it becomes accessible to a virtually unlimited number of people who can download, forward, share, and copy it within seconds. Within days or even hours, that image can dominate a victim's search engine results and be transmitted to the victim's entire personal, social, and professional circle: family, employers, coworkers, and peers (Chiarini 2013). Victims have been stalked,[7] harassed, threatened with sexual assault (Jan-Lim 2017), defamed as sexual predators, terminated by their employers (Ronneburger 2009, p. 9), forced to change schools (Citron and Franks 2014, p. 352), and forced to change their names (Jacobs 2013). Some have committed suicide (Bazelon 2013). According to researcher Samantha Bates,

> The negative mental health consequences of revenge porn for female survivors are similar in nature to the negative mental health outcomes that rape survivors experience. Rape survivors frequently experience PTSD, anxiety, and depression, all of which participants in this study experienced. In terms of coping mechanisms, participants engaged in avoidance/denial and self-medication in attempt to avoid feelings of despair and distress regarding their victimization. (Bates 2017, p. 34)

Victims suffer each time a person views or shares their intimate images, and the traffic in such images increases the demand and the pervasiveness of such images. As one victim expressed it, "I am not victimized one time. I am victimized every time someone types my name into the computer. The crime scene is right before everyone's eyes, played out again and again" (Mathen 2014, p. 531). Victims report that one of the worst aspects of nonconsensual pornography is the "unending uncertainty about who has viewed the material" (Bates 2017, p. 33). Sports reporter Erin Andrews, who was surreptitiously filmed by a stalker while she undressed in her hotel room, stated months after the incident, "I haven't stopped being victimized—I'm going to have to live with this forever .... When I have kids and they have kids, I'll have to explain to them why this is on the Internet" (Citron and Franks 2014, pp. 361–365).

A previous survey conducted by CCRI in 2013 produced suggestive findings about the impact of nonconsensual pornography on victims.[8] In nearly half of all cases, respondents said that identifying information about them was posted along with intimate material, including details such as their full name, social network information, email address, phone number, home address, work address, and even, in some cases, Social Security number. The publication of these details helps explain why half of all victims reported being stalked or harassed online by people who viewed their material, and one-third reported offline stalking or harassment. Nearly all victims reported suffering significant emotional distress as a consequence of victimization. More specifically, 82 percent said they suffered significant impairment in social, occupational, or other functioning; more than half experienced suicidal thoughts; and 42 percent had sought psychological help (Cyber Civil Rights Initiative 2013).

Victims also reported serious effects on their professional, educational, and intimate relationships. More than half experienced difficulty concentrating at work or school due to the experience. Almost half feared the loss of a current or future partner if that partner learns of the disclosure, and more than half feared that the material will be discovered by their current or future children. Forty-two percent of victims were forced to explain the situation to professional or academic supervisors, coworkers, or colleagues. More than one-third of victims responded that the experience jeopardized their relationships with family and friends. More than one-quarter of victims left work or school for a period of time as a result of the abuse, while a number of victims were fired from their jobs or expelled from school. Thirteen percent reported that a relationship with a significant other had ended due to their victimization (Cyber Civil Rights Initiative 2013).

Victims often limited their use of social media in the wake of their experience. A quarter of victims shut down an email address; a quarter shut down their Facebook accounts; and a significant number closed their Twitter and LinkedIn accounts. Forty-two percent of victims considered legally changing their name and three percent of victims, including CCRI founder Holly Jacobs, did so (Cyber Civil Rights Initiative 2013).

While nonconsensual pornography affects both male and female individuals, available evidence to date indicates not only that the majority of victims are women and girls, but that women and girls often face more serious consequences as a result of their victimization (Citron 2012; Citron and Franks 2014, pp. 353–354; Filipovic 2013). Nonconsensual pornography often plays a role in crimes that disproportionately affect women, including intimate partner violence, sexual assault, and sex trafficking. Domestic abusers use the threat of disclosure as a way to keep their partners from leaving or reporting their abuse to law enforcement (Chiarini 2013; Simpson 2014). Rapists have recorded their attacks not only to further humiliate their victims, but also to discourage them from reporting sexual assaults (Culp-Ressler 2014). Traffickers and pimps have used nonconsensual pornography to coerce unwilling individuals into sex trade or prevent them from exiting it (Bartow 2008, 818; Brooks 2013). The disclosure of intimate images—or the threat of such disclosure—is often used to punish and discourage outspoken or successful women (Gray 2014).

These points demonstrate how nonconsensual pornography harms not only individual victims, but imposes larger expressive harms on society as a whole (Anderson and Pildes 2000, p. 1527). Nonconsensual pornography is *disciplinary*: it warns women, in particular, that the cost of displeasing men— whether by exiting a relationship, being sexually unattainable, or simply acting with autonomy—may be sexual exposure against their will. It sends the message that sexual exploitation is an acceptable way to punish or intimidate women. It is no coincidence that many female targets of nonconsensual pornography are successful women, from Hollywood celebrities to judges to PhD students to politicians (Mendelson 2014). Along with other gender-based violence such as rape, sexual harassment, and voyeurism, nonconsensual pornography reinforces the pernicious belief that men have the right to use women and girls sexually without their consent. Like those forms of abuse, nonconsensual pornography is rarely punished, frequently trivialized, and often celebrated.

Objections to Criminalization

Some people take the harm of nonconsensual pornography very seriously, so much so that it was a common assumption that "revenge porn" already was a crime in the United States before the wave of legislative reform began in 2013. However, there are many voices opposing criminalization. The objections to criminalizing nonconsensual pornography generally fall into three categories: belief in the sufficiency of existing laws, First Amendment objections, and concerns about overcriminalization.[9]

Sufficiency of Existing Law

Much of the criticism of the legislative reform movement is based on the claim that adequate legal remedies already exist. The existing remedies that are most frequently cited include criminal laws addressing conduct that sometimes accompanies nonconsensual pornography, including laws prohibiting hacking, voyeurism, extortion, identity theft, stalking, or harassment, as well as non-criminal remedies such as copyright and tort actions. While existing legal remedies can and should be used when possible to aid victims of nonconsensual pornography, they are not in themselves sufficient to address the problem.

Criminal Law

Some critics of criminalization believe that there is no need for new criminal laws against nonconsensual pornography because existing criminal laws already adequately address it. While it is true that some existing criminal laws can be useful in nonconsensual pornography cases, including laws prohibiting hacking, voyeurism, extortion, identity theft, stalking, and harassment, none of these provide an adequate remedy for the problem. These laws, in addition to being generally underused, require special circumstances beyond the unauthorized distribution of sexually explicit imagery that is not present in a significant portion of nonconsensual pornography cases.

The successful prosecution of notorious "revenge porn" site operator Hunter Moore has been invoked to demonstrate the supposed sufficiency of existing criminal laws. In December 2013, federal prosecutors indicted Moore for conspiring to hack into people's computers to steal their nude images. According to the indictment, Moore paid a computer hacker to access women's password-protected computers and email accounts to steal their nude photos for financial gain—profits from his revenge porn site Is Anyone Up. The prosecution of Moore, while justly celebrated, does not provide evidence that existing laws are sufficient to address revenge porn. The fact that one revenge porn site owner may have violated numerous federal laws in running a revenge porn website does not change the fact that he faced no charges for publishing the content itself and that the next revenge porn entrepreneur will no doubt learn not to make the same mistakes as Hunter Moore (Citron and Franks 2014, pp. 365–368).

Both federal and state laws against harassment and stalking are notoriously underenforced, even in clear-cut cases that involve identifiable individuals, in-person contact, and physical violence (Citron 2014, p. 85). The idea that they can and will be applied successfully in cases that often involve online pseud-onyms, complex computer forensics, no physical contact, and moral judgments about women's sexual behavior is either wishful thinking or bad faith.

What is more, harassment and stalking laws are inapplicable to many non-consensual pornography cases. These laws require that perpetrators be moti-vated by the intent to harm or harass; as noted earlier, many perpetrators do not have such motivations. According to the 2017 CCRI study, 79 percent of people who admitted to engaging in nonconsensual pornography stated that they did not act out of a desire to hurt the person whose images they disclosed. Perpetrators have a variety of motives, including greed, notoriety, reputation enhancement, or to provide entertainment. Additionally, noncon-sensual pornography often involves both primary and secondary distributors. In a common scenario, an ex-boyfriend submits an intimate image of his former partner to a "revenge porn" site. The owner of the site publishes the image, making it accessible to thousands or even millions of people, any of whom can further distribute the image by forwarding or linking to it. Existing federal and state criminal laws have limited applications to primary distribu-tors of nonconsensual pornography and even less application to secondary distributors.

Criminal harassment and stalking laws only apply to defendants who engage in repeated harassing acts. The federal cyberstalking statute,[10] for example, pro-hibits the use of any "interactive computer service" to engage in a "course of conduct" intended to harass or intimidate someone in another state that either places that person in reasonable fear of serious bodily injury or death or that would reasonably be expected to cause the person to suffer "substantial emo-tional distress." A single posting of someone's name, address, and sexually explicit image would likely not amount to a harassing "course of conduct," despite the fact that it can cause serious damage.[11]

An additional problem is that many state harassment laws only apply to repeated abuse communicated directly to victims. In 2014, a New York state court dismissed charges against a man who posted his ex-girlfriend's nude pho-tos on Twitter and sent them to her employer and sister in part because he did not send them to the woman herself (Donaghue 2014).[12] Nonconsensual por-nography posted on social media and other third-party sites would not be pro-hibited under harassment statutes that require direct contact with victims.

Even when nonconsensual pornography does fit the definition of criminal harassment, law enforcement often declines to get involved because it is cate-gorized as a minor offense. Victims are often told that the behavior is not seri-ous enough for an in-depth investigation. Holly Jacobs' experience is an illustrative example. Jacobs' intimate photos were featured on hundreds of porn and revenge porn sites next to her contact information, with some posts falsely claiming that she would have sex for money and that she had slept with her students. Law enforcement officers told Jacobs that her ex-boyfriend could do whatever he wanted with the photos because she had voluntarily shared them with him. While the State Attorney's office did finally charge her ex with a misdemeanor count of cyberstalking, and investigators traced one of the posts to her ex's IP address, he claimed that he had been hacked. The state needed a warrant to search his computer for further evidence, a warrant they claimed they could not justify seeking for a misdemeanor case. The charge was dropped (Citron and Franks 2014).

Non-criminal Law: Tort and Copyright

As a general rule, civil actions place a heavy burden on the victim. Civil litigation of any kind generally requires money, time, and access to legal resources. It also often requires further dissemination of the very material that harms the victim (Adams 2014). The irony of privacy actions is that they generally require further breaches of privacy to be effective. Additionally, in many cases the party responsible will not have enough financial resources to make litigation worthwhile.

This is connected to another difficulty in bringing civil claims for nonconsensual pornography: it can be very difficult to find a party to sue. Given the ease with which individual purveyors of nonconsensual pornography can access or distribute images anonymously, it is difficult to identify and prove who they are (McKenna 2017). Victims are barred from making most civil claims against the websites that distribute this material because of Section 230 of the Communications Decency Act (CDA).[13] CDA § 230 has been interpreted to grant website owners and operators far-ranging immunity for tortious material submitted by third-party users.

Copyright law is more promising for some victims of nonconsensual pornography because CDA § 230 does not immunize websites from intellectual property claims. If a victim took the image or video herself, she owns the copyright and can in theory take action against unauthorized use of it. This strategy has proven successful in some cases (Dewey 2014). However, this option will not be of use to the many victims who do not take the images or videos themselves. Moreover, similar problems of publicity, time, and resources that accompany tort claims hinder copyright claims. Even in cases where the victim does hold the copyright and submits a proper Digital Millenium Copyright Act (DMCA) notice and takedown request, many site owners will ignore it (Matorin 2013; Roberts 2014). Even when a site owner does honor a takedown request, the image will often pop up on another site or even the same site after a short time (Roberts 2014).

Current civil law remedies, including copyright remedies, are an ineffective deterrent to revenge porn. Among the reasons that civil litigation is ineffective is that most disclosers know they are unlikely ever to be sued. Most victims do not have either the time or money to bring claims, and litigation may make little sense even for those who can afford to sue if perpetrators have few assets. In the words of Mitchell Matorin, an attorney who has represented revenge porn victims, "In the real world, civil lawsuits are no remedy at all" (Matorin 2013).

Non-criminal legal remedies require money, time, and resources that many victims simply do not have, and the chances of success are low. Even when plaintiffs are successful, civil remedies cannot truly address the harm created by revenge porn. Even victims who win damages or obtain injunctions against the original poster cannot halt the continued circulation of their images. Of course, criminal remedies are similarly limited, but they offer greater potential for deterrence before the fact than the vague and unlikely threat of civil action. This is not to suggest that civil remedies cannot or should not be pursued but to underscore the point that non-criminal responses are not, by themselves, sufficient as a response to nonconsensual pornography.

First Amendment Objections

The First Amendment implications of nonconsensual pornography laws are complex, and I have discussed them in detail in previous work (Franks 2017). Here I offer a brief summary of the key issues.

First Amendment objections to the criminalization of nonconsensual pornography rest fundamentally on the presumption that the unauthorized distribution of private, sexually explicit images is constitutionally protected expression. However, the Supreme Court has never held that the unauthorized publication of private, intimate images is protected by the First Amendment. Indeed, if nonconsensual pornography is categorically protected by the First Amendment, then it is not only the new and specific criminal laws that would be unconstitutional—so would all the existing criminal or civil laws so often cited as proof that nonconsensual pornography is already against the law. While some critics of criminalization claim that First Amendment consequences of criminal laws are substantially different, and more serious, than civil laws,[14] this is not true. The distinction between criminal and civil law is largely irrelevant for First Amendment purposes. As the Supreme Court noted in *New York Times v. Sullivan*, "What a State may not constitutionally bring about by means of a criminal statute is likewise beyond the reach of its civil law of libel."[15] The Court has suggested, in fact, that criminal actions pose a lesser risk to First Amendment freedoms because of the heightened procedural safeguards of criminal law.[16]

Nonconsensual pornography laws are, in essence, privacy laws. Privacy laws are commonly presumed to be constitutional and commonsensical, both by the general public and by scholars (Richards 2015, p. 1505). That is, there is general agreement that protecting sensitive information such as medical records, Social Security numbers, and driver's license information is something the law can and should do. Naked photos are a form of intensely sensitive information that, barring exceptional circumstances, the public has no legitimate interest in accessing. It is notable that while most people would balk at the idea of a First Amendment right to publish driver's license records without consent, some seem to seriously entertain the idea that there is a First Amendment right to publish naked pictures without consent.

Like other privacy violations, nonconsensual pornography is not amenable to "counter-speech." Whatever the merits of the belief that the best answer to bad speech is more speech in other contexts, it is meaningless as a response to privacy violations. One cannot "speak back" to the exposure of one's private information, whether it be medical records, Social Security numbers, or naked photos. Nonconsensual pornography is a form of unanswerable speech.

While the Supreme Court has never squarely faced the particular issue of nonconsensual pornography, it has indicated in multiple cases that the publication of private, sexually explicit imagery receives little or no protection under the First Amendment. The Court has acknowledged that the protection of intimate privacy is essential to the protection of free expression. Accordingly, laws acknowledging the extreme and in many cases irreversible harms inflicted by the knowing or reckless distribution of such images—which include chilling effects on intimate expression in addition to severe physical, professional, and psychological harm—should be viewed as vindicating, rather than threatening, the values of the First Amendment.

The Supreme Court has "long recognized that not all speech is of equal First Amendment importance." Speech on "matters of public concern" is "at the heart of the First Amendment's protection," whereas "speech on matters of purely private concern is of less First Amendment concern."[17] Sexually explicit images intended either for no one's viewing or only for viewing by an intimate partner is a matter of purely private concern. While the disclosure of some matters of private concern may qualify for First Amendment protection, there must be some legitimate public interest in these matters for this to be the case.[18] Prohibiting the nonconsensual disclosure of private, sexually explicit images of individuals poses "no threat to the free and robust debate of public issues; there is no potential interference with a meaningful dialogue of ideas concerning self-government; and there is no threat of liability causing a reaction of self-censorship by the press."[19] The Court has recognized that distribution of homemade sexually explicit material "does not qualify as a matter of public concern under any view."[20]

With all First Amendment objections, it is important to bear in mind that extreme assertions regarding the constitutionality of new laws rely on the fiction that First Amendment doctrine is either coherent or predictable. As Professor Robert Post has written, "contemporary First Amendment doctrine is ... striking chiefly for its superficiality, its internal incoherence, its distressing failure to facilitate constructive judicial engagement with significant contemporary social issues connected with freedom of speech" (Post 1995, pp. 1249–1250). It is difficult to say with confidence what any court will do if and when it is faced with a question about the constitutionality of a given nonconsensual pornography statute. Courts might consider revenge porn to receive no First Amendment protection at all, in which case nonconsensual pornography laws would raise no First Amendment issues. Alternatively, courts might determine that nonconsensual pornography laws trigger minimal First Amendment scrutiny. Another possibility is that courts might decide that such laws trigger but survive strict scrutiny.[21] While it is possible that courts will decide that such laws trigger and do not survive strict scrutiny, this seems like the least likely possibility based on Supreme Court precedent.

Overcriminalization

Concerns about overcriminalization are often related to the belief that existing laws are sufficient to address a social ill. As discussed earlier, existing laws are not in fact adequate to address the problem of nonconsensual pornography.

But overcriminalization concerns can also be grounded in an independent and well-founded distrust of the criminal justice system. In recent years, a growing bipartisan consensus has maintained that the United States has an overcriminalization problem (Will 2015). Overcriminalization concerns tend to be closely associated with concerns about mass incarceration, although the two are distinct phenomena. The American criminal justice system has recently undergone a "dramatic expansion in the substantive criminal law and the extraordinary rise in the use of punishment" (Husak 2009, p. 3). The objection to "overcriminalization" is really a set of intertwined objections: too many harmless acts are being treated as harmful; too many people are being convicted too easily; and too many people who are not dangerous to society are being locked up. These are all legitimate critiques of the American criminal justice system. Not only are too many people incarcerated for nonviolent offenses, but institutionalized bias regarding race and class afflicts the criminal justice system as a whole (Alexander 2010).

None of this, however, is a compelling reason not to criminalize nonconsensual pornography. One can denounce the excesses and prejudices of the criminal justice system without renouncing the value of criminal law altogether. Criminalization is not synonymous with incarceration; incarceration is not synonymous with mandatory minimums or lengthy sentences; and neither criminalization nor incarceration is synonymous with racially biased applications of criminal law. One can simultaneously support the criminalization of serious harms while criticizing the flaws of our current criminal justice system.

Some "overcriminalization" concerns amount to little more than the sense that "there are just too many damn laws." While the proliferation of criminal laws may be cause for concern, it should be the *quality* rather than the *quantity* of laws that is truly at issue. As Professor Citron and I wrote in our 2014 article, *Criminalizing Revenge Porn*:

> To argue that our society should not criminalize certain behavior because too many other kinds of behavior are already criminalized is at best a non sequitur. Only the shallowest of thinkers would suggest that the question whether nonconsensual pornography should be criminalized—indeed, whether any conduct should be criminalized—should turn on something as contingent and arbitrary as

the number of existing laws. Rather, the question of criminalization should be a question about the seriousness of the harm caused and whether such harm is adequately conceptualized as a harm only to individuals, for which tort remedies are sufficient, or should be conceptualized as a harm to both individuals and society as a whole for which civil penalties are not adequate, thus warranting criminal penalties. (Citron and Franks 2014, p. 362)

When one turns to the substantive questions of what forms of abuse deserve criminal punishment, it becomes clear that undercriminalization poses at least as much danger as overcriminalization. It is possible for a society to simultaneously suffer from over- and undercriminalization (Husak 2009, p. 18). This is a point demonstrated in Jill Leovy's book *Ghettoside: A True Story of Murder in America*, which details how minority communities are both over- and under-policed: over-policed as perpetrators of minor crimes and under-policed as victims of major crimes, such as murder (Leovy 2015).

Our society also tends to under-police harms disproportionately affecting women. In particular, our society undercriminalizes male violence against women. Until the mid-1800s, wife-beating was widely considered a natural exercise of a husband's privilege (Siegel 1996, pp. 2122–2124). In the United States, the criminalization of domestic violence did not take hold until the 1970s (Erez 2002). Even after legislative reform, police officers were trained to treat domestic violence as a "private" matter that should be dealt with outside the legal system if at all possible. This "arrest avoidance" stemmed not from concerns for the welfare of victims and their children, but rather from the belief that male violence against intimate partners was an inevitable and not particularly unfortunate reality. Even today, the actions of the victims of violence all too often receive more scrutiny and more opprobrium than the actions of the perpetrators (Marshall and Power 2014).

The criminalization of rape follows a similar pattern. Like domestic violence, rape was treated as a husband's privilege for most of Western history. The last US state to abolish the "marital rape" exemption did not do so until 1993, and many legal vestiges of the exemption remain (National Center for Victims of Crime 2004). Modern definitions of rape still tend to focus on "force" instead of lack of consent, meaning that acquaintance rapes (which make up the vast majority of rapes) are the least likely to be prosecuted (Caplan-Bricker 2014). Narrow definitions of rape, along with humiliating treatment by law enforcement, help explain why more than 80 percent of sexual assaults go unreported (Kruttschnitt et al. 2014, p. 36).

Male violence, particularly white male violence and violence against minority women, is under-, not over-criminalized, in the United States. When gendered and racialized abuse goes unpunished, it has a negative impact on society as a whole. Gendered abuse in particular validates and promotes views of male superiority, male sexual entitlement, and female subordination, which undermines the principle of equality (Franks 2016).

THE CASE FOR CRIMINALIZATION[22]

Criminalizing nonconsensual pornography is, despite the objections and concerns discussed, both justifiable and desirable. The unauthorized disclosure of private, sexually explicit images harms not only individual victims but society as a whole. The abuse violates multiple democratic values: privacy, freedom of expression, bodily autonomy, and gender equality. While non-criminal remedies are also important and necessary, the immediate and often irreparable nature of the harm of "revenge porn" requires the maximum deterrence potential and moral force of criminal law. Criminal prohibition is one of the most powerful and effective ways for society to acknowledge and condemn serious wrongdoing (Citron and Franks 2014, p. 349). Criminal laws are appropriate against conduct that causes severe and irreversible harm to both individuals and society. Laws prohibiting nonconsensual pornography reinforce the importance of sexual privacy to individual dignity and autonomy. They serve to ensure that all individuals retain the fundamental right to control who is allowed to view their naked bodies, a right recognized by long-standing prohibitions against trespass, voyeurism, and surveillance.

Protecting Privacy

The criminalization of privacy invasions has a distinguished pedigree. In their groundbreaking 1890 article *The Right to Privacy*, Samuel Warren and Louis Brandeis maintained that "the privacy of the individual should receive the added protection of the criminal law ... [T]hat the community has an interest in preventing such invasions of privacy, sufficiently strong to justify the introduction of such a remedy, cannot be doubted" (Warren and Brandeis 1890). Over the past 100 years, state and federal legislators have taken Warren and Brandeis' admonitions seriously (Citron and Franks 2014). The Privacy Act of 1974 includes criminal penalties for the disclosure of agency records containing individually identifiable information to any person or agency not entitled to receive it. Federal laws against identity theft criminalize, among other things, the transfer or use of another person's means of identification in connection with any state felony or violation of federal law. Federal laws also prohibit the wrongful disclosure of individually identifiable health information.

A year after the publication of Warren and Brandeis' *Right to Privacy*, Supreme Court Justice Horace Gray wrote that "[t]he inviolability of the person is as much invaded by a compulsory stripping and exposure as by a blow. To compel any one ... to lay bare the body, or to submit it to the touch of a stranger, without lawful authority, is an indignity, an assault, and a trespass." Federal and state criminal laws regarding voyeurism demonstrate that physical contact is not necessary for sexual exposure to cause harm. The federal Video Voyeurism Prevention Act of 2004 bans intentionally recording or broadcasting an image of another person in a state of undress without that person's consent under circumstances in which the person enjoys a reasonable expectation of privacy. Many state voyeurism laws criminalize the viewing or recording of a person's intimate parts without permission. Video voyeurism laws punish the nonconsensual recording of a person in a state of undress in places where individuals enjoy a reasonable expectation of privacy. Criminal laws prohibiting voyeurism rest on the commonly accepted assumption that observing a person in a state of undress or engaged in sexual activity without that person's consent not only inflicts dignitary harms upon the individual observed, but also inflicts a social harm serious enough to warrant criminal prohibition and punishment.

Gender Equality

In the United States, sexual privacy has not been protected to the same extent as other forms of privacy. Laws protecting victims from unauthorized disclosures of their financial, legal, or medical information have a much longer, and mostly uncontroversial, history than laws protecting sexual privacy. A combination of factors is at work in this disparity: in addition to misunderstandings of First Amendment doctrine described earlier, there is also a lack of understanding about the gravity, scope, and dynamics of sexual privacy violations; historical indifference and hostility to women's autonomy; and inconsistent conceptions of contextual privacy.

The public has only recently begun to get a sense of how widespread and serious the problem of nonconsensual pornography is. Like victims of domestic violence and sexual assault, victims of this abuse risk negative consequences for speaking out, including increased exposure and further reputational harm. Despite this, revenge porn victims like Chiarini and Jacobs have publicly shared their stories in order to raise awareness of the abuse. The fact that nonconsensual pornography so often involves issues of constantly evolving technology creates even more challenges for public comprehension of mechanics of the abuse and its devastating impact.

As Professor Citron and I detailed in our 2014 law review article, our society has a poor track record in addressing harms that disproportionately burden women and girls (Citron and Franks 2014). Though great strides have been made toward gender equality in recent years, most social, legal, and political power still remains in the hands of men. The fight to recognize domestic violence, sexual assault, and sexual harassment as serious issues has been long and difficult, and the tendency to tolerate, trivialize, or dismiss these harms persists. It is not surprising that nonconsensual pornography, which affects women and girls more frequently than men and boys and often creates more serious consequences for them, is treated similarly.

At the heart of not only nonconsensual pornography, but other forms of nonconsensual sexual activity, is a tendency to treat sexual consent as different from other kinds of consent, especially women's consent. The commonly expressed belief that a woman who consensually shares sexually explicit photos with one trusted partner has effectively given consent for those images to be shared with a wider audience exposes troubling attitudes about women's sexual autonomy and contextual consent. It is the same attitude that underlies much sexual harassment and sexual assault: the notion that women who have voluntarily participated in some form of sexual activity lose their right to set boundaries about other forms of sexual activity.

Outside of sexual practices, however, most people easily understand that consent is context specific. Privacy regulations, affecting everything from medical records to drivers' licenses, make clear that permission to disclose information to one person in one context does not equate to granting permission to all for use in all contexts. The nonconsensual sharing of an individual's intimate photos should be no different; consent within a particular relationship does not equal consent outside of that relationship.

It can and has been argued that photos exchanged within an intimate relationship should be considered "gifts" from one party to the other, gifts that the recipient is permitted to use any way he sees fit. Questions have been raised about the difference between naked photos and, say, love letters, which are sometimes published by their recipients without consent from the giver. Whether such publication can be considered legally or morally justified is a question beyond the scope of this project; suffice it to say that even if it is permissible to publish writings of another person without their consent in some circumstances, photos and videos are fundamentally different. As indicated earlier, nonconsensual pornography is a form of unanswerable speech. Publishing a private, intimate image of a person inflicts an injury far greater than the publication of a person's private words, which can be contextualized, supplemented, and in some cases denied. As Roland Barthes writes, "pictures, to be sure, are more imperative than writing, they impose meaning at one stroke, without analyzing or diluting it" (Barthes 1972, p. 110).

Some criticize the criminalization of nonconsensual pornography on the grounds that it *undermines* gender equality by reinforcing the perception that women should be ashamed of their bodies or of sexual activity. This criticism, too, is unfounded. First, nonconsensual pornography laws are not gender-specific. They protect every person's right not to have their bodies exposed without consent, not just women's. Second, this protection has nothing to do with shame and everything to do with autonomy and bodily integrity. Nonconsensual pornography laws do not prohibit voluntary exposure of one's body any more than rape laws prohibit voluntary sexual activity.

Drying Up the Market

The market for private nude photos is unlike the market for other private information. We do not (yet) live in a world where thousands of websites are devoted to revealing private medical records, credit card numbers, or even love letters. By contrast, "revenge porn" is featured on thousands of websites, in addition to being distributed through social media, blogs, emails, and texts. There is a demand for private nude photos that is unlike the demand for any other form of private information. While nonconsensual pornography is not a new phenomenon, its prevalence, reach, and impact have increased in recent years in part because technology and social media make it possible to "crowdsource" abuse, as well as make it possible for unscrupulous individuals to profit from it. Dedicated "revenge porn" sites and other forums openly solicit private intimate images and expose them to millions of viewers, while allowing the posters themselves to hide in the shadows (Love 2013).

The trafficking of this material increases the demand for images and videos that exploit the individuals portrayed. As the Supreme Court has held in the context of child pornography, "The most expeditious if not the only practical method of law enforcement may be to dry up the market for this material by imposing severe criminal penalties on persons selling, advertising, or otherwise promoting the product" (New York v. Ferber).

Deterrence

Given the nature and severity of the harm caused by nonconsensual pornography, legal intervention must focus primarily on deterrence. Unlike, for example, victims of property crimes, victims of nonconsensual pornography can never truly be compensated or made whole. There is no undoing a violation of privacy; there is only damage control. Accordingly, legal intervention should seek to prevent the harm from occurring in the first place.

One of the merits of criminalization is that the fear of jail time is far more salient to the average would-be perpetrator than the remote possibility of being sued (Wright 2010). The ideal effect of a criminal law is to discourage perpetrators from becoming perpetrators in the first place. Solid empirical evidence of the deterrent effect of criminalization is admittedly hard to come by. It is always difficult to discern why people do not engage in crime. But we do know that certainty, more so than severity, of punishment does factor into deterrence, and it is generally acknowledged that most people fear jail more than lawsuits. CCRI's 2017 national study on victimization and perpetration of nonconsensual pornography also provides useful insight here. The survey asked respondents who admitted to having engaged in nonconsensual pornography what might have stopped them from doing so. Out of more than a dozen possible factors, the majority of respondents (60 percent) indicated that harsh criminal penalties would have been the most effective deterrent (Eaton et al. 2017, p. 22).

DEFINING THE CRIME

To argue in favor of criminalizing nonconsensual pornography is not to blindly support any and all efforts to make it illegal. Laws should be clear, specific, and narrowly drawn to protect the right to privacy without unduly interfering with freedom of expression. The following summarizes the specific features an effective law should include, as well as features to avoid.[23]

It is a basic principle of US criminal law that crimes include three basic components: an actus reus ("guilty act"), mens rea ("guilty mind"), and social harm. The social harm of nonconsensual pornography is, as has been detailed in the foregoing sections, the invasion of sexual privacy. The following discussion offers a description of what the other components of the crime should look like.

Actus Reus

The elements of a crime should clearly reflect the fundamental social harm of the conduct, namely, the violation of privacy. Nonconsensual pornography *can* involve harassment, extortion, or identity theft; the harm it inflicts *can* be psychological, physical, financial, reputational, professional, educational, or discriminatory. But what nonconsensual pornography *always* involves is an invasion of privacy, and the harm it *always* inflicts is a loss of privacy. Accordingly, the basic elements of the crime should be (1) the disclosure of private, sexually explicit photos or videos of an identifiable[24] person (2) without the consent of the person depicted.

Mens Rea

The law should also clearly state the requisite mens rea for each element of the crime. It is an axiom of criminal law that a person cannot be guilty "unless the mind be guilty; that is unless the intention be criminal."[25] Mens rea, or "guilty mind," refers to the mental state the defendant must have had with regard to the "social harm" elements set out in the definition of the offense.[26] At common law, the terms for mens rea were numerous and often ill-defined. The Model Penal Code (MPC), by contrast, uses just four terms for mens rea: purpose, knowledge, recklessness, and negligence.[27] Many states have adopted the MPC approach to mens rea (Dressler and Garvey 2016, pp. 168–169).

The mens rea for the first element, disclosure, should be purpose or knowledge. The distinction between the two is not bright in most circumstances, and in the context of disclosures it amounts effectively to the same thing. The primary point is to ensure that purely accidental disclosures would not be punishable.

The mens rea for the second element, lack of consent, should by contrast be no higher than recklessness. In some nonconsensual pornography cases, the perpetrator is explicitly aware that the depicted individual did not consent. Imposing liability on such perpetrators is relatively uncontroversial. However, to restrict liability only to actors who act knowingly is too narrow. In many cases, the perpetrator has not been expressly informed that the depicted individual does not consent to disclosure of the image. Many intimate partners never have a specific conversation in which they set the boundaries of who has access to intimate photos; they instead presume that the images will be kept private between them. A discloser who is not in a relationship with the depicted individual—say, a hacker of celebrity photos—will likely not have been expressly told that he does not have consent to distribute images, and he may even think that it is possible that the depicted individual did consent.

If a discloser truly has no idea that the person in the image did not consent, then punishing him arguably is too harsh a response.[28] But in many cases, disclosers have, to use the Model Penal Code's language in defining recklessness, "consciously disregarded a substantial and unjustifiable risk,"[29] namely, the risk that the depicted individual has not consented. When their uncertainty is weighed against the potentially catastrophic consequences of nonconsensual disclosure, it is clear that such individuals should also face liability.

Under a recklessness analysis, only "substantial and unjustifiable" risks are punishable. The "substantial" prong indicates that the risk must be weighty in both a quantitative and a qualitative sense: risks that are extremely unlikely to result in harm, or risks that are likely only to result in trivial harms, are not "substantial." The first prong is moreover informed by the second, "unjustifiable" prong. The analysis of justification requires a calculation of the social utility of the risk. Speeding on a busy highway involves substantial risk both in terms of the probability and in terms of the severity of the harm; car accidents are common and pose a grave risk of serious injury or death. But the analysis of the risk is affected by the reason for speeding. If a person speeds to get home in time to watch a favorite TV show, there is little social utility and thus little to justify in the taking of that risk; if a person speeds to get a seriously ill child to the hospital, there is much greater social utility and thus justification in the taking of that risk. It is appropriate to criminally punish actors who act recklessly, in addition to those who act purposely or knowingly, when they know that the social utility of the risk they take is far outweighed by the social harm that is likely to result.

With regard to nonconsensual pornography, the potential social harm is both highly likely and highly destructive. The likelihood of negative consequences resulting from the public disclosure of personal photos and videos depicting nudity or sexual conduct, especially for women and girls, is extremely high. As discussed earlier, these consequences include psychological trauma severe enough to lead many to contemplate, and some to commit, suicide; threats of sexual assault; harassment; stalking; loss of employment; loss of educational opportunities; loss of intimate and family relationships; and many other harms. The social utility of the risky activity—disclosing a sexually explicit photo or video of a person without verifying consent—is extremely low. Refraining from such disclosures absent clear consent cannot be a burden in the way that refraining from other risky but socially useful activities, such as driving, would.

This is not only because the social utility of disclosing sexually explicit images is so much lower, but also because the elimination of the risk in most cases will be minimally burdensome. All that is required to avoid the risk of nonconsensual disclosure is to confirm consent when there is doubt or refrain from disclosure when consent cannot be ascertained. The decision to disclose sexually explicit images rarely, if ever, requires split-second decision-making that would make verification impossible or impractical. Contemporary communication technology makes it possible for confirmation to be both easy and quick.

Exceptions

The law should include exceptions for sexually explicit images voluntarily exposed in public or commercial settings. These exceptions are important to ensure that recording and reporting unlawful activity in public places (such as indecent exposure), reporting on newsworthy public events (such as topless protests), or forwarding or linking to commercial pornography are not criminalized.

The law should also include narrow exceptions for disclosures made in public interest, including the lawful and common practices of law enforcement or medical treatment. As Warren and Brandeis wrote, "The right to privacy does not prohibit any publication of matter which is of public or general interest" (Warren and Brandeis 1890, p. 214). Law enforcement officers and medical professionals often have to deal with intimate materials, such as visual records of injuries from domestic violence or rape. While it is vital that such materials be kept out of the public eye, the law should not burden the necessary flow of evidence or medical records that takes place in professional settings. Outside of law enforcement and medical practices, the public interest exception might apply, for example, to situations in which a concerned partner or parent of a victim of nonconsensual pornography contacts an advocacy organization or social media platform and includes links to or copies of the content in the hopes of having it removed or otherwise obtaining assistance, without getting express permission from the victim to do so. While the term "public interest" is not without ambiguity, the dictionary definition of the term—"the welfare or well-being of the general public"[30]—provides considerable guidance, as does the case law illustrating its boundaries, discussed in more detail later.

Other Issues

Other pitfalls to avoid in drafting an effective nonconsensual pornography law include overly expansive definitions of nudity; for example, definitions that include the depiction of buttocks or female nipples visible through gauzy or wet fabric or covered male genitals in a "discernibly turgid state."[31] Such definitions have the potential to criminalize innocuous conduct, such as parents sharing baby photos with family members that depict infants taking baths (Bhattacharjee 2013). On the other hand, the law should not be so narrowly drafted as to apply only to images featuring nudity, as an image can be sexually explicit without containing nudity (Goldberg 2014). The law should not be so narrowly drafted as to only apply to disclosures made online or through social media, as nonconsensual pornography can also take "low-tech" forms such as printed photographs and DVDs (Phillips 2013).

State laws should also reflect an understanding of Section 230 of the Communications Decency Act. Section 230 currently protects online entities from liability when they merely provide platforms for third-party content. Given that Section 230 trumps any state law that conflicts with it,[32] state laws should not be drafted in a way that creates unnecessary confusion about this fact.[33] However, state legislators should also take care not to broaden immunity for online entities beyond what is provided by Section 230, which only applies to the extent that these entities serve as intermediaries for third-party content. To the extent that online entities act as codevelopers or cocreators of content, Section 230 is not a bar to state criminal prosecution (Franks 2013).[34]

EVALUATION OF THE CURRENT LEGAL LANDSCAPE

The social, technological, and legal landscape of "revenge porn" has undergone a dramatic transformation in recent years. In addition to receiving extensive attention in the popular press, "revenge porn" has been banned by most major social media platforms and Internet companies. Between 2013 and 2019, the number of states that criminalize nonconsensual pornography has increased from 3 to 46, plus Washington, D.C. The push to criminalize "revenge porn" has achieved tremendous success, at least on paper.

However, these laws vary widely in terms of definitions, scope, effectiveness, remedies, categorization, and constitutional implications. The most serious problem is that the majority of these laws include "intent to harass" requirements, which, as discussed earlier, reflect a fundamental misunderstanding of the nature of the harm. Other serious problems include the classification of the crime as a minor misdemeanor, the limitation of the law to online postings, over- or under-inclusive definitions of nudity and sexual conduct, and a lack of appropriate exceptions.

The responsibility for the first problem can be laid largely at the door of the American Civil Liberties Union (ACLU). The ACLU has led the effort to defeat or dilute criminal legislation against nonconsensual pornography, often joined by the Electronic Frontier Foundation, the Media Coalition, the Motion Picture Association of America, and in some cases, tech companies such as Google. The ACLU has pressured legislators in many states to include intent to harass requirements, falsely stating that such requirements are necessary to ensure compliance with the First Amendment. As a result, the majority of states include this limitation, rendering the laws useless for most victims.

In 2013, when the criminalization movement was just beginning, the ACLU attempted to claim that *any* law criminalizing nonconsensual pornography would violate the First Amendment. When California passed its law late that year, the Northern California chapter of the ACLU responded with a letter declaring that the law violated the First Amendment but provided no relevant case law in support of this conclusion. When pressed for clarification, an ACLU spokesman reversed course, stating "that the ACLU had no objections to the

[California] bill" and "could not offer any explanation for why the initial objection letter was sent" (Schulzke 2013; Halloran 2014).

The ACLU shifted strategies from denial to dilution in 2014, as the criminalization movement began to pick up steam. In May 2014, Arizona passed a law criminalizing nonconsensual pornography. The bill's drafters had worked closely with CCRI, and the final bill strongly resembled CCRI's model statute, with the exception that it lacked the public interest exception that CCRI urged. The statute made it illegal "to intentionally disclose, display, distribute, publish, advertise or offer a photograph, videotape, film or digital recording of another person in a state of nudity or engaged in specific sexual activities if the person knows or should have known that the depicted person has not consented to the disclosure" (Franks 2017, pp. 1327–1329). The statute included exceptions for "lawful and common practices of law enforcement, reporting unlawful activity, or when permitted or required by law or rule in legal proceedings," "lawful and common practices of medical treatment" and "images involving voluntary exposure in a public or commercial setting."

In September 2014, the ACLU initiated a lawsuit challenging the law on behalf of itself and a group of booksellers. In a letter to Arizona lawmakers, the ACLU demanded that the state redefine the crime, asserting that any law criminalizing "revenge porn" must be limited to circumstances where:

(1) a person who was or is in an intimate relationship with another person and who,
(2) during and as a result of that relationship, obtained a recognizable image of such other person in a state of nudity,
(3) where such other person had a reasonable expectation of privacy and an understanding that such image would remain private,
(4) to display such image
(5) without the consent of such other person,
(6) with the intent to harass, humiliate, embarrass, or otherwise harm such other person, and
(7) where there is no public or newsworthy purpose for the display.[35]

The ACLU offered no justification for why the crime should be defined in these narrow terms or on what basis the organization had either the authority or the competence to make such a determination.

Arizona presented a clash of definitions as described in Part II: nonconsensual pornography versus "revenge porn" or, to put it another way, "revenge porn-as-privacy-violation" versus "revenge porn-as-harassment." One the one side was the state's definition, produced through intense consultation with victims, advocates, and First Amendment scholars and enacted into law through the democratic process. On the other was a definition created by a powerful civil liberties organization and a coalition of media lobbyists. The state of Arizona backed down in the face of the ACLU's pressure, withdrawing the law and replacing it with one drafted to meet the ACLU's specifications.

This conflict in many ways set the stage for the national debate over criminalization. The ACLU and its partners in the film, technology, and bookselling industries have used their considerable financial and political resources to thwart the movement by grassroots victims' rights organizations and legal scholars to criminalize the unauthorized distribution of private, sexually explicit images. While the coalition has not been able to stop the wave of legislative reform that led to nearly every state passing a criminal law on the issue, it has been able to render a majority of these laws practically useless by pressuring states to include "intent to harass" requirements and categorize the crime as a minor misdemeanor.

The ACLU's definition of the crime would allow any person who disclosed private, sexually explicit material for profit, reputation enhancement, entertainment, or "satire" to act with impunity (Franks 2017). When Pennsylvania enacted its nonconsensual pornography law in 2014, it hewed closely to the ACLU's definition.[36] The law is restricted to those who, "with intent to harass, annoy or alarm a current or former sexual or intimate partner … disseminate[ ] a visual depiction of the current or former sexual or intimate partner in a state of nudity or engaged in sexual conduct."[37] A 2015 case involving the Penn State chapter of the Kappa Delta Rho (KDR) fraternity illustrates the consequences of this position. In that case, fraternity brothers posted photos of naked, unconscious women to a members-only Facebook page. The women were not, apparently, the current or former intimate partners of the disclosers. What is more, the fact that the fraternity brothers distributed the photos secretly among themselves undermined any claim that they had acted with the "intent to harass, annoy or alarm" anyone. As a KDR member stated in the group's defense, "It wasn't malicious whatsoever. It wasn't intended to hurt anyone. It wasn't intended to demean anyone."[38] The perpetrators were unsurprisingly not charged with violating Pennsylvania's nonconsensual pornography law.

The ACLU's position on nonconsensual pornography laws is in tension with its own positions on other measures to protect privacy rights. The ACLU supports laws that protect many forms of private information, such as Social Security numbers, genetic information, and even geolocation data. Both state and federal criminal laws prohibit the unauthorized disclosure of material such as medical records,[39] financial data,[40] and cell phone usage information.[41] None of these statutes require that perpetrators act with the intent to harass their victims, and certainly none require that the perpetrator and victim be intimate partners. These laws reflect the century-old understanding that, in the words of Warren and Brandeis, "the absence of 'malice' in the publisher does not afford a defence" to privacy violations; "[p]ersonal ill-will is not an ingredient of the offence, any more than in an ordinary case of trespass to person or to property" (Warren and Brandeis 1890, p. 217). The ACLU clearly recognizes in most contexts that protecting privacy does not demand the addition of "intent to harass" requirements and does not violate the First Amendment.

Treating nonconsensual pornography as a harassment issue instead of a privacy issue demotes the harm it causes from an invasion of privacy to something more akin to hurt feelings. Not only is this a misguided and patronizing approach to nonconsensual pornography, but it also renders nonconsensual pornography laws more vulnerable to constitutional attack.

Conclusion

The criminalization of "revenge porn" is necessary to protect essential democratic values of privacy, freedom of expression, bodily autonomy, and equality. The wave of legislative reform since 2013 is a welcome development, but the majority of state criminal laws are hamstrung by mischaracterization of the social harm of the abuse. Nonconsensual pornography is most fundamentally a violation of privacy causing irreversible harm to victims and society as a whole. State and federal laws that clearly express this are necessary to ensure just and effective remedies for victims and deter potential perpetrators.

Notes

1. While this chapter focuses on the United States, several other countries have also moved to criminalize nonconsensual pornography, including Canada, England, Israel, Japan, New Zealand, Northern Ireland, Philippines, Scotland, and Wales (Franks 2017).
2. In addition to being a member of CCRI's founding board of directors, I have served as CCRI's Legislative and Tech Policy Director since 2014 and was named its President in July 2018. I drafted the first model criminal statute on nonconsensual pornography, which has served as the template for several state laws as well as for federal legislation on the issue.
3. A previous nationwide study by the Data & Society Research Institute indicated a somewhat lower level of prevalence, finding that 1 in 25 American Internet users—around 10 million people—had been a victim of or threatened with the disclosure of intimate images. The discrepancy appears to be largely due to the latter study's narrower definition of the abuse and differences in methodology. The Data and Society study was limited to nude or nearly nude depictions disclosed without consent with the intention to hurt or embarrass the victim and was conducted via telephone survey (Data and Society 2016, p. 5). The CCRI study addressed all nonconsensual, sexually explicit disclosures and was conducted through Facebook polling (Eaton et al. 2017, p. 608).
4. Victim takedown request list made available to the Cyber Civil Rights Initiative (on file with author). This number is a considerable increase from 2014, when around 3000 websites were believed to feature nonconsensual pornography (Economist 2014).
5. Uhl et al.'s research revealed that "nearly 92% of victims featured on included websites were women" (Uhl et al. 2013). Whitmarsh's study examined 396 posts to a revenge porn website, of which 378 depicted women versus 18 depicting men (Whitmarsh 2015).

6. The Data and Society Research study did find that men and women were roughly equally likely to have their intimate material posted, as opposed to being threatened with posting—an intriguing finding. Ibid. However, this study does not appear to have distinguished between unsolicited and solicited images and does not provide information about where, how, and with what information these postings were made. This may be relevant, as some studies have shown that men send more sexually explicit images than women do (Scientific American): "[61] percent of men partake in sexting and suggestive photo taking, while 48 percent of women do." Many of these images are what are commonly referred to as "dick pics," are often unsolicited, and often do not include identifying information about the sender (Thompson 2016). Many recipients of such images consider them to be a form of harassment. *See* ibid. It is not uncommon for women uncomfortable with such unsolicited images to publicize these images in an effort to shame or deter the sender, often without revealing identifying details about the sender (Titlow 2016). I take the position that the publication of nude or sexually explicit photos in which the sender cannot be identified should not be considered nonconsensual pornography for purposes of legal prohibition. The sending of unsolicited nude photos should, in many cases, be considered a form of harassment and, in some cases, a form of public exposure in which the sender does not retain an expectation of privacy.

7. For detailed cases, see United States v. Osinger, 753 F.3d 939 (9th Cir. 2014); United States v. Petrovic, 701 F.3d 849 (8th Cir. 2012); U.S. v. Sayer, 748 F.3d 425 (1st Cir. 2014).

8. The study included 1606 total respondents, 361 of whom self-identified as victims. See 2013 NCP Study Results, Cyber Civil Rights Initiative, https://www.cybercivilrights.org/ncpstats/ (last visited May 21, 2017). All of the information provided in this section comes from this study unless otherwise noted.

9. Much of the discussion in this section is drawn from my previous work (Franks 2017).

10. 18 U.S.C. § 2261A.

11. N.Y. Penal Law § 120.50 (McKinney 2017); *Id.* § 240.25.

12. People v. Barber, 2014 N.Y. Slip. Op. 50193(U) (N.Y. Sup. Ct. Feb. 18, 2014).

13. "No provider or user of an interactive computer service shall be treated as the publisher or speaker of any information provided by another information content provider" (47 U.S.C. § 230(c)(1) (2012)).

14. For example, Brill writes, "[T]he First Amendment presents support for the argument that one should not be arrested, let alone imprisoned, for publicizing its speech—in the form of these photographs or images. In fact, some suggest that the criminal law is the inappropriate venue in which to deal with this conduct. After all, the conduct is non-violent and a mere example of a somewhat harsh freedom of expression. Instead, perhaps the better course of action is to file a civil suit for the damages this conduct may cause" (Brill 2014).

15. 376 U.S. 254, 277 (1964).

16. Ibid. "Presumably a person charged with violation of this statute enjoys ordinary criminal-law safeguards such as the requirements of an indictment and of proof beyond a reasonable doubt. These safeguards are not available to the defendant in a civil action."

17. Dun & Bradstreet, Inc. v. Greenmoss Builders, Inc., 472 U.S. 749, 758–60 (1985) (internal citations omitted).

18. Connick v. Myers, 461 U.S. 138, 147 (1983). The Court has observed that while it endorses the "absolute defense of truth 'where discussion of public affairs is concerned,'" it has left "unsettled the constitutional implications of truthfulness 'in the discrete area of purely private libels'" and have "pointedly refused to answer even the less sweeping question 'whether truthful publications may ever be subjected to civil or criminal liability' for invading 'an area of privacy'" given its respect for "the fact that press freedom and privacy rights are both plainly rooted in the traditions and significant concerns of our society…" The Fla. Star v. B.J.F., 491 U.S. 524, 532–332 (1989) (internal citations omitted).

19. In Snyder v. Phelps, 131 S.Ct. 1207, 1215 (2011) (internal citations omitted), the Court suggested that a matter is "purely private" if it does not contribute to "the free and robust debate of public issues" or the "meaningful dialogue of ideas."

20. City of San Diego v. Roe, 543 U.S. 77, 84 (2004) (*per curiam*). *See also* The Fla. Star v. B.J.F., 491 U.S. 524, 541 (1989) ("We do not hold that truthful publication is automatically constitutionally protected, or that there is no zone of personal privacy within which the State may protect the individual from intrusion by the press…"). As the Ninth Circuit recently held in upholding a conviction for harassing and intimidating conduct, unauthorized "sexually explicit publications concerning a private individual" are not "afforded First Amendment protection." United States v. Osinger, 753 F.3d 939, 948 (9th Cir. 2014); *see also* United States v. Petrovic, 701 F.3d 849, 855–56 (8th Cir. 2012) (rejecting a First Amendment challenge by a defendant convicted under federal stalking law for distributing a victim's private nude photos and information).

21. As indeed the Supreme Court of Vermont held in State v. VanBuren, 2018 VT 95 (Vt. Aug. 31, 2018).

22. Much of the discussion in this section is drawn from my previous work (Citron and Franks 2014; Franks 2017).

23. The following is based on a document I prepared for legislators (Franks 2014). Ideally, laws would also include a severability clause, so that in the event that some provision might be declared invalid, the rest of the provision would remain effective.

24. The designation of an "identifiable" person makes clear that the statute will not apply to photos or videos that merely depict body parts or sexual activity and provide no indication of who the subjects might be.

25. Mens Rea, Black's Law Dictionary (4th ed. 1951).

26. United States v. Cordoba-Hincapie, 825 F. Supp. 485, 489 (E.D.N.Y. 1993).

27. Model Penal Code § 2.02(2) (Am. Law Inst. 2016).

28. Ibid.

29. Model Penal Code § 2.02(2)(c) (Am. Law Inst. 2016).

30. *Public Interest*, Dictionary.com, http://www.dictionary.com/browse/public-interest (last visited May 21, 2017).

31. *See*, e.g., Ga. Code Ann. § 16-11-90(a) (2016) (defining "nudity" as "(A) The showing of the human male or female genitals, pubic area, or buttocks without any covering or with less than a full opaque covering; (B) The showing of the female breasts without any covering or with less than a full opaque covering; or (C) The depiction of covered male genitals in a discernibly turgid state").

32. § 230(e)(3) ("No cause of action may be brought and no liability may be imposed under any State or local law that is inconsistent with this section").

33. By the same token, criticisms to the effect that a state "revenge porn" law can deprive Internet entities of their Section 230 immunity are unfounded.

34. Fair Hous. Council of San Fernando Valley v. Roommates.com, LLC, 521 F.3d 1157, 1162–63 (9th Cir. 2008).

35. Email from American Civil Liberties Union, to Ariz. Lawmakers & Ariz. House of Representatives Standing Comm. on the Judiciary (Feb. 10, 2015), https://drive.google.com/file/d/0B2LoKN1jK5BNX0NsZUdOUng5ZlE/view?usp=sharing

36. 18 Pa. Cons. Stat. § 3131 (2017).

37. 18 Pa. Cons. Stat. § 3131.

38. Ibid.

39. 42 U.S.C. § 1320d-6 (2012).

40. Tex. Penal Code Ann. § 31.17 (2015).

41. 47 U.S.C. § 222 (2012).

REFERENCES

Ga. Code Ann. § 16-11-90(a) (2016).

Model Penal Code § 2.02(2) (Am. Law Inst. 2016).

N.Y. Penal Law § 120.50 (McKinney 2017).

Tex. Penal Code Ann. § 31.17 (2015).

H.R. 5896, 114th Cong. (2016).

18 Pa. Cons. Stat. § 3131 (2017).

18 U.S.C. § 2261A.

47 U.S.C. § 230(c)(1) (2012).

42 U.S.C. § 1320d-6 (2012).

47 U.S.C. § 222 (2012).

City of San Diego v. Roe, 543 U.S. 77, 84 (2004).

Connick v. Myers, 461 U.S. 138, 147 (1983).

Dun & Bradstreet, Inc. v. Greenmoss Builders, Inc., 472 U.S. 749, 758–60 (1985).

Fair Hous. Council of San Fernando Valley v. Roommates.com, LLC, 521 F.3d 1157, 1162–63 (9th Cir. 2008).

The Fla. Star v. B.J.F., 491 U.S. 524, 532–332 (1989).

New York v. Ferber, 458 U.S. 747 (1982).

New York Times v. Sullivan, 376 U.S. 254, 277 (1964).

People v. Barber, 2014 N.Y. Slip. Op. 50193(U) (N.Y. Sup. Ct. Feb. 18, 2014).

Snyder v. Phelps, 131 S.Ct. 1207, 1215 (2011).

State v. VanBuren, 2018 VT 95 (Vt. Aug. 31, 2018).

United States v. Cordoba-Hincapie, 825 F. Supp. 485, 489 (E.D.N.Y. 1993).

United States v. Osinger, 753 F.3d 939 (9th Cir. 2014).

United States v. Petrovic, 701 F.3d 849 (8th Cir. 2012).

United States v. Sayer, 748 F.3d 425 (1st Cir. 2014).

Adams, Rebecca. 2014. For victims of sexual assault, there's little incentive to come forward – Besides "justice." *Huffington Post*. http://www.huffingtonpost.com/2014/12/15/victims-sexual-assault-come-forward-justice_n_6294152.html. Accessed 5 Jan 2015.

Alexander, Michelle. 2010. *The new Jim Crow: Mass incarceration in the age of color-blindness*. New York: The New Press.

Anderson, Elizabeth S., and Richard H. Pildes. 2000. Expressive theories of law: A general restatement. *University of Pennsylvania Law Review* 148: 1503–1575.

Barthes, Roland. 1972. *Mythologies*. New York: Hill & Wang.

Bartow, Ann. 2008. Pornography, coercion, and copyright law 2.0. *Vanderbilt Journal of Entertainment & Technology Law* 10: 799–840.

Bates, Samantha. 2017. Revenge porn and mental health: A qualitative analysis of the mental health effects of revenge porn on female survivors. *Feminist Criminology* 12: 22–42.

Bazelon, Emily. 2013. Another sexting tragedy. *Slate*. http://www.slate.com/articles/double_x/doublex/2013/04/audrie_pott_and_rehtaeh_parsons_how_should_the_legal_system_treat_nonconsensual.html. Accessed 15 Apr 2014.

Bhattacharjee, Riya. 2013. Florida pushes bill to criminalize "revenge porn." *MSN News*. http://news.msn.com/us/florida-pushes-bill-to-criminalize-revenge-porn. Accessed 9 Nov 2013.

Brill, Steven. 2014. The growing trend of "revenge porn" and the criminal laws that may follow. *Huffington Post*. http://www.huffingtonpost.com/steven-brill/the-growing-trend-of-revenge-porn_b_4849990.html. Accessed 15 May 2014.

Brooks, Marion. 2013. The world of human trafficking: One woman's story. *NBC Chicago*. http://www.nbcchicago.com/investigations/human-trafficking-alex-campbell-192415731.html. Accessed 22 Feb 2013.

Cambridge Dictionary. Entry for "revenge porn." https://dictionary.cambridge.org/us/dictionary/english/revenge-porn. Accessed 23 Feb 2019.

Caplan-Bricker, Nora. 2014. There's a legal war over the definition of rape. *New Republic*. https://newrepublic.com/article/117630/jed-rubenfeld-rape-law-feminists-debate-force-versus-non-consent. Accessed 6 May 2014.

Chiarini, Annmarie. 2013. I was a victim of revenge porn. *Guardian*. http://www.theguardian.com/commentisfree/2013/nov/19/revenge-porn-victim-maryland-law-change. Accessed 14 Dec 2013.

Citron, Danielle. 2012. Cyber stalking and cyber harassment, a devastating and endemic problem. *Concurring Opinions*. http://www.concurringopinions.com/archives/2012/03/cyber-stalking-and-cyber-harassment-a-devastating-and-endemic-problem.html. Accessed 16 Mar 2012.

Citron, Danielle Keats. 2014. *Hate crimes in cyberspace*. Cambridge, MA: Harvard University Press.

Citron, Danielle Keats, and Mary Anne Franks. 2014. Criminalizing revenge porn. *Wake Forest Law Review* 49: 345–391.

Culp-Ressler, Tara. 2014. 16-Year-Old's rape goes viral on social media: "No human being deserved this." *ThinkProgress*. http://thinkprogress.org/health/2014/07/10/3458564/rape-viral-social-media-jada/. Accessed 10 July 2014.

Cyber Civil Rights Initiative. 2013. 2013 NCP study results. *CCRI Website*. https://www.cybercivilrights.org/ncpstats/. Accessed 21 May 2017.

Data and Society Research Institute. 2016. New report shows that 4% of U.S. internet users have been a victim of "revenge porn." *Data & Soc'y: Blog*. https://datasociety.net/blog/2016/12/13/nonconsensual-image-sharing/. Accessed 13 Dec 2016.

Dewey, Caitlin. 2014. How copyright became the best defense against revenge porn. *Washington Post*. https://www.washingtonpost.com/news/the-intersect/

wp/2014/09/08/how-copyright-became-the-best-defense-against-revenge-porn/?utm_term=.68fd101e3aff. Accessed 8 Sep 2014.

Donaghue, Erin. 2014. Judge throws out New York revenge porn case. *CBS*. http://www.cbsnews.com/news/judge-throws-out-new-york-revenge-porn-case/. Accessed 25 Feb 2014.

Dressler, Joshua, and Stephen Garvey. 2016. *Criminal law: Cases and materials*, American casebook series. 7th ed. St. Paul: West Academic Publishing.

Eaton, Asia A., Holly Jacobs, and Yanet Ruvalcaba. 2017. 2017 Nationwide online study of nonconsensual porn victimization and perpetration: A summary report. *Cyber Civil Rights Initiative*. https://www.cybercivilrights.org/wp-content/uploads/2017/06/CCRI-2017-Research-Report.pdf. Accessed 12 June 2017.

Economist. 2014. Misery merchants: How should the online publication of explicit images without their subjects' consent be punished? *Economist*. http://www.economist.com/news/international/21606307-how-should-online-publication-explicit-images-without-their-subjects-consent-be. Accessed 5 July 2014.

Erez, Edna. 2002. Domestic violence and the criminal justice system: An Overview. *Online Journal of Issues in Nursing* 7. www.nursingworld.org/ojin/MainMenuCategories/ANAMarketplace/ANAPeriodicals/OJIN/TableofContents/Volume72002/No1Jan2002/DomesticViolenceandCriminalJustice.aspx. Accessed 15 Jan 2014.

Filipovic, Jill. 2013. "Revenge porn" is about degrading women sexually and professionally. *Guardian*. https://www.theguardian.com/commentisfree/2013/jan/28/revenge-porn-degrades-women. Accessed 28 Jan 2013.

Franks, Mary Anne. 2013. The lawless internet? Myths and misconceptions about CDA section 230. *Huffington Post*. http://www.huffingtonpost.com/mary-anne-franks/section-230-the-lawless-internet_b_4455090.html. Accessed 18 Dec 2013.

———. 2014. Drafting an effective "revenge porn" law: A guide for legislators. *Cyber Civil Rights Initiative*. http://www.cybercivilrights.org/guide-to-legislation/. Accessed 21 May 2017.

———. 2016. Men, women, and optimal violence. *University of Illinois Law Review* 3: 929–968.

———. 2017. "Revenge porn" reform: A view from the front lines. *Florida Law Review* 69: 1251–1337.

Goldberg, Carrie. 2014. Seven reasons Illinois is leading the fight against revenge porn. *Cyber Civil Rights Initiative*. http://www.cybercivilrights.org/seven-reasons-illinois-leading-fight-revenge-porn. Accessed 31 Dec 2014.

Gray, Emma. 2014. The Emma Watson threats were a hoax, but women face similar intimidation online every day. *Huffington Post*. http://www.huffingtonpost.com/2014/09/26/emma-watson-hoax-women-online-threats_n_5887712.html. Accessed 26 Sep 2014.

Halloran, Liz. 2014. Race to stop "revenge porn" raises free speech worries. *NPR*. http://www.npr.org/blogs/itsallpolitics/2014/03/06/286388840/race-to-stop-revenge-porn-raises-free-speech-worries. Accessed 6 Mar 2014.

Hopkins, Nick, and Olivia Solon. 2017. Facebook flooded with 'sextortion' and revenge porn, files reveal. *Guardian*. https://www.theguardian.com/news/2017/may/22/facebook-flooded-with-sextortion-and-revenge-porn-files-reveal. Accessed 22 May 2017.

Husak, Douglas. 2009. *Overcriminalization: The limits of the criminal law*. Oxford: Oxford University Press.

Jacobs, Holly. 2013. Being a victim of revenge porn forced me to change my name. *XO Jane.* http://www.xojane.com/it-happened-to-me/revenge-porn-holly-jacobs. Accessed 13 Nov 2013.

Jan-Lim, Clarissa. 2017. Meet the women waging war on revenge porn. *A Plus.* https://aplus.com/a/meet-the-women-waging-war-on-revenge-porn?no_monetization=true. Accessed 22 Feb 2017.

Kruttschnitt, Candace, et al. 2014. *Estimating the incidence of rape and sexual assault.* Washington, DC: National Research Council.

Leovy, Jill. 2015. *Ghettoside: A true story of murder in America.* New York: Spiegel & Grau.

Love, Dylan. 2013. It will be hard to stop the rise of revenge porn. *Business Insider.* http://www.businessinsider.com/revenge-porn-2013-2. Accessed 8 Feb 2013.

Marshall, Olivia, and Lis Power. 2014. Right-wing media blames Ray Rice's victim. *Media Matters.* http://mediamatters.org/research/2014/09/08/right-wing-media-blames-ray-rices-victim/200684. Accessed 8 Sep 2014.

Mathen, Carissima. 2014. Crowdsourcing sexual objectification. *Laws* 3: 529–552.

Matorin, Mitchell J. 2013. In the real world, revenge porn is far worse than making it illegal. *TPM.* http://talkingpointsmemo.com/cafe/our-current-law-is-completely-inadequate-for-dealing-with-revenge-porn. Accessed 18 Oct 2013.

McKenna, Kate. 2017. Non-consensual distribution of nude images "a real issue for Canadians." *CBC News.* http://www.cbc.ca/news/canada/montreal/porn-site-reax-montreal-1.3953167. Accessed 26 Jan 2017.

Mendelson, Scott. 2014. Jennifer Lawrence nude photo leak isn't a "scandal." It's a sex crime. *Forbes.* http://www.forbes.com/sites/scottmendelson/2014/09/01/jennifer-lawrence-nude-photo-leak-isnt-a-scandal-its-a-sex-crime/. Accessed 1 Sep 2014.

National Center for Victims of Crime. 2004. Spousal rape laws: 20 years later. http://www.njep-ipsacourse.org/PDFs/NCVCspousalrapelaws.pdf. Accessed 23 Feb 2019.

Phillips, Nicholas. 2013. Sext fiend: Jovica Petrovic tried to embarrass his ex-wife to death, and revenge porn was the name of the game. *Riverfront Times.* http://www.riverfronttimes.com/2013-04-18/news/sext-fiend/full/. Accessed 28 Apr 2013.

Post, Robert. 1995. Recuperating First Amendment doctrine. *Stanford Law Review* 47: 1249–1281.

Richards, Neil M. 2015. Why data privacy law is (mostly) constitutional. *William & Mary Law Review* 56: 1501–1533.

Roberts, Jeff. 2014. No, copyright is not the answer to revenge porn. *Gigaom.* https://gigaom.com/2014/02/06/no-copyright-is-not-the-answer-to-revenge-porn/. Accessed 6 Feb 2014.

Ronneburger, Ariel. 2009. Sex, privacy, and webpages: Creating a legal remedy for victims of porn 2.0. *Syracuse Science & Technology Law Report* 21: 1–34.

Roy, Jessica. 2015. How tech companies are fighting revenge porn—and winning. *New York Magazine.* http://nymag.com/thecut/2015/06/how-tech-companies-are-fighting-revenge-porn.html. Accessed 24 June 2015.

Schulzke, Eric. 2013. California lawmakers target "revenge porn" but miss, critics say. *Deseret News.* http://www.deseretnews.com/article/865586019/California-lawmakers-target-revenge-porn-but-miss-critics-say.html. Accessed 8 Sep 2013.

Scientific American. Sext much? If so, you're not alone. *Scientific American.* https://www.scientificamerican.com/article/sext-much-if-so-youre-not-alone/. Accessed 23 Feb 2019.

Siegel, Reva B. 1996. "The rule of love": Wife beating as prerogative and privacy. *Yale Law Journal* 105: 2117–2207.

Simpson, Jack. 2014. Revenge porn: What is it and how widespread is the problem? *The Independent.* http://www.independent.co.uk/news/uk/home-news/what-is-revenge-porn-9580251.html. Accessed 2 July 2014.

Speier, Jackie. 2016. Fellow members of Congress take on nonconsensual pornography, AKA revenge porn. https://speier.house.gov/media-center/press-releases/congresswoman-speier-fellow-members-congress-take-nonconsensual. Accessed 14 July 2016.

Steinmetz, Katy. 2016. Merriam-Webster adds "FOMO," "Mx." and About 2,000 Other Words. *TIME.* http://time.com/4299634/merriam-webster-fomo-mx-dox-update/. Accessed 20 Apr 2016.

Thompson, Laura. 2016. Exposing yourself is illegal – So why should the law tolerate cyber-flashing on online dating apps? *Independent.* http://www.independent.co.uk/life-style/love-sex/exposing-yourself-is-illegal-so-why-do-online-dating-app-users-think-cyber-flashing-is-ok-a6852761.html. Accessed 4 Feb 2016.

Titlow, John Paul. 2016. This woman wants Facebook to ban unsolicited dick pics. *Fast Company.* https://www.fastcompany.com/3060703/this-woman-wants-facebook-to-ban-unsolicited-dick-pics. Accessed 7 June 2016.

Uhl, Carolyn A., et al. 2013. An examination of nonconsensual pornography websites. *Feminism & Psychology* 28: 50–68.

Warren, Samuel, and Louis Brandeis. 1890. The right to privacy. *Harvard Law Review* 4: 193–220.

Will, George. 2015. America desperately needs to fix its overcriminalization problem. *National Review.* http://www.nationalreview.com/article/416674/. Accessed 8 Apr 2015.

Whitmarsh, Abby. 2015. Analysis of 28 days of data scraped from a "Revenge pornography" website'. 13 April. https://everlastingstudent.wordpress.com

Wright, Valerie. 2010. The sentencing project, deterrence in criminal justice: Evaluating certainty vs. severity of punishment 1. *The Sentencing Project.* http://www.sentencingproject.org/wp-content/uploads/2016/01/Deterrence-in-Criminal-Justice.pdf. Accessed 23 Feb 2019.

PART XXVII

Role Morality

CHAPTER 29

Role Morality

Leo Katz and Alvaro Sandroni

Role morality refers to the obligations associated with occupying a particular role—that of a lawyer, doctor, journalist, government official, parent and friend, to name just a few contexts in which the phenomenon has typically been examined. Among the miscellany of problems role morality has been thought to give rise to, three stand out and will be explored here: (1) the complicity problem, (2) the moral combat problem and (3) the entity problem.

THE COMPLICITY PROBLEM

This is surely the central problem of role morality and nowhere does it emerge as clearly as in the relationship between the lawyer and his client. The client, we suppose, wants to do something immoral or at least something which would make many people queasy: dodge a debt by invoking the statute of limitations, prevail against a criminal accusation by impeaching the credibility of a witness he knows to be telling the truth, withhold information from the other side in a negotiation and rely on caveat emptor even though they are going to feel betrayed when they find out the truth and put pressure on a legitimate claimant by prolonging the discovery process until the claimant's ability to bear the legal expense has been exhausted. All of these are stratagems many people would not really want to pursue in their own behalf and would resent others in using against them. Nevertheless, this is what a client routinely expects of his lawyer and what most lawyers unhesitatingly will supply and feel obliged to supply.

L. Katz (✉)
University of Pennsylvania, Philadelphia, PA, USA
e-mail: lkatz@law.upenn.edu

A. Sandroni
Kellogg School of Management, Northwestern University, Evanston, IL, USA

© The Author(s) 2019
L. Alexander, K. K. Ferzan (eds.), *The Palgrave Handbook of Applied Ethics and the Criminal Law*, https://doi.org/10.1007/978-3-030-22811-8_29

All lawyers? Well, it's a large profession and undoubtedly there are some who wouldn't. But everyone else will judge them to be eccentrics and probably worse. If they already took the case, they will probably be found guilty of not heeding the duty of zealous representation, and if they decline to take it because of what it entails, as just not being properly respectful of the professional ideal of taking on all clients one is competent to represent.

This duty to zealously represent an immoral position raises a puzzle because of the way we ordinarily judge interactions between a principal and his agent. Ordinarily we are inclined to say that if something is immoral to do, it remains so even when someone hires an agent to do it for him. Neither the agent nor the principal should get off the hook in this way. Each is complicitous in the outcome. And yet that seems to be precisely what is happening with the lawyer (the agent) and his client (the principal). The lawyer generally feels let off the hook by the fact that he is doing this on behalf of a client, and the client, though perhaps to a somewhat lesser extent, feels let off the hook because he is acting through a lawyer. And this is not just a matter of feeling. The law fully supports this view. In the context of litigation, both lawyer and client are entitled to recklessly inflict harm on others that would not be permissible in most other contexts.

The most extreme and absurd-looking version of this is presented at the very beginning of David Luban's *Lawyers and Justice*, in which a lawyer, hired to represent the false claimant to a fortune, agrees to bring a made-up murder charge against the true claimant to get him convicted, executed and thus out of the way. The telling part of the exchange is this:

> Pray now, when my Lord Anglesea said to you, That he did not care if it cost him 10,000 pounds to get [his nephew, the true claimant] hanged, did you understand that it was his resolution to destroy him if you could?—I did, Sir. Did you advise my Lord Anglesea not to carry on that prosecution?—I did not advise him not to carry it on; I did not presume to advise him....
>
> Did you not apprehend it to be a bad purpose to lay out money to compass the death of another man?—I make a distinction between carrying on a prosecution, and compassing the death of a man. (Luban 1989, p. 5)

Lawyers aren't the only group where this odd phenomenon arises. Many other principal-agent relationships exhibit it. Soldiers asked to follow questionable orders. Judges asked to enforce immoral laws. Politicians asked to champion repellent causes by their constituents. Authors tempted into disclosing embarrassing family secrets for the sake of "art." Marketers who don't particularly believe in the products they promote. The phenomenon sometimes goes by a different name, such as the "dirty hands problem." And it gains added complexity in the context of what is sometimes called "transitional justice," when those filling out the roles of a since delegitimized order are called to account for what they did. But the lawyer, in whatever legal regime he operates, represents the dilemma in the most common and inescapable way.

David Luban, in his agenda-setting *Lawyers and Justice,* explores several consequentialist and non-consequentialist arguments for exonerating the lawyer from complicity in his client's immorality and finds them all wanting (Luban 1989).

The first three arguments are of a consequentialist variety. The first is the argument that partisanship of this sort promotes truth. It is an argument that rather quickly collapses. To begin with, even in cases where truth is exactly what is at stake, it does not seem all that likely that the adversary method is particularly likely to get at it. Luban offers the following telling analogy: suppose you hire some private investigators to figure out the answer to a question and suppose money were no object. Would you feel you would most likely get at the truth by telling one to assume the answer is X and try to do everything to prove it to be so and telling another to assume the answer is non-X and try to do everything to prove *that* to be the case? Probably not. In addition, and perhaps more importantly, the argument really has no application in the many adversarial proceedings in which truth is not the issue: such as whether the statute of limitations bars a contract enforcement action. If the lawyer has qualms about this defense in his own behalf, arguments about truth are not going to help explain to him why he need not have these qualms when acting on someone else's behalf.

The second consequentialist argument is what Luban calls the argument of legal rights. Legal rights are most likely to be vindicated, it is said, if each side is represented by a lawyer aggressively defending them. That sounds better when put abstractly than when tested out in a specific case—such as our statute of limitations contract case. How desirable is it that the debtor's rights, such as they are, with respect to the statute of limitations, be vindicated?

The third consequentialist argument is the ethical-division-of-labor argument, really an appeal to a market analogy. Let each participant in the proceeding selfishly pursue his ends and laissez-faire will produce a good outcome. The problem is that markets that produce optimal outcomes are very special constellations that even more ordinary markets often don't resemble, let alone an adversarial legal proceeding that resembles a market only in the most metaphorical sense. And indeed the outcomes of partisan representation, even if we are accepting of them, rarely feel particularly optimal in anything like the sense of optimality economists have in mind.

Luban also considers and is unpersuaded by non-consequentialist arguments. The first is Charles Fried's friend-in-need argument: people in trouble deserve a friend, and the lawyer is that to them. The argument would have more appeal if the role in question were not that of a lawyer but a therapist or even if the defendant were a criminal dealing with the overwhelming power of the prosecuting state. But someone pursuing a class action on behalf of consumers of a drug which only highly questionable studies have suggested might be responsible for certain mild adverse effects or our previous debtor vigorously resisting legitimate claims on technical grounds—what kind of a friendship is it that is owed here and by a stranger to boot?

The other non-consequentialist argument he rejects is that the adversarial role of the lawyer is part of our social fabric, the Burkean-inspired thought that "[r]egardless of whether the adversary system is efficacious, it is an integral part of our culture, and that fact by itself justifies it." The problem, as Luban sees it, is that it really isn't. Quoting another legal ethicist, William Simon, he says "I think the argument will seem rather out of proportion to the subject ... It is like making a Burkean argument against no-fault or social security" (Luban 1989, p. 91).

So does Luban propose abolishing the adversary system and abolishing role morality? No, not quite. He endorses its basic set-up as not inferior to any other one might come up with but would severely limit the immunities the lawyer and client should enjoy under it:

> The adversary system possesses only slight moral force, and thus appealing to it can excuse only slightly moral wrongs. Anything else that is morally wrong for a nonlawyer to do on behalf of another person is morally wrong for a lawyer to do as well. The lawyer's role carries no moral privileges and immunities. This does not mean that zealous advocacy is immoral, not even when it frustrates the search for truth or violates legal rights. Sometimes frustrating the search for truth may be a morally worthy thing to do, and sometimes moral rights are ill-served by legal rights. *All I am insisting on is that the standards by which such judgments are made are the same for lawyers and for nonlawyers.* If a lawyer is permitted to puff, bluff, or threaten on certain occasions, this is not because of the adversary system ... but because, in such circumstances, anyone would be permitted to do these things. Nothing justifies doing them in behalf of a predator ... The adversary system and the system of professional obligation it mandates are justified only in that, lacking a clearly superior alternative, they should not be replaced. This implies, I have argued, a presumption in favor of professional obligation, but one that any serious and countervailing moral obligation rebuts. Thus, when professional and serious moral obligations conflict, moral obligations take precedence. When they don't conflict, professional obligations rule the day [Italics mine.] (Luban 2007, p. 63)

That may not abolish role morality entirely but certainly leaves very little room for it.

Several prominent legal ethicists—Arthur Applbaum, William Simon and Bradley Wendel, among others—have reached the same conclusion, bolstering Luban's case with a variety of further considerations (Applbaum 1999; Simon 1998; Wendel 2010).

Vigorously coming out swinging on the other side of this are Daniel Markovitz and Tim Dare (Markovitz 2011; Dare 2009). A legal system without a right, indeed an obligation, on the part of lawyers to do a considerable amount of lying and cheating, as part of a dutifully zealous representation of their clients, is nearly inconceivable, they argue. These "lawyerly vices," as Markovitz calls them, "are not [mere] artifacts of one or another contingent (and misguided) elaboration of the adversary ideal in the positive law but are instead inscribed in the genetic structure of adversary advocacy in all its forms... [L]awyers come under professional duties to lie and to cheat ... [A]ny constraints that are consistent with the adversary ideal will necessarily be unable to purge the legal profession of the lawyerly vices.... The foundations of adversary advocacy remain constant across all forms of adversary legal practice and therefore do not depend on any particular formulation of positive law" (Markovitz 2011, pp. 4–5).

To be sure, that is more of a descriptive observation than an argument, though descriptions of such a widespread phenomenon surely carry some normative force. But he goes further, giving Fried's friend-in-need argument an ingenious twist. He makes an unlikely seeming but in the end quite appealing analogy between a poet and a lawyer. Adapting for his purposes, an observation of John Keats that describes the poet as a creature of "negative capability," someone who, through a sensibility capable of exquisite self-abnegation, manages to inhabit and sympathetically convey the nature of other things, be they people or objects of nature. "Keats argued that the negatively capable poet is unusually able to efface himself, maintaining no identity of his own ... and to work continually as a medium, filling some other body—the Sun, the Moon, the Sea 'and rendering this extraordinarily mute body articulate.' Thus the lawyer as the client's mouthpiece." What Luban sees as immoral complicity, Markovitz sees as a highly moral act or self-subordination to a client deserving to have sympathetically rendered whatever it is that he wants to put forth (Markovitz 2011, p. 93).

THE MORAL COMBAT PROBLEM

The moral combat problem is best illustrated with an example. D's friend F has been accused of a gruesome murder. The punishment for what he has done is likely to be a death sentence. The evidence against F is overwhelming. D has known F for a long time. Given what he knows, he is able to conclude, even with the seemingly compelling evidence the prosecution has presented, that the chance is very small that D is actually guilty. How can he be so sure? Through a perfectly rational updating of reasonable priors, as the lingo has it, in other words, the sensible consolidation of prior beliefs with the evidence supplied by the prosecution. There is nothing eccentric about what he is doing. Any reasonable person in his position could not fail to reach the same conclusion. Now he could of course try to make this special knowledge he has of his friend available to judge and jury, but he knows that that would be pointless. They too are reasonable people and as such will heavily discount anything exculpatory he tells them about F, if he even would be allowed to testify about the diffuse facts he knows about F that lead him to his conclusion. For that matter, there aren't actually many such facts. There is simply his belief based on evidence that like most such evidence is no longer accessible to him.

Because he "knows" his friend to be innocent and seemingly doomed by the evidence against him, he comes up with the one and only maneuver he can think of to save him: he makes up an alibi and testifies to it so convincingly that F is acquitted. Sometime later, though after F would have been executed, had he been convicted, more evidence surfaces that reveals the full truth, namely, that F is innocent *but also that D fabricated his alibi.*

D is prosecuted for perjury and the question arises whether he should be convicted. He invokes the defense of necessity.

The hypothetical illustrates a phenomenon that plagues role morality, the possibility, nay, the likelihood, of colliding role obligations. The judge is obligated by his role as a judge to administer the law as it is written, which will frequently be over- and underinclusive in the sense of requiring him to do something that is somewhat regrettable from the point of view of doing justice and here will require him to convict the perjurer. D, however, by virtue of his role as F's friend, is obligated to try to rescue him from being executed for a crime he did not commit.

Heidi Hurd, pretty much the first person to identify this problem in its full generality, has called such situations *Moral Combat* and devoted a brilliant book (by the same title) to exploring such situations (Hurd 2011). In it she strongly inclines toward the conclusion that any reasonable moral system must avoid letting such situations arise, must subscribe to what she calls the correspondence thesis: "The correspondence thesis asserts a moral claim about correspondent actions. It holds that the justifiability of an action determines the justifiability of permitting or preventing that action. According to the correspondence thesis, if Smith is justified in killing [a] hoodlum as a means of self defense, then Jones is not justified in intervening to prevent that killing, and hence Long is justified in restraining Jones's intervention" (Hurd 2011, p. 3). In other words, if X is entitled to do something, then Y may not hinder him in doing it and Z may help him, among other things, by preventing Y from hindering him. (There are some refinements and qualifications she allows, but we can ignore those here.) How then does she propose that morality deal with the case of D's perjurious testimony? While she does not address this specific case, she discusses many like it, and it seems pretty clear how she would analyze it.

She actually provides two different resolutions depending on whether one embraces a consequentialist or a non-consequentialist approach to morality. If one is a consequentialist, she would suggest analyzing the case as follows. The judge, evaluating the matter from a consequentialist point of view, needs to consider what would happen in the long run if he acquitted this admittedly sympathetic defendant, the perjurious D. What such a decision to acquit (say, by invoking the defense of necessity) would communicate, he might reason, is that any person in the future should feel entitled to lie, and be able to successfully invoke the necessity defense, if he has reasonable grounds for thinking that that would further the cause of justice in the sense that it makes a just verdict in the case at hand more rather than less likely. If everyone understood that to be the case, everyone would learn to distrust all testimony given a bit more because they would realize that lying under oath has just become more permissible and thus more common. That in turn would lead to a devaluation of evidence which in turn would result in less accurate verdicts, more unjust convictions and more unjust acquittals. Given that, he might well conclude that the injustices resulting from the avoidance of an unjust conviction here and now make it advisable to convict D for perjury.

How should D look at the matter? Not all that differently from the judge, Hurd points out. In deciding whether to perjure himself, and in deciding whether to resist being punished for it, if he did, his vantage point, if consequentialism is to be his guide, is identical to that of the judge. There really is no moral combat here after all.

But notice what has happened to role obligations on this mode of looking at things: they have been made to disappear. If then we use consequentialism to avoid moral combat, it seems that would have to happen at the price of abolishing role morality. This is not something that troubles Hurd: she views perspectivalism, as she calls role morality, as leading ineluctably to violations of the correspondence thesis and therefore wants it done away with.

The same result ensues if we analyze the case from a deontological point of view. If the judge is a deontologist, he might reason as follows: if I convict this defendant here and now, I am avoiding future injustices at the price of committing one here and now. This is exactly what deontology forbids: no killing the one here and now because it saves lives down the road. D, in turn, would view the matter correspondingly: if I don't save my friend now, I am collaborating in a severe injustice for the sake of preventing some future injustices, just exactly what deontology forbids. So, I should lie. Once again, the conflict between the judge and D has been made to disappear (though by a different resolution) but again only by essentially abolishing the role obligations.[1]

It would seem that meaningful role obligations can probably only be sustained at the price of producing moral combat. How intolerable is that price? Hurd thinks it is too high, but we are not so sure. There are many situations that resemble moral combat that we happily tolerate. Let us mention a few. These are cases to which one might give the label "permissible mutual frustration." Take the humble scenario of the famous first-year property case *Pierson v. Post*. Two hunters are in pursuit of a fox. One has it in his sights, another intervenes later on, kills and appropriates the beast. That's all right, the court said, approving conflict rather than seeking to end it, by a premature allocation of property rights. What's more, this approach is emblematic for that taken more generally to the allocation of somewhat fugitive or unassigned resources: oil, gas, water, ideas. Competition is endorsed until a fairly advanced moment of clear appropriation and the driving of a stake into the metaphysical ground has occurred. And then there is a plethora of more distantly related examples, such as (1) takeovers: consider all the defensive maneuvers by which an incumbent board is entitled to frustrate the efforts of a would-be acquirer and the aggressive maneuvers by which the acquirer is entitled to try to counter them. (2) Hostile First Amendment-protected interactions between protesters and counterprotesters. (3) Perhaps most illuminatingly, cases like the first-year torts case of *Ploof v. Putnam*: in an emergency, with a storm impending, a boat owner seeks to avail himself of another person's dock. The dock's owner unties the boat, fearing damage to his dock, and is held liable for the damage that then comes to the boat. Where things get interesting is if we imagine in the wake of this decision another dock owner acting with greater prescience by disassembling the dock before the boat even shows up. Presumably that would be all right. Here too then the law seems to have created a zone of mutually permissible frustration. All of that tends to argue in favor of role obligations and against the correspondence thesis.

THE ENTITY PROBLEM

Role obligations are often said to be owed to institutions rather than people. The lawyer is said to be the lawyer for the presidency not the president, for the corporation and not the corporation's CEO who hired him or even the shareholders who ostensibly own the company. The judge is said to owe his duty to the office rather than individual people.

But there lurks a puzzle which is not so easy to articulate, but the essence of which can be conveyed with the example of what Meir Dan-Cohen dubbed the "personless corporation." We start with a run-of-the-mill corporation and then gradually start eliminating most of its human participants. Shareholders are eliminated by buying back their shares. Bondholders are paid off as well. And the only creditors who remain are the trade creditors, if any, who are paid on an ongoing basis. The corporation's production processes are fully automated and the last remaining human workers eliminated. That leaves the board of directors in charge of this personless corporation. Now to add a potent twist to all of this, let us follow A. Hacker, an early conceiver of this kind of scenario, in imagining that Congress is contemplating adopting some kind of policy that would adversely affect the corporation's profitability (Hacker 1965). The board of directors hires a lobbying firm to launch what proves to be a very successful campaign persuading Congress to move in a different direction than the originally contemplated one. They do nothing the least bit illegal. Still, a number of Congressmen feel somewhat surprised at seeing the corporation's objectives successfully attained and conduct a hearing for which they summon the corporation's directors to testify. After having all the perfectly unobjectionable measures the corporation took to protect its profits explained to them, they inquire with some puzzlement as to who really are the beneficiaries of the corporation's policies. Are there any shareholders left? No, there aren't, the directors explain. Well, what about the workers, are there any? No, there aren't, they are told. Well, does that mean that it is the directors themselves who stand to benefit? No, it turns out their salaries are fixed and no obvious benefit flows to them from preserving the high profitability of the corporation. Well, then who is it that the directors are doing this for? For the corporation, they reply and that of course seems highly perplexing, as illustrated by the concluding exchange at the hearing:

> Senator: Then so far as I can see, all of this political pressure that you applied was really in the interests of yourself and your nine fellow directors. You spent

almost six million dollars of this company's money pursuing your personal predilections.

Director: I am afraid, Senator, that now I must disagree with you. The ten of us pay ourselves annual salaries of $100,000 year in and year out, and none of us receives any bonuses or raises if profits happen to be higher than usual in a given year. All earnings are ploughed back into the company. We feel very strongly about this. In fact, we look on ourselves as a kind of civil servant. Secondly, I could not say that the decision to get into politics was a personal wish on our part. At least eight of the ten of us, as private citizens that is, did not favor the legislation we were supporting. As individuals most of us thought it was wrong, was not in the national interest. But we were acting in the company's interest and in this case we knew that it was the right thing to do.

Senator: And by the company you don't mean stockholders or employees, because you don't have any. And you don't mean the ten directors because you just seem to be salaried managers which the machine [which is how I regard this corporation] hires to run its affairs. In fact, when this machine gets into politics—or indeed any kind of activity—it has interests of its own which can be quite different from the personal interests of its managers. I am afraid, I find all this rather confusing.

Director: It may be confusing to you, Senator, but may I say it has been quite straightforward to us at American Electric. We are just doing the job for which we were hired—to look out for the company's interest. (Hacker 1965, p. 4)

We don't have as of yet any personless corporations. But in testing out the coherence of the idea of obligations owed to an institution, the extreme example is of course useful nonetheless. It seems that if the concept made sense, one should not end up in such an absurd-looking situation. So what gives? Not much of an answer to this aspect of role obligations has as of yet been provided by anyone. Even by those who have recognized the possibility and the oddity of the personless corporation. They simply haven't been much concerned with it in the context of role obligations.

Hints of an Alternative Approach

There may be another way of approaching the role morality phenomenon and solving the outlined problems it poses. This is not the place to be more than sketchy about it since it relies on ideas which we have only begun to develop elsewhere.

There would appear to be a way of looking at law and morality that makes the phenomenon of role morality more natural, less inexplicable, than in the approaches outlined so far. The key difficulty faced by the existing defenses of the idea of role morality is a presupposition that is sometimes expressed, but really only imperfectly captured, by the term "impartiality": if morality is impartial, then it seems to make no sense that two people could have conflicting role obligations to bring about a state of affairs that can be judged impartially as being either right or wrong. A more exact and slightly formal statement of this idea will turn out to prove helpful. One might say that what impartiality comes to is this: there is a set of possible outcomes which we can rank as to their desirability, using possibly utilitarian, possibly rights based (i.e. deontological criteria) or maybe others yet. A decision-maker will then face a choice set in which he has the power to bring about one or another of these outcomes. What he ought to do is to bring about the most highly ranked of these outcomes. In this kind of world there really is no room for role morality: if two people both have it in their power to bring about a certain highly ranked outcome, then they must collaborate in doing so. More concretely: if a legal dispute has a certain just outcome, then both sides in that legal dispute are required to do what they can to bring it about, and the lawyer who frustrates the attainment of that outcome is acting impermissibly. Anyone who does not do this is complicitous in a wrongful endeavor. Moral combat can no longer arise. On this view, the complicity and the moral combat problems have been solved by abolishing role morality. We have called a normative system structured in this way option stratified because all possible options an actor might face are "stratified" rigidly (though there may be many ties) and the actor's only discretion relates to choosing among options that happen to be tied. We think that this more or less captures the position of Luban, Applbaum, Simon, Wendel and Hurd.

Let us call all normative systems that are not like this, somewhat unimaginatively, non-option stratified. As it turns out, the moral and legal systems within which we ordinarily operate are all non-option stratified. What is more, though this is something that requires a lot of effort to demonstrate, any system that is option stratified will have many attributes we could not tolerate, which is why in fact all known legal systems are non-option stratified. To see that this is really so, let us simply consider a fairly ordinary legal doctrine, whose structure however has many counterparts. The defense of duress is available to someone who is pressured into committing a crime with a sufficiently dire threat, typically serious bodily harm. It is not available if the threat merely involves the destruction of property. Now this holds regardless of how much he values that property. It holds even if he values it so much that he might be willing to incur serious bodily harm to protect it from being destroyed. This leads to a ranking of outcomes that is not option stratified. As between committing the crime and enduring great bodily harm, one is permitted to choose either. As between enduring the destruction of a valued piece of property and enduring great bodily harm, one is also permitted to choose either. Put those facts together and they suggest that all three options are ranked equally. But now consider the choice between committing a serious crime or enduring the destruction of the valued piece of property. Now only the latter is permitted, which means that a ranking of the three options is actually not possible.[2]

Non-option-stratified normative systems have a counterintuitive characteristic which then engenders many more counterintuitive features as a result of which they violate most of the canons of rational decision-making of standard decision theory. That counterintuitive characteristic is already fairly evident in the foregoing duress example: it leads to intransitive decision-making. A doctrine like duress might lead a law-abiding citizen to choose suffering bodily injury over losing his property, choose committing a crime over suffering bodily injury but also choose destruction of his property over committing a crime. (In the first of those cases he was able to implement his preferences, in the last one, he had to bow to a legal constraint.)

The first important consequence of intransitivity is that a non-option-stratified normative system cannot be represented by a maximizing function: not a utility function, not a welfare function, since decisions that involve the maximization of such a function can never result in intransitivity. If we are called upon to make each of our decisions in accordance with such a function, namely to choose the alternative which this function deems the best one, it is pretty intuitive that we will never end up doing anything intransitive.

Intransitivity in turn engenders an even more important oddity: it makes what are sometimes called irrelevant alternatives highly significant for the relative ranking of alternatives. In other words, if Actor One has to choose between alternatives x and y, x might be the one he is required to choose, but if Actor Two has to choose between x and y and z, y might be the one he is required to choose. If we conceive of the option set as being the "role" in which he is cast, we can see that we get an outcome that has one of the most troublesome but also characteristic features of role morality: the moral combat feature. Actor One has it in his power to bring about x or y. Actor Two has it in his power to bring about x or y or z. That means One is entitled to steer in the direction of x and Two is allowed to steer in the direction of y.

Intransitivity also engenders another feature which helps deal with what we called the "complicity problem." Where there is intransitivity there will also be two other features that are closely related: path dependence and manipulability. If the law allows one to choose both x and y, if the choice is between the two, and y and z if the choice is between those two, but not both x and z, if the choice is between the last two, one can arrive at the forbidden alternative by simply sequencing one's choices strategically, so that one first chooses y as between x and y, z as between y and z and thus arrives at the alternative z, that one was unable to choose when faced with the choice between z and x. In other words, the path by which one arrives at z matters a lot, and this path dependence can be exploited manipulatively. What that means in practice is that one can avoid being complicitous in a forbidden outcome by rearranging one's relationship to the outcome so that although one is still in a functional sense complicitous, one no longer is complicitous in a legally or morally relevant sense. Actual complicity doctrine offers plenty of examples of this: doctors who treat gangsters are not deemed their accomplices in anticipated future wrongdoing. Sellers of goods who know those goods will be used for criminal purposes probably also escape culpability. In fact the limitations of complicity doctrines are such that even the person who is approached by a would-be ax murderer who demands back the ax that he loaned the defendant so he can use it to murder his victim—whereupon the defendant wags his finger and tells him that he must not do that, but of course the ax is his and he cannot refuse to return it—will escape condemnation as an accomplice. This will look to many like a very odd eccentricity of complicity doctrine but is nothing more than a manifestation of the path dependence of non-option-stratified systems. The lawyer and other role occupant can in this way most likely escape being blamed for the immoral actions he is pursuing on behalf of his client.

This obviously doesn't answer all questions one might have about role morality and does not at all try to deal with the entity question, but a hint toward an alternative approach is all we meant to provide.

Notes

1. She does leave a small window for certain types of perspectivalism in cases in which one of the two actors is excused rather than justified in what he is doing: a prisoner who makes a justifiable jail break because he would otherwise have been killed by a fellow prisoner ends up in a tussle with the prison guard who tries to prevent him from fleeing.
2. The example is merely meant to be illustrative. Various ways of making the duress defense transitive might suggest themselves. Rather than arguing about why those strategies are unattractive, it is more fruitful to establish the general result that feasible legal systems must contain lots of doctrines that work the way the duress doctrine ordinarily works. This we do in Katz and Sandroni (2017). The same applies to other doctrinal illustrations we offer later in this section.

References

Pierson v. Post, 3 Cai. R. 175 (N.Y. 1805).

Ploof v. Putnam, 81 Vt. 471 (1908).

Applbaum, Arthur. 1999. *Ethics for adversaries*. Princeton: Princeton University Press.

Dare, Tim. 2009. *The counsel of rogues*. Burlington: Ashgate.

Hacker, Andrew. 1965. *The corporation take-over*. New York: Doubleday Anchor.

Hurd, Heidi. 2011. *Moral combat*. Cambridge: Cambridge University Press.

Katz, Leo, and Alvaro Sandroni. 2017. The inevitability and ubiquity of cycling in all feasible legal regimes: A formal proof. *The Journal of Legal Studies* 46: 237–281.

Luban, David. 1989. *Lawyers and justice*. Princeton: Princeton University Press.

———. 2007. *Legal ethics and human dignity*. Cambridge: Cambridge University Press.

Markovitz, Daniel. 2011. *A modern legal ethics*. Princeton: Princeton University Press.

Simon, William. 1998. *The practice of justice: A theory of lawyers' ethics*. Cambridge, MA: Harvard University Press.

Wendel, Bradley. 2010. *Lawyers and fidelity to law*. Princeton: Princeton University Press.

PART XXVIII

Sex Offenses and Sexually Violent Predators

CHAPTER 30

Sex Offenses and the Problem of Prevention

Margo Kaplan

Introduction

The past few decades have seen a remarkable increase in laws that seek to prevent sex offenses. These laws are, in large part, a response to horrific and highly publicized cases of sexual assault and murder as well as increasing concern over the unprecedented access that the Internet allows adults to groom minors for sexual abuse. Preventing sexual assault is a laudable goal. Yet these laws that punish or detain individuals who have yet to commit an offense may unjustifiably infringe on the freedom of individuals who have yet to act culpably. In this chapter, I consider two approaches to preventing sexual assault that have expanded significantly in recent years: (1) offenses criminalizing the sexual solicitation and enticement of minors and (2) special civil commitment statutes for those determined to be "sexually violent predators."

As inchoate offenses for the target harm of sexual assault, enticement and solicitation offenses focus on a highly preparatory phase with too tenuous a link to the ultimate target offense. These objections could be resolved by truly making enticement and solicitation complete offenses only if we take seriously the psychological harms to minors that these acts in themselves cause, an approach with both costs and benefits. Sexually violent predator (SVP) offenses also raise significant theoretical and practical problems. Even among scholars who support forms of preventive detention, these statutes' vague requirements and inadequate evidentiary rigor raise legitimate concerns among those who take autonomy seriously.

M. Kaplan (✉)
Rutgers Law School, Camden, NJ, USA
e-mail: margo.kaplan@law.rutgers.edu

© The Author(s) 2019
L. Alexander, K. K. Ferzan (eds.), *The Palgrave Handbook of Applied Ethics and the Criminal Law*, https://doi.org/10.1007/978-3-030-22811-8_30

ENTICEMENT AND SOLICITATION OF MINORS

The Statutes

Statutes intermittently use the words "solicitation" and "enticement" to describe the myriad ways that adults might engage in specific acts that proposition or arrange for sexual acts with minors. I use the term "solicitation" to refer to statutes in which the actor propositions sex, sexual performances, or some type of sexual act (such as undressing) from the minor. In contrast, I use "enticement" to refer to statutes that prohibit requesting, luring, or coercing a minor to meet when the actor intends to have the minor engage in an unlawful sexual act with him or another.[1]

All 50 states and the federal law have some form of enticement or solicitation statute. The federal law, for example, prohibits using interstate commerce (including the Internet) to knowingly persuade, induce, entice, or coerce "any individual who has not attained the age of 18 years, to engage in prostitution or any sexual activity for which any person can be charged with a criminal offense" (18 U.S.C. §2422). Washington's statute is quite broad, prohibiting communicating with a minor, or anyone the actor believes to be a minor, "for immoral purposes" (RCW 9.68a.090). Colorado prohibits individuals from using a computer network to convince a minor who has a certain age difference from the actor to "(a) Expose or touch the child's own or another person's intimate parts or (b) Observe the person's intimate parts while communicating with the person via computer network or system" (C.R.S. 18-3-405.4). Colorado also has separate statute prohibiting individuals four years older than a child under 15 from describing certain sex acts to the child and then persuading or enticing the child to meet for any purpose (C.R.S. 18-3-306).

Violating these statutes may not require direct communication with a minor. The federal solicitation statute allows the solicitation to be communicated through an intermediary even if the defendant has no intention of having sexual contact with the victim. In *U.S. v. Rothenberg*, the defendant communicated over the Internet with another adult who described himself as a 30-year-old adult male with sons aged 8 and 11. Rothenberg provided his counterpart explicit instructions on how to groom his sons and eventually engage in sexual activity with them. The Eleventh Circuit held that because communications can be through an intermediary, Rothenberg's instructions were sufficient to establish a violation of the federal law prohibiting soliciting sex with minors.

Enticement and solicitation statutes are commonly understood to be inchoate offenses; they allow the state to punish an actor before he achieves the target offense of sexual assault. These inchoate sex offenses focus on myriad ways that adults use what might be preparatory methods to engage in unlawful sex with minors. Such inchoate offenses are a primary means through which legislatures use criminal law to prevent sexual offenses. In the past few decades, there has been an enormous expansion of inchoate sex offenses, in particular those related to the sexual abuse of children (Wright 2009, pp. 124–140). This expansion is, in large part, due to concern about the ease with which adults and children can anonymously contact each other through the Internet without parental supervision (Wright 2009, pp. 124–140). Whereas an adult might be reluctant to approach a 13-year-old child in public or ring her doorbell soliciting sex, the Internet allows him[2] ease, anonymity, and an abundance of targets.

Yet state and federal enticement and solicitation statutes are drafted in a way that tends to obscure their inchoate nature. Rather than use general enticement and solicitation statutes to address sexual assault, legislatures instead draft specific statutes that make enticement and solicitation the target offense itself. In New Jersey, for example, an actor is guilty if he attempts to lure or entice a child to appear in any place with the purpose to commit a criminal offense with or against the child (N.J. Stat. Ann. §2C: 13–6). Such a statute presents the enticement as the target offense, for which there could be an inchoate offense, such as an attempt to entice (Robbins 1989, pp. 45–46).

If the primary concern of these statutes is to prevent offense of sexual assault, such statutes should still be considered inchoate offenses and held to those standards, regardless of how they are rephrased. Section "Enticement and Solicitation as Inchoate Offenses" takes this approach and concludes that enticement and solicitation offenses raise substantial concerns for those who take seriously critical tenets of criminal legal theory. Section "Enticement and Solicitation as Complete Offenses" considers the benefits and disadvantages of reconsidering enticement and solicitation as target offenses that protect against the specific harms these interactions directly cause minors.

Enticement and Solicitation as Inchoate Offenses

Solicitation and enticement crimes raise potential problems because they punish an actor who may have the intent of committing an unlawful sex act with a minor, but who may have several steps still within his control before accomplishing the target offense. The offenses require us to consider (1) whether criminal law can punish an inchoate crime in which an individual has an intent to harm but has merely taken steps toward the harmful act; (2) if so, at what point an individual's acts merit punishment; and (3) given the answers to these questions, whether solicitation and enticement offenses appropriately punish individuals as a means of preventing future harm.

Inchoate offenses cause significant debate because they threaten to contravene a critical principle of retributivist theory. The state may only punish an individual for the culpable acts he has already taken—it cannot punish him for ones he might take in the future. It must respect an actor's autonomy leading up to the commission of the offense. Whatever an actor's intent leading up to the crime, he may change his mind and renounce his criminal purpose before completing the target offense (Ohana 2007, pp. 117–118).

Enticement and solicitation both raise material concerns because they are preparatory offenses, occurring even before the actor's conduct would constitute an attempt of the target offense. Such preparatory offenses criminalize conduct that may be quite remote from the target offense. An individual may fall within an enticement statute, for example, if he uses the Internet to invite a minor who lives across the country (and with whom sexual contact would be unlawful) to meet for sex at a later, indeterminate date. There are several acts between the enticement and the completion of the target offense: the minor must accept the invitation, the actor must continue contact with the minor, plan the meeting time and place with the minor, arrange and follow through with all attendant planning and acts to help transport and meet the minor, and finally engage in the sexual act.

Several legal theorists have objected to laws that criminalize conduct so remote to the target offense. Antony Duff, for example, opposes criminalizing "mere preparation," arguing that the state should only punish an individual when his conduct has crossed the line to commencing "the crime proper" (Duff 1997, pp. 385–397). Duff's argument relies on respect for the individual's autonomy; because we cannot punish him for what he *may* do, we must respect him as an autonomous agent who may turn back and choose not to commit the crime. Enticement and solicitation statutes fail to meet Duff's demands, punishing conduct that is far removed from the commencement of target offenses such as sexual assault. As described above, for example, enticement may involve an invitation that requires several steps and significant planning before the target offense occurs. This is particularly true when the individual is miles, or even states, away and must take several steps before consummating the offense, giving him several opportunities between the invitation and the target offense to choose whether to commit the offense. However loathsome the individual's conduct is, it falls short of Duff's requirement of that the actor cross the line to the "crime proper." This is not to say these enticement and solicitation statutes never include circumstances in which an individual acts beyond mere preparation. The statutes themselves, however, are specifically and purposely drafted to reach conduct that is far less proximate to the target offense.

This lack of proximity is also problematic for theorists such as Douglas Husak who provide a different perspective. Unlike Duff, Husak allows what he terms "nonconsummate offenses," that do not achieve the target offense— and because such offenses increase the risk that the harm of the target offense may occur, he does not categorically deny preparatory offenses (Husak 1995, pp. 167–169). Yet he argues that such nonconsummate offenses require proximity between the conduct and the harm of the target offense; the causal contribution of nonconsummate offenses must be sufficiently proximate to the target offense's harm (Husak 1995, pp. 173, 177). Husak is skeptical, for example, of circumstances in which an individual could take a number of intermediate steps in order to minimize the harm, such as an intoxicated individual who might instead call a cab rather than drive home, or a potential burglar who approaches an unoccupied structure but might instead decide not to enter it. Both enticement and solicitation statutes fail to meet this proximity requirement. As discussed earlier, enticement and solicitation statutes often include circumstances highly attenuated from the harms at issue.

Enticement statutes also raise concerns for other theories that allow inchoate offenses where there is risk of harm. Larry Alexander and Kimberly Kessler Ferzan have argued that inchoate offenses do not merit punishment unless the actor has unleashed a risk of harm over which he no longer believes he has complete control (Ferzan 2011a, p. 1278). Alexander, Ferzan, and Stephen J. Morse argue that, where the actor may still change his intent and choose not to complete the target offense, he cannot be punished in relation to that offense until he completes it, no matter how close he comes to accomplishing it (Alexander and Ferzan with Morse 2009, pp. 221–225). The law must respect his autonomy and the possibility that he may change his mind. Enticement clearly should not be punished under this reasoning, as it is far too removed from the target offense (Ferzan 2011a, pp. 1283–1284).

Solicitation of a minor may also raise problems under this theory, albeit more complex ones. Ferzan, Alexander, and Morse accept punishment for solicitation unless the actor's future participation is needed for the offense, in which case the actor still retains control over the risk of harm (Alexander and Ferzan with Morse 2009, p. 225 n. 26). Statutes that merely punish requesting a minor engage in a sex act, such as soliciting a minor to engage in an act over the Internet, where the actor need not participate in the act, would not seem to pose problems under this theory of the law. However, it is possible that in these circumstances, the actor's participation may still be required. If the actor must view the sex act in order for the target offense to be committed, for example, then the actor's future participation is required, and the actor still retains control over the risk of harm.

Even those less skeptical of preparatory crimes may be concerned with this expansion of inchoate offenses. Enticement and solicitation offenses create "double inchoate crimes," offenses that layer one inchoate offense upon another, such as attempt to solicit, or conspiracy to entice (Robbins 1989, pp. 54–58). Double inchoate offenses allow defendants to be punished for actions that are even further removed from the target offense. Double inchoate crimes are controversial; some, such as attempt to conspire, have been rejected by several courts, whereas others, such as attempted burglary, are more widely accepted (Robbins 1989, pp. 48, 54–58). Attempted enticement and attempted solicitation are already widely prosecuted, and as of yet, courts seem untroubled by the double inchoate nature of these offenses (Robbins 1989, pp. 45–46). This may be in part because of their subject. In *Huebner v. State*, a Wisconsin court rejected a challenge to a prosecution for attempted enticement by interpreting the enticement statute as a completed offense rather than an inchoate one (Robbins 1989, pp. 45–46). As Ira P. Robbins notes "Underlying the court's discussion of legislative intent, however, was its concern with protecting society from persons who commit dangerous sex crimes and providing treatment for the dangerous sex offender" (Robbins 1989,

p. 46). Robbins notes that subsequent cases suggest "that the seriousness with which society views the substantive crime of sexual assault of minors induces court[s] to focus on the intent that the defendant displayed rather than on the limitation of the doctrine that every criminal should have fair warning of what the law prohibits" (Robbins 1989, p. 47).

Using enticement and solicitation crimes as inchoate offenses to prevent the harm of sexual assault raises troubling issues. This is particularly poignant the further the actions are removed from the target offense. While these actions may be accomplished by vile individuals with culpable mindsets, criminal law does not, and should not, punish being a vile individual with a culpable mindset alone—it requires a culpable act as well. These statutes clearly punish acts in the preparatory phase and too far from the actual act of sexual assault to merit punishment.

Enticement and Solicitation as Complete Offenses

Perhaps the strongest defense of inchoate offenses pertaining to minors such as solicitation and enticement lies in the argument that they are not inchoate offenses but rather complete offenses. After all, most such statutes are drafted as completed offenses, and the *Huebner* case relied upon this reasoning to support allowing attempted enticement. Enticement and solicitation may be complete offenses because they have the potential to protect minors from the distinct harms they prohibit. The act of soliciting sex from a minor can in itself cause the minor psychological harm. Enticement can cause the minor psychological harm. Both solicitation and enticement contribute to an unhealthy and psychologically dangerous environment for minors to navigate, in which they face—particularly in the context of the Internet—sexual harassment and objectification as well as exposure to language and images that are harmful for their development.

In a 2005 survey, 28% of minors who experienced online solicitation said an incident left them feeling very or extremely upset and 20% felt very or extremely afraid (Wolak et al. 2006, p. 20). Overall, 34% of incidents where the actor attempted additional offline contact with the minor made the minor feel very or extremely upset, and 28% made the minor feel very or extremely afraid (Wolak et al. 2006, p. 20). Minors also commonly reported feeling very or extremely embarrassed in tandem with their distress. In 25% of all solicitation incidents, minors experienced one or more symptoms of stress, including being unable to stop thinking about the incident, feeling jumpy or irritable, losing interest in things, and avoiding the Internet (Wolak et al. 2006, p. 20). While the number of minors exposed to online solicitations has decreased between the 1990s and middle of the millennium, this was largely due to youth avoiding internet chat rooms, which they described as unpleasant places attracting unsavory people hoping to meet youth for sexual reasons (Wolak et al. 2006, p. 7).

As complete offenses, enticement and solicitation statutes do not have a clear analogue. They share some similarities to harassment offenses in the way that unwanted imagery and requests can traumatize minors and intimidate them from using public spaces and the Internet. Unlike harassment, however, solicitation and enticement need not be unwanted. A minor may engage and correspond with the actor—the minor may even seek out the actor or respond willingly to the actor's overtures. Enticement and solicitation statutes must therefore recognize the unique psychological and developmental harm that these communications have on minors and place the state in parens patriae to prevent it on their behalf. In this way, enticement and solicitation statutes are similar to offenses that prohibit exposure of minors to pornography or contributing to the delinquency of minors.

Reconceptualizing solicitation and enticement statutes provides an opportunity for the criminal law to acknowledge and take action against a largely ignored harm to minors, which requires a substantial degree of research and analysis. If these offenses punish the risk of psychological and developmental harm that enticement and solicitation cause, then their actus reus must be tailored to target that risk. This should be supported by evidence-based research that is beyond the scope of this chapter. It is useful, however, to provide some examples of how research should inform the actus reus of enticement and solicitation statutes as complete offenses.

Perhaps most evidently, the actus reus must be the one that actually causes substantial harm to the minor. While this may seem apparent, it would likely require states to amend several current statutes. Consider the example of B, a piano teacher, who violates New Jersey's enticement statute against "luring or enticing… to meet," with the purpose to commit a criminal offense with or against the child by instructing his student to meet him while harboring the purpose of committing a sexual offense against her. If the student remains unaware of the teacher's intent, it is arguable that B's instruction to meet for a piano lesson did not cause the student harm. In contrast, psychological harm is much more likely where the adult actor makes their intentions for sex known or when the enticement places the minor in a situation of entering a strange and unsafe place, sneaking out of the home, or even meeting someone older for romantic purposes.

Solicitation statutes are perhaps more obviously linked to psychological harm because they involve directly requesting sexual acts from a minor. The federal solicitation statute prohibits using interstate commerce (including the Internet) to knowingly persuade, induce, entice, or coerce "any individual who has not attained the age of 18 years, to engage in prostitution or any sexual activity for which any person can be charged with a criminal offense" (18 U.S.C. §2422). In doing so, it targets the type of psychological harm that minors face when adults proposition them for sex and persuade—or attempt to persuade—them to engage in sexual activities.[3]

Enticement and solicitation statutes would also need to be tailored to emerging research on how psychological harm is experienced. For example, there is evidence that there is higher risk of distress among younger youth (Mitchell et al. 2001, p. 3013). If research demonstrates that there is a correlation between age and harm, then punishment should reflect the same. There is also evidence that distress is magnified when an adult who solicits sex online also attempts to make offline contact (ibid.). The degree and extent of solicitation might therefore also be considered as part of the severity of the offense.

It is also important to punish enticement and solicitation in proportion with the harms they target. As inchoate offenses, they might be measured in relation to their target offense. But as complete offenses, the punishment must be in proportion to the risk of psychological harm to the minor that the solicitation or enticement in itself causes. The punishment may also vary depending on different variables that affect the risk of harm, as discussed earlier.

Punishment of these harms must also take into account the actor's mental state as to the risk of psychological harm. An individual who intends harm is, of course, more culpable than one who is merely reckless as to the risk of harm or who was ignorant and should have been aware of the risk of harm. In practice, many defendants may claim not to be aware of the harm that enticement and solicitation cause, and they argue that the relationship is healthy. Actors may use a minor's participation against them, claiming solicitation is sexual banter, harmless flirtation, and even enjoyable, for the minor. This may be overcome, however, with expert testimony on minors' capacity and the effects of grooming.

Many actors may genuinely believe, however, that their actions do not cause harm to minors. Those who are truly negligent of the harm their actions cause are less deserving of punishment. These may be, unfortunately, often those from whom society may need the most protection—the ones who may offend again because they see nothing wrong with their actions toward minors. This is not a problem unique to solicitation and enticement, however—the criminal justice system can only punish in accordance with desert, and often that does not align with punishing the most dangerous. Using enticement and solicitation as complete offenses therefore potentially provides weaker protection against future harms than it would as an inchoate offense.

This reflects the underlying sacrifice we make in reconceptualizing enticement and solicitation as complete offenses. As complete offenses, they no longer face the criticisms they did as inchoate offenses. But if they are no longer inchoate offenses related to the prevention of physical sexual abuse, then, of course, they will be less effective in preventing those offenses. It is simply no longer their goal—it is an incidental benefit. If we need these offenses to serve the goal of preventing physical sexual abuse, we sacrifice their effectiveness by making them complete offenses in their own right.

Inchoate offenses are hardly the only means the state uses to prevent future sex offenses; the state often uses preventive measures in order to limit the freedom of a non-culpable individual based on predictions of an offense he will commit in the future. Most scholars distinguish preventive measures from punishment, which looks backwards at acts previously committed and punishes based on desert, whereas preventive measures are forward-looking, based on predictions of harm (Ferzan 2011a, pp. 1275–1277).

The state and federal laws instituted substantial preventive measures limiting the freedom of sex offenders in the past few decades—in particular SVP civil commitment laws. These laws raise significant moral and ethical questions. Legal scholarship is predominately hostile to the concept of preventive detention, skeptical of its justifications, and suspicious of its potential for abuse (Husak 2011, p. 1173; Morse 2004, p. 69). Below, I examine these laws and the theoretical concerns they raise.

Sexually Violent Predator Laws

Sexually Violent Predators in Practice

SVP laws are a special means of civil commitment to detain sex offenders when they cannot be held by the criminal justice system, often after an individual has been convicted of an offense and has completed his sentence (Kaplan 2015, p. 143). These laws vary by jurisdiction but generally require for civil commitment: (1) the actor has been accused of a sexual offense [4]; (2) the actor has a mental abnormality of some sort; (3) that the mental abnormality predisposes the actor to commit sexual offenses; and (4) that the actor has some threshold likelihood to re-offend if released (Kaplan 2015, p. 143).

SVP laws do not extend prison sentences; they invoke civil commitment for those who are being released from the criminal justice system. For an individual convicted of an offense, an SVP law will affect him only when he is due to be released from prison. At this point, he is subject to a hearing to determine whether there is probable cause to believe he is an SVP; if so, he will be transferred to a facility for psychiatric assessment, followed by a civil trial to determine whether he is an SVP. If he is found to be an SVP, he is involuntarily civilly committed to a special commitment center for treatment until he is no longer considered to be a danger to others or can be transferred to less restrictive facilities.

Once committed, the likelihood of release is slim. A comparison of SVP statutes in 2007 found that, since the proliferation of the statutes in the 1990s, 4534 individuals had been committed and only 494 discharged. The majority of discharges were effected when the committed individuals filed special petitions through the courts, rather than on the basis of treatment staff recommendations (Terry 2006, p. 281). As of 2015, Minnesota failed to fully discharge a single individual since it began committing SVPs in the 1990s, with only a handful of people released under tight restrictions (Davey 2015).[5]

The second requirement listed earlier—that the actor has a mental abnormality that predisposes him to commit offenses—differs significantly from ordinary civil commitment standards. Ordinary civil commitment statutes require a showing of a mental disorder that places an individual in danger to himself or others—it ordinarily applies to those who are unable to understand the consequences of their actions or control their behavior, and thus the state must stand in for them because they cannot make appropriate choices for themselves (Zander 2005 pp. 18–19; Schulhofer 1996, p. 70).[6] Civil commitment is an exercise of the state's police and parens patriae powers—it protects the public and stands in for an individual who is unable to appreciate or control the consequences of his actions (Kaplan 2015, p. 139; Klein 2012, pp. 561–562). The New Jersey law, for example, requires an individual to have a "current, substantial disturbance of thought, mood, perception or orientation which significantly impairs judgment, capacity to control behavior or capacity to recognize reality" (N.J. Stat. Ann. §30:4-27.2(r)).

In contrast, most SVP statutes require only some sort of "mental abnormality," "mental dysfunction," or "behavioral abnormality" terms that are not recognized diagnostic terms and seldom defined in the statute (Kaplan 2015, p. 145; Morse 1996, p. 137). The few that require a specific "mental disorder," define it so broadly as to lack any meaning: "a congenital or acquired condition affecting the emotional or volitional capacity" (Kaplan 2015). Unlike traditional civil commitment, SVP laws make gestures toward the concept of mental disorders yet include within their breadth individuals who are able to understand their actions and their consequences (Hamilton 2013, pp. 541–543).

The third and fourth requirements—predisposition to commit offenses and likelihood to re-offend—raise this threshold for commitment, but not nearly to the level of ordinary civil commitment. Courts and legislatures have generally required the state to demonstrate that a potential SVP has difficulty controlling their behavior and is therefore more likely to commit an offense. Federal law requires that an SVP's mental disorder cause "serious difficulty refraining from sexually violent conduct or child molestation" (18 U.S.C. § 4247(a)(6)). Other jurisdictions require that the mental disorder predispose an SVP to commit acts of sexual violence, with a few also requiring that the predisposition must make the individual a danger or menace to the health or safety of others. Some jurisdictions require a likelihood to engage in sexually violent acts, but this likelihood need not be high—most states require only that the individual is "likely" to engage in acts of sexual violence, others that it is "more likely than not."[7] California instructs jurors that likely "does not mean it must be more probable than not that there will be an instance of reoffending" (Cal. Jury Inst. Crim. 4.19).

Lowering the standard for psychologically based civil commitment in order to institute preventive detention is a tempting proposition. Many of the individuals determined to be SVPs are undoubtedly dangerous. One of the cornerstone cases challenging the SVP statutes concerned Leroy Hendricks, who repeatedly sexually assaulted children over the course of decades, refused treatment, and stated that the only way he would stop abusing children was "to die" (Kansas v. Hendricks, 521 U.S. 346, 353–55 (1997)). SVP statutes allow the state to detain men like Hendricks, who are highly likely to sexually abuse a child in the future.

Yet SVP laws, as currently enforced, require little evidence that an individual will offend. Several states do not define "likely to offend," leaving the jury to interpret this phrase. California instructs juries that this does not necessarily mean "more likely than not" to offend, and indeed, this is how many juries may interpret the term without instruction. A Texas survey of SVP jurors found that over half of jurors thought that a 1% chance of offending satisfied the standard of "likely to offend," and 81.7% would accept a 15% chance of offending as "likely to offend" (Knighton et al. 2014). Courts also ignore or confuse established science when determining an individual's dangerousness. For example, SVP commitment proceedings often use pedophilia and other paraphilia diagnoses as de facto evidence that the individual lacks volitional control, when there is no research demonstrating a link between these disorders and impulse control or long-term recidivism (Kaplan 2015, p. 152).

The state also commonly uses the same actuarial assessment tools based on past offenses or personal characteristics similar to a class of offenders who have shown a high degree of recidivism (Terry 2006, p. 282). Actuarial instruments applied to sex offenders are inconsistent in their findings as to who is likely to re-offend (Terry 2006, p. 282). While these models predict the risk of offending better than chance, their "accuracy is generally low to moderate" (Terry 2006, p. 282). Some researchers have argued that these tools do not predict risk, but rather compare an offender's risk level to that of similar groups of offenders (Terry 2006, p. 282). At best, actuarial models predict how groups of people will behave, and what proportion of them will commit an offense; they are useful only to the extent that they accurately measure that group's risk and to the extent that the individual accurately reflects that group's characteristics (Janus 2006, p. 58). Inflexibility in scoring methods, however, may limit the extent to which key information can be integrated (Janus 2006, p. 58). Studies have also shown conflicting levels of reliability for actuarial instruments used in civil commitment; in one study, different evaluators using one of the most trusted actuarial methods assigned different total scores to the same offenders in nearly half the cases (Terry 2006, p. 282).

Sexually Violent Predator Statutes and the Problem of Preventive Action

Sexually Violent Predator Statutes and the Desert-Disease Distinction

Legal scholars have struggled with the question of whether and when the state can use law to preventively detain or otherwise limit the freedom of a responsible individual before he commits an offense. Such measures are ostensibly not punishment, as they do not penalize a previous action, but they do limit the freedom of individuals based on what the state believes they *may* do in the future.

It is widely accepted that the state has limited power to preventively detain those who are not responsible for their actions—this is the foundation of ordinary civil commitment. Such laws are limited to those who lack autonomy—their mental state limits their ability to understand or control their actions. This "disease/desert" distinction differentiates between individuals whom the state does not hold responsible for otherwise criminal actions because of their mental disorder and those whom we hold criminally responsible as autonomous individuals (Morse 2004, pp. 57–58; Alexander and Ferzan 2012, p. 640).

SVP laws defy the desert/disease dichotomy of criminal law theory (Morse 2004). While their phrasing gestures to mental disorders and impulsiveness, their scope includes those with sufficient autonomy to be convicted of an offense—indeed, they are can be used as a means to prevent individuals being released at the end of their sentence. As discussed above, SVPs' standard for commitment, relies upon a broad and vague definition of both mental disorder and volitional impairment that, taken together, encompass individuals who are autonomous decision-makers. SVP laws, therefore, distinguish a group that is responsible enough to be punished yet still can be civilly committed based on volitional impairment due to mental abnormalities. It does not choose between disease and desert—it subjects the individuals to both punishment and civil commitment based on mental abnormality.

SVP statutes therefore use the language of those unable to control their actions because of mental abnormalities while, in reality, preventively detaining those who are morally responsible. The mental condition still serves as the foundation of the civil commitment, but the mental condition need only give one a propensity for sexual assault. This opens the door to "unlimited possibilities" in the context of other offenses, "[o]ne need only give the propensity for dangerous conduct some medicalized label—for example, 'pathological jihadism'—and civil commitment would be available" (Alexander and Ferzan 2012, p. 640; *see also* Morse 1996, p. 138). If legislatures seek to justify SVP civil commitment by claiming that the actor's mental illness volitionally impairs him, then SVP commitment should require proof of mental illness that is sufficiently serious to preclude criminal liability, rather than one that simply makes an individual more likely to choose to commit an offense (Schulhofer 1996, p. 94).

Preventive Detention of Autonomous Decision-Makers

Once the façade of the disease/desert dichotomy is breached, it is far more difficult to justify SVP statutes as preventive detention. The majority of legal theory is hostile to the concept of preventive detention of autonomous individuals (Husak 2011, p. 1173; Morse 2004, p. 69). Interfering with an individual's liberty based on actions they have not yet taken brings us into the dangerous territory of detaining individuals solely based on intentions without actions ("thought crimes") or based on predictions of dangerousness ("Minority Report" territory). Nonetheless, some scholars maintain that preventive action of autonomous individuals is justifiable in limited circumstances.

One of the more interesting theories in favor of preventive detention is that of Kimberly Kessler Ferzan and Larry Alexander, who argue that the state may preventively interfere with the liberty of an individual who has chosen to risk or cause unjustifiable harm to others and has acted in furtherance of that intention (Ferzan 2011a, p. 1274). This argument is based on self-defense principles; when A takes action to harm B, A forfeits his right against preventive action by B; similarly, when C chooses to risk or cause unjustifiable harm to others and acts in furtherance of the intention, C forfeits his right against interference by the state to stop him from proceeding with his criminal act (Ferzan 2011a, pp. 1274–1275, 2011b, pp. 163–176; Alexander and Ferzan 2012, pp. 660–661).

Under Ferzan and Alexander's framework, risk is assessed using the actor's intent to offend. If an individual harbors no intention of offending, his predicted likelihood of offending is immaterial. For example, J may be in prison for sexual abuse of a minor, and actuarial methods (including a psychological profile) may predict a relatively high level of re-offending upon re-release. Ferzan and Alexander argue that the state may not rely on these predictive measures alone. They must demonstrate evidence of J's intent to commit an offense, not merely a likelihood that he will re-offend. Were J to solicit sex from a minor, however, his communication of his intention to have sex with the minor suffices as his action in furtherance of his intention, at which point the state could use civil methods to prevent him from acting (Ferzan 2011b, pp. 176–177). Detention is the most restrictive means of prevention; lesser means might involve, for example, allowing the police to search his computer periodically (Ferzan 2011b, p. 177). The state must use the least restrictive means necessary to prevent J from acting on his intentions, and the restriction is only justified for as long as J harbors the intention to offend (Alexander and Ferzan 2012, p. 663; Ferzan 2011b, p. 191).

SVP statutes fail to uphold Ferzan and Alexander's framework because they do not incorporate its emphasis on the actor's intent. SVP statutes require no evidence of intention, focusing instead on vague notions of mental impairments that make them likely to offend. Ferzan and Alexander specifically reject imposing preventive restrictions of liberty on such "anticipated culpable aggressors," such as a sex offender who has no intention to re-offend "but who is quite likely to form such an intention" (Alexander and Ferzan 2012, p. 666).

Ferzan and Alexander's theory of preventive measures does not prohibit any preventive detention of potential sex offenders. Their framework could have preventively detained, for example, Leroy Hendricks, who expressed intent to re-offend (Kansas v. Hendricks, 521 U.S. 346, 353–55 (1997)). Unlike SVP statutes, however, the state's ability to take preventive measures against Hendricks would be assessed according to whether he harbored an intent to harm a child and performed an act in furtherance of it. Past behavior could be evidence of intent, but propensity to harm and psychology testimony could not be the basis for the state's preventive measures against him (Ferzan 2011b).[8]

Other theories supporting preventive detention would likely find fault with SVP statutes' inadequate standards for demonstrating future dangerousness. As discussed above, SVP statutes use vague standards for assessing an individual's likelihood to offend, allowing juries to interpret this inconsistently.

Moreover, states rely upon actuarial standards that have highly questionable reliability in determining an individual's likelihood to re-offend. Paul H. Robinson argues that SVP laws have the advantage of at least engaging in preventive detention in a way that can be assessed openly rather than "cloaking" it in the criminal justice system where it does not belong (Robinson 2001). He cautions, however, that preventive measures should require the state to periodically prove the detainee's continuing dangerousness (Robinson 2001). Morse, more skeptical of preventive detention, would nonetheless allow it if the risk to others were sufficiently high and predictable (Morse 1996). Morse conditions preventive action upon the availability of excellent predictive technology, adequate due process, and humane and minimally invasive state responses (Morse 2004, p. 69). In their current form, it is doubtful SVP statutes meet either of these standards.

Alec Walen's theory may offer the strongest support for SVP laws. Walen advocates for what he terms the "Autonomy Respecting Model" of detention. This model generally rejects preventing offenses based on predictions that an individual; it holds that the state must respect individuals' autonomy to make choices and—as long as the state has the ability to hold individuals accountable through criminal law—it cannot detain them even if it can predict that they will commit an offense. Walen argues, however, that an individual can be subjected to long-term preventive detention if he has been convicted of a crime for which it is appropriate either to subject them long-term punishment or to punish them by taking away his right not be subjected to long-term preventive detention. Walen therefore allows long-term preventive detention to be provided to those who have already committed an offense and, by doing so, have lost the right not to be subjected to long-term preventive detention in the future (Walen 2011, pp. 880, 908–909). The judgment of whether these individuals should be detained depends on whether their "ongoing detention provides the best balance of liberty and security" (Walen 2011, pp. 908–909).

Walen's Autonomy Respecting Model allows that an individual who has committed a crime can—in addition to losing his liberty—lose his status to be treated like an autonomous and accountable individual. This loss of status can extend past the period of his loss of liberty. While in his "lost status" period, the actor can be subject to long-term preventive detention (Walen 2011).

Walen therefore supports the possibility of SVP laws as a matter of "loss of status." In his words, "if a person violates the law in a serious way and has failed to take steps to guard against his mental disorder, then he might lose the benefit of the presumption of autonomy and accountability." The sex offender's previous offense is important not because it shows he is dangerous, but because it provides a reason to punish him with a loss of status that subjects him to long-term preventive detention (Walen 2011).

SVP statutes may fail to live up to Walen's standards in practice, however. An individual who has lost his status may be detained but detention is not *required*; whether it is appropriate to detain him depends "how dangerous he is thought to be, the strength of his liberty interest, and whether a less restrictive alternative would provide adequate protection against his commission of further crimes" (Walen 2011). SVP statutes' questionable means of assessing dangerousness may undermine their effectiveness in determining whether an individual should be subject to long-term detention.

SVP statutes present an interesting set of questions for Douglas Husak's arguments about preventive detention. While most theorists distinguish preventive detention as nonpunitive because it focuses on future acts rather than past transgressions, Husak counters that preventive measures can indeed be punishment. He defines punishment as containing two essential features: (1) deprivation and (2) stigma, and both must be brought about intentionally by the state. He maintains that preventive detention generally has both, unless an individual has some sort of mental defect or excusing condition. Husak argues that this preventive detention is justified if an individual poses a substantial danger of future harm because has certain characteristics or commits certain acts that pose substantial danger of future harm, as long as those characteristics or acts are within his control (Husak 2011, pp. 1181–1182, 1189).

This raises the interesting question of whether SVP statutes constitute punishment under Husak's interpretation. Husak himself is not certain—while it is clear the state intended deprivation, he leaves open the determination of whether the state intends to stigmatize the SVPs (Husak 2011). There is evidence of the state's intent to stigmatize SVPs in their legislative history. In the 1980s, most states switched from indeterminate to determinate sentencing schemes, just when there was a shift in criminology ideals from rehabilitative to a more conservative "law and order" agenda (Janus 2006, pp. 17–21). This deprived states of their ability to exercise control over offenders deemed too dangerous to release from prison and required them to release them when their sentence ended. By the late 1980s and early 1990s, several of these inmates were eligible for release, including sexual offenders. States prospectively increased sentence lengths of sex offenders, but these increases could not apply retroactively. Highly publicized crimes inflamed public outrage, most notably that of Earl Shriner, who raped, murdered, and mutilated a young boy. Shriner had recently been released from prison for sex offenses after serving his full sentence and was not eligible for ordinary civil commitment (Janus 2006).

States may have used the SVP process as a means to circumvent a sentencing problem—to expand their ability to punish. A Minnesota task force study on the use of civil commitment made this explicit, noting that SVP statutes could compensate for the "comparatively short correctional sentences" of sex offenses (Janus 2006, p. 22). It also noted that civil commitment would allow the state to circumvent many procedural protections it faced in criminal trials, such as prohibitions on hearsay, allowing the confinement of individuals who "may be dangerous but evade conviction due to the high burden of proof required in criminal trials" (Janus 2006, p. 22).

It is also worth noting that the SVP laws distinguish an unpopular group for special treatment in a way that is, without a doubt, stigmatizing. It is premised on the idea of preventing recidivism, yet it singles out a group of offenses for which the rate of recidivism is actually lower than for other offenses, short of murder (Levenson 2003, p. 22).

If SVP statutes do constitute preventive detention as punishment, it is not clear whether Husak's framework would support them. Husak supports preventive measures based on acts or characteristics within the actor's control (Husak 2011). SVP statutes routinely break these rules. They commonly require mental or behavioral abnormalities, characteristics that are likely beyond the individual's control. They also often use actuarial tools that rely on characteristics beyond an individual's control and have limited predictive value.

Conclusion

The expansion of preventive measures to combat sex offenses is an example of the state pursuing a laudable goal with questionable means. Enticement and solicitation offenses attempt to protect a vulnerable population from exploitation and abuse. As inchoate offenses, they punish conduct often so remote that they raise significant questions about their compatibility with important principles of criminal law. One way to resolve this tension is to reconsider these solicitation and enticement as complete offenses that target the harm caused by the communication to the minor. While this would home in on a heretofore underexamined harm, it would undermine the statutes' efficacy in preventing future physical sexual abuse. Sexually violent predator laws present another attempt to protect the population from dangerous individuals. Yet the means expand civil commitment beyond anything before have created broad, vague, and questionably relevant standards for detaining individuals before they act. In sum, even where the individuals and acts involved invoke our strongest feelings of disgust and indignation, legislatures, courts, and scholars must consider preventive measures carefully and critically.

Notes

1. I do not discuss the solicitation of sexual images from minors in this chapter. Child pornography is a crime, and the solicitation of child pornography is soliciting unlawful material. These offenses are therefore justified by distinct legal arguments and do not raise the legal issues of the crimes that are preparatory or inchoate to unlawful sex with a minor. It is worth noting, however, that obtaining sexual images is, in reality, part of the grooming process for child sexual abuse, and it is often then used to blackmail the child (International Centre for Missing and Exploited Children 2017, p. 15). Moreover, many of the arguments above with regard to the creation of psychological harm can almost certainly be explored with regard to solicitation of sexual imagery from a child.
2. Where I do not specify an offender's gender, I use the male pronoun. While both men and women commit sex offenses against both adults and minors, I chose the male pronoun because the majority of those convicted for sex offenses in the United States are men (Hoppe 2016, p. 582).

3. There are, of course, problems with the statute. If the statute is targeting psychological harm, then it is odd that it targets only the harm when a minor is solicited with unlawful sex, which varies depending on who is soliciting what kind of sex and where they are soliciting it. This creates the strange result that the law is targeting the presumed psychological harm of a 17-year-old girl sitting at a computer in Alabama who receives an email from her 18-year-old boyfriend discussing their plans for intercourse in Wisconsin (where all sex with a minor is unlawful) but does nothing to address the psychological harm of a 40-year-old stranger's unsolicited request for sex in New York (where age does not criminalize the act).

4. This can be a conviction but, in some jurisdictions, the actor can merely be charged with the offense, deemed incompetent to stand trial, or can be a minor adjudicated delinquent (Kaplan 2015, p. 144).

5. As a result, 14 individuals have been held under the law filed by a class action lawsuit against the state. The statute was initially held unconstitutional by the federal district court, a ruling that was reversed by the Eighth Circuit Court of Appeals. See Karsjens v. Piper, 845 F.3d 394 (2017).

6. *See also* Foucha v. Louisiana 504 U.S. 71, 77-84 (1992); Addington v. Texas, 441 U.S. 426-32 (1979); O'Connor v. Donaldson, 422 U.S. 563, 574-76 (1975).

7. (See Kaplan 2015) The sole exception to these standards might be New Hampshire, which provides the strongest standard: that the "person has serious difficulty in controlling his or her behavior as to pose a potentially serious likelihood of danger to others" (N.H. Rev. Stat. Ann. § 135-E:2 (2014)).

8. Alexander and Ferzan intend their system of civil preventive measures to replace several types of inchoate offenses for which they believe criminal punishment is inappropriate (Alexander and Ferzan 2012). SVP statutes that complied with their system would therefore supplant, rather than complement, several inchoate sexual offense statutes.

REFERENCES

18 U.S.C. §2422.
18 U.S.C. § 4247(a)(6).
Cal. Jury Inst. Crim. 4.19.
Colo. Rev. Stat. 18-3-306.
Colo. Rev. Stat. 18-3-405.4.
N.H. Rev. Stat. Ann. § 135-E:2.
N.J. Stat. Ann. §2C:13-6.
N.J. Stat. Ann. §30:4-27.2(r).
Rev. Code Wash. 9.68a.090.
Addington v. Texas, 441 U.S. 426–32 (1979).
Foucha v. Louisiana, 504 U.S. 71, 77–84 (1992).
Kansas v. Hendricks, 521 U.S. 346, 353–55 (1997).
Karsjens v. Piper, 845 F.3d 394 (2017).
O'Connor v. Donaldson, 422 U.S. 563, 574–76 (1975).
U.S. v. Rothenberg, 610 F.3d 621 (2010).
Alexander, Larry, and Kimberly Kessler Ferzan. 2009. *Crime and culpability: A theory of criminal law*. Cambridge: Cambridge University Press.

————. 2012. Danger: The ethics of preemptive action. *Ohio State Journal of Criminal Law* 9: 637–667.

Davey, Monica. 2015. States struggle with what to do with sex offenders after prison. *New York Times.* https://www.nytimes.com/2015/10/30/us/states-struggle-with-what-to-do-with-sex-offenders-after-prison.html. Accessed 25 Feb 2019.

Duff, R.A. 1997. *Criminal attempts.* Oxford: Oxford University Press.

Ferzan, Kimberly Kessler. 2011a. Beyond crime and commitment: Justifying liberty deprivations of the dangerous and responsible. *Minnesota Law Review* 96: 141–193.

————. 2011b. Inchoate crimes at the prevention/punishment divide. *San Diego Law Review* 48: 1273–1297.

Hamilton, Melissa. 2013. Adjudicating sex crimes as mental disease. *Pace Law Review* 33: 536–599.

Hoppe, Trevor. 2016. Punishing sex: Sex offenders and the missing punitive turn in sexuality studies. *Law & Social Inquiry* 41: 573–594.

Husak, Douglas. 1995. The nature and justifiability of non-consummate offenses. *Arizona Law Review* 37: 151–183.

————. 2011. Lifting the cloak: Preventive detention as punishment. *San Diego Law Review* 48: 1173–1204.

International Centre for Missing and Exploited Children. 2017. Online grooming of children for sexual purposes: Model legislation and global review. International Centre for Missing and Exploited Children. https://www.icmec.org/wp-content/uploads/2017/09/Online-Grooming-of-Children_FINAL_9-18-17.pdf. Accessed 25 Feb 2019.

Janus, Eric S. 2006. *Failure to protect: America's sexual predator law and the rise of the preventive state.* Ithaca: Cornell University Press.

Kaplan, Margo. 2015. Taking pedophilia seriously. *Washington and Lee Law Review* 72: 75–170.

Klein, Dora W. 2012. When coercion lacks care: Competency to make medical treatment decisions and parens patriae civil commitments. *University of Michigan Journal of Law Reform* 45: 561–593.

Knighton, Jefferson C., Daniel C. Murrie, Marcus T. Boccaccini, and Darrel B. Turner. 2014. How likely is "likely to reoffend" in sex offender civil commitment trials? *Law and Human Behavior* 38: 293–304.

Levenson, Jill S. 2003. Policy interventions designed to combat sexual violence: Community notification and civil commitment. In *Identifying and treating sex offenders: Current approaches, research, and techniques,* ed. Robert Geffner, Kristina Crumpton Franey, Teir Arnold Geffner, and Robert Falconer, 17–52. New York: Haworth Press.

Mitchell, Kimberly J., David Finkelhor, and Janis Wolak. 2001. Risk factors for and impact of online solicitation of youth. *Journal of the American Medical Association* 285: 3011–3014.

Morse, Stephen J. 1996. Blame and danger: An essay on preventive detention. *Boston University Law Review* 76: 113–155.

————. 2004. Preventive confinement of dangerous offenders. *Journal of Law, Medicine, and Ethics* 32: 56–72.

Ohana, Daniel. 2007. Desert and punishment for acts preparatory to the commission of a crime. *Canadian Journal of Law and Jurisprudence* 20: 113–142.

Robbins, Ira P. 1989. Double inchoate Crimes. *Harvard Journal on Legislation* 26: 1–116.

Robinson, Paul H. 2001. Punishing dangerousness: Cloaking preventive detention as criminal justice. *Harvard Law Review* 114: 1429–1456.

Schulhofer, Stephen J. 1996. Two systems of social protection: Comments on the civil-criminal distinction, with particular reference to sexually violent predator laws. *Journal of Contemporary Legal Issues* 7: 69–96.

Terry, Karen J. 2006. *Sexual offenses and offenders: Theory, practice, and policy.* 2nd ed. Belmont: Cengage.

Walen, Alex. 2011. Criminalizing statements of terrorist intent: How to understand the law governing terrorist threats and why it should be used instead of long-term preventive detention. *The Journal of Criminal Law and Criminology* 101: 803–854.

Wolak, Janis, Kimberly J. Mitchell, and David Finkelhor. 2006. Online victimization of youth: Five years later. National Center for Missing & Exploited Children Bulletin #07-06-025. Alexandria, VA.

Wright, Richard G. 2009. Internet sex stings. In *Sex offender laws: Failed policies, new directions*, ed. Richard G. Wright, 115–158. New York: Springer Publishing.

Zander, Thomas K. 2005. Civil commitment without psychosis: The law's reliance on the weakest link in psychodiagnosis. *Journal of Sexual Offender Civil Commitment: Science and the Law* 1: 17–82.

PART XXIX

Stand Your Ground

CHAPTER 31

Stand Your Ground

Kimberly Kessler Ferzan

THE SUBJECT OF OUR INQUIRY

"Stand Your Ground" ("SYG") laws authorize a defender to use deadly force against an aggressor even when the defender can safely retreat. This chapter will examine the moral justifiability of such a provision. The following statute is representative of the legal position that we will be interrogating:

> A person is justified in using or threatening to use deadly force if he or she reasonably believes that using or threatening to use such force is necessary to prevent imminent death or great bodily harm to himself or herself or another or to prevent the imminent commission of a forcible felony. A person who uses or threatens to use deadly force in accordance with this subsection does not have a duty to retreat and has the right to stand his or her ground if the person using or threatening to use the deadly force is not engaged in a criminal activity and is in a place where he or she has a right to be. (Florida Statutes, § 776.012(2))

SYG laws are part of a broader framework. Notably, even in states that do not adopt SYG laws and thereby typically require one to retreat, defenders are not required to leave their homes before using deadly force according to the "castle doctrine" (Dressler 2009, p. 230; Ward 2015, p. 94). In addition, SYG laws do not allow defenders to stand their ground if they provoked the attack (Ward 2015, p. 95). Finally, SYG laws may have peripheral provisions, affecting burdens of proof, immunity, and arrests, but these are outside the scope of this chapter.

K. K. Ferzan (✉)
University of Virginia School of Law, Charlottesville, VA, USA
e-mail: kferzan@law.virginia.edu

© The Author(s) 2019
L. Alexander, K. K. Ferzan (eds.), *The Palgrave Handbook of Applied Ethics and the Criminal Law*, https://doi.org/10.1007/978-3-030-22811-8_31

Our inquiry sidelines some potential justifications for an SYG law that would be based on the benefits of creating a rule out of what would otherwise be a fact-intensive jury question. That is, one potential justification for a rule is the worry that juries will get these inquiries wrong. If we believe that juries are more likely to find that defenders can safely retreat than the facts warrant, thus denying defenders the benefit of self-defense, we might create a bright line rule. So, too, we might create a bright line rule if jurors' hindsight biases will lead them to conclude incorrectly that defenders should have *reasonably* believed they could safely retreat, thus denying defenders an excuse for their mistaken beliefs in the justifying circumstances (Berman 2003, pp. 15–16).

This chapter also will not consider objections based on the possible distributive impacts of these statutes. Some argue that SYG laws embolden white men to more actively pursue black men who are deemed threatening simply because of the color of their skin (Lave 2013, pp. 850–54).[1] Other studies find that SYG laws increase the killing of white men by other white men, with no impact on black men (McCellan and Tekin 2012). There is a further debate as to whether SYG laws entrench aggressive masculine norms (Franks 2014, p. 1127) or whether their absence disadvantages female stalking victims (Kuhns 2017, p. 24).

Other objections outside the scope of our analysis are the potential political motivations for the enactment of these states. SYG laws are typically the handiwork of the National Rifle Association, with the ambition of promoting gun ownership by delineating substantial rights to gun owners (Lave 2013, pp. 836–39; Lerner 2006, p. 340), though that causal story is disputed (Ward 2015, p. 96). Hence, one might ask whether the widespread enactment of these statutes is reflective of an intuitive view that such conduct is permissible or whether it is simply politics.

Irrespective of whether one believes this is the product of politics or, as Renee Lettow Lerner puts it, a "worldwide popular revolt against proportionality" (Lerner 2006), the question remains whether SYG laws are justified. Many theorists find these sorts of statutes unjustifiable, as they allow the defender to kill an aggressor when she could otherwise simply run away. Indeed, a passing glance at the Florida statute reveals what appears to be an internal contradiction. The first sentence permits the use of deadly force to prevent death, grievous bodily harm, and forcible felonies *but only when the attack is imminent and when the force is necessary.* The second claims that the defender may stand her ground instead of leaving. But how can force be necessary and a threat to one's life and limb imminent, if one can simply turn tail and run (Alexander 1999, p. 1480)?[2] And beyond the contradiction, what could normatively ground such a statute? This is the object of our inquiry—to see how such a statute might possibly be justified.

This chapter proceeds as follows. First, it sets forth the parameters of self-defense as understood in the philosophical literature. Next, it focuses on the necessity limitation and questions whether this limitation can be defensibly weakened to accommodate SYG laws. Finding no comfort for SYG statutes in a weakened necessity limitation, the chapter turns to the proportionality constraint and examines approaches that increase the interests that may permissibly be defended as well as approaches that abandon proportionality altogether. Notably, however, SYG laws adopt proportionality requirements; they do not abandon them altogether. Finally, this chapter maintains that the most perspicuous lens through which to view SYG laws is that of law enforcement because what SYG laws actually do is place citizens in the role of police. The justifiability of such enforcement authority turns, then, on two further questions. It must be appropriate for citizens to serve this function. But second, it must be appropriate for the state to stand its ground. This chapter concludes by problematizing this final assumption and claiming that anyone who wishes to justify such behavior by citizens should start by trying to unearth the justification for this behavior by the state.

The Philosophical Approach to Self-Defense

The standard philosophical approach to self-defense is to start with the question of liability. If Bob kills Abe when Abe is trying to kill him intentionally, Bob does not violate Abe's rights (Ferzan 2016). This is often thought to be a form of forfeiture, though unlike the typical view that forfeiture is a permanent loss, liability is a temporary suspension of rights. If Abe threatens to kill Ben on Monday but then recants and poses no threat to Ben, Ben is not permitted to kill Abe on Tuesday as a matter of self-defense (Thomson 1986, pp. 34–36).

Theorists disagree about the basis for liability. Some theorists restrict liability to culpable aggressors (Ferzan 2012). Other theorists broaden the criteria for forfeiture to those actors who take reasonably foreseeable risks of harming another, such that a pedestrian is permitted to kill a conscientious driver whose car unexpectedly malfunctions, or those who are nonnegligently mistaken about whether they are being attacked, such that the person who mistakenly believes she is under attack becomes the aggressor (McMahan 2005a). However, even those who believe that nonculpable aggressors can be liable agree that the rules may be more stringent for killing nonculpable aggressors than culpable ones (McMahan 2009, p. 161; Øverland 2010, p. 338). That is, a defender may need to absorb some risk of harm to avoid killing an innocent attacker (Sangero 2006, p. 192). Because we want to examine the most robust case for SYG laws, I will assume that the aggressor is culpable. Indeed, for ease of exposition, I will assume that the culpable aggressor is intentionally trying to kill the victim.

Most theorists believe that the degree of liability is determined by the threat the culpable aggressor poses (Quong 2015). If Abe only threatens to pinch Ben, Ben may not use deadly force in return. Jeff McMahan calls this "narrow proportionality" (McMahan 2009, pp. 20–21). In contrast to narrow proportionality, "wide proportionality" takes into account injuries to third parties (McMahan 2009, pp. 20–21). If Abe is trying to kill Ben, but for Ben to defend himself successfully he must throw a grenade that will kill Carla and Deena,

Ben's action would be narrowly proportionate (killing to prevent death) but widely disproportionate (killing two innocent bystanders to save one innocent defender). In such a case, Abe would be liable to defensive force, but it would not be all-things-considered permissible to kill him.

Liability may also be limited to those who intend to act defensively (McMahan 2009, p. 10). The idea here is as follows: Abe tries to kill Ben, but Ben does not realize it. Ben decides to shoot Abe. Did Ben act in self-defense? To those who claim that one is only liable to those who act for defensive reasons, Ben wrongs Abe because the rights forfeiture did not apply to Ben. That is, a theorist might think that forfeiture is limited to those who are motivated by, or at least aware of, the justifying circumstances (Ferzan 2016, pp. 249–251).

A final relevant limitation is necessity. There is substantial debate as to whether necessity is internal or external to liability (Frowe 2016, p. 153). Assume Abe tries to kill Ben. Ben can defend by either (a) shooting Abe or (b) yelling "Boo!" which Ben knows will cause Abe to drop the gun and run away. The theorists who take necessity to be internal to liability maintain that Abe is not liable to deadly force and Ben would wrong Abe by killing him, whereas other theorists believe that Abe is liable to deadly force but it remains all-things-considered wrong to kill him if lesser means are available. What internalists (or quasi-internalist (partialist) views) maintain, that externalists deny, is that the aggressor has a complaint against the defender who uses unnecessary force (Quong Forthcoming, p. 122). Both agree that necessity impacts permissibility; it is simply how necessity figures into the equation.

Overlaying all of these inquiries is the question of whether we are taking a fact-relative or evidence-relative approach to justification (Parfit 2011, pp. 159–61). From a fact-relative perspective, an action is only right if it is *in fact* the right thing to do. If Alice does not know that the water she is giving Bob is poisoned, Alice still does the wrong thing by handing it to him. Nevertheless, Alice, who is nonculpably mistaken, is excused. An evidence-relative perspective lets right and wrong turn on the evidence (reasonably) available to the actor. From this perspective, Alice does the right thing. Applying these perspectives to self-defense, if Ben reasonably, but mistakenly, believes Abe is attacking him and he must kill Abe to save himself, when in actuality Abe is rehearsing for a play and believes no one is around him, then from a fact-relative perspective Ben does the wrong thing if he kills Abe but Ben is excused, whereas an evidence-relative perspective yields that Ben did the right thing. Ben is fact-relative unjustified but evidence-relative justified.

Notably, some theorists think one can have one's cake and eat it, too. They approach questions such as Abe and Ben by claiming that there is a perspective by which Ben is justified and a perspective by which he is not (Ferzan 2012, p. 680, n.44). However, it seems odd to think that morality can operate at both levels simultaneously, condemning and condoning the very same behavior as unjustified and justified (Ferzan 2018b). Accordingly, this chapter, in keeping with much of the self-defense literature, will take a fact-relative perspective. It bears noting however that given that SYG laws require "reasonable beliefs," actors will have a defense when they use deadly force when they are actually under attack (and are aware of that) *or* they reasonably believe they are under attack. A fact-relative perspective would simply parse this as the former setting forth a justification and the latter an excuse.[3]

STAND YOUR GROUND AND NECESSITY

With these parameters in mind, let us consider the following case:

> *Stand Your Ground:* Agnes runs at Vera with a knife. Vera can shoot Agnes. However, Vera is also a champion sprinter and can safely outrun Agnes and successfully call the police to apprehend her.

The first thought about such a case is that killing Agnes appears *unnecessary*. The problem appears to be that Vera does not need to kill Agnes to defend herself. At first blush, SYG laws appear to be about the necessity constraint (Quong Forthcoming, p. 122). Killing Agnes is unnecessary for Vera to save herself.

One potential foothold for SYG laws is to reconsider the necessity constraint. If we are permitted to kill people when it is unnecessary, then SYG laws can be justified. Now, most people will stop here, as they will find it unlikely that we are entitled to kill people unnecessarily. However, for the moment, let's take this claim seriously. That is, let's ask whether there really is a necessity requirement.

Although necessity seems extremely attractive, there is reason to doubt that there is a robust, objective necessity requirement for self-defense (Ferzan 2017). The concern is that almost no action is *actually necessary*. It is not just that a defender cannot know whether she must act at the time that she will take preemptive action (Ferzan 2005, p. 715); it is also that there is almost always a lesser harm that the defender could administer if she knew what it was. Unbeknownst to her, the defender can stomp on a loose floorboard such that it hits the attacker in the face, or shoot at an angle where the bullet will graze the attacker's ear and frighten her away, or say just the thing that will distract the attacker with thoughts of her mother. Hence, those who take fact-relative views of justification appear committed to the view that most (all?) defenders act wrongfully most (all?) of the time. And if one takes the view that necessity is internal to liability, then defenders are wronging aggressors all the time.

So, perhaps there is not a robust objective necessity requirement.[4] Nevertheless, even the abandonment of an objective necessity requirement need not yield a relative free-for-all for defenders. Some theorists will shift to thinking that necessity simply requires *reasonable beliefs* in necessity. And even fact relativists may believe that even if there is not a strict objective necessity requirement, defensive actions could still run afoul of the justificatory reason the defender must be aware of (Ferzan 2016, pp. 244–45). The defender who is unsure whether she must shoot (or whether her attacker will miss) still believes that there is some chance her action is necessary. The defender who recognizes that there might be a way to stop the attack that she is unaware of, or incapable of performing, is still aiming to stop an attack the only way she knows how. But none of this is true if the defender knows that all she needs to do is yell "Boo!" at the aggressor. Then, it appears that the killing is simply gratuitous (McMahan 2016, p. 196). If self-defense gives a limited permission to protect our rights, then this permission does not extend to those cases in which we *know* that our actions are not necessary to protect them (Ferzan 2016, pp. 240–43). The grounding of the right's forfeiture does not apply when the defender is well aware of lesser means to protect herself.

Ultimately, even if we weaken the stringency of the necessity requirement, we are unlikely to reach the conclusion that gratuitous killings are authorized. Instead, there will be constraints because the defender must still believe that there is some probability that her defensive action is necessary to thwart the attack.[5] It seems unlikely that defenders of SYG laws want to claim that we can kill people, whether we believe we need to do so or not, simply for sport. Indeed, such an approach would be overinclusive, as SYG laws accept necessity limitations such that one is not permitted to kill in instances in which one could simply yell "Boo!" SYG laws are consistent with a necessity limitation except insofar as the necessity limitation entails a retreat requirement. They do not abandon necessity completely.

STAND YOUR GROUND AND PROPORTIONALITY

But maybe SYG laws aren't truly necessity questions. We should first notice that there is *a cost* to Vera if we require her to retreat. She must relinquish the space where she otherwise has a right to stand. We might then distinguish between *Stand Your Ground* and *Lesser Defense*:

> *Lesser Defense:* Albert threatens to kill Ving with a knife. Ving can stop the attack by either shooting Albert or by yelling, "Boo," the latter of which will cause Albert to drop the knife and run away.

Here, Ving has two options to save himself, and we can assume that each requires the same amount of sacrifice. If we believe that Ving must say "Boo," the necessity principle is doing the work.

In contrast, in *Stand Your Ground*, Vera is not choosing between two ways of defending herself. She is choosing between (a) defending herself and (b) running away and relinquishing where she has a right to be. Her choice is more akin to "your money or your life" than it is to "shoot or say 'Boo.'"

One way to think about this choice would keep it squarely as a question of necessity. This would take the "running away" option off the table because Vera does not have a duty to do so (Leider 2018). Admittedly, the intuitive attractiveness of SYG laws likely lies in something like this rationale.[6] If we are not required to flee from our castles, why should we be required to flee from a space we rightfully occupy? This idea also permeates positions, including the Model Penal Code's, that when faced with "your money or your life," one is entitled to use deadly force (Leider 2018). Simply put, our options don't include things we are not required to do.

Yet, the thought that this option should be taken off the table seems too hasty. If Betty threatens to pinch Alice, and all Alice can do to stop Betty is to shoot her, we would claim that the force was disproportionate to the right that is being protected. We would not allow Alice to simply assert that she has no duty to absorb a pinch. The same would be true if Betty told Alice to walk five spaces or she would kill her. Even if Betty is violating Alice's rights or causing Alice to do something she has no duty to do, the question is whether the use of deadly force is permissible to protect that liberty or autonomy interest.

This means that perhaps the true heavy lifting is not being done by necessity but by narrow proportionality (Sangero 2006, p. 194).[7] That is, the reason why it now seems impermissible for Vera to kill Agnes is because killing is disproportionate to defending the space in which she rightfully stands. And this appears to be true even if we think that individuals have rights to the spaces they rightfully occupy (Quong 2009, p. 528).

If Vera's only goal is to defend "her space," this goal hardly seems proportionate to killing someone. However, there are two distinct ways to try to reconcile SYG laws and proportionality. The first is to increase the number of interests that may permissibly be protected. The second is to abandon proportionality altogether. Let us consider each of these in turn.

Adding Values to the Proportionality Calculus

The question of to what the use of force must be proportionate is tricky. This is because we are less inclined to think that this is a direct comparison of harm to harm. Theorists are inclined to include within the proportionality calculus the fact that the defender will otherwise be wronged and the fact that the defender is culpable (Uniacke 2011; Quong 2015). That is, when we think of why deadly force is permissible to defend against rape, it is not because the harm of rape is the same as death, but because the defender will be *wronged* by the rape. And, in determining how much force one can use, the fact that the attacker is innocent or culpable has bearing for many theorists on the amount of force one can use.

We need not resolve the precise formula for proportionality, however. The question is whether we can get enough values on the table to even come close to rendering it permissible to kill someone. Are there other values that might also be added to "defense of space," such that their aggregate would justify substantially more force? Before setting forth these values, let me give the quick answer of yes and no. Yes, there are additional values that may also be placed on Vera's side of the ledger in *Stand Your Ground*. No, these values cannot, even in the aggregate, justify killing someone.

We should first note that Vera is not just defending her space. After all, this isn't about getting to shoot someone who is about to take the parking space you believe you have claimed with your car's blinker. This is about requiring Vera to move. And, Vera does have an autonomy interest in not being required to move. Indeed, our negative agent claims not to be required to do things are quite robust (Walen and Wasserman 2012, p. 554). Nevertheless, this is then on a par with the aggressor who tells us to hand over a watch—it is both the property interest and the handing over that are at stake. (You could hold up your arm and tell the aggressor to take it after all.)

Honor is another value that can be added to Vera's side of the ledger. The idea behind this is that running away looks timid and weak. This idea is mistakenly attributed to the "true man doctrine," a testosterone-laden title, but this label, originating with Sir Matthew Hale, was not about what "manly men" do but about what blameless people do (Brown 1991, p. 9). Nevertheless, we are assuming that Vera is innocent, and thus, the question is whether it is "dishonorable" to have to run away.

Now, in its current incarnation, "defending honor" seems gendered and potentially outdated, but one hypothetical used to support the intuition looks remarkably different. Imagined by Joanna Mary Firth and Jon Quong, the hypothetical involves Fran, a rape victim, who cannot stop her rapist, Eric, from accomplishing the crime but can break his wrist (Firth and Quong 2012, p. 99). The puzzle presented is that the harm appears unnecessary, because it is not sufficient. Very few people have the intuition that Fran wrongs Eric. And one reason often presented is that Fran is defending her honor (Frowe 2014, pp. 109–13). Elsewhere, I have argued that conceptualizing Fran's conduct as "defending honor" is not quite right (Ferzan 2018a). What is really going on is that not giving up in the face of defeat appears to have expressive value. Likewise, such expression is at work in the value of "mere resistance" articulated by Frances Kamm (2014).

Does this more robust and palatable notion of honor have any play here? I suspect not. Whatever honor we see in Fran fighting back is not the notion on display if Vera decides to kill Agnes when she could simply run away. As I have argued, "There seems to be less poetic expression in shooting Murderer needlessly. One might think that it is, well, dishonorable" (Ferzan 2018a). This means that if we are left with any notion of honor, it is the "I don't want to look weak by running away" notion. (Dsouza 2015, p. 73). We might grant that that is a sufficient value that the law correctly maintains that one need not run away before deploying *nondeadly* force (you get to punch the guy who would otherwise punch you), but it hardly seems to be a strong enough value to justify SYG laws' authorization of deadly force.

However, let us assume that these reasons can aggregate; thus, a defender may employ more force to defend her right to her space, her autonomy interest in not being required to move, and her interest in not being made to appear or feel weak, than she could use to defend any one of these interests individually. What other interests might be added to the calculation to justify more force by Vera?

One potential answer often given in the Fran/Eric case is punishment (Ferzan 2018a). Punishment should be carefully parsed here as we punish for distinct reasons. Retributive desert is one reason to punish. Agnes' threat of killing Vera warrants some retributive desert. However, it is doubtful that Agnes *deserves* death or anything close to it. This is especially true of other felonies that support SYG laws. In Florida, forcible felonies include burglary and robbery. Yet it seems hard to imagine that someone deserves death simply because she pointed a gun at her victim in order to obtain a watch.[8] Still, there is some desert due and owing to Agnes, and this reason arguably should aggregate with the others.

In contrast, although deterrence is also served, one needs an argument that the deterrence reason would aggregate. That is, typically, the fact that you stole a candy bar means that you deserve some punishment (say, one day in jail) and that punishment will deter (say, five days would prove extremely effective), but we do not think that the deterrence reason aggregates with the desert reason (Ferzan 2018b). Rather, punishing more than is deserved is viewed as disproportionate even if effective as deterrence. Hence, you get one day in jail, not six. Likewise, just war theorists have argued that deterrence can reinforce reasons to go to war but cannot itself be a just cause for war (McMahan 2005b, pp. 16–17). This is because deterrence does not increase the rights forfeiture, only desert and liability do this.

We might, though, try to recast the deterrence reason. For instance, Boaz Sangero argues that aggressors threaten the socio-legal order (Sangero 2006, p. 213). Or in the words of Kremnitzer and Ghanayim, a strong requirement of retreat would "grant an unlawful aggressor an advantage over his victim, and could encourage violence" (Kremnitzer and Ghanayim 2004, p. 882). Jake Bronsther views defendants as contributing to "criminality" in a society that undermines security for all (Bronsther 2018). These views would recast the deterrence/punishment rationale as a preventive/self-defense rationale for society generally, thereby placing another interest on the scales to be aggregated.

Of course, the question of whether citizens may permissibly punish is deeply contested. We might worry that even if these reasons exist, they are reasons that are unavailable to the defender (Ferzan 2018a; Wellman 2017, p. 47). However, unlike vigilante conduct, this is state-sanctioned behavior, a wrinkle I will return to below. A principle issue, though, is that even with these values added, it seems hard to believe that the imposition of death is proportionate. Even if these values increase the amount of harm to which Agnes is liable, they pale in comparison to death.

Should We Abandon Narrow Proportionality?

The most sophisticated defense of SYG laws has been leveled by Heidi Hurd, who argues that the proportionality principle should be abandoned.[9] As Hurd throws down the gauntlet, "Of course you should be able to stand your ground when threatened with unjustified aggression. To think otherwise is to subscribe to the view that you must forfeit *your* liberty to an assailant when so doing will be a means of saving *his* life" (Hurd 2016, p. 254).

Hurd casts the "proportionality principle" as she calls it, within the realm of consequentialism, and then argues that five implications of this principle demonstrate "the perversity of strict applications of the proportionality principle" (Hurd 2016, p. 259). Let us consider them in turn.

Hurd's first complaint is that "whenever the harm or indignity with which an innocent victim is threatened is less than the harm that must be inflicted on the assailant to prevent it, the innocent must simply bear that harm" (Hurd 2016, p. 259). It is true that leaving a victim without a right to defend herself, and perhaps uncompensated, is problematic. This implication seems all the more troubling as Hurd requires us to imagine enduring the destruction of "prized family heirlooms," the humiliation of "lascivious groping," and the endurance of "excruciating pain" that leaves no lasting injury (Hurd 2016, p. 259).

Still, we can cite the perverse and counterintuitive implications of going the other way too. A principle that one may use greater force than is proportionate because Right should never give way to Wrong also provides that one may use deadly force to defend against the theft of the old Timex that you never liked, the unwelcome wet willie[10] that your larger brother-in-law plans to give you no matter how much you protest, and the punch in the arm that will not hurt by your feisty colleague who is known to punch people when they mock her. There is no doubt that a proportionality principle is going to pick winners and losers.

What we need, though, is grounds for thinking that when someone attacks you to some extent, they either forfeit their rights proportionate to that attack (which need not be exact parity) or they forfeit their rights writ large. That is, a deontologist can think that rights forfeiture is not always "right to life" forfeiture. Indeed, we see this with punishment, as broad forfeiture doctrines are thought to punish *disproportionately* as, for instance, felony murder rules do. A rule that Right does not give way to Wrong offers no nuance as to wrong, as though we are all either angels or sinners. In contrast, a liability rule could (and in my view should) take into account the degree of wrongdoing on the part of the aggressor. Complete abandonment of proportionality yields that we forfeit our lives whenever we engage in minor infractions.

The second implication Hurd discusses is that if one person is attacked by five culpable aggressors, the aggregation of their numbers means that one may not defend oneself (Hurd 2016, p. 259). Hurd finds it implausible to think that "thugs" are entitled to any weight (Hurd 2016, p. 262). However, as Hurd notes, many deontologists do not agree with this, and a forfeiture principle *does not entail this.* That is, one might think that a culpable aggressor does forfeit his right to life and that one is entitled to use force to prevent that rights violation but that the interest that was protected as a right still has some bearing on what the defender may do (Ferzan 2018a). It is true that if we give the life of a culpable aggressor any weight as an interest (despite not being protected by a right), we might think that their lives could aggregate at some point to outweigh the life of an innocent. But most people think that the aggregation would have to be very substantial indeed.

Hurd's third implication is that "under the proportionality principle, none of us can be thought to be at liberty to act in a manner that we know or even suspect will provoke others to deadly violence" (Hurd 2016, p. 259).[11] We are thus left without recourse to repel "predictable attacks" (Hurd 2016, p. 260). Again, this implication only applies if one is a consequentialist at the outset. But there is no reason to think that deontology might not have more nuanced rules and implications. Liability may only arise at a particular point, such as when the aggressor forms the intention. And, given that aggressors are not liable until that point, their potential wrongdoing cannot restrict others' interests before that intention arises (Quong Forthcoming). Elsewhere, I have argued that provocateurs do forfeit defensive rights (Ferzan 2013). But one is only a provocateur if one instigates at least recklessly, and recklessness requires that one take an unjustifiable risk. So, the question is not whether one can foresee being mugged if one walks in the park at night. The question is whether taking that walk is unjustifiable. And here, the limit to one's liberty in not being allowed to walk through a park is substantial. Ultimately, foreseeability is insufficient for the loss of rights by the defender.

In contrast, Hurd's fourth implication of a proportionality principle is accurate, but it is an implication that we ought to accept. Hurd notes that we may be required to forgo lawful activities if we foresee others' downstream wrongdoing (Hurd 2016, p. 260). Wrongdoing by third parties does impose costs on us, and those limitations of our options are entitled to some weight. Still, we might think that this does not mean that we may do whatever we please willy nilly irrespective of how much harm we can predict a wrongdoer will cause. If you know your friend will use your gun to shoot his girlfriend, then you should put it away (Alexander and Ferzan 2018, pp. 21–26). The question of whether we assume the risk, and forfeit our liberty, is distinct from the question of whether we need to be on the lookout for harm to innocent third parties. Harm to third parties is appropriately an object of our concern (Ibid.).

Hurd's fifth implication is the very claim we have under examination. She notes that the proportionality principle implies that "the loss of liberty that is imposed by such a duty to retreat is thought to be less onerous than is the loss of life that is necessitated if one does not retreat" (Hurd 2016, p. 260). And she claims these five implications "starkly capture why critics of the utility principle have famously complained that it demands too much of people" (Hurd 2016, p. 260).

As noted, however, one can be a deontologist and still believe in a proportionality principle. Retributivists famously fit this bill. There is every reason to think that forfeiture for defensive purposes is likewise sensitive to the degree of wrongdoing.

If one is willing to defend the strong claim that there simply is no proportionality requirement, then SYG laws properly allow you to shoot someone rather than retreat. Still, we have reasons to be skeptical that such a position is justified. Indeed, even jurisdictions that purport to permit disproportionate killings, such as killing an apple thief who is running away, undermine their absolutist rules by finding that such "defenders" have abused their rights (Fletcher and Ohlin 2008, pp. 118–120).

STAND YOUR GROUND AND LAW ENFORCEMENT DELEGATION

The claim that SYG laws are completely opposed to proportionality is over-stated. Notice that even Florida's law does not abandon proportionality. If you threaten to give me a wet willie, I may not kill you. If you threaten to punch me in the nose, I may not kill you. If you threaten to burn my Picasso, then unless it is deemed a forcible felony, I still may not kill you. SYG laws are not a wholesale abandonment of proportionality. Moreover, if I can kill you or (i) step on your toe, (ii) punch you, or (iii) scream "Boo," then I may not kill you either. So, SYG laws don't abandon necessity either. Hence, any move for the outright abandonment of necessity or proportionality would be overinclusive and mischaracterize the actual legal position under consideration.

Instead, these laws simply eliminate one avenue that you might otherwise take. You do not have to leave. And, so, what SYG laws do is essentially turn citizens into law enforcement (West 2014, p. 899). Law enforcement officers are limited by proportionality and necessity, but they are not required to retreat. Indeed, having the cops run away from criminals seems to make for very bad criminal justice policy.

There is not perfect parity here. Law enforcement officials have duties not to retreat. The police are not allowed to see you being attacked by a culpable aggressor and opt to go buy a sandwich. They are required to intervene. And, when they intervene, they are exempted from the usual duty to retreat. Citizens do not become full-fledged law enforcement, as they are still only permitted and not required to aid others, but they are given a permission to stay by SYG laws. My claim is not that the SYG laws are deputizing citizens as cops. The claim is that SYG laws give citizens some police-like rights. But, if SYG rules effectively turn citizens into law enforcement, then we have two separate questions to ask: (1) is law enforcement justified in acting in this manner, and (2) even if this is proper as a form of law enforcement, is "delegation" to citizens proper?

Delegation

Let me start with the delegation question. It is odd to think that if I give power to the state and then it gives it back to me, that the transaction is one of delegation. I may have just never given the power to the state in the first place. On the other hand, the power citizens hold is far more limited, so perhaps "giving back to citizens" is more appropriate than "reserving." Still, for our purposes, nothing turns on this conceptualization or even one's preferred theory of the state.

Doubtless many people would reject that we can or should turn citizens into law enforcement officials. It is rather commonplace to think that the state has a monopoly on force and that vigilantism is problematic (Robinson 2015, p. 406; Dsouza 2015, p. 729). Still, this worry may be overblown. After all, we have privatized many functions of the state, from schools to prisons. Nor can we truly say that this is "state-sanctioned vigilantism," as that is a contradiction in terms—once the state sanctions the conduct, the actor is no longer a vigilante. Moreover, just as police officers are still liable to ex post review of their behavior, so, too, a citizen who employs deadly force can be subject to later review. Hence, we are not placing citizens outside the law. Admittedly, there are statutes that come close to exempting SYG behavior from judicial oversight, but then the error is with the statute and not the underlying delegation of the use of force.

Whatever the theoretical *bona fides* of objections to "citizens turned police" may be, they are utterly out of sync with the actual law on the books. At least in the United States (where these SYG provisions exist), citizens have law enforcement powers. Specifically, little known "citizen's arrest" defenses authorize extraordinarily broad deployment of force by ordinary citizens. Take Florida:

> A private citizen does have the common law right to arrest a person who commits a felony in his presence, or to arrest a person where a felony has been committed, and where the arresting citizen has probable cause to believe, and does believe, the person arrested to be guilty. Even though there was time to obtain a warrant, a private citizen may make such arrest and justify his failure to obtain a warrant by proving the person arrested was actually guilty of the felony (Collins v. Florida).

Moreover, Joshua Dressler notes there is a broad minority rule for crime prevention under which private persons are permitted to use deadly force to stop the commission of any felony (Dressler 2009, p. 278). He notes "an undesirable anomaly: If a defendant kills an intended thief, she may avoid conviction if she claims the defense of crime prevention, but may be convicted of murder if she raises a defense-of-property claim" (Dressler 2009, p. 278).

That is, SYG laws may be, in practice, *redundant*. Citizens already have law enforcement powers. The difference, it appears, is that a citizen without an SYG statute must yell "You are under arrest!" as opposed to "Stop shooting at me or I will kill you!" Earlier, I suggested that justificatory intent may be part of the forfeiture conditions, and thus aggressors do not forfeit their rights to defenders who do not possess the appropriate intent or knowledge. Citizens probably do not intend to arrest that often, primarily because they do not know that this is even an option. Were the right to citizen's arrest more widely known, doubtless the citizens inclined to stand their ground would likewise avail themselves of it. The bottom line is that if someone is shooting at you in Florida, you are permitted to shoot him if necessary to effect an arrest, and when you are arresting, you are never required to retreat. Indeed, you can shoot the person in the back as he is running away if that is the only way to prevent his escape (Nelson v. Howell).

This chapter is not the place to work through the intricacies of the common law defense of the citizen's arrest. There are certainly differences between citizens and law enforcement—for instance, citizens are not bound by the Constitution (and thus their privilege is more permissive), but in many states they are required to get the facts right (and thus have a more restrictive rule than law enforcement's reliance on probable causes) (Griffin 2018). It is enough to state that concerns about delegation of law enforcement authority to citizens need to recognize that SYG laws operate against a background of broad citizen authorization to use force. Indeed, some historians claim that since the nineteenth century, private policing has been cooperative with, as opposed to responsive to a failure by, state law enforcement (Miller 2013).

Now, the fact that citizens have always had this power, that they have retained the power, or that the state has delegated that power does not mean that such a shift to citizens is theoretically justified under our best account of political philosophy. We might worry, as Robin West does, that this weakens civil society (West 2014, p. 200). Arthur Ripstein likewise believes that public officials are uniquely situated to speak on behalf of the public (Ripstein 2017, pp. 9–10). Defenders of SYG laws need to offer a political theory against our presumed backdrop that the state has a monopoly on violence, however mismatched that theory may be to the current laws permitting the use of force by citizens.

Why May the State Stand Its Ground?

But let's assume we think the state may delegate. What is it that the state is delegating? What seems intuitively clear is remarkably difficult to get a handle on. Imagine in our hypothetical world that Vera is a police officer. We now have the framework in which SYG laws exist. But why does Vera get to stand her ground?

The first answer seems to be that she is *defending herself*. But that can't be the answer because our inquiry is why she is permitted to kill rather than retreat. Or, to put the question another way, what values do officers promote by not running away?

Surprisingly, answering this is harder than it first appears. First, let's be clear this is not *punishment*. We are not authorizing the state to administer punishment through its police officers.

Second, it is hard to believe that this is about bringing the aggressor to trial. It hardly seems that making sure someone goes to trial is a good enough reason to kill him. Indeed, as the Supreme Court pointed out in *Tennessee v. Garner* this rationale is a bit self-defeating (Tennessee v. Garner). Moreover, the necessity of the state's laying hands on someone *now* to obtain a later trial appearance is questionable. Many instances of misdemeanor arrests could be replaced with summonses (Harmon 2016),[12] and concerns with unnecessary force also animate our concerns with holding someone in pretrial detention (Duff 2013).

Consider a third potential justification: *dangerousness*. If the cops leave, rather than shooting the aggressor, well, then, he might shoot someone else. It is a future, amorphous defense of others that is doing the work. Indeed, this potential defense of others is the rationale for *Tennessee v. Garner*'s blessing of using deadly force to "capture" certain kinds of fleeing felons (Leider 2018, pp. 982–83). What is curious about this, then, is how attenuated the justification for using force is compared to the value it is said to be protecting. With the no retreat rule, the reason why the police are permitted to stay and shoot is because of some inchoate threat that the aggressor does not currently pose. The cop is not shooting to save herself; she is shooting because standing her ground is a proxy for other values. Self-defense theorists may feel that they are losing their moorings. All of a sudden, liability for a particular threat is doing so little of the work in justifying the defensive harm. This seems like an unpalatable suggestion—cops can shoot you now because you might be dangerous later, even if you haven't formed the intention to commit any other crime.

To rescue this position, we might think that our intuitions are grounded in a substantial concern for Sangero's socio-legal order. If it is permissible for wrongdoers to require the state to stand down, then this truly allows wrongdoing to run rampant. It is ultimately and significantly to put our liberty at the mercy of those who would do us harm.

One might try to make this even more robust. Robert Leider claims that the "the community may resist only certain grave breaches of the community's laws that are tantamount to renouncing one's duty to be subject to the rule of law" (Leider 2018, p. 1013). And Malcolm Thorburn casts the state's use of criminal punishment, not as a useful means to reach an end, but rather "as conceptually required by the state's claim of practical authority itself" (Thorburn Forthcoming). The state's failure to retreat, then, may likewise be part and parcel of what it means to be a state that demands authority.

Ultimately, we need to give more thought to exactly how the state relates to its citizens and why it may stand its ground. And, different answers may present new and different challenges. Consider, for example, two further concerns for the "no duty to retreat" position as it applies to law enforcement and thus would apply to citizens. First, both future dangerousness and harm to the socio-legal order are empirically contingent harms. Sometimes the cops might be able to let someone go, and he'd show up for court later. And maybe society would not become undone for fear of "criminals on the loose" by the police running away on this occasion. If that is true for any given case, then from a fact-relative perspective, killing the criminal would be unnecessary for the interest protected. Our rule of no retreat for police thus occasionally exempts impermissible killings from punishment. As Adil Haque has noted in the law of war context, we need not think that we are permitting the behavior so much as simply creating an immunity from prosecution (Haque 2017, pp. 27–29). So, we create a criminal immunity because on average, we believe that the facts bear out that the police must act in most situations.

Second, at the time of this writing, the standard view of law enforcement is changing. The American Law Institute is putting forth police guidelines that require the police to de-escalate and avoid force. Officers are expected to create barriers, to seek cover, and to create time and distance (American Law Institute 2017, § 5.03 Comment (a)). Hence, SYG laws may find that their justification is being further undermined to the extent that we do not believe that even law enforcement should always stand its ground.

Hence, a defender of SYG laws needs to start with the question of why even the state may stand its ground. Once we have that answer worked out, the intricacies of whether the state may delegate its authority may become clearer. But maybe the answer is that not only should citizens retreat, but also the state should more frequently as well.[13]

NOTES

1. Trayvon Martin's death at the hands of George Zimmerman is often thought to be an example of this. There are two problems, however. If Zimmerman's story is true (that Martin was on top of him prior to the moment Zimmerman used deadly force), he could not have safely retreated. Second, and more importantly, the real problem was the failure to give an initial aggressor/provocateur instruction, partly because Florida improperly conflates provocateurs with initial aggressors (Burke 2013; Ferzan 2013). For a general critique that the focus on SYG laws as the problem with the Zimmerman case is a distraction from more significant racial bias in the criminal justice system, see Gruber (2014).

2. Compare Flanders (2017) with an ecumenical approach that "no retreat" factors into the reasonableness of the defender's belief, such that the import of these provisions is that it creates a jury question.

3. Some theorists would introduce new terminology beyond just justification and excuse. For instance, Antony Duff proposes that a reasonable belief leads to "warranted" conduct (Duff 2007, pp. 271–77).

4. Another way out of this thicket is to think that the reasons that support an action need not be the reasons the defender intends. That is, an action might be defensively unnecessary but justified as punishment. I am sympathetic to this mixing and matching and plan to pursue this question in future work.

5. It is true that there may always be some probability that the defensive mechanism will fail. For instance, Vera may worry that she will be momentarily hoarse when she yells "Boo!" But this insight only leads us to some sort of reasonable belief requirement or probability threshold. It would not justify the outright abandonment of necessity, and that is the question we are considering. The question is whether if Vera believes that her mechanism *will be successful*, she is nevertheless entitled to engage in an action she believes to be unnecessary. No one thinks the King Arthur should kill the Black Knight after Arthur has removed both of the Knight's arms and both of his legs.

6. I thank Jae Lee and Steve Smith for pressing me on this point and Arthur Ripstein for our follow-up conversation.

7. There is a connection between proportionality and necessity that I am simplifying for our purposes here. For discussions of the interconnection, see Ferzan (2016).

8. Use of deadly force in one's dwelling is more complicated, as burglaries, where someone enters your home to commit some sort of felony, are more likely to invoke fear of serious bodily harm, and the statute may reflect a rulified reasonable belief standard.

9. Although I have cast Hurd's attack as on proportionality (as she does), the sorts of arguments she makes would vindicate the approach at the beginning of this section—namely, that one need not cede a space one lawfully occupies and thus the necessity condition does not require one to do so.

10. This is the moistening of one's finger with one's own saliva and the inserting of one's finger into another's ear canal.

11. Larry Alexander presents this as a puzzle of when the duty to retreat arises (Alexander 1999, p. 1480).

12. And, as Rachel Harmon has pointed out, arresting someone has costs: the concomitant fear and humiliation, the opportunities for friction between police and suspects, not to mention the lost opportunity costs for the arrestee while detained (Harmon 2016, pp. 313–316).

13. For comments on this chapter, I thank Larry Alexander, Alli Herzog, Jae Lee, Ken Simons, and Alec Walen. I also thank the participants in the Toronto Legal Theory workshop. I thank Karl Lockhart and Emily Walpole for excellent research assistance.

References

Florida Statutes Annotated § 776.012(2) (2014).

Collins v. State, 143 So.2d 700 (Fl. Ct. App. 1962).

Nelson v. Howell, 455 So.2d 608 (Fl. Ct. App. 1984).

Tennessee v. Garner, 471 U.S. 1 (1985).

Alexander, Larry. 1999. A unified excuse of preemptive self-protection. *Notre Dame Law Review* 74: 1475–1505.

Alexander, Larry, and Kimberly Kessler Ferzan. 2018. *Reflections on crime and culpability: Problems and puzzles*. Cambridge: Cambridge University Press.

American Law Institute. 2017. *Principles of the law policing*. Tentative Draft No. 1, February 27.

Berman, Mitchell N. 2003. Justification and excuse, law and morality. *Duke Law Journal* 53: 1–77.

Bronsther, Jacob. 2018. Two theories of deterrent punishment. *Tulsa Law Review* 53: 461–495.

Brown, Richard Maxwell. 1991. *No duty to retreat: Violence and values in American history and society*. New York/Oxford: Oxford University Press.

Burke, Alafair. 2013. What you may not know about the Zimmerman verdict. The evolution of a jury instruction. *Huffington Post*, September 14. https://www.huffingtonpost.com/alafair-burke/george-zimmerman-jury-instructions_b_3596685.html. Accessed 1 Aug 2018.

Dressler, Joshua. 2009. *Understanding criminal law*. 5th ed. Newark: Matthew Bender.

Dsouza, Mark. 2015. Retreat, submission, and the private use of force. *Oxford Journal of Legal Studies* 35: 727–753.

Duff, R.A. 2007. *Answering for crime*. Oxford: Hart.

———. 2013. Pre-trial detention and the presumption of innocence. In *Prevention and the limits of the criminal law*, ed. Andrew Ashworth, Lucia Zedner, and Patrick Tomlin, 115–132. Oxford: Oxford University Press.

Ferzan, Kimberly Kessler. 2005. Justifying self-defense. *Law and Philosophy* 24: 711–749.

———. 2012. Culpable aggression: The basis for moral liability to defensive killing. *Ohio State Journal of Criminal Law* 9: 669–698.

———. 2013. Provocateurs. *Criminal Law and Philosophy* 7: 597–622.

———. 2016. Forfeiture and self-defense. In *The ethics of self-defense*, ed. Christian Coons and Michael Weber, 233–253. New York: Oxford University Press.

———. 2017. The bluff: The power of insincere actions. *Legal Theory* 23: 168–202.

———. 2018a. Defending honor and beyond: Reconsidering the relationship between seemingly futile defense and permissible harming. *Journal of Moral Philosophy* 15: 683–705.

———. 2018b. Defense and desert: When reasons don't share. *University of San Diego Law Review* 55: 265–289.

Firth, Joanna Mary, and Jonathan Quong. 2012. Necessity, moral liability, and defensive harm. *Law and Philosophy* 31: 673–701.

Flanders, Chad. 2017. Interpreting the new stand your ground rule. *Journal of the Missouri Bar* 73 (1): 20–23.

Fletcher, George P., and Jens David Ohlin. 2008. *Defending humanity: When force is justified and why*. New York: Oxford University Press.

Franks, Mary Anne. 2014. Real men advance, real women retreat: Stand your ground, battered women's syndrome, and violence as male privilege. *University of Miami Law Review* 68: 1099–1128.

Frowe, Helen. 2014. *Defensive killing*. Oxford: Oxford University Press.

———. 2016. The role of necessity in liability to defensive harm. In *The ethics of self-defense*, ed. Christian Coons and Michael Weber, 152–170. New York: Oxford University Press.

Griffin, Thomas J. 2018. Private person's authority, in making arrest for felony, to shoot or kill alleged felon. In *American Law Reports Third*, ed. Thomson West, vol. 32. Eagan: Thomson West.

Gruber, Aya. 2014. Race to incarcerate: Punitive impulse and the bid to repeal stand your ground. *University of Miami Law Review* 68: 961–1023.

Haque, Adil Ahmad. 2017. *Law and morality at war*. Oxford: Oxford University Press.

Harmon, Rachel. 2016. Why arrest? *Michigan Law Review* 115: 307–364.

Hurd, Heidi M. 2016. Stand your ground. In *The ethics of self-defense*, ed. Christian Coons and Michael Weber, 254–273. New York: Oxford University Press.

Kamm, F.M. 2014. Self-defense, resistance and suicide: The Taliban women. In *How we fight: Ethics in war*, ed. Helen Frowe and Gerald Lang, 75–86. Oxford: Oxford University Press.

Kremnitzer, Mordechai, and Khalid Ghanayim. 2004. Proportionality and the aggressor's culpability in self-defense. *Tulsa Law Review* 39: 875–899.

Kuhns, Alicia M. 2017. Why Maryland should stand its ground instead of retreat. *University of Baltimore Legal Forum* 48: 17–33.

Lave, Tamara Rice. 2013. Shoot to kill: A critical look at stand your ground laws. *University of Miami Law Review* 67: 827–860.

Leider, Robert. 2018. Taming self-defense: Using deadly force to prevent escapes. *Florida Law Review* 70: 971–1017.

Lerner, Renee Lettow. 2006. The worldwide popular revolt against proportionality in self-defense law. *Journal of Law, Economics and Policy* 2: 331–364.

McCellan, Chandler B, and Tekin, Erdal. 2012. *Stand your ground laws and homicides.* IZA Discussion Paper No. 6705. Available at https://ssrn.com/abstract=2114885. Accessed 1 Aug 2018.

McMahan, Jeff. 2005a. The basis of moral liability to defensive killing. *Philosophical Issues* 15 (1): 386–405.

———. 2005b. Just cause for war. *Ethics and International Affairs* 19: 1–21.

———. 2009. *Killing in war.* Oxford: Oxford University Press.

———. 2016. The limits of self-defense. In *The ethics of self-defense*, ed. Christian Coons and Michael Weber, 185–210. New York: Oxford University Press.

Miller, Wilbur R. 2013. A state within "the states": Private policing and delegation of power. *Crime, History & Societies* 17 (2): 125–135.

Øverland, Gerhard. 2010. Conditional threats. *Journal of Moral Philosophy* 7: 334–345.

Parfit, Derek. 2011. *On what matters.* Vol. 1. Oxford: Oxford University Press.

Quong, Jonathan. 2009. Killing in self-defense. *Ethics* 119: 507–537.

———. 2015. Proportionality, liability, and defensive harm. *Philosophy and Public Affairs* 43: 144–173.

———. Forthcoming. *The morality of defensive force.* Oxford: Oxford University Press.

Ripstein, Arthur. 2017. Reclaiming proportionality (society for applied philosophy annual lecture 2016). *Journal of Applied Philosophy* 34: 1–18.

Robinson, Paul H. 2015. The moral vigilante and her cousins in the shadows. *University of Illinois Law Review* 2015: 401–478.

Sangero, Boaz. 2006. *Self-defence in criminal law.* Oxford/Portland: Hart.

Thomson, Judith Jarvis. 1986. Self-defense and rights. In *Rights, restitution, and risks: Essays in moral theory*, ed. William Parent, 33–48. Cambridge, MA: Harvard University Press.

Thorburn, Malcolm. Forthcoming. Criminal punishment and the right to rule. *University of Toronto Law Journal.*

Uniacke, Suzanne. 2011. Proportionality and self-defense. *Law and Philosophy* 30: 253–272.

Walen, Alec, and David Wasserman. 2012. Agents, impartiality, and the priority of claims over duties; diagnosing why Thomson still gets the trolley problem wrong by appeal to the "mechanics of claims." *Journal of Moral Philosophy* 9: 545–571.

Ward, Cynthia V. 2015. Stand your ground and self-defense. *American Journal of Criminal Law* 42: 89–138.

Wellman, Christopher Heath. 2017. *Rights forfeiture and punishment.* New York: Oxford University Press.

West, Robin. 2014. A tale of two rights. *Boston University Law Review* 94: 893–912.

PART XXX

Targeted Killing

CHAPTER 32

Targeted Killing and the Criminal Law

Alec Walen

Introduction

"Targeted killing" can be defined as the deliberate killing, by state agents, of individuals who are considered a threat and who do not have the legal privilege to engage in combat.[1] This definition distinguishes it from the act of killing enemy combatants in a traditional battle between opposing forces that are each legally privileged to use lethal force on the other.[2] Targeted killing is normally carried out by states that are in an armed conflict with a non-state actor (NSA) when they decide to deal with that NSA at least in part by seeking to kill a sufficient number of its members and supporters to disable the group.[3]

The obvious ethical problem with targeted killing is that if the killings are not justified, then they are state-directed murder.[4] For these killings to be morally justified, one has to appeal to the idea of self-defense, broadly construed to include other-defense.[5] Thus, the discussion that follows will be largely a discussion of issues in the theory of self-defense.

I set the stage for what follows with a quick survey of two legal issues: (a) the legal authority of a state to engage in targeted killing of suspected members of an NSA if acting without the consent of the state in which the NSAs reside and (b) the significance within the law of armed conflict (LOAC) of the targets functioning as unprivileged enemy combatants. Then I turn to five normative questions. First, what role does forfeiture of the right not to be killed play in justifying targeted killing? Second, may a target be killed simply because of the threat he poses? Third, what does it take for targeted killing to be a necessary

A. Walen (✉)
Rutgers University, New Brunswick, NJ, USA
e-mail: awalen@rutgers.edu

L. Alexander, K. K. Ferzan (eds.), *The Palgrave Handbook of Applied Ethics and the Criminal Law*, https://doi.org/10.1007/978-3-030-22811-8_32

and proportionate response? Fourth, what level of proof must a state agent have that a person really is targetable before she targets him? Finally, what special problems arise when the person targeted is one of many who could equally well have been targeted?[6]

Two Legal Issues

The Legal Right to Use Military Force Against Non-state Actors

Targeted killing is the exercise of a form of military force, and thus, it is fitting to inquire, first, into the use of military force under the LOAC. The legal right to use military force, as established by the Charter of the United Nations, is highly limited. Except under two conditions, military force may not be used "against the territorial integrity or political independence of any state, or in any other manner inconsistent with the Purposes of the United Nations" (Article 2, ¶4). The first exception arises when the Security Council authorizes its use "to maintain or restore international peace and security" (Article 42); the second permits a state to exercise "the inherent right of individual or collective self-defence if an armed attack occurs against a Member of the United Nations, until the Security Council has taken measures necessary to maintain international peace and security" (Article 51).

It is generally agreed that strikes by NSAs can constitute an armed attack; if such an attack were coming from another state, the state that was attacked would have a right to use military force in self-defense under the second exception (Martin 2012, pp. 235–236). But scholars disagree about whether that implies that a state that is attacked by an NSA has a right to use military force in self-defense. To see what is at stake in this dispute, suppose that NSA X maintains a base of operation in country A and launches an attack on country B from that base. If X was sent on its mission "by or one behalf of" A, or if A had a "substantial involvement" in the attack, then B may use self-defense against A.[7] If, however, A was less directly and positively involved in the attack, then disagreement arises. In favor of the right to use force in response, Yoram Dinstein argues:

> The armed bands or terrorists in [A] are not cloaked with a mantle of protection from [B]... Should [A] not grant its consent to [an offer from B] to send military forces into [A's] territory, in order to eliminate the terrorist threat, [A] must be prepared to bear certain unpleasant consequences... [B] may ... dispatch military units into [A's] territory, in order to destroy the bases of the hostile armed bands or terrorists... Although acting beyond the limits of [A's] consent, [B]—in taking these measures—does what [A] itself should have done, had it possessed the means and disposition to perform its duty. (Dinstein 2005, p. 245)

Against this line of reasoning, Craig Martin argues that:

The modern *jus ad bellum* regime is not primarily grounded in [providing remedies for wrongs], or even in a sense of justice, but rather is founded on the profound need to *prevent war* among states. Permitting the use of force against states that have not assisted terrorists acting from within their territory would create a different and far more serious asymmetry, which would … increase the risk of armed conflict among nations. (Martin 2012, p. 242)

I do not propose to try to resolve that conflict, only to highlight it. Nonetheless, in what follows, I will assume that Dinstein is correct and that states have the legal and the moral right to use military force against NSAs in the territory of another state, even without that state's consent, provided that doing so is *otherwise* legally and morally justifiable.

Before moving on, I note that if B has A's consent to attack X on A's territory, then the issue of international armed conflict drops out. The case is then like one in which A uses military force against X within its own territory: the criminal law governing murder and assassination will still be relevant.[8]

Justification by Appeal to Combatant Status

The legal justification for targeted killing, at least in the United States, is that the targets, while not legally entitled to act as combatants, function as combatants and therefore lose their immunity to being killed.[9] This conforms to the LOAC, which allows civilians to be targeted like combatants "for such time as they take a direct part in hostilities" (International Committee of the Red Cross, Rule 6 of Customary International Humanitarian Law). The primary questions, from a legal point of view, are what sort of temporal limit is implied by the "for such time" clause and what does it mean to take "direct part" in hostilities.

This is not the place to engage in a detailed discussion of the views of legal authorities on these questions. But I will offer two cases that allow us to pursue the moral issues in greater depth.

NSA Bomb Maker. X is a bomb maker for an NSA. His bombs have killed citizens of country A, and he is actively working on designing and building new bombs for the NSA.

Civilian Chemist. Y is a chemist working on explosives in country B. She is aware that her work could help people like X, but she does not know that X has actually relied on her work to make better bombs for the NSA.

Legal authorities are split on whether X is taking direct part in the hostilities of the NSA. According to the International Committee of the Red Cross (ICRC), someone whose role is the "design, production [or] shipment of weapons" does not take direct part in hostilities (Melzer 2009, p. 46). But according to the Israeli Supreme Court, "a person who … provides service to [weapons]" takes direct part in hostilities (Public Committee against Torture in Israel, ¶35).

Arguably, a person who designs weapons takes as direct a role in hostilities as someone who services them. And the United States, by its actions—see, for example, the killing, on January 1, 2019, of Jamal al-Badawi, a bomb maker involved in the bombing of the USS Cole in 2000[10]—seems to agree with this last opinion.[11]

Interestingly, no legal authorities take the civilian chemist to be taking direct part in hostilities. Thus, the consensus is that targeting the civilian chemist for killing would violate the LOAC.[12] But it is worth asking whether this reflects a deep moral point about who may be targeted for killing or a prudential legal point to the effect that it is best to limit those who may legally be targeted for killing to those who are *directly* involved in hostilities because otherwise states will abuse the legal license to kill. In what follows, I will argue that the latter is the more plausible moral position. This implies that the empirical matters that govern prudential reasoning might be legitimately reexamined by those interested in modifying the law.

TARGETING AND FORFEITURE

The idea that enemy combatants may be targeted for killing turns on the idea that by becoming combatants they forfeit the right not to be killed. A person forfeits a right by conduct that is inconsistent with retaining it. She need not intend to forfeit a right to do so; in that way, forfeiture is unlike a revocable waiver (e.g., A invites B into her house) or a permanent alienation (e.g., A sells X to B).[13] A paradigmatic example is criminal activity, by which a person forfeits the right not to be punished.[14] Having forfeited that right, treatment (e.g., imprisonment) that would otherwise have wronged her does not wrong her.

The implications of forfeiture include an effect on proportionality. It is commonly thought that it would be proportionate to kill any number of culpable aggressors if doing so is necessary to save the life of an innocent victim. This reflects how little their lives weigh, once they have forfeited their right not to be killed, against the lives of innocent victims in a proportionality analysis.

Forfeiture should not, however, be equated with an absolute loss of rights. It should not be thought of as the equivalent of general exile from the moral community (*see* Ferzan 2016, pp. 245–246). Nor should it be thought irrevocable; an aggressor who ceases to aggress may not be intentionally killed unless his past aggression warrants the death penalty, which many think it never does. Indeed, the right is best thought of as incompletely lost; even a fully culpable aggressor retains a residual right not to be killed for the sake of defending a trivial interest.[15] Moreover, not all of those who forfeit their right to life do so to the same extent as culpable aggressors do.

This last thought brings up a source of disagreement among moral theorists. Some think that merely responsibly choosing to put someone else at risk, even if the choice was perfectly reasonable, can result in forfeiture of the right not to be killed, at least if killing is necessary to protect a proportionate good (*see*, e.g., McMahan 2009, pp. 162–167; Otsuka 1994). Others think that a threat has to engage in at least negligent action to forfeit her right not to be killed (*see*, e.g., Frowe 2014). Others think she has to act with some subjective awareness that she poses a threat that, as a matter of fact, she has no right to pose (*see*, e.g., Ferzan 2012).

In my opinion, this dispute rests on the mistaken idea that there is something called the right to life that must be either forfeited or not. The better view, I think, is that forfeiture comes in degrees. As with criminal law, where the right not to be punished is forfeited to a greater extent the greater one's criminal culpability, so in the case of the right to life, it is forfeited to a greater extent the more one is not only responsible but culpable for having posed a threat that one had no right to pose. The measure of the extent of forfeiture is captured in the way the proportionality analysis weighs the claims of threats not to be killed against the claims of victims to be saved.

Nonetheless, we can see that all three positions on forfeiture would entail that X, the bomb maker, forfeits his right not to be killed, at least if capture is not a relatively promising and low-cost alternative. The question is: how would these theories handle the case of Y, the civilian chemist? There, the different views of forfeiture seem to have different implications. But I also think it is a mistake to treat forfeiture as the key to understanding the permissibility of targeted killing in that case. Focusing exclusively on forfeiture overlooks the way in which a person's claim not to be killed is weakened simply in virtue of contributing to a threat to others when she does something that she has no right to do (*see* Walen 2019).

Threatening and Weakened Claims Not to Be Killed

To explain how merely being a threat can weaken a person's claim not to be killed, I need to introduce a model for talking about rights that I call the *mechanics of claims* (*see* ibid., ch. 3). According to the mechanics of claims, rights are best understood as resulting from a balance of claims that patients make on agents—patients are people affected by the choices of agents—taking into account as well the strength of the claims agents have not to have to act in accordance with the balance of patient claims on them. Claims, in this way of thinking, are pro-tanto rights; they have a normative force that pushes to establish a right in the final analysis.

One central feature of the mechanics of claims is the idea that the strength of patient claims reflects not just the weight of the interest at stake, and not just whether the person has waived or forfeited a claim that he otherwise would have had, but also the way the person is causally connected to others. A patient's claim not to be killed is strongest if he would die as a result of being used as a means of saving others; its strength is weaker, a small multiple (people's intuitions vary on how small) of competing claims to be saved, if he would be killed as a side effect of saving those others. And a threat's claim not to be killed, I argue, is roughly on a par with that of the victims she threatens if she innocently, through no fault of her own, happens to pose a lethal threat to them (*see* ibid., ch. 6–7).

The idea that a threat's claim not to be killed is weaker than the claim a bystander would have not to be killed as a side effect of pursuing some good end reflects the idea that threats have to take some moral responsibility for the fact that they threaten. Even if they have done nothing by which to forfeit their right not to be killed, they still have to take moral ownership of the fact that they are a threat to others. If they have a right to do what threatens others—assuming that they are not in a situation in which competition is morally justified—then they have a right not to be killed to prevent the threat they pose from materializing.[16] But when the agent has no right to threaten, she should take pains to avoid being a threat. And even if she cannot prevent herself from being a threat—if, for example, she is hurtling out of control toward others—she should still accept that her claims not to be harmed are even weaker than the claims of an innocent bystander. Innocent bystanders have no special connection to the welfare of others, except insofar as their presence with claims not to be killed might present a moral obstacle to an agent who might otherwise try to save the others.[17] But a threat who lacks the right to threaten takes on a greater burden and her claim not to be killed is, therefore, correspondingly weaker.

I am agnostic about whether innocent threats, who are not responsible for threatening others, have claims that are weaker or stronger than those of the innocent victims they threaten. If they are weaker, then they may be targeted for killing if doing so is necessary to save their victims—assuming nothing else blocks their being targeted. If they are stronger, then they may not be targeted for killing unless they threaten a larger number of victims. But either way, the mere fact that the civilian chemist is a threat could, in principle, justify targeting her for killing if that was necessary to save a larger number of people from death.

This is just a quick sketch of the view that I defend at length elsewhere. I ignore here complications such as the fact that the civilian chemist does not threaten directly, but only through the actions of others, and that we cannot even assume that she shares their goals or in any way acts in joint agency with them (see ibid., ch. 7). I also ignore here the argument that war is a realm of competition, which would justify targeting people even if they have the right to do what they do (see ibid., ch. 8, § 4). Here, I want to highlight instead a topic that I did not address as well elsewhere, namely the possible interaction between the idea that threats have weaker claims not to be killed simply in virtue of posing threats without the right to do so and forfeiture.

Being a threat who lacks the right to threaten sets a baseline weakening of the claim not to be killed; responsible choice that foreseeably leads one to become such a threat and culpable choice to become such a threat constitute bases for forfeiture that further weaken that claim.[18] Those who responsibly chose to risk imposing threats on others, but who did nothing wrong in doing so, should be taken to have forfeited only a little of the strength of their baseline claim not to be targeted. If an innocent threat has a claim that is roughly on a par with an innocent victim, a person who responsibly chose to risk the welfare of others would have a claim slightly weaker than her potential victim. Insofar as her choice was negligent, her claim would be weaker, and insofar as it was more culpable, it would be weaker still. A malicious, intentional aggressor would have maximally forfeited her claim. But again, this notion of forfeiture builds on a fundamental loss of claim strength that comes from merely being a threat who lacks the right to threaten.

NECESSITY AND PROPORTIONALITY

I have asserted that forfeiture affects the proportionality balance that is relevant to determining when targeted killing is permissible. In this section, I want to say a bit more about proportionality by explaining how it is linked to the concept of necessity and by distinguishing two concepts of proportionality. I also examine the idea that a threat must be imminent before it is permissible to use lethal force to stop it.

Necessity and Comparative Proportionality

Necessity prohibits causing more harm than necessary to achieve some particular good. Proportionality prohibits causing harm that is too large, given the good that would be achieved.[19] These seem like separate considerations: the former compares different options for achieving a good, while the latter seems to focus on weighing the effects of a single option. But in the end, I believe they are just different ways of looking at the same basic commitment to comparative proportionality (*see* Hurka 2005).

I start with necessity. In the context of targeted killing, it holds that it is impermissible to kill a threat if there is some alternative way of protecting the threat's potential victims that promises to be equally effective, would cost the defenders no more, would cause no extra harm to bystanders, and would harm the threat less. For example, suppose the government gets word on where X, the bomb maker is living. Further, suppose it then has two options for neutralizing his threat: send commandoes in to kill him or direct the local authorities, with whom they are cooperating, to arrest him. If both would be equally effective, and neither would expose the actors to more risk or cost more effort, and neither would expose bystanders to more harm, then simply killing him would be unnecessarily harmful and therefore impermissible. Necessity would require that he be arrested.

The problem with appealing to necessity is that it so rarely is the case that an act is, strictly speaking, unnecessarily harmful. This problem arises because the necessity test is very much like a Pareto superiority test, substituting claims of types of individuals (e.g., actor or bystander) for claims of individuals.[20] To see the problem, consider again killing X, the bomb maker. Suppose that arresting X would expose the actors to more risk of getting injured or captured than sending in commandos to kill him. Then we cannot say that killing him is unnecessarily harmful. Rather, it trades off harm to X for safety for the agents. That sort of trade-off is not ruled out by necessity.

Necessity, however, is a special case of a more general norm: comparative proportionality. Comparative proportionality compares the costs and benefits of different acts and asks whether the kind of trade-off just mentioned is justifiable. If the extra risk to the agents is very low, but the difference in outcomes to X is significant, then killing him might still be held to be comparatively disproportionate and, therefore, impermissible. Importantly, to make that calculation, one has to take into account the strength of the claims of the various kinds of parties. If we assume that X is a combatant who has maximally forfeited his right to life, then any appreciable extra risk to the agents would justify killing him rather than arresting him. But those are not the only parties involved. Suppose that killing X would expose bystanders to a substantial risk of harm. If they have done nothing to forfeit their claim not to be killed, then putting them at substantial risk of dying may be comparatively disproportional, given the option of arresting him instead. In that case, targeted killing may be impermissible.

What complicates the comparative proportionality analysis and gives rise to a focus on what seems to be a distinct notion of baseline proportionality—one that focuses on the balance of harm caused versus good achieved in a single act—is that agents often have the right to withdraw the option of putting themselves at risk from consideration. And this gives rise to the thought that the baseline against which an act must be assessed is one in which the agents do not act.

To appreciate this more concretely, suppose you, a private actor, find yourself with the options of arresting X, the bomb maker, killing him, or walking away. And suppose you realize that arresting him is a very risky endeavor. Suppose it would expose you to a 50% risk of death. You would be free to refuse that option. If you thought the risk of death if you tried to kill X were small enough to consider doing that, however, then you would naturally frame the choice as one in which you waive your right not to do that and simply consider the claims all the relevant patients have on you, claims to be helped and claims not to be harmed.[21] That is, you would determine whether the benefits of killing X outweigh the harms, taking both to be filtered through the nature of the claims on you (including both the causal role of those involved and whether anyone has forfeited some of the strength of those claims).

But while baseline proportionality seems to focus simply on the benefits and the harms of acting, in truth, it too is a comparative notion. It reflects the special case in which one of the options is some form of doing nothing. Of course, it is often not clear what "doing nothing" means.[22] Walking away may not have all the same effects as sitting still. Often the baseline really involves action: acting the way one normally acts. But then we need to know what it means to continue doing the same thing. In addition, sometimes the agent has a duty to act and thus does not have a right to withdraw certain options from consideration. Thus, a clearer conception of what is at stake in baseline proportionality is that it compares the options of acting against particular versions of not acting and asks whether acting is permissible.

Taking this back to the case of targeting X, the bomb maker, it may be straightforward that you, the private actor, may choose not to kill him. But if we assume that the collateral damage would be minimal, and that you waive your right not to act, it might be straightforward that killing him passes the test of baseline proportionality. But if you are a military agent, or someone commanding a military agent, you may have a duty to take on some risk for the sake of others (*see* McMahan 2014, pp. 134–135). In that case, you might not be free to take the option of arrest off the table, and the comparison between arrest and targeted killing might show that the latter is banned. Finally, if we shift now to Y, the civilian chemist, her less complete forfeiture of her claim not to be killed might make targeting her impermissible even while the targeting of X is permissible. This could be true even if you are a private actor who is considering only the less risky option of killing. These details matter.

Imminence or Necessity

Insofar as the targets of targeted killing are taken to be combatants, there is no legal need to determine if they pose an imminent threat. But insofar as we are looking for a deeper moral justification for targeted killing, one that rests on the right of self-defense, then there is a normative presumption that the threat must be imminent. In domestic criminal law, the general rule (at least in the United States) is that self-defense may be used only against imminent threats.[23] Likewise, for a state to have just cause to engage in self-defense against another state, the traditional doctrine has required that the threat from the other state must at least be imminent, if not already manifest in an attack (*see* Ferzan 2004, pp. 224–227). Using the imminence standard would present a major obstacle to targeted killing, however, as targeted killing is almost never used in a context in which the threat is imminent.

Consider the threat posed by X, the bomb maker. We are to assume that "he is actively working on designing and building new bombs for the NSA." It is highly unlikely that the government would know when he is just about to finish developing the design of a new bomb. But even if it did, one might argue that the threat is still not imminent until someone is about to deploy it. Insofar as we require the threat to be imminent death of innocent civilians, targeted killing of bomb makers would almost always be ruled out. But even if we allowed his threat to be imminent as soon as he is about to hand off the bomb to someone who would deploy it, it would still be practically impossible to wait until the last minute to target him.

The way around that problem is to realize that imminence is not a fundamental principle governing the permissible use of self-defense; it is a proxy for necessity (or, more accurately, comparative proportionality).[24] As David Rodin put it, the imminence requirement "is simply the application of the necessity requirement subject to epistemic limitations. The point is that we [normally] cannot know with the required degree of certainty that a defensive act is necessary until the infliction of harm is imminent" (Rodin 2002, p. 41; Robinson 1984, pp. 76–78). Imminence is important, in other words, because it reduces the risk that a killing will be unnecessary. But imminence is an imperfect, under-inclusive proxy[25]; it sometimes prohibits the use of self-defense when it is truly necessary. In the context of responding to the threat posed by X, waiting for the threat to be imminent is almost guaranteed to be waiting too long. In such cases, it is appropriate to look directly to necessity.

Importantly, switching from imminence to necessity is not without its costs. The imminence requirement helps to avoid the use of self-help that jumps the gun in terms of necessity and that imposes undue costs on others for the sake of extra security for the defender. Given that imminence is impractical in the context in which targeted killing is up for consideration, some alternative means of avoiding unnecessary killings should be developed. As Andrew Altman observed:

> The number of civilian deaths from drone strikes, particularly over the period 2009–13, makes it difficult to believe that the policy has adequately weighed the harm done to non-US citizens. Instead, US policy appears to have shifted the risks of dealing with al Qaeda to the shoulders of the citizens of other states, with little regard for the interests of those citizens. (Altman 2017, p. 162)

The political pressure to do this is strong. Citizens of other states don't vote in US elections, so US politicians have a strong incentive to save US lives with little concern for the welfare of "aliens." But justice is a stricter master than politics. To do justice, the law must seek to overcome the natural biases that tempt us all. The most obvious way to do so is to put a thumb on the scale in favor of the parties most likely to be the victims of bias: those who are suspected of being members or supporters of NSAs that threaten "us" and bystanders who might be killed along with the targets and who are not part of "us." As noted above, tests like imminence seem to be too rigid. But laws requiring a clear accounting of the basis for the threat assessment (both the evidence that someone is a threat and the magnitude of the threat she poses), of the expected collateral damage caused by targeted killing, and of the risks involved in capture attempts— all to be spelled out to a neutral agency or judge—would be a start. And another helpful move would be requiring an elevated standard of proof—a topic to which I turn now.

Standard of Proof

Ultimately, the justification for targeted killing depends on a number of factors: is the potential target a threat who has no right to threaten? Did she forfeit her claim not to be killed and, if so, how complete was that forfeiture? What alternatives are there to killing her and how effective and how costly might these alternatives be? Uncertainty will infect the assessment of all of these factors. And this raises the question: how certain must one be before one may judge that the targeted killing of a particular person is permissible?

The joke was told in the US State Department, early in the Obama era, that when the Central Intelligence Agency in places like Pakistan or Yemen "sees 'three guys doing jumping jacks,' the agency thinks it is a terrorist training camp" and thinks it is entitled to kill them (Becker and Shane 2012). Granted, this was just a joke. But lest the truest thing be said in jest, it is important that all countries and agencies take the matter of meeting the relevant standard of proof (SOP) very seriously.

Unfortunately, theorizing about what the right SOP should be is a highly underdeveloped area of the law. Even in the context of the criminal law's proof beyond a reasonable doubt standard, the arguments about what it means and why we should use it are far from settled (Yaffe this volume; Walen 2015). In this brief discussion here, I want merely to identify and briefly comment on three fundamentally different ways of approaching the topic and then to suggest how to develop the third.

The first idea is the one with which I ended the previous section, that we should put a thumb on the scales to counter the potential for bias.[26] This presupposes, however, that one knows three things: (a) what the SOP should be if there were no bias, (b) how strong the bias is likely to be in general, and (c) what contextual factors affect the bias in particular cases. I will not try to say anything further about these last two points here; I turn instead to the two strategies one might employ to set the SOP if one were not concerned with bias: a pure consequentialist strategy and a deontologically inflected strategy.

Both strategies start with the same basic thought, namely that the SOP should reflect the values in play. Here is a simple way of putting that point. We should pick a standard so that the expected value of a targeted killing, V_{TK}, is the same as the expected value of refraining from targeted killing, V_{-TK}. That allows us to say that we should have neither more of them nor less of them; we've found the sweet spot.

If we represent V_{TK} as a function of the value of targeted killing when performing it is permissible (a true positive or TP), plus the value (negative value) of performing it when it is impermissible (a false positive or FP), and represent the probability of a TP as P and that of an FP as $1-P$, we get[27]:

$$V_{TK} = P * TP + (1 - P) * FP \qquad (1)$$

Doing the same for V_{-TK} (where FN represents a false negative, TN represents a true negative, and recognizing that a negative is as likely to be false, in a given case, as a positive is to be true, and that a negative is as likely to be true as a positive is to be false), we get:

$$V_{\sim TK} = P * FN + (1 - P) * TN \qquad (2)$$

Setting these two equal to each other, and making the simplifying assumption that whatever value there is in targeted killing when it is permissible is what is lost when it is not carried out (so TP = −FN), and that whatever disvalue there is in targeted killing when it is impermissible is lost when one refrains (so − FP = TN), we can derive the following formula for P or the desired standard of proof:

$$P = 1 / [1 - TP / FP] \qquad (3)$$

This involves, fundamentally, the ratio between the value of a permissible targeted killing and the disvalue of an impermissible targeted killing. We can test this out with three simple cases. All use the simplifying assumption that we value all innocent lives the same and give no value to the loss of life of a person who can permissibly be killed. This last assumption is false and I will revisit it; I use it here just to illustrate the math.

In the first case, we assume that a TP will save one innocent life, and that an FP will cost one innocent life. The ratio of TP/FP = −1. P then is ½ or 50%.

In the second case, we assume that a TP will save two innocent lives, but an FP will cost one innocent life. The ratio of TP/FP = −2. P then is 1/3 or 33%.

In the third case, we assume that targeted killing will cost the life of one innocent bystander, but a TP will save two lives, for a net saving of one innocent life; an FP will involve the loss of two innocent lives. The ratio of TP/FP is −½. P is then 1/1.5 or 67%.

The general lesson is that P goes down, and could go arbitrarily low, as the expected benefits of a justified act of targeted killing go up relative to the expected harms of an unjustified targeted killing, while P goes up, and could go arbitrarily high, as the expected harms of an act of unjustified targeted killing go up relative to the expected benefits of a justified act of targeted killing. If one is a straightforward consequentialist, this may seem to be a perfectly plausible position.

For a deontologist, however, this is worrisome. To make it clear why, suppose we have the chance to kill X, who we think is the bomb maker. If X is who we think he is, then we can stipulate that the expected value of killing him before he kills is 100 saved lives; if he is not who we think he is, then we kill an innocent person.[28] According to this formula, if we are even 1% confident that X is who we think he is, we should feel free to kill him. To a deontologist, this seems crazy.

The question is: what resources are there in deontology to resist this calculation? Adil Haque, citing my work on proof beyond a reasonable doubt, writes "we must first establish a person's liability [forfeiture of his right not to be killed] by sufficient evidence before considering the consequences of killing her" (Haque 2017, p. 121). He suggests that "the appropriate standard … is belief based on decisive epistemic reasons" (ibid.). Unfortunately, that suggestion ducks the question: how strong do reasons have to be to be epistemically decisive (*see* Ferzan 2019)? Moreover, it misses the point I made in the context of my discussion of proof beyond a reasonable doubt, namely that a balance is still called for, even if *some* effects have to be screened off from the balance of considerations that go into the relevant standard of proof.

I suggest that a more ethically sound answer would build on my argument regarding proof beyond a reasonable doubt.[29] With regard to the criminal standard, I argue that we cannot allow the value of a conviction and punishment *if a defendant is guilty* to set the standard of proof for determining *whether* he is guilty. A proper determination of guilt is a precondition for conviction and punishment and for reaping any value from doing so. If we allow the value of punishment in cases in which it would be highly valuable to convict and punish the guilty to set the SOP, then we would do an end around the SOP as a standard for determining *whether* a person is guilty. The same thought has to apply to targeted killing. In targeted killing cases, we should not allow the SOP for determining whether a potential threat may be killed to be lower simply because there would be a lot of value in killing him *if he has lost his right not to be killed*.

Still, we need to find the relevant values to balance to set the SOP. In criminal law, I suggest it's the abstract value of doing retributive justice, which weighs reasonably lightly against the concrete disvalue of the injustice of punishing the innocent. The result is a high burden of proof. In targeted killing, I suggest that the balance reflects the value of saving people from unjust attack *if* the threat lacks the right not to be killed and the value of preventing a person from being unjustly targeted if he retains his right not to be killed. Those are *types* of values, and should be weighed as such; they should not take into account the numbers of people who are expected to be saved or killed; otherwise, we are thrust back into pure consequentialist weighing.

Here is how I see that working out. If we assume the target has fully forfeited his claim not to be killed in the event of a TP, then the values of a TP and an FP will be roughly on a par and the SOP for such a case should be around 50%. If, however, we are considering a case in which the target, even if a threat, has not forfeited his claim not to be killed, then the value of a TP will be relatively low compared to an FP and the SOP will have to be high, near certainty. Other factors could affect the SOP as well. Suppose the threat is potentially threatening not to kill but to beat badly, but that defensive force would be effective only if it aimed to be lethal. Then one would want a higher SOP for using it. Conversely, if nonlethal but damaging force could be used to neutralize a lethal threat, then a lower SOP could be used.[30] And insofar as we are worried about bias against possible targets, then the SOP should be raised accordingly.

THE PROBLEM OF SELECTING AMONG POSSIBLE TARGETS

In this final section, I want to address an intuitive discomfort that arises in cases in which someone is picked out for targeted killing from a group of people who all may justifiably be killed (*see* Waldron Unpublished). This problem could arise in cases in which multiple people are engaged in an activity that makes them a legitimate target for killing. But the problem arises with particular acuity if the target is picked out not for what he is doing at the moment, but because he is taken to be a particular named person who is believed to be a threat.

To see the problem, consider the following case: you are a sniper and you've been told that there are enemy combatants operating out of a hotel 500 yards away. The enemy combatants all wear uniforms, so there is no question that anyone you might target is indeed an enemy combatant. But you are told that you are to kill only two of the ten operating out of the hotel: Smith and Jones, whose photos you have been given. There is something unnerving about this instruction. Why only Smith and Jones? Are they particularly significant because of some special knowledge or skill they possess? If so, that would seem to make the order reasonable. But there are other possibilities that are worrisome. Maybe they were picked out because of their race or religion—that would seem to be objectionable discrimination. Or maybe they had killed people on your side, but in a way that was perfectly legal under the LOAC—that would seem to be objectionably punitive. But suppose you ask your commanding officer and she says that they were picked out because she doesn't like the way they look—they remind her of an old boyfriend—and she thinks that shooting two of them will be enough to cause the others to abandon the hotel. That reason seems arbitrary, but it does not seem to be intrinsically objectionable in quite the same way the second and third reasons were. Yet there's still something problematic about it.

I suggest that the problem is that this is the kind of case in which a lottery is called for. As John Broome wrote, lotteries should be used to decide between people who "have roughly equal claims to [a] good [or harm] that is to be distributed" (Broome 1984, p. 628). Even if combatants have fully forfeited their right not to be killed, they still have a residual claim not to be killed unnecessarily. And I suggest they also have a claim not to be killed unfairly. If some subset of combatants is to be killed, then there must either be a good reason to pick one subset to target over the others, or, failing that, there should be a lottery. The caprice of a commanding officer is a poor substitute for a fair lottery.

But this should not give us general pause regarding cases in which a choice of targets has to be made. It should require only that those who choose have a good reason for targeting some and not others. And, insofar as there is a set of people who are all equally good targets, then some fair lottery should be run to decide which among them should be targeted.

CONCLUSION

If targeted killing is not legal, it is murder. Its legality should depend on whether it can be justified as an act of self-defense. That justification is easier to make, legally, if the targets have lost their legal immunity because they function as enemy combatants. But to rest the justification on more solid normative footing, five fundamental questions must be addressed: (1) Is the targeted person a threat who lacks the right to threaten? (2) Is the justification made easier because the targeted person has also forfeited some of her residual claim not to be killed? (3) Even if the answer to the first two questions is positive, is targeted killing a necessary and proportionate response? (4) Is the evidence in favor of targeted killing high enough to meet the relevant SOP? (5) And insofar as a person is selected for targeting from a larger group of possible targets, is the selection justifiable? The legal justifiability of targeted killing should aim to track, as much as problems of administrability and limiting unwanted effects allow, the answers to those moral questions.[31]

NOTES

1. Compare Craig Martin's definition: "the deliberate killing [by agents of a state] of specifically identified individuals who are not clearly combatants in an armed conflict under international law" (Martin 2012, p. 223, n.1).
2. The Additional Protocol (1) (1977) to the Geneva Conventions states that the combatant privilege is held by people "under a command responsible to that Party for the conduct of its subordinates… [which] shall enforce compliance with the rules of international law applicable in armed conflict" (Article 43, par 1). It is also requires combatants to "distinguish themselves from the civilian population while they are engaged in an attack or in a military operation preparatory to an attack" (Article 44, ¶3).
3. Another interesting problem concerns targeted killing that is justified as a deterrent. That brings up issues of terrorism, broadly understood. It is also core to most military action. As Seth Lazar writes: "Killing in war is always *pour encourager les autres*" (Lazar 2015, p. 71). I leave that issue to the side here but discuss it, at least in passing, in Walen (2019).
4. It may be rare that such murders would ever be prosecuted, but rare does not mean never. For example, if agents enter the territory of another country to carry out a targeted killing, they might be caught and prosecuted. *See* Altman (2017, p. 143) (referring to the risk faced by the Seal Team that killed Osama bin Laden). And even if prosecution is not a significant practical worry in most instances, states and their agents have moral reason to seek to avoid morally unjustifiable killings.
5. The law on self- and other-defense is basically the same. *See* the Model Penal Code, §§ 3.04 and 3.05. The ethics is sometimes thought to be different, because it is often thought that one is allowed to act in self-preferential ways but one is not, outside of certain special relationships, permitted to exercise preference for one over another. I argue against this idea of agent-centered prerogatives in Walen (2019, ch. 2, § 2.1.4).

6. One topic I will not address is the practical value or disvalue of targeted killing; it is an empirical matter on which I am not qualified to opine.

7. The quoted terms are laid out in UN General Assembly Resolution 3314, (XXIX) (1974), Annex, art. 3(g). Martin (2012, p. 238), notes that "'substantial involvement' require[s] more than mere supply."

8. If A or B is a signatory to the Rome Statute establishing the International Criminal Court, then international criminal law will be relevant too. Article 7 of the Rome Statute covers crimes against humanity, including murder; Article 8 covers war crimes including § 2(a) grave breaches of the Geneva Conventions, including willful killing, § 2(b) covers "Other serious violations of the laws and customs applicable in international armed conflict" including 2(b)(i) "Intentionally directing attacks against the civilian population as such or against individual civilians not taking direct part in hostilities"; and 2(c) deals with cases of armed conflict not of an international character, and covers "serious violations of article 3 common to the four Geneva Conventions of 12 August 1949," including 2(c)(i) murder.

9. The White House, in 2013, released a "Fact Sheet" that contained criteria for targeted killing. Among these was "Near certainty that non-combatants will not be injured or killed." That implies that the people targeted are viewed as combatants.

10. *See* Milliken and Stewart (2019). I assume that this was not mere punishment, and that the United States reasonably considered him to be an ongoing threat in al Qaeda's efforts to inflict harm on the United States and its allies.

11. The difference between the ICRC and the Israelis arguably reflects different concerns guiding the interpretation of the LOAC. The ICRC position is that humanitarian law should err on the side of protecting civilians from military attack. *See* Melzer (2009, p. 45) (warning of the need to avoid "erroneous or arbitrary attacks against civilians"). By contrast, the Israeli Court seeks to create "an incentive for civilians to remain as distant from the conflict as possible" (Public Committee against Torture in Israel, ¶34).

12. Despite this, Israel seems to have on multiple occasions engaged in the targeted killing of Iranian nuclear scientists, whose work would have been useful for bomb making but may not have been directly connected to bomb making. *See* Afkhami (2012).

13. Kimberly Ferzan calls it the exercise of a "negative normative power" (Ferzan 2016, p. 234). As it is not about the way one can use one's autonomy to shape one's rights, but rather the way one's rights are affected by what one does, I think a better label is auto-liability.

14. *See* Wellman (2012). Criminal activity may do *more* than forfeit the right not to be punished; retributivists think it also makes it the case that proportional punishment is deserved. *See* Walen (2016).

15. See the Model Penal Code, § 3.04(2)(b), which limits the use of deadly force to situations in which "the actor believes that such force is necessary to protect himself against death, serious bodily harm, kidnapping or sexual intercourse compelled by force or threat."

16. This is a controversial position in just war theory, but I think it is nonetheless true. I call it the agent-patient inference: when competition is not justified, an agent's right to act gives rise to a patient right not to be targeted as a means of interfering with the act. *See* Walen (2019, ch. 8).

17. The phrase "moral obstacle" is Gerard Øverland's. *See* Øverland (2014). I capture the same thought with the concept of "restricting claims."

18. In Walen (2019), I had assumed that forfeiture would arise only on the margins, when dealing with clearly culpable threats. But that was because I assumed that forfeiture had to operate as it does with clearly culpable aggressors, causing their lives to count for very little in the proportionality analysis. I now think it operates more expansively.

19. Whether these concepts are to be judged from an evidence-relative or fact-relative point of view is beyond the scope of this chapter. Seth Lazar argues for an evidence-relative approach in Lazar (2012). I argue, in Walen (2019), Chap. 2, § 2, for a qualified fact-relative account, where the qualification is that the relevant facts cannot be too esoteric. Both views allow us to talk about probabilities.

20. In Walen (2019), Chap. 1, § 2, I mistakenly identified necessity with a Pareto test.

21. Insofar as you are seeking to be impartial, you would presumably also count your own life as having the kind of value a third party would give it.

22. I take this point from Benjamin Bronner.

23. Forty-two US states, the federal criminal code and the District of Columbia require "that the unlawful force or threat be 'imminent' before defense force becomes authorized"; eight states and the Model Penal Code require "that the use of force be 'immediately necessary'" (Robinson et al. 2015, pp. 15–16). These are not the same; the latter can be read to allow the use of force as soon as it is necessary to do so, whether or not the threat itself is imminent.

24. This is not the only account one could give. Sanford Kadish, for example, gave a Hobbesian account according to which individuals give up their right to self-help when the state can be expected to better protect their security, but they recover the right to engage in self-defense when the state cannot adequately provide for their security because the threat is too imminent (Kadish 1976, pp. 884–888). But this Hobbesian account cannot explain why it is impermissible, for example, to use innocent victims as shields when the state is unable to provide for one's defense. According to Hobbes, once an agent is confronted with imminent death, all bets and all limits are off. *See* Walen (1997, p. 1092). *See also* Ferzan (2004, p. 245).

25. Russell Christopher argues that it is also over-inclusive, because even an imminent threat might decide not to complete its attack. Christopher (2012, pp. 261–262). But imminence does not have to swallow up and substitute for all necessity considerations. It can operate as an important test of necessity, while allowing that self-defense is impermissible if it is "unnecessary" for any other reason.

26. This is a strategy some have recommended in defense of the proof beyond a reasonable doubt standard. *See* Lippke (2010, pp. 464–65); Underwood (1977, pp. 1306–1307). I think this is a poor strategy for justifying proof beyond a reasonable doubt for criminal convictions because I think it is less clear what the biases are and there are better ways to fight them. *See* Walen (2015, pp. 388 and 405, n.223). I think the case for countering bias is better in the context of targeted killing.

27. I derive a version of the formulae I develop here, though in terms suited for criminal convictions, in Walen (2015, pp. 406–408). The original development of these formulae was provided in Kaplan (1968).
28. I assume here that we would not simply assume we had killed the right target and reduce security designed to protect against him—contrary to the what happens if the wrong person is convicted of a crime.
29. I was inspired to formulate this idea by reading Ferzan (2019), but the formulation is my own.
30. There might be exceptions if the numbers at stake are truly huge—cases of threshold deontology. *See* Walen (2019, ch. 4, § 3) for a discussion of that idea.
31. I am grateful to Tom Dannenbaum and Adam Kolber for incisive comments on an earlier version of this draft.

References

Public Committee against Torture in Israel v Israel, HCJ 769/02, (2005) IsrSC.

Afkhami, Artin. 2012. Tehran abuzz as book says Israel killed 5 scientists. *New York Times*, July 11.

Altman, Andrew. 2017. Targeting al Qaeda: Law and morality in the US "war on terror". In *The ethics of war*, ed. Saba Bazargan-Forward and Samuel C. Rickless, 141–163. New York: Oxford University Press.

Becker, Jo, and Scott Shane. 2012. Secret "kill list" proves a test of Obama's principles and will. *New York Times*, May 29.

Broome, John. 1984. Uncertainty and fairness. *Economic Journal* 94: 624–632.

Christopher, Russell. 2012. Imminence in justified targeted killing. In *Targeted killing: Law and morality in an asymmetrical world*, ed. Claire Finkelstein, Jens David Ohlin, and Andrew Altman, 253–284. Oxford: Oxford University Press.

Dinstein, Yoram. 2005. *War, aggression and self-defense*. 4th ed. New York: Cambridge University Press.

Ferzan, Kimberly Kessler. 2004. Defending imminence: From battered women to Iraq. *Arizona Law Review* 46: 213–262.

———. 2012. Culpable aggression: The basis for moral liability to defensive killing. *Ohio State Journal of Criminal Law* 9: 669–697.

———. 2016. Forfeiture and self-defense. In *The ethics of self-defense*, ed. Christian Coons and Michael Webber, 233–253. New York: Oxford University Press.

———. 2019. Deontological distinction in war. *Ethics* 129: 603–624.

Frowe, Helen. 2014. *Defensive killing*. Oxford: Oxford University Press.

Haque, Adil. 2017. *Law and morality at war*. Oxford: Oxford University Press.

Hurka, Thomas. 2005. Proportionality in the morality of war. *Philosophy and Public Affairs* 33: 34–66.

International Committee of the Red Cross. Customary international humanitarian law. https://ihl-databases.icrc.org/customaryihl/eng/docs/v1_cha.   Accessed 7 Jan 2019.

Kadish, Sanford. 1976. Respect for life and regard for rights in the criminal law. *California Law Review* 64: 871–901.

Kaplan, John. 1968. Decision theory and the factfinding process. *Stanford Law Review* 20: 1065–1092.

Lazar, Seth. 2012. Necessity in self-defense and war. *Philosophy and Public Affairs* 40: 3–44.

———. 2015. *Sparing civilians*. New York: Oxford University Press.

Lippke, Richard. 2010. Punishing the guilty, not punishing the innocent. *Journal of Moral Philosophy* 7: 462–488.

Martin, Craig. 2012. Going medieval: Targeted killing, self-defense and the *jus ad bellum* regime. In *Targeted killings: Law and morality in an asymmetrical world*, ed. Claire Finkelstein, Jens David Ohlin, and Andrew Altman, 223–252. Oxford: Oxford University Press.

McMahan, Jeff. 2009. *Killing in war*. New York: Oxford University Press.

———. 2014. Self-defense against justified threateners. In *How we fight: Ethics in war*, ed. Helen Frowe and Gerald Lang, 104–137. New York: Oxford University Press.

Melzer, Nils. 2009. Interpretive guidance on the notion of direct participation in hostilities under international humanitarian law. *ICRC*. https://www.icrc.org/eng/assets/files/other/icrc-002-0990.pdf. Accessed 7 Jan 2019.

Milliken, Mary, and Phil Stewart. 2019. U.S. says suspected USS Cole bombing planner killed in Yemen strike. *Reuters*. January 6.

Otsuka, Michael. 1994. Killing the innocent in self-defense. *Philosophy & Public Affairs* 23: 74–94.

Øverland, Gerhard. 2014. Moral obstacles: An alternative to the doctrine of double effect. *Ethics* 124: 481–506.

Robinson, Paul H. 1984. *Criminal law defenses*. Vol. 2. St. Paul: West Publishing.

Robinson, Paul H., Matthew Kussmaul, Camber Stoddard, Ilya Rudyak, and Andreas Kuersten. 2015. *The American criminal code: General defenses*. University of Pennsylvania Legal Scholarship Repository. http://scholarship.law.upenn.edu/faculty_scholarship/1425. Accessed 8 June 2018.

Rodin, David. 2002. *War & self-defense*. New York: Oxford University Press.

Underwood, Barbara. 1977. The thumb on the scales of justice: Burdens of persuasion in criminal cases. *Yale Law Journal* 86: 1299–1348.

Waldron, Jeremy. Unpublished. *Named and targeted*. Public Law Research Paper No. 18-50, NYU School of Law. Available at https://ssrn.com/abstract=3259352. Accessed 2 Jan 2019.

Walen, Alec. 1997. Consensual sex without assuming the risk of carrying an unwanted fetus; another foundation for the right to an abortion. *Brooklyn Law Review* 63: 1051–1140.

———. 2015. Proof beyond a reasonable doubt: A balanced retributive account. *Louisiana Law Review* 76: 355–446.

———. 2016. *Retributive justice*. The Stanford Encyclopedia of Philosophy. https://plato.stanford.edu/archives/win2016/entries/justice-retributive. Accessed 27 Feb 2019.

———. 2019. *The mechanics of claims and permissible killing in war*. New York: Oxford University Press.

Wellman, Christopher, 2012, "The Rights Forfeiture Theory of Punishment." *Ethics* 122: 371–393.

White, House. 2013. *Fact sheet: U.S. policy standards and procedures for the use of force in counterterrorism operations outside the United States and areas of active hostilities*. White House. https://obamawhitehouse.archives.gov/the-press-office/2013/05/23/fact-sheet-us-policy-standards-and-procedures-use-force-counterterrorism. Accessed 7 June 2018.

PART XXXI

War Crimes

CHAPTER 33

War Crimes and Just War Theory

Tom Dannenbaum

International criminal law functions as a system of global moral expression (Drumbl 2007, pp. 3, 12, 61, 173–179; Luban 2010, pp. 575–576; Sloane 2007; *Al Mahdi* 2016, ¶67; *Blaškić* 2004, ¶678). To affix the label "war criminal" to an individual is to identify her or him as a moral outcast—an enemy of humanity (*hostis humani generis*). The perceived moral force of the duty not to commit war crimes is perhaps best exemplified by the notion that it "transcend(s) national obligations of obedience," superseding the domestically valid legal duties of any individual who retains the capacity for "moral choice" (*Göring* 1946, pp. 446, 470).

Given this legal posture, the intellectual ferment in just war theory over the past two decades ought to be of significant interest to war crimes theorists. A growing constituency of philosophers has come to the conclusion that "orthodox" just war theory—articulated most prominently by Michael Walzer (1977)—is beset with fundamental errors. In its place, "revisionist" theory has become philosophically dominant.

Sharpening the significance of this shift is the commonly perceived normative intertwinement of orthodox just war theory and international law. Walzer begins *Just and Unjust Wars* with a careful elaboration of what he calls the "legalist paradigm" (Walzer 1977). Much of what follows in the book provides philosophical support for the moral positions enshrined in that international law framework (albeit with some caveats). So deep are the linkages between the two normative schemes that it has been suggested that orthodox just war theorists "might as readily be called legalists" (Lazar 2017).

In contrast, revisionist principles are often framed as sharply deviating from the law of war. On the account of perhaps the most prominent and prolific

T. Dannenbaum (✉)
The Fletcher School of Law and Diplomacy, Tufts University, Medford, MA, USA
e-mail: tom.dannenbaum@tufts.edu

© The Author(s) 2019
L. Alexander, K. K. Ferzan (eds.), *The Palgrave Handbook of Applied Ethics and the Criminal Law*, https://doi.org/10.1007/978-3-030-22811-8_33

revisionist—Jeff McMahan—this is an appropriate divergence between "deep morality" and morally optimal law, given the need for the latter to accommodate practical and institutional imperatives (McMahan 2008, 2009, pp. 203–235, 2013). However, if revisionist moral theory is right, the breadth of this gap would challenge the credibility of a war crimes regime whose *raison d'être* is the expression of fundamental moral values through criminal sanction.

With that in mind, this chapter focuses on three issues in contemporary just war theory and their implications for criminal law: the normative exceptionalism (or not) of war, the moral (in)equality of combatants, and the moral foundation (or not) of the distinction between civilians and combatants. On each count, the gap between law and revisionist moral theory is narrower than is typically recognized.

Before beginning, a brief comment on scope is in order. The term "war crimes" refers exclusively to serious violations of the international law of armed conflict (also known as the *jus in bello*, law of war, or international humanitarian law [IHL]). This is a broad and diverse category. Among other crimes, it includes targeting civilians, mistreating detainees, destroying cultural property, various forms of sexual violence, the targeting of medical units, faking a surrender or injury in order to kill enemy combatants, using human shields, and enlisting child soldiers.

Its internal breadth notwithstanding, focusing on this code in isolation can lead to confusion regarding the relationship between the law and revisionist moral theory. Avoiding that confusion requires considering two additional criminal categories: aggression (the international crime of waging war in violation of the *jus ad bellum*) and domestic crimes relevant to non-international armed conflict (including both rebellion crimes and ordinary crimes of battery and murder). Whereas war crimes law regulates how belligerents fight, these other criminal law regimes regulate the conditions (if any) under which they may fight in the first place. Addressing these criminal categories together sheds light on aspects of the relationship between the law and morality of war that may otherwise be missed.

NORMATIVE EXCEPTIONALISM

Perhaps the signal premise of orthodox just war theory is the idea that war entails a qualitatively distinct normative context. To apply the morality of ordinary life to a context of armed conflict is, on this view, to make a category error (Walzer 2006; Shue 2008; Finkelstein 2016). As discussed in the next section, the most significant upshot of this exceptionalism is the "moral equality of combatants"—the thesis that combatants fighting in the service of an unjust war ("unjust combatants") and combatants fighting for a just cause ("just combatants") have equal rights to attack and kill one another.

Orthodox theorists offer a range of reasons for war's exceptional status on this and other issues. War is a clash of independent political collectives that creates a "normatively distinct relation" between opposing combatants (Kutz 2005, p. 173). It is a conflict between sovereign equals, with no superior mutual authority (Blum 2010b, pp. 133–134; Finkelstein 2016). In light of that context, the applicable morality governing combatants is best defined by reciprocally beneficial conventions (Benbaji 2011; Mavrodes 1975; Walzer 1977, ch.3, 8). Furthermore, the collective brutality and the "epistemically cloaked choices" (Dill 2013) facing belligerents are deemed "parametric" (Luban 2018, p. 187), defining the normative space in a way that shifts the terms of moral justification and excuse (Dill and Shue 2012).

Philosophically, the notion of an exceptional domain in which ordinary morality does not apply is jarring. In law, on the other hand, the notion of normatively distinct spheres is not uncommon. It is therefore unsurprising that a parallel to war's putative moral exceptionalism was long a feature of international law. Indeed, historically, the entire framework of public international law pivoted on the distinction between war and peace. In war, an entirely separate legal system regulated both the interactions between belligerent states and those between belligerents and third states (Oppenheim 1905, 1906, vols. I & II). No such comprehensive shift occurs today, but the treaties and custom of IHL continue to define a distinct legal code for the regulation of war, applicable only in situations of armed conflict or belligerent occupation. IHL rules governing the killing and detention of combatants, for example, do not apply outside of those contexts. On the most categorical approach (*see*, e.g., Draper 1979), when the conditions of armed conflict obtain, IHL *displaces* international human rights law (IHRL)—the regime with the strongest claim to express the peacetime morality of contemporary international law. On that view, human rights law falls silent in war; individuals are protected exclusively by the qualitatively distinct law of armed conflict.

That strong displacement account of the law is no longer widely accepted. The applicability of human rights law in armed conflict has been affirmed repeatedly by key authorities, including the International Court of Justice (*Nuclear Weapons* 1996, ¶¶24–25; *Wall* 2004, ¶¶102, 105–106), and has been recognized, at least tacitly, by longtime opponents of the theory (U.S. 2011, ¶¶506–507). The primary legal debate is no longer about *whether* human rights law applies in war. It is about *how* it applies in war.

On the view closest to exceptionalism, IHRL is subject to reinterpretation through IHL, as the *lex specialis* in contexts of armed conflict (*Nuclear Weapons* 1996, ¶25; *Wall* 2004, ¶106; *Detainees in Guantanamo Bay* 2002). On this view, although human rights do not simply evaporate, the danger, fog, and collectivizing imperatives that are constitutive of armed conflict require rethinking their demands. In ordinary life, human rights law permits the state to kill or detain an individual only if the action can survive a strict individualized necessity assessment vis-à-vis a narrow range of urgent and limited objectives. In war, however, IHL's classification of persons as combatants or civilians becomes the dominant factor in determining such liability. On the *lex specialis* theory, this classification framework is thought to be the best approximation of what human rights can demand in armed conflict. As Luban puts it, we "cannot will away" the "dramatic differences between war and peace" (Luban 2016, p. 70).

This approach maps relatively well onto a modified version of exceptionalism in orthodox just war theory. Those asserting this view recognize that the basic principles of morality are not displaced in war, but argue nonetheless that the practical, action-guiding instantiation of those principles must be qualitatively distinct in that realm. Thus, "even when the same fundamental moral touchstones are the reference, the differences in the circumstances yield different specific guidelines" (Shue 2008, p. 87).

Revisionists start from a different premise. For them, war is simply a complicated, high-stakes context in which to perform ordinary moral reasoning (McMahan 2009, pp. 35–37, 79–84; Frowe 2014, ch.5). As such, it is perfectly sensible to reason seamlessly across war and peace, relying on common principles and drawing analogies between situations in each realm. The notion that the collective, political nature of war can change this is dismissed as "moral alchemy." (McMahan 2009, p. 82). And yet, in evaluating IHL, revisionists rarely advocate radical legal reform. This conservatism trades in significant part on the aforementioned distinction between "deep morality" and morally justified law.

In response, orthodox theorists have questioned whether there is any "function to be performed by a competing 'morality of war'" when we agree on a "morally justified" framework of the law of war (Shue 2008, p. 89; Walzer 2006). Indeed, some have suggested that a competing deep morality is not just pointless, but dangerous, because it undermines the normative force of a fragile but morally important code without advancing a viable alternative (Waldron 2018).

These responses are unconvincing. In addition to the intrinsic value of deeper understanding, how are we to settle on morally justified laws without first making sense of the underlying principles at stake? How are we to identify the technological and practical conditions under which the morally justified law might change? How are we to grapple with the conditions under which it may be appropriate to break the law? Pointing to the fragility of the code cannot preclude such inquiry. The law of war depends on normative internalization. Protecting it from searching moral analysis is a recipe for the opposite—what Mill would call a "dead dogma" rather than "a living truth" (Mill 1859, p. 103).

Returning to the issue of exceptionalism, it is notable that the legal viability of even a *lex specialis* dichotomy is increasingly in question. It seems particularly ill-suited to address the diversity of contemporary conflict and security scenarios, which include, for example, the intense collective violence of a raging battle, the retaking of a location from an insurgent unit engaged in an isolated attack or hostage-taking operation, the block-by-block security operations of an occupying force, clashes at a military checkpoint, the remote, air-conditioned lethal strikes of a drone operator, the engagement of a sleeper cell a continent away from the conflict motivating its action, and a hacker group's illicit capturing or destruction of the data of a hostile actor.

Although the trends are not unidirectional, there is a growing recognition that human rights remain relevant in war in ways that are not captured by the traditional requirements of IHL (Human Rights Committee 2001, 2004, 2018, ¶¶3, 11, 64 (respectively); Dworkin 2017; Hakimi 2018; Haque 2017, pp. 35–37). In short, as the practice of security operations and war fighting have blurred, the legal exceptionalism of armed conflict has begun to break down. This has criminal law implications. Human rights law requires states to criminalize arbitrary deprivations of life (Human Rights Committee 2018, ¶20; *Osman* 1998, ¶115). The independent application or influence of that regime in war raises the possibility that, under the right conditions, arbitrariness may not be determined exhaustively by IHL. As such, states may have duties to criminalize behaviors that do not themselves violate the law of war. This possibility is discussed further in relation to specific substantive issues below.

THE MORAL EQUALITY OF COMBATANTS

Among the most significant upshots of the orthodox notion of war's exceptionalism is the moral equality of combatants—combatants on both sides are equally liable to targeting, and civilians on both sides are equally protected from targeting. Thus, Walzer argues that a combatant mobilized to fight has thereby "allowed himself to be made into a dangerous man" and thus forfeited his "title to life and liberty," regardless of the cause for which he fights (Walzer 1977, pp. 145, 136). Conversely, as "men and women with rights," civilians "cannot be used for some military purpose, even if it is a legitimate purpose" (Walzer 1977, p. 137).

Having rejected exceptionalism, it should be unsurprising that revisionists also reject moral equality. From the revisionist perspective, orthodox theory can be fairly characterized as asserting the following related and fundamentally implausible positions. First, individuals who have done nothing other than commit to taking justified and proportionate defensive action against a wrongful attack by an aggressor state thereby forfeit their right not to be killed by the agents of that very aggressor. Second, the fact that a political collective (the aggressor state) wrongfully begins a war it has no right to start somehow authorizes its agents to inflict death and violence (including on collaterally harmed civilians) in pursuit of the unjust cause. To state the position concretely: Germany's wrongful invasion of Poland in 1939 somehow gave German soldiers a right they would otherwise lack to target Polish soldiers with lethal force and to kill Polish civilians collaterally. Indeed, the soldiers on either side are thought to stand in a symmetrical moral relationship vis-à-vis one another. As Kutz acknowledges, these propositions seem to be "in contradiction with any rational aspiration of political morality" (Kutz 2008, p. 69).

Supplementing Walzer's theory of rights forfeiture, orthodox theorists have offered a range of arguments to defend moral equality, often interposing quite different claims in a single aggregated account. Soldiers on both sides are described as acting in immediate defense of themselves and their comrades, without control over the macro-policy decisions that placed them in that posture (Anscombe 1958; Finkelstein 2016; Nagel 1972, pp. 138–140; Walzer

1977, p. 145). *Jus-ad-bellum*-determining facts are described as inaccessible to soldiers, precluding individual judgment on the issue and justifying deference to those with such access (Walzer 1977, pp. 35, 39, 289; Estlund 2007). The importance of combatants' obedience to political authority (and particularly civilian, democratic authority) and of their associative duties to serve and protect co-citizens is offered as a basis for their participation in the state's wrongful violence (Estlund 2007; Kutz 2005; Lazar 2013). And it is claimed that the long-run benefits of focusing soldiers exclusively on upholding the *jus in bello* justify a combatant's role morality to that effect (Mavrodes 1975; Dill and Shue 2012; Shue 2013; Waldron 2018) particularly to the extent it can be rooted in a moral contract among soldiers via international law (Benbaji 2008, 2011).

Revisionists have exposed deep flaws in each of these lines of argument (e.g. Fabre 2012; McMahan 2009; Norman 1995; Rodin 2002). Among other things, these rebuttals have spotlighted the ways in which the orthodox arguments variously:

- conflate excuses with justifications (obscuring wrongfulness by establishing individual non-culpability);
- prioritize political over moral obligations without clear grounds for doing so, without an explanation for why the same political priority does not apply to *in bello* crimes (where soldiers are expected to disobey criminal state demands), and despite the lack of a shared political authority between the two sides;
- or assert forms of consent or contracting that are contingent, non-comprehensive in their coverage of war's violence, empirically false, or morally untenable.

Ultimately, revisionists insist, there is no avoiding the simple truth that killing, maiming, and destroying in the service of an unjust cause is necessarily wrongful, whether the victims are combatants or civilians. The wrongfulness of Germany's attack on Poland cannot but contaminate morally the violence inflicted in the pursuit of its success. To suggest instead that such an attack could underpin the legitimation or authorization of the ensuing killing is simply not normatively credible.

Recognizing the force of that rebuttal, some orthodox theorists now acknowledge explicitly that a defense of combatant equality at the level of conduct must rely on soldier non-culpability, or pragmatic imperatives to cabin the normative scope of lower-level decision-making, rather than on a claim that the killing in aggressive war is justified (Benbaji 2011, p. 64; Dill and Shue 2012). In so doing, they concede the moral inequality of combatants at the level of liability to killing and violence.[1]

In law, IHL famously makes no distinction between those fighting with *jus ad bellum* authorization and those fighting without it. In line with Walzerian theory, it appears, on its own terms, to give even unjust combatants the "right" to inflict violence (Additional Protocol I 1977, art. 43). Hence, the perceived chasm between law and revisionist morality.

This putative divide, however, is founded on an overly narrow view of the law. IHL is a regime of prohibitions, not authorizations (Haque 2017, pp. 30–35). Its failure to criminalize the violence inflicted in an illegal war means only that such killing is not criminalized by that legal framework. This entails neither that IHL authorizes that action over the contrary requirements of other regimes nor that the action is not proscribed elsewhere (Dannenbaum 2018, pp. 217–222; Dworkin 2017, p. 481; Greenwood 1983, pp. 223, 228). The "right" of combatants to fight per article 43 of Additional Protocol I does not, and is not meant to, override other requirements of international law. Rather, it underpins the *immunity* of privileged belligerents from punishment for *jus-in-bello*-compliant acts of war in international armed conflicts (IACs) (Dannenbaum 2018, pp. 217–222; Dinstein 2016, p. 45; Haque 2017, p. 34).

Recognizing this is essential because other criminal law frameworks bear upon the issue. In IACs, the most significant of these is the crime of aggression. In non-international armed conflicts (NIACs), domestic criminal law and human rights law combine with significant implications for combatant equality. Consider these in turn.

On what remains the dominant account, aggression is a crime against sovereignty or self-determination (Kahn 2008, pp. 54–55; Luban 1994, pp. 335–341; Solera 2007, p. 427; Stahn 2010, p. 877; Walzer 1977, pp. 58–61). A corollary to this is the common view that "individuals have never been considered victims" of the crime (Pobjie 2016, p. 822). Locating the wrong of aggression at the macro-level and allowing the morality and legality of the constituent acts to be determined exclusively by the *jus in bello*, this conceptualization fits both the moral equality thesis and the notion of IHL as authorizing *jus-in-bello*-compliant violence. However, as an account of the crime of aggression, it is mistaken. Understanding why reveals an underappreciated connection between international criminal law and revisionist just war theory.

The first key problem with the dominant account is that neither sovereignty nor self-determination can explain the contours of the crime of aggression. The move to ban non-defensive war and ultimately criminalize aggression in the early twentieth century granted states legal protection from the harm of armed attack. However, it also restricted severely their sovereign authority to use force to vindicate their other rights (Hathaway and Shapiro 2017, ch.3; Neff 2005, pp. 225–239). The exchange cannot be explained with reference to the greater significance to self-determination or sovereignty of the former because aggressive war is not an exceptionally egregious violation of those rights. A leader that manipulates foreign election results or holds onto foreign territory not taken through illegal force, thereby infringes self-determination, political independence, or territorial integrity more severely and effectively than is even intended (let alone achieved) by potentially criminal uses of force like illegal aerial bombardments. And yet, the former, lacking "armed force," are plainly not international crimes, whereas the latter can be (Statute of the International Criminal Court 2011, art.8*bis*; Dannenbaum 2017, pp. 1270–1272).

What distinguishes aggression as the only criminal violation of sovereignty is not the gravity of its infringement of sovereignty, but the means of that infringement. It alone involves legally unjustified killing and human violence. Indeed, even uses of armed force that do not violate the sovereignty, territorial integrity, or political independence of another state can qualify as criminally aggressive if they are "*otherwise* inconsistent with" the United Nations (UN) Charter, as would be a military campaign against a UN-authorized force on a state's own territory (Dannenbaum 2017, pp. 1275–1278; Institut de Droit International 1971).

Moreover, in the absence of the criminalization of aggression, the *non*-criminality of *jus-in-bello*-compliant killing in an illegal war would be anomalous among other forms of intentional killing in pursuit of an illegal objective, which are all criminal in some other form, whether as crimes against humanity, war crimes, or simply domestic murder (Dannenbaum 2017, pp. 1272–1275; Mégret 2016, pp. 1420–1423; Ohlin 2016, pp. 1455, 1458, 1462). As a crime of unjustified killing and human violence, aggression closes that gap and corrects what might otherwise be considered the "humanitarian laundering" of the *jus in bello* (Mégret 2016, pp. 1420–23). In the landmark aggression case, the prosecutors at Nuremberg asserted its criminality on the grounds that in the absence of *jus ad bellum* authority, there is "nothing to justify the killing" in war, which is therefore equivalent to "murder" (*Shawcross* 1946, p. 433). The judges in the parallel prosecution in Tokyo endorsed precisely this notion (*Araki* 1948, p. 48452).

Understanding the crime in this way also has the virtue of making sense of aggression's place in a human-centered international criminal law regime (Teitel 2011; Meron 2006). It connects directly to the Human Rights Committee's recognition that aggression is fundamentally a widespread and systematic violation of the right to life (Human Rights Committee 2018, ¶71). The notion that aggression is a crime against sovereignty instead isolates aggression as the inexplicably odd crime out, rendering international criminal law confused in its basic normative message (Luban 1994, pp. 335–337, 341; Pobjie 2016, pp. 825–826).

Of course, the *jus in bello* (governing how we fight) and *jus ad bellum* (governing whether and under what circumstances we fight) are independent and separate legal regimes. Since the *jus in bello* is equally permissive and restrictive of killing and violence on both sides, one might think that any prohibition of killing and violence by the aggressor side would amount to a *jus ad bellum* override of the *jus in bello*'s permission. However, independence is not a one-way street. Just as the law on the use of force (on whether and when we fight) cannot override or determine the scope of IHL (on how we fight), so IHL cannot override or determine the scope of the law on the use of force (Dannenbaum 2018, pp. 217–226). Notwithstanding its reference to the "right" of privileged belligerents to fight, Additional Protocol I affirms precisely this in its preamble (1977). The *jus ad bellum* prohibits the infliction of any killing or violence in an illegal war, and the crime of aggression criminalizes that killing and violence. The *jus in bello* additionally, separately, and independently prohibits the infliction of certain kinds of wrong in *any* war—lawful or not—and the war crimes regime criminalizes that killing and violence. Neither authorizes action prohibited by the other.

In short, and in direct contradiction to the orthodox notion that just combatants forfeit their rights not to be killed by an aggressor force, the most coherent understanding of international law affirms that aggression violates those soldiers' human right to life. On the issue of individual liability to be killed, international law adopts the position that unifies revisionists.

Difficulties of jurisdiction, enforcement, and interpretation vis-à-vis the crime of aggression should not be downplayed. Moreover, revisionists are likely to dispute the precise contours of the *jus ad bellum* underlying the crime as currently defined (McMahan 2016). Nonetheless, the crime applies as a matter of customary international law (not just at the International Criminal Court [ICC]), has been affirmed without dissent by both the UN General Assembly and the ICC's Assembly of States Parties, and is codified in the domestic criminal codes of a growing number of states (The Global Campaign 2019). Definitional disputes aside, that alone expresses a fundamentally revisionist normative message. The law recognizes the criminal wrongfulness of both killings in violation of the *jus ad bellum* ("aggression killings") and those in violation of the *jus in bello* ("war crime killings").

And yet, there remains an important distinction. Criminal liability for war crimes, such as the killing of unarmed civilians on any side or torturing detainees, attaches to direct or complicit perpetrators at any level, including those following orders. In contrast, liability for aggression killings, such as the killing of armed and active combatants fighting against an aggressor force, attaches only to those in a position to "control or direct the political or military action" of the aggressor state. This, of course, is at the heart of the confusion regarding the law's posture on aggression killings. It should not be. Even if morality could generally be said to make a pro tanto demand that *all* culpable perpetrators of any given wrong (and not just those most responsible) face criminal punishment, the application and force of that demand in this context is limited.

For both principled and practical reasons, international criminal law is targeted primarily at the gravest wrongdoers. As a matter of principle, the bonds connecting members of the international community are thin. The points of normative consensus are narrow. This limits the standing of that community to condemn wrongdoing, particularly by those acting pursuant to domestic obligations, except when the violation is clear, individual culpability is clear, and the international community has a genuine normative or practical stake in the issue at hand. Pragmatically, whether applied by international courts, such as the ICC, or by domestic courts exercising universal jurisdiction, international criminal law has severely limited resources. It is necessarily selective. Its credibility and perceived fairness depend in part on using those resources relatively evenly across different situations. This in turn precludes pursuing all persons associated with a particular situation of mass-criminality and militates instead in favor of focusing on those most responsible.

Taking the limited scope of international criminal law as a premise, many revisionists would likely accept that criminal liability for aggression should rarely, if ever, attach to lower-level participants. Moreover, they would accept as much not because the law deviates from deep morality, but because, as a matter of deep morality, they recognize that very few of those troops are more than minimally culpable for the wrongs they inflict, for any of the reasons discussed above. Namely, soldiers have limited access to relevant information, are likely unavoidably biased in their interpretation of information, act pursuant to domestic obligations, operate under the threat of punishment, and work in institutions whose functioning is essential to global security.[2] It is plausible to argue that the US-led invasion of Iraq was aggressive, and that the ensuing violence was also wrongful as a result. However, it is less plausible to hold that many of the soldiers who participated in that invasion or the entailed violence against enemy combatants were significantly culpable for those wrongs.

Of course, these factors do not apply to all soldiers in all wars. Thus, some revisionists assert that those unjust combatants who meet the appropriate mens rea thresholds are appropriately liable to some form of punishment for engaging in the violence of a wrongful war (e.g. Chehtman 2018b; Fabre 2016, ch.7). Certainly, assuming such a standard were enshrined in law, those who satisfy standard criminal culpability thresholds "would not be wronged" if so punished (Chehtman 2018b, p. 187). However, the key point here is that a legal system that shields lower-level troops from criminal liability excludes neither victims from vindication by, nor aggressive violence from the condemnation of, criminal law. Rather, it limits the scope of accountability for that violence to those most responsible for it. The fact that vindication and condemnation are channeled, rather than discarded, weakens significantly any concerns that might be raised regarding victims' rights in this context. Moreover, three cumulative reasons favor the immunity of lower-level participants from criminal liability for aggression.

First, identifying the small number of sufficiently culpable participants in a wrongful war would put an extraordinary strain on any system of criminal justice (particularly one as limited in capacity as the system of international criminal law). Since even culpable combatants are almost certainly not as blameworthy or broadly responsible for the wrongful violence of the aggression as are their leaders, and since all of their violence would be condemned in the punishment of the latter, the expressive value to offset that institutional strain is relatively low.

Second, a system of punishment for lower-level participation in aggressive war risks counterproductive incentives. For most combatants, the remote and highly unlikely prospect of liability for aggression would be overwhelmed by the immediacy and force of countervailing incentives to fight. To the extent aggression liability *were* a meaningful prospect for lower-level participants, it would dilute their incentives to comply with the *jus in bello*, to adhere to the requirements of privileged belligerency (including wearing uniforms and carrying arms openly), to surrender, and possibly even to make peace (Dinstein 2012, p. 169; Lauterpacht 1953, p. 220; McMahan 2013). Moreover, such a system could lead to wrongful punishment. In most scenarios, each party to a conflict behaves as though it has *jus ad bellum* authority. Were lower-level troops potentially liable for aggression, that tendency could lead to the unjust side punishing prisoners of war (i.e. just combatants), claiming enemy aggression.

Finally, given *jus ad bellum* ambiguity, a duty to disobey on that basis could trigger erroneous refusals to fight, with detrimental collateral effects on unit cohesion and military functioning in lawful wars. Given the importance of functioning militaries to global deterrence, this, too, may be a cost that exceeds the benefit of punishing the few who deserve it (Dannenbaum 2018, ch.8).

Ultimately, the seemingly gaping chasm between the growing philosophical consensus around a moral inequality of combatants and the posture of contemporary international criminal law is in fact a relatively narrow gap, centered on the question of which individuals are liable for agreed criminal wrongs and rooted in plausible pragmatic considerations rather than deep normative divergence. The law may exclude from criminal liability some participants in wrongful wars who would ordinarily warrant such liability. However, even in those cases, it still provides for the liability of the political and military leaders they obeyed.

Non-international Armed Conflict

Things get more complicated in the realm of non-international armed conflict (NIAC). The vast majority of just war theory and most codified international law continues to focus on international armed conflicts (IACs) (Fabre 2012, p. 131).[3] From an empirical perspective, this is peculiar. Most contemporary conflicts, whether transnational or internal, are between armed groups and states, or between armed groups. Over time, an IHL and war crimes framework for such NIACs has developed, drawing on many (though not all) of the rules and principles of IHL for IACs (*Tadić* 1995, ¶¶96–137; Statute of the International Criminal Court 2011, art.8). As in IACs, there is equal application of this regime to both sides. Targeted attacks on civilians are war crimes and targeted attacks on combatants are not, whichever side perpetrates them.[4] However, there has been no such migration of the crime of aggression, which applies only to wars between states. Indeed, the resort to force in this context is widely considered to be unregulated by international law (Sassòli 2007, p. 254; Schachter 1984, p. 1641).

As in the IAC context, however, equality in IHL does not entail a comprehensive legal equality of combatants. Pursuant to IHL's doctrine of "privileged belligerency," a combatant who fights for the state and meets certain requirements (such as wearing a uniform and operating within a command structure) can kill enemy soldiers in an IAC under an IHL immunity from prosecution for what would otherwise qualify as ordinary domestic murder (Baxter 1951; Dörmann 2003). IHL provides no such protection to those fighting in NIACs.

Thus, when non-state fighters kill enemy forces without an applicable domestic justification or excuse, they commit murder. When their adversary is the state, they may also perpetrate crimes that relate to the illegality of their overall project, such as rebellion, sedition, insurrection, or treason. Even forming an armed group with the unconsummated intention of waging an internal armed conflict would risk domestic criminal liability in many states. This is no less true when the group is motivated by legitimate grievances against the state—including grievances rooted in international human rights law. Indeed, it could be that the state in question has long been in breach of its legal obligations vis-à-vis oppressed subjects, as were at least some of the states that faced uprisings in the "Arab Spring" of 2011. Nonetheless, those who resort to armed force in order to remedy such wrongs perpetrate thereby a range of domestic crimes. With a rarely applicable exception relating to wars of self-determination,[5] international law offers even human-rights-promoting rebels no protection from domestic prosecution.

State troops involved in a NIAC are in a different position. Their side has the monopoly on the legitimate use of force. This accords them fundamentally divergent rights and duties regarding coercion, threatened force, and the use of force. Whereas non-state groups may commit crimes by arming or threatening to use force, state security forces are authorized to be armed and exist partly for the very purpose of providing an ongoing implicit (and sometimes explicit) threat to use force in response to coercive non-state action. This includes the authority to use coercion (i.e. the threat of force) to disarm and neutralize non-state groups in situations in which the latter have valid grievances regarding broader state failings.

To be clear, state actors' legal authority to go beyond a posture of threat and to actually use force internally is not unlimited. At the level of international criminal law, the initiation of a widespread or systematic attack by state forces on a civilian population would be a crime against humanity (Statute of the International Criminal Court 2011, art.7; Dannenbaum 2017, pp. 1272–1273). Such an attack on those engaged in non-violent resistance would clearly fall into this category, but the crime could also extend to an attack on an armed group outside of a state of armed conflict, if not justified on ordinary law-enforcement grounds (Dannenbaum 2017, pp. 1272–1273, n.123). Moreover, although smaller-scale uses of force on the part of state actors prior to crossing the threshold into armed conflict would not amount to international crimes, international human rights law requires the domestic criminalization and punishment of arbitrary killing (and other grave rights violations) by state actors (Human Rights Committee 2018, ¶20; *Osman* 1998, ¶115).

Much as in revisionist theory, human rights law typically considers the use of lethal force to be non-arbitrary for these purposes only if absolutely necessary to defend against wrongful death or similarly grave harms (Heyns et al. 2016, pp. 819–820). To meet this threshold in non-conflict conditions, an operation to arrest or nullify a threat posed by dangerous suspects must be designed from the outset so as to minimize the likelihood that lethal force becomes necessary during its execution (McCann 1995, ¶¶200–213).

These internationally required criminal law constraints on state actors in their actions against non-state armed groups are significant. Nonetheless, they differ from the constraints on such groups, in the sense that state actors have the authority to be armed, to threaten, and to coerce in contexts in which non-state actors do not. State actors do not have unlimited authority, but on the ladder of escalating coercion, they have a legal upper hand.

Once a conflict is fully underway, the legal asymmetry deepens. Perhaps the most startling example of this arises when state forces themselves wrongfully initiate the use of lethal force, either by engaging in an escalating campaign of violence in violation of human rights law or by engaging in a widespread and systematic attack outside the context of an armed conflict. In such circumstances, international law would require that state actors be held criminally liable for the initial attacks, for the reasons noted above. However, as soon as an armed group responds to that attack with anything more organized and comprehensive than what is permitted by ordinary domestic justifications, *its* members would thereby perpetrate the spectrum of domestic crimes discussed above, without any international legal protection from prosecution for so doing.

The criminal regulation required by international law regarding subsequent uses of force by the state is more ambiguous. To the extent human rights law is read in light of IHL (as *lex specialis*), state actors would perpetrate no crimes by targeting the armed group with violence, despite having been the original source of the war. If, on the other hand, human rights law is applied alongside IHL, or in interaction with it, the former's ban on arbitrary deprivations of life would enhance the legal (and ultimately criminal) restrictions on state agents, particularly in areas in which the state exercises great control, or hostilities are limited (Dworkin 2017, p. 499). However, for the most part, IHRL flexibility is likely to accommodate state agent action in suppressing insurrection in ways that closely mirror the requirements of IHL, particularly in areas where hostilities are intense (Dworkin 2017, p. 493; Heyns et al. 2016, p. 822).

This is the area of the criminal regulation of war most apt for critique by legal and moral theorists. Two fundamental questions arise. Are there any conditions (beyond the narrow case of national liberation from oppression by a colonial or racist regime) in which members of a non-state group should *not* be criminally liable merely for fighting? Conversely, are there any conditions, beyond those identified above, in which members of the state forces are, or ought to be, criminally liable for fighting against non-state groups, even if they comply with the *jus in bello*? Although a complete response is beyond the scope of this chapter, it is worth making a few preliminary observations.

First, a blanket assertion of sovereign prerogative in defense of the current asymmetry is difficult to maintain in the human rights era (Lieblich 2016, p. 705). To be clear, there are crucial differences between state and non-state actors on this issue. States are epistemically more sophisticated and more accountable in their uses of force than are non-state groups (Lieblich 2016, p. 747). As is often emphasized in the literature on international uses of force, states can provide immense value as sites of self-determination or collective politics (Walzer 1980; Kutz 2014, pp. 231, 236–237, 241–242). Even when the state is less benign, there are few threats to human welfare and human rights greater than state failure (May 2008, pp. 6–7; Englehart 2009).

The individual rights of persons who will be killed or injured by the resort to collective force set a high justificatory threshold for both state and non-state actors poised to engage in a non-international conflict, just as they do for states using force at the international level. However, unlike its state adversary in a NIAC, a non-state group must *also* establish that the justificatory basis for killing is sufficient to warrant undermining the primary bulwark against state failure—namely, the sovereign's monopoly on internal coercion and the use of force. This is the crux of the imbalance. All else equal, suppressing violent insurgency has the virtue of restoring the monopoly on force, whereas the pursuit of insurgency risks its destruction. This justifies at least some divergence between the thresholds of criminality applicable to each.

Second, and relatedly, political obligation and the obligation not to resort to force are distinct. Individual and communal grievances against the state may be sufficient to undermine the force of political obligation, and yet not sufficient to justify the use of human violence (Lieblich 2016, p. 691; Fabre 2012, p. 136; Finlay 2015, p. 81). Indeed, it is possible that conditions are such that "revolution, as an outcome, would be permitted, but resort to hostilities to achieve it would not" (Lieblich 2016, p. 721). In such circumstances, the domestic criminality of insurgents' *jus-in-bello*-compliant use of force may be appropriate even though their goal is laudable and they commit no war crimes.

Third, these arguments notwithstanding, the extent of the current imbalance in favor of the state is troubling (certainly from a revisionist perspective). Precisely how far it deviates from the demands of morality is an issue on which there remains room for productive debate. One might argue that certain forms of significant political rights violations not including harm to life or limb are sufficient to generate the right to exercise lethal defensive force for at least certain kinds of non-state actor (Bazargan-Forward 2015). Frowe's reductionist argument for the right of states to respond to "political aggression" might be thought to support such a position (Frowe 2014, ch.5). Fabre has argued that although a threat to life or limb is necessary to ground full defensive rights (Fabre 2012, pp. 65–71), non-state actors may, in certain circumstances, assert authority over territory to which they have a legitimate claim as a matter of self-determination, and then gain the right to use force if the state attempts to coerce them out of that posture (thus shifting the imbalance in the ladder of coercive rights discussed above) (Fabre 2012, pp. 140–141). Others hold instead that lethal violence is justified only as a necessary and proportionate response to grave and unjustified harms or threats to life or body (Finlay 2015; McMahan 2004, pp. 75–76). From any of these perspectives, the current legal posture vis-à-vis conflicts initiated by state atrocity is indefensible, both in allowing the state to bootstrap its troops' way into the authority to fight without legal consequence, as long as they comply with the war crimes regime (Jinks 2014, p. 669; Lieblich 2016, p. 735), and in allowing the criminalization of organized non-state armed resistance.

This leads to the fourth point. Eliav Lieblich and Anthony Dworkin have argued that international human rights law has the potential to ground a *jus ad bellum* for state action in NIACs (Dworkin 2017, p. 490; Lieblich 2016, pp. 725–729). Human rights law requires that the state have a legitimate aim in order to limit rights lawfully. In the European Court of Human Rights' analysis of whether certain Russian actions against Chechen rebels met this criterion with respect to the right to life, the available legitimate aim was described as the suppression of an *"illegal* armed insurgency" (*Isayeva* 2005, ¶180). This might be thought to hint at the possibility of a lawful armed insurgency, in response to which any state resort to hostilities would violate the right to life for lack of a legitimate aim (Lieblich 2016, pp. 728–729).

Fifth, the strongest (although not only) candidate for lawful insurgency would surely be war waged to respond to and prevent state atrocities. This would provide an NIAC parallel to the rule that states may use force against one another only in response to severe forms of the illegal application of violence or its immediate threat—that is, armed attacks (Lieblich 2016, p. 742; Dannenbaum 2017, p. 1293; Kreß 2015, p. 41). It would be cognizable through the lens of human rights proportionality analysis (Lieblich 2016, p. 742). And, building on the existing international normative concept of the state's sovereign "responsibility to protect" its people from atrocity, it would rely on an already-recognized threshold in this domain.

To be sure, good faith efforts to use force in response to atrocity can also lead to state failure and long-term humanitarian catastrophe. This is one of the primary justifications for enduring and widespread resistance to claims that the responsibility to protect could underpin the lawfulness of unilateral external intervention. However, these are scenarios in which there is broad consensus that the Security Council would have a positive responsibility to use force against the government and where the African Union has been authorized by its members to do the same (World Summit Outcome 2005, ¶¶138–139; Constitutive Act of the African Union 2000, art. 4(h)). Assuming plausible agent-relative boosts to the justification for using force and the non-state actor's representation of the views of victims (or threatened victims) of state atrocity, it is particularly difficult to defend the criminalization of those who would fight such a government internally.[6]

One might consider the notion of lawful insurgency quixotic. Certainly, it is difficult to imagine a state prosecuting its troops for fighting rebels or granting the legitimacy of the latter. However, the development of international human rights jurisprudence in this direction could underpin legislative codification in states that have no intention of committing atrocity but wish to guard against violations by future regimes. This, after all, is one reason that states ratify the ICC Statute and pass domestic war crimes legislation, despite the constraints it imposes and the vulnerabilities it creates for officials and leaders. A jurisprudence on this at the supranational level could also strengthen the standing of non-state combatants who leave the fight and reach foreign territory to claim refugee status on the grounds that facing punishment for exercising a legal right to resist amounts to persecution (cf. Dinstein 2014, p. 244; von Sternberg 1993).

Given domestic challenges, there may also be a case for an international aggression crime for NIACs (Kreß 2015, pp. 39–41; Mégret 2015, pp. 48–50; Lieblich 2016, p. 739).

WAR CRIMES

The final point of focus in this chapter is that of the international war crimes regime applicable equally to both sides of an armed conflict. Consider two questions in this regard. What is the significance of that regime when applied to those who are already liable for aggression crimes? And, on the other side, is the current configuration of the war crimes regime appropriate for just combatants?

By definition, the war crimes regime is triggered only when the *jus ad bellum* has failed to prevent war. For the very reasons that lower-level participants ought not be criminally liable for aggression killings, it would not make sense for the scope of their liability for war crimes to be determined by the fact of their aggression. The presumption is that these troops fight as if they have the *jus ad bellum* on their side; as such, they are likely to be moved only by constraints applicable to those who do in fact have the *jus ad bellum* on their side (Dill and Shue 2012, p. 324; Shue 2013, pp. 280–281). Were that not the case, liability for aggression itself would be viable. Their receptivity to *jus in bello* constraints, on the other hand, is likely to be far greater, due to their access to relevant knowledge, their degree of influence on compliance, and (typically) the compatibility of compliance with their presumed commitment to fighting.

The war crimes regime is also of practical importance to aggressor leaders, even though the crime of aggression might be thought to cover the full spectrum of violence for which they are responsible. Ambiguities in the *jus ad bellum* status of most interstate wars are such that only a subcategory of wrongful wars will clearly qualify as criminal. Even when the war's status is clear, the culpability of a leader may not be and practical obstacles to punishment at home or abroad anyway make an aggression conviction significantly less likely than a war crimes conviction. Even when an aggression conviction is likely, a leader who orders her troops to commit war crimes in the course of the war would run the risk of triggering their legally required disobedience and would also risk facing additional charges and a longer sentence herself.

Incentives aside, applying the *jus in bello* regime separately to an aggressor force also expresses and condemns the full scope of culpable wrongdoing in such wars. This is most obvious for lower-level participants. Precisely because war crimes are wrongful even when perpetrated in the service of a just war (a point discussed further below), the factors that mitigate or eliminate such individuals' culpability for the *jus ad bellum* do not preclude war crimes culpability. Fighting under the mistaken impression that one's war is justified is no excuse for bombing hospitals or perpetrating rape or torture.

Even for a leader who would be convicted of aggression killings, condemning her war crimes separately is warranted because they entail additional and independent wrongs. Some war crimes involve gratuitous or particularly cruel harm. Others involve harm inflicted for exploitative (as opposed to eliminative, or even opportunistic) reasons.[7] Still others are rooted partly in reciprocal conventions that protect rights and limit the horror of war generally (Mavrodes 1975). Violating any of these rules in the course of an aggressive war involves wrongdoing that is qualitatively distinct from and additional to the ordinary violence of the aggression.

More complex is the question of the degree to which the war crimes regime comports with the deep morality applicable to *just* combatants. Of particular concern to revisionists has been the principle of distinction, which prohibits the targeting of civilians (unless participating directly in hostilities) and allows the targeting of combatants (unless surrendering, captured, or medically incapacitated).

As with the moral (in)equality of combatants issue, the starting revisionist premise here is that the infliction of violence must be justified on the basis of individual liability. Although differing slightly on what precisely that entails, revisionists tend to agree that the combatant/civilian classification system of targeting is difficult to justify on those terms. (Arneson 2006; Frowe 2014, ch.5–6; McMahan 2009, ch.4–5).

Seth Lazar articulates the challenge in the form of a dilemma premised on two observations (Lazar 2010). First, many combatants make "negligible, unnecessary, causal contributions," whether by performing non-fighting roles, such as cooking or mechanical work, or simply by neglecting to inflict or contribute effectively to violence in combat (Lazar 2015, p. 11). Even those who do contribute are often minimally (if at all) culpable vis-à-vis the *jus ad bellum*, due to ignorance, duress, and associative sympathies. Conversely, many civilians work in war-related industries, pay taxes that fund the war, vote in favor of the war, motivate their co-citizens to fight, and give the war domestic legitimacy, any of which may entail contributing more to the wrongful threat than do some combatants, and often with greater culpability (Lazar 2015, p. 13; Lazar 2010, p. 192). The dilemma is this. Either the threshold for liability to defensive killing is low (in terms of threat contribution and responsibility or culpability), in which case some civilians are sufficiently threatening and responsible to be liable. Or the threshold for liability is high, in which case some combatants are not liable, either because they pose no threat or because they fail to meet the responsibility or culpability threshold. The latter path might be thought to lead to contingent pacifism.

Faced with this dilemma, some revisionists have set the responsibility threshold for liability low, thus including most, if not all, unjust combatants (McMahan 2009, p. 166; Frowe 2014, p. 80; Arneson 2017). McMahan argues that an individual is liable to defensive killing in virtue of her *comparative* responsibility (though not necessarily culpability) for an unjust threat vis-à-vis others who could be killed in order to nullify the threat (McMahan 2005, 2009, ch.4). He has also argued that even entirely unthreatening unjust combatants are liable to targeting on the grounds that their responsibility for just combatants' reasonable beliefs that the former are liable is sufficient to forfeit their right not to be attacked (McMahan 2011).

Against McMahan, but still eschewing a culpability theory of liability, Adil Haque argues instead that persons lose the human right not to be attacked "only by posing unjust threats directly, jointly with others, or indirectly through others they effectively control" (Haque 2017, p. 270). This, he argues, better grounds liability in individual rights than does a comparative responsibility approach because it makes liability contingent on what one has done rather than on what others have done to affect the just distribution of harm (Haque 2017, pp. 259–263).

If Haque's threshold is to allow for the targeting of *all* unjust combatants, "jointly" posing a threat must be defined broadly. Along these lines, Bazargan has argued that all unjust combatants are, by definition, jointly responsible for the collective unjust threat, even if they are individually unthreatening (Bazargan 2013). But in what sense is a reluctant 19-year-old conscript who has no intention of firing her weapon, and who makes no significant contribution to the war part of a "joint" threat? And, if she is, why not other members of society who contribute financially, politically, or through their non-military labor? After all, an IAC might be thought to be characterized more fairly as a collective project of the entire state than as a collective project of its military. Bazargan argues that the distinction lies in the prominence of combatant's roles in the overall threat, and thus their greater "inclusive authorship" (Bazargan 2013). This requires placing great moral weight on the significance of a formal role, even when the individuals in question fail to discharge the basic requirements of the role and are non-culpable for the wrongful collective threat.

Alternatively, one might recognize that non-culpable, non-contributing unjust combatants fall below the liability threshold (as do the vast majority of civilians), and yet distinguish the killing of those non-liable combatants from the killing of non-liable civilians on lesser evil grounds. The argument here would accept that the intentional targeting of at least some unjust combatants violates their rights. However, assuming *jus ad bellum* thresholds are surpassed, these rights violations are likely to be justified as the lesser evil, given that some of the arguments above may mitigate the severity of the rights violation, given that most combatants *are* likely to be involved, at least collectively, in posing direct threats, and given that the remaining minority of combatants who are not liable can rarely be distinguished and isolated from liable combatants. The intentional killing of civilians, on the other hand, would be a significantly greater evil, particularly since so few of them are liable. As such, it would be almost impossible to justify, even in service of a just cause.

Substantively, this is probably more plausible than the claim that all unjust combatants are liable to be killed. However, by its very nature, it can avoid the responsibility dilemma only as a contingent matter. After all, an argument can be made for killing civilians as the lesser evil, too (Blum 2010a; Walzer 1977, ch.16). A strong defense of the principle of distinction thus requires showing that the evil of killing non-liable civilians (even for a just cause) is substantially and almost universally greater than the evil of killing non-liable unjust combatants.

Arguing that a line can be drawn here, Lazar contends that one or more of five consistently instantiated and morally salient features distinguish all but a statistically insignificant number of non-liable civilians from non-liable combatants. (Lazar 2015, p. 17). The first is that killing civilians will often fail to advance a military goal and so is typically gratuitous rather than militarily necessary (Lazar 2015, ch.2). Lazar is skeptical of how far this can go, but Chehtman has supplemented the claim, arguing that even in the cases in which killing civilians would advance the war effort, the advantage is rarely proportionate to the evil inflicted (Chehtman 2018a, p. 434). Second, Lazar argues that attacks on even contributing civilians tend to be predominantly exploitative or opportunistic (as is the case when civilians are terrorized so as to reduce support for the aggressive war), whereas attacks on combatants are primarily eliminative (Lazar 2015, ch.3). Third, because a greater proportion of civilians are non-liable, the risk of killing innocents, given the fog of war, is significantly higher in attacks on civilians than it is in attacks on combatants (Lazar 2015, ch.4). As such, attacks on civilians express greater disrespect for the non-liable persons attacked than do attacks on combatants (Lazar 2015, pp. 75–86). Fourth, and less convincingly, Lazar argues that civilians' vulnerability and defenselessness heighten the threshold for attacking them (Lazar 2015, ch.5). Finally, he contends that few combatants take care to comply with the *jus ad bellum*, that their wearing of uniforms and their compliance with IHL imply some level of (heroic) consent to diverting fire from civilians, and their membership in the military grounds obligations to bear costs to remedy the wrongs of the collective (Lazar 2015, ch.6).

Lazar's is perhaps the most comprehensive effort to wrestle with the revisionist difficulty with the principle of distinction. At the theoretical level, it has two vulnerabilities. First, as he admits, the factors are contingent and thus subject to exceptions. Second, as an account of the worseness of attacking non-liable civilians rather than non-liable combatants, it inevitably raises questions of degree and numbers. However, on the level of action-guiding morality, these factors spotlight the difficulty of providing real-world cases in which the targeting of civilians rather than combatants in war would actually be justified. Strengthening the case for the wrongfulness of such targeting is the observation that bright lines on targeting can help to limit the hell of war, since they facilitate monitoring, enforcement, and compliance, as well as strengthening the legality of the rule. Since the distinction between combatants and civilians is perhaps the best feasible approximation of liability, underpinned by a credible lesser evil analysis, and rooted in a convention of long-standing and universal endorsement, it is likely the best available bright line. This, in turn, provides moral reason to uphold the convention, creating a further justificatory threshold past which the killing of a liable civilian must pass.

In short, a war crimes regime built around the principle of distinction is defensible, and ultimately not too far removed from the demands of deep morality. For the rare cases in which the targeting of an unjust combatant is not justified by liability or lesser evil reasoning *and* those involved in the targeting knew enough to be culpable, the prospect of criminal responsibility is currently low, but things are changing. As noted in the discussion on exceptionalism, the rise of individualized targeted killing based on specific intelligence information, the use of such policies outside areas of active hostilities, and the growing prominence of the category of "civilians directly participating in hostilities" as the target class have all been relevant in shifting debates as to the role of human rights law in war and possible adjustments to the *jus in bello*. At least some states engaged in these practices have employed standards (whether by law or policy) that merge the IHL and IHRL frameworks, requiring that even combatants be targeted only when necessary to respond to an imminent threat (U.S. 2016, pp. 24–27 [by policy]; Public Committee Against Torture in Israel 2006, ¶ 40 [by law]). There is growing support for the notion that such an approach either is, or ought to be, legally required—at least in certain circumstances (Blum 2010b; Dworkin 2017; Haque 2017; Luban 2016; Melzer 2009, pp. 78–82).

To be clear, such hybrid IHL/IHRL reasoning may function as a tool of legitimation as much as constraint, and it is open to question whether the claimed standards are adhered to in practice. However, any role for human rights law in this context has the potential to open the door to the development of criminal law standards in at least certain contexts that would prohibit the killing of combatants without individualized justification.

Conclusion

In recent years, revisionists have spotlighted significant blind spots in orthodox just war theory. Given the latter's putatively close relationship to the law of war, one might have thought that this would undermine the normative foundations of the contemporary war crimes regime, particularly given the latter's moralized posture. However, there is more compatibility with revisionist deep morality in the existing criminal law regime than is typically recognized.

The sharp legal distinction between war and peace has begun to erode with the expansion of human rights jurisprudence into that realm. This has been forced in part by the blurring of the boundaries between the two domains. However, it also reflects a normative position that overlaps with the premise of revisionism—individual human rights, by their very nature, cannot be displaced in war; rather, they need to be understood in context.

The current legal regime does not hold that soldiers are equally liable to be killed or harmed, regardless of the side for which they fight. On the contrary, the violence inflicted upon just combatants (unlike that inflicted on their adversaries) is criminal, even if compliant with the *jus in bello*. Where equality does arise is on the question of liability to punishment for aggression killings in IACs, as only leaders are held responsible for the wrongful violence of an aggressive war. However, this limit on the scope of criminal liability is an immunity rooted in widespread non-culpability, the value of encouraging compliance with the war convention, and imperatives of institutional functioning. It should not be mistaken for a legal endorsement of deep equality. The most significant moral difficulty with the law in this realm is, instead, on the question of criminal liability for *jus-in-bello*-compliant killing in NIACs, where the current legal bias in favor of even an atrocity-perpetrating state requires revision.

On the issue of war crimes in the strict sense, revisionist theory raises a number of challenges. It might be thought to demand an articulation of what precisely the *jus in bello* adds to the blanket prohibition on any conduct in furtherance of a wrongful war. More fundamentally, it calls into question some of the moral imprecisions in the principle of distinction, as applied to those fighting a just war. However, although there are areas in which greater legal nuance could be added, the gap between law and morality here is ultimately narrower than some of the critiques suggest and is probably justified overall.

Notes

1. This is not to say that *all* unjust combatants are liable to be killed (a point addressed below). Rather, it is to say that the *jus ad bellum* is a relevant factor in liability.
2. As noted above, many of these features are woven into orthodox thought. The key difference is that revisionists are more likely to identify them as either excuses or limited and contingent grounds for non-attribution.
3. To be clear, the question of whether an action qualifies as an international use of force for the purposes of the *jus ad bellum* does not map perfectly onto whether it qualifies as an international armed conflict for the purpose of IHL—the use of proxy forces in some circumstances may constitute an aggression without creating an IAC—but the basic point holds. On this, see, for example, *Nicaragua* (1986, ¶¶191–195; 228–230).
4. In a technical sense, one might question whether the category "combatants" exists in NIACs. However, there clearly is a classification between civilians protected from attack and persons legally liable to attack in NIACs, whatever terminology one uses to describe the latter.
5. Article 1(4) of Additional Protocol I of 1977 grants the privileges of belligerency to non-state groups fighting wars of self-determination against alien occupation, racist regimes, or colonial domination. This provision has remained entirely dormant, but for the situation of the Polisario Front fighting the Moroccan occupation of Western Sahara (Mačák 2018).
6. On agent-relativity here, see Parry (2017, p. 359); Quong (2009).
7. Killing an agent who poses a lethal threat as the necessary way of eliminating that threat is eliminative. It leaves the killer (or those she is protecting) no better off than had her target never existed. As Lazar puts it, the target is "not a resource" for the killer, but the very "problem that [is] solve[d]" by the killing (Lazar 2015,

p. 60). In contrast, opportunistic forms of killing involve using the target as a resource to achieve the killer's end. Within the latter category, "merely opportunistic" killing targets persons who are in some way responsible (upstream) for the threat the killer now faces, and who may, for that reason, be thought to have forfeited, at least partly, their claim not to be targeted so as to quell that threat (Frowe 2014, p. 179). This may be distinguished from the "exploitative" killing of those who are not responsible at all for the threat, and who cannot be said to have forfeited their right not to be targeted, but who the killer uses as a resource in resisting the threat.

References

Advisory opinion on legal consequences of the construction of a wall in the occupied Palestinian territory. 2004. International Court of Justice. 2004 ICJ Reports 136.

Advisory opinion on the legality of the threat or use of nuclear weapons. 1996. International Court of Justice. 1996 ICJ Reports 226.

Constitutive Act of the African Union. 2000. https://au.int/en/constitutive-act. Accessed 26 Feb 2019.

Human Rights Committee. 2001. General comment 29: States of emergency (article 4). UN Doc. CCPR/C/21/Rev.1/Add.11.

———. 2004. General comment 31: The nature of the general legal obligation on states parties to the Covenant. U.N. Doc. CCPR/C/21/Rev.1/Add.13.

———. 2018. General comment 36: On article 6 of the International Covenant on Civil and Political Rights, on the right to life. U.N. Doc. CCPR/C/GC/36.

Isayava v. Russia. 2005. European Court of Human Rights, application no. 57950/00.

United States et al. v. Göring et. al. 1946. International Military Tribunal (Nuremberg) Judgment. In Vol. 22 of *Trial of the major war criminals before the international military tribunal,* 411.

Shawcross, Hartley. 1946. Closing statement. *United States v. Göring et. al.* In Vol. 19 of *Trial of the major war criminals before the international military tribunal,* 458.

McCann v. United Kingdom. 1995. European Court of Human Rights (Grand Chamber), application no. 18984/91.

Mendez, Juan E. 2002. Detainees in Guantanamo Bay, Cuba. 2002. Inter-American Commission on Human Rights, request for precautionary measures. http://www1.umn.edu/humanrts/cases/guantanamo-2003.html. Accessed 26 Feb 2019.

Nicaragua v. United States. 1986. International Court of Justice. Case concerning military and paramilitary activities in and against Nicaragua (merits). 1986 ICJ Reports 14.

Osman v. United Kingdom. 1998. European Court of Human Rights (Grand Chamber), application no. 23452/94.

Prosecutor v. Al Mahdi. 2016. International Criminal Court. Trial Chamber judgment. Case ICC-01/12–01/15.

Prosecutor v. Blaškić. 2004. International Criminal Tribunal for the former Yugoslavia. Appeals Chamber judgment. Case IT-95-14-A.

Prosecutor v. Tadić. 1995. International Criminal Tribunal for the former Yugoslavia. Appeals Chamber decision on the defence motion for interlocutory (Appeal on jurisdiction). Case IT-94-1-AR72.

Public Committee Against Torture in Israel v. Israel. 2006. Supreme Court of Israel. HCJ 769/02.

Statute of the International Criminal Court. 2011. Doc No. ICC-PIDS-LT-01-002/11_ Eng. Originally: July 17, 1998, 2187 U.N.T.S. 90. Last amended November 29, 2010, depository notification C.N.651.2010.TREATIES-8. https://www.icc-cpi. int/nr/rdonlyres/add16852-aee9-4757-abe7-9cdc7cf02886/283503/romestat-uteng1.pdf. Accessed 26 Feb 2019.

United States Department of State. 2011. Fourth periodic report of the United States to the Human Rights Committee. www.state.gov—179781.htm. Accessed 26 Feb 2019.

———. 2016. Report on the legal and policy frameworks guiding the United States' use of military force and related national security options. https://www.justsecurity. org/wp-content/uploads/2016/12/framework.Report_Final.pdf. Accessed 26 Feb 2019.

United States et al. v. Araki et al. 1948. Repr. in Vol. 22 of *The Tokyo war crimes trial*, ed. John Pritchard and Sonia M. Zaide. New York: Garland. (1981).

World Summit Outcome Document. 2005. United Nations General Assembly Resolution 60/1, September 16.

Anscombe, G.E.M. 1981. Mr. Truman's degree. In *Ethics, religion and politics*, 62–71. Oxford: Blackwell. (Orig. pub. 1958).

Arneson, Richard J. 2006. Just warfare theory and noncombatant immunity. *Cornell International Law Journal* 39: 663–688.

———. 2017. Resolving the responsibility dilemma. In *The ethics of war: Essays*, ed. Saba Bazargan-Forward and Sam Rickless, 67–93. Oxford: Oxford University Press.

Baxter, Richard R. 1951. So-called "unprivileged belligerency". *British Yearbook of International Law* 28: 323–345.

Bazargan, Saba. 2013. Complicitous liability in war. *Philosophical Studies* 165: 177–195.

Bazargan-Forward, Saba. 2015. Review of terrorism and the right to resist: A theory of just revolutionary war. *Ethics* 127: 481–486.

Benbaji, Yitzhak. 2008. A defense of the traditional war convention. *Ethics* 118 (3): 464–495.

———. 2011. The moral power of soldiers to undertake the duty of obedience. *Ethics* 122: 43–73.

Blum, Gabriella. 2010a. The laws of war and the "lesser evil". *Yale Journal of International Law* 35: 1–69.

———. 2010b. The dispensable lives of soldiers. *Journal of Legal Analysis* 2: 115–170.

Chehtman, Alejandro. 2018a. Review of Sparing civilians. *Jurisprudence* 9: 431–437.

———. 2018b. Revisionist just war theory and the concept of war crimes. *Leiden Journal of International Law* 31: 171–194.

Dannenbaum, Tom. 2017. Why have we criminalized aggressive war? *Yale Law Journal* 126: 1242–1318.

———. 2018. *The crime of aggression, humanity, and the soldier.* Cambridge: Cambridge University Press.

Dill, Janina. 2013. Should international law ensure the moral acceptability of war? *Leiden Journal of International Law* 26: 253–270.

Dill, Janina, and Henry Shue. 2012. Limiting the killing in war: Military necessity and the St. Petersburg assumption. *Ethics and International Affairs* 26: 311–333.

Dinstein, Yoram. 2012. *War, aggression, and self-defence.* 5th ed. Cambridge: Cambridge University Press.

———. 2014. *Non-international armed conflicts in international law.* Cambridge: Cambridge University Press.

————. 2016. *The conduct of hostilities under the law of international armed conflict*. 3rd ed. Cambridge: Cambridge University Press.

Dörmann, Knut. 2003. The legal situation of "unlawful/unprivileged combatants". *International Review of the Red Cross* 85 (849): 45–74.

Draper, G.I.A.D. 1979. Humanitarian law and human rights. *Acta Juridica* 1979: 193–206.

Drumbl, Mark. 2007. *Atrocity, punishment and international law*. Cambridge: Cambridge University Press.

Dworkin, Anthony. 2017. Individual, not collective: Justifying the resort to force against members of non-state armed groups. *International Law Studies* 93: 476–525.

Englehart, Neil A. 2009. State capacity, state failure, and human rights. *Journal of Peace Research* 46: 163–180.

Estlund, David. 2007. On following orders in an unjust war. *Journal of Political Philosophy* 15: 213–234.

Fabre, Cécile. 2012. *Cosmopolitan war*. Oxford: Oxford University Press.

————. 2016. *Cosmopolitan peace*. Oxford: Oxford University Press.

Finkelstein, Claire. 2016. Killing in war and the moral equality thesis. *Social Philosophy and Policy* 32 (2): 184–203.

Finlay, Christopher J. 2015. *Terrorism and the right to resist: A theory of just revolutionary war*. Cambridge: Cambridge University Press.

Frowe, Helen. 2014. *Defensive killing*. Oxford: Oxford University Press.

Greenwood, Christopher. 1983. The relationship between jus ad bellum and jus in bello. *Review of International Studies* 9: 221–234.

Hakimi, Monica. 2018. The theory and practice at the intersection between human rights and humanitarian law. *American Journal of International Law* 111: 1063–1074.

Haque, Adil Ahmad. 2017. *Law and morality at war*. Oxford: Oxford University Press.

Hathaway, Oona, and Schott Shapiro. 2017. *The internationalists*. New York: Simon and Schuster.

Heyns, Christof, Dapo Akande, Lawrence Hill-Cawthorne, and Thomas Chengeta. 2016. The international law framework regulating the use of armed drones. *International and Comparative Law Quarterly* 65: 791–827.

Institut de Droit International. 1971. *Conditions of application of humanitarian rules of armed conflict to hostilities in which United Nations forces may be engaged*.

Jinks, Derek. 2014. International human rights law in time of armed conflict. In *The Oxford handbook of international law in armed conflict*, ed. Andrew Clapham and Paola Gaeta, 656–674. Oxford: Oxford University Press.

Kahn, Paul. 2008. *Sacred violence*. Ann Arbor: University of Michigan Press.

Kreß, Claus. 2015. Towards further developing the law of non-international armed conflict: A proposal for a jus in bello interno and a new jus contra bellum internum. *International Review of the Red Cross* 96 (893): 30–44.

Kutz, Christopher. 2005. The difference uniforms make: Collective violence in criminal law and war. *Philosophy and Public Affairs* 33: 148–180.

————. 2008. Fearful symmetry. In *Just and unjust warriors: The moral and legal status of soldiers*, ed. David Rodin and Henry Shue, 69–86. Oxford: Oxford University Press.

————. 2014. What rights may be defended by means of war? In *The morality of defensive war*, ed. Cécile Fabre and Seth Lazar, 229–246. Oxford: Oxford University Press.

Lauterpacht, Hersch. 1953. The limits of the operation of the law of war. *British Yearbook of International Law* 30: 206–243.

Lazar, Seth. 2010. The responsibility dilemma for killing in war: A review essay. *Philosophy and Public Affairs* 38: 180–213.

———. 2013. Associative duties and the ethics of killing in war. *Journal of Practical Ethics.* http://www.jpe.ox.ac.uk/papers/associative-duties-and-the-ethics-of-killing-in-war/. Accessed 26 Feb 2019.

———. 2015. *Sparing civilians.* Oxford: Oxford University Press.

———. 2017. War. The Stanford Encyclopedia of Philosophy. https://plato.stanford.edu/archives/spr2017/entries/war/. Accessed on 26 Feb 2019.

Lieblich, Eliav. 2016. Internal jus ad bellum. *Hastings Law Journal* 67: 687–748.

Luban, David. 1994. *Legal modernism.* Ann Arbor: University of Michigan Press.

———. 2010. Fairness to rightness. In *The philosophy of international law*, ed. Samantha Besson and John Tasioulas, 569–588. Oxford: Oxford University Press.

———. 2016. Human rights thinking and the laws of war. In *Theoretical boundaries of armed conflict and human rights*, ed. Jens David Ohlin, 45–77. Cambridge: Cambridge University Press.

———. 2018. Knowing when not to fight. In *Oxford handbook of the ethics of war*, ed. Seth Lazar and Helen Frowe, 185–203. Oxford: Oxford University Press.

Mačák, Kubo. 2018. Wars of national liberation: The story of one unusual rule II. Oxford University Press Blog. https://blog.oup.com/2018/07/wars-national-liberation-unusual-rule-part-2/. Accessed 26 Feb 2019.

Mavrodes, George I. 1975. Conventions and the morality of war. *Philosophy and Public Affairs.* 4: 117–131.

May, Larry. 2008. *Aggression and crimes against peace.* Cambridge: Cambridge University Press.

McMahan, Jeff. 2004. War as self-defense. *Ethics & International Affairs* 18: 75–80.

———. 2005. The basis of moral liability to defensive killing. *Philosophical Issues* 15: 386–405.

———. 2008. The morality of war and the law of war. In *Just and unjust warriors: The moral and legal status of soldiers*, ed. David Rodin and Henry Shue, 19–43. Oxford: Oxford University Press.

———. 2009. *Killing in war.* Oxford: Oxford University Press.

———. 2011. Who is liable to be killed in war. *Analysis* 71: 544–559.

———. 2013. War crimes and immoral action in war. In *The constitution of criminal law*, ed. Antony Duff, Lindsay Farmer, Sandra Marshall, and Victor Tadros, 151–184. Oxford: Oxford University Press.

———. 2016. Unjust war and the crime of aggression. In *The crime of aggression: A commentary*, ed. Claus Kreß and Stefan Barriga, 1386–1397. Cambridge: Cambridge University Press.

Mégret, Frédéric. 2015. Response to Claus Kreß: Leveraging the privilege of belligerency in non-international armed conflict towards respect for the jus in bello. *International Review of the Red Cross* 96 (893): 44–66.

———. 2016. What is the specific evil of aggression? In *The crime of aggression: A commentary*, ed. Claus Kreß and Stefan Barriga, 1398–1453. Cambridge: Cambridge University Press.

Melzer, Nils. 2009. *Interpretive guidance on the notion of direct participation in hostilities under international humanitarian law.* Geneva: International Committee of the Red Cross.

Meron, Theodor. 2006. *The humanization of international law.* Leiden: Brill.

Mill, John Stuart. 1993. On liberty. In *Utilitarianism, on liberty.* London: Everyman. (Orig. pub. 1859).

Nagel, Thomas. 1972. War and massacre. *Philosophy and Public Affairs* 1: 123–144.

Neff, Stephen C. 2005. *War and the law of nations: A general history*. Cambridge: Cambridge University Press.

Norman, Richard. 1995. *Ethics, killing, and war*. Cambridge: Cambridge University Press.

Ohlin, Jens David. 2016. The crime of bootstrapping. In *The crime of aggression: A commentary*, ed. Claus Kreß and Stefan Barriga, 1454–1479. Cambridge: Cambridge University Press.

Oppenheim, Lassa. 1905, 1906. *International law: A treatise*. Vols. 1 and 2. 1st ed. https://archive.org/details/internationallaw12oppe/page/n5; https://archive.org/details/internationallaw12oppe/page/n671

Parry, Jonathan. 2017. Defensive harm, consent, and intervention. *Philosophy and Public Affairs* 45: 356–396.

Pobjie, Erin. 2016. Victims of the crime of aggression. In *The crime of aggression: A commentary*, ed. Claus Kreß and Stefan Barriga, 816–860. Cambridge: Cambridge University Press.

Quong, Jonathan. 2009. Killing in self-defense. *Ethics* 119: 507–537.

Rodin, David. 2002. *War and self-defense*. Oxford: Oxford University Press.

Sassòli, Marco. 2007. Jus ad bellum and jus in bello—The separation between the legality of the use of force and humanitarian rules to be respected in warfare: Crucial or outdated? In *International law and armed conflict: Exploring the faultlines*, ed. Michael N. Schmitt and Jelena Pejic, 241–264. Leiden: Brill.

Schachter, Oscar. 1984. The right of states to use armed force. *Michigan Law Review* 82: 1620–1646.

Shue, Henry. 2008. Do we need a "morality of war"? In *Just and unjust warriors: The moral and legal status of soldiers*, ed. David Rodin and Henry Shue, 87–111. Oxford: Oxford University Press.

———. 2013. Laws of war, morality, and international politics. *Leiden Journal International Law* 26: 271–292.

Sloane, Robert D. 2007. The expressive capacity of international punishment. *Stanford Journal of International Law* 43: 39–94.

Solera, Oscar. 2007. *Defining the crime of aggression*. London: Cameron May.

Stahn, Carsten. 2010. The "end", the "beginning of the end" or the "end of the beginning"? *Leiden Journal of International Law* 23: 875–882.

Teitel, Ruti. 2011. *Humanity's law*. Oxford: Oxford University Press.

The Global Campaign for Ratification and Implementation of the Kampala Amendments on the Crime of Aggression. 2019. Status of ratification and implementation, update no. 33 (information as of 11 April 2019). https://crimeofaggression.info/the-role-of-states/status-of-ratification-and-implementation/. Accessed 20 Aug 2019.

von Sternberg, Mark R. 1993. Political asylum and the law of internal armed conflict: Refugee status, human rights and humanitarian law concerns. *International Journal of Refugee Law* 5: 153–182.

Waldron, Jeremy. 2018. Deep morality and the laws of war. In *The Oxford handbook of the ethics of war*, ed. Seth Lazar and Helen Frowe, 80–97. Oxford: Oxford University Press.

Walzer, Michael. 1977. *Just and unjust wars*. New York: Basic Books.

———. 1980. The moral standing of states: A response to four critics. *Philosophy and Public Affairs* 9: 209–229.

———. 2006. Response to McMahan's paper. *Philosophia* 34: 43–45.

Index[1]

A
Abernathy, Ralph, 171
Abolitionists and civil disobedience, 170, 173
Abortion
  civil disobedience and protests for and against, 180, 182
  Moral Uncertainty Theory and, 446, 456, 462, 465n2
  Roe v. Wade (1973), 182
ACLU (American Civil Liberties Union), 682–684
Actio in libera causa, 24–26
Act Up (AIDS Coalition to Unleash Power), 167
Actus reus
  in complicity, 199
  in corporate punishment, 217
  enticement and solicitation of minors, 715
  in fraud, 268, 273, 275, 277, 278, 280
  in hate or bias crime laws, 294, 306n17
  reckless behavior and, 652
  in revenge porn, 679
Addiction and responsibility, 13–39
  akrasia (failure to execute one's intention), 29–30, 35–39
  attention issues, 29

automaticity model of addiction (failure to form an intention), 27, 32–33
becoming an addict, 23–26
conceptualizing and defining, 15–23
defense, not currently available as, 13–14, 39n1
disease model of, 18–23, 488
emotion-driven bypassing of intention, addiction as, 27–28, 33–34
erosion of belief and, 28, 34
ignorance and mistakes, 34
incapacitation of addicts by their addiction, 32–39
moral excuse and legal defense, addiction as, 31–39
motivational failure and, 28–29, 35
normative failure (acting and wanting against one's better judgment), 29, 34, 36–37
persistence in continuing to acquire and use substances, 26–31
in prison population, 13
rational choice and, 26–27, 41n21
satisfaction failure and, 30–31
Supreme Court on, 14
as U.S. crisis, 13, 14
willing versus unwilling addicts, 26–27
withdrawal, problem of, 31–32

---

[1] Note: Page numbers followed by 'n' refer to notes.

© The Author(s) 2019
L. Alexander, K. K. Ferzan (eds.), *The Palgrave Handbook of Applied Ethics and the Criminal Law*, https://doi.org/10.1007/978-3-030-22811-8

Printed by Printforce, the Netherlands